ESSENTIAL READINGS IN
WORLD
POLITICS

6TH EDITION

Karen A. Mingst and Jack L. Snyder

W. W. NORTON & COMPANY
New York • London

W. W. Norton & Company has been independent since its founding in 1923, when William Warder Norton and Mary D. Herter Norton first published lectures delivered at the People's Institute, the adult education division of New York City's Cooper Union. The firm soon expanded its program beyond the Institute, publishing books by celebrated academics from America and abroad. By midcentury, the two major pillars of Norton's publishing program—trade books and college texts—were firmly established. In the 1950s, the Norton family transferred control of the company to its employees, and today—with a staff of four hundred and a comparable number of trade, college, and professional titles published each year—W. W. Norton & Company stands as the largest and oldest publishing house owned wholly by its employees.

The text of this book is composed in 10.5/13 Adobe Garamond Pro
with the display set in Neutraface 2 Text.
Book design by Guenet Abraham

Composition and project management by Westchester Publishing Services
Project supervisor: Stephen Barichko

Manufacturing by LSC Harrisonburg
Editor: Peter Lesser
Production Manager: Steven Cestaro
Assistant Editor: Samantha Held

Library of Congress Cataloging-in-Publication Data

Names: Mingst, Karen A., 1947– editor. | Snyder, Jack L., editor.
Title: Essential readings in world politics / edited by Karen A. Mingst and
    Jack L. Snyder.
Description: 6th edition. | New York : W.W. Norton & Company, 2017. |
    Series: The Norton series in world politics | Includes bibliographical references.
Identifiers: LCCN 2016026523 | **ISBN 9780393283662 (pbk.)**
Subjects: LCSH: International relations. | World politics.
Classification: LCC JZ1305 .E85 2017 | DDC 327—dc23 LC record available
    at https://lccn.loc.gov/2016026523

W. W. Norton & Company, Inc.
500 Fifth Avenue, New York, N.Y. 10110
www.wwnorton.com

W. W. Norton & Company Ltd.
15 Carlisle Street, London W1D 3BS

2 3 4 5 6 7 8 9 0

CONTENTS

PREFACE

This reader is the result of a collaborative effort between the two co-editors, with an evolving mix of classic and contemporary selections over six editions.

The articles have been selected to meet several criteria. First, the collection is designed to augment and amplify the core text, *Essentials of International Relations,* Seventh Edition, by Karen A. Mingst and Ivan M. Arreguín-Toft. The chapters in this book follow those in the text. Second, the selections are purposefully eclectic; that is, key theoretical articles are paired with contemporary pieces found in the literature. When possible, articles have been chosen to reflect diverse theoretical perspectives and policy viewpoints. Finally, the articles are intended to be both readable and engaging to undergraduates. The co-editors worked to maintain the integrity of challenging pieces while making them accessible to undergraduates at a variety of colleges and universities, in some cases working closely with authors to translate technical material into highly accessible yet precise prose.

Special thanks go to those individuals who provided reviews of this book and offered suggestions and reflections based on teaching experience. Our product benefited greatly from these evaluations, although had we included all the suggestions, the book would have been thousands of pages! Pete Lesser, our editor at W. W. Norton, guided part of the process, compiling thorough evaluations from users of earlier editions and providing suggestions. Samantha Held kept us "on task" and offered excellent suggestions as the book took final shape. Their professionalism and understanding made this process much more rewarding. We also thank W. W. Norton's copyediting and production staff for their careful work on this book.

GUIDE TO THIS READER

Many of the selections included here are reprinted in their entirety. A number have been excerpted from longer works. A * * * indicates that word(s) or sentence(s) are omitted. A ■ ■ ■ indicates that paragraph(s) or section(s) are omitted. Brackets indicate text added by the editors for purposes of clarification. Complete bibliographic citations are included at the bottom of the first page of each selection. Readers who desire to delve deeper into the source material are encouraged to pursue these citations as well as those cited in the readings.

1 APPROACHES TO INTERNATIONAL RELATIONS

In *Essentials of International Relations*, Seventh Edition, Karen A. Mingst and Ivan M. Arreguín-Toft introduce theories and approaches used to study international relations. The readings in this section of *Essential Readings in World Politics* complement that introduction. Jack Snyder first provides an overview of rival theories and suggests how theories guide decision makers to respond to contemporary events.

Some of the conceptual approaches that shape international relations thinking today have a long track record. Thucydides (460 BCE–c. 395 BCE), in his history of the Peloponnesian War, presents a classic dialogue between Athenian imperialists and their Melian victims. The two sides debate the place of power and principle in international relations. The leaders of Melos ponder the fate of the island, deciding whether to risk defying the Athenians, and whether they can rely on the enemy of Athens, the Lacedaemonians (also known as Spartans), for protection.

Thomas Hobbes's *Leviathan*, published in 1651 at the time of the English Civil War, explains how fear and greed lead to endemic conflict in situations of anarchy, where there is no sovereign power to provide protection and enforce laws. This work expresses a central insight of contemporary realists about the root cause of war.

Immanuel Kant's *Perpetual Peace*, published in 1795, foreshadows the key arguments of today's liberal approach to international relations theory: liberal states with representative governments are unlikely to fight wars against each other, because government policy is accountable to the average citizen who bears the costs of war. This creates the potential to form a cooperative league of liberal states, embodied nowadays in international organizations such as the United Nations, international economic institutions, the North Atlantic Treaty Organization, and the European Union, which were established to a large extent through the efforts of the liberal great powers.

In addition to realism and liberalism, thinking about international politics has also been shaped by radical critiques of global capitalism. These include Marxist-Leninist doctrines propounded by the Soviet Union and theories about dependent economic development advanced by voices in the Global South. Perhaps the most consequential radical theory of international relations is V. I. Lenin's *Imperialism, The Highest Stage of Capitalism*, published in 1917, just months before Lenin's Bolshevik party seized power in the Russian Revolution. Lenin's arguments about global inequality, the privileged position of finance capital, competition for resources and markets, and the consequent armed rivalries between great powers continue to resonate today. Not only leftist radicals but also realists can still find much of interest in Lenin's insights.

Jack Snyder

ONE WORLD, RIVAL THEORIES

The U.S. government has endured several pain-ful rounds of scrutiny as it tries to figure out what went wrong on September 11, 2001. The intel-ligence community faces radical restructuring; the military has made a sharp pivot to face a new enemy; and a vast new federal agency has blos-somed to coordinate homeland security. But did September 11 signal a failure of theory on par with the failures of intelligence and policy? Familiar theories about how the world works still dominate academic debate. Instead of radical change, aca-demia has adjusted existing theories to meet new realities. Has this approach succeeded? Does inter-national relations theory still have something to tell policymakers?

[In 1998], political scientist Stephen M. Walt published a much-cited survey of the field in [*Foreign Policy*] ("One World, Many Theories," Spring 1998). He sketched out three dominant approaches: realism, liberalism, and an updated form of ideal-ism called "constructivism." Walt argued that these theories shape both public discourse and policy analysis. Realism focuses on the shifting distribu-tion of power among states. Liberalism highlights the rising number of democracies and the turbulence of democratic transitions. Idealism illuminates the changing norms of sovereignty, human rights, and international justice, as well as the increased potency of religious ideas in politics.

The influence of these intellectual constructs extends far beyond university classrooms and ten-ure committees. Policymakers and public commen-tators invoke elements of all these theories when articulating solutions to global security dilemmas.

From *Foreign Policy* (Nov./Dec. 2004): 53–62.

President George W. Bush promises to fight terror by spreading liberal democracy to the Middle East and claims that skeptics "who call themselves 'realists' . . . have lost contact with a fundamental reality" that "America is always more secure when freedom is on the march." Striking a more eclectic tone, National Security Advisor Condoleezza Rice, a former Stanford University political science professor, explains that the new Bush doctrine is an amalgam of pragmatic realism and Wilsonian liberal theory. During the recent presidential cam-paign, Sen. John Kerry sounded remarkably sim-ilar: "Our foreign policy has achieved greatness," he said, "only when it has combined realism and idealism."

International relations theory also shapes and informs the thinking of the public intellectuals who translate and disseminate academic ideas. During the summer of 2004, for example, two influential framers of neoconservative thought, columnist Charles Krauthammer and political scientist Fran-cis Fukuyama, collided over the implications of these conceptual paradigms for U.S. policy in Iraq. Backing the Bush administration's Middle East policy, Krauthammer argued for an assertive amal-gam of liberalism and realism, which he called "democratic realism." Fukuyama claimed that Krauthammer's faith in the use of force and the feasibility of democratic change in Iraq blinds him to the war's lack of legitimacy, a failing that "hurts both the realist part of our agenda, by diminishing our actual power, and the idealist portion of it, by undercutting our appeal as the embodiment of certain ideas and values."

Indeed, when realism, liberalism, and idealism enter the policymaking arena and public debate,

Figure 1.1. From Theory to Practice

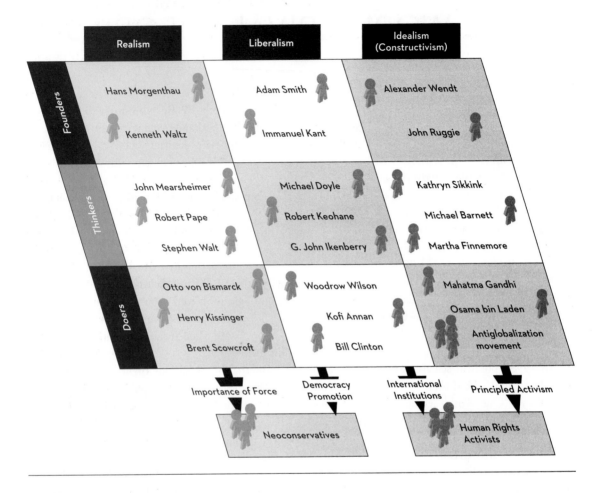

they can sometimes become intellectual window dressing for simplistic worldviews. Properly understood, however, their policy implications are subtle and multifaceted. Realism instills a pragmatic appreciation of the role of power but also warns that states will suffer if they overreach. Liberalism highlights the cooperative potential of mature democracies, especially when working together through effective institutions, but it also notes democracies' tendency to crusade against tyrannies and the propensity of emerging democracies to collapse into violent ethnic turmoil.

Idealism stresses that a consensus on values must underpin any stable political order, yet it also recognizes that forging such a consensus often requires an ideological struggle with the potential for conflict.

Each theory offers a filter for looking at a complicated picture. As such, they help explain the assumptions behind political rhetoric about foreign policy. Even more important, the theories act as a powerful check on each other. Deployed effectively, they reveal the weaknesses in arguments that can lead to misguided policies.

Is Realism Still Realistic?

At realism's core is the belief that international affairs is a struggle for power among self-interested states. Although some of realism's leading lights, notably the late University of Chicago political scientist Hans J. Morgenthau, are deeply pessimistic about human nature, it is not a theory of despair. Clearsighted states can mitigate the causes of war by finding ways to reduce the danger they pose to each other. Nor is realism necessarily amoral; its advocates emphasize that a ruthless pragmatism about power can actually yield a more peaceful world, if not an ideal one.

In liberal democracies, realism is the theory that everyone loves to hate. Developed largely by European émigrés at the end of World War II, realism claimed to be an antidote to the naive belief that international institutions and law alone can preserve peace, a misconception that this new generation of scholars believed had paved the way to war. In recent decades, the realist approach has been most fully articulated by U.S. theorists, but it still has broad appeal outside the United States as well. The influential writer and editor Josef Joffe articulately comments on Germany's strong realist traditions. (Mindful of the overwhelming importance of U.S. power to Europe's development, Joffe once called the United States "Europe's pacifier.") China's current foreign policy is grounded in realist ideas that date back millennia. As China modernizes its economy and enters international institutions such as the World Trade Organization, it behaves in a way that realists understand well: developing its military slowly but surely as its economic power grows, and avoiding a confrontation with superior U.S. forces.

Realism gets some things right about the post-9/11 world. The continued centrality of military strength and the persistence of conflict, even in this age of global economic interdependence, does not surprise realists. The theory's most obvious success is its ability to explain the United States' forceful military response to the September 11 terrorist attacks. When a state grows vastly more powerful than any opponent, realists expect that it will eventually use that power to expand its sphere of domination, whether for security, wealth, or other motives. The United States employed its military power in what some deemed an imperial fashion in large part because it could.

It is harder for the normally state-centric realists to explain why the world's only superpower announced a war against al Qaeda, a nonstate terrorist organization. How can realist theory account for the importance of powerful and violent individuals in a world of states? Realists point out that the central battles in the "war on terror" have been fought against two states (Afghanistan and Iraq), and that states, not the United Nations or Human Rights Watch, have led the fight against terrorism.

Even if realists acknowledge the importance of nonstate actors as a challenge to their assumptions, the theory still has important things to say about the behavior and motivations of these groups. The realist scholar Robert A. Pape, for example, has argued that suicide terrorism can be a rational, realistic strategy for the leadership of national liberation movements seeking to expel democratic powers that occupy their homelands. Other scholars apply standard theories of conflict in anarchy to explain ethnic conflict in collapsed states. Insights from political realism—a profound and wide-ranging intellectual tradition rooted in the enduring philosophy of Thucydides, Niccolò Machiavelli, and Thomas Hobbes—are hardly rendered obsolete because some nonstate groups are now able to resort to violence.

Post-9/11 developments seem to undercut one of realism's core concepts: the balance of power. Standard realist doctrine predicts that weaker states will ally to protect themselves from stronger ones and thereby form and reform a balance of power. So, when Germany unified in the late nineteenth century and became Europe's leading military and industrial power, Russia and France (and later, Britain) soon aligned to counter its power. Yet no combination of states or other powers can challenge the United States militarily, and no balancing coalition is imminent. Realists are scrambling to find a way to fill this hole in the center of their theory. Some theorists speculate that the United States' geographic distance and its relatively benign intentions have tempered the balancing instinct. Second-tier powers tend to worry more about their immediate neighbors and even see the United States as a helpful source of stability in regions such as East Asia. Other scholars insist that armed resistance by U.S. foes in Iraq, Afghanistan, and elsewhere, and foot-dragging by its formal allies actually constitute the beginnings of balancing against U.S. hegemony. The United States' strained relations with Europe offer ambiguous evidence: French and German opposition to recent U.S. policies could be seen as classic balancing, but they do not resist U.S. dominance militarily. Instead, these states have tried to undermine U.S. moral legitimacy and constrain the superpower in a web of multilateral institutions and treaty regimes—not what standard realist theory predicts.

These conceptual difficulties notwithstanding, realism is alive, well, and creatively reassessing how its root principles relate to the post-9/11 world. Despite changing configurations of power, realists remain steadfast in stressing that policy must be based on positions of real strength, not on either empty bravado or hopeful illusions about a world without conflict. In the run-up to the recent Iraq war, several prominent realists signed a public letter criticizing what they perceived as an exercise in American hubris. And in the continuing aftermath of that war, many prominent thinkers called for a return to realism. A group of scholars and public intellectuals (myself included) even formed the Coalition for a Realistic Foreign Policy, which calls for a more modest and prudent approach. Its statement of principles argues that "the move toward empire must be halted immediately." The coalition, though politically diverse, is largely inspired by realist theory. Its membership of seemingly odd bedfellows—including former Democratic Sen. Gary Hart and Scott McConnell, the executive editor of the *American Conservative* magazine—illustrates the power of international relations theory to cut through often ephemeral political labels and carry debate to the underlying assumptions.

The Divided House of Liberalism

The liberal school of international relations theory, whose most famous proponents were German philosopher Immanuel Kant and U.S. President Woodrow Wilson, contends that realism has a stunted vision that cannot account for progress in relations between nations. Liberals foresee a slow but inexorable journey away from the anarchic world the realists envision, as trade and finance forge ties between nations, and democratic norms spread. Because elected leaders are accountable to the people (who bear the burdens of war), liberals expect that democracies will not attack each other and will regard each other's regimes as legitimate and nonthreatening. Many liberals also believe that the rule of law and transparency of democratic processes make it easier to sustain international cooperation, especially when these practices are enshrined in multilateral institutions.

Liberalism has such a powerful presence that the entire U.S. political spectrum, from neoconservatives to human rights advocates, assumes it as largely self-evident. Outside the United States, as well, the liberal view that only elected governments are legitimate and politically reliable has taken hold. So it is no surprise that liberal themes are constantly invoked as a response to today's security dilemmas. But the last several years have also produced a fierce tug-of-war between disparate strains of liberal thought. Supporters and critics of the Bush administration, in particular, have emphasized very different elements of the liberal canon.

For its part, the Bush administration highlights democracy promotion while largely turning its back on the international institutions that most liberal theorists champion. The U.S. National Security Strategy of September 2002, famous for its support of preventive war, also dwells on the need to promote democracy as a means of fighting terrorism and promoting peace. The Millennium Challenge program allocates part of U.S. foreign aid according to how well countries improve their performance on several measures of democratization and the rule of law. The White House's steadfast support for promoting democracy in the Middle East—even with turmoil in Iraq and rising anti-Americanism in the Arab world—demonstrates liberalism's emotional and rhetorical power.

In many respects, liberalism's claim to be a wise policy guide has plenty of hard data behind it. During the last two decades, the proposition that democratic institutions and values help states cooperate with each other is among the most intensively studied in all of international relations, and it has held up reasonably well. Indeed, the belief that democracies never fight wars against each other is the closest thing we have to an iron law in social science.

But the theory has some very important corollaries, which the Bush administration glosses over as it draws upon the democracy-promotion element of liberal thought. Columbia University political scientist Michael W. Doyle's articles on democratic peace warned that, though democracies never fight each other, they are prone to launch messianic struggles against warlike authoritarian regimes to "make the world safe for democracy." It was precisely American democracy's tendency to oscillate between self-righteous crusading and jaded isolationism that prompted early Cold War realists' call for a more calculated, prudent foreign policy.

Countries transitioning to democracy, with weak political institutions, are more likely than other states to get into international and civil wars. In the last fifteen years, wars or large-scale civil violence followed experiments with mass electoral democracy in countries including Armenia, Burundi, Ethiopia, Indonesia, Russia, and the former Yugoslavia. In part, this violence is caused by ethnic groups' competing demands for national self-determination, often a problem in new, multiethnic democracies. More fundamental, emerging democracies often have nascent political institutions that cannot channel popular demands in constructive directions or credibly enforce compromises among rival groups. In this setting, democratic accountability works imperfectly, and nationalist politicians can hijack public debate. The violence that is vexing the experiment with democracy in Iraq is just the latest chapter in a turbulent story that began with the French Revolution.

Contemporary liberal theory also points out that the rising democratic tide creates the presumption that all nations ought to enjoy the benefits of self-determination. Those left out may undertake violent campaigns to secure democratic rights. Some of these movements direct their struggles against democratic or semidemocratic states that they consider occupying powers—such as in Algeria in the 1950s, or Chechnya, Palestine, and the Tamil region of Sri Lanka today. Violence may also be directed at democratic supporters of oppressive regimes, much like the U.S. backing of the governments of Saudi Arabia and Egypt. Democratic regimes make attractive targets for terrorist violence by national liberation movements precisely because they are accountable to a cost-conscious electorate.

Nor is it clear to contemporary liberal scholars that nascent democracy and economic liberalism can always cohabitate. Free trade and the multifaceted globalization that advanced democracies promote often buffet transitional societies. World markets' penetration of societies that run on patronage and protectionism can disrupt social relations and spur strife between potential winners and

Figure 1.2. The Leading Brands

Theories:	Realism	Liberalism	Idealism (Constructivism)
Core Beliefs	Self-interested states compete for power and security	Spread of democracy, global economic ties, and international organizations will strengthen peace	International politics is shaped by persuasive ideas, collective values, culture, and social identities
Key Actors in International Relations	States, which behave similarly regardless of their type of government	States, international institutions, and commercial interests	Promoters of new ideas, transnational activist networks, and nongovernmental organizations
Main Instruments	Military power and state diplomacy	International institutions and global commerce	Ideas and values
Theory's Intellectual Blind Spots	Doesn't account for progress and change in international relations or understanding that legitimacy can be a source of military power	Fails to understand that democratic regimes survive only if they safeguard military power and security; some liberals forget that transitions to democracy are sometimes violent	Does not explain which power structures and social conditions allow for changes in values
What the Theory Explains about the Post-9/11 World	Why the United States responded aggressively to terrorist attacks; the inability of international institutions to restrain military superiority	Why spreading democracy has become such an integral part of current U.S. international security strategy	The increasing role of polemics about values; the importance of transnational political networks (whether terrorists or human rights advocates)
What the Theory Fails to Explain about the Post-9/11 World	The failure of smaller powers to militarily balance the United States; the importance of non-state actors such as al Qaeda; the intense U.S. focus on democratization	Why the United States has failed to work with other democracies through international organizations	Why human rights abuses continue, despite intense activism for humanitarian norms and efforts for international justice

losers. In other cases, universal free trade can make separatism look attractive, as small regions such as Aceh in Indonesia can lay claim to lucrative natural resources. So far, the trade-fueled boom in China has created incentives for improved relations with the advanced democracies, but it has also set the stage for a possible showdown between the relatively wealthy coastal entrepreneurs and the still impoverished rural masses.

While aggressively advocating the virtues of democracy, the Bush administration has shown little patience for these complexities in liberal thought—or for liberalism's emphasis on the importance of international institutions. Far from trying to assure other powers that the United States would adhere to a constitutional order, Bush "unsigned" the International Criminal Court statute, rejected the Kyoto environmental agreement, dictated take-it-or-leave-it arms control changes to Russia, and invaded Iraq despite opposition at the United Nations and among close allies.

Recent liberal theory offers a thoughtful challenge to the administration's policy choices. Shortly before September 11, political scientist G. John Ikenberry studied attempts to establish international order by the victors of hegemonic struggles in 1815, 1919, 1945, and 1989. He argued that even the most powerful victor needed to gain the willing cooperation of the vanquished and other weak states by offering a mutually attractive bargain, codified in an international constitutional order. Democratic victors, he found, have the best chance of creating a working constitutional order, such as the Bretton Woods system after World War II, because their transparency and legalism make their promises credible.

Does the Bush administration's resistance to institution building refute Ikenberry's version of liberal theory? Some realists say it does, and that recent events demonstrate that international institutions cannot constrain a hegemonic power if its preferences change. But international institutions can nonetheless help coordinate outcomes that are in the long-term mutual interest of both the hegemon and the weaker states. Ikenberry did not contend that hegemonic democracies are immune from mistakes. States can act in defiance of the incentives established by their position in the international system, but they will suffer the consequences and probably learn to correct course. In response to Bush's unilateralist stance, Ikenberry wrote that the incentives for the United States to take the lead in establishing a multilateral constitutional order remain powerful. Sooner or later, the pendulum will swing back.

Idealism's New Clothing

Idealism, the belief that foreign policy is and should be guided by ethical and legal standards, also has a long pedigree. Before World War II forced the United States to acknowledge a less pristine reality, Secretary of State Henry Stimson denigrated espionage on the grounds that "gentlemen do not read each other's mail." During the Cold War, such naive idealism acquired a bad name in the Kissingerian corridors of power and among hardheaded academics. Recently, a new version of idealism—called

constructivism by its scholarly adherents—returned to a prominent place in debates on international relations theory. Constructivism, which holds that social reality is created through debate about values, often echoes the themes that human rights and international justice activists sound. Recent events seem to vindicate the theory's resurgence; a theory that emphasizes the role of ideologies, identities, persuasion, and transnational networks is highly relevant to understanding the post-9/11 world.

The most prominent voices in the development of constructivist theory have been American, but Europe's role is significant. European philosophical currents helped establish constructivist theory, and the *European Journal of International Relations* is one of the principal outlets for constructivist work. Perhaps most important, Europe's increasingly legalistic approach to international relations, reflected in the process of forming the European Union out of a collection of sovereign states, provides fertile soil for idealist and constructivist conceptions of international politics.

Whereas realists dwell on the balance of power and liberals on the power of international trade and democracy, constructivists believe that debates about ideas are the fundamental building blocks of international life. Individuals and groups become powerful if they can convince others to adopt their ideas. People's understanding of their interests depends on the ideas they hold. Constructivists find absurd the idea of some identifiable and immutable "national interest," which some realists cherish. Especially in liberal societies, there is overlap between constructivist and liberal approaches, but the two are distinct. Constructivists contend that their theory is deeper than realism and liberalism because it explains the origins of the forces that drive those competing theories.

For constructivists, international change results from the work of intellectual entrepreneurs who proselytize new ideas and "name and shame" actors whose behavior deviates from accepted standards. Consequently, constructivists often study the role of transnational activist networks—such as Human Rights Watch or the International Campaign to Ban Landmines—in promoting change. Such groups typically uncover and publicize information about violations of legal or moral standards at least rhetorically supported by powerful democracies, including "disappearances" during the Argentine military's rule in the late 1970s, concentration camps in Bosnia, and the huge number of civilian deaths from land mines. This publicity is then used to press governments to adopt specific remedies, such as the establishment of a war crimes tribunal or the adoption of a landmine treaty. These movements often make pragmatic arguments as well as idealistic ones, but their distinctive power comes from the ability to highlight deviations from deeply held norms of appropriate behavior.

Progressive causes receive the most attention from constructivist scholars, but the theory also helps explain the dynamics of illiberal transnational forces, such as Arab nationalism or Islamist extremism. Professor Michael N. Barnett's 1998 book *Dialogues in Arab Politics: Negotiations in Regional Order* examines how the divergence between state borders and transnational Arab political identities requires vulnerable leaders to contend for legitimacy with radicals throughout the Arab world—a dynamic that often holds moderates hostage to opportunists who take extreme stances.

Constructivist thought can also yield broader insights about the ideas and values in the current international order. In his 2001 book, *Revolutions in Sovereignty: How Ideas Shaped Modern International Relations*, political scientist Daniel Philpott demonstrates how the religious ideas of the Protestant Reformation helped break down the medieval political order and provided a conceptual basis for the modern system of secular sovereign states. After September 11, Philpott focused on the challenge to the secular international order posed by political Islam. "The attacks and the broader resurgence of public religion," he says, ought to lead international relations scholars to "direct far more

energy to understanding the impetuses behind movements across the globe that are reorienting purposes and policies." He notes that both liberal human rights movements and radical Islamic movements have transnational structures and principled motivations that challenge the traditional supremacy of self-interested states in international politics. Because constructivists believe that ideas and values helped shape the modern state system, they expect intellectual constructs to be decisive in transforming it—for good or ill.

When it comes to offering advice, however, constructivism points in two seemingly incompatible directions. The insight that political orders arise from shared understanding highlights the need for dialogue across cultures about the appropriate rules of the game. This prescription dovetails with liberalism's emphasis on establishing an agreed international constitutional order. And, yet, the notion of cross-cultural dialogue sits awkwardly with many idealists' view that they already know right and wrong. For these idealists, the essential task is to shame rights abusers and cajole powerful actors into promoting proper values and holding perpetrators accountable to international (generally Western) standards. As with realism and liberalism, constructivism can be many things to many people.

Stumped by Change

None of the three theoretical traditions has a strong ability to explain change—a significant weakness in such turbulent times. Realists failed to predict the end of the Cold War, for example. Even after it happened, they tended to assume that the new system would become multipolar ("back to the future," as the scholar John J. Mearsheimer put it). Likewise, the liberal theory of democratic peace is stronger on what happens after states become democratic than in predicting the timing of democratic transitions, let alone prescribing how to make transitions happen peacefully. Constructivists are good at describing changes in norms and ideas, but they are weak on the material and institutional circumstances necessary to support the emergence of consensus about new values and ideas.

With such uncertain guidance from the theoretical realm, it is no wonder that policymakers, activists, and public commentators fall prey to simplistic or wishful thinking about how to effect change by, say, invading Iraq or setting up an International Criminal Court. In lieu of a good theory of change, the most prudent course is to use the insights of each of the three theoretical traditions as a check on the irrational exuberance of the others. Realists should have to explain whether policies based on calculations of power have sufficient legitimacy to last. Liberals should consider whether nascent democratic institutions can fend off powerful interests that oppose them, or how international institutions can bind a hegemonic power inclined to go its own way. Idealists should be asked about the strategic, institutional, or material conditions in which a set of ideas is likely to take hold.

Theories of international relations claim to explain the way international politics works, but each of the currently prevailing theories falls well short of that goal. One of the principal contributions that international relations theory can make is not predicting the future but providing the vocabulary and conceptual framework to ask hard questions of those who think that changing the world is easy.

Thucydides
MELIAN DIALOGUE

Introduction by Suresht Bald

It was the sixteenth year of the Peloponnesian War, but for the last six years the two great feuding empires headed by Athens and Sparta (Lacedaemon) had avoided open hostile action against each other. Ten years into the war they had signed a treaty of peace and friendship; however, this treaty did not dissipate the distrust that existed between them. Each feared the other's hegemonic designs on the Peloponnese and sought to increase its power to thwart the other's ambitions. Without openly attacking the other, each used persuasion, coercion, and subversion to strengthen itself and weaken its rival. This struggle for hegemony by Athens and Sparta was felt most acutely by small, hitherto "independent" states who were now being forced to take sides in the bipolar Greek world of the fifth century B.C. One such state was Melos.

Despite being one of the few island colonies of Sparta, Melos had remained neutral in the struggle between Sparta and Athens. Its neutrality, however, was unacceptable to the Athenians, who, accompanied by overwhelming military and naval power, arrived in Melos to pressure it into submission. After strategically positioning their powerful fleet, the Athenian generals sent envoys to Melos to negotiate the island's surrender.

The commissioners of Melos agreed to meet the envoys in private. They were afraid the Athenians, known for their rhetorical skills, might sway the people if allowed a public forum. The envoys came with an offer that if the Melians submitted

and became part of the Athenian empire, their people and their possessions would not be harmed. The Melians argued that by the law of nations they had the right to remain neutral, and no nation had the right to attack without provocation. Having been a free state for seven hundred years they were not ready to give up that freedom. Thucydides captures the exchange between the Melian commissioners and the Athenian envoys:

* * * The Athenians * * * sent a fleet against the island of Melos. Thirty of the ships were their own, six were from Chios, and two were from Lesbos. Their own troops numbered twelve hundred hoplites, three hundred archers, and twenty mounted archers. There were also about fifteen hundred hoplites from their allies on the islands. The Melians are colonists from Sparta and would not submit to Athenian control like the other islanders. At first, they were neutral and lived peaceably, but they became openly hostile after Athens once tried to compel their obedience by ravaging their land. The generals Cleomedes, son of Lycomedes, and Tisias, son of Tisimachus, bivouacked on Melian territory with their troops, but before doing any injury to the land, they sent ambassadors to hold talks with the Melians. The Melian leadership, however, did not bring these men before the popular assembly. Instead, they asked them to discuss their mission with the council and the privileged voters. The Athenian ambassadors spoke as follows.

"We know that what you are thinking in bringing us before a few voters, and not before the popular assembly, is that now the people won't be deceived after listening to a single long, seductive, and unrefuted speech from us. Well, those of you who are sitting here can make things even safer

From Thucydides, *The Peloponnesian War,* trans. Walter Blanco, ed. Walter Blanco and Jennifer Tolbert Roberts. (New York: W. W. Norton & Co., 1998). Introduction by Suresht Bald, Willamette University.

for yourselves. When we say something that seems wrong, interrupt immediately, and answer, not in a set speech, but one point at a time.—But say first whether this proposal is to your liking."

The Melian councillors said, "There can be no objection to the reasonableness of quiet, instructive talks among ourselves. But this military force, which is here, now, and not off in the future, looks different from instruction. We see that you have come as judges in a debate, and the likely prize will be war if we win the debate with arguments based on right and refuse to capitulate, or servitude if we concede to you."

ATHENIANS

Excuse us, but if you're having this meeting to make guesses about the future or to do anything but look at your situation and see how to save your city, we'll leave. But if that's the topic, we'll keep talking.

MELIANS

It's natural and understandable that in a situation like this, people would want to express their thoughts at length. But so be it. This meeting is about saving our city, and the format of the discussion will be as you have said.

ATHENIANS

Very well.

We Athenians are not going to use false pretenses and go on at length about how we have a right to rule because we destroyed the Persian empire, or about how we are seeking retribution because you did us wrong. You would not believe us anyway. And please do not suppose that you will persuade *us* when you say that you did not campaign with the Spartans although you were their colonists, or that you never did us wrong. No, each of us must exercise what power he really thinks he can, and we know and you know that in the human realm, justice is enforced only among those who can be equally constrained by it, and that those who have power use it, while the weak make compromises.

MELIANS

Since you have ruled out a discussion of justice and forced us to speak of expediency, it would be inexpedient, at least as we see it, for you to eradicate common decency. There has always been a fair and right way to treat people who are in danger, if only to give them some benefit for making persuasive arguments by holding off from the full exercise of power. This applies to you above all, since you would set an example for others of how to take the greatest vengeance if you fall.

ATHENIANS

We're not worried about the end of our empire, if it ever does end. People who rule over others, like the Spartans, are not so bad to their defeated enemies. Anyway, we're not fighting the Spartans just now. What is really horrendous is when subjects are able to attack and defeat their masters.—But you let us worry about all that. We are here to talk about benefiting our empire and saving your city, and we will tell you how we are going to do that, because we want to take control here without any trouble and we want you to be spared for both our sakes.

MELIANS

And just how would it be as much to our advantage to be enslaved, as for you to rule over us?

ATHENIANS

You would benefit by surrendering before you experience the worst of consequences, and we would benefit by not having you dead.

MELIANS

So you would not accept our living in peace, being friends instead of enemies, and allies of neither side?

ATHENIANS

Your hatred doesn't hurt us as much as your friendship. That would show us as weak to our other subjects, whereas your hatred would be a proof of our power.

MELIANS

Would your subjects consider you reasonable if you lumped together colonists who had no connection to you, colonists from Athens, and rebellious colonists who had been subdued?

ATHENIANS

They think there's justice all around. They also think the independent islands are strong, and that we are afraid to attack them. So aside from adding to our empire, your subjugation will also enhance our safety, especially since you are islanders and we are a naval power. Besides, you're weaker than the others—unless, that is, you show that you too can be independent.

MELIANS

Don't you think there's safety in our neutrality? You turned us away from a discussion of justice and persuaded us to attend to what was in your interest. Now it's up to us to tell you about what is to our advantage and to try to persuade you that it is also to yours. How will you avoid making enemies of states that are now neutral, but that look at what you do here and decide that you will go after them one day? How will you achieve anything but to make your present enemies seem more attractive, and to force those who had no intention of opposing you into unwilling hostility?

ATHENIANS

We do not think the threat to us is so much from mainlanders who, in their freedom from fear, will be continually putting off their preparations against us, as from independent islanders, like you, and from those who are already chafing under the restraints of rule. These are the ones who are most likely to commit themselves to ill-considered action and create foreseeable dangers for themselves and for us.

MELIANS

Well then, in the face of this desperate effort you and your slaves are making, you to keep your empire and they to get rid of it, wouldn't we, who are still free, be the lowest of cowards if we didn't try everything before submitting to slavery?

ATHENIANS

No, not if you think about it prudently. This isn't a contest about manly virtue between equals, or about bringing disgrace on yourself. You are deliberating about your very existence, about standing up against a power far greater than yours.

MELIANS

But we know that there are times when the odds in warfare don't depend on the numbers. If we give up, our situation becomes hopeless right away, but if we fight, we can still hope to stand tall.

ATHENIANS

In times of danger, hope is a comfort that can hurt you, but it won't destroy you if you back it up with plenty of other resources. People who gamble everything on it (hope is extravagant by nature, you see) know it for what it really is only after they have lost everything. Then, of course, when you can recognize it and take precautions, it's left you flat. You don't want to experience that. You Melians are weak, and you only have one chance. So don't be like all those people who could have saved themselves by their own efforts, but who abandoned their realistic hopes and turned in their hour of need to invisible powers—to prophecies and oracles and all the other nonsense that conspires with hope to ruin you.

MELIANS

As you well know, we too think it will be hard to fight both your power and the fortunes of war, especially with uneven odds. Still, we believe that our fortune comes from god, and that we will not be defeated because we take our stand as righteous men against men who are in the wrong. And what we lack in power will be made up for by the Spartan League. They will have to help us, if only because of our kinship with them and the disgrace they would feel if they didn't. So it's not totally irrational for us to feel hopeful.

ATHENIANS

Well, when it comes to divine good will, we don't think we'll be left out. We're not claiming anything or doing anything outside man's thinking about the gods or about the way the gods themselves behave. Given what we believe about the gods and know about men, we think that both are always forced by the law of nature to dominate everyone they can. We didn't lay down this law, it was there—and we weren't the first to make use of it. We took it as it was and acted on it, and we will bequeath it as a living thing to future generations, knowing full well that if you or anyone else had the same power as we, you would do the same thing. So we probably don't have to fear any disadvantage when it comes to the gods. And as to this opinion of yours about the Spartans, that you can trust them to help you because of their fear of disgrace—well, our blessings on your innocence, but we don't envy your foolishness. The Spartans do the right thing among themselves, according to their local customs. One could say a great deal about their treatment of others, but to put it briefly, they are more conspicuous than anyone else we know in thinking that pleasure is good and expediency is just. Their mindset really bears no relation to your irrational belief that there is any safety for you now.

MELIANS

But it's exactly because of this expediency that we trust them. They won't want to betray the Melians, their colonists, and prove themselves helpful to their enemies and unreliable to their well-wishers in Greece.

ATHENIANS

But don't you see that expediency is safe, and that doing the right and honorable thing is dangerous? On the whole, the Spartans are the last people to take big risks.

MELIANS

We think they'll take on dangers for us that they wouldn't for others and regard those dangers as less risky, because we are close to the Peloponnese from an operational point of view. Also, they can trust our loyalty because we are kin and we think alike.

ATHENIANS

Men who ask others to come to fight on their side don't offer security in good will but in real fighting power. The Spartans take this kind of thing more into consideration than others, because they have so little faith in their own resources that they even attack their neighbors with plenty of allies. So it's not likely that they'll try to make their way over to an island when we control the sea.

MELIANS

Then maybe they'll send their allies. The sea of Crete is large, and it is harder for those who control the sea to catch a ship than it is for the ship to get through to safety without being noticed. And if that doesn't work, they might turn against your territory or attack the rest of your allies, the ones Brasidas didn't get to. And then the fight would shift from a place where you have no interest to your own land and that of your allies.

ATHENIANS

It's been tried and might even be tried for you—though surely you are aware that we Athenians have never abandoned a siege out of fear of anyone.

But it occurs to us that after saying you were going to talk about saving yourselves, you haven't in any of this lengthy discussion mentioned anything that most people would rely on for their salvation. Your strongest arguments are in the future and depend on hope. What you've actually got is too meager to give you a chance of surviving the forces lined up against you now. You've shown a very irrational attitude—unless, of course, you intend to reach some more prudent conclusion than this after you send us away and begin your deliberations. For surely you don't mean to commit yourselves to that "honor" which has been so destructive to men in clear and present dangers involving "dishonor." Many men who could still see where it was leading them have been drawn on by the allure of this so-called "honor," this word with its seductive power, and fallen with open eyes into irremediable catastrophe, vanquished in their struggle with a fine word, only to achieve a kind of dishonorable honor because they weren't just unlucky, they were fools. You can avoid this, if you think things over carefully, and decide that there is nothing so disgraceful in being defeated by the greatest city in the world, which invites you to become its ally on fair terms—paying us tribute, to be sure, but keeping your land for yourselves. You have been given the choice between war and security. Don't be stubborn and make the wrong choice. The people who are most likely to succeed stand up to their equals, have the right attitude towards their superiors, and are fair to those beneath them.

We will leave now. Think it over, and always remember that you are making a decision about your country. You only have one, and its existence depends on this one chance to make a decision, right or wrong.

Then the Athenians withdrew from the discussion. The Melians, left to themselves, came to the conclusion that had been implied by their responses in the talks. They answered the Athenians as follows: "Men of Athens, our decision is no different from what it was at first. We will not in this brief moment strip the city we have lived in for seven hundred years of its freedom. We will try to save it, trusting in the divine good fortune that has preserved us so far and in the help we expect from the Spartans and from others. We invite you to be our friends, to let us remain neutral, and to leave our territory after making a treaty agreeable to us both."

That was the Melian response. The talks were already breaking up when the Athenians said, "Well, judging from this decision, you seem to us to be the only men who can make out the future more clearly than what you can see, and who gaze upon the invisible with your mind's eye as if it were an accomplished fact. You have cast yourselves on luck, hope, and the Spartans, and the more you trust in them, the harder will be your fall."

Then the Athenian envoys returned to the camp. Since the Melians would not submit, the Athenian generals immediately took offensive action and, after dividing their men according to the cities they came from, began to build a wall around Melos. Later the Athenians left a garrison of their own and allied men to guard the land and sea routes and then withdrew with most of their army. The men who were left behind remained there and carried on the siege.

At about this same time, the Argives invaded the territory of Phlius, where they fell into an ambush set by the Phliasians and the Argive exiles, who killed about eighty of them. The Athenian raiders on Pylos took a great deal of booty from Spartan territory, but despite even this, the Spartans did not renounce the treaty and declare war. They did, however, announce that if any of their people wished to raid Athenian territory, they could do so. The Corinthians made war on the Athenians over some private quarrels, but the rest of the Peloponnesians held their peace. The Melians staged a night attack on the part of the Athenian wall opposite their market and captured it. They killed some men and withdrew into the city carrying grain and as many other useful provisions as they could, taking no further action. The Athenians kept a better watch from then on. And so the summer came to an end.

The following winter, the Spartans were about to march into Argive territory, but the omens from sacrifices made before crossing the border were unfavorable and they turned back. This balked expedition led the Argives to suspect some of their citizens. They arrested some, but others managed to escape. At about the same time, the Melians again captured yet another part of the Athenian wall when only a few men were on guard duty. Because of this, another contingent later came from Athens, under the command of Philocrates, son of Demeas. By now, the Melians were completely cut off, and there were traitors within the city itself. So, on their own initiative, they agreed to terms whereby the Athenians could do with them as they liked. The Athenians thereupon killed all the males of fighting age they could capture and sold the women and children into slavery. The Athenians then occupied the place themselves and later sent out five hundred colonists.

Thomas Hobbes
FROM *LEVIATHAN*

Of the NATURAL CONDITION *of Mankind, as Concerning Their Felicity, and Misery*

Nature hath made men so equal, in the faculties of body, and mind; as that though there be found one man sometimes manifestly stronger in body, or of quicker mind then another; yet when all is reckoned together, the difference between man, and man, is not so considerable, as that one man can thereupon claim to himself any benefit, to which another may not pretend, as well as he. For as to the strength of body, the weakest has strength enough to kill the strongest, either by secret machination, or by confederacy with others, that are in the same danger with himself.

And as to the faculties of the mind (setting aside the arts grounded upon words, and especially that skill of proceeding upon general, and infallible rules, called science; which very few have, and but in few things; as being not a native faculty, born with us; nor attained, (as prudence), while we look after somewhat else), I find yet a greater equality amongst men, than that of strength. For prudence, is but experience; which equal time, equally bestowes on all men, in those things they equally apply themselves unto. That which may perhaps make such equality incredible, is but a vain conceit of one's own wisdom, which almost all men think they have in a greater degree, than the vulgar; that is, than all men but themselves, and a few

others, whom by fame, or for concurring with themselves, they approve. For such is the nature of men, that howsoever they may acknowledge many others to be more witty, or more eloquent, or more learned; yet they will hardly believe there be many so wise as themselves: for they see their own wit at hand, and other men's at a distance. But this proveth rather that men are in that point equal, than unequal. For there is not ordinarily a greater sign of the equal distribution of any thing, than that every man is contented with his share.

From this equality of ability, ariseth equality of hope in the attaining of our ends. And therefore if any two men desire the same thing, which nevertheless they cannot both enjoy, they become enemies; and in the way to their end (which is principally their own conservation, and sometimes their delectation only), endeavour to destroy, or subdue one an other. And from hence it comes to pass, that, where an invader hath no more to fear, than an other man's single power; if one plant, sow, build, or possess a convenient seat, others may probably be expected to come prepared with forces united, to dispossess, and deprive him, not only of the fruit of his labour, but also of his life, or liberty. And the invader again is in the like danger of another.

And from this diffidence of one another, there is no way for any man to secure himself, so reasonable, as anticipation; that is, by force, or wiles, to master the persons of all men he can, so long, till he see no other power great enough to endanger him: And this is no more than his own conservation requireth, and is generally allowed. Also because there be some, that taking pleasure in contemplating their own power in the acts of conquest, which they pursue farther than their security

From Thomas Hobbes, *Leviathan,* ed. A. R. Waller (Cambridge: Cambridge University Press, 1904), 81–86. This excerpt has been edited to contemporary spelling and capitalization.

requires; if others, that otherwise would be glad to be at ease within modest bounds, should not by invasion increase their power, they would not be able, long time, by standing only on their defence, to subsist. And by consequence, such augmentation of dominion over men, being necessary to a man's conservation, it ought to be allowed him.

Again, men have no pleasure (but on the contrary a great deal of grief) in keeping company, where there is no power able to over-awe them all. For every man looketh that his companion should value him, at the same rate he sets upon himself: And upon all signs of contempt, or undervaluing, naturally endeavours, as far as he dares (which amongst them that have no common power to keep them in quiet, is far enough to make them destroy each other), to extort a greater value from his contemners, by dommage; and from others, by the example.

So that in the nature of man, we find three principal causes of quarrel. First, competition; secondly, diffidence; thirdly, glory.

The first, maketh men invade for gain; the second, for safety; and the third, for reputation. The first use violence, to make themselves masters of other men's persons, wives, children, and cattle; the second, to defend them; the third, for trifles, as a word, a smile, a different opinion, and any other sign of undervalue, either direct in their persons, or by reflexion in their kindred, their friends, their nation, their profession, or their name.

Hereby it is manifest, that during the time men live without a common power to keep them all in awe, they are in that condition which is called war; and such a war, as is of every man, against every man. For WAR, consisteth not in battle only, or the act of fighting; but in a tract of time, wherein the will to contend by battle is sufficiently known: and therefore the notion of *time,* is to be considered in the nature of war; as it is in the nature of weather. For as the nature of foul weather, lyeth not in a shower or two of rain; but in an inclination thereto of many days together; So the nature of war, consisteth not in actual fighting; but in the known disposition thereto, during all the *time* there is no assurance to the contrary. All other time is PEACE.

Whatsoever therefore is consequent to a time of war, where every man is enemy to every man; the same is consequent to the time, wherein men live without other security, than what their own strength, and their own invention shall furnish them withal. In such condition, there is no place for industry; because the fruit thereof is uncertain: and consequently no culture of the earth; no navigation, nor use of the commodities that may be imported by sea; no commodious building; no instruments of moving, and removing such things as require much force; no knowledge of the face of the earth; no account of time; no arts; no letters; no society; and which is worst of all, continual fear, and danger of violent death; And the life of man, solitary, poor, nasty, brutish, and short.

It may seem strange to some man, that has not well weighed these things; that nature should thus dissociate, and render men apt to invade, and destroy one another: and he may therefore, not trusting to this inference, made from the passions, desire perhaps to have the same confirmed by experience. Let him therefore consider with himself, when taking a journey, he arms himself, and seeks to go well accompanied; when going to sleep, he locks his doors; when even in his house he locks his chests; and this when he knows there be laws, and public officers, armed, to revenge all injuries shall be done him; what opinion he has of his fellow subjects, when he rides armed; of his fellow citizens, when he locks his doors; and of his children, and servants, when he locks his chests. Does he not there as much accuse mankind by his actions, as I do by my words? But neither of us accuse man's nature in it. The desires, and other passions of man, are in themselves no sin. No more are the actions, that proceed from those passions, till they know a law that forbids them: which till laws be made they cannot know: nor can any law be made, till they have agreed upon the person that shall make it.

It may peradventure be thought, there was never such a time, nor condition of war as this; and I believe it was never generally so, over all the world: but there are many places, where they live so now. For the savage people in many places of *America,* except the government of small families, the concord whereof dependeth on natural lust, have no government at all; and live at this day in that brutish manner, as I said before. Howsoever, it may be perceived what manner of life there would be, where there were no common power to fear; by the manner of life, which men that have formerly lived under a peaceful government, use to degenerate into, in a civil war.

But though there had never been any time, wherein particular men were in a condition of war one against another; yet in all times, kings, and persons of sovereign authority, because of their independency, are in continual jealousies, and in the state and posture of gladiators; having their weapons pointing, and their eyes fixed on one another; that is, their forts, garrisons, and guns upon the frontiers of their kingdoms, and continual spies upon their neighbours; which is a posture of war. But because they uphold thereby, the industry of their subjects; there does not follow from it, that misery, which accompanies the liberty of particular men.

To this war of every man against every man, this also is consequent; that nothing can be unjust. The notions of right and wrong, justice and injustice have there no place. Where there is no common power, there is no law: where no law, no injustice. Force, and fraud, are in war, the two cardinal virtues. Justice, and injustice are none of the faculties neither of the body, nor mind. If they were, they might be in a man that were alone in the world, as well as his senses, and passions. They are qualities, that relate to men in society, not in solitude. It is consequent also to the same condition, that there be no propriety, no dominion, no *mine* and *thine* distinct; but only that to be every man's, that he can get; and for so long, as he can keep it. And thus much for the ill condition, which man by mere nature is actually placed in; though with a possibility to come out of it, consisting partly in the passions, partly in his reason.

The passions that incline men to peace, are fear of death; desire of such things as are necessary to commodious living; and a hope by their industry to obtain them. And reason suggesteth convenient articles of peace, upon which men may be drawn to agreement. These articles, are they, which otherwise are called the laws of nature. * * *

Immanuel Kant
FROM *PERPETUAL PEACE*

The state of peace among men living in close proximity is not the natural state * * *; instead, the natural state is a one of war, which does not just consist in open hostilities, but also in the constant and enduring threat of them. The state of peace must therefore be *established,* for the suspension of hostilities does not provide the security of peace, and unless this security is pledged by one neighbor to another (which can happen only in a state of *lawfulness*), the latter, from whom such security has been requested, can treat the former as an enemy.

First Definitive Article of Perpetual Peace: The Civil Constitution of Every Nation Should Be Republican

The sole established constitution that follows from the idea * * * of an original contract, the one on which all of a nation's just * * * legislation must be based, is republican. For, first, it accords with the principles of the *freedom* of the members of a society (as men), second, it accords with the principles of the *dependence* of everyone on a single, common [source of] legislation (as subjects), and third, it

From Immanuel Kant, *Perpetual Peace and Other Essays on Politics, History, and Morals,* trans. Ted Humphrey (Indianapolis: Hackett Publishing Co., 1983), 107–17. The author's notes have been omitted.

accords with the law of the equality of them all (as citizens). Thus, so far as [the matter of] right is concerned, republicanism is the original foundation of all forms of civil constitution. Thus, the only question remaining is this, does it also provide the only foundation for perpetual peace?

Now in addition to the purity of its origin, a purity whose source is the pure concept of right, the republican constitution also provides for this desirable result, namely, perpetual peace, and the reason for this is as follows: If (as must inevitably be the case, given this form of constitution) the consent of the citizenry is required in order to determine whether or not there will be war, it is natural that they consider all its calamities before committing themselves to so risky a game. (Among these are doing the fighting themselves, paying the costs of war from their own resources, having to repair at great sacrifice the war's devastation, and, finally, the ultimate evil that would make peace itself better, never being able—because of new and constant wars—to expunge the burden of debt.) By contrast, under a nonrepublican constitution, where subjects are not citizens, the easiest thing in the world to do is to declare war. Here the ruler is not a fellow citizen, but the nation's owner, and war does not affect his table, his hunt, his places of pleasure, his court festivals, and so on. Thus, he can decide to go to war for the most meaningless of reasons, as if it were a kind of pleasure party, and he can blithely leave its justification (which decency requires) to his diplomatic corps, who are always prepared for such exercises.

Second Definitive Article for a Perpetual Peace: The Right of Nations Shall Be Based on a Federation of Free States

As nations, peoples can be regarded as single individuals who injure one another through their close proximity while living in the state of nature (i.e., independently of external laws). For the sake of its own security, each nation can and should demand that the others enter into a contract resembling the civil one and guaranteeing the rights of each. This would be a federation *of nations,* but it must not be a nation consisting of nations. The latter would be contradictory, for in every nation there exists the relation of *ruler* (legislator) to *subject* (those who obey, the people); however, many nations in a single nation would constitute only a single nation, which contradicts our assumption (since we are here weighing the rights of *nations* in relation to one another, rather than fusing them into a single nation).

Just as we view with deep disdain the attachment of savages to their lawless freedom—preferring to scuffle without end rather than to place themselves under lawful restraints that they themselves constitute, consequently preferring a mad freedom to a rational one—and consider it barbarous, rude, and brutishly degrading of humanity, so also should we think that civilized peoples (each one united into a nation) would hasten as quickly as possible to escape so similar a state of abandonment. Instead, however, each *nation* sees its majesty * * * to consist in not being subject to any external legal constraint, and the glory of its ruler consists in being able, without endangering himself, to command many thousands to sacrifice themselves for a matter that does not concern them. * * *

Given the depravity of human nature, which is revealed and can be glimpsed in the free relations among nations (though deeply concealed by governmental restraints in law governed civil-society), one must wonder why the word *right* has not been completely discarded from the politics of war as pedantic, or why no nation has openly ventured to declare that it should be. For while Hugo Grotius, Pufendorf, Vattel, and others whose philosophically and diplomatically formulated codes do not and cannot have the slightest legal force (since nations do not stand under any common external constraints), are always piously cited in justification of a war of aggression (and who therefore provide only cold comfort), no example can be given of a nation having foregone its intention [of going to war] based on the arguments provided by such important men. The homage that every nation pays (at least in words) to the concept of right proves, nonetheless, that there is in man a still greater, though presently dormant, moral aptitude to master the evil principle in himself (a principle he cannot deny) and to hope that others will also overcome it. For otherwise the word *right* would never leave the mouths of those nations that want to make war on one another, unless it were used mockingly, as when that Gallic prince declared, "Nature has given the strong the prerogative of making the weak obey them."

Nations can press for their rights only by waging war and never in a trial before an independent tribunal, but war and its favorable consequence, victory, cannot determine the right. And although a *treaty of peace* can put an end to some particular war, it cannot end the state of war (the tendency always to find a new pretext for war). (And this situation cannot straightforwardly be declared unjust, since in this circumstance each nation is judge of its own case.) * * * Nonetheless, from the throne of its moral legislative power, reason absolutely condemns war as a means of determining the right and makes seeking the state of peace a matter of unmitigated duty. But without a contract among nations peace can be neither inaugurated nor guaranteed. A league of a special sort must therefore be established, one that we can call a *league of peace* (*foedus pacificum*), which will be distinguished from a *treaty of peace (pactum pacis)* because the latter seeks merely to stop *one* war, while the former seeks to end *all* wars forever. This league does not seek any power of the sort possessed by nations, but only the maintenance and security of each nation's own freedom, as well as that of the other nations leagued with it, without their having thereby to subject themselves to civil laws and their constraints (as men in the state of nature must do). It can be shown that this *idea of federalism* should eventually include all nations and thus lead to perpetual peace. For if good fortune should so dispose matters that a powerful and enlightened people should form a republic (which by its nature must be inclined to seek perpetual peace), it will provide a focal point for a federal association among other nations that will join it in order to guarantee a state of peace among nations that is in accord with the idea of the right of nations, and through several associations of this sort such a federation can extend further and further.

V. I. Lenin

FROM *IMPERIALISM, THE HIGHEST STAGE OF CAPITALISM*

■ ■ ■

Chapter V

The Division of the World among Capitalist Combines

Monopolist capitalist combines—cartels, syndicates, trusts—divide among themselves, first of all, the whole internal market of a country, and impose their control, more or less completely, upon the industry of that country. But under capitalism the home market is inevitably bound up with the foreign market. Capitalism long ago created a world market. As the export of capital increased, and as the foreign and colonial relations and the "spheres of influence" of the big monopolist combines expanded, things "naturally" gravitated towards an international agreement among these combines, and towards the formation of international cartels.

This is a new stage of world concentration of capital and production, incomparably higher than the preceding stages. Let us see how this super-monopoly develops.

■ ■ ■

From V. I. Lenin, *Imperialism, the Highest Stage Capitalism: A Popular Outline* (New York: International Publishers, 1939). The order of some passages has been changed. The author's notes have been omitted.

Chapter X

The Place of Imperialism in History

We have seen that the economic quintessence of imperialism is monopoly capitalism. This very fact determines its place in history, for monopoly that grew up on the basis of free competition, and precisely out of free competition, is the transition from the capitalist system to a higher social-economic order. We must take special note of the four principal forms of monopoly, or the four principal manifestations of monopoly capitalism, which are characteristic of the epoch under review.

Firstly, monopoly arose out of the concentration of production at a very advanced stage of development. This refers to the monopolist capitalist combines, cartels, syndicates and trusts. We have seen the important part that these play in modern economic life. At the beginning of the twentieth century, monopolies acquired complete supremacy in the advanced countries. And although the first steps towards the formation of the cartels were first taken by countries enjoying the protection of high tariffs (Germany, America), Great Britain, with her system of free trade, was not far behind in revealing the same basic phenomenon, namely, the birth of monopoly out of the concentration of production.

Secondly, monopolies have accelerated the capture of the most important sources of raw materials, especially for the coal and iron industries, which are the basic and most highly cartelised industries in capitalist society. The monopoly of the most important sources of raw materials has enormously increased the power of big capital, and has sharpened the antagonism between cartelised and non-cartelised industry.

Thirdly, monopoly has sprung from the banks. The banks have developed from modest intermediary enterprises into the monopolists of finance capital. Some three or five of the biggest banks in each of the foremost capitalist countries have achieved the "personal union" of industrial and bank capital, and have concentrated in their hands the disposal of thousands upon thousands of millions which form the greater part of the capital and income of entire countries. A financial oligarchy, which throws a close net of relations of dependence over all the economic and political institutions of contemporary bourgeois society without exception—such is the most striking manifestation of this monopoly.

Fourthly, monopoly has grown out of colonial policy. To the numerous "old" motives of colonial policy, finance capital has added the struggle for the sources of raw materials, for the export of capital, for "spheres of influence," *i.e.*, for spheres for profitable deals, concessions, monopolist profits and so on; in fine, for economic territory in general. When the colonies of the European powers in Africa, for instance, comprised only one-tenth of that territory (as was the case in 1876), colonial policy was able to develop by methods other than those of monopoly—by the "free grabbing" of territories, so to speak. But when nine-tenths of Africa had been seized (approximately by 1900), when the whole world had been divided up, there was inevitably ushered in a period of colonial monopoly and, consequently, a period of particularly intense struggle for the division and the redivision of the world.

The extent to which monopolist capital has intensified all the contradictions of capitalism is generally known. It is sufficient to mention the high cost of living and the oppression of the cartels. This intensification of contradictions constitutes the most powerful driving force of the transitional period of history, which began from the time of the definite victory of world finance capital.

Monopolies, oligarchy, the striving for domination instead of the striving for liberty, the exploitation of an increasing number of small or weak nations by an extremely small group of the richest or most powerful nations—all these have given birth to those distinctive characteristics of imperialism which compel us to define it as parasitic or decaying capitalism. More and more prominently there emerges, as one of the tendencies of imperialism, the creation of the "bond-holding" (rentier) state, the usurer state, in which the bourgeoisie lives on the proceeds of capital exports and by clipping coupons. It would be a mistake to believe that this tendency to decay precludes the possibility of the rapid growth of capitalism. It does not. In the epoch of imperialism, certain branches of industry, certain strata of the bourgeoisie and certain countries betray, to a more or less degree, one or other of these tendencies. On the whole, capitalism is growing far more rapidly than before. But this growth is not only becoming more and more uneven in general; its unevenness also manifests itself, in particular, in the decay of the countries which are richest in capital (such as England).

■　　■　　■

When free competition in Great Britain was at its zenith, *i.e.*, between 1840 and 1860, the leading British bourgeois politicians were opposed to colonial policy and were of the opinion that the liberation of the colonies and their complete separation from Britain was inevitable and desirable. M. Beer, in an article, "Modern British Imperialism," published in 1898, shows that in 1852, Disraeli, a statesman generally inclined towards imperialism, declared: "The colonies are millstones round our necks." But at the end of the nineteenth century the heroes of the hour in England were Cecil

Rhodes and Joseph Chamberlain, open advocates of imperialism, who applied the imperialist policy in the most cynical manner.

It is not without interest to observe that even at that time these leading British bourgeois politicians fully appreciated the connection between what might be called the purely economic and the politico-social roots of modern imperialism. Chamberlain advocated imperialism by calling it a "true, wise and economical policy," and he pointed particularly to the German, American and Belgian competition which Great Britain was encountering in the world market. Salvation lies in monopolies, said the capitalists as they formed cartels, syndicates and trusts. Salvation lies in monopolies, echoed the political leaders of the bourgeoisie, hastening to appropriate the parts of the world not yet shared out. The journalist, Stead, relates the following remarks uttered by his close friend Cecil Rhodes, in 1895, regarding his imperialist ideas:

I was in the East End of London yesterday and attended a meeting of the unemployed. I listened to the wild speeches, which were just a cry for "bread," "bread," "bread," and on my way home I pondered over the scene and I became more than ever convinced of the importance of imperialism. . . . My cherished idea is a solution for the social problem, *i.e.,* in order to save the 40,000,000 inhabitants of the United Kingdom from a bloody civil war, we colonial statesmen must acquire new lands to settle the surplus population, to provide new markets for the goods produced by them in the factories and mines. The Empire, as I have always said, is a bread and butter question. If you want to avoid civil war, you must become imperialists.

This is what Cecil Rhodes, millionaire, king of finance, the man who was mainly responsible for the Boer War, said in 1895. * * *

■   ■   ■

* * * The unevenness in the rate of expansion of colonial possessions is very marked. If, for instance, we compare France, Germany and Japan, which do not differ very much in area and population, we will see that the first has annexed almost three times as much colonial territory as the other two combined. In regard to finance capital, also, France, at the beginning of the period we are considering, was perhaps several times richer than Germany and Japan put together. In addition to, and on the basis of, purely economic causes, geographical conditions and other factors also affect the dimensions of colonial possessions. However strong the process of levelling the world, of levelling the economic and living conditions in different countries, may have been in the past decades as a result of the pressure of large-scale industry, exchange and finance capital, great differences still remain; and among the six powers, we see, firstly, young capitalist powers (America, Germany, Japan) which progressed very rapidly; secondly, countries with an old capitalist development (France and Great Britain), which, of late, have made much slower progress than the previously mentioned countries; and, thirdly, a country (Russia) which is economically most backward, in which modern capitalist imperialism is enmeshed, so to speak, in a particularly close network of pre-capitalist relations.

■   ■   ■

Colonial policy and imperialism existed before this latest stage of capitalism, and even before capitalism. Rome, founded on slavery, pursued a colonial policy and achieved imperialism. But "general" arguments about imperialism, which ignore, or put into the background the fundamental difference of social-economic systems, inevitably degenerate into absolutely empty banalities, or into grandiloquent comparisons like "Greater Rome and Greater Britain." Even the colonial policy of capitalism in its *previous* stages is essentially different from the colonial policy of finance capital.

The principal feature of modern capitalism is the domination of monopolist combines of the big capitalists. These monopolies are most firmly established when *all* the sources of raw materials are controlled by the one group. And we have seen with what zeal the international capitalist combines exert every effort to make it impossible for their rivals to compete with them; for example, by buying up mineral lands, oil fields, etc. Colonial possession alone gives complete guarantee of success to the monopolies against all the risks of the struggle with competitors, including the risk that the latter will defend themselves by means of a law establishing a state monopoly. The more capitalism is developed, the more the need for raw materials is felt, the more bitter competition becomes, and the more feverishly the hunt for raw materials proceeds throughout the whole world, the more desperate becomes the struggle for the acquisition of colonies.

■   ■   ■

The bourgeois reformists, and among them particularly the present-day adherents of Kautsky, of course, try to belittle the importance of facts of this kind by arguing that it "would be possible" to obtain raw materials in the open market without a "costly and dangerous" colonial policy; and that it would be "possible" to increase the supply of raw materials to an enormous extent "simply" by improving agriculture. But these arguments are merely an apology for imperialism, an attempt to embellish it, because they ignore the principal feature of modern capitalism: monopoly. Free markets are becoming more and more a thing of the past; monopolist syndicates and trusts are restricting them more and more every day, and "simply" improving agriculture reduces itself to improving the conditions of the masses, to raising wages and reducing profits. Where, except in the imagination of the sentimental reformists, are there any trusts capable of interesting themselves in the condition of the masses instead of the conquest of colonies?

Finance capital is not only interested in the already known sources of raw materials; it is also interested in potential sources of raw materials, because present-day technical development is extremely rapid, and because land which is useless today may be made fertile tomorrow if new methods are applied (to devise these new methods a big bank can equip a whole expedition of engineers, agricultural experts, etc.), and large amounts of capital are invested. This also applies to prospecting for minerals, to new methods of working up and utilising raw materials, etc., etc. Hence, the inevitable striving of finance capital to extend its economic territory and even its territory in general. In the same way that the trusts capitalise their property by estimating it at two or three times its value, taking into account its "potential" (and not present) returns, and the further results of monopoly, so finance capital strives to seize the largest possible amount of land of all kinds and in any place it can, and by any means, counting on the possibilities of finding raw materials there, and fearing to be left behind in the insensate struggle for the last available scraps of undivided territory, or for the repartition of that which has been already divided.

■   ■   ■

The necessity of exporting capital also gives an impetus to the conquest of colonies, for in the colonial market it is easier to eliminate competition, to make sure of orders, to strengthen the necessary "connections," etc., by monoplist methods (and sometimes it is the only possible way).

The non-economic superstructure which grows up on the basis of finance capital, its politics and its ideology, stimulates the striving for colonial conquest. "Finance capital does not want liberty, it wants domination," as Hilferding very truly says. * * *

■　■　■

Since we are speaking of colonial policy in the period of capitalist imperialism, it must be observed that finance capital and its corresponding foreign policy, which reduces itself to the struggle of the Great Powers for the economic and political division of the world, give rise to a number of *transitional* forms of national dependence. The division of the world into two main groups—of colony-owning countries on the one hand and colonies on the other—is not the only typical feature of this period; there is also a variety of forms of dependent countries; countries which, officially, are politically independent, but which are, in fact, enmeshed in the net of financial and diplomatic dependence. We have already referred to one form of dependence—the semi-colony. Another example is provided by Argentina.

"South America, and especially Argentina," writes Schulze-Gaevernitz in his work on British imperialism, "is so dependent financially on London that it ought to be described as almost a British commercial colony."

■　■　■

Chapter VII

Imperialism as a Special Stage of Capitalism

We must now try to sum up and put together what has been said above on the subject of imperialism. Imperialism emerged as the development and direct continuation of the fundamental attributes of capitalism in general. But capitalism only became capitalist imperialism at a definite and very high stage of its development, when certain of its fundamental attributes began to be transformed into their opposites; when the features of a period of transition from capitalism to a higher social and economic system began to take shape and reveal themselves all along the line. Economically, the main thing in this process is the substitution of capitalist monopolies for capitalist free competition. Free competition is the fundamental attribute of capitalism, and of commodity production generally. Monopoly is exactly the opposite of free competition; but we have seen the latter being transformed into monopoly before our very eyes, creating large-scale industry and eliminating small industry, replacing large-scale industry by still larger-scale industry, finally leading to such a concentration of production and capital that monopoly has been and is the result: cartels, syndicates and trusts, and merging with them, the capital of a dozen or so banks manipulating thousands of millions. At the same time monopoly, which has grown out of free competition, does not abolish the latter, but exists over it and alongside of it, and thereby gives rise to a number of very acute, intense antagonisms, friction and conflicts. Monopoly is the transition from capitalism to a higher system.

If it were necessary to give the briefest possible definition of imperialism we should have to say that imperialism is the monopoly stage of capitalism. Such a definition would include what is most important, for, on the one hand, finance capital is the bank capital of a few big monopolist banks, merged with the capital of the monopolist combines of manufacturers; and, on the other hand, the division of the world is the transition from a colonial policy which has extended without hindrance to territories unoccupied by any capitalist power, to a colonial policy of monopolistic possession of the territory of the world which has been completely divided up.

But very brief definitions, although convenient, for they sum up the main points, are nevertheless inadequate, because very important features of the phenomenon that has to be defined have to be especially deduced. And so, without forgetting the conditional and relative value of all definitions, which can never include all the concatenations of a phenomenon in its complete development, we must give a definition of imperialism that will embrace the following five essential features:

1. The concentration of production and capital developed to such a high stage that it created monopolies which play a decisive role in economic life.
2. The merging of bank capital with industrial capital, and the creation, on the basis of this "finance capital," of a "financial oligarchy."
3. The export of capital, which has become extremely important, as distinguished from the export of commodities.
4. The formation of international capitalist monopolies which share the world among themselves.
5. The territorial division of the whole world among the greatest capitalist powers is completed.

Imperialism is capitalism in that stage of development in which the dominance of monopolies and finance capital has established itself; in which the export of capital has acquired pronounced importance; in which the division of the world among the international trusts has begun; in which the division of all territories of the globe among the great capitalist powers has been completed.

■ ■ ■

Another special feature of imperialism, which is connected with the facts we are describing, is the decline in emigration from imperialist countries, and the increase in immigration into these countries from the backward countries where lower wages are paid. As Hobson observes, emigration from Great Britain has been declining since 1884. In that year the number of emigrants was 242,000, while in 1900, the number was only 169,000. German emigration reached the highest point between 1880 and 1890, with a total of 1,453,000 emigrants. In the course of the following two decades, it fell to 544,000 and even to 341,000. On the other hand, there was an increase in the number of workers entering Germany from Austria, Italy, Russia and other countries. According to the 1907 census, there were 1,342,294 foreigners in Germany, of whom 440,800 were industrial workers and 257,329 were agricultural workers. In France, the workers employed in the mining industry are, "in great part," foreigners: Polish, Italian and Spanish. In the United States, immigrants from Eastern and Southern Europe are engaged in the most poorly paid occupations, while American workers provide the highest percentage of overseers or of the better paid workers. Imperialism has the tendency to create privileged sections even among the workers, and to detach them from the main proletarian masses.

It must be observed that in Great Britain the tendency of imperialism to divide the workers, to encourage opportunism among them and to cause temporary decay in the working class movement, revealed itself much earlier than the end of the nineteenth and the beginning of the twentieth centuries; for two important distinguishing features of imperialism were observed in Great Britain in the middle of the nineteenth century, *viz.*, vast colonial possessions and a monopolist position in the world market. Marx and Engels systematically traced this relation between opportunism in the labour movement and the imperialist features of British capitalism for several decades. For example, on October 7, 1858, Engels wrote to Marx:

The English proletariat is becoming more and more bourgeois, so that this most bourgeois of all nations is apparently aiming ultimately at the possession of a bourgeois aristocracy, and a bourgeois proletariat *as well as* a bourgeoisie. For a nation which exploits the whole world— this is, of course, to a certain extent justifiable.

Almost a quarter of a century later, in a letter dated August 11, 1881, Engels speaks of ". . . the worst type of English trade unions which allow themselves to be led by men sold to, or at least, paid by the bourgeoisie." In a letter to Kautsky, dated September 12, 1882, Engels wrote:

You ask me what the English workers think about colonial policy? Well, exactly the same as they think about politics in general. There is no workers' party here, there are only Conservatives and Liberal-Radicals, and the workers merrily share the feast of England's monopoly of the colonies and the world market. . . . [Engels expressed similar ideas in the press in his preface to the second edition of *The Condition of the Working Class in England,* which appeared in 1892.]

We thus see clearly the causes and effects. The causes are: 1) Exploitation of the whole world by this country. 2) Its monopolistic position in the world market. 3) Its colonial monopoly. The effects are: 1) A section of the British proletariat becomes bourgeois. 2) A section of the proletariat permits itself to be led by men sold to, or at least, paid by the bourgeoisie. The imperialism of the beginning of the twentieth century completed the division of the world among a handful of states, each of which today exploits (*i.e.,* draws super-profits from) a part of the world only a little smaller than that which England exploited in 1858. * * *

The distinctive feature of the present situation is the prevalence of economic and political conditions which could not but increase the irreconcilability between opportunism and the general and vital interests of the working class movement. Embryonic imperialism has grown into a dominant system; capitalist monopolies occupy first place in economics and politics; the division of the world has been completed. On the other hand, instead of an undisputed monopoly by Great Britain, we see a few imperialist powers contending for the right to share in this monopoly, and this struggle is characteristic of the whole period of the beginning of the twentieth century. Opportunism, therefore, cannot now triumph in the working class movement of any country for decades as it did in England in the second half of the nineteenth century. But, in a number of countries it has grown ripe, over-ripe, and rotten, and has become completely merged with bourgeois policy in the form of "social-chauvinism."

■　■　■

Chapter IX

The Critique of Imperialism

By the critique of imperialism, in the broad sense of the term, we mean the attiude towards imperialist policy of the different classes of society as part of their general ideology.

The enormous dimensions of finance capital concentrated in a few hands and creating an extremely extensive and close network of ties and relationships which subordinate not only the small and medium, but also even the very small capitalists and small masters, on the one hand, and the intense struggle waged against other national state groups of financiers for the division of the world and domination over other countries, on the other hand, cause the wholesale transition of the possessing classes to the side of imperialism. The signs of the times are a "general" enthusiasm regarding its prospects, a passionate defence of imperialism, and every possible embellishment of its real nature. The imperialist ideology also penetrates the working class. There is no Chinese Wall between it and the other classes. The leaders of the so-called "Social-Democratic" Party of Germany are today justly called "social-imperialists," that is, socialists in words and imperialists in deeds; but as early as 1902, Hobson noted the existence of "Fabian imperialists" who belonged to the opportunist Fabian Society in England.

Bourgeois scholars and publicists usually come out in defence of imperialism in a somewhat veiled form, and obscure its complete domination and its profound roots; they strive to concentrate attention on partial and secondary details and do their very best to distract attention from the main issue by means of ridiculous schemes for "reform," such as police supervision of the trusts and banks, etc. Less frequently, cynical and frank imperialists speak out and are bold enough to admit the absurdity of the idea of reforming the fundamental features of imperialism.

■   ■   ■

2 HISTORICAL CONTEXT

Core ideas about international politics, introduced in Chapter 1 and elaborated in Chapter 3 of *Essentials of International Relations,* Seventh Edition, have emerged as responses to historic diplomatic challenges. The three selections in this chapter were written at the historical and intellectual turning points of the twentieth century: the end of World War I, the end of World War II, and the end of the Cold War. These events spawned many of the ideas and trends that still shape debates about contemporary international politics.

The post–World War I peace process led to a clear statement of the liberal perspective. U.S. President Woodrow Wilson's "Fourteen Points," in an address to Congress in January 1918, summarized some of the key ideas of liberal theory. Wilson blamed power politics, secret diplomacy, and autocratic leaders for the devastating world war. He suggested that with the spread of democracy and the creation of a "league of nations," aggression would be stopped.

The Cold War provides a historical setting for the realist perspective. George F. Kennan, then director of the State Department's Policy Planning Staff, published his famous "Mr. X" article in *Foreign Affairs* in 1947. He assessed Soviet conduct and provided the intellectual justification for Cold War containment policy. Using realist logic, he suggested that counterpressure would have to be applied to prevent Soviet expansion. Today, some argue that challenges to the United States presented by China and Russia could lead to an era that in some respects echoes the containment policies of the Cold War.

At the end of the Cold War in 1989, Francis Fukuyama published a controversial essay, "The End of History," speculating whether the victory of liberal ideas over communism and fascism had left no significant rival ideology in sight. A key question for the future is whether the rise of illiberal China represents a new ideological rival to liberalism based on the principles of national sovereignty, mercantilist economic strategies, cultural conservatism, and authoritarian politics. If so, will these principles attract adherents among other rising powers? Is history beginning again?

Woodrow Wilson
THE FOURTEEN POINTS

It will be our wish and purpose that the processes of peace, when they are begun, shall be absolutely open and that they shall involve and permit henceforth no secret understandings of any kind. The day of conquest and aggrandizement is gone by; so is also the day of secret covenants entered into in the interest of particular governments and likely at some unlooked-for moment to upset the peace of the world. It is this happy fact, now clear to the view of every public man whose thoughts do not still linger in an age that is dead and gone, which makes it possible for every nation whose purposes are consistent with justice and the peace of the world to avow now or at any other time the objects it has in view.

We entered this war because violations of right had occurred which touched us to the quick and made the life of our own people impossible unless they were corrected and the world secured once and for all against their recurrence. What we demand in this war, therefore, is nothing peculiar to ourselves. It is that the world be made fit and safe to live in; and particularly that it be made safe for every peace-loving nation which, like our own, wishes to live its own life, determine its own institutions, be assured of justice and fair dealing by the other people of the world as against force and selfish aggression. All the peoples of the world are in effect partners in this interest, and for our own part we see very clearly that unless justice be done to others it will not be done to us. The program of the world's peace, therefore, is our program; and that program, the only possible program, as we see it, is this:

I. Open covenants of peace, openly arrived at, after which there shall be no private international understandings of any kind but diplomacy shall proceed always frankly and in the public view.

II. Absolute freedom of navigation upon the seas, outside territorial waters, alike in peace and in war, except as the seas may be closed in whole or in part by international action for the enforcement of international covenants.

III. The removal, so far as possible, of all economic barriers and the establishment of an equality of trade conditions among all the nations consenting to the peace and associating themselves for its maintenance.

IV. Adequate guarantees given and taken that national armaments will be reduced to the lowest point consistent with domestic safety.

V. A free, open-minded, and absolutely impartial adjustment of all colonial claims, based upon a strict observance of the principle that in determining all such questions of sovereignty the interests of the populations concerned must have equal weight with the equitable claims of the government whose title is to be determined.

VI. The evacuation of all Russian territory and such a settlement of all questions affecting Russia as will secure the best and freest cooperation of the other nations of the world in obtaining for her

From Woodrow Wilson's address to the U.S. Congress, January 8, 1918.

an unhampered and unembarrassed opportunity for the independent determination of her own political development and national policy and assure her of a sincere welcome into the society of free nations under institutions of her own choosing; and, more than a welcome, assistance also of every kind that she may need and may herself desire. The treatment accorded Russia by her sister nations in the months to come will be the acid test of their good will, of their comprehension of her needs as distinguished from their own interests, and of their intelligent and unselfish sympathy.

VII. Belgium, the whole world will agree, must be evacuated and restored, without any attempt to limit the sovereignty which she enjoys in common with all other free nations. No other single act will serve as this will serve to restore confidence among the nations in the laws which they have themselves set and determined for the government of their relations with one another. Without this healing act the whole structure and validity of international law is forever impaired.

VIII. All French territory should be freed and the invaded portions restored, and the wrong done to France by Prussia in 1871 in the matter of Alsace-Lorraine, which has unsettled the peace of the world for nearly fifty years, should be righted, in order that peace may once more be made secure in the interest of all.

IX. A readjustment of the frontiers of Italy should be effected along clearly recognizable lines of nationality.

X. The peoples of Austria-Hungary, whose place among the nations we wish to see safeguarded and assured, should be accorded the freest opportunity of autonomous development.

XI. Rumania, Serbia, and Montenegro should be evacuated; occupied territories restored; Serbia accorded free and secure access to the sea; and the relations of the several Balkan states to one another determined by friendly counsel along historically established lines of allegiance and nationality; and international guarantees of the political and economic independence and territorial integrity of the several Balkan states should be entered into.

XII. The Turkish portions of the present Ottoman Empire should be assured a secure sovereignty, but the other nationalities which are now under Turkish rule should be assured an undoubted security of life and an absolutely unmolested opportunity of autonomous development, and the Dardanelles should be permanently opened as a free passage to the ships and commerce of all nations under international guarantees.

XIII. An independent Polish state should be erected which should include the territories inhabited by indisputably Polish populations, which should be assured a free and secure access to the sea, and whose political and economic independence and territorial integrity should be guaranteed by international covenant.

XIV. A general association of nations must be formed under specific covenants for the purpose of affording mutual guarantees of political independence and territorial integrity to great and small states alike.

In regard to these essential rectifications of wrong and assertions of right we feel ourselves to be intimate partners of all the governments and peoples associated together against the imperialists. We cannot be separated in interest or divided in purpose. We stand together until the end.

For such arrangements and covenants we are willing to fight and to continue to fight until they are achieved; but only because we wish the right to prevail and desire a just and stable peace such as can be secured only by removing the chief provocations to war, which this program does remove. We have no jealousy of German greatness, and there is nothing in this program that impairs it. We grudge her no achievement or distinction of learning or of pacific enterprise such as have made her record very bright and very enviable. We do not wish to injure her or to block in any way her legitimate influence or power. We do not wish to fight her either with arms or with hostile arrangements of trade if she is willing to associate herself with us and the other peace-loving nations of the world in covenants of justice and law and fair dealing. We wish her only to accept a place of equality among the peoples of the world—the new world in which we now live—instead of a place of mastery.

Neither do we presume to suggest to her any alteration or modification of her institutions. But it is necessary, we must frankly say, and necessary as a preliminary to any intelligent dealings with her on our part, that we should know whom her spokesmen speak for when they speak to us, whether for the Reichstag majority or for the military party and the men whose creed is imperial domination.

We have spoken now, surely, in terms too concrete to admit of any further doubt or question. An evident principle runs through the whole program I have outlined. It is the principle of justice to all peoples and nationalities, and their right to live on equal terms of liberty and safety with one another, whether they be strong or weak. Unless this principle be made its foundation no part of the structure of international justice can stand. The people of the United States could act upon no other principle; and to the vindication of this principle they are ready to devote their lives, their honor, and everything that they possess. The moral climax of this the culminating and final war for human liberty has come, and they are ready to put their own strength, their own highest purpose, their own integrity and devotion to the test.

George F. Kennan ("X")
THE SOURCES OF SOVIET CONDUCT

I

The political personality of Soviet power as we know it today is the product of ideology and circumstances: ideology inherited by the present Soviet leaders from the movement in which they had their political origin, and circumstances of the power which they now have exercised for nearly three decades in Russia. There can be few tasks of psychological analysis more difficult than to try to trace the interaction of these two forces and the relative role of each in the determination of official Soviet conduct. Yet the attempt must be made if that conduct is to be understood and effectively countered.

It is difficult to summarize the set of ideological concepts with which the Soviet leaders came into power. Marxian ideology, in its Russian-Communist projection, has always been in process of subtle evolution. The materials on which it bases itself are extensive and complex. But the outstanding features of Communist thought as it existed in 1916 may perhaps be summarized as follows: (*a*) that the central factor in the life of man, the fact which determines the character of public life and the "physiognomy of society," is the system by which material goods are produced and exchanged; (*b*) that the capitalist system of production is a nefarious one which inevitably leads to the exploitation of the working class by the capital-owning class and is incapable of developing adequately the economic resources of society or of distributing fairly the material goods produced by human labor; (*c*) that capitalism contains the seeds of its own destruction and must, in view of the inability of the capital-owning class to adjust itself to economic change, result eventually and inescapably in a revolutionary transfer of power to the working class; and (*d*) that imperialism, the final phase of capitalism, leads directly to war and revolution.

■ ■ ■

Now it must be noted that through all the years of preparation for revolution, the attention of these men, as indeed of Marx himself, had been centered less on the future form which Socialism[1] would take than on the necessary overthrow of rival power which, in their view, had to precede the introduction of Socialism. Their views, therefore, on the positive program to be put into effect, once power was attained, were for the most part nebulous, visionary and impractical. Beyond the nationalization of industry and the expropriation of large private capital holdings there was no agreed program. The treatment of the peasantry, which according to the Marxist formulation was not of the proletariat, had always been a vague spot in the pattern of Communist thought; and it remained an object of controversy and vacillation for the first ten years of Communist power.

The circumstances of the immediate post-Revolution period—the existence in Russia of civil war and foreign intervention, together with the obvious fact that the Communists represented only a tiny minority of the Russian people—made

From *Foreign Affairs* 25, no. 4 (July 1947): 566–82.

the establishment of dictatorial power a necessity. The experiment with "war Communism" and the abrupt attempt to eliminate private production and trade had unfortunate economic consequences and caused further bitterness against the new revolutionary regime. While the temporary relaxation of the effort to communize Russia, represented by the New Economic Policy, alleviated some of this economic distress and thereby served its purpose, it also made it evident that the "capitalistic sector of society" was still prepared to profit at once from any relaxation of governmental pressure, and would, if permitted to continue to exist, always constitute a powerful opposing element to the Soviet regime and a serious rival for influence in the country. Somewhat the same situation prevailed with respect to the individual peasant who, in his own small way, was also a private producer.

Lenin, had he lived, might have proved a great enough man to reconcile these conflicting forces to the ultimate benefit of Russian society, though this is questionable. But be that as it may, Stalin, and those whom he led in the struggle for succession to Lenin's position of leadership, were not the men to tolerate rival political forces in the sphere of power which they coveted. Their sense of insecurity was too great. Their particular brand of fanaticism, unmodified by any of the Anglo-Saxon traditions of compromise, was too fierce and too jealous to envisage any permanent sharing of power. From the Russian-Asiatic world out of which they had emerged they carried with them a skepticism as to the possibilities of permanent and peaceful coexistence of rival forces. Easily persuaded of their own doctrinaire "rightness," they insisted on the submission or destruction of all competing power. Outside of the Communist Party, Russian society was to have no rigidity. There were to be no forms of collective human activity or association which would not be dominated by the Party. No other force in Russian society was to be permitted to achieve vitality or integrity. Only the Party was to have structure. All else was to be an amorphous mass.

And within the Party the same principle was to apply. The mass of Party members might go through the motions of election, deliberation, decision and action; but in these motions they were to be animated not by their own individual wills but by the awesome breath of the Party leadership and the overbrooding presence of "the world."

Let it be stressed again that subjectively these men probably did not seek absolutism for its own sake. They doubtless believed—and found it easy to believe—that they alone knew what was good for society and that they would accomplish that good once their power was secure and unchallengeable. But in seeking that security of their own rule they were prepared to recognize no restrictions, either of God or man, on the character of their methods. And until such time as that security might be achieved, they placed far down on their scale of operational priorities the comforts and happiness of the peoples entrusted to their care.

Now the outstanding circumstance concerning the Soviet regime is that down to the present day this process of political consolidation has never been completed and the men in the Kremlin have continued to be predominantly absorbed with the struggle to secure and make absolute the power which they seized in November 1917. They have endeavored to secure it primarily against forces at home, within Soviet society itself. But they have also endeavored to secure it against the outside world. For ideology, as we have seen, taught them that the outside world was hostile and that it was their duty eventually to overthrow the political forces beyond their borders. The powerful hands of Russian history and tradition reached up to sustain them in this feeling. Finally, their own aggressive intransigence with respect to the outside world began to find its own reaction; and they were soon forced, to use another Gibbonesque phrase [from Edward Gibbon, *The Decline and Fall of the Roman Empire*], "to chastise the contumacy" which they themselves had provoked. It is an undeniable privilege of every man to prove himself right in the thesis that the world is his enemy; for if he reiterates it frequently enough and makes it the background of his conduct he is bound eventually to be right.

Now it lies in the nature of the mental world of the Soviet leaders, as well as in the character of their ideology, that no opposition to them can be officially recognized as having any merit or justification whatsoever. Such opposition can flow, in theory, only from the hostile and incorrigible forces of dying capitalism. As long as remnants of capitalism were officially recognized as existing in Russia, it was possible to place on them, as an internal element, part of the blame for the maintenance of a dictatorial form of society. But as these remnants were liquidated, little by little, this justification fell away; and when it was indicated officially that they had been finally destroyed, it disappeared altogether. And this fact created one of the most basic of the compulsions which came to act upon the Soviet regime: since capitalism no longer existed in Russia and since it could not be admitted that there could be serious or widespread opposition to the Kremlin springing spontaneously from the liberated masses under its authority, it became necessary to justify the retention of the dictatorship by stressing the menace of capitalism abroad.

■ ■ ■

Now the maintenance of this pattern of Soviet power, namely, the pursuit of unlimited authority domestically, accompanied by the cultivation of the semi-myth of implacable foreign hostility, has gone far to shape the actual machinery of Soviet power as we know it today. Internal organs of administration which did not serve this purpose withered on the vine. Organs which did serve this purpose became vastly swollen. The security of Soviet power came to rest on the iron discipline of the Party, on the severity and ubiquity of the secret police, and on the uncompromising economic monopolism of the state. The "organs of suppression," in which the Soviet leaders had sought security from rival forces, became in large measure the masters of those whom they were designed to serve. Today the major part of the structure of Soviet power is committed to the perfection of the dictatorship and to the maintenance of the concept of Russia as in a state of siege, with the enemy lowering beyond the walls. And the millions of human beings who form that part of the structure of power must defend at all costs this concept of Russia's position, for without it they are themselves superfluous.

As things stand today, the rulers can no longer dream of parting with these organs of suppression. The quest for absolute power, pursued now for nearly three decades with a ruthlessness unparalleled (in scope at least) in modern times, has again produced internally, as it did externally, its own reaction. The excesses of the police apparatus have fanned the potential opposition to the regime into something far greater and more dangerous than it could have been before those excesses began.

But least of all can the rulers dispense with the fiction by which the maintenance of dictatorial power has been defended. For this fiction has been canonized in Soviet philosophy by the excesses already committed in its name; and it is now anchored in the Soviet structure of thought by bonds far greater than those of mere ideology.

II

So much for the historical background. What does it spell in terms of the political personality of Soviet power as we know it today?

Of the original ideology, nothing has been officially junked. Belief is maintained in the basic badness of capitalism, in the inevitability of its destruction, in the obligation of the proletariat to assist in that destruction and to take power into its own hands. But stress has come to be laid primarily on those concepts which relate most specifically to the Soviet regime itself: to its position as the sole truly Socialist regime in a dark and misguided world, and to the relationships of power within it.

The first of these concepts is that of the innate antagonism between capitalism and Socialism. We have seen how deeply that concept has become imbedded in foundations of Soviet power. It has profound implications for Russia's conduct as a member of international society. It means that there can never be on Moscow's side any sincere assumption of a community of aims between the Soviet Union and powers which are regarded as capitalism. It must invariably be assumed in Moscow that the aims of the capitalist world are antagonistic to the Soviet regime and, therefore, to the interests of the peoples it controls. If the Soviet Government occasionally sets its signature to documents which would indicate the contrary, this is to be regarded as a tactical maneuver permissible in dealing with the enemy (who is without honor) and should be taken in the spirit of *caveat emptor* [let the buyer beware]. Basically, the antagonism remains. It is postulated. And from it flow many of the phenomena which we find disturbing in the Kremlin's conduct of foreign policy: the secretiveness, the lack of frankness, the duplicity, the war suspiciousness, and the basic unfriendliness of purpose. These phenomena are there to stay, for the foreseeable future. There can be variations of degree and of emphasis. When there is something the Russians want from us, one or the other of these features of their policy may be thrust temporarily into the background; and when that happens there will always be Americans who will leap forward with gleeful announcements that "the Russians have changed," and some who will even try to take credit for having brought about such "changes." But we should not be misled by tactical maneuvers. These characteristics of Soviet policy, like the postulate from which they flow, are basic to the internal nature of Soviet power, and will be with us, whether in the foreground or the background, until the internal nature of Soviet power is changed.

This means that we are going to continue for a long time to find the Russians difficult to deal with. It does not mean that they should be considered as embarked upon a do-or-die program to overthrow our society by a given date. The theory of the inevitability of the eventual fall of capitalism has the fortunate connotation that there is no hurry about it. * * *

■　■　■

* * * [T]he Kremlin is under no ideological compulsion to accomplish its purposes in a hurry. Like the Church, it is dealing in ideological concepts which are of long-term validity, and it can afford to be patient. It has no right to risk the existing achievements of the revolution for the sake of vain baubles of the future. The very teachings of Lenin himself require great caution and flexibility in the pursuit of Communist purposes. Again, these precepts are fortified by the lessons of Russian history: of centuries of obscure battles between nomadic forces over the stretches of a vast unfortified plain. Here caution, circumspection, flexibility and deception are the valuable qualities; and their value finds natural appreciation in the Russian or the oriental mind. Thus the Kremlin has no compunction about retreating in the face of superior force. And being under the compulsion of no timetable, it does not get panicky under the necessity for such retreat. Its political action is a fluid stream which moves constantly, wherever it is permitted to move, toward a given goal. Its main concern is to make sure that it has filled every nook and cranny available to it in the basin of world power. But if it finds unassailable barriers in its path, it accepts these philosophically and accommodates itself to them. The main thing is that there should always be pressure, increasing constant pressure, toward the desired goal. There is no trace of any feeling in Soviet psychology that the goal must be reached at any given time.

These considerations make Soviet diplomacy at once easier and more difficult to deal with than the diplomacy of individual aggressive leaders like Napoleon and Hitler. On the one hand it is more sensitive to contrary force, more ready to yield on individual sectors of the diplomatic front when that force is felt to be too strong, and thus more rational in the logic and rhetoric of power. On the other hand it cannot be easily defeated or discouraged by a single victory on the part of its opponents. And the patient persistence by which it is animated means that it can be effectively countered not by sporadic acts which represent the momentary whims of democratic opinion but only by intelligent long-range policies on the part of Russia's adversaries—policies no less steady in their purpose, and no less variegated and resourceful in their application, than those of the Soviet Union itself.

In these circumstances it is clear that the main element of any United States policy toward the Soviet Union must be that of a long-term, patient but firm and vigilant containment of Russian expansive tendencies. It is important to note, however, that such a policy has nothing to do with outward histrionics: with threats or blustering or superfluous gestures of outward "toughness." While the Kremlin is basically flexible in its reaction to political realities, it is by no means unamenable to considerations of prestige. Like almost any other government, it can be placed by tactless and threatening gestures in a position where it cannot afford to yield even though this might be dictated by its sense of realism. The Russian leaders are keen judges of human psychology, and as such they are highly conscious that loss of temper and of self-control is never a source of strength in political affairs. They are quick to exploit such evidences of weakness. For these reasons, it is a *sine qua non* of successful dealing with Russia that the foreign government in question should remain at all times cool and collected and that its demands on Russian policy should be put forward in such a manner as to leave the way open for a compliance not too detrimental to Russian prestige.

III

In the light of the above, it will be clearly seen that the Soviet pressure against the free institutions of the Western world is something that can be contained by the adroit and vigilant application of counter-force at a series of constantly shifting geographical and political points, corresponding to the shifts and maneuvers of Soviet policy, but which cannot be charmed or talked out of existence. * * *

■   ■   ■

IV

■   ■   ■

But in actuality the possibilities for American policy are by no means limited to holding the line and hoping for the best. It is entirely possible for the United States to influence by its actions the internal developments, both within Russia and throughout the international Communist movement, by which Russian policy is largely determined. This is not only a question of the modest measure of informational activity which this government can conduct in the Soviet Union and elsewhere, although that, too, is important. It is rather a question of the degree to which the United States can create among the peoples of the world generally the impression of a country which knows what it wants, which is coping successfully with the problems of its internal life and with the responsibilities of a World Power, and which has a spiritual vitality capable of holding its own among the major ideological currents of the time. To the extent that such an impression can be created and maintained, the aims of Russian Communism must appear sterile and quixotic, the hopes and enthusiasm of Moscow's supporters must wane, and added strain must be imposed on the Kremlin's foreign policies. For the palsied decrepitude of the capitalist world is the keystone of Communist philosophy. Even the failure of the United States to experience the early economic depression which the ravens of the Red Square have been predicting with such complacent confidence since hostilities ceased would have deep and important repercussions throughout the Communist world.

By the same token, exhibitions of indecision, disunity and internal disintegration within this country have an exhilarating effect on the whole Communist movement. * * *

* * * [T]he United States has it in its power to increase enormously the strains under which Soviet policy must operate, to force upon the Kremlin a far greater degree of moderation and circumspection than it has had to observe in recent years, and in this way to promote tendencies which must eventually find their outlet in either the break-up or the gradual mellowing of Soviet power. For no mystical, Messianic movement—and particularly not that of the Kremlin—can face frustration indefinitely without eventually adjusting itself in one way or another to the logic of that state of affairs.

■   ■   ■

NOTE

1. Here and elsewhere in this paper "Socialism" refers to Marxist or Leninist Communism. * * *

Francis Fukuyama

THE END OF HISTORY?

In watching the flow of events over the past decade or so, it is hard to avoid the feeling that something very fundamental has happened in world history. The past year has seen a flood of articles commemorating the end of the Cold War, and the fact that "peace" seems to be breaking out in many regions of the world. Most of these analyses lack any larger conceptual framework for distinguishing between what is essential and what is contingent or accidental in world history, and are predictably superficial. If Mr. Gorbachev were ousted from the Kremlin or a new Ayatollah proclaimed the millennium from a desolate Middle Eastern capital, these same commentators would scramble to announce the rebirth of a new era of conflict.

And yet, all of these people sense dimly that there is some larger process at work, a process that gives coherence and order to the daily headlines. The twentieth century saw the developed world descend into a paroxysm of ideological violence, as liberalism contended first with the remnants of absolutism, then bolshevism and fascism, and finally an updated Marxism that threatened to lead to the ultimate apocalypse of nuclear war. But the century that began full of self-confidence in the ultimate triumph of Western liberal democracy seems at its close to be returning full circle to where it started: not to an "end of ideology" or a convergence between capitalism and socialism, as earlier predicted, but to an unabashed victory of economic and political liberalism.

The triumph of the West, of the Western *idea*, is evident first of all in the total exhaustion of viable systematic alternatives to Western liberalism. In the past decade, there have been unmistakable changes in the intellectual climate of the world's two largest communist countries, and the beginnings of significant reform movements in both. But this phenomenon extends beyond high politics and it can be seen also in the ineluctable spread of consumerist Western culture in such diverse contexts as the peasants' markets and color television sets now omnipresent throughout China, the cooperative restaurants and clothing stores opened in the past year in Moscow, the Beethoven piped into Japanese department stores, and the rock music enjoyed alike in Prague, Rangoon, and Tehran.

What we may be witnessing is not just the end of the Cold War, or the passing of a particular period of postwar history, but the end of history as such: that is, the end point of mankind's ideological evolution and the universalization of Western liberal democracy as the final form of human government. This is not to say that there will no longer be events to fill the pages of *Foreign Affairs*'s yearly summaries of international relations, for the victory of liberalism has occurred primarily in the realm of ideas or consciousness and is as yet incomplete in the real or material world. But there are powerful reasons for believing that it is the ideal that will govern the material world *in the long run*. To understand how this is so, we must first consider some theoretical issues concerning the nature of historical change.

I

From *The National Interest* 16 (Summer 1989): 3–18. Some of the author's notes have been omitted.

The notion of the end of history is not an original one. Its best known propagator was Karl Marx, who believed that the direction of historical development was a purposeful one determined by the interplay of material forces, and would come to an end only with the achievement of a communist Utopia that would finally resolve all prior contradictions. But the concept of history as a dialectical process with a beginning, a middle, and an end was borrowed by Marx from his great German predecessor, Georg Wilhelm Friedrich Hegel.

For better or worse, much of Hegel's historicism has become part of our contemporary intellectual baggage. The notion that mankind has progressed through a series of primitive stages of consciousness on his path to the present, and that these stages corresponded to concrete forms of social organization, such as tribal, slave-owning, theocratic, and finally democratic-egalitarian societies, has become inseparable from the modern understanding of man. Hegel was the first philosopher to speak the language of modern social science, insofar as man for him was the product of his concrete historical and social environment and not, as earlier natural right theorists would have it, a collection of more or less fixed "natural" attributes. The mastery and transformation of man's natural environment through the application of science and technology was originally not a Marxist concept, but a Hegelian one. Unlike later historicists whose historical relativism degenerated into relativism *tout court,* however, Hegel believed that history culminated in an absolute moment—a moment in which a final, rational form of society and state became victorious.

It is Hegel's misfortune to be known now primarily as Marx's precursor, and it is our misfortune that few of us are familiar with Hegel's work from direct study, but only as it has been filtered through the distorting lens of Marxism. In France, however, there has been an effort to save Hegel from his Marxist interpreters and to resurrect him as the philosopher who most correctly speaks to our time. Among those modern French interpreters of Hegel, the greatest was certainly Alexandre Kojève, a brilliant Russian emigre who taught a highly influential series of seminars in Paris in the 1930s at the *Ecole Practique des Hautes Etudes*.[1] While largely unknown in the United States, Kojève had a major impact on the intellectual life of the continent. Among his students ranged such future luminaries as Jean-Paul Sartre on the Left and Raymond Aron on the Right; postwar existentialism borrowed many of its basic categories from Hegel via Kojève.

Kojève sought to resurrect the Hegel of the *Phenomenology of Mind*, the Hegel who proclaimed history to be at an end in 1806. For as early as this Hegel saw in Napoleon's defeat of the Prussian monarchy at the Battle of Jena the victory of the ideals of the French Revolution, and the imminent universalization of the state incorporating the principles of liberty and equality. Kojève, far from rejecting Hegel in light of the turbulent events of the next century and a half, insisted that the latter had been essentially correct. The Battle of Jena marked the end of history because it was at that point that the *vanguard* of humanity (a term quite familiar to Marxists) actualized the principles of the French Revolution. While there was considerable work to be done after 1806—abolishing slavery and the slave trade, extending the franchise to workers, women, blacks, and other racial minorities, etc.—the basic *principles* of the liberal democratic state could not be improved upon. The two world wars in this century and their attendant revolutions and upheavals simply had the effect of extending those principles spatially, such that the various provinces of human civilization were brought up to the level of its most advanced outposts, and of forcing those societies in Europe and North America at the vanguard of civilization to implement their liberalism more fully.

The state that emerges at the end of history is liberal insofar as it recognizes and protects through a system of law man's universal right to freedom, and democratic insofar as it exists only with the consent of the governed. For Kojève, this so-called "universal homogenous state" found real-life embodiment in the countries of postwar Western Europe—precisely those flabby, prosperous, self-satisfied, inward-looking, weak-willed states whose grandest project was nothing more heroic than the creation of the Common Market. But this was only to be expected. For human history and the conflict that characterized it was based on the existence of "contradictions": primitive man's quest for mutual recognition, the dialectic of the master and slave, the transformation and mastery of nature, the struggle for the universal recognition of rights, and the dichotomy between proletarian and capitalist. But in the universal homogenous state, all prior contradictions are resolved and all human needs are satisfied. There is no struggle or conflict over "large" issues, and consequently no need for generals or statesmen; what remains is primarily economic activity. * * *

II

For Hegel, the contradictions that drive history exist first of all in the realm of human consciousness, i.e. on the level of ideas—not the trivial election year proposals of American politicians, but ideas in the sense of large unifying world views that might best be understood under the rubric of ideology. Ideology in this sense is not restricted to the secular and explicit political doctrines we usually associate with the term, but can include religion, culture, and the complex of moral values underlying any society as well.

■   ■   ■

For Hegel, all human behavior in the material world, and hence all human history, is rooted in a prior state of consciousness—an idea similar to the one expressed by John Maynard Keynes when he said that the views of men of affairs were usually derived from defunct economists and academic scribblers of earlier generations. * * *

Hegel's idealism has fared poorly at the hands of later thinkers. Marx reversed the priority of the real and the ideal completely, relegating the entire realm of consciousness—religion, art, culture, philosophy itself—to a "superstructure" that was determined entirely by the prevailing material mode of production. Yet another unfortunate legacy of Marxism is our tendency to retreat into materialist or utilitarian explanations of political or historical phenomena, and our disinclination to believe in the autonomous power of ideas. A recent example of this is Paul Kennedy's hugely successful *The Rise and Fall of the Great Powers,* which ascribes the decline of great powers to simple economic overextension. Obviously, this is true on some level: an empire whose economy is barely above the level of subsistence cannot bankrupt its treasury indefinitely. But whether a highly productive modern industrial society chooses to spend 3 or 7 percent of its GNP on defense rather than consumption is entirely a matter of that society's political priorities, which are in turn determined in the realm of consciousness.

■   ■   ■

III

Have we in fact reached the end of history? Are there, in other words, any fundamental "contradictions" in human life that cannot be resolved in the context of modern liberalism, that would be resolvable by an alternative political-economic structure? If we accept the idealist premises laid out above, we must seek an answer to this question in the realm of ideology and consciousness. Our task is not to answer exhaustively the challenges to liberalism promoted by every crackpot messiah around the world, but only those that are embodied in important social or political forces and movements, and which are therefore part of world history. For our purposes, it matters very little what strange thoughts occur to people in Albania or Burkina Faso, for we are interested in what one could in some sense call the common ideological heritage of mankind.

In the past century, there have been two major challenges to liberalism, those of fascism and of communism. The former saw the political weakness, materialism, anomie, and lack of community of the West as fundamental contradictions in liberal societies that could only be resolved by a strong state that forged a new "people" on the basis of national exclusiveness. Fascism was destroyed as a living ideology by World War II. This was a defeat, of course, on a very material level, but it amounted to a defeat of the idea as well. What destroyed fascism as an idea was not universal moral revulsion against it, since plenty of people were willing to endorse the idea as long as it seemed the wave of the future, but its lack of success. After the war, it seemed to most people that German fascism as well as its other European and Asian variants were bound to self-destruct. There was no material reason why new fascist movements could not have sprung up again after the war in other locales, but for the fact that expansionist ultranationalism, with its promise of unending conflict leading to disastrous military defeat, had completely lost its appeal. The ruins of the Reich chancellory as well as the atomic bombs dropped on Hiroshima and Nagasaki killed this ideology on the level of consciousness as well as materially, and all of the proto-fascist movements spawned by the German and Japanese examples like the Peronist movement in Argentina or Subhas Chandra Bose's Indian National Army withered after the war.

The ideological challenge mounted by the other great alternative to liberalism, communism, was far more serious. Marx, speaking Hegel's language, asserted that liberal society contained a fundamental contradiction that could not be resolved within its context, that between capital and labor, and this contradiction has constituted the chief accusation against liberalism ever since. But surely, the class issue has actually been successfully resolved in the West. As Kojève (among others) noted, the egalitarianism of modern America represents the essential achievement of the classless society envisioned by Marx. This is not to say that there are not rich people and poor people in the United States, or that the gap between them has not grown in recent years. But the root causes of economic inequality do not have to do with the underlying legal and social structure of our society, which remains fundamentally egalitarian and moderately redistributionist, so much as with the cultural and social characteristics of the groups that make it up, which are in turn the historical legacy of premodern conditions. Thus black poverty in the United States is not the inherent product of liberalism, but is rather the "legacy of slavery and racism" which persisted long after the formal abolition of slavery.

As a result of the receding of the class issue, the appeal of communism in the developed Western world, it is safe to say, is lower today than any time since the end of the First World War. This can be measured in any number of ways: in the declining membership and electoral pull of the major European communist parties, and their overtly revisionist programs; in the corresponding electoral success of conservative parties from Britain and Germany to the United States and Japan, which are unabashedly pro-market and antistatist; and in an intellectual climate whose most "advanced" members no longer believe that bourgeois society is something that ultimately needs to be overcome. This is not to say that the opinions of progressive intellectuals in Western countries are not deeply pathological in any number of ways. But those who believe that the future must inevitably be socialist tend to be very old, or very marginal to the real political discourse of their societies.

One may argue that the socialist alternative was never terribly plausible for the North Atlantic world, and was sustained for the last several decades primarily by its success outside of this region. But it is precisely in the non-European world that one is most struck by the occurrence of major ideological transformations. Surely the most remarkable changes have occurred in Asia. Due to the strength and adaptability of the indigenous cultures there, Asia became a battleground for a variety of imported Western ideologies early in this century. Liberalism in Asia was a very weak reed in the period after World War I; it is easy today to forget how gloomy Asia's political future looked as recently as ten or fifteen years ago. It is easy to forget as well how momentous the outcome of Asian ideological struggles seemed for world political development as a whole.

The first Asian alternative to liberalism to be decisively defeated was the fascist one represented by Imperial Japan. Japanese fascism (like its German version) was defeated by the force of American arms in the Pacific war, and liberal democracy was imposed on Japan by a victorious United States. Western capitalism and political liberalism when transplanted to Japan were adapted and transformed by the Japanese in such a way as to be scarcely recognizable. Many Americans are now aware that Japanese industrial organization is very different from that prevailing in the United States or Europe, and it is questionable what relationship the factional maneuvering that takes place with the governing Liberal Democratic Party bears to democracy. Nonetheless, the very fact that the essential elements of economic and political liberalism have been so successfully grafted onto uniquely Japanese traditions and institutions guarantees their survival in the long run. More important is the contribution that Japan has made in turn to world history by following in the footsteps of the United States to create a truly universal consumer culture that has become both a symbol and an underpinning of the universal homogenous state. V. S. Naipaul travelling in Khomeini's Iran shortly after the revolution noted the omnipresent signs advertising the products of Sony, Hitachi, and JVC, whose appeal remained virtually irresistible and gave the lie to the regime's pretensions of restoring a state based on the rule of the *Shariah*. Desire for access to the consumer culture, created in large measure by Japan, has played a crucial role in fostering the spread of economic liberalism throughout Asia, and hence in promoting political liberalism as well.

The economic success of the other newly industrializing countries (NICs) in Asia following on the example of Japan is by now a familiar story. What is important from a Hegelian standpoint is that political liberalism has been following economic liberalism, more slowly than many had hoped but with seeming inevitability. Here again we see the victory of the idea of the universal homogenous state. South Korea had developed into a modern, urbanized society with an increasingly large and well-educated middle class that could not possibly be isolated from the larger democratic trends around them. Under these circumstances it seemed intolerable to a large part of this population that it should be ruled by an anachronistic military regime while Japan, only a decade or so ahead in economic terms, had parliamentary institutions for over forty years. Even the former socialist regime in Burma, which for so many decades existed in dismal isolation from the larger trends dominating Asia, was buffeted in the past year by pressures to liberalize both its economy and political system. It is said that unhappiness with strongman Ne Win began when a senior Burmese officer went to Singapore for medical treatment and broke down crying when he saw how far socialist Burma had been left behind by its ASEAN neighbors.

But the power of the liberal idea would seem much less impressive if it had not infected the largest and oldest culture in Asia, China. The simple existence of communist China created an alternative pole of ideological attraction, and as such constituted a threat to liberalism. But the past fifteen years have seen an almost total discrediting of Marxism-Leninism as an economic system. Beginning with the famous third plenum of the Tenth Central Committee in 1978, the Chinese Communist party set about decollectivizing agriculture for the 800 million Chinese who still lived in the countryside. The role of the state in agriculture was reduced to that of a tax collector, while production of consumer goods was sharply increased in order to give peasants a taste of the universal homogenous state and thereby an incentive to work. The reform doubled Chinese grain output in only five years, and in the process created for Deng Xiao-ping a solid political base from which he was able to extend the reform to other parts of the economy. Economic statistics do not begin to describe the dynamism, initiative, and openness evident in China since the reform began.

China could not now be described in any way as a liberal democracy. At present, no more than 20 percent of its economy has been marketized, and most importantly it continues to be ruled by a self-appointed Communist party which has given no hint of wanting to devolve power. Deng has made none of Gorbachev's promises regarding democratization of the political system and there is no Chinese equivalent of *glasnost*. The Chinese leadership has in fact been much more circumspect in criticizing Mao and Maoism than Gorbachev with respect to Brezhnev and Stalin, and the regime continues to pay lip service to Marxism-Leninism as its ideological underpinning. But anyone familiar with the outlook and behavior of the new technocratic elite now governing China knows that Marxism and ideological principle have become virtually irrelevant as guides to policy, and that bourgeois consumerism has a real meaning in that country for the first time since the revolution. The various slowdowns in the pace of reform, the campaigns against "spiritual pollution" and crackdowns on political dissent are more properly seen as tactical adjustments made in the process of managing what is an extraordinarily difficult political transition. By ducking the question of political reform while putting the economy on a new footing, Deng has managed to avoid the breakdown of authority that has accompanied Gorbachev's *perestroika*. Yet

the pull of the liberal idea continues to be very strong as economic power devolves and the economy becomes more open to the outside world. There are currently over 20,000 Chinese students studying in the U.S. and other Western countries, almost all of them the children of the Chinese elite. It is hard to believe that when they return home to run the country they will be content for China to be the only country in Asia unaffected by the larger democratizing trend. The student demonstrations in Beijing that broke out first in December 1986 and recurred recently on the occasion of Hu Yaobang's death were only the beginning of what will inevitably be mounting pressure for change in the political system as well.

What is important about China from the standpoint of world history is not the present state of the reform or even its future prospects. The central issue is the fact that the People's Republic of China can no longer act as a beacon for illiberal forces around the world, whether they be guerrillas in some Asian jungle or middle class students in Paris. Maoism, rather than being the pattern for Asia's future, became an anachronism, and it was the mainland Chinese who in fact were decisively influenced by the prosperity and dynamism of their overseas co-ethnics—the ironic ultimate victory of Taiwan.

Important as these changes in China have been, however, it is developments in the Soviet Union—the original "homeland of the world proletariat"—that have put the final nail in the coffin of the Marxist-Leninist alternative to liberal democracy. It should be clear that in terms of formal institutions, not much has changed in the four years since Gorbachev has come to power: free markets and the cooperative movement represent only a small part of the Soviet economy, which remains centrally planned; the political system is still dominated by the Communist party, which has only begun to democratize internally and to share power with other groups; the regime continues to assert that it is seeking only to modernize socialism and that its ideological basis remains

Marxism-Leninism; and, finally, Gorbachev faces a potentially powerful conservative opposition that could undo many of the changes that have taken place to date. Moreover, it is hard to be too sanguine about the chances for success of Gorbachev's proposed reforms, either in the sphere of economics or politics. But my purpose here is not to analyze events in the short-term, or to make predictions for policy purposes, but to look at underlying trends in the sphere of ideology and consciousness. And in that respect, it is clear that an astounding transformation has occurred.

Emigres from the Soviet Union have been reporting for at least the last generation now that virtually nobody in that country truly believed in Marxism-Leninism any longer, and that this was nowhere more true than in the Soviet elite, which continued to mouth Marxist slogans out of sheer cynicism. The corruption and decadence of the late Brezhnev-era Soviet state seemed to matter little, however, for as long as the state itself refused to throw into question any of the fundamental principles underlying Soviet society, the system was capable of functioning adequately out of sheer inertia and could even muster some dynamism in the realm of foreign and defense policy. Marxism-Leninism was like a magical incantation which, however absurd and devoid of meaning, was the only common basis on which the elite could agree to rule Soviet society.

What has happened in the four years since Gorbachev's coming to power is a revolutionary assault on the most fundamental institutions and principles of Stalinism, and their replacement by other principles which do not amount to liberalism *per se* but whose only connecting thread is liberalism. This is most evident in the economic sphere, where the reform economists around Gorbachev have become steadily more radical in their support for free markets, to the point where some like Nikolai Shmelev do not mind being compared in public to Milton Friedman. There is a virtual consensus among the currently dominant school of Soviet economists now that central planning and the command system of allocation are the root cause of economic inefficiency, and that if the Soviet system is ever to heal itself, it must permit free and decentralized decision-making with respect to investment, labor, and prices. After a couple of initial years of ideological confusion, these principles have finally been incorporated into policy with the promulgation of new laws on enterprise autonomy, cooperatives, and finally in 1988 on lease arrangements and family farming. There are, of course, a number of fatal flaws in the current implementation of the reform, most notably the absence of a thoroughgoing price reform. But the problem is no longer a *conceptual* one: Gorbachev and his lieutenants seem to understand the economic logic of marketization well enough, but like the leaders of a Third World country facing the IMF, are afraid of the social consequences of ending consumer subsidies and other forms of dependence on the state sector.

In the political sphere, the proposed changes to the Soviet constitution, legal system, and party rules amount to much less than the establishment of a liberal state. Gorbachev has spoken of democratization primarily in the sphere of internal party affairs, and has shown little intention of ending the Communist party's monopoly of power; indeed, the political reform seeks to legitimize and therefore strengthen the CPSU's rule. Nonetheless, the general principles underlying many of the reforms—that the "people" should be truly responsible for their own affairs, that higher political bodies should be answerable to lower ones, and not vice versa, that the rule of law should prevail over arbitrary police actions, with separation of powers and an independent judiciary, that there should be legal protection for property rights, the need for open discussion of public issues and the right of public dissent, the empowering of the Soviets as a forum in which the whole Soviet people can participate, and of a political culture that is more tolerant and pluralistic—come from a source fundamentally alien to the USSR's Marxist-Leninist tradition, even if they are incompletely articulated and poorly implemented in practice.

■   ■   ■

If we admit for the moment that the fascist and communist challenges to liberalism are dead, are there any other ideological competitors left? Or put another way, are there contradictions in liberal society beyond that of class that are not resolvable? Two possibilities suggest themselves, those of religion and nationalism.

The rise of religious fundamentalism in recent years within the Christian, Jewish, and Muslim traditions has been widely noted. One is inclined to say that the revival of religion in some way attests to a broad unhappiness with the impersonality and spiritual vacuity of liberal consumerist societies. Yet while the emptiness at the core of liberalism is most certainly a defect in the ideology—indeed, a flaw that one does not need the perspective of religion to recognize—it is not at all clear that it is remediable through politics. Modern liberalism itself was historically a consequence of the weakness of religiously-based societies which, failing to agree on the nature of the good life, could not provide even the minimal preconditions of peace and stability. In the contemporary world only Islam has offered a theocratic state as a political alternative to both liberalism and communism. But the doctrine has little appeal for non-Muslims, and it is hard to believe that the movement will take on any universal significance. Other less organized religious impulses have been successfully satisfied within the sphere of personal life that is permitted in liberal societies.

The other major "contradiction" potentially unresolvable by liberalism is the one posed by nationalism and other forms of racial and ethnic consciousness. It is certainly true that a very large degree of conflict since the Battle of Jena has had its roots in nationalism. Two cataclysmic world wars in this century have been spawned by the nationalism of the developed world in various guises, and if those passions have been muted to a certain extent in postwar Europe, they are still extremely powerful in the Third World. Nationalism has been a threat to liberalism historically in Germany, and continues to be one in isolated parts of "post-historical" Europe like Northern Ireland.

But it is not clear that nationalism represents an irreconcilable contradiction in the heart of liberalism. In the first place, nationalism is not one single phenomenon but several, ranging from mild cultural nostalgia to the highly organized and elaborately articulated doctrine of National Socialism. Only systematic nationalisms of the latter sort can qualify as a formal ideology on the level of liberalism or communism. The vast majority of the world's nationalist movements do not have a political program beyond the negative desire of independence *from* some other group or people, and do not offer anything like a comprehensive agenda for socio-economic organization. As such, they are compatible with doctrines and ideologies that do offer such agendas. While they may constitute a source of conflict for liberal societies, this conflict does not arise from liberalism itself so much as from the fact that the liberalism in question is incomplete. Certainly a great deal of the world's ethnic and nationalist tension can be explained in terms of peoples who are forced to live in unrepresentative political systems that they have not chosen.

While it is impossible to rule out the sudden appearance of new ideologies or previously unrecognized contradictions in liberal societies, then, the present world seems to confirm that the fundamental principles of socio-political organization have not advanced terribly far since 1806. Many of the wars and revolutions fought since that time have been undertaken in the name of ideologies which claimed to be more advanced than liberalism, but whose pretensions were ultimately unmasked by history. In the meantime, they have helped to spread the universal homogenous state to the point where it could have a significant effect on the overall character of international relations.

IV

What are the implications of the end of history for international relations? Clearly, the vast bulk of the Third World remains very much mired in history, and will be a terrain of conflict for many years to come. But let us focus for the time being on the larger and more developed states of the world who after all account for the greater part of world politics. Russia and China are not likely to join the developed nations of the West as liberal societies any time in the foreseeable future, but suppose for a moment that Marxism-Leninism ceases to be a factor driving the foreign policies of these states—a prospect which, if not yet here, the last few years have made a real possibility. How will the overall characteristics of a de-ideologized world differ from those of the one with which we are familiar at such a hypothetical juncture?

The most common answer is—not very much. For there is a very widespread belief among many observers of international relations that underneath the skin of ideology is a hard core of great power national interest that guarantees a fairly high level of competition and conflict between nations. Indeed, according to one academically popular school of international relations theory, conflict inheres in the international system as such, and to understand the prospects for conflict one must look at the shape of the system—for example, whether it is bipolar or multipolar—rather than at the specific character of the nations and regimes that constitute it. This school in effect applies a Hobbesian view of politics to international relations, and assumes that aggression and insecurity are universal characteristics of human societies rather than the product of specific historical circumstances.

Believers in this line of thought take the relations that existed between the participants in the classical nineteenth century European balance of power as a model for what a de-ideologized contemporary world would look like. Charles Krauthammer, for example, recently explained that if as a result of Gorbachev's reforms the USSR is shorn of Marxist-Leninist ideology, its behavior will revert to that of nineteenth century imperial Russia. While he finds this more reassuring than the threat posed by a communist Russia, he implies that there will still be a substantial degree of competition and conflict in the international system, just as there was say between Russia and Britain or Wilhelmine Germany in the last century. This is, of course, a convenient point of view for people who want to admit that something major is changing in the Soviet Union, but do not want to accept responsibility for recommending the radical policy redirection implicit in such a view. But is it true?

In fact, the notion that ideology is a superstructure imposed on a substratum of permanent great power interest is a highly questionable proposition. For the way in which any state defines its national interest is not universal but rests on some kind of prior ideological basis, just as we saw that economic behavior is determined by a prior state of consciousness. In this century, states have adopted highly articulated doctrines with explicit foreign policy agendas legitimizing expansionism, like Marxism-Leninism or National Socialism.

The expansionist and competitive behavior of nineteenth-century European states rested on no less ideal a basis; it just so happened that the ideology driving it was less explicit than the doctrines of the twentieth century. For one thing, most "liberal" European societies were illiberal insofar as they believed in the legitimacy of imperialism, that is, the right of one nation to rule over other nations without regard for the wishes of the ruled. The justifications for imperialism varied from nation to nation, from a crude belief in the legitimacy of force, particularly when applied to non-Europeans, to the White Man's Burden and Europe's

Christianizing mission, to the desire to give people of color access to the culture of Rabelais and Molière. But whatever the particular ideological basis, every "developed" country believed in the acceptability of higher civilizations ruling lower ones—including, incidentally, the United States with regard to the Philippines. This led to a drive for pure territorial aggrandizement in the latter half of the century and played no small role in causing the Great War.

The radical and deformed outgrowth of nineteenth-century imperialism was German fascism, an ideology which justified Germany's right not only to rule over non-European peoples, but over *all* non-German ones. But in retrospect it seems that Hitler represented a diseased bypath in the general course of European development, and since his fiery defeat, the legitimacy of any kind of territorial aggrandizement has been thoroughly discredited. Since the Second World War, European nationalism has been defanged and shorn of any real relevance to foreign policy, with the consequence that the nineteenth-century model of great power behavior has become a serious anachronism. The most extreme form of nationalism that any Western European state has mustered since 1945 has been Gaullism, whose self-assertion has been confined largely to the realm of nuisance politics and culture. International life for the part of the world that has reached the end of history is far more preoccupied with economics than with politics or strategy.

The developed states of the West do maintain defense establishments and in the postwar period have competed vigorously for influence to meet a worldwide communist threat. This behavior has been driven, however, by an external threat from states that possess overtly expansionist ideologies, and would not exist in their absence. To take the "neo-realist" theory seriously, one would have to believe that "natural" competitive behavior would reassert itself among the OECD states were Russia and China to disappear from the face of the earth.

That is, West Germany and France would arm themselves against each other as they did in the 1930s, Australia and New Zealand would send military advisers to block each others' advances in Africa, and the U.S.-Canadian border would become fortified. Such a prospect is, of course, ludicrous: minus Marxist-Leninist ideology, we are far more likely to see the "Common Marketization" of world politics than the disintegration of the EEC into nineteenth-century competitiveness. Indeed, as our experience in dealing with Europe on matters such as terrorism or Libya prove, they are much further gone than we down the road that denies the legitimacy of the use of force in international politics, even in self-defense.

The automatic assumption that Russia shorn of its expansionist communist ideology should pick up where the czars left off just prior to the Bolshevik Revolution is therefore a curious one. It assumes that the evolution of human consciousness has stood still in the meantime, and that the Soviets, while picking up currently fashionable ideas in the realm of economics, will return to foreign policy views a century out of date in the rest of Europe. This is certainly not what happened to China after it began its reform process. Chinese competitiveness and expansionism on the world scene have virtually disappeared: Beijing no longer sponsors Maoist insurgencies or tries to cultivate influence in distant African countries as it did in the 1960s. This is not to say that there are not troublesome aspects to contemporary Chinese foreign policy, such as the reckless sale of ballistic missile technology in the Middle East; and the PRC continues to manifest traditional great power behavior in its sponsorship of the Khmer Rouge against Vietnam. But the former is explained by commercial motives and the latter is a vestige of earlier ideologically-based rivalries. The new China far more resembles Gaullist France than pre–World War I Germany.

The real question for the future, however, is the degree to which Soviet elites have assimilated the consciousness of the universal homogenous state that is post-Hitler Europe. From their writings and from my own personal contacts with them, there is no question in my mind that the liberal Soviet intelligentsia rallying around Gorbachev has arrived at the end-of-history view in a remarkably short time, due in no small measure to the contacts they have had since the Brezhnev era with the larger European civilization around them. "New political thinking," the general rubric for their views, describes a world dominated by economic concerns, in which there are no ideological grounds for major conflict between nations, and in which, consequently, the use of military force becomes less legitimate. As Foreign Minister Shevardnadze put it in mid-1988:

> The struggle between two opposing systems is no longer a determining tendency of the present-day era. At the modern stage, the ability to build up material wealth at an accelerated rate on the basis of front-ranking science and high-level techniques and technology, and to distribute it fairly, and through joint efforts to restore and protect the resources necessary for mankind's survival acquires decisive importance.

The post-historical consciousness represented by "new thinking" is only one possible future for the Soviet Union, however. There has always been a very strong current of great Russian chauvinism in the Soviet Union, which has found freer expression since the advent of *glasnost*. It may be possible to return to traditional Marxism-Leninism for a while as a simple rallying point for those who want to restore the authority that Gorbachev has dissipated. But as in Poland, Marxism-Leninism is dead as a mobilizing ideology: under its banner people cannot be made to work harder, and its adherents have lost confidence in themselves. Unlike the propagators of traditional Marxism-Leninism, however, ultra-nationalists in the USSR believe in their Slavophile cause passionately, and one gets

the sense that the fascist alternative is not one that has played itself out entirely there.

The Soviet Union, then, is at a fork in the road: it can start down the path that was staked out by Western Europe forty-five years ago, a path that most of Asia has followed, or it can realize its own uniqueness and remain stuck in history. The choice it makes will be highly important for us, given the Soviet Union's size and military strength, for that power will continue to preoccupy us and slow our realization that we have already emerged on the other side of history.

V

The passing of Marxism-Leninism first from China and then from the Soviet Union will mean its death as a living ideology of world historical significance. For while there may be some isolated true believers left in places like Managua, Pyongyang, or Cambridge, Massachusetts, the fact that there is not a single large state in which it is a going concern undermines completely its pretensions to being in the vanguard of human history. And the death of this ideology means the growing "Common Marketization" of international relations, and the diminution of the likelihood of large-scale conflict between states.

This does not by any means imply the end of international conflict *per se*. For the world at that point would be divided between a part that was historical and a part that was post-historical. Conflict between states still in history, and between those states and those at the end of history, would still be possible. There would still be a high and perhaps rising level of ethnic and nationalist violence, since those are impulses incompletely played out, even in parts of the post-historical world. Palestinians and Kurds, Sikhs and Tamils, Irish Catholics and Walloons, Armenians and Azeris, will continue to have their unresolved grievances. This implies that terrorism and wars of national liberation will continue to be an important item on the international agenda. But large-scale conflict must involve large states still caught in the grip of history, and they are what appear to be passing from the scene.

The end of history will be a very sad time. The struggle for recognition, the willingness to risk one's life for a purely abstract goal, the worldwide ideological struggle that called forth daring, courage, imagination, and idealism, will be replaced by economic calculation, the endless solving of technical problems, environmental concerns, and the satisfaction of sophisticated consumer demands. In the post-historical period there will be neither art nor philosophy, just the perpetual caretaking of the museum of human history. I can feel in myself, and see in others around me, a powerful nostalgia for the time when history existed. Such nostalgia, in fact, will continue to fuel competition and conflict even in the post-historical world for some time to come. Even though I recognize its inevitability, I have the most ambivalent feelings for the civilization that has been created in Europe since 1945, with its north Atlantic and Asian offshoots. Perhaps this very prospect of centuries of boredom at the end of history will serve to get history started once again.

NOTES

1. Kojève's best-known work is his *Introduction à la lecture de Hegel* (Paris: Editions Gallimard, 1947), which is a transcript of the *Ecole Practique* lectures from the 1930s. This book is available in English entitled *Introduction to the Reading of Hegel* arranged by Raymond Queneau, edited by Allan Bloom, and translated by James Nichols (New York: Basic Books, 1969).

3 INTERNATIONAL RELATIONS THEORIES

Over the past century, the most prominent perspectives for understanding the basic nature of international politics have included realism, liberalism, and various forms of idealism, such as social constructivism. These viewpoints have vied for influence both in public debates and in academic arguments.

The readings in this chapter constitute some of the most concise and important statements of these theoretical traditions. Hans J. Morgenthau, the leading figure in the field of international relations in the period after World War II, presents a realist view of power politics. His influential book, *Politics among Nations* (1948), excerpted here, played a central role in intellectually preparing Americans to exercise global power in the Cold War period and to reconcile power politics with the idealistic ethics that had often dominated American discussions about foreign relations.

In *The Tragedy of Great Power Politics* (2001), John J. Mearsheimer offers a contemporary interpretation of international politics that he calls "offensive realism." The chapter reprinted here describes clearly and concisely international anarchy and its implications. States operate in a self-help system; to ensure their survival in that system, states must strive to become as powerful as possible. This competitive striving for security makes conflict the enduring and dominant feature of international relations, in Mearsheimer's view.

Michael W. Doyle, drawing inspiration from Kant, advances the liberal theory of the democratic peace. His 1986 article in the *American Political Science Review* points out that no two democracies had ever fought a war against each other. This sparked an ongoing debate among academics and public commentators on why this was the case, and whether it meant that the United States and other democracies should place efforts to promote the further spreading of democracy at the head of their foreign policy agendas.

Whereas realists like Mearsheimer argue that the condition of anarchy necessarily causes insecurity and fear among states, social constructivists such as Alexander Wendt insist that behavior in anarchy depends on the ideas, cultures, and identities that people and their states bring to the anarchical situation. The excerpt here is drawn from the seminal piece in that debate, which has spawned influential research on such topics as the taboo against using nuclear weapons, changing norms of humanitarian military intervention, and the rise of powerful transnational human rights networks.

The final selection illustrates currents in the study of international politics that fundamentally challenge the realist, liberal, and radical perspectives. Arguing from a feminist perspective, J. Ann Tickner invokes ironically the title of realist Kenneth Waltz's classic book, *Man, the State, and War*, to argue that the roots of war do indeed lie in the political consequences of the masculine patriarchy that has prevailed to a significant extent in all societies.

Hans J. Morgenthau

A REALIST THEORY OF
INTERNATIONAL POLITICS

This book purports to present a theory of international politics. The test by which such a theory must be judged is not *a priori* and abstract but empirical and pragmatic. The theory, in other words, must be judged not by some preconceived abstract principle or concept unrelated to reality, but by its purpose: to bring order and meaning to a mass of phenomena which without it would remain disconnected and unintelligible. It must meet a dual test, an empirical and a logical one: Do the facts as they actually are lend themselves to the interpretation the theory has put upon them, and do the conclusions at which the theory arrives follow with logical necessity from its premises? In short, is the theory consistent with the facts and within itself?

The issue this theory raises concerns the nature of all politics. The history of modern political thought is the story of a contest between two schools that differ fundamentally in their conceptions of the nature of man, society, and politics. One believes that a rational and moral political order, derived from universally valid abstract principles, can be achieved here and now. It assumes the essential goodness and infinite-malleability of human nature, and blames the failure of the social order to measure up to the rational standards on lack of knowledge and understanding, obsolescent social institutions, or the depravity of certain isolated individuals or groups. It trusts in education, reform, and the sporadic use of force to remedy these defects.

The other school believes that the world, imperfect as it is from the rational point of view, is the result of forces inherent in human nature. To improve the world one must work with those forces, not against them. This being inherently a world of opposing interests and of conflict among them, moral principles can never be fully realized, but must at best be approximated through the ever temporary balancing, of interests and the ever precarious settlement of conflicts. This school, then, sees in a system of checks and balances a universal principle for all pluralist societies. It appeals to historic precedent rather than to abstract principles, and aims at the realization of the lesser evil rather than of the absolute good.

■   ■   ■

*** Principles of Political Realism

*** Political realism believes that politics, like society in general, is governed by objective laws that have their roots in human nature. In order to improve society it is first necessary to understand the laws by which society lives. The operation of these laws being impervious to our preferences, men will challenge them only at the risk of failure.

Realism, believing as it does in the objectivity of the laws of politics, must also believe in the

From Hans J. Morgenthau, *Politics among Nations: The Struggle for Power and Peace* (1948; reprint, New York: Knopf, 1985), 3–5, 12, 31–34, 36–39. Some of the author's notes have been omitted.

possibility of developing a rational theory that reflects, however imperfectly and one-sidedly, these objective laws. It believes also, then, in the possibility of distinguishing in politics between truth and opinion—between what is true objectively and rationally, supported by evidence and illuminated by reason, and what is only a subjective judgment, divorced from the facts as they are and informed by prejudice and wishful thinking.

■　　■　　■

For realism, theory consists in ascertaining facts and giving them meaning through reason. It assumes that the character of a foreign policy can be ascertained only through the examination of the political acts performed and of the foreseeable consequences of these acts. Thus we can find out what statesmen have actually done, and from the foreseeable consequences of their acts we can surmise what their objectives might have been.

Yet examination of the facts is not enough. To give meaning to the factual raw material of foreign policy, we must approach political reality with a kind of rational outline, a map that suggests to us the possible meanings of foreign policy. In other words, we put ourselves in the position of a statesman who must meet a certain problem of foreign policy under certain circumstances, and we ask ourselves what the rational alternatives are from which a statesman may choose who must meet this problem under these circumstances (presuming always that he acts in a rational manner), and which of these rational alternatives this particular statesman, acting under these circumstances, is likely to choose. It is the testing of this rational hypothesis against the actual facts and their consequences that gives theoretical meaning to the facts of international politics.

* * * The main signpost that helps political realism to find its way through the landscape of international politics is the concept of interest defined in terms of power. This concept provides the link between reason trying to understand international politics and the facts to be understood. * * *

We assume that statesmen think and act in terms of interest defined as power, and the evidence of history bears that assumption out. That assumption allows us to retrace and anticipate, as it were, the steps a statesman—past, present, or futures—has taken or will take on the political scene. We look over his shoulder when he writes his dispatches; we listen in on his conversation with other statesmen; we read and anticipate his very thoughts. Thinking in terms of interest defined as power, we think as he does, and as disinterested observers we understand his thoughts and actions perhaps better than he, the actor on the political scene, does himself.

■　　■　　■

* * * Political realism is aware of the moral significance of political action. It is also aware of the ineluctable tension between the moral command and the requirements of successful political action. And it is unwilling to gloss over and obliterate that tension and thus to obfuscate both the moral and the political issue by making it appear as though the stark facts of politics were morally more satisfying than they actually are, and the moral law less exacting that it actually is.

Realism maintains that universal moral principles cannot be applied to the actions of states in their abstract universal formulation, but that they must be filtered through the concrete circumstances of time and place. The individual may say for himself: "*Fiat justitia, pereat mundus* (Let justice be done, even if the world perish)," but the state has no right to say so in the name of those who are in its care. Both individual and state must judge political action by universal moral principles, such as that of liberty. Yet while the individual has a moral right to sacrifice himself in defense of such a moral principle, the state has no right to let its moral disapprobation of the infringement of liberty get in the way of successful political action, itself inspired by the moral principle of national survival. There can be no political morality without prudence; that is, without consideration of the political consequences of seemingly moral action. Realism, then, considers prudence—the weighing of the consequences of alternative political actions—to be the supreme virtue in politics. Ethics in the abstract judges action by its conformity with the moral law; political ethics judges action by its political consequences. * * *

■   ■   ■

POLITICAL POWER

What Is Political Power?

■   ■   ■

International politics, like all politics, is a struggle for power. Whatever the ultimate aims of international politics, power is always the immediate aim. Statesmen and peoples may ultimately seek freedom, security, prosperity, or power itself. They may define their goals in terms of a religious, philosophic, economic, or social ideal. They may hope that this ideal will materialize through its own inner force, through divine intervention, or through the natural development of human affairs. They may also try to further its realization through nonpolitical means, such as technical co-operation with other nations or international organizations. But whenever they strive to realize their goal by means of international politics, they do so by striving for power. The Crusaders wanted to free the holy places from domination by the Infidels; Woodrow Wilson wanted to make the world safe for democracy; the Nazis wanted to open Eastern Europe to German colonization, to dominate Europe, and to conquer the world. Since they all chose power to achieve these ends, they were actors on the scene of international politics.

■   ■   ■

* * * When we speak of power, we mean man's control over the minds and actions of other men. By political power we refer to the mutual relations of control among the holders of public authority and between the latter and the people at large.

Political power is a psychological relation between those who exercise it and those over whom it is exercised. It gives the former control over certain actions of the latter through the impact which the former exert on the latter's minds. That impact derives from three sources: the expectation of benefits, the fear of disadvantage, the respect or love for men or institutions. It may be exerted through orders, threats, the authority or charisma of a man or of an office, or a combination of any of these.

■   ■   ■

Political power must be distinguished from force in the sense, of the actual exercise of physical violence. The threat of physical violence in the form of police action, imprisonment, capital punishment, or war is an intrinsic element of politics. When violence becomes an actuality, it signifies the abdication of political power in favor of military or pseudo-military power. In international politics in particular, armed strength as a threat or a potentiality is the most important material factor making for the political power of a nation. If it becomes an actuality in war, it signifies the substitution of military for political power. The actual exercise of physical violence substitutes for the psychological relation between two minds, which is of the essence of political power, the physical relation between two bodies, one of which is strong enough to dominate the other's movements. It is for this reason that in the exercise of physical violence the psychological element of the political relationship is lost, and that we must distinguish between military and political power.

■   ■   ■

While it is generally recognized that the interplay of the expectation of benefits, the fear of disadvantages, and the respect or love for men or institutions, in ever changing combinations, forms the basis of all domestic politics, the importance of these factors for international politics is less obvious, but no less real. There has been a tendency to reduce political power to the actual application of force or at least to equate it with successful threats of force and with persuasion, to the neglect of charisma. That neglect * * * accounts in good measure for the neglect of prestige as an independent element in international politics. * * *

■   ■   ■

An economic, financial, territorial, or military policy undertaken for its own sake is subject to evaluation in its own terms. Is it economically or financially advantageous? * * *

When, however, the objectives of these policies serve to increase the power of the nation pursuing them with regard to other nations, these policies and their objectives must be judged primarily from the point of view of their contribution to national power. An economic policy that cannot be justified in purely economic terms might nevertheless be undertaken in view of the political policy pursued.

The insecure and unprofitable character of a loan to a foreign nation may be a valid argument against it on purely financial grounds. But the argument is irrelevant if the loan, however unwise it may be from a banker's point of view, serves the political policies of the nation. It may of course be that the economic or financial losses involved in such policies will weaken the nation in its international position to such an extent as to out-weigh the political advantages to be expected. On these grounds such policies might be rejected. In such a case, what decides the issue is not purely economic and financial considerations but a comparison of the political chances and risks involved; that is, the probable effect of these policies upon the power of the nation.

■   ■   ■

The Depreciation of Political Power

The aspiration for power being the distinguishing element of international politics, as of all politics, international politics is of necessity power politics. While this fact is generally recognized in the practice of international affairs, it is frequently denied in the pronouncements of scholars, publicists, and even statesmen. Since the end of the Napoleonic Wars, ever larger groups in the Western world have been persuaded that the struggle for power on the international scene is a temporary phenomenon, a historical accident that is bound to disappear once the peculiar historic conditions that have given rise to it have been eliminated. * * * During the nineteenth century, liberals everywhere shared the conviction that power politics and war were residues of an obsolete system of government, and that the victory of democracy and constitutional government over absolutism and autocracy would assure the victory of international harmony and permanent peace over power politics and war. Of this liberal school of thought, Woodrow Wilson was the most eloquent and most influential spokesman.

In recent times, the conviction that the struggle for power can be eliminated from the international scene has been connected with the great attempts at organizing the world, such as the League of Nations and the United Nations. * * *

* * * [In fact,] the struggle for power is universal in time and space and is an undeniable fact of experience. It cannot be denied that throughout historic time, regardless of social, economic, and political conditions, states have met each other in contests for power. Even though anthropologists have shown that certain primitive peoples seem to be free from the desire for power, nobody has yet shown how their state of mind and the conditions under which they live can be recreated on a world-wide scale so as to eliminate the struggle for power from the international scene.[1] It would be useless and even self-destructive to free one or the other of the peoples of the earth from the desire for power while leaving it extant in others. If the desire for power cannot be abolished everywhere in the world, those who might be cured would simply fall victims to the power of others.

The position taken here might be criticized on the ground that conclusions drawn from the past are unconvincing, and that to draw such conclusions has always been the main stock in trade of the enemies of progress and reform. Though it is true that certain social arrangements and institutions have always existed in the past, it does not necessarily follow that they must always exist in the future. The situation is, however, different when we deal not with social arrangements and institutions created by man, but with those elemental bio-psychological drives by which in turn society is created. The drives to live, to propagate, and to dominate are common to all men.[2] Their relative strength is dependent upon social conditions that may favor one drive and tend to repress another, or that may withhold social approval from certain manifestations of these drives while they encourage others. Thus, to take examples only from the sphere of power, most societies condemn killing as a means of attaining power within society, but all societies encourage the killing of enemies in that struggle for power which is called war. * * *

■ ■ ■

NOTES

1. For an illuminating discussion of this problem, see Malcolm Sharp, "Aggression: A Study of Values and Law," *Ethics*, Vol. 57, No. 4, Part II (July 1947).
2. Zoologists have tried to show that the drive to dominate is found even in animals, such as chickens and monkeys, who create social hierarchies on the basis of will and the ability to dominate. See, e.g., Warder Allee, *Animal Life and Social Growth* (Baltimore: The Williams and Wilkens Company, 1932), and *The Social Life of Animals* (New York: W. W. Norton and Company, Inc., 1938).

John J. Mearsheimer

ANARCHY AND THE STRUGGLE FOR POWER

Great powers, I argue, are always searching for opportunities to gain power over their rivals, with hegemony as their final goal. This perspective does not allow for status quo powers, except for the unusual state that achieves preponderance. Instead, the system is populated with great powers that have revisionist intentions at their core.[1] This chapter presents a theory that explains this competition for power. Specifically, I attempt to show that there is a compelling logic behind my claim that great powers seek to maximize their share of world power. I do not, however, test offensive realism against the historical record in this chapter. That important task is reserved for later chapters.

Why States Pursue Power

My explanation for why great powers vie with each other for power and strive for hegemony is derived from five assumptions about the international system. None of these assumptions alone mandates that states behave competitively. Taken together, however, they depict a world in which states have considerable reason to think and sometimes behave aggressively. In particular, the system encourages states to look for opportunities to maximize their power vis-à-vis other states.

How important is it that these assumptions be realistic? Some social scientists argue that the assumptions that underpin a theory need not conform to reality. Indeed, the economist Milton Friedman maintains that the best theories "will be found to have assumptions that are wildly inaccurate descriptive representations of reality, and, in general, the more significant the theory, the more unrealistic the assumptions."[2] According to this view, the explanatory power of a theory is all that matters. If unrealistic assumptions lead to a theory that tells us a lot about how the world works, it is of no importance whether the underlying assumptions are realistic or not.

I reject this view. Although I agree that explanatory power is the ultimate criterion for assessing theories, I also believe that a theory based on unrealistic or false assumptions will not explain much about how the world works.[3] Sound theories are based on sound assumptions. Accordingly, each of these five assumptions is a reasonably accurate representation of an important aspect of life in the international system.

Bedrock Assumptions

The first assumption is that the international system is anarchic, which does not mean that it is chaotic or riven by disorder. It is easy to draw that conclusion, since realism depicts a world characterized by security competition and war. By itself, however, the realist notion of anarchy has nothing to do with conflict; it is an ordering principle, which says that the system comprises independent states that have no central authority above them.[4] Sovereignty, in other words, inheres in states because there is no

From *The Tragedy of Great Power Politics* (New York: Norton, 2001): 29–54. Some of the author's notes have been edited.

higher ruling body in the international system.[5] There is no "government over governments."[6]

The second assumption is that great powers inherently possess some offensive military capability, which gives them the wherewithal to hurt and possibly destroy each other. States are potentially dangerous to each other, although some states have more military might than others and are therefore more dangerous. A state's military power is usually identified with the particular weaponry at its disposal, although even if there were no weapons, the individuals in those states could still use their feet and hands to attack the population of another state. After all, for every neck, there are two hands to choke it.

The third assumption is that states can never be certain about other states' intentions. Specifically, no state can be sure that another state will not use its offensive military capability to attack the first state. This is not to say that states necessarily have hostile intentions. Indeed, all of the states in the system may be reliably benign, but it is impossible to be sure of that judgment because intentions are impossible to divine with 100 percent certainty.[7] There are many possible causes of aggression, and no state can be sure that another state is not motivated by one of them.[8] Furthermore, intentions can change quickly, so a state's intentions can be benign one day and hostile the next. Uncertainty about intentions is unavoidable, which means that states can never be sure that other states do not have offensive intentions to go along with their offensive capabilities.

The fourth assumption is that survival is the primary goal of great powers. Specifically, states seek to maintain their territorial integrity and the autonomy of their domestic political order. Survival dominates other motives because, once a state is conquered, it is unlikely to be in a position to pursue other aims. Soviet leader Josef Stalin put the point well during a war scare in 1927: "We can and must build socialism in the [Soviet Union]. But in order to do so we first of all have to exist."[9]

States can and do pursue other goals, of course, but security is their most important objective.

The fifth assumption is that great powers are rational actors. They are aware of their external environment and they think strategically about how to survive in it. In particular, they consider the preferences of other states and how their own behavior is likely to affect the behavior of those other states, and how the behavior of those other states is likely to affect their own strategy for survival. Moreover, states pay attention to the long term as well as the immediate consequences of their actions.

As emphasized, none of these assumptions alone dictates that great powers as a general rule *should* behave aggressively toward each other. There is surely the possibility that some state might have hostile intentions, but the only assumption dealing with a specific motive that is common to all states says that their principal objective is to survive, which by itself is a rather harmless goal. Nevertheless, when the five assumptions are married together, they create powerful incentives for great powers to think and act offensively with regard to each other. In particular, three general patterns of behavior result: fear, self-help, and power maximization.

State Behavior

Great powers fear each other. They regard each other with suspicion, and they worry that war might be in the offing. They anticipate danger. There is little room for trust among states. For sure, the level of fear varies across time and space, but it cannot be reduced to a trivial level. From the perspective of any one great power, all other great powers are potential enemies. This point is illustrated by the reaction of the United Kingdom and France to German reunification at the end of the Cold War. Despite the fact that these three states had been close allies for almost forty-five years, both the

United Kingdom and France immediately began worrying about the potential dangers of a united Germany.[10]

The basis of this fear is that in a world where great powers have the capability to attack each other and might have the motive to do so, any state bent on survival must be at least suspicious of other states and reluctant to trust them. Add to this the "911" problem—the absence of a central authority to which a threatened state can turn for help—and states have even greater incentive to fear each other. Moreover, there is no mechanism, other than the possible self-interest of third parties, for punishing an aggressor. Because it is sometimes difficult to deter potential aggressors, states have ample reason not to trust other states and to be prepared for war with them.

The possible consequences of falling victim to aggression further amplify the importance of fear as a motivating force in world politics. Great powers do not compete with each other as if international politics were merely an economic marketplace. Political competition among states is a much more dangerous business than mere economic intercourse; the former can lead to war, and war often means mass killing on the battlefield as well as mass murder of civilians. In extreme cases, war can even lead to the destruction of states. The horrible consequences of war sometimes cause states to view each other not just as competitors, but as potentially deadly enemies. Political antagonism, in short, tends to be intense, because the stakes are great.

States in the international system also aim to guarantee their own survival. Because other states are potential threats, and because there is no higher authority to come to their rescue when they dial 911, states cannot depend on others for their own security. Each state tends to see itself as vulnerable and alone, and therefore it aims to provide for its own survival. In international politics, God helps those who help themselves. This emphasis on self-help does not preclude states from forming alliances.[11] But alliances are only temporary marriages of convenience: today's alliance partner might be tomorrow's enemy, and today's enemy might be tomorrow's alliance partner. For example, the United States fought with China and the Soviet Union against Germany and Japan in World War II, but soon thereafter flip-flopped enemies and partners and allied with West Germany and Japan against China and the Soviet Union during the Cold War.

States operating in a self-help world almost always act according to their own self-interest and do not subordinate their interests to the interests of other states, or to the interests of the so-called international community. The reason is simple: it pays to be selfish in a self-help world. This is true in the short term as well as in the long term, because if a state loses in the short run, it might not be around for the long haul.

Apprehensive about the ultimate intentions of other states, and aware that they operate in a self-help system, states quickly understand that the best way to ensure their survival is to be the most powerful state in the system. The stronger a state is relative to its potential rivals, the less likely it is that any of those rivals will attack it and threaten its survival. Weaker states will be reluctant to pick fights with more powerful states because the weaker states are likely to suffer military defeat. Indeed, the bigger the gap in power between any two states, the less likely it is that the weaker will attack the stronger. Neither Canada nor Mexico, for example, would countenance attacking the United States, which is far more powerful than its neighbors. The ideal situation is to be the hegemon in the system. As Immanuel Kant said, "It is the desire of every state, or of its ruler, to arrive at a condition of perpetual peace by conquering the whole world, if that were possible."[12] Survival would then be almost guaranteed.[13]

Consequently, states pay close attention to how power is distributed among them, and they make a special effort to maximize their share of world power. Specifically, they look for opportunities to alter the balance of power by acquiring additional increments of power at the expense of potential rivals. States employ a variety of means—economic, diplomatic, and military—to shift the balance of power in their favor, even if doing so makes other states suspicious or even hostile. Because one state's gain in power is another state's loss, great powers tend to have a zero-sum mentality when dealing with each other. The trick, of course, is to be the winner in this competition and to dominate the other states in the system. Thus, the claim that states maximize relative power is tantamount to arguing that states are disposed to think offensively toward other states, even though their ultimate motive is simply to survive. In short, great powers have aggressive intentions.[14]

Even when a great power achieves a distinct military advantage over its rivals, it continues looking for chances to gain more power. The pursuit of power stops only when hegemony is achieved. The idea that a great power might feel secure without dominating the system, provided it has an "appropriate amount" of power, is not persuasive, for two reasons.[15] First, it is difficult to assess how much relative power one state must have over its rivals before it is secure. Is twice as much power an appropriate threshold? Or is three times as much power the magic number? The root of the problem is that power calculations alone do not determine which side wins a war. Clever strategies, for example, sometimes allow less powerful states to defeat more powerful foes.

Second, determining how much power is enough becomes even more complicated when great powers contemplate how power will be distributed among them ten or twenty years down the road. The capabilities of individual states vary over time, sometimes markedly, and it is often difficult to predict the direction and scope of change in the balance of power. Remember, few in the West anticipated the collapse of the Soviet Union before it happened. In fact, during the first half of the Cold War, many in the West feared that the Soviet economy would eventually generate greater wealth than the American economy, which would cause a marked power shift against the United States and its allies. What the future holds for China and Russia and what the balance of power will look like in 2020 is difficult to foresee.

Given the difficulty of determining how much power is enough for today and tomorrow, great powers recognize that the best way to ensure their security is to achieve hegemony now, thus eliminating any possibility of a challenge by another great power. Only a misguided state would pass up an opportunity to be the hegemon in the system because it thought it already had sufficient power to survive.[16] But even if a great power does not have the wherewithal to achieve hegemony (and that is usually the case), it will still act offensively to amass as much power as it can, because states are almost always better off with more rather than less power. In short, states do not become status quo powers until they completely dominate the system.

All states are influenced by this logic, which means that not only do they look for opportunities to take advantage of one another, they also work to ensure that other states do not take advantage of them. After all, rival states are driven by the same logic, and most states are likely to recognize their own motives at play in the actions of other states. In short, states ultimately pay attention to defense as well as offense. They think about conquest themselves, and they work to check aggressor states from gaining power at their expense. This inexorably leads to a world of constant security competition, where states are willing to lie, cheat, and use brute force if it helps them gain advantage over their rivals. Peace, if one defines that concept as a state of tranquility or mutual concord, is not likely to break out in this world.

The "security dilemma," which is one of the most well-known concepts in the international relations literature, reflects the basic logic of offensive realism. The essence of the dilemma is that the measures a state takes to increase its own security usually decrease the security of other states. Thus, it is difficult for a state to increase its own chances of survival without threatening the survival of other states. John Herz first introduced the security dilemma in a 1950 article in the journal *World Politics*.[17] After discussing the anarchic nature of international politics, he writes, "Striving to attain security from . . . attack, [states] are driven to acquire more and more power in order to escape the impact of the power of others. This, in turn, renders the others more insecure and compels them to prepare for the worst. Since none can ever feel entirely secure in such a world of competing units, power competition ensues, and the vicious circle of security and power accumulation is on."[18] The implication of Herz's analysis is clear: the best way for a state to survive in anarchy is to take advantage of other states and gain power at their expense. The best defense is a good offense. Since this message is widely understood, ceaseless security competition ensues. Unfortunately, little can be done to ameliorate the security dilemma as long as states operate in anarchy.

It should be apparent from this discussion that saying that states are power maximizers is tantamount to saying that they care about relative power, not absolute power. There is an important distinction here, because states concerned about relative power behave differently than do states interested in absolute power.[19] States that maximize relative power are concerned primarily with the distribution of material capabilities. In particular, they try to gain as large a power advantage as possible over potential rivals, because power is the best means to survival in a dangerous world. Thus, states motivated by relative power concerns are likely to forgo large gains in their own power, if such gains give rival states even greater power, for smaller national gains that nevertheless provide them with a power advantage over their rivals.[20] States that maximize absolute power, on the other hand, care only about the size of their own gains, not those of other states. They are not motivated by balance-of-power logic but instead are concerned with amassing power without regard to how much power other states control. They would jump at the opportunity for large gains, even if a rival gained more in the deal. Power, according to this logic, is not a means to an end (survival), but an end in itself.[21]

Calculated Aggression

There is obviously little room for status quo powers in a world where states are inclined to look for opportunities to gain more power. Nevertheless, great powers cannot always act on their offensive intentions, because behavior is influenced not only by what states want, but also by their capacity to realize these desires. Every state might want to be king of the hill, but not every state has the wherewithal to compete for that lofty position, much less achieve it. Much depends on how military might is distributed among the great powers. A great power that has a marked power advantage over its rivals is likely to behave more aggressively, because it has the capability as well as the incentive to do so.

By contrast, great powers facing powerful opponents will be less inclined to consider offensive action and more concerned with defending the existing balance of power from threats by their more powerful opponents. Let there be an opportunity for those weaker states to revise the balance in their own favor, however, and they will take advantage of it. Stalin put the point well at the end of World War II: "Everyone imposes his own system as far as his army can reach. It cannot be otherwise."[22] States might also have the capability to gain advantage over a rival power but nevertheless decide that the perceived costs of offense are too high and do not justify the expected benefits.

In short, great powers are not mindless aggressors so bent on gaining power that they charge headlong into losing wars or pursue Pyrrhic victories. On the contrary, before great powers take offensive actions, they think carefully about the balance of power and about how other states will react to their moves. They weigh the costs and risks of offense against the likely benefits. If the benefits do not outweigh the risks, they sit tight and wait for a more propitious moment. Nor do states start arms races that are unlikely to improve their overall position. As discussed at greater length in Chapter 3, states sometimes limit defense spending either because spending more would bring no strategic advantage or because spending more would weaken the economy and undermine the state's power in the long run.[23] To paraphrase Clint Eastwood, a state has to know its limitations to survive in the international system.

Nevertheless, great powers miscalculate from time to time because they invariably make important decisions on the basis of imperfect information. States hardly ever have complete information about any situation they confront. There are two dimensions to this problem. Potential adversaries have incentives to misrepresent their own strength or weakness, and to conceal their true aims.[24] For example, a weaker state trying to deter a stronger state is likely to exaggerate its own power to discourage the potential aggressor from attacking. On the other hand, a state bent on aggression is likely to emphasize its peaceful goals while exaggerating its military weakness, so that the potential victim does not build up its own arms and thus leaves itself vulnerable to attack. Probably no national leader was better at practicing this kind of deception than Adolf Hitler.

But even if disinformation was not a problem, great powers are often unsure about how their own military forces, as well as the adversary's, will perform on the battlefield. For example, it is sometimes difficult to determine in advance how new weapons and untested combat units will perform in the face of enemy fire. Peacetime maneuvers and war games are helpful but imperfect indicators of what is likely to happen in actual combat. Fighting wars is a complicated business in which it is often difficult to predict outcomes. Remember that although the United States and its allies scored a stunning and remarkably easy victory against Iraq in early 1991, most experts at the time believed that Iraq's military would be a formidable foe and put up stubborn resistance before finally succumbing to American military might.[25]

Great powers are also sometimes unsure about the resolve of opposing states as well as allies. For example, Germany believed that if it went to war against France and Russia in the summer of 1914, the United Kingdom would probably stay out of the fight. Saddam Hussein expected the United States to stand aside when he invaded Kuwait in August 1990. Both aggressors guessed wrong, but each had good reason to think that its initial judgment was correct. In the 1930s, Adolf Hitler believed that his great-power rivals would be easy to exploit and isolate because each had little interest in fighting Germany and instead was determined to get someone else to assume that burden. He guessed right. In short, great powers constantly find themselves confronting situations in which they have to make important decisions with incomplete information. Not surprisingly, they sometimes make faulty judgments and end up doing themselves serious harm.

Some defensive realists go so far as to suggest that the constraints of the international system are so powerful that offense rarely succeeds, and that aggressive great powers invariably end up being punished.[26] As noted, they emphasize that 1) threatened states balance against aggressors and ultimately crush them, and 2) there is an offense-defense balance that is usually heavily tilted toward the defense, thus making conquest especially difficult. Great powers, therefore, should be content with the existing balance of power and not try to change it by force. After all, it makes little sense for a state to initiate a war that it is likely to lose; that would be self-defeating behavior. It is better to concentrate instead on preserving the balance of power.[27] Moreover, because aggressors seldom succeed, states should understand that security is abundant, and thus there is no good strategic reason for wanting more power in the first place. In a world where conquest seldom pays, states should have relatively benign intentions toward each other. If they do not, these defensive realists argue, the reason is probably poisonous domestic politics, not smart calculations about how to guarantee one's security in an anarchic world.

There is no question that systemic factors constrain aggression, especially balancing by threatened states. But defensive realists exaggerate those restraining forces.[28] Indeed, the historical record provides little support for their claim that offense rarely succeeds. One study estimates that there were sixty-three wars between 1815 and 1980, and the initiator won thirty-nine times, which translates into about a 60 percent success rate.[29] Turning to specific cases, Otto von Bismarck unified Germany by winning military victories against Denmark in 1864, Austria in 1866, and France in 1870, and the United States as we know it today was created in good part by conquest in the nineteenth century. Conquest certainly paid big dividends in these cases. Nazi Germany won wars against Poland in 1939 and France in 1940, but lost to the Soviet Union between 1941 and 1945. Conquest ultimately did not pay for the Third Reich, but if Hitler had restrained himself after the fall of France and had not invaded the Soviet Union, conquest probably would have paid handsomely for the Nazis. In short, the historical record shows that offense sometimes succeeds and sometimes does not. The trick for a sophisticated power maximizer is to figure out when to raise and when to fold.[30]

Hegemony's Limits

Great powers, as I have emphasized, strive to gain power over their rivals and hopefully become hegemons. Once a state achieves that exalted position, it becomes a status quo power. More needs to be said, however, about the meaning of hegemony.

A hegemon is a state that is so powerful that it dominates all the other states in the system.[31] No other state has the military wherewithal to put up a serious fight against it. In essence, a hegemon is the only great power in the system. A state that is substantially more powerful than the other great powers in the system is not a hegemon, because it faces, by definition, other great powers. The United Kingdom in the mid-nineteenth century, for example, is sometimes called a hegemon. But it was not a hegemon, because there were four other great powers in Europe at the time—Austria, France, Prussia, and Russia—and the United Kingdom did not dominate them in any meaningful way. In fact, during that period, the United Kingdom considered France to be a serious threat to the balance of power. Europe in the nineteenth century was multipolar, not unipolar.

Hegemony means domination of the system, which is usually interpreted to mean the entire world. It is possible, however, to apply the concept of a system more narrowly and use it to describe particular regions, such as Europe, Northeast Asia, and the Western Hemisphere. Thus, one can distinguish between *global hegemons*, which dominate the world, and *regional hegemons*, which dominate distinct geographical areas. The United States has been a regional hegemon in the Western Hemisphere for at least the past one hundred years. No other state in the Americas has sufficient military might to challenge it, which is why the United States is widely recognized as the only great power in its region.

My argument, which I develop at length in subsequent chapters, is that except for the unlikely event wherein one state achieves clear-cut nuclear superiority, it is virtually impossible for any state to achieve global hegemony. The principal impediment to world domination is the difficulty of projecting power across the world's oceans onto the territory of a rival great power. The United States, for example, is the most powerful state on the planet today. But it does not dominate Europe and Northeast Asia the way it does the Western Hemisphere, and it has no intention of trying to conquer and control those distant regions, mainly because of the stopping power of water. Indeed, there is reason to think that the American military commitment to Europe and Northeast Asia might wither away over the next decade. In short, there has never been a global hegemon, and there is not likely to be one anytime soon.

The best outcome a great power can hope for is to be a regional hegemon and possibly control another region that is nearby and accessible over land. The United States is the only regional hegemon in modern history, although other states have fought major wars in pursuit of regional hegemony: imperial Japan in Northeast Asia, and Napoleonic France, Wilhelmine Germany, and Nazi Germany in Europe. But none succeeded. The Soviet Union, which is located in Europe and Northeast Asia, threatened to dominate both of those regions during the Cold War. The Soviet Union might also have attempted to conquer the oil-rich Persian Gulf region, with which it shared a border. But even if Moscow had been able to dominate Europe, Northeast Asia, and the Persian Gulf, which it never came close to doing, it still would have been unable to conquer the Western Hemisphere and become a true global hegemon.

States that achieve regional hegemony seek to prevent great powers in other regions from duplicating their feat. Regional hegemons, in other words, do not want peers. Thus the United States, for example, played a key role in preventing imperial Japan, Wilhelmine Germany, Nazi Germany, and the Soviet Union from gaining regional supremacy. Regional hegemons attempt to check aspiring hegemons in other regions because they fear that a rival great power that dominates its own region will be an especially powerful foe that is essentially free to cause trouble in the fearful great power's backyard. Regional hegemons prefer that there be at least two great powers located together in other regions, because their proximity will force them to concentrate their attention on each other rather than on the distant hegemon.

Furthermore, if a potential hegemon emerges among them, the other great powers in that region might be able to contain it by themselves, allowing the distant hegemon to remain safely on the sidelines. Of course, if the local great powers were unable to do the job, the distant hegemon would take the appropriate measures to deal with the threatening state. The United States, as noted, has assumed that burden on four separate occasions in the twentieth century, which is why it is commonly referred to as an "offshore balancer."

In sum, the ideal situation for any great power is to be the only regional hegemon in the world. That state would be a status quo power, and it would go to considerable lengths to preserve the existing distribution of power. The United States is in that enviable position today; it dominates the Western Hemisphere and there is no hegemon in any other area of the world. But if a regional hegemon is confronted with a peer competitor, it would no longer be a status quo power. Indeed, it would go to considerable lengths to weaken and maybe even destroy its distant rival. Of course, both regional hegemons would be motivated by that logic, which would make for a fierce security competition between them.

Power and Fear

That great powers fear each other is a central aspect of life in the international system. But as noted, the level of fear varies from case to case. For example, the Soviet Union worried much less about Germany in 1930 than it did in 1939. How much states fear each other matters greatly, because the amount of fear between them largely determines the severity of their security competition, as well as the probability that they will fight a war. The more profound the fear is, the more intense is the security competition, and the more likely is war. The logic is straightforward: a scared state will look especially hard for ways to enhance its security, and it will be disposed to pursue risky policies to achieve that end. Therefore, it is important to understand what causes states to fear each other more or less intensely.

Fear among great powers derives from the fact that they invariably have some offensive military capability that they can use against each other, and the fact that one can never be certain that other states do not intend to use that power against oneself. Moreover, because states operate in an anarchic system, there is no night watchman to whom they can turn for help if another great power attacks them. Although anarchy and uncertainty about other states' intentions create an irreducible level of fear among states that leads to power-maximizing behavior, they cannot account for why sometimes that level of fear is greater than at other times. The reason is that anarchy and the difficulty of discerning state intentions are constant facts of life, and constants cannot explain variation. The capability that states have to threaten each other, however, varies from case to case, and it is the key factor that drives fear levels up and down. Specifically, the more power a state possesses, the more fear it generates among its rivals. Germany, for example, was much more powerful at the end of the 1930s than it was at the decade's beginning, which is why the Soviets became increasingly fearful of Germany over the course of that decade.

This discussion of how power affects fear prompts the question, What is power? It is important to distinguish between potential and actual power. A state's potential power is based on the size of its population and the level of its wealth. These two assets are the main building blocks of military power. Wealthy rivals with large populations can usually build formidable military forces. A state's actual power is embedded mainly in its army and

the air and naval forces that directly support it. Armies are the central ingredient of military power, because they are the principal instrument for conquering and controlling territory—the paramount political objective in a world of territorial states. In short, the key component of military might, even in the nuclear age, is land power.

Power considerations affect the intensity of fear among states in three main ways. First, rival states that possess nuclear forces that can survive a nuclear attack and retaliate against it are likely to fear each other less than if these same states had no nuclear weapons. During the Cold War, for example, the level of fear between the superpowers probably would have been substantially greater if nuclear weapons had not been invented. The logic here is simple: because nuclear weapons can inflict devastating destruction on a rival state in a short period of time, nuclear-armed rivals are going to be reluctant to fight with each other, which means that each side will have less reason to fear the other than would otherwise be the case. But as the Cold War demonstrates, this does not mean that war between nuclear powers is no longer thinkable; they still have reason to fear each other.

Second, when great powers are separated by large bodies of water, they usually do not have much offensive capability against each other, regardless of the relative size of their armies. Large bodies of water are formidable obstacles that cause significant power-projection problems for attacking armies. For example, the stopping power of water explains in good part why the United Kingdom and the United States (since becoming a great power in 1898) have never been invaded by another great power. It also explains why the United States has never tried to conquer territory in Europe or Northeast Asia, and why the United Kingdom has never attempted to dominate the European continent. Great powers located on the same landmass are in a much better position to attack and conquer each other. That is especially true of states that share a common border. Therefore, great powers separated by water are likely to fear each other less than great powers that can get at each other over land.

Third, the distribution of power among the states in the system also markedly affects the levels of fear.[32] The key issue is whether power is distributed more or less evenly among the great powers or whether there are sharp power asymmetries. The configuration of power that generates the most fear is a multipolar system that contains a potential hegemon—what I call "unbalanced multipolarity."

A potential hegemon is more than just the most powerful state in the system. It is a great power with so much actual military capability and so much potential power that it stands a good chance of dominating and controlling all of the other great powers in its region of the world. A potential hegemon need not have the wherewithal to fight all of its rivals at once, but it must have excellent prospects of defeating each opponent alone, and good prospects of defeating some of them in tandem. The key relationship, however, is the power gap between the potential hegemon and the second most powerful state in the system: there must be a marked gap between them. To qualify as a potential hegemon, a state must have—by some reasonably large margin—the most formidable army as well as the most latent power among all the states located in its region.

Bipolarity is the power configuration that produces the least amount of fear among the great powers, although not a negligible amount by any means. Fear tends to be less acute in bipolarity, because there is usually a rough balance of power between the two major states in the system. Multipolar systems without a potential hegemon, what I call "balanced multipolarity," are still likely to have power asymmetries among their members, although these asymmetries will not be as pronounced as the gaps created by the presence of an aspiring hegemon. Therefore, balanced multipolarity is likely to generate less fear than unbalanced multipolarity, but more fear than bipolarity.

This discussion of how the level of fear between great powers varies with changes in the distribution of power, not with assessments about each other's intentions, raises a related point. When a state surveys its environment to determine which states pose a threat to its survival, it focuses mainly on the offensive *capabilities* of potential rivals, not their intentions. As emphasized earlier, intentions are ultimately unknowable, so states worried about their survival must make worst-case assumptions about their rivals' intentions. Capabilities, however, not only can be measured but also determine whether or not a rival state is a serious threat. In short, great powers balance against capabilities, not intentions.[33]

Great powers obviously balance against states with formidable military forces, because that offensive military capability is the tangible threat to their survival. But great powers also pay careful attention to how much latent power rival states control, because rich and populous states usually can and do build powerful armies. Thus, great powers tend to fear states with large populations and rapidly expanding economies, even if these states have not yet translated their wealth into military might.

The Hierarchy of State Goals

Survival is the number one goal of great powers, according to my theory. In practice, however, states pursue non-security goals as well. For example, great powers invariably seek greater economic prosperity to enhance the welfare of their citizenry. They sometimes seek to promote a particular ideology abroad, as happened during the Cold War when the United States tried to spread democracy around the world and the Soviet Union tried to sell communism. National unification is another goal that sometimes motivates states, as it did with Prussia and Italy in the nineteenth century and Germany after the Cold War. Great powers also occasionally try to foster human rights around the globe. States might pursue any of these, as well as a number of other non-security goals.

Offensive realism certainly recognizes that great powers might pursue these non-security goals, but it has little to say about them, save for one important point: states can pursue them as long as the requisite behavior does not conflict with balance-of-power logic, which is often the case.[34] Indeed, the pursuit of these non-security goals sometimes complements the hunt for relative power. For example, Nazi Germany expanded into eastern Europe for both ideological and realist reasons, and the superpowers competed with each other during the Cold War for similar reasons. Furthermore, greater economic prosperity invariably means greater wealth, which has significant implications for security, because wealth is the foundation of military power. Wealthy states can afford powerful military forces, which enhance a state's prospects for survival. As the political economist Jacob Viner noted more than fifty years ago, "there is a long-run harmony" between wealth and power.[35] National unification is another goal that usually complements the pursuit of power. For example, the unified German state that emerged in 1871 was more powerful than the Prussian state it replaced.

Sometimes the pursuit of non-security goals has hardly any effect on the balance of power, one way or the other. Human rights interventions usually fit this description, because they tend to be small-scale operations that cost little and do not detract from a great power's prospects for survival. For better or for worse, states are rarely willing to expend blood and treasure to protect foreign populations from gross abuses, including genocide. For instance, despite claims that American foreign policy is infused with moralism, Somalia (1992–93) is the only instance during the past one hundred years in which U.S. soldiers were killed in action on a humanitarian mission. And in that case, the loss of a mere eighteen soldiers in an infamous firefight in October 1993 so traumatized American policymakers that they immediately pulled all U.S. troops out of Somalia and then refused to intervene in Rwanda in the spring of 1994, when ethnic Hutu went on a genocidal rampage against their Tutsi neighbors.[36] Stopping that genocide would have been relatively easy and it would have had virtually no effect on the position of the United States in the balance of power.[37] Yet nothing was done. In short, although realism does not prescribe human rights interventions, it does not necessarily proscribe them.

But sometimes the pursuit of non-security goals conflicts with balance-of-power logic, in which case states usually act according to the dictates of realism. For example, despite the U.S. commitment to spreading democracy across the globe, it helped overthrow democratically elected governments and embraced a number of authoritarian regimes during the Cold War, when American policymakers felt that these actions would help contain the Soviet Union.[38] In World War II, the liberal democracies put aside their antipathy for communism and formed an alliance with the Soviet Union against Nazi Germany. "I can't take communism," Franklin Roosevelt emphasized, but to defeat Hitler "I would hold hands with the Devil."[39] In the same way, Stalin repeatedly demonstrated that when his ideological preferences clashed with power considerations, the latter won out. To take the most blatant example of his realism, the Soviet Union formed a non-aggression pact with Nazi Germany in August 1939—the infamous Molotov-Ribbentrop Pact—in hopes that the agreement would at least temporarily satisfy Hitler's territorial ambitions in eastern Europe and turn the Wehrmacht toward France and the United Kingdom.[40] When great powers confront a serious threat, in short, they pay little attention to ideology as they search for alliance partners.[41]

Security also trumps wealth when those two goals conflict, because "defence," as Adam Smith wrote in *The Wealth of Nations,* "is of much more importance than opulence."[42] Smith provides a good illustration of how states behave when forced to choose between wealth and relative power. In 1651, England put into effect the famous Navigation Act, protectionist legislation designed to damage Holland's commerce and ultimately cripple the Dutch economy. The legislation mandated that all goods imported into England be carried either in English ships or ships owned by the country that originally produced the goods. Since the Dutch produced few goods themselves, this measure would badly damage their shipping, the central ingredient in their economic success. Of course, the Navigation Act would hurt England's economy as well, mainly because it would rob England of the benefits of free trade. "The act of navigation," Smith wrote, "is not favorable to foreign commerce, or to the growth of that opulence that can arise from it." Nevertheless, Smith considered the legislation "the wisest of all the commercial regulations of England" because it did more damage to the Dutch economy than to the English economy, and in the mid-seventeenth century Holland was "the only naval power which could endanger the security of England."[43]

Creating World Order

The claim is sometimes made that great powers can transcend realist logic by working together to build an international order that fosters peace and justice. World peace, it would appear, can only enhance a state's prosperity and security. America's political leaders paid considerable lip service to this line of argument over the course of the twentieth century. President Clinton, for example, told an audience at the United Nations in September 1993 that "at the birth of this organization 48 years ago . . . a generation of gifted leaders from many nations stepped forward to organize the world's efforts on behalf of security and prosperity. . . .

Now history has granted to us a moment of even greater opportunity. . . . Let us resolve that we will dream larger. . . . Let us ensure that the world we pass to our children is healthier, safer and more abundant than the one we inhabit today." [44]

This rhetoric notwithstanding, great powers do not work together to promote world order for its own sake. Instead, each seeks to maximize its own share of world power, which is likely to clash with the goal of creating and sustaining stable international orders.[45] This is not to say that great powers never aim to prevent wars and keep the peace. On the contrary, they work hard to deter wars in which they would be the likely victim. In such cases, however, state behavior is driven largely by narrow calculations about relative power, not by a commitment to build a world order independent of a state's own interests. The United States, for example, devoted enormous resources to deterring the Soviet Union from starting a war in Europe during the Cold War, not because of some deep-seated commitment to promoting peace around the world, but because American leaders feared that a Soviet victory would lead to a dangerous shift in the balance of power.[46]

The particular international order that obtains at any time is mainly a by-product of the self-interested behavior of the system's great powers. The configuration of the system, in other words, is the unintended consequence of great-power security competition, not the result of states acting together to organize peace. The establishment of the Cold War order in Europe illustrates this point. Neither the Soviet Union nor the United States intended to establish it, nor did they work together to create it. In fact, each superpower worked hard in the early years of the Cold War to gain power at the expense of the other, while preventing the other from doing likewise.[47] The system that emerged in Europe in the aftermath of World War II was the unplanned consequence of intense security competition between the superpowers.

Although that intense superpower rivalry ended along with the Cold War in 1990, Russia and the

United States have not worked together to create the present order in Europe. The United States, for example, has rejected out of hand various Russian proposals to make the Organization for Security and Cooperation in Europe the central organizing pillar of European security (replacing the U.S.-dominated NATO). Furthermore, Russia was deeply opposed to NATO expansion, which it viewed as a serious threat to Russian security. Recognizing that Russia's weakness would preclude any retaliation, however, the United States ignored Russia's concerns and pushed NATO to accept the Czech Republic, Hungary, and Poland as new members. Russia has also opposed U.S. policy in the Balkans over the past decade, especially NATO's 1999 war against Yugoslavia. Again, the United States has paid little attention to Russia's concerns and has taken the steps it deems necessary to bring peace to that volatile region. Finally, it is worth noting that although Russia is dead set against allowing the United States to deploy ballistic missile defenses, it is highly likely that Washington will deploy such a system if it is judged to be technologically feasible.

For sure, great-power rivalry will sometimes produce a stable international order, as happened during the Cold War. Nevertheless, the great powers will continue looking for opportunities to increase their share of world power, and if a favorable situation arises, they will move to undermine that stable order. Consider how hard the United States worked during the late 1980s to weaken the Soviet Union and bring down the stable order that had emerged in Europe during the latter part of the Cold War.[48] Of course, the states that stand to lose power will work to deter aggression and preserve the existing order. But their motives will be selfish, revolving around balance-of-power logic, not some commitment to world peace.

Great powers cannot commit themselves to the pursuit of a peaceful world order for two reasons. First, states are unlikely to agree on a general formula for bolstering peace. Certainly, international relations scholars have never reached a consensus on what the blueprint should look like. In fact, it seems there are about as many theories on the causes of war and peace as there are scholars studying the subject. But more important, policymakers are unable to agree on how to create a stable world. For example, at the Paris Peace Conference after World War I, important differences over how to create stability in Europe divided Georges Clemenceau, David Lloyd George, and Woodrow Wilson.[49] In particular, Clemenceau was determined to impose harsher terms on Germany over the Rhineland than was either Lloyd George or Wilson, while Lloyd George stood out as the hard-liner on German reparations. The Treaty of Versailles, not surprisingly, did little to promote European stability.

Furthermore, consider American thinking on how to achieve stability in Europe in the early days of the Cold War.[50] The key elements for a stable and durable system were in place by the early 1950s. They included the division of Germany, the positioning of American ground forces in Western Europe to deter a Soviet attack, and ensuring that West Germany would not seek to develop nuclear weapons. Officials in the Truman administration, however, disagreed about whether a divided Germany would be a source of peace or war. For example, George Kennan and Paul Nitze, who held important positions in the State Department, believed that a divided Germany would be a source of instability, whereas Secretary of State Dean Acheson disagreed with them. In the 1950s, President Eisenhower sought to end the American commitment to defend Western Europe and to provide West Germany with its own nuclear deterrent. This policy, which was never fully adopted, nevertheless caused significant instability in Europe, as it led directly to the Berlin crises of 1958–59 and 1961.[51]

Second, great powers cannot put aside power considerations and work to promote international peace because they cannot be sure that their efforts will succeed. If their attempt fails, they are likely to pay a steep price for having neglected the balance of power, because if an aggressor appears at the door there will be no answer when they dial 911. That is a risk few states are willing to run. Therefore, prudence dictates that they behave according to realist logic. This line of reasoning accounts for why collective security schemes, which call for states to put aside narrow concerns about the balance of power and instead act in accordance with the broader interests of the international community, invariably die at birth.[52]

Cooperation among States

One might conclude from the preceding discussion that my theory does not allow for any cooperation among the great powers. But this conclusion would be wrong. States can cooperate, although cooperation is sometimes difficult to achieve and always difficult to sustain. Two factors inhibit cooperation: considerations about relative gains and concern about cheating.[53] Ultimately, great powers live in a fundamentally competitive world where they view each other as real, or at least potential, enemies, and they therefore look to gain power at each other's expense.

Any two states contemplating cooperation must consider how profits or gains will be distributed between them. They can think about the division in terms of either absolute or relative gains (recall the distinction made earlier between pursuing either absolute power or relative power; the concept here is the same). With absolute gains, each side is concerned with maximizing its own profits and cares little about how much the other side gains or loses in the deal. Each side cares about the other only to the extent that the other side's behavior affects its own prospects for achieving maximum profits. With relative gains, on the other hand, each side considers not only its own individual gain, but also how well it fares compared to the other side.

Because great powers care deeply about the balance of power, their thinking focuses on relative gains when they consider cooperating with other states. For sure, each state tries to maximize its absolute gains; still, it is more important for a state to make sure that it does no worse, and perhaps better, than the other state in any agreement. Cooperation is more difficult to achieve, however, when states are attuned to relative gains rather than absolute gains.[54] This is because states concerned about absolute gains have to make sure that if the pie is expanding, they are getting at least some portion of the increase, whereas states that worry about relative gains must pay careful attention to how the pie is divided, which complicates cooperative efforts.

Concerns about cheating also hinder cooperation. Great powers are often reluctant to enter into cooperative agreements for fear that the other side will cheat on the agreement and gain a significant advantage. This concern is especially acute in the military realm, causing a "special peril of defection," because the nature of military weaponry allows for rapid shifts in the balance of power.[55] Such a development could create a window of opportunity for the state that cheats to inflict a decisive defeat on its victim.

These barriers to cooperation notwithstanding, great powers do cooperate in a realist world. Balance-of-power logic often causes great powers to form alliances and cooperate against common enemies. The United Kingdom, France, and Russia, for example, were allies against Germany before and during World War I. States sometimes cooperate to gang up on a third state, as Germany and the Soviet Union did against Poland in 1939.[56] More recently, Serbia and Croatia agreed to conquer and divide Bosnia between them, although the United States and its European allies prevented them from executing their agreement.[57] Rivals as well as allies cooperate. After all, deals can be struck that roughly reflect the distribution of power and satisfy concerns about cheating. The various arms control agreements signed by the superpowers during the Cold War illustrate this point.

The bottom line, however, is that cooperation takes place in a world that is competitive at its core—one where states have powerful incentives to take advantage of other states. This point is graphically highlighted by the state of European politics in the forty years before World War I. The great powers cooperated frequently during this period, but that did not stop them from going to war on August 1, 1914.[58] The United States and the Soviet Union also cooperated considerably during World War II, but that cooperation did not prevent the outbreak of the Cold War shortly after Germany and Japan were defeated. Perhaps most amazingly, there was significant economic and military cooperation between Nazi Germany and the Soviet Union during the two years before the Wehrmacht attacked the Red Army.[59] No amount of cooperation can eliminate the dominating logic of security competition. Genuine peace, or a world in which states do not compete for power, is not likely as long as the state system remains anarchic.

Conclusion

In sum, my argument is that the structure of the international system, not the particular characteristics of individual great powers, causes them to think and act offensively and to seek hegemony.[60] I do not adopt Morgenthau's claim that states invariably behave aggressively because they have a will to power hardwired into them. Instead, I assume that the principal motive behind great-power behavior is survival. In anarchy, however, the desire to survive encourages states to behave aggressively. Nor does my theory classify states as more or less aggressive on the basis of their economic or political systems. Offensive realism makes only a handful of assumptions about great powers, and these assumptions apply equally to all great powers.

Except for differences in how much power each state controls, the theory treats all states alike.

I have now laid out the logic explaining why states seek to gain as much power as possible over their rivals. * * *

NOTES

1. Most realist scholars allow in their theories for status quo powers that are not hegemons. At least some states, they argue, are likely to be satisfied with the balance of power and thus have no incentive to change it. See Randall L. Schweller, "Neorealism's Status-Quo Bias: What Security Dilemma?" *Security Studies* 5, No. 3 (Spring 1996, special issue on "Realism: Restatements and Renewal," ed. Benjamin Frankel), pp. 98–101; and Arnold Wolfers, *Discord and Collaboration: Essays on International Politics* (Baltimore, MD: Johns Hopkins University Press, 1962), pp. 84–86, 91–92, 125–26.

2. Milton Friedman, *Essays in Positive Economics* (Chicago: University of Chicago Press, 1953), p. 14. Also see Kenneth N. Waltz, *Theory of International Politics* (Reading, MA: Addison-Wesley, 1979), pp. 5–6, 91, 119.

3. Terry Moe makes a helpful distinction between assumptions that are simply useful simplifications of reality (i.e., realistic in themselves but with unnecessary details omitted), and assumptions that are clearly contrary to reality (i.e., that directly violate well-established truths). See Moe, "On the Scientific Status of Rational Models," *American Journal of Political Science* 23, No. 1 (February 1979), pp. 215–43.

4. The concept of anarchy and its consequences for international politics was first articulated by G. Lowes Dickinson, *The European Anarchy* (New York: Macmillan, 1916). For a more recent and more elaborate discussion of anarchy, see Waltz, *Theory of International Politics*, pp. 88–93. Also see Robert J. Art and Robert Jervis, eds., *International Politics: Anarchy, Force, Imperialism* (Boston: Little, Brown, 1973), pt. 1; and Helen Milner, "The Assumption of Anarchy in International Relations Theory: A Critique," *Review of International Studies* 17, No. 1 (January 1991), pp. 67–85.

5. Although the focus in this study is on the state system, realist logic can be applied to other kinds of anarchic systems. After all, it is the absence of central authority, not any special characteristic of states, that causes them to compete for power.

6. Inis L. Claude, Jr., *Swords into Plowshares: The Problems and Progress of International Organization*, 4th ed. (New York: Random House, 1971), p. 14.

7. The claim that states might have benign intentions is simply a starting assumption. I argue subsequently that when you combine the theory's five assumptions, states are put in a position in which they are strongly disposed to having hostile intentions toward each other.

8. My theory ultimately argues that great powers behave offensively toward each other because that is the best way for them to guarantee their security in an anarchic world. The assumption here, however, is that there are many reasons besides security for why a state might behave aggressively toward another state. In fact, it is

uncertainty about whether those non-security causes of war are at play, or might come into play, that pushes great powers to worry about their survival and thus act offensively. Security concerns alone cannot cause great powers to act aggressively. The possibility that at least one state might be motivated by non-security calculations is a necessary condition for offensive realism, as well as for any other structural theory of international politics that predicts security competition.

9. Quoted in Jon Jacobson, *When the Soviet Union Entered World Politics* (Berkeley: University of California Press, 1994), p. 271.

10. See Elizabeth Pond, *Beyond the Wall: Germany's Road to Unification* (Washington, DC: Brookings Institution Press, 1993), chap. 12; Margaret Thatcher, *The Downing Street Years* (New York: Harper-Collins, 1993), chaps. 25–26; and Philip Zelikow and Condoleezza Rice, *Germany Unified and Europe Transformed: A Study in Statecraft* (Cambridge, MA: Harvard University Press, 1995), chap. 4.

11. Frederick Schuman introduced the concept of self-help in *International Politics: An Introduction to the Western State System* (New York: McGraw-Hill, 1933), pp. 199–202, 514, although Waltz made the concept famous in *Theory of International Politics*, chap. 6. On realism and alliances, see Stephen M. Walt, *The Origins of Alliances* (Ithaca, NY: Cornell University Press, 1987).

12. Quoted in Martin Wight, *Power Politics* (London: Royal Institute of International Affairs, 1946), p. 40.

13. If one state achieves hegemony, the system ceases to be anarchic and becomes hierarchic. Offensive realism, which assumes international anarchy, has little to say about politics under hierarchy. But as discussed later, it is highly unlikely that any state will become a global hegemon, although regional hegemony is feasible. Thus, realism is likely to provide important insights about world politics for the foreseeable future, save for what goes on inside in a region that is dominated by a hegemon.

14. Although great powers always have aggressive intentions, they are not always *aggressors*, mainly because sometimes they do not have the capability to behave aggressively. I use the term "aggressor" throughout this book to denote great powers that have the material wherewithal to act on their aggressive intentions.

15. Kenneth Waltz maintains that great powers should not pursue hegemony but instead should aim to control an "appropriate" amount of world power. See Waltz, "The Origins of War in Neorealist Theory," in Robert I. Rotberg and Theodore K. Rabb, eds., *The Origin and Prevention of Major Wars* (Cambridge: Cambridge University Press, 1989), p. 40.

16. The following hypothetical example illustrates this point. Assume that American policy-makers were forced to choose between two different power balances in the Western Hemisphere. The first is the present distribution of power, whereby the United States is a hegemon that no state in the region would dare challenge militarily. In the second scenario, China replaces Canada and Germany takes the place of Mexico. Even though the United States would have a significant military advantage over both China and Germany, it is difficult to imagine any American strategist opting for this scenario over U.S. hegemony in the Western Hemisphere.

17. John H. Herz, "Idealist Internationalism and the Security Dilemma," *World Politics* 2, No. 2 (January 1950), pp. 157–80.

Although Dickinson did not use the term "security dilemma," its logic is clearly articulated in *European Anarchy*, pp. 20, 88.

18. Herz, "Idealist Internationalism," p. 157.

19. See Joseph M. Grieco, "Anarchy and the Limits of Cooperation: A Realist Critique of the Newest Liberal Institutionalism," *International Organization* 42, No. 3 (Summer 1988), pp. 485–507; Stephen D. Krasner, "Global Communications and National Power: Life on the Pareto Frontier," *World Politics* 43, No. 3 (April 1991), pp. 336–66; and Robert Powell, "Absolute and Relative Gains in International Relations Theory," *American Political Science Review* 85, No. 4 (December 1991), pp. 1303–20.

20. See Michael Mastanduno, "Do Relative Gains Matter? America's Response to Japanese Industrial Policy," *International Security* 16, No. 1 (Summer 1991), pp. 73–113.

21. Waltz maintains that in Hans Morgenthau's theory, states seek power as an end in itself; thus, they are concerned with absolute power, not relative power. See Waltz, "Origins of War," pp. 40–41; and Waltz, *Theory of International Politics*, pp. 126–27.

22. Quoted in Marc Trachtenberg, *A Constructed Peace: The Making of the European Settlement, 1945–1963* (Princeton, NJ: Princeton University Press, 1999), p. 36.

23. In short, the key issue for evaluating offensive realism is not whether a state is constantly trying to conquer other countries or going all out in terms of defense spending, but whether or not great powers routinely pass up promising opportunities to gain power over rivals.

24. See Richard K. Betts, *Surprise Attack: Lessons for Defense Planning* (Washington, DC: Brookings Institution Press, 1982); James D. Fearon, "Rationalist Explanations for War," *International Organization* 49, No. 3 (Summer 1995), pp. 390–401; Robert Jervis, *The Logic of Images in International Relations* (Princeton, NJ: Princeton University Press, 1970); and Stephen Van Evera, *Causes of War: Power and the Roots of Conflict* (Ithaca, NY: Cornell University Press, 1999), pp. 45–51, 83, 137–42.

25. See Joel Achenbach, "The Experts in Retreat: After-the-Fact Explanations for the Gloomy Predictions," *Washington Post*, February 28, 1991; and Jacob Weisberg, "Gulfballs: How the Experts Blew It, Big-Time," *New Republic*, March 25, 1991.

26. Jack Snyder and Stephen Van Evera make this argument in its boldest form. See Jack Snyder, *Myths of Empire: Domestic Politics and International Ambition* (Ithaca, NY: Cornell University Press, 1991), esp. pp. 1, 307–8; and Van Evera, *Causes of War*, esp. pp. 6, 9.

27. Relatedly, some defensive realists interpret the security dilemma to say that the offensive measures a state takes to enhance its own security force rival states to respond in kind, leaving all states no better off than if they had done nothing, and possibly even worse off. See Charles L. Glaser, "The Security Dilemma Revisited," *World Politics* 50, No. 1 (October 1997), pp. 171–201.

28. Although threatened states sometimes balance efficiently against aggressors, they often do not, thereby creating opportunities for successful offense. Snyder appears to be aware of this problem, as he adds the important qualifier "at least in the long run" to his claim that "states typically form balancing alliances to resist aggressors." *Myths of Empire*, p. 11.

29. John Arquilla, *Dubious Battles: Aggression, Defeat, and the International System* (Washington, DC: Crane Russak, 1992), p. 2. Also see

Bruce Bueno de Mesquita, *The War Trap* (New Haven, CT: Yale University Press, 1981), pp. 21–22; and Kevin Wang and James Ray, "Beginners and Winners: The Fate of Initiators of Interstate Wars Involving Great Powers since 1495," *International Studies Quarterly* 38, No. 1 (March 1994), pp. 139–54.

30. Although Snyder and Van Evera maintain that conquest rarely pays, both concede in subtle but important ways that aggression sometimes succeeds. Snyder, for example, distinguishes between expansion (successful offense) and overexpansion (unsuccessful offense), which is the behavior that he wants to explain. See, for example, his discussion of Japanese expansion between 1868 and 1945 in *Myths of Empire*, pp. 114–16. Van Evera allows for variation in the offense-defense balance, to include a few periods where conquest is feasible. See *Causes of War*, chap. 6. Of course, allowing for successful aggression contradicts their central claim that offense hardly ever succeeds.

31. See Robert Gilpin, *War and Change in World Politics* (Cambridge: Cambridge University Press, 1981), p. 29; and William C. Wohlforth, *The Elusive Balance: Power and Perceptions during the Cold War* (Ithaca, NY: Cornell University Press, 1993), pp. 12–14.

32. In subsequent chapters, the power-projection problems associated with large bodies of water are taken into account when measuring the distribution of power (see Chapter 4). Those two factors are treated separately here, however, simply to highlight the profound influence that oceans have on the behavior of great powers.

33. For an opposing view, see David M. Edelstein, "Choosing Friends and Enemies: Perceptions of Intentions in International Relations," Ph.D. diss., University of Chicago, August 2000; Andrew Kydd, "Why Security Seekers Do Not Fight Each Other," *Security Studies* 7, No. 1 (Autumn 1997), pp. 114–54; and Walt, *Origins of Alliances*.

34. See note 8 in this chapter.

35. Jacob Viner, "Power versus Plenty as Objectives of Foreign Policy in the Seventeenth and Eighteenth Centuries," *World Politics* I, No. 1 (October 1948), p. 10.

36. See Mark Bowden, *Black Hawk Down: A Story of Modern War* (London: Penguin, 1999); Alison Des Forges, *"Leave None to Tell the Story": Genocide in Rwanda* (New York: Human Rights Watch, 1999), pp. 623–25; and Gerard Prunier, *The Rwanda Crisis: History of a Genocide* (New York: Columbia University Press, 1995), pp. 274–75.

37. See Scott R. Feil, *Preventing Genocide: How the Early Use of Force Might Have Succeeded in Rwanda* (New York: Carnegie Corporation, 1998); and John Mueller, "The Banality of 'Ethnic War,'" *International Security* 25, No. 1 (Summer 2000), pp. 58–62. For a less sanguine view of how many lives would have been saved had the United States intervened in Rwanda, see Alan J. Kuperman, "Rwanda in Retrospect," *Foreign Affairs* 79, No. 1 (January–February 2000), pp. 94–118.

38. See David F. Schmitz, *Thank God They're on Our Side: The United States and Right-Wing Dictatorships, 1921–1965* (Chapel Hill: University of North Carolina Press, 1999), chaps. 4–6; Gaddis Smith, *The Last Years of the Monroe Doctrine, 1945–1993* (New York: Hill and Wang, 1994); Tony Smith, *America's Mission: The United States and the Worldwide Struggle for Democracy in the Twentieth Century* (Princeton, NJ: Princeton University Press, 1994); and

Stephen Van Evera, "Why Europe Matters, Why the Third World Doesn't: American Grand Strategy after the Cold War," *Journal of Strategic Studies* 13, No. 2 (June 1990), pp. 25–30.

39. Quoted in John M. Carroll and George C. Herring, eds., *Modern American Diplomacy*, rev. ed. (Wilmington, DE: Scholarly Resources, 1996), p. 122.

40. Nikita Khrushchev makes a similar point about Stalin's policy toward Chinese nationalist leader Chiang Kai-shek during World War II.

41. See Walt, *Origins of Alliances*, pp. 5, 266–68.

42. Adam Smith, *An Inquiry into the Nature and Causes of the Wealth of Nations*, ed. Edwin Cannan (Chicago: University of Chicago Press, 1976), Vol. 1, p. 487. All the quotes in this paragraph are from pp. 484–87 of that book.

43. For an overview of the Anglo-Dutch rivalry, see Jack S. Levy, "The Rise and Decline of the Anglo-Dutch Rivalry, 1609–1689," in William R. Thompson, ed., *Great Power Rivalries* (Columbia: University of South Carolina Press, 1999), pp. 172–200; and Paul M. Kennedy, *The Rise and Fall of British Naval Mastery* (London: Allen Lane, 1976), chap. 2.

44. William J. Clinton, "Address by the President to the 48th Session of the United Nations General Assembly," United Nations, New York, September 27, 1993. Also see George Bush, "Toward a New World Order: Address by the President to a Joint Session of Congress," September 11, 1990.

45. Bradley Thayer examined whether the victorious powers were able to create and maintain stable security orders in the aftermath of the Napoleonic Wars, World War I, and World War II, or whether they competed among themselves for power, as realism would predict. Thayer concludes that the rhetoric of the triumphant powers notwithstanding, they remained firmly committed to gaining power at each other's expense. See Bradley A. Thayer, "Creating Stability in New World Orders," Ph.D. diss., University of Chicago, August 1996.

46. See Melvyn P. Leffler, *A Preponderance of Power: National Security, the Truman Administration, and the Cold War* (Stanford, CA: Stanford University Press, 1992).

47. For a discussion of American efforts to undermine Soviet control of Eastern Europe, see Peter Grose, *Operation Rollback: America's Secret War behind the Iron Curtain* (Boston: Houghton Mifflin, 2000); Walter L. Hixson, *Parting the Curtain: Propaganda, Culture, and the Cold War, 1945–1961* (New York: St. Martin's, 1997); and Gregory Mitrovich, *Undermining the Kremlin: America's Strategy to Subvert the Soviet Bloc, 1947–1956* (Ithaca, NY: Cornell University Press, 2000).

48. For a synoptic discussion of U.S. policy toward the Soviet Union in the late 1980s that cites most of the key sources on the subject, see Randall L. Schweller and William C. Wohlforth, "Power Test: Evaluating Realism in Response to the End of the Cold War," *Security Studies* 9, No. 3 (Spring 2000), pp. 91–97.

49. The editors of a major book on the Treaty of Versailles write, "The resulting reappraisal, as documented in this book, constitutes a new synthesis of peace conference scholarship. The findings call attention to divergent peace aims within the American and Allied camps and underscore the degree to which the negotiators themselves considered the Versailles Treaty a work in progress." Manfred F. Boemeke, Gerald D. Feldman, and Elisabeth Glaser, eds.,

The Treaty of Versailles: A Reassessment after 75 Years (Cambridge: Cambridge University Press, 1998), p. 1.

50. This paragraph draws heavily on Trachtenberg, *Constructed Peace*; and Marc Trachtenberg, *History and Strategy* (Princeton, NJ: Princeton University Press, 1991), chaps. 4–5. Also see G. John Ikenberry, "Rethinking the Origins of American Hegemony," *Political Science Quarterly* 104, No. 3 (Autumn 1989), pp. 375–400.

51. The failure of American policymakers during the early Cold War to understand where the security competition in Europe was leading is summarized by Trachtenberg, "The predictions that were made pointed as a rule in the opposite direction: that Germany could not be kept down forever; that the Federal Republic would ultimately . . . want nuclear forces of her own; that U.S. troops could not be expected to remain in . . . Europe. . . . Yet all these predictions—every single one—turned out to be wrong." Trachtenberg, *History and Strategy*, pp. 231–32. Also see Trachtenberg, *Constructed Peace*, pp. vii–viii.

52. For more discussion of the pitfalls of collective security, see John J. Mearsheimer, "The False Promise of International Institutions," *International Security* 19, No. 3 (Winter 1994–95), pp. 26–37.

53. See Grieco, "Anarchy and the Limits of Cooperation," pp. 498, 500.

54. For evidence of relative gains considerations thwarting cooperation among states, see Paul W. Schroeder, *The Transformation of European Politics, 1763–1848* (Oxford: Clarendon, 1994), chap. 3.

55. Charles Lipson, "International Cooperation in Economic and Security Affairs," *World Politics* 37, No. 1 (October 1984), p. 14.

56. See Randall L. Schweller, "Bandwagoning for Profit: Bringing the Revisionist State Back In," *International Security* 19, No. 1 (Summer 1994), pp. 72–107. See also the works cited in note 59 in this chapter.

57. See Misha Glenny, *The Fall of Yugoslavia: The Third Balkan War*, 3d rev. ed. (New York: Penguin, 1996), p. 149; Philip Sherwell and Alina Petric, "Tudjman Tapes Reveal Plans to Divide Bosnia and Hide War Crimes," *Sunday Telegraph* (London), June 18, 2000; Laura Silber and Allan Little, *Yugoslavia: Death of a Nation*, rev. ed. (New York: Penguin, 1997), pp. 131–32, 213; and Warren Zimmerman, *Origins of a Catastrophe: Yugoslavia and Its Destroyers—America's Last Ambassador Tells What Happened and Why* (New York: Times Books, 1996), pp. 116–17.

58. See John Maynard Keynes, *The Economic Consequences of the Peace* (New York: Penguin, 1988), chap. 2; and J. M. Roberts, *Europe, 1880–1945* (London: Longman, 1970), pp. 239–41.

59. For information on the Molotov-Ribbentrop Pact of August 1939 and the ensuing cooperation between those states, see Alan Bullock, *Hitler and Stalin: Parallel Lives* (London: HarperCollins, 1991), chaps. 14–15; I.C.B. Dear, ed., *The Oxford Companion to World War II* (Oxford: Oxford University Press, 1995), pp. 780–82; Anthony Read and David Fisher, *The Deadly Embrace: Hitler, Stalin, and the Nazi-Soviet Pact, 1939–1941* (New York: Norton, 1988); Geoffrey Roberts, *The Unholy Alliance: Stalin's Pact with Hitler* (Bloomington: Indiana University Press, 1989), chaps. 8–10; and Adam B. Ulam, *Expansion and Coexistence: Soviet Foreign Policy, 1917–1973*, 2d ed. (New York: Holt, Rinehart, and Winston, 1974), chap. 6.

60. Waltz maintains that structural theories can explain international outcomes—i.e., whether war is more likely in bipolar or multipolar systems—but that they cannot explain the foreign policy behavior of particular states. A separate theory of foreign policy, he argues, is needed for that task. See *Theory of International Politics*, pp. 71–72, 121–23.

Michael W. Doyle

LIBERALISM AND WORLD POLITICS

Promoting freedom will produce peace, we have often been told. In a speech before the British Parliament in June of 1982, President Reagan proclaimed that governments founded on a respect for individual liberty exercise "restraint" and "peaceful intentions" in their foreign policy. He then announced a "crusade for freedom" and a "campaign for democratic development" (Reagan, June 9, 1982).

In making these claims the president joined a long list of liberal theorists (and propagandists) and echoed an old argument: the aggressive instincts of authoritarian leaders and totalitarian ruling parties make for war. Liberal states, founded on such individual rights as equality before the law, free speech and other civil liberties, private property, and elected representation are fundamentally against war this argument asserts. When the citizens who bear the burdens of war elect their governments, wars become impossible. Furthermore, citizens appreciate that the benefits of trade can be enjoyed only under conditions of peace. Thus the very existence of liberal states, such as the U.S., Japan, and our European allies, makes for peace.

Building on a growing literature in international political science, I reexamine the liberal claim President Reagan reiterated for us. I look at three distinct theoretical traditions of liberalism, attributable to three theorists: Schumpeter, a brilliant explicator of the liberal pacifism the president invoked;

Machiavelli, a classical republican whose glory is an imperialism we often practice; and Kant.

Despite the contradictions of liberal pacifism and liberal imperialism, I find, with Kant and other liberal republicans, that liberalism does leave a coherent legacy on foreign affairs. Liberal states are different. They are indeed peaceful, yet they are also prone to make war, as the U.S. and our "freedom fighters" are now doing, not so covertly, against Nicaragua. Liberal states have created a separate peace, as Kant argued they would, and have also discovered liberal reasons for aggression, as he feared they might. I conclude by arguing that the differences among liberal pacifism, liberal imperialism, and Kant's liberal internationalism are not arbitrary but rooted in differing conceptions of the citizen and the state.

Liberal Pacifism

There is no canonical description of liberalism. What we tend to call *liberal* resembles a family portrait of principles and institutions, recognizable by certain characteristics—for example, individual freedom, political participation, private property, and equality of opportunity—that most liberal states share, although none has perfected them all. Joseph Schumpeter clearly fits within this family when he considers the international effects of capitalism and democracy.

Schumpeter's "Sociology of Imperialisms," published in 1919, made a coherent and sustained argument concerning the pacifying (in the sense of

From *American Political Science Review* 80, no. 4 (Dec. 1986): 1151–69. The author's notes have been omitted.

nonaggressive) effects of liberal institutions and principles (Schumpeter, 1955; see also Doyle, 1986, pp. 155–59). Unlike some of the earlier liberal theorists who focused on a single feature such as trade (Montesquieu, 1949, vol. I, bk. 20, chap. 1) or failed to examine critically the arguments they were advancing, Schumpeter saw the interaction of capitalism and democracy as the foundation of liberal pacifism, and he tested his arguments in a sociology of historical imperialisms.

He defines *imperialism* as "an objectless disposition on the part of a state to unlimited forcible expansion" (Schumpeter, 1955, p. 6). Excluding imperialisms that were mere "catchwords" and those that were "object-ful" (e.g., defensive imperialism), he traces the roots of objectless imperialism to three sources, each an atavism. Modern imperialism, according to Schumpeter, resulted from the combined impact of a "war machine," warlike instincts, and export monopolism.

Once necessary, the war machine later developed a life of its own and took control of a state's foreign policy: "Created by the wars that required it, the machine now created the wars it required" (Schumpeter, 1955, p. 25). Thus, Schumpeter tells us that the army of ancient Egypt, created to drive the Hyksos out of Egypt, took over the state and pursued militaristic imperialism. Like the later armies of the courts of absolutist Europe, it fought wars for the sake of glory and booty, for the sake of warriors and monarchs—wars *gratia* warriors.

A warlike disposition, elsewhere called "instinctual elements of bloody primitivism," is the natural ideology of a war machine. It also exists independently; the Persians, says Schumpeter (1955, pp. 25–32), were a warrior nation from the outset.

Under modern capitalism, export monopolists, the third source of modern imperialism, push for imperialist expansion as a way to expand their closed markets. The absolute monarchies were the last clear-cut imperialisms. Nineteenth-century imperialisms merely represent the vestiges of the imperialisms created by Louis XIV and Catherine the Great. Thus, the export monopolists are an atavism of the absolute monarchies, for they depend completely on the tariffs imposed by the monarchs and their militaristic successors for revenue (Schumpeter, 1955, p. 82–83). Without tariffs, monopolies would be eliminated by foreign competition.

Modern (nineteenth century) imperialism, therefore, rests on an atavistic war machine, militaristic attitudes left over from the days of monarchical wars, and export monopolism, which is nothing more than the economic residue of monarchical finance. In the modern era, imperialists gratify their private interests. From the national perspective, their imperialistic wars are objectless.

Schumpeter's theme now emerges. Capitalism and democracy are forces for peace. Indeed, they are antithetical to imperialism. For Schumpeter, the further development of capitalism and democracy means that imperialism will inevitably disappear. He maintains that capitalism produces an unwarlike disposition; its populace is "democratized, individualized, rationalized" (Schumpeter, 1955, p. 68). The people's energies are daily absorbed in production. The disciplines of industry and the market train people in "economic rationalism"; the instability of industrial life necessitates calculation. Capitalism also "individualizes"; "subjective opportunities" replace the "immutable factors" of traditional, hierarchical society. Rational individuals demand democratic governance.

Democratic capitalism leads to peace. As evidence, Schumpeter claims that throughout the capitalist world an opposition has arisen to "war, expansion, cabinet diplomacy"; that contemporary capitalism is associated with peace parties; and that the industrial worker of capitalism is "vigorously anti-imperialist." In addition, he points out that the capitalist world has developed means of preventing war, such as the Hague Court and that the least feudal, most capitalist society—the United States—has demonstrated the least imperialistic tendencies (Schumpeter, 1955, pp. 95–96). An example of the lack of imperialistic tendencies in the U.S., Schumpeter thought, was our leaving over half of Mexico unconquered in the war of 1846–48.

Schumpeter's explanation for liberal pacifism is quite simple: Only war profiteers and military aristocrats gain from wars. No democracy would pursue a minority interest and tolerate the high costs of imperialism. When free trade prevails, "no class" gains from forcible expansion because

> foreign raw materials and food stuffs are as accessible to each nation as though they were in its own territory. Where the cultural backwardness of a region makes normal economic intercourse dependent on colonization it does not matter, assuming free trade, which of the "civilized" nations undertakes the task of colonization. (Schumpeter, 1955, pp. 75–76)

Schumpeter's arguments are difficult to evaluate. In partial tests of quasi-Schumpeterian propositions, Michael Haas (1974, pp. 464–65) discovered a cluster that associates democracy, development, and sustained modernization with peaceful conditions. However, M. Small and J. D. Singer (1976) have discovered that there is no clearly negative correlation between democracy and war in the period 1816–1965—the period that would be central to Schumpeter's argument (see also Wilkenfeld, 1968, Wright, 1942, p. 841).

* * * A recent study by R. J. Rummel (1983) of "libertarianism" and international violence is the closest test Schumpeterian pacifism has received. "Free" states (those enjoying political and economic freedom) were shown to have considerably less conflict at or above the level of economic sanctions than "nonfree" states. The free states, the partly free states (including the democratic socialist countries such as Sweden), and the nonfree states accounted for 24%, 26%, and 61%, respectively, of the international violence during the period examined.

These effects are impressive but not conclusive for the Schumpeterian thesis. The data are limited, in this test, to the period 1976 to 1980. It includes, for example, the Russo-Afghan War, the Vietnamese invasion of Cambodia, China's invasion of Vietnam, and Tanzania's invasion of Uganda but just misses the U.S., quasi-covert intervention in Angola (1975) and our not so covert war against Nicaragua (1981–). More importantly, it excludes the cold war period, with its numerous interventions, and the long history of colonial wars (the Boer War, the Spanish-American War, the Mexican Intervention, etc.) that marked the history of liberal, including democratic capitalist, states (Doyle, 1983b; Chan, 1984; Weede, 1984).

The discrepancy between the warlike history of liberal states and Schumpeter's pacifistic expectations highlights three extreme assumptions. First, his "materialistic monism" leaves little room for noneconomic objectives, whether espoused by states or individuals. Neither glory, nor prestige, nor ideological justification, nor the pure power of ruling shapes policy. These nonmaterial goals leave little room for positive-sum gains, such as the comparative advantages of trade. Second, and relatedly, the same is true for his states. The political life of individuals seems to have been homogenized at the same time as the individuals were "rationalized, individualized, and democratized." Citizens—capitalists and workers, rural and urban—seek material welfare. Schumpeter seems to presume that ruling makes no difference. He also presumes that no one is prepared to take those measures (such as stirring up foreign quarrels to preserve a domestic ruling coalition) that enhance one's political power, despite deterimental effects on mass welfare. Third, like domestic politics, world politics are homogenized. Materially monistic and democratically capitalist, all states evolve toward free trade and liberty together. Countries differently constituted seem to disappear from Schumpeter's analysis. "Civilized" nations govern "culturally backward" *regions*. These assumptions are not shared by Machiavelli's theory of liberalism.

Liberal Imperialism

Machiavelli argues, not only that republics are not pacifistic, but that they are the best form of state for imperial expansion. Establishing a republic fit for imperial expansion is, moreover, the best way to guarantee the survival of a state.

Machiavelli's republic is a classical mixed republic. It is not a democracy—which he thought would quickly degenerate into a tyranny—but is characterized by social equality, popular liberty, and political participation (Machiavelli, 1950, bk. 1, chap. 2, p. 112; see also Huliung, 1983, chap. 2; Mansfield, 1970; Pocock, 1975, pp. 198–99; Skinner, 1981, chap. 3). The consuls serve as "kings," the senate as an aristocracy managing the state, and the people in the assembly as the source of strength.

Liberty results from "disunion"—the competition and necessity for compromise required by the division of powers among senate, consuls, and tribunes (the last representing the common people). Liberty also results from the popular veto. The powerful few threaten the rest with tyranny, Machiavelli says, because they seek to dominate. The mass demands not to be dominated, and their veto thus preserves the liberties of the state (Machiavelli, 1950, bk. 1, chap. 5, p. 122). However, since the people and the rulers have different social characters, the people need to be "managed" by the few to avoid having their recklessness overturn or their fecklessness undermine the ability of the state to expand (Machiavelli, 1950, bk. 1, chap. 53, pp. 249–50). Thus the senate and the consuls plan expansion, consult oracles, and employ religion to manage the resources that the energy of the people supplies.

Strength, and then imperial expansion, results from the way liberty encourages increased population and property, which grow when the citizens know their lives and goods are secure from arbitrary seizure. Free citizens equip large armies and provide soldiers who fight for public glory and the common good because these are, in fact, their own (Machiavelli, 1950, bk. 2, chap. 2, pp. 287–90). If you seek the honor of having your state expand, Machiavelli advises, you should organize it as a free and popular republic like Rome, rather than as an aristocratic republic like Sparta or Venice. Expansion thus calls for a free republic.

"Necessity"—political survival—calls for expansion. If a stable aristocratic republic is forced by foreign conflict "to extend her territory, in such a case we shall see her foundations give way and herself quickly brought to ruin"; if, on the other hand, domestic security prevails, "the continued tranquility would enervate her, or provoke internal disensions, which together, or either of them separately, will apt to prove her ruin" (Machiavelli, 1950, bk. 1, chap. 6, p. 129). Machiavelli therefore believes it is necessary to take the constitution of Rome, rather than that of Sparta or Venice, as our model.

Hence, this belief leads to liberal imperialism. We are lovers of glory, Machiavelli announces. We seek to rule or, at least, to avoid being oppressed. In either case, we want more for ourselves and our states than just material welfare (materialistic monism). Because other states with similar aims thereby threaten us, we prepare ourselves for expansion. Because our fellow citizens threaten us if we do not allow them either to satisfy their ambition or to release their political energies through imperial expansion, we expand.

There is considerable historical evidence for liberal imperialism. Machiavelli's (Polybius's) Rome and Thucydides' Athens both were imperial republics in the Machiavellian sense (Thucydides, 1954, bk. 6). The historical record of numerous U.S. interventions in the postwar period supports Machiavelli's argument (* * * Barnet, 1968, chap. 11), but the current record of liberal pacifism, weak as it is, calls some of his insights into question. To the extent that the modern populace actually controls (and thus unbalances) the mixed republic, its diffidence may outweigh elite ("senatorial") aggressiveness.

We can conclude either that (1) liberal pacifism has at least taken over with the further development of capitalist democracy, as Schumpeter predicted it would or that (2) the mixed record of liberalism—pacifism and imperialism—indicates that some liberal states are Schumpeterian democracies while others are Machiavellian republics. Before we accept either conclusion, however, we must consider a third apparent regularity of modern world politics.

Liberal Internationalism

Modern liberalism carries with it two legacies. They do not affect liberal states separately, according to whether they are pacifistic or imperialistic, but simultaneously.

The first of these legacies is the pacification of foreign relations among liberal states. * * *

Beginning in the eighteenth century and slowly growing since then, a zone of peace, which Kant called the "pacific federation" or "pacific union," has begun to be established among liberal societies. More than 40 liberal states currently make up the union. Most are in Europe and North America, but they can be found on every continent, as Appendix 1 indicates.

Here the predictions of liberal pacifists (and President Reagan) are borne out: liberal states do exercise peaceful restraint, and a separate peace exists among them. This separate peace provides a solid foundation for the United States' crucial alliances with the liberal powers, e.g., the North Atlantic Treaty Organization and our Japanese alliance. This foundation appears to be impervious to the quarrels with our allies that bedeviled the Carter and Reagan administrations. It also offers the promise of a continuing peace among liberal states, and as the number of liberal states increases, it announces the possibility of global peace this side of the grave or world conquest.

Of course, the probability of the outbreak of war in any given year between any two given states is low. The occurrence of a war between any two adjacent states, considered over a long period of time, would be more probable. The apparent absence of war between liberal states, whether adjacent or not, for almost 200 years thus may have significance. Similar claims cannot be made for feudal, fascist, communist, authoritarian, or totalitarian forms of rule (Doyle, 1983a, p. 222), nor for pluralistic or merely similar societies. More significant perhaps is that when states are forced to decide on which side of an impending world war they will fight, liberal states all wind up on the same side despite the complexity of the paths that take them there. These characteristics do not prove that the peace among liberals is statistically significant nor that liberalism is the sole valid explanation for the peace. They do suggest that we consider the possibility that liberals have indeed established a separate peace—but only among themselves.

Liberalism also carries with it a second legacy: international "imprudence" (Hume, 1963, pp. 346–47). Peaceful restraint only seems to work in liberals' relations with other liberals. Liberal states have fought numerous wars with nonliberal states. (For a list of international wars since 1816 see Appendix 2.)

Many of these wars have been defensive and thus prudent by necessity. Liberal states have been attacked and threatened by nonliberal states that do not exercise any special restraint in their dealings with the liberal states. Authoritarian rulers both stimulate and respond to an international political environment in which conflicts of prestige, interest, and pure fear of what other states might do all lead states toward war. War and conquest have thus characterized the careers of many authoritarian rulers and ruling parties, from Louis XIV and Napoleon to Mussolini's fascists, Hitler's Nazis, and Stalin's communists.

Yet we cannot simply blame warfare on the authoritarians or totalitarians, as many of our more enthusiastic politicians would have us do. Most wars arise out of calculations and miscalculations of interest, misunderstandings, and mutual suspicions, such as those that characterized the origins of World War I. However, aggression by the liberal state has also characterized a large number of wars. Both France and Britain fought expansionist colonial wars throughout the nineteenth century. The United States fought a similar war with Mexico from 1846 to 1848, waged a war of annihilation against the American Indians, and intervened militarily against sovereign states many times before and after World War II. Liberal states invade weak nonliberal states and display striking distrust in dealings with powerful nonliberal states (Doyle, 1983b).

Neither realist (statist) nor Marxist theory accounts well for these two legacies. While they can account for aspects of certain periods of international stability (* * * Russett, 1985), neither the logic of the balance of power nor the logic of international hegemony explains the separate peace maintained for more than 150 years among states sharing one particular form of governance—liberal principles and institutions. Balance-of-power theory expects—indeed is premised upon—flexible arrangements of geostrategic rivalry that include preventive war. Hegemonies wax and wane, but the liberal peace holds. Marxist "ultra-imperialists" expect a form of peaceful rivalry among capitalists, but only liberal capitalists maintain peace. Leninists expect liberal capitalists to be aggressive toward nonliberal states, but they also (and especially) expect them to be imperialistic toward fellow liberal capitalists.

Kant's theory of liberal internationalism helps us understand these two legacies. * * * *Perpetual Peace*, written in 1795 (Kant, 1970, pp. 93–130), helps us understand the interactive nature of international relations. Kant tries to teach us methodologically that we can study neither the systemic relations of states nor the varieties of state behavior in isolation from each other. Substantively, he anticipates for us the ever-widening pacification of a liberal pacific union, explains this pacification, and at the same time suggests why liberal states are not pacific in their relations with nonliberal states. Kant argues that perpetual peace will be guaranteed by the ever-widening acceptance of three "definitive articles" of peace. When all nations have accepted the definitive articles in a metaphorical "treaty" of perpetual peace he asks them to sign, perpetual peace will have been established.

The First Definitive Article requires the civil constitution of the state to be republican. By *republican* Kant means a political society that has solved the problem of combining moral autonomy, individualism, and social order. A private property and market-oriented economy partially addressed that dilemma in the private sphere. The public, or political, sphere was more troubling. His answer was a republic that preserved juridical freedom—the legal equality of citizens as subjects—on the basis of a representative government with a separation of powers. Juridical freedom is preserved because the morally autonomous individual is by means of representation a self-legislator making laws that apply to all citizens equally, including himself or herself. Tyranny is avoided because the individual is subject to laws he or she does not also administer (Kant, *PP* [*Perpetual Peace*], pp. 99–102 * * *).

Liberal republics will progressively establish peace among themselves by means of the pacific federation, or union (*foedus pacificum*), described in Kant's Second Definitive Article. The pacific union will establish peace within a federation of free states and securely maintain the rights of each state. The world will not have achieved the "perpetual peace" that provides the ultimate guarantor of republican freedom until "a late stage and after many unsuccessful attempts" (Kant, *UH* [*The Idea for a Universal History with a Cosmopolitan Purpose*], p. 47). At that time, all nations will have learned the lessons of peace through right conceptions of the appropriate constitution, great and sad experience, and good will. Only then will individuals enjoy perfect republican rights or the full guarantee of a global and just peace. In the meantime, the "pacific federation" of liberal republics—"an enduring and gradually expanding federation likely to prevent war"—brings within it more and more republics—despite republican collapses, backsliding, and disastrous wars—creating an ever-expanding separate peace (Kant, *PP*, p. 105). Kant emphasizes that

> it can be shown that this idea of federalism, extending gradually to encompass all states and thus leading to perpetual peace, is practicable and has objective reality. For if by good fortune one powerful and enlightened nation can form a republic (which is by nature inclined to seek peace), this will provide a focal point for federal association among other states. These will join up with the first one, thus securing the freedom of each state in accordance with the idea of international right, and the whole will gradually spread further and further by a series of alliances of this kind. (Kant, *PP*, p. 104)

The pacific union is not a single peace treaty ending one war, a world state, nor a state of nations. Kant finds the first insufficient. The second and third are impossible or potentially tyrannical. National sovereignty precludes reliable subservience to a state of nations; a world state destroys the civic freedom on which the development of human capacities rests (Kant, *UH*, p. 50). Although Kant obliquely refers to various classical interstate confederations and modern diplomatic congresses, he develops no systematic organizational embodiment of this treaty and presumably does not find institutionalization necessary (Riley, 1983, chap. 5; Schwarz, 1962, p. 77). He appears to have in mind a mutual nonaggression pact, perhaps a collective security agreement, and the cosmopolitan law set forth in the Third Definitive Article.

The Third Definitive Article establishes a cosmopolitan law to operate in conjunction with the pacific union. The cosmopolitan law "shall be limited to conditions of universal hospitality." In this Kant calls for the recognition of the "right of a foreigner not to be treated with hostility when he arrives on someone else's territory." This "does not extend beyond those conditions which make it possible for them [foreigners] to attempt to enter into relations [commerce] with the native inhabitants" (Kant, *PP*, p. 106). Hospitality does not require extending to foreigners either the right to citizenship or the right to settlement, unless the foreign visitors would perish if they were expelled. Foreign conquest and plunder also find no justification under this right. Hospitality does appear to include the right of access and the obligation of maintaining the opportunity for citizens to exchange goods and ideas without imposing the obligation to trade (a voluntary act in all cases under liberal constitutions).

Perpetual peace, for Kant, is an epistemology, a condition for ethical action, and, most importantly, an explanation of how the "mechanical process of nature visibly exhibits the purposive plan of producing concord among men, even against their will and indeed by means of their very discord" (Kant, *PP*, p. 108; *UH*, pp. 44–45). Understanding history requires an epistemological foundation, for without a teleology, such as the promise of perpetual peace, the complexity of history would overwhelm human understanding (Kant, *UH*, pp. 51–53). Perpetual peace, however, is not merely a heuristic device with which to interpret history. It is guaranteed, Kant explains in the "First Addition" to *Perpetual Peace* ("On the Guarantee of Perpetual Peace"), to result from men fulfilling their ethical duty or, failing that, from a hidden plan. Peace is an ethical duty because it is only under conditions of peace that all men can treat each other as ends, rather than means to an end (Kant, *UH*, p. 50; Murphy, 1970, chap. 3). * * *

In the end, however, our guarantee of perpetual peace does not rest on ethical conduct. * * *

The guarantee thus rests, Kant argues, not on the probable behavior of moral angels, but on that of "devils, so long as they possess understanding" (*PP*, p. 112). In explaining the sources of each of the three definitive articles of the perpetual peace, Kant then tells us how we (as free and intelligent devils) could be motivated by fear, force, and calculated advantage to undertake a course of action whose outcome we could reasonably anticipate to be perpetual peace. Yet while it is possible to conceive of the Kantian road to peace in these terms, Kant himself recognizes and argues that social evolution also makes the conditions of moral behavior less onerous and hence more likely (*CF* [*The Contest of Faculties*], pp. 187–89; Kelly, 1969, pp. 106–13). In tracing the effects of both political and moral development, he builds an account of why liberal states do maintain peace among themselves and of how it will (by implication, has) come about that the pacific union will expand. He also explains how these republics would engage in wars with nonrepublics and therefore suffer the "sad experience" of wars that an ethical policy might have avoided.

■   ■   ■

Kant shows how republics, once established, lead to peaceful relations. He argues that once the aggressive interests of absolutist monarchies are tamed and the habit of respect for individual rights engrained by republican government, wars would appear as the disaster to the people's welfare that he and the other liberals thought them to be. The fundamental reason is this:

> If, as is inevitability the case under this constitution, the consent of the citizens is required to decide whether or not war should be declared, it is very natural that they will have a great hesitation in embarking on so dangerous an enterprise. For this would mean calling down on themselves

all the miseries of war, such as doing the fighting themselves, supplying the costs of the war from their own resources, painfully making good the ensuing devastation, and, as the crowning evil, having to take upon themselves a burden of debts which will embitter peace itself and which can never be paid off on account of the constant threat of new wars. But under a constitution where the subject is not a citizen, and which is therefore not republican, it is the simplest thing in the world to go to war. For the head of state is not a fellow citizen, but the owner of the state, and war will not force him to make the slightest sacrifice so far as his banquets, hunts, pleasure palaces and court festivals are concerned. He can thus decide on war, without any significant reason, as a kind of amusement, and unconcernedly leave it to the diplomatic corps (who are always ready for such proposes) to justify the war for the sake of propriety. (Kant, *PP*, p. 100).

Yet these domestic republican restraints do not end war. If they did, liberal states would not be warlike, which is far from the case. They do introduce republican caution—Kant's "hesitation"—in place of monarchical caprice. Liberal wars are only fought for popular, liberal purposes. The historical liberal legacy is laden with popular wars fought to promote freedom, to protect private property, or to support liberal allies against nonliberal enemies. Kant's position is ambiguous. He regards these wars as unjust and warns liberals of their susceptibility to them (Kant, *PP*, p. 106). At the same time, Kant argues that each nation "can and ought to" demand that its neighboring nations enter into the pacific union of liberal states (*PP*, p. 102). * * *

■   ■   ■

* * * As republics emerge (the first source) and as culture progresses, an understanding of the

legitimate rights of all citizens and of all republics comes into play; and this, now that caution characterizes policy, sets up the moral foundations for the liberal peace. Correspondingly, international law highlights the importance of Kantian publicity. Domestically, publicity helps ensure that the officials of republics act according to the principles they profess to hold just and according to the interests of the electors they claim to represent. Internationally, free speech and the effective communication of accurate conceptions of the political life of foreign peoples is essential to establishing and preserving the understanding on which the guarantee of respect depends. Domestically just republics, which rest on consent, then presume foreign republics also to be consensual, just, and therefore deserving of accommodation. * * * Because nonliberal governments are in a state of aggression with their own people, their foreign relations become for liberal governments deeply suspect. In short, fellow liberals benefit from a presumption of amity; nonliberals suffer from a presumption of enmity. Both presumptions may be accurate; each, however, may also be self-confirming.

Lastly, cosmopolitan law adds material incentives to moral commitments. The cosmopolitan right to hospitality permits the "spirit of commerce" sooner or later to take hold of every nation, thus impelling states to promote peace and to try to avert war. Liberal economic theory holds that these cosmopolitan ties derive from a cooperative international division of labor and free trade according to comparative advantage. Each economy is said to be better off than it would have been under autarky; each thus acquires an incentive to avoid policies that would lead the other to break these economic ties. Because keeping open markets rests upon the assumption that the next set of transactions will also be determined by prices rather than coercion, a sense of mutual security is vital to avoid security-motivated searches for economic autarky. Thus, avoiding a challenge to

another liberal state's security or even enhancing each other's security by means of alliance naturally follows economic interdependence.

A further cosmopolitan source of liberal peace is the international market's removal of difficult decisions of production and distribution from the direct sphere of state policy. A foreign state thus does not appear directly responsible for these outcomes, and states can stand aside from, and to some degree above, these contentious market rivalries and be ready to step in to resolve crises. The interdependence of commerce and the international contacts of state officials help create crosscutting transnational ties that serve as lobbies for mutual accommodation. According to modern liberal scholars, international financiers and transnational and transgovernmental organizations create interests in favor of accommodation. Moreover, their variety has ensured that no single conflict sours an entire relationship by setting off a spiral of reciprocated retaliation * * *. Conversely, a sense of suspicion, such as that characterizing relations between liberal and nonliberal governments, can lead to restrictions on the range of contacts between societies, and this can increase the prospect that a single conflict will determine an entire relationship.

No single constitutional, international, or cosmopolitan source is alone sufficient, but together (and only together) they plausibly connect the characteristics of liberal polities and economies with sustained liberal peace. Alliances founded on mutual strategic interest among liberal and nonliberal states have been broken; economic ties between liberal and nonliberal states have proven fragile; but the political bonds of liberal rights and interests have proven a remarkably firm foundation for mutual nonaggression. A separate peace exists among liberal states.

In their relations with nonliberal states, however, liberal states have not escaped from the insecurity caused by anarchy in the world political system considered as a whole. Moreover, the very constitutional restraint, international respect for individual rights, and shared commercial interests that establish grounds for peace among liberal states establish grounds for additional conflict in relations between liberal and nonliberal societies.

Conclusion

Kant's liberal internationalism, Machiavelli's liberal imperialism, and Schumpeter's liberal pacifism rest on fundamentally different views of the nature of the human being, the state, and international relations. Schumpeter's humans are rationalized, individualized, and democratized. They are also homogenized, pursuing material interests "monistically." Because their material interests lie in peaceful trade, they and the democratic state that these fellow citizens control are pacifistic. Machiavelli's citizens are splendidly diverse in their goals but fundamentally unequal in them as well, seeking to rule or fearing being dominated. Extending the rule of the dominant elite or avoiding the political collapse of their state, each calls for imperial expansion.

Kant's citizens, too, are diverse in their goals and individualized and rationalized, but most importantly, they are capable of appreciating the moral equality of all individuals and of treating other individuals as ends rather than as means. The Kantian state thus is governed publicly according to law, as a republic. Kant's is the state that solves the problem of governing individualized equals, whether they are the "rational devils" he says we often find ourselves to be or the ethical agents we can and should become. Republics tell us that

> in order to organize a group of rational beings who together require universal laws for their survival, but of whom each separate individual

is secretly inclined to exempt himself from them, the constitution must be so designed so that, although the citizens are opposed to one another in their private attitudes, these opposing views may inhibit one another in such a way that the public conduct of the citizens will be the same as if they did not have such evil attitudes. (Kant, *PP*, p. 113)

Unlike Machiavelli's republics, Kant's republics are capable of achieving peace among themselves because they exercise democratic caution and are capable of appreciating the international rights of foreign republics. These international rights of republics derive from the representation of foreign individuals, who are our moral equals. Unlike Schumpeter's capitalist democracies, Kant's republics—including our own—remain in a state of war with nonrepublics. Liberal republics see themselves as threatened by aggression from nonrepublics that are not constrained by representation. Even though wars often cost more than the economic return they generate, liberal republics also are prepared to protect and promote—sometimes forcibly—democracy, private property, and the rights of individuals overseas against nonrepublics, which, because they do not authentically represent the rights of individuals, have no rights to noninterference. These wars may liberate oppressed individuals overseas; they also can generate enormous suffering.

■   ■   ■

Perpetual peace, Kant says, is the end point of the hard journey his republics will take. The promise of perpetual peace, the violent lessons of war, and the experience of a partial peace are proof of the need for and the possibility of world peace. They are also the grounds for moral citizens and statesmen to assume the duty of striving for peace.

Appendix 1. Liberal Regimes and the Pacific Union, 1700–1982

PERIOD	PERIOD	PERIOD
18th Century	Argentina, 1880–	Ireland, 1920–
Swiss Cantons[a]	Chile, 1891–	Mexico, 1928–
French Republie, 1790–1795	Total = 13	Lebanon, 1944–
United States,[a] 1776–		Total = 29
Total = 3	**1900–1945**	
	Switzerland	**1945–[b]**
	United States	Switzerland
1800–1850	Great Britain	United States
Swiss Confederation	Sweden	Great Britain
United States	Canada	Sweden
France, 1830–1849	Greece, –1911; 1928–1936	Canada
Belgium, 1830–	Italy, –1922	Australia
1800–1850 (cont.)	Belgium, –1940	New Zealand
Great Britain, 1832–	Netherlands, –1940	Finland
Netherlands, 1848–	Argentina, –1943	Ireland
Piedmont, 1848–	France, –1940	Mexico
Denmark, 1849–	Chile, –1924; 1932–	Uruguay, –1973
Total = 8	Australia, 1901	Chile, –1973
	Norway, 1905–1940	Lebanon, –1975
1850–1900	New Zealand, 1907–	Costa Rica, –1948; 1953–
Switzerland	Colombia, 1910–1949	Iceland, 1944–
United States	Denmark, 1914–1940	France, 1945–
Belgium	Poland, 1917–1935	Denmark, 1945
Great Britain	Latvia, 1922–1934	Norway, 1945
Netherlands	Germany, 1918–1932	Austria, 1945–
Piedmont, –1861	Austria, 1918–1934	Brazil, 1945–1954; 1955–1964
Italy, 1861–	Estonia, 1919–1934	Belgium, 1946–
Denmark, –1866	Finland, 1919–	Luxembourg, 1946–
Sweden, 1864–	Uruguay, 1919–	Netherlands, 1946–
Greece, 1864–	Costa Rica, 1919–	Italy, 1946–
Canada, 1867–	Czechoslovakia, 1920–1939	Philippines, 1946–1972
France, 1871–		

(continued)

Appendix 1. Liberal Regimes and the Pacific Union, 1700–1982 (Continued)

PERIOD	PERIOD	PERIOD
1945–(cont.)	Turkey, 1950–1960;	Senegal, 1963–
India, 1947–1975; 1977–	1966–1971	Malaysia, 1963–
Sri Lanka, 1948–1961;	Japan, 1951–	Botswana, 1966–
1963–1971; 1978–	Bolivia, 1956–1969; 1982–	Singapore, 1965–
Ecuador, 1948–1963; 1979–	Colombia, 1958–	Portugal, 1976–
Israel, 1949–	Venezuela, 1959–	Spain, 1978–
West Germany, 1949–	Nigeria, 1961–1964;	Dominican Republic, 1978–
Greece, 1950–1967; 1975–	1979–1984	Honduras, 1981–
Peru, 1950–1962; 1963–	Jamaica, 1962–	Papua New Guinea, 1982–
1968; 1980–	Trinidad and Tobago, 1962–	Total = 50
El Salvador, 1950–1961		

Note: I have drawn up this approximate list of "Liberal Regimes" according to the four institutions Kant described as essential: market and private property economies; politics that are externally sovereign; citizens who possess juridical rights; and "republican" (whether republican or parliamentary monarchy), representative government. This latter includes the requirement that the legislative branch have an effective role in public policy and be formally and competitively (either inter- or intra-party) elected. Furthermore, I have taken into account whether male suffrage is wide (i.e., 30%) or, as Kant (*MM* [*The Metaphysics of Morals*], p. 139) would have had it, open by "achievement" to inhabitants of the national or metropolitan territory (e.g., to poll-tax payers or householders). This list of liberal regimes is thus more inclusive than a list of democratic regimes, or polyarchies (Powell, 1982, p. 5). Other conditions taken into account here are that female suffrage is granted within a generation of its being demanded by an extensive female suffrage movement and that representative government is internally sovereign (e.g., including, and especially over military and foreign affairs) as well as stable (in existence for at least three years). Sources for these data are Banks and Overstreet (1983), Gastil (1985), *The Europa Yearbook, 1985* (1985), Langer (1968), U.K. Foreign and Commonwealth Office (1980), and U.S. Department of State (1981). Finally, these lists exclude ancient and medieval "republics," since none appears to fit Kant's commitment to liberal individualism (Holmes, 1979).

[a]There are domestic variations within these liberal regimes: Switzerland was liberal only in certain cantons; the United States was liberal only north of the Mason-Dixon line until 1865, when it became liberal throughout.

[b]Selected list, excludes liberal regimes with populations less than one million. These include all states categorized as "free" by Gastil and those "partly free" (four-fifths or more free) states with a more pronounced capitalist orientation.

Appendix 2. International Wars Listed Chronologically

British-Maharattan (1817–1818)

Greek (1821–1828)

Franco-Spanish (1823)

First Anglo-Burmese (1823–1826)

Javanese (1825–1830)

Russo-Persian (1826–1828)

Russo-Turkish (1828–1829)

First Polish (1831)

First Syrian (1831–1832)

Texas (1835–1836)

(continued)

Appendix 2. International Wars Listed Chronologically (Continued)

First British-Afghan (1838–1842)

Second Syrian (1839–1940)

Franco-Algerian (1839–1847)

Peruvian-Bolivian (1841)

First British-Sikh (1845–1846)

Mexican-American (1846–1848)

Austro-Sardinian (1848–1849)

First Schleswig-Holstein (1848–1849)

Hungarian (1848–1849)

Second British-Sikh (1848–1849)

Roman Republic (1849)

La Plata (1851–1852)

First Turco-Montenegran (1852–1853)

Crimean (1853–1856)

Anglo-Persian (1856–1857)

Sepoy (1857–1859)

Second Turco-Montenegran (1858–1859)

Italian Unification (1859)

Spanish-Moroccan (1859–1860)

Italo-Roman (1860)

Italo-Sicilian (1860–1861)

Franco-Mexican (1862–1867)

Ecuadorian-Colombian (1863)

Second Polish (1863–1864)

Spanish-Santo Dominican (1863–1865)

Second Schleswig-Holstein (1864)

Lopez (1864–1870)

Spanish-Chilean (1865–1866)

Seven Weeks (1866)

Ten Years (1868–1878)

Franco-Prussian (1870–1871)

Dutch-Achinese (1873–1878)

Balkan (1875–1877)

Russo-Turkish (1877–1878)

Bosnian (1878)

Second British-Afghan (1878–1880)

Pacific (1879–1883)

British-Zulu (1879)

Franco-Indochinese (1882–1884)

Mahdist (1882–1885)

Sino-French (1884–1885)

Central American (1885)

Serbo-Bulgarian (1885)

Sino-Japanese (1894–1895)

Franco-Madagascan (1894–1895)

Cuban (1895–1898)

Italo-Ethiopian (1895–1896)

First Philippine (1896–1898)

Greco-Turkish (1897)

Spanish-American (1898)

Second Philippine (1899–1902)

Boer (1899–1902)

Boxer Rebellion (1900)

Ilinden (1903)

Vietnamese-Cambodian (1975–)

Timor (1975–)

Saharan (1975–)

Ogaden (1976–)

Russo-Japanese (1904–1905)

Central American (1906)

Central American (1907)

Spanish-Moroccan (1909–1910)

Italo-Turkish (1911–1912)

First Balkan (1912–1913)

(continued)

Second Balkan (1913)	Palestine (1948–1949)
World War I (1914–1918)	Hyderabad (1948)
Russian Nationalities (1917–1921)	Korean (1950–1953)
Russo-Polish (1919–1920)	Algerian (1954–1962)
Hungarian-Allies (1919)	Russo-Hungarian (1956)
Greco-Turkish (1919–1922)	Sinai (1956)
Riffian (1921–1926)	Tibetan (1956–1959)
Druze (1925–1927)	Sino-Indian (1962)
Sino-Soviet (1929)	Vietnamese (1965–1975)
Manchurian (1931–1933)	Second Kashmir (1965)
Chaco (1932–1935)	Six Day (1967)
Italo-Ethiopian (1935–1936)	Israeli-Egyptian (1969–1970)
Sino-Japanese (1937–1941)	Football (1969)
Changkufeng (1938)	Bangladesh (1971)
Nomohan (1939)	Philippine-MNLF (1972–)
World War II (1939–1945)	Yom Kippur (1973)
Russo-Finnish (1939–1940)	Turco-Cypriot (1974)
Franco-Thai (1940–1941)	Ethiopian-Eritrean (1974–)
Indonesian (1945–1946)	Ugandan-Tanzanian (1978–1979)
Indochinese (1945–1954)	Sino-Vietnamese (1979)
Madagascan (1947–1948)	Russo-Afghan (1979–)
First Kashmir (1947–1949)	Iran-Iraqi (1980–)

Note: This table is taken from Melvin Small and J. David Singer (1982, pp. 79–80). This is a partial list of international wars fought between 1816 and 1980. In Appendices A and B, Small and Singer identify a total of 575 wars during this period, but approxi Note: This table is taken from Melvin Small and J. David Singer (1982, pp. 79–80). This is a partial list of international wars fought between 1816 and 1980. In Appendices A and B, Small and Singer identify a total of 575 wars during this period, but approximately 159 of them appear to be largely domestic, or civil wars. mately 159 of them appear to be largely domestic, or civil wars.

This list excludes covert interventions, some of which have been directed by liberal regimes against other liberal regimes—for example, the United States' effort to destabilize the Chilean election and Allende's government. Nonetheless, it is significant that such interventions are not pursued publicly as acknowledged policy. The covert destabilization campaign against Chile is recounted by the Senate Select Committee to Study Governmental Operations with Respect to Intelligence Activities (1975, *Covert Action in Chile, 1963–73*).

Following the argument of this article, this list also excludes civil wars. Civil wars differ from international wars, not in the ferocity of combat, but in the issues that engender them. Two nations that could abide one another as independent neighbors separated by a border might well be the fiercest of enemies if forced to live together in one state, jointly deciding how to raise and spend taxes, choose leaders, and legislate fundamental questions of value. Notwithstanding these differences, no civil wars that I recall upset the argument of liberal pacification.

REFERENCES

Banks, Arthur, and William Overstreet, eds. 1983. *A Political Handbook of the World; 1982–1983*. New York: McGraw Hill.

Barnet, Richard. 1968. *Intervention and Revolution*. Cleveland: World Publishing Co.

Chan, Steve. 1984. Mirror, Mirror on the Wall . . . : Are Freer Countries More Pacific? *Journal of Conflict Resolution*, 28:617–48.

Doyle, Michael W. 1983a. Kant, Liberal Legacies, and Foreign Affairs: Part 1. *Philosophy and Public Affairs*, 12:205–35.

Doyle, Michael W. 1983b. Kant, Liberal Legacies, and Foreign Affairs: Part 2. *Philosophy and Public Affairs*, 12:323–53.

Doyle, Michael W. 1986. *Empires*. Ithaca: Cornell University Press.

The Europa Yearbook for 1985. 1985. 2 vols. London: Europa Publications.

Gastil, Raymond. 1985. The Comparative Survey of Freedom 1985. *Freedom at Issue*, 82:3–16.

Haas, Michael. 1974. *International Conflict*. New York: Bobbs-Merrill.

Holmes, Stephen. 1979. Aristippus in and out of Athens. *American Political Science Review*, 73:113–28.

Huliung, Mark. 1983. *Citizen Machiavelli*. Princeton: Princeton University Press.

Hume, David. 1963. Of the Balance of Power. *Essays: Moral, Political, and Literary*. Oxford: Oxford University Press.

Kant, Immanuel. 1970. *Kant's Political Writings*. Hans Reiss, ed. H. B. Nisbet, trans. Cambridge: Cambridge University Press.

Kelly, George A. 1969. *Idealism, Politics, and History*. Cambridge: Cambridge University Press.

Langer, William L., ed. 1968. *The Encyclopedia of World History*. Boston: Houghton Mifflin.

Machiavelli, Niccolo. 1950. *The Prince and the Discourses*. Max Lerner, ed. Luigi Ricci and Christian Detmold, trans. New York: Modern Library.

Mansfield, Harvey C. 1970. Machiavelli's New Regime. *Italian Quarterly*, 13:63–95.

Montesquieu, Charles de. 1949. *Spirit of the Laws*. New York: Hafner. (Originally published in 1748.)

Murphy, Jeffrie. 1970. *Kant: The Philosophy of Right*. New York: St. Martins.

Pocock, J. G. A. 1975. *The Machiavellian Moment*. Princeton: Princeton University Press.

Powell, G. Bingham. 1982. *Contemporary Democracies*. Cambridge, MA: Harvard University Press.

Reagan, Ronald. June 9, 1982. Address to Parliament. *New York Times*.

Riley, Patrick. 1983. *Kant's Political Philosophy*. Totowa, NJ: Rowman and Littlefield.

Rummel, Rudolph J. 1983. Libertarianism and International Violence. *Journal of Conflict Resolution*, 27:27–71.

Russett, Bruce. 1985. The Mysterious Case of Vanishing Hegemony. *International Organization*, 39:207–31.

Schumpeter, Joseph. 1955. The Sociology of Imperialism. In *Imperialism and Social Classes*. Cleveland: World Publishing Co. (Essay originally published in 1919.)

Schwarz, Wolfgang. 1962. Kant's Philosophy of Law and International Peace. *Philosophy and Phenomenonological Research*, 23:71–80.

Skinner, Quentin. 1981. *Machiavelli*. New York: Hill and Wang.

Small, Melvin, and J. David Singer. 1976. The War-Proneness of Democratic Regimes. *The Jerusalem Journal of International Relations*, 1(4):50–69.

Small, Melvin, and J. David Singer. 1982. *Resort to Arms*. Beverly Hills: Sage Publications.

Thucydides. 1954. *The Peloponnesian War*. Rex Warner, ed. and trans. Baltimore: Penguin.

U.K. Foreign and Commonwealth Office. 1980. *A Yearbook of the Commonwealth 1980*. London: HMSO.

U.S. Congress. Senate. Select Committee to Study Governmental Operations with Respect to Intelligence Activities. 1975. *Covert Action in Chile, 1963–74*. 94th Cong., 1st sess., Washington, DC: U.S. Government Printing Office.

U.S. Department of State. 1981. *Country Reports on Human Rights Practices*. Washington, DC: U.S. Government Printing Office.

Weede, Erich. 1984. Democracy and War Involvement. *Journal of Conflict Resolution*, 28:649–64.

Wilkenfeld, Jonathan. 1968. Domestic and Foreign Conflict Behavior of Nations. *Journal of Peace Research*, 5:56–69.

Wright, Quincy. 1942. *A Study of History*. Chicago: Chicago University Press.

Alexander Wendt

ANARCHY IS WHAT STATES MAKE OF IT
The Social Construction of Power Politics

The debate between realists and liberals has reemerged as an axis of contention in international relations theory.[1] Revolving in the past around competing theories of human nature, the debate is more concerned today with the extent to which state action is influenced by "structure" (anarchy and the distribution of power) versus "process" (interaction and learning) and institutions. Does the absence of centralized political authority force states to play competitive power politics? Can international regimes overcome this logic, and under what conditions? What in anarchy is given and immutable, and what is amenable to change?

■   ■   ■

* * * I argue that self-help and power politics do not follow either logically or causally from anarchy and that if today we find ourselves in a self-help world, this is due to process, not structure. There is no "logic" of anarchy apart from the practices that create and instantiate one structure of identities and interests rather than another; structure has no existence or causal powers apart from process. Self-help and power politics are institutions, not essential features of anarchy. *Anarchy is what states make of it.*

■   ■   ■

From *International Organization* 46, no. 2 (Spring 1992): 391–425. Some of the author's notes have been omitted.

Anarchy and Power Politics

Classical realists such as Thomas Hobbes, Reinhold Niebuhr, and Hans Morgenthau attributed egoism and power politics primarily to human nature, whereas structural realists or neorealists emphasize anarchy. The difference stems in part from different interpretations of anarchy's causal powers. Kenneth Waltz's work is important for both. In *Man, the State, and War,* he defines anarchy as a condition of possibility for or "permissive" cause of war, arguing that "wars occur because there is nothing to prevent them."[2] It is the human nature or domestic politics of predator states, however, that provide the initial impetus or "efficient" cause of conflict which forces other states to respond in kind.[3] Waltz is not entirely consistent about this, since he slips without justification from the permissive causal claim that in anarchy war is always possible to the active causal claim that "war may at any moment occur."[4] But despite Waltz's concluding call for third-image theory, the efficient causes that initialize anarchic systems are from the first and second images. This is reversed in Waltz's *Theory of International Politics,* in which first- and second-image theories are spurned as "reductionist," and the logic of anarchy seems by itself to constitute self-help and power politics as necessary features of world politics.[5]

This is unfortunate, since whatever one may think of first- and second-image theories, they have the virtue of implying that practices determine the character of anarchy. In the permissive view, only if human or domestic factors cause A to attack B will B have to defend itself. Anarchies may contain dynamics that lead to competitive power politics, but they also may not, and we can argue about when particular structures of identity and interest will emerge. In neorealism, however, the role of practice in shaping the character of anarchy is substantially reduced, and so there is less about which to argue: self-help and competitive power politics are simply given exogenously by the structure of the state system.

I will not here contest the neorealist description of the contemporary state system as a competitive, self-help world;[6] I will only dispute its explanation. I develop my argument in three stages. First, I disentangle the concepts of self-help and anarchy by showing that self-interested conceptions of security are not a constitutive property of anarchy. Second, I show how self-help and competitive power politics may be produced causally by processes of interaction between states in which anarchy plays only a permissive role. In both of these stages of my argument, I self-consciously bracket the first- and second-image determinants of state identity, not because they are unimportant (they are indeed important), but because like Waltz's objective, mine is to clarify the "logic" of anarchy. Third, I reintroduce first- and second-image determinants to assess their effects on identity-formation in different kinds of anarchies.

Anarchy, Self-Help, and Intersubjective Knowledge

Waltz defines political structure on three dimensions: ordering principles (in this case, anarchy), principles of differentiation (which here drop out), and the distribution of capabilities.[7] By itself, this definition predicts little about state behavior. It does not predict whether two states will be friends or foes, will recognize each other's sovereignty, will have dynastic ties, will be revisionist or status quo powers, and so on. These factors, which are fundamentally intersubjective, affect states' security interests and thus the character of their interaction under anarchy. In an important revision of Waltz's theory, Stephen Walt implies as much when he argues that the "balance of threats," rather than the balance of power, determines state action, threats being socially constructed.[8] Put more generally, without assumptions about the structure of identities and interests in the system, Waltz's definition of structure cannot predict the content or dynamics of anarchy. Self-help is one such intersubjective structure and, as such, does the decisive explanatory work in the theory. The question is whether self-help is a logical or contingent feature of anarchy. In this section, I develop the concept of a "structure of identity and interest" and show that no particular one follows logically from anarchy.

A fundamental principle of constructivist social theory is that people act toward objects, including other actors, on the basis of the meanings that the objects have for them.[9] States act differently toward enemies than they do toward friends because enemies are threatening and friends are not. Anarchy and the distribution of power are insufficient to tell us which is which. U.S. military power has a different significance for Canada than for Cuba, despite their similar "structural" positions, just as British missiles have a different significance for the United States than do Soviet missiles. The distribution of power may always affect states' calculations, but how it does so depends on the intersubjective understandings and expectations, on the "distribution of knowledge," that constitute their conceptions of self and other.[10] If society "forgets" what a university is, the powers and practices of professor and student cease to exist; if the United States and Soviet Union decide that they are no longer enemies, "the cold war is over." It is collective meanings that constitute the structures which organize our actions.

Actors acquire identities—relatively stable, role-specific understandings and expectations about self—by participating in such collective meanings.[11]

Identities are inherently relational: "Identity, with its appropriate attachments of psychological reality, is always identity within a specific, socially constructed world," Peter Berger argues.[12] Each person has many identities linked to institutional roles, such as brother, son, teacher, and citizen. Similarly, a state may have multiple identities as "sovereign," "leader of the free world," "imperial power," and so on.[13] The commitment to and the salience of particular identities vary, but each identity is an inherently social definition of the actor grounded in the theories which actors collectively hold about themselves and one another and which constitute the structure of the social world.

Identities are the basis of interests. Actors do not have a "portfolio" of interests that they carry around independent of social context; instead, they define their interests in the process of defining situations.[14] As Nelson Foote puts it: "Motivation . . . refer[s] to the degree to which a human being, as a participant in the ongoing social process in which he necessarily finds himself, defines a problematic situation as calling for the performance of a particular act, with more or less anticipated consummations and consequences, and thereby his organism releases the energy appropriate to performing it."[15] Sometimes situations are unprecedented in our experience, and in these cases we have to construct their meaning, and thus our interests, by analogy or invent them de novo. More often they have routine qualities in which we assign meanings on the basis of institutionally defined roles. When we say that professors have an "interest" in teaching, research, or going on leave, we are saying that to function in the role identity of "professor," they have to define certain situations as calling for certain actions. This does not mean that they will necessarily do so (expectations and competence do not equal performance), but if they do not, they will not get tenure. The absence or failure of roles makes defining situations and interests more difficult, and identity confusion may result. This seems to be happening today in the United States and the former Soviet Union:

without the cold war's mutual attributions of threat and hostility to define their identities, these states seem unsure of what their "interests" should be.

An institution is a relatively stable set or "structure" of identities and interests. Such structures are often codified in formal rules and norms, but these have motivational force only in virtue of actors' socialization to and participation in collective knowledge. Institutions are fundamentally cognitive entities that do not exist apart from actors' ideas about how the world works.[16] This does not mean that institutions are not real or objective, that they are "nothing but" beliefs. As collective knowledge, they are experienced as having an existence "over and above the individuals who happen to embody them at the moment."[17] In this way, institutions come to confront individuals as more or less coercive social facts, but they are still a function of what actors collectively "know." Identities and such collective cognitions do not exist apart from each other; they are "mutually constitutive."[18] On this view, institutionalization is a process of internalizing new identities and interests, not something occurring outside them and affecting only behavior; socialization is a cognitive process, not just a behavioral one. Conceived in this way, institutions may be cooperative or conflictual, a point sometimes lost in scholarship on international regimes, which tends to equate institutions with cooperation. There are important differences between conflictual and cooperative institutions to be sure, but all relatively stable self-other relations—even those of "enemies"—are defined intersubjectively.

Self-help is an institution, one of various structures of identity and interest that may exist under anarchy. Processes of identity-formation under anarchy are concerned first and foremost with preservation or "security" of the self. Concepts of security therefore differ in the extent to which and the manner in which the self is identified cognitively with the other,[19] and, I want to suggest, it is upon this cognitive variation that the meaning of anarchy and the distribution of power depends. Let me illustrate with a standard continuum of security systems.[20]

At one end is the "competitive" security system, in which states identify negatively with each other's security so that ego's gain is seen as alter's loss. Negative identification under anarchy constitutes system of "realist" power politics: risk-averse actors that infer intentions from capabilities and worry about relative gains and losses. At the limit—in the Hobbesian war of all against all—collective action is nearly impossible in such a system because each actor must constantly fear being stabbed in the back.

In the middle is the "individualistic" security system, in which states are indifferent to the relationship between their own and others' security. This constitutes "neoliberal" systems: states are still self-regarding about their security but are concerned primarily with absolute gains rather than relative gains. One's position in the distribution of power is less important, and collective action is more possible (though still subject to free riding because states continue to be "egoists").

Competitive and individualistic systems are both "self-help" forms of anarchy in the sense that states do not positively identify the security of self with that of others but instead treat security as the individual responsibility of each. Given the lack of a positive cognitive identification on the basis of which to build security regimes, power politics within such systems will necessarily consist of efforts to manipulate others to satisfy self-regarding interests.

This contrasts with the "cooperative" security system, in which states identify positively with one another so that the security of each is perceived as the responsibility of all. This is not self-help in any interesting sense, since the "self" in terms of which interests are defined is the community; national interests are international interests.[21] In practice, of course, the extent to which states' identification with the community varies, from the limited form found in "concerts" to the full-blown form seen in "collective security" arrangements.[22] Depending on how well developed the collective self is, it will produce security practices that are in varying degrees altruistic or prosocial. This makes collective action less dependent on the presence of active threats and less prone to free riding.[23] Moreover, it restructures efforts to advance one's objectives, or "power politics," in terms of shared norms rather than relative power.[24]

On this view, the tendency in international relations scholarship to view power and institutions as two opposing explanations of foreign policy is therefore misleading, since anarchy and the distribution of power only have meaning for state action in virtue of the understandings and expectations that constitute institutional identities and interests. Self-help is one such institution, constituting one kind of anarchy but not the only kind. Waltz's three-part definition of structure therefore seems underspecified. In order to go from structure to action, we need to add a fourth: the intersubjectively constituted structure of identities and interests in the system.

This has an important implication for the way in which we conceive of states in the state of nature before their first encounter with each other. Because states do not have conceptions of self and other, and thus security interests, apart from or prior to interaction, we assume too much about the state of nature if we concur with Waltz that, in virtue of anarchy, "international political systems, like economic markets, are formed by the coaction of self-regarding units."[25] We also assume too much if we argue that, in virtue of anarchy, states in the state of nature necessarily face a "stag hunt" or "security dilemma."[26] These claims presuppose a history of interaction in which actors have acquired "selfish" identities and interests; before interaction (and still in abstraction from first- and second-image factors) they would have no experience upon which to base such definitions of self and other. To assume otherwise is to attribute to states in the state of nature qualities that they can only possess in society.[27] Self-help is an institution, not a constitutive feature of anarchy.

What, then, *is* a constitutive feature of the state of nature before interaction? Two things are left if we strip away those properties of the self which presuppose interaction with others. The first is the material substrate of agency, including its intrinsic capabilities. For human beings, this is the body; for states, it is an organizational apparatus of governance. In effect, I am suggesting for rhetorical purposes that the raw material out of which members of the state system are constituted is created by domestic society before states enter the constitutive process of international society,[28] although this process implies neither stable territoriality nor sovereignty, which are internationally negotiated terms of individuality (as discussed further below). The second is a desire to preserve this material substrate, to survive. This does not entail "self-regardingness," however, since actors do not have a self prior to interaction with an other; how they view the meaning and requirements of this survival therefore depends on the processes by which conceptions of self evolve.

This may all seem very arcane, but there is an important issue at stake: are the foreign policy identities and interests of states exogenous or endogenous to the state system? The former is the answer of an individualistic or undersocialized systemic theory for which rationalism is appropriate; the latter is the answer of a fully socialized systemic theory. Waltz seems to offer the latter and proposes two mechanisms, competition and socialization, by which structure conditions state action.[29] The content of his argument about this conditioning, however, presupposes a self-help system that is not itself a constitutive feature of anarchy. As James Morrow points out, Waltz's two mechanisms condition behavior, not identity and interest.[30] This explains how Waltz can be accused of both "individualism" and "structuralism."[31] He is the former with respect to systemic constitutions of identity and interest, the latter with respect to systemic determinations of behavior.

Anarchy and the Social Construction of Power Politics

If self-help is not a constitutive feature of anarchy, it must emerge causally from processes in which anarchy plays only a permissive role.[32] This reflects a second principle of constructivism: that the meanings in terms of which action is organized arise out of interaction.[33] This being said, however, the situation facing states as they encounter one another for the first time may be such that only self-regarding conceptions of identity can survive; if so, even if these conceptions are socially constructed, neorealists may be right in holding identities and interests constant and thus in privileging one particular meaning of anarchic structure over process. In this case, rationalists would be right to argue for a weak, behavioral conception of the difference that institutions make, and realists would be right to argue that any international institutions which are created will be inherently unstable, since without the power to transform identities and interests they will be "continuing objects of choice" by exogenously constituted actors constrained only by the transaction costs of behavioral change.[34] Even in a permissive causal role, in other words, anarchy may decisively restrict interaction and therefore restrict viable forms of systemic theory. I address these causal issues first by showing how self-regarding ideas about security might develop and then by examining the conditions under which a key efficient cause—predation—may dispose states in this direction rather than others.

Conceptions of self and interest tend to "mirror" the practices of significant others over time. This principle of identity-formation is captured by the symbolic interactionist notion of the "looking-glass self," which asserts that the self is a reflection of an actor's socialization.

Consider two actors—ego and alter—encountering each other for the first time.[35] Each wants to survive and has certain material capabilities, but neither actor has biological or domestic imperatives for power, glory, or conquest (still bracketed), and there is no history of security or insecurity between the two. What should they do? Realists would probably argue that each should act on the basis of worst-case assumptions about the other's intentions, justifying such an attitude as prudent in view of the possibility of death from making a mistake. Such a possibility always exists, even in civil society; however, society would be impossible if people made decisions purely on the basis of worst-case possibilities. Instead, most decisions are and should be made on the basis of probabilities, and these are produced by interaction, by what actors *do*.

In the beginning is ego's gesture, which may consist, for example, of an advance, a retreat, a brandishing of arms, a laying down of arms, or an attack.[36] For ego, this gesture represents the basis on which it is prepared to respond to alter. This basis is unknown to alter, however, and so it must make an inference or "attribution" about ego's intentions and, in particular, given that this is anarchy, about whether ego is a threat.[37] The content of this inference will largely depend on two considerations. The first is the gesture's and ego's physical qualities, which are in part contrived by ego and which include the direction of movement, noise, numbers, and immediate consequences of the gesture.[38] The second consideration concerns what alter would intend by such qualities were it to make such a gesture itself. Alter may make an attributional "error" in its inference about ego's intent, but there is also no reason for it to assume a priori—before the gesture—that ego is threatening, since it is only through a process of signaling and interpreting that the costs and probabilities of being wrong can be determined.[39] Social threats are constructed, not natural.

Consider an example. Would we assume, a priori, that we were about to be attacked if we are ever contacted by members of an alien civilization? I think not. We would be highly alert, of course, but whether we placed our military forces on alert or launched an attack would depend on how we interpreted the import of their first gesture for our security—if only to avoid making an immediate enemy out of what may be a dangerous adversary. The possibility of error, in other words, does not force us to act on the assumption that the aliens are threatening: action depends on the probabilities we assign, and these are in key part a function of what the aliens do; prior to their gesture, we have no systemic basis for assigning probabilities. If their first gesture is to appear with a thousand spaceships and destroy New York, we will define the situation as threatening and respond accordingly. But if they appear with one spaceship, saying what seems to be "we come in peace," we will feel "reassured" and will probably respond with a gesture intended to reassure them, even if this gesture is not necessarily interpreted by them as such.[40]

This process of signaling, interpreting, and responding completes a "social act" and begins the process of creating intersubjective meanings. It advances the same way. The first social act creates expectations on both sides about each other's future behavior: potentially mistaken and certainly tentative, but expectations nonetheless. Based on this tentative knowledge, ego makes a new gesture, again signifying the basis on which it will respond to alter, and again alter responds, adding to the pool of knowledge each has about the other, and so on over time. The mechanism here is reinforcement; interaction rewards actors for holding certain ideas about each other and discourages them from holding others. If repeated long enough, these "reciprocal typifications" will create relatively stable concepts of self and other regarding the issue at stake in the interaction.[41]

It is through reciprocal interaction, in other words, that we create and instantiate the relatively enduring social structures in terms of which we define our identities and interests. Jeff Coulter sums up the ontological dependence of structure on process this way: "The parameters of social organization themselves are reproduced only in and through the orientations and practices of members engaged in social interactions over time. . . . Social configurations are not 'objective' like mountains or forests, but neither are they 'subjective' like dreams or flights of speculative fancy. They are, as most social scientists concede at the theoretical level, intersubjective constructions."[42]

The simple overall model of identity- and interest-formation proposed in Figure 3.1 applies to competitive institutions no less than to cooperative ones. Self-help security systems evolve from cycles of interaction in which each party acts in ways that the other feels are threatening to the self, creating expectations that the other is not to be trusted. Competitive or egoistic identities are caused by such insecurity; if the other is threatening, the self is forced to "mirror" such behavior in its conception of the self's relationship to that other.[43] Being treated as an object for the gratification of others precludes the positive identification with others necessary for collective security; conversely, being treated by others in ways that are empathic with respect to the security of the self permits such identification.[44]

Competitive systems of interaction are prone to security "dilemmas," in which the efforts of actors to enhance their security unilaterally threatens the security of the others, perpetuating distrust and alienation. The forms of identity and interest that constitute such dilemmas, however, are themselves ongoing effects of, not exogenous to, the interaction; identities are produced in and through "situated activity."[45] We do not *begin* our relationship with the aliens in a security dilemma; security dilemmas are not given by anarchy or nature. Of course, once institutionalized such a dilemma may be hard to change (I return to this below), but the point remains: identities and interests are

Figure 3.1. The Codetermination of Institutions and Process

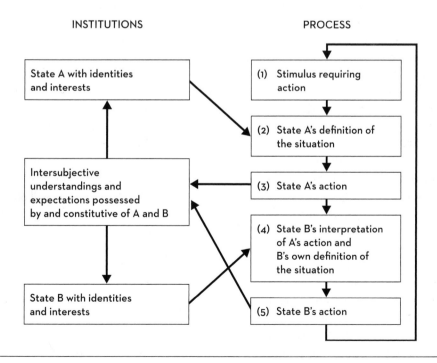

constituted by collective meanings that are always in process. As Sheldon Stryker emphasizes, "The social process is one of constructing and reconstructing self and social relationships."[46] If states find themselves in a self-help system, this is because their practices made it that way. Changing the practices will change the intersubjective knowledge that constitutes the system.

Predator States and Anarchy as Permissive Cause

The mirror theory of identity-formation is a crude account of how the process of creating identities and interests might work, but it does not tell us why a system of states—such as, arguably, our own—would have ended up with self-regarding and not collective identities. In this section, I examine an efficient cause, predation, which, in conjunction with anarchy as a permissive cause, may generate a self-help system. In so doing, however, I show the key role that the structure of identities and interests plays in mediating anarchy's explanatory role.

The predator argument is straightforward and compelling. For whatever reasons—biology, domestic politics, or systemic victimization—some states may become predisposed toward aggression. The aggressive behavior of these predators or "bad apples" forces other states to engage in competitive power politics, to meet fire with fire, since failure to do so may degrade or destroy them. One predator will best a hundred pacifists because anarchy provides no guarantees. This argument is powerful in part because it is so weak: rather than making the strong assumption that all states are inherently power-seeking (a purely reductionist theory of power politics), it assumes that just one is power-seeking and that the others have to follow suit because anarchy permits the one to exploit them.

In making this argument, it is important to reiterate that the possibility of predation does not in itself force states to anticipate it a priori with competitive power politics of their own. The possibility of predation does not mean that "war may at any moment occur"; it may in fact be extremely unlikely. Once a predator emerges, however, it may condition identity- and interest-formation in the following manner.

In an anarchy of two, if ego is predatory, alter must either define its security in self-help terms or pay the price. This follows directly from the above argument, in which conceptions of self mirror treatment by the other. In an anarchy of many, however, the effect of predation also depends on the level of collective identity already attained in the system. If predation occurs right after the first encounter in the state of nature, it will force others with whom it comes in contact to defend themselves, first individually and then collectively *if* they come to perceive a common threat. The emergence of such a defensive alliance will be seriously inhibited if the structure of identities and interests has already evolved into a Hobbesian world of maximum insecurity, since potential allies will strongly distrust each other and face intense collective action problems; such insecure allies are also more likely to fall out amongst themselves once the predator is removed. If collective security identity is high, however, the emergence of a predator may do much less damage. If the predator attacks any member of the collective, the latter will come to the victim's defense on the principle of "all for one, one for all," even if the predator is not presently a threat to other members of the collective. If the predator is not strong enough to withstand the collective, it will be defeated and collective security will obtain. But if it is strong enough, the logic of the two-actor case (now predator and collective) will activate, and balance-of-power politics will reestablish itself.

The timing of the emergence of predation relative to the history of identity-formation in the community is therefore crucial to anarchy's explanatory role as a permissive cause. Predation will always lead victims to defend themselves, but whether defense will be collective or not depends on the history of interaction within the potential collective as much as on the ambitions of the predator. Will the disappearance of the Soviet threat renew old insecurities among the members of the North Atlantic Treaty Organization? Perhaps, but not if they have reasons independent of that threat for identifying their security with one another. Identities and interests are relationship-specific, not intrinsic attributes of a "portfolio"; states may be competitive in some relationships and solidary in others. "Mature" anarchies are less likely than "immature" ones to be reduced by predation to a Hobbesian condition, and maturity, which is a proxy for structures of identity and interest, is a function of process.[47]

The source of predation also matters. If it stems from unit-level causes that are immune to systemic impacts (causes such as human nature or domestic politics taken in isolation), then it functions in a manner analogous to a "genetic trait" in the constructed world of the state system. Even if successful, this trait does not select for other predators in an evolutionary sense so much as it teaches other states to respond in kind, but since traits cannot be unlearned, the other states will continue competitive behavior until the predator is either destroyed or transformed from within. However, in the more likely event that predation stems at least in part from prior systemic interaction—perhaps as a result of being victimized in the past (one thinks here of Nazi Germany or the Soviet Union)—then it is more a response to a learned identity and, as such, might be transformed by future social interaction in the form of appeasement, reassurances that security needs will be met, systemic effects on domestic politics, and so on. In this case, in other words, there is more hope that process can transform a bad apple into a good one.

The role of predation in generating a self-help system, then, is consistent with a systematic focus on process. Even if the source of predation is entirely exogenous to the system, it is what states *do* that determines the quality of their interactions under anarchy. In this respect, it is not surprising

that it is classical realists rather than structural realists who emphasize this sort of argument. The former's emphasis on unit-level causes of power politics leads more easily to a permissive view of anarchy's explanatory role (and therefore to a processual view of international relations) than does the latter's emphasis on anarchy as a "structural cause";[48] neorealists do not need predation because the system is given as self-help.

This raises anew the question of exactly how much and what kind of role human nature and domestic politics play in world politics. The greater and more destructive this role, the more significant predation will be, and the less amenable anarchy will be to formation of collective identities. Classical realists, of course, assumed that human nature was possessed by an inherent lust for power or glory. My argument suggests that assumptions such as this were made for a reason: an unchanging Hobbesian man provides the powerful efficient cause necessary for a relentless pessimism about world politics that anarchic structure alone, or even structure plus intermittent predation, cannot supply. One can be skeptical of such an essentialist assumption, as I am, but it does produce determinate results at the expense of systemic theory. A concern with systemic process over structure suggests that perhaps it is time to revisit the debate over the relative importance of first-, second-, and third-image theories of state identity-formation.[49]

Assuming for now that systemic theories of identity-formation in world politics are worth pursuing, let me conclude by suggesting that the realist-rationalist alliance "reifies" self-help in the sense of treating it as something separate from the practices by which it is produced and sustained. Peter Berger and Thomas Luckmann define reification as follows: "[It] is the apprehension of the products of human activity *as if* they were something else than human products—such as facts of nature, results of cosmic laws, or manifestations of divine will. Reification implies that man is capable of forgetting his own authorship of the human world, and further, that the dialectic between man, the producer, and his products is lost to consciousness. The reified world is . . . experienced by man as a strange facticity, an *opus alienum* over which he has no control rather than as the *opus proprium* of his own productive activity."[50] By denying or bracketing states' collective authorship of their identities and interests, in other words, the realist-rationalist alliance denies or brackets the fact that competitive power politics help create the very "problem of order" they are supposed to solve—that realism is a self-fulfilling prophecy. Far from being exogenously given, the intersubjective knowledge that constitutes competitive identities and interests is constructed every day by processes of "social will formation."[51] It is what states have made of themselves.

Institutional Transformations of Power Politics

Let us assume that processes of identity- and interest-formation have created a world in which states do not recognize rights to territory or existence—a war of all against all. In this world, anarchy has a "realist" meaning for state action: be insecure and concerned with relative power. Anarchy has this meaning only in virtue of collective, insecurity-producing practices, but if those practices are relatively stable, they do constitute a system that may resist change. The fact that worlds of power politics are socially constructed, in other words, does not guarantee they are malleable, for at least two reasons.

The first reason is that once constituted, any social system confronts each of its members as an objective social fact that reinforces certain behaviors and discourages others. Self-help systems, for example, tend to reward competition and punish altruism. The possibility of change depends on whether the exigencies of such competition leave

room for actions that deviate from the prescribed script. If they do not, the system will be reproduced and deviant actors will not.[52]

The second reason is that systemic change may also be inhibited by actors' interests in maintaining relatively stable role identities. Such interests are rooted not only in the desire to minimize uncertainty and anxiety, manifested in efforts to confirm existing beliefs about the social world, but also in the desire to avoid the expected costs of breaking commitments made to others—notably domestic constituencies and foreign allies in the case of states—as part of past practices. The level of resistance that these commitments induce will depend on the "salience" of particular role identities to the actor.[53] The United States, for example, is more likely to resist threats to its identity as "leader of anticommunist crusades" than to its identity as "promoter of human rights." But for almost any role identity, practices and information that challenge it are likely to create cognitive dissonance and even perceptions of threat, and these may cause resistance to transformations of the self and thus to social change.[54]

For both systemic and "psychological" reasons, then, intersubjective understandings and expectations may have a self-perpetuating quality, constituting path-dependencies that new ideas about self and other must transcend. This does not change the fact that through practice agents are continuously producing and reproducing identities and interests, continuously "choosing now the preferences [they] will have later."[55] But it does mean that choices may not be experienced with meaningful degrees of freedom. This could be a constructivist justification for the realist position that only simple learning is possible in self-help systems. The realist might concede that such systems are socially constructed and still argue that after the corresponding identities and interests have become institutionalized, they are almost impossible to transform.

In the remainder of this article, I examine three institutional transformations of identity and security interest through which states might escape a Hobbesian world of their own making. In so doing, I seek to clarify what it means to say that "institutions transform identities and interests," emphasizing that the key to such transformations is relatively stable practice.

Sovereignty, Recognition, and Security

In a Hobbesian state of nature, states are individuated by the domestic processes that constitute them as states and by their material capacity to deter threats from other states. In this world, even if free momentarily from the predations of others, state security does not have any basis in social recognition—in intersubjective understandings or norms that a state has a right to its existence, territory, and subjects. Security is a matter of national power, nothing more.

The principle of sovereignty transforms this situation by providing a social basis for the individuality and security of states. Sovereignty is an institution, and so it exists only in virtue of certain intersubjective understandings and expectations; there is no sovereignty without an other. These understandings and expectations not only constitute a particular kind of state—the "sovereign" state—but also constitute a particular form of community, since identities are relational. The essence of this community is a mutual recognition of one another's right to exercise exclusive political authority within territorial limits. These reciprocal "permissions"[56] constitute a spatially rather than functionally differentiated world—a world in which fields of practice constitute and are organized around "domestic" and "international" spaces rather than around the performance of particular activities.[57] The location of the boundaries between these spaces is of course sometimes contested, war being one practice through which states negotiate the terms of their individuality.

But this does not change the fact that it is only in virtue of mutual recognition that states have "territorial property rights."[58] This recognition functions as a form of "social closure" that disempowers nonstate actors and empowers and helps stabilize interaction among states.[59]

Sovereignty norms are now so taken for granted, so natural, that it is easy to overlook the extent to which they are both presupposed by and an ongoing artifact of practice. When states tax "their" "citizens" and not others, when they "protect" their markets against foreign "imports," when they kill thousands of Iraqis in one kind of war and then refuse to "intervene" to kill even one person in another kind, a "civil" war, and when they fight a global war against a regime that sought to destroy the institution of sovereignty and then give Germany back to the Germans, they are acting against the background of, and thereby reproducing, shared norms about what it means to be a sovereign state.

If states stopped acting on those norms, their identity as "sovereigns" (if not necessarily as "states") would disappear. The sovereign state is an ongoing accomplishment of practice, not a once-and-for-all creation of norms that somehow exist apart from practice.[60] Thus, saying that "the institution of sovereignty transforms identities" is shorthand for saying that "regular practices produce mutually constituting sovereign identities (agents) and their associated institutional norms (structures)." Practice is the core of constructivist resolutions of the agent-structure problem. This ongoing process may not be politically problematic in particular historical contexts and, indeed, once a community of mutual recognition is constituted, its members—even the disadvantaged ones[61]—may have a vested interest in reproducing it. In fact, this is part of what having an identity means. But this identity and institution remain dependent on what actors do: removing those practices will remove their intersubjective conditions of existence.

This may tell us something about how institutions of sovereign states are reproduced through social interaction, but it does not tell us why such a structure of identity and interest would arise in the first place. Two conditions would seem necessary for this to happen: (1) the density and regularity of interactions must be sufficiently high and (2) actors must be dissatisfied with preexisting forms of identity and interaction. Given these conditions, a norm of mutual recognition is relatively undemanding in terms of social trust, having the form of an assurance game in which a player will acknowledge the sovereignty of the others as long as they will in turn acknowledge that player's own sovereignty. Articulating international legal principles such as those embodied in the Peace of Augsburg (1555) and the Peace of Westphalia (1648) may also help by establishing explicit criteria for determining violations of the nascent social consensus.[62] But whether such a consensus holds depends on what states do. If they treat each other as if they were sovereign, then over time they will institutionalize that mode of subjectivity; if they do not, then that mode will not become the norm.

Practices of sovereignty will transform understandings of security and power politics in at least three ways. First, states will come to define their (and our) security in terms of preserving their "property rights" over particular territories. We now see this as natural, but the preservation of territorial frontiers is not, in fact, equivalent to the survival of the state or its people. Indeed, some states would probably be more secure if they would relinquish certain territories—the "Soviet Union" of some minority republics, "Yugoslavia" of Croatia and Slovenia, Israel of the West Bank, and so on. The fact that sovereignty practices have historically been oriented toward producing distinct territorial spaces, in other words, affects states' conceptualization of what they must "secure" to function in that identity, a process that may help account for the "hardening" of territorial boundaries over the centuries.[63]

Second, to the extent that states successfully internalize sovereignty norms, they will be more respectful toward the territorial rights of others.[64] This restraint is *not* primarily because of the costs of violating sovereignty norms, although when violators do get punished (as in the Gulf War) it reminds everyone of what these costs can be, but because part of what it means to be a "sovereign" state is that one does not violate the territorial rights of others without "just cause." A clear example of such an institutional effect, convincingly argued by David Strang, is the markedly different treatment that weak states receive within and outside communities of mutual recognition.[65] What keeps the United States from conquering the Bahamas, or Nigeria from seizing Togo, or Australia from occupying Vanuatu? Clearly, power is not the issue, and in these cases even the cost of sanctions would probably be negligible. One might argue that great powers simply have no "interest" in these conquests, and this might be so, but this lack of interest can only be understood in terms of their recognition of weak states' sovereignty. I have no interest in exploiting my friends, not because of the relative costs and benefits of such action but because they are my friends. The absence of recognition, in turn, helps explain the Western states' practices of territorial conquest, enslavement, and genocide against Native American and African peoples. It is in *that* world that only power matters, not the world of today.

Finally, to the extent that their ongoing socialization teaches states that their sovereignty depends on recognition by other states, they can afford to rely more on the institutional fabric of international society and less on individual national means—especially military power—to protect their security. The intersubjective understandings embodied in the institution of sovereignty, in other words, may redefine the meaning of others' power for the security of the self. In policy terms, this means that states can be less worried about short-term survival and relative power and can thus shift their resources accordingly. Ironically, it is the great powers, the states with the greatest national means, that may have the hardest time learning this lesson; small powers do not have the luxury of relying on national means and may therefore learn faster that collective recognition is a cornerstone of security.

None of this is to say that power becomes irrelevant in a community of sovereign states. Sometimes states *are* threatened by others that do not recognize their existence or particular territorial claims, that resent the externalities from their economic policies, and so on. But most of the time, these threats are played out within the terms of the sovereignty game. The fates of Napoleon and Hitler show what happens when they are not.

Cooperation among Egoists and Transformations of Identity

We began this section with a Hobbesian state of nature. Cooperation for joint gain is extremely difficult in this context, since trust is lacking, time horizons are short, and relative power concerns are high. Life is "nasty, brutish, and short." Sovereignty transforms this system into a Lockean world of (mostly) mutually recognized property rights and (mostly) egoistic rather than competitive conceptions of security, reducing the fear that what states already have will be seized at any moment by potential collaborators, thereby enabling them to contemplate more direct forms of cooperation. A necessary condition for such cooperation is that outcomes be positively interdependent in the sense that potential gains exist which cannot be realized by unilateral action. States such as Brazil and Botswana may recognize each other's sovereignty, but they need further incentives to engage in joint action. One important source of incentives is the growing "dynamic density" of interaction among states in a world with new communications technology, nuclear weapons, externalities from industrial development, and so on.[66] Unfortunately, growing dynamic density does not ensure that states will in fact realize joint gains; interdependence also entails vulnerability and the risk of being "the sucker," which if exploited will become a source of conflict rather than cooperation.

This is the rationale for the familiar assumption that egoistic states will often find themselves facing prisoners' dilemma, a game in which the dominant strategy, if played only once, is to defect. As Michael Taylor and Robert Axelrod have shown, however, given iteration and a sufficient shadow of the future, egoists using a tit-for-tat strategy can escape this result and build cooperative institutions.[67] The story they tell about this process on the surface seems quite similar to George Herbert Mead's constructivist analysis of interaction, part of which is also told in terms of "games."[68] Cooperation is a gesture indicating ego's willingness to cooperate; if alter defects, ego does likewise, signaling its unwillingness to be exploited; over time and through reciprocal play, each learns to form relatively stable expectations about the other's behavior, and through these, habits of cooperation (or defection) form. Despite similar concerns with communication, learning, and habit-formation, however, there is an important difference between the game-theoretic and constructivist analysis of interaction that bears on how we conceptualize the causal powers of institutions.

In the traditional game-theoretic analysis of cooperation, even an iterated one, the structure of the game—of identities and interests—is exogenous to interaction and, as such, does not change.[69] A "black box" is put around identity- and interest-formation, and analysis focuses instead on the relationship between expectations and behavior. The norms that evolve from interaction are treated as rules and behavioral regularities which are external to the actors and which resist change because of the transaction costs of creating new ones. The game-theoretic analysis of cooperation among egoists is at base behavioral.

A constructivist analysis of cooperation, in contrast, would concentrate on how the expectations produced by behavior affect identities and interests. The process of creating institutions is one of internalizing new understandings of self and other, of acquiring new role identities, not just of creating external constraints on the behavior of exogenously constituted actors.[70] Even if not intended as such, in other words, the process by which egoists learn to cooperate is at the same time a process of reconstructing their interests in terms of shared commitments to social norms. Over time, this will tend to transform a positive interdependence of *outcomes* into a positive interdependence of *utilities* or collective interest organized around the norms in question. These norms will resist change because they are tied to actors' commitments to their identities and interests, not merely because of transaction costs. A constructivist analysis of "the cooperation problem," in other words, is at base cognitive rather than behavioral, since it treats the intersubjective knowledge that defines the structure of identities and interests, of the "game," as endogenous to and instantiated by interaction itself.

The debate over the future of collective security in Western Europe may illustrate the significance of this difference. A weak liberal or rationalist analysis would assume that the European states' "portfolio" of interests has not fundamentally changed and that the emergence of new factors, such as the collapse of the Soviet threat and the rise of Germany, would alter their cost-benefit ratios for pursuing current arrangements, thereby causing existing institutions to break down. The European states formed collaborative institutions for good, exogenously constituted egoistic reasons, and the same reasons may lead them to reject those institutions; the game of European power politics has not changed. A strong liberal or constructivist analysis of this problem would suggest that four decades of cooperation may have transformed a positive interdependence of outcomes into a collective "European identity" in terms of which states increasingly define their "self"-interests.[71] Even if egoistic reasons were its starting point, the process of cooperating tends to redefine those reasons by

reconstituting identities and interests in terms of new intersubjective understandings and commitments. Changes in the distribution of power during the late twentieth century are undoubtedly a challenge to these new understandings, but it is not as if West European states have some inherent, exogenously given interest in abandoning collective security if the price is right. Their identities and security interests are continuously in process, and if collective identities become "embedded," they will be as resistant to change as egoistic ones.[72] Through participation in new forms of social knowledge, in other words, the European states of 1990 might no longer be the states of 1950.

Critical Strategic Theory and Collective Security

The transformation of identity and interest through an "evolution of cooperation" faces two important constraints. The first is that the process is incremental and slow. Actors' objectives in such a process are typically to realize joint gains within what they take to be a relatively stable context, and they are therefore unlikely to engage in substantial reflection about how to change the parameters of that context (including the structure of identities and interests) and unlikely to pursue policies specifically designed to bring about such changes. Learning to cooperate may change those parameters, but this occurs as an unintended consequence of policies pursued for other reasons rather than as a result of intentional efforts to transcend existing institutions.

A second, more fundamental, constraint is that the evolution of cooperation story presupposes that actors do not identify negatively with one another. Actors must be concerned primarily with absolute gains; to the extent that antipathy and distrust lead them to define their security in relativistic terms, it will be hard to accept the vulnerabilities that attend cooperation.[73] This is important because it is precisely the "central balance" in the state system that seems to be so often afflicted with such competitive thinking, and realists can therefore argue that the possibility of cooperation within one "pole" (for example, the West) is parasitic on the dominance of competition between poles (the East–West conflict). Relations between the poles may be amenable to some positive reciprocity in areas such as arms control, but the atmosphere of distrust leaves little room for such cooperation and its transformative consequences.[74] The conditions of negative identification that make an "evolution of cooperation" most needed work precisely against such a logic.

This seemingly intractable situation may nevertheless be amenable to quite a different logic of transformation, one driven more by self-conscious efforts to change structures of identity and interest than by unintended consequences. Such voluntarism may seem to contradict the spirit of constructivism, since would-be revolutionaries are presumably themselves effects of socialization to structures of identity and interest. How can they think about changing that to which they owe their identity? The possibility lies in the distinction between the social determination of the self and the personal determination of choice, between what Mead called the "me" and the "I."[75] The "me" is that part of subjectivity which is defined in terms of others; the character and behavioral expectations of a person's role identity as "professor," or of the United States as "leader of the alliance," for example, are socially constituted. Roles are not played in mechanical fashion according to precise scripts, however, but are "taken" and adapted in idiosyncratic ways by each actor.[76] Even in the most constrained situations, role performance involves a choice by the actor. The "I" is the part of subjectivity in which this appropriation and reaction to roles and its corresponding existential freedom lie.

The fact that roles are "taken" means that, in principle, actors always have a capacity for "character planning"—for engaging in critical self-reflection

and choices designed to bring about changes in their lives.[77] But when or under what conditions can this creative capacity be exercised? Clearly, much of the time it cannot: if actors were constantly reinventing their identities, social order would be impossible, and the relative stability of identities and interests in the real world is indicative of our propensity for habitual rather than creative action. The exceptional, conscious choosing to transform or transcend roles has at least two preconditions. First, there must be a reason to think of oneself in novel terms. This would most likely stem from the presence of new social situations that cannot be managed in terms of preexisting self-conceptions. Second, the expected costs of intentional role change—the sanctions imposed by others with whom one interacted in previous roles—cannot be greater than its rewards.

When these conditions are present, actors can engage in self-reflection and practice specifically designed to transform their identities and interests and thus to "change the games" in which they are embedded. Such "critical" strategic theory and practice has not received the attention it merits from students of world politics (another legacy of exogenously given interests perhaps), particularly given that one of the most important phenomena in contemporary world politics, Mikhail Gorbachev's policy of "New Thinking," is arguably precisely that.[78] Let me therefore use this policy as an example of how states might transform a competitive security system into a cooperative one, dividing the transformative process into four stages.

The first stage in intentional transformation is the breakdown of consensus about identity commitments. In the Soviet case, identity commitments centered on the Leninist theory of imperialism, with its belief that relations between capitalist and socialist states are inherently conflictual, and on the alliance patterns that this belief engendered. In the 1980s, the consensus within the Soviet Union over the Leninist theory broke down for a variety of reasons, principal among which seem to have been the state's inability to meet the economic-technological-military challenge from the West, the government's decline of political legitimacy at home, and the reassurance from the West that it did not intend to invade the Soviet Union, a reassurance that reduced the external costs of role change.[79] These factors paved the way for a radical leadership transition and for a subsequent "unfreezing of conflict schemas" concerning relations with the West.[80]

The breakdown of consensus makes possible a second stage of critical examination of old ideas about self and other and, by extension, of the structures of interaction by which the ideas have been sustained. In periods of relatively stable role identities, ideas and structures may become reified and thus treated as things that exist independently of social action. If so, the second stage is one of denaturalization, of identifying the practices that reproduce seemingly inevitable ideas about self and other; to that extent, it is a form of "critical" rather than "problem-solving" theory.[81] The result of such a critique should be an identification of new "possible selves" and aspirations.[82] New Thinking embodies such critical theorizing. Gorbachev wants to free the Soviet Union from the coercive social logic of the cold war and engage the West in far-reaching cooperation. Toward this end, he has rejected the Leninist belief in the inherent conflict of interest between socialist and capitalist states and, perhaps more important, has recognized the crucial role that Soviet aggressive practices played in sustaining that conflict.

Such rethinking paves the way for a third stage of new practice. In most cases, it is not enough to rethink one's own ideas about self and other, since old identities have been sustained by systems of interaction with *other* actors, the practices of which remain a social fact for the transformative agent. In order to change the self, then, it is often necessary to change the identities and interests of the others that help sustain those systems of interaction. The vehicle for inducing such change is one's own practice and, in particular, the practice of "altercasting"—a technique of interactor control in which ego uses tactics of self-presentation and stage management in an attempt to frame alter's definitions of social situations in ways that create the role which ego desires alter to play.[83] In effect, in altercasting ego tries to induce alter to take on a new identity (and thereby enlist alter in ego's effort to change itself) by treating alter *as if* it already had that identity. The logic of this follows directly from the mirror theory of identity-formation, in which alter's identity is a reflection of ego's practices; change those practices and ego begins to change alter's conception of itself.

What these practices should consist of depends on the logic by which the preexisting identities were sustained. Competitive security systems are sustained by practices that create insecurity and distrust. In this case, transformative practices should attempt to teach other states that one's own state can be trusted and should not be viewed as a threat to their security. The fastest way to do this is to make unilateral initiatives and self-binding commitments of sufficient significance that another state is faced with "an offer it cannot refuse."[84] Gorbachev has tried to do this by withdrawing from Afghanistan and Eastern Europe, implementing asymmetric cuts in nuclear and conventional forces, calling for "defensive defense," and so on. In addition, he has skillfully cast the West in the role of being morally required to give aid and comfort to the Soviet Union, has emphasized the bonds of common fate between the Soviet Union and the West, and has indicated that further progress in East–West relations is contingent upon the West assuming the identity being projected onto it. These actions are all dimensions of altercasting, the intention of which is to take away the Western "excuse" for distrusting the Soviet Union, which, in Gorbachev's view, has helped sustain competitive identities in the past.

Yet by themselves such practices cannot transform a competitive security system, since if they are not reciprocated by alter, they will expose ego to a "sucker" payoff and quickly wither on the vine. In order for critical strategic practice to transform competitive identities, it must be "rewarded" by alter, which will encourage more such practice by ego, and so on.[85] Over time, this will institutionalize a positive rather than a negative identification between the security of self and other and will thereby provide a firm intersubjective basis for what were initially tentative commitments to new identities and interests.[86]

Notwithstanding today's rhetoric about the end of the cold war, skeptics may still doubt whether Gorbachev (or some future leader) will succeed in building an intersubjective basis for a new Soviet (or Russian) role identity. There are important domestic, bureaucratic, and cognitive-ideological sources of resistance in both East and West to such a change, not the least of which is the shakiness of the democratic forces' domestic position. But if my argument about the role of intersubjective knowledge in creating competitive structures of identity and interest is right, then at least New Thinking shows a greater appreciation—conscious or not—for the deep structure of power politics than we are accustomed to in international relations practice.

Conclusion

All theories of international relations are based on social theories of the relationship between agency, process, and social structure. Social theories do not determine the content of our international theorizing, but they do structure the questions we ask about world politics and our approaches to answering those questions. The substantive issue at stake in debates about social theory is what kind of foundation offers the most fruitful set of questions and research strategies for explaining the revolutionary changes that seem to be occurring in the late twentieth century international system. Put simply, what should systemic theories of international relations look like? How should they conceptualize the relationship between structure and process? Should they be based exclusively on "microeconomic" analogies in which identities and interests are exogenously given by structure and process is reduced to interactions within those parameters? Or should they also be based on "sociological" and "social psychological" analogies in which identities and interests and therefore the meaning of structure are endogenous to process? Should a behavioral-individualism or a cognitive-constructivism be the basis for systemic theories of world politics?

This article notwithstanding, this question is ultimately an empirical one in two respects. First, its answer depends in part on how important interaction among states is for the constitution of their identities and interests. On the one hand, it may be that domestic or genetic factors, which I have systematically bracketed, are in fact much more important determinants of states' identities and interests than are systemic factors. To the extent that this is true, the individualism of a rationalist approach and the inherent privileging of structure over process in this approach become more substantively appropriate for systemic theory (if not for first- and second-image theory), since identities and interests are *in fact* largely exogenous to interaction among states. On the other hand, if the bracketed factors are relatively unimportant or if the importance of the international system varies historically (perhaps with the level of dynamic density and interdependence in the system), then such a framework would not be appropriate as an exclusive foundation for general systemic theory.

Second, the answer to the question about what systemic theories should look like also depends on how easily state identities and interests can change as a result of systemic interaction. Even if interaction is initially important in constructing identities and interests, once institutionalized its logic may make transformation extremely difficult. If the meaning of structure for state action changes so slowly that it becomes a de facto parameter within which process takes place, then it may again be substantively appropriate to adopt the rationalist assumption that identities and interests are given (although again, this may vary historically).

We cannot address these empirical issues, however, unless we have a framework for doing systemic research that makes state identity and interest an issue for both theoretical and empirical inquiry. Let me emphasize that this is *not* to say we should never treat identities and interests as given. The framing of problems and research strategies should be question-driven rather than method-driven, and if we are not interested in identity- and interest-formation, we may find the assumptions of a rationalist discourse perfectly reasonable. Nothing in this article, in other words, should be taken as an attack on rationalism per se. By the same token, however, we should not let this legitimate analytical stance become a de facto ontological stance with respect to the content of third-image theory, at least not until after we have determined that systemic interaction does not play an important role in processes of state identity- and interest-formation. We should not choose our philosophical anthropologies and social theories prematurely. By arguing that we cannot derive a self-help structure of identity and interest from the principle of anarchy alone—by arguing that anarchy is what states make of it—this article has challenged one important justification for ignoring processes of identity- and interest-formation in world politics. As such, it helps set the stage for inquiry into the empirical issues raised above and thus for a debate about whether communitarian or individualist assumptions are a better foundation for systemic theory.

I have tried to indicate by crude example what such a research agenda might look like. Its objective should be to assess the causal relationship between practice and interaction (as independent variable) and the cognitive structures at the level of individual states and of systems of states which constitute identities and interests (as dependent variable)—that is, the relationship between what actors *do* and what they *are*. We may have some a priori notion that state actors and systemic structures are "mutually constitutive," but this tells us little in the absence of an understanding of how the mechanics of dyadic, triadic, and n-actor interaction shape and are in turn shaped by "stocks of knowledge" that collectively constitute identities and interests and, more broadly, constitute the structures of international life. Particularly important in this respect is the role of practice in shaping attitudes toward the "givenness" of these structures. How and why do actors reify social structures, and under what conditions do they denaturalize such reifications?

The state-centrism of this agenda may strike some, particularly postmodernists, as "depressingly familiar."[87] The significance of states relative to multinational corporations, new social movements, transnationals, and intergovernmental organizations is clearly declining, and "postmodern" forms of world politics merit more research attention than they have received. But I also believe, with realists, that in the medium run sovereign states will remain the dominant political actors in the international system. Any transition to new structures of global political authority and identity—to "postinternational" politics—will be mediated by and path-dependent on the particular institutional resolution of the tension between unity and diversity, or particularism and universality, that is the sovereign state.[88] In such a world there should continue to be a place for theories of anarchic interstate politics, alongside other forms of international theory; to that extent, I am a statist and a realist. I have argued in this article, however, that statism need not be bound by realist ideas about what "state" must mean. State identities and interests can be collectively transformed within an anarchic context by many factors—individual, domestic, systemic, or transnational—and as such are an important dependent variable. Such a reconstruction of state-centric international theory is necessary if we are to theorize adequately about the emerging forms of transnational political identity that sovereign states will help bring into being. To that extent, I hope that statism, like the state, can be historically progressive.

■　　■　　■

NOTES

1. See, for example, Joseph Grieco, "Anarchy and the Limits of Cooperation: A Realist Critique of the Newest Liberal Institutionalism," *International Organization* 42 (Summer 1988), pp. 485–507; Joseph Nye, "Neorealism and Neoliberalism," *World Politics* 40 (January 1988), pp. 235–51; Robert Keohane, "Neoliberal Institutionalism: A Perspective on World Politics," in his collection of essays entitled *International Institutions and State Power* (Boulder, CO: Westview Press, 1989), pp. 1–20; John Mearsheimer, "Back to the Future: Instability in Europe after the Cold War," *International Security* 13 (Summer 1990), pp. 5–56.

2. Kenneth Waltz, *Man, the State, and War* (New York: Columbia University Press, 1959), p. 232.

3. Ibid., pp. 169–70.

4. Ibid., p. 232. This point is made by Hidemi Suganami in "Bringing Order to the Causes of War Debates," *Millennium* 19 (Spring 1990), p. 34, fn. 11.

5. Kenneth Waltz, *Theory of International Politics* (Boston: Addison-Wesley, 1979).

6. The neorealist description is not unproblematic. For a powerful critique, see David Lumsdaine, [*Moral Vision in International Politics:*] *The Foreign Aid Regime, 1949–1989* (Princeton, NJ: Princeton University Press, [1993]).

7. Waltz, *Theory of International Politics,* pp. 79–101.

8. Stephen Walt, *The Origins of Alliances* (Ithaca, NY: Cornell University Press, 1987).

9. See, for example, Herbert Blumer, "The Methodological Position of Symbolic Interactionism," in his *Symbolic Interactionism: Perspective and Method* (Englewood Cliffs, NJ: Prentice-Hall, 1969), p. 2. Throughout this article, I assume that a theoretically productive analogy can be made between individuals and states.

10. The phrase "distribution of knowledge" is Barry Barnes's, as discussed in his work *The Nature of Power* (Cambridge: Polity Press, 1988); see also Peter Berger and Thomas Luckmann, *The Social Construction of Reality* (New York: Anchor Books, 1966).

11. For an excellent short statement of how collective meanings constitute identities, see Peter Berger, "Identity as a Problem in the Sociology of Knowledge," *European Journal of Sociology,* vol. 7, no. 1, 1966, pp. 32–40.

12. Berger, "Identity as a Problem in the Sociology of Knowledge," p. 111.

13. While not normally cast in such terms, foreign policy scholarship on national role conceptions could be adapted to such identity language. See Kal Holsti, "National Role Conceptions in the Study of Foreign Policy," *International Studies Quarterly* 14 (September 1970), pp. 233–309; and Stephen Walker, ed., *Role Theory and Foreign Policy Analysis* (Durham, NC: Duke University Press, 1987). For an important effort to do so, see Stephen Walker, "Symbolic Interactionism and International Politics: Role Theory's Contribution to International Organization," in C. Shih and Martha Cottam, eds., *Contending Dramas: A Cognitive Approach to Post-War International Organizational Processes* (New York: Praeger, [1992]).

14. On the "portfolio" conception of interests, see Barry Hindess, *Political Choice and Social Structure* (Aldershot, UK: Edward Elgar, 1989), pp. 2–3. The "definition of the situation" is a central concept in interactionist theory.

15. Nelson Foote, "Identification as the Basis for a Theory of Motivation," *American Sociological Review* 16 (February 1951), p. 15. Such strongly sociological conceptions of interest have been criticized, with some justice, for being "oversocialized"; see Dennis Wrong, "The Oversocialized Conception of Man in Modern Sociology," *American Sociological Review* 26 (April 1961), pp. 183–93. For useful correctives, which focus on the activation of presocial but nondetermining human needs within social contexts, see Turner, *A Theory of Social Interaction,* pp. 23–69; and Viktor Gecas, "The Self-Concept as a Basis for a Theory of Motivation," in Judith Howard and Peter Callero, eds., *The Self-Society Dynamic* (Cambridge: Cambridge University Press, 1991), pp. 171–87.

16. In neo-Durkheimian parlance, institutions are "social representations." See Serge Moscovici, "The Phenomenon of Social Representations," in Rob Farr and Serge Moscovici, eds., *Social Representations* (Cambridge: Cambridge University Press, 1984), pp. 3–69.

17. Berger and Luckmann, *The Social Construction of Reality,* p. 58.

18. See Giddens, *Central Problems in Social Theory;* and Alexander Wendt and Raymond Duvall, "Institutions and International Order," in Ernst-Otto Czempiel and James Rosenau, eds., *Global Changes and Theoretical Challenges* (Lexington, Mass.: Lexington Books, 1989), pp. 51–74.

19. Proponents of choice theory might put this in terms of "interdependent utilities."

20. Security systems might also vary in the extent to which there is a functional differentiation or a hierarchical relationship between patron and client, with the patron playing a hegemonic role within its sphere of influence in defining the security interests of its clients. I do not examine this dimension here; for preliminary discussion, see Alexander Wendt, "The States System and Global Militarization," Ph.D. diss., University of Minnesota, Minneapolis, 1989; and Alexander Wendt and Michael Barnett, "The International System and Third World Militarization," unpublished manuscript, 1991.

21. This amounts to an "internationalization of the state." For a discussion of this subject, see Raymond Duvall and Alexander Wendt, "The International Capital Regime and the Internationalization of the State," unpublished manuscript, 1987. See also R. B. J. Walker, "Sovereignty, Identity, Community: Reflections on the Horizons of Contemporary Political Practice," in R. B. J. Walker and Saul Mendlovitz, eds., *Contending Sovereignties* (Boulder, CO: Lynne Rienner, 1990), pp. 159–85.

22. On the spectrum of cooperative security arrangements, see Charles Kupchan and Clifford Kupchan, "Concerts, Collective Security,

and the Future of Europe," *International Security* 16 (Summer 1991), pp. 114–61; and Richard Smoke, "A Theory of Mutual Security," in Richard Smoke and Andrei Kortunov, eds., *Mutual Security* (New York: St. Martin's Press, 1991), pp. 59–111. These may be usefully set alongside Christopher Jencks' "Varieties of Altruism," in Jane Mansbridge, ed., *Beyond Self-Interest* (Chicago: University of Chicago Press, 1990), pp. 53–67.

23. On the role of collective identity in reducing collective action problems, see Bruce Fireman and William Gamson, "Utilitarian Logic in the Resource Mobilization Perspective," in Mayer Zald and John McCarthy, eds., *The Dynamics of Social Movements* (Cambridge, MA: Winthrop, 1979), pp. 8–44; Robyn Dawes et al., "Cooperation for the Benefit of Us—Not Me, or My Conscience," in Mansbridge, *Beyond Self-Interest,* pp. 97–110; and Craig Calhoun, "The Problem of Identity in Collective Action," in Joan Huber, ed., *Macro-Micro Linkages in Sociology* (Beverly Hills, CA: Sage, 1991), pp. 51–75.

24. See Thomas Risse-Kappen, "Are Democratic Alliances Special?" unpublished manuscript, Yale University, New Haven, CT, 1991.

25. Waltz, *Theory of International Politics,* p. 91.

26. See Waltz, *Man, the State, and War;* and Robert Jervis, "Cooperation Under the Security Dilemma," *World Politics* 30 (January 1978), pp. 167–214.

27. My argument here parallels Rousseau's critique of Hobbes. For an excellent critique of realist appropriations of Rousseau, see Michael Williams, "Rousseau, Realism, and Realpolitik," *Millennium* 18 (Summer 1989), pp. 188–204. Williams argues that far from being a fundamental starting point in the state of nature, for Rousseau the stag hunt represented a stage in man's fall. On p. 190, Williams cites Rousseau's description of man prior to leaving the state of nature: "Man only knows himself; he does not see his own well-being to be identified with or contrary to that of anyone else; he neither hates anything nor loves anything; but limited to no more than physical instinct, he is no one, he is an animal." For another critique of Hobbes on the state of nature that parallels my constructivist reading of anarchy, see Charles Landesman, "Reflections on Hobbes: Anarchy and Human Nature," in Peter Caws, ed., *The Causes of Quarrel* (Boston: Beacon, 1989), pp. 139–48.

28. Empirically, this suggestion is problematic, since the process of decolonization and the subsequent support of many Third World states by international society point to ways in which even the raw material of "empirical statehood" is constituted by the society of states. See Robert Jackson and Carl Rosberg, "Why Africa's Weak States Persist: The Empirical and the Juridical in Statehood," *World Politics* 35 (October 1982), pp. 1–24.

29. Waltz, *Theory of International Politics,* pp. 74–77.

30. See James Morrow, "Social Choice and System Structure in World Politics," *World Politics* 41 (October 1988), p. 89. Waltz's behavioral treatment of socialization may be usefully contrasted with the more cognitive approach taken by Ikenberry and the Kupchans in the following articles: G. John Ikenberry and Charles Kupchan, "Socialization and Hegemonic Power," *International Organization* 44 (Summer 1989), pp. 283–316; and Kupchan and Kupchan, "Concerts, Collective Security, and the Future of Europe." Their approach is close to my own, but they define socialization as an elite strategy to induce value change in others, rather than as a ubiquitous feature of interaction in terms of which all identities and interests get produced and reproduced.

31. Regarding individualism, see Richard Ashley, "The Poverty of Neorealism," *International Organization* 38 (Spring 1984), pp. 225–86; Wendt, "The Agent-Structure Problem in International Relations Theory"; and David Dessler, "What's at Stake in the Agent-Structure Debate?" *International Organization* 43 (Summer 1989), pp. 441–74. Regarding structuralism, see R. B. J. Walker, "Realism, Change, and International Political Theory," *International Studies Quarterly* 31 (March 1987), pp. 65–86; and Martin Hollis and Steven Smith, *Explaining and Understanding International Relations* (Oxford: Clarendon Press, 1989).

32. The importance of the distinction between constitutive and causal explanations is not sufficiently appreciated in constructivist discourse. See Wendt, "The Agent-Structure Problem in International Relations Theory," pp. 362–65; Wendt, "The States System and Global Militarization," pp. 110–13; and Wendt, "Bridging the Theory/Meta-Theory Gap in International Relations," *Review of International Studies* 17 (October 1991), p. 390.

33. See Blumer, "The Methodological Position of Symbolic Interactionism," pp. 2–4.

34. See Robert Grafstein, "Rational Choice: Theory and Institutions," in Kristen Monroe, ed., *The Economic Approach to Politics* (New York: Harper Collins, 1991), pp. 263–64. A good example of the promise and limits of transaction cost approaches to institutional analysis is offered by Robert Keohane in his *After Hegemony* (Princeton, NJ: Princeton University Press, 1984).

35. This situation is not entirely metaphorical in world politics, since throughout history states have "discovered" each other, generating an instant anarchy as it were.

36. Mead's analysis of gestures remains definitive. See Mead's *Mind, Self, and Society.* See also the discussion of the role of signaling in the "mechanics of interaction" in Turner's *A Theory of Social Interaction,* pp. 74–79 and 92–115.

37. On the role of attribution processes in the interactionist account of identity-formation, see Sheldon Stryker and Avi Gottlieb, "Attribution Theory and Symbolic Interactionism," in John Harvey et al., eds., *New Directions in Attribution Research,* vol. 3 (Hillsdale, NJ: Lawrence Erlbaum, 1981), pp. 425–58; and Kathleen Crittenden, "Sociological Aspects of Attribution," *Annual Review of Sociology,* vol. 9, 1983, pp. 425–46. On attributional processes in international relations, see Shawn Rosenberg and Gary Wolfsfeld, "International Conflict and the Problem of Attribution," *Journal of Conflict Resolution* 21 (March 1977), pp. 75–103.

38. On the "stagecraft" involved in "presentations of self," see Erving Goffman, *The Presentation of Self in Everyday Life* (New York: Doubleday, 1959). On the role of appearance in definitions of the situation, see Gregory Stone, "Appearance and the Self," in Arnold Rose, ed., *Human Behavior and Social Processes* (Boston: Houghton Mifflin, 1962), pp. 86–118.

39. This discussion of the role of possibilities and probabilities in threat perception owes much to Stewart Johnson's comments on an earlier draft of my article.

40. On the role of "reassurance" in threat situations, see Richard Ned Lebow and Janice Gross Stein, "Beyond Deterrence," *Journal of Social Issues,* vol. 43, no. 4, 1987, pp. 5–72.

41. On "reciprocal typifications," see Berger and Luckmann, *The Social Construction of Reality,* pp. 54–58.

42. Jeff Coulter, "Remarks on the Conceptualization of Social Structure," *Philosophy of the Social Sciences* 12 (March 1982), pp. 42–43.

43. The following articles by Noel Kaplowitz have made an important contribution to such thinking in international relations: "Psychopolitical Dimensions of International Relations: The Reciprocal Effects of Conflict Strategies," *International Studies Quarterly* 28 (December 1984), pp. 373–406; and "National Self-Images, Perception of Enemies, and Conflict Strategies: Psychopolitical Dimensions of International Relations," *Political Psychology* 11 (March 1990), pp. 39–82.

44. These arguments are common in theories of narcissism and altruism. See Heinz Kohut, *Self-Psychology and the Humanities* (New York: Norton, 1985); and Martin Hoffmann, "Empathy, Its Limitations, and Its Role in a Comprehensive Moral Theory," in William Kurtines and Jacob Gewirtz, eds., *Morality, Moral Behavior, and Moral Development* (New York: Wiley, 1984), pp. 283–302.

45. See C. Norman Alexander and Mary Glenn Wiley, "Situated Activity and Identity Formation," in Morris Rosenberg and Ralph Turner, eds., *Social Psychology: Sociological Perspectives* (New York: Basic Books, 1981), pp. 269–89.

46. Sheldon Stryker, "The Vitalization of Symbolic Interactionism," *Social Psychology Quarterly* 50 (March 1987), p. 93.

47. On the "maturity" of anarchies, see Barry Buzan, *People, States, and Fear* (Chapel Hill: University of North Carolina Press, 1983).

48. A similar intuition may lie behind Ashley's effort to reappropriate classical realist discourse for critical international relations theory. See Richard Ashley, "Political Realism and Human Interests," *International Studies Quarterly* 38 (June 1981), pp. 204–36.

49. Waltz has himself helped open up such a debate with his recognition that systemic factors condition but do not determine state actions. See Kenneth Waltz, "Reflections on *Theory of International Politics:* A Response to My Critics," in Robert Keohane, ed., *Neorealism and Its Critics* (New York: Columbia University Press, 1986), pp. 322–45. The growing literature on the observation that "democracies do not fight each other" is relevant to this question, as are two other studies that break important ground toward a "reductionist" theory of state identity: William Bloom's *Personal Identity, National Identity and International Relations* (Cambridge: Cambridge University Press, 1990) and Lumsdaine's *Ideals and Interests.*

50. See Berger and Luckmann, *The Social Construction of Reality,* p. 89. See also Douglas Maynard and Thomas Wilson, "On the Reification of Social Structure," in Scott McNall and Gary Howe, eds., *Current Perspectives in Social Theory,* vol. 1 (Greenwich, CT: JAI Press, 1980), pp. 287–322.

51. See Richard Ashley, "Social Will and International Anarchy," in Hayward Alker and Richard Ashley, eds., *After Realism,* work in progress, Massachusetts Institute of Technology, Cambridge, and Arizona State University, Tempe, 1992.

52. See Ralph Turner, "Role-Taking: Process Versus Conformity," in Rose, *Human Behavior and Social Processes,* pp. 20–40; and Judith

Howard, "From Changing Selves toward Changing Society," in Howard and Callero, *The Self-Society Dynamic,* pp. 209–37.

53. On the relationship between commitment and identity, see Foote, "Identification as the Basis for a Theory of Motivation"; Howard Becker, "Notes on the Concept of Commitment," *American Journal of Sociology* 66 (July 1960), pp. 32–40; and Stryker, *Symbolic Interactionism.* On role salience, see Stryker, ibid.

54. On threats to identity and the types of resistance that they may create, see Glynis Breakwell, *Coping with Threatened Identities* (London: Methuen, 1986); and Terrell Northrup, "The Dynamic of Identity in Personal and Social Conflict," in Louis Kreisberg et al., eds., *Intractable Conflicts and Their Transformation* (Syracuse, NY: Syracuse University Press, 1989), pp. 55–82. For a broad overview of resistance to change, see Timur Kuran, "The Tenacious Past: Theories of Personal and Collective Conservatism," *Journal of Economic Behavior and Organization* 10 (September 1988), pp. 143–71.

55. James March, "Bounded Rationality, Ambiguity, and the Engineering of Choice," *Bell Journal of Economics* 9 (Autumn 1978), p. 600.

56. Haskell Fain, *Normative Politics and the Community of Nations* (Philadelphia: Temple University Press, 1987).

57. This is the intersubjective basis for the principle of functional nondifferentiation among states, which "drops out" of Waltz's definition of structure because the latter has no explicit intersubjective basis. In international relations scholarship, the social production of territorial space has been emphasized primarily by poststructuralists. See, for example, Richard Ashley, "The Geopolitics of Geopolitical Space: Toward a Critical Social Theory of International Politics," *Alternatives* 12 (October 1987), pp. 403–34; and Simon Dalby, *Creating the Second Cold War* (London: Pinter, 1990). But the idea of space as both product and constituent of practice is also prominent in structurationist discourse. See Giddens, *Central Problems in Social Theory;* and Derek Gregory and John Urry, eds., *Social Relations and Spatial Structures* (London: Macmillan, 1985).

58. See John Ruggie, "Continuity and Transformation in the World Polity: Toward a Neorealist Synthesis," *World Politics* 35 (January 1983), pp. 261–85.

59. For a definition and discussion of "social closure," see Raymond Murphy, *Social Closure* (Oxford: Clarendon Press, 1988).

60. See Richard Ashley, "Untying the Sovereign State: A Double Reading of the Anarchy Problematique," *Millennium* 17 (Summer 1988), pp. 227–62.

61. See, for example, Mohammed Ayoob, "The Third World in the System of States: Acute Schizophrenia or Growing Pains?" *International Studies Quarterly* 33 (March 1989), pp. 67–80.

62. See William Coplin, "International Law and Assumptions about the State System," *World Politics* 17 (July 1965), pp. 615–34.

63. See Anthony Smith, "States and Homelands: The Social and Geopolitical Implications of National Territory," *Millennium* 10 (Autumn 1981), pp. 187–202.

64. This assumes that there are no other, competing, principles that organize political space and identity in the international system and coexist with traditional notions of sovereignty; in fact, of course, there are. On "spheres of influence" and "informal empires," see Jan Triska, ed., *Dominant Powers and Subordinate States* (Durham, NC:

Duke University Press, 1986); and Ronald Robinson, "The Excentric Idea of Imperialism, With or Without Empire," in Wolfgang Mommsen and Jurgen Osterhammel, eds., *Imperialism and After: Continuities and Discontinuities* (London: Allen & Unwin, 1986), pp. 267–89. On Arab conceptions of sovereignty, see Michael Barnett, "Sovereignty, Institutions, and Identity: From Pan-Arabism to the Arab State System," unpublished manuscript, University of Wisconsin, Madison, 1991.

65. David Strang, "Anomaly and Commonplace in European Expansion: Realist and Institutional Accounts," *International Organization* 45 (Spring 1991), pp. 143–62.

66. On "dynamic density," see Ruggie, "Continuity and Transformation in the World Polity"; and Waltz, "Reflections on *Theory of International Politics.*" The role of interdependence in conditioning the speed and depth of social learning is much greater than the attention to which I have paid it. On the consequences of interdependence under anarchy, see Helen Milner, "The Assumption of Anarchy in International Relations Theory: A Critique," *Review of International Studies* 17 (January 1991), pp. 67–85.

67. See Michael Taylor, *Anarchy and Cooperation* (New York: Wiley, 1976); and Robert Axelrod, *The Evolution of Cooperation* (New York: Basic Books, 1984).

68. Mead, *Mind, Self, and Society.*

69. Strictly speaking, this is not true, since in iterated games the addition of future benefits to current ones changes the payoff structure of the game at T1, in this case from prisoners' dilemma to an assurance game. This transformation of interest takes place entirely within the actor, however, and as such is not a function of interaction with the other.

70. In fairness to Axelrod, he does point out that internalization of norms is a real possibility that may increase the resilience of institutions. My point is that this important idea cannot be derived from an approach to theory that takes identities and interests as exogenously given.

71. On "European identity," see Barry Buzan et al., eds., *The European Security Order Recast* (London: Pinter, 1990), pp. 45–63.

72. On "embeddedness," see John Ruggie, "International Regimes, Transactions, and Change: Embedded Liberalism in a Postwar Economic Order," in Krasner, *International Regimes,* pp. 195–232.

73. See Grieco, "Anarchy and the Limits of Cooperation."

74. On the difficulties of creating cooperative security regimes given competitive interests, see Robert Jervis, "Security Regimes," in Krasner, *International Regimes,* pp. 173–94; and Charles Lipson, "International Cooperation in Economic and Security Affairs," *World Politics* 37 (October 1984), pp. 1–23.

75. See Mead, *Mind, Self, and Society.*

76. Turner, "Role-Taking."

77. On "character planning," see Jon Elster, *Sour Grapes: Studies in the Subversion of Rationality* (Cambridge: Cambridge University Press, 1983), p. 117.

78. For useful overviews of New Thinking, see Mikhail Gorbachev, *Perestroika: New Thinking for Our Country and the World* (New York: Harper & Row, 1987); and Allen Lynch, *Gorbachev's International Outlook: Intellectual Origins and Political Consequences* (New York: Institute for East–West Security Studies, 1989).

79. For useful overviews of these factors, see Jack Snyder, "The Gorbachev Revolution: A Waning of Soviet Expansionism?" *World Politics* 12 (Winter 1987–88), pp. 93–121; and Stephen Meyer, "The Sources and Prospects of Gorbachev's New Political Thinking on Security," *International Security* 13 (Fall 1988), pp. 124–63.

80. See Daniel Bar-Tal et al., "Conflict Termination: An Epistemological Analysis of International Cases," *Political Psychology* 10 (June 1989), pp. 233–55.

81. See Robert Cox, "Social Forces, States and World Orders: Beyond International Relations Theory," in Keohane, *Neorealism and Its Critics,* pp. 204–55. See also Brian Fay, *Critical Social Science* (Ithaca, NY: Cornell University Press, 1987).

82. Hazel Markus and Paula Nurius, "Possible Selves," *American Psychologist* 41 (September 1986), pp. 954–69.

83. See Goffman, *The Presentation of Self in Everyday Life;* Eugene Weinstein and Paul Deutschberger, "Some Dimensions of Altercasting," *Sociometry* 26 (December 1963), pp. 454–66; and Walter Earle, "International Relations and the Psychology of Control: Alternative Control Strategies and Their Consequences," *Political Psychology* 7 (June 1986), pp. 369–75.

84. See Volker Boge and Peter Wilke, "Peace Movements and Unilateral Disarmament: Old Concepts in a New Light," *Arms Control* 7 (September 1986), pp. 156–70; Zeev Maoz and Daniel Felsenthal, "Self-Binding Commitments, the Inducement of Trust, Social Choice, and the Theory of International Cooperation," *International Studies Quarterly* 31 (June 1987), pp. 177–200; and V. Sakamoto, "Unilateral Initiative as an Alternative Strategy," *World Futures,* vol. 24, nos. 1–4, 1987, pp. 107–34.

85. On rewards, see Thomas Milburn and Daniel Christie, "Rewarding in International Politics," *Political Psychology* 10 (December 1989), pp. 625–45.

86. The importance of reciprocity in completing the process of structural transformation makes the logic in this stage similar to that in the "evolution of cooperation." The difference is one of prerequisites and objective: in the former, ego's tentative redefinition of self enables it to try and change alter by acting "as if" both were already playing a new game; in the latter, ego acts only on the basis of given interests and prior experience, with transformation emerging only as an unintended consequence.

87. Yale Ferguson and Richard Mansbach, "Between Celebration and Despair: Constructive Suggestions for Future International Theory," *International Studies Quarterly* 35 (December 1991), p. 375.

88. For excellent discussions of this tension, see Walker, "Sovereignty, Identity, Community"; and R. B. J. Walker, "Security, Sovereignty, and the Challenge of World Politics," *Alternatives* 15 (Winter 1990), pp. 3–27. On institutional path dependencies, see Stephen Krasner, "Sovereignty: An Institutional Perspective," *Comparative Political Studies* 21 (April 1988), pp. 66–94.

J. Ann Tickner

MAN, THE STATE, AND WAR
Gendered Perspectives on National Security

It is not in giving life but in risking life that man is raised above the animal: that is why superiority has been accorded in humanity not to the sex that brings forth but to that which kills.
                              —SIMONE DE BEAUVOIR

If we do not redefine manhood, war is inevitable.
                              —PAUL FUSSELL

In the face of what is generally perceived as a dangerous international environment, states have ranked national security high in terms of their policy priorities. According to international relations scholar Kenneth Waltz, the state conducts its affairs in the "brooding shadow of violence," and therefore war could break out at any time.[1] In the name of national security, states have justified large defense budgets, which take priority over domestic spending, military conscription of their young adult male population, foreign invasions, and the curtailment of civil liberties. The security of the state is perceived as a core value that is generally supported unquestioningly by most citizens, particularly in time of war. While the role of the state in the twentieth century has expanded to include the provision of domestic social programs, national security often takes precedence over the social security of individuals.

When we think about the provision of national security we enter into what has been, and continues to be, an almost exclusively male domain. While most women support what they take to be legitimate calls for state action in the interests of international security, the task of defining, defending, and advancing the security interests of the state is a man's affair, a task that, through its association with war, has been especially valorized and rewarded in many cultures throughout history. As Simone de Beauvoir's explanation for male superiority suggests, giving one's life for one's country has been considered the highest form of patriotism, but it is an act from which women have been virtually excluded. While men have been associated with defending the state and advancing its international interests as soldiers and diplomats, women have typically been engaged in the "ordering" and "comforting" roles both in the domestic sphere, as mothers and basic needs providers, and in the caring professions, as teachers, nurses, and social workers.[2] The role of women with respect to national security has been ambiguous: defined as those whom the state and its men are protecting, women have had little control over the conditions of their protection.

■   ■   ■

From *Gender in International Relations: Feminist Perspectives on Achieving Global Security* (New York: Columbia University Press, 1992): 27–66, 147–53.

A Gendered Perspective on National Security

Morgenthau, Waltz, and other realists claim that it is possible to develop a rational, objective theory of international politics based on universal laws that operate across time and space. In her feminist critique of the natural sciences, Evelyn Fox Keller points out that most scientific communities share the "assumption that the universe they study is directly accessible, represented by concepts shaped not by language but only by the demands of logic and experiment." The laws of nature, according to this view of science, are beyond the relativity of language.[3] Like most contemporary feminists, Keller rejects this positivist view of science that, she asserts, imposes a coercive, hierarchical, and conformist pattern on scientific inquiry. Since most contemporary feminist scholars believe that knowledge is socially constructed, they are skeptical of finding an unmediated foundation for knowledge that realists claim is possible. Since they believe that it is language that transmits knowledge, many feminists suggest that the scholarly claims about the neutral uses of language and about objectivity must continually be questioned.[4]

I shall now investigate the individual, the state, and the international system—the three levels of analysis that realists use in their analysis of war and national security—and examine how they have been constructed in realist discourse. I shall argue that the language used to describe these concepts comes out of a Western-centered historical worldview that draws almost exclusively on the experiences of men. Underneath its claim to universality this worldview privileges a view of security that is constructed out of values associated with hegemonic masculinity.

"Political Man"

In his *Politics among Nations,* a text rich in historical detail, Morgenthau has constructed a world almost entirely without women. Morgenthau claims that individuals are engaged in a struggle for power whenever they come into contact with one another, for the tendency to dominate exists at all levels of human life: the family, the polity, and the international system; it is modified only by the conditions under which the struggle takes place.[5] Since women rarely occupy positions of power in any of these arenas, we can assume that, when Morgenthau talks about domination, he is talking primarily about men, although not all men.[6] His "political man" is a social construct based on a partial representation of human nature abstracted from the behavior of men in positions of public power.[7] Morgenthau goes on to suggest that, while society condemns the violent behavior that can result from this struggle for power within the polity, it encourages it in the international system in the form of war.

While Morgenthau's "political man" has been criticized by other international relations scholars for its essentializing view of human nature, the social construction of hegemonic masculinity and its opposition to a devalued femininity have been central to the way in which the discourse of international politics has been constructed more generally. In Western political theory from the Greeks to Machiavelli, traditions upon which contemporary realism relies heavily for its analysis, this socially constructed type of masculinity has been projected onto the international behavior of states. The violence with which it is associated has been legitimated through the glorification of war.

■　　■　　■

The International System: The War of Everyman Against Everyman

According to Richard Ashley, realists have privileged a higher reality called "the sovereign state" against which they have posited anarchy understood in a negative way as difference, ambiguity, and contingency—as a space that is external and dangerous.[8] All these characteristics have also been attributed to women. Anarchy is an actual or potential site of war. The most common metaphor that realists employ to describe the anarchical international system is that of the seventeenth-century English philosopher Thomas Hobbes's depiction of the state of nature. Although Hobbes did not write much about international politics, realists have applied his description of individuals' behavior in a hypothetical precontractual state of nature, which Hobbes termed the war of everyman against everyman, to the behavior of states in the international system.[9]

Carole Pateman argues that, in all contemporary discussions of the state of nature, the differentiation between the sexes is generally ignored, even though it was an important consideration for contract theorists themselves.[10] Although Hobbes did suggest that women as well as men could be free and equal individuals in the state of nature, his description of human behavior in this environment refers to that of adult males whose behavior is taken as constitutive of human nature as a whole by contemporary realist analysis. According to Jane Flax, the individuals that Hobbes described in the state of nature appeared to come to full maturity without any engagement with one another; they were solitary creatures lacking any socialization in interactive behavior. Any interactions they did have led to power struggles that resulted in domination or submission. Suspicion of others' motives led to behavior characterized by aggression, self-interest, and the drive for autonomy.[11] In a similar vein, Christine Di

Stephano uses feminist psychoanalytic theory to support her claim that the masculine dimension of atomistic egoism is powerfully underscored in Hobbes's state of nature, which, she asserts, is built on the foundation of denied maternity. "Hobbes' abstract man is a creature who is self-possessed and radically solitary in a crowded and inhospitable world, whose relations with others are unavoidably contractual and whose freedom consists in the absence of impediments to the attainment of privately generated and understood desires."[12]

As a model of human behavior, Hobbes's depiction of individuals in the state of nature is partial at best; certain feminists have argued that such behavior could be applicable only to adult males, for if life was to go on for more than one generation in the state of nature, women must have been involved in activities such as reproduction and child rearing rather than in warfare. Reproductive activities require an environment that can provide for the survival of infants and behavior that is interactive and nurturing.

■   ■   ■

* * * [W]ar is central to the way we learn about international relations. * * * War is a time when male and female characteristics become polarized; it is a gendering activity at a time when the discourse of militarism and masculinity permeates the whole fabric of society.[13]

As Jean Elshtain points out, war is an experience to which women are exterior; men have inhabited the world of war in a way that women have not.[14] The history of international politics is therefore a history from which women are, for the most part, absent. Little material can be found on women's roles in wars; generally they are seen as victims, rarely as agents. While war can be a time of advancement for women as they step in to do men's jobs, the battlefront takes precedence, so the hierarchy remains and women are urged to step aside once peace is restored. When women themselves engage in violence, it is often portrayed as a mob or a food riot that is out of control.[15] Movements for peace, which are also part of our history, have not been central to the conventional way in which the evolution of the Western state system has been presented to us. International relations scholars of the early twentieth century, who wrote positively about the possibilities of international law and the collective security system of the League of Nations, were labeled "idealists" and not taken seriously by the more powerful realist tradition.

Metaphors, such as Hobbes's state of nature, are primarily concerned with representing conflictual relations between great powers. The images used to describe nineteenth-century imperialist projects and contemporary great power relations with former colonial states are somewhat different. Historically, colonial people were often described in terms that drew on characteristics associated with women in order to place them lower in a hierarchy that put their white male colonizers on top. As the European state system expanded outward to conquer much of the world in the nineteenth century, its "civilizing" mission was frequently described in stereotypically gendered terms. Colonized peoples were often described as being effeminate, masculinity was an attribute of the white man, and colonial order depended on Victorian standards of manliness. Cynthia Enloe suggests that the concept of "ladylike behavior" was one of the mainstays of imperialist civilization. Like sanitation and Christianity, feminine respectability was meant to convince colonizers and colonized alike that foreign conquest was right and necessary. Masculinity denoted protection of the respectable lady; she stood for the civilizing mission that justified the colonization of benighted peoples.[16] Whereas the feminine stood for danger and disorder for Machiavelli, the European female, in contrast to her colonial counterpart, came to represent a stable, civilized order in nineteenth-century representations of British imperialism.

An example of the way in which these gender identities were manipulated to justify Western policy with respect to the rest of the world can also be seen in attitudes toward Latin America prevalent in the United States in the nineteenth century. According to Michael Hunt, nineteenth-century American images of Latin society depicted a (usually black) male who was lazy, dishonest, and corrupt. A contrary image that was more positive—a Latin as redeemable—took the form of a fair-skinned senorita living in a marginalized society, yet escaping its degrading effects. Hunt suggests that Americans entered the twentieth century with three images of Latin America fostered through legends brought back by American merchants and diplomats. These legends, perpetuated through school texts, cartoons, and political rhetoric, were even incorporated into the views of policymakers. The three images pictured the Latin as a half-breed brute, feminized, or infantile. In each case, Americans stood superior; the first image permitted a predatory aggressiveness, the second allowed the United States to assume the role of ardent suitor, and the third justified America's need to provide tutelage and discipline. All these images are profoundly gendered: the United States as a civilizing warrior, a suitor, or a father, and Latin America as a lesser male, a female, or a child.[17]

Such images, although somewhat muted, remain today and are particularly prevalent in the thinking of Western states when they are dealing with the Third World. * * *

■   ■   ■

Feminist Perspectives on National Security

Women Define Security

It is difficult to find definitions by women of national security. While it is not necessarily the case that women have not had ideas on this subject, they are not readily accessible in the literature of international relations. When women speak or write about national security, they are often dismissed as being naive or unrealistic. An example of this is the women in the United States and Europe who spoke out in the early years of the century for a more secure world order. Addressing the International Congress of Women at the Hague during World War I, Jane Addams spoke of the need for a new internationalism to replace the self-destructive nationalism that contributed so centrally to the outbreak and mass destruction of that war. Resolutions adopted at the close of the congress questioned the assumption that women, and civilians more generally, could be protected during modern war. The conference concluded that assuring security through military means was no longer possible owing to the indiscriminate nature of modern warfare, and it called for disarmament as a more appropriate course for ensuring future security.[18]

At the Women's International Peace Conference in Halifax, Canada, in 1985, a meeting of women from all over the world, participants defined security in various ways depending on the most immediate threats to their survival; security meant safe working conditions and freedom from the threat of war or unemployment or the economic squeeze of foreign debt. Discussions of the meaning of security revealed divisions between Western middle-class women's concerns with nuclear war, concerns that were similar to those of Jane Addams and her colleagues, and Third World women who defined insecurity more broadly in terms of the structural violence associated with imperialism, militarism, racism, and sexism. Yet all agreed that security meant nothing if it was built on others' insecurity.[19]

The final document of the World Conference to Review and Appraise the Achievements of the United Nations Decade for Women, held in Nairobi in 1985, offered a similarly multidimensional definition of security. The introductory chapter of the document defined peace as "not only the absence of war, violence and hostilities at the national and international levels but also the enjoyment of economic and social justice."[20] All these definitions of security take issue with realists' assumptions that security is zero-sum and must therefore be built on the insecurity of others.

■   ■   ■

Citizenship Redefined

Building on the notion of hegemonic masculinity, the notion of the citizen-warrior depends on a devalued femininity for its construction. In international relations, this devalued femininity is bound up with myths about women as victims in need of protection; the protector/protected myth contributes to the legitimation of a militarized version of citizenship that results in unequal gender relations that can precipitate violence against women. Certain feminists have called for the construction of an enriched version of citizenship that would depend less on military values and more on an equal recognition of women's contributions to society. Such a notion of citizenship cannot come about, however, until myths that perpetuate views of women as victims rather than agents are eliminated.

One such myth is the association of women with peace, an association that has been invalidated through considerable evidence of women's support for men's wars in many societies.[21] In spite of a gender gap, a plurality of women generally support war and national security policies; Bernice Carroll suggests that the association of women and peace is one that has been imposed on women by their disarmed condition.[22] In the West, this association grew out of the Victorian ideology of women's moral superiority and the glorification of motherhood. This ideal was expressed by feminist Charlotte Perkins Gilman whose book *Herland* was first serialized in *The Forerunner* in 1915. Gilman glorified women as caring and nurturing mothers whose private sphere skills could benefit the world at large.[23] Most turn-of-the-century feminists shared Gilman's ideas. But if the implication of this view was that women were disqualified from participating in the corrupt world of political and economic power by virtue of their moral superiority, the result could only be the perpetuation of male dominance. Many contemporary feminists see dangers in the continuation of these essentializing myths that can only result in the perpetuation of women's subordination and reinforce dualisms that serve to make men more powerful. The association of femininity with peace lends support to an idealized masculinity that depends on constructing women as passive victims in need of protection. It also contributes to the claim that women are naive in matters relating to international politics. An enriched, less militarized notion of citizenship cannot be built on such a weak foundation.

While women have often been willing to support men's wars, many women are ambivalent about fighting in them, often preferring to leave that task to men. Feminists have also been divided on this issue; some argue, on the grounds of equality, that women must be given equal access to the military, while others suggest that women must resist the draft in order to promote a politics of peace. * * *

■   ■   ■

In spite of many women's support for men's wars, a consistent gender gap in voting on defense-related issues in many countries suggests that women are less supportive of policies that rest on the use of direct violence. Before the outbreak of the Persian Gulf war in 1990, women in the United States were overwhelmingly against the use of force and, for the first time, women alone turned the public opinion polls against opting for war.[24] During the 1980s, when the Reagan administration was increasing defense budgets, women were less likely to support defense at the expense of social programs, a pattern that, in the United States, holds true for women's behavior more generally.

Explanations for this gender gap, which in the United States appears to be increasing as time goes on, range from suggestions that women have not been socialized into the practice of violence to claims that women are increasingly voting their own interests. While holding down jobs, millions of women also care for children, the aged, and the sick—activities that usually take place outside the economy. When more resources go to the military, additional burdens are placed on such women as public sector resources for social services shrink. While certain women are able, through access to the military, to give service to their country, many more are serving in these traditional care-giving roles. A feminist challenge to the traditional definition of patriotism should therefore question the meaning of service to one's country.[25] In contrast to a citizenship that rests on the assumption that it is more glorious to die than to live for one's state, Wendy Brown suggests that a more constructive view of citizenship could center on the courage to sustain life.[26] In similar terms, Jean Elshtain asserts the need to move toward a politics that shifts the focus of political loyalty and identity from sacrifice to responsibility.[27] Only when women's contributions to society are seen as equal to men's can these reconstructed visions of citizenship come about.

Feminist Perspectives on States' Security-Seeking Behavior

Realists have offered us an instrumental version of states' security-seeking behavior, which, I have argued, depends on a partial representation of human behavior associated with a stereotypical hegemonic masculinity. Feminist redefinitions of citizenship allow us to envisage a less militarized version of states' identities, and feminist theories can also propose alternative models for states' international security-seeking behavior, extrapolated from a more comprehensive view of human behavior.

Realists use state-of-nature stories as metaphors to describe the insecurity of states in an anarchical international system. I shall suggest an alternative story, which could equally be applied to the behavior of individuals in the state of nature. Although frequently unreported in standard historical accounts, it is a true story, not a myth, about a state of nature in early nineteenth-century America. Among those present in the first winter encampment of the 1804–1806 Lewis and Clark expedition into the Northwest territories was Sacajawea, a member of the Shoshone tribe. Sacajawea had joined the expedition as the wife of a French interpreter; her presence was proving invaluable to the security of the expedition's members, whose task it was to explore uncharted territory and establish contact with the native inhabitants to inform them of claims to these territories by the United States. Although unanticipated by its leaders, the presence of a woman served to assure the native inhabitants that the expedition was peaceful since the Native Americans assumed that war parties would not include women: the expedition was therefore safer because it was not armed.[28]

This story demonstrates that the introduction of women can change the way humans are assumed to behave in the state of nature. Just as Sacajawea's presence changed the Native Americans' expectations about the behavior of intruders into their territory, the introduction of women into our state-of-nature myths could change the way we think about the behavior of states in the international system. The use of the Hobbesian analogy in international relations theory is based on a partial view of human nature that is stereotypically masculine; a more inclusive perspective would see human nature as both conflictual and cooperative, containing elements of social reproduction and interdependence as well as domination and separation. Generalizing from this more comprehensive view of human nature, a feminist perspective would assume that the potential for international community also exists and that an atomistic, conflictual view of the international system is only a partial representation of reality. Liberal individualism, the instrumental rationality of the marketplace, and the defector's self-help approach in Rousseau's stag hunt *** are all, in analogous ways, based on a partial masculine model of human behavior.[29]

■   ■   ■

Feminist perspectives on national security take us beyond realism's statist representations. They allow us to see that the realist view of national security is constructed out of a masculinized discourse that, while it is only a partial view of reality, is taken as universal. Women's definitions of security are multilevel and multidimensional. Women have defined security as the absence of violence whether it be military, economic, or sexual. Not until the hierarchical social relations, including gender relations, that have been hidden by realism's frequently depersonalized discourse are brought to light can we begin to construct a language of national security that speaks out of the multiple experiences of both women and men. ***

NOTES

I owe the title of this chapter to Kenneth Waltz's book *Man, the State, and War.*

De Beauvoir epigraph from *The Second Sex* (New York: Knopf, 1972), p. 72. De Beauvoir's analysis suggests that she herself endorsed this explanation for male superiority; *** Fussell epigraph quoted by Anna Quindlen in *The New York Times,* February 7, 1991, p. A25.

1. [Kenneth N.] Waltz, *Theory of International Politics* (Boston: Addison-Wesley, 1979), p. 102.
2. While heads of state, all men, discussed the "important" issues in world politics at the Group of Seven meeting in London in July

1991, Barbara Bush and Princess Diana were pictured on the *CBS Evening News* (July 17, 1991) meeting with British AIDS patients.

3. [Evelyn Fox] Keller, *Reflections on Gender and Science* (New Haven: Yale University Press 1985), p. 130.

4. For example, see Donna Haraway, *Primate Visions* (New York: Routledge, 1989), ch. 1. Considering scientific practice from the perspective of the way its factual findings are narrated, Haraway provocatively explores how scientific theories produce and are embedded in particular kinds of stories. This allows her to challenge the neutrality and objectivity of scientific facts. She suggests that texts about primates can be read as science fictions about race, gender, and nature.

5. [Hans J.] Morgenthau, *Politics among Nations* (New York: Knopf, 1973), p. 34.

6. Morgenthau does talk about dominating mothers-in-law, but as feminist research has suggested, it is generally men, legally designated as heads of households in most societies, who hold the real power even in the family and certainly with respect to the family's interaction with the public sphere.

7. For an extended discussion of Morgenthau's "political man," see J. Ann Tickner, "Hans Morgenthau's Principles of Political Realism," [*Millennium* 17(3):429–40]. In neorealism's depersonalized structural analysis, Morgenthau's depiction of human nature slips out of sight.

8. [Richard K.] Ashley, "Untying the Sovereign State" [*Millennium* 17(2) (1988)], p. 230.

9. Hobbes, *Leviathan*, part 1, ch. 13, quoted in Vasquez, ed., *Classics of International Relations*, pp, 213–15.

10. [Carole] Pateman, *The Sexual Contract* (Stanford: Stanford University Press, 1988), p. 41.

11. [Jane] Flax, "Political Philosophy and the Patriarchal Unconscious: A Psychoanalytic Perspective on Epistemology and Metaphysics," in Harding and Hintikka, eds., *Discovering Reality* (Dordrecht, Holland: D. Reidel, 1983), pp. 245–81.

12. [Christine] Di Stephano, "Masculinity as Ideology in Political Theory," [*Women's Studies International Forum* 6(6) (1983) 633–44]. Carole Pateman has disputed some of Di Stephano's assumptions about Hobbes's characterizations of women and the family in the state of nature. But this does not deny the fact that Di Stephano's characterization of men is the one used by realists in their depiction of the international system. See Pateman, " 'God Hath Ordained to Man a Helper': Hobbes, Patriarchy, and Conjugal Right."

13. [Margaret Randolph] Higonnet et al., *Behind the Lines* (New Haven: Yale University Press, 1987), introduction.

14. [Jean Bethke] Elshtain, *Women and War* (New York: Basic Books, 1987), p. 194.

15. Ibid., p. 163.

16. [Cynthia] Enloe, *Bananas, Beaches, and Bases* (Berkeley: University of California Press, 1990), pp. 48–49.

17. [Michael H.] Hunt, *Ideology and U.S. Foreign Policy* (New Haven: Yale University Press, 1987), pp. 58–62.

18. [Jane] Addams et al., *Women at the Hague* (New York: Macmillan, 1916), pp. 150ff.

19. [Anne Sisson] Runyan, "Feminism, Peace, and International Politics" (Ph.D. diss., American University, 1988), ch. 6.

20. "Forward-looking Strategies for the Advancement of Women Towards the Year 2000." Quoted in [Hilkka] Pietilä and [Jeanne] Vickers, *Making Women Matter* (London: Zed Books, 1990), pp. 46–47.

21. See Elshtain, *Women and War*, ch. 3.

22. Carroll, "Feminism and Pacifism: Historical and Theoretical Connections," in [Ruth Roach] Pierson, ed., *Women and Peace* (London: Croom Helm, 1987), pp. 2–28.

23. Margaret Hobbs, "The Perils of 'Unbridled Masculinity': Pacifist Elements in the Feminist and Socialist Thought of Charlotte Perkins Gilman," in Pierson, ed., *Women and Peace*, pp. 149–69.

24. The *New York Times* of December 12, 1990 (p. A35) reported that while men were about evenly split on attacking Iraqi forces in Kuwait, women were 73 percent against and 22 percent in favor.

25. Suzanne Gordon, "Another Enemy," *Boston Globe,* March 8, 1991, p. 15.

26. [Wendy] Brown, *Manhood and Politics* [Totowa, NJ: Rowman and Littlefield, 1988), p. 206.

27. Elshtain, "Sovereignty, Identity, Sacrifice," in [V. Spike] Peterson, ed., *Gendered States* (Boulder: Lynne Rienner, 1992).

28. I am grateful to Michael Capps, historian at the Lewis and Clark Museum in St. Louis, Missouri, for this information. The story of Sacajawea is told in one of the museum's exhibits.

29. In *Man, the State, and War* (New York: Columbia University Press, 1959), Kenneth N. Waltz argues that "in the stag-hunt example, the will of the rabbit-snatcher was rational and predictable from his own point of view" (p. 183), while "in the early state of nature, men were sufficiently dispersed to make any pattern of cooperation unnecessary" (p. 167). Neorealist revisionists, such as Snidal [see "Relative Gains and the Pattern of International Cooperation"] do not question the masculine bias of the stag hunt metaphor. Like Waltz and Rousseau, they also assume the autonomous, adult male (unparented and in an environment without women or children) in their discussion of the stag hunt; they do not question the rationality of the rabbit-snatching defector or the restrictive situational descriptions implied by their payoff matrices. Transformations in the social nature of an interaction are very hard to represent using such a model. Their reformulation of Waltz's position is instead focused on the exploration of different specifications of the game payoff in less conflictual ways (i.e., as an assurance game) and on inferences concerning the likely consequences of relative gain-seeking behavior in a gamelike interaction with more than two (equally autonomous and unsocialized) players.

4 THE INTERNATIONAL SYSTEM

The different theoretical traditions offer different conceptions of the international system. Realist Hans J. Morgenthau writes in *Politics among Nations* that the international system is characterized by competition among states, each seeking to enhance its power. As a consequence of this competition, a balance of power tends to emerge. In this selection, Morgenthau discusses what states can do to stabilize the balance.

What are the characteristics of the contemporary international system? G. John Ikenberry explains the origins and workings of the American-led liberal international order. Despite challenges from illiberal powers and what he sees as some recent missteps in U.S. strategy, Ikenberry argues that astute U.S. leadership can sustain a thriving liberal, rule-based, multilateral system.

Thomas J. Christensen, an academic China specialist and a prominent theorist of international relations, served as Deputy Assistant Secretary of State for East Asian and Pacific Affairs with responsibility for relations with China from 2006 to 2008. In *The China Challenge* he draws on both his experience in government and his scholarly roots to argue in favor of a balanced strategy that will "channel China's nationalist ambitions into cooperation rather than coercion." In presenting his case, Christensen makes use of the arguments of some contributors to *Essential Readings in World Politics*, including Thomas Schelling and Robert Jervis, and rebuts the arguments of others, such as John J. Mearsheimer.

Hans J. Morgenthau

THE BALANCE OF POWER

The aspiration for power on the part of several nations, each trying either to maintain or overthrow the status quo, leads of necessity to a configuration that is called the balance of power[1] and to policies that aim at preserving it. We say "of necessity" advisedly. For here again we are confronted with the basic misconception that has impeded the understanding of international politics and has made us the prey of illusions. This misconception asserts that men have a choice between power politics and its necessary outgrowth, the balance of power, on the one hand, and a different, better kind of international relations on the other. It insists that a foreign policy based on the balance of power is one among several possible foreign policies and that only stupid and evil men will choose the former and reject the latter.

It will be shown * * * that the international balance of power is only a particular manifestation of a general social principle to which all societies composed of a number of autonomous units owe the autonomy of their component parts; that the balance of power and policies aiming at its preservation are not only inevitable but are an essential stabilizing factor in a society of sovereign nations; and that the instability of the international balance of power is due not to the faultiness of the principle but to the particular conditions under which the principle must operate in a society of sovereign nations.

From Hans J. Morgenthau, *Politics among Nations: The Struggle for Power and Peace* (1948; reprint, New York: Knopf, 1985), pp. 187–89, 198–201, 213–14, 222, 227–28. Some of the author's notes have been omitted.

Social Equilibrium

Balance of Power as Universal Concept

The concept of "equilibrium" as a synonym for "balance" is commonly employed in many sciences—physics, biology, economics, sociology, and political science. It signifies stability within a system composed of a number of autonomous forces. Whenever the equilibrium is disturbed either by an outside force or by a change in one or the other elements composing the system, the system shows a tendency to re-establish either the original or a new equilibrium. Thus equilibrium exists in the human body. While the human body changes in the process of growth, the equilibrium persists as long as the changes occurring in the different organs of the body do not disturb the body's stability. This is especially so if the quantitative and qualitative changes in the different organs are proportionate to each other. When, however, the body suffers a wound or loss of one of its organs through outside interference, or experiences a malignant growth or a pathological transformation of one of its organs, the equilibrium is disturbed, and the body tries to overcome the disturbance by re-establishing the equilibrium either on the same or a different level from the one that obtained before the disturbance occurred.[2]

The same concept of equilibrium is used in a social science, such as economies, with reference to the relations between the different elements of the economic system, e.g., between savings and investments, exports and imports, supply and demand, costs and prices. Contemporary capitalism itself has been described as a system of "countervailing power."[3] It also applies to society as a whole. Thus we search for a proper balance between different geographical regions, such as the East and the West, the North and the South; between different kinds of activities, such as agriculture and industry, heavy and light industries, big and small businesses, producers and consumers, management and labor; between different functional groups, such, as city and country, the old, the middle-aged, and the young, the economic and the political sphere, the middle classes and the upper and lower classes.

Two assumptions are at the foundation of all such equilibriums: first, that the elements to be balanced are necessary for society or are entitled to exist and, second, that without a state of equilibrium among them one element will gain ascendancy over the others, encroach upon their interests and rights, and may ultimately destroy them. Consequently, it is the purpose of all such equilibriums to maintain the stability of the system without destroying the multiplicity of the elements composing it. If the goal were stability alone, it could be achieved by allowing one element to destroy or overwhelm the others and take their place. Since the goal is stability plus the preservation of all the elements of the system, the equilibrium must aim at preventing any element from gaining ascendancy over the others. The means employed to maintain the equilibrium consist in allowing the different elements to pursue their opposing tendencies up to the point where the tendency of one is not so strong as to overcome the tendency of the others, but strong enough to prevent the others from overcoming its own. * * *

■   ■   ■

DIFFERENT METHODS OF THE BALANCE OF POWER

The balancing process can be carried on either by diminishing the weight of the heavier scale or by increasing the weight of the lighter one.

Divide and Rule

The former method has found its classic manifestation, aside from the imposition of onerous conditions in peace treaties and the incitement to treason and revolution, in the maxim "divide and rule." It has been resorted to by nations who tried to make or keep their competitors weak by dividing them or keeping them divided. The most consistent and important policies of this kind in modern times are the policy of France with respect to Germany and the policy of the Soviet Union with respect to the rest of Europe. From the seventeenth century to the end of the Second World War, it has been an unvarying principle of French foreign policy either to favor the division of the German Empire into a number of small independent states or to prevent the coalescence of such states into one unified nation. * * * Similarly, the Soviet Union from the twenties to the present has consistently opposed all plans for the unification of Europe, on the assumption that the pooling of the divided strength of the European nations into a "Western bloc" would give the enemies of the Soviet Union such power as to threaten the latter's security.

The other method of balancing the power of several nations consists in adding to the strength of the weaker nation. This method can be carried out by two different means: Either B can increase its power sufficiently to offset, if not surpass, the power of A, and vice versa; or B can pool its power with the power of all the other nations that pursue identical policies with regard to A, in which case A will pool its power with all the nations pursuing identical policies with respect to B. The former alternative is exemplified by the policy of compensations and the armament race as well as by disarmament; the latter, by the policy of alliances.

Compensations

Compensations of a territorial nature were a common device in the eighteenth and nineteenth centuries for maintaining a balance of power which had been, or was to be, disturbed by the territorial acquisitions of one nation. The Treaty of Utrecht of 1713, which terminated the War of the Spanish Succession, recognized for the first time expressly the principle of the balance of power by way of territorial compensations. It provided for the division of most of the Spanish possessions, European and colonial, between the Hapsburgs and the Bourbons *"ad conservandum in Europa equilibrium,"* as the treaty put it.

■   ■   ■

In the latter part of the nineteenth and the beginning of the twentieth century, the principle of compensations was again deliberately applied to the distribution of colonial territories and the delimitation of colonial or semicolonial spheres of influence. Africa, in particular, was during that period the object of numerous treaties delimiting spheres of influence for the major colonial powers. Thus the competition between France, Great Britain, and Italy for the domination of Ethiopia was provisionally resolved * * * by the treaty of 1906, which divided the country into three spheres of influence for the purpose of establishing in that region a balance of power among the nations concerned. * * *

Even where the principle of compensations is not deliberately applied, however, * * * it is nowhere absent from political arrangements, territorial or other, made within a balance-of-power system. For, given such a system, no nation will agree to concede political advantages to another nation without the expectation, which may or may not be well founded, of receiving proportionate advantages in return. The bargaining of diplomatic negotiations, issuing in political compromise, is but the principle of compensations in its most general form, and as such it is organically connected with the balance of power.

Armaments

The principal means, however, by which a nation endeavors with the power at its disposal to maintain or re-establish the balance of power are armaments. The armaments race in which Nation A tries to keep up with, and then to outdo, the armaments of Nation B, and vice versa, is the typical instrumentality of an unstable, dynamic balance of power. The necessary corollary of the armaments race is a constantly increasing burden of military preparations devouring an ever greater portion of the national budget and making for ever deepening fears, suspicions, and insecurity. The situation preceding the First World War, with the naval competition between Germany and Great Britain and the rivalry of the French and German armies, illustrates this point.

It is in recognition of situations such as these that, since the end of the Napoleonic Wars, repeated attempts have been made to create a stable balance of power, if not to establish permanent peace, by means of the proportionate disarmament of competing nations. The technique of stabilizing the balance of power by means of a proportionate reduction of armaments is somewhat similar to the technique of territorial compensations. For both techniques require a quantitative evaluation of the influence that the arrangement is likely to exert on the respective power of the individual nations. The difficulties in making such a quantitative evaluation—in correlating, for instance, the military strength of the French army of 1932 with the military power represented by the industrial potential of Germany—have greatly contributed to the failure of most attempts at creating a stable balance of power by means of disarmament. The only outstanding success of this kind was the Washington Naval Treaty of 1922, in which Great Britain, the United States, Japan, France, and Italy agreed to a proportionate reduction and limitation of naval armaments. Yet it must be noted that this treaty was part of an overall political and territorial settlement in the Pacific which sought to stabilize the power relations in that region on the foundation of Anglo-American predominance.

Alliances

The historically most important manifestation of the balance of power, however, is to be found not in the equilibrium of two isolated nations but in the relations between one nation or alliance of nations and another alliance.

■   ■   ■

Alliances are a necessary function of the balance of power operating within a multiple-state system. Nations A and B, competing with each other, have three choices in order to maintain and improve their relative power positions. They can increase their own power, they can add to their own power

the power of other nations, or they can withhold the power of other nations from the adversary. When they make the first choice, they embark upon an armaments race. When they choose the second and third alternatives, they pursue a policy of alliances.

Whether or not a nation shall pursue a policy of alliances is, then, a matter not of principle but of expediency. A nation will shun alliances if it believes that it is strong enough to hold its own unaided or that the burden of the commitments resulting from the alliance is likely to outweigh the advantages to be expected. It is for one or the other or both of these reasons that, throughout the better part of their history, Great Britain and the United States have refrained from entering into peacetime alliances with other nations.

■   ■   ■

The "Holder" of the Balance

Whenever the balance of power is to be realized by means of an alliance—and this has been generally so throughout the history of the Western world—two possible variations of this pattern have to be distinguished. To use the metaphor of the balance, the system may consist of two scales, in each of which are to be found the nation or nations identified with the same policy of the status quo or of imperialism. The continental nations of Europe have generally operated the balance of power in this way.

The system may, however, consist of two scales plus a third element, the "holder" of the balance or the "balancer." The balancer is not permanently identified with the policies of either nation or group of nations. Its only objective within the system is the maintenance of the balance, regardless of the concrete policies the balance will serve. In consequence, the holder of the balance will throw its weight at one time in this scale, at another time in the other scale, guided only by one consideration—the relative position of scales. Thus it will put its weight always in the scale that seems to be higher than the other because it is lighter. The balancer may become in a relatively short span of history consecutively the friend and foe of all major powers, provided they all consecutively threaten the balance by approaching predominance over the others and are in turn threatened by others about to gain such predominance. To paraphrase a statement of Palmerston: While the holder of the balance has no permanent friends, it has no permanent enemies either; it has only the permanent interest of maintaining the balance of power itself.

The balancer is in a position of "splendid isolation." It is isolated by its own choice; for, while the two scales of the balance must vie with each other to add its weight to theirs in order to gain the overweight necessary for success, it must refuse to enter into permanent ties with either side. The holder of the balance waits in the middle in watchful detachment to see which scale is likely to sink. Its isolation is "splendid"; for, since its support or lack of support is the decisive factor in the struggle for power, its foreign policy, if cleverly managed, is able to extract the highest price from those whom it supports. But since this support, regardless of the price paid for it, is always uncertain and shifts from one side to the other in accordance with the movements of the balance, its policies are resented and subject to condemnation on moral grounds. Thus it has been said of the outstanding balancer in

modern times, Great Britain, that it lets others fight its wars, that it keeps Europe divided in order to dominate the continent, and that the fickleness of its policies is such as to make alliances with Great Britain impossible. "Perfidious Albion" has become a byword in the mouths of those who either were unable to gain Great Britain's support, however hard they tried, or else lost it after they had paid what seemed to them too high a price.

The holder of the balance occupies the key position in the balance-of-power system, since its position determines the outcome of the struggle for power. It has, therefore, been called the "arbiter" of the system, deciding who will win and who will lose. By making it impossible for any nation or combination of nations to gain predominance over the others, it preserves its own independence as well as the independence of all the other nations, and is thus a most powerful factor in international politics.

The holder of the balance can use this power in three different ways. It can make its joining one or the other nation or alliance dependent upon certain conditions favorable to the maintenance or restoration of the balance. It can make its support of the peace settlement dependent upon similar conditions. It can, finally, in either situation see to it that the objectives of its own national policy, apart from the maintenance of the balance of power, are realized in the process of balancing the power of others.

■　　■　　■

EVALUATION OF THE BALANCE OF POWER

■ ■ ■

The Unreality of the Balance of Power

[The] uncertainty of all power calculations not only makes the balance of power incapable of practical application but leads also to its very negation in practice. Since no nation can be sure that its calculation of the distribution of power at any particular moment in history is correct, it must at least make sure that its errors, whatever they may be, will not put the nation at a disadvantage in the contest for power. In other words, the nation must try to have at least a margin of safety which will allow it to make erroneous calculations and still maintain the balance of power. To that effect, all nations actively engaged in the struggle for power must actually aim not at balance—that is, equality—of power, but at superiority of power in their own behalf. And since no nation can foresee how large its miscalculations will turn out to be, all nations must ultimately seek the maximum of power obtainable under the circumstances. Only thus can they hope to attain the maximum margin of safety commensurate with the maximum of errors they might commit. The limitless aspiration for power, potentially always present * * * in the power drives of nations, finds in the balance of power a mighty incentive to transform itself into an actuality.

Since the desire to attain a maximum of power is universal, all nations must always be afraid that their own miscalculations and the power increases of other nations might add up to an inferiority for themselves which they must at all costs try to avoid. Hence all nations who have gained an apparent edge over their competitors tend to consolidate that advantage and use it for changing the distribution of power permanently in their favor. This can be done through diplomatic pressure by bringing the full weight of that advantage to bear upon the other nations, compelling them to make the concessions that will consolidate the temporary advantage into a permanent superiority. It can also be done by war. Since in a balance-of-power system all nations live in constant fear lest their rivals deprive them, at the first opportune moment, of their power position, all nations have a vital interest in anticipating such a development and doing unto the others what they do not want the others to do unto them. * * *

NOTES

1. The term "balance of power" is used in the text with four different meanings: (1) as a policy aimed at a certain state of affairs, (2) as an actual state of affairs, (3) as an approximately equal distribution of power, (4) as any distribution of power. Whenever the term is used without qualification, it refers to an actual state of affairs in which power is distributed among several nations with approximate equality. * * *

2. Cf., for instance, the impressive analogy between the equilibrium in the human body and in society in Walter B. Cannon, *The Wisdom of the Body* (New York: W. W. Norton and Company, 1932), pp. 293, 294: "At the outset it is noteworthy that the body politic itself exhibits some indications of crude automatic stabilizing processes. In the previous chapter I expressed the postulate that a certain degree of constancy in a complex system is itself evidence that agencies are acting or are ready to act to maintain that constancy. And moreover, that when a system remains steady it does so because any tendency towards change is met by increased effectiveness of the factor or factors which resist the change. Many familiar facts prove

that these statements are to some degree true for society even in its present unstabilized condition. A display of conservatism excites a radical revolt and that in turn is followed by a return to conservatism. Loose government and its consequences bring the reformers into power, but their tight reins soon provoke restiveness and the desire for release. The noble enthusiasms and sacrifices of war are succeeded by moral apathy and orgies of self-indulgence. Hardly any strong tendency in a nation continues to the stage of disaster; before that extreme is reached corrective forces arise which check the tendency and they commonly prevail to such an excessive degree as themselves to cause a reaction. A study of the nature of these social swings and their reversal might lead to valuable understanding and possibly to means of more narrowly limiting the disturbances. At this point, however, we merely note that the disturbances are roughly limited, and that this limitation suggests, perhaps, the early stages of social homeostasis." (Reprinted by permission of the publisher. Copyright 1932, 1939, by Walter B. Cannon.)

3.   John K. Galbraith, *American Capitalism, the Concept of Countervailing Power* (Boston: Houghton Mifflin, 1952).

G. John Ikenberry

FROM *LIBERAL LEVIATHAN*
The Origins, Crisis, and Transformation of the American World Order

Crisis of the Old Order

Introduction

One of the great dramas of world politics over the last two hundred years has been the rise of liberal democratic states to global dominance. This liberal ascendancy has involved the extraordinary growth of the Western democracies—from weakness and minority status in the late eighteenth century to wealth and predominance in the late twentieth century. This rise occurred in fits and starts over the course of the modern era. In the nineteenth century, Great Britain was the vanguard of the liberal ascendancy, becoming the leading industrial and naval power of its day. In the twentieth century, the United States was transformed from inwardness and isolation into the dominant world power. During these decades, world wars and geopolitical struggles pitted the liberal democracies against rival autocratic, fascist, and totalitarian great powers. The Cold War was a grand struggle between alternative ideologies of rule and pathways to modern development. With the sudden collapse of the Soviet Union and the end of the Cold War,

the liberal ascendancy reaches a worldwide crescendo. The United States and a far-flung alliance of liberal democracies stood at the center of world politics—rich, powerful, and dominant.

The Western democracies did not just grow powerful and rich. They also made repeated efforts to build liberal international order—that is, order that is relatively open, rule-based, and progressive. Led by Great Britain and the United States, they championed free trade and took steps to create multilateral rules and institutions of various sorts. Open markets, international institutions, cooperative security, democratic community, progressive change, collective problem solving, shared sovereignty, the rule of law—all are aspects of the liberal vision that have made appearances in various combinations and changing ways over the decades and centuries.

In the decades after World War II, the United States engaged in the most ambitious and far-reaching liberal order building the world had yet seen. It was a distinctive type of liberal international order—a liberal hegemonic order. The United States did not just encourage open and rule-based order. It became the hegemonic organizer and manager of that order. The American political system—and its alliances, technology, currency, and markets—became fused to the wider liberal order. In the shadow of the Cold War, the United States became the "owner and operator" of the liberal capitalist political systems—supporting the rules and institutions of liberal internationalism but also enjoying

From G. John Ikenberry, *Liberal Leviathan: The Origins, Crisis, and Transformation of the American World Order* (Princeton, NJ: Princeton University Press): 1–32. Some of the author's notes have been edited.

special rights and privileges. It organized and led an extended political system built around multilateral institutions, alliances, strategic partners, and client states. This order is built on strategic understandings and hegemonic bargains. The United States provided "services" to other states through the provision of security and its commitment to stability and open markets.

In the fifty years following World War II, this American-led liberal hegemonic order has been remarkably successful. It provided a stable foundation for decades of Western and global growth and advancement. The United States and its partners negotiated agreements and built mechanisms that reopened the world economy, ushering in a golden era of economic growth. West Germany and Japan were transformed from enemies into strategic partners, ultimately becoming the second- and third-largest economies in the world. The Western powers also bound themselves together in pacts of mutual restraint and commitment, finding a solution to the centuries-old problem of how Germany, France, and the rest of Europe could exist in peace—the great "quiet revolution" of the twentieth century. In later decades, non-Western countries made transitions to democracy and market economy and integrated into this expanding liberal hegemonic system. The Cold War ended peacefully and on terms favorable to the West. The Western allies were able to both outperform the Soviet system and find ways to signal restraint and accommodation as Soviet leaders made difficult choices to end hostilities with old rivals. By the 1990s, this American-led order was at a zenith. Ideological and geopolitical rivals to American leadership had disappeared. The United States stood at the center of it all as the unipolar power. Its dynamic bundle of oversized capacities, interests, and ideals constituted a remarkable achievement in the unfolding drama of the liberal international project.

* * * I explore the logic and character of this American liberal hegemonic order. What are its inner workings and moving parts? How can we identify and understand the specific organizational logic of this liberal hegemonic order in the context of earlier efforts to build liberal international order and the wider varieties of global and regional orders? How is it different—if it is—from imperial forms of order? If it is a hierarchical order with liberal characteristics, how do we make sense of its distinctive blend of command and reciprocity, coercion and consent?

Today, the American-led liberal hegemonic order is troubled. Conflicts and controversies have unsettled it. The most obvious crisis of this order unfolded during the George W. Bush administration. Its controversial "war on terror," invasion of Iraq, and skepticism about multilateral rules and agreements triggered a global outpouring of criticism. Anti-Americanism spread and gained strength. Even old and close allies started to question the merits of living in a world dominated by a unipolar America. This sentiment was expressed in a particularly pointed fashion by the then French president Jacques Chirac, who argued that the world must be turned back into a multipolar one because "any community with only one dominant power is always a dangerous one and provokes reactions."[1]

If the crisis of the old American-led order is reducible to the Bush administration's policies, the crisis may now have passed. The Obama administration has made the restoration of American liberal hegemonic leadership—or what Secretary of State Clinton has called a "multipartner world"—the centerpiece of its foreign policy agenda.[2] But if the crisis was generated by the inherent tensions and insecurities that flow from a unipolar distribution of power, the crisis will surely persist. It may be that a hierarchical order with liberal characteristics is simply not sustainable in a unipolar world—either because others will inevitably resist it or because the hegemon will inevitably become increasingly imperialistic.

Other observers argue that the problems with the American-led order run in a different direction. The crisis of the old is not about American unipolarity; it is about the passing of the American era of dominance. The conflicts and controversies are a struggle by states to shape what comes next, after unipolarity. This great shift is being triggered by a return to multipolarity and the rise of rival global powers with their own order-building agendas.[3] In this view, the 2008 financial crisis and subsequent world economic downturn—the most severe since the Great Depression—was an especially stark demonstration of the pressures on the American-led liberal system. Unlike past postwar economic crises, this one had its origins in the United States, and it has served to tarnish the American model of liberal capitalism and raised new doubts about the capacities of the United States to act as the global leader in the provision of economic stability and advancement.[4] With the decline of American unipolarity, we are witnessing the beginning of a struggle over leadership and dominance.

Still other observers accept this view of declining American power and go on to argue that it is liberal international order itself that is ending. The rise of new power centers will come with new agendas for organizing the basic logic and principles of international order. China is the obvious protagonist in this emerging grand drama. Rather than becoming a stakeholder in the existing order, China will use its growing power to push world politics in an illiberal direction.[5] It is the underlying openness and rule-based character of international order that is in transition.

These various claims prompt basic questions about the nature of the troubles that beset the American-led postwar order. Did the Bush administration simply mishandle or mismanage the leadership of the American liberal hegemonic order? Or is the struggle deeper than this, rooted in disagreements over the virtues and liabilities of the American hegemonic organization of liberal international order? Or is it even deeper still, rooted in a breakdown of consensus among leading states—old Western states and rising non-Western states—in the virtues of liberal internationalism as a way of organizing international relations?

* * * I argue that the crisis of the old order transcends controversies generated by recent American foreign policy or even the ongoing economic crisis. It is a crisis of authority *within* the old hegemonic organization of liberal order, *not* a crisis in the deep principles of the order itself. It is a crisis of governance.

This crisis stems from the fact that the underlying foundations of the old order have been transformed. Changes include shifts in power, contested norms of sovereignty, threats related to nonstate actors, and the scope of participating states. America's hegemonic leadership of the liberal international order was made acceptable to other states during the postwar decades because it provided security and other "system services" to a wide range of states. That authority is now less securely established. This does not mean the inevitable end of liberal order. But it does raise a basic challenge for that order: establishing legitimate authority for concerted international action on behalf of the global community, doing so at a time when old relations of authority are eroding.

Although the old American-led hegemonic system is troubled, what is striking about liberal internationalism is its durability. The last decade has brought remarkable upheavals in the global system—the emergence of new powers, financial crises, a global recession, and bitter disputes among allies over American unipolar ambitions. Despite these upheavals, liberal international order as an organizational logic of world politics has proven resilient. It is still in demand. Appealing alternatives to an open and rule-based order simply have not crystallized. On the contrary, the rise of non-Western powers and the growth of economic and security interdependence are creating new constituencies and pressures for liberal international order.

Ironically, the old order has, in some ways, been the victim of its own success. It successfully defeated the threat—Communist expansionism—that, in part, drove its creation. It succeeded in creating a relatively open and robust system of trade and investment. The demise of the Soviet Union has reduced the importance of American military guarantees in Western Europe and East Asia. Economic growth in countries like China and India has created new centers of global power. These and other developments have led to profound questions about the American-centered nature of the old order. That has led not to a rejection per se of liberal order but to a call to renegotiate authority among the United States and other key stakeholders. In short, we need a new bargain, not a new system. And if this constitutes a crisis of authority, it is worth remembering that liberal international order has encountered crises in the past and evolved as a result. I believe it will again.

There are four central claims in this book. First, a distinctive type of international order was constructed after World War II. At its core, it was a hierarchical order with liberal characteristics. America played the leading role in the provision of rule and stability in that order. It was a hierarchical system that was built on both American power dominance and liberal principles of governance. The United States was the dominant state, but its power advantages were muted and mediated by an array of postwar rules, institutions, and reciprocal political processes—backed up by shared strategic interests and political bargains. Weaker and secondary states were given institutionalized access to the exercise of American power. The United States provided public goods and operated within a loose system of multilateral rules and institutions. American hegemonic power and liberal international order were fused—indeed they each were dependent on the other. But the strategic bargains and institutional foundations of this liberal hegemonic order have eroded, and as a result, the authority with which the United States has wielded power in this system has also diminished.

Second, there are deep sources for this authority crisis, rooted in the transformation of the Westphalian organization of the state system. The rise of American unipolarity and the erosion of norms of state sovereignty—along with other deep shifts in the global system—have eroded the foundations of the old order and thrown the basic terms of order and rule of world politics into dispute. In a bipolar or multipolar system, powerful states "rule" in the process of leading a coalition of states to balance against other states. When the system shifts to unipolarity, this logic of rule disappears. Rule is no longer based on leadership of a balancing coalition or on the resulting equilibrium of power but on the predominance of one state. This is new and different—and potentially threatening to weaker and secondary states. As a result, the power of the leading state is thrown into the full light of day.

The end of the Cold War ushered in a world system characterized by unipolarity and globalization. Relations between poles and peripheries shifted. During the Cold War, the liberal order was built primarily within the Western advanced industrial world. It existed within one half of the larger bipolar global system. With the collapse of the Soviet Union and the end of bipolarity, the "inside" Western system became the "outside" order. This large-scale expansion of the liberal order set new players and issues into motion. More recently, the rise of new security threats has brought into question the logic of alliance and security partnerships. After September 11, 2001, America showed itself to be not the satisfied protector of the old order but a threatened and insecure power that resisted the bargains and restraints of its own postwar order. As a result, in the decades of the new century, the character of rule in world politics has been thrown into question.

Third, to understand the nature of this crisis and the future of liberal international order, we need to understand the types of international order—and the sources of rule and authority, power, and legitimacy within them. In the first instance, this means identifying the various logics of liberal order and the ways in which sovereignty, rules, and hierarchy can be arrayed. Our most invoked theories of world politics begin with the assumption that the global system is anarchical—organized around the diffusion and decentralization of power among competing sovereign states. In other words, our theories tend to focus on the "logic of anarchy." But in a global system in which one state is so powerful and a balancing or equilibrium of power does not obtain, it is necessary to understand the logic of relations between superordinate and subordinate states. We need, in effect, to illuminate the "logic of hierarchy" that operates within the system.

I offer a basic distinction between imperial and liberal hegemonic forms of hierarchy. After this, I explore the ways in which shifts from bipolarity to unipolarity alter the incentives and forms in which leading states make institutional bargains and agree to operate within rule-based order. The rise of unipolarity has altered—and to some extent diminished—the incentives that the United States has to bind itself to global rules and institutions. But it has not negated those incentives. To the extent that the United States sees that its unipolar position of power is or will wane, the incentives to renegotiate postwar hegemonic bargains actually increase.

Fourth, the liberal ascendancy is not over. It is evolving and there are multiple pathways of change. There are pressures for the reallocation of authority and leadership within the system. But there are also constituencies that support a continued—if renegotiated—American hegemonic role. Various features of the contemporary global system reinforce the continuity of liberal international order. The disappearance of great-power war removes a classic mechanism for the overturning of order. The growth and sheer geopolitical heft of the world's liberal democracies creates a certain stability to the existing order. Moreover, liberal international order—hegemonic or otherwise—tends to be unusually integrative. It is an order that is easy

to join and hard to overturn. Countries such as China and Russia are not fully embedded in the liberal international order, but they nonetheless profit from its existence. These states may not soon or ever fully transform into liberal states, but the expansive and integrative logic of liberal international order creates incentives for them to do so—and it forecloses opportunities to create alternative global orders.

In the end, it is the United States itself that will be critical in shaping the evolving character of liberal internationalism. If the United States wants to remain the leading purveyor of global order, it will need to rediscover and adapt its old strategy of liberal order building. The United States will need to renegotiate its relationship with the rest of the world and this will inevitably mean giving up some of the rights and privileges that it has had in the earlier hegemonic era. In the twentieth century, the United States became a "liberal Leviathan." Indeed, American global authority was built on Hobbesian grounds—that is, other countries, particularly in Western Europe and later in East Asia, handed the reigns of power to Washington, just as Hobbes's individuals in the state of nature voluntarily construct and hand over power to the Leviathan. Today, amidst long-term transformations in power and interdependence, there is a widespread view that no one elected the United States to its position of privilege—or at least that only the Europeans and Japanese did, and other states that are now rising in power did not. The reestablishment of the United States as a liberal Leviathan involves the voluntary granting of that status by other states. For this to happen, the United States again needs to search for and champion practical and consensual functioning global rules and institutions. In the twenty-first century, this will involve sharing authority among a wider coalition of liberal democratic states, advanced and developing, rising and declining, Western and non-Western. It is this liberal complex of states that is the ultimate guardian of the rules, institutions, and progressive purposes of the liberal order.

* * * I first look at the enduring problem of international order. Next, I look at the rise and transformation of liberal international order. After this, I look at the logic of hierarchical political order and its imperial and liberal variants. * * *

The Rise and Fall of International Order

Over the centuries, world politics has been marked by repeated historical dramas of order creation and destruction. International order has risen and fallen, come and gone. At periodic moments, leading states have found themselves seeking to create and maintain rules and institutions of order. The most basic questions about world politics are on the table: who commands and who benefits? The struggle over order has tended to be, first and foremost, a struggle over how leading states can best provide security for themselves. It is a search for a stable peace. But states engaged in order building have also gone beyond this and attempted to establish a wider array of political and economic rules and principles of order. They have sought to create a congenial environment in which to pursue their interests. Along the way, the rights, roles, and authority relations that define the system are established. In all these ways, struggles over international order are moments when states grapple over the terms by which the global system will be governed, if it is to be governed at all.

We can look more closely at these underlying questions about international order. What is international order? How has it been created and destroyed? And how has it varied in terms of its logic and character?

In every era, great powers have risen up to build rules and institutions of relations between states, only to see those ordering arrangements eventually break down or transform. In the past, the restructuring of the international system has tended to occur after major wars. "At the end of every war since the end of the eighteenth century," as F. H. Hinsley notes, "the leading states made a concerted effort, each one more radical than the last, to reconstruct the system on lines that would enable them, or so they believed, to avoid a further war."[6] The violence of great-power war tears apart the old order. The war itself strips the rules and arrangements of the prewar system of its last shreds of legitimacy. Indeed, great-power war is perhaps the ultimate sign that an international order has failed. Revisionist states seek to overturn it through aggression, while status quo states cannot defend it short of war. And in the aftermath of war, victors are empowered to organize a new system with rules and arrangements that accord with their interests. Armistice agreements and peace conferences provide opportunities to lay down new rules and principles of international order.[7]

In this way, the settlements of great-power conflicts have become ordering moments when the rules and institutions of the international order are on the table for negotiation and change. The major powers are forced to grapple with and come to agreement on the general principles and arrangements of international order. These ordering moments not only ratify the outcome of the war, they also lay out common understandings, rules and expectations, and procedures for conflict resolution. They play a sort of constitutional function, providing a framework in which the subsequent flow of international relations takes place.[8]

International order is manifest in the settled rules and arrangements between states that define and guide their interaction.[9] War and upheaval between states—that is, disorder—is turned into order when stable rules and arrangements are established by agreement, imposition, or otherwise. Order exists in the patterned relations between states. States operate according to a set of organizational principles that define roles and the terms of their interaction.[10] International order breaks down or enters into crisis when the settled rules and arrangements are thrown into dispute or when the forces that perpetuate order no longer operate.

International orders can be distinguished and compared in many ways. Some international orders are regional, others global. Some are highly institutionalized, others not. Some are hierarchical. The distribution of power in international orders can also vary. Power can be centralized or decentralized. Order can be organized around various "poles" of power—multipolar, bipolar, or unipolar. The challenge for scholars is to use these various features or dimensions to capture the alternative logics and characteristics of international order.

At the outset, it is useful to characterize and compare types of international order in terms of the ways in which stable order is maintained. Generally speaking, international order can be established and rendered stable in one of three ways: through balance, command, or consent. Each involves a different mechanism—or logic—for the establishment and maintenance of order. In different times and places, international order has been organized around each of these mechanisms or by a combination of these mechanisms. As we shall see, the American-led liberal hegemonic order has relied in important ways on all three.

In an international order based on balance, order is maintained through an equilibrium of power among the major states. No one state dominates or controls the system. Order emerges from a power stalemate. States amass power, build alliances, and maneuver to prevent a strong and threatening state from establishing dominance. The specific ways in which balance can be achieved can vary widely. Through this ongoing balancing process, international order is rendered stable. Order based on a balance of power was manifest in Europe in the eighteenth century, and as a concert of powers in Europe after 1815; during the Cold War, international order took the shape of a bipolar balance-of-power system. But in each of these historical eras, order was established through the presence of an equilibrium of power among major states. Leading states or coalitions of states formed counterbalancing poles that checked and restrained each other.

In an order based on command, a powerful state organizes and enforces order. Order is hierarchical and maintained through the dominance of the leading state. States are integrated vertically in superordinate and subordinate positions. Command-based order can vary widely in terms of the degree to which the hierarchical terms of order are enforced through coercion or are also moderated by elements of autonomy, bargaining, and reciprocity. The great empires of the ancient and modern world were hierarchical orders, manifesting various strategies of rule and "repertories of imperial power."[11] The British and American-led international orders were also hierarchical—each, as we shall see, with a distinct mix of imperial and liberal characteristics.

Finally, order based on consent is organized around agreed-upon rules and institutions that allocate rights and limits on the exercise of power. Frameworks of rules and arrangements are constructed that provide authoritative arrangements for international relations. State power is not extinguished in a consent-based order, but it is circumscribed by agreed-upon rules and institutions. Disparities of power between states may still matter in the structuring of consensual, rule-based order, but the rules and institutions nonetheless reflect reciprocal and negotiated agreements between states. The British and American-led liberal orders have been built in critical respects around consent. The contemporary European Union is also a political order of this sort.

■　■　■

Liberal International Order

Over the last two hundred years, international order has been profoundly influenced by the rise of liberal democratic states. This liberal ascendancy has been manifest in the rise in the power, influence, and global reach of liberal great powers—and in the international order that they have built. Through the Victorian era and into the twentieth century, the fortunes of liberal democratic states flourished—and with the growth and expansion of this liberal core of states and its organizing principles, world politics increasingly took a liberal internationalist cast. This liberal ascendancy took a dramatic jump forward in the hands of the United States after World War II, when the United States built postwar order within the Western world—and extending outward—on liberal ideas and principles.

The liberal ascendancy has moved through two great historical eras dominated, respectively, by Great Britain and the United States. Each emerged as the leading power of its day and pushed and pulled other states in a liberal direction, looking after the overall stability and openness of the system. In the nineteenth century, Great Britain led in giving shape to an international order marked by great power, imperial, and liberal arrangements. In the decades following the Napoleonic war, the major states of Europe agreed on a set of rules and expectations that guided great-power relations. Great Britain and the other major states also pursued empire in Africa, Asia, and other parts of the world. At the same time, Great Britain—beginning with its famous repeal of the Corn Laws in 1846—oversaw the expansion of a global system of commerce organized around open trade, the gold standard, and freedom of the seas.

In the twentieth century, liberal order building became more explicit and ambitious. At different moments over these decades, the United States made efforts to create or expand the architecture of an open and rule-based order. Woodrow Wilson brought a vision of a liberal world order to the post–World War I settlement, anchored in the proposal for a League of Nations, although it failed to take hold. When the United States found itself again in a position to build international order in the 1940s, Franklin Roosevelt and Harry Truman extended and ultimately reinvented the liberal international project. During the postwar decades, this order itself evolved as the United States and the other Western liberal states waged the Cold War, modernized their societies, and rebuilt and expanded economic and security relations across the democratic capitalist world. After the Cold War, America's international liberal project evolved yet again. The bipolar world order gave way to a global system dominated by the Western capitalist states. If liberal order was built after World War II primarily within the West, the end of the Cold War turned that order into a sprawling global system. States in all the regions of the world made democratic transitions and pursued market strategies of economic development. Trade and investment expanded across the international system.[12]

■   ■   ■

Following from this, it is possible to make several general observations about the rise of liberal states and liberal order building.

First, liberal international order can be seen as a distinctive type of international order. As noted earlier, liberal international order is defined as order that is open and loosely rule-based. Openness is manifest when states trade and exchange on the basis of mutual gain. Rules and institutions operate as mechanisms of governance—and they are at least partially autonomous from the exercise of state power. In its ideal form, liberal international order creates a foundation in which states can engage in reciprocity and institutionalized cooperation. As such, liberal international order can be contrasted with closed and non-rule-based relations—whether geopolitical blocs, exclusive regional spheres, or closed imperial systems.[13]

In ideal form, liberal international order is sustained through consent rather than balance or command. States voluntarily join the order and operate within it according to mutually agreed-upon rules and arrangements. The rule of law, rather than crude power politics, is the framework of interstate relations. But of course, the real-world liberal international political formations have been more complex orders where power balance and hierarchy intervene in various ways to shape and constrain relations.

Second, the more specific features of liberal international order vary widely. The liberal vision is wide ranging, and the ideas associated with liberal internationalism have evolved over the last two centuries. In the nineteenth century, liberal international order was understood primarily as a commitment to open trade, the gold standard, and great power accommodation. In the twentieth century, it has been understood to entail more elaborate forms of rules and institutional cooperation. Notions of cooperative security, democratic community, collective problem solving, universal rights, and shared sovereignty have also evolved over the last century to inform the agenda of liberal order building.

Generally speaking, liberal international order in the twentieth century has traveled through two phases—marked by the two world wars. After World War I, Woodrow Wilson and other liberals pushed for an international order organized around a global collective security body in which sovereign states would act together to uphold a system of territorial peace. Open trade, national self-determination, and a belief in progressive global change also undergirded the Wilsonian worldview—a "one world" vision of nation-states that trade and interact in a multilateral system of laws creating an orderly international community. "What we seek," Wilson declared at Mount Vernon on July 4, 1918, "is the reign of law, based on the consent of the governed and sustained by the organized opinion of mankind." Despite its great ambition, the Wilsonian plan for liberal international order entailed very little in the way of institutional machinery or formal great-power management of the system. It was a "thin" liberal order in which states would primarily act cooperatively through the shared embrace of liberal ideas and principles.[14] In the end, this experiment in liberal order building failed, and the world soon entered an interwar period of closed economic systems and rival imperial blocs.

When the Roosevelt administration found itself in a position to shape the global system after World War II, it initially sought to pursue order building along Wilsonian lines. It embraced the vision of an open trading system and a world organization in which the great powers would cooperate to keep the peace. Beyond this, American architects of postwar orders—drawing lessons from the Wilsonian failure and incorporating ideas from the New Deal period—also advanced more ambitious ideas about economic and political cooperation embodied in the Bretton Woods institutions. But the weakness of postwar Europe and rising tensions with the Soviet Union pushed liberal order building toward a much more American-led and Western-centered system. As the Cold War unfolded, the United States took command of organizing and running the system. In both the security and economic realms, the United States found itself taking on new commitments and functional roles. Its own economic and political system became, in effect, the central component of the larger liberal hegemonic order.

In these instances, we can distinguish various features of liberal international order. Liberal order can be relatively flat, as it was envisaged by Wilson after 1919, or built around institutionalized hierarchical relations, as it eventually came to be after 1945. Liberal international order can be universal in scope or operate as a regional or an exclusive grouping. It can be constructed between Western democracies or within the wider global system. Liberal international order can affirm and embody principles of state sovereignty and national-self-determination or champion more supranational forms of shared sovereignty. It can be highly institutionalized with formal legal rules, or it can operate with more informally structured expectations and commitments. Liberal international order can be narrowly drawn as a security order—as the League of Nations was on collective security—or developed as a more ambitious system of cooperative security and shared rights and obligations.[15]

Third, liberal international order—and the successive waves of liberal order building—has been built upon the modern states system and evolving frameworks for managing great power relations. That is, liberal order, in each of its nineteenth- and twentieth-century formations, has been built on realist foundations. This is true in two respects. Most generally, over the last two centuries, the construction of open and rule-based relations has been pursued by liberal great powers as they operated in the wider system of states. At a deep or foundational level in the modern era, the Westphalian system of states has prevailed, defined in terms of the multipolar or bipolar organization of great powers and shared norms of state sovereignty. It has been leading states, operating within this system of states, that have pursued liberal order building.

Over the last two centuries, the great powers within this Westphalian system have evolved principles and practices to manage and stabilize their relations. Beginning in 1815, successful settlements were increasingly understood to be based on a set of principles of restraint and accommodation. Embodying this "society of states" approach to international order, the Vienna settlement integrated the defeated French, recognized legitimate French national and security interests, and put in place a diplomatic process for resolving emerging problems on the basis of shared principles and understandings.[16] The resulting Concert of Europe is widely seen as a model of a stable and successful international order. The failure of the Versailles settlement in 1919 to embody these restraint and accommodation principles is widely seen as a critical source of the instability and war that followed. In contrast, in the settlement of World War II, the United States undertook the comprehensive reconstruction of Germany and Japan as liberal democratic states and their integration into the postwar American-led liberal international order—incorporating principles and practices of great-power restraint and accommodation brought forward from earlier eras of order building within the Westphalian system.[17]

Taken together, we can see several distinct eras of liberal order building, and across these eras we can trace evolving ideas and practices of liberal international order. The American-led liberal hegemonic order is only one type of liberal order. Liberal international order itself has been pursued on the foundation of a state system in which the great powers have evolved principles and practices of restraint and conflict management. These various "waves" and "layers" of international order coexist within the contemporary global system.

Imperial and Liberal Rule

The United States emerged in the mid-twentieth century as the world's most powerful state. It had the power not just to pursue its interests but to shape its global environment. It made strategic choices, deployed power, built institutions, forged partnerships, and produced a sprawling order. * * *

But what sort of order was it? If the American postwar order has been a mix of command and consent, what is the nature of this mix and how has it changed over time? Is the American political formation an empire, or do its liberal features give it a shape and organization that is distinct from the great empires of the past? Put simply, has the United States been engaged in imperial rule or liberal rule?

The empire debate is an old one—shadowing the rise of American power itself. In the early postwar years, in the 1960s, and again in the post–Cold War decades, scholars and commentators have debated the character of American domination, arguing about whether it is a modern form of empire.[18] The British writer and labor politician Harold Laski evoked a looming American empire in 1947 when he said that "America bestrides the world like a colossus; neither Rome at the height of its power nor Great Britain in the period of economic supremacy enjoyed an influence so direct, so profound, or so pervasive.[19] Later, during the Vietnam War, critics and revisionist historians traced what was seen as a deep-rooted impulse toward militarism and empire through the history of American foreign policy. Some writers saw the underlying motive for empire as essentially economic, tracing this impulse back to the Open Door policy of the turn of the nineteenth century.[20] Others saw imperial ambition rooted in a logic of security and geopolitical control, given impetus by the Cold War. * * *

In recent years, the empire debate has returned, focusing on America's global ambitions under conditions of unipolarity. With the collapse of the Soviet Union, geopolitical rivals to the United States all but disappeared. Yet, a half century after their occupation, the United States still provides security for Japan and Germany—until recently, the world's second- and third-largest economies. American military bases and carrier battle groups project power into all corners of the world—and indeed the United States possesses a near monopoly on the use of force internationally. Upon this unipolar foundation, the Bush administration came to power and, after the attacks of September 11, 2001, pursued a "war on terror," invaded Afghanistan and Iraq, expanded the military budget, and put forward a controversial 2002 National Security Strategy articulating a doctrine of military preemption in the face of self-defined threats. American power was once again thrust into the light of day—and it deeply unsettled much of the world. Not surprisingly, the concept of empire was invoked again to describe America's global ambitions and exercise of power in a one-superpower world.[21]

But is the American political formation—in the postwar decades or more recently—really an empire? The term "empire" refers to the political control by a dominant state of the domestic and foreign policies of weaker peoples or politics. The European colonial empires of the late nineteenth century were the most direct, formal kind. The Soviet "sphere of influence" in Eastern Europe entailed an equally coercive but less direct form of control. The British Empire included both direct colonial rule and informal empire. If empire is defined loosely, as a hierarchical system of political relationships in which the most powerful state exercises decisive influence, then the American-led order indeed qualifies.

What the American postwar political formation shares with empires is that it is an order organized, at least loosely, around hierarchical relations of domination and subordination. But the American postwar order is multifaceted. The most salient aspect of American domination in the postwar era is its mixed character. The United States built hierarchical relations but also mutually agreed-upon rules and institutions. There are both command-based and consent-based logics embedded in the postwar American-led order. * * * Thus, it is useful to think of hierarchical political orders as existing on a continuum between imperial and liberal hegemonic ideal types.[22]

Empires are hierarchical political systems in which the dominant state exercises direct or indirect sovereign control over the decisions of subordinate states. "Empire," as Napoleon's foreign minister, Charles Maurice de Talleyrand, said, is "the art of putting men in their place." Political control is extensive. The imperial state asserts control over both the internal and external policies of subordinate states—or at least it maintains the right to do so. At the same time, the imperial state imposes the rules of hierarchical order but is itself not bound by those rules. In an empire, the dominating state has the final say over the terms of the relationship—its control may be disguised and obscured, but it has ultimate and sovereign control over the subordinate units within the order. Historically, imperial systems have been manifest in a wide variety of ways, ranging from direct colonial rule to looser types of informal empire.[23]

In contrast, liberal hegemony is hierarchical order built around political bargains, diffuse reciprocity, provision of public goods, and mutually agreeable institutions and working relationships. The liberal hegemonic state asserts more limited control over subordinate states, primarily directed at shaping the terms of their external policies. The liberal hegemonic state dominates the order by establishing and maintaining its rules and institutions—but in doing so, it operates to a greater or lesser extent within those rules and institutions. The liberal hegemonic state establishes its rule within the order by shaping the milieu in which other states operate.

In the case of the American postwar order, * * * there are several features that—at least in its ideal form—give it a more consensual and agreed-upon character than imperial systems. One is the sponsorship and support of a loose system of rules and institutions that it has itself operated within. Another is its leadership in the provision of public goods—including security and maintenance of an open economic system. As an open system organized around leading liberal democratic states, states that operated within it have opportunities to consult, bargain, and negotiate with the United States. In effect, subordinate states have access to decision making at the center. Institutions for joint or concerted leadership span the liberal hegemonic landscape. These features of the American-led order do not eliminate hierarchy or the exercise of power, but they mute the imperial form of hierarchy and infuse it with liberal characteristics.

To be sure, variations in hierarchy exist across the various regional realms of American domination. Liberal characteristics of hegemonic order are most extensive within the advanced liberal democratic world, particularly in U.S. relations with Western Europe and Japan. In other parts of East Asia and across the developing world, American-led order is hierarchical but with much fainter liberal characteristics. While American hegemony within the Western world tends to be organized around agreed-upon multilateral rules and institutions, American hegemony in East Asia is organized around a "hub-and-spoke" security system of client states. In some parts of the developing world—including in Latin America and the Middle East—American involvement has often been crudely imperial.

If this liberal hegemonic order is in crisis, can the bargains and institutions that support it be renegotiated and reestablished? This is in part a question about American willingness and capacity to continue to operate within a liberal hegemonic framework—providing public goods, supporting and abiding by agreed-upon rules and institutions, and adjusting policies within an ongoing system of political bargaining and reciprocity. It is also a question of the interests and ambitions of other established and rising states in the system. Was the American liberal hegemonic order a historical artifact of the long postwar era, now breaking down and giving way to a different type of international order? Or can it be reorganized and renegotiated for the next era of world politics?

■   ■   ■

In the end, I argue that despite America's imperial temptation, it is not doomed to abandon rule-based order—and rising states are not destined to reject the basic features of liberal international order. The United States ultimately will want to wield its power legitimately in a world of rules and institutions. It will also have incentives to build and strengthen regional and global institutions in preparation for a future after unipolarity. The rising power of China, India, and other non-Western states presents a challenge to the old American-led order that will require new, expanded, and shared international governance arrangements.

If America is smart and plays its foreign policy "cards" right, twenty years from now, it can still be at the center of a one-world system defined in terms of open markets, democratic community, cooperative security, and rule-based order. This future can be contrasted with less-desirable alternatives familiar from history: great-power-balancing orders, regional blocs, or bipolar rivalries. The United States should seek to consolidate a global order where other countries "bandwagon" rather than balance against it—and where it remains at the center of a prosperous and secure democratic-capitalist order, which in turn provides the architecture and axis points around which the wider global system turns. But to reestablish this desired world order, the United States must work to re-create the basic governance institutions of the system—investing in alliances, partnerships, multilateral institutions, special relationships, great-power concerts, cooperative security pacts, and democratic security communities.

NOTES

1. See interviews with Chirac by James Graff and Bruce Crumley, "France Is Not a Pacifist Country," *Time*, 24 February 2003, 32–33; and James Hoagland, "Chirac's 'Multipolar World,'" *Washington Post,* 4 February 2004, A23.

2. Signaling a return to America's postwar liberal-oriented leadership, the Obama administration's *National Security Strategy* asserts that the United States "must pursue a rules-based international system that can advance our own interests by serving mutual interests." Office of the President, *National Security Strategy* (Washington, DC: White House, May 2010).

3. On anticipations of a return to multipolarity and the end of American dominance, see Charles Kupchan, *The End of the American Era: U.S. Foreign Policy and the Geopolitics of the Twenty-First Century* (New York: Knopf, 2003); Kishore Mahbubani, *The New Asian Hemisphere: The Irresistible Shift in Global Power to the East* (New York: Public Affairs, 2009); and Fareed Zakaria, *The Post-American World* (New York: Norton, 2009).

4. For arguments about the impact of the world economic crisis on the American neoliberal model and Washington's leadership capacities, see Joseph Stiglitz, *America, Free Markets, and the Sinking of the World Economy* (New York: Norton, 2010); and J. Bradford Lelong and Stephen S. Cohen, *The End of Influence: What Happens When Other Countries Have the Money* (New York: Basic, 2010).

5. See Martin Jacques, *When China Rules the World: The End of the Western World and the Birth of a New Global Order* (New York: Penguin, 2009). On the rise of ideological competition in world politics, see Steven Weber and Bruce W. Jentleson, *The End of Arrogance: America in the Global Competition of Ideas* (Cambridge: Cambridge University Press, 2010).

6. F. H. Hinsley, "The Rise and Fall of the Modern International System," *Review of International Studies* (January 1982), 4.

7. On the politics and ideas of order building after major wars, see G. John Ikenberry, *After Victory: Institutions, Strategic Restraint, and the Rebuilding of Order after Major War* (Princeton, NJ: Princeton University Press, 2001).

8. On the notion of postwar settlements as "constitutional" moments of order building, see Ikenberry, "Constitutional Politics in International Relations," *European Journal of International Relations* 4, no. 2, (June 1998), 147–77; and Daniel Philpott, *Revolutions in Sovereignty: How Ideas Shaped Modern International Relations* (Princeton, NJ: Princeton University Press, 2001).

9. In his classic study, Hedley Bull distinguished between world order and international order. World order is composed of all peoples and the totality of relations between them, and international order is composed of the rules and settled expectations between states. See Bull, *The Anarchical Society: A Study of Order in World Politics* (London: Macmillan, 1977).

10. International order in this sense involved shared and stable expectations among states about how they will interact with each other, or as Janice Mattern suggests, it is a "relationship among specific states that produces and reinforces shared understandings of expectations and behaviors with respect to each other." Mattern, *Ordering International Politics: Identity, Crisis, and Representational Force* (New York: Routledge, 2005), 30.

11. Jane Burbank and Frederick Cooper, *Empires in World History: Power and the Politics of Difference* (Princeton, NJ: Princeton University Press, 2010), chap. 1.

12. For explorations of the rise and spread of Anglo-American liberal internationalism, see Mark R. Brawley, *Liberal Leadership: Great Powers and Their Challengers in Peace and War* (Ithaca, NY: Cornell University Press, 1993); Tony Smith, *America's Mission: The United States and the Worldwide Struggle for Democracy in the Twentieth Century* (Princeton, NJ: Princeton University Press, 1994); Michael Mandelbaum, *The Ideas That Conquered the World: Peace, Democracy, and Free Markets in the Twenty-First Century* (New York: Public Affairs, 2002); Walter Russell Mead, *God and Gold: Britain, America, and the Making of the Modern World* (New York: Knopf, 2007); and David Ekbladh, *The Great American Mission: Modernization and the Construction of an American World Order* (Princeton, NJ: Princeton University Press, 2010).

13. For a survey of types of international orders, including nonliberal varieties, see essays in Greg Fry and Jocinta O'Hagan, eds., *Contending Images of World Politics* (New York: St. Martin's/Macmillan, 2000).

14. See Thomas Knock, *To End All Wars: Woodrow Wilson and the Quest for a New World Order* (New York: Oxford University Press, 1992); Lloyd E. Ambrosius, *Wilsonianism: Woodrow Wilson and His Legacy in American Foreign Relations* (New York: Palgrave, 2002); and John Milton Cooper, Jr., *Breaking the Heart of the World: Woodrow Wilson and the Fight for the League of Nations* (New York: Cambridge University Press, 2001).

15. These various dimensions of liberal order are explored in G. John Ikenberry, "Liberal Internationalism 3.0: America and the Dilemmas of Liberal World Order," *Perspectives on Politics* 7, no. 1, (March 2009), 71–87.

16. On the society-of-states approach to international order, see Hedley Bull, *The Anarchical Society*.

17. For a discussion of principles of great-power restraint and accommodation as they were manifest in the Cold War settlement, see Daniel Deudney and G. John Ikenberry, "The Unraveling of the Cold War Settlement," *Survival* (December/January 2009–10).

18. For surveys of these waves of empire debate, see Michael Cox, "Empire in Denial? Debating U.S. Power," *Security Dialogue* 35, no. 2 (2004), 228–36; and Cox, "The Empire's Back in Town—Or America's Imperial Temptation—Again," *Millennium* 32, no. 1 (2003), 1–27.

19. Harold Laski., quoted in Niall Ferguson, *Colossus: The Rise and Fall of the American Empire* (New York: Penguin, 2004), 68.

20. See the works by William Appleman Williams, especially *The Tragedy of American Diplomacy* (New York: Norton, 1959).

21. The historian Niall Ferguson captured this widely held view, noting that "the British Empire is the most commonly cited precedent for the global power currently wielded by the United States. America is heir to the Empire in both senses: offspring in the colonial era, successor today." Ferguson, *Empire: The Rise and Demise of the British World Order and the Lessons for Global Power* (New York: Basic Books, 2002), xii. For surveys of the large and growing list of books and essays on the United States as global empire, see G. John Ikenberry, "The Illusions of Empire," *Foreign Affairs* 82, no. 2 (March/April 2004), 144–54; Alexander J. Motyl, "Is Empire Everything? Is Everything Empire?" *Comparative Politics* 39 (2006), pp. 229–49; and Charles S. Maier, "Empire Without End: Imperial Achievements and Ideologies," *Foreign Affairs* 89, no. 4 (July/August 2010), 153–59.

22. See David Lake, *Entangling Relations: American Foreign Policy in Its Century* (Princeton, NJ: Princeton University Press, 1999); and Lake, "Anarchy, Hierarchy and the Variety of International Relations," *International Organization* 50, no. 1 (1996), 1–35.

23. For studies of the logic of empire, see Michael Doyle, *Empires* (Ithaca, NY: Cornell University Press, 1984); and Herfried Munkler, *Empires: The Logic of World Domination from Ancient Rome to the United States* (London: Polity, 2007).

Thomas J. Christensen

FROM *THE CHINA CHALLENGE*
Shaping the Choices of a Rising Power

■ ■ ■

As the leading State Department official focusing on China [from 2006 to 2008], I often testified before congressional committees and congressionally mandated commissions about China's rise and the U.S. response. My message was consistent and reflected a broad consensus in the interagency process: the goal of the United States, its allies, and all like-minded states should not be to contain China but to shape Beijing's choices so as to channel China's nationalist ambitions into cooperation rather than coercion. If we can demonstrate that Chinese nationalist greatness can best be achieved in the new century through participation in global projects, we will have accomplished this strategic goal. * * *

■ ■ ■

China's Rise: Why It Is Real

China's rise in wealth, diplomatic influence, and military power since 1978 is real and it's stunning. For all the scars on his personal political history—from support for the disastrous Great Leap Forward in the late 1950s to the Tiananmen massacre in 1989—Deng Xiaoping will be

From Thomas J. Christensen, *The China Challenge: Shaping the Choices of a Rising Power* (New York: W. W. Norton & Co., 2015). Some of the author's notes have been omitted.

remembered most by historians for launching the program of Reform and Opening. That program pulled hundreds of millions of people out of grinding poverty and allowed China to become a potent international actor for the first time since the first half of the Qing Dynasty, which spanned the mid-seventeenth to the early nineteenth centuries.

Deng's market reforms unleashed the pent-up economic energy of the Chinese people, who had suffered for more than two decades under Mao's postmodern version of Communism. Under Mao, market laws of supply and demand and basic economic concepts such as diminishing returns on investment were dismissed as bourgeois, imperialist myths. Expertise and management skills were valued much less than blind loyalty to Mao and devotion to the bizarre economic model he created in the late 1950s. Mao communized agriculture, localized industry, and commanded unrealistic production targets. He mobilized the population around Utopian Communist economics and radical political activism. His goal was to have China catch up with the Soviet Union and the United States in a short time frame and position the People's Republic of China as the leader of the international Communist movement. But his Great Leap of the 1950s and the Great Proletarian Cultural Revolution of the 1960s led instead to domestic economic disaster, international isolation, and the premature deaths of some forty million Chinese citizens. In the late 1970s Deng Xiaoping would restore market incentives and place an emphasis on skill and practicality rather than ideological purity in professional promotion. Practical control of agricultural land, if not ownership, was taken away from communes and given to farmers. The reform program also injected market-based pricing and incentives into the Chinese economy and opened China up to foreign trade and investment. Officials, engineers, and scientists were chosen for being expert, not "red." The resulting growth brought some three hundred million people—about the size of the U.S. population today—above the threshold of poverty as measured by international organizations: an income of less than one dollar per day.

These results are unprecedented in world history. For the past thirty-six years, China's economy has grown on an average of about 10 percent per annum in real terms (meaning adjusted for inflation). Accordingly, the gross domestic product (GDP) of China has almost doubled every seven years since 1979. And with a Chinese population of 1.3 billion, the economy has moved from one that was poor but still large to one that is now much less poor and truly gargantuan. China's per capita income is still very modest compared to the wealthiest countries of the world, but the change is nonetheless astonishing. Official per capita income rose from $220 USD in 1978 to $4,940 in 2011,[1] and according to some measures using "purchase power parity," China's per capita income was $9,300 in 2012 (an impressive figure, though it is notable that the per capita income of the United States, by comparison, was $50,700).[2] While still a developing country, China surpassed Japan in 2010 to become the world's second largest economy, a feat simply unimaginable in the early years of the reform era. At that time Americans were fretting about the economic recession of the early 1980s and Japan was seen as the great power likely to surpass the United States in the next cycle in the "rise and fall of the great powers," to use Yale professor Paul Kennedy's famous phrase.

The economic reforms have had more than just economic results. The individual citizen's life is incomparably more energetic and free in China today than in the pre-reform period. My first trip to China was in the summer of 1987, the eighth year of the reform era. The anesthetic grip of socialism was still very strong on Chinese society. At midday, cities like Beijing and Shanghai, moving at a slow pace already, ground to a halt as the population rested and often slept for two hours, wherever they might be. This was the *xiuxi* period, a designated siesta for urban Chinese citizens, many of whom still worked in inefficient state-owned work units. By contrast, the energy on the contemporary streets of Beijing and Shanghai is palpable and sometimes overwhelming. Cranes rotate at construction sites in every direction, and one is more likely to find oneself stuck in stultifying traffic at midday than stepping around a slumbering deliveryman sleeping on his bicycle's flatbed. The slowly rolling bicycles of the 1980s urban landscape have been replaced by the twenty-first-century traffic of young professionals in new and relatively sturdy automobiles. In fact, China has become the largest market for new cars in the world and the lifeline of companies like GM facing declining domestic sales.

The government's often impressive efforts to build an infrastructure capable of handling this new burden has kept world-famous equipment companies like Caterpillar in the black despite diminishing demand in wealthier countries. Still, the growth in the new Chinese middle class has outstripped the growth of new roads; epic traffic jams in Chinese cities are a regular occurrence. Beijing now ranks alongside Mexico City as the worst in the world for traffic. In less thoughtful moments, the experienced traveler almost yearns for the slower but more predictable pace of Beijing's bicycle lanes, where coal couriers and relatively unstressed citizens spat out the sand and industrial dust blown downwind from the manufacturing centers and the Gobi desert.

Marketization has had a big impact on personal freedoms in China as well and thus constitutes what the political scientist Harry Harding aptly described as the People's Republic's Second Revolution.[3] In Mao's China, the Party secretaries in charge of state-owned enterprises had a degree of power over the workers that Americans simply cannot imagine. Local Party chiefs had near total control over the lives of their charges from cradle to cremation. They had authority over not only salary and career promotion but also education, health care, housing, retirement, and even permission to marry. Marketization changed this to a large degree by creating both a vibrant private sector outside of the state-owned enterprise system, to which disgruntled workers could escape from meddling Party chiefs, and a new standard of success—market competitiveness—for the state-owned enterprises themselves. The combination meant that Party chiefs in those enterprises needed to focus on something other than micromanaging the personal lives of their workers and could ill afford to alienate their most able staff lest they jump ship to the private sector. The personal individual space created by this process, even space to privately express disappointment with the state itself, moved China very quickly from what Ambassador Jeane Kirkpatrick had categorized in the Cold War as a totalitarian state to what she described as a typical authoritarian one. Nations living under the latter suffer from lack of democracy, free press, freedom of assembly, and often rule of law, but the life of the individual on a day-to-day basis is still much freer than under the ever-present thumb of totalitarianism. Along the same lines, the hope for positive future economic and political change in China is also much greater now than it was in the totalitarian Mao era, and hope for a better future may be one of the most underappreciated human rights of all.

■ ■ ■

This Time Should Be Different: China's Rise in a Globalized World

When great power rise, there is often real trouble. The examples are both numerous and horrific. Modern German history alone provides a series of demonstrations. The punctuated and violent rise of Bismarck's Prussia and the German successor states helped cause several great power wars in the late nineteenth and early twentieth centuries, including the two most brutal armed conflicts in world history. In Asia, the rise of Japan after the Meiji Restoration also led to several wars from the 1880s to 1945 involving Japan, China, Russia, Great Britain, and the United States.

There have been partial exceptions to what seems like a general rule of international relations. The rise of the United States and the decline of Great Britain as a global leader in the late nineteenth and early twentieth centuries did not lead to conflict between the two democracies. In fact, they would be allied together in two subsequent world wars against a rising Germany, in the Cold War that followed, and ever since. But even in that instance, structural transition was not truly peaceful. As I argued with Columbia professor Richard Betts in 2000, if China handles disputes with its neighbors as poorly as the United States did in the late nineteenth century, East Asia is in for a very rocky ride.[4] Racism under the thin academic patina of social Darwinism and the yellow journalism of a jingoistic press helped spark the Spanish-American war over Cuba, which in turn placed the U.S. military in a costly counterinsurgency war in the Philippines. The ostensible reason for conflict was a nebulous naval incident in Havana Harbor with American casualties that became a national rallying cry for war ("Remember the *Maine,* to hell with Spain!").

It does not take great imagination to see how similar factors could contribute to Chinese belligerence as it pursues expansive maritime claims against rivals like Japan, Vietnam, and the Philippines. Those nations are often treated with derision, condescension, or both in Chinese nationalist circles. The prospect of U.S. intervention in such disputes and in relations across the Taiwan Strait could eventually lead China to mimic another nineteenth-century American concept, the Monroe Doctrine, which sought to prevent further European imperial incursions in the Western Hemisphere. In fact, some U.S. scholars like Princeton's Aaron Friedberg already ascribe to China the goal of "extruding," or expelling, the United States from its regional bases in neighboring countries. Friedberg and others believe China plans to target the United States and its regional allies and security partners with a combination of economic and military coercion and diplomatic persuasion to achieve this goal. In this scenario, either the United States would leave of its own volition, fearing conflict with a rising China or, more likely, would be deprived of regional partners because no Asian actor would want to run the risk of alienating or provoking Beijing by maintaining traditional security ties with the United States.[5]

Friedberg lays out his argument with typical intelligence and care. While I find scant evidence in Chinese strategic writings to support this claim about Beijing's intentions at present, it is definitely a real and dangerous possibility for the future. Avoiding such a turn in Chinese doctrine and ensuring its failure if it were adopted, in that order, should be priority goals for U.S. policy in the region. If such a doctrine were actually adopted by China and proved successful, the decline of American power would be severe indeed. But even a failed attempt by China to expel the United States from the region would likely be fraught with crises and military conflicts. For this reason, University of Chicago professor John Mearsheimer has adopted an even more pessimistic stance than Friedberg, declaring that China's rise cannot be peaceful because it is inevitable that China will pursue what Friedberg calls extrusion, whether such an effort proves successful or not.[6]

Despite these dreary historic precedents and prognostications, there are reasons to be more sanguine that the rise of China can be managed in a way that preserves both American power in East Asia and regional peace and stability. Two related arguments about the destabilizing effects of the rise and fall of great powers predict that China's rise will hurt regional and global stability. I hope to show that both are wrong. The first is a purely structural argument, based in the strategic history of past disasters associated with the rise of new challengers in the international system. The rise of new rivals destabilizes the international system by creating opportunities for territorial expansion and leads to intense spirals of tension among the great powers. The greed and fear created by these shifts in the distribution of great power capabilities result in crises among the great powers that lead to large-scale war and massive suffering.

The second argument is a corollary of the first and has less to do with material power and more to do with the international norms, institutions, and rules of the road. Scholars of institutions like the UN and the International Monetary Fund (IMF) often claim that the international rules and institutions in place at any time were previously set by the leading power at the apex of its hegemony over the system. The more cynical version of this theory suggests that such a hegemonic leader would only set up institutions that disproportionately benefit itself, not the system as a whole. When the leader's power declines in comparison to a rising rival, it is only natural, then, that the up-and-coming rival would want to revise or even overturn the existing rules and create new institutions that disproportionally benefit the rising state. So at the close of World War II, the United States sought the end of European colonial preferences in trade and finance and the creation of free trade regimes and a global financial system. According to the most cynical interpretation, Washington did not do so altruistically to create a more prosperous and stable world but rather because the United States was economically much more competitive than the remaining European great powers after World War II. In the current day, if China wanted to undercut existing international institutions in order to foster new ones that benefited itself more and the United States less, the process of change could damage near-term global cooperation on economics, security matters, humanitarian crises, and environmental problems and thus prove fundamentally destabilizing.

Fortunately, in the case of China's ongoing rise, there are several reasons to doubt these two arguments. The kinds of temptations that led to great power wars during previous power transitions are much less prominent in Asia today than they were in the Western Hemisphere and Asia in the past. Substantial changes in global economics and politics have made the current international system more robust than previous systems. Broader economic trends have made territorial conquest of colonies less tempting, and changes in both economics and weaponry have decreased the need for invasion and conquest of either peer competitors or their smaller allies. Furthermore, the institutions set up by the United States and its allies after World War II were beneficial not just to themselves but to all states willing to open up their economies to a rule-based global order. No country has benefited from that global order more than China, particularly since it joined the World Trade Organization (WTO) in 2001. Since domestic stability is paramount for the CCP and the maintenance of that stability depends in large part on economic growth, I can see few reasons why China would intentionally seek conflict with its trade and investment partners or undercut the institutional framework that has enabled its historic economic development.

■　■　■

Why Chinese Power Will Not Surpass U.S. Power Anytime Soon

China's rise is real, as discussed [earlier]. And for reasons that will be discussed [later], China's increased military, economic, and political power poses challenges for U.S. national security and regional stability in Asia. But we need not panic. Not only does China have many disincentives for aggression, but it is not likely to catch up or surpass the United States in terms of comprehensive national power anytime soon.

There is a growing chorus that portrays China as being on a clear path to economic, military, and diplomatic supremacy. For example, Martin Jacques predicts China's impending hegemony in the title of his book *When China Rules the World.*[7] * * *

Pessimistic commentators like Jacques * * * ignore too many sources of Chinese weakness and American strength. In addition to viewing trade and investment in the developing world as a realpolitik competition between great powers, a highly questionable proposition, these studies often exaggerate the political leverage enjoyed by countries that are purchasing raw materials. Moreover, there are several negative factors for China's reputation in these areas. China's extractive business practices have led to resentment of Chinese companies, including some high-profile instances of violence in Africa. Democratization in Latin America and Africa has led to a political backlash against China's support for states like Zimbabwe. The Arab Spring in the Middle East has also complicated Beijing's relations with some members of the Arab League as Beijing joins Russia in blocking the international community from pressuring Assad's regime in Syria.

In military matters, China's defense modernization does pose real problems for the United States, but the scope of that newfound military power is often exaggerated by scholars and public officials. Too often these observers approach military net assessments as if they are tallying a sports score, with each country getting a certain number of points for each counted asset. But even though the United States still does well in such a competition with China, numbers are not everything. A more sophisticated analysis would take into account the quality of systems, the quality of personnel, and the wartime experience of the two militaries. Such a study reveals that China is unlikely to have the military wherewithal to become a global peer competitor of the United States for decades to come. Chinese strategic writings, even those not meant for foreign consumption, seem to recognize China's shortcomings. They often refer to the need to develop strategies that overcome China's relative military weakness in comparison to a potential great power foe. While they discuss closing the gap in overall military power, there is almost no sense that such a goal will be achieved anytime soon. It seems then that Americans often give the Chinese higher grades and aspirations than Chinese military officers themselves are willing to accept.

For similar reasons, China is also unlikely to have the wherewithal to deny the United States access to the western Pacific, a goal that the Pentagon believes China is pursuing under the distinctly American concept of "anti-access/area denial" (or A2AD in DoD-speak). As with Friedberg's concept of extrusion, I have seen in my research no Chinese-language equivalent to these terms in authoritative strategic writings. The closest Chinese term is "counterintervention," but this concept has more to do with raising the costs to intervening foreign forces than to physically preventing their entry in the first place. This does not mean that China will not adopt such a strategy of exclusion, only that it currently seems to lack the capability and intention to do so.

■　■　■

Why China Still Poses Strategic Challenges

Enjoying superior power is preferable to the alternatives, but it is no guarantor of peace. Nor does superior economic and political power guarantee that a nation's political goals will be achieved. A China that lags behind the United States in terms of economics, soft power, military capabilities, and alliances can still pose major challenges to U.S. security interests, particularly in East Asia. Weaker powers have often challenged stronger ones. As John Arquilla has argued, the initiator of great power wars has more often than not proven to be the loser.[8] Arquilla's work challenges the realist notion that superior powers should deter aggression from weaker states. Leaders in weaker states often miscalculate the balance of power and overestimate their prospects for success—or they understand the distribution of overall capabilities but challenge stronger ones anyway. They might do so because they believe that they can achieve limited political aims: to coerce stronger powers into concessions on some specific set of issues. Often the calculus takes into account the political willpower of the two sides to pay costs over a contested issue and the perceived importance of the issue. Leaders' perceptions of those realities are more important than the physical and political realities in determining whether a nation will initiate a limited conflict.

Most of international security politics involves political battles over limited political and territorial aims. Brute force struggles such as the two world wars are important, but they are the exception, not the rule. The struggles for national survival in the late nineteenth and early twentieth centuries informed realist balance-of-power theories developed in the mid-twentieth century. But even in that dark period, there were many crises and limited wars involving coercive diplomacy. And during the Cold War, the United States often found itself in combat with weaker actors with high degrees of resolve, such as in Korea and Vietnam. More recently, we have witnessed a vastly superior U.S. military confront difficulties in the face of insurgencies in post-invasion Iraq and Afghanistan. With that historic backdrop, consider the strategic challenges posed by a modernizing Chinese military today. Although China is hardly a military peer competitor of the United States, the United States has fought no military since World War II that is anywhere near as impressive as Chinese forces are today. And even in World War II, the formidable axis powers—Germany, Japan, and Italy—did not have nuclear weapons that could strike the United States. Contemporary China does, and that fact could, in specific circumstances, limit the willingness of a U.S. president to exercise all aspects of U.S. conventional military superiority.

China's military modernization concerns American strategists because Beijing has intelligently focused its development on new capabilities that expose U.S. forces deployed far from the United States and close to China to various risks. By doing so, Chinese elites might gain confidence that they have increased coercive leverage against Washington or against its allies and security partners. The United States relies on bases in those places and cooperation provided by regional actors for power projection not just in Asia but around the world. In this sense, while the U.S. alliance system is a great source of U.S. power and has no equivalent in the Chinese security portfolio, it is also a source of vulnerability to Chinese punishment: China can try to dissuade those allies from cooperating with the United States or can strike directly at U.S. forces at bases relatively close to China to cause pain to the more distant United States. Chinese coercive strategies can thus raise the costs of U.S. intervention in the region even if China cannot prevail in a full-scale conflict. So, while responsible Chinese elites might view the Chinese military as weaker than the United States, and their strategic writings suggest that they almost

universally do, they might still be emboldened by certain new coercive capabilities under development. This is particularly true if they believe that the issues at stake matter more to China than to the United States. Chinese leaders might believe they have greater resolve regarding sovereignty disputes, for example, even if their military is not as powerful as that of the United States. Observers around the world have noted U.S. withdrawal from Vietnam, Somalia, and Afghanistan when costs to the United States were raised by significantly weaker actors. By endangering American and allied military assets in the region, Beijing can raise the prospective costs of U.S. intervention. The strategic goals would be to deter U.S. intervention, delay effective deployment of U.S. forces until local actors have been subdued, or compel U.S. withdrawal if the United States decides to intervene in an extended conflict with China.

In such a campaign, military pressure might be brought to bear against not only the United States but also key U.S. allies and security partners such as Japan, South Korea, Taiwan, the Philippines, Thailand, Singapore, and Australia. Beijing has invested an impressive amount of resources, especially since the late 1990s, in military capabilities designed to project power offshore and strike the assets of the United States and its allies. Many hundreds of accurate, conventionally tipped ballistic missiles threaten Taiwan's fixed assets. A smaller number of these missiles can reach U.S. bases in Japan and the western Pacific as well. According to the Pentagon, one version of an intermediate-range ballistic missile, the DF-21, can hunt and kill large capital ships at sea by using terminal guidance, the ability to steer a warhead toward its target after it reenters the earth's atmosphere from space. If deployed and integrated into China's existing doctrine, the DF-21D or antiship ballistic missile (ASBM) could threaten American aircraft carriers, home to several thousand American service personnel and a tremendous amount of firepower and ammunition, making it both an attractive coercive target and an important military target.[9]

To challenge American sea power, the Chinese navy has developed a large number of submarines armed with advanced torpedoes, cruise missiles, and sea mines. These would be supplemented with a large fleet of smaller naval and civilian surface vessels, including the Houbei-class fast missile boat, that could be used to fire cruise missiles, lay mines, and help locate U.S. forces for targeting by other Chinese assets. China has also invested in a large fleet of fourth-generation fighter planes and advanced air defenses to try to offset the qualitative and quantitative advantages enjoyed by the United States. Chinese surface ships and aircraft can also launch cruise missiles at ships at sea and against fixed targets on land. In 2007 and 2009 China demonstrated the ability to strike satellites in low earth orbit. Along with electronic warfare and cyber attack capabilities, these assets could also serve to reduce America's clear advantage in the realm of what the Department of Defense calls Command, Control, Communications, Computers, Intelligence, Surveillance, and Reconnaissance (C4ISR). In combination with the other weapons systems listed above, these assets can be force multipliers that allow the Chinese military to threaten a greater number of American and allied soldiers, sailors, and airmen. Such perceived coercive capability might embolden the Chinese leadership in potential standoffs.[10]

It is important to remember that these capabilities do not give Chinese leaders confidence that they can prevail in an all-out struggle with technologically more sophisticated militaries like the United States. On the contrary, Chinese strategic writings assume that Chinese forces are likely to be weaker and less technologically sophisticated than those of unnamed, advanced great power enemies. Chinese strategists hold little hope of closing the gap of overall military power with the United States anytime soon, but this is hardly a cause for passivity among Chinese strategists. Instead they write about the "inferior defeating the superior under high-tech conditions" through a combination of skill, timely strikes on key targets, and superior political resolve.[11] The goals of the proposed attacks on a physically superior enemy are as much to affect the psychology of the enemy and the cohesion of its regional alliances as they are to denude the enemy's physical capacity to fight over the long run.

In Washington security circles, I often encounter melodramatic language about the threat to U.S. access to the western Pacific. Such talk might be good for securing budgets for the Pentagon and, in particular, for the U.S. Navy and Air Force. But the hyperbole is intellectually inaccurate and politically counterproductive in several ways. In recent years, the Department of Defense has coined a new term, anti-access/area denial, or A2AD, to describe Beijing's newfound capabilities and the doctrines that accompany them. The idea is that China is trying to deny the United States military access to the waters and airspace near China's coastline. But while DoD descriptors have changed, my research and conversations in China over several years suggest that the current Chinese strategy has been in place since the 1990s at the latest. I outlined that strategy in a 2001 article in the journal *International Security* entitled "Posing Problems without Catching Up."[12] China has long sought to affect the psychology of a militarily superior United States and its regional allies by posing potentially costly military challenges to forward-deployed U.S. forces. What has changed in the interim is not so much China's strategy but its capability to execute that strategy. Starting from a humble base, China has for the first time developed the ability to project naval and airpower offshore in a serious way. Defense budgets have grown even faster than China's rapidly expanding economy. But China could not physically deny military access to the western Pacific should the United States resolve to go there. The only area in which China might have a technological edge is with the antiship ballistic missile. The United States has eschewed production of such a weapons system not because it cannot build them but because to do so could violate certain Cold War–era arms control agreements and because Washington has other more effective methods than ballistic missiles to strike at distant moving targets.

Ironically, perhaps, the phrase A2AD and other buzzwords ascribe to China more coercive leverage than Beijing has earned during its impressive military modernization. If the Chinese military modernization campaign is aimed as much at affecting American psychology as it is at crippling American forces—and everything we know from Chinese doctrinal writings suggests that it is—then Beijing has already scored a direct hit. When the United States discusses publicly the notion that there are areas of the world its military cannot penetrate, it has the potential to undercut not only U.S. resolve but also allied resolve, since third parties would naturally wonder if China can actually physically prevent the United States from intervening on their behalf in a regional crisis. This perfectly serves China's doctrinal purposes.

A second problem is that, by using terms like A2AD, the likes of which I have never seen in the Chinese military literature, the United States is suggesting that U.S. forces would have to fight hard and early simply to gain access to what would otherwise be a closed theater of operations. Since access is a prerequisite for any coercive diplomatic role, such an exaggerated view of China's capabilities could have devastating escalatory implications in a real crisis. In other words, rather than adopting a more measured approach, U.S. commanders may decide to launch large-scale electronic warfare and precision strike operations merely to get U.S. forces into the theater. Some U.S. strategists have even publicly discussed a nascent U.S. doctrinal concept, "air-sea battle," some versions of which call for large-scale kinetic and blinding operations against China's "kill chain"—missile sites, command and control nodes, submarines, submarine bases, et cetera—to be launched early in a conflict to protect forward-deployed U.S. forces.[13]

Even against a conventionally armed weaker power, such an early escalation of conflict would be frightening, particularly to U.S. allies within range of Chinese missiles and conventional forces. Moreover, the United States might appear the aggressor and China the victim, reducing U.S. political advantages with both allies and neutral states alike. But there is a more basic issue: the United States has never in its history launched such a robust conventional attack against the homeland of a nuclear-armed state. Since the 1980s China has had a small and backward force of liquid-fueled missiles capable of reaching the continental United States (according to public reports, China has about twenty such missiles). Since they are relatively small in number and the missiles would require a good deal of time to be fueled and mated to warheads during a crisis, many inside and outside of China have doubted whether or not Beijing possessed what in nuclear parlance is a "secure second strike": the ability to level unacceptable damage against an adversary even after absorbing the most concerted preemptive attack (or first strike). We are not sure how Chinese leaders themselves viewed the survivability of the traditional Chinese nuclear deterrent, particularly in a world in which the United States has developed much better conventional strike weapons, greater reconnaissance capability, and missile defenses as a partial insurance policy against missiles that might survive a U.S. preemptive strike. But China is developing a significantly larger set of solid-fueled mobile missiles, and each potentially could have multiple warheads. This would provide a much bigger challenge for U.S. targeting units and even bigger risks for a U.S. president if he or she wanted to contemplate a first strike on China's nuclear weapons.[14]

On the opposite side of this strategic equation, a more robust second-strike nuclear capability for China should foster greater confidence among China's leaders during a crisis than they have enjoyed in crises in the past. In coercive diplomacy—or military engagements short of full-scale wars of survival—psychology and perceptions are even more important than military reality, So even if U.S. leaders were already sufficiently wary about China's traditional nuclear deterrent to eschew first-strike options, and even if they view the modernization program in China as merely an upgrade of China's preexisting deterrent, we cannot be sure whether Chinese leaders sincerely believed that the older arsenal could have survived a first strike. Any added confidence Chinese leaders gain by the nuclear modernization might give them added resolve in a crisis.

One could posit that talk of nuclear escalation is simply Cold War science fiction. After all, both sides have nuclear arsenals. So even if China has for the first time established a secure nuclear retaliatory capability against the United States, it would never have any rational incentive to use it unless the United States were to attempt a massive nuclear first strike against China out of the blue, an extremely unlikely scenario. Such a scenario is rendered even less likely, so the logic goes, by U.S. conventional superiority and the options that such advantage provides U.S. leaders short of the nuclear threshold.

Assessing Chinese nuclear modernization recalls Cold War–era debates about the role of nuclear weapons in deterring superpower aggression. During the Cold War, hawkish theorists in the United States claimed that there was something called the "stability-instability paradox," meaning that since both the United States and the Soviet Union enjoyed secure nuclear arsenals that could obliterate each other, nuclear weapons, in effect, simply canceled one another out. By this logic, stability at the nuclear level—known as mutually assured destruction (MAD)—allegedly fostered a robust rivalry at the conventional level. The argument ran that a conventionally superior power would know that its conventionally inferior rival would never have a rational reason to escalate to the nuclear level because such escalation would lead to an unacceptably devastating nuclear retaliation. This was a hawkish analysis in Cold War America because it was widely believed that the Soviets and their allies enjoyed conventional superiority over NATO forces in central Europe. U.S. hawks believed that Soviet conventional superiority posed a danger that strategic nuclear weapons could not neutralize because of the stability-instability paradox. So the Soviets might be emboldened by allied weakness unless conventional NATO forces were beefed up and/or bolstered by tactical and theater nuclear weapons that could be used short of a full-scale nuclear war to offset those Soviet conventional advantages.[15]

Less hawkish Cold War critics of this viewpoint, such as Robert Jervis and Thomas Schelling, believed that nuclear deterrence cast a much larger shadow over the behavior of nuclear-armed states than the hawks allowed. They believed that attackers seeking to change the status quo would have to consider the threat of escalation from conventional war to nuclear war. Defenders of the status quo could manipulate what Schelling famously, called the "threat that leaves something to chance": the dangerous prospect that limited, conventional warfare could escalate at "time $t+1$" in ways such that no one could accurately predict at "time t," and that escalation to the nuclear level could occur as the tensions spiraled. In other words, an actor could not easily exploit its conventional superiority for fear of unleashing an unintended escalatory process that would end in nuclear conflict. That both superpowers deployed tactical and theater nuclear weapons to the European theater bolstered this analysis. Those deployments provided a slippery slope between conventional and nuclear combat that the Soviets could hardly ignore when plotting a conventional attack.[16]

It is important to remember that the U.S. and NATO, while possessing inferior conventional forces, were defending the recognized status quo in western Europe. And one of the underappreciated stabilizing factors in the Cold

War was that—with the notable exceptions of volatile areas like West Berlin—the geographic lines between the two ideological camps in Europe were fairly clear and mutually accepted. Schelling and Jervis theorized that this made for relatively stable superpower relations in the Cold War, an analysis consistent with psychological theories developed by Amos Tversky and Nobel laureate Daniel Kahneman. Tversky and Kahneman's work on prospect theory demonstrates that, in general, humans accept higher risks and pay greater costs to defend what they believe to be rightfully theirs than they will to acquire new possessions.[17] Applying these findings to Cold War Europe, Jervis asserted that, even if the United States and NATO could not prevail in a conventional physical struggle with the Soviets and the Warsaw Pact, they could successfully deter the Soviets from invading western Europe by raising the prospect that they would exact unacceptable costs on the Soviets to defend the status quo in this geostrategic game of chicken.[18]

■   ■   ■

Given the arguments laid out by Jervis and Schelling, one could take comfort in the notion that only a very aggressive China would want to unleash dangerous forces by challenging the status quo in the East Asian region. For reasons laid out [earlier], some new aspects of modern international politics and economics should dissuade Beijing from such brazen adventurism. But one must curb unalloyed optimism because in contemporary East Asia there are many sovereignty disputes, particularly in the maritime domain. Indeed, there is nothing close to a mutually accepted territorial status quo among potential belligerents. China itself has active disputes with many of its neighbors, including U.S. allies and security partners such as Japan, the Philippines, and Taiwan and important nonallied states such as Vietnam, Malaysia, and Brunei.[19] In addition, China has overlapping exclusive economic zones (EEZ) at sea under the UN Convention of the Law of the Sea (UNCLOS) with even more states, including South Korea, another U.S. ally, and Indonesia.

Such disputes are dangerous because all potential belligerents can believe that they are defending sovereign territory and the status quo. There does not need to be a clear aggressor for there to be trouble. Per Tversky and Kahneman's prospect theory, if both sides believe they own the disputed territories, then the game of chicken is much more likely to lead to a head-on collision than if one side is trying to change the status quo.

Such tendencies among individual humans can become even more pronounced for governments, which have to worry about the strategic and domestic political consequences of appearing not to defend the status quo. On strategic grounds, if a nation is willing to back down on an issue related to one's proclaimed sovereign territory, that nation will lose face, thus undermining its positions on other matters. So, in any given dispute, a country like China or Japan, with multiple island disputes, has to worry about the implications for future negotiations not only with the rival disputant but with third-party onlookers (Japan also has island disputes with South Korea and Russia; the PRC has disputes with Taiwan and four other countries in the South China Sea).

The situation only looks worse when one factors in the domestic political interests of governments, who are loath to look weak on issues that touch on nationalistic pride. If a state fails to defend its sovereign claims, then its own people can hold it to task. This is true everywhere but is particularly salient in East Asia, where the national ideology of states like Vietnam, the Philippines, Malaysia, and China itself are steeped in postcolonial resentment and the narrative of liberation from foreign bullying. When all the actors involved have such emotional and strategic incentives to stand firm, the mix becomes very volatile—perhaps volatile enough that fishing and energy

Figure 4.1. South China Sea Territorial Claims

The map outlines the identical claim of the People's Republic of China and the Republic of China (Taiwan) and the claims of the four other nations in the dispute.

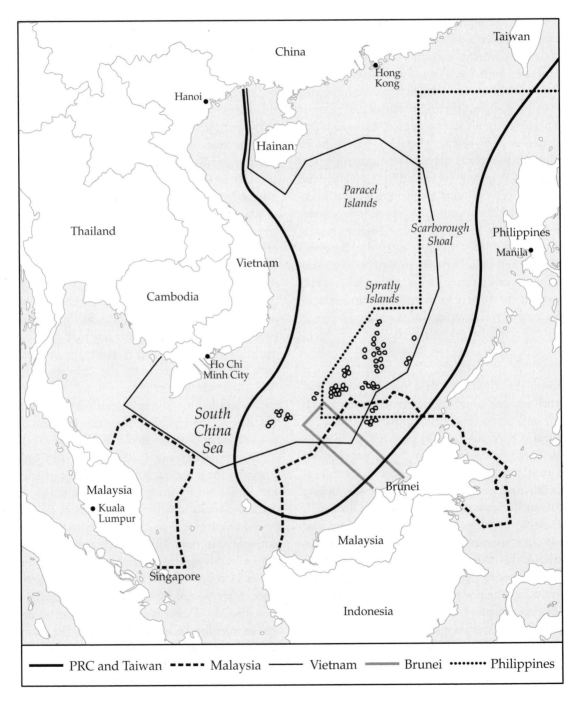

Source: http://www.southchinasea.org/files/2014/09/China-claims-a-big-backyard.png.

Editor: David Rosenberg

Figure 4.2. East China Sea Territorial Claims

The map outlines the overlapping claims of China and Japan in the East China Sea, and the known oil and gas fields in and around those overlapping claims.

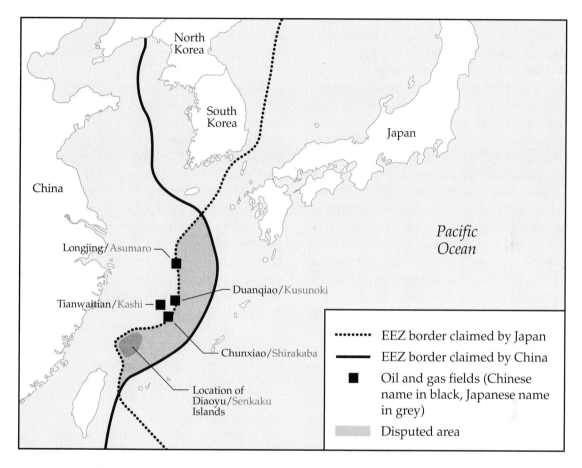

Source: "East China Sea," U.S. Energy Information Administration (EIA), September 25, 2012, http://www.eia.gov/countries/regions-topics .cfm?fips=ECS.

disputes over uninhabited rocks in the East and South China Seas can escalate to shooting wars.

In China, continued Party rule is the top security goal. If there is any doubt about this, please note that the People's Liberation Army is dedicated not to China as a nation but to the Chinese Communist Party. This has always been the case since the days of the revolution, and if the rhetoric of Xi Jinping and the recently selected leadership of the Party is any indication, it is not going to change anytime soon. One major problem for the Party in recent years has been the increase in "mass social incidents" (protests and riots) and the suggestion that Chinese society is increasingly unstable. Before the government stopped publicly discussing the number of such incidents in the middle of the past decade, it was already reporting as many as 87,000 per year.[20] Extrapolating from those trends, some analysts estimate that there are more than 100,000 of these every year in China today; one Chinese academic study in 2010 put the number as high as 180,000.[21] There is little doubt from my many recent trips to China that the public and the government alike are concerned about the long-term stability of China in a way that they have not been since the years immediately following the Tiananmen protests and massacre of 1989. Citizens seem frustrated by official corruption, eminent domain problems related to the fast-paced growth of cities and infrastructure, environmental degradation, and the unbalanced distribution of wealth. Adding to the unease of Chinese elites are uncertainties about the sources of future Chinese economic growth, particularly since the financial crisis called into question the reliability of markets abroad. There is, therefore, a growing consensus that China needs to restructure its economy to become less dependent on trade and investment and to increase the role of domestic consumption, but there is no consensus on how to achieve this transformation or at what pace.[22] All of these changes can create new controversies and dashed expectations, thus sparking new challenges to social and political stability.

Since jettisoning Maoist Communist ideology in the reform period, the nominally Communist CCP has legitimized itself through fast-paced economic growth and by nationalism. It portrays itself as an increasingly capable protector of Chinese interests and national honor. The ways that the, CCP has managed domestic dissent in China renders nationalist issues such as Taiwan or other sovereignty disputes particularly delicate. The central government in China has successfully ridden the waves of popular discontent by keeping protests local and small and keeping the protestors out of the Party. The higher authorities have often been able to paint themselves as the solution to local problems by coming in to quell protests, making arrests when necessary, firing and replacing local officials, and paying off some of the aggrieved citizens. Still, the increasing frequency of the protests is alarming to Chinese officials.

One reason potential nationalist humiliation is so worrisome to the central government is that people angry at the state for other reasons can take the opportunity of such a humiliation, to criticize government policies using politically correct slogans fostered for decades by the government's own "patriotic education" campaigns. Take, for example, the urban protests that arose across China over a nationalist issue: Japan's central government had purchased the disputed Senkaku Islands from a private Japanese family in 2012. One angry Chinese man held a placard that read: "Oppose Japan, Oppose America, Oppose Price Inflation!" (*Fan Ri, Fan Mei, Fan Zhangjia!*) In so doing, he was linking a serious domestic concern with protests over international humiliation. Even when the topics of protests appear to remain international in nature, they can have dangerous domestic repercussions for the Chinese economy and political stability. So protestors targeting "Little Japan" (*Xiao Riben*) often call on their Chinese compatriots to boycott Japanese products (*Dizhi Rihuo!*). But a boycott, if enacted, would severely harm China's own economy. Many products in China bearing Japanese brands are made in-country by Chinese workers in Japanese-invested factories. Many other domestic and international firms operating in China depend on Japanese parts in their transnational production chains. Chinese officials are well aware of the irony. Anti-Japanese protestors in China often carry portraits of Chairman Mao, indirectly criticizing contemporary leaders for their lack of fortitude on the international stage in comparison to Mao.

Popular calls for national action have grown all the more dangerous for the central government as individuals and disgruntled groups around the nation can increasingly communicate through social media. Furthermore, as with most governments and militaries, there is plenty of sincere nationalism within the CCP regime. Protestors in the future then might find sympathetic ears inside the state security mechanism. Moreover, military or civilian elites who are unhappy with their colleagues' lack of fortitude on international issues could stir up popular protest through expanding media channels to pressure more moderate leaders to change policy or, at the extreme, to help drive them from office. In fact, frustration with insufficiently robust resistance to the United States, Japan, and Vietnam, for example, has already been expressed in the mainstream press in China, sometimes by active duty or recently retired military officers. (More broadly, that press, although more open than in earlier decades, is still ultimately controlled by the state.) For these reasons, nationalist humiliation, particularly as it pertains to issues such as Japan or Taiwan independence, is the third rail of Chinese Communist politics.

Of course, China has no regional monopoly on nationalism or domestic political concerns related to foreign policy. Strong strands of postcolonial nationalism run through Filipino, Vietnamese, and Malaysian politics. And citizens in these countries are no less certain than those Chinese protestors that their countries are the rightful owners of disputed islands. Japanese prime ministers have sat atop extremely shaky coalition governments for the past ten years while the Japanese public believes that the Senkaku Islands are rightfully Japanese and that China only became interested in the islands after natural resources were discovered in the seabed around them in the late 1960s. While only a few Japanese rightists seem eager for a fight over the islands, no Japanese leader wants to appear ineffective or weak in the face of Chinese pressure. If all sides are willing to run high risks to avoid humiliation and defend national honor, then coercive diplomatic crises become very dangerous games indeed.

The United States finds itself in the unenviable position of having alliances or security relationships with three of the actors with which China has territorial disputes (Japan, the Philippines, and Taiwan) but no position on any of the sovereignty disputes themselves. In the case of Taiwan, the U.S. legal position on its sovereignty has been "undetermined" since the U.S. decision to enter the Korean War on June 27, 1950. The consistent U.S. government demand since the 1970s has been that the two sides of the Strait should work out their differences peacefully and that each side of the Strait should avoid actions that unilaterally change the status quo in cross-Strait relations without the acquiescence of the other. In general this means that the United States opposes mainland China's use of force or the threat of force to compel Taiwan into unification against the will of the Taiwan people, and it opposes actions by Taiwan that move the island in the direction of permanent legal independence from the broader Chinese nation without the consent of Beijing. In the case of the largely uninhabited islands, rocks, and reefs in the South China Sea (Paracels and Spratlys) disputed by China, Taiwan, the Philippines, Vietnam, Malaysia, and Brunei as well as the case of the uninhabited rocks in the East China Sea disputed by Japan and China (Diaoyu in Chinese and Senkaku in Japanese), the United States takes no position on the sovereignty of the islands, even those claimed by U.S. allies. This is part of a global maritime legal policy in which the United States takes no position on disputed islands but simply insists that disputes be settled peacefully and in accordance with prevailing international law so as not to disturb freedom of navigation. The only Partial exception is the Senkakus. In 1971, the United States transferred control of the islands to postwar Japan as part of the reversion of Okinawa. The Americans did this despite the protests of mainland China and Taiwan. The United States never recognized Japan's sovereignty over the Senkaku islands, however, just its administrative control. But it is notable that the United States claims that the islands fall under the purview of Article V of the U.S.–Japan Security Treaty in a way that the United States has never asserted for any of the Filipino claims in the South China Sea.

While Washington enjoys military superiority over China, it is increasingly the case that China enjoys military superiority over most, if not all, of the United States' regional friends and allies. It may be this factor, above all others, that proves China's rise is real. So when, exactly, would the United States choose to intervene in support of its friends and allies? The question is complicated by Washington's status as a nonclaimant on the sovereignty issues. For its part, China has somewhat cleverly, if at times clumsily, deployed maritime security forces and civilian ships instead of PLA Navy assets to assert and protect China's claims. This puts the onus of escalation on the other disputant and places Washington in the extremely uncomfortable position of urging restraint on its ally while trying to dissuade China from continued provocations and manipulation of risk. The United States has its own reputational reasons not to appear indifferent or weak in the region, but it also has reputational and other strategic reasons not to allow its weaker allies to drag it into a conflict, especially a conflict over uninhabited rocks!

One can see how the real world of international security politics can diverge sharply from the predictions and concerns of the allegedly "realist" balance-of-power theories. One can also see why a China with inferior conventional and nuclear capabilities in comparison to the United States can still pose serious problems for the United States and its regional friends and allies. Unlike a brute-force struggle for regional or global supremacy, coercive diplomacy is a bargaining process. As Thomas Schelling argued during the Cold War, for coercive diplomacy to work, the target of one's efforts must not only understand the credibility of one's own threat of intervention and punishment but must also be credibly reassured that if it forgoes aggression or some other transgression it will not be punished anyway. Otherwise, it has no incentive to comply with the demands being leveled. So in the context of U.S.–China relations, the United States needs to credibly threaten to defend its own interests and the interests of its allies without at the same time suggesting to Beijing that Washington is preparing the means with which to harm China's security interests regardless of Beijing's behavior. This is no easy task, particularly given the ambiguous nature of the maritime sovereignty disputes. Any U.S. military units capable of intervening in the region could, from a Chinese perspective, also be used to promote revisionist goals at the expense of China. Along the same lines, it is a challenge for China to develop coercive capabilities designed to protect what it sees as legitimate interests without, in the process, appearing to those actors to be threatening, aggressive, and destabilizing.

The combination of ambiguous and contested political claims, geography, and military technology make managing East Asia while China rises a complex task, particularly since there are more than two actors involved. In the Taiwan context, for example, any combination of U.S., Taiwanese, or Japanese military power that could be used to deter China from forcing Taiwan into unification with the mainland against its will might also be used for the purpose of protecting Taiwan's moves toward permanent legal independence from mainland China. Similarly, any combination of PRC coercive capabilities designed to deter Taiwan's unilateral declaration of formal independence from the mainland could also be used to compel unification with the mainland against Taiwan's will. The fact that both Taiwan and the mainland can adopt political initiatives deemed provocative by the other side only makes the headaches in Washington all the greater. The same applies to Japan and the Philippines, formal U.S. allies with whom China has maritime disputes.

The United States needs to balance its deterrence of mainland aggression against the need to reassure China that Washington does not seek to promote provocative policies by its allies nor change its own neutrality policy. The challenges in this may become even more difficult as China's own rise exacerbates tensions with the United States and its neighbors and, along with the discovery of energy resources in the seabeds around the islands, accelerates other claimants' timetables for pursuing and consolidating their claims.

Global Governance: The Biggest Challenge of All

Deterring Chinese aggression toward its neighbors and the United States will be increasingly challenging, but there are many reasons to be hopeful. China has major incentives to avoid unnecessary conflict, and after decades of a global Cold War, the United States government is highly experienced in the practice of coercive diplomacy. But no government has experience tackling the least appreciated challenge: persuading a uniquely large developing country with enormous domestic challenges and a historical chip on its national shoulder to cooperate actively with the international community. For the many reasons already offered, China has an interest in the stability of the current international system, but that does not easily translate into China helping to pay the costs to maintain that system.

Two stark facts underpin this challenge. First, China is by far the most influential developing country in world history. Second, globalization has made the world so interconnected that the behavior of every great power has become very consequential. As a result, China is being asked to do more at present than any developing country has in the past. Moreover, the intensity and diversity of those requests are only going to increase with the continuing rise of China and the deepening of globalization. If China actively tries to block efforts at improved global governance, many international problems will be extremely difficult to solve. But

even if China simply tries to lie low and ride free on the efforts of others, we will have great difficulty managing some of the globe's biggest security, economic, environmental and humanitarian problems.

There are a number of reasons why it will be so difficult to convince China to assert itself in the role of responsible stakeholder described by then–Deputy Secretary Robert Zoellick in his thoughtful and influential September 2005 speech. Zoellick correctly argued that China had benefited greatly from the security and prosperity created by a stable, rule-based international economic and political order.[23] But China had contributed a disproportionally small amount to maintain that order. Zoellick recognized that one of the great challenges facing diplomats in the United States, Europe, and Japan was to persuade China to do more to contribute to the global commons. So far the record of this effort is at best mixed, and there are real reasons to be concerned that the other great powers will continue to have a difficult time encouraging China to do more.

The goal here is analysis, not moral judgment. China's postcolonial nationalism often leads Chinese commentators to level over-the-top accusations against the United States and other great powers, suggesting that their entreaties to cooperation have some nefarious intent. But Chinese analysts and officials also make more thoughtful, logical, and compelling arguments for why China should be treated differently than advanced industrial nations. Compared to all other great powers and medium powers, China's per capita GDP is quite small and its social and political challenges incomparably larger than any other great power. China's per capita GDP in 2013 was the same as Ecuador's. Nobody is expecting Ecuadorians to contribute greatly to global governance—not so for the Chinese. While China has the largest holdings of foreign reserves in the world and has run a current account surplus with the developed world for decades, it also has a nascent and underdeveloped social security system at home and more than 100 million people still living in abject poverty. So when, for instance, it is asked to use its foreign exchange reserves on a large scale abroad to prop up economies in Europe, many in China wonder about the social justice in such a proposal. Why should a developing country with the frailest of safety nets bail out rich social democracies with per capita GDPs several times China's simply because those states are now realizing the results of many years of profligate government spending?

China, the world's largest emitter of greenhouse gases, also needs to burn carbon to continue to grow. Developed countries dispersed massive amounts of CO_2 into the atmosphere as they industrialized and have only in the past two or three decades turned their attention to the negative results of that behavior. But the world's most advanced economies have also become much more service-oriented, so the realization comes at a relatively convenient time in their economic histories. Chinese leaders and scholars also correctly point out that those same advanced countries benefit from consuming the cheap products manufactured in China's coastal greenhouse gas belt, often by firms owned in the countries complaining most loudly about Beijing's emissions.

China is a major importer of natural resources and has energy firms that are entering the global marketplace relatively late in the game. Chinese officials and commentators argue that China cannot be so finicky as to turn down oil and gas partnerships with regimes considered unsavory in Washington, Tokyo, and European capitals simply because those partnerships might serve to undercut global humanitarian or non-proliferation efforts. So China does lots of business with perpetrators of mass killings in Sudan, supporters of terrorism and violators of the Nuclear Nonproliferation Treaty in Iran, and other questionable suppliers. Chinese leaders can also point to the long history of close relations between unsavory oil-producing regimes and the United States, Great Britain, and France. With its own authoritarian rule, its recent history of the use of military force against civilians, and its own recent experience with international sanctions and condemnation, Beijing is also predictably less comfortable than the capitals of the advanced liberal democracies with condemning, sanctioning, and intervening in authoritarian regimes in the developing world.

Fortunately, there are solid responses to these Chinese arguments, some of which are accepted by segments of China's elite. All are based in long-term thinking and a recognition that China has benefited and continues to benefit greatly from the economic stability and security of the current international system. Nuclear proliferation, terrorists finding safe haven in poorly governed states, financial instability in its export markets, and potentially catastrophic changes in the global climate would all affect China at least as much as they do any of the advanced democracies. But such a holistic, over-the-horizon approach to current issues is difficult to market in any country, democratic or authoritarian. It is a particularly hard sell in a country like China with very pressing near-term challenges. * * *

Diplomats from the United States and its allies have enjoyed limited success in convincing China to make near-term sacrifices. Such entreaties might appear to be a trap designed to undercut China's overall national power. * * *

* * * [M]any Chinese commentators view Zoellick's challenge to China as a ruse to get China to foot the bill for something that will benefit the United States and other countries much more than China. Rather than accepting Zoellick's arguments that global governance is a shared mission of all the great powers, they wonder why China should "help" the United States with its problems. After all, Washington continues to sell weapons to Taiwan and support Japanese military enhancements. Since

Chinese elites are worried about regime stability and personal promotion within the CCP, they are likely more concerned about the domestic political need for near-term job creation at home than the future effects of long-term global warming. * * *

The reality, however, is that those countries have little choice but to foster Chinese activism. China's sheer size and its deep connections to the global economy as both a producer and an importer mean that the world cannot afford to give China a pass. China is the world's largest trader of manufactured goods, one of the world's largest importers of natural resources, the world's largest emitter of greenhouse gases, a close diplomatic and economic partner of several of the world's worst proliferators and failed states, and the holder of the largest reserves of foreign currency. When the other great powers seek cooperation from China on international security and humanitarian, economic, and environmental problems, China can undercut the efforts without even intentionally doing so. It is in this sense that China is too big to fail to pull its weight on global governance.

■   ■   ■

The Post-9/11 World, 2001–2008

When the George W. Bush administration took office in January 2001, it inherited the bilateral U.S.–PRC tension from the Clinton era. The legacies of the Kosovo War and the early 2000 election of a pro-independence president, Chen Shui-bian, in Taiwan complicated the bilateral relationship. Moreover, the Bush campaign had labeled China a "strategic competitor" and implied Clinton and Gore had been too soft toward Beijing. Just as Clinton had done eight years before, the Bush administration entered office emphasizing confrontation, not partnership with China.

A Very Rocky Ride in 2001

One month before the 2000 presidential elections, future Deputy Secretary of State Richard Armitage issued a report on behalf of a bipartisan group calling for a strengthened U.S.–Japan alliance and a more assertive Japanese role within that alliance. The so-called Armitage Report urged Japan to shed some of the historical and legal constraints on collective self-defense and on Japan's ability to project power abroad. Japan should become an ally more akin to Great Britain, the authors believed. The new Bush team also wanted to improve Taiwan's defensive capabilities and streamline arms sales decisions. Chinese analysts predictably distrusted the new administration's defense orientation.

Less than three months into the Bush presidency, the U.S.–China relationship fell into crisis. On April 1, 2001, a Chinese fighter jet clipped a U.S. EP-3 surveillance aircraft in international airspace near China's coast. The Chinese pilot, who was killed in the collision, apparently miscalculated distances while buzzing the lumbering U.S. propeller plane as part of a common intercept. The severely damaged U.S. plane made a miraculous emergency landing on China's Hainan Island with no loss of life. The brave and physically powerful Navy pilot, a former Nebraska high school football linebacker, controlled the plane by applying his considerable leg strength to foot pedals unaided by hydraulics, guiding the plane to the Chinese tarmac and saving the lives of his approximately two dozen crewmembers. He also saved U.S.–China relations from the the specter of American deaths caused by the aggressive act of a Chinese pilot over international waters. While things could have been worse, they also could have been much better. Beijing handled the diplomacy of the crisis in a ham-fisted manner, initially blaming the United States for the collision and then holding the crew for ten days and the plane, packed with U.S. surveillance technology, for much longer. This approach ensured an extended period of distrust, especially between the military establishments of the two countries.[24]

The air crew was released following the procurement of a carefully worded nonapology by U.S. officials about recent occurrences that they "regretted." This allowed Chinese leaders to tell their public and Party brethren that the United States had apologized while allowing the Bush administration to tell its public and its allies the opposite. As long as neither side explicitly corrected the other, all would be fine. Such mutual nondenial is often the stuff of diplomatic compromise.

In the same month, the Bush administration created new tensions with Beijing by announcing its offer to Taiwan of a very large arms sale package (worth over $12 billion USD). President Bush also stated in a television interview that the United States would "do whatever it takes" to help Taiwan defend itself.[25] U.S.–PRC relations regressed to their worst level since the May 1999 U.S. bombing of the PRC's Belgrade Embassy.

■ ■ ■

Coercive Diplomacy: U.S. Alliances and Relations Across the Taiwan Strait

While relations improved after 9/11, distrust remained. Beijing still worried that the Bush administration would offer unconditional support to the independence-leaning government in Taiwan. When President Bush, in a speech at Tsinghua University during a February 2002 trip to China, mentioned the Taiwan Relations Act but not the three joint communiqués negotiated with Beijing as the basis of U.S. policy toward Taiwan, Chinese elites took note. Such an omission might

simply have been a mistake. But many in Beijing see nefarious plots in Washington's every utterance. For them it would be hard to accept the notion that Bush's truncated version of the American "one China" policy was simply a gaffe. Perhaps more controversial was the invitation of Taiwan Defense Minister Tang Yao-ming to Florida for a mid-March 2002 defense industry meeting attended by Deputy Secretary of Defense Paul Wolfowitz and Assistant Secretary of State for East Asia James Kelly, among other top officials. Beijing branded this a violation of the 1979 U.S.–PRC normalization agreement (the second joint communiqué).[26]

Other regional developments affected Chinese perceptions. The September 11, 2001, attacks and the wars that followed would provide Japan with military opportunities to support U.S. forces far from the island nation, including noncombat roles in Iraq and in the Indian Ocean near Afghanistan. Under Prime Minister Junichiro Koizumi, Japan also expressed frank concerns about China's regional defense buildup. Newspaper articles in China singled out the United States and Japan for opportunistically exploiting September 11 to bolster their military presence around China. The underlying themes of many Chinese articles in 2002 were that Tokyo had planned to break out of the constraints of its peacetime constitution and the United States had planned to increase its military presence in Central and Southeast Asia even before September 11. The terrorist attacks on New York City and Washington simply provided a pretext for Japan and the United States to implement those plans, the authors argued. One major focus of this criticism was Japan's decision to send Maritime Self Defense Force ships to the Indian Ocean in logistical support of the U.S.-led effort there.[27]

Increased Japanese military activities would have caused concerns in China under any Japanese leadership. But conservative and nationalist trends in Japanese politics seemed to be confirming some elements of the overblown conspiracy theories in China about Japan's long-term strategic intentions. Perhaps most galling to China were yearly visits by Prime Minister Koizumi to the Yasukuni Shrine, a Shinto memorial paying homage to Japan's historical war dead, including fourteen Class-A war criminals from World War II. A museum next to the shrine offers a cartoonish history in which Japan was driven into war by a scheming United States. According to the museum, Roosevelt allegedly provoked the otherwise avoidable war to kickstart the U.S. economy and create jobs as a way out of the Great Depression. Japan, the story goes, was only trying to assist its brethren in mainland Asia in warding off threats from Europeans and Americans, a version of history that is deeply offensive to the many victims of Japanese aggression in the region, not just in China. Koizumi's trips to the shrine soured Japan's relations with China (and with South Korea) and precluded high-level summits and bilateral confidence-building measures between Beijing and Tokyo.

The bilateral Sino-Japanese relationship would be further strained by unruly anti-Japanese nationalism in Chinese society. In August 2004 soccer riots broke out in the wake of the Japanese victory over China in the Asian Cup Soccer Final in Beijing. I attended the match with friends after scalping tickets from a Beijing street merchant who, with a signature sleeveless T-shirt rolled up at the belly, looked somewhat more authentic and less likely than his competitors to sell us some of the many counterfeit ones circulating at the time. Our instincts having been proven correct, we entered the stadium to the sight of official signage above the field hailing regional harmony and peace. But the massive Chinese crowd soon struck up loud and truly obscene chants about the Japanese team, revealing another emotion altogether. The government had ordered security personnel positioned around the stadium. They wore full battle gear in stifling August humidity, making it clear that the government lacked confidence that the

propaganda message it had created for the games had taken root in the Chinese crowd. They were right to be worried. When Japan won on a controversial goal and vandalism started outside the stadium after the game, security forces were already in place to limit the scope of the disturbance. Unfortunately for China–Japan relations, this was hardly an isolated event. When Japan pursued membership in the UN Security Council in early 2005, millions of Chinese signed an online anti-Japanese petition against the proposal, street protests filled with invective, and vandalism followed in Shanghai and other Chinese cities.[28]

TAIWAN REASSURANCE

The strengthening of the U.S. military alliance system in Asia under George W. Bush and the demonstration of U.S. resolve to use force on the battlefield helped bolster U.S. deterrence of any PRC military aggression against Taiwan or its other neighbors. But, as discussed [earlier], resolve, or the "credibility of threat," is only one part of successful coercive diplomacy. Measures that bolster the credibility of threat can unintentionally undercut coercive diplomacy if they seem provocative and are not accompanied by assurances that the key interests of the target will not be harmed if the target forgoes the use of force. In a period in which Taiwan's leadership was making fairly frequent verbal assertions of Taiwan's independent sovereignty and promoting a series of policy measures to weaken historical links between itself and the mainland, Beijing could have concluded that a demonstration of force was necessary to avoid further erosion of its long-term position in cross-Strait relations, regardless of the degree of U.S. resolve to resist such a move. In his first few years in office, President Chen made several statements that touched upon Taiwan's sovereignty. And, along the same lines, he pushed policy agendas such as public referendums on aspects of cross-Strait relations that suggested he might seek populist means to break out of Taiwan's constitutional constraints on permanent separation from mainland China.

Chen's initiatives and statements often caught the Bush administration by surprise and seemed to violate Chen's private promises to Washington to avoid provoking Beijing in his first term. Strangely, however, Chen's potentially destabilizing antics proved an asset for Washington in its dealings with Beijing. After all, if Washington (and Tokyo) were looking for a chance to wrest Taiwan away from the mainland forever, as many Chinese nationalists had long suspected and U.S. leaders had long denied, President Chen provided a clear opportunity to do so. But the Bush administration eschewed such an opportunity at every turn and, at times, actively opposed Chen's actions. This built a basic foundation of assurance in U.S.–China relations that bolstered U.S. coercive diplomacy significantly and established trust that was useful in other areas.

In April 2002 then–Vice President Hu Jintao would make an important trip to Washington as he prepared to ascend to the CCP's top spot later in the year. By all accounts, his meetings with his counterpart, Vice President Dick Cheney, went well, and the U.S. government was able to convey the message that it still supported Washington's traditional "one China" policy.

The Bush administration's message would be underscored dramatically in August 2002 during Deputy Secretary of State Armitage's trip to Beijing. Three weeks earlier, Chen Shui-bian had made a speech that asserted Taiwan's sovereignty. On August 3, Chen described relations across the Taiwan Strait as "one country on each side" (*yi bian yi guo*) and suggested that he would pursue a popular referendum to determine Taiwan's status. Chen's formulation went considerably further than Lee Teng-hui's characterization of relations across the Taiwan Strait as "special state-to-state relations" (*teshu de guo yu guo guanxi*). Because the Chinese term *guo* can be translated as either "state" or "nation/country," Lee's formulation could be interpreted as two governments negotiating on an equal basis inside one nation. But Chen's speech referred to China and Taiwan separately, suggesting that he viewed Taiwan as an independent country. If there were any remaining doubt, his government offered the official English translation of the speech with the word *guo* given as "country," not "state."[29] For our purposes, it is also notable that Chen's speech was made in a teleconference with Taiwan compatriots in Japan, a fact that linked Japan to Taiwan independence and, by association, Japan's treaty ally, the United States.

During his August 2002 Beijing visit, Deputy Secretary Armitage distanced himself from Chen's statements. When answering questions to the press about the speech, Armitage replied simply and firmly that the United States "does not support Taiwan independence." Also of importance, during his trip Armitage treated China as a partner in the War on Terror by publicly designating the East Turkestan Islamic Movement (ETIM) an international terrorist organization with links to al Qaeda. ETIM is a radical organization that seeks independence for the PRC's Xinjiang region. The designation suggested that the United States was not exploiting China's ethnic and geographic splits.[30]

At the Crawford Summit in October 2002, President Bush would have another chance to explain to President Jiang that his administration was not seeking to change the historical U.S. "one China" policy. Then, in the lead-up to the 2004 Taiwan presidential elections, President Bush made the clearest statement yet that Washington actively opposed Chen's unilateral moves in the direction of Taiwan independence. On the campaign trail in Taiwan in late 2003, President Chen had suggested that he would pursue "defensive referenda" on aspects of Taiwan's relationship with the mainland during the presidential election of March 2004. He also suggested the need for constitutional reform and made various verbal assertions of Taiwan's sovereign independence from mainland China. With the visiting PRC premier Wen Jiabao at his side in Washington in December 2003, President Bush asserted that he opposed actions by either side of the Taiwan Strait to unilaterally change the status quo, then criticized President Chen's recent actions and statements. Bush's statement was extremely well received in Beijing.[31]

President Chen won a second term in a much-disputed electoral process that included an apparent eleventh-hour assassination attempt on him and his vice president, Annette Lu. The result dismayed Beijing. The reelected President Chen would return to divisive rhetoric as he campaigned for his party's candidates in the legislative elections in December 2004. China's leadership responded by having the National People's Congress draft and eventually pass an antisecession law, which outlined conditions under which the mainland might use "nonpeaceful" means against Taiwan.[32]

Contributing to China's concerns about regional security in this period were trends in Japanese politics and in U.S.–Japan alliance relations. In Japan, Prime Minister Koizumi continued his yearly visits to the Yasukuni Shrine, aggravating nationalist sentiments in both China and South Korea. And the United States and Japan continued to strengthen the U.S.–Japan alliance pursuant to the 2000 Armitage Report. In February 2005, the leading diplomats and defense officials from both Japan and the United States issued their "2+2" report, which declared a mutual interest in peaceful and stable relations across the Taiwan Strait.[33] From an American perspective, it is only natural that Japan would be concerned about cross-Strait stability and that U.S. bases in Japan would be essential to military intervention if the president were to decide to launch such an effort. But in China any suggestion that Japan might be directly involved in a cross-Strait conflict is politically very sensitive given the bitter history of Japanese imperialism and Taiwan's central role at the beginning (1895) and end (1945) of that saga.

In a revealing 2005 article, an influential Shanghai-based scholar, Wu Xinbo, outlined China's concerns and hopes for the U.S.–Japan alliance. Rather than present the usual diatribe, the article notes that the U.S.–Japan alliance had in the past prevented a more assertive and independent Japanese security policy. Wu saw three key issues of concern: nationalist political trends in Japan under Koizumi; the perception in some quarters in Japan of China's rise as a threat; and Japan's apparent growing attention to and interest in Taiwan, as evidenced by the February 2005 2+2 statement. Wu claimed, however, that these negative reactions had been tempered in the past and could be tempered in the future by proactive diplomacy in Washington and Tokyo to distance those capitals from Chen Shui-bian's gambits on Taiwan and to encourage trilateral dialogue between the United States, Japan, and China.[34]

From 2005 to 2007 the United States and Japan would take actions consistent with the prescriptions in Wu's article. The Bush administration adopted policies that clearly ran counter to any containment strategy, and Washington engaged Beijing in high-level security dialogues at which Beijing was invited to take a larger role on the international stage. This approach took on doctrinal stature through Deputy Secretary Robert Zoellick's speech at the National Committee on U.S.–China Relations gala on September 21, 2005. Zoellick invited China to become a "responsible stakeholder" on the international stage and outlined the philosophy behind the U.S.–PRC Senior Dialogue on Security and Political Affairs (hereafter referred to as the "Strategic Dialogue," the name preferred by China and eventually adopted by the Obama administration). Cooperation and collaboration among China, the United States, and two U.S. allies, Japan and the ROK, during the Six Party Talks on Korean denuclearization would continue and intensify, especially following the North Korean nuclear test of late 2006. Beyond North Korea, Washington would continue to engage in productive bilateral discussions with Beijing about how the United States and the PRC could better coordinate the two countries' responses to challenges around the world.[35] The same spirit of U.S.–PRC cooperation and the same rejection of a zero-sum mentality in bilateral relations underpinned the late 2006 initiative to create the Strategic Economic Dialogue, headed by Treasury Secretary Henry Paulson, on improving economic conditions within and between the two nations.[36]

Perhaps the most important instances of confidence-building among the United States, Japan, and the PRC were Washington's and Tokyo's policies toward relations across the Taiwan Strait in the lead-up to the March 2008 Taiwan presidential election. President Chen's Democratic Progressive Party created a popular referendum to apply to the United Nations under the name Taiwan, rather than the Republic of China, the constitutional name of the government in Taipei. The referendum, which was held in conjunction with the presidential election, was partly a campaign strategy for the DPP. Passage of the referendum could not change Taiwan's status on the international stage and it certainly would not have led to Taiwan's admission to the United Nations. But the referendum's passage would have given Chen and his party a quasilegal foundation from which to launch further pro-independence policies. Beijing elites were particularly concerned that Chen might push for an extraconstitutional declaration of independence since he would have two months in office between the election and the inauguration of his successor, even if his party were to lose the election, to implement such a radical strategy.

After repeated efforts at private diplomacy failed to dissuade Chen and the DPP from pursuing the referendum, the Bush administration opposed it publicly. This campaign was carried out in a series of high-level statements in late summer 2007 by Deputy Secretary of State John Negroponte, Deputy National Security Advisor James Jeffrey, and the National Security Council Senior Director for East Asian Affairs Dennis Wilder.[37] In December, Secretary Condoleezza Rice again rejected the referendum as "provocative" in a press briefing.[38]

As part of this process, in my capacity as Deputy Assistant Secretary of State for East Asian and Pacific Affairs, I gave a lengthy speech on September 11, 2007, at a high-level U.S.–Taiwan defense conference. My gifted deputy Clifford Hart, the director of the Taiwan Coordination Office at State, contributed greatly to the drafting of the speech. We then had it cleared around Washington in what was a surprisingly smooth and speedy interagency process. The speech was not free of controversy because it criticized a fellow democracy for holding a specific referendum. But after a long series of statements and actions by President Chen that ran against U.S. policy interests, a broad consensus had formed in the Bush administration that something needed to be done to distance the United States from Chen in the eyes of the Taiwan public. In the speech, entitled "A Strong and Moderate Taiwan," I emphasized that while Taiwan's security required a strong military, it also required Taipei to avoid unnecessary, frivolous, and dangerous provocations of nationalism in the PRC. I stated:

> As long as Taiwan maintains a credible defensive capability, the chief threats to its welfare are political actions by Taipei itself that could trigger Beijing's use of force. The United States has repeatedly made clear that the use of force would be unacceptable, and we have repeatedly called on Beijing . . . to reduce its armed threat to Taiwan. But as much as we oppose Beijing's threat to use force, we also take it seriously, and Taipei cannot afford to do otherwise. . . . Responsible leadership in Taipei has to anticipate potential Chinese red lines and reactions and avoid unnecessary and unproductive provocations. . . . The United States has neither the power nor the right to tell the Taiwan people what they can and cannot do. As friends, however, we feel it is our obligation to warn that the content of this particular referendum is ill conceived and potentially quite harmful. Bad public policy initiatives are made no better for being wrapped in the flag of "democracy." . . . We

anticipate that Taiwan's perceptive, intelligent citizens will see through the rhetoric and make a sound judgment that the referendum does not serve their interests because it will be fundamentally harmful to Taiwan's external relations.[39]

The speech was widely covered and analyzed in Taiwan's public media. The intended audience had been reached.

■　■　■

The consistency of U.S. and Japanese support for the "one China" policy paid dividends. In fact, several weeks after conservative president Ma Ying-jeou's electoral victory in Taipei, President Hu made the first trip to Japan by a Chinese leader in more than ten years. In the days leading up to the trip, an influential Chinese scholar at the CCP Central Party School, Gong Li, pointed out that relations between the two sides were much improved thanks to Japan's rejection of Taiwan's UN referendum and Prime Minister Fukuda's trip to China.[40]

■　■　■

The China Challenge

■　■　■

A sophisticated and constructive strategy toward China combines two elements not normally associated with each other: a very strong U.S. military presence in East Asia with a consistent diplomatic posture that invites China to participate in regional and global governance. Without a reassuring diplomatic mission, many inside and outside China might see the strong U.S. military presence as containment—the dawn of a new cold war. With a strong presence in place, Washington should suggest peaceful channels through

which the United States and China can cooperate regionally and globally and thereby reduce bilateral tensions while still allowing for increasing Chinese power and prestige. Without the strong presence, however, many in China might view U.S. entreaties for cooperation and confidence-building as signs of U.S. weakness, and Beijing might be more tempted to settle its differences through coercion. The combined effect of a military and a diplomatic presence should be to show China that such a campaign of coercion would not only fail but also further the outcome that Chinese strategists fear most: the encirclement of China by countries aligned with a mobilized and adversarial United States.

For U.S. leaders, the regional security challenges and the global governance challenges created by China's rise are linked. Success in one area could breed success in the other. Serious failure in one, however, could also spoil the prospects of success in the other. One of the best ways to foster Sino-American mutual trust is to find areas for cooperation outside of East Asia, where mutual suspicions between Washington and Beijing should be lower than they are over sensitive territorial issues like Taiwan or the Senkaku Islands. If global governance issues are handled deftly, China may become more assertive internationally and more constructive at the same time. If China does improve its performance on global governance and the response from the United States is positive, strategic mistrust of a rising China in Washington and in East Asian capitals should decline, and at the same time, Chinese citizens hoping for a more prominent role in world affairs should be satisfied. Getting China's foreign policy to improve—to be assertive without being aggressive—may be the greatest challenge facing the next few generations of U.S. diplomats.

■　■　■

NOTES

1. World Bank, http://data.worldbank.org/indicator/NY.GNP .PCAP.CD.

2. GDP per capita (PPP) in 2012. CIA World Factbook, https://www .cia.gov/library/publications/the-world-factbook/geos/us.html.

3. Harry Harding, *China's Second Revolution: Reform After Mao* (Washington, DC: Brookings Institution, 1987).

4. Richard K. Betts and Thomas J. Christensen, "China: Getting the Questions Right," *The National Interest,* Winter 2000–2001.

5. Aaron L. Friedberg, *A Contest for Supremacy: China, America, and the Struggle for Mastery in Asia* (New York: Norton, 2011).

6. John J. Mearsheimer, "China's Unpeaceful Rise," *Current History,* April 2006.

7. Martin Jacques, *When China Rules the World: The End of the Western World and the Birth of a New Global Order* (New York: Penguin Books, 2009).

8. John Arquilla, *Dubious Battles: Aggression, Defeat, and the International System* (Washington, DC: Taylor & Francis, 1992).

9. For a review of Chinese coercive capabilities, including the DF-21D, see Department of Defense, *Annual Report to Congress on the Military Power of the People's Republic of China*, 2009, 2010, and 2011.

10. Ibid.

11. Lieutenant General Wang Houqing and Major General Zhang Xingye, chief eds., *Zhanyi Xue* [Military Campaign Studies] (Beijing: National Defense University Press, May 2000), military circulation only, 28. The authors, writing in 2000, state, "Our weaponry has improved greatly in comparison to the past, but in comparison to the militaries of the advanced countries *[fada guojia]*, there will still be a large gap not only now but long into the future. Therefore we not only must accelerate our development of advanced weapons, thus shrinking the gap to the fullest extent possible, but also [we must] use our current weapons to defeat enemies. . . . [We must] explore the art of the inferior defeating the superior under high-tech conditions." A more recent doctrinal work for China's rocket forces, the Second Artillery, that is classified in the Chinese system but is now available outside China similarly discussed China's modernizing nuclear arsenal and conventional rocket forces as a means to confront enemies with superior conventional and nuclear forces; see Yu Xijun, ed., *Di Er Pao Bing Zhanyi Xue* [The Science of Second Artillery Campaigns] (Beijing: PLA Press, 2004). This fascinating doctrinal volume has become available from Chinese-language booksellers outside the PRC and at libraries at George Washington University, Harvard University, Oxford University, and the U.S. Naval War College.

12. Thomas J. Christensen, "Posing Problems without Catching Up," *International Security* 25, no. 4 (Spring 2001), 5–40.

13. Andrew F. Krepinevich, *Why AirSea Battle?* (Washington, DC: CSBA, 2010), especially p. 24.

14. For a review of China's nuclear modernization, see Senior Colonel Yao Yunzhu, "China's Perspective on Nuclear Deterrence," *Air and Space Power Journal*, March 2010.

15. For the work that originally coined the term "stability-instability paradox," see Glenn Snyder, "The Balance of Power and the Balance of Terror," in *The Balance of Power,* ed. Paul Seabury (San Francisco: Chandler Publishers, 1965), 184–201.

16. See [Robert] Jervis, *The Meaning of the Nuclear Revolution,* [the *Prospect of Armageddon* (Ithaca, NY: Cornell University Press, 1989),] chapter 3; and Thomas Schelling, *Arms and Influence* (New Haven, CT: Yale University Press, 1967), 18–25.

17. Amos Tversky and Daniel Kahneman, "Prospect Theory: An Analysis of Decision under Risk," *Econometrica* 47, no. 2 (March 1979), 263–91. For interesting applications of the theory to international relations, see Rose McDermott, *Risk Taking in International Relations: Prospect Theory in Post-War American Foreign Policy* (Ann Arbor: University of Michigan Press, 1998); Barbara Farnham, ed., *Avoiding Losses/Taking Risks: Prospect Theory and International Conflict* (Ann Arbor: University of Michigan Press, 1994); and James W. Davis, *Threats and Promises: The Pursuit of International Influence* (Baltimore, MD: Johns Hopkins University Press, 2000), 32–35.

18. Jervis, *The Meaning of the Nuclear Revolution*, 168–73.

19. For a masterful overview of China's historical handling of its sovereignty disputes on land and at sea, see Taylor Fravel, *Strong Borders, Secure Nation: Cooperation and Conflict in China's Territorial Disputes* (Princeton, NJ: Princeton University Press, 2008). For analysis of China's most assertive recent reactions to Japanese and Filipino behavior in the South China Sea and East China Sea, see Taylor Fravel, "China's Island Strategy: 'Redefine the Status Quo,'" *The Diplomat*, November 1, 2012, http://thediplomat.com/china -power/chinas-island-strategy-redefine-the-status-quo/.

20. See Kevin O'Brien and Rachel E. Stern, "Introduction: Studying Contention in Contemporary China," in *Popular Protests in China,* ed. Kevin O'Brien (Cambridge, MA: Harvard University Press, 2008), 12.

21. Kathrin Hille, "China: Citizens United," *Financial Times,* July 29, 2013, citing the work of Professor Sun Liping of Tsinghua University.

22. For a good summation of the challenges facing the Xi Jinping government, see Bruce Dickson, "Revising Reform: China's New Leaders and the Challenges of Governance," *China: An International Journal* 10, no. 2 (August 2012), 34–51.

23. Robert B. Zoellick, "Whither China: From Membership to Responsibility?" Remarks to the National Committee of U.S–China Relations, New York City, September 21, 2005, http://2001-2009.state .gov/s/d/former/zoellick/rem/53682.htm.

24. The best coverage of the EP-3 crisis is by a major player in the events at the U.S. Embassy in Beijing, John Keefe, who was special assistant to Ambassador Joseph Prueher at the time. See his monograph, *Anatomy of the EP-3 Incident, April 2001* (Alexandria, VA: Center for Naval Analyses, 2001).

25. President Bush made this comment in a televised interview with Charlie Gibson of ABC News on April 25, 2001.

26. For official CCP reaction to the visit of ROC Minister of Defense Tang Yao-ming, see "China Summons U.S. Ambassador to Make Representations," Xinhua News Agency, March 16, 2002; and "U.S.–Taiwan Secret Talks on Arms-Sales: Analysis," *People's Daily* Online, March 18, 2002, FBIS CPP-2002-0118-000088.

27. For Chinese press reactions to U.S. basing in Central Asia, see, for example, Gao Qiufu, "U.S. Wishful Thinking on Its Military

Presence in Central Asia and Real Purpose," Beijing *Liaowang*, April 29, 2002, FBIS CPP-2002-0506-000066.

28. Robert Marquand, "Anti-Japan Protests Jar an Uneasy Asia: Demonstrations Spread from Beijing to Several Southern Cities Sunday," *Christian Science Monitor,* April 11, 2005, http://www .csmonitor.com/2005/0411/p01s04-woap.html. For a novel political analysis of the anti-Japanese protests in China, see Jessica Chen Weiss, *Powerful Patriots: Nationalist Protest in China's Foreign Relations* (New York: Oxford University Press, 2014).

29. "Chen Stresses Urgency for Referendum Legislation for Taiwan's Future," Taipei Central News Agency, August 3, 2002; and Taipei Office of the President, "Apparent Text of Chen Shui-bian's Speech on Taiwan's Future, Referendum" (in Chinese), August 3, 2002, FBIS CPP-2002-080-3000098. For the CCP's official reaction, see "Text of Taiwan Affairs Spokesman's Remarks on Chen's Call for Referendum," Xinhua News Agency (in Chinese), August 5, 2002, FBIS CPP-2002-0805-00002.

30. Alan D. Romberg, *Rein In at the Brink of the Precipice: American Policy toward Taiwan and U.S.–PRC Relations* (Washington, DC: Henry L. Stimson Center, 2003), 207–208.

31. For the very positive reaction in China to Bush's statement, see John Pomfret, "China Lauds Bush for Comments on Taiwan," *Washington Post,* December 11, 2003.

32. For coverage of the political tensions in the lead-up to the December 2004 legislative elections and the creation of the antisecession law, see Thomas J. Christensen, "Taiwan's Legislative Yuan Elections and Cross-Strait Relations: Reduced Tensions and Remaining Challenges," *China Leadership Monitor,* no. 13 (Winter 2005), http://media.hoover.org/documents/clm13_tc.pdf.

33. For an assessment of the U.S.–Japan joint statement, see Yuki Tatsumi, "U.S.–Japan Security Consultative Committee: An Assessment," *Pacific Forum* 10, http://www.csis.org.

34. Wu Xinbo, "The End of the Silver Lining: A Chinese View of the U.S.–Japan Alliance," *Washington Quarterly* 29, no. 1, 119–30.

35. For an overview of U.S.–China relations in this period, see Thomas J. Christensen, "Shaping the Choices of a Rising China: Some Recent Lessons for the Obama Administration," *Washington Quarterly* 32, no. 3 (July 2009), 89–104.

36. For the text of the speech, see "Whither China: From Membership to Responsibility?," Robert B. Zoellick, Deputy Secretary of State, remarks to the National Committee on U.S.–China Relations, September 21, 2005, New York City, http://www.ncuscr.org /articlesandspeeches/Zoellick.htm.

37. For expert coverage of the U.S.–PRC–Taiwan triangle in this period, see Alan Romberg, "Applying to the U.N. in the Name of Taiwan," *China Leadership Monitor,* no. 22 (Fall 2008), http:// media.hoover.org/documents/CLM22AR.pdf.

38. Thom Shanker and Helene Cooper, "Rice Has Sharp Words for Taiwan, as Gates Does for China," *New York Times,* December 22, 2007, http://www.nytimes.com/2007/12/22/world/asia/22diplo. html.

39. "A Strong and Moderate Taiwan," Thomas J. Christensen, Deputy Assistant Secretary of State for East Asian and Pacific Affairs, speech to the U.S.–Taiwan Business Council's Defense Industry Conference, Annapolis, Maryland, September 11, 2007, http://2001 -2009.state.gov/eap/rls/rm/2007/91979.htm.

40. Ma Hao-liang, "China–Japan Relations Will Usher in a Period of Relative Stability," *Ta Kung Pao,* Internet version, May 3, 2008, FBIS T08:50:47Z.

5 THE STATE

S tates are key actors in international relations, and how they act depends, in part, on domestic political considerations, as explained in Chapter 5 of *Essentials of International Relations*. In a widely cited article, Robert D. Putnam explains the entanglements between international and domestic factors during negotiations, using the metaphor and the language of the two-level game. Negotiators consider not only what the other state wants, but also what the domestic constituencies in each state will accept. This approach connects the disciplines of international relations and comparative politics.

The penetration of a state's domestic authority by other states challenges one of the basic rules of the system of states, that of state sovereignty. Political scientist Stephen D. Krasner discusses the principles of sovereignty, which have long been bent by hypocritical and flexible practices. In the contemporary world, Krasner says, pragmatic adaptation to the realities of failed states requires new options, including sharing the state's sovereignty with outside powers and de facto trusteeship in which the international community holds ultimate authority in the state.

Religion is posing a different kind of challenge to states. In one of the most widely discussed articles ever written about international relations, political scientist Samuel P. Huntington predicted in 1993 that the future international system would be characterized by a clash between Western and non-Western, particularly Islamic, civilizations. In Huntington's subsequent book, *The Clash of Civilizations and the Remaking of the World Order* (1996), he somewhat modified his earlier claim, acknowledging that conflicts within civilizations remained more common than conflicts between them. Despite criticism from many scholarly experts and political analysts, his thesis attracted huge attention, seemed relevant in an era of rising terrorist attacks, and appealed even to some non-Westerners, such as Chinese nationalists who agreed that a clash of civilizations was coming.

Susanne and Lloyd Rudolph point out that hatred between religiously defined groups might appear to be based on ancient ideas of the sacred, but in fact they are often sparked by modern social movements seeking political goals in response to mundane grievances. The Rudolphs show that in this case the grievances are directed at the Indian state's affirmative action policies favoring disadvantaged minorities.

Robert D. Putnam

DIPLOMACY AND DOMESTIC POLITICS
The Logic of Two-Level Games

Introduction: The Entanglements of Domestic and International Politics

Domestic politics and international relations are often somehow entangled, but our theories have not yet sorted out the puzzling tangle. It is fruitless to debate whether domestic politics really determine international relations, or the reverse. The answer to that question is clearly "Both, sometimes." The more interesting questions are "When?" and "How?" This article offers a theoretical approach to this issue, but I begin with a story that illustrates the puzzle.

One illuminating example of how diplomacy and domestic politics can become entangled culminated at the Bonn summit conference of 1978.[1] In the mid-1970s, a coordinated program of global reflation, led by the "locomotive" economies of the United States, Germany, and Japan, had been proposed to foster Western recovery from the first oil shock.[2] This proposal had received a powerful boost from the incoming Carter administration and was warmly supported by the weaker countries, as well as the Organization for Economic

Co-operation and Development (OECD) and many private economists, who argued that it would overcome international payments imbalances and speed growth all around. On the other hand, the Germans and the Japanese protested that prudent and successful economic managers should not be asked to bail out spendthrifts. Meanwhile, Jimmy Carter's ambitious National Energy Program remained deadlocked in Congress, while Helmut Schmidt led a chorus of complaints about the Americans' uncontrolled appetite for imported oil and their apparent unconcern about the falling dollar. All sides conceded that the world economy was in serious trouble, but it was not clear which was more to blame, tight-fisted German and Japanese fiscal policies or slack-jawed U.S. energy and monetary policies.

At the Bonn summit, however, a comprehensive package deal was approved, the clearest case yet of a summit that left all participants happier than when they arrived. Helmut Schmidt agreed to additional fiscal stimulus, amounting to 1 percent of GNP, Jimmy Carter committed himself to decontrol domestic oil prices by the end of 1980, and Takeo Fukuda pledged new efforts to reach a 7 percent growth rate. Secondary elements in the Bonn accord included French and British acquiescence in the Tokyo Round trade negotiations; Japanese undertakings to foster import growth and restrain exports; and a generic American promise to fight inflation. All in all, the Bonn summit produced a balanced agreement of unparalleled breadth and specificity.

From *International Organization* 42, no. 3 (Summer 1988), 427–60. Some of the author's notes have been omitted.

More remarkably, virtually all parts of the package were actually implemented.

Most observers at the time welcomed the policies agreed to at Bonn, although in retrospect there has been much debate about the economic wisdom of this package deal. However, my concern here is not whether the deal was wise economically, but how it became possible politically. My research suggests, first, that the key governments at Bonn adopted policies different from those that they would have pursued in the absence of international negotiations, but second, that agreement was possible only because a powerful minority within each government actually favored on domestic grounds the policy being demanded internationally.

Within Germany, a political process catalyzed by foreign pressures was surreptitiously orchestrated by expansionists inside the Schmidt government. Contrary to the public mythology, the Bonn deal was not forced on a reluctant or "altruistic" Germany. In fact, officials in the Chancellor's Office and the Economics Ministry, as well as in the Social Democratic party and the trade unions, had argued privately in early 1978 that further stimulus was domestically desirable, particularly in view of the approaching 1980 elections. However, they had little hope of overcoming the opposition of the Finance Ministry, the Free Democratic party (part of the government coalition), and the business and banking community, especially the leadership of the Bundesbank. Publicly, Helmut Schmidt posed as reluctant to the end. Only his closest advisors suspected the truth: that the chancellor "let himself be pushed" into a policy that he privately favored, but would have found costly and perhaps impossible to enact without the summit's package deal.

Analogously, in Japan a coalition of business interests, the Ministry of Trade and Industry (MITI), the Economic Planning Agency, and some expansion-minded politicians within the Liberal Democratic Party pushed for additional domestic stimulus, using U.S. pressure as one of their prime arguments against the stubborn resistance of the Ministry of Finance (MOF). Without internal divisions in Tokyo, it is unlikely that the foreign demands would have been met, but without the external pressure, it is even more unlikely that the expansionists could have overridden the powerful MOF. "Seventy percent foreign pressure, 30 percent internal politics," was the disgruntled judgment of one MOF insider. "Fifty-fifty," guessed an official from MITI.[3]

In the American case, too, internal politicking reinforced, and was reinforced by, the international pressure. During the summit preparations American negotiators occasionally invited their foreign counterparts to put more pressure on the Americans to reduce oil imports. Key economic officials within the administration favored a tougher energy policy, but they were opposed by the president's closest political aides, even after the summit. Moreover, congressional opponents continued to stymie oil price decontrol, as they had under both Nixon and Ford. Finally, in April 1979, the president decided on gradual administrative decontrol, bringing U.S. prices up to world levels by October 1981. His domestic advisors thus won a postponement of this politically costly move until after the 1980 presidential election, but in the end, virtually every one of the pledges made at Bonn was fulfilled. Both proponents and opponents of decontrol agree that the summit commitment was at the center of the administration's heated intramural debate during the winter of 1978–79 and instrumental in the final decision.[4]

In short, the Bonn accord represented genuine international policy coordination. Significant policy changes were pledged and implemented by the key participants. Moreover—although this counterfactual claim is necessarily harder to establish—those policy changes would very probably not have been pursued (certainly not the same scale and within the same time frame) in the absence of the international agreement. Within each country, one faction supported the policy shift being demanded of its country internationally, but that faction was initially outnumbered. Thus, international pressure was a necessary condition for these policy shifts. On the other hand, without domestic resonance, international forces would not have sufficed to produce the accord, no matter how balanced and intellectually persuasive the overall package. In the end, each leader believed that what he was doing was in his nation's interest— and probably in his own political interest, too, even though not all his aides agreed.[5] Yet without the summit accord he probably would not (or could not) have changed policies so easily. In that sense, the Bonn deal successfully meshed domestic and international pressures.

Neither a purely domestic nor a purely international analysis could account for this episode. Interpretations cast in terms either of domestic causes and international effects ("Second Image"[6]) or of international causes and domestic effects ("Second Image Reversed"[7]) would represent merely "partial equilibrium" analyses and would miss an important part of the story, namely, how the domestic politics of several countries became entangled via an international negotiation. The events of 1978 illustrate that we must aim instead for "general equilibrium" theories that account simultaneously for the interaction of domestic and international factors. This article suggests a conceptual framework for understanding how diplomacy and domestic politics interact.

Domestic-International Entanglements: The State of the Art

Much of the existing literature on relations between domestic and international affairs consists either of ad hoc lists of countless "domestic influences" on foreign policy or of generic

observations that national and international affairs are somehow "linked."[8]

■ ■ ■

We need to move beyond the mere observation that domestic factors influence international affairs and vice versa, and beyond simple catalogs of instances of such influence, to seek theories that integrate both spheres, accounting for the areas of entanglement between them.

Two-Level Games: A Metaphor for Domestic-International Interactions

Over two decades ago Richard E. Walton and Robert B. McKersie offered a "behavioral theory" of social negotiations that is strikingly applicable to international conflict and cooperation.[9] They pointed out, as all experienced negotiators know, that the unitary-actor assumption is often radically misleading. As Robert Strauss said of the Tokyo Round trade negotiations: "During my tenure as Special Trade Representative, I spent as much time negotiating with domestic constituents (both industry and labor) and members of the U.S. Congress as I did negotiating with our foreign trading partners."[10]

The politics of many international negotiations can usefully be conceived as a two-level game. At the national level, domestic groups pursue their interests by pressuring the government to adopt favorable policies, and politicians seek power by constructing coalitions among those groups. At the international level, national governments seek to maximize their own ability to satisfy domestic pressures, while minimizing the adverse consequences of foreign developments. Neither of the two games can be ignored by central decision-makers, so long as their countries remain interdependent, yet sovereign.

Each national political leader appears at both game boards. Across the international table sit his foreign counterparts, and at his elbows sit diplomats and other international advisors. Around the domestic table behind him sit party and parliamentary figures, spokespersons for domestic agencies, representatives of key interest groups, and the leader's own political advisors. The unusual complexity of this two-level game is that moves that are rational for a player at one board (such as raising energy prices, conceding territory, or limiting auto imports) may be impolitic for that same player at the other board. Nevertheless, there are powerful incentives for consistency between the two games. Players (and kibitzers) will tolerate some differences in rhetoric between the two games, but in the end either energy prices rise or they don't.

The political complexities for the players in this two-level game are staggering. Any key player at the international table who is dissatisfied with the outcome may upset the game board, and conversely, any leader who fails to satisfy his fellow players at the domestic table risks being evicted from his seat. On occasion, however, clever players will spot a move on one board that will trigger realignments on other boards, enabling them to achieve otherwise unattainable objectives. This "two-table" metaphor captures the dynamics of the 1978 negotiations better than any model based on unitary national actors.

* * * Probably the most interesting empirically based theorizing about the connection between domestic and international bargaining is that of Glenn Snyder and Paul Diesing. Though working in the neo-realist tradition with its conventional assumption of unitary actors, they found that, in fully half of the crises they studied, top decision-makers were *not* unified. They concluded that prediction of international outcomes is significantly improved by understanding internal bargaining, especially with respect to minimally acceptable compromises.[11]

Metaphors are not theories, but I am comforted by Max Black's observation that "perhaps every science must start with metaphor and end with algebra; and perhaps without the metaphor there would never have been any algebra."[12] Formal analysis of any game requires well-defined rules, choices, payoffs, players, and information, and even then, many simple two-person, mixed-motive games have no determinate solution. Deriving analytic solutions for two-level games will be a difficult challenge. In what follows I hope to motivate further work on that problem.

Towards a Theory of Ratification: The Importance of "Win-Sets"

Consider the following stylized scenario that might apply to any two-level game. Negotiators representing two organizations meet to reach an agreement between them, subject to the constraint that any tentative agreement must be ratified by their respective organizations. The negotiators might be heads of government representing nations, for example, or labor and management representatives, or party leaders in a multiparty coalition, or a finance minister negotiating with an IMF team, or leaders of a House-Senate conference committee, or ethnic-group leaders in a consociational democracy. For the moment, we shall presume that each side is represented by a single leader or "chief negotiator," and that this individual has no independent policy preferences, but seeks simply to achieve an agreement that will be attractive to his constituents.[13]

It is convenient analytically to decompose the process into two stages:

1. bargaining between the negotiators, leading to a tentative agreement; call that Level I.
2. separate discussions within each group of constituents about whether to ratify the agreement; call that Level II.

This sequential decomposition into a negotiation phase and a ratification phase is useful for purposes of exposition, although it is not descriptively accurate. In practice, expectational effects will be quite important. There are likely to be prior consultations and bargaining at Level II to hammer out an initial position for the Level I negotiations. Conversely, the need for Level II ratification is certain to affect the Level I bargaining. In fact, expectations of rejection at Level II may abort negotiations at Level I without any formal action at Level II. For example, even though both the American and Iranian governments seem to have favored an arms-for-hostages deal, negotiations collapsed as soon as they became public and thus liable to de facto "ratification." In many negotiations, the two-level process may be iterative, as the negotiators try out possible agreements and probe their constituents' views. In more complicated cases, as we shall see later, the constituents' views may themselves evolve in the course of the negotiations. Nevertheless, the requirement that any Level I agreement must, in the end, be ratified at Level II imposes a crucial theoretical link between the two levels.

"Ratification" may entail a formal voting procedure at Level II, such as the constitutionally required two-thirds vote of the U.S. Senate for ratifying treaties, but I use the term generically to refer to any decision-process at Level II that is required to endorse or implement a Level I agreement, whether formally or informally. It is sometimes convenient to think of ratification as a parliamentary function, but that is not essential. The actors at Level II may represent bureaucratic agencies, interest groups, social classes, or even "public opinion." For example, if labor unions in a debtor country withhold necessary cooperation from an austerity program that the government has negotiated with the IMF, Level II ratification of the agreement may be said to have failed; ex ante expectations about that prospect will surely influence the Level I negotiations between the government and the IMF.

Domestic ratification of international agreements might seem peculiar to democracies. As the German Finance Minister recently observed, "The limit of expanded cooperation lies in the fact that we are democracies, and we need to secure electoral majorities at home."[14] However, ratification need not be "democratic" in any normal sense. For example, in 1930 the Meiji Constitution was interpreted as giving a special role to the Japanese military in the ratification of the London Naval Treaty;[15] and during the ratification of any agreement between Catholics and Protestants in Northern Ireland, presumably the IRA would throw its power onto the scales. We need only stipulate that, for purposes of counting "votes" in the ratification process, different forms of political power can be reduced to some common denominator.

The only formal constraint on the ratification process is that since the identical agreement must be ratified by both sides, a preliminary Level I agreement cannot be amended at Level II without reopening the Level I negotiations. In other words, final ratification must be simply "voted" up or down; any modification to the Level I agreement counts as a rejection, unless that modification is approved by all other parties to the agreement.[16] Congresswoman Lynn Martin captured the logic of ratification when explaining her support for the 1986 tax reform bill as it emerged from the conference committee: "As worried as I am about what this bill does, I am even more worried about the current code. The choice today is not between this bill and a perfect bill; the choice is between this bill and the death of tax reform."[17]

Given this set of arrangements, we may define the "win-set" for a given Level II constituency as the set of all possible Level I agreements that would "win"—that is, gain the necessary majority among the constituents—when simply voted up or down.[18] For two quite different reasons, the contours of the Level II win-sets are very important for understanding Level I agreements.

First, **larger win-sets make Level I agreement more likely**, *ceterls paribus*.[19] By definition, any successful agreement must fall within the Level II win-sets of each of the parties to the accord. Thus, agreement is possible only if those win-sets overlap, and the larger each win-set, the more likely they are to overlap. Conversely, the smaller the win-sets, the greater the risk that the negotiations will break down. For example, during the prolonged pre-war Anglo-Argentine negotiations over the Falklands/Malvinas, several tentative agreements were rejected in one capital or the other for domestic political reasons; when it became clear that the initial British and Argentine win-sets did not overlap at all, war became virtually inevitable.[20]

■　　■　　■

The second reason why win-set size is important is that **the relative size of the respective Level II win-sets will affect the distribution of the joint gains from the international bargain**. The larger the perceived win-set of a negotiator, the more he can be "pushed around" by the other Level I negotiators. Conversely, a small domestic win-set can be a bargaining advantage: "I'd like to accept your proposal, but I could never get it accepted at home." Lamenting the domestic constraints under which one must operate is (in the words of one experienced British diplomat) "the natural thing to say at the beginning of a tough negotiation."[21]

This general principle was, of course, first noted by Thomas Schelling nearly thirty years ago:

> The power of a negotiator often rests on a manifest inability to make concessions and meet demands. . . . When the United

States Government negotiates with other governments . . . if the executive branch negotiates under legislative authority, with its position constrained by law, . . . then the executive branch has a firm position that is visible to its negotiating partners. . . . [Of course, strategies such as this] run the risk of establishing an immovable position that goes beyond the ability of the other to concede, and thereby provoke the likelihood of stalemate or breakdown.[22]

Writing from a strategist's point of view, Schelling stressed ways in which win-sets may be manipulated, but even when the win-set itself is beyond the negotiator's control, he may exploit its leverage. A Third World leader whose domestic position is relatively weak (Argentina's Alfonsin?) should be able to drive a better bargain with his international creditors, other things being equal, than one whose domestic standing is more solid (Mexico's de la Madrid?).[23] The difficulties of winning congressional ratification are often exploited by American negotiators. During the negotiation of the Panama Canal Treaty, for example, "the Secretary of State warned the Panamanians several times . . . that the new treaty would have to be acceptable to at least sixty-seven senators," and "Carter, in a personal letter to Torrijos, warned that further concessions by the United States would seriously threaten chances for Senate ratification."[24] Precisely to forestall such tactics, opponents may demand that a negotiator ensure himself "negotiating room" at Level II before opening the Level I negotiations.

■　　■　　■

Determinants of the Win-Set

It is important to understand what circumstances affect win-set size. Three sets of factors are especially important:

- Level II preferences and coalitions
- Level II institutions
- Level I negotiators' strategies

Let us consider each in turn.

1. *The size of the win-set depends on the distribution of power, preferences, and possible coalitions among Level II constituents.*

Any testable two-level theory of international negotiation must be rooted in a theory of domestic politics, that is, a theory about the power and preferences of the major actors at Level II. This is not the occasion for even a cursory evaluation of the relevant alternatives, except to note that the two-level conceptual framework could in principle be married to such diverse perspectives as Marxism, interest group pluralism, bureaucratic politics, and neo-corporatism. For example, arms negotiations might be interpreted in terms of a bureaucratic politics model of Level II politicking, while class analysis or neo-corporatism might be appropriate for analyzing international macroeconomic coordination.

Abstracting from the details of Level II politics, however, it is possible to sketch certain principles that govern the size of the win-sets. For example, the lower the cost of "no-agreement" to constituents, the smaller the win-set.[25] Recall that ratification pits the proposed agreement, *not* against an array of other (possibly attractive) alternatives, but only against "no-agreement."[26] No-agreement often represents the status quo, although in some cases no-agreement may in fact lead to a worsening situation; that might be a reasonable description of the failed ratification of the Versailles Treaty.

Some constituents may face low costs from no-agreement, and others high costs, and the former will be more skeptical of Level I agreements than the latter. * * * The size of the win-set (and thus the negotiating room of the Level I negotiator) depends on the relative size of the "isolationist" forces (who oppose international cooperation in general) and the "internationalists" (who offer "all-purpose" support). All-purpose support for international agreements is probably greater in smaller, more dependent countries with more open economies, as compared to more self-sufficient countries, like the United States, for most of whose citizens the costs of no-agreement are generally lower. *Ceteris paribus*, more self-sufficient states with smaller win-sets should make fewer international agreements and drive harder bargains in those that they do make.

In some cases, evaluation of no-agreement may be the *only* significant disagreement among the Level II constituents, because their interests are relatively homogeneous. For example, if oil imports are to be limited by an agreement among the consuming nations—the sort of accord sought at the Tokyo summit of 1979, for example—then presumably every constituent would prefer to maximize his nation's share of the available supply, although some constituents may be more reluctant than others to push too hard, for fear of losing the agreement entirely. * * * Other international examples in which domestic interests are relatively homogeneous except for the evaluation or no-agreement might include the SALT talks, the Panama Canal Treaty negotiations, and the Arab-Israeli conflict. A negotiator is unlikely to face criticism at home that a proposed agreement reduces the opponents' arms too much, offers too little compensation for foreign concessions, or contains too few security guarantees for the other side, although in each case opinions may differ on how much to risk a negotiating deadlock in order to achieve these objectives.

The distinctive nature of such "homogeneous" issues is thrown into sharp relief by contrasting them to cases in which constituents' preferences are more heterogeneous, so that any Level I agreement bears unevenly on them. Thus, an internationally coordinated reflation may encounter domestic opposition *both* from those who think it goes too far (bankers, for example) *and* from those who think it does not go far enough (unions, for example). In 1919, some Americans opposed the Versailles Treaty because it was too harsh on the defeated powers and others because it was too lenient.[27] Such patterns are even more common, as we shall shortly see, where the negotiation involves multiple issues, such as an arms agreement that involves tradeoffs between seaborne and airborne weapons, or a labor agreement that involves tradeoffs between take-home pay and pensions. (Walton and McKersie term these "factional" conflicts, because the negotiator is caught between contending factions within his own organization.)

The problems facing Level I negotiators dealing with a *homogeneous* (or "boundary") conflict are quite different from those facing negotiators dealing with a *heterogeneous* (or "factional") conflict. In the former case, the more the negotiator can win at Level I—the higher his national oil allocation, the deeper the cuts in Soviet throwweight, the lower the rent he promises for the Canal, and so on—the better his odds of winning ratification. In such cases, the negotiator may use the implicit threat from his own hawks to maximize his gains (or minimize his losses) at Level I, as Carter and Vance did in dealing with the Panamanians. Glancing over his shoulder at Level II, the negotiator's main problem in a homogeneous conflict is to manage the discrepancy between his constituents' expectations and the negotiable outcome. Neither negotiator is likely to find much sympathy for the enemy's demands among his own constituents, nor much support for his constituents' positions in the enemy camp. The effect of domestic division, embodied in hard-line opposition from hawks, is to raise the risk of involuntary defection and thus to impede agreement at Level I. The common belief that domestic politics is inimical to international cooperation no doubt derives from such cases.

The task of a negotiator grappling instead with a heterogeneous conflict is more complicated, but potentially more interesting. Seeking to maximize the chances of ratification, he cannot follow a simple "the more, the better" rule of thumb; imposing more severe reparations on the Germans in 1919 would have gained some votes at Level II but lost others, as would hastening the decontrol of domestic oil prices in 1978. In some cases, these lines of cleavage within the Level II constituencies will cut across the Level I division, and the Level I negotiator may find silent allies at his opponent's domestic table. German labor unions might welcome foreign pressure on their own government to adopt a more expansive fiscal policy, and Italian bankers might welcome international demands for a more austere Italian monetary policy. Thus transnational alignments may emerge, tacit or explicit, in which domestic interests pressure their respective governments to adopt mutually supportive policies. This is, of course, my interpretation of the 1978 Bonn summit accord.

In such cases, domestic divisions may actually improve the prospects for international cooperation. * * *

Thus far we have implicitly assumed that all eligible constituents will participate in the ratification process. In fact, however, participation rates vary across groups and across issues, and this variation often has implications for the size of the win-set. For example, when the costs and/or benefits of a proposed agreement are relatively concentrated, it is reasonable to expect that those constituents whose interests are most affected will exert special influence on the ratification process.[28] One reason why Level II games are more important for trade negotiations than in monetary matters is that the "abstention rate" is higher on international monetary issues than on trade issues.[29]

The composition of the active Level II constituency (and hence the character of the win-set) also varies with the politicization of the issue.

Politicization often activates groups who are less worried about the costs of no-agreement, thus reducing the effective win-set. For example, politicization of the Panama Canal issue seems to have reduced the negotiating flexibility on both sides of the diplomatic table.[30] This is one reason why most professional diplomats emphasize the value of secrecy to successful negotiations. However, Woodrow Wilson's transcontinental tour in 1919 reflected the opposite calculation, namely, that by expanding the active constituency he could ensure ratification of the Versailles Treaty, although in the end this strategy proved fruitless.[31]

Another important restriction of our discussion thus far has been the assumption that the negotiations involve only one issue. Relaxing this assumption has powerful consequences for the play at both levels.[32] Various groups at Level II are likely to have quite different preferences on the several issues involved in a multi-issue negotiation. As a general rule, the group with the greatest interest in a specific issue is also likely to hold the most extreme position on that issue. In the Law of the Sea negotiations, for example, the Defense Department felt most strongly about sea-lanes, the Department of the Interior about sea-bed mining rights, and so on.[33] If each group is allowed to fix the Level I negotiating position for "its" issue, the resulting package is almost sure to be "non-negotiable" (that is, non-ratifiable in opposing capitals).[34]

Thus, the chief negotiator is faced with tradeoffs across different issues: how much to yield on mining rights in order to get sea-lane protection, how much to yield on citrus exports to get a better deal on beef, and so on. * * * The central point is simple: the possibility of package deals opens up a rich array of strategic alternatives for negotiators in a two-level game.

One kind of issue linkage is absolutely crucial to understanding how domestic and international politics can become entangled.[35] Suppose that a majority of constituents at Level II oppose a given policy (say, oil price decontrol), but that some members of that majority would be willing to switch their vote on that issue in return for more jobs (say, in export industries). If bargaining is limited to Level II, that tradeoff is not technically feasible, but if the chief negotiator can broker an international deal that delivers more jobs (say, via faster growth abroad), he can, in effect, overturn the initial outcome at the domestic table. Such a transnational issue linkage was a crucial element in the 1978 Bonn accord.

Note that this strategy works not by changing the preferences of any domestic constituents, but rather by creating a policy option (such as faster export growth) that was previously beyond domestic control. Hence, I refer to this type of issue linkage at Level I that alters the feasible outcomes at Level II as *synergistic linkage*. For example, "in the Tokyo Round . . . nations used negotiation to achieve internal reform in situations where constituency pressures would otherwise prevent action without the pressure (and tradeoff benefits) that an external partner could provide."[36] Economic interdependence multiplies the opportunities for altering domestic coalitions (and thus policy outcomes) by expanding the set of feasible alternatives in this way—in effect, creating political entanglements across national boundaries. Thus, we should expect synergistic linkage (which is, by definition, explicable only in terms of two-level analysis) to become more frequent as interdependence grows.

2. *The size of the win-set depends on the Level II political institutions.*

Ratification procedures clearly affect the size of the win-set. For example, if a two-thirds vote is required for ratification, the win-set will almost certainly be smaller than if only a simple majority is required. As one experienced observer has written: "Under the Constitution, thirty-four of the one hundred senators can block ratification of any treaty. This is an unhappy and unique feature of our democracy. Because of the effective veto power of a small group, many worthy agreements have been rejected, and many treaties are never considered for ratification."[37] As noted earlier, the U.S. separation of powers imposes a tighter constraint on the American win-set than is true in many other countries. This increases the bargaining power of American negotiators, but it also reduces the scope for international cooperation. It raises the odds for involuntary defection and makes potential partners warier about dealing with the Americans.

■   ■   ■

Not all significant ratification practices are formalized; for example, the Japanese propensity for seeking the broadest possible domestic consensus before acting constricts the Japanese win-set, as contrasted with majoritarian political cultures. Other domestic political practices, too, can affect the size of the win-set. Strong discipline within the governing party, for example, increases the win-set by widening the range of agreements for which the Level I negotiator can expect to receive backing. For example, in the 1986 House-Senate conference committee on tax reform, the final bill was closer to the Senate version, despite (or rather, *because of*) Congressman Rostenkowski's greater control of his delegation, which increased the House win-set. Conversely, a weakening of party discipline across the major Western nations would, *ceteris paribus*, reduce the scope for international cooperation.

The recent discussion of "state strength" and "state autonomy" is relevant here. The greater the autonomy of central decision-makers from their Level II constituents, the larger their win-set and thus the greater the likelihood of achieving international agreement. For example, central bank insulation from domestic political pressures in effect increases the win-set and thus the odds for international monetary cooperation; recent

proposals for an enhanced role for central bankers in international policy coordination rest on this point.[38] However, two-level analysis also implies that, *ceteris paribus*, the stronger a state is in terms of autonomy from domestic pressures, the weaker its relative bargaining position internationally. For example, diplomats representing an entrenched dictatorship are less able than representatives of a democracy to claim credibly that domestic pressures preclude some disadvantageous deal.[39] This is yet another facet of the disconcerting ambiguity of the notion of "state strength."

■   ■   ■

3.   *The size of the win-set depends on the strategies of the Level I negotiators.*

Each Level I negotiator has an unequivocal interest in maximizing the other side's win-set, but with respect to his own win-set, his motives are mixed. The larger his win-set, the more easily he can conclude an agreement, but also the weaker his bargaining position vis-à-vis the other negotiator. This fact often poses a tactical dilemma. For example, one effective way to demonstrate commitment to a given position in Level I bargaining is to rally support from one's constituents (for example, holding a strike vote, talking about a "missile gap," or denouncing "unfair trading practices" abroad). On the other hand, such tactics may have irreversible effects on constituents' attitudes, hampering subsequent ratification of a compromise agreement.[40] Conversely, preliminary consultations at home, aimed at "softening up" one's constituents in anticipation of a ratification struggle, can undercut a negotiator's ability to project an implacable image abroad.

Nevertheless, disregarding these dilemmas for the moment and assuming that a negotiator wishes to expand his win-set in order to encourage ratification of an agreement, he may exploit both conventional side-payments and generic "good will," The use of side-payments to attract marginal supporters is, of course, quite familiar in game theory, as well as in practical politics. For example, the Carter White House offered many inducements (such as public works projects) to help persuade wavering Senators to ratify the Panama Canal Treaty.[41] In a two-level game the side-payments may come from unrelated domestic sources, as in this case, or they may be received as part of the international negotiation.

The role of side-payments in international negotiations is well known. However, the two-level approach emphasizes that the value of an international side-payment should be calculated in terms of its marginal contribution to the likelihood of ratification, rather than in terms of its overall value to the recipient nation. What counts at Level II is not total national costs and benefits, but their *incidence, relative to existing coalitions and proto-coalitioins.* An across-the-board trade concession (or still worse, a concession on a product of interest to a committed free-trade congressman) is less effective than a concession (even one of lesser intrinsic value) that tips the balance with a swing voter. Conversely, trade retaliation should be targeted, neither at free-traders nor at confirmed protectionists, but at the uncommitted.

An experienced negotiator familiar with the respective domestic tables should be able to maximize the cost-effectiveness (to him and his constituents) of the concessions that he must make to ensure ratification abroad, as well as the cost-effectiveness of his own demands and threats, by targeting his initiatives with an eye to their Level II incidence, both at home and abroad. In this endeavor Level I negotiators are often in collusion, since each has an interest in helping the other to get the final deal ratified. In effect, they are moving jointly towards points of tangency between their respective political indifference curves. The empirical frequency of such targeting in trade negotiations and trade wars, as well as in other international negotiations, would be a crucial test of the relative merits of conventional unitary-actor analysis and the two-level approach proposed here.[42]

In addition to the use of specific side-payments, a chief negotiator whose political standing at home is high can more easily win ratification of his foreign initiatives. Although generic good will cannot guarantee ratification, as Woodrow Wilson discovered, it is useful in expanding the win-set and thus fostering Level I agreement, for it constitutes a kind of "all-purpose glue" for his supporting coalition. * * *

Note that each Level I negotiator has a strong interest in the popularity of his opposite number, since Party A's popularity increases the size of his win-set, and thus increases both the odds of success and the relative bargaining leverage of Party B. Thus, negotiators should normally be expected to try to reinforce one another's standing with their respective constituents.

Partly for this reason and partly because of media attention, participation on the world stage normally gives a head of government a special advantage vis-à-vis his or her domestic opposition. Thus, although international policy coordination is hampered by high transaction costs, heads of government may also reap what we might term "transaction benefits." Indeed, the recent evolution of Western summitry, which has placed greater emphasis on publicity than on substance, seems designed to appropriate these "transaction benefits" without actually seeking the sort of agreements that might entail transaction costs.[43]

Higher status negotiators are likely to dispose of more side-payments and more "good will" at home, and hence foreigners prefer to negotiate with a head of government than with a lower official. In purely distributive terms, a nation might have a bargaining advantage if its chief negotiator were a mere clerk. Diplomats are acting rationally, not merely symbolically, when they refuse to negotiate with a counterpart of inferior rank. America's negotiating partners have reason for concern whenever the American president is domestically weakened.

Uncertainty and Bargaining Tactics

Level I negotiators are often badly misinformed about Level II politics, particularly on the opposing side. In 1978, the Bonn negotiators were usually wrong in their assessments of domestic politics abroad; for example, most American officials did not appreciate the complex domestic game that Chancellor Schmidt was playing over the issue of German reflation. Similarly, Snyder and Diesing report that "decision makers in our cases only occasionally attempted such assessments, and when they tried they did pretty miserably. . . . Governments generally do not do well in analyzing each other's internal politics in crises [and, I would add, in normal times], and indeed it is inherently difficult."[44] Relaxing the assumption of perfect information to allow for uncertainty has many implications for our understanding of two-level games. Let me illustrate a few of these implications.

Uncertainty about the size of a win-set can be both a bargaining device and a stumbling block in two-level negotiation. In purely distributive Level I bargaining, negotiators have an incentive to understate their own win-sets. Since each negotiator is likely to know more about his own Level II than his opponent does, the claim has some plausibility. * * *

On the other hand, uncertainty about the opponent's win-set increases one's concern about the risk of involuntary defection. Deals can only be struck if each negotiator is convinced that the proposed deal lies within his opposite number's win-set and thus will be ratified. Uncertainty about party A's ratification lowers the expected value of the agreement to party B, and thus party B will demand more generous side-payments from party A than would be needed under conditions of certainty. In fact, party B has an incentive to feign doubt about party A's ability to deliver, precisely in order to extract a more generous offer.[45]

Thus, a utility-maximizing negotiator must seek to convince his opposite number that his own win-set is "kinky," that is, that the proposed deal is certain to be ratified, but that a deal slightly more favorable to the opponent is unlikely to be ratified. * * *

The analysis of two-level games offers many illustrations of Zartman's observation that all negotiation involves "the controlled exchange of partial information."[46]

Restructuring and Reverberation

Formally speaking, game-theoretic analysis requires that the structure of issues and payoffs be specified in advance. In reality, however, much of what happens in any bargaining situation involves attempts by the players to restructure the game and to alter one another's perceptions of the costs of no-agreement and the benefits of proposed agreements. Such tactics are more difficult in two-level games than in conventional negotiations, because it is harder to reach constituents on the other side with persuasive messages. Nevertheless, governments do seek to expand one another's win-sets. Much ambassadorial activity—wooing opinion leaders, establishing contact with opposition parties, offering foreign aid to a friendly, but unstable government, and so on—has precisely this function. When Japanese officials visit Capitol Hill, or British diplomats lobby Irish-American leaders, they are seeking to relax domestic constraints that might otherwise prevent the administration from cooperating with their governments.

■ ■ ■

In some instances, perhaps even unintentionally, international pressures "reverberate" within domestic politics, tipping the domestic balance and thus influencing the international negotiations. Exactly this kind of reverberation characterized the 1978 summit negotiations. Dieter Hiss, the German sherpa and one of those who believed that a stimulus program was in Germany's own interest, later wrote that summits change national policy

> only insofar as they mobilize and/or change public opinion and the attitude of political groups. . . . Often that is enough, if the balance of opinion is shifted, providing a bare majority for the previously stymied actions of a strong minority. . . . No country violates its own interests, but certainly the definition of its interests can change through a summit with its possible tradeoffs and give-and-take.[47]

From the point of view of orthodox social-choice theory, reverberation is problematic, for it implies a certain interconnectedness among the utility functions of independent actors, albeit across different levels of the game. Two rationales may be offered to explain reverberation among utility-maximizing egoists. First, in a complex, interdependent, but often unfriendly world, offending foreigners may be costly in the long run. "To get along, go along" may be a rational maxim. This rationale is likely to be more common the more dependent (or interdependent) a nation, and it is likely to be more persuasive to Level II actors who are more exposed internationally, such as multinational corporations and international banks.

A second rationale takes into account cognitive factors and uncertainty. It would be a mistake for political scientists to mimic most economists' disregard for the suasive element in negotiations.[48] Given the pervasive uncertainty that surrounds many international issues, messages from abroad can change minds, move the undecided, and hearten those in the domestic minority. * * * Suasive reverberation is more likely among countries with close relations and is probably more frequent in economic than in political–military

negotiations. Communiqués from the Western summits are often cited by participants to domestic audiences as a way of legitimizing their policies. After one such statement by Chancellor Schmidt, one of his aides privately characterized the argument as "not intellectually valid, but politically useful." Conversely, it is widely believed by summit participants that a declaration contrary to a government's current policy could be used profitably by its opponents. Recent congressional proposals to ensure greater domestic publicity for international commentary on national economic policies (including hitherto confidential IMF recommendations) turn on the idea that reverberation might increase international cooperation.[49]

Reverberation as discussed thus far implies that international pressure expands the domestic win-set and facilitates agreement. However, reverberation can also be negative, in the sense that foreign pressure may create a domestic backlash. Negative reverberation is probably less common empirically than positive reverberation, simply because foreigners are likely to forgo public pressure if it is recognized to be counterproductive. Cognitive balance theory suggests that international pressure is more likely to reverberate negatively if its source is generally viewed by domestic audiences as an adversary rather than an ally. Nevertheless, predicting the precise effect of foreign pressure is admittedly difficult, although empirically, reverberation seems to occur frequently in two-level games.

■ ■ ■

The Role of the Chief Negotiator

In the stylized model of two-level negotiations outlined here, the chief negotiator is the only formal link between Level I and Level II. Thus far, I have assumed that the chief negotiator has no independent policy views, but acts merely as an honest broker, or rather as an agent on behalf of his constituents. That assumption powerfully simplifies the analysis of two-level games. However, as principal-agent theory reminds us, this assumption is unrealistic.[50] Empirically, the preferences of the chief negotiator may well diverge from those of his constituents. Two-level negotiations are costly and risky for the chief negotiator, and they often interfere with his other priorities, so it is reasonable to ask what is in it for him.

The motives of the chief negotiator include:

1. Enhancing his standing in the Level II game by increasing his political resources or by minimizing potential losses. * * *
2. Shifting the balance of power at Level II in favor of domestic policies that he prefers for exogenous reasons. International negotiations sometimes enable government leaders to do what they privately wish to do, but are powerless to do domestically. * * *
3. To pursue his own conception of the national interest in the international context. * * *

It is reasonable to presume, at least in the international case of two-level bargaining, that the chief negotiator will normally give primacy to his domestic calculus, if a choice must be made, not least because his own incumbency often depends on his standing at Level II. Hence, he is more likely to present an international agreement for ratification, the less of his own political capital he expects to have to invest to win approval, and the greater the likely political returns from a ratified agreement.

This expanded conception of the role of the chief negotiator implies that he has, in effect, a veto over possible agreements. Even if a proposed deal lies within his Level II win-set, that deal is unlikely to be struck if he opposes it.[51] Since this proviso applies on both sides of the Level I table,

the actual international bargaining set may be narrower—perhaps much narrower—than the overlap between the Level II win-sets. Empirically, this additional constraint is often crucial to the outcome of two-level games. One momentous example is the fate of the Versailles Treaty. The best evidence suggests, first, that perhaps 80 percent of the American public *and* of the Senate in 1919 favored ratification of the treaty, if certain reservations were attached, and second, that those reservations were acceptable to the other key signatories, especially Britain and France. In effect, it was Wilson himself who vetoed this otherwise ratifiable package, telling the dismayed French Ambassador, "I shall consent to nothing."[52]

Yet another constraint on successful two-level negotiation derives from the leader's existing domestic coalition. Any political entrepreneur has a fixed investment in a particular pattern of policy positions and a particular supporting coalition. If a proposed international deal threatens that investment, or if ratification would require him to construct a different coalition, the chief negotiator will be reluctant to endorse it, even if (judged abstractly) it could be ratified. Politicians may be willing to risk a few of their normal supporters in the cause of ratifying an international agreement, but the greater the potential loss, the greater their reluctance.

In effect, the fixed costs of coalition-building thus imply this constraint on the win-set: How great a realignment of prevailing coalitions at Level II would be required to ratify a particular proposal? For example, a trade deal may expand export opportunities for Silicon Valley, but harm Aliquippa. This is fine for a chief negotiator (for example, Reagan?) who can easily add Northern California yuppies to his support coalition and who has no hope of winning Aliquippa steelworkers anyhow. But a different chief negotiator with a different support coalition (for example, Mondale?) might find it costly or even impossible to convert the gains from the same agreement into politically usable form. * * *

Relaxing the assumption that the chief negotiator is merely an honest broker, negotiating on behalf of his constituents, opens the possibility that the constituents may be more eager for an agreement (or more worried about "no-agreement") than he is. Empirical instances are not hard to find: in early 1987, European publics were readier to accept Gorbachev's "double-zero" arms control proposal than European leaders, just as in the early 1970s the American public (or at least the politically active public) was more eager for a negotiated end to the Vietnam War than was the Nixon administration. As a rule, the negotiator retains a veto over any proposed agreement in such cases. However, if the negotiator's own domestic standing (or indeed, his incumbency) would be threatened if he were to reject an agreement that falls within his Level II win-set, and if this is known to all parties, then the other side at Level I gains considerable leverage. Domestic U.S. discontent about the Vietnam War clearly affected the agreement reached at the Paris talks.[53] Conversely, if the constituents are (believed to be) hard-line, then a leader's domestic weakness becomes a diplomatic asset. * * *

■ ■ ■

Conclusion

The most portentous development in the fields of comparative politics and international relations in recent years is the dawning recognition among practitioners in each field of the need to take into account entanglements between the two. Empirical illustrations of reciprocal influence between domestic and international affairs abound. What we need now are concepts and theories that will help us organize and extend our empirical observations.

Analysis in terms of two-level games offers a promising response to this challenge. Unlike state-centric theories, the two-level approach recognizes the inevitability of domestic conflict about what the "national interest" requires. Unlike the "Second Image" or the "Second Image Reversed," the two-level approach recognizes that central decision-makers strive to reconcile domestic and international imperatives simultaneously. As we have seen, statesmen in this predicament face distinctive strategic opportunities and strategic dilemmas.

This theoretical approach highlights several significant features of the links between diplomacy and domestic politics, including:

■ the important distinction between voluntary and involuntary defection from international agreements;
■ the contrast between issues on which domestic interests are homogeneous, simply pitting hawks against doves, and issues on which domestic interests are more heterogeneous, so that domestic cleavage may actually foster international cooperation;
■ the possibility of synergistic issue linkage, in which strategic moves at one game-table facilitate unexpected coalitions at the second table;
■ the paradoxical fact that institutional arrangements which strengthen decision-makers at home may weaken their international bargaining position, and vice versa;
■ the importance of targeting international threats, offers, and side-payments with an eye towards their domestic incidence at home and abroad;
■ the strategic uses of uncertainty about domestic politics, and the special utility of "kinky win-sets";
■ the potential reverberation of international pressures within the domestic arena;
■ the divergences of interest between a national leader and those on whose behalf he is negotiating, and in particular, the international implications of his fixed investments in domestic politics.

Two-level games seem a ubiquitous feature of social life, from Western economic summitry to diplomacy in the Balkans and from coalition politics in Sri Lanka to legislative maneuvering on Capitol Hill. Far-ranging empirical research is needed now to test and deepen our understanding of how such games are played.

NOTES

1. The following account is drawn from Robert D. Putnam and C. Randall Henning, "The Bonn Summit of 1978: How Does International Economic Policy Coordination Actually Work?" *Brookings Discussion Papers in International Economics,* no. 53 (Washington, DC: Brookings Institution, October 1986), and Robert D. Putnam and Nicholas Bayne, *Hanging Together: Cooperation and Conflict in the Seven-Power Summits,* rev. ed. (Cambridge, MA: Harvard University Press, 1987), pp. 62–94.

2. Among interdependent economies, most economists believe, policies can often be more effective if they are internationally coordinated. For relevant citations, see Putnam and Bayne, *Hanging Together,* p. 24.

3. For a comprehensive account of the Japanese story, see I. M. Destler and Hisao Mlisuyu, "Locomotives on Different Tracks; Macroeconomic Diplomacy, 1977–1979," in I. M. Destler and Hideo Sato, eds., *Coping with U.S.-Japanese Economic Conflicts* (Lexington, MA: Heath, 1982).

4. For an excellent account of U.S. energy policy during this period, see G. John Ikenberry, "Market Solutions for State Problems: The International and Domestic Politics of American Oil Decontrol," *International Organization* 42 (Winter 1988).

5. It is not clear whether Jimmy Carter fully understood the domestic implications of his Bonn pledge at the time. See Putnam and Henning, "The Bonn Summit," and Ikenberry, "Market Solutions for State Problems."

6. Kenneth N. Waltz, *Man, the State, and War: A Theoretical Analysis* (New York: Columbia University Press, 1959).

7. Peter Gourevitch, "The Second Image Reversed: The International Sources of Domestic Politics," *International Organization* 32 (Autumn 1978), pp. 881–911.

8. I am indebted to Stephen Haggard for enlightening discussions about domestic influences on international relations.

9. Richard E. Walton and Robert B. McKersie, *A Behavioral Theory of Labor Negotiations: An Analysis of a Social Interaction System* (New York: McGraw-Hill, 1965).

10. Robert S. Strauss, "Foreword," in Joan E. Twiggs, *The Tokyo Round of Multilateral Trade Negotiations: A Case Study in Building Domestic Support for Diplomacy* (Washington, DC: Georgetown University Institute for the Study of Diplomacy, 1987), p. vii. Former Secretary of Labor John Dunlop is said to have remarked that "bilateral negotiations usually require three agreements—one across the lable and one on each side of the table," as cited in Howard Raiffa, *The Art and Science of Negotiation* (Cambridge, MA: Harvard University Press, 1982), p. 166.

11. Glenn H. Snyder and Paul Diesing, *Conflict Among Nations: Bargaining, Decision Making, and System Structure in International Crises* (Princeton: Princeton University Press, 1977), pp. 510–25.

12. Max Black, *Models and Metaphors* (Ithaca, NY: Cornell University Press, 1962), p. 242, as cited in Duncan Snidal, "The Game Theory of International Politics," *World Politics* 38 (October 1985), p. 36n.

13. To avoid unnecessary complexity, my argument throughout is phrased in terms of a single chief negotiator, although in many cases some of his responsibilities may be delegated to aides. Later in this article I relax the assumption that the negotiator has no independent preferences.

14. Gerhardt Stoltenberg, *Wall Street Journal Europe,* 2 October 1986, as cited in C. Randall Henning, *Macroeconomic Diplomacy in the 1980s: Domestic Politics and International Conflict Among the United States, Japan, and Europe,* Atlantic Paper No. 65 (New York: Croom Helm, for the Atlantic Institute for International Affairs, 1987), p. 1.

15. Ito Takashi, "Conflicts and Coalition in Japan, 1930: Political Groups and the London Naval Disarmament Conference," in Sven Groennings et al., eds., *The Study of Coalition Behavior* (New York: Holt, Rinehart, & Winston, 1970); Kobayashi Tatsuo, "The London Naval Treaty, 1930," in James W. Morley, ed., *Japan Erupts: The London Naval Conference and the Manchurian Incident, 1928–1932* (New York: Columbia University Press, 1984), pp. 11–117. I am indebted to William Jarosz for this example.

16. This stipulation is, in fact, characteristic of most real-world ratification procedures, such as House and Senate action on conference committee reports, although it is somewhat violated by the occasional practice of appending "reservations" to the ratification of treaties.

17. *New York Times,* 26 September 1986.

18. For the conception of win-set, see Kenneth A. Shepsle and Barry R. Weingast, "The Institutional Foundations of Committee Power," *American Political Science Review* 81 (March 1987), pp, 85–104. I am indebted to Professor Shepsle for much help on this topic.

19. To avoid tedium, I do not repeat the "other things being equal" proviso in each of the propositions that follow. Under some circumstances an expanded win-set might actually make practicable some outcome that could trigger a dilemma of collective action. See Vincent P. Crawford, "A Theory of Disagreement in Bargaining." *Econometrica* 50 (May 1982), pp. 607–37.

20. The Sunday Times Insight Team, *The Falklands War* (London: Sphere, 1982); Max Hastings and Simon Jenkins, *The Battle for the Falklands* (New York: Norton, 1984); Alejandro Dabai and Luis Lorenzano, *Argentina: The Malvinas and the End of Military Rule* (London: Verso, 1984). I am indebted to Louise Richardson for these citations.

21. Geoffrey W. Harrison, in John C. Campbell, ed., *Successful Negotiation: Trieste 1954* (Princeton: Princeton University Press, 1976), p. 62.

22. Thomas C. Schelling, *The Strategy of Conflict* (Cambridge, MA: Harvard University Press, 1960), pp. 19–28.

23. I am grateful to Lara Putnam for this example. For supporting evidence, see Robert R. Kaufman, "Democratic and Authoritarian Responses to the Debt Issue: Argentina, Brazil, Mexico," *International Organization* 39 (Summer 1985), pp. 473–503.

24. W. Mark Habeeb and I. William Zartman, *The Panama Canal Negotiations* (Washington, DC: Johns Hopkins Foreign Policy Institute, 1986), pp. 40, 42.

25. Thomas Romer and Howard Rosenthal, "Political Resource Allocation, Controlled Agendas, and the Status Quo," *Public Choice* 33 (no. 4, 1978), pp. 27–44.

26. In more formal treatments, the no-agreement outcome is called the "reversion point." A given constituent's evaluation of no-agreement corresponds to what Raiffa terms a seller's "walk-away price," that is, the price below which ho would prefer "no deal." (Raiffa, *Art and Science of Negotiation*.) No-agreement is equivalent to what Snyder and Diesing term "breakdown," or the expected cost of war. (Snyder and Diesing, *Conflict Among Nations*.)

27. Thomas A. Bailey, *Woodrow Wilson and the Great Betrayal* (New York: Macmillan, 1945), pp. 16–37.

28. See James Q. Wilson, *Political Organization* (New York: Basic Books, 1975) on how the politics of an issue are affected by whether the costs and the benefits are concentrated or diffuse.

29. Another factor fostering abstention is the greater complexity and opacity of monetary issues; as Gilbert R. Winham ("Complexity in International Negotiation," in Daniel Druckman, ed., *Negotiations: A Social-Psychological Perspective* [Beverly Hills: Sage, 1977], p. 363) observes, "complexity can strengthen the hand of a negotiator vis-à-vis the organization he represents."

30. Habeeb and Zariman, *Panama Canal Negotiations.*

31. Bailey, *Wilson and the Great Betrayal.*

32. I am grateful to Ernst B. Haas and Robert O. Keohane for helpful advice on this point.

33. Ann L. Hollick, *U.S. Foreign Policy and the Law of the Sea* (Princeton: Princeton University Press, 1981), especially pp. 208–37, and James K. Sebenius, *Negotiating the Law of the Sea* (Cambridge, MA: Harvard University Press, 1984), especially pp. 74–78.

34. Raiffa, *Art and Science of Negotiation*, p. 175.

35. I am grateful to Henry Brady for clarifying this point for me.

36. Gilbert R. Winham, "The Relevance of Clausewitz to a Theory of International Negotiation," prepared for delivery at the 1987 annual meeting of the American Political Science Association.

37. Jimmy Carter, *Keeping Faith: Memoirs of a President* (New York: Bantam Books, 1982), p. 225.

38. Michael Artis and Sylvia Ostry, *International Economic Policy Coordination*, Chatham House Papers: 30 (London: Routledge & Kegan Paul, 1986), pp. 75–76. Of course, whether this is desirable in terms of democratic values is quite another matter.

39. Schelling, *Strategy of Conflict*, p. 28.

40. Walton and McKersie, *A Behavioral Theory of Labor Negotiations*, p. 345.

41. Carter, *Keeping Faith*, p. 172. See also Raiffa, *Art and Science of Negotiation*, p. 183.

42. The strategic significance of targeting at Level II is illustrated in John Conybeare, "Trade Wars: A Comparative Study of Anglo-Hanse, Franco-Italian, and Hawley-Smoot Conflicts," *World Politics* 38 (October 1985), p. 157. Retaliation in the Anglo-Hanse trade wars did not have the intended deterrent effect, because it was not (and perhaps could not have been) targeted at the crucial members of the opposing Level II coalition. Compare Snyder and Diesing, *Conflict Among Nations*, p. 552: "If one faces a coercive opponent, but the opponent's majority coalition includes a few wavering members inclined to compromise, a compromise proposal that suits their views may cause their defection and the formation of a different majority coalition. Or if the opponent's strategy is accommodative, based on a tenuous soft-line coalition, one knows that care is required in implementing one's own coercive strategy to avoid the opposite kind of shift in the other state."

43. Transaction benefits may be enhanced if a substantive agreement is reached, although sometimes leaders can benefit domestically by loudly rejecting a proffered international deal.

44. Snyder and Diesing, *Conflict Among Nations*, pp. 516, 522–23. Analogous misperceptions in Anglo-American diplomacy are the focus of Richard E. Neustadt, *Alliance Politics* (New York: Columbia University Press, 1970).

45. I am grateful to Robert O. Keohane for pointing out the impact of uncertainty on the expected value of proposals.

46. William Zartman, *The 50% Solution* (Garden City, NJ: Anchor Books, 1976), p. 14. The present analysis assumes that constituents are myopic about the other side's Level II, an assumption that is not unrealistic empirically. However, a fully informed constituent would consider the preferences of key players on the other side, for if the current proposal lies well within the other side's win-set, then it would be rational for the constituent to vote against it, hoping for a second-round proposal that was more favorable to him and still ratifiable abroad; this might be a reasonable interpretation of Senator Lodge's position in 1919 (Bailey, *Wilson and the Great Betrayal*). Consideration of such strategic voting at Level II is beyond the scope of this article.

47. Dieter Hiss, "Weitwirtschaftsgipfel: Betrachtungen eines Insiders [World Economic Summit: Observations of an Insider]," in Joachim Frohn and Reiner Staeglin, eds., *Empirische Wirtschaftsforschung* (Berlin: Duncker and Humblot, 1980), pp. 286–87.

48. On cognitive and communications explanations of international cooperation, see, for example, Ernst B. Haas, "Why Collaborate? Issue-Linkage and International Regimes," *World Politics* 32 (April 1980), pp. 357–405; Richard N. Cooper, "International Cooperation in Public Health as a Prologue to Macroeconomic Cooperation," *Brookings Discussion Papers in International Economics* 44 (Washington, DC: Brookings Institution, 1986); and Zartman, *50% Solution*, especially Part 4.

49. Henning, *Macroeconomic Diplomacy in the 1980s*, pp. 62–63.

50. For overviews of this literature, see Terry M. Moe, "The New Economics of Organization," *American Journal of Political Science* 28 (November 1984), pp. 739–77; John W. Prati and Richard J. Zeckhauser, eds., *Principals and Agents: The Structure of Business* (Boston, MA: Harvard Business School Press, 1985); and Barry M. Mitnick, "The Theory of Agency and Organizational Analysis," prepared for delivery at the 1986 annual meeting of the American Political Science Association. This literature is only indirectly relevant to

our concerns here, for it has not yet adequately addressed the problems posed by multiple principals (or constituents, in our terms). For one highly formal approach to the problem of multiple principals, see R. Douglas Bernheim and Michael D. Whinston, "Common Agency," *Econometrica* 54 (July 1986), pp. 923–42.

51. This power of the chief negotiator is analogous to what Shepsle and Weingast term the "penultimate" or "ex post veto" power of the members of a Senate-House conference committee. (Shepsle and Weingast, "Institutional Foundations of Committee Power.")

52. Bailey, *Wilson and the Great Betrayal*, quotation at p. 15.

53. I. William Zartman, "Reality, Image, and Detail: The Paris Negotiations, 1969–1973," in Zartman, *50% Solution*, pp. 372–98.

Stephen D. Krasner

SHARING SOVEREIGNTY
New Institutions for Collapsed and Failing States

Conventional sovereignty assumes a world of autonomous, internationally recognized, and well-governed states. Although frequently violated in practice, the fundamental rules of conventional sovereignty—recognition of juridically independent territorial entities and nonintervention in the internal affairs of other states—have rarely been challenged in principle. But these rules no longer work, and their inadequacies have had deleterious consequences for the strong as well as the weak. The policy tools that powerful and well-governed states have available to "fix" badly governed or collapsed states—principally governance assistance and transitional administration (whether formally authorized by the United Nations or engaged in by a coalition of the willing led by the United States)—are inadequate. In the future, better domestic governance in badly governed, failed, and occupied polities will require the transcendence of accepted rules, including the creation of shared sovereignty in specific areas. In some cases, decent governance may require some new form of trusteeship, almost certainly de facto rather than de jure.[1]

Many countries suffer under failed, weak, incompetent, or abusive national authority structures. The best that people living in such countries can hope for is marginal improvement in their material well-being; limited access to social services, including health care and education; and a

moderate degree of individual physical security. At worst they will confront endemic violence, exploitative political leaders, falling life expectancy, declining per capita income, and even state-sponsored genocide. In the Democratic Republic of Congo (formerly Zaire), for example, civil wars that have persisted for more than two decades have resulted in millions of deaths. In Zimbabwe the policies of President Robert Mugabe, who was determined to stay in office regardless of the consequences for his country's citizens, led to an economic debacle that began in 2000 with falling per capita income, inflation above 500 percent, and the threat of mass starvation. In Colombia much of the territory is controlled by the Revolutionary Armed Forces of Colombia (FARC), a Marxist rebel group that derives most of its income from drug trafficking. In Rwanda more than 700,000 people were slaughtered in a matter of weeks in 1994 as a result of a government-organized genocide.

The consequences of failed and inadequate governance have not been limited to the societies directly affected. Poorly governed societies can generate conflicts that spill across international borders. Transnational criminal and terrorist networks can operate in territories not controlled by the internationally recognized government. Humanitarian disasters not only prick the conscience of political leaders in advanced democratic societies but also leave them with no policy options that are appealing to voters.

From *International Security* 29, no. 2 (Fall 2004): 85–120. Some of the author's notes have been omitted.

Challenges related to creating better governance also arise where national authority structures have collapsed because of external invasion and occupation rather than internal conflict. The availability of weapons of mass destruction and the presence of transnational terrorism have created a historically unprecedented situation in which polities with very limited material capability can threaten the security of much more powerful states. These polities can be conquered and occupied with relative ease, leaving the occupying power with the more challenging task of establishing an acceptable domestic governing structure. Contemporary Afghanistan and Iraq are the obvious cases in point.

Left to their own devices, collapsed and badly governed states will not fix themselves because they have limited administrative capacity, not least with regard to maintaining internal security.[2] Occupying powers cannot escape choices about what new governance structures will be created and sustained. To reduce international threats and improve the prospects for individuals in such polities, alternative institutional arrangements supported by external actors, such as de facto trusteeships and shared sovereignty, should be added to the list of policy options.

The current menu of policy instruments for dealing with collapsed and failing states is paltry, consisting primarily of transitional administration and foreign assistance to improve governance, both of which assume that in more or less short order, targeted states can function effectively on their own. Nation-building or state-building efforts are almost always described in terms of empowering local authorities to assume the responsibilities of conventional sovereignty. The role of external actors is understood to be limited with regard to time, if not scope, in the case of transitional administration exercising full executive authority. Even as the rules of conventional sovereignty are de facto violated if not de jure challenged, and it is evident that in many cases effective autonomous national government is far in the future, the language of diplomacy, the media, and the street portrays nothing other than a world of fully sovereign states.

The next section of this article describes the basic elements that constitute the conventional understanding of sovereignty and provides a taxonomy of alternative institutional forms. It is followed by a discussion of the ways in which conventional sovereignty has failed in some states, threatening the well-being of their own citizens and others. The inadequacy of the current repertoire of policy options for dealing with collapsed, occupied, and badly governed states—governance assistance and transitional administration—is then assessed. The possibilities for new institutional forms—notably shared sovereignty and some de facto form of trusteeship—are examined. Included is a discussion of why such arrangements might be accepted by political leaders in target as well as intervening states.

Conventional Sovereignty and Some Alternatives

Conventional sovereignty has three elements: international legal sovereignty, Westphalian/Vatellian sovereignty, and domestic sovereignty.[3] The basic rule of international legal sovereignty is to recognize juridically independent territorial entities. These entities then have the right to freely decide which agreements or treaties they will enter into. In practice, this rule has been widely but not universally honored. Some entities that are not juridically independent have been recognized (e.g., Byelorussia and the Ukraine during the Cold War), and some entities that are juridically independent have not been recognized (e.g., the People's Republic of China from 1949 to the 1970s).

The fundamental rule of Westphalian/Vatellian sovereignty is to refrain from intervening in the internal affairs of other states. Each state has the right to determine its own domestic authority structures. In practice, Westphalian/Vatellian sovereignty has frequently been violated.

Domestic sovereignty does not involve a norm or a rule, but is rather a description of the nature of domestic authority structures and the extent to which they are able to control activities within a state's boundaries. Ideally, authority structures would ensure a society that is peaceful, protects human rights, has a consultative mechanism, and honors a rule of law based on a shared understanding of justice.

In the ideal sovereign state system, international legal sovereignty, Westphalian/Vatellian sovereignty, and domestic sovereignty are mutually supportive. Recognized authorities within territorial entities regulate behavior, enjoy independence from outside interference, and enter into mutually beneficial contractual relations (treaties) with other recognized entities. This is the conventional world of international politics in which state-to-state relations are what count. One of the most striking aspects of the contemporary world is the extent to which domestic sovereignty has faltered so badly in states that still enjoy international legal, and sometimes even Westphalian/Vatellian, sovereignty. Somalia, for instance, is still an internationally recognized entity, even though it has barely any national institutions; and external actors have not, in recent years, tried to do much about Somalia's domestic sovereignty, or the lack thereof.

Conventional sovereignty was not always the hegemonic structure for ordering political life. Obviously, the basic rules of medieval Europe or the pre-nineteenth-century Sinocentric world were very different. But even in the nineteenth century, by which time conventional sovereignty had become a well-recognized structure, there were also legitimated and accepted alternatives. Protectorates were one alternative to conventional sovereignty; the rulers of a protectorate relinquished control over foreign policy to a more powerful state but retained authority over domestic affairs. For instance, in 1899 the ruler of Kuwait signed an agreement that gave Britain control of most elements of his country's foreign policy because he needed external support against threats from both Iraq and members of his own family.[4] In nineteenth-century China the major powers established treaty ports where British, French, German, and Japanese authorities regulated commerce and exercised extraterritorial authority over their own citizens and sometimes Chinese as well.[5] Within the British Empire, Australia, Canada, and South Africa became dominions that enjoyed almost complete control over their domestic affairs, recognized the British ruler as the head of state, but to some extent deferred to Britain in matters of foreign policy. Finally, colonization was a legitimated practice in the nineteenth century that allowed powerful states to assume international legal sovereignty and regulate the domestic authority structures of far-flung territories.

Conventional sovereignty is currently the only fully legitimated institutional form, but unfortunately, it does not always work. Honoring Westphalian/Vatellian sovereignty (and sometimes international legal sovereignty as well) makes it impossible to secure decent and effective domestic sovereignty, because the autochthonous political incentives facing political leaders in many failed, failing, or occupied states are perverse. These leaders are better able to enhance their own power and wealth by making exclusionist ethnic appeals or undermining even the limited legal routinized administrative capacity that might otherwise be available.

To secure decent domestic governance in failed, failing, and occupied states, new institutional forms are needed that compromise Westphalian/Vatellian sovereignty for an indefinite period. Shared sovereignty, arrangements under which individuals chosen by international organizations, powerful states, or ad hoc entities would share authority with nationals over some aspects of

Table 5.1. Alternative Institutional Arrangements

	International Legal Sovereignty		Westphalian/Vatellian Sovereignty			Duration of Rule Violation		
	NO	YES	NONE	SOME	FULL	SHORT	MEDIUM	LONG
Conventional sovereignty		X			X	n/a	n/a	n/a
Colony	X		X					X
Transitional administration with full foreign executive authority	X		X			X		
Trusteeship	X		X or X			X	X	
Shared sovereignty		X		X				X
Nineteenth-century protectorate	X			X				X

domestic sovereignty, would be a useful addition to the policy repertoire. Ideally, shared sovereignty would be legitimated by a contract between national authorities and an external agent. In other cases, external interveners may conclude that the most attractive option would be the establishment of a de facto trusteeship or protectorate. Under such an arrangement, the Westphalian/Vatellian sovereignty of the target polity would be violated, executive authority would be vested primarily with external actors, and international legal sovereignty would be suspended. There will not, however, be any effort to formalize through an international convention or treaty a general set of principles for such an option.[6] (For a summary of these different institutional possibilities, see Table 5.1.)

Failures of Conventional Sovereignty

Failed, inadequate, incompetent, or abusive national authority structures have sabotaged the economic well-being, violated the basic human rights, and undermined the physical security of their countries' populations. In some cases, state authority has collapsed altogether for an extended period, although such instances are rare. Afghanistan in the early 1990s before the Taliban consolidated power, Liberia for much of the 1990s, and the Democratic Republic of Congo and Sierra Leone in the late 1990s are just a few of the examples. Governance challenges have also arisen in Afghanistan and Iraq, where authority structures collapsed as a result of external invasion rather than internal conflict. The occupying powers, most obviously the United States, were then confronted with the challenge of fashioning decent governance structures in both countries.

In some parts of the world, disorder (including civil war) has become endemic. For the period 1955 to 1998, the State Failure Task Force identified 136 occurrences of state failure in countries with populations larger than 500,000. The task force operationalized state failure as one of four kinds of internal political crisis: revolutionary war, ethnic war, "adverse regime change," or genocide. In 1955 fewer than 6 percent of the countries were in failure. In the early 1990s the figure had risen to almost 30 percent, falling to about 20 percent in 1998, the last year of the study. Adverse regime change was the most common form of state failure, followed by ethnic war, revolutionary war, and genocide. The task force identified partial democracy, trade closure, and low levels of economic well-being as indicated by high infant mortality rates as the primary causes of state failure. James Fearon and David Laitin show that internal strife is more likely in countries suffering from poverty, recent decolonization, high population, and mountainous terrain. These conditions allow even relatively small guerrilla bands to operate successfully because recognized governments do not have the administrative competence to engage in effective rural policing and counterinsurgency operations.[7]

States that experience failure or poor governance more generally are beset by many problems. In such states, infrastructure deteriorates; corruption is widespread; borders are unregulated; gross domestic product is declining or stagnant; crime is rampant; and the national currency is not widely accepted. Armed groups operate within the state's boundaries but outside the control of the government. The writ of the central government, the entity that exercises the prerogatives of international legal sovereignty (e.g., signing treaties and sending delegates to international meetings), may not extend to the whole country; in some cases, it may not extend beyond the capital. Authority may be exercised by local entities in other parts of the country, or by no one at all.

Political leaders operating in an environment in which material and institutional resources are limited have often chosen policies that make a bad situation even worse. For some leaders, disorder and uncertainty are more attractive than order and stability because they are better able to extract resources from a disorderly society. Decisions affecting the distribution of wealth are based on personal connections rather than bureaucratic regulations or the rule of law. Leaders create multiple armed units that they can play off against each other. They find it more advantageous to take a bigger piece of a shrinking pie than a smaller piece of a growing pie.

The largest number of poorly governed states is found on the continent of Africa. Since the mid-1950s about a third of African states have been in failure.[8] In constant 1995 U.S. dollars, gross domestic product per capita for all of sub-Saharan Africa fell from $660 in 1980 to $587 in 1990 to $563 in 2000. Out of the sub-Saharan states for which data are available from the World Bank, eighteen had increases in their per capita gross domestic product from 1990 to 2000, seven had decreases of less than 5 percent, and seventeen experienced decreases of more than 5 percent. With the exception of the former Soviet Union, no other area of the world fared so badly with regard to economic performance.[9]

■　■　■

Thus, for many countries domestic sovereignty is not working, and the situation is not improving in any substantive way. Although the number and percentage of countries suffering from civil war declined during the 1990s, the per capita gross national income in current U.S. dollars of the least developed countries continued to drop, falling by

9 percent from 1990 to 2000, a period of robust growth for the world as a whole.

Why Sovereignty Failures Matter

In the contemporary world, powerful states have not been able to ignore governance failures. Polities where domestic authority has collapsed or been inadequate have threatened the economic and security interests of these states. Humanitarian crises have engaged electorates in advanced democracies and created no-win situations for political leaders who are damned if they intervene and damned if they do not. And, most obviously, when a state has been invaded, the occupiers have been confronted with the problem of establishing effective domestic sovereignty.

The availability of weapons of mass destruction, the ease of movement across borders, and the emergence of terrorist networks have attenuated the relationship between the underlying capabilities of actors and the ability to kill large numbers of people. In the past, state and nonstate actors with limited resources could not threaten the security of states with substantial resources. The killing power of a nation's military depended on the underlying wealth of the country. Nonstate actors such as anarchist groups in the nineteenth century could throw bombs that might kill fifty or even several hundred people, but not more. This is no longer true. States with limited means can procure chemical and biological weapons. Nuclear weapons demand more resources, but they are not out of reach of even a dismally poor country such as North Korea. Weapons of mass destruction can be delivered in myriad ways, not only by missiles but also by commercial ships, trucks, planes, and even envelopes. Failed or weak states may provide terrorists with territory in which they can operate freely.

Moreover, political leaders who have effective control within their borders but limited resources to defend or deter an invasion present a tempting target if they adopt policies that threaten the core security interests of powerful states. For instance, throughout his rule Saddam Hussein sought and sometimes used weapons of mass destruction, and even when faced with invasion, failed to fully cooperate with UN inspectors. In Afghanistan the Taliban supported al-Qa'ida, which had already demonstrated that it could strike core targets in the United States. Neither Iraq nor Afghanistan could defend itself against, or deter, a U.S. attack. When the threat is high and invasion is easy, powerful states are likely to use military force to bring down a menacing regime. When, however, the old regime has collapsed, the occupiers confront the challenge of creating effective and decent domestic sovereignty.

Sovereignty failures may also present problems in the area of transnational criminality. Drug trafficking is difficult to control under any circumstances, but such activities are more likely to flourish where domestic sovereignty is inadequate. About 95 percent of illicit drug production takes place in areas of civil strife. Colombia, where the FARC controls a large part of the territory, has been one of the major sources of such drugs for the United States. In the late 1990s Afghanistan cultivated 75 percent of the world's opium poppies, and despite a ban by the Taliban at the end of its rule, production revived after the regime was overthrown because the new government in Kabul had only limited control over much of the country. Transnational trafficking in persons is more likely, although not limited to, countries where domestic authority and control are weak or ineffective. A 2004 State Department report lists ten countries—Bangladesh, Burma, Cuba, Ecuador, Equatorial Guinea, Guyana, North Korea, Sierra Leone, Sudan, and Venezuela—that have not met minimum efforts to control trafficking in persons. Most of the ten are failed or badly governed states.[10] In addition, it is more difficult to trace and punish the perpetrators of transnational financial fraud in countries where the police and judiciary do not function well.

Finally, gross violations of human rights present unpleasant political choices for democratic leaders in powerful states. There have been a number of humanitarian catastrophes in recent years, with the killings in Rwanda in the mid-1990s being one of the most appalling and most widely reported. Millions of people have died in other countries as well at the hands of their own government or rival political groups. These and other humanitarian disasters have engaged attentive elites. The Canadian ministry of foreign affairs, for instance, organized the International Commission on Intervention and State Sovereignty in 2000 in response to UN Secretary-General Kofi Annan's appeal for a new consensus on the right of humanitarian intervention. The commission, composed of twelve eminent persons, produced a widely circulated report entitled *The Responsibility to Protect.* The report defends the principle of humanitarian intervention when governments abuse or fail to protect their own citizens. Samantha Power's book, *A Problem from Hell: America and the Age of Genocide,* which describes the failure of the United States to act either to prevent or to mitigate a number of genocides throughout the twentieth century, won a Pulitzer Prize in 2003.[11]

■   ■   ■

Humanitarian crises, then, present decisionmakers in democratic countries with a no-win situation. If they fail to intervene and a humanitarian disaster occurs, they may lose the votes of citizens who are attentive to and care about the fate of particular countries, regions, ethnic groups, or principled issues in general. On the other hand, if a political leader does intervene, the costs in terms of soldiers killed will be readily apparent, but the number of lives saved can never be demonstrated with certainty.

The Existing Institutional Repertoire: Governance Assistance and Transitional Administration

Political leaders in powerful and weak states have been reluctant to challenge the conventional norms of sovereignty. The policy options currently available to repair occupied or badly governed states—governance assistance and transitional administration—are consistent with these norms. They have made some limited contribution to improving governance in badly run and collapsed states, but policymakers would be better served if they had a wider repertoire of policy choices.

Governance Assistance

For the last decade international organizations, the United States, and other donor countries have devoted substantial resources to promoting better governance. U.S. foreign aid has been given to train judges, rewrite criminal codes, increase fiscal transparency, professionalize the police, encourage an open media, strengthen political parties, and monitor elections. In 2004 President George W. Bush's administration launched a new foreign aid initiative, the Millennium Challenge Account (MCA), which, if fully funded, will increase U.S. foreign assistance by 50 percent and provide these resources to a relatively small number of poor countries that have demonstrated good governance in the areas of promoting economic freedom, governing justly, and investing in people.[12]

Since the 1950s, international financial institutions have been involved in questions of policy and sometimes institutional reform in borrowing countries. The conditions attached to lending by the World Bank and the International Monetary Fund (IMF) have covered a wide range of issues such as aggregate credit expansion, subsidies, number of government employees, indexation of salaries, tariffs, tax rates, and institution building. International financial institutions have placed their own personnel in key bureaus.[13] * * *

Foreign assistance to improve governance in weak states does not usually contradict the rules of conventional sovereignty. Governments contract with external agencies (e.g., countries, multilateral organizations, and nongovernmental organizations [NGOs]) to provide training in various areas. Such contracting is a manifestation of international legal sovereignty and is consistent with Westphalian/Vatellian sovereignty, so long as the influence of external actors on domestic authority structures is limited to specific policies or improvements in the capabilities of government employees. When bargaining power is highly asymmetric, as may be the case in some conditionality agreements between international financial institutions and borrowing countries, Westphalian/Vatellian sovereignty can be compromised. External actors can influence not just policies but also institutional arrangements in target states. The borrowing country is better off with the agreement, conditions or no, than it would have been without it; otherwise it would not have signed. Nevertheless, political leaders may accept undesired and intrusive engagement from external actors because the alternative is loss of access to international capital markets.

The effectiveness of governance assistance will always be limited. Some leaders will find the exploitation of their own populations more advantageous than the introduction of reforms. The leverage of external actors will usually be constrained. International financial institutions are in the business of lending money; they cannot put too stringent restrictions on their loans lest their customers disappear. Many IMF agreements are renegotiated, sometimes several times. Small social democratic countries in Europe have been committed, because of the views of their electorates, to assisting the poor; they will be loath to allow their funding levels to drop below the generally recognized target of 0.7 percent of national income. The wealthier countries also routinely provide humanitarian assistance, regardless of the quality of governance in a particular country.

Moreover, those providing governance assistance are likely to adopt formulas that reflect their own domestic experience and that may be ill suited to the environments of particular target countries. The United States, for instance, has emphasized elections and independent legislatures. Interest groups have been regarded as independent of the state, whereas in European social democratic countries, they are legitimated by and sometimes created by the state.

Transitional Administration

Transitional administration is the one recognized alternative to conventional sovereignty that exists in the present international environment, but it is explicitly not meant as a challenge to the basic norms of sovereignty. The scope of transitional administration or peacekeeping and peacebuilding operations has ranged from the full assertion of executive authority by the UN for some period of time, East Timor being an example, to more modest efforts involving monitoring the implementation of peace agreements, as was the case in Guatemala in the 1990s. Transitional administration, usually authorized by the UN Security Council, has always been seen as a temporary, transitional measure designed to create the conditions under which conventional sovereignty can be restored. The U.S. occupation of Iraq has followed the same script, albeit without any UN endorsement of the occupation itself, although the Security Council did validate the restoration of international legal sovereignty in June 2004. Westphalian/Vatellian sovereignty and sometimes international legal sovereignty are violated in the short term so that they can be restored in the longer term; at least that is the standard explanation.

The record of peacebuilding efforts since World War II has been mixed. One recent study identified 124 cases of peacebuilding by the international community. Of these, 43 percent were judged to be successful based on the absence of hostilities. If progress toward democracy is added as a measure of success, only 35 percent were successful.[14]

More extensive peacekeeping operations, those that might accurately be called "transitional administration" because they involve the assertion of wide-ranging or full executive authority by the UN (or the United States), are difficult: the demands are high; advance planning, which must prejudge outcomes, is complicated, especially for the UN; and resources—economic, institutional, and military—are often limited. UN missions have run monetary systems, enforced laws, appointed officials, created central banks, decided property claims, regulated businesses, and operated public utilities. The resources to undertake these tasks have rarely been adequate. Each operation has been ad hoc; no cadres of bureaucrats, police, soldiers, or judges permanently committed to transitional administration exist; and there is a tension between devolving authority to local actors and having international actors assume responsibility for all governmental functions because, at least at the outset, this latter course is seen as being more efficient.[15]

Transitional administration is particularly problematic in situations where local actors disagree about basic objectives among themselves and with external actors. Under these circumstances, as opposed to situations in which local actors agree on goals but need external monitoring to provide reassurances about the behavior of their compatriots, the inherently temporary character of transitional administration increases the difficulty of creating stable institutions. If indigenous groups disagree about the distribution of power and the constitutional structure of the new state, then the optimal strategy for their political leaders is to strengthen their own position in anticipation of the departure of external actors. They do so by maximizing support among their followers rather than backing effective national institutions. Alternatively, local leaders who become dependent on external actors during a transitional administration, but who lack support within their own country, do not have an incentive to invest in the development of new institutional arrangements that would allow their external benefactors to leave at an earlier date.[16]

Multiple external actors with varying interests and little reason to coordinate their activities have exacerbated the problems associated with transitional administration. The bureaucratic and financial interests of international organizations are not necessarily complementary. NGOs need to raise money and make a mark. The command structures for security and civilian activities have been separated. The permanent members of the Security Council, to whom UN peacekeeping authorities are ultimately responsible, have not always had the same interests.[17]

■　　■　　■

Transitional administration has been most effective when the level of violence in a country has been low, where there has been involvement by major powers, and where the contending parties within the country have reached a mutually acceptable agreement. The key role for the transitional administration is then to monitor the implementation of the agreement. For instance, in Namibia the contact group, comprising Canada, France, Germany, Great Britain, and the United States, was involved in UN discussions about the constitutional structure for an independent Namibia beginning in 1978. All of the major contending parties consented to the UN Transition Assistance Group (UNTAG) that was sent in 1989, allowing the lightly armed mission to play a neutral role between South Africa and Namibia. The strength of the major potential spoilers, hard-line whites, was undermined by the collapse of apartheid in South Africa. The major responsibility of UNTAG was to supervise the elections for the government that assumed power when Namibia secured international legal sovereignty.[18]

There were also successful missions in Central America in the 1990s. In both Guatemala and Nicaragua, government and rebel groups had reached a mutually acceptable settlement. Peace-keeping missions contributed to stability by supervising elections, helping to demobilize combatants, and training police.[19]

In sum, transitional administration has worked best for the easiest cases, those where the key actors have already reached a mutually acceptable agreement. In these situations, the transitional administration plays a monitoring role. It can be truly neutral among the contending parties. The mission does not have to be heavily armed. Transitional administration, however, is much more difficult in cases such as Bosnia, Kosovo, Afghanistan, and Iraq—that is, where local leaders have not reached agreement on what the ultimate outcome for their polity should be and where they must think about positioning themselves to win support from parochial constituencies when transitional administration, along with its large foreign military force, comes to an end.

New Institutional Options: De Facto Trusteeships and Shared Sovereignty

Given the limitations of governance assistance and transitional administration, other options for dealing with countries where international legal sovereignty and Westphalian/Vatellian sovereignty are inconsistent with effective and responsible domestic sovereignty need to be explored. At least two such arrangements would add to the available tool kit of policy options. The first would be to revive the idea of trusteeship or protectorate, probably de facto rather than de jure. The second would be to explore possibilities for shared sovereignty in which national rulers would use their international legal sovereignty to legitimate institutions within their states in which authority was shared between internal and external actors.

De Facto Trusteeships

In a prescient article published in 1993, Gerald Helman and Steven Ratner argued that in extreme cases of state failure, the establishment of trusteeships under the auspices of the UN Security Council would be necessary. By the end of the 1990s, such suggestions had become more common. Analysts have noted that de facto trusteeships have become a fact of international life. In a monograph published in 2002, Richard Caplan argues, "An idea that once enjoyed limited academic currency at best—international trusteeship for failed states and contested territories—has become a reality in all but name." Martin Indyk, an assistant secretary of state during President Bill Clinton's administration, has argued that the most attractive path to permanent peace in the Middle East would be to establish a protectorate in Palestine, legitimated by the United Nations and with the United States playing a key role in security and other areas. Even if final status talks were completed, the trusteeship would remain in place until a responsible Palestinian government was established.[20]

Despite these recent observations, developing an alternative to conventional sovereignty, one that explicitly recognizes that international legal sovereignty will be withdrawn and that external actors will control many aspects of domestic sovereignty for an indefinite period of time, will not be easy. * * *

Codifying a general set of principles and rules for some new kind of trusteeship or protectorate would involve deciding who would appoint the authority and oversee its activities: the UN Security Council? A regional organization such as the European Union? A coalition of the willing? A single state? A treaty or convention would have to define the possible scope of authority of the governing entity. * * *

The most substantial barrier to a general international treaty codifying a new form of trusteeship or protectorate is that it will not receive support from either the powerful, who would have to implement it, or the weak, who might be subject to it. There is widespread sentiment for the proposition that Westphalian/Vatellian sovereignty is not absolute and can be breached in cases of massive human rights violations. UN Secretary-General Annan expressed this view in 1999 to widespread international acclaim.[21] But arguing that Westphalian/Vatellian sovereignty is not absolute is quite different from codifying an explicit alternative that would deprive states of their international legal sovereignty as well as control over their domestic affairs. * * * For states in the third world, any successor to the mandate system of the League of Nations, or the trusteeship system of the UN, would smell if not look too much like colonialism.[22]

Shared Sovereignty

Shared sovereignty would involve the engagement of external actors in some of the domestic authority structures of the target state for an indefinite period of time. Such arrangements would be legitimated by agreements signed by recognized national authorities. National actors would use their international legal sovereignty to enter into agreements that would compromise their Westphalian/Vatellian sovereignty with the goal of improving domestic sovereignty. One core element of sovereignty—voluntary agreements—would be preserved, while another core element—the principle of autonomy—would be violated.

National leaders could establish shared sovereignty through either treaties or unilateral commitments. To be effective, such arrangements would have to create self-enforcing equilibria involving either domestic players alone or some combination of domestic and international actors. Political elites in the target state would have to believe that they would be worse off if the shared sovereignty arrangement were violated.

For policy purposes, it would be best to refer to shared sovereignty as "partnerships." This would more easily let policymakers engage in organized hypocrisy, that is, saying one thing and doing another. Shared sovereignty or partnerships would allow political leaders to embrace sovereignty, because these arrangements would be legitimated by the target state's international legal sovereignty, even though they violate the core principle of Westphalian/Vatellian sovereignty: autonomy. Organized hypocrisy is not surprising in an environment such as the international system where there are competing norms (e.g., human rights vs. Westphalian/Vatellian sovereignty), power differentials that allow strong actors to pursue policies that are inconsistent with recognized rules, and exceptional complexity that makes it impossible to write any set of rules that could provide optimal outcomes under all conditions. Shared sovereignty or partnerships would make no claim to being an explicit alternative to conventional sovereignty. It would allow actors to obfuscate the fact that their behavior would be inconsistent with their principles.

HISTORICAL EXAMPLES OF SHARED SOVEREIGNTY

Shared sovereignty agreements have been used in the past. There are several late nineteenth-century shared sovereignty arrangements in which external actors assumed control over part of the revenue-generating stream of a state that had defaulted on its debt. The state wanted renewed access to international capital markets. The lenders wanted assurance that they would be repaid. Direct control over the collection of specific taxes provided greater confidence than other available measures.

For example, a shared sovereignty arrangement between external lenders and the Porte (the government of the Ottoman Empire) was constructed for some parts of the revenue system of the empire during the latter part of the nineteenth century. The empire entered international capital markets in the 1850s to fund military expenditures associated with the Crimean War. By 1875, after receiving more than a dozen new loans, the empire was unable to service its foreign debt. To again secure access to international capital markets, the Ottomans agreed in 1881 to create, through government decree, the Council of the Public Debt. The members of the council—two from France; one each from Austria, Germany, Italy, and the Ottoman Empire itself; and one from Britain and the Netherlands together—were selected by foreign creditors. Until the debt was liquidated, the Porte gave control of several major sources of revenue to the council and authorized it to take initiatives that would increase economic activity. The council promoted, for instance, the export of salt (the tax on which it controlled) to India and introduced new technologies for the silk and wine industries. It increased the confidence of foreign investors in the empire's railways by collecting revenues that the government had promised to foreign companies. In the decade before World War I, the council controlled about one-quarter of the empire's revenue. It was disbanded after the war.[23]

Unlike classic gunboat diplomacy, where the governments of foreign creditors took over control of customs houses to secure repayment of loans, in the case of the Ottoman Council of the Public Debt, the norm of international legal sovereignty was honored, at least in form. The council was established by an edict issued by the Ottoman Empire at the behest of foreign creditors. International legal sovereignty was honored; Westphalian/ Vatellian sovereignty was ignored. This arrangement was durable because if the empire had revoked its decree, it would have lost access to international capital markets.

■   ■   ■

The shared sovereignty arrangements established by the United States after World War II were more successful. Germany is the prime example. The Western allies wanted to internationally legitimate the Federal Republic of Germany (FRG or West Germany) but at the same time constrain its freedom of action. The Bonn agreements, signed in 1952 by the FRG, France, the United Kingdom, and the United States and revised in Paris in 1954, gave West Germany full authority over its internal and external affairs but with key exceptions in the security area. Not only did the FRG renounce its right to produce chemical, biological, and nuclear weapons; it also signed a status of forces agreement that gave the allies expansive powers. These included exclusive jurisdiction over the members of their armed forces and the right to patrol public areas including roads, railways, and restaurants. Allied forces could take any measures necessary to ensure order and discipline.[24] West Germany's military was fully integrated into NATO. Article 5(2) of the Convention on Relations gave the Western powers the right to declare a state of emergency until FRG officials obtained adequate powers enabling them to take effective action to protect the security of the foreign forces.[25] Without a clear definition of these adequate powers, the Western allies formally retained the right to resume their occupation of the Federal Republic until 1990, when the 1990 Treaty on the Final Settlement with Respect to Germany terminated the Bonn agreements.

The United States succeeded in the West German case because most Germans supported democracy, a market economy, and constraints on the FRG's security policies. Obviously the strength of this support reflected many factors, including the long-term economic success of the West relative to the Soviet bloc. Shared sovereignty arrangements for security in the FRG contributed to effective domestic governance by taking a potentially explosive issue off the table both within and, more important, without West Germany. Security dilemmas that might have strengthened undemocratic forces in the FRG never occurred because the Bonn government did not have exclusive control of the country's defense.

■   ■   ■

INCENTIVES FOR SHARED SOVEREIGNTY

Shared sovereignty arrangements can work only if they create a self-enforcing equilibrium, which might include external as well as domestic players. There are at least four circumstances that might make shared sovereignty arrangements attractive for political decision-makers, those who hold international legal sovereignty, in target states: avarice, postconflict occupation, desperation, and elections.

NATURAL RESOURCES AND AVARICE   Rulers salivate at the wealth and power that natural resources, most notably oil, can bring them. Their bargaining position, however, depends on the acceptance of the precepts of conventional sovereignty: the state owns the oil and has the right to sign contracts and set rules governing its exploitation. Neither companies, nor consuming states, nor international organizations have challenged the property rights of the state. No one, at least no one in a position of authority, has suggested, for instance, that oil in badly governed states ought to be declared part of the common heritage of mankind and placed under the control of perhaps the World Bank.

For poorly governed countries, however, natural resources, especially oil, have been a curse that has feathered the nests of rulers and undermined democracy and economic growth. Oil concentrates resources in the hands of the state. The road to wealth and power for any ambitious individual leads through the offices of the central government, not through individual enterprise or productive economic activity. With oil wealth, the state can buy off dissenters and build military machines that can be used to repress those who cannot be bought off.[26]

Shared sovereignty arrangements for extractive industries would offer an alternative to conventional practices that would provide better governance in oil-abundant states, more benefits for their people, and fewer incentives for corruption and conflict. Such arrangements would depend on the willingness of wealthier democratic states to constrain the options available to political leaders in poorly governed resource-rich states. Conventional sovereignty would not be challenged in principle but would be compromised in practice. Political leaders in host countries would then be confronted with a choice between nothing and something, although much less than they might have at their private disposal under conventional practices.

A shared sovereignty arrangement for natural resources could work in the following way. An agreement between the host country and, say, the World Bank would create a trust. The trust would be domiciled in an advanced industrialized country with effective rule of law. All funds generated by the natural resources project would be placed in an international escrow account controlled by the trust. All disbursements from the account would have to be approved by a majority of the directors of the trust. Half of the board of directors of the trust would be appointed by the host government, the other half by the World Bank; the bank could name directors from any country but would not designate its own employees. Directors would have to believe that their success depended on the success of the trust.

The trust agreement would stipulate that a large part of these funds would be used for social welfare programs, although specific allocations for, say, health care or education would be left to the host government. The trust would refuse to dispense funds that did not conform with these commitments. The trust might even be charged with implementing programs using the resources of the escrow account if the government failed to act expeditiously.

The laws of the advanced democracy in which the trust was incorporated would hold accountable the directors of the trust. Legislation enacted by the country in which the trust was domiciled would back the firms' responsibility to pay revenues into the escrow account, and only the escrow account.

No doubt the leaders of oil-rich or other natural resource–rich countries would cringe at such arrangements. They would have much more difficulty putting billions of dollars in foreign bank accounts, as did Sani Abacha, the late Nigerian military dictator. It would be hard to spend half a billion dollars on a European vacation as did some members of the Saudi royal family in 2002. But if the major democracies passed legislation requiring that any imported oil be governed by a trust arrangement, avarice might induce political leaders in resource-rich countries to accept shared sovereignty, because without shared sovereignty they would get nothing.[27]

POSTCONFLICT OCCUPATION Postconflict occupation might also be conducive to creating shared sovereignty arrangements. When there is military intervention and occupation, local leaders have limited choice. In Afghanistan, Bosnia, East Timor, Iraq, and Kosovo, the local leaders have been dependent to some extent on external actors. They have had to accept the presence of nonnationals. Foreigners have been running many of the ministries in Bosnia. In Kosovo joint implementation for administrative structures has been the norm: there are twenty administrative departments and four independent agencies, all of which are codirected by a Kosovar and a senior UNMIK staff person.[28] In Afghanistan and Iraq, security has been provided in part by foreign forces.

Shared sovereignty contracts would make such arrangements permanent, not transitional. The presence of external actors would not be the result of a unilateral decision by an external administrator but rather of a contract between external and domestic actors who would be granted international legal sovereignty. Because the contract would have no termination date, local actors could no longer assume that they could simply wait for the foreigners to leave. Some local leaders might still decide that acting as a spoiler might maximize their interests, but others would see cooperation as more likely to enhance their long-term prospects.

Such arrangements could be successful in the long run only if they were supported by a winning coalition in the host country. Unlike oil trusts, external enforcement mechanisms would be difficult to create. External actors might bolster domestic agents committed to shared sovereignty or threaten to impose sanctions or cut foreign assistance if the agreement were violated, but there could not be an ironclad guarantee of success.

Still, shared sovereignty arrangements would be more promising than constitution writing, which has been the center of attention in recent occupations. The problem with relying on a constitution or any other legal commitments made under pressure at a particular moment in time is that once the occupying power leaves, the incentives for domestic actors to honor their earlier commitments can radically change. Shared sovereignty, in contrast, could generate a self-enforcing equilibrium if it provided benefits to a large enough group of domestic actors.

Monetary policy is one area where shared sovereignty might work in a postconflict or even a more benign environment. Controlling inflation can be a daunting problem. A few countries, East Timor being one example, have simply resorted to using the U.S. dollar. Others have tried to engineer credible commitments through domestic institutions, such as independent central banks. Appointment of the governors of the central bank by both government and external actors could enhance the credibility of such arrangements. In this regard, the IMF might be the right partner. Nonnational governors could be of any nationality. They would not be IMF employees. The fund would sign a contract with the host country setting up shared sovereignty on a permanent basis or until both parties agreed to end the arrangement. If the national government unilaterally abrogated the arrangement, it would be a clear signal to external actors that the government was abandoning the path of monetary responsibility. If the central bank were successful in constraining inflation, the arrangement would generate support from domestic actors. Like oil trusts, one major attraction of such an agreement is that it would not be costly for the IMF or any other external actor.

Commercial courts might be another area where shared sovereignty could be productive. Again, the opportunities in this area would not be limited to postconflict situations. In a state where the rule of law has been sketchy, the international legal sovereign would conclude a contract with an external entity—for instance, a regional organization such as the EU or the Organization of American States—to establish a separate commercial court system. The judges in these courts would be appointed by both the national government and its external partner. The expectation would be that local business interests would find this court system attractive. It would provide a venue in which they could resolve disagreements more effectively than would be the case within existing national institutions. The presence of such a court system might even attract higher levels of foreign investment. Like oil trusts and central banks, such an arrangement would not involve substantial costs for the external actor. The national government, or even to some extent the litigants, could fund commercial courts.

■ ■ ■

Conclusion

During the twentieth century, the norms of international legal sovereignty and Westphalian/Vatellian sovereignty became universally accepted. It has often been tacitly assumed that these norms would be accompanied by effective domestic sovereignty, that is, by governance structures that exercised competent and ideally constructive control over their countries' populations and territory. This assumption has proven false. Poor, even malevolent, governance is a widespread problem. Badly governed states have become a threat to the interests of much more powerful actors: weapons of mass destruction have broken the connection between resources and the ability to do grievous harm; genocides leave political leaders in democratic polities with uncomfortable choices; and transnational disease and crime are persistent challenges.

The policy tools available to external actors—governance assistance and transitional administration—are inadequate, even when foreign powers have militarily occupied a country. Governance assistance can have positive results in occupied or badly governed states, but the available evidence suggests that the impact is weak. Transitional administration, which aims to restore conventional sovereignty in a relatively short time frame, can be effective only if indigenous political leaders believe that they will be better off allying with external actors not only while these actors are present but also after they leave.

The menu of options to deal with failing and collapsed states could be expanded in at least two ways. First, major states or regional or international organizations could assume some form of de facto trusteeship or protectorate responsibility for specific countries, even if there is no general international convention defining such arrangements. In a trusteeship, international actors would assume control over local functions for an indefinite period of time. They might also eliminate the international legal sovereignty of the entity or control treaty-making powers in whole or in part (e.g., in specific areas such as security or trade). There would be no assumption of a withdrawal in the short or medium term.

Second, domestic sovereignty in collapsed or poorly governed states could be improved through shared sovereignty contracts. These contracts would create joint authority structures in specific areas. They would not involve a direct assault on sovereignty norms because they would be formally consistent with international legal sovereignty, even though they would violate Westphalian/Vatellian sovereignty. Natural resources trusts, whose directors were appointed by national and nonnational entities, would be one possibility; central banks whose boards of governors comprised citizens and noncitizens would be another.

■　　■　　■

De facto trusteeships or protectorates and shared sovereignty hardly exhaust the possibilities for improving domestic sovereignty in poorly governed states. Leaders in some polities have already used private firms to carry out some activities that have traditionally been in the hands of state officials. Indonesia, for instance, used a Swiss firm to collect its customs for more than eleven years. Other governments have hired private military companies (PMCs). Perhaps with stronger accountability mechanisms enforced by advanced industrial states, such as the ability to prosecute PMCs and their employees for abuses, the results might be more consistently salutary.

There is no panacea for domestic sovereignty failures. Even with the best of intentions and substantial resources, external actors cannot quickly eliminate the causes of these failures: poverty, weak indigenous institutions, insecurity, and the raw materials curse. But the instruments currently available to policy-makers to deal with places such as Congo, Liberia, and Iraq are woefully inadequate. De facto trusteeships, and especially shared

sovereignty, would offer political leaders a better chance of bringing peace and prosperity to the populations of badly governed states and reduce the threat that such polities present to the wider international community.

NOTES

1. For a discussion of the requirements for successful international engagement that complements many of the points made in this article, see James D. Fearon and David D. Laitin, "Neotrusteeship and the Problem of Weak States," *International Security*, Vol. 28, No. 4 (Spring 2004), pp. 5–43.

2. See ibid., especially pp. 36–37.

3. Although the principle of nonintervention is traditionally associated with the Peace of Westphalia of 1648, the doctrine was not explicitly articulated until a century later by the Swiss jurist Emmerich de Vattel in his *The Law of Nations or Principles of the Law of Nature Applied to the Conduct and Affairs of Nations and Sovereigns*, originally published in French in 1758.

4. Mary Ann Tetreault, "Autonomy, Necessity, and the Small State: Ruling Kuwait in the Twentieth Century," *International Organization*, Vol. 45, No. 4 (Autumn 1991), pp. 565–91.

5. In Shanghai, for instance, the British established a municipal council that regulated the activities of Chinese living within Shanghai as well as non-Chinese. See Jean Chesneaux, Marianne Bastid, and Marie-Claire Bergere, *China from the Opium Wars to the 1911 Revolution* (Hassocks, Sussex, UK: Harvester, 1977), pp. 61–68.

6. For two very similar analyses, see Robert O. Keohane, "Political Authority after Intervention: Gradations in Sovereignty," in J.L. Holzgrefe and Keohane, eds., *Humanitarian Intervention: Ethical, Legal, and Political Dilemmas* (Cambridge: Cambridge University Press, 2003), pp. 276–77; and Gerald B. Helman and Steven R. Ratner, "Saving Failed States," *Foreign Policy*, No. 89 (Winter 1993), pp. 3–21. Keohane argues that there should be gradations of sovereignty. Helman and Ratner suggest that there are three forms of what they call "guardianship": governance assistance, the delegation of government authority, and trusteeship. They also suggest the term "conservatorship" as an alternative to trusteeship.

7. James D. Fearon and David D. Laitin, "Ethnicity, Insurgency, and Civil War," *American Political Science Review*, Vol. 97, No. 1 (March 2003), pp. 1–17; and Fearon and Laitin, "Neotrusteeship and the Problem of Weak States," pp. 36–37.

8. Goldstone et al., *State Failure Task Force Report*, p. 21.

9. These figures are derived from data found at World Bank, *WDI Online*, http://devdata.worldbank.org/dataonline/.

10. U.S. Department of State, *Trafficking in Persons Report* (Washington, DC: U.S. Department of State, June 2004), http://www.state.gov/documents/organization/33614.pdf.

11. International Commission on Intervention and State Sovereignty, *The Responsibility to Protect* (Ottawa: International Development Research Centre, 2001), http://www.dfait-maeci.gc.ca/icissciise/pdf/Commission-Report.pdf. See also Gareth Evans and

Mohamed Sahnoun, "The Responsibility to Protect," *Foreign Affairs*, Vol. 81, No. 6 (November/December 2002), pp. 99–110.

12. For the White House description of the MCA, see http://www.whitehouse.gov/infocus/developingnations/millennium.html. For a list of the first set of countries to receive funding from the MCA, see MCA, press release, "The Millennium Challenge Corporation Names MCA Eligible Countries," May 6, 2004, http://www.usaid.gov/mca/Documents/PR_Eligible.pdf. For a discussion of the World Bank's governance assistance programs, see http://www.worldbank.org/wbi/governance/about.html. See also Arthur A. Goldsmith, "Foreign Aid and Statehood in Africa," *International Organization*, Vol. 55, No. 1 (Winter 2000), pp. 135–36.

13. International Monetary Fund, Fiscal Affairs Department, *Fund-Supported Programs, Fiscal Policy, and Income Distribution*, Occasional Paper No. 46 (Washington, DC: International Monetary Fund, 1986), p. 40; and Robin Broad, *Unequal Alliance: The World Bank, the International Monetary Fund, and the Philippines* (Berkeley: University of California Press, 1988), pp. 51–53, Table 12.

14. Michael W. Doyle and Nicholas Sambanis, "International Peacebuilding: A Theoretical and Quantitative Analysis," *American Political Science Review*, Vol. 94, No. 4 (December 2000), pp. 779–802. For a second study with a different database but comparable findings, see George Downs and Stephen John Stedman, "Evaluating Issues in Peace Implementation," in Stedman, Donald Rothchild, and Elizabeth M. Cousens, eds., *Ending Civil Wars: The Implementation of Peace Agreements* (Boulder, CO: Lynne Rienner, 2002), pp. 50–52.

15. Richard Caplan, *A New Trusteeship? The International Administration of War-torn Territories* (London: International Institute for Strategic Studies, 2002), pp. 8–9, 50–51; United Nations, *Report of the Panel on United Nations Peace Operations* (Brahimi report) (New York: United Nations, 2000), pp. 7, 14. In June 2003 Secretary of Defense Donald Rumsfeld discussed the possibility of a standing international peacekeeping force under the leadership of the United States. Ester Schrader, "U.S. Looks at Organizing Global Peacekeeping Force," *Los Angeles Times*, June 27, 2003, p. A1.

16. Fearon and Laitin, "Neotrusteeship and the Problem of Weak States," p. 37. See also David M. Edelstein, "Occupational Hazards: Why Military Occupations Succeed or Fail," *International Security*, Vol. 29, No. 1 (Summer 2004), pp. 49–81.

17. Michael Ignatieff points to the possibly negative consequences of competition among NGOs. Ignatieff, "State Failure and Nation-Building," p. 27.

18. For Namibia, see Downs and Stedman, "Evaluating Issues in Peace Implementation," pp. 59–61; and Roland Paris, *At War's End? Building Peace after Civil Conflict* (Cambridge: Cambridge University Press, 2004), chap. 8.

19. Downs and Stedman, "Evaluating Issues in Peace Implementation," pp. 62–63; and Paris, *At War's End*, chap. 7.

20. Helman and Ratner, "Saving Failed States," pp. 3–21; Caplan, *A New Trusteeship?* p. 7; Ignatieff, "State Failure and

Nation-Building," p. 308; and Martin Indyk, "A Trusteeship for Palestine?" *Foreign Affairs*, Vol. 82, No. 3 (May/June 2003), pp. 51–66.

21. Kofi Annan, "The Legitimacy to Intervene: International Action to Uphold Human Rights Requires a New Understanding of State and Individual Sovereignty," *Financial Times*, December 31, 1999.

22. Fearon and Laitin have suggested that "neotrusteeship" is the most appropriate term for arrangements that could cope with the postconflict security problems afflicting states suffering from weak administrative capacity, poverty, and rough terrain. Because such states are unlikely to be able to conduct effective policing and counterinsurgency operations on their own, maintaining security will require the engagement of external actors for an extended period of time. The authors do not, however, argue that neotrusteeship would involve a loss of international legal sovereignty. See Fearon and Laitin, "Neotrusteeship and the Problem of Weak States," especially pp. 24–41.

23. Donald C. Blaisdell, *European Financial Control in the Ottoman Empire: A Study of the Establishment, Activities, and Significance of the Administration of the Ottoman Public Debt* (New York: Columbia University Press, 1929), pp. 90–120, 124–30; Herbert Feis, *Europe, the World's Banker, 1870–1914: An Account of European Foreign Investment and the Connection of World Finance with Diplomacy before World War I* (New York: W. W. Norton, 1965), pp. 332–41; Bernard Lewis, *The Middle East: A Brief History of the Last 2,000 Years* (New York: Scribner, 1995), pp. 298–99; and Roger Owen, *The Middle East in the World Economy, 1800–1914* (Cambridge: Cambridge University Press, 1981), p. 101.

24. "Revised NATO SOFA Supplementary Agreement," articles 19, 22, 28. The full text of the agreement is available at http://www.oxc.army.mil/others/Gca/files%5Cgermany.doc.

25. "Convention on Relations between the Three Powers and the Federal Republic of Germany," *American Journal of International Law*, Vol. 49, No. 3 (July 1955), pp. 57–69. For a detailed examination of the retained rights of the Western powers, see Joseph W. Bishop Jr., "The 'Contractual Agreements' with the Federal Republic of Germany," *American Journal of International Law*, Vol. 49, No. 2 (April 1955), pp. 125–47. For a general analysis of Germany's situation after World War II, see Peter J. Katzenstein, *Policy and Politics in West Germany: The Growth of a Semisovereign State* (Philadelphia: Temple University Press, 1987).

26. Michael Lewin Ross, "Does Oil Hinder Democracy?" *World Politics*, Vol. 53, No. 3 (April 2001), pp. 325–61.

27. This proposal assumes that oil could be exploited only by companies domiciled in advanced democratic polities interested in supporting good governance and that these countries cooperate with each other. Absent these conditions, the host country could play one oil company against another and avoid the constraints that would come with a shared sovereignty trust.

28. Caplan, *A New Trusteeship?* p. 39.

Samuel P. Huntington

THE CLASH OF CIVILIZATIONS?

The Next Pattern of Conflict

World politics is entering a new phase, and intellectuals have not hesitated to proliferate visions of what it will be—the end of history, the return of traditional rivalries between nation states, and the decline of the nation state from the conflicting pulls of tribalism and globalism, among others. Each of these visions catches aspects of the emerging reality. Yet they all miss a crucial, indeed a central, aspect of what global politics is likely to be in the coming years.

It is my hypothesis that the fundamental source of conflict in this new world will not be primarily ideological or primarily economic. The great divisions among humankind and the dominating source of conflict will be cultural. Nation states will remain the most powerful actors in world affairs, but the principal conflicts of global politics will occur between nations and groups of different civilizations. The clash of civilizations will dominate global politics. The fault lines between civilizations will be the battle lines of the future.

Conflict between civilizations will be the latest phase in the evolution of conflict in the modern world. For a century and a half after the emergence of the modern international system with the Peace of Westphalia, the conflicts of the Western world were largely among princes—emperors, absolute monarchs, and constitutional monarchs attempting to expand their bureaucracies, their armies, their mercantilist economic strength, and,

From *Foreign Affairs* 72, no. 3 (Summer 1993): 22–49.

most important, the territory they ruled. In the process they created nation states, and beginning with the French Revolution the principal lines of conflict were between nations rather than princes. * * * [A]s a result of the Russian Revolution and the reaction against it, the conflict of nations yielded to the conflict of ideologies, first among communism, fascism-Nazism, and liberal democracy, and then between communism and liberal democracy. During the Cold War, this latter conflict became embodied in the struggle between the two superpowers, neither of which was a nation state in the classical European sense and each of which defined its identity in terms of its ideology.

* * * With the end of the Cold War, international politics moves out of its Western phase, and its centerpiece becomes the interaction between the West and non-Western civilizations and among non-Western civilizations. In the politics of civilizations, the peoples and governments of non-Western civilizations no longer remain the objects of history as targets of Western colonialism but join the West as movers and shapers of history.

The Nature of Civilizations

During the Cold War the world was divided into the First, Second, and Third Worlds. Those divisions are no longer relevant. It is far more meaningful now to group countries not in terms of their political or economic systems or in terms of their level of economic development but rather in terms of their culture and civilization.

What do we mean when we talk of a civilization? A civilization is a cultural entity. Villages, regions, ethnic groups, nationalities, religious groups, all have distinct cultures at different levels of cultural heterogeneity. The culture of a village in southern Italy may be different from that of a village in northern Italy, but both will share in a common Italian culture that distinguishes them from German villages. European communities, in turn, will share cultural features that distinguish them from Arab or Chinese communities. Arabs, Chinese, and Westerners, however, are not part of any broader cultural entity. They constitute civilizations. A civilization is thus the highest cultural grouping of people and the broadest level of cultural identity people have short of that which distinguishes humans from other species. It is defined both by common objective elements, such as language, history, religion, customs, institutions, and by the subjective self-identification of people. * * *

* * * Civilizations are nonetheless meaningful entities, and while the lines between them are seldom sharp, they are real. Civilizations are dynamic; they rise and fall; they divide and merge. And, as any student of history knows, civilizations disappear and are buried in the sands of time.

Westerners tend to think of nation states as the principal actors in global affairs. They have been that, however, for only a few centuries. The broader reaches of human history have been the history of civilizations. In *A Study of History*, Arnold Toynbee identified 21 major civilizations; only six of them exist in the contemporary world.

Why Civilizations Will Clash

Civilization identity will be increasingly important in the future, and the world will be shaped in large measure by the interactions among seven or eight major civilizations. These include Western, Confucian, Japanese, Islamic, Hindu, Slavic-Orthodox, Latin American, and possibly African civilization. The most important conflicts of the future will occur along the cultural fault lines separating these civilizations from one another.

Why will this be the case?

First, differences among civilizations are not only real; they are basic. Civilizations are differentiated from each other by history, language, culture, tradition and, most important, religion. The people of different civilizations have different views on the relations between God and man, the individual and the group, the citizen and the state, parents and children, husband and wife, as well as differing views of the relative importance of rights and responsibilities, liberty and authority, equality and hierarchy. These differences are the product of centuries. They will not soon disappear. * * *

Second, the world is becoming a smaller place. The interactions between peoples of different civilizations are increasing; these increasing interactions intensify civilization consciousness and awareness of differences between civilizations and commonalities within civilizations. * * *

Third, the processes of economic modernization and social change throughout the world are separating people from longstanding local identities. They also weaken the nation state as a source of identity. In much of the world, religion has moved in to fill this gap, often in the form of movements that are labeled "fundamentalist." Such movements are found in Western Christianity, Judaism, Buddhism, and Hinduism, as well as in Islam. * * * The "unsecularization of the world," George Weigel has remarked, "is one of the dominant social facts of life in the late twentieth century." * * *

Fourth, the growth of civilization-consciousness is enhanced by the dual role of the West. On the one hand, the West is at a peak of power. At the same time, however, and perhaps as a result, a return to the roots phenomenon is occurring among non-Western civilizations. Increasingly one hears references to trends toward a turning inward and "Asianization" in Japan, the end of the Nehru legacy and the "Hinduization" of India, the failure of Western ideas of socialism and nationalism and hence "re-Islamization" of the Middle East, and now a debate over Westernization versus Russianization in Boris Yeltsin's country. A West at the peak of its power confronts non-Wests that increasingly have the desire, the will, and the resources to shape the world in non-Western ways.

■ ■ ■

Fifth, cultural characteristics and differences are less mutable and hence less easily compromised and resolved than political and economic ones. In the former Soviet Union, communists can become democrats, the rich can become poor and the poor rich, but Russians cannot become Estonians and Azeris cannot become Armenians. * * * Even more than ethnicity, religion discriminates sharply and exclusively among people. A person can be half-French and half-Arab and simultaneously even a citizen of two countries. It is more difficult to be half-Catholic and half-Muslim.

Finally, economic regionalism is increasing. * * * On the one hand, successful economic regionalism will reinforce civilization-consciousness. On the other hand, economic regionalism may succeed only when it is rooted in a common civilization. The European Community rests on the shared foundation of European culture and Western Christianity. The success of the North American Free Trade Area depends on the convergence now underway of Mexican, Canadian, and American cultures. Japan, in contrast, faces difficulties in creating a comparable economic entity in East Asia because Japan is a society and civilization unique to itself. * * *

■ ■ ■

As people define their identity in ethnic and religious terms, they are likely to see an "us" versus "them" relation existing between themselves and people of different ethnicity or religion. The end of ideologically defined states in Eastern Europe and the former Soviet Union permits traditional ethnic identities and animosities to come to the fore. Differences in culture and religion create differences over policy issues, ranging from human rights to immigration to trade and commerce to the environment. * * * Most important, the efforts of the West to promote its values of democracy and liberalism as universal values, to maintain its military predominance and to advance its economic interests engender countering responses from other civilizations. * * *

The clash of civilizations thus occurs at two levels. At the micro-level, adjacent groups along the fault lines between civilizations struggle, often violently, over the control of territory and each other. At the macro-level, states from different civilizations compete for relative military and economic power, struggle over the control of international institutions and third parties, and competitively promote their particular political and religious values.

The Fault Lines between Civilizations

The fault lines between civilizations are replacing the political and ideological boundaries of the Cold War as the flash points for crisis and bloodshed. The Cold War began when the Iron Curtain divided Europe politically and ideologically. The Cold War ended with the end of the Iron Curtain. As the ideological division of Europe has disappeared, the cultural division of Europe between Western Christianity, on the one hand, and Orthodox Christianity and Islam, on the other, has reemerged. The most significant dividing line in Europe, as William Wallace has suggested, may well be the eastern boundary of Western Christianity in the year 1500. This line runs along what are now the boundaries between Finland and

Russia and between the Baltic states and Russia, cuts through Belarus and Ukraine separating the more Catholic western Ukraine from Orthodox eastern Ukraine, swings westward separating Transylvania from the rest of Romania, and then goes through Yugoslavia almost exactly along the line now separating Croatia and Slovenia from the rest of Yugoslavia. In the Balkans this line, of course, coincides with the historic boundary between the Hapsburg and Ottoman empires. The peoples to the north and west of this line are Protestant or Catholic; they shared the common experiences of European history—feudalism, the Renaissance, the Reformation, the Enlightenment, the French Revolution, the Industrial Revolution; they are generally economically better off than the peoples to the east; and they may now look forward to increasing involvement in a common European economy and to the consolidation of democratic political systems. The peoples to the east and south of this line are Orthodox or Muslim; they historically belonged to the Ottoman or Tsarist empires and were only lightly touched by the shaping events in the rest of Europe; they are generally less advanced economically; they seem much less likely to develop stable democratic political systems. The Velvet Curtain of culture has replaced the Iron Curtain of ideology as the most significant dividing line in Europe. As the events in Yugoslavia show, it is not only a line of difference; it is also at times a line of bloody conflict.

Conflict along the fault line between Western and Islamic civilizations has been going on for 1,300 years. * * *

■   ■   ■

This centuries-old military interaction between the West and Islam is unlikely to decline. It could become more virulent. The Gulf War left some Arabs feeling proud that Saddam Hussein had attacked Israel and stood up to the West. It also left many feeling humiliated and resentful of the West's military presence in the Persian Gulf, the West's overwhelming military dominance, and their apparent inability to shape their own destiny. Many Arab countries, in addition to the oil exporters, are reaching levels of economic and social development where autocratic forms of government become inappropriate and efforts to introduce democracy become stronger. Some openings in Arab political systems have already occurred. The principal beneficiaries of these openings have been Islamist movements. * * *

Those relations are also complicated by demography. The spectacular population growth in Arab countries, particularly in North Africa, has led to increased migration to Western Europe. The movement within Western Europe toward minimizing internal boundaries has sharpened political sensitivities with respect to this development. * * *

■   ■   ■

Historically, the other great antagonistic interaction of Arab Islamic civilization has been with the pagan, animist, and now increasingly Christian black peoples to the south. In the past, this antagonism was epitomized in the image of Arab slave dealers and black slaves. It has been reflected in the on-going civil war in the Sudan between Arabs and blacks, the fighting in Chad between Libyan-supported insurgents and the government, the tensions between Orthodox Christians and Muslims in the Horn of Africa, and the political conflicts, recurring riots and communal violence between Muslims and Christians in Nigeria. The modernization of Africa and the spread of Christianity are likely to enhance the probability of violence along this fault line. Symptomatic of the intensification of this conflict was the Pope John Paul II's speech in Khartoum in February 1993 attacking the actions of the Sudan's Islamist government against the Christian minority there.

On the northern border of Islam, conflict has increasingly erupted between Orthodox and

Muslim peoples, including the carnage of Bosnia and Sarajevo, the simmering violence between Serb and Albanian, the tenuous relations between Bulgarians and their Turkish minority, the violence between Ossetians and Ingush, the unremitting slaughter of each other by Armenians and Azeris, the tense relations between Russians and Muslims in Central Asia. * * *

The conflict of civilizations is deeply rooted elsewhere in Asia. The historic clash between Muslim and Hindu in the subcontinent manifests itself now not only in the rivalry between Pakistan and India but also in intensifying religious strife within India between increasingly militant Hindu groups and India's substantial Muslim minority. The destruction of the Ayodhya mosque in December 1992 brought to the fore the issue of whether India will remain a secular democratic state or become a Hindu one. * * *

■　　■　　■

Groups or states belonging to one civilization that become involved in war with people from a different civilization naturally try to rally support from other members of their own civilization. * * *

■　　■　　■

Civilization rallying to date has been limited, but it has been growing, and it clearly has the potential to spread much further. As the conflicts in the Persian Gulf, the Caucasus, and Bosnia continued, the positions of nations and the cleavages between them increasingly were along civilizational lines. Populist politicians, religious leaders, and the media have found it a potent means of arousing mass support and of pressuring hesitant governments. In the coming years, the local conflicts most likely to escalate into major wars will be those, as in Bosnia and the Caucasus, along the fault lines between civilizations. The next world war, if there is one, will be a war between civilizations.

The West versus the Rest

The West is now at an extraordinary peak of power in relation to other civilizations. Its superpower opponent has disappeared from the map. Military conflict among Western states is unthinkable, and Western military power is unrivaled. Apart from Japan, the West faces no economic challenge. It dominates international political and security institutions and with Japan international economic institutions. Global political and security issues are effectively settled by a directorate of the United States, Britain, and France, world economic issues by a directorate of the United States, Germany, and Japan, all of which maintain extraordinarily close relations with each other to the exclusion of lesser and largely non-Western countries. Decisions made at the U.N. Security Council or in the International Monetary Fund that reflect the interests of the West are presented to the world as reflecting the desires of the world community. The very phrase "the world community" has become the euphemistic collective noun (replacing "the Free World") to give global legitimacy to actions reflecting the interests of the United States and other Western powers.[1] * * *

■　　■　　■

* * * V. S. Naipaul has argued that Western civilization is the "universal civilization" that "fits all men." At a superficial level much of Western culture has indeed permeated the rest of the world. At a more basic level, however, Western concepts differ fundamentally from those prevalent in other civilizations. Western ideas of individualism, liberalism, constitutionalism, human rights, equality, liberty, the rule of law, democracy, free markets, the separation of church and state often have little resonance in Islamic, Confucian, Japanese, Hindu, Buddhist, or Orthodox cultures. Western efforts to propagate such ideas produce instead a reaction against "human rights imperialism" and a reaffirmation of

indigenous values, as can be seen in the support for religious fundamentalism by the younger generation in non-Western cultures. The very notion that there could be a "universal civilization" is a Western idea, directly at odds with the particularism of most Asian societies and their emphasis on what distinguishes one people from another. Indeed, the author of a review of 100 comparative studies of values in different societies concluded that "the values that are most important in the West are least important worldwide."[2] In the political realm, of course, these differences are most manifest in the efforts of the United States and other Western powers to induce other peoples to adopt Western ideas concerning democracy and human rights. Modern democratic government originated in the West. When it has developed in non-Western societies it has usually been the product of Western colonialism or imposition.

The central axis of world politics in the future is likely to be, in Kishore Mahbubani's phrase, the conflict between "the West and the Rest" and the responses of non-Western civilizations to Western power and values.[3] Those responses generally take one or a combination of three forms. At one extreme, non-Western states can, like Burma and North Korea, attempt to pursue a course of isolation, to insulate their societies from penetration or "corruption" by the West, and, in effect, to opt out of participation in the Western-dominated global community. The costs of this course, however, are high, and few states have pursued it exclusively. A second alternative, the equivalent of "bandwagoning" in international relations theory, is to attempt to join the West and accept its values and institutions. The third alternative is to attempt to "balance" the West by developing economic and military power and cooperating with other non-Western societies against the West, while preserving indigenous values and institutions; in short, to modernize but not to Westernize.

■   ■   ■

Implications for the West

This article does not argue that civilization identities will replace all other identities, that nation states will disappear, that each civilization will become a single coherent political entity, that groups within a civilization will not conflict with and even fight each other. This paper does set forth the hypotheses that differences between civilizations are real and important; civilization-consciousness is increasing; conflict between civilizations will supplant ideological and other forms of conflict as the dominant global form of conflict; international relations, historically a game played out within Western civilization, will increasingly be de-Westernized and become a game in which non-Western civilizations are actors and not simply objects; successful political, security, and economic international institutions are more likely to develop within civilizations than across civilizations; conflicts between groups in different civilizations will be more frequent, more sustained, and more violent than conflicts between groups in the same civilization; violent conflicts between groups in different civilizations are the most likely and most dangerous source of escalation that could lead to global wars; the paramount axis of world politics will be the relations between "the West and the Rest"; the elites in some torn non-Western countries will try to make their countries part of the West, but in most cases face major obstacles to accomplishing this; a central focus of conflict for the immediate future will be between the West and several Islamic-Confucian states.

This is not to advocate the desirability of conflicts between civilizations. It is to set forth descriptive hypotheses as to what the future may be like. If these are plausible hypotheses, however, it is necessary to consider their implications for Western policy. These implications should be divided between short-term advantage and long-term accommodation. In the short term it is clearly in the interest of the West to promote greater cooperation and unity within its own civilization, particularly between its European and North American components; to incorporate into the West societies in Eastern Europe, and Latin America whose cultures are close to those of the West; to promote and maintain cooperative relations with Russia and Japan; to prevent escalation of local inter-civilization conflicts into major inter-civilization wars; to limit the expansion of the military strength of Confucian and Islamic states; to moderate the reduction of Western military capabilities and maintain military superiority in East and Southwest Asia; to exploit differences and conflicts among Confucian and Islamic states; to support in other civilizations groups sympathetic to Western values and interests; to strengthen international institutions that reflect and legitimate Western interests and values and to promote the involvement of non-Western states in those institutions.

In the longer term other measures would be called for. Western civilization is both Western and modern. Non-Western civilizations have attempted to become modern without becoming Western. To date only Japan has fully succeeded in this quest. Non-Western civilizations will continue to attempt to acquire the wealth, technology, skills, machines, and weapons that are part of being modern. They will also attempt to reconcile this modernity with their traditional culture and values. Their economic and military strength

relative to the West will increase. Hence the West will increasingly have to accommodate these non-Western modern civilizations whose power approaches that of the West but whose values and interests differ significantly from those of the West. This will require the West to maintain the economic and military power necessary to protect its interests in relation to these civilizations. It will also, however, require the West to develop a more profound understanding of the basic religious and philosophical assumptions underlying other civilizations and the ways in which people in those civilizations see their interests. It will require an effort to identify elements of commonality between Western and other civilizations. For the relevant future, there will be no universal civilization, but instead a world of different civilizations, each of which will have to learn to coexist with the others.

NOTES

1. Almost invariably Western leaders claim they are acting on behalf of "the world community." One minor lapse occurred during the run-up to the Gulf War. In an interview on "Good Morning America," Dec. 21, 1990, British Prime Minister John Major referred to the actions "the West" was taking against Saddam Hussein. He quickly corrected himself and subsequently referred to "the world community." He was, however, right when he erred.

2. Harry C. Triandis, *The New York Times*, Dec. 25, 1990, p. 41, and "Cross-Cultural Studies of Individualism and Collectivism," Nebraska Symposium on Motivation, vol. 37, 1989, pp. 41–133.

3. Kishore Mahbubani, "The West and the Rest," *The National Interest*, Summer 1992, pp. 3–13.

Susanne Hoeber Rudolph and Lloyd I. Rudolph

MODERN HATE

How ancient animosities get invented

On Inauguration Day, Bill Clinton told the country and the world a story about how "a generation raised in the shadows of the Cold War assumes new responsibilities in a world warmed by the sunshine of freedom but threatened still by ancient hatreds." The new president seemed to have in mind such things as ethnic cleansing and religious fundamentalism, the first a deceptive metaphor invented by extreme nationalist Serbs, the second a ubiquitous term that relieves politicians, news anchors, and policy intellectuals from thinking about the complexities of the "other."

One event that fed the country's growing preoccupation with ancient hatreds occurred last December, when "Hindu fundamentalists" tore down a mosque built in the sixteenth century by the first Mughal emperor, Babur, in Ayodhya, a small town in eastern Uttar Pradesh, India's most populous state. Its destruction was the climax of three tumultuous years during which the Hindu nationalist Bharatiya Janata Party piqued emotions over the mosque. It held that Babur had destroyed a temple on Lord Rama's birthsite in order to build what came to be known as the Babri Masjid (Babur's Mosque); thus, Hindus should reclaim their heritage by building a new temple to Lord Rama on the site of the mosque. More than 2,500 people were killed in the retaliatory violence that followed the destruction of the Babri Masjid. In January violence erupted again in

From *The New Republic*, March 22, 1993, 24–29.

Bombay, where the police openly abetted burning and vandalism. At the end of February, the BJP attempted to hold a mass rally in New Delhi to bring down the Congress party government.

But recent news accounts that depict the violence as an outgrowth of old animosities are misleading. Hindus and Muslims in India under the Mughal emperor Akbar, the nationalistic leadership of Mahatma Gandhi, and the Congress governments of Jawaharlal Nehru have gotten along more often than they have gone for each other's throats. So did Serbs, Croats, and Muslims under Tito in Yugoslavia. Clinton and others too easily invoke "ancient hatreds" to explain what are really contemporary conflicts. The question, in other words, is not why old conflicts are flaring up anew, but rather why traditionally harmonious mosaics have been shattered.

Before Christmas, the Hanukkah card section of the University of Chicago bookstore featured a seasonal card depicting two Santas, one with a white beard, one with a brown one, the first carrying the regulation Santa bag, the second carrying a menorah. A scholar of India looks at that card and says, "How Indian!" St. Nicholas integrated into a Jewish festival! Societies with a plurality of religions can and often do work out symbolic settlements. Until recently, the ability to reach such settlements was the dominant theme in Indian history and in its postindependence politics. Friendships are as "ancient" as hatreds. The face we see depends on what human agents cause us to see.

Looking at that Hanukkah card, we were reminded of a friend of ours, an observant Muslim, one of the numerous South Asian diaspora in Chicago. As a child in India, she was once asked to participate in a small community drama about the life of Lord Krishna. Krishna is the blue "Hindu" god adored by shepherdesses, who dance for his pleasure. They exemplify through their human passion the quest of the devout soul for the lord. Not exactly a Muslim monotheist's theme. She was invited to dance as a shepherdess with other schoolgirls. Her father forbade it: Muslims don't dance. In that case, said the drama's director, we will cast you as Krishna. All you have to do is stand there in the usual Krishna pose, a flute at your mouth. Her father consented. She played Krishna.

Line-crossing seemed as natural to that Krishna-playing child as it did to Mahatma Gandhi. In his autobiography, *The Story of My Experiments with Truth*, he recalls that his devout mother regularly visited the tomb of a Muslim *pir* and followed Jain ideas about self-suffering and nonviolence. Her un-self-conscious ecumenism was common in Gandhi's birthplace, Kathiawad, a cosmopolitan entrepôt area bordering the Arabian sea. Gandhi began his historic career in South Africa, working for migrant Muslim businessmen from the same region.

With about 110 million Muslim citizens, India is the second-largest Muslim country in the world, after Indonesia. Islam takes many forms, from the most severe monotheism to a Sufi mysticism and devotion that features worship of saints and their relics—practices repugnant to a more austere orthodoxy. Sufi *pirs* and their magnificent tombs attract Hindu as well as Muslim pilgrims from all parts of the subcontinent. None is more renowned than the Dargah at Ajmer, the burial place of Kwaja Nuin-ud-din Chisti, founder in the twelfth century of a family of saints and courtiers, a shrine second only to Mecca in the eyes of South Asian Muslims. Cultural practices mingle and mix. Hindu practices persist among converts to Islam—dietary laws are followed, marriage boundaries observed, festivals celebrated. Aristocratic north Indian culture, its language and manners, its music and cuisine, remained distinctively Persian at least until the time of Nehru, embodying the idioms of Mughal court culture. The region's leading performers of Hindu devotional music, the Dagar brothers, are Muslims. Village Muslims, like their urban brothers, share in local or neighborhood *Ramayana* performances and watch as eagerly as the rest of the nation when Doordarshan, Indian state-run television, airs the eighteen-month-long megaseries on the ("Hindu") *Ramayana* and *Mahabharata*.

But not all practices promote a composite culture and unity in diversity. Hindu and Muslim religious sensibilities have vacillated between tendencies to naturalize and demonize differences. Political language in the nationalist era sometimes used religious symbols to make politics meaningful to common people for whom religion was a natural idiom. Religious language, however, is capable of many different forms of expression.

Some nationalists used Hindu religious symbolism that excluded Muslims. B. G. Tilak, India's most influential popular leader before Mahatma Gandhi, led the way in inventing "communalism," the term Indians use for community exclusivism and chauvinism. In the 1890s, keen to build a mass following, he revived a Maharashtrian festival commemorating the birth of Shiva's elephant-headed son, Ganesh, Hinduism's most beloved deity. For ten days each year villagers poured into cities and towns to celebrate and hear recitations of Hindu epic poetry. Ganapati festivals became occasions for clashes with Muslims when paramilitary "Ganesh guards" directed noisy parades past mosques at prayer time. Muslims began to retaliate by acts of profanation and desacralization, "killing cows" and cutting auspicious peepul trees. Bengali nationalists wrote plays and songs that alienated Muslims by using the theme of opposition to Muslim kings as a surrogate for opposition to British rule.

Secular nationalism took different forms: Nehru maintained that science should ask and answer all questions; Gandhi believed that spiritual truth could be found in all religions. At Gandhi's prayer meetings, the Gita, the Koran, and the Bible were read. He favored a national language—Hindustani—which could accommodate Urdu, the language of North Indian Muslims, and Hindi, the language of North Indian Hindus.

"Ancient hatreds" are thus made as much as they are inherited. To call them ancient is to pretend they are primordial forces, outside of history and human agency, when often they are merely synthetic antiques. Intellectuals, writers, artists, and politicians "make" hatreds. Films and videos, texts and textbooks, certify stories about the past, the collective memories that shape perceptions and attitudes.

Before democracy, modernization, and the nation-state, Hinduism was loose, open, and diverse, a web of local and regional sectarian groupings defined by a sacred geography of places and events, deities and temples. The very term "Hinduism" was an abstraction, a word used by outsiders to describe a place and a people, not an institutionalized religion. Travelers—Hsuan Tsang, the seventh-century Chinese Buddhist pilgrim, and Alberuni, the eleventh-century Arab savant accompanying Mahmud of Ghazni—designated trans-Indus peoples as Hindus.

Instead of Hindus, there were followers of saints (sants): Kabir followers and Dadu followers, Vaishnavites in Gujarat and Bengal, Lingayats in Karnataka, and Shivites in Tamilnadu, pursuing distinctive doctrines and practices. It is a truism to say Hinduism had no church. There was no pope, no ecclesia, no bishops to enunciate what

was orthodox and heterodox, much less heretical or blasphemous. Great debates at Banaras reverberated through the centuries. Great teachers such as Shankara in the eighth century and Ramanuja in the twelfth were revered. But there was no all-India, transhistorical authority. Even today a local religious teacher in Jaipur or Bangalore is likely to be the person of greatest authority for her followers; no one is in a position to discipline her or to question her doctrine or ritual practices.

If there was no standard version of Hinduism until yesterday, then when and how did the day before yesterday end? How did it happen that the Bharatiya Janata Party was able to hijack Hinduism, replacing its diversity multivocality and generativity with a monotheistic Ram cult? An answer can be found in the history of storytelling. The ancient legend of Ram, the virtuous god-king, incarnation of Vishnu, who wandered in exile for twelve years with his wife Sita before vanquishing the Southern demon Ravana, can be found all over India. It is a moral tale, exemplifying what right conduct should be between a king and his subjects and among generations, genders, and relatives. Ram was an intimate deity, his representations infinitely diverse by region and locale. He was the subject of thousands of *Ramayanas* in many languages, of village drama cycles, of stories told by grandmothers, and today of epic comic books.

In time, Ram stories became consolidated. In *The Life of a Text: Performing the Ramcaritmanas of Tulsidas,* Philip Lutgendorf writes that this sixteenth-century *Ramayana* was regarded "not merely as the greatest modern Indian epic, but as something like a living sum of Indian culture." Lutgendorf details how during the nineteenth century the recitations of the *Ramayana* became the vehicle for the "rise of the eternal religion" and how, through the *manas,* Hindus became a "people of the book." In 1984 the vastly popular recitals of the text, boxed in a set of eight audiocassettes, was the "hottest-selling recording in the thriving cassette stalls of Banaras," hotter even than the immensely popular cassettes of Hindi film music.

In January 1987 an eighteen-month-long serial of the *Ramayana* based on the *manas* began airing at 9:30 AM, prime time, on state-run TV *Ramayana* episodes quickly became the most popular program ever shown, attracting an estimated 100 million viewers, roughly the size of the audience for presidential debates in America. On Sundays streets were deserted throughout India. Everyone was watching, even knots of cycle rickshaw drivers crowded in front of TV store windows.

The *Ramayana* "megaseries" took advantage of a new space for religious discourse in India, Pakistan, Iran, Oman, and elsewhere, a public space outside the private arenas of family and village, temple, and mosque. In this space a new public culture is being created and consumed. Distant persons, strangers, create representations of public culture for anonymous viewers. Values and symbols, meaning systems and metaphors, can be standardized for national consumption.

And what did the series do to grandmother's version of the Rama tale? Or to the village performance? In Gatiali, located in the state of Rajasthan, the local village production of *Ramayana* wasn't performed in 1989. Village leaders who watched the television version had been impressed. The local version seemed to them amateurish by comparison. Why take the trouble and expense to put on an unworthy, moth-eaten version? Other Hinduish megaseries followed—such as the great epic *Mahabharata, Chanakya,* a Hindu nationalist reinvention of the Mauryan empire's cunning prime minister. Together they helped stamp out diversity and localism, replacing them with a national, standardized version of Hinduism, what historian and social critic Romila Thapar has characterized as syndicated, semitized Hinduism,

a Hinduism of one God, one book, one place, one people, a religion resembling exclusivist versions of Judaism, Christianity, and Islam.

Ten months after the *Ramayana* megaseries, the Vishua Hindu Parishad (World Hindu Council) called on Hindus throughout India to make holy bricks, inscribed with Rama's name, for use at Ayodhya. There, at the site of Rama's birth, and on the place of the Babri Masjid, they would build a temple to Rama. Construction was deferred during the national elections of 1989. The Bharatiya Janata Party, which had captured only two seats with 8 percent of the vote in 1984, now garnered eighty-six seats with 11 percent. Its modest 3 percentage point increase in electoral votes suggests that the party gained eighty-four seats more by virtue of making electoral alliances than by an increase in popular support, but its electoral gains put religion in the political spotlight. After another two years the BJP emerged from the May–June 1991 election as India's second-largest party, its vote share bounding upward from 11 percent to 20 percent and its seats in Parliament increasing from eighty-six to 118. L. K. Advani told India's electorate that if the countries of Western Europe and the United States can call themselves Christian. India should be free to call itself Hindu.

One of the ways to think about the recent savaging of the Babri Masjid by young Hindu men is to see it as a renegotiation of political and economic power and status, or rather as a sign of the pathology of renegotiation. The youths we saw standing on the domes of the doomed mosque were wearing city clothes, shirts and trousers, not the *kuria* and *dhotis* of villagers or the urban poor. They looked like clerks, boys from urban lower-middle-class families. They are the educated unemployed, not the poor and illiterate. Frustrated by the lack of good jobs and opportunities, they are victims of modernization, seeking to victimize others—like "pampered" Muslims.

In an India where, despite its problems, the number of persons under the poverty line has been declining and entrepreneurship expanding exponentially, their expectations have run well ahead of available opportunities.

Social mobility in India has become a widespread phenomenon. Liberalization and economic growth have enormously expanded the opportunities for many Indians. The '80s witnessed the highest economic growth rates of the last five decades. Green revolutionaries have grown prosperous on high-yielding varieties of wheat; doctors and engineers educated at government expense find public sector jobs; craftspeople who have parleyed workshops into lucrative enterprises supply large manufacturers. Such mobility is unhinging a severely hierarchical asociety, creating social stress bred of envy and resentment. Old, established Hindu middle classes, mostly from the upper literate and landed castes, suddenly see a whole range of Johnny-come-latelies at their side who only yesterday were their inferiors in status and income, both low-caste folk and Muslims. The hatred that led Nathuram Godse to kill Mahatma Gandhi was bred in the resentment of upper castes on the way down. Gandhi had mobilized the periphery against the center, the lower castes and village poor against Brahmanical orthodoxy. These are conflicts generated by individuals using the opportunities of recent history.

The short-lived Janata party government of 1990, under V. P. Singh, recognized the political implications of the emergence into politics and social power of these new forces, forging an alliance of the "Backward Classes" (a *raj* euphemism for the disadvantaged lower castes) and Muslims. The Backward Classes, many of them agricultural castes who have profited from the green revolution, have been demanding quotas in government jobs and education for decades. Their demands threaten the position of urban upper castes who respond to an appeal to Hindu identity, whose long traditions of literacy have given them the advantage in merit-based competitions, and who disproportionately control such jobs.

How is that relevant to the position of Muslims? They do not have such quotas, either in government jobs or in education. The main "privilege" they have in independent India is immunity for their religiously based family law, which allows "privileges" such as multiple marriages for men and easy divorce. Muslims also have had tacit guarantees, imperfectly enforced, from state and federal governments to be represented in Cabinet and party posts. These may not be substantial privileges, but to the upper castes in the midst of backlash against their slipping position, it is easier to resent minority "privileges" for Muslims than for other minorities. At 11 percent, Muslims are a more vulnerable target than the proportionately more numerous and politically more powerful "Backwards."

North India's Muslim population was decapitated at independence in 1947, when Muslim landowners and educated professionals, many descendants of Mughal court families, went to Pakistan. They left behind silk weavers in Banaras, gem cutters in Jaipur, poor cultivators and unskilled laborers, hewers of wood and drawers of water. But in recent years Muslims have found new opportunities through migratory labor to the Middle East.

A major component of India's foreign exchange has come from remittances of guest workers in the Gulf, Iraq, and other Middle East countries. When several hundred thousand fled the Gulf War in early 1991, the precipitous fall in remittances that followed triggered a foreign exchange crisis that drove India into the arms of the International Monetary Fund and the World Bank. A large proportion of India's guest workers were (and are again) Muslims. For years they sent their earnings home to poor relatives scattered all over India. Their relatives built fancy houses and mosques cheek by jowl with the ostentatious homes and temples of newly rich Hindu neighbors. As Muslim youths joined the sons of green revolution farmers in sporting jeans and sunglasses, as their parents joined Hindu traders in wearing terrycotton bush suits and driving Rajiv Gandhi's car of choice, the "Gypsy" off-road vehicle, newly rich Muslims elbowed their way ahead rather than lagging respectfully behind.

Prosperity has also bred resentment and anger among those in North India. Kerala and Bombay accustomed to Muslim invisibility and deference. Hindu professionals and businessmen expect Muslims to serve them as tailors and bakers. Industrial and office workers seeking jobs, better pay, or promotions expect them to stick to their traditional occupations—weaving, gem cutting, brass tooling. Hindus often respond to Muslim mobility and wealth by challenging Nehru-style secularism that offers special protection to Islam and Muslims. They decry it as privileging Muslim communalism and stigmatizing Hindu communalism. The Hindu backlash to minority protectionism asks, whose country is this anyway? In Bombay in early January, a month after the destruction of the Babri Masjid, the militantly Hindu, Muslim-hating Shiv Sena acted out the fiery images and language of its campaign videos by torching Muslim homes and shops. The Bombay elite's sense of being in charge and safe in India's most cosmopolitan city was shattered when roving bands searched for Muslim names in elegant apartments along hitherto sacrosanct Marine Drive, Club Road, and Malabar Hill.

The prospect that the aspiring poor might receive yet another boost from government action helped precipitate the Ayodhya crisis. In August 1990 Prime Minister Singh's minority government implemented the Mandal Commission report. The report recommended "reservations"—quotas—in federal government employment for Backward Classes. Singh, who had campaigned on the issue, announced that 27 percent of federal jobs were to

be reserved for Backward Classes. Together with the current 15 percent for untouchables (those at the bottom of the caste system) and the 7 percent for tribals, roughly their proportions of the population, reservations now totaled 49 percent, a ceiling set by the Supreme Court to maintain the credibility of the equal opportunity clause of the constitution.

Singh's minority government had been held in place by support from a number of left and right parties, including the Hindu-oriented BJP. The BJP leaders, who had not been consulted on the implementation, thought that Singh was ditching their party's support with a view to holding a midterm election that would give him a clear majority. He would appeal to the "minorities"—untouchables, lower castes, Muslims, tribals who together constituted some 60 percent of India's population. The BJP set out to trump Singh's social justice platform, which pitted the disadvantaged against the advantaged, with a Hindu communal unity appeal.

Indian politics began to polarize around *mandir* (temple) versus Mandal. Within a week, anti-Mandal, anti-reservation violence backed by the Congress Party and the BJP began in New Delhi and spread throughout northern India. Upper-caste students, fearful of lost job opportunities, protested the job reservations by blocking traffic, burning buses, forcing shopkeepers to close their businesses, and staging immolation rituals that sometimes ended in tragedy. Building on the discontents, BJP president L. K. Advani set out on a 10,000-kilometer chariot pilgrimage to arrive at Ayodhya for the proposed construction of a Ram temple. The country was convulsed as pro- and anti-pilgrimage violence joined anti-reservation violence and refocused attention from Mandal to *mandir*. Advani was arrested on October 23, 1990, and the BJP formally withdrew its support of Singh's government, which fell on November 7. Advani had succeeded in polarizing Indian politics on communal rather than caste-class lines.

The Babri Masjid destruction and the ensuing violence tells us something about the making of "ancient" hatreds: that they are being made in Lebanon, Bosnia, the republics of the former Soviet Union, Iraq, Israel, South-Central Los Angeles, and Crown Heights—all those places where neighbors and friends have turned into foreigners and enemies. The enlightenment's vision prophesied human progress, modernization predicted affluence with equality, and democracy promised fellow feeling and shared citizenship. Together they foretold a world in which Santa Claus would join the menorah in Hanukkah cards, WASPs eat pizza and Anglos tacos, Muslim performers sing Hindu devotional music, and Colin Powell could be chairman of the Joint Chiefs of Staff.

Thinking people are less sanguine about rationality, modernization, and democracy reducing ethnic and religious solidarities to harmless dietary differences. Religion has not retreated with increasing media exposure and political participation. The reverse seems to be the case. Religion is on the rise everywhere, from the religious right in Colorado Springs to Islamic fundamentalism in Tehran. It exhibits benign enthusiasm, spiritual exaltation, and neo-communitarianism on the one hand, exclusionary and even deadly intolerance on the other. As political ideology recedes with the collapse of communism, the politics of identity and community, of religion, ethnicity, and gender have begun to occupy the space vacated by political ideology. Directly and indirectly, religion, ethnicity, and gender increasingly define what politics is about, from the standing of Muslim personal law and monuments in India to Muslim and Christian Serbs and Croats sharing sovereignty in Bosnia to the Clinton administration's effort to appoint a government that "looks like America."

Which identities become relevant for politics is not predetermined by some primordial ancientness. They are crafted in benign and malignant ways in print and electronic media, in textbooks and advertising, in India's TV megaseries and America's talk shows, in campaign strategies, in all the places and all the ways that self and other, us and them, are represented in an expanding public culture. The struggle in India between Mandal and *mandir,* between quota government and Hindu nationalism, reminds us that in America, too, the politics of interest is being overtaken by cultural politics, the politics of gender, family values, race, and sexual orientation. When TV talking heads and op-ed contributors portray "mobs" as "frenzied" and believers as "fanatic," they have given up the task of discerning the human inducements and political calculations that make politics happen. They have given up making motives visible and showing how they are transformed. "Ancient hatreds" function like the "evil empire." That term, too, was a projection on a scrim, obscuring the motives and practice that lay behind it. The doctrine of ancient hatreds may become the post–Cold War's most robust mystification, a way of having an enemy and knowing evil that deceives as it satisfies. The hatred is modern, and may be closer than we think.

6 THE INDIVIDUAL

Individual psychology is also important in shaping international relations. Individuals include not only foreign policy elites—the leaders who move the world—but also the diplomats, warriors, activists, and voters whose attitudes and perceptions animate the politics of international issues. In a now-classic piece originally published in 1968, Robert Jervis articulates hypotheses on the origins of misperceptions. Drawing heavily on psychology, he suggests strategies for decision makers to mitigate the effects of misperception.

One of the most consequential tasks of political judgment is inferring the intentions of a state's adversaries. In her article "In the Eye of the Beholder," Keren Yarhi-Milo surveys three theories of how leaders and their intelligence services approach this problem. The first two are based on variants of a rational theory of decision making: the first posits that actors base their judgments on the adversary's costly behavior, ignoring "cheap talk," while the second expects them to focus mainly on the adversary's capabilities. Yarhi-Milo proposes a third theory based on psychological research about selective attention to information. In case studies of the Carter administration's response to the Soviet invasion of Afghanistan and the Reagan administration's response to Mikhail Gorbachev's diplomacy, she finds that leaders focus inordinately on vivid information gained in personal encounters, whereas intelligence services focus narrowly on data that can be compiled routinely, such as weapons capabilities.

Robert Jervis

HYPOTHESES ON MISPERCEPTION

In determining how he will behave, an actor must try to predict how others will act and how their actions will affect his values. The actor must therefore develop an image of others and of their intentions. This image may, however, turn out to be an inaccurate one; the actor may, for a number of reasons, misperceive both others' actions and their intentions. * * * I wish to discuss the types of misperceptions of other states' intentions which states tend to make. * * *

■   ■   ■

Theories—Necessary and Dangerous

* * * The evidence from both psychology and history overwhelmingly supports the view (which may be labeled Hypothesis 1) that decision-makers tend to fit incoming information into their existing theories and images. Indeed, their theories and images play a large part in determining what they notice. In other words, actors tend to perceive what they expect. Furthermore (Hypothesis 1a), a theory will have greater impact on an actor's interpretation of data (a) the greater the ambiguity of the data and (b) the higher the degree of confidence with which the actor holds the theory.[1]

■   ■   ■

From *World Politics* 20, no. 3 (April 1968), 454–79. Some of the author's notes have been omitted.

* * * Hypothesis 2: scholars and decision-makers are apt to err by being too wedded to the established view and too closed to new information, as opposed to being too willing to alter their theories. Another way of making this point is to argue that actors tend to establish their theories and expectations prematurely. In politics, of course, this is often necessary because of the need for action. But experimental evidence indicates that the same tendency also occurs on the unconscious level. * * *

However, when we apply these and other findings to politics and discuss kinds of misperception, we should not quickly apply the label of cognitive distortion. We should proceed cautiously for two related reasons. The first is that the evidence available to decision-makers almost always permits several interpretations. It should be noted that there are cases of visual perception in which different stimuli can produce exactly the same pattern on an observer's retina. Thus, for an observer using one eye the same pattern would be produced by a sphere the size of a golf ball which was quite close to the observer, by a baseball-sized sphere that was further away, or by a basketball-sized sphere still further away. Without other clues, the observer cannot possibly determine which of these stimuli he is presented with, and we would not want to call his incorrect perceptions examples of distortion. Such cases, relatively rare in visual perception, are frequent in international relations. The evidence available to decision-makers is almost always very ambiguous since accurate clues to others' intentions are surrounded by noise[2] and deception.

In most cases, no matter how long, deeply, and "objectively" the evidence is analyzed, people can differ in their interpretations, and there are no general rules to indicate who is correct.

The second reason to avoid the label of cognitive distortion is that the distinction between perception and judgment, obscure enough in individual psychology, is almost absent in the making of inferences in international politics. Decision-makers who reject information that contradicts their views—or who develop complex interpretations of it—often do so consciously and explicitly. Since the evidence available contains contradictory information, to make any inferences requires that much information be ignored or given interpretations that will seem tortuous to those who hold a different position.

Indeed, if we consider only the evidence available to a decision-maker at the time of decision, the view later proved incorrect may be supported by as much evidence as the correct one—or even by more. Scholars have often been too unsympathetic with the people who were proved wrong. On closer examination, it is frequently difficult to point to differences between those who were right and those who were wrong with respect to their openness to new information and willingness to modify their views. Winston Churchill, for example, did not open-mindedly view each Nazi action to see if the explanations provided by the appeasers accounted for the data better than his own beliefs. Instead, like Chamberlain, he fitted each bit of ambiguous information into his own hypotheses. That he was correct should not lead us to overlook the fact that his methods of analysis and use of theory to produce cognitive consistency did not basically differ from those of the appeasers.

A consideration of the importance of expectations in influencing perception also indicates that the widespread belief in the prevalence of "wishful thinking" may be incorrect, or at least may be based on inadequate data. The psychological literature on the interaction between affect and perception is immense and cannot be treated here,

but it should be noted that phenomena that at first were considered strong evidence for the impact of affect on perception often can be better treated as demonstrating the influence of expectations.[3] Thus, in international relations, cases like the United States' misestimation of the political climate in Cuba in April 1961, which may seem at first glance to have been instances of wishful thinking, may instead be more adequately explained by the theories held by the decision-makers (e.g., Communist governments are unpopular). Of course, desires may have an impact on perception by influencing expectations, but since so many other factors affect expectations, the net influence of desires may not be great.

There is evidence from both psychology[4] and international relations that when expectations and desires clash, expectations seem to be more important. The United States would like to believe that North Vietnam is about to negotiate or that the USSR is ready to give up what the United States believes is its goal of world domination, but ambiguous evidence is seen to confirm the opposite conclusion, which conforms to the United States' expectations. Actors are apt to be especially sensitive to evidence of grave danger if they think they can take action to protect themselves against the menace once it has been detected.

Safeguards

Can anything then be said to scholars and decision-makers other than "Avoid being either too open or too closed, but be especially aware of the latter danger"? Although decision-makers will always be faced with ambiguous and confusing evidence and will be forced to make inferences about others which will often be inaccurate, a number of safeguards may be suggested which could enable them to minimize their errors. First, and most obvious, decision-makers should be aware that they do not make "unbiased" interpretations of each new bit of incoming information, but rather are inevitably heavily influenced by the theories they expect to be verified. They should know that what may appear to them as a self-evident and unambiguous inference often seems so only because of their preexisting beliefs. To someone with a different theory the same data may appear to be unimportant or to support another explanation. Thus many events provide less independent support for the decision-makers' images than they may at first realize. Knowledge of this should lead decision-makers to examine more closely evidence that others believe contradicts their views.

Second, decision-makers should see if their attitudes contain consistent or supporting beliefs that are not logically linked. These may be examples of true psycho-logic. While it is not logically surprising nor is it evidence of psychological pressures to find that people who believe that Russia is aggressive are very suspicious of any Soviet move, other kinds of consistency are more suspect. For example, most people who feel that it is important for the United States to win the war in Vietnam also feel that a meaningful victory is possible. And most people who feel defeat would neither endanger U.S. national security nor be costly in terms of other values also feel that we cannot win. Although there are important logical linkages between the two parts of each of these views (especially through theories of guerrilla warfare), they do not seem strong enough to explain the degree to which the opinions are correlated. Similarly, in Finland in the winter of 1939, those who felt that grave consequences would follow Finnish agreement to give Russia a military base also believed that the Soviets would withdraw their demand if Finland stood firm. And those who felt that concessions would not lead to loss of major values also believed that Russia would fight if need be.[5] In this country, those who favored a nuclear test ban tended to argue that fallout was very harmful, that only limited improvements in technology would flow from further testing, and that a test ban would increase the chances for peace and security. Those who opposed the test ban were apt to disagree on all three points. This does not mean, of course, that the people holding such sets of supporting views were necessarily wrong in any one element. The Finns who wanted to make concessions to the USSR were probably correct in both parts of their argument. But decision-makers should be suspicious if they hold a position in which elements that are not logically connected support the same conclusion. This condition is psychologically comfortable and makes decisions easier to reach (since competing values do not have to be balanced off against each other). The chances are thus considerable that at least part of the reason why a person holds some of these views is related to psychology and not to the substance of the evidence.

Decision-makers should also be aware that actors who suddenly find themselves having an important shared interest with other actors have a tendency to overestimate the degree of common interest involved. This tendency is especially strong for those actors (e.g., the United States, at least before 1950) whose beliefs about international relations and morality imply that they can cooperate only with "good" states and that with those states there will be no major conflicts. On the other hand, states that have either a tradition of limited cooperation with others (e.g., Britain) or a strongly held theory that differentiates occasional from permanent allies[6] (e.g., the Soviet Union) find it easier to resist this tendency and need not devote special efforts to combating its danger.

A third safeguard for decision-makers would be to make their assumptions, beliefs, and the predictions that follow from them as explicit as possible. An actor should try to determine, before events occur, what evidence would count for and against his theories. By knowing what to expect he would know what to be surprised by, and surprise could indicate to that actor that his beliefs needed reevaluation.[7]

A fourth safeguard is more complex. The decision-maker should try to prevent individuals and organizations from letting their main task, political future, and identity become tied to specific theories and images of other actors.[8] If this occurs, subgoals originally sought for their contribution to higher ends will take on value of their own, and information indicating possible alternative routes to the original goals will not be carefully considered. For example, the U.S. Forest Service was unable to carry out its original purpose as effectively when it began to see its distinctive competence not in promoting the best use of lands and forests but rather in preventing all types of forest fires.[9]

Organizations that claim to be unbiased may not realize the extent to which their definition of their role has become involved with certain beliefs about the world. Allen Dulles is a victim of this lack of understanding when he says, "I grant that we are all creatures of prejudice, including CIA officials, but by entrusting intelligence coordination to our central intelligence service, which is excluded from policy-making and is married to no particular military hardware, we can avoid, to the greatest possible extent, the bending of facts obtained through intelligence to suit a particular occupational viewpoint."[10] This statement overlooks the fact that the CIA has developed a certain view of international relations and of the cold war which maximizes the importance of its information-gathering, espionage, and subversive activities. Since the CIA would lose its unique place in the government if it were decided that the "back alleys" of world politics were no longer vital to U.S. security, it is not surprising that the organization interprets information in a way that stresses the continued need for its techniques.

Fifth, decision-makers should realize the validity and implications of Roberta Wohlstetter's argument that "a willingness to play with material from different angles and in the context of unpopular as well as popular hypotheses is an essential ingredient of a good detective, whether the end is the solution of a crime or an intelligence estimate."[11] However, it is often difficult, psychologically and politically, for any one person to do this. Since a decision-maker usually cannot get "unbiased" treatments of data, he should instead seek to structure conflicting biases into the decision-making process. The decision-maker, in other words, should have devil's advocates around. Just as, as Neustadt points out,[12] the decision-maker will want to create conflicts among his subordinates in order to make appropriate choices, so he will also want to ensure that incoming information is examined from many different perspectives with many different hypotheses in mind. To some extent this kind of examination will be done automatically through the divergence of goals, training, experience, and information that exists in any large organization. But in many cases this divergence will not be sufficient. The views of those analyzing the data will still be too homogeneous, and the decision-maker will have to go out of his way not only to cultivate but to create differing viewpoints.

While all that would be needed would be to have some people examining the data trying to validate unpopular hypotheses, it would probably be more effective if they actually believed and had a stake in the views they were trying to support. If in 1941 someone had had the task of proving the view that Japan would attack Pearl Harbor, the government might have been less surprised by the attack. And only a person who was out to show that Russia would take objectively great risks would have been apt to note that several ships with especially large hatches going to Cuba were riding high in the water, indicating the presence of a bulky but light cargo that was not likely to be anything other than strategic missiles. And many people who doubt the wisdom of the administration's Vietnam policy would be somewhat reassured if there were people in the government who searched the statements and actions of both sides in an effort to prove that North Vietnam was willing to negotiate and that the official interpretation of such moves as the Communist activities during the Tết truce of 1967 was incorrect.

Of course all these safeguards involve costs. They would divert resources from other tasks and would increase internal dissension. Determining whether these costs would be worth the gains would depend on a detailed analysis of how the suggested safeguards might be implemented. Even if they were adopted by a government, of course, they would not eliminate the chance of misperception. However, the safeguards would make it more likely that national decision-makers would make conscious choices about the way data were interpreted rather than merely assuming that they can be seen in only one way and can mean only one thing. Statesmen would thus be reminded of alternative images of others just as they are constantly reminded of alternative policies.

These safeguards are partly based on Hypothesis 3: actors can more easily assimilate into their established image of another actor information contradicting that image if the information is transmitted and considered bit by bit than if it comes all at once. In the former case, each piece of discrepant data can be coped with as it arrives and each of the conflicts with the prevailing view will be small enough to go unnoticed, to be dismissed as unimportant, or to necessitate at most a slight modification of the image (e.g., addition of exceptions to the rule). When the information arrives in a block, the contradiction between it and the prevailing view is apt to be much clearer and the probability of major cognitive reorganization will be higher.

Sources of Concepts

An actor's perceptual thresholds—and thus the images that ambiguous information is apt to produce—are influenced by what he has experienced and learned about.[13] If one actor is to perceive that another fits in a given category he must first have, or develop, a concept for that category. We can usefully distinguish three levels at which a concept can be present or absent. First, the concept can be completely missing. The actor's cognitive structure may not include anything corresponding to the phenomenon he is encountering. This situation can occur not only in science fiction, but also in a world of rapid change or in the meeting of two dissimilar systems. Thus China's image of the Western world was extremely inaccurate in the mid-nineteenth century, her learning was very slow, and her responses were woefully inadequate. The West was spared a similar struggle only because it had the power to reshape the system it encountered. Once the actor clearly sees one instance of the new phenomenon, he is apt to recognize it much more quickly in the future.[14] Second, the actor can know about a concept but not believe that it reflects an actual phenomenon. Thus Communist and Western decision-makers are each aware of the other's explanation of how his system functions, but do not think that the concept corresponds to reality. Communist elites, furthermore, deny that anything *could* correspond to the democracies' description of themselves. Third, the actor may hold a concept, but not believe that another actor fills it at the present moment. Thus the British and French statesmen of the 1930's held a concept of states with unlimited ambitions. They realized that Napoleons were possible, but they did not think Hitler belonged in that category. Hypothesis 4 distinguishes these three cases: misperception is most difficult to correct in the case of a missing concept and least difficult to correct in the case of a recognized but presumably unfilled concept. All other things being equal (e.g., the degree to which the concept is central to the actor's cognitive structure), the first case requires more cognitive reorganization than does the second, and the second requires more reorganization than the third.

However, this hypothesis does not mean that learning will necessarily be slowest in the first case, for if the phenomena are totally new the actor may make such grossly inappropriate responses that he will quickly acquire information clearly indicating that he is faced with something he does not understand. And the sooner the actor realizes that things are not—or may not be—what they seem, the sooner he is apt to correct his image.[15]

Three main sources contribute to decision-makers' concepts of international relations and of other states and influence the level of their perceptual thresholds for various phenomena. First, an actor's beliefs about his own domestic political system are apt to be important. In some cases, like that of the USSR, the decision-makers' concepts are tied to an ideology that explicitly provides a frame of reference for viewing foreign affairs. Even where this is not the case, experience with his own system will partly determine what the actor is familiar with and what he is apt to perceive in others. Louis Hartz claims, "It is the absence of the experience of social revolution which is at the heart of the whole American dilemma. . . . In a whole series of specific ways it enters into our difficulty of communication with the rest of the world. We find it difficult to understand Europe's 'social question'. . . . We are not familiar with the deeper social struggles of Asia and hence tend to interpret even reactionary regimes as 'democratic.'"[16] Similarly, George Kennan argues that in World War I the Allied powers, and especially America, could not understand the bitterness and violence of others' internal conflicts: ". . . The inability of the Allied statesmen to picture to themselves the passions of the Russian civil war [was partly caused by the fact that] we represent . . . a society in which the manifestations of evil have been carefully buried and sublimated in the social behavior of people, as in their very consciousness. For this reason, probably, despite our widely traveled and outwardly cosmopolitan lives, the mainsprings of political behavior in such a country as Russia tend to remain concealed from our vision."[17]

Second, concepts will be supplied by the actor's previous experiences. An experiment from another field illustrates this. Dearborn and Simon presented business executives from various divisions (e.g., sales, accounting, production) with the same hypothetical data and asked them for an analysis and recommendations from the standpoint of what would be best for the company as a whole. The executives' views heavily reflected their departmental perspectives.[18] William W. Kaufmann shows how the perceptions of Ambassador Joseph Kennedy were affected by his past: "As befitted a former chairman of the Securities Exchange and Maritime Commissions, his primary interest lay in economic matters. . . . The revolutionary character of the Nazi regime was not a phenomenon that he could easily grasp. . . . It was far simpler, and more in accord with his own premises, to explain German aggressiveness in economic terms. The Third Reich was dissatisfied, authoritarian, and expansive largely because her economy was unsound."[19] Similarly it has been argued that Chamberlain was slow to recognize Hitler's intentions partly because of the limiting nature of his personal background and business experiences. The impact of training and experience seems to be demonstrated when the background of the appeasers is compared to that of their opponents. One difference stands out: "A substantially higher percentage of the anti-appeasers (irrespective of class origins) had the kind of knowledge which comes from close acquaintance, mainly professional, with foreign affairs."[20] Since members of the diplomatic corps are responsible for meeting threats to the nation's security before these grow to major proportions and since they have learned about cases in which aggressive states were not recognized as such until very late, they may be prone to interpret ambiguous data as showing that others are aggressive. It should be stressed that we cannot say that the professionals of the 1930s were more apt to make accurate judgments of other states. Rather, they may have been more sensitive to the chance that others were aggressive. They would then rarely take an aggressor for a status-quo power, but would more often make the opposite error. Thus in the years before World War I the permanent officials in the British Foreign Office overestimated German aggressiveness.[21]

A parallel demonstration in psychology of the impact of training on perception is presented by an experiment in which ambiguous pictures were shown to both advanced and beginning police-administration students. The advanced group perceived more violence in the pictures than did the beginners. The probable explanation is that "the law enforcer may come to accept crime as a familiar personal experience, one which he himself is not surprised to encounter. The acceptance of crime as a familiar experience in turn increases the ability or readiness to perceive violence where clues to it are potentially available."[22] This experiment lends weight to the view that the British diplomats' sensitivity to aggressive states was not totally a product of personnel selection procedures.

A third source of concepts, which frequently will be the most directly relevant to a decision-maker's perception of international relations, is international history. As Henry Kissinger points out, one reason why statesmen were so slow to recognize the threat posed by Napoleon was that previous events had accustomed them only to actors who wanted to modify the existing system, not overthrow it."[23] The other side of the coin is even more striking: historical traumas can heavily influence future perceptions. They can either establish a state's image of the other state involved or can be used as analogies. An example of the former case is provided by the fact that for at least ten years after the Franco-Prussian War most of Europe's statesmen felt that Bismarck had aggressive plans when in fact his main goal was to protect the status quo. Of course the evidence was ambiguous. The post-1871 Bismarckian maneuvers, which were designed to keep peace, looked not unlike the pre-1871 maneuvers designed to set the stage for war. But that the post-1871 maneuvers were seen as indicating aggressive plans is largely attributable to the impact of Bismarck's earlier actions on the statesmen's image of him.

A state's previous unfortunate experience with a type of danger can sensitize it to other examples of that danger. While this sensitivity may lead the state to avoid the mistake it committed in the past, it may also lead it mistakenly to believe that the present situation is like the past one. Santayana's maxim could be turned around: "Those who remember the past are condemned to make the opposite mistakes." As Paul Kecskemeti shows, both defenders and critics of the unconditional surrender plan of the Second World War thought in terms of the conditions of World War I.[24] Annette Baker Fox found that the Scandinavian countries' neutrality policies in World War II were strongly influenced by their experiences in the previous war, even though vital aspects of the two situations were different. Thus "Norway's success [during the First World War] in remaining non-belligerent though pro-Allied gave the Norwegians confidence that their country could again stay out of war."[25] And the lesson drawn from the unfortunate results of this policy was an important factor in Norway's decision to join NATO.

The application of the Munich analogy to various contemporary events has been much commented on, and I do not wish to argue the substantive points at stake. But it seems clear that the probabilities that any state is facing an aggressor who has to be met by force are not altered by the career of Hitler and the history of the 1930s. Similarly the probability of an aggressor's announcing his plans is not increased (if anything, it is decreased) by the fact that Hitler wrote *Mein Kampf.* Yet decision-makers are more sensitive to these possibilities, and thus more apt to perceive ambiguous evidence as indicating they apply to a given case, than they would have been had there been no Nazi Germany.

Historical analogies often precede, rather than follow, a careful analysis of a situation (e.g., Truman's initial reaction to the news of the invasion of South Korea was to think of the Japanese invasion of Manchuria). Noting this precedence, however, does not show us which of many analogies will come to a decision-maker's mind. Truman could have thought of nineteenth-century European wars that were of no interest to the United States. Several factors having nothing to do with the event under consideration influence what analogies a decision-maker is apt to make. One factor is the number of cases similar to the analogy with which the decision-maker is familiar. Another is the importance of the past event to the political system of which the decision-maker is a part. The more times such an event occurred and the greater its consequences were, the more a decision-maker will be sensitive to the particular danger involved and the more he will be apt to see ambiguous stimuli as indicating another instance of this kind of event. A third factor is the degree of the decision-maker's personal involvement in the past case—in time, energy, ego, and position. The last-mentioned variable will affect not only the event's impact on the decision-maker's cognitive structure, but also the way he perceives the event and the lesson he draws. Someone who was involved in getting troops into South Korea after the attack will remember the Korean War differently from someone who was involved in considering the possible use of nuclear weapons or in deciding what messages should be sent to the Chinese. Greater personal involvement will usually give the event greater impact, especially if the decision-maker's own views were validated by the event. One need not accept a total application of learning theory to nations to believe that "nothing fails like success."[26] It also seems likely that if many critics argued at the time that the decision-maker was wrong, he will be even more apt to see other situations in terms of the original event. For example, because Anthony Eden left the government on account of his views and was later shown to have been correct, he probably was more apt to see as Hitlers other leaders with whom he had conflicts (e.g., Nasser). A fourth factor is the degree to which the analogy is compatible with the rest of his belief system. A fifth is the absence of alternative concepts and analogies. Individuals and states vary in the amount of direct or indirect political experience they have had which can provide different ways of interpreting data. Decision-makers who are aware of multiple possibilities of states' intentions may be less likely to seize on an analogy prematurely. The perception of citizens of nations like the United States which have relatively little history of international politics may be more apt to be heavily influenced by the few major international events that have been important to their country.

The first three factors indicate that an event is more apt to shape present perceptions if it occurred in the recent rather than the remote past. If it occurred recently, the statesman will then know about it at first hand even if he was not involved in the making of policy at the time. Thus if generals are prepared to fight the last war, diplomats may be prepared to avoid the last war. Part of the Anglo-French reaction to Hitler can be explained by the prevailing beliefs that the First World War was to a large extent caused by misunderstandings and could have been avoided by farsighted and nonbelligerent diplomacy. And part of the Western perception of Russia and China can be explained by the view that appeasement was an inappropriate response to Hitler.[27]

The Evoked Set

The way people perceive data is influenced not only by their cognitive structure and theories about other actors but also by what they are concerned with at the time they receive the information. Information is evaluated in light of the small part of the person's memory that is presently active—the "evoked set." My perceptions of the dark streets I pass walking home from the movies will be different if the film I saw had dealt with spies than if it had been a comedy. If I am working on aiding a country's education system and I hear someone talk about the need for economic development in that state, I am apt to think he is concerned with education, whereas if I had been working on, say, trying to achieve political stability in that country, I would have placed his remarks in that framework.[28]

Thus Hypothesis 5 states that when messages are sent from a different background of concerns and information than is possessed by the receiver, misunderstanding is likely. Person A and person B will read the same message quite differently if A has seen several related messages that B does not know about. This difference will be compounded if, as is frequently the case, A and B each assume that the other has the same background he does. This means that misperception can occur even when deception is neither intended nor expected. Thus Roberta Wohlstetter found not only that different parts of the United States government had different perceptions of data about Japan's intentions and messages partly because they saw the incoming information in very different contexts, but also that officers in the field misunderstood warnings from Washington: "Washington advised General Short [in Pearl Harbor] on November 27 to expect 'hostile action' at any moment, by which it meant 'attack on American possessions from without,' but General Short understood this phrase to mean 'sabotage.'"[29] Washington did not realize the extent to which Pearl Harbor considered the danger of sabotage to be primary, and furthermore it incorrectly believed that General Short had received the intercepts of the secret Japanese diplomatic messages available in Washington which indicated that surprise attack was a distinct possibility. Another implication of this hypothesis is that if important information is known to only part of the government of state A and part of the government of state B, international messages may be misunderstood by those parts of the receiver's government that do not match, in the information they have, the part of the sender's government that dispatched the message.[30]

Two additional hypotheses can be drawn from the problems of those sending messages. Hypothesis 6 states that when people spend a great deal of time drawing up a plan or making a decision, they tend to think that the message about it they wish to convey will be clear to the receiver.[31] Since they are aware of what is to them the important pattern in their actions, they often feel that the pattern will be equally obvious to others, and they overlook the degree to which the message is apparent to them only because they know what to look for. Those who have not participated in the endless meetings may not understand what information the sender is trying to convey. George Quester has shown how the German and, to a lesser extent, the British desire to maintain target limits on bombing in the first eighteen months of World War II was undermined partly by the fact that each side knew the limits it was seeking and its own reasons for any apparent "exceptions" (e.g., the German attack on Rotterdam) and incorrectly felt that these limits and reasons were equally clear to the other side.[32]

Hypothesis 7 holds that actors often do not realize that actions intended to project a given image may not have the desired effect because the actions themselves do not turn out as planned. Thus even without appreciable impact of different cognitive structures and backgrounds, an action may convey an unwanted message. For example, a country's representatives may not follow instructions and so may give others impressions contrary to those the home government wished to convey. The efforts of Washington and Berlin to settle their dispute over Samoa in the late 1880s were complicated by the provocative behavior of their agents on the spot. These agents not only increased the intensity of the local conflict, but led the decision-makers to become more suspicious of the other state because they tended to assume that their agents were obeying instructions and that the actions of the other side represented official policy. In such cases both sides will believe that the other is reading hostility into a policy of theirs which is friendly. Similarly, Quester's study shows that the attempt to limit bombing referred to above failed partly because neither side was able to bomb as accurately as it thought it could and thus did not realize the physical effects of its actions.[33]

Further Hypotheses from the Perspective of the Perceiver

From the perspective of the perceiver several other hypotheses seem to hold. Hypothesis 8 is that there is an overall tendency for decision-makers to see other states as more hostile than they are.[34] There seem to be more cases of statesmen incorrectly believing others are planning major acts against their interest than of statesmen being lulled by a potential aggressor. There are many reasons for this which are too complex to be treated here (e.g., some parts of the bureaucracy feel it is their responsibility to be suspicious of all other states; decision-makers often feel they are "playing it safe" to believe and act as though the other state were hostile in questionable cases; and often, when people do not feel they are a threat to others, they find it difficult to believe that others may see them as a threat). It should be noted, however, that decision-makers whose perceptions are described by this hypothesis would not necessarily further their own values by trying to correct for this tendency. The values of possible outcomes as well as their probabilities must be considered, and it may be that the probability of an unnecessary arms-tension cycle arising out of misperceptions, multiplied by the costs of such a cycle, may seem less to decision-makers than the probability of incorrectly believing another state is friendly, multiplied by the costs of this eventuality.

Hypothesis 9 states that actors tend to see the behavior of others as more centralized, disciplined, and coordinated than it is. This hypothesis holds true in related ways. Frequently, too many complex events are squeezed into a perceived pattern. Actors are hesitant to admit or even see that particular incidents cannot be explained by their theories.[35] Those events not caused by factors that are important parts of the perceiver's image are often seen as though they were. Further, actors see others as more internally united than they in fact are and generally overestimate the degree to which others are following a coherent policy. The degree to which the other side's policies are the product of internal bargaining,[36] internal misunderstandings, or subordinates' not following instructions is underestimated. This is the case partly because actors tend to be unfamiliar with the details of another state's policy-making processes. Seeing only the finished product, they find it simpler to try to construct a rational explanation for the policies, even though they know that such an analysis could not explain their own policies.[37]

Familiarity also accounts for Hypothesis 10: because a state gets most of its information about the other state's policies from the other's foreign office, it tends to take the foreign office's position for the stand of the other government as a whole. In many cases this perception will be an accurate one, but when the other government is divided or when the other foreign office is acting without specific authorization, misperception may result. For example, part of the reason why in 1918 Allied governments incorrectly thought "that the Japanese were preparing to take action [in Siberia], if need be, with agreement with the British and French alone, disregarding the absence of American consent,"[38] was that Allied ambassadors had talked mostly with Foreign Minister Motono, who was among the minority of the Japanese favoring this policy. Similarly, America's NATO allies may have gained an inaccurate picture of the degree to which the American government was committed to the MLF because they had greatest contact with parts of the government that strongly favored the MLF. And states that tried to get information about Nazi foreign policy from German diplomats were often misled because these officials were generally ignorant of or out of sympathy with Hitler's plans. The Germans and the Japanese sometimes purposely misinformed their own ambassadors in order to deceive their enemies more effectively.

Hypothesis 11 states that actors tend to overestimate the degree to which others are acting in response to what they themselves do when the others behave in accordance with the actor's desires; but when the behavior of the other is undesired, it is usually seen as derived from internal forces. If the *effect* of another's action is to injure or threaten the first side, the first side is apt to believe that such was the other's *purpose*. An example of the first part of the hypothesis is provided by Kennan's account of the activities of official and unofficial American representatives who protested to the new Bolshevik government against several of its actions. When the Soviets changed their position, these representatives felt it was largely because of their influence.[39] This sort of interpretation can be explained not only by the fact that it is gratifying to the individual making it, but also, taking the other side of the coin mentioned in Hypothesis 9, by the fact that the actor is most familiar with his own input into the other's decision and has less knowledge of other influences. The second part of Hypothesis 11 is illustrated by the tendency of actors to believe that the hostile behavior of others is to be explained by the other side's motives and not by its reaction to the first side. Thus Chamberlain did not see that Hitler's behavior was related in part to his belief that the British were weak. More common is the failure to see that the other side is reacting out of fear of the first side, which can lead to self-fulfilling prophecies and spirals of misperception and hostility.

This difficulty is often compounded by an implication of Hypothesis 12: when actors have intentions that they do not try to conceal from others, they tend to assume that others accurately perceive these intentions. Only rarely do they believe that others may be reacting to a much less favorable image of themselves than they think they are projecting.[40]

For state A to understand how state B perceives A's policy is often difficult because such understanding may involve a conflict with A's image of itself. Raymond Sontag argues that Anglo-German relations before World War I deteriorated partly because "the British did not like to think of themselves as selfish, or unwilling to tolerate 'legitimate' German expansion. The Germans did not like to think of themselves as aggressive, or unwilling to recognize 'legitimate' British vested interest."[41]

Hypothesis 13 suggests that if it is hard for an actor to believe that the other can see him as a menace, it is often even harder for him to see that issues important to him are not important to others. While he may know that another actor is on an opposing team, it may be more difficult for him to realize that the other is playing an entirely different game. This is especially true when the game he is playing seems vital to him.[42]

The final hypothesis, Hypothesis 14, is as follows: actors tend to overlook the fact that evidence consistent with their theories may also be consistent with other views. When choosing between two theories we have to pay attention only to data that cannot be accounted for by one of the theories. But it is common to find people claiming as proof of their theories data that could also support alternative views. This phenomenon is related to the point made earlier that any single bit of information can be interpreted only within a framework of hypotheses and theories. And while it is true that "we may without a vicious circularity accept some datum as a fact because it conforms to the very law for which it counts as another confirming instance, and reject an allegation of fact because it is already excluded by law,"[43] we should be careful lest we forget that a piece of information seems in many cases to confirm a certain hypothesis only because we already believe that hypothesis to be correct and that the information can with as much validity support a different hypothesis. For example, one of the reasons why the German attack on Norway took both that country and England by surprise, even though they had detected German ships moving toward Norway, was that they expected not an attack but an attempt by the Germans to break through the British blockade and reach the Atlantic. The initial course of the ships was consistent with either plan, but the British and Norwegians took this course to mean that their predictions were being borne out.[44] This is not to imply, that the interpretation made was foolish, but only that the decision-makers should have been aware that the evidence was also consistent with an invasion and should have had a bit less confidence in their views.

The longer the ships would have to travel the same route whether they were going to one or another of two destinations, the more information would be needed to determine their plans. Taken as a metaphor, this incident applies generally to the treatment of evidence. Thus as long as Hitler made demands for control only of ethnically German areas, his actions could be explained either by the hypothesis that he had unlimited ambitions or by the hypothesis that he wanted to unite all the Germans. But actions against non-Germans (e.g., the takeover of Czechoslovakia in March 1938) could not be accounted for by the latter hypothesis. And it was this action that convinced the appeasers that Hitler had to be stopped. It is interesting to speculate on what the British reaction would have been had Hitler left Czechoslovakia alone for a while and instead made demands on Poland similar to those he eventually made in the summer of 1939.

The two paths would then still not have diverged, and further misperception could have occurred.

NOTES

1. Floyd Allport, *Theories of Perception and the Concept of Structure* (New York 1955), 382; Ole Holsti, "Cognitive Dynamics and Images of the Enemy," in David Finlay, Ole Holsti, and Richard Fagen, *Enemies in Politics* (Chicago 1967), 70.

2. For a use of this concept in political communication, see Roberta Wohlstetter, *Pearl Harbor* (Stanford 1962).

3. See, for example, Donald Campbell, "Systematic Error on the Part of Human Links in Communications Systems," *Information and Control*, 1 (1958), 346–50; and Leo Postman, "The Experimental Analysis of Motivational Factors in Perception," in Judson S. Brown, ed., *Current Theory and Research in Motivation* (Lincoln, Neb., 1953), 59–108.

4. Dale Wyatt and Donald Campbell, "A Study of Interviewer Bias as Related to Interviewer's Expectations and Own Opinions," *International Journal of Opinion and Attitude Research*, IV (Spring 1950), 77–83.

5. Max Jacobson, *The Diplomacy of the Winter War* (Cambridge, MA, 1961), 136–39.

6. Raymond Aron, *Peace and War* (Garden City 1966), 29.

7. [Thomas] Kuhn, *The Structure of Scientific Revolution* [(Chicago 1964)], 65.

8. See Philip Selznick, *Leadership in Administration* (Evanston 1957).

9. Ashley Schiff, *Fire and Water: Scientific Heresy in the Forest Service* (Cambridge, MA, 1962).

10. *The Craft of Intelligence* (New York 1963), 53.

11. P. 302. See Beveridge, 93, for a discussion of the idea that the scientist should keep in mind as many hypotheses as possible when conducting and analyzing experiments.

12. *Presidential Power* (New York 1960).

13. Most psychologists argue that this influence also holds for perception of shapes. For data showing that people in different societies differ in respect to their predisposition to experience certain optical illusions and for a convincing argument that this difference can be explained by the societies' different physical environments, which have led their people to develop different patterns of drawing inferences from ambiguous visual cues, see Marshall Segall, Donald Campbell, and Melville Herskovits, *The Influence of Culture on Visual Perceptions* (Indianapolis 1966).

14. Thus when Bruner and Postman's subjects first were presented with incongruous playing cards (i.e., cards in which symbols and colors of the suits were not matching, producing red spades or black diamonds), long exposure times were necessary for correct identification. But once a subject correctly perceived the card and added this type of card to his repertoire of categories, he was able to identify other incongruous cards much more quickly. For an analogous example—in this case, changes in the analysis of aerial reconnaissance photographs of an enemy's secret weapons-testing facilities produced by the belief that a previously unknown object may he

present—see David Irving, *The Mare's Nest* (Boston 1964), 66–67, 274–75.

15. [Jerome Bruner and Leo Postman, "On the Perceptions of Incongruity: A Paradigm," in Jerome Bruner and David Krech, eds., *Perception and Personality* (Durham, NC, 1949)].

16. *The Liberal Tradition in America* (New York 1955), 306.

17. *Russia and the West Under Lenin and Stalin* (New York 1962), 142–43.

18. DeWitt Dearborn and Herbert Simon, "Selective Perception: A Note on the Departmental Identification of Executives," *Sociometry*, XXI (June 1958), 140–44.

19. "Two American Ambassadors: Bullitt and Kennedy," in [Gordon Craig and Felix Gilbert, eds., *The Diplomats*, Vol. 3 (New York 1963)], 358–59.

20. [Donald Lammers, *Explaining Munich* (Stanford 1966)], 15.

21. George Monger, *The End of Isolation* (London 1963).

22. Hans Toch and Richard Schulte, "Readiness to Perceive Violence as a Result of Police Training," *British Journal of Psychology*, LII (November 1961), 392 (original italics omitted). It should be stressed that one cannot say whether or not the advanced police students perceived the pictures "accurately." The point is that their training predisposed them to see violence in ambiguous situations. * * * For an experiment showing that training can lead people to "recognize" an expected stimulus even when that stimulus is in fact not shown, see Israel Goldiamond and William F. Hawkins, "Vexierversuch: The Log Relationship Between Word-Frequency and Recognition Obtained in the Absence of Stimulus Words," *Journal of Experimental Psychology*, LVI (December 1958), 457–63.

23. *A World Restored* (New York 1964), 2–3.

24. *Strategic Surrender* (New York 1964), 215–41.

25. *The Power of Small States* (Chicago 1959), 81.

26. William Inge, *Outspoken Essays,* First Series (London 1923), 88.

27. Of course, analogies themselves are not "unmoved movers." The interpretation of past events is not automatic and is informed by general views of international relations and complex judgments. And just as beliefs about the past influence the present, views about the present influence interpretations of history. It is difficult to determine the degree to which the United States' interpretation of the reasons it went to war in 1917 influenced American foreign policy in the 1920s and 1930s and how much the isolationism of that period influenced the histories of the war.

28. For some psychological experiments on this subject, see Jerome Bruner and A. Leigh Minturn, "Perceptual Identification and Perceptual Organization," *Journal of General Psychology*, LIII (July 1955), 22–28; Seymour Feshbach and Robert Singer, "The Effects of Fear Arousal and Suppression of Fear Upon Social Perception," *Journal of Abnormal and Social Psychology*, LV (November 1957), 283–88; and Elsa Sippoal, "A Group Study of Some Effects of Preparatory Sets," *Psychology Monographs*, XLVI, No. 210 (1935), 27–28. For a general discussion of the importance of the perceiver's evoked set, see Postman, 87.

29. Pp. 73–74.

30. For example, Roger Hilsman points out, "Those who knew of the peripheral reconnaissance flights that probed Soviet air defenses during the Eisenhower administration and the U-2 flights over the Soviet Union itself . . . were better able to understand some of the things the Soviets were saying and doing than people who did not know of these activities" (*To Move a Nation* [Garden City 1967], 66). But it is also possible that those who knew about the U-2 flights at times misinterpreted Soviet messages by incorrectly believing that the sender was influenced by, or at least knew of, these flights.

31. I am grateful to Thomas Schelling for discussion on this point.

32. *Deterrence Before Hiroshima* (New York 1966), 105–22.

33. Ibid.

34. For a slightly different formulation of this view, see [Ole Holsti, "Cognitive Dynamics and Images of the Enemy," in David Finlay, Ole Holsti, and Richard Fagen, *Enemies in Politics* (Chicago 1967)], 27.

35. The Soviets consciously hold an extreme version of this view and seem to believe that nothing is accidental. See the discussion in Nathan Leites, *A Study of Bolshevism* (Glencoe 1953), 67–73.

36. A. W. Marshall criticizes Western explanations of Soviet military posture for failing to take this into account. See his "Problems of Estimating Military Power," a paper presented at the 1966 Annual Meeting of the American Political Science Association, 16.

37. It has also been noted that in labor-management disputes both sides may be apt to believe incorrectly that the other is controlled from above, either from the international union office or from the company's central headquarters (Robert Blake, Herbert Shepard, and Jane Mouton, *Managing Intergroup Conflict in Industry* [Houston 1964], 182). It has been further noted that both Democratic and Republican members of the House tend to see the other party as the one that is more disciplined and united (Charles Clapp, *The Congressman* [Washington 1963], 17–19).

38. George Kennan, *Russia Leaves the War* (New York 1967), 484.

39. Ibid., 404, 408, 500.

40. Herbert Butterfield notes that these assumptions can contribute to the spiral of "Hobbesian fear. . . . You yourself may vividly feel the terrible fear that you have of the other party, but you cannot enter into the other man's counter-fear, or even understand why he should be particularly nervous. For you know that you yourself mean him no harm, and that you want nothing from him save guarantees for your own safety; and it is never possible for you to realize or remember properly that since he cannot see the inside of your mind, he can never have the same assurance of your intentions that you have" (*History and Human Conflict* [London 1951], 20).

41. *European Diplomatic History 1871–1932* (New York 1933), 125. It takes great mental effort to realize that actions which seem only the natural consequence of defending your vital interests can look to others as though you are refusing them any chance of increasing their influence. In rebutting the famous Crowe "balance of power" memorandum of 1907, which justified a policy of "containing" Germany on the grounds that she was a threat to British national security, Sanderson, a former permanent undersecretary in the Foreign Office, wrote, "It has sometimes seemed to me that to a foreigner reading our press the British Empire must appear in the light of some huge giant sprawling all over the globe, with gouty fingers and toes stretching in every direction, which cannot be approached without eliciting a scream" (quoted in Monger, 315).

But few other Englishmen could be convinced that others might see them this way.

42. George Kennan makes clear that in 1918 this kind of difficulty was partly responsible for the inability of either the Allies or the new Bolshevik government to understand the motivations of the other side: "There is . . . nothing in nature more egocentrical than the embattled democracy. . . . It . . . tends to attach to its own cause an absolute value which distorts its own vision of everything else. . . . It will readily be seen that people who have got themselves into this frame of mind have little understanding for the issues of any contest other than the one in which they are involved. The idea of people wasting time and substance on any *other* issue seems to them preposterous" (*Russia and the West*, 11–12).

43. [Abraham Kaplan, *The Conduct of Inquiry* (San Francisco 1964)], 89.

44. Johan Jorgen Hoist, "Surprise, Signals, and Reaction: The Attack on Norway," *Cooperation and Conflict*, No. 1 (1966), 34. The Germans made a similar mistake in November 1942 when they interpreted the presence of an Allied convoy in the Mediterranean as confirming their belief that Malta would be resupplied. They thus were taken by surprise when landings took place in North Africa (William Langer, *Our Vichy Gamble* [New York 1966], 365).

Keren Yarhi-Milo

IN THE EYE OF THE BEHOLDER
How Leaders and Intelligence Communities Assess the Intentions of Adversaries

How do policymakers infer the long-term political intentions of their states' adversaries? This question has important theoretical, historical, and political significance. If British decisionmakers had understood the scope of Nazi Germany's intentions for Europe during the 1930s, the twentieth century might have looked very different. More recently, a Brookings report observes that "[t]he issue of mutual distrust of long-term intentions . . . has become a central concern in U.S.–China relations."[1] Statements by U.S. and Chinese officials confirm this suspicion. U.S. Ambassador to China Gary Locke noted "a concern, a question mark, by people all around the world and governments all around the world as to what China's intentions are."[2] Chinese officials, similarly, have indicated that Beijing regards recent U.S. policies as a "sophisticated ploy to frustrate China's growth."[3]

Current assessments of the threat posed by a rising China—or for that matter, a possibly nuclear-armed Iran, or a resurgent Russia—depend on which indicators observers use to derive predictions about a potential adversary's intentions. Surprisingly, however, little scholarship exists to identify which indicators leaders and the state's intelligence apparatus tasked with estimating threats use to assess intentions. For example, disputes among American analysts over the military capabilities of the Soviet Union dominated debates on the Soviet threat throughout the Cold

War, yet there has been little examination of the extent to which such calculations shaped or reflected U.S. political decisionmakers' assessments of Soviet intentions. Analyzing how signals are filtered and interpreted by the state's decisionmakers and its intelligence apparatus can lead to better understanding of the types of signals that tend to prompt changes in relations with adversaries, as well as help to develop useful advice for policymakers on how to deter or reassure an adversary more effectively.

In this article, I compare two prominent rationalist approaches in international relations theory about how observers can be expected to infer adversaries' political intentions, with a third approach that I develop and term the "selective attention thesis." First, the behavior thesis asserts that observers refer to certain noncapability-based actions—such as the adversary's decision to withdraw from a foreign military intervention or join binding international organizations—to draw conclusions regarding that adversary's intentions. This approach focuses on the role of costly information in influencing state behavior. Actions are considered costly if they require the state to expend significant, unrecoverable resources or if they severely constrain its future decisionmaking. The basic intuition behind this approach is that an action that costs nothing could equally be taken by actors with benign or with malign intentions, and thus it provides no credible information about the actor's likely plans.[4] Observers

From *International Security* 38, No. 1 (Summer 2013): 7–51.

should therefore ignore "cheap talk."[5] Second, the capabilities thesis, drawing on insights from realism as well as costly signaling, asserts that states should consider an adversary's military capabilities in assessing its intentions. Of particular importance would be significant changes in armament policies, such as a unilateral reduction in military capabilities. Such changes reveal credible information about an adversary's ability to engage in warfare and thus its intention to do so.[6]

Drawing on insights from psychology, neuroscience, and organizational theory, I develop a third approach, the selective attention thesis. This thesis posits that individual perceptual biases and organizational interests and practices influence which types of indicators observers regard as credible signals of the adversary's intentions. Thus, the thesis predicts differences between a state's political leaders and its intelligence community in their selection of which signals to focus on and how to interpret those signals. In particular, decision-makers often base their interpretations on their own theories, expectations, and needs, sometimes ignoring costly signals and paying more attention to information that, though less costly, is more vivid (i.e., personalized and emotionally involving). The thesis also posits that organizational affiliations and roles matter: intelligence organizations predictably rely on different indicators than civilian decisionmakers do to determine an adversary's intentions. In intelligence organizations, the collection and analysis of data on the adversary's military inventory typically receive priority. Over time, intelligence organizations develop substantial knowledge of these material indicators that they then use to make predictions about an adversary's intentions.

To test the competing theses, I examined * * * U.S. assessments of Soviet intentions under the administration of President Jimmy Carter (a period when détente collapsed) [and] U.S. assessments of Soviet intentions in the years leading to the end of the Cold War during the second administration of President Ronald Reagan. * * *

My findings are based on review of more than 30,000 archival documents and intelligence reports, as well as interviews with former decisionmakers and intelligence officials. The cases yield findings more consistent with the selective attention thesis than with either the behavior or capabilities thesis, as I explain in the conclusion.

Before proceeding, it is important to note what lies outside the scope of this study. First, I am concerned primarily with the perceptions of an adversary's long-term political intentions because these are most likely to affect a state's foreign policy and strategic choices. Second, I do not address whether observers correctly identified the intentions of their adversaries. Addressing this question would require that we first establish what the leaders of * * * the Soviet Union during the periods examined here genuinely believed their own intentions to be at the time. Third, elsewhere I address the effects of perceived intentions on the collective policies of the states.[7] Rather, the focus of this article is on the indicators that leaders and intelligence organizations tend to privilege or ignore in their assessments of an adversary's political intentions.

The next section of this article describes the dependent variable—perceived political intentions—and lays out the three theses. The following section outlines the research design. Then, three cases offer empirical tests of the theoretical explanations. The last section discusses the implications of my findings for international relations theory and practice.

Theories of Intentions and the Problem of Attention

The three theses I outline below provide different explanations as to how observers reach their assessments about the adversary's political intentions. The term "political intentions" refers to beliefs about the foreign policy plans of the adversary with regard to the status quo.[8] I divide assessments of political intentions into three simple categories: expansionist, opportunistic, or status quo.[9] Expansionist adversaries exhibit strong determination to expand their power and influence beyond their territorial boundaries. Opportunistic states desire a favorable change in the distribution of power with either a limited or an unlimited geographical scope, but do not actively seek change. They may have contingent plans to seize opportunities to achieve this objective, but they will not pursue their revisionist goals when the cost of doing so appears high.[10] Status quo powers want only to maintain their relative power position.

The Selective Attention Thesis

Information about intentions can be complex, ambiguous, and potentially deceptive, and thus requires much interpretive work. Cognitive, affective, and organizational practices impede individuals' ability to process this information. To distinguish between signals and noise, individuals use a variety of heuristic inference strategies.[11] These simplified models of reality, however, can have the unintended effect of focusing excessive attention on certain pieces of information and away from others. The selective attention thesis recognizes that individual decisionmakers and bureaucratic organizations, such as an intelligence community, process information differently. The thesis yields two hypotheses: the subjective credibility hypothesis explains the inference process of decisionmakers, and the organizational expertise hypothesis describes that of intelligence organizations.

THE SUBJECTIVE CREDIBILITY HYPOTHESIS

The subjective credibility hypothesis predicts that decisionmakers will not necessarily detect or interpret costly actions as informative signals.[12]

This psychology-based theory posits that both the degree of credence given to evidence and the interpretation of evidence deemed credible will depend on a decisionmaker's expectations about the links between the adversary's behavior and its underlying characteristics; his or her own theories about which signals are indicative of the adversary's type; and the vividness of the information.[13]

First, the attention paid to costly actions hinges on observers' expectations about the adversary.[14] Observers are likely to vary in their prior degree of distrust toward an adversary and the extent to which they believe its intentions are hostile. This variation in decisionmakers' beliefs and expectations affects their selection and reading of signals in predictable ways. Given cognitive assimilation mechanisms and the human tendency to try to maintain cognitive consistency, decisionmakers who already hold relatively more hawkish views about the adversary's intentions when they assume power are less likely to perceive and categorize even costly reassuring actions as credible signals of benign intent. They are likely to reason, for example, that the adversary's actions are intended to deceive observers into believing that it harbors no malign intentions. Or they may believe that the adversary's reassuring signals merely reflect its economic or domestic political interests, and thus should not be seen as signaling more benign foreign policy goals. In contrast, those with relatively less hawkish views of an adversary's intentions are more likely to interpret reassuring signals as conforming with their current beliefs and, therefore, are more likely to see such signals as benign. Hawks are likely to focus on costly actions that indicate malign intentions, because such actions are consistent with their existing beliefs about the adversary's intentions.[15]

Second, decisionmakers' interpretations are also guided by their theories about the relationship between an adversary's behavior and its underlying characteristics. As Robert Jervis points out, different observers will interpret even costly behavior differently, "because some of them saw a certain correlation while others either saw none or believed that the correlation was quite different."[16] If, for instance, a decisionmaker believes in the logic of diversionary war, he or she is likely to pay attention to indicators of an adversary state's domestic social unrest and see them as evidence that its leadership is about to embark on a revisionist foreign policy. Thus, social unrest serves as an index of intention, one that the adversary is unlikely to manipulate to project a false image. Those within the administration who do not share this theory of diversionary war will view social unrest as an unreliable indicator of future intentions.

Third, the subjective credibility hypothesis expects decisionmakers to focus on information that, even if perhaps costless, is vivid. Vividness refers to the "emotional interest of information, the concreteness and imaginability of information, and the sensory, spatial, and temporal proximity of information."[17] One "vivid" indicator that is particularly salient to the issues studied in this article consists of a decisionmaker's impressions from personal interactions with members of the adversary's leadership.[18] Recent work in psychology and political science has shown that our emotional responses in face-to-face meetings shape the certainty of our beliefs and preferences for certain choices.[19] As Eugene Borgida and Richard Nisbett argued, "[T]here may be a kind of 'eyewitness' principle of the weighing of evidence, such that firsthand, sense-impression data is assigned greater validity."[20] Accordingly, information about intentions that is vivid, personalized, and emotionally involving is more likely to be remembered, and hence to be disproportionately available for influencing inferences. Conversely, decisionmakers will be reluctant to rely on evidence that is abstract, colorless, objective, or less tangible—such as measurements of the adversary's weapon inventory or the contents of its doctrinal manuals—even if such evidence could be regarded as extremely reliable. This kind of information is not nearly as engaging as the vivid, salient, and often emotionally laden personal responses that leaders take away from meeting with their opponents.[21]

A few clarifications about the selective attention thesis are in order. First, the importance of prior beliefs in assimilating new information is central to both psychological and some rationalist approaches.[22] In Bayesian learning models, observers evaluating new evidence are not presumed to possess identical prior beliefs. The prediction that distinguishes Bayesian models from biased-learning models concerns whether observers with identical prior beliefs and levels of uncertainty will be similarly affected by new information revealed by costly signals.[23] In contrast, the subjective credibility hypothesis claims that a process of updating might not occur even in the face of costly signals, and that vivid, noncostly actions can also be seen as informative. Further, the concept of Bayesian updating suggests that disconfirming data will always lead to some belief change, or at least to lowered confidence. The subjective credibility hypothesis, however, recognizes that some decisionmakers will not revise their beliefs even when confronted with valuable and costly information for reasons described above, such as a strong confirmation bias, the colorless nature of the information, or incongruity with the decisionmaker's theories. This study also asks a set of questions about the importance of costly actions that Bayesian models tend to ignore: that is, do different observers select different kinds of external indicators to update their beliefs?

THE ORGANIZATIONAL EXPERTISE HYPOTHESIS

The bureaucratic-organizational context in which intelligence analysts operate has specific effects that do not apply to political decisionmakers. As a collective, intelligence organizations tend to analyze their adversary's intentions through the prism of their relative expertise. Intelligence organizations tend to devote most of their resources to the collection, production, and analysis of information about the military inventory of the adversary, which can be known and tracked over time. As Mark Lowenthal writes, "[T]he regularity and precision that govern each nation's military make it susceptible to intelligence collection."[24] Quantified inventories can also be presented in a quasi-scientific way to decisionmakers.

Over time, the extensive monitoring of the adversary's military inventory creates a kind of narrow-mindedness that influences the inference process. To use Isaiah Berlin's metaphor, extensive monitoring creates hedgehogs: "[T]he intellectually aggressive hedgehogs knew one big thing and sought, under the banner of parsimony, to expand the explanatory power of that big thing to 'cover' new cases."[25] This is not to argue that intelligence organizations know only how to count an adversary's missiles and military divisions. Rather, the organizational expertise hypothesis posits that, because analyzing intentions is one central issue with which intelligence organizations are explicitly tasked, and because there is no straightforward or easy way to predict the adversary's intentions, a state's intelligence apparatus has strong incentives to use the relative expertise that it has, which emphasizes careful empirical analysis of military capabilities. Unlike the capabilities thesis, the organizational expertise hypothesis sees the logic of relying on capabilities as arising from bureaucratic and practical reasons specific to intelligence organizations.[26]

The Capabilities Thesis

The capabilities thesis posits that observers should infer an adversary's intentions based on indexes of its military power. This thesis draws on several realist theories that suggest that a state's intentions reveal, or are at least constrained by, its military capabilities. Two pathways link military power and perceived intentions.[27] First, according to John Mearsheimer's theory of offensive realism,

decisionmakers in an anarchic international system must "assume the worst" about adversaries' intentions.[28] How aggressive a state can (or will) be is essentially a function of its power. A second pathway relies on the logic of costly actions, according to which the size of an incremental increase or decrease in an adversary's military capabilities, in combination with how powerful the observing country sees it to be, can serve as a credible signal of aggressive or benign intentions.[29]

Drawing on these insights, the capabilities hypothesis predicts that observers in a state will infer an adversary's intentions from perceived trends in the level of the adversary's military capabilities compared with its own military capabilities. Under conditions of uncertainty about states' intentions, a perception that an adversary is devoting more resources to building up its military capabilities is likely to be seen as a costly signal of hostile intentions. As Charles Glaser puts it, "[A] state's military buildup can change the adversary's beliefs about the state's motives, convincing the adversary that the state is inherently more dangerous than it had previously believed. More specifically, the state's buildup could increase the adversary's assessment of the extent to which it is motivated by the desire to expand for reasons other than security."[30] Conversely, a perception of a freeze or a decrease in the adversary's military capabilities or its investment in them is likely to be seen as a costly and reassuring signal of more benign intentions. At the same time, realists have long emphasized that a state's perception of security or threat depends on how its military power compares with the power of the adversary, that is, on the balance of military power. Thus, in the process of discerning intentions, assessments of the balance of military capabilities are also likely to affect interpretations of benign or hostile intent. For example, if the adversary already enjoys military superiority over the observer, then observers will perceive an increase in the adversary's military capabilities as clear evidence of hostile intentions.

The Behavior Thesis

The behavior thesis posits that certain kinds of noncapability-based actions are also useful in revealing information about political intentions, because undertaking them requires the adversary either to sink costs or to commit itself credibly by tying its own hands. I evaluate the potential causal role of three types of such "costly" actions. The first is a state's decision to join or withdraw from binding international institutions.[31] Some institutions can impose significant costs on states, and they are thus instrumental in allowing other states to discern whether a state has benign or malign intentions.[32] The structural version of the democratic peace, for instance, posits that the creation of democratic domestic institutions—because of their constraining effects, transparency, and ability to generate audience costs—should make it easier for others to recognize a democratic state's benign intentions.[33]

The second costly signal involves foreign interventions in the affairs of weaker states, or withdrawals from such interventions. A state's decision to spill blood and treasure in an effort to change the status quo, for example, is likely to be viewed as a costly, hence credible, signal of hostile intentions.

A third type of behavioral signal involves arms control agreements. Scholars have pointed out that, when offensive and defensive weapons are distinguishable, arms control agreements—especially those that limit offensive deployment and impose effective verification—provide an important and reassuring signal of benign intentions.[34] Cheating or reneging on arms control agreements would lead others to question the intentions of that state. It is important to differentiate indicators such as the signing of arms control agreements as a behavioral signal of intentions from indicators associated with the capabilities thesis. Although both theses ultimately deal with the relationship between a state's military policy and others' assessments of its intentions, they have different predictions. If the capabilities thesis is correct, a change in perceived intentions should occur only when the implementation of the agreement results in an actual decrease in the adversary's capabilities. Policymakers should refer to the actual change in capabilities as the reason for a change in their perceptions of the adversary's intentions. If the behavior thesis is correct, perceptions of intentions should shift when the arms control agreement is signed, and policymakers should refer to the action of signing the agreement as a critical factor. Evidence indicating that changes in assessments of intentions occurring at the time of the signing of a treaty in response to expectations of future shifts in capabilities, or reasoning pointing to both the symbolic and the actual value of a treaty, confirms both theses.

Summary of Predictions

Table 6.1 highlights the most significant differences in the observable implications of the selective attention, capabilities, and behavior theses. Each of the four questions in the table addresses how to test the predictions of the three theories against the empirical evidence.

Research Design

To evaluate the selective attention, capabilities, and behavior theses, I examine, first, the perceptions of key decisionmakers and their closest senior advisers on the foreign policy of a particular adversary and, second, the coordinated assessments of the intelligence community.[35] In addition to variation on the dependent variable—perceptions of political intentions—the cases also provide useful variation on the explanatory variables.

To test the propositions offered by the selective attention thesis, I examine how the primary

Table 6.1. Summary of Predictions

	Selective Attention Thesis	Capabilities Thesis	Behavior Thesis
Do observers vary in how they assess the adversary's political intentions?	Yes, decisionmakers and the intelligence community will rely on different indicators.	Not necessarily	Not necessarily
What is the key set of variables guiding observers' assessments of political intentions?	Decisionmakers will focus on vivid information that addresses what they subjectively judge as informative. Intelligence community will prioritize information in which it has the most expertise, which in most cases will pertain to the adversary's military capabilities.	Influential variables are costly changes in the quantity of the adversary's military capabilities.	Influential variables are costly noncapabilities-based actions by the adversary.
When do assessments about political intentions change?	Decisionmakers will update in response to vivid information and subjective reading of credible indicators. Intelligence community will update in response to changes in relative expertise; in most cases, in response to the perceived military capabilities of the adversary.	Assessments change in response to costly changes in the perceived quantity of the adversary's military capabilities.	Assessments change when the adversary undertakes particular costly actions.
How do observers explain their assessments of political intentions?	Decisionmakers reason with reference to information that they perceive as vivid or subjectively perceive as credible. Intelligence community reasons with reference to information on which it has the most expertise, usually about the adversary's military capabilities.	Observers reason with reference to the quantity of the adversary's military capabilities.	Observers reason with reference to the costly behavior of the adversary.

decisionmakers—President Jimmy Carter [and] President Ronald Reagan * * * and their senior advisers—varied in their initial assessments of the enemy. Also, all three key decisionmakers were engaged in personal meetings with the adversary's leadership, albeit to various degrees.

The cases also allow testing of the capabilities thesis, because both the initial balance of capabilities and the magnitude of change in the adversary's capabilities during the period of interaction vary across the cases. Both Cold War cases assume relative equality in military capabilities between the superpowers with a moderate increase (the collapse of détente case) or decrease (the end of the Cold War case) in Soviet capabilities during the interaction period. In contrast, the German military was vastly inferior to the British military, but an unprecedented increase in German military capabilities during the mid-to-late 1930s shifted the balance of power in Germany's favor. Thus, the interwar case should be an easy test case for the capabilities thesis, as the dramatic increase in German military capabilities and the shift in the balance of power during the period should have led observers to focus on this indicator as a signal of intentions.

The cases are also useful in testing the predictions of the behavior thesis. In particular, the end of the Cold War case is an easy test for the behavior thesis, given that the Soviet leader, Mikhail Gorbachev, took a series of extremely costly actions. This should have had a significant reassuring influence on observers' perceptions.

In each case, I subject the evidence to two probes. First, I look for covariance between changes in the independent variables cited in each thesis and changes in the dependent variable of perceptions of intentions. A finding of no correlation between the predictions of a thesis and the time or direction in which perceptions of intentions change is evidence against that thesis. Second, through process tracing, I examine whether decisionmakers or collective intelligence reports explicitly cited the adversary's capabilities or its behavior, for example, as relevant evidence in their assessments of the adversary's intentions. This step provides a further check against mistaking correlation for causation. Third, in each case I test the predictions of the selective attention framework by comparing decisionmakers' assessments with those of the intelligence communities, as well as by tracing the process by which the selective attention criteria account for the variation among decisionmakers in how they categorized credible signals, and the timing of changes in their perceived intentions.

The Collapse of Détente, 1977–80

Jimmy Carter began his presidency with great optimism about relations with the Soviet Union. But by his last year in office, the U.S.-Soviet détente had collapsed: Carter did not meet with Soviet leaders; he increased the defense budget; he withdrew the Strategic Arms Limitation Talks (SALT) II Treaty from Senate consideration; and he announced the Carter Doctrine, which warned against interference with U.S. interests in the Middle East. In this case, I briefly outline trends in Soviet military capabilities and costly actions during that period that inform the capabilities and behavior theses, respectively. Then I show how the main decisionmakers in the Carter administration—President Jimmy Carter, National Security Adviser Zbigniew Brzezinski, and Secretary of State Cyrus Vance[36]—assessed Soviet intentions in a manner that is most consistent with the subjective credibility hypothesis of the selective attention thesis. This is followed by a discussion of the U.S. intelligence community's assessments which, I argue, are in line with both the capabilities thesis and the selective attention thesis's organizational expertise hypothesis.

The U.S. consensus during this period was that the Soviet Union was building up and modernizing its military capabilities and that the correlation of military forces was shifting in its favor.[37] The Soviets were expanding their already large conventional ground and theater air forces and introducing modern systems that were equal or superior to those of NATO.[38] The deployment of Soviet intermediate-range ballistic missiles in Europe produced a growing concern over the potential threat of Soviet continental strategic superiority.[39] While the United States maintained what it called "asymmetric equivalence" with the Soviet Union,[40] the U.S. defense establishment was especially worried about increases in Soviet nuclear counterforce capability. The Soviets were steadily improving the survivability and flexibility of their strategic forces, which had reached the potential to destroy about four-fifths of the U.S. Minuteman silos by 1980 or 1981.[41] In mid-1979, the National Security Council (NSC) cautioned that the strategic nuclear balance was deteriorating faster than the United States had expected two years earlier, and would get worse into the early 1980s.

The Soviets took two kinds of costly actions that fit the criteria of the behavior thesis. The first was signing the SALT II Treaty in June 1979, which called for reductions in U.S. and Soviet strategic forces to 2,250 in all categories of delivery vehicles.[42] The second was Soviet interventions in crises around the world. The Soviets intervened in twenty-six conflicts during 1975–80.[43] Unlike previous interventions during that period, however, the 1978 Soviet intervention in Ethiopia was direct, not simply through Cuban proxies, and the Soviet invasion of Afghanistan in late 1979 was a full-scale application of Soviet military power. The United States feared that the pattern of Soviet actions would expand beyond the "arc of crisis" to include additional regions and countries more important to U.S. interests. The Soviet invasion of Afghanistan, in particular, significantly intensified this fear, because it was the first direct use of Soviet force beyond the Warsaw Pact nations to restore a pro-Soviet regime.

In addition to these two interventions, reports in 1979 that the Soviets had placed a combat brigade in Cuba created a sense of panic in Washington that subsided only when American decisionmakers realized that the brigade had been in Cuba since 1962.[44]

Carter Administration Assessments of Soviet Intentions

In what follows I show that, consistent with the subjective credibility hypothesis derived from the selective attention thesis, Carter and his advisers did not agree on the informative value of Soviet costly actions. Rather, they debated the importance of various indicators in inferring intentions, and interpreted costly Soviet behavior markedly differently from one another. Specifically, their initial beliefs and theories about the Soviet Union affected the degree of credibility that each of the three decisionmakers attached to various Soviet actions.

Prior to becoming national security adviser, Brzezinski had held a more negative impression of the Soviet Union than either Carter or Vance.[45] During their first year in office, Carter and Vance perceived Soviet intentions as, at worst, opportunistic.[46] Brzezinski's private weekly memoranda to Carter reveal that, even though he was more skeptical than the president about Soviet intentions, he, too, was hopeful that the Soviets would remain relatively cooperative.[47] As conflicts in the third world grew in scope, intensity, and importance throughout 1978, however, Brzezinski concluded that the Soviet involvement in Africa was expansionist, not merely opportunistic. In January 1978, he maintained that "either by design or simply as a response to an apparent opportunity, the Soviets have stepped up their efforts to exploit African turbulence to their own advantage."[48] Soon after, he cautioned Carter that the "Soviet leaders may be acting merely in response to an apparent opportunity, or the Soviet actions may be part of a wider strategic design."[49] On February 17, Brzezinski provided Carter with a rare, explicit account of his impressions of Soviet intentions, including a table that divided Soviet behavior into three categories: benign, neutral, and malignant.[50] Brzezinski described Soviet objectives as seeking "selective détente,"[51] and explained that his revised assessments about Soviet intentions "emerge from Soviet behavior and statements since the election."[52] The table is particularly illuminating because it provides no mention of Soviet military capabilities, only of Soviet behavior, although the latter was not confined to Soviet interventionism or costly actions alone. During February and March, Cuban and Soviet forces backed the government of Ethiopia in its effort to expel the defeated Somali army; Brzezinski believed that the Soviet Union was in Ethiopia "because it has a larger design in mind."[53] He reiterated these conclusions in subsequent reports to the president.[54]

In contrast, Secretary of State Vance believed that the Soviet Union's actions in Africa were not "part of a grand Soviet plan, but rather attempts to exploit targets of opportunity,"[55] and that they were "within the bounds of acceptable competition."[56] Alarmed by Carter's growing skepticism about Soviet motivations and objectives, Vance requested a formal review of U.S.–Soviet relations in May 1978. "Many are asking whether this Administration has decided to make a sharp shift in its foreign policy priorities," Vance noted, expressing alarm about the more hawkish Brzezinski's influence on the president's view of the Soviet Union.[57] Indeed, Carter's growing distrust of Soviet intentions, ignited by the Soviet involvement in the Horn of Africa, had become apparent in a series of public statements depicting the Soviets as less trustworthy and calling for the adoption of a harsher U.S. stance.[58] Yet Carter continued to see the Soviet Union's actions in the Horn as opportunistic.[59]

By mid-1978, Brzezinski and Vance found themselves in opposing camps while Carter vacillated. Brzezinski summarized the differences:

One view . . . was that "the Soviets have stomped all over the code of détente." They continue to pursue a selective détente. Their action reflects growing assertiveness in Soviet foreign policy generally. Brezhnev's diminished control permits the natural, historical, dominating impulse of the regime to assert itself with less restraint.

Another view . . . was that the record of Soviet action is much more mixed and has to be considered case-by-case. The Soviets are acting on traditional lines and essentially reacting to U.S. steps.[60]

Convinced by early 1979 that the Soviets were pursuing an expansionist "grand design," Brzezinski continued to press Carter to act more assertively. He wrote to Carter that the recent pattern in Soviet interventions revealed revisionist intentions.[61] Although alarmed, the president continued to reject Brzezinski's calls to "deliberately toughen both the tone and the substance of our foreign policy."[62] The issue of Soviet intentions resurfaced in the fall of 1979 during the uproar over the Soviet brigade in Cuba. Brzezinski saw this as another credible indicator of Soviet expansionist intentions, but Carter and Vance were unpersuaded.[63]

The Soviet invasion of Afghanistan in December 1979 caused Carter to re-evaluate his perceptions of Soviet intentions. On January 20, 1980, he declared that it had made "a more dramatic change in my opinion of what the Soviets' ultimate goals are than anything they've done in the previous time that I've been in office."[64] Carter now viewed the Soviet Union as expansionist, not necessarily because of the financial or political costs incurred by the Soviets, but because the invasion represented a qualitative shift in Soviet behavior. Explaining this shift, Carter adopted Brzezinski's line of reasoning, saying, "[I]t is obvious that the Soviets' actual invasion of a previously nonaligned country, an independent, freedom-loving country, a deeply religious country, with their own massive troops is a radical departure from the policy or actions that the Soviets have pursued since the Second World War."[65] Consequently, he warned that the invasion of Afghanistan was "an extremely serious threat to peace because of the threat of further Soviet expansion into neighboring countries."[66]

The invasion was seen as an informative indicator of intention not solely because it was a "costly" action, but also because of the emotional response it invoked in Carter. Indeed, the reason he saw the invasion as indicative of Soviet intentions can also be explained, as Richard Ned Lebow and Janice Stein point out, by the "egocentric bias" that led Carter to exaggerate the extent to which he, personally, was the target of Soviet actions.[67] In particular, the invasion contradicted the frank rapport and the understanding that he felt he had achieved with Brezhnev during their meeting in June 1979 in Vienna.[68] Indeed, during that summit meeting, Carter spoke of "continuing cooperation and honesty in our discussions," and upon his return he had proudly reported to Congress that "President Brezhnev and I developed a better sense of each other as leaders and as men."[69] Brezhnev's justification for the invasion—which asserted that the Soviet troops were sent in response to requests by the Afghan government—infuriated Carter, as he interpreted it as an "insult to his intelligence."[70] Finally, Brezhnev's betrayal also suggested that the Soviet leader could not be trusted to be a partner for détente. As Carter explained, "[T]his is a deliberate aggression that calls into question détente and the way we have been doing business with the Soviets for the past decade. It raises grave questions about Soviet intentions and destroys any chance of getting the SALT Treaty through the Senate. And that makes the prospects for nuclear war even greater."[71] Carter wrote in his diary, "[T]he Soviet invasion sent a clear indication that they were not to be trusted."[72]

Vance's reactions to and interpretation of the Soviet invasion differed dramatically from Carter's. He did not see the invasion as significant and costly, and thus informative of Soviet intentions. Rather, he considered it an "aberration" from past behavior, and "largely as an expedient reaction to opportunities rather than as a manifestation of a more sustained trend."[73] Vance understood why others might view the invasion as a significant signal of expansionist intentions, but he believed that "the primary motive for the Soviet actions was defensive, [and] that the Soviets do not have long-term regional ambitions beyond Afghanistan."[74] Indeed, Vance continued to view Soviet intentions as opportunistic long after the invasion of Afghanistan.[75]

In sum, the evidence presented provides strong support for the selective attention thesis. The support for the capabilities thesis is weak: the significant Soviet military buildup did not lead all U.S. observers to see Soviet intentions as becoming more hostile throughout this period. More important, none of the decisionmakers referred to the Soviet military buildup in explaining his assessment of Soviet political intentions. Brzezinski's writings rarely discussed the recent Soviet military buildup, even though it would have bolstered the hawkish case.[76] The evidence for the behavior thesis is moderate. Both Carter and Brzezinski used Soviet military interventions to infer political intentions. Yet the behavior thesis does not explain why, unlike Brzezinski, Carter and Vance did not infer hostile or expansionist motives from Soviet involvement in the Horn of Africa; it also does not explain why the invasion of Afghanistan triggered such a dramatic change in Carter's beliefs about Soviet intentions but had no such effect on Vance. Finally, the behavior thesis fails to account for the differences between the decisionmakers' inference processes—which largely relied on assessments of Soviet actions, albeit not necessarily "costly" ones—and the U.S. intelligence community's inference process, which, as described in the next section, largely relied on assessments of Soviet capabilities.

U.S. Intelligence Community Assessments of Soviet Intentions

The bulk of the integrated national intelligence estimates (NIEs) on the Soviet Union throughout the Cold War focused on aspects of the Soviet military arsenal. As Raymond Garthoff stated, "Estimates of Soviet capabilities were the predominant focus of attention and received virtually all of the intelligence collection, analysis, and estimative effort."[77] Former Director of Central Intelligence George Tenet noted that "from the mid-1960s on to the Soviet collapse, we knew roughly how many combat aircraft or warheads the Soviets had, and where. But why did they need that many or that kind? What did they plan to do with them? To this day, Intelligence is always much better at counting heads than divining what is going on inside them. That is, we are very good at gauging the size and location of militaries and weaponry. But for obvious reasons, we can never be as good at figuring out what leaders will do with them."[78]

During the mid-to-late 1970s, various agencies within the U.S. intelligence community held differing views about Soviet intentions. For example, the State Department's Bureau of Intelligence and Research and the Central Intelligence Agency (CIA) saw the Soviets as opportunistic. The military intelligence agencies and the Defense Intelligence Agency (part of the Department of Defense) viewed Soviet intentions as expansionist. The reasoning described in the integrated NIEs shows that all U.S. intelligence agencies viewed measures of Soviet current and projected strategic power as the most important indicator of Soviet political intentions. For example, NIE 11-4-78 estimated that "more assertive Soviet international behavior" was "likely to persist as long as the USSR perceives that Western strength is declining and its own strength is steadily increasing." It judged that "if the new [Soviet] leaders believe the 'correlation of forces' to be favorable, especially if they are less impressed than Brezhnev with U.S. military might and more impressed with their own, they might employ military power even more assertively in pursuit of their global ambitions."[79] The centrality of Soviet capabilities and the balance of capabilities as indicators of intentions also dominated NIE 11-3/8-79, in which Director of Central Intelligence Stansfield Turner asserted that "as they [the Soviets] see this [military] superiority increase during the next three to five years, they will probably attempt to secure maximum political advantage from their military arsenal in anticipation of U.S. force modernization programs."[80] * * *

Interagency disagreements about Soviet military strength and the evolving correlation of forces shaped readings of Soviet intentions. Agencies that perceived the Soviet Union as highly confident in its power also predicted that Soviet foreign policy would become more aggressive. Agencies that perceived Soviet capabilities as weaker also saw Soviet intentions as less aggressive and Soviet objectives as more moderate.[81] Bureaucratic interests did sometimes influence interpretations of Soviet capabilities and intentions, but whatever the parochial motives of analysts from different agencies and in spite of their disagreements about Soviet intentions, all of the intelligence agencies grounded their estimates of intentions in Soviet capabilities. Furthermore, in stark contrast to the Carter administration's decisionmakers, the intelligence community made almost no references to presumably costly noncapabilities-based actions to support the inferences they were drawing about their political intentions.[82]

In sum, the review of the NIEs on the Soviet Union reveals that unlike Carter, Brzezinski, and Vance, the U.S. intelligence community did not assess Soviet political intentions on the basis of behavioral or vivid indicators, but rather on their reading of Soviet military capabilities. This finding is consistent with both the capabilities thesis and the selective attention thesis's organizational expertise hypothesis. The marked differences between evaluations by the civilian decisionmakers and those of the intelligence community, as well as the substantial number of NIEs dedicated to assessing Soviet military capabilities, provide further support for the selective attention thesis.

The End of the Cold War, 1985–88

During his first term, President Ronald Reagan perceived Soviet intentions as expansionist. His views changed dramatically, however, during his second administration. Following the Moscow summit in May 1988, Reagan asserted that his characterization of the Soviet Union five years earlier as an "evil empire" belonged to "another time, another era."[83] When asked if he could declare the Cold War over, the president responded, "I think right now, of course."[84] This section explores the indicators that President Reagan, Secretary of State George Shultz, and Secretary of Defense Caspar Weinberger used to assess Soviet political intentions during Reagan's second term, and how the U.S. intelligence community analyzed similar indicators to infer Gorbachev's intentions during the same period. The discussion that follows begins with some background information about trends in Soviet capabilities and costly action. This is followed by an analysis of how Reagan and his advisers perceived Soviet intentions. The final section evaluates the inference process that the coordinated assessments of the U.S. intelligence community used to judge Soviet intentions during the same period.

Realist accounts of the end of the Cold War point to the decline in Soviet power relative to that of the United States during the late 1980s.[85] Yet archival documents show that at this time, the U.S. defense establishment estimated that the Soviet Union's military power was growing; that the Soviets were modernizing their strategic force comprehensively;[86] and that the Warsaw Pact had a strong advantage over NATO in almost all categories of forces as a result of its continuing weapons production.[87] In addition, prior to the signing of the Intermediate Nuclear Forces (INF) Treaty, the United States perceived the theater nuclear balance of power as extremely threatening, given the Soviet Union's vigorous modernization and initial deployment of intermediate-range ballistic missiles in Europe. Although the INF Treaty, which took effect in June 1988, substantially limited Soviet medium-range and intermediate-range ballistic missile forces, the U.S. intelligence community believed that it did not diminish the Soviets' ability to wage a nuclear war.[88] Then, in December 1988, Soviet Head of State Mikhail Gorbachev announced a unilateral and substantial reduction in Soviet conventional forces in Eastern Europe. Even so, U.S. perceptions of the balance of capabilities did not change until late 1989, following initial implementation of the Soviet force reductions. The announcement itself did not result in U.S. recognition of any significant diminution of Soviet capabilities in either size or quality.[89]

As for Soviet behavioral signals, Gorbachev's proposals during 1985 and 1986 were not sufficiently "costly."[90] During 1987 and 1988, however, the Soviet Union offered additional and significant reassurances to the United States. Especially costly were the Soviet acceptance of asymmetric reductions in the INF in 1987, the withdrawal of Soviet troops from Afghanistan announced publicly in February 1988,[91] and a series of other actions that Gorbachev undertook throughout 1988 aimed at restructuring the political system in the Soviet Union.[92]

Second Reagan Administration's Assessments of Soviet Intentions

A review of the historical record shows that Reagan, Shultz, and Weinberger disagreed on which Soviet actions they categorized as costly. Their interpretation of signals was shaped by their expectations, theories, and vivid, costless information.

To be sure, all three decisionmakers shared similar hawkish views of the Soviet Union, but they exhibited important differences in outlook. Weinberger held much more hawkish views than Reagan and Shultz at the start of Reagan's second administration.[93] Shultz was far less hawkish and did not believe, prior to 1985, that the Soviet Union desired global domination. Reagan's views were closer to those of Weinberger than Shultz. During his first term, Reagan had repeatedly referred to the Soviet Union as an ideologically motivated power bent on global hegemony.[94] Until mid-1987, Reagan continued to view Soviet intentions as expansionist. In December 1985, Reagan stated both in public and in private his belief that Gorbachev was still dedicated to traditional Soviet goals and that he had yet to see a break from past Soviet behavior.[95] In 1986, although Reagan had begun to view Gorbachev's policies as signaling a positive change in attitude, he still asserted that he had no illusions about the Soviets or their ultimate intentions."[96]

Reagan and Shultz began to gradually reevaluate their perceptions of Gorbachev's intentions during 1987. The Soviet leader's acceptance of the U.S. proposal on INF was a major contributing factor. In 1987 Reagan reflected on his evolving characterization of the Soviet Union: "With regard to the evil empire. I meant it when I said it [in 1983], because under previous leaders they have made it evident that . . . their program was based on expansionism."[97] Still, neither Reagan nor Shultz expected Gorbachev to signal a genuine change in Soviet foreign policy objectives. Reagan wrote, "[I]n the spring of 1987 we were still facing a lot of uncertainty regarding the Soviets. . . . It was evident something was up in the Soviet Union, but we still didn't know what it was."[98]

Two events in the spring of 1988 persuaded Reagan and Shultz of a change in Soviet intentions. First, the initial Soviet withdrawal from Afghanistan in April symbolized to both that the Brezhnev Doctrine was dead.[99] Shultz explained that the dominant perception in the administration was that "if the Soviets left Afghanistan, the Brezhnev Doctrine would be breached, and the principle of 'never letting go' would be violated."[100] In a private conversation with Gorbachev, Reagan acknowledged that the withdrawal "was a tangible step in the right direction," and took note of Gorbachev's statement that "the settlement could serve as a model for ending other regional conflict."[101] The second event occurred during the 19th Communist Party Conference, at which Gorbachev proposed major domestic reforms such as the establishment of competitive elections with secret ballots; term limits for elected officials; separation of powers with an independent judiciary; and provisions for freedom of speech, assembly, conscience, and the press. The proposals signaled to many in the Reagan administration that Gorbachev's domestic reforms were meant to make revolutionary and irreversible changes. Ambassador Jack Matlock described these proposals as "nothing short of revolutionary in the Soviet context," adding that they "provided evidence that Gorbachev was finally prepared to cross the Rubicon and discard the Marxist ideology that had defined and justified the Communist Party dictatorship in the Soviet Union."[102]

Reagan also paid significant attention to some "costless" actions and viewed them as credible signals of changed intentions given their vividness. Reagan repeatedly cited his positive impressions of Gorbachev from their private interactions in four summit meetings as persuading him that Gorbachev was genuinely seeking to reduce U.S.-Soviet tensions.[103] Emphasizing his growing conviction of Gorbachev's trustworthiness.[104] Reagan began increasingly to refer to Gorbachev as a friend who was "very sincere about the progressive ideas that he is introducing there [in the Soviet Union] and the changes that he thinks should be made."[105] * * * The president wrote, "It's clear that there was a chemistry between Gorbachev and me that produced something very close to a friendship. He was a tough, hard bargainer. . . . I liked Gorbachev even though he was a dedicated Communist."[106] * * *

Other members of Reagan's administration noticed the importance of vivid information in shaping his views. Matlock thus notes, "Once he [Reagan] and Shultz started meeting with Gorbachev they relied on their personal impressions and personal instincts." * * * Reagan's personality—specifically his openness to contradictory information, his belief in his power of persuasion, and his emotional intelligence[107]—allowed him to rely heavily on his personal impressions of Gorbachev. As Barbara Farnham puts it, for Reagan, "[p]ersonal experience counted for everything."[108] Reagan's confidants have pointed to his tendency to reduce issues to personalities: "If he liked and trusted someone, he was more prone to give credence to the policies they espoused."[109]

■   ■   ■

As for the role of Soviet capabilities, both Reagan and Shultz saw a connection between the Soviet Union's capabilities, its actions, and its political intentions. In their eyes, Soviet expansionist conduct during the 1970s occurred at a time when the United States had lost its superiority over the Soviet Union in strategic nuclear weapons.[110] They made it clear, however, that it was Soviet behavior during that period, rather than the Soviet military buildup, that was the decisive evidence of Soviet aggressive intentions. In fact, one of Reagan's favorite quotations was that "nations do not mistrust each other because they are armed; they are armed because they mistrust each other."[111] Reagan similarly acknowledged that the adversary's capabilities by themselves are not good indicators of its intentions; instead they are a by-product of how each state perceives the other's intentions.

■   ■   ■

In conclusion, the series of Gorbachev's costly actions should make this an easy case for the behavior thesis, yet, the empirical evidence lends only moderate support. While Reagan and Shultz relied on costly behavior signals to infer intentions, they also focused significantly on behavioral actions such as their own personal impressions of Gorbachev. Further, the behavior thesis fails to explain Weinberger's inference process: the secretary of defense stated explicitly that he did not regard any of Gorbachev's costly actions as credible reassuring indicators of intentions. As a result, his assessments of Soviet intentions did not change at all, even after leaving office. These aspects in the inference processes underscore the subjective nature of credibility. The support for the capabilities thesis is weak. Given the perceived trends in Soviet capabilities described at the beginning of this section, one would have expected the perceived intentions of the Soviet Union to have remained hostile until mid-1988. This thesis, therefore, cannot explain the radical change in Reagan's and Shultz's perceptions, and why the president and his secretary of state rarely focused on the Soviet military arsenal as an indicator that shaped their assessments of Soviet political intentions during the period under examination.

U.S. Intelligence Community's Assessment of Soviet Intentions

The U.S. intelligence community's National Intelligence Estimates focused on markedly different indicators of Soviet intentions from 1985 to 1988 than did Reagan, Shultz, and Weinberger.[112] It gave greatest weight to the Soviet Union's military capabilities in judging Soviet political intentions. The U.S. intelligence community, as is now known, overestimated Soviet strategic forces and defense spending during the 1980s; this overestimation was an important contributing factor to the community's tendency to overstate Soviet hostility.[113]

Intelligence estimates from 1985 to 1987 concluded that Gorbachev was seeking détente with the West to reduce U.S. challenges to Soviet interests and to decrease U.S. defense efforts. His long-term goal was said to be to "preserve and advance the USSR's international influence and its relative military power."[114] Recognition by the Soviet leadership that the correlation of forces would soon shift against the Soviet Union and a relative decline in Soviet economic power were offered as the leading explanations for Gorbachev's cooperative initiatives.[115] A 1985 NIE stated, "Moscow has long believed that arms control must first and foremost protect the capabilities of Soviet military forces relative to their opponents. The Soviets seek to limit U.S. force modernization through both the arms control process and any resulting agreements."[116] A Special NIE in 1986 pointed to Soviet concerns about the Reagan administration's Strategic Defense Initiative as the primary motive behind Gorbachev's pursuit of a détente-like policy vis-à-vis the West. The NIEs portrayed Gorbachev's arms control initiatives as propaganda aimed at bolstering his campaign of deception.[117] The intelligence community's working assumption was that, despite serious economic problems since the mid-1970s, Soviet objectives remained unchanged.[118]

By mid-1988, Reagan's and Shultz's assessments of Soviet intentions had undergone a fundamental change, but the available NIEs indicate that the U.S. intelligence community did not revise its estimates of Soviet objectives until mid-1989.[119] Throughout 1987 and 1988, the community continued to hold that Gorbachev's foreign policy initiatives were merely tactical, and that no significant discontinuity in Soviet traditional goals and expectations could be anticipated.[120] For instance, in describing Gorbachev's "ultimate goal[s]," a late-1987 NIE repeated earlier assertions that Gorbachev was pursuing a clever plan to pursue communism, not through the use of blunt force, but through a deceiving posture of accommodation with the West that was intended to win more friends in the underdeveloped world.[121]

Soviet modernization efforts toward greater "war-fighting" capabilities, coupled with calculations as to how economic difficulties would affect the strategic balance of power, were said to provide the most reliable guides to Soviet objectives.[122]

In conclusion, consistent with the expectations of the selective attention thesis's organizational expertise hypothesis, as well as with those of the capabilities thesis, the intelligence community's NIEs inferred Soviet political intentions primarily from its military capabilities. Throughout this period, the community did not update its assessments in response to Gorbachev's costly actions of reassurance, and it rarely used costly Soviet behavior to draw inferences about Soviet foreign policy goals. It saw Gorbachev's policies on arms limitations, for example, as rooted in the need to increase Soviet relative economic capabilities, a task that could be accomplished only by reducing pressure to allocate more resources to defense. Engaging NATO in arms control agreements was merely a ploy to undercut support in the West for NATO's weapons modernization efforts.[123] Thus, the support for the behavior thesis is weak.

Interestingly, the intelligence community's reluctance to revise its estimates of Soviet intentions led to repeated clashes between Director of Central Intelligence Robert Gates and Secretary of State Shultz, the latter saying later that he had little confidence in the community's intelligence reports on the Soviet Union.[124] Nevertheless, intelligence assessments had only limited impact on Reagan and Shultz, who drew conclusions about Soviet intentions largely from their personal impressions and insights from meetings with Gorbachev. As Matlock explains, "They are very experienced people and experienced politicians and it meant much more to them what they were experiencing."[125] Paul Pillar contends that Reagan and his advisers, apart from Shultz, "brushed aside as irrelevant any careful analysis of Soviet intentions, just as Carter and Brzezinski had brushed aside the question of the Soviets' reason for intervening in Afghanistan."[126]

■ ■ ■

Conclusion

The selective attention framework fills important gaps in scholars' understanding of the effectiveness of signals. This approach sees the interaction of signals with perceptual and organizational filters as central. In particular, several patterns emerge from the analysis. First, the subjective credibility hypothesis of the selective attention thesis receives strong support in all three cases examined in this study. At the heart of this hypothesis lies the idea that "credibility depends on how observers assess evidence and on what evidence they decide to assess."[127] Decisionmakers' own explicit or implicit theories or beliefs about how the world operates and their expectations significantly affect this selection and interpretation of signals. Decisionmakers in * * * the Carter administration and the second Reagan administration debated what to make of different indicators of intentions. To a large extent, their reading of signals was influenced by what they expected to see. Those decisionmakers with relatively hawkish views, such as * * * Zbigniew Brzezinski, were quicker to read Soviet actions, respectively, as evidence of malign intentions. Some clung to their original beliefs and interpreted all incoming information through the prism of those beliefs. Thus, Caspar Weinberger did not revise his beliefs about the expansionist nature of Soviet intentions even when faced with costly reassuring actions. Similarly, Cyrus Vance interpreted Soviet actions in the Horn and in Afghanistan consistently with his existing belief that the Soviets were merely opportunistic.

Second, consistent with the selective attention thesis, * * * American decisionmakers repeatedly and explicitly relied on their personal insights to derive conclusions about their adversary's intentions. They monitored and responded not only to what the adversary's leader promised or threatened behind closed doors, but also to how he delivered the message: tone of voice, mannerisms, and mood were critical pieces of intelligence in their eyes. * * * Personal impressions gleaned from private meetings with Mikhail Gorbachev * * * played a critical role in transforming President Ronald Reagan's assessments of Soviet intentions. In sum, personal diplomatic communication may leave strong emotional impressions (positive or negative) on leaders, who then use these impressions as evidence of intentions. This inference process is, in some sense, rational, but it may cause leaders to act in ways that do not serve their best interests. Rather than debate the concept of rationality in a vacuum, scholars need to understand that vividness, or an affect heuristics, more generally, is essential for rationality.[128]

At times, vividness and costly signaling jointly produced a drastic change in decisionmakers' beliefs. The analysis has shown that vivid information provided the context for understanding Gorbachev's costly signals, leading to a transformation in Reagan's views. Similarly, the Soviet invasion of Afghanistan, because of its magnitude, its salience, and the emotional toll it exerted on President Carter, induced a drastic change in his beliefs. * * *

A third point has to do with the second hypothesis of the selective attention thesis pertaining to the filters that intelligence organizations use in estimating intentions. Collective intelligence assessments in the United States * * * were consistent in their preference for military indicators over other types of indicators in their analysis of intentions. * * * NIEs on the Soviet Union also carefully tracked changes in Soviet military inventories and future capabilities. They did not always recognize the tautological logic they were using: that is, in estimating capabilities, these coordinated intelligence reports used certain assumptions about Soviet intentions while the resulting estimates of Soviet capabilities were used to infer future political intentions.

These divergent uses of information point to a weakness in the relationship between decisionmakers and intelligence organizations.[129] For example, according to Brzezinski, intelligence assessments of the Soviet Union were "weak on the level of 'politology,' and thus "did not provide much help to the President . . . in determining what the Soviets, in general, were trying to do."[130] Intelligence analysts were painfully aware of this criticism, and saw the task of analyzing Soviet intentions as the "biggest single trap."[131] Director of Intelligence Stansfield Turner explained that, "sometimes they [decision-makers] have better information than you do. I mean, whenever I briefed President Carter, I always had to keep in the back of my mind that 'he met with Brezhnev last week.' I'd never met with Brezhnev, so if he interpreted what Brezhnev was going to do tomorrow differently than we interpreted what Brezhnev might do tomorrow, I had to give him credit that maybe he understood Brezhnev better than we."[132] * * *

Of the alternative theses, the capabilities thesis has its greatest support in describing the practice of a state's intelligence organization. The Soviet Union's nuclear buildup and modernization efforts served as the main indicator the U.S. intelligence community used to estimate Soviet intentions during the 1970s, as well as the 1980s. * * * The capabilities thesis does a poorer job, however, at explaining how civilian decisionmakers read and interpret intentions. To be sure, armament efforts also had important "framing effects," because they forced decision-makers to raise questions about the adversary's long-term objectives. Nevertheless, in none of the three episodes were these indicators regarded by the state's civilian leadership as primary evidence of the adversary's long-term intentions. This inference process implies that decisionmakers do not always assume the worst about intentions, as offensive realists would say that they should. More consistent with defensive realism, decisionmakers see estimating intentions as a central task of statecraft, and they attempt to detect important signals, which may reduce or exacerbate the security dilemma. What the realist logic neglects, however, is that decisionmakers' beliefs about the adversary's intentions are not necessarily driven by changes in the adversary's military forces. Thus, the policy prescription of rationalist security-dilemma scholars who identify changes in armament policies as a way of signaling intentions may not be effective.

The behavior thesis performs better than the capabilities thesis in explaining how decisionmakers gauge intentions. Indeed, for some * * * U.S. decisionmakers, contemporary costly actions such as observed shifts in Soviet behavior induced changes in beliefs about the adversary's intentions. Still, the empirical analysis provides many examples that contradict the causal mechanisms and underlying logic of the behavior thesis. Significantly, decisionmakers rarely agreed on what constituted a truly "credible" signal even when it was "costly." Members of the Carter administration disagreed on the significance of Soviet military involvement in the Horn of Africa. Some officials, such as Vance, did not treat the Soviet invasion of Afghanistan as a diagnostic indicator of Soviet expansionist intentions, despite its considerable scale and cost. Even at the end of the Cold War, a relatively easy test of the behavior thesis, one finds that some Reagan officials, including Weinberger, did not regard Gorbachev's costly actions as informative signals of reassurance. Indeed, neither Weinberger nor Vance updated his beliefs during his time in office, even when faced with hostile signals that would otherwise be categorized as "costly."[133] * * *

Moreover, the assumption that the informational value of "costless" (and even private) communication will be discounted does not withstand empirical scrutiny.[134] Leaders explicitly drew on their personal insights about the sincerity and intentions of adversarial leaders. * * * Finally, the behavior thesis does not explain why intelligence organizations ignored or dismissed those costly noncapabilities-based actions that civilian decisionmakers relied upon, a practice especially pronounced in the collective NIEs during the 1980s. These findings appear to challenge the empirical validity of the behavior thesis, but they do not negate the logic of costly signaling, as there is some evidence that certain "costly" behavioral signals were seen as informative in the eyes of some decisionmakers.

Taken together, the logic of the costly signaling approach deserves more scrutiny. Although certain costly actions do receive more attention than others, decisionmakers' inference processes diverge significantly from those predicted by that approach. Nonetheless, this study should not be seen as dismissing the costly signaling concept entirely. Rather, it reveals significant shortcomings and ambiguities in how one should translate this concept of a costly signal from economic theory, where it originated, into a testable proposition in international politics. The literature should be clearer about the inferences that observers are expected to draw from a costly action. Finally, decisionmakers often must interpret multiple signals, some of which may suggest that the adversary's intentions are becoming more benign, whereas others may suggest the opposite. Rationalist accounts are silent as to which costly signals perceivers are likely to notice and which they are likely to ignore.

In sum, the findings imply that any study on the efficacy of signals that fails to consider how signals are perceived and interpreted may be of little use to policymakers seeking to deter or reassure an adversary. They also suggest that policymakers should not assume that their costly signals will be understood clearly by their state's adversaries. They should not fear that others are necessarily making worst-case assumptions about their intentions on the basis of their military capabilities, but they should be aware that the adversary's intelligence apparatus is likely to view such an indicator as a credible signal of intentions. Decisionmakers' inclination to rely on their own judgments and subjective reading of signals to infer political intentions is pervasive and universal, but these individuals should be wary: getting inside the mind of the adversary is perhaps one of the most difficult tasks facing intelligence organizations, and perhaps most susceptible to bias and bureaucratic interests. * * *

NOTES

1. Kenneth Lieberthal and Wang Jisi, "Addressing U.S.-China Strategic Distrust" (Washington, DC: Brookings Institution, 2012), p. vi.

2. Gary Locke, "China Is a Country of Great Contrasts," National Public Radio, January 18, 2012, http://www.npr.org/2012/01/18/145384412/ambassador-locke-shares-his-impressions-of-china.

3. Jeffrey A. Bader, Obama and China's Rise: An Insider's Account of America's Asia Strategy (Washington, DC: Brookings Institution Press, 2012). See also Calum McLeod, "Some Cast Obama Trip as Effort to Contain China's Influence," USA Today, November 20, 2011, http://www.usatoday.com/news/world/story/2011-11-21/China-US-relations-Obama/51321096/1.

4. In the context of foreign policy intentions, see James D. Fearon, "Signaling Foreign Policy Interests: Tying Hands versus Sinking Costs," Journal of Conflict Resolution, Vol. 41, No. 1 (February 1997), pp. 68–90; Andrew Kydd, Trust and Mistrust in International Relations (Princeton, NJ: Princeton University Press, 2005); and Robert F. Trager, "Diplomatic Calculus in Anarchy: How Communication Matters," American Political Science Review, Vol. 104, No. 2 (May 2010), pp. 347–68. I exclude from the analysis public statements that can generate "audience costs," because they are typically seen as relevant in crisis situations. James D. Fearon, "Domestic Political Audiences and the Escalation of International Disputes," American Political Science Review, Vol. 88, No. 3 (September 1994), pp. 577–92. For an empirical analysis of audience costs, see Jack Snyder and Erica D. Borghard, "The Cost of Empty Threats: A Penny, Not a Pound," American Political Science Review, Vol. 105, No. 3 (November 2011), pp. 437–56; and Marc Trachtenberg, "Audience Costs: An Historical Analysis," Security Studies, Vol. 21, No. 1 (2012), pp. 3–42.

5. Thomas C. Schelling, The Strategy of Conflict (Cambridge, Mass.: Harvard University Press, 1980); and Fearon, "Signaling Foreign Policy Interests." On when and how "cheap talk" could matter, see Trager, "Diplomatic Calculus in Anarchy"; Vincent P. Crawford and Joel Sobel, "Strategic Information Transmission," Econometrica, Vol. 50, No. 6 (November 1982), pp. 1431–451; Joseph Farrell and Robert Gibbons, "Cheap Talk Can Matter in Bargaining," Journal of Economic Theory, Vol. 48, No. 1 (June 1989), pp. 221–37; and Anne E. Sartori, Deterrence by Diplomacy (Princeton, NJ: Princeton University Press, 2005).

6. Charles L. Glaser, Rational Theory of International Politics: The Logic of Competition and Cooperation (Princeton, NJ: Princeton University Press, 2010).

7. For the effects of perceived intentions on policies, see Keren Yarhi-Milo, Knowing Thy Adversary: Leaders, Intelligence, and Assessments of Intentions in International Relations (Princeton, NJ: Princeton University Press, forthcoming).

8. Intention should be distinguished from states' motives for keeping or changing the status quo. On motives, see Glaser, Rational Theory of International Politics, pp. 38–39.

9. The scope of the revisionist intentions in expansionist and opportunistic states can be limited or unlimited. For a similar typology, see Keith L. Shimko, Images and Arms Control: Perceptions of the Soviet

Union in the Reagan Administration (Ann Arbor: University of Michigan Press, 1991).

10. Douglas Seay, "What Are the Soviets' Objectives in Their Foreign, Military, and Arms Control Policies?" in Lynn Eden and Steven E. Miller, eds., *Nuclear Arguments: Understanding the Strategic Nuclear Arms and Arms Control Debates* (Ithaca, NY: Cornell University Press, 1989), pp. 47–108; and Robert Jervis, *Perception and Misperception in International Politics* (Princeton, NJ: Princeton University Press, 1976).

11. Amos Tversky and Daniel Kahneman, "Availability: A Heuristic for Judging Frequency and Probability," *Cognitive Psychology,* Vol. 5, No. 2 (September 1973), pp. 207–32; and Thomas Gilovich, Dale Griffin, and Daniel Kahneman, eds., *Heuristics and Biases: The Psychology of Intuitive Judgment* (Cambridge: Cambridge University Press, 2002).

12. Robert Jervis, "Signaling and Perception: Drawing Inferences and Projecting Images," in Kristen Monroe, ed., *Political Psychology* (Mahwah, NJ: Lawrence Erlbaum, 2002); and Jonathan Mercer, "Emotional Beliefs," *International Organization,* Vol. 64, No. 1 (January 2010), pp. 1–31.

13. The literature on such biases is vast. For important works and good summaries, see Jervis, *Perception and Misperception in International Politics;* Ole Holsti, "The Belief System and National Images: A Case Study," *Journal of Conflict Resolution,* Vol. 6, No. 3 (September 1962), pp. 244–52; and Philip E. Tetlock, "Social Psychology and World Politics," in Susan T. Fiske, Daniel T. Gilbert, and Gardner Lindzey, eds., *Handbook of Social Psychology,* 4th ed. (New York: McGraw-Hill, 1998), pp. 868–914.

14. Robert Jervis, "Understanding Beliefs," *Political Psychology,* Vol. 27, No. 5 (October 2006), pp. 641–63.

15. This hypothesis cannot indicate a priori when observers will change their assessments about intentions, but it can predict the possibility of change in perceived intentions relative to those of other observers on the basis of their initial beliefs about the intentions of the adversary.

16. Peer Schouten, "Theory Talk #12: Robert Jervis on Nuclear Weapons, Explaining the Non-Realist Politics of the Bush Administration and U.S. Military Presence in Europe," *Theory Talks,* January 24, 2008, http://www.theory-talks.org/2008/07/theory-talk-12.html.

17. Richard E. Nisbett and Lee Ross, *Human Inference: Strategies and Shortcomings of Social Judgment* (Englewood Cliffs, NJ: Prentice Hall, 1980), p. 62. See also Eugene Borgida and Richard E. Nisbett, "The Differential Impact of Abstract vs. Concrete Information on Decisions," *Journal of Applied Social Psychology,* Vol. 7, No. 3 (September 1977), pp. 258–71; Chaim D. Kaufmann, "Out of the Lab and into the Archives: A Method for Testing Psychological Explanations of Political Decision Making," *International Studies Quarterly,* Vol. 38, No. 4 (December 1994), pp. 557–86; and Tversky and Kahneman, "Availability."

18. On the importance of personal meetings in inferring leaders' sincerity, see Todd Hall and Keren Yarhi-Milo, "The Personal Touch: Leaders' Impressions, Costly Signaling, and Assessments of Sincerity in International Affairs," *International Studies Quarterly,* Vol. 56, No. 3 (September 2012), pp. 560–73.

19. See, for example, Mercer, "Emotional Beliefs"; and Rose McDermott, "The Feeling of Rationality: The Meaning of Neuroscientific

Advances for Political Science," *Perspectives on Politics,* Vol. 2, No. 4 (December 2004), pp. 691–706.

20. Borgida and Nisbett, "Differential Impact of Abstract vs. Concrete Information," p. 269.

21. Nisbett and Ross, *Human Inference,* pp. 188–91; Fiske and Taylor, *Social Cognition,* pp. 278–79; Tversky and Kahneman, "Availability"; Kaufmann, "Out of the Lab and into the Archives"; and Rose McDermott, Jonathan Cowden, and Stephen Rosen, "The Role of Hostile Communications in a Simulated Crisis Game," *Peace and Conflict: Journal of Peace Psychology,* Vol. 14, No. 2 (2008), p. 156.

22. For a debate on the role of "common prior beliefs" in bargaining models, see Alastair Smith and Allan Stam, "Bargaining and the Nature of War." *Journal of Conflict Resolution,* Vol. 50, No. 6 (December 2004), pp. 783–813; and Mark Fey and Kristopher W. Ramsay, "The Common Priors Assumption: A Comment on 'Bargaining and the Nature of War,'" *Journal of Conflict Resolution,* Vol. 50, No. 4 (2006), pp. 607–13.

23. Alan Gerber and Donald P. Green, "Rational Learning and Partisan Attitudes," *American Journal of Political Science,* Vol. 42, No. 3 (July 1998), pp. 189–210; and Charles S. Taber and Milton Lodge, "Motivated Skepticism in the Evaluation of Political Beliefs," *American Journal of Political Science,* Vol. 50, No. 3 (July 2006), pp. 755–69.

24. As Mark M. Lowenthal writes, "Deployed conventional and strategic forces . . . are difficult to conceal, as they tend to exist in identifiable garrisons and must exercise from time to time. They also tend to be garrisoned or deployed in large numbers, which makes hiding them or masking them impractical at best." Lowenthal, *Intelligence: From Secrets to Policy* (Washington, DC: CQ Press, 2009), pp. 234–35.

25. Philip E. Tetlock, *Expert Political Judgment: How Good Is It? How Can We Know?* (Princeton, NJ: Princeton University Press, 2005), pp. 20–21.

26. For analyses of how organizations influence information processes, see Martha S. Feldman and James G. March, "Information in Organizations as Signal and Symbol," *Administrative Science Quarterly,* Vol. 26, No. 2 (June 1981), pp. 171–86; Yaacov Y. I. Vertzberger, *The World in Their Minds: Information Processing, Cognition, and Perception in Foreign Policy Decisionmaking* (Stanford, CA: Stanford University Press, 1990); and Isaiah Berlin, *The Hedgehog and the Fox: An Essay on Tolstoy's View of History* (London: Weidenfeld and Nicolson, 1953).

27. A third pathway concerns the offensive or defensive nature of the military capabilities as a signal of intentions. On the little impact that such indicators had on the inference processes of decision-makers during these periods, see Yarhi-Milo, *Knowing Thy Adversary.*

28. John J. Mearsheimer, *The Tragedy of Great Power Politics* (New York: W. W. Norton, 2001), p. 31.

29. Kydd, *Trust and Mistrust in International Relations;* and Glaser, *Rational Theory of International Politics.*

30. Charles L. Glaser, "The Security Dilemma Revisited," *World Politics,* Vol. 50, No. 1 (October 1997), p. 178.

31. On the role of institutions in signaling intentions, see Robert O. Keohane, *After Hegemony: Cooperation and Discord in the World Political Economy* (Princeton, NJ: Princeton University Press,

1984); G. John Ikenberry, *After Victory: Institutions, Strategic Restraint, and the Rebuilding of Order after Major Wars* (Princeton, NJ: Princeton University Press, 2001); Seth Weinberger, "Institutional Signaling and the Origins of the Cold War," *Security Studies,* Vol. 12, No. 4 (Summer 2003), pp. 80–115.

32. The usefulness of international institutions in revealing information about intentions depends on institutional characteristics such as the nature of enforcement, the effects of veto points on state decision-making, and the institution's effects on member states' domestic political institutions.

33. For a summary of how domestic institutions can be a signal of intentions, see Mark L. Haas, "The United States and the End of the Cold War: Reactions to Shifts in Soviet Power, Policies, or Domestic Politics?" *International Organization,* Vol. 61, No. 1 (Winter 2007), p. 152; and James D. Fearon, "Domestic Political Audiences and the Escalation of International Disputes," *American Political Science Review,* Vol. 88, No. 3 (September 1994), pp. 577–92.

34. Glaser, "The Security Dilemma Revisited"; and Charles L. Glaser, *Analyzing Strategic Nuclear Policy* (Princeton, NJ: Princeton University Press, 1991).

35. For the U.S. cases, I use the declassified National Intelligence Estimates (NIEs) on the Soviet Union. NIEs, which are produced by the National Intelligence Council, are the most authoritative product of the intelligence community. The community regularly assessed Soviet intentions in the 11-4 and 11-8 series of NIEs, supplemented by occasional Special NIEs (SNIEs). In all NIEs, I analyze only those sections that deal with the question of intentions. In the British case, the main focus of the analysis is the coordinated Chiefs of Staff reports and memoranda, because these represent the integrated analysis of all three military service intelligence agencies. As such, they provide a useful guide to the evolution of perceptions of the German threat at the level of the British intelligence community as a whole.

36. On the relationship between the three decisionmakers, see Jerel A. Rosati, *The Carter Administration's Quest for Global Community: Beliefs and Their Impact on Behavior* (Columbia: University of South Carolina Press. 1987); and Betty Glad, *An Outsider in the White House: Jimmy Carter, His Advisors, and the Making of American Foreign Policy* (Ithaca, NY: Cornell University Press, 2009).

37. Zbigniew Brzezinski, memo, "Comprehensive Net Assessment, 1978," p. 8; and Harold Brown, "Report of Secretary of Defense Harold Brown to the Congress on the FY 1979 Budget, FY Authorization Request, and FY 1979–1983 Defense Programs," January 23, 1978, pp. 65–66.

38. Office of Strategic Research, "The Development of Soviet Military Power: Trends since 1965 and Prospects for the 1980s," SR 81-10035X (Washington, DC: National Foreign Research Center, April 1981), pp. xiii–xv.

39. NIE 11-6-78, pp. 2–3.

40. National Security Council (NSC) meeting, June 4, 1979, quoted in Zbigniew Brzezinski, *Power and Principle: Memoirs of the National Security Advisor, 1977–1981* (New York: Farrar, Straus and Giroux, 1983), pp. 334–36. The conventional military balance in Europe was perceived as favoring the Warsaw Pact forces. See National Foreign Assessment Center, "The Balance of Nuclear Forces in Central Europe," SR 78-10004 (Washington,

DC: Central Intelligence Agency, January 1978); and "Comprehensive Net Assessment, 1978."

41. NIE 11-3/8-79, pp. 2, 4. Soviet damage-limitation capabilities were, however, still judged to be poor despite a large, ongoing Soviet investment. NIE 11-3/8-78, pp. 5–6, 11. See also Harold Brown, "Report of Secretary of Defense Harold Brown, on the FY 1979 Budget," pp. 65–66; and Harold Brown, "Department of Defense Annual Report, Fiscal Year 1980," January 25, 1979, p. 70.

42. As a result of the Soviet invasion of Afghanistan, Carter decided to table SALT II. NSC Weekly Report 123, December 28, 1979.

43. The Soviet Union had low-level involvement in eleven crises and conducted covert or semi-military activities in thirteen crises, in addition to using direct military force in Ethiopia and Afghanistan. See International Conflict Behavior Project dataset, http://www .cidcm.umd.edu/icb/.

44. On the episode of the Soviet brigade in Cuba, see Cyrus R. Vance, *Hard Choices: Critical Years in America's Foreign Policy* (New York: Simon and Schuster, 1983), pp. 360–61; Brzezinski, *Power and Principle,* p. 347; and NSC Weekly Report 98, May 25, 1979; NSC Weekly Report 103, July 20, 1979; NSC Weekly Report 104, July 27, 1979; and NSC Weekly Report 109, September 13, 1979.

45. Rosati, *The Carter Administration's Quest for Global Community;* Melchiore Laucella, "A Cognitive-Psychodynamic Perspective to Understanding Secretary of State Cyrus Vance's Worldview," *Presidential Studies Quarterly,* Vol. 34, No. 2 (June 2004), pp. 227–71; and Steven Jay Campbell, "Brzezinski's Image of the USSR: Inferring Foreign Policy Beliefs from Multiple Sources Over Time," Ph.D. dissertation, University of South Carolina, 2003, pp. 74–75.

46. See, for example, *Public Papers of the President of the United States* [hereafter *PPP*] (Washington, DC: Government Printing Office, June 30, 1977), p. 1198; and *PPP,* December 15, 1977, p. 2119.

47. NSC Weekly Report 18, June 24, 1977.

48. NSC Weekly Report 42, January 13, 1978.

49. Quoted in Brzezinski, *Power and Principle,* p. 181.

50. NSC Weekly Report 47, February 17, 1978.

51. Ibid.

52. NSC Weekly Report 2, February 26, 1977.

53. Zbigniew Brzezinski, memo for the president, "The Soviet Union and Ethiopia: Implications for U.S. Soviet Relations," March 3, 1978.

54. NSC Weekly Report 55, April 21, 1978; and NSC Weekly Report 57, May 5, 1978.

55. Vance, *Hard Choices*, p. 84.

56. Ibid., p. 101.

57. Vance, memo to President Jimmy Carter, May 29, 1978. Document released to author under the Freedom of Information Act, July 2007.

58. *PPP,* May 20, 1978, pp. 872, 940; and *PPP,* May 25, 1978, p. 977. See also Brzezinski, *Power and Principle,* pp. 188–89; and Richard C. Thornton, *The Carter Years: Toward a New Global Order* (New York: Paragon House, 1991), p. 185.

59. *PPP,* November 13, 1978, p. 2017.

60. NSC Weekly Report 65, June 30, 1978.

61. NSC Weekly Report 84, January 12, 1979.

62. NSC Weekly Report 109, September 13, 1979.

63. Brzezinski, *Power and Principle,* pp. 347–51.

64. Jimmy Carter, interview, *Meet the Press,* January 20, 1980. See also Jimmy Carter, *Keeping Faith: Memoirs of a President* (Fayetteville: University of Arkansas Press, 1995), p. 480; "Message for Brezhnev from Carter Regarding Afghanistan," December 28, 1979; and Brzezinski, *Power and Principle,* p. 429.

65. *PPP,* January 20, 1980, p. 11. For a similar line of reasoning, see also pp. 308, 329.

66. *U.S. Department of State Bulletin (DSB),* Vol. 80, No. 2034 (January 1980).

67. Richard Ned Lebow and Janice Gross Stein, "Afghanistan, Carter, and Foreign Policy Change: The Limits of Cognitive Models," in Dan Caldwell and Timothy J. McKeown, eds., *Diplomacy, Force, and Leadership: Essays in Honor of Alexander L. George* (Boulder, CO: Westview, 1993), p. 112.

68. Raymond L. Garthoff, *Détente and Confrontation: American-Soviet Relations from Nixon to Reagan,* rev. ed. (Washington, DC: Brookings Institution Press, 1994), p. 1059.

69. Quoted in ibid.

70. Ibid.

71. Hamilton Jordan, *Crisis: The Last Year of the Carter Presidency* (New York: G. P. Putnam's Sons, 1982), p. 99.

72. Jimmy Carter, *White House Diary* (New York: Farrar, Straus and Giroux, 2010), p. 383.

73. Ibid. For a similar logic, see Marshall Shulman, memorandum for Warren Christopher, "Notes on SU/Afghanistan," January 22, 1980; and Vance, *Hard Choices,* p. 388.

74. NSC Weekly Report 134, March 28, 1980.

75. See interviews with Vance and Shulman in Melchiore Laucella, "Cyrus Vance's Worldview: The Relevance of the Motivated Perspective," Ph.D. dissertation, Union Institute, 1996.

76. In only a few statements did the decisionmakers link Soviet intentions to the buildup. For example, in a report to Carter, Brzezinski wrote: "Soviet defense programs are going beyond the needs of legitimate deterrence and are increasingly pointing towards the acquisition of something which might approximate a war-fighting capability. While we do not know why the Soviets are doing this (intentions?), we do know that their increased capabilities have consequences for our national security." This statement does not, however, lend support to the capabilities thesis, as Brzezinski explicitly says that he cannot infer Soviet intentions from these indicators. Brzezinski also addressed capabilities in other reports, but he did not link them—implicitly or explicitly—to an assessment of Soviet political intentions. NSC Weekly Report 33, October 21, 1977; and NSC Weekly Report 108, September 6, 1979.

77. In this section, I rely in part on interviews I conducted with William Odom, head of the National Security Agency at the time, and Fritz Ermarth, Raymond Garthoff, Melvin Goodman, and Douglas MacEachin, all former CIA analysts of the Soviet Union. Raymond L. Garthoff, "Estimating Soviet Intentions and Capabilities," in Gerald K. Haines and Robert E. Leggett, eds., *Watching the Bear: Essays on CIA's Analysis of the Soviet Union* (Washington, DC: Center for the Study of Intelligence Publications, 2003), chap. 5, https://www.cia.gov/library/center-for-the-study-of

-intelligence/csi-publications/books-and-monographs/watching-the -bear-essays-on-cias-analysis-of-the-soviet-union.

78. "Speeches Delivered at the Conference," in ibid., chap. 8.

79. NIE 11-4-78, p. 6.

80. NIE 11-3/8-79, p. 4.

81. See, for example, NIE 11-4-77; NIE 11-3/8-79; and NIE 11-3/8-80.

82. NIE 11-4-78 made some references to current Soviet actions with respect to SALT and détente. This line of reasoning, however, was rarely invoked. NIE 4-1-78, pp. ix, x, 17.

83. Quoted in Raymond L. Garthoff, *The Great Transition: American-Soviet Relations and the End of the Cold War* (Washington, DC: Brookings Institution Press, 1994), p. 352.

84. President's news conference, Spaso House, Moscow, *DSB,* June 1988, p. 32.

85. William C. Wohlforth, "Realism and the End of the Cold War," *International Security,* Vol. 19, No. 3 (Winter 1994/95), pp. 91–129.

86. See, for example, NIE 11-3/8-86; NIE 11-3/8-87; and NIE 11-3/8-88.

87. Frank Carlucci, "Annual Report to the President and Congress, 1989" (Washington, DC: Government Printing Office, February 18, 1988), p. 29.

88. NIE 11-3/8-88, p. 5. The Department of Defense reached a similar conclusion. U.S. Department of Defense, Office of the Secretary of Defense, "Soviet Military Power" (Washington, DC: U.S. Department of Defense, 1989), p. 7; and U.S. Department of Defense, Office of the Secretary of Defense, "Soviet Military Power" (Washington, DC: Government Printing Office, 1990), pp. 54–55.

89. National Intelligence Council (NIC), "Status of Soviet Unilateral Withdrawal," M 89-10003 (Washington, DC: NIC, October 1989).

90. Jack F. Matlock, *Reagan and Gorbachev: How the Cold War Ended* (New York: Random House, 2004), pp. 275–76; and Garthoff, *The Great Transition,* p. 334. For an analysis of Gorbachev's costly actions and their effects on perceived intentions, see Haas, "The United States and the End of the Cold War"; and Kydd, *Trust and Mistrust in International Relations.*

91. Soviet Foreign Minister Eduard Shevardnadze informed Shultz of the decision to withdraw from Afghanistan in September 1987. Gorbachev publicly confirmed this decision in February 1988.

92. Some decisionmakers in the United States did recognize the significance of Gorbachev's efforts to institute glasnost (openness, or transparency) within the Soviet Union during 1987. It was only from mid-1988, however, that his actions seemed aimed at fundamental institutional change. Both Shultz and Matlock argue that Gorbachev's actions had not, as of the end of 1987, signified fundamental reforms. George Shultz, *Turmoil and Triumph: My Years as Secretary of State* (New York: Charles Scribner's Sons, 1993), p. 1081; and Matlock, *Reagan and Gorbachev,* pp. 295–96. By mid-1988, however, Reagan had begun to praise Gorbachev for initiating true "democratic reform." He said that Gorbachev's efforts were "cause for shaking the head in wonder," leading him to view Gorbachev as "a serious man seeking serious reform." *DSB,* Vol. 2137 (1988), pp. 37–38.

93. In his comprehensive study on perceptions of the Soviet Union during the Reagan administration, Keith Shimko noted that "Weinberger's views of the Soviet Union were about as hard-line as one could get." Shimko, *Images and Arms Control,* p. 233.

94. Ibid., pp. 235–37. According to Shimko, however, Reagan exhibited a rather superficial understanding of the Soviet Union, and his beliefs about the Soviet Union may not have formed a coherent image.

95. See, for example, *DSB,* November 1985, p. 11; and *PPP,* 1985, p. 415.

96. *PPP,* 1986, p. 1369.

97. *PPP,* 1987, pp. 1508–09.

98. Ronald Reagan, *An American Life* (New York: Simon and Schuster, 1990), p. 683.

99. The Brezhnev Doctrine, announced in 1968, asserted the Soviet Union's right to use Warsaw Pact forces to intervene in any Eastern bloc nation that was seen as compromising communist rule and Soviet domination, either by trying to leave the Soviet sphere of influence or even by attempting to moderate Moscow's policies.

100. Shultz, *Turmoil and Triumph,* p. 1086.

101. Transcripts of the Washington Summit, June 1, 1988, 10:05 A.M.–11:20 A.M.; and *PPP,* 1988, pp. 632, 726.

102. Matlock, *Reagan and Gorbachev,* pp. 295–96.

103. Reagan and Gorbachev interacted during four summit meetings: the Geneva Summit (November 1985), the Reykjavik Summit (October 1986), the Washington Summit (December 1987), and the Moscow Summit (May 1988). During these summits, the two held long, private meetings, as a result of which Reagan gained a positive impression of the Soviet leader. Yarhi-Milo, *Knowing Thy Adversary.*

104. *PPP,* June 1, 1987, pp. 594–95; *PPP,* June 11, 1987, p. 624; *PPP,* June 12, 1987, pp. 635–36; *PPP,* August 29, 1987, p. 988; and *PPP,* September 16, 1987, p. 1038.

105. *PPP,* May 24, 1988, p. 649.

106. Reagan, *An American Life,* p. 707.

107. For an excellent analysis of Reagan's personality traits that allowed him to revise his beliefs about the Soviet threat, see Barbara Farnham, "Reagan and the Gorbachev Revolution: Perceiving the End of Threat," *Political Science Quarterly,* Vol. 116, No. 2 (Summer 2001), pp. 225–52; and Fred I. Greenstein, "Ronald Reagan, Mikhail Gorbachev, and the End of the Cold War: What Difference Did They Make?" in William C. Wolforth, ed., *Witnesses to the End of the Cold War* (Baltimore, MD: Johns Hopkins University Press, 1996).

108. Farnham, "Reagan and the Gorbachev Revolution," p. 248.

109. "Leadership and the End of the Cold War," in Richard K. Herrmann and Richard Ned Lebow, eds., *Ending the Cold War: Interpretations, Causation, and the Study of International Relations* (Basingstoke, UK: Palgrave Macmillan, 2004), p. 183.

110. *PPP,* 1985, pp. 650, 1287–88.

111. See, for example, Ronald Reagan, speech given at Moscow State University, May 31, 1988; and *DSB,* August 1988.

112. In addition to NIEs, I relied on the interviews that I conducted with Ermath, Garthoff, Goodman, MacEachin, and Odom.

113. The CIA's Office of Soviet Analysis had become increasingly concerned that estimates of projected Soviet strategic weapons systems were inflated. See, for example, MacEachin, memorandum to deputy director for intelligence, "Force Projections," NIE 11-3/8, April 22, 1986.

114. SNIE 11-9-86, p. 4; and NIE 11-18-87, pp. 3–4.

115. NIE 11-3/8-86; NIE 11-8-87; SNIE 11-16-88; and NIE 11-3/8-88.

116. NIE 11-3/8-85, p. 18. This line of reasoning is repeated in NIE 11-16-85, pp. 3–9.

117. See NIE 11-16-85, p. 13; and SNIE 11-8-86, pp. 15–17.

118. NIE 11-3/8-86, pp. 2, 18.

119. In an estimate published five days after the fall of the Berlin Wall, the intelligence community still viewed Warsaw Pact intentions as hostile, and warned of the possibility of an unprovoked attack on Western Europe. NIE 11-14-89, p. iii.

120. "NIE 11-18-87; SNIE, "Soviet Policy during the Next Phase of Arms Control in Europe"; Robert Gates, memorandum, "Gorbachev's Gameplan: The Long View," November 24, 1987; and NIE 11-3-8-88.

121. NIE 11-3/8-88.

122. Ibid. On the INF Treaty, see ibid., p. 6.

123. Shultz, *Turmoil and Triumph,* p. 864. See also "Nomination of Robert M. Gates," p. 481.

124. Author phone interview with Jack Matlock.

125. Paul Pillar, *Intelligence and U.S. Foreign Policy: Iraq, 9/11, and Misguided Reform* (New York: Columbia University Press, 2011), p. 116.

126. Mercer, "Emotional Beliefs," p. 14.

127. Paul Slovic, Melissa Finucane, Ellen Peters, and Donald G. MacGregor, "The Affect Heuristic," in Gilovich, Griffin, and Kahneman, *Heuristics and Biases,* pp. 397–420; and A. R. Damasio, *Descartes' Error: Emotion, Reason, and the Human Brain* (New York: Avon, 1994).

128. The evidence I have presented suggests that in neither of the Cold War episodes did U.S. decisionmakers use the NIEs to derive conclusions about their adversary's intentions. During the interwar period, British decision makers appear to have relied on human intelligence reports of the Secret Intelligence Services, but much less on the COS strategic reports, to reach conclusions about Germany's political intentions. Future studies should disaggregate the intelligence community and look beyond the coordinated reports in order to examine which and when individual intelligence agencies (or officials) tend to have a stronger influence on decisionmakers' assessments of the intentions of their state's adversary.

129. Quoted in Haines and Leggett, *Watching the Bear,* chap. 8.

130. Robert Gates, "The CIA and Foreign Policy," *Foreign Affairs,* Vol. 66, No. 2 (Winter 1987/88), pp. 225–26.

131. Interview with Turner, "Episode 21: Spies." *National Security Archive,* December 18, 1997, http://www.gwu.edu/~nsarchiv /coldwar/interviews/episode-21/turnerl.html.

132. Quoted in Donald C. Watt, "British Intelligence and the Coming of the Second World War in Europe," in Ernest May, ed., *Knowing One's Enemies: Intelligence Assessment before the Two World Wars* (Princeton, NJ: Princeton University Press, 1984), p. 268.

133. I also do not find support for the proposition that these decision makers' assessments of intentions were epiphenomenal to the interests of the bureaucracies they headed at the time. Both Weinberger and Vance continued to defend their assessments of Soviet intentions long after leaving office.

134. On the credibility of secret assurances, see Keren Yarhi-Milo, "Tying Hands behind Closed Doors: The Logic and Practice of Secret Reassurance," *Security Studies*, Vol. 22, No. 3 (2013).

7

INTERGOVERNMENTAL ORGANIZATIONS, INTERNATIONAL LAW, AND NONGOVERNMENTAL ORGANIZATIONS

International organizations such as the United Nations (UN) are major actors in international relations. Samantha Power argued in her Pulitzer Prize–winning book *A Problem from Hell,* as excerpted here from *The Atlantic,* that one of the key tasks of international organizations and powerful states should be to prevent massive atrocities. This policy objective, called "The Responsibility to Protect," or R2P, has subsequently been formally adopted by the United Nations. Power explains why neither the UN nor the United States did more to stop the 1994 genocide in Rwanda. Despite the adoption of R2P, some of her explanations still resonate in light of the international community's more recent failure to intervene to stop atrocities in the Syrian civil war.

What explains how international institutions facilitate cooperation more generally? Robert O. Keohane, in his highly influential book *After Hegemony: Cooperation and Discord in the World Political Economy* (1984), lays out the theory of liberal institutionalism to explain how such institutions make cooperation possible despite the absence of a sovereign enforcement power standing above states. He explains that international institutions (or "international regimes") establish rules around which expectations converge. Rules reduce the costs of transactions, facilitate bargaining across different issue areas, and provide information that reduces the risk of cheating. By way of contrast, John J. Mearsheimer, the quintessential realist, is skeptical about the impact of international institutions. He delineates the flaws of liberal institutionalist theory, arguing that international institutions exert no independent influence of their own because they simply reflect the underlying power and interests of states.

In addition to intergovernmental organizations (IGOs) and international law, research on nongovernmental organizations (NGOs), social movements, and transnational advocacy networks has expanded since the 1990s. Using a constructivist approach, Margaret E. Keck and Kathryn Sikkink, in an excerpt from their award-winning book *Activists beyond Borders: Advocacy Networks in International Politics*

(1998), show how such networks develop by "building new links among actors in civil societies, states, and international organizations."

Finally, Michael N. Barnett and Martha Finnemore draw on constructivism to study the "pathologies" of international organizations that can lead to unintended consequences.

Samantha Power

BYSTANDERS TO GENOCIDE
Why the United States Let the Rwandan Tragedy Happen

I. People Sitting in Offices

In the course of a hundred days in 1994 the Hutu government of Rwanda and its extremist allies very nearly succeeded in exterminating the country's Tutsi minority. Using firearms, machetes, and a variety of garden implements, Hutu militiamen, soldiers, and ordinary citizens murdered some 800,000 Tutsi and politically moderate Hutu. It was the fastest, most efficient killing spree of the twentieth century.

A few years later, in a series in *The New Yorker,* Philip Gourevitch recounted in horrific detail the story of the genocide and the world's failure to stop it. President Bill Clinton, a famously avid reader, expressed shock. He sent copies of Gourevitch's articles to his second-term national-security adviser, Sandy Berger. The articles bore confused, angry, searching queries in the margins. "Is what he's saying true?" Clinton wrote with a thick black felt-tip pen beside heavily underlined paragraphs. "How did this happen?" he asked, adding, "I want to get to the bottom of this." The President's urgency and outrage were oddly timed. As the terror in Rwanda had unfolded, Clinton had shown virtually no interest in stopping the genocide, and his Administration had stood by as the death toll rose into the hundreds of thousands.

Why did the United States not do more for the Rwandans at the time of the killings? Did the President really not know about the genocide, as

From *The Atlantic* (Sept. 2001), 84–108.

his marginalia suggested? Who were the people in his Administration who made the life-and-death decisions that dictated U.S. policy? Why did they decide (or decide not to decide) as they did? Were any voices inside or outside the U.S. government demanding that the United States do more? If so, why weren't they heeded? And most crucial, what could the United States have done to save lives?

So far people have explained the U.S. failure to respond to the Rwandan genocide by claiming that the United States didn't know what was happening, that it knew but didn't care, or that regardless of what it knew there was nothing useful to be done. The account that follows is based on a three-year investigation involving sixty interviews with senior, mid-level, and junior State Department, Defense Department, and National Security Council officials who helped to shape or inform U.S. policy. It also reflects dozens of interviews with Rwandan, European, and United Nations officials and with peacekeepers, journalists, and nongovernmental workers in Rwanda. Thanks to the National Security Archive (www.nsarchive.org), a nonprofit organization that uses the Freedom of Information Act to secure the release of classified U.S. documents, this account also draws on hundreds of pages of newly available government records. This material provides a clearer picture than was previously possible of the interplay among people, motives, and events. It reveals that the U.S. government knew enough about the genocide early on to save lives, but passed up countless opportunities to intervene.

In March of 1998, on a visit to Rwanda, President Clinton issued what would later be known as the "Clinton apology," which was actually a carefully hedged acknowledgment. He spoke to the crowd assembled on the tarmac at Kigali Airport: "We come here today partly in recognition of the fact that we in the United States and the world community did not do as much as we could have and should have done to try to limit what occurred" in Rwanda.

This implied that the United States had done a good deal but not quite enough. In reality the United States did much more than fail to send troops. It led a successful effort to remove most of the UN peacekeepers who were already in Rwanda. It aggressively worked to block the subsequent authorization of UN reinforcements. It refused to use its technology to jam radio broadcasts that were a crucial instrument in the coordination and perpetuation of the genocide. And even as, on average, 8,000 Rwandans were being butchered each day, U.S. officials shunned the term "genocide," for fear of being obliged to act. The United States in fact did virtually nothing "to try to limit what occurred." Indeed, staying out of Rwanda was an explicit U.S. policy objective.

With the grace of one grown practiced at public remorse, the President gripped the lectern with both hands and looked across the dais at the Rwandan officials and survivors who surrounded him. Making eye contact and shaking his head, he explained, "It may seem strange to you here, especially the many of you who lost members of your family, but all over the world there were people like me sitting in offices, day after day after day, who *did not fully appreciate* [pause] the depth [pause] and the speed [pause] with which you were being engulfed by this *unimaginable* terror."

Clinton chose his words with characteristic care. It was true that although top U.S. officials could not help knowing the basic facts—thousands of Rwandans were dying every day—that were being reported in the morning papers, many did not

"fully appreciate" the meaning. In the first three weeks of the genocide the most influential American policymakers portrayed (and, they insist, perceived) the deaths not as astrocities or the components and symptoms of genocide but as wartime "casualties"—the deaths of combatants or those caught between them in a civil war.

Yet this formulation avoids the critical issue of whether Clinton and his close advisers might reasonably have been expected to "fully appreciate" the true dimensions and nature of the massacres. During the first three days of the killings U.S. diplomats in Rwanda reported back to Washington that well-armed extremists were intent on eliminating the Tutsi. And the American press spoke of the door-to-door hunting of unarmed civilians. By the end of the second week informed nongovernmental groups had already begun to call on the Administration to use the term "genocide," causing diplomats and lawyers at the State Department to begin debating the word's applicability soon thereafter. In order not to appreciate that genocide or something close to it was under way, U.S. officials had to ignore public reports and internal intelligence and debate.

The story of U.S. policy during the genocide in Rwanda is not a story of willful complicity with evil. U.S. officials did not sit around and conspire to allow genocide to happen. But whatever their convictions about "never again," many of them did sit around, and they most certainly did allow genocide to happen. In examining how and why the United States failed Rwanda, we see that without strong leadership the system will incline toward risk-averse policy choices. We also see that with the possibility of deploying U.S. troops to Rwanda taken off the table early on—and with crises elsewhere in the world unfolding—the slaughter never received the top-level attention it deserved. Domestic political forces that might have pressed for action were absent. And most U.S. officials opposed to American involvement in Rwanda were firmly convinced that they were doing all they could—and, most important, all they *should*—in light of competing American interests and a highly circumscribed understanding of what was "possible" for the United States to do.

One of the most thoughtful analyses of how the American system can remain predicated on the noblest of values while allowing the vilest of crimes was offered in 1971 by a brilliant and earnest young foreign-service officer who had just resigned from the National Security Council to protest the 1970 U.S. invasion of Cambodia. In an article in *Foreign Policy*, "The Human Reality of Realpolitik," he and a colleague analyzed the process whereby American policymakers with moral sensibilities could have waged a war of such immoral consequence as the one in Vietnam. They wrote,

> The answer to that question begins with a basic intellectual approach which views foreign policy as a lifeless, bloodless set of abstractions. "Nations," "interests," "influence," "prestige"—all are disembodied and dehumanized terms which encourage easy inattention to the real people whose lives our decisions affect or even end.

Policy analysis excluded discussion of human consequences. "It simply is not *done*," the authors wrote. "Policy—good, steady policy—is made by the 'tough-minded.' To talk of suffering is to lose 'effectiveness,' almost to lose one's grip. It is seen as a sign that one's 'rational' arguments are weak."

In 1994, fifty years after the Holocaust and twenty years after America's retreat from Vietnam, it was possible to believe that the system had changed and that talk of human consequences had become admissible. Indeed, when the machetes were raised in Central Africa, the White House official primarily responsible for the shaping of U.S. foreign policy was one of the authors of that 1971 critique: Anthony Lake, President Clinton's first-term national-security adviser. The genocide in Rwanda presented Lake and the rest of the Clinton team with an opportunity to prove that "good, steady policy" could be made in the interest of saving lives.

II. The Peacekeepers

Rwanda was a test for another man as well: Romeo Dallaire, then a major general in the Canadian army who at the time of the genocide was the commander of the UN Assistance Mission in Rwanda. If ever there was a peacekeeper who believed wholeheartedly in the promise of humanitarian action, it was Dallaire. A broad-shouldered French-Canadian with deep-set sky-blue eyes, Dallaire has the thick, calloused hands of one brought up in a culture that prizes soldiering, service, and sacrifice. He saw the United Nations as the embodiment of all three.

Before his posting to Rwanda Dallaire had served as the commandant of an army brigade that sent peacekeeping battalions to Cambodia and Bosnia, but he had never seen actual combat himself. "I was like a fireman who has never been to a fire, but has dreamed for years about how he would fare when the fire came," the fifty-five-year-old Dallaire recalls. When, in the summer of 1993, he received the phone call from UN headquarters offering him the Rwanda posting, he was ecstatic. "It was answering the aim of my life," he says. "It's *all* you've been waiting for."

Dallaire was sent to command a UN force that would help to keep the peace in Rwanda, a nation the size of Vermont, which was known as "the land of a thousand hills" for its rolling terrain. Before Rwanda achieved independence from Belgium, in 1962, the Tutsi, who made up 15 percent of the populace, had enjoyed a privileged status. But independence ushered in three decades of Hutu rule, under which Tutsi were systematically discriminated against and periodically subjected to waves of killing and ethnic cleansing. In 1990 a group of armed exiles, mainly Tutsi, who had been clustered on the Ugandan border, invaded

Rwanda. Over the next several years the rebels, known as the Rwandan Patriotic Front, gained ground against Hutu government forces. In 1993 Tanzania brokered peace talks, which resulted in a power-sharing agreement known as the Arusha Accords. Under its terms the Rwandan government agreed to share power with Hutu opposition parties and the Tutsi minority. UN peacekeepers would be deployed to patrol a cease-fire and assist in demilitarization and demobilization as well as to help provide a secure environment, so that exiled Tutsi could return. The hope among moderate Rwandans and Western observers was that Hutu and Tutsi would at last be able to coexist in harmony.

Hutu extremists rejected these terms and set out to terrorize Tutsi and also those Hutu politicians supportive of the peace process. In 1993 several thousand Rwandans were killed, and some 9,000 were detained. Guns, grenades, and machetes began arriving by the planeload. A pair of international commissions—one sent by the United Nations, the other by an independent collection of human-rights organizations—warned explicitly of a possible genocide.

But Dallaire knew nothing of the precariousness of the Arusha Accords. When he made a preliminary reconnaissance trip to Rwanda, in August of 1993, he was told that the country was committed to peace and that a UN presence was essential. A visit with extremists, who preferred to eradicate Tutsi rather than cede power, was not on Dallaire's itinerary. Remarkably, no UN officials in New York thought to give Dallaire copies of the alarming reports from the international investigators.

The sum total of Dallaire's intelligence data before that first trip to Rwanda consisted of one encyclopedia's summary of Rwandan history, which Major Brent Beardsley, Dallaire's executive assistant, had snatched at the last minute from his local public library. Beardsley says, "We flew to Rwanda with a Michelin road map, a copy of the Arusha agreement, and that was it. We were under the impression that the situation was quite straightforward: there was one cohesive government side and one cohesive rebel side, and they had come together to sign the peace agreement and had then requested that we come in to help them implement it."

Though Dallaire gravely underestimated the tensions brewing in Rwanda, he still felt that he would need a force of 5,000 to help the parties implement the terms of the Arusha Accords. But when his superiors warned him that the United States would never agree to pay for such a large deployment, Dallaire reluctantly trimmed his written request to 2,500. He remembers, "I was told, 'Don't ask for a brigade, because it ain't there.'"

Once he was actually posted to Rwanda, in October of 1993, Dallaire lacked not merely intelligence data and manpower but also institutional support. The small Department of Peacekeeping Operations in New York, run by the Ghanaian diplomat Kofi Annan, now the UN secretary general, was overwhelmed. Madeleine Albright, then the U.S. ambassador to the UN, recalls, "The global nine-one-one was always either busy or nobody was there." At the time of the Rwanda deployment, with a staff of a few hundred, the UN was posting 70,000 peacekeepers on seventeen missions around the world. Amid these widespread crises and logistical headaches the Rwanda mission had a very low status.

Life was not made easier for Dallaire or the UN peacekeeping office by the fact that American patience for peacekeeping was thinning. Congress owed half a billion dollars in UN dues and peacekeeping costs. It had tired of its obligation to foot a third of the bill for what had come to feel like an insatiable global appetite for mischief and an equally insatiable UN appetite for missions. The Clinton Administration had taken office better disposed toward peacekeeping than any other Administration in U.S. history. But it felt that the Department of Peacekeeping Operations needed fixing and demanded that the UN "learn to say no" to chancy or costly missions.

Every aspect of the UN Assistance Mission in Rwanda was run on a shoestring. UNAMIR (the acronym by which it was known) was equipped with hand-me-down vehicles from the UN's Cambodia mission, and only eighty of the 300 that turned up were usable. When the medical supplies ran out, in March of 1994, New York said there was no cash for resupply. Very little could be procured locally, given that Rwanda was one of Africa's poorest nations. Replacement spare parts, batteries, and even ammunition could rarely be found. Dallaire spent some 70 percent of his time battling UN logistics.

Dallaire had major problems with his personnel, as well. He commanded troops, military observers, and civilian personnel from twenty-six countries. Though multinationality is meant to be a virtue of UN missions, the diversity yielded grave discrepancies in resources. Whereas Belgian troops turned up well armed and ready to perform the tasks assigned to them, the poorer contingents showed up "bare-assed," in Dallaire's words, and demanded that the United Nations suit them up. "Since nobody else was offering to send troops, we had to take what we could get," he says. When Dallaire expressed concern, he was instructed by a senior UN official to lower his expectations. He recalls, "I was told, 'Listen, General, you are NATO-trained. This is not NATO.'" Although some 2,500 UNAMIR personnel had arrived by early April of 1994, few of the soldiers had the kit they needed to perform even basic tasks.

The signs of militarization in Rwanda were so widespread that even without much of an intelligence-gathering capacity, Dallaire was able to learn of the extremists' sinister intentions. In January of 1994 an anonymous Hutu informant, said to be high up in the inner circles of the Rwandan government, had come forward to describe the rapid arming and training of local militias. In what is now referred to as the "Dallaire fax," Dallaire relayed to New York the informant's claim that Hutu extremists "had been ordered to register all the Tutsi in Kigali." "He suspects it is for their extermination," Dallaire wrote. "Example he gave was that in 20 minutes his personnel could kill up to 1000 Tutsis." "Jean-Pierre," as the informant became known, had said that the militia planned first to provoke and murder a number of Belgian peacekeepers, to "thus guarantee Belgian withdrawal from Rwanda." When Dallaire notified Kofi Annan's office that UNAMIR was poised to raid Hutu arms caches, Annan's deputy forbade him to do so. Instead Dallaire was instructed to notify the Rwandan President, Juvénal Habyarimana, and the Western ambassadors of the informant's claims. Though Dallaire battled by phone with New York, and confirmed the reliability of the informant, his political masters told him plainly and consistently that the United States in particular would not support aggressive peace-keeping. (A request by the Belgians for reinforcements was also turned down.) In Washington, Dallaire's alarm was discounted. Lieutenant Colonel Tony Marley, the U.S. military liaison to the Arusha process, respected Dallaire but knew he was operating in Africa for the first time. "I thought that the neophyte meant well, but I questioned whether he knew what he was talking about," Marley recalls.

III. The Early Killings

On the evening of April 6, 1994, Romeo Dallaire was sitting on the couch in his bungalow residence in Kigali, watching CNN with Brent Beardsley. Beardsley was preparing plans for a national Sports Day that would match Tutsi rebel soldiers against Hutu government soldiers in a soccer game. Dallaire said, "You know, Brent, if the shit ever hit the fan here, none of this stuff would really matter, would it?" The next instant the phone rang. Rwandan President Habyarimana's Mystère Falcon jet, a gift from French President François Mitterrand, had just been shot down, with

Habyarimana and Burundian President Cyprien Ntaryamira aboard. Dallaire and Beardsley raced in their UN jeep to Rwandan army headquarters, where a crisis meeting was under way.

Back in Washington, Kevin Aiston, the Rwanda desk officer, knocked on the door of Deputy Assistant Secretary of State Prudence Bushnell and told her that the Presidents of Rwanda and Burundi had gone down in a plane crash. "Oh, shit," she said. "Are you sure?" In fact nobody was sure at first, but Dallaire's forces supplied confirmation within the hour. The Rwandan authorities quickly announced a curfew, and Hutu militias and government soldiers erected roadblocks around the capital.

Bushnell drafted an urgent memo to Secretary of State Warren Christopher. She was concerned about a probable outbreak of killing in both Rwanda and its neighbor Burundi. The memo read,

> If, as it appears, both Presidents have been killed, there is a strong likelihood that widespread violence could break out in either or both countries, particularly if it is confirmed that the plane was shot down. Our strategy is to appeal for calm in both countries, both through public statements and in other ways.

A few public statements proved to be virtually the only strategy that Washington would muster in the weeks ahead.

Lieutenant General Wesley Clark, who later commanded the NATO air war in Kosovo, was the director of strategic plans and policy for the Joint Chiefs of Staff at the Pentagon. On learning of the crash, Clark remembers, staff officers asked, "Is it Hutu and Tutsi or Tutu and Hutsi?" He frantically called for insight into the ethnic dimension of events in Rwanda. Unfortunately, Rwanda had never been of more than marginal concern to Washington's most influential planners.

America's best-informed Rwanda observer was not a government official but a private citizen,

Alison Des Forges, a historian and a board member of Human Rights Watch, who lived in Buffalo, New York. Des Forges had been visiting Rwanda since 1963. She had received a Ph.D. from Yale in African history, specializing in Rwanda, and she could speak the Rwandan language, Kinyarwanda. Half an hour after the plane crash Des Forges got a phone call from a close friend in Kigali, the human-rights activist Monique Mujawamariya. Des Forges had been worried about Mujawamariya for weeks, because the Hutu extremist radio station, Radio Mille Collines, had branded her "a bad patriot who deserves to die." Mujawamariya had sent Human Rights Watch a chilling warning a week earlier: "For the last two weeks, all of Kigali has lived under the threat of an instantaneous, carefully prepared operation to eliminate all those who give trouble to President Habyarimana."

Now Habyarimana was dead, and Mujawamariya knew instantly that the hard-line Hutu would use the crash as a pretext to begin mass killing. "This is it," she told Des Forges on the phone. For the next twenty-four hours Des Forges called her friend's home every half hour. With each conversation Des Forges could hear the gunfire grow louder as the militia drew closer. Finally the gunmen entered Mujawamariya's home. "I don't want you to hear this," Mujawamariya said softly. "Take care of my children." She hung up the phone.

Mujawamariya's instincts were correct. Within hours of the plane crash Hutu militiamen took command of the streets of Kigali. Dallaire quickly grasped that supporters of the Arusha peace process were being targeted. His phone at UNAMIR headquarters rang constantly as Rwandans around the capital pleaded for help. Dallaire was especially concerned about Prime Minister Agathe Uwilingiyimana, a reformer who with the President's death had become the titular head of state. Just after dawn on April 7 five Ghanaian and ten Belgian peacekeepers arrived at the Prime Minister's home in order to deliver her to Radio Rwanda, so that she could broadcast an emergency appeal for calm.

Joyce Leader, the second-in-command at the U.S. embassy, lived next door to Uwilingiyimana. She spent the early hours of the morning behind the steel-barred gates of her embassy-owned house as Hutu killers hunted and dispatched their first victims. Leader's phone rang. Uwilingiyimana was on the other end. "Please hide me," she begged.

Minutes after the phone call a UN peacekeeper attempted to hike the Prime Minister over the wall separating their compounds. When Leader heard shots fired, she urged the peacekeeper to abandon the effort. "They can see you!" she shouted. Uwilingiyimana managed to slip with her husband and children into another compound, which was occupied by the UN Development Program. But the militiamen hunted them down in the yard, where the couple surrendered. There were more shots. Leader recalls, "We heard her screaming and then, suddenly, after the gunfire the screaming stopped, and we heard people cheering." Hutu gunmen in the Presidential Guard that day systematically tracked down and eliminated Rwanda's moderate leadership.

The raid on Uwilingiyimana's compound not only cost Rwanda a prominent supporter of the Arusha Accords; it also triggered the collapse of Dallaire's mission. In keeping with the plan to target the Belgians which the informant Jean-Pierre had relayed to UNAMIR in January, Hutu soldiers rounded up the peacekeepers at Uwilingiyimana's home, took them to a military camp, led the Ghanaians to safety, and then killed and savagely mutilated the ten Belgians. In Belgium the cry for either expanding UNAMIR's mandate or immediately withdrawing was prompt and loud.

In response to the initial killings by the Hutu government, Tutsi rebels of the Rwandan Patriotic Front—stationed in Kigali under the terms of the Arusha Accords—surged out of their barracks and resumed their civil war against the Hutu regime.

But under the cover of that war were early and strong indications that systematic genocide was taking place. From April 7 onward the Hutu-controlled army, the gendarmerie, and the militias worked together to wipe out Rwanda's Tutsi. Many of the early Tutsi victims found themselves specifically, not spontaneously, pursued: lists of targets had been prepared in advance, and Radio Mille Collines broadcast names, addresses, and even license-plate numbers. Killers often carried a machete in one hand and a transistor radio in the other. Tens of thousands of Tutsi fled their homes in panic and were snared and butchered at checkpoints. Little care was given to their disposal. Some were shoveled into landfills. Human flesh rotted in the sunshine. In churches bodies mingled with scattered hosts. If the killers had taken the time to tend to sanitation, it would have slowed their "sanitization" campaign.

IV. The "Last War"

The two tracks of events in Rwanda—simultaneous war and genocide—confused policymakers who had scant prior understanding of the country. Atrocities are often carried out in places that are not commonly visited, where outside expertise is limited. When country-specific knowledge is lacking, foreign governments become all the more likely to employ faulty analogies and to "fight the last war." The analogy employed by many of those who confronted the outbreak of killing in Rwanda was a peacekeeping intervention that had gone horribly wrong in Somalia.

On October 3, 1993, ten months after President Bush had sent U.S. troops to Somalia as part of what had seemed a low-risk humanitarian mission, U.S. Army Rangers and Delta special forces in Somalia attempted to seize several top advisers to the warlord Mohammed Farah Aideed. Aideed's faction had ambushed and killed two dozen Pakistani peacekeepers, and the United States was striking back. But in the firefight that ensued the Somali militia killed eighteen Americans, wounded seventy-three, and captured one Black Hawk helicopter pilot. Somali television broadcast both a video interview with the trembling, disoriented pilot and a gory procession in which the corpse of a U.S. Ranger was dragged through a Mogadishu street.

On receiving word of these events, President Clinton cut short a trip to California and convened an urgent crisis-management meeting at the White House. When an aide began recapping the situation, an angry President interrupted him. "Cut the bullshit," Clinton snapped. "Let's work this out." "Work it out" meant walk out. Republican Congressional pressure was intense. Clinton appeared on American television the next day, called off the manhunt for Aideed, temporarily reinforced the troop presence, and announced that all U.S. forces would be home within six months. The Pentagon leadership concluded that peacekeeping in Africa meant trouble and that neither the White House nor Congress would stand by it when the chips were down.

Even before the deadly blowup in Somalia the United States had resisted deploying a UN mission to Rwanda. "Anytime you mentioned peacekeeping in Africa," one U.S. official remembers, "the crucifixes and garlic would come up on every door." Having lost much of its early enthusiasm for peacekeeping and for the United Nations itself, Washington was nervous that the Rwanda mission would sour like so many others. But President Habyarimana had traveled to Washington in 1993 to offer assurances that his government was committed to carrying out the terms of the Arusha Accords. In the end, after strenuous lobbying by France (Rwanda's chief diplomatic and military patron), U.S. officials accepted the proposition that UNAMIR could be the rare "UN winner." On October 5, 1993, two days after the Somalia firefight, the United States reluctantly voted in the Security Council to authorize Dallaire's mission.

Even so, U.S. officials made it clear that Washington would give no consideration to sending U.S. troops to Rwanda. Somalia and another recent embarrassment in Haiti indicated that multilateral initiatives for humanitarian purposes would likely bring the United States all loss and no gain.

Against this backdrop, and under the leadership of Anthony Lake, the national-security adviser, the Clinton Administration accelerated the development of a formal U.S. peacekeeping doctrine. The job was given to Richard Clarke, of the National Security Council, a special assistant to the President who was known as one of the most effective bureaucrats in Washington. In an interagency process that lasted more than a year, Clarke managed the production of a presidential decision directive, PDD-25, which listed sixteen factors that policymakers needed to consider when deciding whether to support peacekeeping activities: seven factors if the United States was to vote in the UN Security Council on peace operations carried out by non-American soldiers, six additional and more stringent factors if U.S. forces were to participate in UN peacekeeping missions, and three final factors if U.S. troops were likely to engage in actual combat. In the words of Representative David Obey, of Wisconsin, the restrictive checklist tried to satisfy the American desire for "zero degree of involvement, and zero degree of risk, and zero degree of pain and confusion." The architects of the doctrine remain its strongest defenders. "Many say PDD-25 was some evil thing designed to kill peacekeeping, when in fact it was there to save peacekeeping," Clarke says. "Peacekeeping was almost dead. There was no support for it in the U.S. government, and the peacekeepers were not effective in the field." Although the directive was not publicly released until May 3, 1994, a month into the genocide, the considerations encapsulated in the doctrine and the Administration's frustration with peacekeeping greatly influenced the thinking of U.S. officials involved in shaping Rwanda policy.

V. The Peace Processors

Each of the American actors dealing with Rwanda brought particular institutional interests and biases to his or her handling of the crisis. Secretary of State Warren Christopher knew little about Africa. At one meeting with his top advisers, several weeks after the plane crash, he pulled an atlas off his shelf to help him locate the country. Belgian Foreign Minister Willie Claes recalls trying to discuss Rwanda with his American counterpart and being told, "I have other responsibilities." Officials in the State Department's Africa Bureau were, of course, better informed. Prudence Bushnell, the deputy assistant secretary, was one of them. The daughter of a diplomat, Bushnell had joined the foreign service in 1981, at the age of thirty-five. With her agile mind and sharp tongue, she had earned the attention of George Moose when she served under him at the U.S. embassy in Senegal. When Moose was named the assistant secretary of state for African affairs, in 1993, he made Bushnell his deputy. Just two weeks before the plane crash the State Department had dispatched Bushnell and a colleague to Rwanda in an effort to contain the escalating violence and to spur the stalled peace process.

Unfortunately, for all the concern of the Americans familiar with Rwanda, their diplomacy suffered from three weaknesses. First, ahead of the plane crash diplomats had repeatedly threatened to pull out UN peacekeepers in retaliation for the parties' failure to implement Arusha. These threats were of course counterproductive, because the very Hutu who opposed power-sharing wanted nothing more than a UN withdrawal. One senior U.S. official remembers, "The first response to trouble is 'Let's yank the peacekeepers.' But that is like believing that when children are misbehaving, the proper response is 'Let's send the baby-sitter home.'"

Second, before and during the massacres U.S. diplomacy revealed its natural bias toward states and toward negotiations. Because most official contact occurs between representatives of states, U.S. officials were predisposed to trust the assurances of Rwandan officials, several of whom were plotting genocide behind the scenes. Those in the U.S. government who knew Rwanda best viewed the escalating violence with a diplomatic prejudice that left them both institutionally oriented toward the Rwandan government and reluctant to do anything to disrupt the peace process. An examination of the cable traffic from the U.S. embassy in Kigali to Washington between the signing of the Arusha agreement and the downing of the presidential plane reveals that setbacks were perceived as "dangers to the peace process" more than as "dangers to Rwandans." American criticisms were deliberately and steadfastly leveled at "both sides," though Hutu government and militia forces were usually responsible.

The U.S. ambassador in Kigali, David Rawson, proved especially vulnerable to such bias. Rawson had grown up in Burundi, where his father, an American missionary, had set up a Quaker hospital. He entered the foreign service in 1971. When, in 1993, at age fifty-two, he was given the embassy in Rwanda, his first, he could not have been more intimate with the region, the culture, or the peril. He spoke the local language—almost unprecedented for an ambassador in Central Africa. But Rawson found it difficult to imagine the Rwandans who surrounded the President as conspirators in genocide. He issued pro forma demarches over Habyarimana's obstruction of power-sharing, but the cable traffic shows that he accepted the President's assurances that he was doing all he could. The U.S. investment in the peace process gave rise to a wishful tendency to see peace "around the corner." Rawson remembers, "We were naive policy optimists, I suppose. The fact that negotiations can't work is almost not one of the options open to people who care about peace. We were looking for the hopeful signs, not the dark signs. In fact, we were looking away from the dark signs . . . One of the things I learned and should have already known is that once you launch a process, it takes on its own momentum. I had said, 'Let's try this, and then if it doesn't work, we can back away.' But bureaucracies don't allow that. Once the Washington side buys into a process, it gets pursued, almost blindly." Even after the Hutu government began exterminating Tutsi, U.S. diplomats focused most of their efforts on "re-establishing a cease-fire" and "getting Arusha back on track."

The third problematic feature of U.S. diplomacy before and during the genocide was a tendency toward blindness bred by familiarity: the few people in Washington who were paying attention to Rwanda before Habyarimana's plane was shot down were those who had been tracking Rwanda for some time and had thus come to expect a certain level of ethnic violence from the region. And because the U.S. government had done little when some 40,000 people had been killed in Hutu-Tutsi violence in Burundi in October of 1993, these officials also knew that Washington was prepared to tolerate substantial bloodshed. When the massacres began in April, some U.S. regional specialists initially suspected that Rwanda was undergoing "another flare-up" that would involve another "acceptable" (if tragic) round of ethnic murder.

Rawson had read up on genocide before his posting to Rwanda, surveying what had become a relatively extensive scholarly literature on its causes. But although he expected internecine killing, he did not anticipate the scale at which it occurred. "Nothing in Rwandan culture or history could have led a person to that forecast," he says. "Most of us thought that if a war broke out, it would be quick, that these poor people didn't have the resources, the means, to fight a sophisticated war. I couldn't have known that they would do each other in with the most economic means." George Moose agrees: "We were psychologically and imaginatively too limited."

◾ ◾ ◾

VII. Genocide?
What Genocide?

Just when did Washington know of the sinister Hutu designs on Rwanda's Tutsi? Writing in *Foreign Affairs* last year [2000], Alan Kuperman argued that President Clinton "could not have known that a nationwide genocide was under way" until about two weeks into the killing. It is true that the precise nature and extent of the slaughter was obscured by the civil war, the withdrawal of U.S. diplomatic sources, some confused press reporting, and the lies of the Rwandan government. Nonetheless, both the testimony of U.S. officials who worked the issue day to day and the declassified documents indicate that plenty was known about the killers' intentions.

A determination of genocide turns not on the numbers killed, which is always difficult to ascertain at a time of crisis, but on the perpetrators' intent: Were Hutu forces attempting to destroy Rwanda's Tutsi? The answer to this question was available early on. "By eight AM the morning after the plane crash we knew what was happening, that there was systematic killing of Tutsi," Joyce Leader recalls. "People were calling me and telling me who was getting killed. I knew they were going door to door." Back at the State Department she explained to her colleagues that three kinds of killing were going on: war, politically motivated murder, and genocide. Dallaire's early cables to New York likewise described the armed conflict that had resumed between rebels and government forces, and also stated plainly that savage "ethnic cleansing" of Tutsi was occurring. U.S. analysts warned that mass killings would increase. In an April 11 memo prepared for Frank Wisner, the undersecretary of defense for policy, in advance of a dinner with Henry Kissinger, a key talking point was "Unless both sides can be convinced to return to the peace process, a massive (hundreds of thousands of deaths) bloodbath will ensue."

Whatever the inevitable imperfections of U.S. intelligence early on, the reports from Rwanda were severe enough to distinguish Hutu killers from ordinary combatants in civil war. And they certainly warranted directing additional U.S. intelligence assets toward the region—to snap satellite photos of large gatherings of Rwandan civilians or of mass graves, to intercept military communications, or to infiltrate the country in person. Though there is no evidence that senior policymakers deployed such assets, routine intelligence continued to pour in. On April 26 an unattributed intelligence memo titled "Responsibility for Massacres in Rwanda" reported that the ringleaders of the genocide, Colonel Théoneste Bagosora and his crisis committee, were determined to liquidate their opposition and exterminate the Tutsi populace. A May 9 Defense Intelligence Agency report stated plainly that the Rwandan violence was not spontaneous but was directed by the government, with lists of victims prepared well in advance. The DIA observed that an "organized parallel effort of *genocide* [was] being implemented by the army to destroy the leadership of the Tutsi community."

From April 8 onward media coverage featured eyewitness accounts describing the widespread targeting of Tutsi and the corpses piling up on Kigali's streets. American reporters relayed stories of missionaries and embassy officials who had been unable to save their Rwandan friends and neighbors from death. On April 9 a front-page *Washington Post* story quoted reports that the Rwandan employees of the major international relief agencies had been executed "in front of horrified expatriate staffers." On April 10 a *New York Times* front-page article quoted the Red Cross claim that "tens of thousands" were dead, 8,000 in Kigali alone, and that corpses were "in the houses, in the streets, everywhere." The *Post* the same day led its front-page story with a description of "a pile of corpses six feet high" outside the main hospital. On April 14 the *New York Times* reported the shooting and hacking to death of nearly 1,200

men, women, and children in the church where they had sought refuge. On April 19 Human Rights Watch, which had excellent sources on the ground in Rwanda, estimated the number of dead at 100,000 and called for use of the term "genocide." The 100,000 figure (which proved to be a gross underestimate) was picked up immediately by the Western media, endorsed by the Red Cross, and featured on the front page of the *Washington Post*. On April 24 the *Post* reported how "the heads and limbs of victims were sorted and piled neatly, a bone-chilling order in the midst of chaos that harked back to the Holocaust." President Clinton certainly could have known that a genocide was under way, if he had wanted to know.

Even after the reality of genocide in Rwanda had become irrefutable, when bodies were shown choking the Kagera River on the nightly news, the brute fact of the slaughter failed to influence U.S. policy except in a negative way. American officials, for a variety of reasons, shunned the use of what became known as "the g-word." They felt that using it would have obliged the United States to act, under the terms of the 1948 Genocide Convention. They also believed, understandably, that it would harm U.S. credibility to name the crime and then do nothing to stop it. A discussion paper on Rwanda, prepared by an official in the Office of the Secretary of Defense and dated May 1, testifies to the nature of official thinking. Regarding issues that might be brought up at the next interagency working group, it stated,

> 1. Genocide Investigation: Language that calls for an international investigation of human rights abuses and possible violations of the genocide convention. *Be Careful. Legal at State was worried about this yesterday—Genocide finding could commit [the U.S. government] to actually "do something."* [Emphasis added.]

At an interagency teleconference in late April, Susan Rice, a rising star on the NSC who worked under Richard Clarke, stunned a few of the officials present when she asked, "If we use the word 'genocide' and are seen as doing nothing, what will be the effect on the November [congressional] election?" Lieutenant Colonel Tony Marley remembers the incredulity of his colleagues at the State Department. "We could believe that people would wonder that," he says, "but not that they would actually voice it." Rice does not recall the incident but concedes, "If I said it, it was completely inappropriate, as well as irrelevant."

The genocide debate in U.S. government circles began the last week of April, but it was not until May 21, six weeks after the killing began, that Secretary Christopher gave his diplomats permission to use the term "genocide"—sort of. The UN Human Rights Commission was about to meet in special session, and the U.S. representative, Geraldine Ferraro, needed guidance on whether to join a resolution stating that genocide had occurred. The stubborn U.S. stand had become untenable internationally.

The case for a label of genocide was straightforward, according to a May 18 confidential analysis prepared by the State Department's assistant secretary for intelligence and research, Toby Gati: lists of Tutsi victims' names and addresses had reportedly been prepared; Rwandan government troops and Hutu militia and youth squads were the main perpetrators; massacres were reported all over the country; humanitarian agencies were now "claiming from 200,000 to 500,000 lives" lost. Gati offered the intelligence bureau's view: "We believe 500,000 may be an exaggerated estimate, but no accurate figures are available. Systematic killings began within hours of Habyarimana's death. Most of those killed have been Tutsi civilians, including women and children." The terms of the Genocide Convention had been met. "We weren't quibbling about these numbers," Gati says. "We can never know precise figures, but our analysts had been reporting huge numbers of deaths for weeks. We were basically saying, 'A rose by any other name . . .'"

Despite this straightforward assessment, Christopher remained reluctant to speak the obvious truth. When he issued his guidance, on May 21, fully a month after Human Rights Watch had put a name to the tragedy, Christopher's instructions were hopelessly muddied.

> The delegation is authorized to agree to a resolution that states that "acts of genocide" have occurred in Rwanda or that "genocide has occurred in Rwanda." Other formulations that suggest that some, but not all of the killings in Rwanda are genocide . . . e.g. "genocide is taking place in Rwanda"—are authorized. Delegation is not authorized to agree to the characterization of any specific incident as genocide or to agree to any formulation that indicates that all killings in Rwanda are genocide.

Notably, Christopher confined permission to acknowledge full-fledged genocide to the upcoming session of the Human Rights Commission. Outside that venue State Department officials were authorized to state publicly only that *acts* of genocide had occurred.

Christine Shelly, a State Department spokesperson, had long been charged with publicly articulating the U.S. position on whether events in Rwanda counted as genocide. For two months she had avoided the term, and as her June 10 exchange with the Reuters correspondent Alan Elsner reveals, her semantic dance continued.

ELSNER: How would you describe the events taking place in Rwanda?

SHELLY: Based on the evidence we have seen from observations on the ground, we have every reason to believe that acts of genocide have occurred in Rwanda.

ELSNER: What's the difference between "acts of genocide" and "genocide"?

SHELLY: Well, I think the—as you know, there's a legal definition of this . . . clearly not all of the killings that have taken place in Rwanda are killings to which you might apply that label . . . But as to the distinctions between the words, we're trying to call what we have seen so far as best as we can; and based, again, on the evidence, we have every reason to believe that acts of genocide have occurred.

ELSNER: How many acts of genocide does it take to make genocide?

SHELLY: Alan, that's just not a question that I'm in a position to answer.

The same day, in Istanbul, Warren Christopher, by then under severe internal and external pressure, relented: "If there is any particular magic in calling it genocide, I have no hesitancy in saying that."

VIII. "Not Even a Sideshow"

Once the Americans had been evacuated, Rwanda largely dropped off the radar of most senior Clinton Administration officials. In the situation room on the seventh floor of the State Department a map of Rwanda had been hurriedly pinned to the wall in the aftermath of the plane crash, and eight banks of phones had rung off the hook. Now, with U.S. citizens safely home, the State Department chaired a daily interagency meeting, often by teleconference, designed to coordinate mid-level diplomatic and humanitarian responses. Cabinet-level officials focused on crises elsewhere. Anthony Lake recalls, "I was obsessed with Haiti and Bosnia during that period, so Rwanda was, in William Shawcross's words, a 'sideshow,' but not even a sideshow—a no-show." At the NSC the person who managed Rwanda policy was not Lake, the national-security adviser, who happened to know Africa, but Richard Clarke, who oversaw peace-keeping policy, and for whom the news from Rwanda only confirmed a deep skepticism about the viability of UN deployments. Clarke believed that another UN failure could doom relations

between Congress and the United Nations. He also sought to shield the President from congressional and public criticism. Donald Steinberg managed the Africa portfolio at the NSC and tried to look out for the dying Rwandans, but he was not an experienced infighter and, colleagues say, he "never won a single argument" with Clarke.

■　■　■

During the entire three months of the genocide Clinton never assembled his top policy advisers to discuss the killings. Anthony Lake likewise never gathered the "principals"—the Cabinet-level members of the foreign-policy team. Rwanda was never thought to warrant its own top-level meeting. When the subject came up, it did so along with, and subordinate to, discussions of Somalia, Haiti, and Bosnia. Whereas these crises involved U.S. personnel and stirred some public interest, Rwanda generated no sense of urgency and could safely be avoided by Clinton at no political cost. The editorial boards of the major American newspapers discouraged U.S. intervention during the genocide. They, like the Administration, lamented the killings but believed, in the words of an April 17 *Washington Post* editorial, "The United States has no recognizable national interest in taking a role, certainly not a leading role." Capitol Hill was quiet. Some in Congress were glad to be free of the expense of another flawed UN mission. Others, including a few members of the Africa subcommittees and the Congressional Black Caucus, eventually appealed tamely for the United States to play a role in ending the violence—but again, they did not dare urge U.S. involvement on the ground, and they did not kick up a public fuss. Members of Congress weren't hearing from their constituents. Pat Schroeder, of Colorado, said on April 30, "There are some groups terribly concerned about the gorillas . . . But—it sounds terrible—people just don't know what can be done about the people." Randall Robinson, of the nongovernmental organization TransAfrica, was preoccupied, staging a hunger strike to protest the U.S. repatriation of Haitian refugees. Human Rights Watch supplied exemplary intelligence and established important one-on-one contacts in the Administration, but the organization lacks a grassroots base from which to mobilize a broader segment of American society.

IX. The UN Withdrawal

When the killing began, Romeo Dallaire expected and appealed for reinforcements. Within hours of the plane crash he had cabled UN headquarters in New York: "Give me the means and I can do more." He was sending peacekeepers on rescue missions around the city, and he felt it was essential to increase the size and improve the quality of the UN's presence. But the United States opposed the idea of sending reinforcements, no matter where they were from. The fear, articulated mainly at the Pentagon but felt throughout the bureaucracy, was that what would start as a small engagement by foreign troops would end as a large and costly one by Americans. This was the lesson of Somalia, where U.S. troops had gotten into trouble in an effort to bail out the beleaguered Pakistanis. The logical outgrowth of this fear was an effort to steer clear of Rwanda entirely and be sure others did the same. Only by yanking Dallaire's entire peacekeeping force could the United States protect itself from involvement down the road.

One senior U.S. official remembers, "When the reports of the deaths of the ten Belgians came in, it was clear that it was Somalia redux, and the sense was that there would be an expectation everywhere that the U.S. would get involved. We thought leaving the peacekeepers in Rwanda and having them confront the violence would take us where we'd been before. It was a foregone conclusion that the United States wouldn't intervene and that the concept of UN peacekeeping could not be sacrificed again."

A foregone conclusion. What is most remarkable about the American response to the Rwandan genocide is not so much the absence of U.S. military action as that during the entire genocide the possibility of U.S. military intervention was never even debated. Indeed, the United States resisted intervention of any kind.

The bodies of the slain Belgian soldiers were returned to Brussels on April 14. One of the pivotal conversations in the course of the genocide took place around that time, when Willie Claes, the Belgian Foreign Minister, called the State Department to request "cover." "We are pulling out, but we don't want to be seen to be doing it alone," Claes said, asking the Americans to support a full UN withdrawal. Dallaire had not anticipated that Belgium would extract its soldiers, removing the backbone of his mission and stranding Rwandans in their hour of greatest need. "I expected the excolonial white countries would stick it out even if they took casualties," he remembers. "I thought their pride would have led them to stay to try to sort the place out. The Belgian decision caught me totally off guard. I was truly stunned."

Belgium did not want to leave ignominiously, by itself. Warren Christopher agreed to back Belgian requests for a full UN exit. Policy over the next month or so can be described simply: no U.S. military intervention, robust demands for a withdrawal of all of Dallaire's forces, and no support for a new UN mission that would challenge the killers. Belgium had the cover it needed.

On April 15 Christopher sent one of the most forceful documents to be produced in the entire three months of the genocide to Madeleine Albright at the UN—a cable instructing her to demand a full UN withdrawal. The cable, which was heavily influenced by Richard Clarke at the NSC, and which bypassed Donald Steinberg and was never seen by Anthony Lake, was unequivocal about the next steps. Saying that he had "fully" taken into account the "humanitarian reasons put forth for retention of UNAMIR elements in Rwanda,"

Christopher wrote that there was "insufficient justification" to retain a UN presence.

> The international community must give highest priority to full, orderly withdrawal of all UNAMIR personnel as soon as possible . . . We will oppose any effort at this time to preserve a UNAMIR presence in Rwanda . . . Our opposition to retaining a UNAMIR presence in Rwanda is firm. It is based on our conviction that the Security Council has an obligation to ensure that peacekeeping operations are viable, that they are capable of fulfilling their mandates, and that UN peacekeeping personnel are not placed or retained, knowingly, in an untenable situation.

"Once we knew the Belgians were leaving, we were left with a rump mission incapable of doing anything to help people," Clarke remembers. "They were doing nothing to stop the killings."

But Clarke underestimated the deterrent effect that Dallaire's very few peacekeepers were having. Although some soldiers hunkered down, terrified, others scoured Kigali, rescuing Tutsi, and later established defensive positions in the city, opening their doors to the fortunate Tutsi who made it through roadblocks to reach them. One Senegalese captain saved a hundred or so lives single-handedly. Some 25,000 Rwandans eventually assembled at positions manned by UNAMIR personnel. The Hutu were generally reluctant to massacre large groups of Tutsi if foreigners (armed or unarmed) were present. It did not take many UN soldiers to dissuade the Hutu from attacking. At the Hotel des Mille Collines ten peacekeepers and four UN military observers helped to protect the several hundred civilians sheltered there for the duration of the crisis. About 10,000 Rwandans gathered at the Amohoro Stadium under light UN cover. Brent Beardsley, Dallaire's executive assistant, remembers, "If there was any determined resistance at close quarters, the government guys tended to back

off." Kevin Aiston, the Rwanda desk officer at the State Department, was keeping track of Rwandan civilians under UN protection. When Prudence Bushnell told him of the U.S. decision to demand a UNAMIR withdrawal, he turned pale. "We can't," he said. Bushnell replied, "The train has already left the station."

On April 19 the Belgian Colonel Luc Marchal delivered his final salute and departed with the last of his soldiers. The Belgian withdrawal reduced Dallaire's troop strength to 2,100. More crucially, he lost his best troops. Command and control among Dallaire's remaining forces became tenuous. Dallaire soon lost every line of communication to the countryside. He had only a single satellite phone link to the outside world.

The UN Security Council now made a decision that sealed the Tutsi's fate and signaled the militia that it would have free rein. The U.S. demand for a full UN withdrawal had been opposed by some African nations, and even by Madeleine Albright; so the United States lobbied instead for a dramatic drawdown in troop strength. On April 21, amid press reports of some 100,000 dead in Rwanda, the Security Council voted to slash UNAMIR's forces to 270 men. Albright went along, publicly declaring that a "small, skeletal" operation would be left in Kigali to "show the will of the international community."

After the UN vote Clarke sent a memorandum to Lake reporting that language about "the safety and security of Rwandans under UN protection had been inserted by US/UN at the end of the day to prevent an otherwise unanimous UNSC from walking away from the at-risk Rwandans under UN protection as the peacekeepers drew down to 270." In other words, the memorandum suggested that the United States was *leading* efforts to ensure that the Rwandans under UN protection were not abandoned. The opposite was true.

Most of Dallaire's troops were evacuated by April 25. Though he was supposed to reduce the size of his force to 270, he ended up keeping 503 peacekeepers. By this time Dallaire was trying to deal with a bloody frenzy. "My force was standing knee-deep in mutilated bodies, surrounded by the guttural moans of dying people, looking into the eyes of children bleeding to death with their wounds burning in the sun and being invaded by maggots and flies," he later wrote. "I found myself walking through villages where the only sign of life was a goat, or a chicken, or a songbird, as all the people were dead, their bodies being eaten by voracious packs of wild dogs."

Dallaire had to work within narrow limits. He attempted simply to keep the positions he held and to protect the 25,000 Rwandans under UN supervision while hoping that the member states on the Security Council would change their minds and send him some help while it still mattered.

By coincidence Rwanda held one of the rotating seats on the Security Council at the time of the genocide. Neither the United States nor any other UN member state ever suggested that the representative of the genocidal government be expelled from the council. Nor did any Security Council country offer to provide safe haven to Rwandan refugees who escaped the carnage. In one instance Dallaire's forces succeeded in evacuating a group of Rwandans by plane to Kenya. The Nairobi authorities allowed the plane to land, sequestered it in a hangar, and, echoing the American decision to turn back the *S.S. St. Louis* during the Holocaust, then forced the plane to return to Rwanda. The fate of the passengers is unknown.

Throughout this period the Clinton Administration was largely silent. The closest it came to a public denunciation of the Rwandan government occurred after personal lobbying by Human Rights Watch, when Anthony Lake issued a statement calling on Rwandan military leaders by name to "do everything in their power to end the violence immediately." When I spoke with Lake six years later, and informed him that human-rights groups and U.S. officials point to this statement as the sum total of official public attempts to shame the Rwandan

government in this period, he seemed stunned. "You're kidding," he said. "That's truly pathetic."

At the State Department the diplomacy was conducted privately, by telephone. Prudence Bushnell regularly set her alarm for 2:00 AM and phoned Rwandan government officials. She spoke several times with Augustin Bizimungu, the Rwandan military chief of staff. "These were the most bizarre phone calls," she says. "He spoke in perfectly charming French. 'Oh, it's so nice to hear from you,' he said. I told him, 'I am calling to tell you President Clinton is going to hold you accountable for the killings.' He said, 'Oh, how nice it is that your President is thinking of me.'"

X. The Pentagon "Chop"

The daily meeting of the Rwanda interagency working group was attended, either in person or by teleconference, by representatives from the various State Department bureaus, the Pentagon, the National Security Council, and the intelligence community. Any proposal that originated in the working group had to survive the Pentagon "chop." "Hard intervention," meaning U.S. military action, was obviously out of the question. But Pentagon officials routinely stymied initiatives for "soft intervention" as well.

The Pentagon discussion paper on Rwanda, referred to earlier, ran down a list of the working group's six short-term policy objectives and carped at most of them. The fear of a slippery slope was persuasive. Next to the seemingly innocuous suggestion that the United States "support the UN and others in attempts to achieve a cease-fire" the Pentagon official responded, "Need to change 'attempts' to 'political efforts'—without 'political' there is a danger of signing up to troop contributions."

The one policy move the Defense Department supported was a U.S. effort to achieve an arms embargo. But the same discussion paper acknowledged the ineffectiveness of this step: "We do not envision it will have a significant impact on the killings because machetes, knives and other hand implements have been the most common weapons."

Dallaire never spoke to Bushnell or to Tony Marley, the U.S. military liaison to the Arusha process, during the genocide, but they all reached the same conclusions. Seeing that no troops were forthcoming, they turned their attention to measures short of full-scale deployment which might alleviate the suffering. Dallaire pleaded with New York, and Bushnell and her team recommended in Washington, that something be done to "neutralize" Radio Mille Collines.

The country best equipped to prevent the genocide planners from broadcasting murderous instructions directly to the population was the United States. Marley offered three possibilities. The United States could destroy the antenna. It could transmit "counter-broadcasts" urging perpetrators to stop the genocide. Or it could jam the hate radio station's broadcasts. This could have been done from an airborne platform such as the Air Force's Commando Solo airplane. Anthony Lake raised the matter with Secretary of Defense William Perry at the end of April. Pentagon officials considered all the proposals non-starters. On May 5 Frank Wisner, the undersecretary of defense for policy, prepared a memo for Sandy Berger, then the deputy national-security adviser. Wisner's memo testifies to the unwillingness of the U.S. government to make even financial sacrifices to diminish the killing.

> We have looked at options to stop the broadcasts within the Pentagon, discussed them interagency and concluded jamming is an ineffective and expensive mechanism that will not accomplish the objective the NSC Advisor seeks.
>
> International legal conventions complicate airborne or ground based jamming and the mountainous terrain reduces the effectiveness of either option. Commando Solo, an Air National Guard asset, is the only suitable DOD jamming platform. It costs approximately $8500 per flight hour and requires a semi-secure area of operations due to its vulnerability and limited self-protection.
>
> I believe it would be wiser to use air to assist in Rwanda in the [food] relief effort . . .

The plane would have needed to remain in Rwandan airspace while it waited for radio transmissions to begin. "First we would have had to figure out whether it made sense to use Commando Solo," Wisner recalls. "Then we had to get it from where it was already and be sure it could be moved. Then we would have needed flight clearance from all the countries nearby. And then we would need the political go-ahead. By the time we got all this, weeks would have passed. And it was not going to solve the fundamental problem, which was one that needed to be addressed militarily." Pentagon planners understood that stopping the genocide required a military solution. Neither they nor the White House wanted any part in a military solution. Yet instead of undertaking other forms of intervention that might have at least saved some lives, they justified inaction by arguing that a military solution was required.

Whatever the limitations of radio jamming, which clearly would have been no panacea, most of the delays Wisner cites could have been avoided if senior Administration officials had followed through. But Rwanda was not their problem. Instead justifications for standing by abounded. In early May the State Department Legal Advisor's Office issued a finding against radio jamming, citing international broadcasting agreements and the American commitment to free speech. When Bushnell raised radio jamming yet again at a meeting, one Pentagon official chided her for naiveté: "Pru, radios don't kill people. *People* kill people!"

■   ■   ■

However significant and obstructionist the role of the Pentagon in April and May, Defense Department officials were stepping into a vacuum. As one U.S. official put it, "Look, nobody senior was paying any attention to this mess. And in the absence of any political leadership from the top, when you have one group that feels pretty strongly about what *shouldn't* be done, it is extremely likely they are going to end up shaping U.S. policy." Lieutenant General Wesley Clark looked to the White House for leadership. "The Pentagon is always going to be the last to want to intervene," he says. "It is up to the civilians to tell us they want to do something and we'll figure out how to do it."

■ ■ ■

XI. PDD-25 in Action

No sooner had most of Dallaire's forces been withdrawn, in late April, than a handful of nonpermanent members of the Security Council, aghast at the scale of the slaughter, pressed the major powers to send a new, beefed-up force (UNAMIR II) to Rwanda.

When Dallaire's troops had first arrived, in the fall of 1993, they had done so under a fairly traditional peacekeeping mandate known as a Chapter VI deployment—a mission that assumes a ceasefire and a desire on both sides to comply with a peace accord. The Security Council now had to decide whether it was prepared to move from peacekeeping to peace *enforcement*—that is, to a Chapter VII mission in a hostile environment. This would demand more peacekeepers with far greater resources, more-aggressive rules of engagement, and an explicit recognition that the UN soldiers were there to protect civilians.

Two proposals emerged. Dallaire submitted a plan that called for joining his remaining peacekeepers with about 5,000 well-armed soldiers he hoped could be gathered quickly by the Security Council. He wanted to secure Kigali and then fan outward to create safe havens for Rwandans who had gathered in large numbers at churches and schools and on hillsides around the country. The United States was one of the few countries that could supply the rapid airlift and logistic support needed to move reinforcements to the region. In a meeting with UN Secretary General Boutros Boutros-Ghali on May 10, Vice President Al Gore pledged U.S. help with transport.

Richard Clarke, at the NSC, and representatives of the Joint Chiefs challenged Dallaire's plan. "How do you plan to take control of the airport in Kigali so that the reinforcements will be able to land?" Clarke asked. He argued instead for an "outside-in" strategy, as opposed to Dallaire's "inside-out" approach. The U.S. proposal would have created protected zones for refugees at Rwanda's borders. It would have kept any U.S. pilots involved in airlifting the peacekeepers safely out of Rwanda. "Our proposal was the most feasible, doable thing that could have been done in the short term," Clarke insists. Dallaire's proposal, in contrast, "could not be done in the short term and could not attract peacekeepers." The U.S. plan—which was modeled on Operation Provide Comfort, for the Kurds of northern Iraq—seemed to assume that the people in need were refugees fleeing to the border, but most endangered Tutsi could not make it to the border. The most vulnerable Rwandans were those clustered together, awaiting salvation, deep inside Rwanda. Dallaire's plan would have had UN soldiers move to the Tutsi in hiding. The U.S. plan would have required civilians to move to the safe zones, negotiating murderous roadblocks on the way. "The two plans had very different objectives," Dallaire says. "My mission was to save Rwandans. Their mission was to put on a show at no risk."

America's new peacekeeping doctrine, of which Clarke was the primary architect, was unveiled on May 3, and U.S. officials applied its criteria zealously. PDD-25 did not merely circumscribe U.S. participation in UN missions; it also limited U.S.

support for other states that hoped to carry out UN missions. Before such missions could garner U.S. approval, policymakers had to answer certain questions: Were U.S. interests at stake? Was there a threat to world peace? A clear mission goal? Acceptable costs? Congressional, public, and allied support? A working cease-fire? A clear command-and-control arrangement? And, finally, what was the exit strategy?

The United States haggled at the Security Council and with the UN Department of Peacekeeping Operations for the first two weeks of May. U.S. officials pointed to the flaws in Dallaire's proposal without offering the resources that would have helped him to overcome them. On May 13 Deputy Secretary of State Strobe Talbott sent Madeleine Albright instructions on how the United States should respond to Dallaire's plan. Noting the logistic hazards of airlifting troops into the capital, Talbott wrote, "The U.S. is not prepared at this point to lift heavy equipment and troops into Kigali." The "more manageable" operation would be to create the protected zones at the border, secure humanitarian-aid deliveries, and "promot[e] restoration of a ceasefire and return to the Arusha Peace Process." Talbott acknowledged that even the minimalist American proposal contained "many unanswered questions":

> Where will the needed forces come from; how will they be transported . . . where precisely should these safe zones be created; . . . would UN forces be authorized to move out of the zones to assist affected populations not in the zones . . . will the fighting parties in Rwanda agree to this arrangement . . . what conditions would need to obtain for the operation to end successfully?

Nonetheless, Talbott concluded, "We would urge the UN to explore and refine this alternative and present the Council with a menu of at least two options in a formal report from the [Secretary General] along with cost estimates before the Security Council votes on changing UNAMIR's mandate." U.S. policymakers were asking valid questions. Dallaire's plan certainly would have required the intervening troops to take risks in an effort to reach the targeted Rwandans or to confront the Hutu militia and government forces. But the business-as-usual tone of the American inquiry did not seem appropriate to the unprecedented and utterly unconventional crisis that was under way.

On May 17, by which time most of the Tutsi victims of the genocide were already dead, the United States finally acceded to a version of Dallaire's plan. However, few African countries stepped forward to offer troops. Even if troops had been immediately available, the lethargy of the major powers would have hindered their use. Though the Administration had committed the United States to provide armored support if the African nations provided soldiers, Pentagon stalling resumed. On May 19 the UN formally requested fifty American armored personnel carriers. On May 31 the United States agreed to send the APCs from Germany to Entebbe, Uganda. But squabbles between the Pentagon and UN planners arose. Who would pay for the vehicles? Should the vehicles be tracked or wheeled? Would the UN buy them or simply lease them? And who would pay the shipping costs? Compounding the disputes was the fact that Department of Defense regulations prevented the U.S. Army from preparing the vehicles for transport until contracts had been signed. The Defense Department demanded that it be reimbursed $15 million for shipping spare parts and equipment to and from Rwanda. In mid-June the White House finally intervened. On June 19, a month after the UN request, the United States began transporting the APCs, but they were missing the radios and heavy machine guns that would be needed if UN troops came under fire. By the time the APCs arrived, the genocide was over—halted by Rwandan Patriotic Front forces under the command of the Tutsi leader, Paul Kagame.

XII. The Stories We Tell

It is not hard to conceive of how the United States might have done things differently. Ahead of the plane crash, as violence escalated, it could have agreed to Belgian pleas for UN reinforcements. Once the killing of thousands of Rwandans a day had begun, the President could have deployed U.S. troops to Rwanda. The United States could have joined Dallaire's beleaguered UNAMIR forces or, if it feared associating with shoddy UN peace-keeping, it could have intervened unilaterally with the Security Council's backing, as France eventually did in late June. The United States could also have acted without the UN's blessing, as it did five years later in Kosovo. Securing congressional support for U.S. intervention would have been extremely difficult, but by the second week of the killing Clinton could have made the case that something approximating genocide was under way, that a supreme American value was imperiled by its occurrence, and that U.S. contingents at relatively low risk could stop the extermination of a people.

Alan Kuperman wrote in *Foreign Affairs* that President Clinton was in the dark for two weeks; by the time a large U.S. force could deploy, it would not have saved "even half of the ultimate victims." The evidence indicates that the killers' intentions were known by mid-level officials and knowable by their bosses within a week of the plane crash. Any failure to fully appreciate the genocide stemmed from political, moral, and imaginative weaknesses, not informational ones. As for what force could have accomplished, Kuperman's claims are purely speculative. We cannot know how the announcement of a robust or even a limited U.S. deployment would have affected the perpetrators' behavior. It is worth noting that even Kuperman concedes that belated intervention would have saved 75,000 to 125,000—no small achievement. A more serious challenge comes from the U.S. officials who argue that no amount of leadership from the White House would have overcome congressional opposition to sending U.S. troops to Africa. But even if that highly debatable point was true, the United States still had a variety of options. Instead of leaving it to mid-level officials to communicate with the Rwandan leadership behind the scenes, senior officials in the Administration could have taken control of the process. They could have publicly and frequently denounced the slaughter. They could have branded the crimes "genocide" at a far earlier stage. They could have called for the expulsion of the Rwandan delegation from the Security Council. On the telephone, at the UN, and on the Voice of America they could have threatened to prosecute those complicit in the genocide, naming names when possible. They could have deployed Pentagon assets to jam—even temporarily—the crucial, deadly radio broadcasts.

Instead of demanding a UN withdrawal, quibbling over costs, and coming forward (belatedly) with a plan better suited to caring for refugees than to stopping massacres, U.S. officials could have worked to make UNAMIR a force to contend with. They could have urged their Belgian allies to stay and protect Rwandan civilians. If the Belgians insisted on withdrawing, the White House could have done everything within its power to make sure that Dallaire was immediately reinforced. Senior officials could have spent U.S. political capital rallying troops from other nations and could have supplied strategic airlift and logistic support to a coalition that it had helped to create. In short, the United States could have led the world.

Why did none of these things happen? One reason is that all possible sources of pressure—U.S. allies, Congress, editorial boards, and the American people—were mute when it mattered for Rwanda. American leaders have a circular and deliberate relationship to public opinion. It is circular because public opinion is rarely if ever aroused by foreign crises, even genocidal ones, in the absence of political leadership, and yet at the same time, American leaders continually cite the absence of public support as grounds for inaction. The relationship is deliberate because American leadership is not absent in such circumstances: it was present regarding Rwanda, but devoted mainly to suppressing public outrage and thwarting UN initiatives so as to avoid acting.

Strikingly, most officials involved in shaping U.S. policy were able to define the decision not to stop genocide as ethical and moral. The Administration employed several devices to keep down enthusiasm for action and to preserve the public's sense—and, more important, its own—that U.S. policy choices were not merely politically astute but also morally acceptable. First, Administration officials exaggerated the extremity of the possible responses. Time and again U.S. leaders posed the choice as between staying out of Rwanda and "getting involved everywhere." In addition, they often presented the choice as one between doing nothing and sending in the Marines. On May 25, at the Naval Academy graduation ceremony, Clinton described America's relationship to ethnic trouble spots: "We cannot turn away from them, but our interests are not sufficiently at stake in so many of them to justify a commitment of our folks."

Second, Administration policymakers appealed to notions of the greater good. They did not simply frame U.S. policy as one contrived in order to advance the national interest or avoid U.S. casualties. Rather, they often argued against intervention from the standpoint of people committed to protecting human life. Owing to recent failures in UN peacekeeping, many humanitarian interventionists in the U.S. government were concerned about the future of America's relationship with the United Nations generally and peacekeeping specifically. They believed that the UN and humanitarianism could not afford another Somalia. Many internalized the belief that the UN had more to lose by sending reinforcements and failing than by allowing the killings to proceed. Their chief priority, after the evacuation of the Americans, was looking after UN peacekeepers, and they justified the withdrawal of the peacekeepers on the grounds that it would ensure a future for humanitarian intervention. In other words, Dallaire's peacekeeping mission in Rwanda had to be destroyed so that peacekeeping might be saved for use elsewhere.

A third feature of the response that helped to console U.S. officials at the time was the sheer flurry of Rwanda-related activity. U.S. officials with a special concern for Rwanda took their solace from mini-victories—working on behalf of specific individuals or groups (Monique Mujawamariya; the Rwandans gathered at the hotel). Government officials involved in policy met constantly and remained "seized of the matter"; they neither appeared nor felt indifferent. Although little in the way of effective intervention emerged from midlevel meetings in Washington or New York, an abundance of memoranda and other documents did.

Finally, the almost willful delusion that what was happening in Rwanda did not amount to genocide created a nurturing ethical framework for inaction. "War" was "tragic" but created no moral imperative.

What is most frightening about this story is that it testifies to a system that in effect worked. President Clinton and his advisers had several aims. First, they wanted to avoid engagement in a conflict that posed little threat to American interests, narrowly defined. Second, they sought to appease a restless Congress by showing that they were cautious in their approach to peacekeeping. And third, they hoped to contain the political costs and avoid the moral stigma associated with allowing genocide. By and large, they achieved all three objectives. The normal operations of the foreign-policy bureaucracy and the international community permitted an illusion of continual deliberation, complex activity, and intense concern, even as Rwandans were left to die.

Robert O. Keohane

FROM *AFTER HEGEMONY*
Cooperation and Discord in the World Political Economy

Realism, Institutionalism, and Cooperation

Impressed with the difficulties of cooperation, observers have often compared world politics to a "state of war." In this conception, international politics is "a competition of units in the kind of state of nature that knows no restraints other than those which the changing necessities of the game and the shallow conveniences of the players impose" (Hoffmann, 1965, p. vii). It is anarchic in the sense that it lacks an authoritative government that can enact and enforce rules of behavior. States must rely on "the means they can generate and the arrangements they can make for themselves" (Waltz, 1979, p. 111). Conflict and war result, since each state is judge in its own cause and can use force to carry out its judgments (Waltz, 1959, p. 159). The discord that prevails is accounted for by fundamental conflicts of interest (Waltz, 1959; Tucker, 1977).

Were this portrayal of world politics correct, any cooperation that occurs would be derivative from overall patterns of conflict. Alliance cooperation would be easy to explain as a result of the operation of a balance of power, but system-wide patterns of cooperation that benefit many countries without being tied to an alliance system

From Robert O. Keohane, *After Hegemony: Cooperation and Discord in the World Political Economy* (Princeton, NJ: Princeton University Press, 1984), Chaps. 1, 6, 7. Some of the author's notes have been omitted.

directed against an adversary would not. If international politics were a state of war, institutionalized patterns of cooperation on the basis of shared purposes should not exist except as part of a larger struggle for power. The extensive patterns of international agreement that we observe on issues as diverse as trade, financial relations, health, telecommunications, and environmental protection would be absent.

At the other extreme from these "Realists" are writers who see cooperation as essential in a world of economic interdependence, and who argue that shared economic interests create a demand for international institutions and rules (Mitrany, 1975). Such an approach, which I refer to as "Institutionalist" because of its adherents' emphasis on the functions performed by international institutions, runs the risk of being naive about power and conflict. Too often its proponents incorporate in their theories excessively optimistic assumptions about the role of ideals in world politics, or about the ability of statesmen to learn what the theorist considers the "right lessons." But sophisticated students of institutions and rules have a good deal to teach us. They view institutions not simply as formal organizations with headquarters buildings and specialized staffs, but more broadly as "recognized patterns of practice around which expectations converge" (Young, 1980, p. 337). They regard these patterns of practice as significant because they affect state behavior. Sophisticated institutionalists do not expect cooperation always to prevail, but they are aware of the malleability of interests and they argue that interdependence creates interests in cooperation.

During the first twenty years or so after World War II, these views, though very different in their intellectual origins and their broader implications about human society, made similar predictions about the world political economy, and particularly about the subject of this [discussion], the political economy of the advanced market-economy countries. Institutionalists expected successful cooperation in one field to "spill over" into others (Haas, 1958). Realists anticipated a relatively stable international economic order as a result of the dominance of the United States. Neither set of observers was surprised by what happened, although they interpreted events differently.

Institutionalists could interpret the liberal international arrangements for trade and international finance as responses to the need for policy coordination created by the fact of interdependence. These arrangements, which we will call "international regimes," contained rules, norms, principles, and decisionmaking procedures. Realists could reply that these regimes were constructed on the basis of principles espoused by the United States, and that American power was essential for their construction and maintenance. For Realists, in other words, the early postwar regimes rested on the *political hegemony* of the United States. Thus Realists and Institutionalists could both regard early postwar developments as supporting their theories.

After the mid-1960s, however, U.S. dominance in the world political economy was challenged by the economic recovery and increasing unity of Europe and by the rapid economic growth of Japan. Yet economic interdependence continued to grow, and the pace of increased U.S. involvement in the world economy even accelerated after 1970. At this point, therefore, the Institutionalist and Realist predictions began to diverge. From a strict Institutionalist standpoint, the increasing need for coordination of policy, created by interdependence, should have led to more cooperation. From a Realist perspective, by contrast, the diffusion of power should have undermined the ability of anyone to create order.

On the surface, the Realists would seem to have made the better forecast. Since the late 1960s there have been signs of decline in the extent and efficacy of efforts to cooperate in the world political economy. As American power eroded, so did international regimes. The erosion of these regimes after World War II certainly refutes a naive version of the Institutionalist faith in interdependence as a solvent of conflict and a creator of cooperation. But it does not prove that only the Realist emphasis on power as a creator of order is valid. It might be possible, after the decline of hegemonic regimes, for more symmetrical patterns of cooperation to evolve after a transitional period of discord. Indeed, the persistence of attempts at cooperation during the 1970s suggests that the decline of hegemony does not necessarily sound cooperation's death knell.

International cooperation and discord thus remain puzzling. Under what conditions can independent countries cooperate in the world political economy? In particular, can cooperation take place without hegemony and, if so, how? This [project] is designed to help us find answers to these questions. I begin with Realist insights about the role of power and the effects of hegemony. But my central arguments draw more on the Institutionalist tradition, arguing that cooperation can under some conditions develop on the basis of complementary interests, and that institutions, broadly defined, affect the patterns of cooperation that emerge.

Hegemonic leadership is unlikely to be revived in this century for the United States or any other country. Hegemonic powers have historically only emerged after world wars; during peacetime, weaker countries have tended to gain on the hegemon rather than vice versa (Gilpin, 1981). It is difficult to believe that world civilization, much less a complex international economy, would survive such a war in the nuclear age. Certainly no prosperous hegemonic power is likely to emerge from such a cataclysm. As long as a world political economy persists, therefore, its central political dilemma will be how to organize cooperation without hegemony.

■ ■ ■

A Functional Theory of International Regimes

* * * [I]nternational regimes could be created and emphasized their value for overcoming what could be called "political market failure." * * * [Following is a] detailed examination of this argument by exploring why political market failure occurs and how international regimes can help to overcome it. This investigation will help us understand both why states often comply with regime rules and why international regimes can be maintained even after the conditions that facilitated their creation have disappeared. The functional theory developed in this chapter will therefore suggest some reasons to believe that even if U.S. hegemonic leadership may have been a crucial factor in the creation of some contemporary international economic regimes, the continuation of hegemony is not necessarily essential for their continued viability.

Political Market Failure and the Coase Theorem

Like imperfect markets, world politics is characterized by institutional deficiencies that inhibit mutually advantageous cooperation. * * * [I]n this self-help system, [there are] conflicts of interest between actors. In economic terms, these conflicts can be regarded as arising in part from the existence of externalities: actors do not bear the full costs, or receive the full benefits, of their own actions.[1] Yet in a famous article Ronald Coase (1960) argued that the presence of externalities alone does not necessarily prevent effective coordination among independent actors. Under certain conditions, declared Coase, bargaining among these actors could lead to solutions that are Pareto-optimal regardless of the rules of legal liability.

To illustrate the Coase theorem and its counter-intuitive result, suppose that soot emitted by a paint factory is deposited by the wind onto clothing hanging outdoors in the yard of an old-fashioned laundry. Assume that the damage to the laundry is greater than the $20,000 it would cost the laundry to enclose its yard and install indoor drying equipment; so if no other alternative were available, it would be worthwhile for the laundry to take these actions. Assume also, however, that it would cost the paint factory only $10,000 to eliminate its emissions of air pollutants. Social welfare would clearly be enhanced by eliminating the pollution rather than by installing indoor drying equipment, but in the absence of either governmental enforcement or bargaining, the egoistic owner of the paint factory would have no incentive to spend anything to achieve this result.

It has frequently been argued that this sort of situation requires centralized governmental authority to provide the public good of clean air. Thus if the laundry had an enforceable legal right to demand compensation, the factory owner would have an incentive to invest $10,000 in pollution control devices to avoid a $20,000 court judgment. Coase argued, however, that the pollution would be cleaned up equally efficiently even if the laundry had no such recourse. If the law, or the existence of a decentralized self-help system, gave the factory a right to pollute, the laundry owner could simply pay the factory owner a sum greater than $10,000, but less than $20,000, to install anti-soot equipment. Both parties would agree to some such bargain, since both would benefit.

In either case, the externality of pollution would be eliminated. The key difference would not be one of economic efficiency, but of distribution of benefits between the factory and the laundry. In a self-help system, the laundry would have to pay between $10,000 and $20,000 and the factory would reap a profit from its capacity to pollute. But if legal liability rules were based on "the polluter pays principle," the laundry would pay nothing and the factory would have to invest $10,000 without reaping a financial return. Coase did not dispute that rules of liability could be evaluated on grounds of fairness, but insisted that, given his assumptions, efficient arrangements could be consummated even where the rules of liability favored producers of externalities rather than their victims.

The Coase theorem has frequently been used to show the efficacy of bargaining without central authority, and it has occasionally been applied specifically to international relations (Conybeare, 1980). The principle of sovereignty in effect establishes rules of liability that put the burden of externalities on those who suffer from them. The Coase theorem could be interpreted, therefore, as predicting that problems of collective action could easily be overcome in international politics through bargaining and mutual adjustment—that is, through cooperation * * * The further inference could be drawn that the discord observed must be the result of fundamental conflicts of interest rather than problems of coordination. The Coase theorem, in other words, could be taken as minimizing the importance of [Mancur] Olson's [1965] perverse logic of collective action or of the problems of coordination emphasized by game theory. However, such a conclusion would be incorrect for two compelling sets of reasons.

In the first place, Coase specified three crucial conditions for his conclusion to hold. These were: a legal framework establishing liability for actions, presumably supported by governmental authority; perfect information; and zero transaction costs (including organization costs and the costs of making side-payments). It is absolutely clear that none of these conditions is met in world politics. World government does not exist, making property rights and rules of legal liability fragile; information is extremely costly and often held unequally by different actors; transaction costs, including costs of organization and side-payments, are often very high. Thus an *inversion* of the Coase theorem would seem more appropriate to our subject. In the absence of the conditions that Coase specified, coordination will often be thwarted by dilemmas of collective action.

Second, recent critiques of Coase's argument reinforce the conclusion that it cannot simply be applied to world politics, and suggest further interesting implications about the functions of international regimes. It has been shown on the basis of game theory that, with more than two participants, the Coase theorem cannot necessarily be demonstrated. Under certain conditions, there will be no stable solution: any coalition that forms will be inferior, for at least one of its members, to another possible coalition. The result is an infinite regress. In game-theoretic terminology, the "core" of the game is empty. When the core is empty, the assumption of zero transaction costs means that agreement is hindered rather than facilitated: "in a world of zero transaction costs, the inherent instability of all coalitions could result in endless recontracting among the firms" (Aivazian and Callen, 1981, p. 179; Veljanovski, 1982).

What do Coase and his critics together suggest about the conditions for international cooperation through bargaining? First, it appears that approximating Coase's first two conditions—that is, having a clear legal framework establishing property rights and low-cost information available in a roughly equal way to all parties—will tend to facilitate cooperative solutions. But the implications of reducing transaction costs are more complex. If transaction costs are too high, no bargains will take place; but if they are too low, under certain conditions an infinite series of unstable coalitions may form.

Inverting the Coase theorem allows us to analyze international institutions largely as responses to problems of property rights, uncertainty, and transaction costs. Without consciously designed institutions, these problems will thwart attempts to cooperate in world politics even when actors' interests are complementary. From the deficiency of the "self-help system" (even from the perspective of purely self-interested national actors) we derive a need for international regimes. Insofar as they fill this need, international regimes perform the functions of establishing patterns of legal liability, providing relatively symmetrical information, and arranging the costs of bargaining so that specific agreements can more easily be made. Regimes are developed in part because actors in world politics believe that with such arrangements they will be able to make mutually beneficial agreements that would otherwise be difficult or impossible to attain.

This is to say that the architects of regimes anticipate that the regimes will facilitate cooperation. Within the functional argument being constructed here, these expectations explain the formation of the regimes: the *anticipated effects* of the regimes account for the actions of governments that establish them. Governments believe that *ad hoc* attempts to construct particular agreements, without a regime framework, will yield inferior results compared to negotiations within the framework of regimes. Following our inversion of the Coase theorem, we can classify the reasons for this belief under the categories of legal liability (property rights), transaction costs, and problems of uncertainty. We will consider these issues in turn.

LEGAL LIABILITY

Since governments put a high value on the maintenance of their own autonomy, it is usually impossible to establish international institutions that exercise authority over states. This fact is widely recognized by officials of international organizations and their advocates in national governments as well as by scholars. It would therefore be mistaken to regard international regimes, or the organizations that constitute elements of them, as characteristically unsuccessful attempts to institutionalize centralized authority in world politics. They cannot establish patterns of legal liability that are as solid as those developed within well-ordered societies, and their architects are well aware of this limitation.

Of course, the lack of a hierarchical structure of world politics does not prevent regimes from developing bits and pieces of law (Henkin, 1979, pp. 13–22). But the principal significance of international regimes does not lie in their formal legal status, since any patterns of legal liability and property rights established in world politics are subject to being overturned by the actions of sovereign states. International regimes are more like the "quasi-agreements" that William Fellner (1949) discusses when analyzing the behavior of oligopolistic firms than they are like governments. These quasi-agreements are legally unenforceable but, like contracts, help to organize relationships in mutually beneficial ways (Lowry, 1979, p. 276). Regimes also resemble conventions: practices, regarded as common knowledge in a community, that actors conform to not because they are uniquely best, but because others conform to them as well (Hardin, 1982; Lewis, 1969; Young, 1983). What these arrangements have in common is that they are designed not to implement centralized enforcement of agreements, but rather to establish stable mutual expectations about others' patterns of behavior and to develop working relationships that will allow the parties to adapt their practices to new situations. Contracts, conventions, and quasi-agreements provide information and generate patterns of transaction costs: costs of reneging on commitments are increased, and the costs of operating within these frameworks are reduced.

Both these arrangements and international regimes are often weak and fragile. Like contracts and quasi-agreements, international regimes are frequently altered: their rules are changed, bent, or broken to meet the exigencies of the moment. They are rarely enforced automatically, and they are not self-executing. Indeed, they are often matters for negotiation and renegotiation. As [Donald] Puchala has argued, "attempts to enforce EEC regulations open political cleavages up and down the supranational-to-local continuum and spark intense politicking along the cleavage lines" (1975, p. 509).

TRANSACTION COSTS

Like oligopolistic quasi-agreements, international regimes alter the relative costs of transactions. Certain agreements are forbidden. Under the provisions of the General Agreement on Tariffs and Trade (GATT), for instance, it is not permitted to make discriminatory trade arrangements except under specific conditions. Since there is no centralized government, states can nevertheless implement such actions, but their lack of legitimacy means that such measures are likely to be costly. Under GATT rules, for instance, retaliation against such behavior is justified. By elevating injunctions to the level of principles and rules, furthermore, regimes construct linkages between issues. No longer does a specific discriminatory agreement constitute merely a particular act without general significance; on the contrary, it becomes a "violation of GATT" with serious implications for a large number of other issues. In the terms of Prisoners' Dilemma, the situation has been transformed from a single-play to an iterated game. In market-failure terms, the transaction costs of certain possible bargains have been increased, while the costs of others have been reduced. In either case, the result is the same: incentives to violate regime principles are reduced. International regimes reduce transaction costs of legitimate bargains and increase them for illegitimate ones.

International regimes also affect transaction costs in the more mundane sense of making it cheaper for governments to get together to negotiate agreements. It is more convenient to make agreements within a regime than outside of one. International economic regimes usually incorporate international organizations that provide forums for meetings and secretariats that can act as catalysts for agreement. Insofar as their principles and rules can be applied to a wide variety of particular issues, they are efficient: establishing the rules and principles at the outset makes it unnecessary to renegotiate them each time a specific question arises.

International regimes thus allow governments to take advantage of potential economics of scale. Once a regime has been established, the marginal cost of dealing with each additional issue will be lower than it would be without a regime. * * * [I]f a policy area is sufficiently dense, establishing a regime will be worthwhile. Up to a point there may even be what economists call "increasing returns to scale." In such a situation, each additional issue could be included under the regime at lower cost than the previous one. As [Paul] Samuelson notes, in modern economies, "increasing returns is the prime case of deviations from perfect competition" (1967, p. 117). In world politics, we should expect increasing returns to scale to lead to more extensive international regimes.

In view of the benefits of economies of scale, it is not surprising that specific agreements tend to be "nested" within regimes. For instance, an agreement by the United States, Japan, and the European Community in the Multilateral Trade Negotiations to reduce a particular tariff will be affected by the rules and principles of GATT—that is, by the trade regime. The trade regime, in turn, is nested within a set of other arrangements, including those for monetary relations, energy, foreign investment, aid to developing countries, and other issues, which together constitute a complex and interlinked pattern of relations among the advance market-economy countries. These, in turn, are related to military-security relations among the major states.[2]

The nesting patterns of international regimes affect transaction costs by making it easier or more difficult to link particular issues and to arrange side-payments, giving someone something on one issue in return for her help on another.[3] Clustering of issues under a regime facilitates side-payments among these issues: more potential *quids* are available for the *quo*. Without international regimes linking clusters of issues to one another, side-payments and linkages would be difficult to arrange in world politics; in the absence of a price system for the exchange of favors, institutional barriers would hinder the construction of mutually beneficial bargains.

Suppose, for instance, that each issue were handled separately from all others, by a different governmental bureau in each country. Since a side-payment or linkage always means that a government must give up something on one dimension to get something on another, there would always be a bureaucratic loser within each government. Bureaus that would lose from proposed side-payments, on issues that matter to them, would be unlikely to bear the costs of these linkages willingly on the basis of other agencies' claims that the national interest required it.

Of course, each issue is not considered separately by a different governmental department or bureau. On the contrary, issues are grouped together, in functionally organized departments such as Treasury, Commerce, and Energy (in the United States). Furthermore, how governments organize themselves to deal with foreign policy is affected by how issues are organized internationally; issues considered by different regimes are often dealt with by different bureaucracies at home. Linkages and side-payments among issues grouped in the same regime thus become easier, since the necessary internal tradeoffs will tend to take place within

rather than across bureaus; but linkages among issues falling into different regimes will remain difficult, or even become more so (since the natural linkages on those issues will be with issues within the same regime).

Insofar as issues are dealt with separately from one another on the international level, it is often hard, in simply bureaucratic terms, to arrange for them to be considered together. There are bound to be difficulties in coordinating policies of different international organizations—GATT, the IMF [International Monetary Fund], and the IEA [International Energy Agency] all have different memberships and different operating styles—in addition to the resistance that will appear to such a move within member governments. Within regimes, by contrast, side-payments are facilitated by the fact that regimes bring together negotiators to consider sets of issues that may well lie within the negotiators' bureaucratic bailiwicks at home. GATT negotiations, as well as deliberations on the international monetary system, have been characterized by extensive bargaining over side-payments and the politics of issue-linkage (Hutton, 1975). The well-known literature on "spillover" in bargaining, relating to the European Community and other integration schemes, can also be interpreted as concerned with side-payments. According to these writings, expectations that an integration arrangement can be expanded to new issue-areas permit the broadening of potential side-payments, thus facilitating agreement (Haas, 1958).

We conclude that international regimes affect the costs of transactions. The value of a potential agreement to its prospective participants will depend, in part, on how consistent it is with principles of legitimacy embodied in international regimes. Transactions that violate these principles will be costly. Regimes also affect bureaucratic costs of transactions: successful regimes organize issue-areas so that productive linkages (those that facilitate agreements consistent with the principles of the regime) are facilitated, while destructive linkages and bargains that are inconsistent with regime principles are discouraged.

UNCERTAINTY AND INFORMATION

From the perspective of market-failure theories, the informational functions of regimes are the most important of all. * * * [W]hat Akerlof [1970] called "quality uncertainty" was the crucial problem in [a] "market for lemons" example. Even in games of pure coordination with stable equilibria, this may be a problem. Conventions—commuters meeting under the clock at Grand Central Station, suburban families on a shopping trip "meeting at the car"—become important. But in simple games of coordination, severe information problems are not embedded in the structure of relationships, since actors have incentives to reveal information and their own preferences fully to one another. In these games the problem is to reach some point of agreement; but it may not matter much which of several possible points is chosen (Schelling, 1960/1978). Conventions are important and ingenuity may be required, but serious systemic impediments to the acquisition and exchange of information are lacking (Lewis, 1969; Young, 1983).

Yet as we have seen in * * * discussions of collective action and Prisoners' Dilemma, many situations—both in game theory and in world politics—are characterized by conflicts of interest as well as common interests. In such situations, actors have to worry about being deceived and double-crossed, just as the buyer of a used car has to guard against purchasing a "lemon." The literature on market failure elaborates on its most fundamental contention—that, in the absence of appropriate institutions, some mutually advantageous bargains will not be made because of uncertainty—by pointing to three particularly important sources of difficulty: *asymmetrical information; moral hazard;* and *irresponsibility.*

ASYMMETRICAL INFORMATION   Some actors may know more about a situation than others. Expecting that the resulting bargains would be unfair, "outsiders" will be reluctant to make agreements with "insiders" (Williamson, 1975, pp. 31–33). This is essentially the problem of "quality uncertainty" as discussed by Akerlof. Recall that this is a problem not merely of insufficient information, but rather of *systematically biased* patterns of information, which are recognized in advance of any agreement both by the holder of more information (the seller of the used car) and by its less well-informed prospective partner (the potential buyer of the "lemon" or "creampuff," as the case may be). Awareness that others have greater knowledge than oneself, and are therefore capable of manipulating a relationship or even engaging successful deception and double-cross, is a barrier to making agreements. When this suspicion is unfounded—that is, the agreement would be mutually benefical—it is an obstacle to improving welfare through cooperation.

This problem of asymmetrical information only appears when dishonest behavior is possible. In a society of saints, communication would be open and no one would take advantage of superior information. In our imperfect world, however, asymmetries of information are not rectified simply by communication. Not all communication reduces uncertainty, since communication may lead to asymmetrical or unfair bargaining outcomes as a result of deception. Effective communication is not measured well by the amount of talking that used-car salespersons do to customers or that governmental officials do to one another in negotiating international regimes! The information that is required in entering into an international regime is not merely information about other governments' resources and formal negotiating positions, but also accurate knowledge of their future positions. In part, this is a matter of estimating whether they will keep their commitments. As the "market for lemons" example suggests, and as we will see in more detail below, a government's reputation therefore becomes an important asset in persuading others to enter into agreements with it. International regimes help governments to assess others' reputations by providing standards of behavior against which performance can be measured, by linking these standards to specific issues, and by providing forums, often through international organizations, in which these evaluations can be made.[4] Regimes may also include international organizations whose secretariats act not only as mediators but as providers of unbiased information that is made available, more or less equally to all members. By reducing asymmetries of information through a process of upgrading the general level of available information, international regimes reduce uncertainty. Agreements based on misapprehension and deception may be avoided; mutually beneficial agreements are more likely to be made.

Regimes provide information to members, thereby reducing risks of making agreements. But the information provided by a regime may be insufficiently detailed. A government may require precise information about its prospective partners' internal evaluations of a particular situation, their intentions, the intensity of their preferences, and their willingness to adhere to an agreement even in adverse future circumstances. Governments also need to know whether other participants will follow the spirit as well as the letter of agreements, whether they will share the burden of adjustment to unexpected adverse change, and whether they are likely to seek to strengthen the regime in the future.

The significance of asymmetrical information and quality uncertainty in theories of market failure therefore calls attention to the importance not only of international regimes but also of variations in the degree of closure of different states' decisionmaking processes. Some governments maintain secrecy much more zealously than others. American officials, for example, often lament that the U.S. government leaks information "like a sieve" and claim that this openness puts the United States at a disadvantage vis-à-vis its rivals.

Surely there are disadvantages in openness. The real or apparent incoherence in policy that often accompanies it may lead the open government's partners to view it as unreliable because its top leaders, whatever their intentions, are incapable of carrying out their agreements. A cacophony of messages may render all of them uninterpretable. But some reflection on the problem of making agreements in world politics suggests that there are advantages for the open government that cannot be duplicated by countries with more tightly closed bureaucracies. Governments that cannot provide detailed and reliable information about their intentions—for instance, because their decisionmaking processes are closed to the outside world and their officials are prevented from developing frank informal relationships with their foreign counterparts—may be unable convincingly to persuade their potential partners of their commitment to the contemplated arrangements. Observers from other countries will be uncertain about the genuineness of officials' enthusiasm or the depth of their support for the cooperative scheme under consideration. These potential partners will therefore insist on discounting the value of prospective agreements to take account of their uncertainty. As in the "market for lemons," some potential agreements, which would be beneficial to all parties, will not be made because of "quality uncertainty"—about the quality of the closed government's commitment to the accord.[5]

MORAL HAZARD Agreements may alter incentives in such a way as to encourage less cooperative behavior. Insurance companies face this problem of "moral hazard." Property insurance, for instance, may make people less careful with their property and therefore increase the risk of loss (Arrow, 1974). The problem of moral hazard arises quite sharply in international banking. The solvency of a major country's largest banks may be essential to its financial system, or even to the stability of the entire international banking network. As a result, the country's central bank may have to intervene if one of these banks is threatened. The U.S. Federal Reserve, for instance, could hardly stand idly by while the Bank of America or Citibank became unable to meet its liabilities. Yet this responsibility creates a problem of moral hazard, since the largest banks, in effect, have automatic insurance against disastrous consequences of risky but (in the short-run at least) profitable loans. They have incentives to follow risk-seeking rather than risk-averse behavior at the expense of the central bank (Hirsch, 1977).

IRRESPONSIBILITY Some actors may be irresponsible, making commitments that they may not be able to carry out. Governments or firms may enter into agreements that they intend to keep, assuming that the environment will continue to be benign; if adversity sets in, they may be unable to keep their commitments. Banks regularly face this problem, leading them to devise standards of creditworthiness. Large governments trying to gain adherents to international agreements may face similar difficulties: countries that are enthusiastic about cooperation are likely to be those that expect to gain more, proportionately, than they contribute. This is a problem of self-selection, as discussed in the market-failure literature. For instance, if rates are not properly adjusted, people with high risks of heart attack will seek life insurance more avidly than those with longer life expectancies; people who purchased "lemons" will tend to sell them earlier on the used-car market than people with "creampuffs" (Akerlof, 1970; Arrow, 1974). In international politics, self-selection means that for certain types of activities—such as sharing research and development information—weak states (with much to gain but little to give) may have more incentive to participate than strong ones, but less incentive actually to spend funds on research and developments.[6] Without the strong states, the enterprise as a whole will fail.

From the perspective of the outside observer, irresponsibility is an aspect of the problem of public goods and free-riding; but from the standpoint of the actor trying to determine whether to rely on a potentially irresponsible partner, it is a problem of uncertainty. Either way, informational costs and asymmetries may prevent mutually beneficial agreement.

REGIMES AND MARKET FAILURE

International regimes help states to deal with all of these problems. As the principles and rules of a regime reduce the range of expected behavior, uncertainty declines, and as information becomes more widely available, the asymmetry of its distribution is likely to lessen. Arrangements within regimes to monitor actors' behavior * * * mitigate problems of moral hazard. Linkages among particular issues within the context of regimes raise the costs of deception and irresponsibility, since the consequences of such behavior are likely to extend beyond the issue on which they are manifested. Close ties among officials involved in managing international regimes increase the ability of governments to make mutually beneficial agreements, because intergovernmental relationships characterized by ongoing communication among working-level officials, informal as well as formal, are inherently more conducive to exchange of information than are traditional relationships between closed bureaucracies. In general, regimes make it more sensible to cooperate by lowering the likelihood of being double-crossed. Whether we view this problem through the lens of game theory or that of market failure, the central conclusion is the same: international regimes can facilitate cooperation by reducing uncertainty. Like international law, broadly defined, their function is "to make human actions conform to predictable patterns so that contemplated actions can go forward with some hope of achieving a rational relationship between means and ends" (Barkun, 1968, p. 154).

Thus international regimes are useful to governments. Far from being threats to governments (in which case it would be hard to understand why they exist at all), they permit governments to attain objectives that would otherwise be unattainable. They do so in part by facilitating intergovernmental agreements. Regimes facilitate agreements by raising the anticipated costs of violating others' property rights, by altering transaction costs through the clustering of issues, and by providing reliable information to members. Regimes are relatively efficient institutions, compared with the alternative of having a myriad of unrelated agreements, since their principles, rules, and institutions create linkages among issues that give actors incentives to reach mutually beneficial agreements. They thrive in situations where states have common as well as conflicting interests on multiple, overlapping issues and where externalities are difficult but not impossible to deal with through bargaining. Where these conditions exist, international regimes can be of value to states.

We have seen that it does not follow from this argument that regimes necessarily increase global welfare. They can be used to pursue particularistic and parochial interests as well as more widely shared objectives. Nor should we conclude that all potentially valuable regimes will necessarily be instituted. * * * [E]ven regimes that promise substantial overall benefits may be difficult to invent.

■   ■   ■

Bounded Rationality and Redefinitions of Self-Interest

The perfectly rational decisionmaker * * * may face uncertainty as a result of the behavior of others, or the forces of nature, but she is assumed to make her own calculations costlessly. Yet this individual, familiar in textbooks, is not made of human flesh and blood. Even the shrewdest speculator or the most brilliant scientist faces limitations on her capacity for calculation. To imagine that all available information will be used by a decisionmaker is to exaggerate the intelligence of the human species.

Decisionmakers are in practice subject to limitations on their own cognitive abilities, quite apart from the uncertainties inherent in their environments. Herbert Simon has made this point with his usual lucidity (1982, p. 162):

> Particularly important is the distinction between those theories that locate all the conditions and constraints in the environment, outside the skin of the rational actor, and those theories that postulate important constraints arising from the limitations of the actor himself as an information processor. Theories that incorporate constraints on the information-processing capacities of the actor may be called *theories of bounded rationality*.

Actors subject to bounded rationality cannot maximize in the classical sense, because they are not capable of using all the information that is potentially available. They cannot compile exhaustive lists of alternative courses of action, ascertaining the value of each alternative and accurately judging the probability of each possible outcome (Simon, 1955/1979a, p. 10). It is crucial to emphasize that the source of their difficulties in calculation lies not merely in the complexity of the external world, but in their own cognitive limitations. In this respect, behavioral theories of bounded rationality are quite different from recent neoclassical theories, such as the theories of market failure * * *, which retain the assumption of perfect maximization:

> [In new neoclassical theories] limits and costs of information are introduced, not as psychological

characteristics of the decision maker, but as part of his technological environment. Hence, the new theories do nothing to alleviate the computational complexities facing the decision maker—do not see him coping with them by heroic approximation, simplifying and satisficing, but simply magnify and multiply them. Now he needs to compute not merely the shapes of his supply and demand curves, but in addition, the costs and benefits of computing those shapes to greater accuracy as well. Hence, to some extent, the impression that these new theories deal with the hitherto ignored phenomena of uncertainty and information transmission is illusory. (Simon, 1979b, p. 504)

In Simon's own theory, people "satisfice" rather than maximize. That is, they economize on information by searching only until they find a course of action that falls above a satisfactory level—their "aspiration level." Aspiration levels are adjusted from time to time in response to new information about the environment (Simon, 1972, p. 168). In view of people's knowledge of their own cognitive limitations, this is often a sensible strategy; it is by no means irrational and may well be the best way to make most decisions.

In ordinary life, we satisfice all the time. We economize on information by developing habits, by devising operating rules to simplify calculation in situations that repeat themselves, and by adopting general principles that we expect, in the long run, to yield satisfactory results. I do not normally calculate whether to brush my teeth in the morning, whether to hit a tennis ball directed at me with my backhand or my forehand, or whether to tell the truth when asked on the telephone whether Robert Keohane is home. On the contrary, even apart from any moral scruples I might have (for instance, about lying), I assume that my interests will be furthered better by habitually brushing my teeth, applying the rule "when in doubt, hit it with your forehand because you have a lousy backhand," and adopting the general principle of telling the truth than by calculating the costs and benefits of every alternative in each case. I do not mean to deny that I might occasionally be advantaged by pursuing a new idea at my desk rather than brushing my teeth, hitting a particular shot with my backhand, or lying to an obnoxious salesman on the telephone. If I could costlessly compute the value of each alternative, it might indeed be preferable to make the necessary calculations each time I faced a choice. But since this is not feasible, given the costs of processing information, it is in my long-run interest to eschew calculation in these situations.

Simon's analysis of bounded rationality bears some resemblance to the argument made for rule-utilitarianism in philosophy, which emphasizes the value of rules in contributing to the general happiness.[7] Rule-utilitarianism was defined by John Austin in a dictum: "Our rules would be fashioned on utility; our conduct, on our rules" (Mackie, 1977, p. 136). The rule-utilitarian adopts these rules, or "secondary principles," in John Stuart Mill's terms, in the belief that they will lead, in general, to better results than a series of *ad hoc* decisions based each time on first principles.[8] A major reason for formulating and following such rules is the limited calculating ability of human beings. In explicating his doctrine of utilitarianism, Mill therefore anticipated much of Simon's argument about bounded rationality (1861/1951, p. 30):

> Nobody argues that the art of navigation is not founded on astronomy, because sailors cannot wait to calculate the Nautical Almanack. Being rational creatures, they go to sea with it ready calculated; and all rational creatures go out upon the sea of life with their minds made up on the common questions of right and wrong, as well as on many of the far more difficult questions of wise and foolish. And this, as long as foresight is a human quality, it is to be presumed they will continue to do.

If individuals typically satisfice rather than maximize, all the more so do governments and other large organizations (Allison, 1971; Steinbruner, 1974; Snyder and Diesing, 1977). Organizational decision-making processes hardly meet the requirements of classical rationality. Organizations have multiple goals, defined in terms of aspiration levels; they search until satisfactory courses of action are found; they resort to feedback rather than systematically forecasting future conditions; and they use "standard operating procedures and rules of thumb" to make and implement decisions (Cyert and March, 1963, p. 113; March and Simon, 1958).

The behavioral theory of the firm has made it clear that satisficing does not constitute aberrant behavior that should be rectified where possible; on the contrary, it is intelligent. The leader of a large organization who demanded that the organization meet the criteria of classical rationality would herself be foolish, perhaps irrationally so. An organization whose leaders behaved in this way would become paralyzed unless their subordinates found ways to fool them into believing that impossible standards were being met. This assertion holds even more for governments than for business firms, since governments' constituencies are more varied, their goals more diverse (and frequently contradictory), and success or failure more difficult to measure. Assumptions of unbounded rationality, however dear they may be to the hearts of classical Realist theorists (Morgenthau, 1948/1966) and writers on foreign policy, are idealizations. A large, complex government would tie itself in knots by "keeping its options open," since middle-level bureaucrats would not know how to behave and the top policymakers would be overwhelmed by minor problems. The search for complete flexibility is as quixotic as looking for the Holy Grail or the fountain of youth.

If governments are viewed as constrained by bounded rationality, what are the implications for the functional argument * * * about the value of international regimes? * * * [U]nder rational-choice assumptions, international regimes are valuable to governments because they reduce transaction costs and particularly because they reduce uncertainty in the external environment. Each government is better able, with regimes in place, to predict that its counterparts will follow predictably cooperative policies. According to this theory, governments sacrifice the ability to maximize their myopic self-interest by making calculations on each issue as it arises, in return for acquiring greater certainty about others' behavior.

Under bounded rationality, the inclination of governments to join or support international regimes will be reinforced by the fact that the alternatives to regimes are less attractive than they would be if the assumptions of classical rationality were valid. Actors laboring under bounded rationality cannot calculate the costs and benefits of each alternative course of action on each issue. On the contrary, they need to simplify their own decisionmaking processes in order to function effectively at all. The rules of thumb they devise will not yield better, and will generally yield worse, results (apart from decisionmaking costs) than classically rational action—whether these rules of thumb are adopted unilaterally or as part of an international regime. Thus a comparison between the value of a unilateral rule of thumb and that of a regime rule will normally be more favorable to the regime rule than a comparison between the value of costless, perfectly rational calculation and the regime rule.

When we abandon the assumption of classical rationality, we see that it is not international regimes that deny governments the ability to make classically rational calculations. The obstacle is rather the nature of governments as large, complex organizations composed of human beings with limited problem-solving capabilities. The choice that governments actually face with respect to international regimes is not whether to adhere to regimes at the expense of maximizing utility through continuous calculation, but rather on what rules of thumb to rely. Normally, unilateral rules will fit the individual country's situation better than rules devised multilaterally. Regime rules, however, have the advantage of constraining the actions of others. The question is whether the value of the constraints imposed on others justifies the costs of accepting regime rules in place of the rules of thumb that the country would have adopted on its own.

Thus if we accept that governments must adopt rules of thumb, the costs of adhering to international regimes appear less severe than they would be if classical rationality were a realistic possibility. Regimes merely substitute multilateral rules (presumably somewhat less congenial per se) for unilateral ones, with the advantage that other actors' behavior thereby becomes more predictably cooperative. International regimes neither enforce hierarchical rules on governments nor substitute their own rules for autonomous calculation; instead, they provide rules of thumb in place of those that governments would otherwise adopt.

* * * [W]e can see how different our conception of international regimes is from the self-help system that is often taken as revealing the essence of international politics. In a pure self-help system, each actor calculates its interests on each particular issue, preserving its options until that decision has been made. The rational response to another actor's distress in such a system is to take advantage of it by driving a hard bargain, demanding as much as "the traffic will bear" in return for one's money, one's oil, or one's military support. Many such bargains are in fact struck in world politics, especially among adversaries; but one of the key features of international regimes is that they limit the ability of countries in a particularly strong bargaining position (however transitory) to take advantage of that situation. This limitation, as we have stressed, is not the result of altruism but of the fact that joining a regime changes calculations of long-run self-interest. To a government that values its ability to make future agreements, reputation is a crucial resource; and the most important aspect of an actor's reputation in world politics is the belief of others that it will keep its future commitments even when a particular situation, myopically viewed, makes it appear disadvantageous to do so. Thus even classically rational governments will sometimes join regimes and comply with their rules. To a government seeking to economize on decisionmaking costs, the regime is also valuable for providing rules of thumb; discarding it would require establishing a new set of rules to guide one's bureaucracy. The convenience of rules of thumb combines with the superiority of long-run calculations of self-interest over myopic ones to reinforce adherence to rules by egoistic governments, particularly when they labor under the constraints of bounded rationality.

■   ■   ■

NOTES

1. For an elaborated version of this definition, see Davis and North (1971, p. 16).

2. For the idea of "nesting," I am indebted to Aggarwal (1981). Snidal (1981) also relies on this concept, which was used in a similar context some years ago by Barkun (1968, p. 17).

3. On linkage, see especially the work of Kenneth A. Oye (1979, 1983). See also Stein (1980) and Tollison and Willett (1979).

4. This point was suggested to me by reading Elizabeth Colson's account of how stateless societies reach consensus on the character of individuals: through discussions and gossip that allow people to "apply the standards of performance in particular roles in making an overall judgement about the total person; this in turn allows them to predict future behavior" (1974, p. 53).

5. In 1960 Thomas Schelling made a similar argument about the problem of surprise attack. Asking how we would prove that we were not planning a surprise attack if the Russians suspected we were, he observed that "evidently it is not going to be enough just to tell the truth. . . . There has to be some way of authenticating certain facts, the facts presumably involving the disposition of forces" (p. 247). To authenticate facts requires becoming more open to external monitoring as a way of alleviating what Akerlof [1970] later called "quality uncertainty."

6. Bobrow and Kudrle found evidence of severe problems of collective goods in the IEA's energy research and development program, suggesting that "commercial interests and other national rivalries

appear to have blocked extensive international cooperation" (1979, p. 170).

7. In philosophy, utilitarianism refers to an ethical theory that purports to provide generalizable principles for moral human action. Since my argument here is a positive one, seeking to explain the behavior of egoistic actors rather than to develop or criticize an ethical theory, its relationship to rule-utilitarianism in philosophy, as my colleague Susan Okin has pointed out to me, is only tangential.

8. John Mackie argues that even act-utilitarians "regularly admit the use of rules of thumb," and that whether one follows rules therefore does not distinguish act- from rule-utilitarianism (1977, p. 137). Conversely, Joseph Nye has pointed out to me that even rule-utilitarians must depart at some point from their rules for consequentialist reasons. The point here is not to draw a hard-and-fast dichotomy between the two forms of utilitarianism, but rather to point out the similarities between Mill's notion of relying on rules and Simon's conception of bounded rationality. If all utilitarians have to resort to rules of thumb to some extent, this only strengthens the point I am making about the importance of rules in affecting, but not determining, the behavior of governments. For a succinct discussion of utilitarianism in philosophy, see Urmson (1968).

BIBLIOGRAPHY

* * * *Where a date is given for an original as well as a later edition, the latter was used; page references in the text refer to it.*

Aggarwal, Vinod, 1981. Hanging by a Thread: International Regime Change in the Textile/Apparel System, 1950–1979 (Ph.D. dissertation. Stanford University).

Aivazian, Varouj A., and Jeffrey L. Callen, 1981. The Coase theorem and the empty core. *Journal of Law and Economics*, vol. 24, no. 1 (April), pp. 175–81.

Akerlof, George A., 1970. The market for "lemons." *Quarterly Journal of Economics*, vol. 84, no. 3 (August), pp. 488–500.

Allison, Graham, 1971. *Essence of Decision: Explaining the Cuban Missile Crisis* (Boston: Little, Brown).

Arrow, Kenneth J., 1974. *Essays in the Theory of Risk-Bearing* (New York: North-Holland/American Elsevier).

Barkun, Michael, 1968. *Law without Sanctions: Order in Primitive Societies and the World Community* (New Haven: Yale University Press).

Bobrow, Davis W., and Robert Kudrle, 1979. Energy R & D: in tepid pursuit of collective goods. *International Organization*, vol. 33, no. 2 (Spring), pp. 149–76.

Coase, Ronald, 1960. The problem of social cost. *Journal of Law and Economics*, vol. 3, pp. 1–44.

Colson, Elizabeth, 1974. *Tradition and Contract: The Problem of Order* (Chicago: Aldine Publishing Company).

Conybeare, John A.C., 1980. International organization and the theory of property rights. *International Organization*, vol. 34, no. 3 (Summer), pp. 307–34.

Cyert, Richard, and James G. March, 1963. *The Behavioral Theory of the Firm* (Englewood Cliffs, NJ: Prentice-Hall).

Davis, Lance, and Douglass C. North, 1971. *Institutional Change and American Economic Growth* (Cambridge: Cambridge University Press).

Fellner, William, 1949. *Competition among the Few* (New York: Knopf).

Gilpin, Robert, 1981. *War and Change in World Politics* (Cambridge: Cambridge University Press).

Haas, Ernst B., 1958. *The Uniting of Europe* (Stanford: Stanford University Press).

Hardin, Russell, 1982. *Collective Action* (Baltimore: The Johns Hopkins University Press for Resources for the Future).

Henkin, Louis, 1979. *How Nations Behave: Law and Foreign Policy*, 2nd edition (New York: Columbia University Press for the Council on Foreign Relations).

Hirsch, Fred, 1977. The Bagehot problem. *The Manchester School*, vol. 45, no. 3 (September), pp. 241–57.

Hoffmann, Stanley, 1965. *The State of War: Essays on the Theory and Practice of International Politics* (New York: Praeger).

Hutton, Nicholas, 1975. The salience of linkage in international economic negotiations. *Journal of Common Market Studies*, vol. 13, nos. 1–2, pp. 136–60.

Lewis, David K., 1969. *Convention: A Philosophical Study* (Cambridge: Harvard University Press).

Lowry, S. Todd. 1979. Bargain and contract theory in law and economics. In Samuels, 1979, pp. 261–82.

Mackie, J. L., 1977. *Ethics: Inventing Right and Wrong* (Harmondsworth, England: Penguin Books).

March, James G., and Herbert Simon, 1958. *Organizations* (New York: John Wiley & Sons).

Mill, John Stuart, 1861/1951. *Utilitarianism* (New York: E. P. Dutton).

Mitrany, David, 1975. *The Functional Theory of Politics* (London: St. Martin's Press for the London School of Economics and Political Science).

Morgenthau, Hans J., 1948/1966. *Politics among Nations*, 4th edition (New York: Knopf).

Olson, Mancur, 1965, *The Logic of Collective Action* (Cambridge: Harvard University Press).

Oye, Kenneth A., 1979. The domain of choice. In Oye et al., 1979, pp. 3–33.

Oye, Kenneth A., 1983 Belief Systems, Bargaining and Breakdown: International Political Economy 1929–1934 (Ph.D. dissertation, Harvard University).

Puchala, Donald J., 1975. Domestic politics and regional harmonization in the European Communities. *World Politics*, vol. 27, no. 4 (July), pp. 496–520.

Samuelson, Paul A., 1967. The monopolistic competition revolution. In R. E. Kuenne, ed., *Monopolistic Competition Theory* (New York: John Wiley & Sons).

Schelling, Thomas C., 1960/1980. *The Strategy of Conflict* (Cambridge: Harvard University Press).

Schelling, Thomas C., 1978. *Micromotives and Macrobehavior* (New York: W. W. Norton).

Simon, Herbert A., 1955. A behavioral model of rational choice. *Quarterly Journal of Economics*, vol. 69, no. 1 (February), pp. 99–118. Reprinted in Simon, 1979a, pp. 7–19.

Simon, Herbert A., 1972. Theories of bounded rationality. In Radner and Radner, 1972, pp. 161–76. Reprinted in Simon, 1982, pp. 408–23.

Simon, Herbert A., 1979a. *Models of Thought* (New Haven: Yale University Press).

Simon, Herbert A., 1979b. Rational decision making in business organizations. *American Economic Review*, vol. 69, no. 4 (September), pp. 493–513. Reprinted in Simon, 1982, pp. 474–94.

Simon, Herbert A., 1982. *Models of Bounded Rationality*, 2 vols. (Cambridge: MIT Press).

Snidal, Duncan, 1981. Interdependence, Regimes and International Cooperation (unpublished manuscript).

Snyder, Glenn H., and Paul Diesing, 1977. *Conflict among Nations: Bargaining, Decision making, and System Structure in International Crises* (Princeton: Princeton University Press).

Stein, Arthur A., 1980. The politics of linkage. *World Politics*, vol. 33, no. 1 (October), pp. 62–81.

Steinbruner, John D., 1974. *The Cybernetic Theory of Decision: New Dimensions of Political Analysis* (Princeton: Princeton University Press).

Tollison, Robert D., and Thomas D. Willett, 1979. An economic theory of mutually advantageous issue linkages in international negotiations. *International Organization*, vol. 33, no. 4 (Autumn), pp. 425–49.

Tucker, Robert W., 1977. *The Inequality of Nations* (New York: Basic Books).

Urmson, J. O., 1968. Utilitarianism. *International Encyclopedia of the Social Sciences* (New York: Macmillan), pp. 224–29.

Veljanovski, Cento G., 1982. The Coase theorems and the economic theory of markets and law. *Kyklos*, vol. 35, fasc. 1, pp. 53–74.

Waltz, Kenneth, 1959. *Man, the State and War* (New York: Columbia University Press).

Waltz, Kenneth, 1979. *Theory of World Politics* (Reading, MA: Addison-Wesley).

Williamson, Oliver, 1975. *Markets and Hierarchies: Analysis and Anti-Trust Implications* (New York: The Free Press).

Young, Oran R., 1980. International regimes: problems of concept formation. *World Politics*, vol. 32, no. 3 (April), pp. 331–56.

Young, Oran R., 1983. Regime dynamics: the rise and fall of international regimes. In Krasner, 1983, pp. 93–114.

John J. Mearsheimer

THE FALSE PROMISE OF INTERNATIONAL INSTITUTIONS

■ ■ ■

What Are Institutions?

There is no widely-agreed upon definition of institutions in the international relations literature.[1] The concept is sometimes defined so broadly as to encompass all of international relations, which gives it little analytical bite.[2] For example, defining institutions as "recognized patterns of behavior or practice around which expectations converge" allows the concept to cover almost every regularized pattern of activity between states, from war to tariff bindings negotiated under the General Agreement on Tariffs and Trade (GATT), thus rendering it largely meaningless.[3] Still, it is possible to devise a useful definition that is consistent with how most institutionalist scholars employ the concept.

I define institutions as a set of rules that stipulate the ways in which states should cooperate and compete with each other.[4] They prescribe acceptable forms of state behavior, and proscribe unacceptable kinds of behavior. These rules are negotiated by states, and according to many prominent theorists, they entail the mutual acceptance of higher norms, which are "standards of behavior defined in terms of rights and obligations."[5] These rules are typically formalized in international agreements, and are usually embodied in organizations with their own personnel and budgets.[6] Although rules are usually incorporated into a formal international

organization, it is not the organization *per se* that compels states to obey the rules. Institutions are not a form of world government. States themselves must choose to obey the rules they created. Institutions, in short, call for the "decentralized cooperation of individual sovereign states, without any effective mechanism of command."[7]

■ ■ ■

Institutions in a Realist World

Realists * * * recognize that states sometimes operate through institutions. However, they believe that those rules reflect state calculations of self-interest based primarily on the international distribution of power. The most powerful states in the system create and shape institutions so that they can maintain their share of world power, or even increase it. In this view, institutions are essentially "arenas for acting out power relationships."[8] For realists, the causes of war and peace are mainly a function of the balance of power, and institutions largely mirror the distribution of power in the system. In short, the balance of power is the independent variable that explains war; institutions are merely an intervening variable in the process.

NATO provides a good example of realist thinking about institutions. NATO is an institution, and it certainly played a role in preventing World War III and helping the West win the Cold War. Nevertheless, NATO was basically a manifestation of the bipolar distribution of power in Europe during the

From *International Security* 19, no. 3 (Winter 1994/95): 5–49.
Some of the author's notes have been edited.

Cold War, and it was that balance of power, not NATO *per se*, that provided the key to maintaining stability on the continent. NATO was essentially an American tool for managing power in the face of the Soviet threat. Now, with the collapse of the Soviet Union, realists argue that NATO must either disappear or reconstitute itself on the basis of the new distribution of power in Europe.[9] NATO cannot remain as it was during the Cold War.

■　■　■

Liberal Institutionalism

Liberal institutionalism does not directly address the question of whether institutions cause peace, but instead focuses on the less ambitious goal of explaining cooperation in cases where state interests are not fundamentally opposed.[10] Specifically, the theory looks at cases where states are having difficulty cooperating because they have "mixed" interests; in other words, each side has incentives both to cooperate and not to cooperate.[11] Each side can benefit from cooperation, however, which liberal institutionalists define as "goal-directed behavior that entails mutual policy adjustments so that all sides end up better off than they would otherwise be."[12] The theory is of little relevance in situations where states' interests are fundamentally conflictual and neither side thinks it has much to gain from cooperation. In these circumstances, states aim to gain advantage over each other. They think in terms of winning and losing, and this invariably leads to intense security competition, and sometimes war. But liberal institutionalism does not deal directly with these situations, and thus says little about how to resolve or even ameliorate them.

Therefore, the theory largely ignores security issues and concentrates instead on economic and, to a lesser extent, environmental issues.[13] In fact, the theory is built on the assumption that international politics can be divided into two realms—security and political economy—and that liberal institutionalism mainly applies to the latter, but not the former. * * *

■　■　■

According to liberal institutionalists, the principal obstacle to cooperation among states with mutual interests is the threat of cheating.[14] The famous "prisoners' dilemma," which is the analytical centerpiece of most of the liberal institutionalist literature, captures the essence of the problem that states must solve to achieve cooperation.[15] Each of two states can either cheat or cooperate with the other. Each side wants to maximize its own gain, but does not care about the size of the other side's gain; each side cares about the other side only so far as the other side's chosen strategy affects its own prospects for maximizing gain. The most attractive strategy for each state is to cheat and hope the other state pursues a cooperative strategy. In other words, a state's ideal outcome is to "sucker" the other side into thinking it is going to cooperate, and then cheat. But both sides understand this logic, and therefore both sides will try to cheat the other. Consequently, both sides will end up worse off than if they had cooperated, since mutual cheating leads to the worst possible outcome. Even though mutual cooperation is not as attractive as suckering the other side, it is certainly better than the outcome when both sides cheat.

The key to solving this dilemma is for each side to convince the other that they have a collective interest in making what appear to be short-term sacrifices (the gain that might result from successful cheating) for the sake of long-term benefits (the substantial payoff from mutual long-term cooperation). This means convincing states to accept the second-best outcome, which is mutual collaboration. The principal obstacle to reaching this cooperative outcome will be fear of getting suckered, should the other side cheat. This, in a nutshell, is the problem that institutions must solve.

To deal with this problem of "political market failure," institutions must deter cheaters and protect victims.[16] Three messages must be sent to potential cheaters: you will be caught, you will be punished immediately, and you will jeopardize future cooperative efforts. Potential victims, on the other hand, need early warning of cheating to avoid serious injury, and need the means to punish cheaters.

Liberal institutionalists do not aim to deal with cheaters and victims by changing fundamental norms of state behavior. Nor do they suggest transforming the anarchical nature of the international system. They accept the assumption that states operate in an anarchic environment and behave in a self-interested manner.[17] * * * Liberal institutionalists instead concentrate on showing how rules can work to counter the cheating problem, even while states seek to maximize their own welfare. They argue that institutions can change a state's calculations about how to maximize gains. Specifically, rules can get states to make the short-term sacrifices needed to resolve the prisoners' dilemma and thus to realize long-term gains. Institutions, in short, can produce cooperation.

Rules can ideally be employed to make four major changes in "the contractual environment."[18] First, rules can increase the number of transactions between particular states over time.[19] This *institutionalized iteration* discourages cheating in three ways. It raises the costs of cheating by creating the prospect of future gains through cooperation, thereby invoking "the shadow of the future" to deter cheating today. A state caught cheating would jeopardize its prospects of benefiting from future cooperation, since the victim would probably retaliate. In addition, iteration gives the victim the opportunity to pay back the cheater: it allows for reciprocation, the tit-for-tat strategy, which works to punish cheaters and not allow them to get away with their transgression. Finally, it rewards states that develop a reputation for faithful adherence to agreements, and punishes states that acquire a reputation for cheating.[20]

Second, rules can tie together interactions between states in different issue areas. *Issue-linkage* aims to create greater interdependence between states, who will then be reluctant to cheat in one issue area for fear that the victim—and perhaps other states as well—will retaliate in another issue area. It discourages cheating in much the same way as iteration: it raises the costs of cheating and provides a way for the victim to retaliate against the cheater.

Third, a structure of rules can increase the amount of *information* available to participants in cooperative agreements so that close monitoring is possible. Raising the level of information discourages cheating in two ways: it increases the likelihood that cheaters will be caught, and more importantly, it provides victims with early warning of cheating, thereby enabling them to take protective measures before they are badly hurt.

Fourth, rules can reduce the *transaction costs* of individual agreements.[21] When institutions perform the tasks described above, states can devote less effort to negotiating and monitoring cooperative agreements, and to hedging against possible defections. By increasing the efficiency of international cooperation, institutions make it more profitable and thus more attractive for self-interested states.

Liberal institutionalism is generally thought to be of limited utility in the security realm, because fear of cheating is considered a much greater obstacle to cooperation when military issues are at stake.[22] There is the constant threat that betrayal will result in a devastating military defeat. This threat of "swift, decisive defection" is simply not present when dealing with international economics. Given that "the costs of betrayal" are potentially much graver in the military than the economic sphere, states will be very reluctant to accept the "one step backward, two steps forward" logic which underpins the tit-for-tat strategy of conditional cooperation. One step backward in the security realm might mean destruction, in which case there will be no next step—backward or forward.[23]

* * * There is an important theoretical failing in the liberal institutionalist logic, even as it applies

to economic issues. The theory is correct as far as it goes: cheating can be a serious barrier to cooperation. It ignores, however, the other major obstacle to cooperation: relative-gains concerns. As Joseph Grieco has shown, liberal institutionalists assume that states are not concerned about relative gains, but focus exclusively on absolute gains.[24] * * *

This oversight is revealed by the assumed order of preference in the prisoners' dilemma game: each state cares about how its opponent's strategy will affect its own (absolute) gains, but not about how much one side gains relative to the other. In other words, each side simply wants to get the best deal for itself, and does not pay attention to how well the other side fares in the process.[25] Nevertheless, liberal institutionalists cannot ignore relative-gains considerations, because they assume that states are self-interested actors in an anarchic system, and they recognize that military power matters to states. A theory that explicitly accepts realism's core assumptions—and liberal institutionalism does that—must confront the issue of relative gains if it hopes to develop a sound explanation for why states cooperate.

One might expect liberal institutionalists to offer the counterargument that relative-gains logic applies only to the security realm, while absolute-gains logic applies to the economic realm. Given that they are mainly concerned with explaining economic and environmental cooperation, leaving relative-gains concerns out of the theory does not matter.

There are two problems with this argument. First, if cheating were the only significant obstacle to cooperation, liberal institutionalists could argue that their theory applies to the economic, but not the military realm. In fact, they do make that argument. However, once relative-gains considerations are factored into the equation, it becomes impossible to maintain the neat dividing line between economic and military issues, mainly because military might is significantly dependent on economic might. The relative size of a state's economy has profound consequences for its standing in the international balance of military power. Therefore,

relative-gains concerns must be taken into account for security reasons when looking at the economic as well as military domain. The neat dividing line that liberal institutionalists employ to specify when their theory applies has little utility when one accepts that states worry about relative gains.[26]

Second, there are non-realist (i.e., non-security) logics that might explain why states worry about relative gains. Strategic trade theory, for example, provides a straightforward economic logic for why states should care about relative gains.[27] It argues that states should help their own firms gain comparative advantage over the firms of rival states, because that is the best way to insure national economic prosperity. There is also a psychological logic, which portrays individuals as caring about how well they do (or their state does) in a cooperative agreement, not for material reasons, but because it is human nature to compare one's progress with that of others.[28]

Another possible liberal institutionalist counterargument is that solving the cheating problem renders the relative-gains problem irrelevant. If states cannot cheat each other, they need not fear each other, and therefore, states would not have to worry about relative power. The problem with this argument, however, is that even if the cheating problem were solved, states would still have to worry about relative gains because gaps in gains can be translated into military advantage that can be used for coercion or aggression. And in the international system, states sometimes have conflicting interests that lead to aggression.

There is also empirical evidence that relative-gains considerations mattered during the Cold War even in economic relations among the advanced industrialized democracies in the Organization for Economic Cooperation and Development (OECD). One would not expect realist logic about relative gains to be influential in this case: the United States was a superpower with little to fear militarily from the other OECD states, and those states were unlikely to use a relative-gains advantage to threaten the United States.[29] Furthermore, the OECD states were important American allies during the Cold War, and thus the United States benefited strategically when they gained substantially in size and strength.

Nonetheless, relative gains appear to have mattered in economic relations among the advanced industrial states. Consider three prominent studies. Stephen Krasner considered efforts at cooperation in different sectors of the international communications industry. He found that states were remarkably unconcerned about cheating but deeply worried about relative gains, which led him to conclude that liberal institutionalism "is not relevant for global communications." Grieco examined American and EC efforts to implement, under the auspices of GATT, a number of agreements relating to non-tariff barriers to trade. He found that the level of success was not a function of concerns about cheating but was influenced primarily by concern about the distribution of gains. Similarly, Michael Mastanduno found that concern about relative gains, not about cheating, was an important factor in shaping American policy towards Japan in three cases: the FSX fighter aircraft, satellites, and high-definition television.[30]

I am not suggesting that relative-gains considerations make cooperation impossible; my point is simply that they can pose a serious impediment to cooperation and must therefore be taken into account when developing a theory of cooperation among states. This point is apparently now recognized by liberal institutionalists. Keohane, for example, acknowledges that he "did make a major mistake by underemphasizing distributive issues and the complexities they create for international cooperation."[31]

CAN LIBERAL INSTITUTIONALISM BE REPAIRED?

Liberal institutionalists must address two questions if they are to repair their theory. First, can institutions facilitate cooperation when states seriously care about relative gains, or do institutions only matter when states can ignore relative-gains considerations and focus instead on absolute gains?

I find no evidence that liberal institutionalists believe that institutions facilitate cooperation when states care deeply about relative gains. They apparently concede that their theory only applies when relative-gains considerations matter little or hardly at all.[32] Thus the second question: when do states not worry about relative gains? The answer to this question would ultimately define the realm in which liberal institutionalism applies.

Liberal institutionalists have not addressed this important question in a systematic fashion, so any assessment of their efforts to repair the theory must be preliminary. * * *

■   ■   ■

PROBLEMS WITH THE EMPIRICAL RECORD

Although there is much evidence of cooperation among states, this alone does not constitute support for liberal institutionalism. What is needed is evidence of cooperation that would not have occurred in the absence of institutions because of fear of cheating, or its actual presence. But scholars have provided little evidence of cooperation of that sort, nor of cooperation failing because of cheating. Moreover, as discussed above, there is considerable evidence that states worry much about relative gains not only in security matters, but in the economic realm as well.

This dearth of empirical support for liberal institutionalism is acknowledged by proponents of that theory.[33] The empirical record is not completely blank, however, but the few historical cases that liberal institutionalists have studied provide scant support for the theory. Consider two prominent examples.

Keohane looked at the performance of the International Energy Agency (IEA) in 1974–81, a period that included the 1979 oil crisis.[34] This case does not appear to lend the theory much support. First, Keohane concedes that the IEA failed outright when put to the test in 1979: "regime-oriented efforts at cooperation do not always succeed, as the fiasco of IEA actions in 1979 illustrates."[35] He claims, however, that in 1980 the IEA had a minor success "under relatively favorable conditions" in responding to the outbreak of the Iran-Iraq War. Although he admits it is difficult to specify how much the IEA mattered in the 1980 case, he notes that "it seems clear that 'it [the IEA] leaned in the right direction,'" a claim that hardly constitutes strong support for the theory.[36] Second, it does not appear from Keohane's analysis that either fear of cheating or actual cheating hindered cooperation in the 1979 case, as the theory would predict. Third, Keohane chose the IEA case precisely because it involved relations among advanced Western democracies with market economies, where the prospects for cooperation were excellent.[37] The modest impact of institutions in this case is thus all the more damning to the theory.

Lisa Martin examined the role that the European Community (EC) played during the Falklands War in helping Britain coax its reluctant allies to continue economic sanctions against Argentina after military action started.[38] She concludes that the EC helped Britain win its allies' cooperation by lowering transaction costs and facilitating issue linkage. Specifically, Britain made concessions on the EC budget and the Common Agricultural Policy (CAP); Britain's allies agreed in return to keep sanctions on Argentina.

This case, too, is less than a ringing endorsement for liberal institutionalism. First, British efforts to maintain EC sanctions against Argentina were not impeded by fears of possible cheating, which the theory identifies as the central impediment to cooperation. So this case does not present an important test of liberal institutionalism, and thus the cooperative outcome does not tell us much about the theory's explanatory power. Second, it was relatively easy for Britain and her allies to strike a deal in this case. Neither side's core interests were threatened, and neither side had to make significant sacrifices to reach an agreement. Forging an accord to continue sanctions was not a

difficult undertaking. A stronger test for liberal institutionalism would require states to cooperate when doing so entailed significant costs and risks. Third, the EC was not essential to an agreement. Issues could have been linked without the EC, and although the EC may have lowered transaction costs somewhat, there is no reason to think these costs were a serious impediment to striking a deal.[39] It is noteworthy that Britain and America were able to cooperate during the Falklands War, even though the United States did not belong to the EC.

There is also evidence that directly challenges liberal institutionalism in issue areas where one would expect the theory to operate successfully. The studies discussed above by Grieco, Krasner, and Mastanduno test the institutionalist argument in a number of different political economy cases, and each finds the theory has little explanatory power. More empirical work is needed before a final judgment is rendered on the explanatory power of liberal institutionalism. Nevertheless, the evidence gathered so far is unpromising at best.

In summary, liberal institutionalism does not provide a sound basis for understanding international relations and promoting stability in the post–Cold War world. It makes modest claims about the impact of institutions, and steers clear of war and peace issues, focusing instead on the less ambitious task of explaining economic cooperation. Furthermore, the theory's causal logic is flawed, as proponents of the theory now admit. Having overlooked the relative-gains problem, they are now attempting to repair the theory, but their initial efforts are not promising. Finally, the available empirical evidence provides little support for the theory.

Conclusion

■   ■   ■

The attraction of institutionalist theories for both policymakers and scholars is explained, I believe, not by their intrinsic value, but by their relationship to realism, and especially to core elements of American political ideology. Realism has long been and continues to be an influential theory in the United States.[40] Leading realist thinkers such as George Kennan and Henry Kissinger, for example, occupied key policymaking positions during the Cold War. The impact of realism in the academic world is amply demonstrated in the institutionalist literature, where discussions of realism are pervasive.[41] Yet despite its influence, Americans who think seriously about foreign policy issues tend to dislike realism intensely, mainly because it clashes with their basic values. The theory stands opposed to how most Americans prefer to think about themselves and the wider world.[42]

There are four principal reasons why American elites, as well as the American public, tend to regard realism with hostility. First, realism is a pessimistic theory. It depicts a world of stark and harsh competition, and it holds out little promise of making that world more benign. Realists, as Hans Morgenthau wrote, are resigned to the fact that "there is no escape from the evil of power, regardless of what one does."[43] Such pessimism, of course, runs up against the deep-seated American belief that with time and effort, reasonable individuals can solve important social problems. Americans regard progress as both desirable and possible in politics, and they are therefore uncomfortable with realism's claim that security competition and war will persist despite our best efforts to eliminate them.[44]

Second, realism treats war as an inevitable, and indeed sometimes necessary, form of state activity. For realists, war is an extension of politics by other means. Realists are very cautious in their prescriptions about the use of force: wars should not be fought for idealistic purposes, but instead for balance-of-power reasons. Most Americans, however, tend to think of war as a hideous enterprise that should ultimately be abolished. For the time being, however, it can only justifiably be used for lofty moral goals, like "making the world safe for democracy"; it is morally incorrect to fight wars to change or preserve the balance of power. This makes the realist conception of warfare anathema to many Americans.

Third, as an analytical matter, realism does not distinguish between "good" states and "bad" states, but essentially treats them like billiard balls of varying size. In realist theory, all states are forced to seek the same goal: maximum relative power.[45] A purely realist interpretation of the Cold War, for example, allows for no meaningful difference in the motives behind American and Soviet behavior during that conflict. According to the theory, both sides must have been driven by concerns about the balance of power, and must have done what was necessary to try to achieve a favorable balance. Most Americans would recoil at such a description of the Cold War, because they believe the United States was motivated by good intentions while the Soviet Union was not.[46]

Fourth, America has a rich history of thumbing its nose at realism. For its first 140 years of existence, geography and the British navy allowed the United States to avoid serious involvement in the power politics of Europe. America had an isolationist foreign policy for most of this period, and its rhetoric explicitly emphasized the evils of entangling alliances and balancing behavior. Even as the United States finally entered its first European war in 1917, Woodrow Wilson railed against realist thinking. America has a long tradition of anti-realist rhetoric, which continues to influence us today.

Given that realism is largely alien to American culture, there is a powerful demand in the United States for alternative ways of looking at the world, and especially for theories that square with basic American values. Institutionalist theories nicely meet these requirements, and that is the main source of their appeal to policymakers and scholars. Whatever else one might say about these theories, they have one undeniable advantage in the eyes of their supporters: they are not realism. Not only do institutionalist theories offer an alternative to realism, but they explicitly seek to undermine it. Moreover, institutionalists offer arguments that reflect basic American values. For example, they are optimistic about the possibility of greatly reducing, if not eliminating, security competition among states and creating a more peaceful world. They certainly do not accept the realist stricture that war is politics by other means. Institutionalists, in short, purvey a message that Americans long to hear.

There is, however, a downside for policymakers who rely on institutionalist theories: these theories do not accurately describe the world, hence policies based on them are bound to fail. The international system strongly shapes the behavior of states, limiting the amount of damage that false faith in institutional theories can cause. The constraints of the system notwithstanding, however, states still have considerable freedom of action, and their policy choices can succeed or fail in protecting American national interests and the interests of vulnerable people around the globe. The failure of the League of Nations to address German and Japanese aggression in the 1930s is a case in point. The failure of institutions to prevent or stop the war in Bosnia offers a more recent example. These cases illustrate that institutions have mattered rather little in the past; they also suggest that the false belief that institutions matter has mattered more, and has had pernicious effects. Unfortunately, misplaced reliance on institutional solutions is likely to lead to more failures in the future.

NOTES

1. Regimes and institutions are treated as synonymous concepts in this article. They are also used interchangeably in the institutionalist literature. See Robert O. Keohane, "International Institutions: Two Approaches," *International Studies Quarterly,* Vol. 32, No. 4 (December 1988), p. 384; Robert O. Keohane, *International Institutions and State Power: Essays in International Relations Theory* (Boulder, CO: Westview Press, 1989), pp. 3–4; and Oran R. Young, *International Cooperation: Building Regimes for Natural Resources and the Environment* (Ithaca, NY: Cornell University Press, 1989),

chaps. 1 and 8. The term "multilateralism" is also virtually synonymous with institutions.

2. See Arthur A. Stein, *Why Nations Cooperate: Circumstance and Choice in International Relations* (Ithaca, NY: Cornell University Press, 1990), pp. 25–27. Also see Susan Strange, "*Cave! Hic Dragones:* A Critique of Regime Analysis," in Stephen D. Krasner, ed., *International Regimes,* special issue of *International Organization,* Vol. 36, No. 2 (Spring 1982), pp. 479–96.

3. Oran R. Young, "Regime Dynamics: The Rise and Fall of International Regimes," in Krasner, *International Regimes,* p. 277.

4. See Douglass C. North and Robert P. Thomas, "An Economic Theory of the Growth of the Western World," *The Economic History Review,* 2nd series, Vol. 23, No. 1 (April 1970), p. 5.

5. Krasner, *International Regimes,* p. 186. Non-realist institutions are often based on higher norms, while few, if any, realist institutions are based on norms. The dividing line between norms and rules is not sharply defined in the institutionalist literature. See Robert O. Keohane, *After Hegemony: Cooperation and Discord in the World Political Economy* (Princeton, NJ: Princeton University Press, 1984), pp. 57–58. For example, one might argue that rules, not just norms, are concerned with rights and obligations. The key point, however, is that for many institutionalists, norms, which are core beliefs about standards of appropriate state behavior, are the foundation on which more specific rules are constructed. This distinction between norms and rules applies in a rather straightforward way in the subsequent discussion. Both collective security and critical theory challenge the realist belief that states behave in a self-interested way, and argue instead for developing norms that require states to act more altruistically. Liberal institutionalism, on the other hand, accepts the realist view that states act on the basis of self-interest, and concentrates on devising rules that facilitate cooperation among states.

6. International organizations are public agencies established through the cooperative efforts of two or more states. These administrative structures have their own budget, personnel, and buildings. John Ruggie defines them as "palpable entities with headquarters and letterheads, voting procedures, and generous pension plans." Ruggie, "Multilateralism[: The Anatomy of an Institution]," [*International Organization,* Vol. 46, No. 3 (Summer 1992),] p. 573. Once rules are incorporated into an international organization, "they may seem almost coterminous," even though they are "distinguishable analytically." Keohane, *International Institutions and State Power,* p. 5.

7. Charles Lipson, "Is the Future of Collective Security Like the Past?" in George W. Downs, ed., *Collective Security beyond the Cold War* (Ann Arbor: University of Michigan Press), p. 114.

8. Tony Evans and Peter Wilson, "Regime Theory and the English School of International Relations: A Comparison," *Millennium: Journal of International Studies,* Vol. 21, No. 3 (Winter 1992), p. 330.

9. See Gunther Hellmann and Reinhard Wolf, "Neorealism, Neoliberal Institutionalism, and the Future of NATO," *Security Studies,* Vol. 3, No. 1 (Autumn 1993), pp. 3–43.

10. Among the key liberal institutionalist works are: Robert Axelrod and Robert O. Keohane, "Achieving Cooperation under Anarchy:

Strategies and Institutions," *World Politics,* Vol. 38, No. 1 (October 1985), pp. 226–54; Keohane, *After Hegemony;* Keohane, "International Institutions: Two Approaches," pp. 379–96; Keohane, *International Institutions and State Power,* chap. 1; Lisa L. Martin, *Coercive Cooperation: Explaining Multilateral Economic Sanctions* (Princeton, NJ: Princeton University Press, 1992); Kenneth A. Oye, "Explaining Cooperation Under Anarchy: Hypotheses and Strategies," *World Politics,* Vol. 38, No. 1 (October 1985), pp. 1–24; and Stein, *Why Nations Cooperate.*

11. Stein, *Why Nations Cooperate,* chap. 2. Also see Keohane, *After Hegemony,* pp. 6–7, 12–13, 67–69.

12. Milner, "International Theories of Cooperation [among Nations: Strengths and Weakness]," [*World Politics,* Vol. 44, No. 3 (April 1992),] p. 468.

13. For examples of the theory at work in the environmental realm, see Peter M. Haas, Robert O. Keohane, and Marc A. Levy, eds., *Institutions for the Earth: Sources of Effective International Environmental Protection* (Cambridge, MA: MIT Press, 1993), especially chaps. 1 and 9.

14. Cheating is basically a "breach of promise." Oye, "Explaining Cooperation Under Anarchy," p. 1. It usually implies unobserved non-compliance, although there can be observed cheating as well. Defection is a synonym for cheating in the institutionalist literature.

15. The centrality of the prisoners' dilemma and cheating to the liberal institutionalist literature is clearly reflected in virtually all the works cited in footnote 10. As Helen Milner notes in her review essay on this literature: "The focus is primarily on the role of regimes [institutions] in solving the defection [cheating] problem." Milner, "International Theories of Cooperation," p. 475.

16. The phrase is from Keohane. *After Hegemony,* p. 85.

17. Kenneth Oye, for example, writes in the introduction to an issue of *World Politics* containing a number of liberal institutionalist essays: "Our focus is on non-altruistic cooperation among states dwelling in international anarchy." Oye, "Explaining Cooperation Under Anarchy," p. 2. Also see Keohane, "International Institutions: Two Approaches," pp. 380–81; and Keohane, *International Institutions and State Power,* p. 3.

18. Haas, Keohane, and Levy, *Institutions for the Earth,* p. 11. For general discussions of how rules work, which inform my subsequent discussion of the matter, see Keohane, *After Hegemony,* chaps. 5–6; Lisa L. Martin, "Institutions and Cooperation: Sanctions During the Falkand Islands Conflict," International Security, Vol. 16, No. 4 (Spring 1992), pp. 143–78; and Milner, "International Theories of Cooperation," pp. 474–78.

19. See Axelrod and Keohane, "Achieving Cooperation Under Anarchy," pp. 248–50; [Charles] Lipson, "International Cooperation [in Economic and Security Affairs]," [*World Politics,* Vol. 37, No. 1 (October 1984),] pp. 4–18.

20. Lipson, "International Cooperation," p. 5.

21. See Keohane, *After Hegemony,* pp. 89–92.

22. This point is clearly articulated in Lipson, "International Cooperation," especially pp. 12–18. The subsequent quotations in this paragraph are from ibid. Also see Axelrod and Keohane, "Achieving Cooperation Under Anarchy," pp. 232–33.

23. See Roger B. Parks, "What if 'Fools Die'? A Comment on Axelrod," Letter to *American Political Science Review,* Vol. 79, No. 4 (December 1985), pp. 1173–74.

24. See Grieco, "Anarchy and the Limits of Cooperation[: A Realist Critique of the Newest Liberal Institutionalism,]" [*International Organization,* Vol. 42, No. 3 (Summer 1988)]. Other works by Grieco bearing on the subject include: Joseph M. Grieco, *Cooperation among Nations: Europe, America, and Non-Tariff Barriers to Trade* (Ithaca, NY: Cornell University Press, 1990).

25. Lipson writes: "The Prisoner's Dilemma, in its simplest form, involves two players. Each is assumed to be a self-interested, self-reliant maximizer of his own utility, an assumption that clearly parallels the Realist conception of sovereign states in international politics." Lipson, "International Cooperation," p. 2. Realists, however, do not accept this conception of international politics and, not surprisingly, have questioned the relevance of the prisoners' dilemma (at least in its common form) for explaining much of international relations. See Stephen D. Krasner, "Global Communications and National Power: Life on the Pareto Frontier," *World Politics,* Vol. 43, No. 3 (April 1991), pp. 336–66.

26. My thinking on this matter has been markedly influenced by Sean Lynn-Jones, in his June 19, 1994, correspondence with me.

27. For a short discussion of strategic trade theory, see Robert Gilpin, *The Political Economy of International Relations* (Princeton, NJ: Princeton University Press, 1987), pp. 215–21. The most commonly cited reference on the subject is Paul R. Krugman, ed., *Strategic Trade Policy and the New International Economics* (Cambridge, MA: MIT Press, 1986).

28. See Robert Axelrod, *The Evolution of Cooperation* (New York: Basic Books, 1984), pp. 110–13.

29. Grieco maintains in *Cooperation among Nations* that realist logic should apply here. Robert Powell, however, points out that "in the context of negotiations between the European Community and the United States . . . it is difficult to attribute any concern for relative gains to the effects that a relative loss may have on the probability of survival." Robert Powell, "Absolute and Relative Gains in International Relations Theory," *American Political Science Review,* Vol. 85, No. 4 (December 1991), p. 1319, footnote 26. I agree with Powell. It is clear from Grieco's response to Powell that Grieco includes non-military logics like strategic trade theory in the realist tent, whereas Powell and I do not. See Grieco's contribution to "The Relative-Gains Problem for International Relations," *American Political Science Review,* Vol. 87, No. 3 (September 1993), pp. 733–35.

30. Krasner, "Global Communications and National Power," pp. 336–66; Grieco, *Cooperation among Nations;* and Michael Mastanduno, "Do Relative Gains Matter? America's Response to Japanese Industrial Policy," *International Security,* Vol. 16, No. 1 (Summer 1991), pp. 73–113.

31. Keohane, "Institutional Theory and the Realist Challenge," [in Baldwin, *Neorealism and Neoliberalism,*] p. 292.

32. For example, Keohane wrote after becoming aware of Grieco's argument about relative gains: "Under specified conditions—where mutual interests are low and relative gains are therefore particularly important to states—neoliberal theory expects neorealism to

explain elements of state behavior." Keohane, *International Institutions and State Power*, pp. 15–16.

33. For example, Lisa Martin writes that "scholars working in the realist tradition maintain a well-founded skepticism about the empirical impact of institutional factors on state behavior. This skepticism is grounded in a lack of studies that show precisely how and when institutions have constrained state decisionmaking." Martin, "Institutions and Cooperation," p. 144.

34. Keohane, *After Hegemony*, chap. 10.

35. Ibid., p. 16.

36. Ibid., p. 236. A U.S. Department of Energy review of the IEA's performance in the 1980 crisis concluded that it had "failed to fulfill its promise." Ethan B. Kapstein, *The Insecure Alliance: Energy Crises and Western Politics Since 1944* (New York: Oxford University Press, 1990), p. 198.

37. Keohane, *After Hegemony*, p. 7.

38. Martin, "Institutions and Cooperation." Martin looks closely at three other cases in *Coercive Cooperation* to determine the effect of institutions on cooperation. I have concentrated on the Falklands War case, however, because it is, by her own admission, her strongest case. See ibid., p. 96.

39. Martin does not claim that agreement would not have been possible without the EC. Indeed, she appears to concede that even without the EC, Britain still could have fashioned "separate bilateral agreements with each EEC member in order to gain its cooperation, [although] this would have involved much higher transaction costs." Martin, "Institutions and Cooperation," pp. 174–75. However, transaction costs among the advanced industrial democracies are not very high in an era of rapid communications and permanent diplomatic establishments.

40. See Michael J. Smith, *Realist Thought from Weber to Kissinger* (Baton Rouge: Louisiana State University Press, 1986), chap. 1.

41. Summing up the autobiographical essays of 34 international relations scholars, Joseph Kruzel notes that "Hans Morgenthau is more frequently cited than any other name in these memoirs." Joseph Kruzel, "Reflections on the Journeys," in Joseph Kruzel and James N. Rosenau, eds., *Journeys through World Politics: Autobiographical Reflections of Thirty-four Academic Travelers* (Lexington, MA: Lexington Books, 1989), p. 505. Although "Morgenthau is often cited, many of the references in these pages are negative in tone. He seems to have inspired his critics even more than his supporters." Ibid.

42. See Keith L. Shimko, "Realism, Neorealism, and American Liberalism," *Review of Politics*, Vol. 54, No. 2 (Spring 1992), pp. 281–301.

43. Hans J. Morgenthau, *Scientific Man vs. Power Politics* (Chicago: University of Chicago Press, 1974), p. 201. Nevertheless, Keith Shimko convincingly argues that the shift within realism, away from Morgenthau's belief that states are motivated by an unalterable will to power, and toward Waltz's view that states are motivated by the desire for security, provides "a residual, though subdued optimism, or at least a possible basis for optimism [about international politics]. The extent to which this optimism is stressed or suppressed varies, but it is there if one wants it to be." Shimko, "Realism, Neorealism, and American Liberalism," p. 297. Realists like Stephen Van Evera, for example, point out that although states operate in a dangerous world, they can take steps to dampen security competition and minimize the danger of war. See Van Evera, *Causes of War* [Vol. II: *National Misperception and the Origins of War*, forthcoming].

44. See Reinhold Niebuhr, *The Children of Light and the Children of Darkness: A Vindication of Democracy and a Critique of Its Traditional Defense* (New York: Charles Scribner's, 1944), especially pp. 153–90. See also Samuel P. Huntington, *The Soldier and the State: The Theory and Politics of Civil-Military Relations* (New York: Vintage Books, 1964).

45. It should be emphasized that many realists have strong moral preferences and are driven by deep moral convictions. Realism is not a normative theory, however, and it provides no criteria for moral judgment. Instead, realism merely seeks to explain how the world works. Virtually all realists would prefer a world without security competition and war, but they believe that goal is unrealistic given the structure of the international system. See, for example, Robert G. Gilpin, "The Richness of the Tradition of Political Realism," in Keohane, ed., *Neorealism and Its Critics* [New York: Columbia University Press, 1986], p. 321.

46. Realism's treatment of states as billiard balls of different sizes tends to raise the hackles of comparative politics scholars, who believe that domestic political and economic factors matter greatly for explaining foreign policy behavior.

Margaret E. Keck and Kathryn Sikkink

TRANSNATIONAL ADVOCACY NETWORKS IN INTERNATIONAL POLITICS

World politics at the end of the twentieth century involves, alongside states, many nonstate actors that interact with each other, with states, and with international organizations. These interactions are structured in terms of networks, and transnational networks are increasingly visible in international politics. [Networks are forms of organization characterized by voluntary, reciprocal, and horizontal patterns of communication and exchange.] Some involve economic actors and firms. Some are networks of scientists and experts whose professional ties and shared causal ideas underpin their efforts to influence policy.[1] Others are networks of activists, distinguishable largely by the centrality of principled ideas or values in motivating their formation.[2] We will call these *transnational advocacy networks.* [A transnational advocacy network includes those relevant actors working internationally on an issue who are bound together by shared values, a common discourse, and dense exchanges of information and services.]

Advocacy networks are significant transnationally and domestically. By building new links among actors in civil societies, states, and international organizations, they multiply the channels of access to the international system. In such issue areas as the environment and human rights, they

From Margaret E. Keck and Kathryn Sikkink, *Activists beyond Borders: Advocacy Networks in International Politics* (Ithaca, NY: Cornell University Press, 1998), Chaps. 1, 3.

also make international resources available to new actors in domestic political and social struggles. By thus blurring the boundaries between a state's relations with its own nationals and the recourse both citizens and states have to the international system, advocacy networks are helping to transform the practice of national sovereignty.

■   ■   ■

Transnational advocacy networks are proliferating, and their goal is to change the behavior of states and of international organizations. Simultaneously principled and strategic actors, they "frame" issues to make them comprehensible to target audiences, to attract attention and encourage action, and to "fit" with favorable institutional venues.[3] Network actors bring new ideas, norms, and discourses into policy debates, and serve as sources of information and testimony. * * *

They also promote norm implementation, by pressuring target actors to adopt new policies, and by monitoring compliance with international standards. Insofar as is possible, they seek to maximize their influence or leverage over the target of their actions. In doing so they contribute to changing perceptions that both state and societal actors may have of their identities, interests, and preferences, to transforming their discursive positions, and ultimately to changing procedures, policies, and behavior.[4]

Networks are communicative structures. To influence discourse, procedures, and policy, activists may engage and become part of larger policy communities that group actors working on an issue from a variety of institutional and value perspectives. Transnational advocacy networks must also be understood as political spaces, in which differently situated actors negotiate—formally or informally—the social, cultural, and political meanings of their joint enterprise.

■   ■   ■

Major actors in advocacy networks may include the following: (1) international and domestic nongovernmental research and advocacy organizations; (2) local social movements; (3) foundations; (4) the media; (5) churches, trade unions, consumer organizations, and intellectuals; (6) parts of regional and

Table 7.1. International Nongovernmental Social Change Organizations (Categorized by the Major Issue Focus of their Work)

ISSUE AREA (N)	1953 (N = 110)	1963 (N = 141)	1973 (N = 183)	1983 (N = 348)	1993 (N = 631)
Human rights	33	38	41	79	168
	30.0%	27.0%	22.4%	22.7%	26.6%
World order	8	4	12	31	48
	7.3%	2.8%	6.6%	8.9%	7.6%
International law	14	19	25	26	26
	12.7%	13.4%	13.7%	7.4%	4.1%
Peace	11	20	14	22	59
	10.0%	14.2%	7.7%	6.3%	9.4%
Women's rights	10	14	16	25	61
	9.1%	9.9%	8.7%	7.2%	9.7%
Environment	2	5	10	26	90
	1.8%	3.5%	5.5%	7.5%	14.3%
Development	3	3	7	13	34
	2.7%	2.1%	3.8%	3.7%	5.4%
Ethnic unity/ Group rts.	10	12	18	37	29
	9.1%	8.5%	9.8%	10.6%	4.6%
Esperanto	11	18	28	41	54
	10.0%	12.8%	15.3%	11.8%	8.6%

Source: Union of International Associations, *Yearbook of International Organizations* (1953, 1963, 1973, 1983, 1993). We are indebted to Jackie Smith, University of Notre Dame, for the use of her data from 1983 and 1993, and the use of her coding form and codebook for our data collection for the period 1953–73.

international intergovernmental organizations; and (7) parts of the executive and/or parliamentary branches of governments. Not all these will be present in each advocacy network. Initial research suggests, however, that international and domestic NGOs play a central role in all advocacy networks, usually initiating actions and pressuring more powerful actors to take positions. NGOs introduce new ideas, provide information, and lobby for policy changes.

Groups in a network share values and frequently exchange information and services. The flow of information among actors in the network reveals a dense web of connections among these groups, both formal and informal. The movement of funds and services is especially notable between foundations and NGOs, and some NGOs provide services such as training for other NGOs in the same and sometimes other advocacy networks. Personnel also circulate within and among networks, as relevant players move from one to another in a version of the "revolving door."

■   ■   ■

We cannot accurately count transnational advocacy networks to measure their growth over time, but one proxy is the increase in the number of international NGOs committed to social change. Because international NGOs are key components of any advocacy network, this increase suggests broader trends in the number, size, and density of advocacy networks generally. Table 7.1 suggests that the number of international nongovernmental social change groups has increased across all issues, though to varying degrees in different issue areas. There are five times as many organizations working primarily on human rights as there were in 1950, but proportionally human rights groups have remained roughly a quarter of all such groups. Similarly, groups working on women's rights accounted for 9 percent of all groups in 1953 and in 1993. Transnational environmental organizations have

grown most dramatically in absolute and relative terms, increasing from two groups in 1953 to ninety in 1993, and from 1.8 percent of total groups in 1953 to 14.3 percent in 1993. The percentage share of groups in such issue areas as international law, peace, ethnic unity, and Esperanto, has declined.[5]

■   ■   ■

How Do Transnational Advocacy Networks Work?

Transnational advocacy networks seek influence in many of the same ways that other political groups or social movements do. Since they are not powerful in a traditional sense of the word, they must use the power of their information, ideas, and strategies to alter the information and value contexts within which states make policies. The bulk of what networks do might be termed persuasion or socialization, but neither process is devoid of conflict. Persuasion and socialization often involve not just reasoning with opponents, but also bringing pressure, arm-twisting, encouraging sanctions, and shaming. * * *

Our typology of tactics that networks use in their efforts at persuasion, socialization, and pressure includes (1) *information politics*, or the ability to quickly and credibly generate politically usable information and move it to where it will have the most impact; (2) *symbolic politics*, or the ability to call upon symbols, actions, or stories that make sense of a situation for an audience that is frequently far away;[6] (3) *leverage politics*, or the ability to call upon powerful actors to affect a situation where weaker members of a network are unlikely to have influence; and (4) *accountability politics*, or the effort to hold powerful actors to their previously stated policies or principles.

A single campaign may contain many of these elements simultaneously. For example, the human rights network disseminated information about human rights abuses in Argentina in the period 1976–83. The Mothers of the Plaza de Mayo marched in circles in the central square in Buenos Aires wearing white handkerchiefs to draw symbolic attention to the plight of their missing children. The network also tried to use both material and moral leverage against the Argentine regime, by pressuring the United States and other governments to cut off military and economic aid, and by efforts to get the UN and the Inter-American Commission on Human Rights to condemn Argentina's human rights practices. Monitoring is a variation on information politics, in which activists use information strategically to ensure accountability with public statements, existing legislation and international standards.

■ ■ ■

Network members actively seek ways to bring issues to the public agenda by framing them in innovative ways and by seeking hospitable venues. Sometimes they create issues by framing old problems in new ways; occasionally they help transform other actors' understanding of their identities and their interests. Land use rights in the Amazon, for example, took on an entirely different character and gained quite different allies viewed in a deforestation frame than they did in either social justice or regional development frames. In the 1970s and 1980s many states decided for the first time that promotion of human rights in other countries was a legitimate foreign policy goal and an authentic expression of national interest. This decision came in part from interaction with an emerging global human rights network. We argue that this represents not the victory of morality over self-interest, but a transformed understanding of national interest, possible in part because of structured interactions between state components and networks. * * *

■ ■ ■

Under What Conditions Do Advocacy Networks Have Influence?

To assess the influence of advocacy networks we must look at goal achievement at several different levels. We identify the following types or stages of network influence: (1) issue creation and agenda setting; (2) influence on discursive positions of states and international organizations; (3) influence on institutional procedures; (4) influence on policy change in "target actors" which may be states, international organizations like the World Bank, or private actors like the Nestlé Corporation; and (5) influence on state behavior.

Networks generate attention to new issues and help set agendas when they provoke media attention, debates, hearings, and meetings on issues that previously had not been a matter of public debate. Because values are the essence of advocacy networks, this stage of influence may require a modification of the "value context" in which policy debates takes place. The UN's theme years and decades, such as International Women's Decade and the Year of Indigenous Peoples, were international events promoted by networks that heightened awareness of issues.

Networks influence discursive positions when they help persuade states and international organizations to support international declarations or to change stated domestic policy positions. The role environmental networks played in shaping state positions and conference declarations at the 1992 "Earth Summit" in Rio de Janeiro is an example of this kind of impact. They may also pressure states to make more binding commitments by signing conventions and codes of conduct.

The targets of network campaigns frequently respond to demands for policy change with changes in procedures (which may affect policies in the future). The multilateral bank campaign is largely responsible for a number of changes in internal bank directives mandating greater NGO and local participation in discussions of projects. It also opened access to formerly restricted information, and led to the establishment of an independent inspection panel for World Bank projects. Procedural changes can greatly increase the opportunity for advocacy organizations to develop regular contact with other key players on an issue, and they sometimes offer the opportunity to move from outside to inside pressure strategies.

A network's activities may produce changes in policies, not only of the target states, but also of other states and/or international institutions. Explicit policy shifts seem to denote success, but even here both their causes and meanings may be elusive. We can point with some confidence to network impact where human rights network pressures have achieved cutoffs of military aid to repressive regimes, or a curtailment of repressive practices. Sometimes human rights activity even affects regime stability. But we must take care to distinguish between policy change and change in behavior; official policies regarding timber extraction in Sarawak, Malaysia, for example, may say little about how timber companies behave on the ground in the absence of enforcement.

We speak of stages of impact, and not merely types of impact, because we believe that increased attention, followed by changes in discursive positions, make governments more vulnerable to the claims that networks raise. (Discursive changes can also have a powerfully divisive effect on networks themselves, splitting insiders from outsiders, reformers from radicals.[7]) A government that claims to be protecting indigenous areas or ecological reserves is potentially more vulnerable to charges that such areas are endangered than one that makes no such claim. At that point the effort is not to make governments change their position but to hold them to their word. Meaningful policy change is thus more likely when the first three types or stages of impact have occurred.

Both issue characteristics and actor characteristics are important parts of our explanation of how networks affect political outcomes and the conditions under which networks can be effective. Issue characteristics such as salience and resonance within existing national or institutional agendas can tell us something about where networks are likely to be able to insert new ideas and discourses into policy debates. Success in influencing policy also depends on the strength and density of the network and its ability to achieve leverage. * * *

■ ■ ■

Toward a Global Civil Society?

Many other scholars now recognize that "the state does not monopolize the public sphere,"[8] and are seeking, as we are, ways to describe the sphere of international interactions under a variety of names: transnational relations, international civil society, and global civil society.[9] In these views, states no longer look unitary from the outside. Increasingly dense interactions among individuals, groups, actors from states, and international institutions appear to involve much more than representing interests on a world stage.

We contend that the advocacy network concept cannot be subsumed under notions of transnational social movements or global civil society. In particular, theorists who suggest that a global civil society will inevitably emerge from economic globalization or from revolutions in communication and transportation technologies ignore the issues of agency and political opportunity that we find central for understanding the evolution of new international institutions and relationships.

■ ■ ■

We lack convincing studies of the sustained and specific processes through which individuals and organizations create (or resist the creation of) something resembling a global civil society. Our research leads us to believe that these interactions involve much more agency than a pure diffusionist perspective suggests. Even though the implications of our findings are much broader than most political scientists would admit, the findings themselves do not yet support the strong claims about an emerging global civil society.[10] We are much more comfortable with a conception of transnational civil society as an arena of struggle, a fragmented and contested area where "the politics of transnational civil society is centrally about the way in which certain groups emerge and are legitimized (by governments, institutions, and other groups)."[11]

■ ■ ■

HUMAN RIGHTS ADVOCACY NETWORKS IN LATIN AMERICA

Argentina

Even before the military coup of March 1976, international human rights pressures had influenced the Argentine military's decision to cause political opponents to "disappear," rather than imprisoning them or executing them publicly.[12] (The technique led to the widespread use of the verb "to disappear" in a transitive sense.) The Argentine military believed they had "learned" from the international reaction to the human rights abuses after the Chilean coup. When the Chilean military executed and imprisoned large numbers of people, the ensuing uproar led to the international isolation of the regime of Augusto Pinochet. Hoping to maintain a moderate international image, the Argentine military decided to secretly kidnap, detain, and execute its victims, while denying any knowledge of their whereabouts.[13]

Although this method did initially mute the international response to the coup, Amnesty International and groups staffed by Argentine political exiles eventually were able to document and condemn the new forms of repressive practices. To counteract the rising tide of criticism, the Argentina junta invited AI for an on-site visit in 1976. In March 1977, on the first anniversary of the military coup, AI published the report on its visit, a well-documented denunciation of the abuses of the regime with emphasis on the problem of the disappeared. Amnesty estimated that the regime had taken six thousand political prisoners, most without specifying charges, and had abducted between two and ten thousand people. The report helped demonstrate that the disappearances were part of a deliberate government policy by which the military and the police kidnapped perceived opponents, took them to secret detention centers where they tortured, interrogated, and killed them, then secretly disposed of their bodies.[14] Amnesty International's denunciations of the Argentine regime were legitimized when it won the Nobel Peace Prize later that year.

Such information led the Carter administration and the French, Italian, and Swedish governments to denounce rights violations by the junta. France, Italy, and Sweden each had citizens who had been victims of Argentine repression, but their concerns extended beyond their own citizens. Although the Argentine government claimed that such attacks constituted unacceptable intervention in their internal affairs and violated Argentine sovereignty, U.S. and European officials persisted. In 1977 the U.S. government reduced the planned level of military aid for Argentina because of human rights abuses. Congress later passed a bill eliminating all military assistance to Argentina, which went into effect on 30 September 1978.[15] A number of high-level U.S. delegations met with junta members during this period to discuss human rights.

Early U.S. action on Argentina was based primarily on the human rights documentation provided by AI and other NGOs, not on information received through official channels at the embassy or the State Department.[16] For example, during a 1977 visit, Secretary of State Cyrus Vance carried a list of disappeared people prepared by human rights NGOs to present to members of the junta.[17] When Patricia Derian met with junta member Admiral Emilio Massera during a visit in 1977, she brought up the navy's use of torture. In response to Massera's denial, Derian said she had seen a rudimentary map of a secret detention center in the Navy Mechanical School, where their meeting was being held, and asked whether perhaps under their feet someone was being tortured. Among Derian's key sources of information were NGOs and especially the families of the disappeared, with whom she met frequently during her visits to Buenos Aires.[18]

Within a year of the coup, Argentine domestic human rights organizations began to develop significant external contacts. Their members traveled frequently to the United States and Europe, where they met with human rights organizations, talked to the press, and met with parliamentarians and government officials. These groups sought foreign contacts to publicize the human rights situation, to fund their activities, and to help protect themselves from further repression by their government, and

they provided evidence to U.S. and European policymakers. Much of their funding came from European and U.S.-based foundations.[19]

Two key events that served to keep the case of Argentine human rights in the minds of U.S. and European policymakers reflect the impact of transnational linkages on policy. In 1979 the Argentine authorities released Jacobo Timerman, whose memoir describing his disappearance and torture by the Argentine military helped human rights organizations, members of the U.S. Jewish community, and U.S. journalists to make his case a cause célèbre in U.S. policy circles.[20] Then in 1980 the Nobel Peace Prize was awarded to an Argentine human rights activist, Adolfo Pérez Esquivel. Peace and human rights groups in the United States and Europe helped sponsor Pérez Esquivel's speaking tour to the United States exactly at the time that the OAS was considering the IACHR report on Argentina and Congress was debating the end of the arms embargo to Argentina.

The Argentine military government wanted to avoid international human rights censure. Scholars have long recognized that even authoritarian regimes depend on a combination of coercion and consent to stay in power. Without the legitimacy conferred by elections, they rely heavily on claims about their political efficacy and on nationalism.[21] Although the Argentine military mobilized nationalist rhetoric against foreign criticism, a sticking point was that Argentines, especially the groups that most supported the military regime, thought of themselves as the most European of Latin American countries. The military junta claimed to be carrying out the repression in the name of "our Western and Christian civilization."[22] But the military's intent to integrate Argentina more fully into the liberal global economic order was being jeopardized by deteriorating relations with countries most identified with that economic order, and with "Western and Christian civilization."

The junta adopted a sequence of responses to international pressures. From 1976 to 1978 the military pursued an initial strategy of denying the legitimacy of international concern over human rights in Argentina. At the same time it took actions that appear to have contradicted this strategy, such as permitting the visit of the Amnesty International mission to Argentina in 1976. The "failure" of the Amnesty visit, from the military point of view, appeared to reaffirm the junta's resistance to human rights pressures. This strategy was most obvious at the UN, where the Argentine government worked to silence international condemnation in the UN Commission on Human Rights. Ironically, the rabidly anticommunist Argentine regime found a diplomatic ally in the Soviet Union, an importer of Argentine wheat, and the two countries collaborated to block UN consideration of the Argentine human rights situation.[23] Concerned states circumvented this blockage by creating the UN Working Group on Disappearances in 1980. Human rights NGOs provided information, lobbied government delegations, and pursued joint strategies with sympathetic UN delegations.

By 1978 the Argentine government recognized that something had to be done to improve its international image in the United States and Europe, and to restore the flow of military and economic aid.[24] To these ends the junta invited the Inter-American Commission on Human Rights for an on-site visit, in exchange for a U.S. commitment to release Export-Import Bank funds and otherwise improve U.S.-Argentine relations.[25] During 1978 the human rights situation in Argentina improved significantly. [T]he practice of disappearance as a tool of state policy was curtailed only after 1978, when the government began to take the "international variable" seriously.[26]

The value of the network perspective in the Argentine case is in highlighting the fact that international pressures did not work independently, but rather in coordination with national actors. Rapid change occurred because strong domestic human rights organizations documented abuses and protested against repression, and international pressures helped protect domestic monitors and open spaces for their protest. International groups amplified both information and symbolic politics of domestic groups and projected them onto an international stage, from which they echoed back into Argentina. This classic boomerang process was executed nowhere more skillfully than in Argentina, in large part due to the courage and ability of domestic human rights organizations.

Some argue that repression stopped because the military had finally killed all the people that they thought they needed to kill. This argument disregards disagreements within the regime about the size and nature of the "enemy." International pressures affected particular factions within the military regime that had differing ideas about how much repression was "necessary." Although by the military's admission 90 percent of the *armed* opposition had been eliminated by April 1977, this did not lead to an immediate change in human rights practices.[27] By 1978 there were splits within the military about what it should do in the future. One faction was led by Admiral Massera, a right-wing populist, another by Generals Carlos Suarez Mason and Luciano Menéndez, who supported indefinite military dictatorship and unrelenting war against the left, and a third by Generals Jorge Videla and Roberto Viola, who hoped for eventual political liberalization under a military president. Over time, the Videla-Viola faction won out, and by late 1978 Videla had gained increased control over the Ministry of Foreign Affairs, previously under the influence of the navy.[28] Videla's ascendancy in the fall of 1978, combined with U.S. pressure, helps explain his ability to deliver on his promise to allow the Inter-American Commission on Human Rights visit in December.

The Argentine military government thus moved from initial refusal to accept international human rights interventions, to cosmetic cooperation with the human rights network, and eventually to concrete improvements in response to increased international pressures. Once it had invited IACHR and discovered that the commission could not be co-opted or confused, the government ended the practice of disappearance, released political prisoners, and restored some semblance of political participation. Full restoration of human rights in Argentina did not come until after the Malvinas War and the transition to democracy in 1983, but after 1980 the worst abuses had been curtailed.

In 1985, after democratization, Argentina tried the top military leaders of the juntas for human rights abuses, and a number of key network members testified: Theo Van Boven and Patricia Derian spoke about international awareness of the Argentine human rights situation, and a member of the IACHR delegation to Argentina discussed the OAS report. Clyde Snow and Eric Stover provided information about the exhumation of cadavers from mass graves. Snow's testimony, corroborated by witnesses, was a key part of the prosecutor's success in establishing that top military officers were guilty of murder.[29] A public opinion poll taken during the trials showed that 92 percent of Argentines were in favor of the trials of the military juntas.[30] The tribunal convicted five of the nine defendants, though only two—ex-president Videla, and Admiral Massera—were given life sentences. The trials were the first of their kind in Latin America, and among the very few in the world ever to try former leaders for human rights abuses during their rule. In 1990 President Carlos Menem pardoned the former officers. By the mid-1990s, however, democratic rule in Argentina was firmly entrenched, civilian authority over the military was well established, and the military had been weakened by internal disputes and severe cuts in funding.[31]

The Argentine case set important precedents for other international and regional human rights action, and shows the intricate interactions of groups and individuals within the network and the repercussions of these interactions. The story of the Grandmothers of the Plaza de Mayo is an exemplar of network interaction and unanticipated effects. The persistence of the Grandmothers helped create a new profession—what one might call "human rights forensic science." (The scientific skills existed before, but they had never been put to the service of human rights.) Once the Argentine case had demonstrated that forensic science could illuminate mass murder and lead to convictions, these skills were diffused and legitimized. Eric Stover, Clyde Snow, and the Argentine forensic anthropology team they helped create were the prime agents of international diffusion. The team later carried out exhumations and training in Chile, Bolivia, Brazil, Venezuela, and Guatemala.[32] Forensic science is being used to prosecute mass murderers in El Salvador, Honduras, Rwanda, and Bosnia. By 1996 the UN International Criminal Tribunal for the former Yugoslavia had contracted with two veterans of the Argentine forensic experiment, Stover and Dr. Robert Kirschner, to do forensic investigations for its war crimes tribunal. "'A war crime creates a crime scene,' said Dr. Kirschner, 'That's how we treat it. We recover forensic evidence for prosecution and create a record which cannot be successfully challenged in court.'"[33]

■   ■   ■

Conclusions

A realist approach to international relations would have trouble attributing significance either to the network's activities or to the adoption and implementation of state human rights policies. Realism offers no convincing explanation for why relatively weak nonstate actors could affect state policy, or why states would concern themselves with the internal human rights practices of other states even when doing so interferes with the pursuit of other goals. For example, the U.S. government's pressure on Argentina on human rights led Argentina to defect from the grain embargo of the Soviet Union. Raising human rights issues with Mexico could have undermined the successful completion of the free trade agreement and cooperation with Mexico on antidrug operations. Human rights pressures have costs, even in strategically less important countries of Latin America.

In liberal versions of international relations theory, states and nonstate actors cooperate to realize joint gains or avoid mutually undesirable outcomes when they face problems they cannot resolve alone. These situations have been characterized as cooperation or coordination games with particular payoff structures.[34] But human rights issues are not easily modeled as such. Usually states can ignore the internal human rights practices of other states without incurring undesirable economic or security costs.

In the issue of human rights it is primarily principled ideas that drive change and cooperation. We cannot understand why countries, organizations, and individuals are concerned about human rights or why countries respond to human rights pressures without taking into account the role of norms and ideas in international life. Jack Donnelly has argued that such moral interests are as real as material interests, and that a sense of moral interdependence has led to the emergence of human rights regimes.[35] For human rights * * * the primary movers behind this form of principled international action are international networks.

NOTES

1. Peter Haas has called these "knowledge-based" or "epistemic communities." See Peter Haas, "Introduction: Epistemic Communities and International Policy Coordination," *Knowledge, Power and International Policy Coordination,* special issue, *International Organization* 46 (Winter 1992), pp. 1–36.

2. Ideas that specify criteria for determining whether actions are right and wrong and whether outcomes are just or unjust are shared principled beliefs or values. Beliefs about cause-effect relationships are shared casual beliefs. Judith Goldstein and Robert Keohane, eds., *Ideas and Foreign Policy: Beliefs, Institutions, and*

Political Change (Ithaca: Cornell University Press, 1993), pp. 8–10.

3. David Snow and his colleagues have adapted Erving Goffman's concept of framing. We use it to mean "conscious strategic efforts by groups of people to fashion shared understandings of the world and of themselves that legitimate and motivate collective action." Definition from Doug McAdam, John D. McCarthy, and Mayer N. Zald, "Introduction," *Comparative Perspectives on Social Movements: Political Opportunities, Mobilizing Structures, and Cultural Framings,* ed. McAdam, McCarthy, and Zald (New York: Cambridge University Press, 1996), p. 6. See also Frank Baumgartner and Bryan Jones, "Agenda Dynamics and Policy Subsystems," *Journal of Politics* 53:4 (1991): 1044–74.

4. With the "constructivists" in international relations theory, we take actors and interests to be constituted in interaction. See Martha Finnemore, *National Interests in International Society* (Ithaca: Cornell University Press, 1996), who argues that "states are embedded in dense networks of transnational and international social relations that shape their perceptions of the world and their role in that world. States are *socialized* to want certain things by the international society in which they and the people in them live" (p. 2).

5. Data from a collaborative research project with Jackie G. Smith. We thank her for the use of her data from the period 1983–93, whose results are presented in Jackie G. Smith, "Characteristics of the Modern Transnational Social Movement Sector," in Jackie G. Smith, et al., eds. *Transnational Social Movements and World Politics: Solidarity beyond the State* (Syracuse: Syracuse University Press 1997), and for permission to use her coding form and codebook for our data collection for the period 1953–73. All data were coded from Union of International Associations, *The Yearbook of International Organizations,* 1948–95 (published annually).

6. Alison Brysk uses the categories "information politics" and "symbolic politics" to discuss strategies of transnational actors, especially networks around Indian rights. See "Acting Globally: Indian Rights and International Politics in Latin America," in *Indigenous Peoples and Democracy in Latin America,* ed. Donna Lee Van Cott (New York: St. Martin's Press/Inter-American Dialogue, 1994), pp. 29–51; and "Hearts and Minds: Bringing Symbolic Politics Back In," *Polity* 27 (Summer 1995): 559–85.

7. We thank Jonathan Fox for reminding us of this point.

8. M. J. Peterson, "Transnational Activity, International Society, and World Politics," *Millennium* 21:3 (1992): 375–76.

9. See, for example, Ronnie Lipschutz, "Reconstructing World Politics: The Emergence of Global Civil Society," *Millennium* 21:3 (1992): 389–420; Paul Wapner, "Politics beyond the State: Environmental Activism and World Civic Politics," *World Politics* 47 (April 1995): 311–40; and the special issue of *Millennium* on social movements and world politics, 23:3 (Winter 1994).

10. Sidney Tarrow, *Power in Movement: Social Movements and Contentious Politics,* rev. ed. (Cambridge: Cambridge University Press 1998), Chapter 11. An earlier version appeared as "Fishnets, Internets and Catnets: Globalization and Transnational Collective Action," Instituto Juan March de Estudios e Investigaciones, Madrid: Working Papers 1996/78, March 1996; and Peterson, "Transnational Activity."

11. Andrew Hurrell and Ngaire Woods, "Globalisation and Inequality," *Millennium* 24:3 (1995), p. 468.

12. This section draws upon some material from an earlier co-authored work: Lisa L. Martin and Kathryn Sikkink, "U.S. Policy and Human Rights in Argentina and Guatemala, 1973–1980," in *Double-Edged Diplomacy: International Bargaining and Domestic Politics,* ed., Peter B. Evans, Harold K. Jacobson, and Robert D. Putnam (Berkeley: University of California Press, 1993), pp. 330–62.

13. See Emilio Mignone, *Derechos humanos y sociedad: el caso argentino* (Buenos Aires: Ediciones del Pensamiento Nacional and Centro de Estudios Legales y Sociales, 1991), p. 66; Claudio Uriarte, *Almirante Cero: Biografía No Autorizada de Emilio Eduardo Massera* (Buenos Aires: Planeta, 1992), p. 97; and Carlos H. Acuña and Catalina Smulovitz, "Adjusting the Armed Forces to Democracy: Successes, Failures, and Ambiguities in the Southern Cone," in *Constructing Democracy: Human Rights, Citizenship, and Society in Latin America,* ed. Elizabeth Jelin and Eric Hershberg (Boulder, CO: Westview, 1993), p. 15.

14. Amnesty International, *Report of an Amnesty International Mission to Argentina* (London: Amnesty International, 1977).

15. Congressional Research Service, Foreign Affairs and National Defense Division, *Human Rights and U.S. Foreign Assistance: Experiences and Issues in Policy Implementation (1977–1978),* report prepared for U.S. Senate Committee on Foreign Relations, November 1979, p. 106.

16. After the 1976 coup, Argentine political exiles set up branches of the Argentine Human Rights Commission (CADHU) in Paris, Mexico, Rome, Geneva, and Washington, DC. In October two of its members testified on human rights abuses before the U.S. House Subcommittee on Human Rights and International Organization. Iain Guest, *Behind the Disappearances: Argentina's Dirty War against Human Rights and the United Nations* (Philadelphia: University of Pennsylvania Press, 1990), pp. 66–67.

17. Interview with Robert Pastor, Wianno, Massachusetts, 28 June 1990.

18. Testimony given by Patricia Derian to the National Criminal Appeals Court in Buenos Aires during the trials of junta members. "Massera sonrió y me dijo: Sabe qué pasó con Poncio Pilatos . . . ?" *Diario del Juicio,* 18 June 1985, p. 3; Guest, *Behind the Disappearances,* pp. 161–63. Later it was confirmed that the Navy Mechanical School was one of the most notorious secret torture and detention centers. *Nunca Más: The Report of the Argentine National Commission for the Disappeared* (New York: Farrar Straus & Giroux, 1986), pp. 79–84.

19. The Mothers of the Plaza de Mayo received grants from Dutch churches and the Norwegian Parliament, and the Ford Foundation provided funds for the Center for Legal and Social Studies (CELS) and the Grandmothers of the Plaza de Mayo.

20. Jacobo Timerman, *Prisoner without a Name, Cell without a Number* (New York: Random House, 1981).

21. See Guillermo O'Donnell, "Tensions in the Bureaucratic Authoritarian State and the Question of Democracy," in *The New Authoritarianism in Latin America,* ed. David Collier (Princeton: Princeton University Press, 1979), pp. 288, 292–94.

22. Daniel Frontalini and Maria Cristina Caiati, *El Mito de la Guerra Sucia* (Buenos Aires: Centro de Estudios Legales y Sociales, 1984), p. 24.

23. Guest, *Behind the Disappearances,* pp. 118–19, 182–83.

24. *Carta Política,* a news magazine considered to reflect the junta's views concluded in 1978 that "the principal problem facing the Argentine State has now become the international siege (*cerco internacional*)." "Cuadro de Situación," *Carta Política* 57 (August 1978): 8.

25. Interviews with Walter Mondale, Minneapolis, Minnesota, 20 June 1989, and Ricardo Yofre, Buenos Aires, 1 August 1990.

26. See Asamblea Permanente por los Derechos Humanos, *Las Cifras de la Guerra Sucia* (Buenos Aires, 1988), pp. 26–32.

27. According to a memorandum signed by General Jorge Videla, the objectives of the military government "go well beyond the simple defeat of subversion." The memorandum called for a continuation and intensification of the "general offensive against subversion," including "intense military action." "Directivo 504," 20 April 1977, in "La orden secreta de Videla," *Diario del Juicio* 28 (3 December 1985): 5–8.

28. David Rock, *Argentina, 1516–1987: From Spanish Colonization to Alfonsín* (Berkeley: University of California Press, 1985), pp. 370–71; Timerman, *Prisoner without a Name,* p. 163.

29. *Diario del Juicio* 1 (27 May 1985), and 9 (23 July 1985).

30. *Diario del Juicio* 25 (12 November 1985).

31. Acuña and Smulovitz, "Adjusting the Armed Forces to Democracy," pp. 20–21.

32. Cohen Salama, *Tumbas anónimas [informe sobre la identificación de restos de víctimas de la represión* (Buenos Aires: Catálogos Editora, 1992)], p. 275.

33. Mike O'Connor, "Harvesting Evidence in Bosnia's Killing Fields," *New York Times,* 7 April 1996, p. E3.

34. See, e.g., Arthur A. Stein, "Coordination and Collaboration: Regimes in an Anarchic World," *International Organization* 36:2 (Spring 1982): 299–324.

35. Donnelly, *Universal Human Rights [in Theory and Practice* (Ithaca: Cornell University Press, 1989)], pp. 211–12.

Michael N. Barnett and Martha Finnemore

THE POLITICS, POWER, AND PATHOLOGIES OF INTERNATIONAL ORGANIZATIONS

Do international organizations really do what their creators intend them to do? In the past century the number of international organizations (IOs) has increased exponentially, and we have a variety of vigorous theories to explain why they have been created. Most of these theories explain IO creation as a response to problems of incomplete information, transaction costs, and other barriers to Pareto efficiency and welfare improvement for their members. Research flowing from these theories, however, has paid little attention to how IOs actually behave after they are created. Closer scrutiny would reveal that many IOs stray from the efficiency goals these theories impute and that many IOs exercise power autonomously in ways unintended and unanticipated by states at their creation. Understanding how this is so requires a reconsideration of IOs and what they do.

In this article we develop a constructivist approach rooted in sociological institutionalism to explain both the power of IOs and their propensity for dysfunctional, even pathological, behavior. Drawing on long-standing Weberian arguments about bureaucracy and sociological institutionalist approaches to organizational behavior, we argue that the rational-legal authority that IOs embody gives them power independent of the states that created them and channels that power in particular directions. Bureaucracies, by definition, make rules, but in so doing they also create social knowledge.

From *International Organization* 53, no. 4 (Autumn 1999): 699–732.

They define shared international tasks (like "development"), create and define new categories of actors (like "refugee"), create new interests for actors (like "promoting human rights"), and transfer models of political organization around the world (like markets and democracy). However, the same normative valuation on impersonal, generalized rules that defines bureaucracies and makes them powerful in modern life can also make them unresponsive to their environments, obsessed with their own rules at the expense of primary missions, and ultimately lead to inefficient, self-defeating behavior. We are not the first to suggest that IOs are more than the reflection of state preferences and that they can be autonomous and powerful actors in global politics.[1] Nor are we the first to note that IOs, like all organizations, can be dysfunctional and inefficient.[2] However, our emphasis on the way that characteristics of bureaucracy as a generic cultural form shape IO behavior provides a different and very broad basis for thinking about how IOs influence world politics.[3]

Developing an alternative approach to thinking about IOs is only worthwhile if it produces significant insights and new opportunities for research on major debates in the field. Our approach allows us to weigh in with new perspectives on at least three such debates. First, it offers a different view of the power of IOs and whether or how they matter in world politics. This issue has been at the core of the neoliberal-institutionalists' debate with neorealists for years.[4] We show in this article how neoliberal-institutionalists actually disadvantage themselves in their argument with realists by looking at only one facet of IO power. Global organizations do more than just facilitate cooperation by helping states to overcome market failures, collective action dilemmas, and problems associated with interdependent social choice. They also create actors, specify responsibilities and authority among them, and define the work these actors should do, giving it meaning and normative value. Even when they lack material resources, IOs exercise power as they constitute and construct the social world.[5]

Second and related, our perspective provides a theoretical basis for treating IOs as autonomous actors in world politics and thus presents a challenge to the statist ontology prevailing in international relations theories. Despite all their attention to international institutions, one result of the theoretical orientation of neoliberal institutionalists and regimes theorists is that they treat IOs the way pluralists treat the state. IOs are mechanisms through which others (usually states) act; they are not purposive actors. The regimes literature is particularly clear on this point. Regimes are "principles, norms, rules, and decision-making procedures"; they are not actors.[6] Weber's insights about the normative power of the rational-legal authority that bureaucracies embody and its implications for the ways bureaucracies produce and control social knowledge provide a basis for challenging this view and treating IOs as agents, not just as structure.

Third, our perspective offers a different vantage point from which to assess the desirability of IOs. While realists and some policymakers have taken up this issue, surprisingly few other students of IOs have been critical of their performance or desirability.[7] Part of this optimism stems from central tenets of classical liberalism, which has long viewed IOs as a peaceful way to manage rapid technological change and globalization, far preferable to the obvious alternative—war.[8] Also contributing to this uncritical stance is the normative judgment about IOs that is built into the theoretical assumptions of most neoliberal and regimes scholars and the economic organization theories on which they draw. IOs exist, in this view, only because they are Pareto improving and solve problems for states. Consequently, if an IO exists, it must be because it is more useful than other alternatives since, by theoretical axiom, states will pull the plug on any IO that does not perform. We find this assumption unsatisfying. IOs often produce undesirable and even self-defeating outcomes repeatedly, without punishment much less dismantlement, and we, as theorists, want to understand why. International relations scholars are familiar with principal-agent problems and the ways in which bureaucratic politics can compromise organizational effectiveness, but these approaches have rarely been applied to IOs. Further, these approaches by no means exhaust sources of dysfunction. We examine one such source that flows from the same rational-legal characteristics that make IOs authoritative and powerful. Drawing from research in sociology and anthropology, we show how the very features that make bureaucracies powerful can also be their weakness.

The claims we make in this article flow from an analysis of the "social stuff" of which bureaucracy is made. We are asking a standard constructivist question about what makes the world hang together or, as Alexander Wendt puts it, "how are things in the world put together so that they have the properties they do."[9] In this sense, our explanation of IO behavior is constitutive and differs from most other international relations approaches. This approach does not make our explanation "mere description," since understanding the constitution of things does essential work in explaining how those things behave and what causes outcomes. Just as understanding how the double-helix DNA molecule is constituted materially makes possible causal arguments about genetics, disease, and other biological processes, so understanding how bureaucracies are constituted socially allows us to hypothesize about the behavior of IOs and the effects this social form might have in world politics. This type of constitutive explanation does not allow us to offer law-like statements such as "if *X* happens, then *Y* must follow." Rather, by providing a more complete understanding of what bureaucracy is, we can provide explanations of how certain kinds of bureaucratic behavior are possible, or even probable, and why.[10]

We begin by examining the assumptions underlying different branches of organization theory and exploring their implications for the study of IOs. We argue that assumptions drawn from economics that undergird neoliberal and neorealist treatments of IOs do not always reflect the empirical situation of most IOs commonly studied by political scientists. Further, they provide research hypotheses about only some aspects of IOs (like why they are created) and not others (like what they do). We then introduce sociological arguments that help remedy these problems.

In the second section we develop a constructivist approach from these sociological arguments to examine the power wielded by IOs and the sources of their influence. Liberal and realist theories only make predictions about, and consequently only look for, a very limited range of welfare-improving effects caused by IOs. Sociological theories, however, expect and explain a much broader range of impacts organizations can have and specifically highlight their role in constructing actors, interests, and social purpose. We provide illustrations from the UN system to show how IOs do, in fact, have such powerful effects in contemporary world politics. In the third section we explore the dysfunctional behavior of IOs, which we define as behavior that undermines the stated goals of the organization. International relations theorists are familiar with several types of theories that might explain such behavior. Some locate the source of dysfunction in material factors, others focus on cultural factors. Some theories locate the source of dysfunction outside the organization, others locate it inside. We construct a typology, mapping these theories according to the source of dysfunction they emphasize, and show that the same internally generated cultural forces that give IOs their power and autonomy can also be a source of dysfunctional behavior. We use the term *pathologies* to describe such instances when IO dysfunction can be traced to bureaucratic culture. We conclude by discussing how our perspective helps to widen the research agenda for IOs.

Theoretical Approaches to Organizations

Within social science there are two broad strands of theorizing about organizations. One is economistic and rooted in assumptions of instrumental rationality and efficiency concerns; the other is sociological and focused on issues of legitimacy and power.[11] The different assumptions embedded within each type of theory focus attention on different kinds of questions about organizations and provide insights on different kinds of problems.

The economistic approach comes, not surprisingly, out of economics departments and business schools for whom the fundamental theoretical problem, laid out first by Ronald Coase and more recently by Oliver Williamson, is why we have business firms. Within standard microeconomic logic, it should be much more efficient to conduct all transactions through markets rather than "hierarchies" or organizations. Consequently, the fact that economic life is dominated by huge organizations (business firms) is an anomaly. The body of theory developed to explain the existence and power of firms focuses on organizations as efficient solutions to contracting problems, incomplete information, and other market imperfections.[12]

This body of organization theory informs neoliberal and neorealist debates over international institutions. Following Kenneth Waltz, neoliberals and neorealists understand world politics to be analogous to a market filled with utility-maximizing competitors.[13] Thus, like the economists, they see organizations as welfare-improving solutions to problems of incomplete information and high transaction costs.[14] Neoliberals and realists disagree about the degree to which constraints of anarchy, an interest in relative versus absolute gains, and fears of cheating will scuttle international institutional arrangements or hobble their effectiveness, but both agree, implicitly or explicitly, that IOs help states further their interests where they are allowed to work.[15] State power may be exercised in political battles inside IOs over where, on the Pareto frontier, political bargains fall, but the notion that IOs are instruments created to serve state interests is not much questioned by neorealist or neoliberal scholars.[16] After all, why else would states set up these organizations and continue to support them if they did not serve state interests?

Approaches from sociology provide one set of answers to this question. They provide reasons why, in fact, organizations that are not efficient or effective servants of member interests might exist. In so doing, they lead us to look for kinds of power and sources of autonomy in organizations that economists overlook. Different approaches within sociology treat organizations in different ways, but as a group they stand in sharp contrast to the economists' approaches in at least two important respects: they offer a different conception of the relationship between organizations and their environments, and they provide a basis for understanding organizational autonomy.

IOS AND THEIR ENVIRONMENT

The environment assumed by economic approaches to organizations is socially very thin and devoid of social rules, cultural content, or even other actors beyond those constructing the organization. Competition, exchange, and consequent pressures for efficiency are the dominant environmental characteristics driving the formation and behavior of organizations. Sociologists, by contrast, study organizations in a wider world of nonmarket situations, and, consequently, they begin with no such assumptions. Organizations are treated as "social facts" to be investigated; whether they do what they claim or do it efficiently is an empirical question, not a theoretical assumption of these approaches. Organizations respond not only to other actors pursuing material interests in the environment but also to normative and cultural forces that shape how organizations see the world and conceptualize their own missions. Environments can "select" or favor organizations for reasons other than efficient or responsive behavior. For example, organizations may be created and supported for reasons of legitimacy and normative fit rather than efficient output; they may be created not for what they do but for what they are—for what they represent symbolically and the values they embody.[17]

Empirically, organizational environments can take many forms. Some organizations exist in competitive environments that create strong pressures for efficient or responsive behavior, but many do not. Some organizations operate with clear criteria for "success" (like firms that have balance sheets), whereas others (like political science departments) operate with much vaguer missions, with few clear criteria for success or failure and no serious threat of elimination. Our point is simply that when we choose a theoretical framework, we should choose one whose assumptions approximate the empirical conditions of the IO we are analyzing, and that we should be aware of the biases created by those assumptions. Economistic approaches make certain assumptions about the environment in which IOs are embedded that drive researchers who use them to look for certain kinds of effects and not others. Specifying different or more varied environments for IOs would lead us to look for different and more varied effects in world politics.[18]

IO AUTONOMY

Following economistic logic, regime theory and the broad range of scholars working within it generally treat IOs as creations of states designed to further state interests.[19] Analysis of subsequent IO behavior focuses on processes of aggregating member state preferences through strategic interaction within the structure of the IO. IOs, then, are simply epiphenomena of state interaction; they are, to quote Waltz's definition of reductionism, "understood by knowing the attributes and the interactions of [their] parts."[20]

These theories thus treat IOs as empty shells or impersonal policy machinery to be manipulated by other actors. Political bargains shape the machinery at its creation, states may politick hard within the machinery in pursuit of their policy goals, and the machinery's norms and rules may constrain what states can do, but the machinery itself is passive. IOs are not purposive political actors in their own right and have no ontological independence. To the extent that IOs do, in fact, take on a life of their own, they breach the "limits of realism" as well as of neoliberalism by violating the ontological structures of these theories.[21]

The regimes concept spawned a huge literature on interstate cooperation that is remarkably consistent in its treatment of IOs as structure rather than agents. Much of the neoliberal institutionalist literature has been devoted to exploring the ways in which regimes (and IOs) can act as intervening variables, mediating between states' pursuit of self-interest and political outcomes by changing the structure of opportunities and constraints facing states through their control over information, in particular.[22] Although this line of scholarship accords IOs some causal status (since they demonstrably change outcomes), it does not grant them autonomy and purpose independent of the states that comprise them. Another branch of liberalism has recently divorced itself from the statist ontology and focuses instead on the preferences of social groups as the causal engine of world politics, but, again, this view simply argues for attention to a different group of agents involved in the construction of IOs and competing for access to IO mechanisms. It does not offer a fundamentally different conception of IOs.[23]

The relevant question to ask about this conceptualization is whether it is a reasonable approximation of the empirical condition of most IOs. Our reading of detailed empirical case studies of IO activity suggests not. Yes, IOs are constrained by states, but the notion that they are passive mechanisms with no independent agendas of their own is not borne out by any detailed empirical study of an IO that we have found. Field studies of the European Union provide evidence of independent roles for "eurocrats."[24] Studies of the World Bank consistently identify an independent culture and agendas for action.[25] Studies of recent UN peacekeeping and reconstruction efforts similarly document a UN agenda that frequently leads to conflict with member states.[26] Accounts of the UN High Commission on Refugees (UNHCR) routinely note how its autonomy and authority has grown over the years. Not only are IOs independent actors with their own agendas, but they may embody multiple agendas and contain multiple sources of agency—a problem we take up later.

Principal-agent analysis, which has been increasingly employed by students of international relations to examine organizational dynamics, could potentially provide a sophisticated approach to understanding IO autonomy.[27] Building on theories of rational choice and of representation, these analysts understand IOs as "agents" of states ("principals"). The analysis is concerned with whether agents are responsible delegates of their principals, whether agents smuggle in and pursue their own preferences, and how principals can construct various mechanisms to keep their agents honest.[28] This framework provides a means of treating IOs as actors in their own right with independent interests and capabilities. Autonomous action by IOs is to be expected in this perspective. It would also explain a number of the nonresponsive and pathological behaviors that concern us because we know that monitoring and shirking problems are pervasive in these principal-agent relationships and that these relationships can often get stuck at suboptimal equilibria.

The problem with applying principal-agent analysis to the study of IOs is that it requires a priori theoretical specification of what IOs want. Principal-agent dynamics are fueled by the disjuncture between what agents want and what principals want. To produce any insights, those two sets of interests cannot be identical. In economics this type of analysis is usually applied to preexisting agents and principals (clients hiring lawyers, patients visiting doctors) whose ongoing independent existence makes specification of independent interests relatively straightforward. The lawyer or the doctor would probably be in business even if you and I did not take our problems to them. IOs, on the other hand, are often created by the principals (states) and given mission statements written by the principals. How, then, can we impute independent preferences a priori?

Scholars of American politics have made some progress in producing substantive theoretical propositions about what U.S. bureaucratic agencies want. Beginning with the pioneering work of William Niskanen, scholars theorized that bureaucracies had interests defined by the absolute or relative size of their budget and the expansion or protection of their turf. At first these interests were imputed, and later they became more closely investigated, substantiated, and in some cases modified or rejected altogether.[29]

Realism and liberalism, however, provide no basis for asserting independent utility functions for IOs. Ontologically, these are theories about states. They provide no basis for imputing interests to IOs beyond the goals states (that is, principals) give them. Simply adopting the rather battered Niskanen hypothesis seems less than promising

given the glaring anomalies—for example, the opposition of many NATO and OSCE (Organization for Security and Cooperation in Europe) bureaucrats to those organizations' recent expansion and institutionalization. There are good reasons to assume that organizations care about their resource base and turf, but there is no reason to presume that such matters exhaust or even dominate their interests. Indeed, ethnographic studies of IOs describe a world in which organizational goals are strongly shaped by norms of the profession that dominate the bureaucracy and in which interests themselves are varied, often in flux, debated, and worked out through interactions between the staff of the bureaucracy and the world in which they are embedded.[30]

Various strands of sociological theory can help us investigate the goals and behavior of IOs by offering a very different analytical orientation than the one used by economists. Beginning with Weber, sociologists have explored the notion that bureaucracy is a peculiarly modern cultural form that embodies certain values and can have its own distinct agenda and behavioral dispositions. Rather than treating organizations as mere arenas or mechanisms through which other actors pursue interests, many sociological approaches explore the social content of the organization—its culture, its legitimacy concerns, dominant norms that govern behavior and shape interests, and the relationship of these to a larger normative and cultural environment. Rather than assuming behavior that corresponds to efficiency criteria alone, these approaches recognize that organizations also are bound up with power and social control in ways that can eclipse efficiency concerns.

The Power of IOs

IOs can become autonomous sites of authority, independent from the state "principals" who may have created them, because of power flowing from at least two sources: (1) the legitimacy of the rational-legal authority they embody, and (2) control over technical expertise and information. The first of these is almost entirely neglected by the political science literature, and the second, we argue, has been conceived of very narrowly, leading scholars to overlook some of the most basic and consequential forms of IO influence. Taken together, these two features provide a theoretical basis for treating IOs as autonomous actors in contemporary world politics by identifying sources of support for them, independent of states, in the larger social environment. Since rational-legal authority and control over expertise are part of what defines and constitutes any bureaucracy (a bureaucracy would not be a bureaucracy without them), the autonomy that flows from them is best understood as a constitutive effect, an effect of the way bureaucracy is constituted, which, in turn, makes possible (and in that sense causes) other processes and effects in global politics.

Sources of IO Autonomy and Authority

To understand how IOs can become autonomous sites of authority we turn to Weber and his classic study of bureaucratization. Weber was deeply ambivalent about the increasingly bureaucratic world in which he lived and was well-attuned to the vices as well as the virtues of this new social form of authority.[31] Bureaucracies are rightly considered a grand achievement, he thought. They provide a framework for social interaction that can respond to the increasingly technical demands of modern life in a stable, predictable, and nonviolent way; they exemplify rationality and are technically superior to previous forms of rule because they bring precision, knowledge, and continuity to increasingly complex social tasks.[32] But such technical and rational achievements, according to Weber, come at a steep price. Bureaucracies are

political creatures that can be autonomous from their creators and can come to dominate the societies they were created to serve, because of both the normative appeal of rational-legal authority in modern life and the bureaucracy's control over technical expertise and information. We consider each in turn.

Bureaucracies embody a form of authority, rational-legal authority, that modernity views as particularly legitimate and good. In contrast to earlier forms of authority that were invested in a leader, legitimate modern authority is invested in legalities, procedures, and rules and thus rendered impersonal. This authority is "rational" in that it deploys socially recognized relevant knowledge to create rules that determine how goals will be pursued. The very fact that they embody rationality is what makes bureaucracies powerful and makes people willing to submit to this kind of authority. According to Weber,

> in legal authority, submission does not rest upon the belief and devotion to charismatically gifted persons . . . or upon piety toward a personal lord and master who is defined by an ordered tradition. . . . Rather submission under legal authority is based upon an *impersonal* bond to the generally defined and functional "duty of office." The official duty—like the corresponding right to exercise authority: the "jurisdictional competency"—is fixed by *rationally established* norms, by enactments, decrees, and regulations in such a manner that the legitimacy of the authority becomes the legality of the general rule, which is purposely thought out, enacted, and announced with formal correctness.[33]

When bureaucrats do something contrary to your interests or that you do not like, they defend themselves by saying "Sorry, those are the rules" or "just doing my job." "The rules" and "the job" are the source of great power in modern society. It is because bureaucrats in IOs are performing "duties of office" and implementing "rationally established norms" that they are powerful.

A second basis of autonomy and authority, intimately connected to the first, is bureaucratic control over information and expertise. A bureaucracy's autonomy derives from specialized technical knowledge, training, and experience that is not immediately available to other actors. While such knowledge might help the bureaucracy carry out the directives of politicians more efficiently, Weber stressed that it also gives bureaucracies power over politicians (and other actors). It invites and at times requires bureaucracies to shape policy, not just implement it.[34]

The irony in both of these features of authority is that they make bureaucracies powerful precisely by creating the appearance of depoliticization. The power of IOs, and bureaucracies generally, is that they present themselves as impersonal, technocratic, and neutral—as not exercising power but instead as serving others; the presentation and acceptance of these claims is critical to their legitimacy and authority.[35] Weber, however, saw through these claims. According to him, the depoliticized character of bureaucracy that legitimates it could be a myth: "Behind the functional purposes [of bureaucracy], of course, 'ideas of culture-values' usually stand."[36] Bureaucracies always serve some social purpose or set of cultural values. That purpose may be normatively "good," as Weber believed the Prussian nationalism around him was, but there was no a priori reason to assume this.

In addition to embodying cultural values from the larger environment that might be desirable or not, bureaucracies also carry with them behavioral dispositions and values flowing from the rationality that legitimates them as a cultural form. Some of these, like the celebration of knowledge and expertise, Weber admired. Others concerned him greatly, and his descriptions of bureaucracy as an "iron cage" and bureaucrats as "specialists without spirit" are hardly an endorsement of the bureaucratic form.[37] Bureaucracy can undermine personal freedom in important ways. The very impersonal, rule-bound character that empowers bureaucracy also dehumanizes it. Bureaucracies often exercise their power in repressive ways, in the name of general rules because rules are their raison d'être. This tendency is exacerbated by the way bureaucracies select and reward narrowed professionals seeking secure careers internally—people who are "lacking in heroism, human spontaneity, and inventiveness."[38] Following Weber, we investigate rather than assume the "goodness" of bureaucracy.

Weber's insights provide a powerful critique of the ways in which international relations scholars have treated IOs. The legitimacy of rational-legal authority suggests that IOs may have an authority independent of the policies and interests of states that create them, a possibility obscured by the technical and apolitical treatment of IOs by both realists and neoliberals. * * *

Examples of the ways in which IOs have become autonomous because of their embodiment of technical rationality and control over information are not hard to find. The UN's peacekeepers derive part of their authority from the claim that they are independent, objective, neutral actors who simply implement Security Council resolutions. UN officials routinely use this language to describe their role and are explicit that they understand this to be the basis of their influence. As a consequence, UN officials spend considerable time and energy attempting to maintain the image that they are not the instrument of any great power and must be seen as representatives of "the international community" as embodied in the rules and resolutions of the UN.[39] The World Bank is widely recognized to have exercised power over development policies far greater than its budget, as a percentage of North/South aid flows, would suggest because of the expertise it houses. While competing sites of expertise in development have proliferated in recent years, for decades after its founding the World Bank was a magnet for the "best and brightest" among "development experts." Its staff had and continues to have impressive credentials from the most prestigious universities and the elaborate models, reports, and research groups it has sponsored over the years were widely influential among the "development experts" in the field. This expertise, coupled with its claim to "neutrality" and its "apolitical" technocratic decision-making style, have given the World Bank an authoritative voice with which it has successfully dictated the content, direction, and scope of global development over the past fifty years.[40] Similarly, official standing and long experience with relief efforts have endowed the UNHCR with "expert" status and consequent authority in refugee matters. This expertise, coupled with its role in implementing international refugee conventions and law ("the rules" regarding refugees), has allowed the UNHCR to make life and death decisions about refugees without consulting the refugees, themselves, and to compromise the authority of states in various ways in setting up refugee camps.[41] Note that, as these examples show, technical knowledge and expertise need not be "scientific" in nature to create autonomy and power for IOs.

The Power of IOs

If IOs have autonomy and authority in the world, what do they do with it? A growing body of research in sociology and anthropology has examined ways in which IOs exercise power by virtue of their culturally constructed status as sites of authority; we distill from this research three broad types of IO power. We examine how IOs (1) classify the world, creating categories of actors and action; (2) fix meanings in the social world; and (3) articulate and diffuse new norms, principles, and actors around the globe. All of these sources of power flow from the ability of IOs to structure knowledge.[42]

CLASSIFICATION

An elementary feature of bureaucracies is that they classify and organize information and knowledge. This classification process is bound up with power. "Bureaucracies," writes Don Handelman, "are ways of making, ordering, and knowing social worlds." They do this by "moving persons among social categories or by inventing and applying such categories."[43] The ability to classify objects, to shift their very definition and identity, is one of bureaucracy's greatest sources of power. This power is frequently treated by the objects of that power as accomplished through caprice and without regard to their circumstances but is legitimated and justified by bureaucrats with reference to the rules and regulations of the bureaucracy. Consequences of this bureaucratic exercise of power may be identity defining, or even life threatening.

Consider the evolving definition of "refugee." The category "refugee" is not at all straightforward and must be distinguished from other categories of individuals who are "temporarily" and "involuntarily" living outside their country of origin—displaced persons, exiles, economic migrants, guest workers, diaspora communities, and those seeking political asylum. The debate over the meaning of "refugee" has been waged in and around the UNHCR. The UNHCR's legal and operational definition of the category strongly influences decisions about who is a refugee and shapes UNHCR staff decisions in the field—decisions that have a tremendous effect on the life circumstance of thousands of people.[44] These categories are not only political and legal but also discursive, shaping a view among UNHCR officials that refugees must, by definition, be powerless, and that as powerless actors they do not have to be consulted in decisions such as asylum and repatriation that will directly and dramatically affect them.[45] Guy Gran similarly describes how the World Bank sets up criteria to define someone as a peasant in order to distinguish them from a farmer, day laborer, and other categories. The classification matters because only certain classes of people are recognized by the World Bank's development machinery as having knowledge that is relevant in solving development problems.[46] Categorization and classification are a ubiquitous feature of bureaucratization that has potentially important implications for those being classified. To classify is to engage in an act of power.

THE FIXING OF MEANINGS

IOs exercise power by virtue of their ability to fix meanings, which is related to classification.[47] Naming or labeling the social context establishes the parameters, the very boundaries, of acceptable action. Because actors are oriented toward objects and objectives on the basis of the meaning that they have for them, being able to invest situations with a particular meaning constitutes an important source of power.[48] IOs do not act alone in this regard, but their organizational resources contribute mightily to this end.

There is strong evidence of this power from development studies. Arturo Escobar explores how the institutionalization of the concept of "development" after World War II spawned a huge international apparatus and how this apparatus has now spread its tentacles in domestic and international politics through the discourse of development. The discourse of development, created and arbitrated in large part by IOs, determines not only what constitutes the activity (what development is) but also who (or what) is considered powerful and privileged, that is, who gets to do the developing (usually the state or IOs) and who is the object of development (local groups).[49]

Similarly, the end of the Cold War encouraged a reexamination of the definition of security.[50] IOs have been at the forefront of this debate, arguing that security pertains not only to states but also to individuals and that the threats to security may be economic, environmental, and political as well as military.[51] In forwarding these alternative definitions of security, officials from various IOs are empowering a different set of actors and legitimating an alternative set of practices. Specifically, when security meant safety from invading national armies, it privileged state officials and invested power in military establishments. These alternative definitions of security shift attention away from states and toward the individuals who are frequently threatened by their own government, away from military practices and toward other features of social life that might represent a more immediate and daily danger to the lives of individuals.

One consequence of these redefined meanings of development and security is that they legitimate, and even require, increased levels of IO intervention in the domestic affairs of states—particularly Third World states. This is fairly obvious in the realm of development. The World Bank, the International Monetary Fund (IMF), and other development institutions have established a web of interventions that affect nearly every phase of the economy and polity in many Third World states. As "rural development," "basic human needs," and "structural adjustment" became incorporated into the meaning of development, IOs were permitted, even required, to become intimately involved in the domestic workings of developing polities by posting in-house "advisors" to run monetary policy, reorganizing the political economy of entire rural regions, regulating family and reproductive practices, and mediating between governments and their citizens in a variety of ways.[52]

■ ■ ■

DIFFUSION OF NORMS

Having established rules and norms, IOs are eager to spread the benefits of their expertise and often act as conveyor belts for the transmission of norms and models of "good" political behavior.[53] There is nothing accidental or unintended about this role.

Officials in IOs often insist that part of their mission is to spread, inculcate, and enforce global values and norms. They are the "missionaries" of our time. Armed with a notion of progress, an idea of how to create the better life, and some understanding of the conversion process, many IO elites have as their stated purpose a desire to shape state practices by establishing, articulating, and transmitting norms that define what constitutes acceptable and legitimate state behavior. To be sure, their success depends on more than their persuasive capacities, for their rhetoric must be supported by power, sometimes (but not always) state power. But to overlook how state power and organizational missionaries work in tandem and the ways in which IO officials channel and shape states' exercise of power is to disregard a fundamental feature of value diffusion.[54]

Consider decolonization as an example. The UN Charter announced an intent to universalize sovereignty as a constitutive principle of the society of states at a time when over half the globe was under some kind of colonial rule; it also established an institutional apparatus to achieve that end (most prominently the Trusteeship Council and the Special Committee on Colonialism). These actions had several consequences. One was to eliminate certain categories of acceptable action for powerful states. Those states that attempted to retain their colonial privileges were increasingly viewed as illegitimate by other states. Another consequence was to empower international bureaucrats (at the Trusteeship Council) to set norms and standards for "stateness." Finally, the UN helped to ensure that throughout decolonization the sovereignty of these new states was coupled with territorial inviolability. Colonial boundaries often divided ethnic and tribal groups, and the UN was quite concerned that in the process of "self-determination," these governments containing "multiple" or "partial" selves might attempt to create a whole personality through territorial adjustment—a fear shared by many of these newly decolonized states. The UN encouraged the acceptance of the norm of sovereignty-as-territorial-integrity through resolutions, monitoring devices, commissions, and one famous peacekeeping episode in Congo in the 1960s.[55]

Note that, as with other IO powers, norm diffusion, too, has an expansionary dynamic. Developing states continue to be popular targets for norm diffusion by IOs, even after they are independent. The UN and the European Union are now actively involved in police training in non-Western states because they believe Western policing practices will be more conducive to democratization processes and the establishment of civil society. But having a professional police establishment assumes that there is a professional judiciary and penal system where criminals can be tried and jailed; and a professional judiciary, in turn, presupposes that there are lawyers that can come before the court. Trained lawyers presuppose a code of law. The result is a package of reforms sponsored by IOs aimed at transforming non-Western societies into Western societies.[56] Again, while Western states are involved in these activities and therefore their values and interests are part of the reasons for this process, international bureaucrats involved in these activities may not see themselves as doing the bidding for these states but rather as expressing the interests and values of the bureaucracy.

Other examples of this kind of norm diffusion are not hard to find. The IMF and the World Bank are explicit about their role as transmitters of norms and principles from advanced market economies to less-developed economies.[57] The IMF's Articles of Agreement specifically assign it this task of incorporating less-developed economies into the world economy, which turns out to mean teaching them how to "be" market economies. The World Bank, similarly, has a major role in arbitrating the meaning of development and norms of behavior appropriate to the task of developing oneself, as was discussed earlier. The end of the Cold War has opened up a whole new set of states to this kind of norm diffusion task for IOs. According to former Secretary of Defense William Perry, one of the functions of NATO expansion is to inculcate "modern" values and norms into the Eastern European countries and their militaries.[58]

■ ■ ■

The Pathologies of IOs

Bureaucracies are created, propagated, and valued in modern society because of their supposed rationality and effectiveness in carrying out social tasks. These same considerations presumably also apply to IOs. Ironically, though, the folk wisdom about bureaucracies is that they are inefficient and unresponsive. Bureaucracies are infamous for creating and implementing policies that defy rational logic, for acting in ways that are at odds with their stated mission, and for refusing requests of and turning their backs on those to whom they are officially responsible.[59] Scholars of U.S. bureaucracy have recognized this problem and have devoted considerable energy to understanding a wide range of undesirable and inefficient bureaucratic behaviors caused by bureaucratic capture and slack and to exploring the conditions under which "suboptimal equilibria" may arise in organizational structures. Similarly, scholars researching foreign policy decision making and, more recently, those interested in learning in foreign policy have investigated organizational dynamics that produce self-defeating and inefficient behavior in those contexts.[60]

IOs, too, are prone to dysfunctional behaviors, but international relations scholars have rarely investigated this, in part, we suspect, because the theoretical apparatus they use provides few grounds for expecting undesirable IO behavior.[61] The state-centric utility-maximizing frameworks most international relations scholars have borrowed from economics simply assume that IOs are reasonably responsive to state interests (or, at least, more responsive than alternatives), otherwise states would withdraw from them. This assumption, however, is a necessary theoretical axiom of these frameworks; it is rarely treated as a hypothesis subject to empirical investigation.[62] With little theoretical reason to expect suboptimal or self-defeating behavior in IOs, these scholars do not look for it and have had little to say about it. Policymakers, however, have been quicker to perceive and address these problems and are putting them on the political agenda. It is time for scholars, too, to begin to explore these issues more fully.

In this section we present several bodies of theorizing that might explain dysfunctional IO behavior, which we define as behavior that undermines the IO's stated objectives. Thus our vantage point for judging dysfunction (and later pathology) is the publicly proclaimed mission of the organization. There may be occasions when overall organizational dysfunction is, in fact, functional for certain members or others involved in the IO's work, but given our analysis of the way claims of efficiency and effectiveness act to legitimate rational-legal authority in our culture, whether organizations actually do what they claim and accomplish their missions is a particularly important issue to examine. Several bodies of theory provide some basis for understanding dysfunctional behavior by IOs, each of which emphasizes a different locus of causality for such behavior. Analyzing these causes, we construct a typology of these explanations that locates them in relation to one another. Then, drawing on the work of James March and Johan Olsen, Paul DiMaggio, and Walter Powell, and other sociological institutionalists, we elaborate how the same sources of bureaucratic power, sketched earlier, can cause dysfunctional behavior. We term this particular type of dysfunction *pathology*.[63] We identify five features of bureaucracy that might produce pathology, and using examples from the UN system we illustrate the way these might work in IOs.

Extant theories about dysfunction can be categorized in two dimensions: (1) whether they locate the cause of IO dysfunction inside or outside the organization, and (2) whether they trace the causes to material or cultural forces. Mapping theories on these dimensions creates the typology shown in Figure 7.1.

Within each cell we have identified a representative body of theory familiar to most international relations scholars. Explanations of IO dysfunction that emphasize the pursuit of material interests within an organization typically examine how competition among subunits over material resources leads the organization to make decisions and engage in behaviors that are inefficient or undesirable as judged against some ideal policy that would better allow the IO to achieve its stated goals. Bureaucratic politics is the best-known theory here, and though current scholars of international politics have not widely adopted this perspective to explain IO behavior, it is relatively well developed in the older IO literature.[64] Graham Allison's central argument is that the "name of the game is politics: bargaining along regularized circuits among players positioned hierarchically within the government. Government behavior can thus be understood as . . . results of these bargaining games."[65] In this view, decisions are not made after a rational decision process but rather through a competitive bargaining process over turf,

budgets, and staff that may benefit parts of the organization at the expense of overall goals.

Another body of literature traces IO dysfunctional behavior to the material forces located outside the organization. Realist and neoliberal theories might posit that state preferences and constraints are responsible for understanding IO dysfunctional behavior. In this view IOs are not to blame for bad outcomes, states are. IOs do not have the luxury of choosing the optimal policy but rather are frequently forced to chose between the bad and the awful because more desirable policies are denied to them by states who do not agree among themselves and/or do not wish to see the IO fulfill its mandate in some particular instance. As Robert Keohane observed, IOs often engage in policies not because they are strong and have autonomy but because they are weak and have none.[66] The important point of these theories is that they trace IO dysfunctional behavior back to the environmental conditions established by, or the explicit preferences of, states.

Cultural theories also have internal and external variants. We should note that many advocates of cultural theories would reject the claim that an organization can be understood apart from its environment or that culture is separable from the material world. Instead they would stress how the

Figure 7.1. Theories of International Organization Dysfunction

	Internal	External
Material	Bureaucratic politics	Realism/ neoliberal institutionalism
Cultural	Bureaucratic culture	World polity model

organization is permeated by that environment, defined in both material and cultural terms, in which it is embedded. Many are also quite sensitive to the ways in which resource constraints and the material power of important actors will shape organizational culture. That said, these arguments clearly differ from the previous two types in their emphasis on ideational and cultural factors and clearly differ among themselves in the motors of behavior emphasized. For analytical clarity we divide cultural theories according to whether they see the primary causes of the IO's dysfunctional behavior as deriving from the culture of the organization (internal) or of the environment (external).

The world polity model exemplifies theories that look to external culture to understand an IO's dysfunctional behavior. There are two reasons to expect dysfunctional behavior here. First, because IO practices reflect a search for symbolic legitimacy rather than efficiency, IO behavior might be only remotely connected to the efficient implementation of its goals and more closely coupled to legitimacy criteria that come from the cultural environment.[67] For instance, many arms-export control regimes now have a multilateral character not because of any evidence that this architecture is the most efficient way to monitor and prevent arms exports but rather because multilateralism has attained a degree of legitimacy that is not empirically connected to any efficiency criteria.[68] Second, the world polity is full of contradictions; for instance, a liberal world polity has several defining principles, including market economics and human equality, that might conflict at any one moment. Thus, environments are often ambiguous about missions and contain varied, often conflicting, functional, normative, and legitimacy imperatives.[69] Because they are embedded in that cultural environment, IOs can mirror and reproduce those contradictions, which, in turn, can lead to contradictory and ultimately dysfunctional behavior.

Finally, organizations frequently develop distinctive internal cultures that can promote dysfunctional behavior, behavior that we call "pathological." The basic logic of this argument flows directly from our previous observations about the nature of bureaucracy as a social form. Bureaucracies are established as rationalized means to accomplish collective goals and to spread particular values. To do this, bureaucracies create social knowledge and develop expertise as they act upon the world (and thus exercise power). But the way bureaucracies are constituted to accomplish these ends can, ironically, create a cultural disposition toward undesirable and ultimately self-defeating behavior.[70] Two features of the modern bureaucratic form are particularly important in this regard. The first is the simple fact that bureaucracies are organized around rules, routines, and standard operating procedures designed to trigger a standard and predictable response to environmental stimuli. These rules can be formal or informal, but in either case they tell actors which action is appropriate in response to a specific stimuli, request, or demand. This kind of routinization is, after all, precisely what bureaucracies are supposed to exhibit—it is what makes them effective and competent in performing complex social tasks. However, the presence of such rules also compromises the extent to which means-ends rationality drives organizational behavior. Rules and routines may come to obscure overall missions and larger social goals. They may create "ritualized behavior" in bureaucrats and construct a very parochial normative environment within the organization whose connection to the larger social environment is tenuous at best.[71]

Second, bureaucracies specialize and compartmentalize. They create a division of labor on the logic that because individuals have only so much time, knowledge, and expertise, specialization will allow the organization to emulate a rational decision-making process.[72] Again, this is one of the virtues of bureaucracy in that it provides a way of overcoming the limitations of individual rationality and knowledge by embedding those individuals in a structure that takes advantage of their competencies without having to rely on their weaknesses. However, it, too, has some negative consequences. Just as rules can eclipse goals, concentrated expertise and specialization can (and perhaps must) limit bureaucrats' field of vision and create subcultures within bureaucracy that are distinct from those of the larger environment. Professional training plays a particularly strong role here since this is one widespread way we disseminate specialized knowledge and credential "experts." Such training often gives experts, indeed is designed to give them, a distinctive worldview and normative commitments, which, when concentrated in a subunit of an organization, can have pronounced effects on behavior.[73]

Once in place, an organization's culture, understood as the rules, rituals, and beliefs that are embedded in the organization (and its subunits), has important consequences for the way individuals who inhabit that organization make sense of the world. It provides interpretive frames that individuals use to generate meaning.[74] This is more than just bounded rationality; in this view, actors' rationality itself, the very means and ends that they value, are shaped by the organizational culture.[75] Divisions and subunits within the organization may develop their own cognitive frameworks that are consistent with but still distinct from the larger organization, further complicating this process.

All organizations have their own culture (or cultures) that shape their behavior. The effects of bureaucratic culture, however, need not be dysfunctional. Indeed, specific organizational cultures may be valued and actively promoted as a source of "good" behavior, as students of business culture know very well. Organizational culture is tied to "good" and "bad" behavior, alike, and the effects of organizational culture on behavior are an empirical question to be researched.

To further such research, we draw from studies in sociology and anthropology to explore five mechanisms by which bureaucratic culture can breed pathologies in IOs: the irrationality of rationalization, universalism, normalization of deviance, organizational insulation, and cultural contestation.

The first three of these mechanisms all flow from defining features of bureaucracy itself. Consequently, we expect them to be present in any bureaucracy to a limited degree. Their severity may be increased, however, by specific empirical conditions of the organization. Vague mission, weak feedback from the environment, and strong professionalism all have the potential to exacerbate these mechanisms and to create two others, organizational insulation and cultural contestation, through processes we describe later. Our claim, therefore, is that the very nature of bureaucracy—the "social stuff" of which it is made—creates behavioral predispositions that make bureaucracy prone to these kinds of behaviors.[76] But the connection between these mechanisms and pathological behavior is probabilistic, not deterministic, and is consistent with our constitutive analysis. Whether, in fact, mission-defeating behavior occurs depends on empirical conditions. We identify three such conditions that are particularly important (mission, feedback, and professionals) and discuss how they intensify these inherent predispositions and activate or create additional ones.

IRRATIONALITY OF RATIONALIZATION

Weber recognized that the "rationalization" processes at which bureaucracies excelled could be taken to extremes and ultimately become irrational if the rules and procedures that enabled bureaucracies to do their jobs became ends in themselves. Rather than designing the most appropriate and efficient rules and procedures to accomplish their missions, bureaucracies often tailor their missions to fit the existing, well-known, and comfortable rulebook.[77] Thus, means (rules and procedures) may become so embedded and powerful that they determine ends and the way the organization defines its goals. One observer of the World Bank noted how, at an operational level, the bank did not decide on development goals and collect data necessary to pursue them. Rather, it continued to use existing data-collection procedures and formulated goals and development plans from those data alone.[78] UN-mandated elections may be another instance where means become ends in themselves. The "end" pursued in the many troubled states where the UN has been involved in reconstruction is presumably some kind of peaceful, stable, just government. Toward that end, the UN has developed a repertoire of instruments and responses that are largely intended to promote something akin to a democratic government. Among those various repertoires, elections have become privileged as a measure of "success" and a signal of an operation's successful conclusion. Consequently, UN (and other IO) officials have conducted elections even when evidence suggests that such elections are either premature or perhaps even counterproductive (frequently acknowledged as much by state and UN officials).[79] In places like Bosnia elections have ratified precisely the outcome the UN and Outside powers had intervened to prevent—ethnic cleansing—and in places like Africa elections are criticized as exacerbating the very ethnic tensions they were ostensibly designed to quell.

■ ■ ■

BUREAUCRATIC UNIVERSALISM

A second source of pathology in IOs derives from the fact that bureaucracies "orchestrate numerous local contexts at once."[80] Bureaucrats necessarily flatten diversity because they are supposed to generate universal rules and categories that are, by design, inattentive to contextual and particularistic concerns. Part of the justification for this, of course, is the bureaucratic view that technical knowledge is transferable across circumstances. Sometimes this is a good assumption, but not always; when particular circumstances are not appropriate to the generalized knowledge being applied, the results can be disastrous.[81]

Many critics of the IMF's handling of the Asian financial crises have argued that the IMF inappropriately applied a standardized formula of budget cuts plus high interest rates to combat rapid currency depreciation without appreciating the unique and local causes of this depreciation. These governments were not profligate spenders, and austerity policies did little to reassure investors, yet the IMF prescribed roughly the same remedy that it had in Latin America. The result, by the IMF's later admission, was to make matters worse.[82]

■ ■ ■

NORMALIZATION OF DEVIANCE

We derive a third type of pathology from Diane Vaughan's study of the space shuttle *Challenger* disaster in which she chronicles the way exceptions to rules (deviance) over time become routinized and normal parts of procedures.[83] Bureaucracies establish rules to provide a predictable response to environmental stimuli in ways that safeguard against decisions that might lead to accidents and faulty decisions. At times, however, bureaucracies make small, calculated deviations from established rules because of new environmental or institutional developments, explicitly calculating that bending the rules in this instance does not create excessive risk of policy failure. Over time, these exceptions can become the rule—they become normal, not exceptions at all: they can become institutionalized to the point where deviance is "normalized." The result of this process is that what at time t_1 might be weighed seriously and debated as a potentially unacceptable risk or dangerous procedure comes to be treated as normal at time t_n. Indeed, because of staff turnover, those making decisions at a later point in time might be unaware that the now-routine behavior was ever viewed as risky or dangerous.

We are unaware of any studies that have examined this normalization of deviance in IO decision making, though one example of deviance normalization comes to mind. Before 1980 the UNHCR viewed repatriation as only one of three durable solutions to refugee crises (the others being third-country asylum and host-country integration). In its view, repatriation had to be both safe and voluntary because forced repatriation violates the international legal principle of nonrefoulement, which is the cornerstone of international refugee law and codified in the UNHCR's convention. Prior to 1980, UNHCR's discussions of repatriation emphasized that the principles of safety and voluntariness must be safeguarded at all costs. According to many commentators, however, the UNHCR has steadily lowered the barriers to repatriation over the years. Evidence for this can be found in international protection manuals, the UNHCR Executive Committee resolutions, and discourse that now weighs repatriation and the principle of nonrefoulement against other goals such a peace building. This was a steady and incremental development as initial deviations from organizational norms accumulated over time and led to a normalization of deviance. The result was a lowering of the barriers to repatriation and an increase in the frequency of involuntary repatriation.[84]

INSULATION

Organizations vary greatly in the degree to which they receive and process feedback from their environment about performance. Those insulated from such feedback often develop internal cultures and worldviews that do not promote the goals and expectations of those outside the organization who created it and whom it serves. These distinctive worldviews can create the conditions for pathological behavior when parochial classification and categorization schemes come to define reality—how bureaucrats understand the world—such that they routinely ignore information that is essential to the accomplishment of their goals.[85]

Two causes of insulation seem particularly applicable to IOs. The first is professionalism. Professional training does more than impart technical knowledge. It actively seeks to shape the normative orientation and worldviews of those who are trained. Doctors are trained to value life

above all else, soldiers are trained to sacrifice life for certain strategic objectives, and economists are trained to value efficiency. Bureaucracies, by their nature, concentrate professionals inside organizations, and concentrations of people with the same expertise or professional training can create an organizational worldview distinct from the larger environment. Second, organizations for whom "successful performance" is difficult to measure—that is, they are valued for what they represent rather than for what they do and do not "compete" with other organizations on the basis of output—are protected from selection and performance pressures that economistic models simply assume will operate. The absence of a competitive environment that selects out inefficient practices coupled with already existing tendencies toward institutionalization of rules and procedures insulates the organization from feedback and increases the likelihood of pathologies.

■   ■   ■

Conclusion

■   ■   ■

Viewing IOs through a constructivist or sociological lens, as we suggest here, reveals features of IO behavior that should concern international relations scholars because they bear on debates central to our field—debates about whether and how international institutions matter and debates about the adequacy of a statist ontology in an era of globalization and political change. Three implications of this alternative approach are particularly important. First, this approach provides a basis for treating IOs as purposive actors. Mainstream approaches in political science that are informed by economic theories have tended to locate agency in the states that comprise IO membership and treat IOs as mere arenas in which states pursue their policies. By exploring the normative support for bureaucratic authority in the broader international culture and the way IOs use that authority to construct the social world, we provide reasons why IOs may have autonomy from state members and why it may make sense analytically to treat them as ontologically independent. Second, by providing a basis for that autonomy we also open up the possibility that IOs are powerful actors who can have independent effects on the world. We have suggested various ways to think about how IOs are powerful actors in global politics, all of which encourage greater consideration of how IOs affect not only discrete outcomes but also the constitutive basis of global politics.

Third, this approach also draws attention to normative evaluations of IOs and questions what appears to us to be rather uncritical optimism about IO behavior. Contemporary international relations scholars have been quick to recognize the positive contributions that IOs can make, and we, too, are similarly impressed. But for all their desirable qualities, bureaucracies can also be inefficient, ineffective, repressive, and unaccountable. International relations scholars, however, have shown little interest in investigating these less savory and more distressing effects. The liberal Wilsonian tradition tends to see IOs as promoters of peace, engines of progress, and agents for emancipation. Neoliberals have focused on the impressive way in which IOs help states to overcome collective action problems and achieve durable cooperation. Realists have focused on their role as stabilizing forces in world politics. Constructivists, too, have tended to focus on the more humane and other-regarding features of IOs, but there is nothing about social construction that necessitates "good" outcomes. We do not mean to imply that IOs are "bad"; we mean only to point out theoretical reasons why undesirable behavior may occur and suggest that normative evaluation of IO behavior should be an empirical and ethical matter, not an analytic assumption.

NOTES

1. For Gramscian approaches, see Cox 1980, 1992, and 1996; and Murphy 1994. For Society of States approaches, see Hurrell and Woods 1995. For the epistemic communities literature, see Haas 1992. For IO decision-making literature, see Cox et al. 1974; Cox and Jacobson 1977; Cox 1996; and Ness and Brechin 1988. For a rational choice perspective, see Snidal 1996.
2. Haas 1990.
3. Because the neorealist and neoliberal arguments we engage have focused on intergovernmental organizations rather than nongovernmental ones, and because Weberian arguments from which we draw deal primarily with public bureaucracy, we, too, focus on intergovernmental organizations in this article and use the term *international organizations* in that way.
4. Baldwin 1993.
5. See Finnemore 1993 and 1996b; and McNeely 1995.
6. Krasner 1983b.
7. See Mearsheimer 1994; and Helms 1996.
8. See Commission on Global Governance 1995; Jacobson 1979, 1; and Doyle 1997.
9. See Ruggie 1998; and Wendt 1998.
10. Wendt 1998.
11. See Powell and DiMaggio 1991, chap. 1; and Grandori 1993.
12. See Williamson 1975 and 1985; and Coase 1937.
13. Waltz 1979.
14. See Vaubel 1991, 27; and Dillon, Ilgen, and Willett 1991.
15. Baldwin 1993.
16. Krasner 1991.
17. See DiMaggio and Powell 1983; Scott 1992; Meyer and Scott 1992, 1–5; Powell and DiMaggio 1991; Weber 1994; and Finnemore 1996a.
18. Researchers applying these economistic approaches have become increasingly aware of the mismatch between the assumptions of their models and the empirics of IOs. See Snidal 1996.
19. Note that empirically this is not the case; most IOs now are created by other IOs. See Shanks, Jacobson, and Kaplan 1996.
20. Waltz 1979, 18.
21. Krasner 1983a, 355–68; but see Finnemore 1996b; and Rittberger 1993.
22. See Keohane 1984; and Baldwin 1993.
23. Moravcsik 1997.
24. See Pollack 1997; Ross 1995; and Zabusky 1995; but see Moravcsik 1999.
25. See Ascher 1983; Ayres 1983; Ferguson 1990; Escobar 1995; Wade 1996; Nelson 1995; and Finnemore 1996a.
26. Joint Evaluation of Emergency Assistance to Rwanda 1996.
27. See Pollack 1997; Lake 1996; Vaubel 1991; and Dillon, Ilgen, and Willett 1991.
28. See Pratt and Zeckhauser 1985; and Kiewit and McCubbins 1991.
29. See Niskanen 1971; Miller and Moe 1983; Weingast and Moran 1983; Moe 1984; and Sigelman 1986.
30. See Ascher 1983; Zabusky 1995; Barnett 1997b; and Wade 1996.
31. See Weber 1978, 196–97; Weber 1947; Mouzelis 1967; and Beetham 1985 and 1996.

32. See Schaar 1984, 120; Weber 1978, 973; and Beetham 1985, 69.

33. Gerth and Mills 1978, 299 (italics in original).

34. See Gerth and Mills 1978, 233; Beetham 1985, 74–75; and Schaar 1984, 120.

35. We thank John Boli for this insight. Also see Fisher 1997; Ferguson 1990; Shore and Wright 1997; and Burley and Mattli 1993.

36. Gerth and Mills 1978, 199.

37. See Weber [1930] 1968, 181–83; and Clegg 1994a, 152–55.

38. Gerth and Mills 1978, 216, 50, 299. For the extreme manifestation of this bureaucratic characteristic, see Arendt 1977.

39. See David Rieff, "The Institution that Saw No Evil," *The New Republic,* 12 February 1996, 19–24; and Barnett 1997b.

40. See Wade 1996; Ayres 1983; Ascher 1983; Finnemore 1996b; and Nelson 1995.

41. See Malkki 1996; Hartigan 1992; and Harrell-Bond 1989.

42. See Foucault 1977, 27; and Clegg 1994b, 156–59. International relations theory typically disregards the negative side of the knowledge and power equation. For an example, see Haas 1992.

43. Handelman 1995, 280. See also Starr 1992; and Wright 1994, 22.

44. See Weiss and Pasic 1997; Goodwin-Gill 1996; and Anonymous 1997.

45. See Harrell-Bond 1989; Walkup 1997; and Malkki 1996.

46. Gran 1986.

47. See Williams 1996; Clegg 1994b; Bourdieu 1994; Carr [1939] 1964; and Keeley 1990.

48. Blumer 1969.

49. See Gupta 1998; Escobar 1995; Cooper and Packard 1998; Gran 1986; Ferguson 1990; and Wade 1996.

50. See Matthews 1989; and Krause and Williams 1996.

51. See UN Development Program 1994; and Boutros-Ghali 1995.

52. See Escobar 1995; Ferguson 1990; and Feldstein 1998.

53. See Katzenstein 1996; Finnemore 1996b; and Legro 1997.

54. See Alger 1963, 425; and Claude 1966, 373.

55. See McNeely 1995; and Jackson 1993.

56. Call and Barnett forthcoming.

57. Wade 1996.

58. See Perry 1996; and Ruggie 1996.

59. March and Olsen 1989, chap. 5.

60. See Haas 1990; Haas and Haas 1995; and Sagan 1993.

61. Two exceptions are Gallaroti 1991; and Snidal 1996.

62. Snidal 1996.

63. Karl Deutsch used the concept of pathology in a way similar to our usage. We thank Hayward Alker for this point. Deutsch 1963, 170.

64. See Allison 1971; Haas 1990; Cox et al. 1974; and Cox and Jacobson 1977.

65. See Allison 1971, 144; and Bendor and Hammond 1992.

66. Personal communication to the authors.

67. See Meyer and Rowan 1977; Meyer and Zucker 1989; Weber 1994; and Finnemore 1996a.

68. Lipson 1999.

69. McNeely 1995.

70. See Vaughan 1996; and Lipartito 1995.

71. See March and Olsen 1989, 21–27; and Meyer and Rowan 1977.

72. See March and Olsen 1989, 26–27; and March 1997.

73. See DiMaggio and Powell 1983; and Schien 1996.

74. See Starr 1992, 160; Douglas 1986; and Berger and Luckmann 1966, chap. 1.

75. See Campbell 1998, 378; Alvesson 1996; Burrell and Morgan 1979; Dobbin 1994; and Immergut 1998, 14–19.

76. Wendt 1998.

77. Beetham 1985, 76.

78. See Ferguson 1990; and Nelson 1995.

79. Paris 1997.

80. Heyman 1995, 262.

81. Haas 1990, chap. 3.

82. See Feldstein 1998; Radelet and Sach 1999; and Kapur 1998.

83. Vaughan 1996.

84. See Chimni 1993, 447; Amnesty International 1997a,b; Human Rights Watch 1997; Zieck 1997, 433, 434, 438–39; and Barbara Crossette, "The Shield for Exiles Is Lowered, *The New York Times,* 22 December 1996, 4–1."

85. See Berger and Luckmann 1966, chap. 1; Douglas 1986; Bruner 1990; March and Olsen 1989; and Starr 1992.

REFERENCES

Alger, Chadwick. 1963. United Nations Participation as a Learning Process. *Public Opinion Quarterly* 27 (3):411–26.

Allison, Graham. 1971. *Essence of Decision.* Boston: Little, Brown.

Alvesson, Mats. 1996. *Cultural Perspectives on Organizations.* New York: Cambridge University Press.

Amnesty International. 1997a. In Search of Safety: The Forcibly Displaced and Human Rights in Africa. AI Index, 20 June, AFR 01/05/97. Available from www.amnesty.org/ailib/aipub/1997 /10100597.htm.

———. 1997b. Rwanda: Human Rights Overlooked in Mass Repatriation. Available from www.amnesty.org/ailib/aipub/1997 /AFR/147002797.htm.

Anonymous. 1997. The UNHCR Note on International Protection You Won't See. *International Journal of Refugee Law* 9 (2):267–73.

Arendt, Hannah. 1977. *Eichmann in Jerusalem: A Report on the Banality of Evil.* New York: Penguin.

Ascher, William. 1983. New Development Approaches and the Adaptability of International Agencies: The Case of the World Bank. *International Organization* 37 (3):415–39.

Ayres, Robert L. 1983. *Banking on the Poor: The World Bank and World Poverty.* Cambridge, MA: MIT Press.

Baldwin, David, ed. 1993. *Neorealism and Neoliberalism.* New York: Columbia University Press.

Barnett, Michael, 1997a. The Politics of Indifference at the United Nations and Genocide in Rwanda and Bosnia. In *This Time We Knew: Western Responses to Genocide in Bosnia,* edited by Thomas Cushman and Stjepan Mestrovic, 128–62. New York: New York University Press.

———. 1997b. The UN Security Council, Indifference, and Genocide in Rwanda. *Cultural Anthropology* 12 (4):55–78.

Beetham, David. 1985. *Max Weber and the Theory of Modern Politics.* New York: Polity.

———. 1996. *Bureaucracy.* 2d ed. Minneapolis: University of Minnesota Press.

Bendor, Jonathan, and Thomas Hammond. 1992. Rethinking Allison's Models. *American Political Science Review* 82 (2):301–22.

Berger, Peter, and Thomas Luckmann. 1966. *The Social Construction of Reality.* New York: Doubleday.

Blumer, Herbert. 1969. *Symbolic Interactionism: Perspective and Method.* Englewood Cliffs, NJ: Prentice-Hall.

Bourdieu, Pierre. 1994. On Symbolic Power. In *Language and Symbolic Power,* edited by Pierre Bourdieu, 163–70. Chicago: University of Chicago Press.

Boutros-Ghali, Boutros. 1995. *Agenda for Peace.* 2d ed. New York: UN Press.

Bruner, Jerome. 1990. *Acts of Meaning.* Cambridge, MA: Harvard University Press.

Burley, Anne-Marie, and Walter Mattli. 1993. Europe Before the Court: A Political Theory of Integration. *International Organization* 47 (1):41–76.

Burrell, Gibson, and Gareth Morgan. 1979. *Sociological Paradigms and Organizational Analysis.* London: Heinemann.

Call, Chuck, and Michael Barnett. Forthcoming. Looking for a Few Good Cops: Peacekeeping, Peace-building, and U.N. Civilian Police. *International Peacekeeping.*

Campbell, John. 1998. Institutional Analysis and the Role of Ideas in Political Economy. *Theory and Society* 27:377–409.

Carr, Edward H. [1939] 1964. *The Twenty Year's Crisis.* New York: Harper Torchbooks.

Chimni, B. 1993. The Meaning of Words and the Role of UNHCR in Voluntary Repatriation. *International Journal of Refugee Law* 5 (3):442–60.

Claude, Inis L., Jr. 1966. Collective Legitimization as a Political Function of the United Nations. *International Organization* 20 (3):337–67.

Clegg, Stewart. 1994a. Power and Institutions in the Theory of Organizations. In *Toward a New Theory of Organizations*, edited by John Hassard and Martin Parker, 24–49. New York: Routledge.

———. 1994b. Weber and Foucault: Social Theory for the Study of Organizations. *Organization* 1 (1): 149–78.

Coase, Ronald. 1937. The Nature of the Firm. *Economica* 4 (November):386–405.

Commission on Global Governance. 1995. *Our Global Neighborhood.* New York: Oxford University Press.

Cooper, Frederick, and Randy Packard, eds. 1998. *International Development and the Social Sciences.* Berkeley: University of California Press.

Cox, Robert. 1980. The Crisis of World Order and the Problem of International Organization in the 1980s. *International Journal* 35 (2):370–95.

———. 1992. Multilateralism and World Order. *Review of International Studies* 18 (2):161–80.

———. 1996. The Executive Head: An Essay on Leadership in International Organization. In *Approaches to World Order*, edited by Robert Cox, 317–48. New York: Cambridge University Press.

Cox, Robert, and Harold Jacobson. 1977. Decision Making. *International Social Science Journal* 29 (1):115–33.

Cox, Robert, Harold Jacobson, Gerard Curzon, Victoria Curzon, Joseph Nye, Lawrence Scheinman, James Sewell, and Susan Strange. 1974.

The Anatomy of Influence: Decision Making in International Organization. New Haven, CT: Yale University Press.

Deutsch, Karl. 1963. *The Nerves of Government: Models of Political Communication and Control.* Glencoe. IL: Free Press.

Dillon, Patricia, Thomas Ilgen, and Thomas Willett. 1991. Approaches to the Study of International Organizations: Major Paradigms in Economics and Political Science. In *The Political Economy of International Organizations: A Public Choice Approach,* edited by Ronald Vaubel and Thomas Willett, 79–99. Boulder, CO: Westview Press.

DiMaggio, Paul J., and Walter W. Powell. 1983. The Iron Cage Revisited: Institutional Isomorphism and Collective Rationality in Organizational Fields. *American Sociological Review* 48:147–60.

Dobbin, Frank. 1994. Cultural Models of Organization: The Social Construction of Rational Organizing Principles. In *The Sociology of Culture,* edited by Diana Crane, 117–42. Boston: Basil Blackwell.

Douglas, Mary. 1986. *How Institutions Think.* Syracuse, NY: Syracuse University Press.

Doyle, Michael. 1997. *Ways of War and Peace.* New York: Norton.

Escobar, Arturo. 1995. *Encountering Development: The Making and Unmaking of the Third World.* Princeton, NJ: Princeton University Press.

Feld, Werner J., and Robert S. Jordan, with Leon Hurwitz. 1988. *International Organizations: A Comparative Approach.* 2d ed. New York: Praeger.

Feldstein, Martin. 1998. Refocusing the IMF. *Foreign Affairs* 77 (2):20–33.

Ferguson, James. 1990. *The Anti-Politics Machine: "Development," Depoliticization, and Bureaucratic Domination in Lesotho.* New York: Cambridge University Press.

Finnemore, Martha. 1993. International Organizations as Teachers of Norms: The United Nations Educational, Scientific, and Cultural Organization and Science Policy. *International Organization* 47:565–97.

———. 1996a. Norms, Culture, and World Politics: Insights from Sociology's Institutionalism. *International Organization* 50 (2):325–47.

———. 1996b. *National Interests in International Society.* Ithaca, NY: Cornell University Press.

Fisher, William. 1997. Doing Good? The Politics and Antipolitics of NGO Practices. *Annual Review of Anthropology* 26:439–64.

Foucault, Michel. 1977. *Discipline and Punish.* New York: Vintage Press.

Gallaroti, Guilio. 1991. The Limits of International Organization. *International Organization* 45 (2):183–220.

Gerth, H. H., and C. Wright Mills. 1978. *From Max Weber: Essays in Sociology.* New York: Oxford University Press.

Goodwin-Gill, Guy. 1996. *Refugee in International Law.* New York: Oxford Clarendon.

Gran, Guy. 1986. Beyond African Famines: Whose Knowledge Matters? *Alternatives* 11:275–96.

Grandori, Anna. 1993. Notes on the Use of Power and Efficiency Constructs in the Economics and Sociology of Organizations. In *Interdisciplinary Perspectives on Organizational Studies*, edited by S. Lindenberg and H. Schreuder, 61–78. New York: Pergamon.

Gupta, Akhil. 1998. *Postcolonial Developments: Agriculture in the Making of Modern India.* Durham, NC: Duke University Press.

Haas, Ernst. 1990. *When Knowledge Is Power.* Berkeley: University of California Press.

Haas, Ernst, and Peter Haas. 1995. Learning to Learn: Improving International Governance. *Global Governance* 1 (3):255–85.

Haas, Peter, ed. 1992. Epistemic Communities. *International Organization* 46 (1). Special issue.

Handelman, Don. 1995. Comment. *Current Anthropology* 36 (2):280–8l.

Harrell-Bond, Barbara. 1989. Repatriation: Under What Conditions Is It the Most Desirable Solution for Refugees? *African Studies Review* 32 (1):41–69.

Hartigan, Kevin. 1992. Matching Humanitarian Norms with Cold, Hard Interests: The Making of Refugee Policies in Mexico and Honduras, 1980–89. *International Organization* 46:709–30.

Helms, Jesse. 1996. Saving the UN. *Foreign Affairs* 75 (5):2–7.

Heyman, Josiah McC. 1995. Putting Power in the Anthropology of Bureaucracy. *Current Anthropology* 36 (2):261–77.

Hirsch, John, and Robert Oakley. 1995. *Somalia and Operation Restore Hope: Reflections on Peacemaking and Peacekeeping.* Washington, DC: USIP Press.

Human Rights Watch. 1997. Uncertain Refuge: International Failures to Protect Refugees. Vol. 1, no. 9 (April).

Hurrell, Andrew, and Ngaire Woods. 1995. Globalisation and Inequality. *Millennium* 24 (3):447–70.

Immergut, Ellen. 1998. The Theoretical Core of the New Institutionalism. *Politics and Society* 26 (1):5–34.

Jackson, Robert. 1993. The Weight of Ideas in Decolonization: Normative Change in International Relations. In *Ideas and Foreign Policy,* edited by Judith Goldstein and Robert O. Keohane, 111–38. Ithaca, NY: Cornell University Press.

Jacobson, Harold. 1979. *Networks of Interdependence.* New York: Alfred A. Knopf.

Joint Evaluation of Emergency Assistance to Rwanda. 1996. *The International Response to Conflict and Genocide: Lessons from the Rwanda Experience.* 5 vols. Copenhagen: Steering Committee of the Joint Evaluation of Emergency Assistance to Rwanda.

Kapur, Devesh. 1998. The IMF: A Cure or a Curse? *Foreign Policy* 111:114–29.

Katzenstein, Peter J., ed. 1996. *The Culture of National Security: Identity and Norms in World Politics.* New York: Columbia University Press.

Keeley, James. 1990. Toward a Foucauldian Analysis of International Regimes. *International Organization* 44 (1):83–105.

Keohane, Robert O. 1984. *After Hegemony.* Princeton, NJ: Princeton University Press.

Kiewiet, D. Roderick, and Matthew McCubbins. 1991. *The Logic of Delegation.* Chicago: University of Chicago Press.

Krasner, Stephen D. 1991. Global Communications and National Power: Life on the Pareto Frontier. *World Politics* 43 (3):336–66.

———. 1983a. Regimes and the Limits of Realism: Regimes as Autonomous Variables. In *International Regimes,* edited by Stephen Krasner, 355–68. Ithaca, NY: Cornell University Press.

Krasner, Stephen D., ed. 1983b. *International Regimes.* Ithaca, NY: Cornell University Press.

Krause, Keith, and Michael Williams. 1996. Broadening the Agenda of Security Studies: Politics and Methods. *Mershon International Studies Review* 40 (2):229–54.

Lake, David. 1996. Anarchy, Hierarchy, and the Variety of International Relations. *International Organization* 50 (1):1–34.

Legro, Jeffrey. 1997. Which Norms Matter? Revisiting the "Failure" of Internationalism. *International Organization* 51 (1):31–64.

Lipartito, Kenneth. 1995. Culture and the Practice of Business History. *Business and Economic History* 24 (2):1–41.

Lipson, Michael. 1999. International Cooperation on Export Controls: Nonproliferation, Globalization, and Multilateralism. Ph.D. diss., University of Wisconsin, Madison.

Malkki, Liisa. 1996. Speechless Emissaries: Refugees, Humanitarianism, and Dehistoricization. *Cultural Anthropology* 11 (3):377–404.

March, James. 1988. *Decisions and Organizations.* Boston: Basil Blackwell.

———. 1997. Understanding How Decisions Happen in Organizations. In *Organizational Decision Making,* edited by Z. Shapira, 9–33. New York: Cambridge University Press.

March, James, and Johan P. Olsen. 1989. *Rediscovering Institutions: The Organizational Basis of Politics.* New York: Free Press.

Matthews, Jessica Tuchman. 1989. Redefining Security. *Foreign Affairs* 68 (2):162–77.

McNeely, Connie. 1995. *Constructing the Nation-State: International Organization and Prescriptive Action.* Westport, CT: Greenwood Press.

Mearsheimer, John. 1994. The False Promise of International Institutions. *International Security* 19 (3):5–49.

Meyer, John W., and Brian Rowan. 1977. Institutionalized Organizations: Formal Structure as Myth and Ceremony. *American Journal of Sociology* 83:340–63.

Meyer, John W., and W. Richard Scott. 1992. *Organizational Environments: Ritual and Rationality.* Newbury Park, CA: Sage.

Meyer, Marshall, and Lynne Zucker. 1989. *Permanently Failing Organizations.* Newbury Park: Sage Press.

Miller, Gary, and Terry M. Moe. 1983. Bureaucrats, Legislators, and the Size of Government. *American Political Science Review* 77 (June):297–322.

Moe, Terry M. 1984. The New Economics of Organization. *American Journal of Political Science* 28: 739–77.

Moravcsik, Andrew. 1997. Taking Preferences Seriously: Liberal Theory and International Politics. *International Organization* 51 (4):513–54.

———. 1999. A New Statecraft? Supranational Entrepreneurs and International Cooperation. *International Organization* 53 (2):267–306.

Mouzelis, Nicos. 1967. *Organization and Bureaucracy.* Chicago: Aldine.

Murphy, Craig. 1994. *International Organizations and Industrial Change.* New York: Oxford University Press.

Nelson, Paul. 1995. *The World Bank and Non-Governmental Organizations.* New York: St. Martin's Press.

Ness, Gayl, and Steven Brechin. 1988. Bridging the Gap: International Organizations as Organizations. *International Organization* 42 (2):245–73.

Niskanen, William A. 1971. *Bureaucracy and Representative Government.* Chicago: Aldine.

Paris, Roland. 1997. Peacebuilding and the Limits of Liberal Internationalism. *International Security* 22 (2):54–89.

Perry, William. 1996. Defense in an Age of Hope. *Foreign Affairs* 75 (6):64–79.

Pollack, Mark. 1997. Delegation, Agency, and Agenda-Setting in the European Community. *International Organization* 51 (1):99–134.

Powell, Walter W., and Paul J. DiMaggio, eds. 1991. *The New Institutionalism in Organizational Analysis.* Chicago: University of Chicago Press.

Pratt, John, and Richard J. Zeckhauser. 1985. *Principals and Agents: The Structure of Business.* Boston: Harvard Business School Press.

Radelet, Steven, and Jeffrey Sach. 1999. What Have We Learned, So Far, from the Asian Financial Crisis? Harvard Institute for International Development, 4 January. Available from www.hiid.harvard.edu/pub /other/aea122.pdf.

Rittberger, Volker, ed. 1993. *Regime Theory and International Relations.* Oxford: Clarendon Press.

Ross, George. 1995. *Jacques Delors and European Integration.* New York: Oxford University Press.

Ruggie, John. 1996. *Winning the Peace.* New York: Columbia University Press.

———. 1998. What Makes the World Hang Together. *International Organization* 52 (3):855–86.

Sagan, Scott. 1993. *The Limits of Safety: Organizations, Accidents, and Nuclear Weapons.* Princeton, NJ: Princeton University Press.

Schaar, John. 1984. Legitimacy in the Modern State. In *Legitimacy and the State,* edited by William Connolly, 104–33. Oxford: Basil Blackwell.

Schien, Edgar. 1996. Culture: The Missing Concept in Organization Studies. *Administrative Studies Quarterly* 41:229–40.

Scott, W. Richard. 1992. *Organizations: Rational, Natural, and Open Systems.* 3d ed. Englewood Cliffs, NJ: Prentice-Hall.

Shanks, Cheryl, Harold K. Jacobson, and Jeffrey H. Kaplan. 1996. Inertia and Change in the Constellation of Intergovernmental Organizations, 1981–1992. *International Organization* 50 (4):593–627.

Shapira, Zur, ed. 1997. *Organizational Decision.* New York: Cambridge University Press.

Shore, Cris, and Susan Wright. 1997. Policy: A New Field of Anthropology. In *Anthropology of Policy: Critical Perspectives on Governance and Power,* edited by Cris Shore and Susan Wright, 3–41. New York: Routledge Press.

Sigelman, Lee. 1986. The Bureaucratic Budget Maximizer: An Assumption Examined. *Public Budgeting and Finance* (spring):50–59.

Snidal, Duncan. 1996. Political Economy and International Institutions. *International Review of Law and Economics* 16:121–37.

Starr, Paul. 1992. Social Categories and Claims in the Liberal State. In *How Classification Works: Nelson Goodman Among the Social Sciences,* edited by Mary Douglas and David Hull, 154–79. Edinburgh: Edinburgh University Press.

UN Development Program. 1994. *Human Development Report 1994.* New York: Oxford University Press.

UN Peacekeeping Missions. 1994. The Lessons from Cambodia. Asia Pacific Issues, Analysis from the East-West Center, No. 11, March.

Vaubel, Roland. 1991. A Public Choice View of International Organization. In *The Political Economy of International Organizations,* edited by Roland Vaubel and Thomas Willett, 27–45. Boulder, CO: Westview Press.

Vaughan, Diane. 1996. *The Challenger Launch Decision.* Chicago: University of Chicago Press.

Wade, Robert. 1996. Japan, the World Bank, and the Art of Paradigm Maintenance: The East Asian Miracle in Political Perspective. *New Left Review* 217:3–36.

Walkup, Mark. 1997. Policy Dysfunction in Humanitarian Organizations: The Role of Coping Strategies, Institutions, and Organizational Culture. *Journal of Refugee Studies* 10 (1):37–60.

Waltz, Kenneth. 1979. *Theory of International Politics.* Reading, MA: Addison-Wesley.

Weber, Max. 1947. *Theory of Social and Economic Organization.* New York: Oxford University Press.

———.[1930] 1968. *The Protestant Ethic and the Spirit of Capitalism.* New York: Routledge.

———. 1978. Bureaucracy. In *From Max Weber: Essays in Sociology,* edited by H. H. Gerth and C. Wright Mills. New York: Oxford

Weber, Steven. 1994. Origins of the European Bank for Reconstruction and Development. *International Organization* 48 (1):1–38.

Weingast, Barry R., and Mark Moran. 1983. Bureaucratic Discretion or Congressional Control: Regulatory Policymaking by the Federal Trade Commission. *Journal of Political Economy* 91 (October):765–800.

Weiss, Thomas. 1996. Collective Spinelessness: U.N. Actions in the Former Yugoslavia. In *The World and Yugoslavia's Wars,* edited by Richard Ullman, 59–96. New York: Council on Foreign Relations Press.

Weiss, Tom, and Amir Pasic. 1997. Reinventing UNHCR: Enterprising Humanitarians in the Former Yugoslavia, 1991–95. *Global Governance* 3 (1):41–58.

Wendt, Alexander. 1995. Constructing International Politics. *International Security* 20 (1):71–81.

———. 1998. Constitution and Causation in International Relations. *Review of International Studies* 24 (4):101–17. Special issue.

Williams, Michael. 1996. Hobbes and International Relations: A Reconsideration. *International Organization* 50 (2):213–37.

Williamson, Oliver. 1975. *Markets and Hierarchies, Analysis and Antitrust Implications: A Study in the Economics of Internal Organization.* New York: Free Press.

———. 1985. *The Economic Institutions of Capitalism: Firms, Markets, Relational Contracting.* New York: Free Press.

Wright, Susan. 1994. "Culture" in Anthropology and Organizational Studies. In *Anthropology of Organizations,* edited by Susan Wright, 1–31. New York: Routledge.

Zabusky, Stacia. 1995. *Launching Europe.* Princeton, NJ: Princeton University Press.

Zieck, Marjoleine. 1997. *UNHCR and Voluntary Repatriation of Refugees: A Legal Analysis.* The Hague: Martinus Nijhoff.

8 WAR AND STRIFE

Warfare and military intervention continue to be central problems of international relations. Two of the readings in this section address a core issue: the relationship between the use of force and politics. Excerpts from classic books by Carl von Clausewitz, *On War* (originally published in the 1830s), and Thomas C. Schelling, *Arms and Influence* (1966), remind us that warfare is not simply an exercise of brute force; war needs to be understood as a continuation of political bargaining. In the most influential treatise on warfare ever written, Prussian general Clausewitz reminded the generation that followed the devastating Napoleonic wars that armed conflict should not be considered a blind, all-out struggle governed by the logic of military operations. Rather, he said, the conduct of war had to be subordinated to its political objectives. These ideas resonated strongly with American strategic thinkers of Schelling's era, who worried that military plans for total nuclear war would outstrip the ability of political leaders to control them. Schelling, a Harvard professor who also advised the U.S. Air Force on its nuclear weapons strategy, explained that political bargaining and risk-taking, not military victory, lay at the heart of the use and threat of force in the nuclear era.

Like Schelling, Robert Jervis drew on game theory and theories of bargaining in his influential 1978 article on the "security dilemma," which explains how war can arise even among states that seek only to defend themselves. Like the realists, Schelling and Jervis analysts are interested in studying how states' strategies for survival can lead to tragic results. However, they go beyond the realists in examining how differences in bargaining tactics and perceptions can intensify or mitigate the struggle for security.

James D. Fearon's 1995 article, "Rationalist Explanations for War," explores the puzzle of why two rational states would ever fight a costly war rather than settle their dispute more cheaply through peaceful bargaining. He shows that three problems can hinder the achievement of bargains that would benefit both sides: first, states may have private information (such as their military capabilities) that leads the sides to make different estimates as to who would prevail in a fight; second, side A may be unable to convince side B that it would live up to their bargain in the future; third, it may be impossible to divide up the stakes that lie at the heart of the dispute.

The advent of nuclear weapons has led to a lively debate over the relationship between nuclear proliferation and international system stability. The debate has been fueled by the emergence of nuclear states in South Asia and fears over nuclearization in both Iran and North Korea. Kenneth N. Waltz takes a contrarian position in this debate: a nuclear Iran would lead to a more stable Middle East. He derives this from his long-held, theoretically grounded view that "when it comes to nuclear weapons, now as ever, more may be better."

While terrorism has long been used as a means of achieving political objectives, the attention of the international community has been drawn to this phenomenon following the September 11, 2001, attacks. Andrew H. Kydd and Barbara F. Walter explore the types of goals that terrorists seek, the strategies terrorists use to achieve those goals, the counterstrategies that can be used against terrorist tactics, and the conditions under which such strategies will or will not work. Virginia Page Fortna brings an exemplary research design to bear on the latter question in "Do Terrorists Win?"

The proliferation of terrorism and of humanitarian emergencies has reprised an old debate on when it is right to fight when states do not protect their own populations. How has the notion of humanitarian intervention evolved over time? This is discussed by Martha Finnemore in her book *The Purpose of Intervention: Changing Beliefs about the Use of Force* (2003). In this constructivist piece, Finnemore shows how changes in international system-level norms explain why states choose to intervene in the affairs of other states, even when no national interests are at stake.

Carl von Clausewitz

WAR AS AN INSTRUMENT OF POLICY

■ ■ ■

*** *War is only a part of political intercourse, therefore by no means an independent thing in itself.*

We know, certainly, that War is only called forth through the political intercourse of Governments and Nations; but in general it is supposed that such intercourse is broken off by War, and that a totally different state of things ensues, subject to no laws but its own.

We maintain, on the contrary, that War is nothing but a continuation of political intercourse, with a mixture of other means. We say mixed with other means in order thereby to maintain at the same time that this political intercourse does not cease by the War itself, is not changed into something quite different, but that, in its essence, it continues to exist, whatever may be the form of the means which it uses, and that the chief lines on which the events of the War progress, and to which they are attached, are only the general features of policy which run all through the War until peace takes place. And how can we conceive it to be otherwise? Does the cessation of diplomatic notes stop the political relations between different Nations and Governments? Is not War merely another kind of writing and language for political thoughts? It has certainly a grammar of its own, but its logic is not peculiar to itself.

Accordingly, War can never be separated from political intercourse, and if, in the consideration of the matter, this is done in any way, all the threads of the different relations are, to a certain extent, broken, and we have before us a senseless thing without an object.

This kind of idea would be indispensable even if War was perfect War, the perfectly unbridled element of hostility, for all the circumstances on which it rests, and which determine its leading features, viz. our own power, the enemy's power, Allies on both sides, the characteristics of the people and their Governments respectively, etc.— are they not of a political nature, and are they not so intimately connected with the whole political intercourse that it is impossible to separate them? But this view is doubly indispensable if we reflect that real War is no such consistent effort tending to an extreme, as it should be according to the abstract idea, but a half-and-half thing, a contradiction in itself; that, as such, it cannot follow its own laws, but must be looked upon as a part of another whole—and this whole is policy.

Policy in making use of War avoids all those rigorous conclusions which proceed from its nature; it troubles itself little about final possibilities, confining its attention to immediate probabilities. If such uncertainty in the whole action ensues therefrom, if it thereby becomes a sort of game, the policy of each Cabinet places its confidence in the belief that in this game it will surpass its neighbour in skill and sharp-sightedness.

Thus policy makes out of the all-overpowering element of War a mere instrument, changes the tremendous battle-sword, which should be lifted with both hands and the whole power of the body

From Carl von Clausewitz, *On War* (Harmondsworth: Penguin Books, 1968), Bk. 5, Chap. 6. The author's notes have been omitted.

to strike once for all, into a light handy weapon, which is even sometimes nothing more than a rapier to exchange thrusts and feints and parries.

Thus the contradictions in which man, naturally timid, becomes involved by War may be solved, if we choose to accept this as a solution.

If War belongs to policy, it will naturally take its character from thence. If policy is grand and powerful, so also will be the War, and this may be carried to the point at which War attains to *its absolute form*.

In this way of viewing the subject, therefore, we need not shut out of sight the absolute form of War, we rather keep it continually in view in the background.

Only through this kind of view War recovers unity; only by it can we see all Wars as things of *one* kind; and it is only through it that the judgement can obtain the true and perfect basis and point of view from which great plans may be traced out and determined upon.

It is true the political element does not sink deep into the details of War. Vedettes are not planted, patrols do not make their rounds from political considerations; but small as is its influence in this respect, it is great in the formation of a plan for a whole War, or a campaign, and often even for a battle.

For this reason we were in no hurry to establish this view at the commencement. While engaged with particulars, it would have given us little help, and, on the other hand, would have distracted our attention to a certain extent; in the plan of a War or campaign it is indispensable.

There is, upon the whole, nothing more important in life than to find out the right point of view from which things should be looked at and judged of, and then to keep to that point; for we can only apprehend the mass of events in their unity from *one* standpoint; and it is only the keeping to one point of view that guards us from inconsistency.

If, therefore, in drawing up a plan of a War, it is not allowable to have a two-fold or three-fold point of view, from which things may be looked at, now with the eye of a soldier, then with that of an administrator, and then again with that of a politician, etc., then the next question is, whether *policy* is necessarily paramount and everything else subordinate to it.

That policy unites in itself, and reconciles all the interests of internal administrations, even those of humanity, and whatever else are rational subjects of consideration is presupposed, for it is nothing in itself, except a mere representative and exponent of all these interests towards other States. That policy may take a false direction, and may promote unfairly the ambitious ends, the private interests, the vanity of rulers, does not concern us here; for, under no circumstances can the Art of War be regarded as its preceptor, and we can only look at policy here as the representative of the interests generally of the whole community.

The only question, therefore, is whether in framing plans for a War the political point of view should give way to the purely military (if such a point is conceivable), that is to say, should disappear altogether, or subordinate itself to it, or whether the political is to remain the ruling point of view and the military to be considered subordinate to it.

That the political point of view should end completely when War begins is only conceivable in contests which are Wars of life and death, from pure hatred: as Wars are in reality, they are, as we before said, only the expressions or manifestations of policy itself. The subordination of the political point of view to the military would be contrary to common sense, for policy has declared the War; it is the intelligent faculty, War only the instrument, and not the reverse. The subordination of the military point of view to the political is, therefore, the only thing which is possible.

If we reflect on the nature of real War, and call to mind what has been said, *that every War should be viewed above all things according to the probability of its character, and its leading features as they are to be deduced from the political forces and proportions,* and that often—indeed we may safely affirm, in our days, *almost* always—War is to be regarded as an organic whole, from which the single branches are not to be separated, in which therefore every individual activity flows into the whole, and also has its origin in the idea of this whole, then it becomes certain and palpable to us that the superior standpoint for the conduct of the War, from which its leading lines must proceed, can be no other than that of policy.

From this point of view the plans come, as it were, out of a cast; the apprehension of them and the judgement upon them become easier and more natural, our convictions respecting them gain in force, motives are more satisfying and history more intelligible.

At all events from this point of view there is no longer in the nature of things a necessary conflict between the political and military interests, and where it appears it is therefore to be regarded as imperfect knowledge only. That policy makes demands on the War which it cannot respond to, would be contrary to the supposition that it knows the instrument which it is going to use, therefore, contrary to a natural and indispensable supposition. But if policy judges correctly of the march of military events, it is entirely its affair to determine what are the events and what the direction of events most favourable to the ultimate and great end of the War.

In one word, the Art of War in its highest point of view is policy, but, no doubt, a policy which fights battles instead of writing notes.

According to this view, to leave a great military enterprise or the plan for one, to *a purely military judgement and decision* is a distinction which cannot be allowed, and is even prejudicial; indeed, it is an irrational proceeding to consult professional soldiers on the plan of a War, that they may give a *purely military opinion* upon what the Cabinet ought to do; but still more absurd is the demand of Theorists that a statement of the available means of War should be laid before the General, that he may draw out a purely military plan for the War or for a campaign in accordance with those means. Experience in general also teaches us that notwithstanding the multifarious branches and scientific character of military art in the present day, still the leading outlines of a War are always determined by the Cabinet, that is, if we would use technical language, by a political not a military organ.

This is perfectly natural. None of the principal plans which are required for a War can be made without an insight into the political relations; and, in reality, when people speak, as they often do, of the prejudicial influence of policy on the conduct of a War, they say in reality something very different to what they intend. It is not this influence but the policy itself which should be found fault with. If policy is right, that is, if it succeeds in hitting the object, then it can only act with advantage on the War. If this influence of policy causes a divergence from the object, the cause is only to be looked for in a mistaken policy.

It is only when policy promises itself a wrong effect from certain military means and measures, an effect opposed to their nature, that it can exercise a prejudicial effect on War by the course it prescribes. Just as a person in a language with which he is not conversant sometimes says what he does not intend, so policy, when intending right, may often order things which do not tally with its own views.

This has happened times without end, and it shows that a certain knowledge of the nature of War is essential to the management of political intercourse.

But before going further, we must guard ourselves against a false interpretation of which this is very susceptible. We are far from holding the opinion that a War Minister smothered in official papers, a scientific engineer, or even a soldier who has been well tried in the field, would, any of them, necessarily make the best Minister of State where the Sovereign does not act for himself; or, in other words, we do not mean to say that this acquaintance with the nature of War is the principal qualification for a War Minister; elevation, superiority of mind, strength of character, these are the principal qualifications which he must possess; a knowledge of War may be supplied in one way or the other. * * *

■   ■   ■

We shall now conclude with some reflections derived from history.

In the last decade of the past century, when that remarkable change in the Art of War in Europe took place by which the best Armies found that a part of their method of War had become utterly unserviceable, and events were brought about of a magnitude far beyond what any one had any previous conception of, it certainly appeared that a false calculation of everything was to be laid to the charge of the Art of War. * * *

■   ■   ■

But is it true that the real surprise by which men's minds were seized was confined to the conduct of War, and did not rather relate to policy itself? That is: Did the ill success proceed from the influence of policy on the War, or from a wrong policy itself?

The prodigious effects of the French Revolution abroad were evidently brought about much less through new methods and views introduced by the French in the conduct of War than through the changes which it wrought in state-craft and civil administration, in the character of Governments, in the condition of the people, etc. That other Governments took a mistaken view of all these things; that they endeavoured, with their ordinary means, to hold their own against forces of a novel kind and overwhelming in strength—all that was a blunder in policy.

Would it have been possible to perceive and mend this error by a scheme for the War from a purely military point of view? Impossible. For if there had been a philosophical strategist, who merely from the nature of the hostile elements had foreseen all the consequences, and prophesied remote possibilities, still it would have been practically impossible to have turned such wisdom to account.

If policy had risen to a just appreciation of the forces which had sprung up in France, and of the new relations in the political state of Europe, it might have foreseen the consequences which must follow in respect to the great features of War, and it was only in this way that it could arrive at a correct view of the extent of the means required as well as of the best use to make of those means.

We may therefore say, that the twenty years' victories of the Revolution are chiefly to be ascribed to the erroneous policy of the Governments by which it was opposed.

It is true these errors first displayed themselves in the War, and the events of the War completely disappointed the expectations which policy entertained. But this did not take place because policy neglected to consult its military advisers. That Art of War in which the politician of the day could believe, namely, that derived from the reality of War at that time, that which belonged to the policy of the day, that familiar instrument which policy had hitherto used—*that* Art of War, I say, was naturally involved in the error of policy, and therefore could not teach it anything better. It is true that War itself underwent important alterations both in its nature and forms, which brought it nearer to its absolute form; but these changes were not brought about because the French Government had, to a certain extent, delivered itself from the leading-strings of policy; they arose from an altered policy, produced by the French Revolution, not only in France, but over the rest of Europe as well. This policy had called forth other means and other powers, by which it became possible to conduct War with a degree of energy which could not have been thought of otherwise.

Therefore, the actual changes in the Art of War are a consequence of alterations in policy; and, so far from being an argument for the possible separation of the two, they are, on the contrary, very strong evidence of the intimacy of their connexion.

Therefore, once more: War is an instrument of policy; it must necessarily bear its character, it must measure with its scale: the conduct of War, in its great features, is therefore policy itself, which takes up the sword in place of the pen, but does not on that account cease to think according to its own laws.

Thomas C. Schelling
THE DIPLOMACY OF VIOLENCE

The usual distinction between diplomacy and force is not merely in the instruments, words or bullets, but in the relation between adversaries—in the interplay of motives and the role of communication, understandings, compromise, and restraint. Diplomacy is bargaining: it seeks outcomes that, though not ideal for either party, are better for both than some of the alternatives. In diplomacy each party somewhat controls what the other wants, and can get more by compromise, exchange, or collaboration than by taking things in his own hands and ignoring the other's wishes. The bargaining can be polite or rude, entail threats as well as offers, assume a status quo or ignore all rights and privileges, and assume mistrust rather than trust. But whether polite or impolite, constructive or aggressive, respectful or vicious, whether it occurs among friends or antagonists and whether or not there is a basis for trust and goodwill, there must be some common interest, if only in the avoidance of mutual damage, and an awareness of the need to make the other party prefer an outcome acceptable to oneself.

With enough military force a country may not need to bargain. Some things a country wants it can take, and some things it has it can keep, by sheer strength, skill and ingenuity. It can do this *forcibly*, accommodating only to opposing strength, skill, and ingenuity and without trying to appeal to an enemy's wishes. Forcibly a country can repel and expel, penetrate and occupy, seize, exterminate, disarm and disable, confine, deny access, and directly frustrate intrusion or attack. It can, that is, if it has enough strength. "Enough" depends on how much an opponent has.

There is something else, though, that force can do. It is less military, less heroic, less impersonal, and less unilateral; it is uglier, and has received less attention in Western military strategy. In addition to seizing and holding, disarming and confining, penetrating and obstructing, and all that, military force can be used *to hurt*. In addition to taking and protecting things of value it can *destroy* value. In addition to weakening an enemy militarily it can cause an enemy plain suffering.

Pain and shock, loss and grief, privation and horror are always in some degree, sometimes in terrible degree, among the results of warfare; but in traditional military science they are incidental, they are not the object. If violence can be done incidentally, though, it can also be done purposely. The power to hurt can be counted among the most impressive attributes of military force.

Hurting, unlike forcible seizure or self-defense, is not unconcerned with the interest of others. It is measured in the suffering it can cause and the victims' motivation to avoid it. Forcible action will work against weeds or floods as well as against armies, but suffering requires a victim that can feel pain or has something to lose. To inflict suffering gains nothing and saves nothing directly; it can only make people behave to avoid it. The only purpose, unless sport or revenge, must be to influence somebody's behavior, to coerce his decision or choice. To be coercive, violence has to be anticipated. And it has to be avoidable by accommodation. The power to hurt is bargaining power. To exploit it is diplomacy—vicious diplomacy, but diplomacy.

The Contrast of Brute Force with Coercion

There is a difference between taking what you want and making someone give it to you, between fending off assault and making someone afraid to assault you, between holding what people are trying to take and making them afraid to take it, between losing what someone can forcibly take and giving it up to avoid risk or damage. It is the difference between defense and deterrence, between brute force and intimidation, between conquest and blackmail, between action and threats. It is the difference between the unilateral, "undiplomatic" recourse to strength, and coercive diplomacy based on the power to hurt.

The contrasts are several. The purely "military" or "undiplomatic" recourse to forcible action is concerned with enemy strength, not enemy interests; the coercive use of the power to hurt, though, is the very exploitation of enemy wants and fears. And brute strength is usually measured relative to enemy strength, the one directly opposing the other, while the power to hurt is typically not reduced by the enemy's power to hurt in return. Opposing strengths may cancel each other, pain and grief do not. The willingness to hurt, the credibility of a threat, and the ability to exploit the power to hurt will indeed depend on how much the adversary can hurt in return; but there is little or nothing about an adversary's pain or grief that directly reduces one's own. Two sides cannot both overcome each other with superior strength; they may both be able to hurt each other. With strength they can dispute objects of value; with sheer violence they can destroy them.

And brute force succeeds when it is used, whereas the power to hurt is most successful when held in reserve. It is the *threat* of damage, or of more damage to come, that can make someone yield or comply. It is *latent* violence that can influence someone's choice—violence that can still be withheld or inflicted, or that a victim believes can be withheld or inflicted. The threat of pain tries to structure someone's motives, while brute force tries to overcome his strength. Unhappily, the power to hurt is often communicated by some performance of it. Whether it is sheer terroristic violence to induce an irrational response, or cool premeditated violence to persuade somebody that you mean it and may do it again, it is not the pain and damage itself but its influence on somebody's behavior that matters. It is the expectation of *more* violence that gets the wanted behavior, if the power to hurt can get it at all.

To exploit a capacity for hurting and inflicting damage one needs to know what an adversary treasures and what scares him and one needs the adversary to understand what behavior of his will cause the violence to be inflicted and what will cause it to be withheld. The victim has to know what is wanted, and he may have to be assured of what is not wanted. The pain and suffering have to appear *contingent* on his behavior; it is not alone the threat that is effective—the threat of pain or loss if he fails to comply—but the corresponding assurance, possibly an implicit one, that he can avoid the pain or loss if he does comply. The prospect of certain death may stun him, but it gives him no choice.

Coercion by threat of damage also requires that our interests and our opponent's not be absolutely opposed. If his pain were our greatest delight and our satisfaction his greatest woe, we would just proceed to hurt and to frustrate each other. It is when his pain gives us little or no satisfaction compared with what he can do for us, and the action or inaction that satisfies us costs him less than the pain we can cause, that there is room for coercion. Coercion requires finding a bargain, arranging for him to be better off doing what we want—worse off not doing what we want—when he takes the threatened penalty into account.

It is this capacity for pure damage, pure violence, that is usually associated with the most vicious labor disputes, with racial disorders, with civil uprisings and their suppression, with racketeering. It is also the power to hurt rather than brute force that we use in dealing with criminals; we hurt them afterward, or threaten to, for their misdeeds rather than protect ourselves with cordons of electric wires, masonry walls, and armed guards. Jail, of course, can be either forcible restraint or threatened privation; if the object is to keep criminals out of mischief by confinement, success is measured by how many of them are gotten behind bars, but if the object is to *threaten* privation, success will be measured by how few have to be put behind bars and success then depends on the subject's understanding of the consequences. Pure damage is what a car threatens when it tries to hog the road or to keep its rightful share, or to go first through an intersection. A tank or a bulldozer can force its way regardless of others' wishes; the rest of us have to threaten damage, usually mutual damage, hoping the other driver values his car or his limbs enough to give way, hoping he sees us, and hoping he is in control of his own car. The threat of pure damage will not work against an unmanned vehicle.

This difference between coercion and brute force is as often in the intent as in the instrument. To hunt down Comanches and to exterminate them was brute force; to raid their villages to make them behave was coercive diplomacy, based on the power to hurt. The pain and loss to the Indians might have looked much the same one way as the other; the difference was one of purpose and effect. If Indians were killed because they were in the way, or somebody wanted their land, or the authorities despaired of making them behave and could not confine them and decided to exterminate them, that was pure unilateral force. If *some* Indians were killed to make *other* Indians behave, that was coercive violence—or intended to be, whether or not it was effective. The Germans at Verdun perceived themselves to be chewing up hundreds of thousands of French soldiers in a gruesome "meat-grinder." If the purpose was to eliminate a military

obstacle—the French infantryman, viewed as a military "asset" rather than as a warm human being—the offensive at Verdun was a unilateral exercise of military force. If instead the object was to make the loss of young men—not of impersonal "effectives," but of sons, husbands, fathers, and the pride of French manhood—so anguishing as to be unendurable, to make surrender a welcome relief and to spoil the foretaste of an Allied victory, then it was an exercise in coercion, in applied violence, intended to offer relief upon accommodation. And of course, since any use of force tends to be brutal, thoughtless, vengeful, or plain obstinate, the motives themselves can be mixed and confused. The fact that heroism and brutality can be either coercive diplomacy or a contest in pure strength does not promise that the distinction will be made, and the strategies enlightened by the distinction, every time some vicious enterprise gets launched.

The contrast between brute force and coercion is illustrated by two alternative strategies attributed to Genghis Khan. Early in his career he pursued the war creed of the Mongols: the vanquished can never be the friends of the victors, their death is necessary for the victor's safety. This was the unilateral extermination of a menace or a liability. The turning point of his career, according to Lynn Montross, came later when he discovered how to use his power to hurt for diplomatic ends. "The great Khan, who was not inhibited by the usual mercies, conceived the plan of forcing captives—women, children, aged fathers, favorite sons—to march ahead of his army as the first potential victims of resistance."[1] Live captives have often proved more valuable than enemy dead; and the technique discovered by the Khan in his maturity remains contemporary. North Koreans and Chinese were reported to have quartered prisoners of war near strategic targets to inhibit bombing attacks by United Nations aircraft. Hostages represent the power to hurt in its purest form.

Coercive Violence in Warfare

This distinction between the power to hurt and the power to seize or hold forcibly is important in modern war, both big war and little war, hypothetical war and real war. For many years the Greeks and the Turks on Cyprus could hurt each other indefinitely but neither could quite take or hold forcibly what they wanted or protect themselves from violence by physical means. The Jews in Palestine could not expel the British in the late 1940s but they could cause pain and fear and frustration through terrorism, and eventually influence somebody's decision. The brutal war in Algeria was more a contest in pure violence than in military strength; the question was who would first find the pain and degradation unendurable. The French troops preferred—indeed they continually tried—to make it a contest of strength, to pit military force against the nationalists' capacity for terror, to exterminate or disable the nationalists and to screen off the nationalists from the victims of their violence. But because in civil war terrorists commonly have access to victims by sheer physical propinquity, the victims and their properties could not be forcibly defended and in the end the French troops themselves resorted, unsuccessfully, to a war of pain.

Nobody believes that the Russians can take Hawaii from us, or New York, or Chicago, but nobody doubts that they might destroy people and buildings in Hawaii, Chicago, or New York. Whether the Russians can conquer West Germany in any meaningful sense is questionable; whether they can hurt it terribly is not doubted. That the United States can destroy a large part of Russia is universally taken for granted; that the United States can keep from being badly hurt, even devastated, in return, or can keep Western Europe from being devastated while itself destroying Russia, is at best arguable; and it is virtually out of the question that we could conquer Russia territorially and use its economic assets unless it were by threatening disaster and inducing compliance. It is the power to hurt, not military strength in the traditional sense, that inheres in our most impressive military capabilities at the present time [1966]. We have a Department of *Defense* but emphasize *retaliation*—"to return evil for evil" (synonyms: requital, reprisal, revenge, vengeance, retribution). And it is pain and violence, not force in the traditional sense, that inheres also in some of the least impressive military capabilities of the present time—the plastic bomb, the terrorist's bullet, the burnt crops, and the tortured farmer.

War appears to be, or threatens to be, not so much a contest of strength as one of endurance, nerve, obstinacy, and pain. It appears to be, and threatens to be, not so much a contest of military strength as a bargaining process—dirty, extortionate, and often quite reluctant bargaining on one side or both—nevertheless a bargaining process.

The difference cannot quite be expressed as one between the *use* of force and the *threat* of force. The actions involved in forcible accomplishment, on the one hand, and in fulfilling a threat, on the other, can be quite different. Sometimes the most effective direct action inflicts enough cost or pain on the enemy to serve as a threat, sometimes not. The United States threatens the Soviet Union with virtual destruction of its society in the event of a surprise attack on the United States; a hundred million deaths are awesome as pure damage, but they are useless in stopping the Soviet attack—especially if the threat is to do it all afterward anyway. So it is worth while to keep the concepts distinct—to distinguish forcible action from the threat of pain—recognizing that some actions serve as both a means of forcible accomplishment and a means of inflicting pure damage, some do not. Hostages tend to entail almost pure pain and damage, as do all forms of reprisal after the fact. Some modes of self-defense may exact so little in blood or treasure as to entail negligible violence; and some forcible actions entail so much violence that their threat can be effective by itself.

The power to hurt, though it can usually accomplish nothing directly, is potentially more versatile than a straightforward capacity for forcible accomplishment. By force alone we cannot even lead a horse to water—we have to drag him—much less make him drink. Any affirmative action, any collaboration, almost anything but physical exclusion, expulsion, or extermination, requires that an opponent or a victim *do* something, even if only to stop or get out. The threat of pain and damage may make him want to do it, and anything he can do is potentially susceptible to inducement. Brute force can only accomplish what requires no collaboration. The principle is illustrated by a technique of unarmed combat: one can disable a man by various stunning, fracturing, or killing blows, but to take him to jail one has to exploit the man's own efforts. "Come-along" holds are those that threaten pain or disablement, giving relief as long as the victim complies, giving him the option of using his own legs to get to jail.

We have to keep in mind, though, that what is pure pain, or the threat of it, at one level of decision can be equivalent to brute force at another level. Churchill was worried, during the early bombing raids on London in 1940, that Londoners might panic. Against people the bombs were pure violence, to induce their undisciplined evasion; to Churchill and the government, the bombs were a cause of inefficiency, whether they spoiled transport and made people late to work or scared people and made them afraid to work. Churchill's decisions were not going to be coerced by the fear of a few casualties. Similarly on the battlefield: tactics that frighten soldiers so that they run, duck their heads, or lay down their arms and surrender represent coercion based on the power to hurt; to the top command, which is frustrated but not coerced, such tactics are part of the contest in military discipline and strength.

The fact that violence—pure pain and damage—can be used or threatened to coerce and to deter, to intimidate and to blackmail, to demoralize and to paralyze, in a conscious process of dirty bargaining, does not by any means imply that violence is not often wanton and meaningless or, even when purposive, in danger of getting out of hand. Ancient wars were often quite "total" for the loser, the men being put to death, the women sold as slaves, the boys castrated, the cattle slaughtered, and the buildings leveled, for the sake of revenge, justice, personal gain, or merely custom. If an enemy bombs a city, by design or by carelessness, we usually bomb his if we can. In the excitement and fatigue of warfare, revenge is one of the few satisfactions that can be savored; and justice can often be construed to demand the enemy's punishment, even if it is delivered with more enthusiasm than justice requires. When Jerusalem fell to the Crusaders in 1099 the ensuing slaughter was one of the bloodiest in military chronicles. "The men of the West literally waded in gore, their march to the church of the Holy Sepulcher being gruesomely likened to 'treading out the wine press'. . . . ," reports Montross (p. 138), who observes that these excesses usually came at the climax of the capture of a fortified post or city. "For long the assailants have endured more punishment than they were able to inflict; then once the walls are breached, pent up emotions find an outlet in murder, rape and plunder, which discipline is powerless to prevent." The same occurred when Tyre fell to Alexander after a painful siege, and the phenomenon was not unknown on Pacific islands in the Second World War. Pure violence, like fire, can be harnessed to a purpose; that does not mean that behind every holocaust is a shrewd intention successfully fulfilled.

But if the occurrence of violence does not always bespeak a shrewd purpose, the absence of pain and destruction is no sign that violence was idle. Violence is most purposive and most successful when it is threatened and not used. Successful threats are those that do not have to be carried out. By European standards, Denmark was virtually unharmed in the Second World War; it was violence that made the Danes submit. Withheld violence—successfully threatened violence—can look clean, even merciful. The fact that a kidnap victim is returned unharmed, against receipt of ample ransom, does not make kidnapping a nonviolent enterprise. * * *

■ ■ ■

The Strategic Role of Pain and Damage

Pure violence, nonmilitary violence, appears most conspicuously in relations between unequal countries, where there is no substantial military challenge and the outcome of military engagement is not in question. Hitler could make his threats contemptuously and brutally against Austria; he could make them, if he wished, in a more refined way against Denmark. It is noteworthy that it was Hitler, not his generals, who used this kind of language; proud military establishments do not like to think of themselves as extortionists. Their favorite job is to deliver victory, to dispose of opposing military force and to leave most of the civilian violence to politics and diplomacy. But if there is no room for doubt how a contest in strength will come out, it may be possible to bypass the military stage altogether and to proceed at once to the coercive bargaining.

A typical confrontation of unequal forces occurs at the *end* of a war, between victor and vanquished. Where Austria was vulnerable before a shot was fired, France was vulnerable after its military shield had collapsed in 1940. Surrender negotiations are the place where the threat of civil violence can come to the fore. Surrender negotiations are often so one-sided, or the potential violence so unmistakable, that bargaining succeeds and the violence remains in reserve. But the fact that most of the actual damage was done during the military stage of the war, prior to victory and defeat, does not mean that violence was idle in the aftermath, only that it was latent and the threat of it successful.

Indeed, victory is often but a prerequisite to the exploitation of the power to hurt. When Xenophon was fighting in Asia Minor under Persian leadership, it took military strength to disperse enemy soldiers and occupy their lands; but land was not what the victor wanted, nor was victory for its own sake.

> Next day the Persian leader burned the villages to the ground, not leaving a single house standing, so as to strike terror into the other tribes to show them what would happen if they did not give in. . . . He sent some of the prisoners into the hills and told them to say that if the inhabitants did not come down and settle in their houses to submit to him, he would burn up their villages too and destroy their crops, and they would die of hunger.[2]

Military victory was but the *price of admission*. The payoff depended upon the successful threat of violence.

■ ■ ■

The Nuclear Contribution to Terror and Violence

Man has, it is said, for the first time in history enough military power to eliminate his species from the earth, weapons against which there is no conceivable defense. War has become, it is said, so destructive and terrible that it ceases to be an instrument of national power. "For the first time in human history," says Max Lerner in a book whose title, *The Age of Overkill,* conveys the point, "men have bottled up a power . . . which they have thus far not dared to use."[3] And Soviet military authorities, whose party dislikes having to accommodate an entire theory of history to a single technological event, have had to reexamine a set of principles that had been given the embarrassing name of "permanently operating factors" in warfare. Indeed, our era is epitomized by words like "the first time in human history," and by the abdication of what was "permanent."

For dramatic impact these statements are splendid. Some of them display a tendency, not at all necessary, to belittle the catastrophe of earlier wars. They may exaggerate the historical novelty of deterrence and the balance of terror. More important, they do not help to identify just what is new about war when so much destructive energy can be packed in warheads at a price that permits advanced countries to have them in large numbers. Nuclear warheads are incomparably more devastating than anything packaged before. What does that imply about war?

It is not true that for the first time in history man has the capability to destroy a large fraction, even the major part, of the human race. Japan was defenseless by August 1945. With a combination of bombing and blockade, eventually invasion, and if necessary the deliberate spread of disease, the United States could probably have exterminated the population of the Japanese islands without nuclear weapons. It would have been a gruesome, expensive, and mortifying campaign; it would have taken time and demanded persistence. But we had the economic and technical capacity to do it; and, together with the Russians or without them, we could have done the same in many populous parts of the world. Against defenseless people there is not much that nuclear weapons can do that cannot be done with an ice pick. And it would not have strained our Gross National Product to do it with ice picks.

It is a grisly thing to talk about. We did not do it and it is not imaginable that we would have done it. We had no reason; if we had had a reason, we would not have the persistence of purpose, once the fury of war had been dissipated in victory and we had taken on the task of executioner. If we and our enemies might do such a thing to each other now, and to others as well, it is not because nuclear weapons have for the first time made it feasible.

■   ■   ■

* * * In the past it has usually been the victors who could do what they pleased to the enemy. War has often been "total war" for the loser. With deadly monotony the Persians, Greeks, or Romans "put to death all men of military age, and sold the women and children into slavery," leaving the defeated territory nothing but its name until new settlers arrived sometime later. But the defeated could not do the same to their victors. The boys could be castrated and sold only after the war had been won, and only on the side that lost it. The power to hurt could be brought to bear only after military strength had achieved victory. The same sequence characterized the great wars of this century; for reasons of technology and geography, military force has usually had to penetrate, to exhaust, or to collapse opposing military force—to achieve military victory—before it could be brought to bear on the enemy nation itself. The Allies in World War I could not inflict coercive pain and suffering directly on the Germans in a decisive way until they could defeat the German army; and the Germans could not coerce the French people with bayonets unless they first beat the Allied troops that stood in their way. With two-dimensional warfare, there is a tendency for troops to confront each other, shielding their own lands while attempting to press into each other's. Small penetrations could not do major damage to the people; large penetrations were so destructive of military organization that they usually ended the military phase of the war.

Nuclear weapons make it possible to do monstrous violence to the enemy without first achieving victory. With nuclear weapons and today's means of delivery, one expects to penetrate an enemy homeland without first collapsing his military force. What nuclear weapons have done, or appear to do, is to promote this kind of warfare to first place. Nuclear weapons threaten to make war less military, and are responsible for the lowered status of "military victory" at the present time. *Victory is no longer a prerequisite for hurting the enemy.* And it is no assurance against being terribly hurt. One need not wait until he has won the war before inflicting "unendurable" damages on his enemy. One need not wait until he has lost the war. There was a time when the assurance of victory—false or genuine assurance—could make national leaders not just willing but sometimes enthusiastic about war. Not now.

Not only *can* nuclear weapons hurt the enemy before the war has been won, and perhaps hurt decisively enough to make the military engagement academic, but it is widely assumed that in a major war that is *all* they can do. Major war is often discussed as though it would be only a contest in national destruction. If this is indeed the case—if the destruction of cities and their populations has become, with nuclear weapons, the primary object in an all-out war—the sequence of war has been reversed. Instead of destroying enemy forces as a prelude to imposing one's will on the enemy nation, one would have to destroy the nation as a means or a prelude to destroying the enemy forces. If one cannot disable enemy forces without virtually destroying the country, the victor does not even have the option of sparing the conquered nation. He has already destroyed it. Even with blockade and strategic bombing it could be supposed that a country would be defeated before it was destroyed, or would elect surrender before annihilation had gone far. In the Civil War it could be hoped that the South would become too weak to fight before it became too weak to survive. For "all-out" war, nuclear weapons threaten to reverse this sequence.

So nuclear weapons do make a difference, marking an epoch in warfare. The difference is not just in the amount of destruction that can be accomplished but in the role of destruction and in the decision process. Nuclear weapons can change the speed of events, the control of events, the sequence of events, the relation of victor to vanquished, and the relation of homeland to fighting front. Deterrence rests today on the threat of pain and extinction, not just on the threat of military defeat. We may argue about the wisdom of announcing "unconditional surrender" as an aim in the last major war, but seem to expect "unconditional destruction" as a matter of course in another one.

Something like the same destruction always *could* be done. With nuclear weapons there is an expectation that it *would* be done. It is not "overkill" that is new; the American army surely had enough 30 caliber bullets to kill everybody in the world in 1945, or if it did not it could have bought them without any strain. What is new is plain "kill"—the idea that major war might be just a contest in the killing of countries, or not even a contest but just two parallel exercises in devastation.

That is the difference nuclear weapons make. At least they *may* make that difference. They also may not. If the weapons themselves are vulnerable to attack, or the machines that carry them, a successful surprise might eliminate the opponent's means of retribution. That an enormous explosion can be packaged in a single bomb does not by itself guarantee that the victor will receive deadly punishment. Two gunfighters facing each other in a Western town had an unquestioned capacity to kill one another; that did not guarantee that both would die in a gunfight—only the slower of the two. Less deadly weapons, permitting an injured one to shoot back before he died, might have been more conducive to a restraining balance of terror, or of caution. The very efficiency of nuclear weapons could make them ideal for starting war, if they can suddenly eliminate the enemy's capability to shoot back.

And there is a contrary possibility: that nuclear weapons are not vulnerable to attack and prove not to be terribly effective against each other, posing no need to shoot them quickly for fear they will be destroyed before they are launched, and with no task available but the systematic destruction of the enemy country and no necessary reason to do it fast rather than slowly. Imagine that nuclear destruction *had* to go slowly—that the bombs could be dropped only one per day. The prospect would look very different, something like the most terroristic guerilla warfare on a massive scale. It happens that nuclear war does not have to go slowly; but it may also not have to go speedily. The mere existence of nuclear weapons does not itself determine that everything must go off in a blinding flash, any more than that it must go slowly. Nuclear weapons do not simplify things quite that much.

■　■　■

War no longer looks like just a contest of strength. War and the brink of war are more a contest of nerve and risk-taking, of pain and endurance. Small wars embody the threat of a larger war; they are not just military engagements but "crisis diplomacy." The threat of war has always been somewhere underneath international diplomacy, but for Americans it is now much nearer the surface. Like the threat of a strike in industrial relations, the threat of divorce in a family dispute, or the threat of bolting the party at a political convention, the threat of violence continuously circumscribes international politics. Neither strength nor goodwill procures immunity.

Military strategy can no longer be thought of, as it could for some countries in some eras, as the science of military victory. It is now equally, if not more, the art of coercion, of intimidation and deterrence. The instruments of war are more punitive than acquisitive. Military strategy, whether we like it or not, has become the diplomacy of violence.

NOTES

1. Lynn Montross, *War Through the Ages* (3d ed. New York, Harper and Brothers, 1960), p. 146.
2. Xenophon, *The Persian Expedition*, Rex Warner, transl. (Baltimore, Penguin Books, 1949), p. 272. "The 'rational' goal of the threat of violence," says H. L. Nieburg, "is an accommodation of interests, not the provocation of actual violence. Similarly the 'rational' goal of actual violence is demonstration of the will and capability of action, establishing a measure of the credibility of future threats, not the exhaustion of that capability in unlimited conflict." "Uses of Violence," *Journal of Conflict Resolution, 7* (1963), 44.
3. New York, Simon and Schuster, 1962, p. 47.

Robert Jervis

COOPERATION UNDER THE SECURITY DILEMMA

I. Anarchy and the Security Dilemma

The lack of an international sovereign not only permits wars to occur, but also makes it difficult for states that are satisfied with the status quo to arrive at goals that they recognize as being in their common interest. Because there are no institutions or authorities that can make and enforce international laws, the policies of cooperation that will bring mutual rewards if others cooperate may bring disaster if they do not. Because states are aware of this, anarchy encourages behavior that leaves all concerned worse off than they could be, even in the extreme case in which all states would like to freeze the status quo. This is true of the men in Rousseau's "Stag Hunt." If they cooperate to trap the stag, they will all eat well. But if one person defects to chase a rabbit—which he likes less than stag—none of the others will get anything. Thus, all actors have the same preference order, and there is a solution that gives each his first choice: (1) cooperate and trap the stag (the international analogue being cooperation and disarmament); (2) chase a rabbit while others remain at their posts (maintain a high level of arms while others are disarmed); (3) all chase rabbits (arms competition and high risk of war); and (4) stay at the original position while another chases a rabbit (being disarmed while others are armed). Unless

From *World Politics* 30, no. 2 (Jan. 1978), 167–214. Some of the author's notes have been omitted.

each person thinks that the others will cooperate, he himself will not. And why might he fear that any other person would do something that would sacrifice his own first choice? The other might not understand the situation, or might not be able to control his impulses if he saw a rabbit, or might fear that some other member of the group is unreliable. If the person voices any of these suspicions, others are more likely to fear that he will defect, thus making them more likely to defect, thus making it more rational for him to defect. Of course in this simple case—and in many that are more realistic—there are a number of arrangements that could permit cooperation. But the main point remains: although actors may know that they seek a common goal, they may not be able to reach it.

Even when there is a solution that is everyone's first choice, the international case is characterized by three difficulties not present in the Stag Hunt. First, to the incentives to defect given above must be added the potent fear that even if the other state now supports the status quo, it may become dissatisfied later. No matter how much decision makers are committed to the status quo, they cannot bind themselves and their successors to the same path. Minds can be changed, new leaders can come to power, values can shift, new opportunities and dangers can arise.

The second problem arises from a possible solution. In order to protect their possessions, states often seek to control resources or land outside their own territory. Countries that are not self-sufficient must try to assure that the necessary supplies will continue to flow in wartime. This was part of the explanation for Japan's drive into China and Southeast Asia before World War II. If there were an international authority that could guarantee access, this motive for control would disappear. But since there is not, even a state that would prefer the status quo to increasing its area of control may pursue the latter policy.

When there are believed to be tight linkages between domestic and foreign policy or between the domestic politics of two states, the quest for security may drive states to interfere pre-emptively in the domestic politics of others in order to provide an ideological buffer zone. * * *

More frequently, the concern is with direct attack. In order to protect themselves, states seek to control, or at least to neutralize, areas on their borders. But attempts to establish buffer zones can alarm others who have stakes there, who fear that undesirable precedents will be set, or who believe that their own vulnerability will be increased. When buffers are sought in areas empty of great powers, expansion tends to feed on itself in order to protect what is acquired. * * *

Though this process is most clearly visible when it involves territorial expansion, it often operates with the increase of less tangible power and influence. The expansion of power usually brings with it an expansion of responsibilities and commitments; to meet them, still greater power is required. The state will take many positions that are subject to challenge. It will be involved with a wide range of controversial issues unrelated to its core values. And retreats that would be seen as normal if made by a small power would be taken as an index of weakness inviting predation if made by a large one.

The third problem present in international politics but not in the Stag Hunt is the security dilemma: many of the means by which a state tries to increase its security decrease the security of others. In domestic society, there are several ways to increase the safety of one's person and property without endangering others. One can move to a safer neighborhood, put bars on the windows, avoid dark streets, and keep a distance from suspicious-looking characters. Of course these measures are not convenient, cheap, or certain of success. But no one save criminals need be alarmed if a person takes them. In international politics, however, one state's gain in security often inadvertently threatens others. In explaining British policy on naval disarmament in the interwar period to the Japanese, Ramsey MacDonald said that "Nobody wanted Japan to be insecure."[1] But the problem was not with British desires, but with the consequences of her policy. In earlier periods, too, Britain had needed a navy large enough to keep the shipping lanes open. But such a navy could not avoid being a menace to any other state with a coast that could be raided, trade that could be interdicted, or colonies that could be isolated. When Germany started building a powerful navy before World War I, Britain objected that it could only be an offensive weapon aimed at her. As Sir Edward Grey, the Foreign Secretary, put it to King Edward VII: "If the German Fleet ever becomes superior to ours, the German Army can conquer this country. There is no corresponding risk of this kind to Germany; for however superior our Fleet was, no naval victory could bring us any nearer to Berlin." The English position was half correct: Germany's navy was an anti-British instrument. But the British often overlooked what the Germans knew full well: "in every quarrel with England, German colonies and trade were . . . hostages for England to take." Thus, whether she intended it or not, the British Navy constituted an important instrument of coercion.[2]

II. What Makes Cooperation More Likely?

Given this gloomy picture, the obvious question is, why are we not all dead? Or, to put it less

Figure 8.1. Stag Hunt and Prisoner's Dilemma

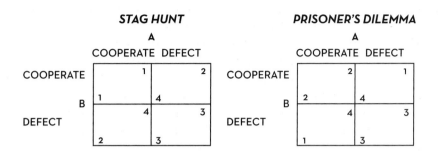

starkly, what kinds of variables ameliorate the impact of anarchy and the security dilemma? The working of several can be seen in terms of the Stag Hunt or repeated plays of the Prisoner's Dilemma.[3] The Prisoner's Dilemma differs from the Stag Hunt in that there is no solution that is in the best interests of all the participants; there are offensive as well as defensive incentives to defect from the coalition with the others; and, if the game is to be played only once, the only rational response is to defect [Figure 8.1]. But if the game is repeated indefinitely, the latter characteristic no longer holds and we can analyze the game in terms similar to those applied to the Stag Hunt. It would be in the interest of each actor to have others deprived of the power to defect; each would be willing to sacrifice this ability if others were similarly restrained. But if the others are not, then it is in the actor's interest to retain the power to defect.[4] The game theory matrices for these two situations are given below, with the numbers in the boxes being the order of the actor's preferences.

We can see the logical possibilities by rephrasing our question: "Given either of the above situations, what makes it more or less likely that the players will cooperate and arrive at CC?" The chances of achieving this outcome will be increased by: (1) anything that increases incentives to cooperate by increasing the gains of mutual cooperation (CC) and/or decreasing the costs the actor will pay if he cooperates and the other does not (CD); (2) anything that decreases the incentives for defecting by decreasing the gains of taking advantage of the other (DC) and/or increasing the costs of mutual noncooperation (DD); (3) anything that increases each side's expectation that the other will cooperate.[5]

The Costs of Being Exploited (CD)

The fear of being exploited (that is, the cost of CD) most strongly drives the security dilemma; one of the main reasons why international life is not more nasty, brutish, and short is that states are not as vulnerable as men are in a state of nature. People are easy to kill, but as Adam Smith replied to a friend who feared that the Napoleonic Wars would ruin England, "Sir, there is a great deal of ruin in a nation."[6] The easier it is to destroy a state, the greater the reason for it either to join a larger and more secure unit, or else to be especially suspicious of others, to require a large army, and, if conditions are favorable, to attack at the slightest provocation rather than wait to be attacked. If the failure to eat that day—be it venison or rabbit—means that he will starve, a person is likely to defect in the Stag Hunt even if he really likes venison and has a high level of trust in his colleagues. (Defection is especially likely if the others are also starving or if they know that he is.) By contrast, if the costs of CD are lower, if people are well-fed or states are resilient, they can afford to take a more relaxed view of threats.

A relatively low cost of CD has the effect of transforming the game from one in which both players make their choices simultaneously to one in which an actor can make his choice after the other has moved. He will not have to defect out of fear that the other will, but can wait to see what the other will do. States that can afford to be cheated in a bargain or that cannot be destroyed by a surprise attack can more easily trust others and need not act at the first, and ambiguous, sign of menace. Because they have a margin of time and error, they need not match, or more than match, any others' arms in peacetime. They can mobilize in the prewar period or even at the start of the war itself, and still survive. For example, those who opposed a crash program to develop the H-bomb felt that the U.S. margin of safety was large enough so that even if Russia managed to gain a lead in the race, America would not be endangered. The program's advocates disagreed: "If we let the Russians get the super first, catastrophe becomes all but certain."[7]

When the costs of CD are tolerable, not only is security easier to attain but, what is even more important here, the relatively low level of arms and relatively passive foreign policy that a status-quo power will be able to adopt are less likely to threaten others. Thus it is easier for status-quo states to act on their common interests if they are hard to conquer. All other things being equal, a world of small states will feel the effects of anarchy much more than a world of large ones. Defensible borders, large size, and protection against sudden attack not only aid the state, but facilitate cooperation that can benefit all states.

Of course, if one state gains invulnerability by being more powerful than most others, the problem will remain because its security provides a base from which it can exploit others. When the price a state will pay for DD is low, it leaves others with few hostages for its good behavior. Others who are more vulnerable will grow apprehensive, which will lead them to acquire more arms and will reduce the chances of cooperation. The best situation is one in which a state will not suffer greatly if others exploit it, for example, by cheating on an arms control agreement (that is, the costs of CD are low); but it will pay a high long-run price if cooperation with the others breaks down—for example, if agreements cease functioning or if there is a long war (that is, the costs of DD are high). The state's invulnerability is then mostly passive; it provides some protection, but it cannot be used to menace others. As we will discuss below, this situation is approximated when it is easier for states to defend themselves than to attack others, or when mutual deterrence obtains because neither side can protect itself.

The differences between highly vulnerable and less vulnerable states are illustrated by the contrasting policies of Britain and Austria after the Napoleonic Wars. Britain's geographic isolation and political stability allowed her to take a fairly relaxed view of disturbances on the Continent. Minor wars and small changes in territory or in the distribution of power did not affect her vital interests. An adversary who was out to overthrow the system could be stopped after he had made his intentions clear. And revolutions within other states were no menace, since they would not set off unrest within England. Austria, surrounded by strong powers, was not so fortunate; her policy had to be more closely attuned to all conflicts. By the time an aggressor-state had clearly shown its colors, Austria would be gravely threatened. And foreign revolutions, be they democratic or nationalistic, would encourage groups in Austria to upset the existing order. So it is not surprising that Metternich propounded the doctrine summarized earlier, which defended Austria's right to interfere in the internal affairs of others, and that British leaders rejected this view. Similarly, Austria wanted the Congress system to be a relatively tight one, regulating most disputes. The British favored a less centralized system. In other words, in order to protect herself, Austria had either to threaten or to harm others, whereas Britain did not. For Austria and her neighbors the security dilemma was acute; for Britain it was not.

The ultimate cost of CD is of course loss of sovereignty. This cost can vary from situation to situation. The lower it is (for instance, because the two states have compatible ideologies, are similar ethnically, have a common culture, or because the citizens of the losing state expect economic benefits), the less the impact of the security dilemma; the greater the costs, the greater the impact of the dilemma. Here is another reason why extreme differences in values and ideologies exacerbate international conflict.

■   ■   ■

SUBJECTIVE SECURITY DEMANDS

Decision makers act in terms of the vulnerability they feel, which can differ from the actual situation; we must therefore examine the decision makers' subjective security requirements. Two dimensions are involved. First, even if they agree about the objective situation, people can differ about how much security they desire—or, to put it more precisely, about the price they are willing to pay to gain increments of security. The more states value their security above all else (that is, see a prohibitively high cost in CD), the more they are likely to be sensitive to even minimal threats, and to demand high levels of arms. And if arms are positively valued because of pressures from a military-industrial complex, it will be especially hard for status-quo powers to cooperate. By contrast, the security dilemma will not operate as strongly when pressing domestic concerns increase the opportunity costs of armaments. In this case, the net advantage of exploiting the other (DC)

will be less, and the costs of arms races (that is, one aspect of DD) will be greater; therefore the state will behave as though it were relatively invulnerable.

The second aspect of subjective security is the perception of threat (that is, the estimate of whether the other will cooperate). A state that is predisposed to see either a specific other state as an adversary, or others in general as a menace, will react more strongly and more quickly than a state that sees its environment as benign. Indeed, when a state believes that another not only is not likely to be an adversary, but has sufficient interests in common with it to be an ally, then it will actually welcome an increase in the other's power.

■   ■   ■

Geography, Commitments, Beliefs, and Security through Expansion

* * * Situations vary in the ease or difficulty with which all states can simultaneously achieve a high degree of security. The influence of military technology on this variable is the subject of the next section. Here we want to treat the impact of beliefs, geography, and commitments (many of which can be considered to be modifications of geography, since they bind states to defend areas outside their homelands). In the crowded continent of Europe, security requirements were hard to mesh. Being surrounded by powerful states, Germany's problem—or the problem created by Germany—was always great and was even worse when her relations with both France and Russia were bad, such as before World War I. In that case, even a status-quo Germany, if she could not change the political situation, would almost have been forced to adopt something like the Schlieffen Plan. Because she could not hold off both of her enemies, she had

to be prepared to defeat one quickly and then deal with the other in a more leisurely fashion. If France or Russia stayed out of a war between the other state and Germany, they would allow Germany to dominate the Continent (even if that was not Germany's aim). They therefore had to deny Germany this ability, thus making Germany less secure. Although Germany's arrogant and erratic behavior, coupled with the desire for an unreasonably high level of security (which amounted to the desire to escape from her geographic plight), compounded the problem, even wise German statesmen would have been hard put to gain a high degree of security without alarming their neighbors.

■ ■ ■

III. Offense, Defense, and the Security Dilemma

Another approach starts with the central point of the security dilemma—that an increase in one state's security decreases the security of others—and examines the conditions under which this proposition holds. Two crucial variables are involved: whether defensive weapons and policies can be distinguished from offensive ones, and whether the defense or the offense has the advantage. The definitions are not always clear, and many cases are difficult to judge, but these two variables shed a great deal of light on the question of whether status-quo powers will adopt compatible security policies. All the variables discussed so far leave the heart of the problem untouched. But when defensive weapons differ from offensive ones, it is possible for a state to make itself more secure without making others less secure. And when the defense has the advantage over the offense, a large increase in one state's security only slightly decreases the security of the others, and status-quo powers can all enjoy a high level of security and largely escape from the state of nature.

Offense-Defense Balance

When we say that the offense has the advantage, we simply mean that it is easier to destroy the other's army and take its territory than it is to defend one's own. When the defense has the advantage, it is easier to protect and to hold than it is to move forward, destroy, and take. If effective defenses can be erected quickly, an attacker may be able to keep territory he has taken in an initial victory. Thus, the dominance of the defense made it very hard for Britain and France to push Germany out of France in World War I. But when superior defenses are difficult for an aggressor to improvise on the battlefield and must be constructed during peacetime, they provide no direct assistance to him.

The security dilemma is at its most vicious when commitments, strategy, or technology dictate that the only route to security lies through expansion. Status-quo powers must then act like aggressors; the fact that they would gladly agree to forego the opportunity for expansion in return for guarantees for their security has no implications for their behavior. Even if expansion is not sought as a goal in itself, there will be quick and drastic changes in the distribution of territory and influence. Conversely, when the defense has the advantage, status-quo states can make themselves more secure without gravely endangering others.[8] Indeed, if the defense has enough of an advantage and if the states are of roughly equal size, not only will the security dilemma cease to inhibit status-quo states from cooperating, but aggression will be next to impossible, thus rendering international anarchy relatively unimportant. If states cannot conquer each other, then the lack of sovereignty, although it presents problems of collective goods in a number of areas, no longer forces states to devote their primary attention to self-preservation. Although, if force were not usable, there would be fewer restraints on the use of nonmilitary instruments, these are rarely powerful enough to threaten the vital interests of a major state.

Two questions of the offense-defense balance can be separated. First, does the state have to spend more or less than one dollar on defensive forces to offset each dollar spent by the other side on forces that could be used to attack? If the state has one dollar to spend on increasing its security, should it put it into offensive or defensive forces? Second, with a given inventory of forces, is it better to attack or to defend? Is there an incentive to strike first or to absorb the other's blow? These two aspects are often linked: if each dollar spent on offense can overcome each dollar spent on defense, and if both sides have the same defense budgets, then both are likely to build offensive forces and find it attractive to attack rather than to wait for the adversary to strike.

These aspects affect the security dilemma in different ways. The first has its greatest impact on arms races. If the defense has the advantage, and if the status-quo powers have reasonable subjective security requirements, they can probably avoid an arms race. Although an increase in one side's arms and security will still decrease the other's security, the former's increase will be larger than the latter's decrease. So if one side increases its arms, the other can bring its security back up to its previous level by adding a smaller amount to its forces. And if the first side reacts to this change, its increase will also be smaller than the stimulus that produced it. Thus a stable equilibrium will be reached. Shifting from dynamics to statics, each side can be quite secure with forces roughly equal to those of the other. Indeed, if the defense is much more potent than the offense, each side can be willing to have forces much smaller than the other's, and can be indifferent to a wide range of the other's defense policies.

The second aspect—whether it is better to attack or to defend—influences short-run stability. When the offense has the advantage, a state's reaction to international tension will increase the chances of war. The incentives for pre-emption and the "reciprocal fear of surprise attack" in this situation have been made clear by analyses of the dangers that exist when two countries have first-strike capabilities.[9] There is no way for the state to increase its security without menacing, or even attacking, the other. Even Bismarck, who once called preventive war "committing suicide from fear of death," said that "no government, if it regards war as inevitable even if it does not want it, would be so foolish as to leave to the enemy the choice of time and occasion and to wait for the moment which is most convenient for the enemy."[10] In another arena, the same dilemma applies to the policeman in a dark alley confronting a suspected criminal who appears to be holding a weapon. Though racism may indeed be present, the security dilemma can account for many of the tragic shootings of innocent people in the ghettos.

Beliefs about the course of a war in which the offense has the advantage further deepen the security dilemma. When there are incentives to strike first, a successful attack will usually so weaken the other side that victory will be relatively quick, bloodless, and decisive. It is in these periods when conquest is possible and attractive that states consolidate power internally—for instance, by destroying the feudal barons—and expand externally. There are several consequences that decrease the chance of cooperation among status-quo states. First, war will be profitable for the winner. The costs will be low and the benefits high. Of course, losers will suffer; the fear of losing could induce states to try to form stable cooperative arrangements, but the temptation of victory will make this particularly difficult. Second, because wars are expected to be both frequent and short, there will be incentives for high levels of arms, and quick and strong reaction to the other's increases in arms. The state cannot afford to wait until there is unambiguous evidence that the other is building new weapons. Even large states that have faith in their economic strength cannot wait, because the war will be over before their products can reach the army. Third, when wars are quick, states will have to recruit allies in advance.[11] Without the opportunity for bargaining and re-alignments during the opening stages of hostilities, peacetime diplomacy loses a degree of the fluidity that facilitates balance-of-power policies. Because alliances must be secured during peacetime, the international system is more likely to become bipolar. It is hard to say whether war therefore becomes more or less likely, but this bipolarity increases tension between the two camps and makes it harder for status-quo states to gain the benefits of cooperation. Fourth, if wars are frequent, statesmen's perceptual thresholds will be adjusted accordingly and they will be quick to perceive ambiguous evidence as indicating that others are aggressive. Thus, there will be more cases of status-quo powers arming against each other in the incorrect belief that the other is hostile.

When the defense has the advantage, all the foregoing is reversed. The state that fears attack does not pre-empt—since that would be a wasteful use of its military resources—but rather prepares to receive an attack. Doing so does not decrease the security of others, and several states can do it simultaneously; the situation will therefore be stable, and status-quo powers will be able to cooperate. * * *

More is involved than short-run dynamics. When the defense is dominant, wars are likely to become stalemates and can be won only at enormous cost. Relatively small and weak states can hold off larger and stronger ones, or can deter attack by raising the costs of conquest to an unacceptable level. States then approach equality in what they can do to each other. Like the .45-caliber pistol in the American West, fortifications were the "great equalizer" in some periods. Changes in the status quo are less frequent and cooperation is more common wherever the security dilemma is thereby reduced.

Many of these arguments can be illustrated by the major powers' policies in the periods preceding the two world wars. Bismarck's wars surprised statesmen by showing that the offense had the advantage, and by being quick, relatively cheap, and quite decisive. Falling into a common error, observers projected this pattern into the future. The resulting expectations had several effects. First, states sought semi-permanent allies. In the early stages of the Franco-Prussian War, Napoleon III had thought that there would be plenty of time to recruit Austria to his side. Now, others were not going to repeat this mistake. Second, defense budgets were high and reacted quite sharply to increases on the other side. * * * Third, most decision makers thought that the next European war would not cost much blood and treasure.[12] That is one reason why war was generally seen as inevitable and why mass opinion was so bellicose. Fourth, once war seemed likely, there were strong pressures to pre-empt. Both sides believed that whoever moved first could penetrate the other deep enough to disrupt mobilization and thus gain an insurmountable advantage. (There was no such belief about the use of naval forces. Although Churchill made an ill-advised speech saying that if German ships "do not come out and fight in time of war they will be dug out like rats in a hole,"[13] everyone knew that submarines, mines, and coastal fortifications made this impossible. So at the start of the war each navy prepared to defend itself rather than attack, and the short-run destabilizing forces that launched the armies toward each other did not operate.)[14] Furthermore, each side knew that the other saw the situation the same way, thus increasing the perceived danger that the other would attack, and giving each added reasons to precipitate a war if conditions seemed favorable. In the long and the short run, there were thus both offensive and defensive incentives to strike. This situation casts light on the common question about German motives in 1914: "Did Germany unleash the war deliberately to become a world power or did she support Austria merely to defend a weakening ally," thereby protecting her own position?[15] To some extent, this question is misleading. Because of the perceived advantage of the offense, war was seen as the best route both to gaining expansion and to avoiding drastic loss of influence. There seemed to be no way for Germany merely to retain and safeguard her existing position.

Of course the war showed these beliefs to have been wrong on all points. Trenches and machine guns gave the defense an overwhelming advantage. The fighting became deadlocked and produced horrendous casualties. It made no sense for the combatants to bleed themselves to death. If they had known the power of the defense beforehand, they would have rushed for their own trenches rather than for the enemy's territory. Each side could have done this without increasing the other's incentives to strike. War might have broken out anyway, * * * but at least the pressures of time and the fear of allowing the other to get the first blow would not have contributed to this end. And, had both sides known the costs of the war, they would have negotiated much more seriously. The obvious question is why the states did not seek a negotiated settlement as soon as the shape of the war became clear. Schlieffen had said that if his plan failed, peace should be sought.[16] The answer is complex, uncertain, and largely outside of the scope of our concerns. But part of the reason was the hope and sometimes the expectation that breakthroughs could be made and the dominance of the offensive restored. Without that hope, the political and psychological pressures to fight to a decisive victory might have been overcome.

The politics of the interwar period were shaped by the memories of the previous conflict and the belief that any future war would resemble it. Political and military lessons reinforced each other in ameliorating the security dilemma. Because it was believed that the First World War had been a mistake that could have been avoided by skillful conciliation, both Britain and, to a lesser extent, France were highly sensitive to the possibility that interwar Germany was not a real threat to peace,

and alert to the danger that reacting quickly and strongly to her arms could create unnecessary conflict. And because Britain and France expected the defense to continue to dominate, they concluded that it was safe to adopt a more relaxed and non-threatening military posture.[17] Britain also felt less need to maintain tight alliance bonds. The Allies' military posture then constituted only a slight danger to Germany; had the latter been content with the status quo, it would have been easy for both sides to have felt secure behind their lines of fortifications. Of course the Germans were not content, so it is not surprising that they devoted their money and attention to finding ways out of a defense-dominated stalemate. *Blitzkrieg* tactics were necessary if they were to use force to change the status quo.

The initial stages of the war on the Western Front also contrasted with the First World War. Only with the new air arm were there any incentives to strike first, and these forces were too weak to carry out the grandiose plans that had been both dreamed and feared. The armies, still the main instrument, rushed to defensive positions. Perhaps the allies could have successfully attacked while the Germans were occupied in Poland.[18] But belief in the defense was so great that this was never seriously contemplated. Three months after the start of the war, the French Prime Minister summed up the view held by almost everyone but Hitler: on the Western Front there is "deadlock. Two Forces of equal strength and the one that attacks seeing such enormous casualties that it cannot move without endangering the continuation of the war or of the aftermath."[19] The Allies were caught in a dilemma they never fully recognized, let alone solved. On the one hand, they had very high war aims; although unconditional surrender had not yet been adopted, the British had decided from the start that the removal of Hitler was a necessary condition for peace.[20] On the other hand, there were no realistic plans or instruments for allowing the Allies to impose their will on the other side. The British Chief of the Imperial General Staff noted, "The French have no intention of carrying out an offensive for years, if at all"; the British were only slightly bolder.[21] So the Allies looked to a long war that would wear the Germans down, cause civilian suffering through shortages, and eventually undermine Hitler. There was little analysis to support this view—and indeed it probably was not supportable—but as long as the defense was dominant and the numbers on each side relatively equal, what else could the Allies do?

To summarize, the security dilemma was much less powerful after World War I than it had been before. In the later period, the expected power of the defense allowed status-quo states to pursue compatible security policies and avoid arms races. Furthermore, high tension and fear of war did not set off short-run dynamics by which each state, trying to increase its security, inadvertently acted to make war more likely. The expected high costs of war, however, led the Allies to believe that no sane German leader would run the risks entailed in an attempt to dominate the Continent, and discouraged them from risking war themselves.

TECHNOLOGY AND GEOGRAPHY

Technology and geography are the two main factors that determine whether the offense or the defense has the advantage. As Brodie notes, "On the tactical level, as a rule, few physical factors favor the attacker but many favor the defender. The defender usually has the advantage of cover. He characteristically fires from behind some form of shelter while his opponent crosses open ground."[22] Anything that increases the amount of ground the attacker has to cross, or impedes his progress across it, or makes him more vulnerable while crossing, increases the advantage accruing to the defense. When states are separated by barriers that produce these effects, the security dilemma is eased, since both can have forces adequate for defense without being able to attack. * * *

Oceans, large rivers, and mountain ranges serve the same function as buffer zones. Being hard to cross, they allow defense against superior numbers. The defender has merely to stay on his side of the barrier and so can utilize all the men he can bring up to it. The attacker's men, however, can cross only a few at a time, and they are very vulnerable when doing so. If all states were self-sufficient islands, anarchy would be much less of a problem. A small investment in shore defenses and a small army would be sufficient to repel invasion. Only very weak states would be vulnerable, and only very large ones could menace others. As noted above, the United States, and to a lesser extent Great Britain, have partly been able to escape from the state of nature because their geographical positions approximated this ideal.

Although geography cannot be changed to conform to borders, borders can and do change to conform to geography. Borders across which an attack is easy tend to be unstable. States living within them are likely to expand or be absorbed. Frequent wars are almost inevitable since attacking will often seem the best way to protect what one has. This process will stop, or at least slow down, when the state's borders reach—by expansion or contraction—a line of natural obstacles. Security without attack will then be possible. Furthermore, these lines constitute salient solutions to bargaining problems and, to the extent that they are barriers to migration, are likely to divide ethnic groups, thereby raising the costs and lowering the incentives for conquest.

Attachment to one's state and its land reinforce one quasi-geographical aid to the defense. Conquest usually becomes more difficult the deeper the attacker pushes into the other's territory. Nationalism spurs the defenders to fight harder; advancing not only lengthens the attacker's supply lines, but takes him through unfamiliar and often devastated lands that require troops for garrison duty. These stabilizing dynamics will not operate, however, if the defender's war materiel is situated near its borders, or if the people do not care about their state, but only about being on the winning side. * * *

■   ■   ■

The other major determinant of the offense-defense balance is technology. When weapons are highly vulnerable, they must be employed before they are attacked. Others can remain quite invulnerable in their bases. The former characteristics are embodied in unprotected missiles and many kinds of bombers. (It should be noted that it is not vulnerability *per se* that is crucial, but the location of the vulnerability. Bombers and missiles that are easy to destroy only after having been launched toward their targets do not create destabilizing dynamics.) Incentives to strike first are usually absent for naval forces that are threatened by a naval attack. Like missiles in hardened silos, they are usually well protected when in their bases. Both sides can then simultaneously be prepared to defend themselves successfully.

In ground warfare under some conditions, forts, trenches, and small groups of men in prepared positions can hold off large numbers of attackers. * * *

■   ■   ■

Concerning nuclear weapons, it is generally agreed that defense is impossible—a triumph not of the offense, but of deterrence. Attack makes no sense, not because it can be beaten off, but because the attacker will be destroyed in turn. In terms of the questions under consideration here, the result is the equivalent of the primacy of the defense. First, security is relatively cheap. Less than one percent of the GNP is devoted to deterring a direct attack on the United States; most of it is spent on acquiring redundant systems to provide a lot of insurance against the worst conceivable contingencies. Second, both sides can simultaneously gain security in the form of second-strike capability. Third, and related to the foregoing, second-strike capability can be maintained in the face of wide variations in the other side's military posture. There is no purely military reason why each side has to react quickly and strongly to the other's increases in arms. Any spending that the other devotes to trying to achieve first-strike capability can be neutralized by the state's spending much smaller sums on protecting its second-strike capability. Fourth, there are no incentives to strike first in a crisis.

■   ■   ■

Offense-Defense Differentiation

The other major variable that affects how strongly the security dilemma operates is whether weapons and policies that protect the state also provide the capability for attack. If they do not, the basic postulate of the security dilemma no longer applies. A state can increase its own security without decreasing that of others. The advantage of the defense can only ameliorate the security dilemma. A differentiation between offensive and defensive stances comes close to abolishing it. Such differentiation does not mean, however, that all security problems will be abolished. If the offense has the advantage, conquest and aggression will still be possible. And if the offense's advantage is great enough, status-quo powers may find it too expensive to protect themselves by defensive forces and decide to procure offensive weapons even though this will menace others. Furthermore, states will still have to worry that even if the other's military posture shows that it is peaceful now, it may develop aggressive intentions in the future.

Assuming that the defense is at least as potent as the offense, the differentiation between them allows status-quo states to behave in ways that are clearly different from those of aggressors. Three beneficial consequences follow. First, status-quo powers can identify each other, thus laying the foundations for cooperation. Conflicts growing out of the mistaken belief that the other side is expansionist will be less frequent. Second, status-quo states will obtain advance warning when others plan aggression. Before a state can attack, it has to develop and deploy offensive weapons. If procurement of these weapons cannot be disguised and takes a fair amount of time, as it almost always does, a status-quo state will have the time to take countermeasures. It need not maintain a high level of defensive arms as long as its potential adversaries are adopting a peaceful posture. * * *

■　　■　　■

* * * [I]f all states support the status quo, an obvious arms control agreement is a ban on weapons that are useful for attacking. As President Roosevelt put it in his message to the Geneva Disarmament Conference in 1933: "If all nations will agree wholly to eliminate from possession and use the weapons which make possible a successful attack, defenses automatically will become impregnable, and the frontiers and independence of every nation will become secure."[23] The fact that such treaties have been rare * * * shows either that states are not always willing to guarantee the security of others, or that it is hard to distinguish offensive from defensive weapons.

■　　■　　■

IV. Four Worlds

The two variables we have been discussing—whether the offense or the defense has the advantage, and whether offensive postures can be distinguished from defensive ones—can be combined to yield four possible worlds.

The first world is the worst for status-quo states. There is no way to get security without menacing others, and security through defense is terribly difficult to obtain. Because offensive and defensive postures are the same, status-quo states acquire the same kind of arms that are sought by aggressors. And because the offense has the advantage over the defense, attacking is the best route to protecting what you have; status-quo states will therefore behave like aggressors. The situation will be unstable. Arms races are likely. Incentives to strike first will turn crises into wars. Decisive victories and conquests will be common. States will grow and shrink rapidly, and it will be hard for any state to maintain its size and influence without trying to increase them. Cooperation among status-quo powers will be extremely hard to achieve.

There are no cases that totally fit this picture, but it bears more than a passing resemblance to Europe before World War I. Britain and Germany, although in many respects natural allies, ended up as enemies. Of course much of the explanation lies in Germany's ill-chosen policy. And from the perspective of our theory, the powers' ability to avoid war in a series of earlier crises cannot be easily explained. Nevertheless, much of the behavior in this period was the product of technology and beliefs that magnified the security dilemma. Decision makers thought that the offense had a big advantage and saw little difference between offensive and defensive military postures. The era was characterized by arms races. And once war seemed likely, mobilization races created powerful incentives to strike first.

In the nuclear era, the first world would be one in which each side relied on vulnerable weapons that were aimed at similar forces and each side understood the situation. In this case, the incentives to strike first would be very high—so high that status-quo powers as well as aggressors would be sorely tempted to pre-empt. And since the forces could be used to change the status quo as well as to preserve it, there would be no way for both sides to increase their security simultaneously. Now the familiar logic of deterrence leads both sides to see the dangers in this world.

Figure 8.2. The Security Dilemma

	Offense Has the Advantage	Defense Has the Advantage
Offensive Posture Not Distinguishable from Defensive One	1 Doubly dangerous.	2 Security dilemma, but security requirements may be compatible.
Offensive Posture Distinguishable from Defensive One	3 No security dilemma, but aggression possible. Status-quo states can follow different policy than aggressors. Warning given.	4 Doubly stable.

Indeed, the new understanding of this situation was one reason why vulnerable bombers and missiles were replaced. Ironically, the 1950s would have been more hazardous if the decision makers had been aware of the dangers of their posture and had therefore felt greater pressure to strike first. This situation could be recreated if both sides were to rely on MIRVed ICBMs.

In the second world, the security dilemma operates because offensive and defensive postures cannot be distinguished; but it does not operate as strongly as in the first world because the defense has the advantage, and so an increment in one side's strength increases its security more than it decreases the other's. So, if both sides have reasonable subjective security requirements, are of roughly equal power, and the variables discussed earlier are favorable, it is quite likely that status-quo states can adopt compatible security policies. * * *

This world is the one that comes closest to matching most periods in history. Attacking is usually harder than defending because of the strength of fortifications and obstacles. But purely defensive postures are rarely possible because fortifications are usually supplemented by armies and mobile guns which can support an attack. In the nuclear era, this world would be one in which both sides relied on relatively invulnerable ICBMs and believed that limited nuclear war was impossible. * * *

In the third world there may be no security dilemma, but there are security problems. Because states can procure defensive systems that do not threaten others, the dilemma need not operate. But because the offense has the advantage, aggression is possible, and perhaps easy. If the offense has enough of an advantage, even a status-quo state may take the initiative rather than risk being attacked and defeated. If the offense has less of an advantage, stability and cooperation are likely because the status-quo states will procure defensive forces. They need not react to others who are similarly armed, but can wait for the warning they would receive if others started to deploy offensive weapons. But each state will have to watch the others carefully, and there is room for false suspicions. The costliness of the defense and the allure of the offense can lead to unnecessary mistrust, hostility, and war, unless some of the variables discussed earlier are operating to restrain defection.

■ ■ ■

The fourth world is doubly safe. The differentiation between offensive and defensive systems permits a way out of the security dilemma; the advantage of the defense disposes of the problems discussed in the previous paragraphs. There is no reason for a status-quo power to be tempted to procure offensive forces, and aggressors give notice of their intentions by the posture they adopt. Indeed, if the advantage of the defense is great enough, there are no security problems. The loss of the ultimate form of the power to alter the status quo would allow greater scope for the exercise of non-military means and probably would tend to freeze the distribution of values.

■ ■ ■

NOTES

1. Quoted in Gerald Wheeler, *Prelude to Pearl Harbor* (Columbia: University of Missouri Press 1963), 167.

2. Quoted in Leonard Wainstein, "The Dreadnought Gap," in Robert Art and Kenneth Waltz, eds., *The Use of Force* (Boston: Little, Brown 1971), 155. * * *

3. In another article, Jervis says: "International politics sometimes resembles what is called a Prisoner's Dilemma (PD). In this scenario, two men have been caught red-handed committing a minor crime. The district attorney knows that they are also guilty of a much more serious offense. He tells each of them separately that if he confesses and squeals on his buddy, he will go free and the former colleague will go to jail for thirty years. If both of them refuse to give any information, they will be prosecuted for the minor crime and be jailed for thirty days; if they both squeal, plea-bargaining will get them ten years. In other words, as long as each criminal cares only about himself, he will confess to the more serious crime no matter what he thinks his colleague will do. If he confesses and his buddy does not, he will get the best possible outcome (freedom); if he confesses and his buddy also does so, the outcome will not be good (ten years in jail), but it will be better than keeping silent and going to jail for thirty years. Since both can see this, both will confess. Paradoxically, if they had both been irrational and kept quiet, they would have gone to jail for only a month." (Robert Jervis, "A Political Science Perspective on the Balance of Power and the Concert," *American Historical Review* 97, no. 3 (June 1992): 720.)

4. Experimental evidence for this proposition is summarized in James Tedeschi, Barry Schlenker, and Thomas Bonoma, *Conflict, Power, and Games* (Chicago: Aldine 1973), 135–41.

5. The results of Prisoner's Dilemma games played in the labouratory support this argument. See Anatol Rapoport and Albert Chammah, *Prisoner's Dilemma* (Ann Arbor: University of Michigan Press 1965), 33–50. Also see Robert Axelrod, *Conflict of Interest* (Chicago: Markham 1970), 60–70.

6. Quoted in Bernard Brodie, *Strategy in the Missile Age* (Princeton: Princeton University Press 1959), 6.

7. Herbert York, *The Advisors: Oppenheimer, Teller, and the Superbomb* (San Francisco: Freemar, 1976), 56–60.

8. Thus, when Wolfers [*Discord and Collaboration* (Baltimore: Johns Hopkins Press 1962),] 126, argues that a status-quo state that settles for rough equality of power with its adversary, rather than seeking preponderance, may be able to convince the other to reciprocate by showing that it wants only to protect itself, not menace the other, he assumes that the defense has an advantage.

9. Schelling, [*The Strategy of Conflict* (New York: Oxford University Press 1963),] chap. 9.

10. Quoted in Fritz Fischer, *War of Illusions* (New York: Norton 1975), 377, 461.

11. George Quester, *Offense and Defense in the International System* (New York: John Wiley 1977), 105–06; Sontag [*European Diplomatic History, 1871–1932* (New York: Appleton-Century-Crofts 1933)], 4–5.

12. Some were not so optimistic. Gray's remark is well-known: "The lamps are going out all over Europe; we shall not see them lit again in our life-time." The German Prime Minister, Bethmann Hollweg, also feared the consequences of the war. But the controlling view was that it would certainly pay for the winner.

13. Quoted in Martin Gilbert, *Winston S. Churchill*, III, *The Challenge of War, 1914–1916* (Boston: Houghton Mifflin 1971), 84.

14. Quester (fn. 33), 98–99. Robert Art, *The Influence of Foreign Policy on Seapower*, II (Beverly Hills: Sage Professional Papers in International Studies Series, 1973), 14–18, 26–28.

15. Konrad Jarausch, "The Illusion of Limited War: Chancellor Bethmann Hollweg's Calculated Risk, July 1914," *Central European History*, II (March 1969), 50.

16. Brodie (fn. 6), 58.

17. President Roosevelt and the American delegates to the League of Nations Disarmament Conference maintained that the tank and mobile heavy artillery had re-established the dominance of the offensive, thus making disarmament more urgent (Boggs, [*Attempts to Define and. Limit "Aggressive" Armament in Diplomacy and Strategy* (Columbia: University of Missouri Studies, XVI, No. 1, 1941)], pp. 31, 108), but this was a minority position and may not even have been believed by the Americans. The reduced prestige and influence of the military, and the high pressures to cut government spending throughout this period also contributed to the lowering of defense budgets.

18. Jon Kimche, *The Unfought Battle* (New York: Stein 1968); Nicholas William Bethell, *The War Hitler Won: The Fall of Poland, September 1939* (New York: Holt 1972); Alan Alexandroff and Richard Rosecrance, "Deterrence in 1939," *World Politics,* XXIX (April 1977), 404–24.

19. Roderick Macleod and Denis Kelly, eds., *Time Unguarded: The Ironside Diaries, 1937–1940* (New York: McKay 1962), 173.

20. For a short time, as France was falling, the British Cabinet did discuss reaching a negotiated peace with Hitler. The official history ignores this, but it is covered in P.M.H. Bell, *A Certain Eventuality* (Farnborough, England: Saxon House 1974), 40–48.

21. Macleod and Kelly (fn. 19), 174. In flat contradiction to common sense and almost everything they believed about modern warfare, the Allies planned an expedition to Scandinavia to cut the supply of iron ore to Germany and to aid Finland against the Russians. But the dominant mood was the one described above.

22. Brodie (fn. 6), 179.

23. Quoted in Merze Tate, *The United States and Armaments* (Cambridge: Harvard University Press 1948), 108.

James D. Fearon

RATIONALIST EXPLANATIONS FOR WAR

The central puzzle about war, and also the main reason we study it, is that wars are costly but nonetheless wars recur. Scholars have attempted to resolve the puzzle with three types of argument. First, one can argue that people (and state leaders in particular) are sometimes or always irrational. They are subject to biases and pathologies that lead them to neglect the costs of war or to misunderstand how their actions will produce it. Second, one can argue that the leaders who order war enjoy its benefits but do not pay the costs, which are suffered by soldiers and citizens. Third, one can argue that even rational leaders who consider the risks and costs of war may end up fighting nonetheless.

This article focuses on arguments of the third sort, which I will call rationalist explanations.[1] Rationalist explanations abound in the literature on international conflict, assuming a great variety of specific forms. Moreover, for at least two reasons many scholars have given rationalist explanations a certain pride of place. First, historians and political scientists who have studied the origins of particular wars often have concluded that war can be a rational alternative for leaders who are acting in their states' interest—they find that the expected benefits of war sometimes outweigh the expected costs, however unfortunate this may be. Second, the dominant paradigm in international relations theory, neorealism, is thought to advance or even to depend on rationalist arguments about the causes of war. Indeed, if no rationalist explanation for war is theoretically or empirically tenable, then neither is neorealism. The causes of war would then lie in the defects of human nature or particular states rather than in the international system, as argued by neorealists. What I refer to here as "rationalist explanations for war" could just as well be called "neorealist explanations."[2]

This article attempts to provide a clear statement of what a rationalist explanation for war is and to characterize the full set of rationalist explanations that are both theoretically coherent and empirically plausible. It should be obvious that this theoretical exercise must take place prior to testing rationalist explanations against alternatives—we cannot perform such tests unless we know what a rationalist explanation really is. Arguably, the exercise is also foundational for neorealism. Despite its prominence, neorealist theory lacks a clearly stated and fully conceived explanation for war. As I will argue below, it is not enough to say that under anarchy nothing stops states from using force, or that anarchy forces states to rely on self-help, which engenders mutual suspicion and (through spirals or the security dilemma) armed conflict. Neither do diverse references to miscalculation, deterrence failure because of inadequate forces or incredible threats, preventive and preemptive considerations, or free-riding in alliances amount to theoretically coherent rationalist explanations for war.

From *International Organization* 49, no. 3 (Summer 1995), 379–410. Bracketed editorial insertions are the author's and three asterisks (***) are used to mark places where technical material has been omitted. Some notes and a technical appendix have been omitted.

My main argument is that on close inspection none of the principal rationalist arguments advanced in the literature holds up as an explanation because none addresses or adequately resolves the central puzzle, namely, that war is costly and risky, so rational states should have incentives to locate negotiated settlements that all would prefer to the gamble of war. The common flaw of the standard rationalist arguments is that they fail either to address or to explain adequately what prevents leaders from reaching *ex ante* (prewar) bargains that would avoid the costs and risks of fighting. A coherent rationalist explanation for war must do more than give reasons why armed conflict might appear an attractive option to a rational leader under some circumstances—it must show why states are unable to locate an alternative outcome that both would prefer to a fight.

To summarize what follows, the article will consider five rationalist arguments accepted as tenable in the literature on the causes of war. Discussed at length below, these arguments are given the following labels: (1) anarchy; (2) expected benefits greater than expected costs; (3) rational preventive war; (4) rational miscalculation due to lack of information; and (5) rational miscalculation or disagreement about relative power. I argue that the first three arguments simply do not address the question of what prevents state leaders from bargaining to a settlement that would avoid the costs of fighting. The fourth and fifth arguments do address the question, holding that rational leaders may miss a superior negotiated settlement when lack of information leads them to miscalculate relative power or resolve. However, as typically stated, neither argument explains what prevents rational leaders from using diplomacy or other forms of communication to avoid such costly miscalculations.

If these standard arguments do not resolve the puzzle on rationalist terms, what does? I propose that there are three defensible answers, which take the form of general mechanisms, or causal logics, that operate in a variety of more specific international contexts.[3] In the first mechanism, rational leaders may be unable to locate a mutually preferable negotiated settlement due to *private information* about relative capabilities or resolve and *incentives to misrepresent* such information. Leaders know things about their military capabilities and willingness to fight that other states do not know, and in bargaining situations they can have incentives to misrepresent such private information in order to gain a better deal. I show that given these incentives, communication may not allow rational leaders to clarify relative power or resolve without generating a real risk of war. This is not simply a matter of miscalculation due to poor information but rather of specific strategic dynamics that result from the combination of asymmetric information and incentives to dissemble.

Second, rationally led states may be unable to arrange a settlement that both would prefer to war due to *commitment problems,* situations in which mutually preferable bargains are unattainable because one or more states would have an incentive to renege on the terms. While anarchy (understood as the absence of an authority capable of policing agreements) is routinely cited as a cause of war in the literature, it is difficult to find explanations for exactly why the inability to make commitments should imply that war will sometimes occur. That is, what are the specific, empirically identifiable mechanisms by which the inability to commit makes it impossible for states to strike deals that would avoid the costs of war? I identify three such specific mechanisms, arguing in particular that preventive war between rational states stems from a commitment problem rather than from differential power growth per se.

The third sort of rationalist explanation I find less compelling than the first two, although it is logically tenable. States might be unable to locate a peaceful settlement both prefer due to *issue indivisibilities.* Perhaps some issues, by their very natures, simply will not admit compromise.

Though neither example is wholly convincing, issues that might exhibit indivisibility include abortion in domestic politics and the problem of which prince sits on the throne of, say, Spain, in eighteenth- or nineteenth-century international politics. Issue indivisibility could in principle make war rational for the obvious reason that if the issue allows only a finite number of resolutions, it might be that none falls within the range that both prefer to fighting. However, the issues over which states bargain typically are complex and multidimensional; side-payments or linkages with other issues typically are possible; and in principle states could alternate or randomize among a fixed number of possible solutions to a dispute. War-prone international issues may often be *effectively* indivisible, but the cause of this indivisibility lies in domestic political and other mechanisms rather than in the nature of the issues themselves.

In the first section of the article I discuss the puzzle posed by the fact that war is costly. Using a simple formalization of the bargaining problem faced by states in conflict, I show that under very broad conditions bargains will exist that genuinely rational states would prefer to a risky and costly fight. The second section argues that rational miscalculations of relative power and resolve must be due to private information and then considers how war may result from the combination of private information and incentives to misrepresent that information in bargaining. In the third section, I discuss commitment problems as the second class of defensible rationalist explanations for war. Throughout, I specify theoretical arguments with simple game-theoretic representations and assess plausibility with historical examples.

Before beginning, I should make it clear that I am not presenting either commitment problems or private information and incentives to misrepresent as wholly novel explanations for war that are proposed here for the first time. The literature on

the causes of war is massive, and these ideas, mixed with myriad others, can be found in it in various guises. The main theoretical task facing students of war is not to add to the already long list of arguments and conjectures but instead to take apart and reassemble these diverse arguments into a coherent theory fit for guiding empirical research. Toward this end, I am arguing that when one looks carefully at the problem of explaining how war could occur between genuinely rational, unitary states, one finds that there are really only two ways to do it. The diverse rationalist or neorealist explanations commonly found in the literature fail for two reasons. First, many do not even address the relevant question—what prevents states from locating a bargain both sides would prefer to a fight? They do not address the question because it is widely but incorrectly assumed that rational states can face a situation of deadlock, wherein no agreements exist that both sides would prefer to a war.[4] Second, the rationalist arguments that do address the question—such as (4) and (5) above—do not go far enough in answering it. When fully developed, they prove to be one of the two major mechanisms developed here, namely, either a commitment problem or a problem arising from private information and incentives to misrepresent. These two mechanisms, I will argue, provide the foundations for a rationalist or neorealist theory of war.

The Puzzle

Most historians and political scientists who study war dismiss as naive the view that all wars must be unwanted because they entail destruction and suffering. Instead, most agree that while a few wars may have been unwanted by the leaders who brought them about—World War I is sometimes given as an example—many or perhaps most wars were simply wanted. The leaders involved viewed war as a costly but worthwhile gamble.[5]

Moreover, many scholars believe that wanted wars are easily explained from a rationalist perspective. Wanted wars are thought to be Pareto-efficient—they occur when no negotiated settlements exist that both sides would prefer to the gamble of military conflict. Conventional wisdom holds that while this situation may be tragic, it is entirely possible between states led by rational leaders who consider the costs and risks of fighting. Unwanted wars, which take place despite the existence of settlements both sides preferred to conflict, are thought to pose more of a puzzle, but one that is resolvable and also fairly rare.

The conventional distinction between wanted and unwanted wars misunderstands the puzzle posed by war. The reason is that the standard conception does not distinguish between two types of efficiency—*ex ante* and *ex post*. As long as both sides suffer some costs for fighting, then war is always inefficient *ex post*—both sides would have been better off if they could have achieved the same final resolution without suffering the costs (or by paying lower costs). This is true even if the costs of fighting are small, or if one or both sides viewed the potential benefits as greater than the costs, since there are still costs. Unless states enjoy the activity of fighting for its own sake, as a consumption good, then war is inefficient *ex post*.

From a rationalist perspective, the central puzzle about war is precisely this *ex post* inefficiency. Before fighting, both sides know that war will entail some costs, and even if they expect offsetting benefits they still have an incentive to avoid the costs. The central question, then, is what prevents states in a dispute from reaching an *ex ante* agreement that avoids the costs they know will be paid *ex post* if they go to war? Giving a rationalist explanation for war amounts to answering this question.

Three of the most common and widely employed rationalist arguments in the literature do not directly address or answer the question. These are arguments from anarchy, preventive war, and positive expected utility.

Anarchy

Since Kenneth Waltz's influential *Man, the State, and War,* the anarchical nature of the international realm is routinely cited as a root cause of or explanation for the recurrence of war. Waltz argued that under anarchy, without a supranational authority to make and enforce law, "war occurs because there is nothing to prevent it. . . . Among states as among men there is no automatic adjustment of interests. In the absence of a supreme authority there is then the constant possibility that conflicts will be settled by force."[6]

The argument focuses our attention on a fundamental difference between domestic and international politics. Within a well-ordered state, organized violence as a strategy is ruled out—or at least made very dangerous—by the potential reprisals of a central government. In international relations, by contrast, no agency exists that can credibly threaten reprisal for the use of force to settle disputes.[7] The claim is that without such a credible threat, war will sometimes appear the best option for states that have conflicting interests.

While I do not doubt that the condition of anarchy accounts for major differences between domestic and international politics, and that anarchy encourages both fear of and opportunities for military conflict, the standard framing of the argument is not enough to explain why wars occur and recur. Under anarchy, nothing stops states from using force if they wish. But if using force is a costly option regardless of the outcome, then why is it ever employed? How exactly does the lack of a central authority prevent states from negotiating agreements both sides would prefer to fighting? As it is typically stated, the argument that anarchy provides a rationalist explanation for war does not address this question and so does not solve the problem posed by war's *ex post* inefficiency.

Neither, it should be added, do related arguments invoking the security dilemma, the fact that under anarchy one state's efforts to make itself more secure can have the undesired but unavoidable effect of making another state less secure.[8] By itself this fact says nothing about the availability or feasibility of peaceful bargains that would avoid the costs of war. More elaborate arguments are required, and those that are typically given do not envision bargaining and do not address the puzzle of costs. Consider, for instance, a spiral scenario in which an insecure state increases its arms, rendering another so insecure that it decides to attack. If the first state anticipated the reaction producing war, then by itself this is a deadlock argument; I argue against these below. If the first state did not anticipate war and did not want it, then the problem would seem to be miscalculation rather than anarchy, and we need to know why signaling and bargaining could not have solved it. As Robert Jervis has argued, anarchy and the security dilemma may well foster arms races and territorial competition.[9] But with the exception of occasional references to the preemptive war problem, the standard security dilemma arguments do not explicitly address the question of why the inability to make commitments should necessarily make for war between rational states.[10]

Below I will argue that anarchy is indeed implicated as a cause of specific sorts of military conflict (e.g., preventive and preemptive war and in some cases war over strategic territory). In contrast to the standard arguments, however, showing how anarchy figures in a coherent rationalist explanation entails describing the specific mechanism by which states' inability to write enforceable contracts makes peaceful bargains both sides would prefer unattainable.

Preventive War

It frequently is argued that if a declining power expects it might be attacked by a rising power in the future, then a preventive war in the present may be rational. Typically, however, preventive war arguments do not consider whether the rising and declining powers could construct a bargain, perhaps across time, that would leave both sides better off than a costly and risky preventive war would.[11] The incentives for such a deal surely exist. The rising state should not want to be attacked while it is relatively weak, so what stops it from offering concessions in the present and the future that would make the declining state prefer not to attack? Also, if war is inefficient and bargains both sides prefer to a fight will exist, why should the declining power rationally fear being attacked in the future? The standard argument supposes that an anticipated shift in the balance of power can by itself be enough to make war rational, but this is not so.

Positive Expected Utility

Perhaps the most common informal rationalist explanation found in the literature is that war may occur when two states each estimate that the expected benefits of fighting outweigh the expected costs. As Bruce Bueno de Mesquita argued in an influential formalization of this claim, war can be rational if both sides have positive expected utility for fighting; that is, if the expected utility of war (expected benefits less costs) is greater than the expected utility of remaining at peace.[12]

Informal versions of the expected utility argument typically fail to address the question of how or under what conditions it can be possible for two states both to prefer the costly gamble of war to any negotiated settlement. Formal versions have tended to avoid the question by making various restrictive and sometimes nonrationalist assumptions. To support these claims, I need to be more precise about the expected utility argument.

When Will There Exist Bargains Both Sides Prefer to War?

This section considers the question of whether and when two rationally led states could both prefer war to any negotiated settlement.

Consider two states, A and B, who have preferences over a set of issues represented by the interval $X = [0, 1]$. State A prefers issue resolutions closer to 1, while B prefers outcomes closer to 0. For concreteness we might think of x as representing the proportion of all territory between A and B that is controlled by A. [Thus, a point X in the interval represents the situation where state A controls all the territory from ϕ to X, while state B controls all the territory from X to 1.][13]

In order to say whether the set X contains negotiated settlements that both sides would prefer to conflict, it must be possible to say how the states evaluate the military option versus those outcomes. Almost all analysts of war have stressed that war is a gamble whose outcome may be determined by random or otherwise unforeseeable events.[14] As Bueno de Mesquita argued, this makes expected utility a natural candidate.[15] Suppose that if the states fight a war, state A prevails with probability $p \in [0, 1]$, and that the winner gets to choose its favorite outcome in the issue space. * * * [Thus, A's expected utility for war is $p - c$, since A gets all the territory, which is worth 1, with probability p, loses everything with probability $1 - p$, and pays a cost for fighting c_A in either event.] Similarly, state B's expected utility for war will be $1 - p - c_B$. Since we are considering rationalist theories for war, we assume that c_A and c_B are both positive. War is thus represented as a costly lottery.[16]

We can now answer the question posed above. The following result is easily demonstrated: given the assumptions stated in the last two paragraphs, there always exists a set of negotiated settlements that both sides prefer to fighting. * * *

[For example, in the special case where each state's value for an additional increment of territory is constant, the two states will both prefer any division of territory in the range from $p - c_A$ to $p + c_B$ over fighting a war. This interval represents the bargaining range, with $p - c_A$ and $p + c_B$ as the reservation levels that delimit it. This case of "risk neutral" states is depicted in Figure 8.3.]

This simple but important result is worth belaboring with some intuition. Suppose that two people (or states) are bargaining over the division of $100—if they can agree on a split they can keep what they agree to. However, in contrast to the usual economic scenarios, in this international relations example the players also have an outside option.[17] For a price of $20, they can go to war, in which case each player has a 50-percent chance of winning the whole $100. This implies that the expected value of the war option is $30 ($0.5 \cdot 100 + 0.5 \cdot 0 - 20$) for each side, so that if the players are risk-neutral, then neither should be willing to accept less than $30 in the bargaining. But notice that there is still a range of peaceful, bargained outcomes from ($31, $69) to ($69, $31) that make both sides strictly better off than the war option. Risk aversion will tend to increase the range yet further; indeed, even if the leaders pay no costs for war, a set of agreements both sides prefer to a fight will still exist provided both are risk-averse over the issues. In effect, the costs and risks of fighting open up a "wedge" of bargained solutions that risk-neutral or risk-averse states will prefer to the gamble of conflict. The existence of this *ex ante* bargaining range derives from the fact that war is inefficient *ex post*.

Three substantive assumptions are needed for the result, none of which seems particularly strong. First, the states know that there is some true probability p that one state would win in a military contest. As discussed below, it could be that the states have conflicting estimates of the likelihood of victory, and if both sides are optimistic about their chances this can obscure the bargaining range.

Figure 8.3. The Bargaining Range

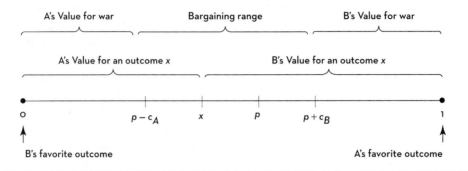

But even if the states have private and conflicting estimates of what would happen in a war, if they are rational, they should know that there can be only one true probability that one or the other will prevail (perhaps different from their own estimate). Thus rational states should know that there must in fact exist a set of agreements all prefer to a fight.

Second, it is assumed that the states are risk-averse or risk-neutral over the issues. Because risk attitude is defined relative to an underlying metric (such as money in economics), the substantive meaning of this assumption depends on the bargaining context. Loosely, it says that the states prefer a fifty-fifty split or share of whatever is at issue (in whatever metric it comes, if any) to a fifty-fifty chance at all or nothing, where this refers to the value of winning or losing a war. In effect, the assumption means that leaders do not like gambling when the downside risk is losing at war, which seems plausible given the presumption that state leaders normally wish to retain territory and power. A risk-acceptant leader is analogous to a compulsive gambler—willing to accept a sequence of gambles that has the expected outcome of eliminating the state and regime. Even if we admitted such a leader as rational, it seems doubtful that many have held such preferences (Hitler being a possible exception).

Finally, it was assumed that a continuous range of peaceful settlements (from 0 to 1) exists. In other words, the issues in dispute are perfectly divisible, so that there are always feasible bargains between the states' reservation levels $p - c_A$ and $p + c_B$. This third assumption immediately suggests a tenable rationalist explanation for war. Perhaps something about the nature of some international issues, such as which successor will sit on a throne, does not admit finely graded divisions and compromise. If so, then small costs for fighting and bad luck may make for rational war over such issues.

But we would immediately like to know what about the nature of an issue makes it impossible to divide up. On more thought, this seems empirically implausible. In the first place, most issues states negotiate over are quite complex—they have many dimensions of concern and allow many possible settlements. Second, if states can simply pay each other sums of money or goods (which they can, in principle), or make linkages with other issues, then this should have the effect of making any issues in dispute perfectly divisible. Before the age of nationalism, princes often bought, sold, and partitioned land.[18] In the nineteenth century the United States purchased the Louisiana Territory from France, and Alaska from Russia, and as late as 1898 President McKinley explored the possibility of buying Cuba from Spain in order to avoid a war over it.[19] Third, if something about the nature of an issue means that it can be settled in only, say, two ways, then some sort of random allocation or alternation between the two resolutions could in principle serve to create intermediate bargains. Mafia dons, for example, apparently have avoided costly internal wars by using lotteries to allocate construction contracts among families.[20]

In practice, creating intermediate settlements with cash, with linkages to other issues, or with randomization or alternation often seems difficult or impossible for states engaged in a dispute. For example, the immediate issue that gave rise to the Franco–Prussian war was a dispute over which prince would take the Spanish throne. It doubtless occurred to no one to propose that the two candidates alternate year by year, or three years for the Hapsburg and one for the Hohenzollern, or whatever. In this case as in many others, the issue could in principle have been made more continuous and was not for other reasons—here, alternating kings would have violated so many conventions and norms as to have been domestically unworkable. To give a more realistic example, nineteenth- and twentieth-century leaders cannot divide up and trade territory in international negotiations as easily as could rulers in the seventeenth and eighteenth centuries, due in part to domestic political consequences of the rise of nationalism; contrast, for example, the Congress of Vienna with the negotiations following World War I.

So in principle the indivisibility of the issues that are the subject of international bargaining can provide a coherent rationalist explanation for war. However, the real question in such cases is what prevents leaders from creating intermediate settlements, and the answer is likely to be other mechanisms (often domestic political) rather than the nature of the issues themselves.[21] Both the intrinsic complexity and richness of most matters over which states negotiate and the availability of linkages and side-payments suggest that intermediate bargains typically will exist.

It is thus not sufficient to say that positive expected utility by itself supplies a coherent or compelling rationalist explanation for war. Provided that the issues in dispute are sufficiently divisible, or that side-payments are possible, there should exist a set of negotiated agreements that have greater utility for both sides than the gamble of war does. The reason is that the *ex post* inefficiency of war opens up an *ex ante* bargaining range.

So, to explain how war could occur between rationally led states, we need to answer the following question. Given the existence of an *ex ante* bargaining range, why might states fail either to locate or to agree on an outcome in this range, so avoiding the costs and risks of war?

War Due to Private Information and Incentives to Misrepresent

Two commonly employed rationalist explanations in the literature directly address the preceding question. Both turn on the claim that war can be and often is the product of rational miscalculation. One explanation holds that a state's leaders may rationally overestimate their chance of military victory against an adversary, so producing a disagreement about relative power that only war can resolve. The other argues that rationally led states may lack information about an adversary's willingness to fight over some interest and so may challenge in the mistaken belief that war will not follow.

In this section I argue that while these ideas point toward a tenable rationalist explanation for war, neither goes far enough and neither works by itself. Both neglect the fact that states can in principle communicate with each other and so avoid a costly miscalculation of relative power or will. The cause of war cannot be simply lack of information, but whatever it is that prevents its disclosure. I argue that the fact that states have incentives to misrepresent their positions is crucial here, explaining on rationalist terms why diplomacy may not allow rational states to clarify disagreements about relative power or to avoid the miscalculation of resolve.

The mainstream international relations literature recognizes the existence of both private information and incentives to misrepresent, but typically views them as background conditions to be taken for granted rather than as key elements of an explanation of how rationally led states might end up at war. For example, Jack Levy's impressive review of the literature on the causes of war contains nothing on the role of incentives to misrepresent and discusses private information largely in the context of misperceptions of other states' intentions (which are linked to psychological biases). This is an accurate reflection of where these factors stand in the mainstream literature.[22]

Disagreements about Relative Power

Geoffrey Blainey's well-known and often-cited argument is that "wars usually begin when two nations disagree on their relative strength."[23] It is easy to see how a disagreement about relative strength—understood as conflicting estimates of the likelihood of military victory—can eliminate any *ex ante* bargaining range. Recall the example given above, where two states bargain over the division of $100, and each has the outside option of going to war. If each expects that it surely would prevail at war, then each side's expected value for the war option is $80 ($1 \cdot 100 + 0 \cdot 0 - 20$). So given these expectations, neither side will accept less than $80 in the bargaining, implying that no negotiated outcome is mutually preferred to war. More generally, suppose that state A expects to win with probability p, state B expects to win

with probability r, and p and r sum to greater than one. Such conflicting expectations will certainly shrink and could eliminate any *ex ante* bargaining range.

But how could rationally led states have conflicting expectations about the likely outcome of military conflict? In the extreme case, how could both sides rationally expect to win? The literature barely addresses this question in explicit terms. Blainey, whom the literature views as advancing a rationalist explanation for war, in fact explains disagreements about relative power as a consequence of human *ir*rationality. He says that mutual optimism about victory in war is the product of "moods which cannot be grounded in fact" and which "permeate what appear to be rational assessments of the relative military strength of two contending powers." Mutual optimism is said to result from a "process by which nations evade reality," which hardly sounds like a rationalist explanation.[24]

Conflicting expectations about the likely outcome of military conflict may be explained in three ways. First, as Blainey suggests, emotional commitments could irrationally bias leaders' military estimates. They might, for instance, come to believe nationalist rhetoric holding that their soldiers are more courageous and spirited than those of the adversary.[25] Second, the world is a very complex place, and for this reason military analysts in different states could reach different conclusions about the likely impact of different technologies, doctrines, and tactics on the expected course of battle. Third, state leaders might have private information about militarily relevant factors—military capabilities, strategy, and tactics; the population's willingness to prosecute a long war; or third-state intentions. If a state has superior (and so private) information about any such factor, then its estimate of the probable course of battle may differ from that of an adversary.

Under a strict but standard definition of rationality, only the third explanation qualifies as an account of how rationally led states could have conflicting estimates of the probability of winning in war. As argued by John Harsanyi, if two rational agents have the same information about an uncertain event, then they should have the same beliefs about its likely outcome.[26] The claim is that given identical information, truly rational agents should reason to the same conclusions about the probability of one uncertain outcome or another. Conflicting estimates should occur only if the agents have different (and so necessarily private) information.[27]

It follows that the second explanation for disagreements about relative power listed above—the complexity of the world—is not a rationalist account. Instead, it is an account that explains conflicting military estimates as a consequence of bounded rationality. In this view, leaders or military analysts with the same information about military technology, strategy, political will, etc., might reason to different conclusions about the likely course of a war because of differential ability to cope with complexity of the problem. This is entirely plausible, but it is a bounded rationality explanation rather than a fully rationalist one.[28]

The rationalist account of how disagreements about the probability of winning might arise also seems empirically plausible. States certainly have private information about factors affecting the likely course of battle—for example, they jealously guard military secrets and often have superior information about what an ally will or will not fight for. Nonetheless, while private information about militarily relevant capabilities provides a first step, it does not provide a coherent rationalist explanation for war. The problem is that even if leaders have such private information, they should understand that their own estimates based on this information are suspect because they do not know the other side's private information. In principle, both sides could gain by sharing information, which would yield a consensus military estimate (absent bounded rationality). And, as shown above, doing so could not help but reveal bargains that both would prefer to a fight.[29]

So the question of how rationally led states can disagree about relative power devolves to the question of what prevents states from sharing private information about factors that might affect the course of battle. Before turning to this question, I will consider the second common explanation for how a rational miscalculation may produce war.

War Due to the Miscalculation of an Opponent's Willingness to Fight

Many wars have been given the following so-called rationalist explanation: state A transgressed some interest of state B in the erroneous belief that B would not fight a war over the matter. Though rationally led, state A lacked information about B's willingness to fight and simply happened to guess wrong, causing a war. Thus, some say that Germany miscalculated Russian and/or British willingness to fight in 1914; Hitler miscalculated Britain and France's willingness to resist his drive to the east; Japanese leaders in 1941 miscalculated U.S. willingness to fight a long war over control in the South Pacific; North Korea miscalculated U.S. willingness to defend South Korea; the United States miscalculated China's willingness to defend North Korea; and so on. In each case, the argument would hold that lack of information led a more-or-less rational actor to guess wrong about the extent of the bargaining range.

Blainey has argued that if states agree on relative power they are very unlikely to go to war against each other.[30] It is worth pointing out that in the preceding argument, war can occur despite complete agreement on relative power across states. To show how and for later use, I will introduce a simple model of international bargaining. As in the empirical examples just mentioned, in the model one state unilaterally chooses some revision of the status quo. The second state can then either acquiesce to the revision or can go to war to reverse it.

Formally, suppose there is a status quo resolution of the issues, [represented as number q between 0 and 1,] and that state A has the opportunity to chose any outcome x [between 0 and 1], presenting state B with a fait accompli. On observing what state A did (which might be nothing, i.e., $x = q$), state B can choose whether to go to war or to acquiesce to A's revision of the status quo.

If neither state has any private information, so that all payoffs are common knowledge, state A does best to push the outcome just up to B's reservation level $p + c_B$, which makes B just willing to acquiesce rather than go to war. With complete information, then, the states avoid the inefficient outcome of war.[31] On the other hand, if state B has private information about either its capabilities (which affect p) or its value for the issues at stake relative to the costs of conflict (c_B), then state A may not know whether a particular "demand" x will yield war or peace. Lacking this information, state A faces a trade-off in deciding whether and how much territory to "grab": The larger the grab, the greater the risk of war, but the better off A will be if state B acquiesces.

Suppose, for example, that A and B share a common estimate of p—they agree about relative power—but that A is unsure about B's costs for fighting. Under very broad conditions, if A cannot learn B's private information and if A's own costs are not too large, then state A's optimal grab produces a positive chance of war. Intuitively, if A is not too fearful of the costs of war relative to what might be gained in bargaining, it will run some risk of war in hopes of gaining on the ground. So Blainey's suggestion that a disagreement about relative power is necessary for war is incorrect—all that is necessary is that the states in dispute be unable to locate or agree on some outcome in the bargaining range. Since the bargaining range is determined not just by relative power but also by states' values for the issues at stake relative to the costs of fighting, uncertainty about the latter can (and apparently does) produce war.

Once again, it is entirely plausible that state leaders have private information about their value for various international interests relative to their costs of fighting over them.[32] Thus it seems we have a second tenable rationalist explanation for war, again based on the concept of private information. But as in the case of disagreements about relative power, the explanation fails as given because it does not explain why states cannot avoid miscalculating a potential opponent's willingness to fight. In the model, why cannot state A simply ask state B whether it would fight rather than acquiesce to a particular demand? To give a concrete example, why did German leaders in 1914 not simply ask their British and Russian counterparts what they would do if Austria were to attack Serbia? If they could have done so and if the answers could have been believed, the Germans might not have miscalculated concerning Russian and, more importantly, British willingness to fight. In consequence they might have avoided the horrendous costs of World War I.

To recap, I have argued that in a rationalist framework, disagreements about relative power and uncertainty about a potential opponent's willingness to fight must have the same source: leaders' private information about factors affecting the likely course of a war or their resolve to fight over specific interests. In order to avoid war's *ex post* inefficiency, leaders have incentives to share any such private information, which would have the effect of revealing peaceful settlements that lie within the bargaining range. So, to explain how war could occur between states led by rational leaders who consider the costs of fighting, we need to explain what would prevent them from sharing such private information.

Incentives to Misrepresent in Bargaining

Prewar bargaining may fail to locate an outcome in the bargaining range because of strategic incentives to withhold or misrepresent private information. While states have an incentive to avoid the costs of war, they also wish to obtain a favorable resolution of the issues. This latter desire can give them an incentive to exaggerate their true willingness or capability to fight, if by doing so they might deter future challenges or persuade the other side to make concessions. States can also have an incentive to conceal their capabilities or resolve, if they are concerned that revelation would make them militarily (and hence politically) vulnerable or would reduce the chances for a successful first strike. Similarly, states may conceal their true willingness to fight in order to avoid appearing as the aggressor.

Combined with the fact of private information, these various incentives to misrepresent can explain why even rational leaders may be unable to avoid the miscalculations of relative will and power that can cause war. This section first considers why this is so theoretically and then discusses two empirical examples.

A drawback of the simple bargaining model given above was that state B had no opportunity to try to communicate its willingness to fight to state A. It is easy to imagine that if communication were possible—say, if B could announce what interests in X it considered vital enough to fight over—this might at least lower the chance of war by miscalculation. To check this, we give state B an initial opportunity to make a foreign policy announcement f, which can be any statement about its foreign policy or what it considers to be vital or peripheral interests. (Assume as before that A is uncertain about B's capabilities or costs for fighting.)

If the announcement itself has no effect on either side's payoffs, then it can be shown that in any equilibrium in which state A does not choose randomly among demands, A will make the same demand regardless of what state B says, and the *ex ante* risk of war will remain the same as in the game without communication by state B. To gain an intuition for these results, suppose that A conditioned its behavior on f, grabbing more or less depending on what B announced. Then regardless of B's true willingness to fight, B does best to make the announcement that leads to the smallest grab by A—that is, B has an incentive to misrepresent its actual willingness to resist. But then A learns nothing from the announcement.[33]

This conclusion is slightly altered if the leaders of B can render the announcement f costly to make.[34] In practice, five common methods include building weapons, mobilizing troops, signing alliance treaties, supporting troops in a foreign land, and creating domestic political costs that would be paid if the announcement proves false. Of course, signaling by means of domestic political audience costs lies outside a purely unitary rational-actor framework, since this presumes a state run by an agent on behalf of a principal (the "audience") rather than a unitary state with a perfectly secure leadership. In the latter case, leaders may be able to make foreign policy announcements credible only by engaging an international reputation, taking financially costly mobilization measures, or bearing the costs and risks of limited military engagements.[35]

Even when the signal is costly, however, this will not in general completely eliminate all risk of war by miscalculation—indeed, it may even increase it. The reason concerns the nature of the signals that states have incentives to send. To be genuinely informative about a state's actual willingness or ability to fight, a signal must be costly in such a way that a state with lesser resolve or capability might not wish to send it. Actions that generate a real risk of war—for example, troop mobilizations that engage a leadership's reputation before international or domestic audiences—can easily satisfy this constraint, since states with high resolve are less fearful of taking them. In other words, a rational state may choose to run a real risk of (inefficient) war in order to signal that it will fight if not given a good deal in bargaining.[36]

The July crisis of World War I provides several examples of how incentives to misrepresent can make miscalculations of resolve hard to dispel. Soon after German leaders secretly endorsed Austrian plans to crush Serbia, they received both direct and indirect verbal indications from St. Petersburg that Russia would fight rather than acquiesce.[37] For example, on 21 July, the Russian Foreign Minister told the German ambassador that "Russia would not be able to tolerate Austria-Hungary's using threatening language to Serbia or taking military measures."[38] Such verbal statements had little effect on German leaders' beliefs, however, since they knew Russian leaders had a strategic incentive to misrepresent. On 18 July in a cable explaining Berlin's policy to Ambassador Lichnowsky in London, Secretary of State Jagow wrote that "there is certain to be some blustering in St. Petersburg."[39] Similarly, when on 26 July Lichnowsky began to report that Britain might join with France and Russia in the event of war, German Chancellor Bethmann Hollweg told his personal assistant of the "danger that France and England will commit their support to Russia in order not to alienate it, perhaps without really believing that for us mobilization means war, thinking of it as a bluff which they answer with a counterbluff."[40]

At the same time, the Chancellor had an incentive to misrepresent the strength and nature of German support for Austria's plans. Bethmann correctly anticipated that revealing this information would make Germany appear the aggressor, which might undermine Social Democratic support for his policies in Germany as well as turn British public opinion more solidly against his state.[41] This incentive led the Chancellor to avoid making direct or pointed inquiries about England's

attitude in case of war. The incentive also led him to pretend to go along with the British Foreign Secretary's proposals for a conference to mediate the dispute.[42] In consequence, Lord Grey may not have grasped the need for a stronger warning to Germany until fairly late in the crisis (on 29 July), by which time diplomatic and military actions had made backing off more difficult for both Austria and Germany.

In July 1914, incentives to misrepresent private information fostered and supported miscalculations of willingness to fight. Miscalculations of relative power can arise from this same source. On the one hand, states at times have an incentive to exaggerate their capabilities in an attempt to do better in bargaining. On the other hand, they can also have the well-known incentive to withhold information about capabilities and strategy. Presumably because of the strongly zero-sum aspect of military engagements, a state that has superior knowledge of an adversary's war plans may do better in war and thus in prewar bargaining—hence, states rarely publicize war plans. While the theoretical logic has not been worked out, it seems plausible that states' incentives to conceal information about capabilities and strategy could help explain some disagreements about relative power.

The 1904 war between Japan and Russia serves to illustrate this scenario. On the eve of the war, Russian leaders believed that their military could almost certainly defeat Japan.[43] In this conviction they differed little from the view of most European observers. By contrast, at the imperial council of 4 February that decided for war, the Japanese chief of staff estimated a fifty-fifty chance of prevailing, if their attack began immediately.[44] Thus Japanese and Russian leaders disagreed about relative power—their estimates of the likelihood of victory summed to greater than 1.

Moreover, historical accounts implicate this disagreement as a major cause of the war: Russia's refusal to compromise despite repeated offers by the Japanese was motivated in large measure by their belief that Japan would not dare attack them. The Japanese Cabinet finally decided for war after the Tsar and his advisers failed to make any real compromises over Korea or Manchuria in a series of proposals exchanged in 1903. The Tsar and his top advisers were hardly eager to fight, not because they expected to lose but because they saw an Asian war as a costly diversion of resources to the wrong theater.[45] Nonetheless, they refused to make concessions from what they viewed as a position of great military strength. They believed that Japan would have to settle for less, given its relative military weakness.[46]

The disagreement arose in substantial part from Japanese private information about their military capabilities and how they compared with Russia's. A far superior intelligence service had provided the Japanese military with a clear picture of Russian strengths and weaknesses in Northeast Asia and enabled them to develop an effective offensive strategy. According to John Albert White, due to this intelligence "the Japanese government apparently faced the war with a far more accurate conception of their task than their enemy had."[47] In addition, compared with the Russians or indeed with any European power, Japanese leaders had much better knowledge of the fighting ability of the relatively untested Japanese army and of the effect of the reforms, training, and capital development of the previous decade.[48]

If by communicating this private information the Japanese could have led the Russians to see that their chances of victory were smaller than expected, they might have done so. Almost all historians who have carefully examined the case agree that the Japanese government was not bent on war for its own sake—they were willing to compromise if the Russians would as well.[49] However, it was unthinkable for the Japanese to reveal such information or convince the Russians even if they did. In the first place, the Japanese could not simply make announcements about the quality of their forces, since the Russians would have had no reason to believe them. Second, explaining how they planned to win a war might seriously compromise any such attempt by changing the likelihood that they would win; there is a trade-off between revealing information about resolve or capabilities to influence bargaining and reducing the advantages of a first strike.

In sum, the combination of private information about relative power or will and the strategic incentive to misrepresent these afford a tenable rationalist explanation for war. While states always have incentives to locate a peaceful bargain cheaper than war, they also always have incentives to do well in the bargaining. Given the fact of private information about capabilities or resolve, these incentives mean that states cannot always use quiet diplomatic conversations to discover mutually preferable settlements. It may be that the only way to surmount this barrier to communication is to take actions that produce a real risk of inefficient war.

This general mechanism operates in at least two other empirically important ways to produce conflict in specific circumstances. First, private information about the costs of fighting or the value leaders place on international interests can give them an incentive to cultivate a reputation for having lower costs or more far-flung vital interests than they actually do. If cutting a deal in one dispute would lead other states to conclude the leader's costs for using force are high, then the leader might choose a costly war rather than suffer the depredations that might follow from making concessions. The U.S. interventions in Korea and Vietnam are sometimes explained in these terms, and states surely have worried about such inferences drawn by other states for a long time.[50] The same logic operates when a small state or group (for example, Finland or the Chechens) chooses to fight a losing war against a larger one (for example, the Soviet Union or Russia) in order to develop a reputation for being hard to subjugate. In both cases, states employ war itself as a costly signal of privately known and otherwise unverifiable information about willingness to fight.

Second, since incentives to misrepresent military strength can undermine diplomatic signaling, states may be forced to use war as a credible means to reveal private information about their military capabilities. Thus, a rising state may seek out armed conflict in order to demonstrate that it is more powerful than others realize, while a state in apparent decline may fight in hope of revealing that its capabilities remain better than most believe. In both instances, the inefficient outcome of war derives from the fact that states have private information about their capabilities and a strategic incentive to misrepresent it to other states.

War as a Consequence of Commitment Problems

This section considers a second and quite different rationalist mechanism by which war may occur even though the states in dispute share the same assessment of the bargaining range. Even if private information and incentives to misrepresent it do not tempt states into a risky process of discovery or foster costly investments in reputation, states may be unable to settle on an efficient bargained outcome when for structural reasons they cannot trust each other to uphold the deal.

In this class of explanations, the structural condition of anarchy reemerges as a major factor, although for nonstandard reasons. In the conventional argument, anarchy matters because no hegemonic power exists to threaten states with "jail" if they use force. Without this threat, states become suspicious and worried about other states' intentions; they engage in self-help by building weapons; and somehow uncertainty-plus-weapons leads them ultimately to attack each other (the security dilemma or spiral model). Below, I show that anarchy does indeed matter but for more specific

reasons and in more specific contexts. Anarchy matters when an unfortunate combination of state preferences and opportunities for action imply that one or both sides in a dispute have incentives to renege on peaceful bargains which, if they were enforceable, would be mutually preferred to war. I will consider three such unfortunate situations that can claim some empirical plausibility.

It should be stressed that in standard security dilemma and spiral model arguments the suspicions and lack of trust engendered by anarchy are understood to originate either from states' inability to observe each other's motivations (that is, from private information about greed or desire for conquest) or from the knowledge that motivations can change.[51] By contrast, in the arguments given below, states have no private information and motivations never change; thus states understand each other's motivations perfectly. This is not to argue that private information about the value a leadership places on expansion is unimportant in international politics—it surely is. Indeed, private information about motivation and various incentives to misrepresent it might exacerbate any of the three specific commitment problems discussed below. However, when they do so this is a matter of an interaction between informational and commitment problems rather than of anarchy per se. Our first task should be to isolate and specify the mechanisms by which anarchy itself might cause war.

Preemptive War and Offensive Advantages

Consider the problem faced by two gunslingers with the following preferences. Each would most prefer to kill the other by stealth, facing no risk of retaliation, but each prefers that both live in peace to a gunfight in which each risks death. There is a bargain here that both sides prefer to "war"—namely, that each leaves the other alone—but without the enforcement capabilities of a third party, such as an effective sheriff, they may not be able to attain it. Given their preferences, neither person can credibly commit not to defect from the bargain by trying to shoot the other in the back. Note that no matter how far the shadow of the future extends, iteration (or repeat play) will not make cooperation possible in strategic situations of this sort. Because being the "sucker" here may mean being permanently eliminated, strategies of conditional cooperation such as tit-for-tat are infeasible.[52] Thus, if we can find a plausible analogy in international relations, this example might afford a coherent rationalist explanation for war.

Preemptive war scenarios provide the analogy. If geography or military technology happened to create large first-strike or offensive advantages, then states might face the same problem as the gunslingers. To demonstrate this theoretically, I consider how offensive advantages affect the bargaining range between two states engaged in a dispute.

There are at least three ways of interpreting offensive advantages in a formal context. First, an offensive advantage might mean that a state's odds of winning are better if it attacks rather than defends. Second, an offensive advantage might mean that the costs of fighting are lower for an attacking state than for a defending state. It can be shown that no commitment problem operates in this second case, although lowering the costs of war for attackers does narrow the de facto bargaining range. Third, offensive advantages might mean that military technology and doctrine increase the variance of battlefield outcomes. That is, technology and doctrine might make total victory or total defeat more likely, while rendering stalemate and small territorial changes less likely. In this case, offensive advantages can actually reduce the expected utility of war for both sides, thus increasing the bargaining range and perhaps making war less rather than more likely. Intuitively, if states care most of all about security (understood as survival), then offensive advantages make war less safe by increasing the risk of total defeat.[53]

A commitment problem of the sort faced by the gunslingers arises only under the first interpretation, in which "offensive advantage" refers to an increase in a state's military prospects if it attacks rather than defends. To demonstrate this, let p_f be the probability that state A wins a war if A attacks; p_s the probability that A wins if A strikes second or defends; and p the chance that A wins if both states mobilize and attack at the same time. Thus, an offensive advantage exists when $p_f > p > p_s$.

Since states can always choose to attack if they wish, a peaceful resolution of the issues is feasible only if neither side has an incentive to defect unilaterally by attacking. * * * [It is easy to show that there will exist stable outcomes both sides prefer to conflict only if there is a de facto bargaining range represented by issue resolutions between $p_f - c_A$ and $p_s + c_B$. One end of the range is determined by A's value for attacking with a first strike advantage, and the other by B's.]

Notice that as p_f increases above p, and p_s decreases below it, this interval shrinks and may even disappear. Thus, first-strike advantages narrow the de facto bargaining range, while second-strike (or defensive) advantages increase it. The reason is that when first-strike advantages are large, both states must be given more from the peacetime bargain in order to allay the greater temptation of unilateral attack.

In the extreme case, [if the first-strike advantage is sufficiently large relative to the total costs of fighting,] no self-enforcing peaceful outcomes exist [$p_f - c_A$ is greater than $p_s + c_B$]. This does not mean that no bargains exist that both sides would prefer to war. Since by definition both states cannot enjoy the advantage of going first, agreements that both sides prefer to fighting are always available in principle. The problem is that under anarchy, large enough first-strike incentives (relative to cost-benefit ratios) can make all of these agreements unenforceable and incredible as bargains.

Does this prisoners' dilemma logic provide an empirically plausible explanation for war? Though I lack the space to develop the point, I would argue that first-strike and offensive advantages probably are an important factor making war more likely in a few cases, but not because they make mobilization and attack a dominant strategy, as in the extreme case above. In the pure preemptive war scenario leaders reason as follows: "The first-strike advantage is so great that regardless of how we resolve any diplomatic issues between us, one side will always want to attack the other in an effort to gain the (huge) advantage of going first." But even in July 1914, a case in which European leaders apparently held extreme views about the advantage of striking first, we do not find leaders thinking in these terms.[54] It would be rather surprising if they did, since they had all lived at peace but with the same military technology prior to July 1914. Moreover, in the crisis itself military first-strike advantages did not become a concern until quite late, and right to the end competed with significant political (and so strategic) disadvantages to striking first.[55]

Rather than completely eliminating enforceable bargains and so causing war, it seems more plausible that first-strike and offensive advantages exacerbate other causes of war by narrowing the bargaining range. If for whatever reason the issues in dispute are hard to divide up, then war will be more likely the smaller the set of enforceable agreements both sides prefer to a fight. Alternatively, the problems posed by private information and incentives to misrepresent may be more intractable when the de facto bargaining range is small.[56] For example, in 1914 large perceived first-strike advantages meant that relatively few costly signals of intent were sufficient to commit both sides to war (chiefly, for Germany/Austria and Russia). Had leaders thought defense had the advantage, the set of enforceable agreements both would have preferred would have been larger, and this may have made costly signaling less likely to have destroyed the bargaining range.

I should note that scholars have sometimes portrayed the preemptive war problem differently, assuming that neither state would want to attack unilaterally but that each would want to attack if the other was expected to also. This is a coordination problem known as "stag hunt" that would seem easily resolved by communication. At any rate, it seems farfetched to think that small numbers of states (typically dyads) would have trouble reaching the efficient solution here, if coordination were really the only problem.[57]

Preventive War as a Commitment Problem

Empirically, preventive motivations seem more prevalent and important than preemptive concerns. In his diplomatic history of Europe from 1848 to 1918, A.J.P. Taylor argued that "every war between the Great Powers [in this period] started as a preventive war, not a war of conquest."[58] In this subsection I argue that within a rationalist framework, preventive war is properly understood as arising from a commitment problem occasioned by anarchy and briefly discuss some empirical implications of this view.[59]

The theoretical framework used above is readily adapted for an analysis of the preventive war problem. Whatever their details, preventive war arguments are necessarily dynamic—they picture state leaders who think about what may happen in the future. So, we must modify the bargaining model to make it dynamic as well. Suppose state A will have the opportunity to choose the resolution of the issues in each of an infinite number of successive periods. For periods $t = 1, 2, \ldots$, state A can attempt a fait accompli to revise the status quo, choosing a demand x_t. On seeing the demand x_t, state B can either acquiesce or go to war, which state A is assumed to win with probability p_t. * * *

This model extends the one-period bargaining game considered above to an infinite-horizon case in which military power can vary over time. An important observation about the multiperiod model is that war remains a strictly inefficient outcome. It is straightforward to show that there will always exist peaceful settlements in X such that both states would prefer to see one of these settlements implemented in every period from t forward rather than go to war.[60]

The strategic dilemma is that without some third party capable of guaranteeing agreements, state A may not be able to commit itself to future foreign policy behavior that makes B prefer not to attack at some point. Consider the simple case in which A's chance of winning a war begins at p_1 and then will increase to $p_2 > p_1$ in the next period, where it will remain for all subsequent periods. Under anarchy, state A cannot commit itself not to exploit the greater bargaining leverage it will have starting in the second period. * * * [At that time, A will choose a resolution of the issues that makes state B just willing to acquiesce, given the new distribution of military power. This means that in the first period, when state B is still relatively strong, B is choosing between going to war and acquiescing to A's first period demand, which gives it some value today plus the issue equivalent of fighting a war at a disadvantage in the next period. The most state A could possibly do for B in the first period would be to cede B's most preferred outcome ($x_1 = 0$). However, if the change in relative military power is large enough, this concession can still be too small to make accepting it worthwhile for state B. B may prefer to "lock in" what it gets from war when it is relatively strong, to one period of concessions followed by a significantly worse deal when it is militarily weaker. In sum,] if B's expected decline in military power is too large relative to B's costs for war, then state A's inability to commit to restrain its foreign policy demands after it gains power makes preventive attack rational for state B.[61] Note also that A's commitment problem meshes with a parallel problem facing B. If B could commit to fight in the second period rather than accept the rising state's increased demands, then B's bargaining power would not fall in the second period, so that preventive war would be unnecessary in the first.

Several points about this rationalist analysis of preventive war are worth stressing. First, preventive war occurs here despite (and in fact partially because of) the states' agreement about relative power. Preventive war is thus another area where Blainey's argument misleads. Second, contrary to the standard formulation, the declining state attacks not because it fears being attacked in the future but because it fears the peace it will have to accept after the rival has grown stronger. To illustrate, even if Iraq had moved from Kuwait to the conquest of Saudi Arabia, invasion of the United States would not have followed. Instead, the war for Kuwait aimed to prevent the development of an oil hegemon that would have had considerable bargaining leverage due to U.S. reliance on oil.[62]

Third, while preventive war arises here from states' inability to trust each other to keep to a bargain, the lack of trust is not due to states' uncertainty about present or future motivations, as in typical security-dilemma and spiral-model accounts. In my argument, states understand each other's motivations perfectly well—there is no private information—and they further understand that each would like to avoid the costs of war— they are not ineluctably greedy. Lack of trust arises here from the situation, a structure of preferences and opportunities, that gives one party an incentive to renege. For example, regardless of expectations about Saddam Hussein's future motivation or intentions, one could predict with some confidence that decreased competition among sellers of oil would have led to higher prices. My claim is not that uncertainty about intentions is unimportant in such situations—it surely is—but that commitment and informational problems are distinct mechanisms and that a rationalist preventive war argument turns crucially on a commitment problem.

Finally, the commitment problem behind preventive war may be undermined if the determinants of military power can reliably be transferred between states. In the model, the rising state can actually have an incentive to transfer away or otherwise limit the sources of its new strength, since by doing so it may avoid being attacked. While such transfers might seem implausible from a realist perspective, the practice of "compensation" in classical balance-of-power politics may be understood in exactly these terms: states that gained territory by war or other means were expected to (and sometimes did) allow compensating gains in order to reduce the incentive for preventive war against them.[63]

Preventive motivations figured in the origins of World War I and are useful to illustrate these points. One of the reasons that German leaders were willing to run serious risks of global conflict in 1914 was that they feared the consequences of further growth of Russian military power, which appeared to them to be on a dangerous upward trajectory.[64] Even if the increase in Russian power had not led Russia to attack Austria and Germany at some point in the future—war still being a costly option—greater Russian power would have allowed St. Petersburg to pursue a more aggressive foreign policy in the Balkans and the Near East, where Austria and Russia had conflicting interests. Austrian and German leaders greatly feared the consequences of such a (pro-Slav) Russian foreign policy for the domestic stability of the Austro-Hungarian Empire, thus giving them incentives for a preventive attack on Russia.[65]

By the argument made above, the states should in principle have had incentives to cut a multiperiod deal both sides would have preferred to preventive war. For example, fearing preventive attack by Austria and Germany, Russian leaders might have wished to have committed themselves not to push so hard in the Balkans as to endanger the Dual Monarchy. But such a deal would be so obviously unenforceable as to not be worth proposing.

Leaving aside the serious monitoring difficulties, once Russia had become stronger militarily, Austria would have no choice but to acquiesce to a somewhat more aggressive Russian policy in the Balkans. And so Russia would be drawn to pursue it, regardless of its overall motivation or desire for conquest of Austria-Hungary.

While German leaders in July 1914 were willing to accept a very serious risk that Russia might go to war in support of Serbia, they seem to have hoped at the start of the crisis that Russia would accept the Austrian demarche.[66] Thus, it is hard to argue that the preventive logic itself produced the war. Rather, as is probably true for other cases in which these concerns appear, the preventive logic may have made war more likely in combination with other causes, such as private information, by making Berlin much more willing to risk war.[67] How preventive concerns impinge on international bargaining with private information is an important topic for future research.

Commitment, Strategic Territory, and the Problem of Appeasement

The objects over which states bargain frequently are themselves sources of military power. Territory is the most important example, since it may provide economic resources that can be used for the military or be strategically located, meaning that its control greatly increases a state's chances for successful attack or defense. Territory is probably also the main issue over which states fight wars.[68]

In international bargaining on issues with this property, a commitment problem can operate that makes mutually preferable negotiated solutions unattainable. The problem is similar to that underlying preventive war. Here, both sides might prefer some package of territorial concessions to a fight, but if the territory in question is strategically vital or economically important, its transfer could radically increase one side's future bargaining leverage (think of the Golan Heights). In principle, one state might prefer war to the status quo but be unable to commit not to exploit the large increase in bargaining leverage it would gain from limited territorial concessions. Thus the other state might prefer war to limited concessions (appeasement), so it might appear that the issues in dispute were indivisible. But the underlying cause of war in this instance is not indivisibility per se but rather the inability of states to make credible commitments under anarchy.[69]

As an example, the 1939 Winter War between Finland and the Soviet Union followed on the refusal of the Finnish government to cede some tiny islands in the Gulf of Finland that Stalin seems to have viewed as necessary for the defense of Leningrad in the event of a European war. One of the main reasons the Finns were so reluctant to grant these concessions was that they believed they could not trust Stalin not to use these advantages to pressure Finland for more in the future. So it is possible that Stalin's inability to commit himself not to attempt to carry out in Finland the program he had just applied in the Baltic states may have led or contributed to a costly war both sides clearly wished to avoid.[70]

Conclusion

The article has developed two major claims. First, under broad conditions the fact that fighting is costly and risky implies that there should exist negotiated agreements that rationally led states in dispute would prefer to war. This claim runs directly counter to the conventional view that rational states can and often do face a situation of deadlock, in which war occurs because no mutually preferable bargain exists.

Second, essentially two mechanisms, or causal logics, explain why rationally led states are sometimes unable to locate or agree on such a bargain:

(1) the combination of private information about resolve or capability and incentives to misrepresent these, and (2) states' inability, in specific circumstances, to commit to uphold a deal. Historical examples were intended to suggest that both mechanisms can claim empirical relevance.

I conclude by anticipating two criticisms. First, I am not saying that explanations for war based on irrationality or "pathological" domestic politics are less empirically relevant. Doubtless they are important, but we cannot say how so or in what measure if we have not clearly specified the causal mechanisms making for war in the "ideal" case of rational unitary states. In fact, a better understanding of what the assumption of rationality really implies for explaining war may actually raise our estimate of the importance of particular irrational and second-image factors.

For example, once the distinction is made clear, bounded rationality may appear a more important cause of disagreements about relative power than private information about military capabilities. If private information about capabilities was often a major factor influencing the odds of victory, then we would expect rational leaders to update their war estimates during international crises; a tough bargaining stand by an adversary would signal that the adversary was militarily stronger than expected. Diplomatic records should then contain evidence of leaders reasoning as follows: "The fact that the other side is not backing down means that we are probably less likely to win at war than we initially thought." I do not know of a single clear instance of this sort of updating in any international crisis, even though updating about an opponent's resolve, or willingness to fight, is very common.

Second, one might argue that since both anarchy and private information plus incentives to misrepresent are constant features of international politics, neither can explain why states fail to strike a bargain preferable to war in one instance but not another. This argument is correct. But the task of specifying the causal mechanisms that explain the occurrence of war must precede the identification of factors that lead the mechanisms to produce one outcome rather than another in particular settings. That is, specific models in which commitment or information problems operate allow one to analyze how different variables (such as power shifts and cost-benefit ratios in the preventive war model) make for war in some cases rather than others.

This is the sense in which these two general mechanisms provide the foundations for a coherent rationalist or neorealist theory of war. A neorealist explanation for war shows how war could occur given the assumption of rational and unitary ("billiard ball") states, the assumption made throughout this article. Consider any particular factor argued in the literature to be a cause of war under this assumption—for example, a failure to balance power, offensive advantages, multipolarity, or shifts in relative power. My claim is that showing how any such factor could cause war between rational states requires showing how the factor can occasion an unresolvable commitment or information problem in specific empirical circumstances. Short of this, the central puzzle posed by war, its costs, has not been addressed.

NOTES

1. Of course, arguments of the second sort may and often do presume rational behavior by individual leaders; that is, war may be rational for civilian or military leaders if they will enjoy various benefits of war without suffering costs imposed on the population. While I believe that "second-image" mechanisms of this sort are very important empirically, I do not explore them here. A more accurate label for the subject of the article might be "rational unitary-actor explanations," but this is cumbersome.

2. For the founding work of neorealism, see Kenneth Waltz, *Theory of International Politics* (Reading, MA: Addison-Wesley, 1979). For examples of theorizing along these lines, see Robert Jervis, "Cooperation Under the Security Dilemma," *World Politics* 30 (January 1978), pp. 167–214; Stephen Walt, *The Origins of Alliances* (Ithaca, NY: Cornell University Press, 1987); John J. Mearsheimer, "Back to the Future: Instability in Europe After the Cold War," *International Security* 15 (Summer 1990), pp. 5–56; and Charles Glaser, "Realists as Optimists: Cooperation as Self-Help," *International Security* 19 (Winter 1994/95), pp. 50–90.

3. The sense of "mechanism" is similar to that proposed by Elster, although somewhat broader. See Jon Elster, *Political Psychology* (Cambridge: Cambridge University Press, 1993), pp. 1–7; and Jon Elster, *Nuts and Bolts for the Social Sciences* (Cambridge: Cambridge University Press, 1989), chap. 1.

4. For an influential example of this common assumption see Glenn Snyder and Paul Diesing, *Conflict among Nations* (Princeton, NJ: Princeton University Press, 1977).

5. See, for examples, Geoffry Blainey, *The Causes of War* (New York: Free Press, 1973); Michael Howard, *The Causes of Wars* (Cambridge, MA: Harvard University Press, 1983), especially chap. 1; and Arthur Stein, *Why Nations Cooperate: Circumstance and Choice in International Relations* (Ithaca, NY: Cornell University Press, 1990), pp. 60–64. Even the case of World War I is contested; an important historical school argues that this was a wanted war. See Fritz Fisher, *Germany's Aims in the First World War* (New York: Norton, 1967).

6. The quotation is drawn from Kenneth Waltz, *Man, the State, and War: A Theoretical Analysis* (New York: Columbia University Press, 1959), p. 188.

7. For a careful analysis and critique of this standard argument on the difference between the international and domestic arenas, see R. Harrison Wagner, "The Causes of Peace," in Roy A. Licklider, ed., *Stopping the Killing: How Civil Wars End* (New York: New York University Press, 1993), pp. 235–68 and especially pp. 251–57.

8. See John H. Herz, "Idealist Internationalism and the Security Dilemma," *World Politics* 2 (January 1950), pp. 157–80; and Jervis, "Cooperation Under the Security Dilemma." Anarchy is implicated in the security dilemma externality by the following logic: but for anarchy, states could commit to use weapons only for nonthreatening, defensive purposes.

9. Jervis, "Cooperation under the Security Dilemma."

10. For an analysis of the security dilemma that takes into account signaling, see Andrew Kydd, "The Security Dilemma, Game Theory, and World War I," paper presented at the annual meeting of the American Political Science Association, Washington, DC, 2–5 September 1993.

11. The most developed exception I know of is found in Stephen Van Evera, "Causes of War," Ph.D. diss., University of California, Berkeley, 1984, pp. 61–64.

12. See Bruce Bueno de Mesquita, *The War Trap* (New Haven, CT: Yale University Press, 1981), and "The War Trap Revisited: A Revised Expected Utility Model," *American Political Science Review* 79 (March 1985), pp. 157–76. For a generalization that introduces the idea of a bargaining range, see James D. Morrow, "A Continuous-Outcome Expected Utility Theory of War," *Journal of Conflict Resolution* 29 (September 1985), pp. 473–502. Informal versions of the expected utility argument are everywhere. For example, Waltz's statement that "A state will use force to attain its goals if, after assessing the prospects for success, it values those goals more than it values the pleasures of peace" appears in different ways in a great many works on war. See Waltz, *Man, the State, and War*, p. 60.

13. Let the states' utilities for the outcome $x \in X$ be $u_A(x)$ and $u_B(1-x)$, and assume for now that $u_A(\cdot)$ and $u_B(\cdot)$ are continuous, increasing,

and weakly concave (that is, risk-neutral or risk-averse). Without losing any generality, we can set $u_i(1) = 1$ and $u_i(0) = 0$ for both states ($i = A, B$).

14. See, for classic examples, Thucydides, *The Peloponnesian War* (New York: Modern Library, 1951), pp. 45 and 48; and Carl von Clausewitz, *On War* (Princeton, NJ: Princeton University Press, 1984), p. 85.

15. Bueno de Mesquita, *The War Trap.*

16. Note that in this formulation the terms c_A and c_B capture not only the states' values for the costs of war but also the value they place on winning or losing on the issues at stake. That is, c_A reflects state A's costs for war relative to any possible benefits. For example, if the two states see little to gain from winning a war against each other, then c_A and c_B would be large even if neither side expected to suffer much damage in a war.

17. On the theory of bargaining with outside options, see Martin J. Osborne and Ariel Rubinstein, *Bargaining and Markets* (New York: Academic Press, 1990), chap. 3; Motty Perry, "An Example of Price Formation in Bilateral Situations," *Econometrica* 50 (March 1986), pp. 313–21; and Robert Powell, "Bargaining in the Shadow of Power" (University of California, Berkeley, 1993, mimeographed). See also the analyses in R. Harrison Wagner, "Peace, War, and the Balance of Power," *American Political Science Review* 88 (September 1994), pp. 593–607; and Wagner, "The Causes of Peace."

18. See, for example, Evan Luard, *War in International Society* (New Haven, CT: Yale University Press, 1992), p. 191. Schroeder notes that "patronage, bribes, and corruption" were "a major element" of eighteenth-century international relations. See Paul Schroeder, *The Transformation of European Politics, 1763–1848* (Oxford: Oxford University Press, 1994), p. 579.

19. On Cuba, see Ernest May, *Imperial Democracy* (New York: Harper and Row, 1961), pp. 149–50. On the Louisiana Purchase, military threats raised in the U.S. Senate apparently made Napoleon more eager to negotiate the sale. See E. Wilson Lyon, *Louisiana in French Diplomacy* (Norman: University of Oklahoma Press, 1934), pp. 179 and 214ff.

20. Diego Gambetta, *The Sicilian Mafia: The Business of Private Protection* (Cambridge, MA: Harvard University Press, 1993), p. 214.

21. In one of the only articles on this problem, Morrow proposes a private information explanation for states' failures to link issues in many disputes. See James D. Morrow, "Signaling Difficulties with Linkage in Crisis Bargaining," *International Studies Quarterly* 36 (June 1992), pp. 153–72.

22. See Jack Levy, "The Causes of War: A Review of Theories and Evidence," in Philip E. Tetlock et al., eds., *Behavior, Society, and Nuclear War*, vol. 1 (Oxford: Oxford University Press, 1989), pp. 209–333. Recent work using limited-information game theory to analyze crisis bargaining places the strategic consequences of private information at the center of the analysis. See, for examples, Bruce Bueno de Mesquita and David Lalman, *War and Reason* (New Haven, CT: Yale University Press, 1992); James D. Fearon, "Domestic Political Audiences and the Escalation of International Disputes," *American Political Science Review* 88 (September 1994), pp. 577–92; James D. Morrow, "Capabilities, Uncertainty, and Resolve: A Limited Information Model of Crisis Bargaining,"

American Journal of Political Science 33 (November 1989), pp. 941–72; Barry Nalebuff, "Brinkmanship and Nuclear Deterrence: The Neutrality of Escalation," *Conflict Management and Peace Science* 9 (Spring 1986), pp. 19–30; and Robert Powell, *Nuclear Deterrence Theory: The Problem of Credibility* (Cambridge: Cambridge University Press, 1990).

23. Blainey, *The Causes of War*, p. 246.

24. Ibid., p. 54. Blainey also blames patriotic and nationalistic fervor, leaders' (irrational) tendency to surround themselves with yes-men, and crowd psychology.

25. See Ralph K. White, *Nobody Wanted War: Misperception in Vietnam and Other Wars* (New York: Doubleday/Anchor, 1970), chap. 7; Blainey, *The Causes of War*, p. 54; and Richard Ned Lebow, *Between Peace and War: The Nature of International Crises* (Baltimore, MD: Johns Hopkins University Press, 1981), p. 247.

26. John C. Harsanyi, "Games with Incomplete Information Played by 'Bayesian' Players, Part III," *Management Science* 14 (March 1968), pp. 486–502.

27. Aumann observed an interesting implication of this doctrine: genuinely rational agents cannot "agree to disagree," in the sense that it cannot be commonly known that they are rational and that they hold different estimates of the likelihood of some uncertain event. See Robert Aumann, "Agreeing to Disagree," *The Annals of Statistics* 4 (November 1976), pp. 1236–39. Emerson Niou, Peter Ordeshook, and Gregory Rose note that this implies that rational states cannot agree to disagree about the probability that one or the other would win in a war in *The Balance of Power: Stability in the International System* (Cambridge: Cambridge University Press, 1989), p. 59.

28. On bounded rationality, see Herbert A. Simon, "A Behavioral Model of Rational Choice," *Quarterly Journal of Economics* 69 (February 1955), pp. 99–118.

29. This analysis runs exactly parallel to work in law and economics on pretrial bargaining in legal disputes. Early studies explained costly litigation as resulting from divergent expectations about the likely trial outcome, while in more recent work such expectations derive from private information about the strength of one's case. For a review and references, see Robert D. Cooter and Daniel L. Rubinfeld, "Economic Analysis of Legal Disputes and Their Resolution," *Journal of Economic Literature* 27 (September 1989), pp. 1067–97.

30. Blainey, *The Causes of War.*

31. This take-it-or-leave-it model of international bargaining is proposed and analyzed under conditions of both complete and incomplete information in James D. Fearon, "Threats to Use Force: The Role of Costly Signals in International Crises," Ph.D. diss., University of California, Berkeley, 1992, chap. 1. Similar results for more elaborate bargaining structures are given in my own work in progress. See James D. Fearon, "Game-Theoretic Models of International Bargaining: An Overview," University of Chicago, 1995. Powell has analyzed an alternative model in which both sides must agree if the status quo is to be revised. See Powell, "Bargaining in the Shadow of Power."

32. For examples and discussion on this point, see Fearon, "Threats to Use Force," chap. 3.

33. * * * Cheap talk announcements can affect outcomes in some bargaining contexts. For an example from economics, see Joseph

Farrell and Robert Gibbons, "Cheap Talk Can Matter in Bargaining," *Journal of Economic Theory* 48 (June 1989), pp. 221–37. These authors show how cheap talk might credibly signal a willingness to negotiate seriously that then affects subsequent terms of trade. For an example from international relations, see James D. Morrow, "Modeling the Forms of International Cooperation: Distribution Versus Information," *International Organization* 48 (Summer 1994), pp. 387–423.

34. The conclusion is likewise altered if the possibility of repeated interactions in sufficiently similar contexts is great enough that reputation building can be supported.

35. On signaling costs in crises and audience costs in particular, see Fearon, "Threats to Use Force," and "Domestic Political Audiences and the Escalation of International Disputes." For an excellent analysis of international signaling in general, see Robert Jervis, *The Logic of Images in International Relations* (Princeton, NJ: Princeton University Press, 1970).

36. For developed models that make this point, see James Fearon, "Deterrence and the Spiral Model: The Role of Costly Signals in Crisis Bargaining," paper presented at the annual meeting of the American Political Science Association, 30 August–2 September 1990, San Francisco, Calif.; Fearon, "Domestic Political Audiences and the Escalation of International Disputes"; Morrow, "Capabilities, Uncertainty, and Resolve"; Nalebuff, "Brinkmanship and Nuclear Deterrence"; and Powell, *Nuclear Deterrence Theory.*

37. Luigi Albertini, *The Origins of the War of 1914,* vol. 2 (London: Oxford University Press, 1953), pp. 183–87.

38. Ibid., p. 187.

39. Ibid., p. 158. For the full text of the cable, see Karl Kautsky, comp., *German Documents Relating to the Outbreak of the World War* (New York: Oxford University Press, 1924), doc. no. 71, p. 130.

40. Konrad Jarausch, "The Illusion of Limited War: Chancellor Bethmann Hollweg's Calculated Risk," *Central European History* 2 (March 1969), pp. 48–76. The quotation is drawn from p. 65.

41. See L. C. F. Turner, *Origins of the First World War* (New York: Norton, 1970), p. 101; and Jarausch, "The Illusion of Limited War," p. 63. Trachtenberg writes that "one of Bethmann's basic goals was for Germany to avoid coming across as the aggressor." See Marc Trachtenberg, *History and Strategy* (Princeton, NJ: Princeton University Press, 1991), p. 90.

42. Albertini concludes that "on the evening of the 27th all the Chancellor sought to do was to throw dust in the eyes of Grey and lead him to believe that Berlin was seriously trying to avert a conflict, that if war broke out it would be Russia's fault and that England could therefore remain neutral." See Albertini, *The Origins of the War of 1914,* vol. 1, pp. 444–45. See also Turner, *Origins of the First World War,* p. 99.

43. See J. A. White, *The Diplomacy of the Russo–Japanese War* (Princeton, NJ: Princeton University Press, 1964), pp. 142–43; and Ian Nish, *The Origins of the Russo–Japanese War* (London: Longman, 1985), pp. 241–42.

44. J. N. Westwood, *Russia against Japan, 1904–5: A New Look at the Russo–Japanese War* (Albany: State University of New York Press, 1986), p. 22. Estimates varied within the Japanese leadership, but with the exception of junior-level officers, few seem to have been highly confident of victory. For example, as the decision for war was taken the Japanese navy requested a two-week delay to allow it to even the odds at sea. See Nish, *The Origins of the Russo–Japanese War,* pp. 197–200 and 206–7.

45. See, for example, David Walder, *The Short Victorious War: The Russo–Japanese Conflict, 1904–5* (London: Hutchinson, 1973), pp. 53–56; and Nish, *The Origins of the Russo–Japanese War,* p. 253.

46. See White, *The Diplomacy of the Russo–Japanese War,* chaps. 6–8; Nish, *The Origins of the Russo–Japanese War,* p. 241; and Lebow, *Between Peace and War,* pp. 244–46.

47. White, *The Diplomacy of the Russo–Japanese War,* p. 139. Nish writes that "many Russians certainly took a view of [the Japanese military] which was derisory in comparison with themselves. It may be that this derived from a deliberate policy of secrecy and concealment which the Japanese army applied because of the historic coolness between the two countries." See Nish, *The Origins of the Russo–Japanese War,* p. 241.

48. The British were the major exception, who as recent allies of Japan had better knowledge of its capabilities and level of organization. See Nish, *The Origins of the Russo–Japanese War,* p. 241.

49. See, for example, William Langer, "The Origins of the Russo–Japanese War," in Carl Schorske and Elizabeth Schorske, eds., *Explorations in Crisis* (Cambridge, MA: Harvard University Press, 1969), p. 44.

50. For some examples, see Fearon, "Threats to Use Force," chap. 3. For a formal version of reputational dynamics due to private information, see Barry Nalebuff, "Rational Deterrence in an Imperfect World," *World Politics* 43 (April 1991), pp. 313–35.

51. See, for examples, Robert Jervis, *Perception and Misperception in International Politics* (Princeton, NJ: Princeton University Press, 1976), pp. 62–67; Barry Posen, *The Sources of Military Doctrine* (Ithaca, NY: Cornell University Press, 1984), pp. 16–17; and Charles Glaser, "The Political Consequences of Military Strategy," *World Politics* 44 (July 1992), p. 506.

52. For dynamic game models that demonstrate this, see Robert Powell, "Absolute and Relative Gains in International Relations Theory," *American Political Science Review* 85 (December 1991), pp. 1303–20; and James D. Fearon, "Cooperation and Bargaining Under Anarchy," (University of Chicago, 1994, mimeographed). On tit-for-tat and the impact of the shadow of the future, see Robert Axelrod, *The Evolution of Cooperation* (New York: Basic Books, 1984); and Kenneth Oye, ed., *Cooperation under Anarchy* (Princeton, NJ: Princeton University Press, 1986).

53. This argument about military variance runs counter to the usual hypothesis that offensive advantages foster war. For a discussion and an empirical assessment, see James D. Fearon, "Offensive Advantages and War since 1648," paper presented at the annual meeting of the International Studies Association, 21–25 February 1995. On the offense–defense balance and war, see Jervis, "Cooperation under the Security Dilemma"; and Van Evera, "Causes of War," chap. 3.

54. For the argument about leaders' views on first-strike advantages in 1914, see Stephen Van Evera, "The Cult of the Offensive and the Origins of the First World War," *International Security* 9 (Summer 1984), pp. 58–107.

55. See, for example, Trachtenberg, *History and Strategy,* p. 90.

56. This is suggested by results in Roger Myerson and Mark Satterthwaite, "Efficient Mechanisms for Bilateral Trading," *Journal of Economic Theory* 29 (April 1983), pp. 265–81.

57. Schelling suggested that efficient coordination in stag hunt-like preemption problems might be prevented by a rational dynamic of "reciprocal fear of surprise attack." See Thomas Schelling, *The Strategy of Conflict* (Cambridge, MA: Harvard University Press, 1960), chap. 9. Powell has argued that no such dynamic exists between rational adversaries. See Robert Powell, "Crisis Stability in the Nuclear Age," *American Political Science Review* 83 (March 1989), pp. 61–76.

58. Taylor, *The Struggle for Mastery in Europe, 1848–1918* (London: Oxford University Press, 1954), p. 166. Carr held a similar view: "The most serious wars are fought in order to make one's own country militarily stronger or, more often, to prevent another country from becoming militarily stronger." See E. H. Carr, *The Twenty Years' Crisis, 1919–1939* (New York: Harper and Row, 1964), pp. 111–12.

59. To my knowledge, Van Evera is the only scholar whose treatment of preventive war analyzes at some length how issues of credible commitment intervene. The issue is raised by both Snyder and Levy. See Van Evera, "Causes of War," pp. 62–64; Jack Snyder, "Perceptions of the Security Dilemma in 1914," in Robert Jervis, Richard Ned Lebow, and Janice Gross Stein, eds., *Psychology and Deterrence* (Baltimore, MD: Johns Hopkins University Press, 1985), p. 160; and Jack Levy, "Declining Power and the Preventive Motivation for War," *World Politics* 40 (October 1987), p. 96.

60. If the states go to war in period t, expected payoffs from period t on are $(p_t /(1 - \delta)) - c_A$ for state A and $((1 - p_t)/ (1 - \delta)) - c_B$ for state B where δ is the time discount factor that both states apply to payoffs to be received in the next period.

61. The formal condition for preventive war is δ

$$p_2 - p_1 > c_B (1 - \delta)^2.$$

62. According to Hiro, President Bush's main concern at the first National Security Council meeting following the invasion of Kuwait was the potential increase in Iraq's economic leverage and its likely influence on an "already gloomy" U.S. economy.

See Dilip Hiro, *Desert Shield to Desert Storm: The Second Gulf War* (London: Harper-Collins, 1992), p. 108.

63. On compensation, see Edward V. Gulick, *Europe's Classical Balance of Power* (New York: Norton, 1955), pp. 70–72; and Paul W. Schroeder, *The Transformation of European Politics, 1763–1848,* pp. 6–7.

64. See Trachtenberg, *History and Strategy,* pp. 56–59; Albertini, *The Origins of the War of 1914,* vol. 2, pp. 129–30; Turner, *Origins of the First World War,* chap. 4; James Joll, *The Origins of the First World War* (London: Longman, 1984), p. 87; and Van Evera, "The Cult of the Offensive and the Origins of the First World War," pp. 79–85.

65. Samuel Williamson, "The Origins of World War I," *Journal of Interdisciplinary History* (Spring 1988), pp. 795–818 and pp. 797–805 in particular; and D. C. B. Lieven, *Russia and the Origins of the First World War* (New York: St. Martins, 1983), pp. 38–49.

66. Jack S. Levy, "Preferences, Constraints, and Choices in July 1914," *International Security* 15 (Winter 1990/91), pp. 234–36.

67. Levy argues that preventive considerations are rarely themselves sufficient to cause war. See Levy, "Declining Power and the Preventive Motivation for War."

68. See, for example, Kalevi J. Holsti, *Peace and War: Armed Conflicts and International Order 1648–1989* (Cambridge: Cambridge University Press, 1991); and John Vasquez, *The War Puzzle* (Cambridge: Cambridge University Press, 1993).

69. The argument is formalized in work in progress by the author, where it is shown that the conditions under which war will occur are restrictive: the states must be unable to continuously adjust the odds of victory by dividing up and trading the land. In other words, the smallest feasible territorial transfer must produce a discontinuously large change in a state's military chances for war to be possible. See also Wagner, "Peace, War, and the Balance of Power," p. 598, on this commitment problem.

70. See Max Jakobson, *The Diplomacy of the Winter War: An Account of the Russo-Finnish Conflict, 1939–1940* (Cambridge, MA: Harvard University Press, 1961), pp. 135–39; and Van Evera, "Causes of War," p. 63. Private information and incentives to misrepresent also caused problems in the bargaining here. See Fearon, "Threats to Use Force," chap. 3.

Kenneth N. Waltz

WHY IRAN SHOULD GET THE BOMB
Nuclear Balancing Would Mean Stability

The past several months have witnessed a heated debate over the best way for the United States and Israel to respond to Iran's nuclear activities. As the argument has raged, the United States has tightened its already robust sanctions regime against the Islamic Republic, and the European Union announced in January that it will begin an embargo on Iranian oil on July 1. Although the United States, the EU, and Iran have recently returned to the negotiating table, a palpable sense of crisis still looms.

It should not. Most U.S., European, and Israeli commentators and policymakers warn that a nuclear-armed Iran would be the worst possible outcome of the current standoff. In fact, it would probably be the best possible result: the one most likely to restore stability to the Middle East.

Power Begs to Be Balanced

The crisis over Iran's nuclear program could end in three different ways. First, diplomacy coupled with serious sanctions could convince Iran to abandon its pursuit of a nuclear weapon. But this outcome is unlikely: the historical record indicates that a country bent on acquiring nuclear weapons can rarely be dissuaded from doing so. Punishing a state through economic sanctions does not inexorably derail its nuclear program. Take North Korea, which succeeded in building its weapons despite countless rounds of sanctions and UN Security Council resolutions. If Tehran determines that its security depends on possessing nuclear weapons, sanctions are unlikely to change its mind. In fact, adding still more sanctions now could make Iran feel even more vulnerable, giving it still more reason to seek the protection of the ultimate deterrent.

The second possible outcome is that Iran stops short of testing a nuclear weapon but develops a breakout capability, the capacity to build and test one quite quickly. Iran would not be the first country to acquire a sophisticated nuclear program without building an actual bomb. Japan, for instance, maintains a vast civilian nuclear infrastructure. Experts believe that it could produce a nuclear weapon on short notice.

Such a breakout capability might satisfy the domestic political needs of Iran's rulers by assuring hard-liners that they can enjoy all the benefits of having a bomb (such as greater security) without the downsides (such as international isolation and condemnation). The problem is that a breakout capability might not work as intended.

The United States and its European allies are primarily concerned with weaponization, so they might accept a scenario in which Iran stops short of a nuclear weapon. Israel, however, has made it clear that it views a significant Iranian enrichment capacity alone as an unacceptable threat. It is possible, then, that a verifiable commitment from Iran

From *Foreign Affairs* 91, no. 4 (July/August 2012), 2–5.

to stop short of a weapon could appease major Western powers but leave the Israelis unsatisfied. Israel would be less intimidated by a virtual nuclear weapon than it would be by an actual one and therefore would likely continue its risky efforts at subverting Iran's nuclear program through sabotage and assassination—which could lead Iran to conclude that a breakout capability is an insufficient deterrent, after all, and that only weaponization can provide it with the security it seeks.

The third possible outcome of the standoff is that Iran continues its current course and publicly goes nuclear by testing a weapon. U.S. and Israeli officials have declared that outcome unacceptable, arguing that a nuclear Iran is a uniquely terrifying prospect, even an existential threat. Such language is typical of major powers, which have historically gotten riled up whenever another country has begun to develop a nuclear weapon of its own. Yet so far, every time another country has managed to shoulder its way into the nuclear club, the other members have always changed tack and decided to live with it. In fact, by reducing imbalances in military power, new nuclear states generally produce more regional and international stability, not less.

Israel's regional nuclear monopoly, which has proved remarkably durable for the past four decades, has long fueled instability in the Middle East. In no other region of the world does a lone, unchecked nuclear state exist. It is Israel's nuclear arsenal, not Iran's desire for one, that has contributed most to the current crisis. Power, after all, begs to be balanced. What is surprising about the Israeli case is that it has taken so long for a potential balancer to emerge.

Of course, it is easy to understand why Israel wants to remain the sole nuclear power in the region and why it is willing to use force to secure that status. In 1981, Israel bombed Iraq to prevent a challenge to its nuclear monopoly. It did the same to Syria in 2007 and is now considering similar action against Iran. But the very acts that have allowed Israel to maintain its nuclear edge in the

short term have prolonged an imbalance that is unsustainable in the long term. Israel's proven ability to strike potential nuclear rivals with impunity has inevitably made its enemies anxious to develop the means to prevent Israel from doing so again. In this way, the current tensions are best viewed not as the early stages of a relatively recent Iranian nuclear crisis but rather as the final stages of a decades-long Middle East nuclear crisis that will end only when a balance of military power is restored.

Unfounded Fears

One reason the danger of a nuclear Iran has been grossly exaggerated is that the debate surrounding it has been distorted by misplaced worries and fundamental misunderstandings of how states generally behave in the international system. The first prominent concern, which undergirds many others, is that the Iranian regime is innately irrational. Despite a widespread belief to the contrary, Iranian policy is made not by "mad mullahs" but by perfectly sane ayatollahs who want to survive just like any other leaders. Although Iran's leaders indulge in inflammatory and hateful rhetoric, they show no propensity for self-destruction. It would be a grave error for policymakers in the United States and Israel to assume otherwise.

Yet that is precisely what many U.S. and Israeli officials and analysts have done. Portraying Iran as irrational has allowed them to argue that the logic of nuclear deterrence does not apply to the Islamic Republic. If Iran acquired a nuclear weapon, they warn, it would not hesitate to use it in a first strike against Israel, even though doing so would invite massive retaliation and risk destroying everything the Iranian regime holds dear.

Although it is impossible to be certain of Iranian intentions, it is far more likely that if Iran desires nuclear weapons, it is for the purpose of providing for its own security, not to improve its offensive capabilities (or destroy itself). Iran may be intransigent at the negotiating table and defiant in the face of sanctions, but it still acts to secure its own preservation. Iran's leaders did not, for example, attempt to close the Strait of Hormuz despite issuing blustery warnings that they might do so after the EU announced its planned oil embargo in January. The Iranian regime clearly concluded that it did not want to provoke what would surely have been a swift and devastating American response to such a move.

Nevertheless, even some observers and policy-makers who accept that the Iranian regime is rational still worry that a nuclear weapon would embolden it, providing Tehran with a shield that would allow it to act more aggressively and increase its support for terrorism. Some analysts even fear that Iran would directly provide terrorists with nuclear arms. The problem with these concerns is that they contradict the record of every other nuclear weapons state going back to 1945. History shows that when countries acquire the bomb, they feel increasingly vulnerable and become acutely aware that their nuclear weapons make them a potential target in the eyes of major powers. This awareness discourages nuclear states from bold and aggressive action. Maoist China, for example, became much less bellicose after acquiring nuclear weapons in 1964, and India and Pakistan have both become more cautious since going nuclear. There is little reason to believe Iran would break this mold.

As for the risk of a handoff to terrorists, no country could transfer nuclear weapons without running a high risk of being found out. U.S. surveillance capabilities would pose a serious obstacle, as would the United States' impressive and growing ability to identify the source of fissile material. Moreover, countries can never entirely control or even predict the behavior of the terrorist groups they sponsor. Once a country such as Iran acquires a nuclear capability, it will have every reason to maintain full control over its arsenal. After all, building a bomb is costly and dangerous. It would make little sense to transfer the product of that investment to parties that cannot be trusted or managed.

Another oft-touted worry is that if Iran obtains the bomb, other states in the region will follow suit, leading to a nuclear arms race in the Middle East. But the nuclear age is now almost 70 years old, and so far, fears of proliferation have proved to be unfounded. Properly defined, the term "proliferation" means a rapid and uncontrolled spread. Nothing like that has occurred; in fact, since 1970, there has been a marked slowdown in the emergence of nuclear states. There is no reason to expect that this pattern will change now. Should Iran become the second Middle Eastern nuclear power since 1945, it would hardly signal the start of a landslide. When Israel acquired the bomb in the 1960s, it was at war with many of its neighbors. Its nuclear arms were a much bigger threat to the Arab world than Iran's program is today. If an atomic Israel did not trigger an arms race then, there is no reason a nuclear Iran should now.

Rest Assured

In 1991, the historical rivals India and Pakistan signed a treaty agreeing not to target each other's nuclear facilities. They realized that far more worrisome than their adversary's nuclear deterrent was the instability produced by challenges to it. Since then, even in the face of high tensions and risky provocations, the two countries have kept the peace. Israel and Iran would do well to consider this precedent. If Iran goes nuclear, Israel and Iran will deter each other, as nuclear powers always have. There has never been a full-scale war between two nuclear-armed states. Once Iran crosses the nuclear threshold, deterrence will apply, even if the Iranian arsenal is relatively small. No other country in the region will have an incentive to acquire its own nuclear capability, and the current crisis will finally dissipate, leading to a Middle East that is more stable than it is today.

For that reason, the United States and its allies need not take such pains to prevent the Iranians from developing a nuclear weapon. Diplomacy between Iran and the major powers should continue, because open lines of communication will make the Western countries feel better able to live with a nuclear Iran. But the current sanctions on Iran can be dropped: they primarily harm ordinary Iranians, with little purpose.

Most important, policymakers and citizens in the Arab world, Europe, Israel, and the United States should take comfort from the fact that history has shown that where nuclear capabilities emerge, so, too, does stability. When it comes to nuclear weapons, now as ever, more may be better.

Andrew H. Kydd and Barbara F. Walter
THE STRATEGIES OF TERRORISM

Terrorism often works. Extremist organizations such as al-Qaida, Hamas, and the Tamil Tigers engage in terrorism because it frequently delivers the desired response. The October 1983 suicide attack against the U.S. Marine barracks in Beirut, for example, convinced the United States to withdraw its soldiers from Lebanon.[1] The United States pulled its soldiers out of Saudi Arabia two years after the terrorist attacks of September 11, 2001, even though the U.S. military had been building up its forces in that country for more than a decade.[2] The Philippines recalled its troops from Iraq nearly a month early after a Filipino truck driver was kidnapped by Iraqi extremists.[3] In fact, terrorism has been so successful that between 1980 and 2003, half of all suicide terrorist campaigns were closely followed by substantial concessions by the target governments.[4] Hijacking planes, blowing up buses, and kidnapping individuals may seem irrational and incoherent to outside observers, but these tactics can be surprisingly effective in achieving a terrorist group's political aims.

Despite the salience of terrorism today, scholars and policymakers are only beginning to understand how and why it works. Much has been written on the origins of terror, the motivations of terrorists, and counterterror responses, but little has appeared on the strategies terrorist organizations employ and the conditions under which these strategies succeed or fail. Alan Krueger, David Laitin, Jitka Maleckova, and Alberto Abadie, for example, have traced the effects of poverty, education, and political freedom on terrorist recruitment.[5] Jessica Stern has examined the grievances that give rise to

terrorism and the networks, money, and operations that allow terrorist organizations to thrive.[6] What is lacking, however, is a clear understanding of the larger strategic games terrorists are playing and the ways in which state responses help or hinder them.

Effective counterstrategies cannot be designed without first understanding the strategic logic that drives terrorist violence. Terrorism works not simply because it instills fear in target populations, but because it causes governments and individuals to respond in ways that aid the terrorists' cause. The Irish Republican Army (IRA) bombed pubs, parks, and shopping districts in London because its leadership believed that such acts would convince Britain to relinquish Northern Ireland. In targeting the World Trade Center and the Pentagon on September 11, al-Qaida hoped to raise the costs for the United States of supporting Israel, Saudi Arabia, and other Arab regimes, and to provoke the United States into a military response designed to mobilize Muslims around the world. That so many targeted governments respond in the way that terrorist organizations intend underscores the need for understanding the reasoning behind this type of violence.

In this article we seek answers to four questions. First, what types of goals do terrorists seek to achieve? Second, what strategies do they pursue to achieve these goals? Third, why do these strategies work in some cases but not in others? And fourth, given these strategies, what are the targeted governments' best responses to prevent terrorism and protect their countries from future attacks?

The core of our argument is that terrorist violence is a form of costly signaling. Terrorists are too

From International Security 31, no. 1 (Summer 2006), 49–80.

weak to impose their will directly by force of arms. They are sometimes strong enough, however, to persuade audiences to do as they wish by altering the audience's beliefs about such matters as the terrorist's ability to impose costs and their degree of commitment to their cause. Given the conflict of interest between terrorists and their targets, ordinary communication or "cheap talk" is insufficient to change minds or influence behavior. If al-Qaida had informed the United States on September 10, 2001, that it would kill 3,000 Americans unless the United States withdrew from Saudi Arabia, the threat might have sparked concern, but it would not have had the same impact as the attacks that followed. Because it is hard for weak actors to make credible threats, terrorists are forced to display publicly just how far they are willing to go to obtain their desired results.

There are five principal strategic logics of costly signaling at work in terrorist campaigns: (1) attrition, (2) intimidation, (3) provocation, (4) spoiling, and (5) outbidding. In an attrition strategy, terrorists seek to persuade the enemy that the terrorists are strong enough to impose considerable costs if the enemy continues a particular policy. Terrorists using intimidation try to convince the population that the terrorists are strong enough to punish disobedience and that the government is too weak to stop them, so that people behave as the terrorists wish. A provocation strategy is an attempt to induce the enemy to respond to terrorism with indiscriminate violence, which radicalizes the population and moves them to support the terrorists. Spoilers attack in an effort to persuade the enemy that moderates on the terrorists' side are weak and untrustworthy, thus undermining attempts to reach a peace settlement. Groups engaged in outbidding use violence to convince the public that the terrorists have greater resolve to fight the enemy than rival groups, and therefore are worthy of support. Understanding these five distinct strategic logics is crucial not only for understanding terrorism but also for designing effective antiterror policies.[7]

The article is divided into two main sections. The first discusses the goals terrorists pursue and examines the forty-two groups currently on the U.S. State Department's list of foreign terrorist organizations (FTOs).[8] The second section develops the costly signaling approach to terrorism, analyzes the five strategies that terrorists use to achieve their goals, discusses the conditions in which each of these strategies is likely to be successful, and draws out the implications for the best counterterror responses.

The Goals of Terrorism

For years the press has portrayed terrorists as crazy extremists who commit indiscriminate acts of violence, without any larger goal beyond revenge or a desire to produce fear in an enemy population. This characterization derives some support from statements made by terrorists themselves. For example, a young Hamas suicide bomber whose bomb failed to detonate said, "I know that there are other ways to do jihad. But this one is sweet—the sweetest. All martyrdom operations, if done for Allah's sake, hurt less than a gnat's bite!"[9] Volunteers for a suicide mission may have a variety of motives—obtaining rewards in the afterlife, avenging a family member killed by the enemy, or simply collecting financial rewards for their descendants. By contrast, the goals driving terrorist organizations are usually political objectives, and it is these goals that determine whether and how terrorist campaigns will be launched.

We define "terrorism" as the use of violence against civilians by nonstate actors to attain political goals.[10] These goals can be conceptualized in a variety of ways. Individuals and groups often have hierarchies of objectives, where broader goals lead to more proximate objectives, which then become specific goals in more tactical analyses.[11] For the sake of simplicity, we adopt the common distinction between goals (or ultimate

Table 8.1. Foreign Terrorist Organizations and their Goals

NAME	ULTIMATE GOALS	RC	TC	PC	SC	SQM
Abu Nidal Organization	Destroy Israel; establish Palestinian state	X	X			
Abu Sayyaf Group	Secede from Philippines		X			
Al-Aqsa Martyrs' Brigade	Destroy Israel; establish Palestinian state	X	X			
Ansar al-Islam	Evict United States from Iraq; establish Islamic state	X		X		
Armed Islamic Group	Establish Islamic state in Algeria	X				
Asbat al-Ansar	Establish Islamic state in Lebanon	X				
Aum Shinrikyo	Seize power in Japan; hasten the Apocalypse	X				
Basque Fatherland and Liberty (ETA)	Secede from Spain		X			
Communist Party of the Philippines/ New People's Army	Establish Communist state in Philippines	X				
Continuity Irish Republican Army	Evict Britain from Northern Ireland; unite with Eire		X			
Al-Gama'a al-Islamiyya (Islamic Group)	Establish Islamic state in Egypt	X				
Hamas (Islamic Resistance Movement)	Destroy Israel; establish Palestinian Islamic state	X	X			
Harakat ul-Mujahidin	Evict India from Kashmir; unite with Pakistan		X			
Hezbollah (Party of God)	Originally: evict Israel from Lebanon; now: destroy Israel and establish Palestinian Islamic state	X	X			
Islamic Jihad Group	Establish Islamic state in Uzbekistan; reduce U.S. influence	X		X		
Islamic Movement of Uzbekistan	Establish Islamic state in Uzbekistan	X				
Jaish-e-Mohammed (Army of Mohammed)	Evict India from Kashmir; unite with Pakistan		X			

Organization	Goal				
Jemaah Islamiya	Establish Islamic state in Indonesia	X			
Al-Jihad (Egyptian Islamic Jihad)	Establish Islamic state in Egypt	X			
Kahane Chai (Kach)	Expand Israel				X
Kongra-Gel (formerly Kurdistan Workers' Party)	Secede from Turkey				X
Lashkar-e Tayyiba (Army of the Righteous)	Evict India from Kashmir; unite with Pakistan				X
Lashkar i Jhangvi	Establish Islamic state in Pakistan	X			
Liberation Tigers of Tamil Eelam	Secede from Sri Lanka				X
Libyan Islamic Fighting Group	Establish Islamic state in Libya	X			
Moroccan Islamic Combatant Group	Establish Islamic state in Morocco	X			
Mujahedin-e Khalq Organization	Overthrow Iranian government	X			
National Liberation Army	Establish Marxist government in Colombia	X			
Palestine Liberation Front	Destroy Israel; establish Palestinian state	X			X
Palestinian Islamic Jihad	Destroy Israel; establish Palestinian state	X			X
Popular Front for the Liberation of Palestine	Destroy Israel; establish Palestinian state	X			X
Popular Front for the Liberation of Palestine—General Command	Destroy Israel; establish Palestinian state	X			X
Al-Qaida	Establish Islamic states in Middle East; destroy Israel; reduce U.S. influence	X		X	X
Al-Qaida in Iraq (Zarqawi group)	Evict United States from Iraq; establish Islamic state	X			X
Real Irish Republican Army	Evict Britain from Northern Ireland; unite with Eire	X			X
Revolutionary Armed Forces of Colombia	Establish Marxist state in Colombia	X			

(continued)

Table 8.1. Foreign Terrorist Organizations and their Goals (Continued)

NAME	ULTIMATE GOALS	RC	TC	PC	SC	SQM
Revolutionary Nuclei (formerly Revolutionary People's Struggle)	Establish Marxist state in Greece	X				
Revolutionary Organization 7 November	Establish Marxist state in Greece	X				
Revolutionary People's Liberation Party/Front	Establish Marxist state in Turkey	X				
Salafist Group for Call and Combat	Establish Islamic state in Algeria	X				
Shining Path (Sendero Luminoso)	Establish Marxist state in Peru	X				
United Self-Defense Forces of Colombia	Preserve Colombian state					X
Total		31	19	4	0	1

NOTE: RC: regime change; TC: territorial change; PC: policy change; SC: social control; and SQM: status quo maintenance. Coding of goals is the authors'.

SOURCE: Office of Counterterrorism, U.S. Department of State, "Foreign Terrorist Organizations," fact sheet, October 11, 2005.

desires) and strategies (or plans of action to attain the goals).

Although the ultimate goals of terrorists have varied over time, five have had enduring importance: regime change, territorial change, policy change, social control, and status quo maintenance. Regime change is the overthrow of a government and its replacement with one led by the terrorists or at least one more to their liking.[12] Most Marxist groups, including the Shining Path (Sendero Luminoso) in Peru have sought this goal. Territorial change is taking territory away from a state either to establish a new state (as the Tamil Tigers seek to do in Tamil areas of Sri Lanka) or to join another state (as Lashkar-e Tayyiba would like to do by incorporating Indian Kashmir into Pakistan). Policy change is a broader category of lesser demands, such as al-Qaida's demand that the United States drop its support for Israel and corrupt Arab regimes such as Saudi Arabia. Social control constrains the behavior of individuals, rather than the state. In the United States, the Ku Klux Klan sought the continued oppression of African Americans after the Civil War. More recently, antiabortion groups have sought to kill doctors who perform abortions to deter other doctors from providing this service. Finally, status quo maintenance is the support of an existing regime or a territorial arrangement against political groups that seek to change it. Many right-wing paramilitary organizations in Latin America, such as the United Self-Defense Force of Colombia, have sought this goal.[13] Protestant paramilitary groups in Northern Ireland supported maintenance of the territorial status quo (Northern Ireland as British territory) against IRA demands that the territory be transferred to Ireland.[14]

Some organizations hold multiple goals and may view one as facilitating another. For instance, by seeking to weaken U.S. support for Arab regimes (which would represent a policy change by the United States), al-Qaida is working toward the overthrow of those regimes (or regime change). As another example, Hamas aims to drive Israel out of the occupied territories (territorial change) and then to overthrow it (regime change).

A cross section of terrorist organizations listed in Table 8.1 illustrates the range of goals and their relative frequency. Of the forty-two groups currently designated as FTOs by the U.S. State Department, thirty-one seek regime change, nineteen seek territorial change, four seek policy change, and one seeks to maintain the status quo.[15] The list is neither exhaustive nor representative of all terrorist groups, and it does not reflect the frequency of goals in the universe of cases. None of the FTOs appear to pursue social control, but some domestic groups, which are by definition not on the list, are more interested in this goal.[16] What Table 8.1 reveals, however, is the instrumental nature of terrorist violence and some of the more popular political objectives being sought.

The Strategies of Terrorist Violence

To achieve their long-term objectives, terrorists pursue a variety of strategies. Scholars have suggested a number of typologies of terrorist strategies and tactics over the years. In a pathbreaking early analysis of terrorism, Thomas Thornton offered five proximate objectives: morale building, advertising, disorientation (of the target population), elimination of opposing forces, and provocation.[17] Martha Crenshaw also identifies advertising and provocation as proximate objectives, along with weakening the government, enforcing obedience in the population, and outbidding.[18] David Fromkin argues that provocation is *the* strategy of terrorism.[19] Edward Price writes that terrorists must delegitimize the regime and impose costs on occupying forces, and he identifies kidnapping, assassination, advertising, and provocation as tactics.[20] Although these analyses are helpful in identifying strategies of terrorism, they fail to derive them from a coherent framework, spell out their logic in detail, and consider best responses to them.

A fruitful starting point for a theory of terrorist strategies is the literature on uncertainty, conflict, and costly signaling. Uncertainty has long been understood to be a cause of conflict. Geoffrey Blainey argued that wars begin when states disagree about their relative power, and they end when states agree again.[21] James Fearon and other theorists built upon this insight and showed that uncertainty about a state's willingness to fight can cause conflict.[22] If states are unsure what other states will fight for, they may demand too much in negotiations and end up in conflict. This uncertainty could reflect a disagreement about power, as Blainey understood, or a disagreement over resolve, willpower, or the intensity of preferences over the issue. The United States and North Vietnam did not disagree over their relative power, but the United States fatally underestimated North Vietnamese determination to achieve victory.

Uncertainty about trustworthiness or moderation of preferences can also cause conflict. Thomas Hobbes argued that if individuals mistrust each other, they have an incentive to initiate an attack rather than risk being attacked by surprise.[23] John Herz, Robert Jervis, and others have developed this concept in the international relations context under the heading of the security dilemma and the spiral model.[24] States are often uncertain about each other's ultimate ambitions, intentions, and preferences. Because of this, anything that increases one side's belief that the other is deceitful, expansionist, risk acceptant, or hostile increases incentives to fight rather than cooperate.

If uncertainty about power, resolve, and trustworthiness can lead to violence, then communication on these topics is the key to preventing (or instigating) conflict. The problem is that simple verbal statements are often not credible, because actors frequently have incentives to lie

and bluff. If by saying "We're resolved," the North Vietnamese could have persuaded the United States to abandon the South in 1965, then North Vietnam would have had every incentive to say so even if it was not that resolute. In reality, they had to fight a long and costly war to prove their point. Similarly, when Mikhail Gorbachev wanted to reassure the West and end the Cold War, verbal declarations of innocent intentions were insufficient, because previous Soviet leaders had made similar statements. Instead, real arms reductions, such as the 1987 Intermediate-Range Nuclear Forces Treaty, were necessary for Western opinion to change.

Because talk is cheap, states and terrorists who wish to influence the behavior of an adversary must resort to costly signals.[25] Costly signals are actions so costly that bluffers and liars are unwilling to take them.[26] In international crises, mobilizing forces or drawing a very public line in the sand are examples of strategies that less resolved actors might find too costly to take.[27] War itself, or the willingness to endure it, can serve as a forceful signal of resolve and provide believable information about power and capabilities.[28] Costly signals separate the wheat from the chaff and allow honest communication, although sometimes at a terrible price.

To obtain their political goals, terrorists need to provide credible information to the audiences whose behavior they hope to influence. Terrorists play to two key audiences: governments whose policies they wish to influence and individuals on the terrorists' own side whose support or obedience they seek to gain.[29] The targeted governments are central because they can grant concessions over policy or territory that the terrorists are seeking. The terrorists' domestic audience is also important, because they can provide resources to the terrorist group and must obey its edicts on social or political issues.

Figure 8.4 shows how the three subjects of uncertainty (power, resolve, and trustworthiness)

Figure 8.4. Strategies of Terrorist Violence

		Target of Persuasion	
		Enemy	Own Population
Subject of Uncertainty	Power	attrition	intimidation
	Resolve		outbidding
	Trustworthiness	spoiling	provocation

combine with the two targets of persuasion (the enemy government and the domestic population) to yield a family of five signaling strategies. These strategies form a theoretically cohesive set that we believe represents most of the commonly used strategies in important terrorist campaigns around the world today.[30] A terrorist organization can of course pursue more than one strategy at a time. The September 11 terrorist attacks, for example, were probably part of both an attrition strategy and a provocation strategy. By targeting the heart of the United States' financial district, al-Qaida may have been attempting to increase the cost of the U.S. policy of stationing soldiers in Saudi Arabia. But by targeting prominent symbols of American economic and military power, al-Qaida may also have been trying to goad the United States into an extreme military response that would serve al-Qaida's larger goal of radicalizing the world's Muslim population. The challenge for policymakers in targeted countries is to calibrate their responses in ways that do not further any of the terrorists' goals.

Below we analyze the five terrorist strategies in greater detail, discuss the conditions under which each is likely to succeed, and relate these conditions to the appropriate counterterrorism strategies.

Attrition: A Battle of Wills

The most important task for any terrorist group is to persuade the enemy that the group is strong and resolute enough to inflict serious costs, so that the enemy yields to the terrorists' demands.[31] The attrition strategy is designed to accomplish this task.[32] In an attrition campaign, the greater the costs a terrorist organization is able to inflict, the more credible its threat to inflict future costs, and the more likely the target is to grant concessions. During the last years of the British Empire, the Greeks in Cyprus, Jews in Palestine, and Arabs in Aden used a war of attrition strategy against their colonizer. By targeting Britain with terrorist attacks, they eventually convinced the political leadership that maintaining control over these territories would not be worth the cost in British lives.[33] Attacks by Hezbollah and Hamas against Israel, particularly during the second intifada, also appear to be guided by this strategy. In a letter written in the early 1990s to the leadership of Hamas, the organization's master bomb maker, Yahya Ayyash, said, "We paid a high price when we used only sling-shots and stones. We need to exert more pressure, make the cost of the occupation that much more expensive in human lives, that much more unbearable."[34]

Robert Pape presents the most thorough exposition of terrorism as a war of attrition in his analysis of suicide bombing.[35] Based on a data set of all suicide attacks from 1980 to 2003 (315 in total), Pape argues that suicide terrorism is employed by weak actors for whom peaceful tactics have failed and conventional military tactics are infeasible because of the imbalance of power. The strategy is to inflict costs on the enemy until it withdraws its occupying forces: the greater the costs inflicted, the more likely the enemy is to withdraw. Pape asserts that terrorists began to recognize the effectiveness of suicide terrorism with the 1983 Hezbollah attack against U.S. Marines in Beirut that killed 241 people. Since then, suicide terrorism has been employed in nationalist struggles around the world.

CONDITIONS FAVORABLE TO ATTRITION

A war of attrition strategy is more effective against some targets than others. Three variables are likely to figure in the outcome: the state's level of interest in the issue under dispute, the constraints on its ability to retaliate, and its sensitivity to the costs of violence.

The first variable, the state's degree of interest in the disputed issue, is fundamental. States with only peripheral interests at stake often capitulate to terrorist demands; states with more important interests at stake rarely do. The United States withdrew from Lebanon following the bombing of the marine barracks because it had only a marginal interest in maintaining stability and preventing Syrian domination of that country. In that case, the costs of the attack clearly outweighed the U.S. interests at stake. Similarly, Israel withdrew from southern Lebanon in 2000 because the costs of the occupation outstripped Israel's desire to maintain a buffer zone in that region. In contrast,

the United States responded to the September 11 attacks by launching offensive wars in Afghanistan and Iraq rather than withdrawing U.S. troops from the region, as al-Qaida demanded (though U.S. troops did ultimately leave Saudi Arabia for Iraq). Similarly, Israel is unlikely to withdraw from East Jerusalem, much less allow itself to become an Islamic state as Hamas has demanded.

The second variable, constraints on retaliation, affects the costs paid by the terrorists for pursuing a war of attrition. Terrorist organizations almost always are weaker than the governments they target and, as a result, are vulnerable to government retaliation. The more constrained the government is in its use of force, the less costly an attrition strategy is, and the longer the terrorists can hold out in the hopes of achieving their goal. For instance, the Israelis have the military means to commit genocide against the Palestinian people or to expel them to surrounding Arab countries. Israel, however, depends for its long-term survival on close ties with Europe and the United States. Western support for Israel would plummet in response to an Israeli strategy designed to inflict mass casualties, making such a strategy prohibitively costly. This constraint makes a war of attrition strategy less costly (and more attractive) for the Palestinians.

Democracies may be more constrained in their ability to retaliate than authoritarian regimes. Pape finds that suicide bombers target democracies exclusively and argues that this is in part because of constraints on their ability to strike back.[36] Capable authoritarian regimes are able to gather more information on their populations than democracies and can more easily round up suspected terrorists and target those sympathetic to them. They are also less constrained by human rights considerations in their interrogation and retaliation practices.[37]

The ease with which a terrorist organization can be targeted also influences a country's ability to retaliate forcefully. Terrorist organizations such as al-Qaida that are widely dispersed, difficult to identify, or otherwise hard to target are at an advantage in a war of attrition because their enemies will have difficulty delivering punishment. Israel has, through superior intelligence gathering, been able to assassinate top members of Hamas's leadership at will, including its founder and spiritual leader, Sheik Ahmed Yassin, as well as his successor, Abdel Aziz Rantisi. The United States, by contrast, has been unable to locate Osama bin Laden and his top deputy, Ayman al-Zawahiri.

The third variable is a target's cost tolerance. Governments that are able to absorb heavier costs and hold out longer are less inviting targets for an attrition strategy. Terrorist organizations are likely to gauge a target's cost tolerance based on at least two factors: the target's regime type and the target's past behavior toward other terrorists. Regime type is important because democracies may be less able to tolerate the painful effects of terrorism than non-democracies. Citizens of democracies, their fears stoked by media reports and warnings of continued vulnerability, are more likely to demand an end to the attacks. In more authoritarian states, the government exerts more control over the media and can disregard public opinion to a greater extent. The Russian government's heavy-handed response to hostage situations, for example, suggests a higher tolerance for casualties than a more fully democratic government would have. Additionally, because terrorist organizations operate more freely in democracies and politicians must interact with the public to maintain political support, terrorists have an easier time targeting prominent individuals for assassination. Of four leaders assassinated by terrorists in the past quarter century—Indira Gandhi, Rajiv Gandhi, Yitzak Rabin, and Anwar Sadat—three were leaders of democracies.

Among democratic states, sensitivity to costs may vary with the party in power. When more dovish parties are in charge, the target may be perceived to have lower cost tolerances than if a more hawkish party were at the helm. The dove-hawk dimension may correlate with the left-right dimension in domestic politics, leading left-wing parties to be more likely to grant terrorist demands. This traditional divide between peace and security has characterized Israeli politics for years. Labor Party Prime Minister Ehud Barak was elected on a platform of withdrawing Israeli forces from Lebanon and making peace with the Palestinians; in contrast, Likud Party Prime Minister Ariel Sharon was elected on a platform of meeting terrorists with military force. Hoping for greater concessions, terrorists may preferentially attack dovish parties.

The number of prior concessions made to other terrorists is also likely to influence perceptions of the target's cost tolerance. Governments that have already yielded to terrorist demands are more likely to experience additional terrorist attacks. Evidence abounds that terrorists explicitly consider the prior behavior of states and are encouraged by signs of weakness. Israel's precipitous withdrawal from southern Lebanon in May 2000 convinced Hamas that the Israeli leadership's resolve was weakening and encouraged Hamas leaders to initiate the second intifada in September 2000.[38] Israelis fear the same inference will be drawn from their withdrawal from Gaza. A Hamas leader interviewed in October 2005 declared, "When we took up arms and launched [the second intifada], we succeeded in less than five years to force the Israelis to withdraw from the Gaza Strip. This fulfilled everyone's dream. I think we have to benefit from this experience by applying it accordingly to the West Bank and other occupied areas."[39] The past behavior of a targeted government, therefore, also provides important information to terrorist groups about its likely future behavior and the success of this particular strategy.

Perhaps the most important example of a terrorist group pursuing an attrition strategy is al-Qaida's war with the United States. In a November 2004 broadcast, bin Laden boasted, "We gained experience in guerilla and attritional warfare in our struggle against the great oppressive superpower, Russia, in which we and the mujahidin ground it down for ten years until it went bankrupt, and decided to withdraw in defeat. . . . We are continuing to make America bleed to the point of bankruptcy."[40] Al-Qaida's goal—policy change—is well suited to an attrition strategy. Bin Laden has frequently argued that the United States lacks the resolve to fight a long attritional war, as in his February 1996 declaration of jihad:

> Where was this false courage of yours when the explosion in Beirut took place in 1983 A.D.? You were transformed into scattered bits and pieces; 241 soldiers were killed, most of them Marines. And where was this courage of yours when two explosions made you leave Aden in less than twenty-four hours!
>
> But your most disgraceful case was in Somalia; where, after vigorous propaganda about the power of the U.S. and its post–cold war leadership of the new world order, you moved tens of thousands of international forces, including twenty-eight thousand American soldiers, into Somalia. However, when tens of your soldiers were killed in minor battles and one American pilot was dragged in the streets of Mogadishu, you left the area in disappointment, humiliation, and defeat, carrying your dead with you. Clinton appeared in front of the whole world threatening and promising revenge, but these threats were merely a preparation for withdrawal. You had been disgraced by Allah and you withdrew; the extent of your impotence and weaknesses became very clear.[41]

Although difficult to prove, it also appears that bin Laden believed that he and his organization would be hard to target with counterattacks, making a war of attrition strategy even more appealing. In 2001 the Taliban was on the verge of eliminating armed resistance in northern Afghanistan; and, as a landlocked country, Afghanistan must have seemed relatively invulnerable to a U.S. invasion. The United States had bombed al-Qaida camps before to no effect. Even if the United States invaded, Afghanistan was both costly and difficult to conquer, as the Soviets discovered in the 1980s. In the end, of course, the Taliban would have been well advised to insist that the September 11 attacks be delayed until the Northern Alliance was defeated, but the latter's dramatic success with U.S. help was perhaps difficult to anticipate.

BEST RESPONSES TO ATTRITION

There are at least five counterstrategies available to a state engaged in a war of attrition. First, the targeted government can concede inessential issues in exchange for peace, a strategy that we believe is frequently pursued though rarely admitted.[42] In some cases, the terrorists will genuinely care more about the disputed issue and be willing to outlast the target. In such cases, concessions are likely to be the state's best response. Other potential challengers, however, may perceive this response as a sign of weakness, which could lead them to launch their own attacks. To reduce the damage to its reputation, the target can vigorously fight other wars of attrition over issues it cares more deeply about, thus signaling a willingness to bear costs if the matter is of sufficient consequence.

Second, where the issue under dispute is important enough to the targeted state that it does not want to grant any concessions, the government may engage in targeted retaliation. Retaliation can target the leadership of the terrorist group, its followers, their assets, and other objects of value. Care must be taken, however, that the retaliation is precisely targeted, because the terrorist organization could simultaneously be pursuing a strategy of provocation. A harsh, indiscriminate response might make a war of attrition more costly for the terrorists, but it would also harm innocent civilians who might then serve as willing recruits for the terrorists. The Israeli policy of assassination of terrorist leaders is shaped by this concern.

Third, a state can harden likely targets to minimize the costs the terrorist organization can inflict. If targeted governments can prevent most attacks from being executed, a war of attrition strategy will not be able to inflict the costs necessary to convince the target to concede. The wall separating Israel from the West Bank and Gaza is a large-scale example of this counterstrategy. The United States has been less successful in hardening its own valuable targets, such as nuclear and chemical plants and the container shipping system, despite the creation of the Department of Homeland Security.[43] Protecting these types of targets is essential if one seeks to deter additional attacks and discourage the use of attrition.

Fourth, states should seek to deny terrorists access to the most destructive weapons, especially nuclear and biological ones. Any weapon that can inflict enormous costs will be particularly attractive to terrorists pursuing a war of attrition. The greater the destruction, the higher the likelihood that the target will concede increasingly consequential issues. Particular attention should be placed on securing Russian stockpiles of fissile material and on halting the spread of uranium enrichment technology to Iran and North Korea. No other country has as much material under so little government control as Russia, and Iran and North Korea are vital because of the links both countries have to terrorist organizations.[44]

Finally, states can strive to minimize the psychological costs of terrorism and the tendency people have to overreact. John Mueller has noted that the risks associated with terrorism are actually quite small; for the average U.S. citizen, the likelihood of being a victim of a terrorist attack is about the same as that of being struck by light[n]ing.[45] Government public education programs should therefore be careful not to overstate the threat, for this plays into the hands of the terrorists. If Americans become convinced that terrorism, while a deadly problem, is no more of a health risk than drunk driving, smoking, or obesity, then al-Qaida's attrition strategy will be undercut. What the United States should seek to avoid are any unnecessary costs associated with wasteful and misguided counterterror programs. The more costs the United States inflicts on itself in the name of counterterrorism policies of dubious utility, the more likely a war of attrition strategy is to succeed.

Intimidation: The Reign of Terror

Intimidation is akin to the strategy of deterrence, preventing some undesired behavior by means of threats and costly signals.[46] It is most frequently used when terrorist organizations wish to overthrow a government in power or gain social control over a given population. It works by demonstrating that the terrorists have the power to punish whoever disobeys them, and that the government is powerless to stop them.

Terrorists are often in competition with the government for the support of the population. Terrorists who wish to bring down a government must somehow convince the government's defenders that continued backing of the government will be costly. One way to do this is to provide clear evidence that the terrorist organization can kill those individuals who continue to sustain the regime. By targeting the government's more visible agents and supporters, such as mayors, police, prosecutors, and pro-regime citizens, terrorist organizations demonstrate that they have the ability to hurt their opponents and that the government is too weak to punish the terrorists or protect future victims.

Terrorists can also use an intimidation strategy to gain greater social control over a population. Terrorists may turn to this strategy in situations where a government has consistently refused to implement a policy a terrorist group favors and where efforts to change the state's policy appear futile. In this case, terrorists use intimidation to impose the desired policy directly on the population, gaining compliance through selective violence and the threat of future reprisals. In the United States, antiabortion activists have bombed clinics to prevent individuals from performing or seeking abortions, and in the 1960s racist groups burned churches to deter African Americans from claiming their civil rights. In Afghanistan, the Taliban beheaded the principal of a girls school to deter others from providing education for girls.[47]

An intimidation strategy can encompass a range of actions—from assassinations of individuals in positions of power to car bombings of police recruits, such as those carried out by the Zarqawi group in Iraq. It can also include massacres of civilians who have cooperated with the government or rival groups, such as the 1957 massacre at Melouza by the National Liberation Front during the Algerian war for independence.[48] This strategy was taken to an extreme by the Armed Islamic Group in Algeria's civil war of the 1990s. In that war, Islamist guerrillas massacred thousands of people suspected of switching their allegiance to the government. Massacres were especially common in villages that had once been under firm rebel control but that the army was attempting to retake and clear of rebels. Stathis Kalyvas argues that these conditions pose extreme dilemmas for the local inhabitants, who usually wish to support whoever will provide security, but are often left exposed when the government begins to retake an area but has not established effective control.[49]

CONDITIONS FAVORABLE TO INTIMIDATION

When the goal is regime change, weak states and rough terrain are two factors that facilitate intimidation. James Fearon and David Laitin argue that civil wars are likely to erupt and continue where the government is weak and the territory is large and difficult to traverse. These conditions allow small insurgent groups to carve out portions of a country as a base for challenging the central government.[50] Intimidation is likely to be used against civilians on the fault lines between rebel and government control to deter individuals from supporting the government.

When the goal is social control, weak states again facilitate intimidation. When the justice system is too feeble to effectively prosecute crimes associated with intimidation, people will either live in fear or seek protection from non-state actors such as local militias or gangs. Penetration of the justice system by sympathizers of a terrorist group also facilitates an intimidation strategy, because police and courts will be reluctant to prosecute crimes and may even be complicit in them.

BEST RESPONSES TO INTIMIDATION

When the terrorist goal is regime change, the best response to intimidation is to retake territory from the rebels in discrete chunks and in a decisive fashion. Ambiguity about who is in charge should be minimized, even if this means temporarily ceding some areas to the rebels to concentrate resources on selected sections of territory. This response is embodied in the "clear-and-hold strategy" that U.S. forces are employing in Iraq. The 2005 National Strategy for Victory in Iraq specifically identifies intimidation as the "strategy of our enemies."[51] The proper response, as Secretary of State Condoleezza Rice stated in October 2005, "is to clear, hold, and build: clear areas from insurgent control, hold them securely, and build durable national Iraqi institutions."[52] If rebels control their own zone and have no access to the government zone, they will have no incentive to kill the civilians they control and no ability to kill the civilians the government controls. In this situation, there is no uncertainty about who is in control;

the information that would be provided by intimidation is already known. The U.S. military developed the clear-and-hold strategy during the final years of U.S. involvement in Vietnam. A principal strategy of the Vietcong was intimidation—to prevent collaboration with the government and build up control in the countryside. In the early years of the war, the United States responded with search and destroy missions, essentially an attrition strategy. Given that the insurgents were not pursuing an attrition strategy, and were not particularly vulnerable to one, this initial counterstrategy was a mistake. Clear-and-hold was the more appropriate response because it limited the Vietcong's access to potential targets and thus undercut its strategy.[53]

Clear-and-hold has its limitations. It is usually impossible to completely deny terrorists entry into the government-controlled zones. In 2002 Chechen terrorists were able to hold a theater audience of 912 people hostage in the heart of Moscow, and 130 were killed in the operation to retake the building. The Shining Path frequently struck in Lima, far from its mountain strongholds. In such situations, a more effective counterstrategy would be to invest in protecting the targets of attacks. In most states, most of the time, the majority of state agents do not need to worry about their physical security, because no one wants to harm them. However, certain state agents, such as prosecutors of organized crime, are more accustomed to danger, and procedures have been developed to protect them. These procedures should be applied to election workers, rural officials and police, community activists, and any individual who plays a visible role in the support and functioning of the embattled government.

When the terrorist goal is social control, the best response is strengthening law enforcement. This may require more resources to enable the government to effectively investigate and prosecute crimes. More controversial, it may mean using national agencies such as the Federal Bureau of Investigation to bypass local officials who are sympathetic to the terrorist group and investigating law enforcement agencies to purge such sympathizers if they obstruct justice. The state can also offer additional protection to potential targets and increase penalties for violence against them. For instance, the 1994 federal Freedom of Access to Clinic Entrances Act, passed in the wake of the 1993 killing of a doctor at an abortion clinic in Florida, prohibits any violence designed to prevent people from entering such clinics.

Provocation: Lighting the Fuse

A provocation strategy is often used in pursuit of regime change and territorial change, the most popular goals of the FTOs listed by the State Department. It is designed to persuade the domestic audience that the target of attacks is evil and untrustworthy and must be vigorously resisted.

Terrorist organizations seeking to replace a regime face a significant challenge: they are usually much more hostile to the regime than a majority of the state's citizens. Al-Qaida may wish to topple the House of Saud, but if a majority of citizens do not support this goal, al-Qaida is unlikely to achieve it. Similarly, if most Tamils are satisfied living in a united Sri Lanka, the Tamil Tigers' drive for independence will fail. To succeed, therefore, a terrorist organization must first convince moderate citizens that their government needs to be replaced or that independence from the central government is the only acceptable outcome.

Provocation helps shift citizen support away from the incumbent regime. In a provocation strategy, terrorists seek to goad the target government into a military response that harms civilians within the terrorist organization's home territory.[54] The aim is to convince them that the government is so evil that the radical goals of the terrorists are justified and support for their organization is warranted.[55] This is what the Basque Fatherland and

Liberty group (ETA) sought to do in Spain. For years, Madrid responded to ETA attacks with repressive measures against the Basque community, mobilizing many of its members against the government even if they did not condone those attacks. As one expert on this conflict writes, "Nothing radicalizes a people faster than the unleashing of undisciplined security forces on its towns and villages."[56]

David Lake argues that moderates are radicalized because government attacks provide important information about the type of leadership in power and its willingness to negotiate with more moderate elements.[57] Ethan Bueno de Mesquita and Eric Dickson develop this idea and show that if the government has the ability to carry out a discriminating response to terrorism but chooses an undiscriminating one, it reveals itself to be unconcerned with the welfare of the country's citizens. Provocation, therefore, is a way for terrorists to force an enemy government to reveal information about itself that then helps the organization recruit additional members.[58]

CONDITIONS FAVORABLE TO PROVOCATION

Constraints on retaliation and regime type are again important in determining when provocation is successful. For provocation to work, the government must be capable of middling levels of brutality. A government willing and able to commit genocide makes a bad target for provocation, as the response will destroy the constituency the terrorists represent. At the opposite pole, a government so committed to human rights and the rule of law that it is incapable of inflicting indiscriminate punishment also makes a bad target, because it cannot be provoked. Such a government might be an attractive target for an attrition strategy if it is not very good at stopping attacks, but provocation will be ineffective.

What explains why a government would choose a less discriminating counterstrategy over a more

precise one? In some instances, a large-scale military response will enhance the security of a country rather than detract from it. If the target government is able to eliminate the leadership of a terrorist organization and its operatives, terrorism is likely to cease or be greatly reduced even if collateral damage radicalizes moderates to some extent. A large-scale military response may also enhance the security of a country, despite radicalizing some moderates, if it deters additional attacks from other terrorist groups that may be considering a war of attrition. Target governments may calculate that the negative consequences of a provocation strategy are acceptable under these conditions.

Domestic political considerations are also likely to influence the type of response that the leadership of a target state chooses. Democracies may be more susceptible to provocation than nondemocracies. Populations that have suffered from terrorist violence will naturally want their government to take action to stop terrorism. Unfortunately, many of the more discriminating tools of counterterrorism, such as infiltrating terrorist cells, sharing intelligence with other countries, and arresting individuals, are not visible to the publics these actions serve to protect. Bueno de Mesquita has argued that democratic leaders may have to employ the more public and less discriminating counterterror strategies to prove that their government is taking sufficient action against terrorists, even if these steps are provocative.[59] Pressure for a provocative counterresponse may also be particularly acute for more hard-line administrations whose constituents may demand greater action.[60] Counterstrategies, therefore, are influenced in part by the political system from which they emerge.

The United States in September 2001 was ripe for provocation, and al-Qaida appears to have understood this. The new administration of George W. Bush was known to be hawkish in its foreign policy and in its attitude toward the use of military power. In a November 2004 videotape, bin Laden bragged that al-Qaida found it "easy for us to provoke this administration."[61] The strategy appears to be working. A 2004 Pew survey found that international trust in the United States had declined significantly in response to the invasion of Iraq.[62] Similarly, a 2004 report by the International Institute for Strategic Studies found that al-Qaida's recruitment and fundraising efforts had been given a major boost by the U.S. invasion of Iraq.[63] In the words of Shibley Telhami, "What we're seeing now is a disturbing sympathy with al-Qaida coupled with resentment toward the United States."[64] The Bush administration's eagerness to overthrow Saddam Hussein, a desire that predated the September 11 attacks, has, in the words of bin Laden, "contributed to these remarkable results for al-Qaida."[65]

BEST RESPONSES TO PROVOCATION

The best response to provocation is a discriminating strategy that inflicts as little collateral damage as possible. Countries should seek out and destroy the terrorists and their immediate backers to reduce the likelihood of future terror attacks, but they must carefully isolate these targets from the general population, which may or may not be sympathetic to the terrorists.[66] This type of discriminating response will require superior intelligence capabilities. In this regard, the United States' efforts to invest in information-gathering abilities in response to September 11 have been underwhelming. Even the most basic steps, such as developing a deeper pool of expertise in the regional languages, have been slow in coming.[67] This stands in contrast to U.S. behavior during the Cold War, when the government sponsored research centers at top universities to analyze every aspect of the Soviet economic, military, and political system. The weakness of the U.S. intelligence apparatus has been most clearly revealed in the inability of the United States to eliminate bin Laden and al-Zawahiri, and in the United States' decision to invade Iraq.[68] Faulty U.S. intelligence

has simultaneously protected al-Qaida leaders from death and led to the destruction of thousands of Muslim civilians—exactly the response al-Qaida was likely seeking.

Spoiling: Sabotaging the Peace

The goal of a spoiling strategy is to ensure that peace overtures between moderate leaders on the terrorists' side and the target government do not succeed.[69] It works by playing on the mistrust between these two groups and succeeds when one or both parties fail to sign or implement a settlement. It is often employed when the ultimate objective is territorial change.

Terrorists resort to a spoiling strategy when relations between two enemies are improving and a peace agreement threatens the terrorists' more far-reaching goals. Peace agreements alarm terrorists because they understand that moderate citizens are less likely to support ongoing violence once a compromise agreement between more moderate groups has been reached. Thus, Iranian radicals kidnapped fifty-two Americans in Tehran in 1979 not because relations between the United States and Iran were becoming more belligerent, but because three days earlier Iran's relatively moderate prime minister, Mehdi Bazargan, met with the U.S. national security adviser, Zbigniew Brzezinski, and the two were photographed shaking hands. From the perspective of the radicals, a real danger of reconciliation existed between the two countries, and violence was used to prevent this.[70] A similar problem has hampered Arab-Israeli peace negotiations, as well as talks between Protestants and Catholics in Northern Ireland.

A spoiling strategy works by persuading the enemy that moderates on the terrorists' side cannot be trusted to abide by a peace deal. Whenever two sides negotiate a peace agreement, there is uncertainty about whether the deal is self-enforcing. Each side fears that even if it honors its commitments, the other side may not, catapulting it back to war on disadvantageous terms. Some Israelis, for example, feared that if Israel returned an additional 13 percent of the West Bank to the Palestinians, as mandated by the 1998 Wye accord, the Palestinian Authority would relaunch its struggle from an improved territorial base. Extremists understand that moderates look for signs that their former enemy will violate an agreement and that targeting these moderates with violence will heighten their fears that they will be exploited. Thus terrorist attacks are designed to persuade a targeted group that the seemingly moderate opposition with whom it negotiated an agreement will not or cannot stop terrorism, and hence cannot be trusted to honor an agreement.

Terrorist acts are particularly effective during peace negotiations because opposing parties are naturally distrustful of each other's motives and have limited sources of information about each other's intentions. Thus, even if moderate leaders are willing to aggressively suppress extremists on their side, terrorists know that isolated violence might still convince the target to reject the deal. A reason for this is that the targeted group may not be able to readily observe the extent of the crackdown and must base its judgments primarily on whether terrorism occurs or not. Even a sincere effort at self-policing, therefore, will not necessarily convince the targeted group to proceed with a settlement if a terrorist attack occurs.

CONDITIONS FAVORABLE TO SPOILING

Terrorists pursuing a spoiling strategy are likely to be more successful when the enemy perceives moderates on their side to be strong and therefore more capable of halting terrorism.[71] When an attack occurs, the target cannot be sure whether moderates on the other side can suppress their own extremists but choose not to, or are weak and lack the ability to stop them. Israelis, for example, frequently questioned whether Yasser Arafat was simply unable to

stop terrorist attacks against Israel or was unwilling to do so. The weaker the moderates are perceived to be, the less impact a terrorist attack will have on the other side's trust, and the less likely such an attack is to convince them to abandon a peace agreement.

The Israeli-Palestinian conflict, and in particular the Oslo peace process, has been plagued by spoilers. On the Palestinian side, Hamas's violent attacks coincided with the ratification and implementation of accords—occasions when increased mistrust could thwart progress toward peace. Hamas also stepped up its attacks prior to Israeli elections in 1996 and 2001, in which Labor was the incumbent party, in an effort to persuade Israeli voters to cast their votes for the less cooperative and less trusting hard-line Likud Party.[72] Terrorism was especially effective after Arafat's 1996 electoral victory, when it became clear to the Israelis that Arafat was, at the time, a popular and powerful leader within the Palestinian community.[73] This in turn suggested to the Israelis that Arafat was capable of cracking down aggressively on terrorist violence but was unwilling to do so, a sign that he could not be trusted to keep the peace.

BEST RESPONSES TO SPOILING

When mutual trust is high, a peace settlement can be implemented despite ongoing terrorist acts and the potential vulnerabilities the agreement can create. Trust, however, is rarely high after long conflicts, which is why spoilers can strike with a reasonable chance that their attack will be successful. Strategies that build trust and reduce vulnerability are, therefore, the best response to spoiling.

Vulnerabilities emerge in peace processes in two ways. Symmetric vulnerabilities occur during the implementation of a deal because both sides must lower their guard. The Israelis, for example, have had to relax controls over the occupied territories, and the Palestinians were obligated to disarm militant groups. Such symmetric vulnerabilities can be eased by third-party monitoring and verification of the peace implementation process. Monitoring can help reduce uncertainty regarding the behavior of the parties. Even better, third-party enforcement of the deal can make reneging more costly, increasing confidence in the deal and its ultimate success.[74]

Vulnerabilities can also be longer term and asymmetric. In any peace deal between Israel and the Palestinians, the ability of the Palestinians to harm Israel will inevitably grow as Palestinians build their own state and acquire greater military capabilities. This change in the balance of power can make it difficult for the side that will see an increase in its power to credibly commit not to take advantage of this increase later on. This commitment problem can cause conflicts to be prolonged even though there are possible peace agreements that both sides would prefer to war.[75]

The problem of shifting power can be addressed in at least three ways. First, agreements themselves can be crafted in ways that limit the post-treaty shift in power. Power-sharing agreements such as that between the Liberals and Conservatives to create a single shared presidency in Colombia in 1957 are one example of this. Allowing the defeated side to retain some military capabilities, as Confederate officers were allowed to do after the surrender at Appomattox, is another example.[76] Second, peace settlements can require the side about to be advantaged to send a costly signal of its honorable intentions, such as providing constitutional protections of minority rights. An example is the Constitutional Law on National Minorities passed in Croatia in 2002, which protects the right of minorities to obtain an education in their own language. Finally, parties can credibly commit to an agreement by participating in international institutions that insist on the protection of minority rights. A government that is willing to join the European Union effectively constrains itself from exploiting a minority group because of the high costs to that government of being ejected from the group.

Outbidding: Zealots versus Sellouts

Outbidding arises when two key conditions hold: two or more domestic parties are competing for leadership of their side, and the general population is uncertain about which of the groups best represents their interests.[77] The competition between Hamas and Fatah is a classic case where two groups vie for the support of the Palestinian citizens and where the average Palestinian is uncertain about which side he or she ought to back.

If citizens had full information about the preferences of the competing groups, an outbidding strategy would be unnecessary and ineffective; citizens would simply support the group that best aligned with their own interests. In reality, however, citizens cannot be sure if the group competing for power truly represents their preferences. The group could be a strong and resolute defender of the cause (zealots) or weak and ineffective stooges of the enemy (sellouts). If citizens support zealots, they get a strong champion but with some risk that they will be dragged into a confrontation with the enemy that they end up losing. If citizens support sellouts, they get peace but at the price of accepting a worse outcome than might have been achieved with additional armed struggle. Groups competing for power have an incentive to signal that they are zealots rather than sellouts. Terrorist attacks can serve this function by signaling that a group has the will to continue the armed struggle despite its costs.

Three reasons help to explain why groups are likely to be rewarded for being more militant rather than less. First, in bargaining contexts, it is often useful to be represented by an agent who is more hard-line than oneself. Hard-line agents will reject deals that one would accept, which will force the adversary to make a better offer than one would get by representing oneself in the negotiations.[78] Palestinians might therefore prefer Hamas as a negotiating agent with Israel because it has a reputation for resolve and will reject inferior deals.

Second, uncertainty may also exist about the type of adversary the population and its competing groups are facing. If the population believes there is some chance that their adversary is untrustworthy (unwilling to compromise under any condition), then they know that conflict may be inevitable, in which case being represented by zealots may be advantageous.[79]

A third factor that may favor outbidding is that office-holding itself may produce incentives to sell out. Here, the problem lies with the benefits groups receive once in office (i.e., income and power). Citizens fear that their leaders, once in office, may betray important principles and decide to settle with the enemy on unfavorable terms. They know that holding office skews one's preferences toward selling out, but they remain unsure about which of their leaders is most likely to give in. Terrorist organizations exploit this uncertainty by using violence to signal their commitment to a cause. Being perceived as more extreme than the median voter works to the terrorists' benefit because it balances out the "tempering effect" of being in office.

An interesting aspect of the outbidding strategy is that the enemy is only tangentially related to the strategic interaction. In fact, an attack motivated by outbidding may not even be designed to achieve any goal related to the enemy, such as inducing a concession or scuttling a peace treaty. The process is almost entirely concerned with the signal it sends to domestic audiences uncertain about their own leadership and its commitment to a cause. As such, outbidding provides a potential explanation for terrorist attacks that continue even when they seem unable to produce any real results.

CONDITIONS FAVORABLE TO OUTBIDDING

Outbidding will be favored when multiple groups are competing for the allegiance of a similar demographic base of support. In Peru, the 1970s saw the development of a number of leftist groups seeking to represent the poor and indigenous population. When the military turned over power to an elected government in 1980, the Shining Path took up an armed struggle to distinguish itself from groups that chose to pursue electoral politics.[80] It also embarked on an assassination campaign designed to weaken rival leftist groups and intimidate their followers. When organizations encounter less competition for the support of their main constituents, outbidding will be less appealing.

BEST RESPONSES TO OUTBIDDING

One solution to the problem of outbidding would be to eliminate the struggle for power by encouraging competing groups to consolidate into a unified opposition. If competition among resistance groups is eliminated, the incentive for outbidding also disappears. The downside of this counterstrategy is that a unified opposition may be stronger than a divided one. United oppositions, however, can make peace and deliver, whereas divided ones may face greater structural disincentives to do so.

An alternative strategy for the government to pursue in the face of outbidding is to validate the strategy chosen by nonviolent groups by granting them concessions and attempting to satisfy the demands of their constituents. If outbidding can be shown to yield poor results in comparison to playing within the system, groups may be persuaded to abandon the strategy. As in the case of the Shining Path, this may require providing physical protection to competing groups in case the outbidder turns to intimidation in its competition with less violent rivals. In general, any steps that can be taken to make the non-outbidding groups seem successful (e.g., channeling resources and government services to their constituents) will also help undermine the outbidders. The high turnout in the December 2005 Iraqi election in Sunni-dominated regions may indicate that outbidding is beginning to fail in the communities most strongly opposed to the new political system.[81]

Conclusion

Terrorist violence is a form of costly signaling by which terrorists attempt to influence the beliefs of their enemy and the population they represent or wish to control. They use violence to signal their strength and resolve in an effort to produce concessions from their enemy and obedience and support from their followers. They also attack both to sow mistrust between moderates who might want to make peace and to provoke a reaction that makes the enemy appear barbarous and untrustworthy.

In this article, we have laid out the five main goals terrorist organizations seek and the five most important terrorist strategies, and we have outlined when they are likely to be tried and what the best counterstrategies might look like. What becomes clear in this brief analysis is that a deeper study of each of the five strategies is needed to reveal the nuanced ways in which terrorism works, and to refine responses to it. We conclude by highlighting two variables that will be important in any such analysis, and by a final reflection on counterterror policies that are strategically independent or not predicated on the specific strategy being used.

The first variable is information. It has long been a truism that the central front in counterinsurgency warfare is the information front. The same is true in terrorism. Costly signaling is pointless in the absence of uncertainty on the part of the recipient of the signal. Attrition is designed to convince the target that the costs of maintaining a policy are not worth the gains; if the target already knew this, it would have ceded the issue without an attack being launched. Provocation is designed to goad the target into retaliating indiscriminately (because it lacks information to discriminate), which will persuade the population that the target is malevolent (because it is uncertain of the target's intentions). The other strategies are similarly predicated on uncertainty, intelligence, learning, and communication. Thus, it bears emphasizing that the problem of terrorism is not a problem of applying force per se, but one of acquiring intelligence and affecting beliefs. With the right information, the proper application of force is comparatively straightforward. The struggle against terrorism is, therefore, not usefully guided by the metaphor of a "war on terrorism" any more than policies designed to alleviate poverty are usefully guided by the metaphor of a "war on poverty" or narcotics policy by a "war on drugs." The struggle against terrorism can more usefully be thought of as a struggle to collect and disseminate reliable information in environments fraught with uncertainty.

The second important variable is regime type. Democracies have been the sole targets of attritional suicide bombing campaigns, whereas authoritarian regimes such as those in Algeria routinely face campaigns by rebel groups pursuing an intimidation strategy. Democracies also seem to be more susceptible to attrition and provocation strategies. This type of variation cries out for deeper analysis of the strengths and weakness of different regime types in the face of different terrorist strategies. Our analysis suggests that democracies are more likely to be sensitive to the costs of terrorist attacks, to grant concessions to terrorists so as to limit future attacks, to be constrained in their ability to pursue a lengthy attritional campaign against an organization, but also to be under greater pressure to "do something." This does not mean that all democracies will behave incorrectly in the face of terrorist attacks all the time. Democratic regimes may possess certain structural features, however, that make them attractive targets for terrorism.

Finally, we realize that our discussion is only a beginning and that further elaboration of each of the strategies and their corresponding counterstrategies awaits future research. We also understand that not all counterterrorism policies are predicated on the specific strategy terrorists pursue. Our analysis is at the middling level of strategic interaction. At the tactical level are all the tools of intelligence gathering and target defense that make sense no matter what the terrorist's strategy is. At the higher level are the primary sources of terrorism such as poverty, education, international conflict, and chauvinistic indoctrination that enable terrorist organizations to operate and survive in the first place. Our aim in this article has been to try to understand why these organizations choose certain forms of violence, and how this violence serves their larger purposes. The United States has the ability to reduce the likelihood of additional attacks on its territory and citizens. But it will be much more successful if it first understands the goals terrorists are seeking and the underlying strategic logic by which a plane flying into a skyscraper might deliver the desired response.

NOTES

1. Thomas L. Friedman, "Marines Complete Beirut Pullback: Moslems Move In," *New York Times*, February 27, 2004.

2. Don Van Natta Jr., "The Struggle for Iraq: Last American Combat Troops Quit Saudi Arabia," *New York Times*, September 22, 2003.

3. James Glanz, "Hostage Is Freed after Philippine Troops Are Withdrawn from Iraq," *New York Times*, July 21, 2004.

4. Robert A. Pape, *Dying to Win: The Strategic Logic of Suicide Terrorism* (New York: Random House, 2005), p. 65.

5. Alan B. Krueger and David D. Laitin, "Kto Kogo? A Cross-Country Study of the Origins and Targets of Terrorism," Princeton University and Stanford University, 2003; Alan B. Krueger and Jitka Maleckova, "Education, Poverty, and Terrorism: Is There a Causal Connection?" *Journal of Economic Perspectives*, Vol. 17, No. 4 (November 2003), pp. 119–44; and Alberto Abadie, "Poverty, Political Freedom, and the Roots of Terrorism," Faculty Research Working Papers Series, RWP04-043 (Cambridge, MA: John F. Kennedy School of Government, Harvard University, 2004).

6. Jessica Stern, *Terror in the Name of God: Why Religious Militants Kill* (New York: Ecco-HarperCollins, 2003).

7. Of course, terrorists will also be seeking best responses to government responses. A pair of strategies that are best responses to each other constitutes a Nash equilibrium, the fundamental prediction tool of game theory.

8. Office of Counterterrorism, U.S. Department of State, "Foreign Terrorist Organizations," fact sheet, October 11, 2005, http://www.state.gov/s/ct/rls/fs/3719.htm.

9. Quoted in Nasra Hassan, "An Arsenal of Believers: Talking to the 'Human Bombs,'" *New Yorker*, November 19, 2001, p. 37.

10. For discussion of differing definitions of terrorism, see Alex P. Schmid and Albert J. Jongman, *Political Terrorism: A New Guide to Actors, Authors, Concepts, Data Bases, Theories, and Literature* (New Brunswick, NJ: Transaction, 1988), pp. 1–38. We do not focus on state terrorism because states face very different opportunities and constraints in their use of violence, and we do not believe the two cases are similar enough to be profitably analyzed together.

11. For the distinction between goals and strategies, see David A. Lake and Robert Powell, eds., *Strategic Choice and International Relations* (Princeton, NJ: Princeton University Press, 1999), especially chap. 1.

12. On revolutionary terrorism, see Martha Crenshaw Hutchinson, "The Concept of Revolutionary Terrorism," *Journal of Conflict Resolution*, Vol. 16, No. 3 (September 1972), pp. 383–96; Martha Crenshaw Hutchinson, *Revolutionary Terrorism: The FLN in Algeria, 1954–1962* (Stanford, CA: Hoover Institution Press, 1978); and H. Edward Price Jr., "The Strategy and Tactics of Revolutionary Terrorism," *Comparative Studies in Society and History*, Vol. 19, No. 1 (January 1977), pp. 52–66.

13. This group has recently surrendered its weapons.

14. Some analysts argue that many terrorist organizations have degenerated into little more than self-perpetuating businesses that primarily seek to enhance their own power and wealth, and only articulate political goals for rhetorical purposes. See, for example, Stern, *Terror in the Name of God*, pp. 235–36. This suggests that power and wealth should be considered goals in their own right. All organizations, however, seek power and wealth to further their political objectives, and these are better viewed as instrumental in nature.

15. A difficult coding issue arises in determining when a group is a nonstate actor engaged in status quo maintenance and when it is simply a covert agent of the state. Some death squads were linked to elements in the armed forces, yet were not necessarily responsive to the chief executive of the country. Others were tied to right-wing parties and are more clearly nonstate, unless that party is the party in power. See Bruce D. Campbell and Arthur D. Brenner, eds., *Death Squads in Global Perspective: Murder with Deniability* (New York: Palgrave Macmillan, 2002).

16. The Taliban, which is not listed, does pursue social control; and the Israeli group Kach, which seeks to maintain the subordinate status of Palestinians in Israel and eventually to expel them, may also be considered to seek it. The Memorial Institute for the Prevention of Terrorism maintains a database of terrorist organizations that includes more than forty groups based in the United States. Some of these can be considered to seek social control, such as the Army of God, which targets doctors who provide abortions. See http://www.tkb.org.

17. Thomas Perry Thornton, "Terror as a Weapon of Political Agitation," in Harry Eckstein, ed., *Internal War: Problems and Approaches* (London: Free Press of Glencoe, 1964), p. 87.

18. Martha Crenshaw, "The Causes of Terrorism," *Comparative Politics*, Vol. 13, No. 4 (July 1981), pp. 379–99.

19. David Fromkin, "The Strategy of Terrorism," *Foreign Affairs*, Vol. 53, No. 4 (July 1975), pp. 683–98.

20. Price, "The Strategy and Tactics of Revolutionary Terrorism," pp. 54–58. Other related discussions include Paul Wilkinson, "The Strategic Implications of Terrorism," in M. L. Sondhi, ed., *Terrorism and Political Violence: A Sourcebook* (New Delhi: Har-anand Publications, 2000); Paul Wilkinson, *Terrorism and the Liberal State* (New York: New York University Press, 1986), pp. 110–18; and Schmid and Jongman, *Political Terrorism*, pp. 50–59.

21. Geoffrey Blainey, *The Causes of War*, 3d ed. (New York: Free Press, 1988), p. 122.

22. James D. Fearon, "Rationalist Explanations for War," *International Organization*, Vol. 49, No. 3 (Summer 1995), pp. 379–414; and Robert Powell, "Bargaining Theory and International Conflict," *Annual Review of Political Science*, Vol. 5 (June 2002), pp. 1–30.

23. Thomas Hobbes, *Leviathan* (New York: Penguin, [1651] 1968), p. 184.

24. John H. Herz, "Idealist Internationalism and the Security Dilemma," *World Politics*, Vol. 2, No. 2 (January 1950), pp. 157–80; Robert Jervis, *Perception and Misperception in International Politics* (Princeton, NJ: Princeton University Press, 1976); Robert Jervis, "Cooperation under the Security Dilemma," *World Politics*, Vol. 30, No. 2 (January 1978), pp. 167–214; and Charles L. Glaser, "The Security Dilemma Revisited," *World Politics*, Vol. 50, No. 1 (October 1997), pp. 171–202.

25. Andrew H. Kydd, *Trust and Mistrust in International Relations* (Princeton, NJ: Princeton University Press, 2005).

26. John G. Riley, "Silver Signals: Twenty-five Years of Screening and Signaling," *Journal of Economic Literature*, Vol. 39, No. 2 (June 2001), pp. 432–78.

27. James D. Fearon, "Signaling Foreign Policy Interests: Tying Hands vs. Sunk Costs," *Journal of Conflict Resolution*, Vol. 41, No. 1 (February 1977), pp. 68–90.

28. Dan Reiter, "Exploring the Bargaining Model of War," *Perspectives on Politics*, Vol. 1, No. 1 (March 2003), pp. 27–43; and Robert Powell, "Bargaining and Learning While Fighting," *American Journal of Political Science*, Vol. 48, No. 2 (April 2004), pp. 344–61.

29. Rival terrorist or moderate groups are also important, but terrorism is not often used to signal such groups. Sometimes rival groups are targeted in an effort to eliminate them, but this violence is usually thought of as internecine warfare rather than terrorism. The targeted government may also be divided into multiple actors, but these divisions are not crucial for a broad understanding of terrorist strategies.

30. This list is not exhaustive. In particular, it omits two strategies that have received attention in the literature: advertising and retaliation. Advertising may play a role in the beginning of some conflicts, but it does not sustain long-term campaigns of terrorist violence. Retaliation is a motivation for some terrorists, but terrorism would continue even if the state did not strike at terrorists, because terrorism is designed to achieve some goal, not just avenge counterterrorist attacks.

31. Per Baltzer Overgaard, "The Scale of Terrorist Attacks as a Signal of Resources," *Journal of Conflict Resolution*, Vol. 38, No. 3 (September 1994), pp. 452–78; and Harvey E. Lapan and Todd Sandler, "Terrorism and Signaling," *European Journal of Political Economy*, Vol. 9, No. 3 (August 1993), pp. 383–98.

32. J. Maynard Smith, "The Theory of Games and Evolution in Animal Conflicts," *Journal of Theoretical Biology*, Vol. 47 (1974), pp. 209–11; John J. Mearsheimer, *Conventional Deterrence* (Ithaca, NY: Cornell University Press, 1983), pp. 33–35; and James D. Fearon, "Bargaining, Enforcement, and International Cooperation," *International Organization*, Vol. 52, No. 2 (Spring 1998), pp. 269–305.

33. Bernard Lewis, "The Revolt of Islam," *New Yorker*, November 19, 2001, p. 61.

34. Quoted in Hassan, "An Arsenal of Believers," p. 38.

35. Robert A. Pape, "The Strategic Logic of Suicide Terrorism," *American Political Science Review*, Vol. 97, No. 3 (August 2003), pp. 343–61; and Pape, *Dying to Win*.

36. Pape, *Dying to Win*, p. 44. Krueger and Laitin also find that targets of terrorism tend to be democratic. See Krueger and Laitin, "Kto Kogo?"

37. The U.S. program of extraordinary rendition, for example, is an effort to evade the restrictions usually faced by democracies by outsourcing the dirty work.

38. Debate Goes On Over Lebanon Withdrawal, *Haaretz*, May 23, 2001; and Daoud Kuttab, "The Lebanon Lesson," *Jerusalem Post*, May 25, 2000.

39. Interview with Mahmoud Khalid al-Zahar, *Al Jazeera*, October 22, 2005.

40. Osama bin Laden, *Messages to the World: The Statements of Osama bin Laden*, trans. James Howarth, ed. Bruce Lawrence (London: Verso, 2005), pp. 241–42.

41. Osama bin Laden, "Declaration of War against the Americans Occupying the Land of the Two Holy Places," *Al-Quds Al-Arabi*, August 1996, http://www.pbs.org/newshour/terrorism/international/fatwa_1996.html.

42. Peter C. Sederberg, "Conciliation as Counter-terrorist Strategy," *Journal of Peace Research*, Vol. 32, No. 3 (August 1995), pp. 295–312.

43. Stephen Flynn, *America the Vulnerable: How Our Government Is Failing to Protect Us from Terrorism* (New York: HarperCollins, 2004).

44. Graham T. Allison, Owen R. Coté Jr., Richard A. Falkenrath, and Steven E. Miller, *Avoiding Nuclear Anarchy: Containing the Threat of Loose Russian Nuclear Weapons and Fissile Material* (Cambridge, MA: MIT Press, 1996); and Graham Allison, *Nuclear Terrorism: The Ultimate Preventable Catastrophe* (New York: Times Books, 2004).

45. John Mueller, "Six Rather Unusual Propositions about Terrorism," *Terrorism and Political Violence*, Vol. 17, No. 4 (Winter 2005), pp. 487–505.

46. The literature on deterrence is vast. See, for example, Thomas C. Schelling, *Arms and Influence* (New Haven, CT: Yale University Press, 1966); and Christopher H. Achen and Duncan Snidal, "Rational Deterrence Theory and Comparative Case Studies," *World Politics*, Vol. 41, No. 2 (January 1989), pp. 143–69.

47. Noor Khan, "Militants Behead Afghan Principal for Educating Girls," *Boston Globe*, January 5, 2006.

48. Crenshaw Hutchinson, "The Concept of Revolutionary Terrorism," p. 390.

49. Stathis N. Kalyvas, "Wanton and Senseless? The Logic of Massacres in Algeria," *Rationality and Society*, Vol. 11, No. 3 (August 1999), pp. 243–85.

50. James D. Fearon and David D. Laitin, "Ethnicity, Insurgency, and Civil War," *American Political Science Review*, Vol. 97, No. 1 (February 2003), pp. 75–90.

51. United States National Security Council, *National Strategy for Victory in Iraq* (Washington, DC: White House, November 2005), p. 7.

52. Secretary of State Condoleezza Rice, "Iraq and U.S. Policy," testimony before the U.S. Senate Committee on Foreign Relations, October 19, 2005, 109th Cong., 1st sess., http://www.foreign.senate.gov/testimony/2005/RiceTestimony051019.pdf.

53. See Lewis Sorley, *A Better War: The Unexamined Victories and the Final Tragedy of America's Last Years in Vietnam* (New York: Harcourt, 1999). This thesis is not without controversy. See Matt Steinglass, "Vietnam and Victory," *Boston Globe*, December 18, 2005.

54. Fromkin, "The Strategy of Terrorism."

55. Crenshaw, "The Causes of Terrorism," p. 387; and Price, "The Strategy and Tactics of Revolutionary Terrorism," p. 58.

56. Paddy Woodworth, "Why Do They Kill? The Basque Conflict in Spain," *World Policy Journal*, Vol. 18, No. 1 (Spring 2001), p. 7.

57. David A. Lake, "Rational Extremism: Understanding Terrorism in the Twenty-first Century," *Dialog-IO*, Vol. 56, No. 2 (Spring 2002), pp. 15–29.

58. Ethan Bueno de Mesquita and Eric S. Dickson, "The Propaganda of the Deed: Terrorism, Counterterrorism, and Mobilization," Washington University and New York University, 2005. Bueno de Mesquita and Dickson also argue that government violence lowers economic prosperity, which favors extremists in their competition with moderates.

59. Ethan Bueno de Mesquita, "Politics and the Suboptimal Provision of Counterterror," *International Organization* [Vol. 61, No. 1 (Winter 2007), pp. 9–36].

60. On the other hand, more dovish regimes might feel political pressure to take strong visible actions, whereas a regime with hawkish credentials could credibly claim that it was pursuing effective but nonvisible tactics. For a similar logic, see Kenneth A. Schultz, "The Politics of Risking Peace: Do Hawks or Doves Deliver the Olive Branch?" *International Organization*, Vol. 59, No. 1 (Winter 2005), pp. 1–38.

61. Bin Laden, *Messages to the World*, pp. 241–42.

62. Pew Research Center for the People and the Press, Pew Global Attitudes Project: Nine-Nation Survey, "A Year after the Iraq War: Mistrust of America in Europe Ever Higher, Muslim Anger Persists," March 16, 2004.

63. See International Institute for Strategic Studies, *Strategic Survey, 2003/4: An Evaluation and Forecast of World Affairs* (London: Routledge, 2005).

64. Quoted in Dafna Linzer, "Poll Shows Growing Arab Rancor at U.S.," *Washington Post*, July 23, 2004.

65. Bob Woodward, *Plan of Attack* (New York: Simon and Schuster, 2004), pp. 21–23; and bin Laden, *Messages to the World*, pp. 241–42.

66. A program of economic and social assistance to these more moderate elements would provide counterevidence that the target is not malicious or evil as the terrorist organizations had claimed.

67. Farah Stockman, "Tomorrow's Homework: Reading, Writing, and Arabic," *Boston Globe*, January 6, 2006.

68. For an analysis of obstacles to innovation in U.S. intelligence agencies, see Amy B. Zegart, "September 11 and the Adaptation Failure of U.S. Intelligence Agencies," *International Security*, Vol. 29, No. 4 (Spring 2005), pp. 78–111.

69. Stephen John Stedman, "Spoiler Problems in Peace Processes," *International Security*, Vol. 22, No. 2 (Fall 1997), pp. 5–53.

70. Lewis, "The Revolt of Islam," p. 54.

71. Andrew H. Kydd and Barbara F. Walter, "Sabotaging the Peace: The Politics of Extremist Violence," *International Organization*, Vol. 56, No. 2 (Spring 2002), pp. 263–96.

72. Claude Berrebi and Esteban F. Klor, "On Terrorism and Electoral Outcomes: Theory and Evidence from the Israeli-Palestinian Conflict," Princeton University and Hebrew University of Jerusalem, 2004.

73. Kydd and Walter, "Sabotaging the Peace," pp. 279–89.

74. Barbara F. Walter, *Committing to Peace: The Successful Settlement of Civil Wars* (Princeton, NJ: Princeton University Press, 2002); and Holger Schmidt, "When (and Why) Do Brokers Have to Be Honest? Impartiality and Third-Party Support for Peace Implementation after Civil Wars, 1945–1999," Georgetown University, 2004.

75. Fearon, "Rationalist Explanations for War"; James D. Fearon, "Commitment Problems and the Spread of Ethnic Conflict," in David A. Lake and Donald Rothchild, eds., *The International Spread of Ethnic Conflict: Fear, Diffusion, and Escalation* (Princeton, NJ: Princeton University Press, 1998); and Robert Powell, "The Inefficient Use of Power: Costly Conflict with Complete Information," *American Political Science Review*, Vol. 98, No. 2 (May 2004), pp. 231–41.

76. As part of the terms of surrender, Confederate officers were allowed to keep their sidearms and personal property (including their horses) and return home.

77. For the most extensive treatment of terrorism and outbidding, see Mia Bloom, *Dying to Kill: The Allure of Suicide Terrorism* (New York: Columbia University Press, 2005). See also Stuart J. Kaufman, "Spiraling to Ethnic War: Elites, Masses, and Moscow in Moldova's Civil War," *International Security*, Vol. 21, No. 2 (Fall 1996), pp. 108–38.

78. Abhinay Muthoo, *Bargaining Theory with Applications* (Cambridge: Cambridge University Press, 1999), p. 230.

79. Rui J.P. de Figueiredo Jr. and Barry R. Weingast, "The Rationality of Fear: Political Opportunism and Ethnic Conflict," in Barbara F. Walter and Jack Snyder, eds., *Civil Wars, Insecurity, and Intervention* (New York: Columbia University Press, 1999), pp. 261–302.

80. James Ron, "Ideology in Context: Explaining Sendero Luminoso's Tactical Escalation," *Journal of Peace Research*, Vol. 38, No. 5 (September 2001), p. 582.

81. Dexter Filkins, "Iraqis, Including Sunnis, Vote in Large Numbers on Calm Day," *New York Times*, December 16, 2005.

Virginia Page Fortna

DO TERRORISTS WIN? REBELS' USE OF TERRORISM AND CIVIL WAR OUTCOMES

■ ■ ■

How effective is terrorism? This question has generated lively scholarly debate and is of obvious importance to policymakers. However, most existing studies of terrorism are not well equipped to answer this question for a simple reason—they lack an appropriate comparison. Few studies of terrorism have compared conflicts in which terrorism is used with those in which it is not. This article examines the outcomes of civil wars to assess whether rebel groups that use terrorism fare better than those who eschew this tactic.[1] I argue that terrorism is not a particularly effective tactic for winning outright, nor for obtaining concessions at the bargaining table. On balance, terrorists undermine rather than enhance their military effectiveness by attacking civilians indiscriminately. If it does not help rebels achieve their ultimate political goals, one might reasonably ask why rebels ever employ terrorism? A second finding of this research provides a possible answer. Wars in which terrorism is used last longer than others, suggesting that terrorism enhances rebel organizations' survival. Rebels thus appear to face a dilemma: what helps them survive comes at the expense of the larger political goals for which they ostensibly fight.

In the next section I review the literature and debate over the effectiveness of terrorism and argue that civil wars provide a fruitful testing ground for evaluating the relative success of terrorism. I then present definitions and explain how "terrorist" rebel groups are distinguished from others, as well as how I use war outcomes to gauge "success." Next I examine the strategic uses of terrorism to evaluate theoretically its advantages and disadvantages, and to generate hypotheses about its effects on war outcomes. In the following section I discuss how selection effects and endogeneity issues affect this study. After describing the data, I turn to empirical findings. * * * The data support hypotheses that although civil wars involving terrorism last longer than other wars, terrorist rebel groups are less likely than those who eschew terrorism to achieve outright victory or concessions at the negotiating table. Terrorism may be somewhat less ineffective against democracies, but even in this context, terrorists do not win.

State of the Debate

A number of authors have argued that terrorism works. Pape, for example, argues that suicide terrorism is on the rise because terrorists have learned that it pays, generating "gains for the terrorists' political cause" about half the time.[2] Similarly, Kydd and Walter argue that terrorism

From *International Organization* 69 (Summer 2015): 519–56.
Some of the author's notes have been omitted.

more generally "is a form of costly signaling" and that "terrorism often works."[3] Thomas argues that terrorism gives rebels the "power to hurt," inducing governments to negotiate and make concessions.[4] Some scholars suggest that although terrorism can sometimes backfire and effects may be nonlinear, it is, on balance, effective.[5]

Others, however, maintain that terrorism is not particularly effective. Abrahms argues that the prevailing view of terrorism as a potent coercive strategy rests on scant empirical footing, and that campaigns of violence that primarily target civilians almost never succeed.[6] Jones and Libicki conclude that "there is rarely a causal link between the use of terrorism and the achievement of [group] goals."[7] Merari and Cronin both argue that, although terrorist groups may achieve partial or tactical (for example, recruitment) objectives, they almost never achieve their strategic goals in full.[8]

Some of this debate hinges on what one counts as success: only full achievement of the group's goals, or any political concession, or achievement of intermediate goals meant eventually to help a group achieve its goals?—an issue I return to below.[9] Whether terrorism is considered effective also depends on what the chances of success, however defined, are if terrorism is not used. Not surprisingly, terrorists achieve higher levels of success when groups have limited objectives that do not impinge on the core interests of the target state.[10] So perhaps terrorism only "works" when achieving political change is relatively easy. Success rates cannot be judged without some sort of context.

Claims that terrorism "works" or "does not work" reflect a causal argument; that terrorism leads, or does not lead, to political change in favor of the group using it. Implicit in any causal argument is an argument about variation: using terrorism leads to more change (or no more change) than not using terrorism. But few empirical studies examine variation on the independent variable; most look only at terrorist organizations, with no comparison with otherwise similar groups that do not use terrorism.[11]

I use data on civil wars to introduce variation. Civil wars represent a universe of cases in which a group has a serious enough perceived grievance against the state to launch a violent rebellion in which some groups choose to use terrorism as part of their repertoire of tactics whereas others do not. Data on civil wars are relatively well developed, allowing me to explore and control for a number of factors that are likely to affect both this tactical choice and the outcome I wish to explain.

The study of terrorism and the study of civil wars have generally proceeded in isolation from one another.[12] However, if one thinks of prominent cases such as the LTTE in Sri Lanka, the PLO or Hamas in Palestine, the IRA in Northern Ireland, the PKK in Turkey, or the MNLF and MILF in the Philippines, it is clear that much terrorism takes place in the context of civil war. Indeed, the vast majority—75 to 85 percent by most estimates—of all terrorism is domestic.[13] This article merges insights from the two literatures.

This raises the thorny question of the definition of terrorism, however, because some scholars maintain that in the Venn diagram of political violence, terrorism and civil war do not overlap, whereas for others they overlap completely.

Definitions

"Terrorist" Rebel Groups

Defining terrorism is notoriously difficult; as the cliché goes, one person's terrorist is another's freedom fighter, and this is particularly true in the context of civil wars. Because it is such a loaded term, its definition is highly contested.[14] I define *terrorist rebel groups* as those who employ a systematic campaign of indiscriminate violence against public civilian targets to influence a wider audience. The ultimate aim of this type of violence is to coerce the government to make political concessions, up to and including conceding outright defeat. This definition allows for distinctions among rebel groups and does not include in the definition other variables whose relationship to terrorism I wish to examine.[15]

For many scholars of terrorism, though by no means all,[16] a defining characteristic of terrorism is that it deliberately attacks civilians.[17] This distinguishes terrorism from "normal" rebel attacks on military targets. However, civilian targeting is ubiquitous; almost all rebel groups (and almost all governments involved in civil wars) target individuals as a form of "control" to force cooperation and deter civilians from providing aid to the opponents.[18] Violence against civilians is thus too broad a criterion by itself to distinguish terrorist rebel groups from others. Moreover, this type of selective violence against civilians to punish or deter collaboration with the other side is not what most people think of when they think of "terrorism."

By narrowing the definition to deliberately indiscriminate violence, I exclude this more common form of violence and focus on that which makes terrorism so terrifying: its randomness; and so outrageous: the intentional targeting of innocent civilians (as opposed to collaborators). This definition also captures what the literature often refers to as the "symbolic" nature of terrorism: that it aims not to influence the victims of the violence but to send a political message to a wider audience.[19] Stanton distinguishes strategies of "coercion" from the above-mentioned control by focusing on "the use of violence as a means of forcing the opponent to take a particular desired action—to agree to negotiations, to reduce its war aims, to make concessions, to surrender." This strategy is "intended not to coerce civilians themselves, but to coerce *the opponent* into making concessions."[20] An attack on a public market, for example, is intended to influence the government, not shoppers.

Stanton's strategies of "destabilization" and "cleansing," which she distinguishes from coercion, also sound like terrorism to some degree. These involve attacks on civilians intended to destabilize a country or to force people to flee by terrorizing the population. However, Stanton's operational coding of these strategies involve massacres and "scorched earth" campaigns (burning homes and crops), which, although terrifying to their victims are farther from our intuitive understanding of terrorism than the indiscriminate attacks she codes under coercion.[21] Thus, not all who "terrify" a population are "terrorist" as I use the term here—groups such as the RUF in Sierra Leone or the Lord's Resistance Army in Uganda are not coded as terrorist under my definition, for example. Some terrorist groups (such as the FMLN or the IRA, depending on one's political leanings) might thus be considered morally preferable to some nonterrorist groups.[22] Indeed, it is important not to let judgments of the morality of a group's cause influence the use of the term *terrorism*.

War Outcomes and Relative Success

Civil wars end in one of four ways: either the government or the rebels win outright, or they reach a peace agreement of some sort, or the rebellion peters out. These possibilities can be thought of as representing a continuum of success for the rebel group. Government victory and rebel victory obviously he at opposite ends of this continuum, as depicted in Figure 8.5. Peace agreements represent a second-best outcome from the rebels' perspective. Agreements entail concessions and compromise by both sides, but since rebels fight to change the status quo, whereas governments fight to maintain it, government concessions represent at least partial political victory for rebels. Moreover, agreements require the government to accept rebels as legitimate negotiating partners, itself a significant concession. Indeed,

Figure 8.5. A Continuum of Rebel Political Success

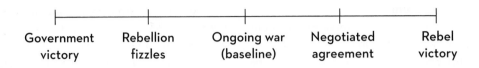

| Government victory | Rebellion fizzles | Ongoing war (baseline) | Negotiated agreement | Rebel victory |

many civil wars coded as ending in an agreement could easily be considered rebel victories in political if not military terms. For example, the peace agreement between South Africa and the ANC represented the fulfillment of that group's primary goal, the end of apartheid.[23]

Second worst from the rebels' perspective are wars that end when a formerly full-scale rebellion fizzles out with violence ending or dropping to such low levels that the conflict is no longer considered ongoing. Although the rebel group may still exist, it is not causing much trouble at this low level of violence. Most rebellions in this category have been largely defeated, though not eliminated outright.[24] Examples include Sendero Luminoso in Peru, which ended its fight after the capture of its leader; and the MQM in Pakistan, which "decided to pursue a peaceful strategy rather than a violent one" after the Pakistani military dealt "a serious blow to the militants."[25]

Scholars in the effectiveness debate differ on how to treat conflicts that have not yet ended. Should ongoing conflict count as failure because rebels have not yet achieved their goals,[26] or success because they have avoided defeat?[27] In relation to a group's ultimate political objectives, one can treat ongoing conflict as a baseline category of intermediate success; neither side has been able to defeat the other, no significant concessions have been agreed to, and the rebels continue to inflict pain on the country. However, rebel groups are organizations, and as such they seek to survive.[28] Ongoing war therefore represents success on that dimension. As I shall show, the goals of political change and organizational survival may be in tension.

Advantages and Disadvantages of Terrorism

Terrorism has both advantages and disadvantages. I argue that the advantages tend to help rebels survive rather than to win, whereas the disadvantages make it harder for terrorists to achieve political concessions or to win outright. Much of the literature considers the usefulness of terrorism in isolation. The implicit comparison is thus effectiveness relative to doing nothing. But how effective is terrorism relative to other tactics a rebel organization could employ? All rebel groups attack military targets; terrorist rebel groups, as defined here, are distinguished by the fact that they also purposively attack civilians indiscriminately to influence a wider audience.[29]

There are several potential audiences to consider. The primary audience is the government, which rebels hope to induce to make concessions or to give up the fight. There are also secondary audiences, those whose support rebels attempt to win, and those rebels hope to induce to put pressure on the government. Within the country, there is an "aggrieved" population on whose behalf the rebel organization claims to fight.[30] There are also civilians on the other side of the conflict—those who support the government or generally consent to be governed by it. For lack of a better term, I refer to this group as the "mainstream." It includes both those who benefit from and support the state and its use of violence against the rebel group and "fence-sitters." Finally, there are international audiences—particularly those (great or regional powers, neighboring states, relevant diasporas) in a position to aid or pressure either side of the conflict.

Terrorism has obvious disadvantages as a military tactic. Attacking civilians indiscriminately in public places is not useful for taking or holding territory or the capital. It is thus much less effective than other tactics for winning outright. Unlike attacks on the government's military forces, or even other types of attacks on civilians (such as ethnic cleansing of territory, or attacks to prevent collaboration with the enemy), indiscriminate attacks on public targets such as markets or buses have no direct military value.

The terrorism literature identifies a number of less direct ways through which it is thought to "work." These include (1) attrition, (2) advertising the cause, (3) provocation, (4) outbidding, and (5) spoiling.[31] Of these, attrition is arguably the most important because it entails the most direct (or least indirect) link between rebel actions and the achievement of political goals. The other strategies aim at intermediate goals, including mobilizing support, and/or preserving organizational survival, often in competition among groups claiming to represent the same aggrieved population. I discuss each of these strategies in turn, considering both the advantages and disadvantages of terrorism for the rebels' larger military effort.[32]

Attrition

Terrorism is used as part of an attrition strategy, meant to inflict pain on the other side so as to undermine the adversary's will, rather than its capacity, to fight.[33] However, terrorist attacks are not the only way to fight a war of attrition. Insurgency or guerrilla warfare tactics classically employ hit-and-run attacks to dog the adversary's forces and undermine its will to continue the fight. Unlike other forms of insurgency, terrorism, by definition, does not target military forces,

and thus does not degrade the government's military capacity.

Terrorist attacks do entail some advantages in their sheer ability to inflict pain in a cost-effective manner. It is less costly (in material terms) to attack "soft" civilian targets than "hard" military ones. Because terrorism attacks targets that are inherently hard to defend, preventing every single attack is difficult. As Condoleezza Rice described counterterrorism efforts (paraphrasing the IRA): "They only have to be right once. We have to be right 100 percent of the time."[34] It takes relatively few people to organize and carry out a terrorist attack, making full elimination of terrorist groups difficult; mere remnants can continue to inflict damage.

Terrorism is also a relatively cheap way to impose costs on civilians such that the mainstream population pressures its government to give in to terrorist demands. There is some evidence that this can be effective, up to a point,[35] perhaps particularly so in democracies (see hypothesis 4). However, terrorism can also induce pressure on the government not to concede by rallying the mainstream population around the flag. Moreover, many governments have a stated policy never to negotiate with terrorists. This is often observed only in the breach, and governments are always reluctant to negotiate with and grant concessions to any rebel group. The rhetoric of nonnegotiation with terrorists can nonetheless make it especially politically difficult to do so.

Terrorism is also thought to be a communication device, meant to signal strength and resolve, to convince the opponent that the war of attrition will be long and costly.[36] Compared with not attacking at all, terrorism may indeed be effective as a costly signal, but compared with attacks against the military, the effectiveness of terrorism as a signal of resolve is unclear at best, whereas terrorism signals weakness rather than strength.

Terrorism signals a willingness to use extreme tactics that violate widely held norms and this may be interpreted as a signal of resolve. However, extremism and resolve are not necessarily the same thing. Willingness to attack civilians signals willingness to impose these costs in the future. To the extent that the government cares more about the loss of civilian life than the loss of soldiers' lives, this may provide a signaling advantage to terrorist tactics.

There are also downsides to sending such signals, however. By deliberately violating the norm against targeting noncombatants, terrorists place themselves beyond the pale, painting themselves as untrustworthy—likely to break their promises rather than abide by a negotiated agreement.[37] The targets of terrorism may also infer from the extreme nature of the tactics used that the groups' demands are also extreme; that terrorists seek to destroy their society.[38] Opponents will therefore view negotiations as an act of appeasement. Use of extreme tactics may credibly signal resolve to carry on the fight, but it undermines the credibility of promises to reward concessions with peace.

Terrorism can also make it harder for rebels to accept concessions. Terrorist rebel groups may be particularly suspicious of the government in any potential negotiations to end the conflict. This may be, in part, because of a selection effect if only particularly hardline groups choose terrorist tactics. But it could also be induced by this choice. Having committed terrorist attacks, rebels may not believe that they will be accepted into a peaceful postwar political order.[39] Government promises of amnesty or of a power-sharing role for rebels may therefore not be credible to terrorist rebel groups. Mistrust and problems of credible commitment plague all civil wars,[40] but terrorism makes them even worse. For a number of reasons, then, signaling extremism can make one's would-be negotiating partner less, rather than more, willing to make political concessions.

As a signal of strength, moreover, terrorist attacks are clearly inferior. Despite the empirical (non)finding presented shortly, the deeply embedded conventional wisdom is that terrorism is a "weapon of the weak." To be credible, signals have to be costly. Precisely because it is less costly to attack "soft" civilian targets than hardened military ones, terrorism signals military impotence rather than strength.

In sum, terrorism is a cheap way to inflict costs in a war of attrition, and is hard to eliminate fully, fostering organizational survival. On the other hand, it creates pressures on the government not to concede, and its very affordability undermines its value as a credible signal.

Rebellion, particularly insurgency or guerrilla warfare, as Mao famously stressed, requires a supportive population.[41] Though Mao would disagree, the terrorism literature generally maintains that terrorism is a strategy used to mobilize support.[42] Do indiscriminate attacks on civilians enhance or undermine popular support?[43]

Advertising the Cause

One way terrorism is thought to mobilize support is by publicizing grievances—"propaganda of the deed"—to put the cause on the political agenda.[44] Because they are more outrageous, terrorist attacks usually generate more publicity than attacks against the military. This attention can create a sense of urgency about resolving a political issue.

At whom is such a strategy aimed? Publicizing grievances probably plays less of a role in situations that have escalated to the level of civil war than in lower-level conflicts. In civil wars, both the aggrieved and the mainstream population are already aware of the grievances. Terrorism can, however, publicize grievances to international audiences; or in some conflicts over secession or autonomy, to advertise the plight of an aggrieved population whose lives are quite remote to citizens in other parts of the country.

The disadvantages of targeting civilians to generate their support are obvious. Those who see such attacks as justified given their view of the righteousness of the cause, are those most likely already to support the rebellion. Terrorism "preaches to the choir." Those potential supporters who remain to be mobilized—less radical or politicized members of the aggrieved population, "fence-sitters," and the international community—are more likely to feel revulsion at the taking of innocent life.[45] Moreover, as Abrahms argues, the publicity gained by terrorism often focuses on the "senseless" or irrational nature of the violence rather than the grievances or demands the terrorist group wishes to make.[46] In the battle for legitimacy and "hearts and minds," terrorism is counterproductive.[47]

Provocation

The literature also suggests that terrorism can be used to mobilize support by provoking the state to overreact.[48] This strategy hopes to induce the government to crack down on the aggrieved population, creating new grievances and exacerbating old ones, causing an increase in support for the rebel organization. Because they violate norms of warfare, terrorist attacks may be more likely than attacks on military targets to provoke an overreaction. However, using terrorism for this purpose is risky for two reasons. First, successful provocation requires that the aggrieved will blame the government for the crackdown, rather than the rebel group that provoked it.[49] Second, by attacking civilians, terrorist attacks make it easier for the government to justify—both domestically and internationally—draconian measures to crush the rebellion. The opprobrium directed against a government that employs extreme measures will be lower when it is fighting a terrorist rebel group than a nonterrorist rebel group.[50] For provocation to work, the rebels must be able to goad the government into a "middling level of brutality."[51] A government strongly committed to human rights is difficult to provoke, whereas one willing to employ extreme brutality in its fight will be able to wipe out the rebels and the constituency they claim to represent.[52] In this Goldilocks equation, terrorism may induce governments to move from "too soft" to "just right," but can also make governments "too hard," allowing them to justify measures to crush the rebels rather than creating a backlash of support in their favor.

Outbidding

Terrorism is thought useful as a means of competing with other rival groups that claim to represent the same aggrieved population. Outbidding is intended to mobilize popular support for a group by demonstrating commitment to the cause and ability to fight for the interests of the aggrieved.[53] But why should the aggrieved population support groups that use terrorism over those who do not? Kydd and Walter respond that it is advantageous to be represented by an agent who will drive a harder bargain than oneself, and extreme tactics signal a tougher negotiating stance.[54] This argument discounts the cost of continued conflict to the aggrieved population, however. Supporting a group whose reservation price is higher than one's own by definition rules out settlements one would prefer to ongoing conflict. If one fears the government will never compromise (Kydd and Walter's second answer), then one should prefer not a more extreme agent, but a militarily more competent one. Given that terrorism signals military weakness rather than strength, it is unclear how attacking civilians rather than military targets might win political support.[55] Although competition among groups and factions is undoubtedly an important motive for rebel behavior, it is questionable how terrorism serves these competitive purposes better than other tactics.

Spoiling

Spoiling is another manifestation of competition among rebel groups. It occurs when a more extreme group is threatened by the prospect of peace between the government and a more moderate group. By launching a terrorist attack and inducing doubt about the moderates' ability or willingness to control terrorism, extremists can derail peace.[56] This can help ensure the survival of an extremist group that might otherwise become obsolete in the face of peace. Spoilers presumably hope for an eventual outcome more favorable to their cause than the one moderates were willing to accept, but spoiling does nothing to ensure this more favorable outcome rather than a less favorable one. Terrorism driven by spoiling thus contributes to survival but does nothing to help a group achieve its political goals.

Hypotheses

This evaluation of the pros and cons of terrorism relative not to inaction but to other types of attacks (notably attacks on military targets), leads to several hypotheses. On balance, terrorism generally undermines military effectiveness. It has no direct value for winning the war outright; it does not degrade the government's military capability, nor can it be used to take and hold territory. It is a cheap way to inflict costs on the enemy and may help signal resolve, but its low cost also signals weakness. It may help advertise the cause, but it also drives potential supporters away. It can provoke a government into self-destructive overreaction, but it can also help the government justify draconian measures in their fight against rebels.

H1:   Terrorist rebels are less likely than nonterrorist rebels to achieve military victory.

Terrorism also makes the second-best outcome for rebels less likely. Governments will grant fewer concessions to a less militarily effective opponent. Moreover, rebels' use of extreme tactics makes it harder for the government to negotiate an agreement and exacerbates the problems of trust and credible commitment that plague all civil wars.

H2:   Rebels using terrorism are less likely than those who eschew terrorism to achieve negotiated settlements.

There are, however, some advantages to terrorism for organizational survival. Terrorist rebel groups are hard to eliminate entirely, and spoiling can prevent peace with more moderate groups from making extremist groups obsolete. For both these reasons, and because terrorism prevents negotiated settlements that would otherwise end the war more quickly, terrorism should increase civil war duration.

H3:   Wars involving terrorist rebels are likely to last longer than those involving nonterrorist rebels.

I argue that terrorism is, on balance, ineffective for achieving political goals. But there are several reasons to think that terrorism might be relatively more effective against democracies than against autocracies. First, democratic governments are likely more sensitive to civilian loss of life.[57] If terrorism works by inflicting pain on civilians who then pressure their government to make concessions, then it stands to reason that the more accountable the government is to popular pressure, the more likely this strategy will work.

Second, democracies are thought to have trouble repressing or preventing and policing terrorist groups.[58] Because they start on the "soft" end of the spectrum, democracies should be more likely provoked into the "just right" level of brutality discussed earlier, whereas nondemocracies will be provoked into a response that is "too hard" and that brutally but effectively represses rebellion.

Terrorism may also be less likely to backfire by undermining support among the aggrieved when its victims are seen as "complicitous" in government policy because they have voted the government into power in democratic elections.[59]

H4: *Terrorism will be more effective against democratic governments than against nondemocratic governments.*

Selection and Potential Confounders

Because I look at the use of terrorism only in the context of civil wars, this study does not cover all terrorist organizations, raising issues of selection bias. The analysis excludes transnational terrorist groups that attack primarily across borders rather than in their home state.[60] It also excludes organizations involved in conflicts that do not meet the standard 1,000 battle death threshold of a civil war.[61] The smallest and weakest groups are thus excluded.[62] Focusing on the deadliest groups is defensible on policy grounds and is necessary for empirical comparison with nonterrorist groups. It does, however, limit generalizability because I evaluate terrorism by only groups capable of mounting civil war, not terrorism relative to other options for those without this capability. The notion that terrorism is used only by those with no other option is belied, however, by the terrorist rebel groups examined in this study, who by definition can mount a civil war.

The selection of organizations involved in civil wars likely overrepresents ethno-nationalist organizations, which are more likely to have clear political or territorial goals that are more easily negotiable than the goals of other types of terrorist organizations.[63] The data used here also exclude coups,[64] which are quite unlikely to involve terrorism and which may be more often successful than other types of rebellion. All of these selection issues bias the study toward finding terrorism successful, and against my own argument.

The temporal bounds of the data used in this study (post-1989) do not cover the era of decolonization, and therefore exclude a set of highly successful rebellions; virtually all of these cases led to independence. Some notable cases of terrorist success (for example, Algeria) are thus omitted. If terrorism was used disproportionally in anticolonial wars of this era (an open empirical question), excluding this era will bias the results away from finding terrorism effective. On the other hand, anticolonial struggles enjoyed particular legitimacy; relationships in that era may not apply to more recent conflicts.

Arguably more important as a concern than selection bias are the thorny issues of endogeneity and spuriousness for although terrorism inflicts random violence, it is not a tactic chosen at random. To assess its effectiveness accurately, I must therefore pay particular attention to any variables that might affect both the use of terrorism and the outcome of the war. The literature on the causes of terrorism, particularly on why terrorism appears in some places rather than others, suggests several potential confounders. I explore the relationships between these factors and the use of terrorism in greater depth elsewhere, but I discuss them briefly here.[65]

The most obvious potential confounding variable is the strength of the rebel group relative to the government. If, as is commonly asserted, terrorism is a "weapon of the weak,"[66] failure to take this into account will make terrorism look less effective than it really is.

The relationship between democracy and terrorism has generated significant theoretical and empirical debate.[67] Many see a positive relationship between democracy and terrorism, in part because terrorism is thought to be more effective against democracies, as discussed earlier.

Terrorism is also thought to be a tactic used by groups with particularly extreme aims. This argument is often tautological: groups that use extreme tactics such as terrorism are considered extremist, therefore extremist groups use terrorism. But it is possible to assess group aims independent of their tactics by focusing on how far rebels' stated aims are from the status quo. I argue elsewhere that in wars over a particular region, secessionist rebels can be considered more extreme than those fighting for autonomy, whereas in wars over control of the state, those who seek to transform society in fundamental ways (for example, by instituting Sharia in a secular state, or communism in a capitalist state, or vice versa) are more extreme than those merely engaged in a power struggle to take the reins of power (the fight between Lissouba and Sassou Nguesso in Congo–Brazzaville is a good example).[68]

Secessionist aims are particularly important to consider because scholars such as Pape and Stanton suggest that terrorism should be especially likely in secessionist conflicts.[69] Fazal suggests just the opposite, however; because separatists desire to become accepted members of the international system, they have incentives to avoid targeting civilians indiscriminately.[70] Scholars have also noted links between religious conflict and terrorism,[71] and between population and/or gross domestic product (GDP) per capita and terrorism.[72] Terrorism as defined here may be less likely in Africa than elsewhere,[73] and may be more likely where rebels do not have the advantage of rough terrain that enables other forms of insurgency.[74] The outbidding argument suggests that terrorism is more likely when there are several rebel groups active as part of the same struggle.[75]

This set of variables by no means exhausts the list of factors that might make rebel groups more likely to choose terrorism—this is obviously an important questions in its own right. For the purposes of this article, however, my focus is on variables that likely also affect the outcome of war,

and whose omission could thus lead to spurious findings about the effectiveness of terrorism.[76]

The Data

The data analyzed here consist of 104 rebel groups involved in full-scale civil wars active between 1989 and 2004. Much of the data come from Cunningham, Gleditsch, and Salehyan's Non-State Actor data set (hereafter CGS),[77] which builds on and expands the well-known Uppsala-PRIO Armed Conflict Data (hereafter UCDP)[78] by identifying each nonstate (or rebel) actor.[79] These data are particularly useful for several reasons. First, the unit of analysis is the government-rebel group dyad, rather than the conflict as is common in many data sets on civil war. Second, the relative strength of the government and each rebel group is coded. The CGS data are time varying, allowing for variables that change over the course of the conflict, for example, changes in the relative strength of the actors, or changes in democracy or economic variables.

The dependent variable is war outcome for each dyad, covering the five possibilities discussed here: government victory, rebel victory, agreement (including peace agreements and ceasefire agreements), wars that fizzle out to "low or no activity" by dropping below twenty-five battle deaths per year, and ongoing conflicts. Outcomes data are from UCDP through 2003; I updated through 2009 and corrected a few cases based on case-specific research.[80]

The measure of the main independent variable, whether a rebel group uses terrorist tactics, comes from Stanton's coding of "high casualty terrorism," a measure of a group's systematic use of "small-scale bombs . . . to attack unambiguously civilian targets" excluding attacks on infrastructure (for example, power stations, pipelines, bridges) which impose costs on civilians, but in which casualties are rare.[81] I use this more restrictive, high-casualty-only measure of terrorism because it best captures the deliberate and indiscriminate killing of civilians on which my definition and theory focus. Of the 104 cases examined here, twenty-four (23 percent) use high-casualty terrorism.

This measure captures groups generally classified as "terrorist" by other sources, such as the LTTE in Sri Lanka, the Taliban in Afghanistan (after 2003), the FARC in Colombia, the Provisional IRA in Northern Ireland, and so on. One advantage of Stanton's data over databases more commonly used in the terrorism literature is that this minimizes some of the well-known geographical biases in the terrorism data, particularly their overrepresentation of terrorism in Western democracies and underrepresentation or spotty coverage of groups in Africa and other strategically less important (to the US) places. The main disadvantage of this measure is that it is limited to full-scale civil wars active between 1989 and 2004, thus providing the bounds of the empirical analysis. Merging the Stanton and time varying CGS data yields 104 cases and 566 observations over time.[82] * * *

Stanton found surprisingly little variation over time within conflicts in the types of strategies rebels and governments used in terms of targeting civilians. With very few exceptions, groups that used terrorism did so throughout the conflict, whereas those who eschewed the tactic early on continued to avoid it later.[83] This in itself is quite interesting, and suggests that rebel organizations' choices about using terrorism are remarkably "sticky."

The CGS data include a five-point indicator of rebel group strength relative to the government, ranging from much weaker to much stronger. This variable summarizes assessments of the rebel group's ability to mobilize supporters, arms procurement ability, and fighting capacity, which Cunningham and colleagues argue capture the rebel group's ability to target government forces,

or "offensive strength."[84] To capture the effects of war aims, I include two dummy variables. The first marks whether the group seeks full independence and is taken from Coggins's data on secessionist movements.[85] The second differentiates among groups fighting for control of the center, marking those who aim to transform society in fundamental ways. This I coded myself, based on case descriptions in the CGS data coding notes, Minorities at Risk (MAR), START's Terrorist Organization Profiles (TOPs), UCDP's case summaries, and case-specific sources.[86] Together, the independence and transform society dummy variables can be compared with an omitted category of relatively "moderate" rebels who aim either for autonomy, or who are engaged in power struggles at the top without a desire to transform society.[87] Because this is a newly coded variable, Figures 8.6 and 8.7 provide information about its relationship with both terrorism and war outcomes, respectively. From this bivariate look at the data, we see that moderate rebels appear to be less likely to use terrorism and more likely to succeed, making inclusion of this variable particularly important to avoid spuriousness.

■ ■ ■

Which Groups Use Terrorism?

Before turning to tests of the hypotheses, I take a brief detour to address the issue of spuriousness, examining the effects of potentially confounding variables on the use of terrorism. Of the rebel groups examined in this study, fewer than a quarter used terrorism as a tactic in their fight against the government, whereas the rest did not. What accounts for this variation? Table 1 [not shown in this excerpt] shows the results of logistic analysis with terrorist rebel group as the dependent variable.

Figure 8.6. War Aims and Percent Terrorist

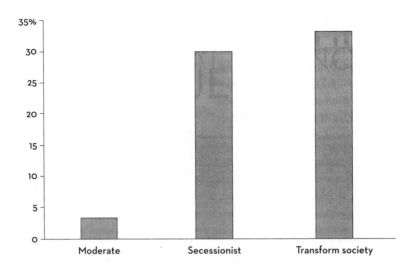

Figure 8.6. War Aims and Percent Terrorist

* * * Analysis of terrorism as the dependent variable, rather than the independent variable as it is in the rest of the article, suggests that terrorism is most likely in civil wars in democracies, where rebels face governments representing a different religion, and is seldom seen in Africa (indeed in the data used in this study, there are no cases of high-casualty terrorism by African rebel groups).[88]

Given how deeply entrenched it is, the conventional wisdom that terrorism is more likely to be used by weaker groups receives surprisingly weak support. The relationship between relative strength and terrorism is negative, but it is never statistically significant.[89] I also find that the apparent link between a group's war aims and its use of terrorism seen in Figure 8.6 disappears once other variables are controlled for. Those fighting for secession are, if anything, less likely to use terrorism, whereas those aiming to transform society appear more likely to do so, but neither effect is significant. Together, these findings indicate that the extremity of a group's aims are not necessarily associated with the extremity of its tactics. * * *

Do Terrorist Rebels Win? The Effects of Terrorism on War Outcomes

Figure 8.8 shows the percentage of terrorist and nonterrorist rebellions ending in each outcome. Although these bivariate relationships obviously do not yet take into account potentially confounding variables, the figures do suggest preliminary support for H1 to H3. Most tellingly, of the groups examined here none of those that deliberately killed large numbers of civilians through terrorist attacks won its fight outright.[90] Peace agreements, which I argue represent significant concessions to the rebel cause, are also much less frequent when rebels use terrorism. Meanwhile, government victories and wars ending through low or no activity are slightly more common in civil wars involving terrorism. Wars in which rebels used terror were much more likely to be ongoing as of 2009 than were wars with nonterrorist rebels, suggesting that terrorism makes wars particularly difficult to terminate.

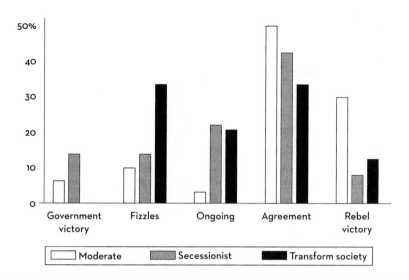

Figure 8.7. War Aims and Percent in Each War Outcome

* * * Figure 8.9 depict[s] the survival function for wars in which terrorism is and is not used.[91] As expected, civil wars in which rebels use terrorism last longer than those in which rebels do not; terrorism contributes to organizational survival.

■   ■   ■

The basic pattern in the bivariate analysis represented in Figure 8.8 generally holds, even when potential confounders are controlled for. Although there is no significant difference between ongoing war (the omitted baseline category) and rebel defeat or wars that fizzle out, the "good" outcomes for rebels—peace agreements and rebel victory—are both significantly less likely, relative to ongoing war, when rebels employ terrorism as a tactic, supporting H1 and H2. * * * The predicted probability of a war ending in an agreement is 6.6 percent for rebels that do not resort to terrorism, but only 1 percent for those who do. The predicted probability of a rebel victory is low for all rebellions, but drops from 3.4 to 0 percent for those who employ terrorism.

I also test these hypotheses with a competing risks model. * * * This analysis indicates that the use of terrorism increases the risk of government defeat by more than four times. Unlike the multinomial logit results, this effect is statistically significant. Terrorism has no appreciable effect on the likelihood of war fizzling out. Meanwhile, the use of terrorism reduces the likelihood that rebels reach a negotiated agreement by 80 percent, and given that there are no cases of rebel victories by terrorist rebels, the competing risks model predicts that terrorism reduces the chance of a rebel victory to zero; both results easily pass tests of statistical significance. In other words, I again find strong support for H1 and H2.

■   ■   ■

Figure 8.10 shows the results of the competing risks analysis graphically, plotting the cumulative incidence rate of each outcome over time for terrorist and nonterrorist rebels, holding other variables at their mean or modal values. As can

Figure 8.8. Terrorism and Percent in Each War Outcome

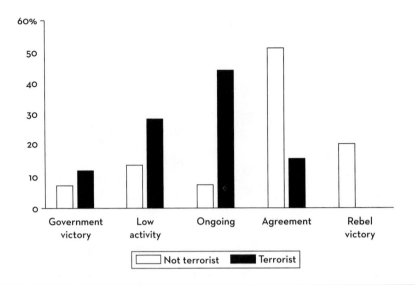

be seen, the incidence of the best outcomes for rebels, negotiated agreement and rebel victory, are lower for those who resort to terrorism, whereas the worst outcome, government victory, is higher for terrorist rebels. In sum, rebel groups who deliberately and indiscriminately kill civilians are, all else equal, much less likely to win outright or to achieve concessions in the form of an agreement than are nonterrorist rebel groups, but are no less likely to fizzle out or be defeated rather than to live to fight another day.

I turn, finally, to analysis of the relative effects of terrorism against democratic and nondemocratic governments. An initial look at the cases is consistent with H4; of the terrorist rebel groups that succeeded in reaching a negotiated agreement, three out of four fought democratic governments.[92] * * *

■   ■   ■

[However,] I find only mixed support for H4 overall. The negative effects of terrorism are smaller against democracies, but not always significantly so.

Terrorist rebels may be somewhat more likely to succeed against democratic governments than nondemocratic governments, but they are still less likely to succeed than rebels who do not use terrorism.

Conclusion

Research on terrorism has exploded since 2001 for obvious reasons. However, the ability of this literature to answer fundamental questions has been hampered by a lack of variation on the phenomenon. This project uses variation within civil wars, namely the fact that some rebel groups use terrorism whereas others do not, to help resolve the debate about the effectiveness of terrorism.

I argue that when it comes to achieving a rebel group's political goals, the disadvantages of terrorism generally outweigh its advantages. It is a cheap way to inflict pain on the other side, and terrorist groups are hard to eliminate completely, but it is useless for taking or holding territory. It may help signal commitment to a cause, but because it is

Figure 8.9. Terrorism and the Duration of War

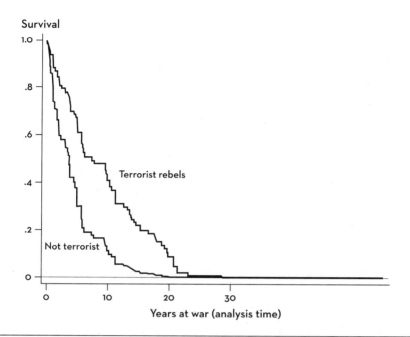

cheap, it signals weakness rather than strength. It may be useful for provoking an overreaction by the government, but it also helps justify draconian measures to crush the rebellion. Its outrageous nature may help bring attention to a cause, but it also undermines legitimacy and alienates potential supporters. Terrorism may help achieve tactical results, but these apparently do not translate into strategic success. It may also be useful at lower levels of conflict or for groups that do not have the ability to wage full-scale war (a question I cannot yet address with available data). Empirically, I find much more support for the argument that terrorism is likely to backfire than for the notion that it is effective. Rebels who use terrorism do not win outright, and they are less likely to achieve concessions in a negotiated outcome. This negative effect may be somewhat attenuated when rebels fight against democracies rather than autocracies. But even in democratic states, terrorist rebel groups do not achieve victory and are unlikely to obtain concessions at the

negotiating table. The short answer to the question "Do terrorist rebels win?" is "No."

If terrorism is so ineffective, one might reasonably ask why rebel groups use it, especially rebels who are not fighting democratic governments.[93] The answer may lie in the finding that civil wars in which terrorism is used last significantly longer than others. The use of terrorism contributes to rebels' organizational survival. Rebels thus appear to face a dilemma—using terrorism as a tactic is good for the immediate goal of survival, but comes at the expense of the long-term political goals for which they are, ultimately (or ostensibly) fighting.

This study begins to shed light on the causes of terrorism, as well as its effects. I examine this question only briefly in this article, focusing on variables that might also affect war outcomes, to avoid spurious results. The results are intriguing, however. They cast doubt on the conventional wisdom that terrorism is a "weapon of the weak." Among rebels fighting full-fledged civil wars, there is surprisingly

Figure 8.10. Terrorism and War Outcomes (Competing Risks)

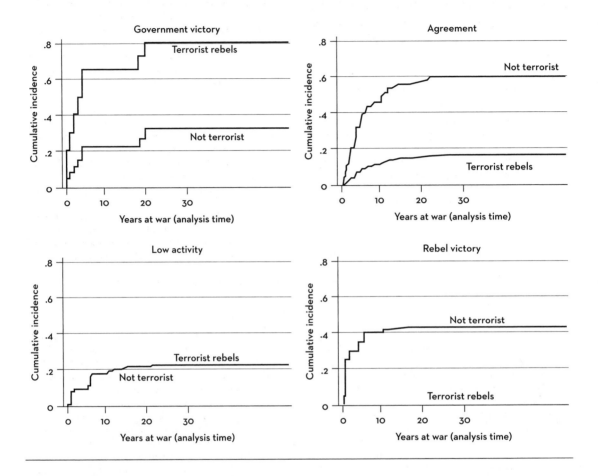

little evidence that weaker groups are more likely to use terrorism than stronger ones. Nor is terrorism more likely, again contrary to conventional wisdom, in secessionist wars, or when rebels profess extreme aims. Terrorism is more likely, however, in civil wars in democracies, as many have argued, and where religion divides rebels from the government they fight. It is much less likely to be used in Africa, a finding that remains to be explained theoretically. Expanding the analysis of why some groups turn to terrorism whereas others do not is an obvious avenue for further research.

Extensions of this study to further our understanding both of where terrorism arises, and how successful it is, will require new data. Data are currently available for only a relatively short period (1989–2004) and for full-fledged civil wars. Extending the analysis temporally before the end of the Cold War and to include more recent conflicts, and especially to lower level conflicts will strengthen the analysis, and in particular allow fuller testing, for example, of the notion that terrorism is a "weapon of the weak." Further research is also needed to establish how rebel groups navigate the tradeoff between organizational survival and political efficacy.

In the meantime, the empirical evidence presented in this study suggests that terrorism is likely to be a persistent problem—elongating the destruction and suffering that civil wars entail—but not a potent force for political change. Terrorism may help rebel groups survive, but it does not help them get what they want politically.

NOTES

1. This study examines only rebels' use of terrorism, not governments' use of such tactics (state terrorism), thus sidestepping the question of whether the definition of terrorism should be limited to nonstate actors.

2. Pape 2003, 351. Pape is ambiguous on whether his argument applies to terrorism more broadly, arguing that suicide terrorism is to terrorism as lung cancer is to cancer—a particularly virulent strain. Author discussion with Pape, 11 November 2010; and Pape and Feldman 2010.

3. Kydd and Walter 2006, 49–50.

4. Thomas 2014, 807–9.

5. See Bueno de Mesquita and Dickson 2007; Gould and Klor 2010; and Wood and Kathman 2014.

6. See Abrahms 2005, 2006, 43, and 2012.

7. Jones and Libicki 2008, 32–33.

8. See Merari 1993, 238–39; and Cronin 2009, 11. See also Acosta 2014.

9. See Krause 2013.

10. See Jones and Libicki 2008, 34; Abrahms 2006, 53–54; and Pape 2003, 355.

11. Wood and Kathman 2014; and Thomas 2014 are exceptions. Abrahms's work is a partial exception, however because he examines only groups designated as "foreign terrorist organizations" by the U.S. State Department, variation on the independent variable is truncated.

12. Exceptions include Sambanis 2008; Findley and Young 2012a; and Boulden 2009.

13. See Enders, Sandler, and Gaibulloev 2011, 323; LaFree and Dugan 2007, 187; and Asal and Rethemeyer 2008a, 447.

14. McCormick 2003, 473. For a good discussion of definitions, see Merari 1993.

15. Some draw a distinction, often based on group size or strength or even the regime type of the opponent, between terrorism and guerrilla warfare or insurgency. These definitions exclude all rebel groups, and preclude the examination of the relationship, for example, between terrorism and group strength. See Schmid and Jongman 1988, especially 13–18; Silke 1996; Cronin 2006, 31–32; and Sambanis 2008.

16. Many definitions in the literature are so broad as arguably to encompass all rebel groups in all civil wars. Indeed, much of the terrorism literature could easily substitute *rebellion* or *insurgency* for *terrorism*. See, for example, Hoffman 2006, 40.

17. Cronin 2003, 32–33.

18. See Stanton 2009, 31. Kydd and Walter 2006, 66–69, refer to this as "intimidation." See also Kalyvas 2006.

19. See Crenshaw 1981, 379; and McCormick 2003, 474.

20. See Stanton 2009, 34–35, emphasis in the original. In more recent work, Stanton refers to this strategy as "terrorism." Stanton 2013.

21. Ibid., 8–9, 90–93. Some of the groups that engage in these strategies also engage in coercion (Stanton's strategies are not mutually exclusive), so are captured under my definition in any case. Investigating the causes and effectiveness of these other types of strategies of violence against civilians is beyond the scope of this article.

22. On the relative morality of terrorism, see Crenshaw 1983, 3; and Merari 1993, 227–31.

23. Some agreements are reached when rebels are largely defeated (for example, the RUF in Sierra Leone), but in the vast majority of cases, agreements represent political gains for the rebels. Terrorism is also sometimes used to prevent agreements between the government and another more moderate group (see my discussion on spoiling). Kydd and Walter 2002. However, an agreement represents a relatively successful outcome for the group that negotiates it.

24. Some conflicts admittedly fizzle out because rebel demands have been partially met (for example, de facto autonomy for Kurds in Iraq after the Persian Gulf War). However, in most low/no activity cases, rebels were all but defeated militarily, making this category a reasonable proxy.

25. Cunningham, Gleditsch, and Salehyan 2009b, 350.

26. Abrahms 2006.

27. Jones and Libicki 2008.

28. See Wilson 1974, 10; and Acosta 2014.

29. Terrorist groups may also attack civilians in other more discriminating ways, as discussed earlier (for example, to punish collaboration with the enemy). Groups that attack only civilians and no military targets do not reach the threshold of civil war—on selection effects, see section on selection effects.

30. Bueno de Mesquita and Dickson 2007, 369.

31. See Kydd and Walter 2006; Thornton 1964; and Crenshaw 1981 and 2011. Kydd and Walter also discuss intimidation, which as I explained is not considered terrorism in this study.

32. See also Goodwin 2006, especially 2038.

33. See Pape 2003, 346; and Kydd and Walter 2006. See also Arreguín-Toft 2001, especially 105.

34. Quoted in Nina Easton, "Condi: The Should-Be Face of the GOP," *Fortune* (Internet ed.), 22 September 2009.

35. Gould and Klor 2010.

36. See Kydd and Walter 2006, 59–60; Merari 1993; and Wood and Kathman 2014.

37. Bapat 2006, 214.

38. Abrahms 2012, 22.

39. This can make terrorism a self-perpetuating tactic. Laitin and Shapiro 2008, 222–23.

40. Walter 2002.

41. Mao 1937. See also Arreguín-Toft 2001, 104.

42. See, for example, Pape 2003; Bueno de Mesquita and Dickson 2007; and DeNardo 1985.

43. To my knowledge, there is no empirical work supporting the contention that terrorism mobilizes support more effectively than other forms of resistance.

44. See Crenshaw 2011, 118; and Thornton 1964, 82–83.

45. The international reaction may be particularly pronounced after 11 September 2001 and the US-led strengthening of the norm against terrorism.

46. Abrahms 2012, 21.

47. Cronin 2009, 93. Stephan and Chenoweth 2008 argue that violence in general decreases legitimacy and discourages broad-based participation.

48. See Kydd and Walter 2006, especially 69–72; Lake 2002; and Crenshaw 2011, 119.

49. Bueno de Mesquita and Dickson suggest that the aggrieved cannot credibly threaten to punish "extremists" for provoking the government's crackdown because the crackdown itself (by diminishing economic opportunities) makes the population inclined toward direct struggle. Bueno de Mesquita and Dickson 2007, 375. But why should the population react to diminished opportunities brought on by the conflict by choosing to continue it, rather than settle?

50. Hence the attempt by almost all governments to label rebels as "terrorists" whether they employ terrorist tactics or not.

51. Kydd and Walter 2006, 70.

52. Arreguín-Toft 2001, 109.

53. Bloom 2005.

54. Kydd and Walter 2006.

55. Terrorist attacks are likely to signal lack of popular support to the aggrieved, rather than strength. Laitin and Shapiro 2008, 216.

56. Kydd and Walter 2002.

57. See Stanton 2009; and Heger 2010.

58. See Cronin 2006, 31; Crenshaw 1981, 383; Pape 2003, 349–50; and Eubank and Weinberg 1994. But see also Lyall 2010.

59. Goodwin 2006, 2027.

60. It is not clear what the equivalent nonterrorist actors would be for a comparison with transnational terrorist groups.

61. Battle deaths exclude civilian deaths, so this could in theory exclude highly lethal terrorist groups that did not also engage in significant attacks on military targets. I checked the Global Terrorism Database to ensure that no domestic terrorist group responsible for 1,000 deaths was omitted from the study. LaFree and Dugan 2007.

62. In some terrorism databases, the majority of "terrorist" groups have never killed anyone. See Asal and Rethemeyer 2008b; and Sánchez-Cuenca and de la Calle 2009, 35.

63. Cronin 2003, 39–40.

64. Cunningham, Gleditsch, and Salehyan 2009a.

65. Fortna 2014.

66. Among many examples, see Crenshaw 1981, 387; McCormick 2003, 483; Merari 1993, 231; Pape 2003, 349; Sánchez-Cuenca and de la Calle 2009; and DeNardo 1985, 230. Little empirical work has tested this conventional wisdom directly, however. The few existing studies come to contradictory conclusions. See Stanton 2009 and 2013; Goodwin 2006; and Metelits 2010.

67. For a good overview, see Chenoweth 2010 and 2013.

68. Fortna 2014.

69. See Pape 2005, 23; and Stanton 2009, especially chapter 5.

70. Fazal 2013.

71. See Pape 2005, 22; Svensson 2007; Asal and Rethemeyer 2008a; Stanton 2013; and Satana, Inman, and Birnir 2013.

72. See Chenoweth 2010; Sánchez-Cuenca and de la Calle 2009; Burgoon 2006; Li and Schaub 2004; and Abadie 2006.

73. Boulden 2009, 13.

74. Laitin and Shapiro 2008, 213.

75. See Lawrence 2010; Bloom 2005; and Nemeth 2014. But see also Findley and Young 2012b; and Stanton 2009, 232–33.

76. On the relationship between these variables and war outcomes, see Cunningham, Gleditsch, and Salehyan 2009a; DeRouen and Sobek 2004; Fortna 2008; Balch-Lindsay, Enterline, and Joyce 2008; and Mason, Weingarten, and Fett 1999.

77. Cunningham, Gleditsch, and Salehyan 2009a, version 2.4.

78. See Gleditsch et al. 2002.

79. Note that although the overall conflict must reach the 1,000 battle death threshold, it is not the case that each rebel group/government dyad included in this study reaches this threshold.

80. For example, I updated Sri Lanka versus LTTE to reflect the government victory in 2009. This updating introduces possible inconsistencies since some variables are coded only through 2003. I also recoded cases in which a peace agreement was reached shortly after UCDP codes a war as terminated in low activity (for example, the Good Friday Agreement settling the Northern Ireland conflict). This change improves the outcomes for two terrorist rebel groups (Provisional IRA and the MNLF in the Philippines) thus working against the argument made here. I also corrected two clearly miscoded cases: Burundi versus CNDD, and UK versus Real IRA. Cases affected by these changes are dropped in robustness tests.

81. Stanton 2013, 1014–15. For further discussion, see also Stanton 2009. In some cases, Stanton's coding for a single case was applicable to more than one dyad in the CGS data (for example, Stanton codes Fatah and Hamas together in a single conflict against Israel).

82. Because thirty-four cases involve wars that began before 1989, there are another 449 observations in the data that are used for some robustness checks.

83. The PKK turned to terrorism after 1993 (a shift reflected in the time-varying data used here). The MILF (Philippines) did so after 1986 (before the start of the data). E-mail correspondence with Stanton, 25 July 2008. The Taliban did not use terrorism in its fight against the Rabbani government of Afghanistan in the 1990s, but used terrorism against the Karzai government and its Western backers in the 2000s. These are treated as separate conflicts here.

84. Cunningham, Gleditsch, and Salehyan 2009a, 574–75.

85. Coggins 2011.

86. See Minorities at Risk Project 2009; National Consortium for the Study of Terrorism and Responses to Terrorism 2008; and Uppsala Conflict Data Program 2012. Detailed coding notes available from the author.

87. This moderate category is dominated by power struggle cases, of which there are twenty-three, because there are only a handful (five) of cases of rebel groups fighting for autonomy only.

88. More recent use of terrorism in Nigeria and Somalia may, unfortunately, temper this finding.

89. This could be the result of selection effects; this analysis covers only the strongest opposition groups, those involved in full-scale civil

wars. However, among these relatively strong groups, it is clearly not the case that only weak groups resort to terrorism.

90. See Fortna 2014.

91. Nor have any of the cases of terrorist rebel groups that were ongoing as of 2010 ended in rebel victory since then (at least as of this writing [January 2015]).

92. These include Fatah versus Israel, IRA versus the UK, and the MNLF versus Philippines (all in 1993). The only case of an agreement with terrorist rebels in a nondemocracy is the CPN-M/UPF versus Nepal in 2003.

93. Forty-two percent of the rebels who use terrorism were engaged in civil war in a nondemocratic state (measured in the year the war started).

■   ■   ■

REFERENCES

Abadie, Alberto. 2006. Poverty, Political Freedom, and the Roots of Terrorism. *American Economic Review* 96 (2):50–56.

Abrahms, Max. 2005. Review of *Dying to Win: The Strategic Logic of Suicide Terrorism* by Robert A. Pape. *Middle East Policy* 12 (4):176–78.

———. 2006. Why Terrorism Does Not Work. *International Security* 31 (2):42–78.

———. 2012. The Political Effectiveness of Terrorism Revisited. *Comparative Political Studies* 45 (3): 366–93.

Acosta, Benjamin. 2014. Live to Win Another Day: Why Many Militant Organizations Survive yet Few Succeed. *Studies in Conflict and Terrorism* 37 (2):135–61.

Arreguín-Toft, Ivan. 2001. How the Weak Win Wars: A Theory of Asymmetric Conflict. *International Security* 26 (1):93–128.

Asal, Victor, and R. Karl Rethemeyer. 2008a. The Nature of the Beast: Organizational Structures and the Lethality of Terrorist Attacks. *Journal of Politics* 70 (2):437–49.

———. 2008b. Dilettantes, Ideologues, and the Weak: Terrorists Who Don't Kill. *Conflict Management and Peace Science* 25 (3):244–63.

Balch-Lindsay, Dylan, Andrew J. Enterline, and Kyle A. Joyce. 2008. Third-Party Intervention and the Civil War Process. *Journal of Peace Research* 45 (3):345–63.

Bapat, Navin A. 2006. State Bargaining with Transnational Terrorist Groups. *International Studies Quarterly* 50 (1):213–29.

Bloom, Mia. 2005. *Dying to Kill: The Allure of Suicide Terror.* New York: Columbia University Press.

Boulden, Jane. 2009. Terrorism and Civil Wars. *Civil Wars* 11 (1):5–21.

Bueno de Mesquita, Ethan, and Eric S. Dickson. 2007. The Propaganda of the Deed: Terrorism, Counterterrorism, and Mobilization. *American Journal of Political Science* 51 (2):364–81.

Burgoon, Brian. 2006. On Welfare and Terror: Social Welfare Policies and Political-Economic Roots of Terrorism. *Journal of Conflict Resolution* 50 (2):176–203.

Chenoweth, Erica. 2010. Democratic Competition and Terrorist Activity. *Journal of Politics* 72 (1):16–30.

———. 2013. Terrorism and Democracy. *Annual Review of Political Science* 16:355–78.

Coggins, Bridget. 2011. Friends in High Places: International Politics and the Emergence of States from Secessionism. *International Organization* 65 (3):433–67.

Crenshaw, Martha. 1981. The Causes of Terrorism. *Comparative Politics* 13 (4):379–99.

———. 1983. *Terrorism, Legitimacy, and Power: The Consequences of Political Violence.* Middletown, CT: Wesleyan University Press.

———. 2011. *Explaining Terrorism: Causes, Processes, and Consequences.* New York: Routledge.

Cronin, Audrey K. 2003. Behind the Curve: Globalization and International Terrorism. *International Security* 27 (3):30–58.

———. 2006. How al-Qaida Ends: The Decline and Demise of Terrorist Groups. *International Security* 31 (1):7–48.

———. 2009. *How Terrorism Ends: Understanding the Decline and Demise of Terrorist Campaigns.* Princeton, NJ: Princeton University Press.

Cunningham, David E., Kristian Skrede Gleditsch, and Idean Salehyan. 2009a. It Takes Two: A Dyadic Analysis of Civil War Duration and Outcome. *Journal of Conflict Resolution* 53 (4):570–97. Data available at http://privatewww.essex.ac.uk/~ksg/eacd.html Version 2.4. Accessed 13 January 2010.

———. 2009b. Data Coding Notes. Available at http://jcr.sagepub.com /content/53/4/570/suppl/DC1. Accessed 25 January 2010.

DeNardo, James. 1985. *Power in Numbers: The Political Strategy of Protest and Rebellion.* Princeton, NJ: Princeton University Press.

DeRouen, Karl, and David Sobek. 2004. The Dynamics of Civil War Duration and Outcome. *Journal of Peace Research* 41 (3):303–20.

Dow, Jay K., and James W. Endersby. 2004. Multinomial Probit and Multinomial Logit: A Comparison of Choice Models for Voting Research. *Electoral Studies* 23 (1):107–22.

Enders, Walter, Todd Sandler, and Khusrav Gaibulloev. 2011. Domestic Versus Transnational Terrorism: Data, Decomposition, and Dynamics. *Journal of Peace Research* 48 (3):319–37.

Eubank, William L., and Leonard Weinberg. 1994. Does Democracy Encourage Terrorism? *Terrorism and Political Violence* 6 (4):417–63.

Fazal, Tanisha M. 2013. Secessionism and Civilian Targeting. Paper presented at the 2013 Annual Meeting of the American Political Science Association, August, Chicago.

Findley, Michael G., and Joseph K. Young. 2012a. Terrorism and Civil War: A Spatial and Temporal Approach to a Conceptual Problem. *Perspectives on Politics* 10 (2):285–305.

———. 2012b. More Combatant Groups, More Terror? Empirical Tests of an Outbidding Logic. *Terrorism and Political Violence* 24 (5):706–21.

Fortna, Virginia Page. 2008. *Does Peacekeeping Work? Shaping Belligerents' Choices after Civil War.* Princeton, NJ: Princeton University Press.

———. 2014. Choosing Terror: Rebels' Use of Terrorism in Internal Armed Conflict, 1970–2010. Unpublished manuscript, Columbia University, New York.

Gleditsch, Nils P., Peter Wallensteen, Mikael Eriksson, Margareta Sollenberg, and Hoavard Strand. 2002. Armed Conflict 1946–2001: A New Dataset. *Journal of Peace Research* 39 (5):615–37. Data available at http://www.pcr.uu.se/research/ucdp/datasets /ucdp_prio_armed_conflict_dataset/. Accessed 1 April 2010.

Goodwin, Jeff. 2006. A Theory of Categorical Terrorism. *Social Forces* 84 (4):2027–46.

Gould, Eric D., and Esteban F. Klor. 2010. Does Terrorism Work? *Quarterly Journal of Economics* 125 (4):1459–510.

Heger, Lindsay L. 2010. In the Crosshairs: Explaining Violence Against Civilians. PhD diss., University of California, San Diego.

Hoffman, Bruce. 2006. *Inside Terrorism.* New York: Columbia University Press.

Jones, Seth G., and Martin C. Libicki. 2008. *How Terrorist Groups End: Lessons for Countering al Qa'ida.* Santa Monica, CA: Rand Corporation.

Kalyvas, Stathis N. 2006. *The Logic of Violence in Civil War.* New York: Cambridge University Press.

Krause, Peter. 2013. The Political Effectiveness of Non-State Violence: A Two-Level Framework to Transform a Deceptive Debate. *Security Studies* 22 (2):259–94.

Kydd, Andrew H., and Barbara F. Walter. 2002. Sabotaging the Peace: The Politics of Extremist Violence. *International Organization* 56 (2):263–96.

———. 2006. The Strategies of Terrorism. *International Security* 31 (1):49–80.

LaFree, Gary, and Laura Dugan. 2007. Introducing the Global Terrorism Database. *Terrorism and Political Violence* 19 (2):181–204.

Laitin, David D., and Jacob N. Shapiro. 2008. The Political, Economic, and Organizational Sources of Terrorism. In *Terrorism, Economic Development, and Political Openness,* edited by Philip Keefer and Norman Loayza, 209–32. New York: Cambridge University Press.

Lake, David A. 2002. Rational Extremism: Understanding Terrorism in the Twenty-First Century. *Dialogue IO* 1 (1):15–29.

Lawrence, Adria S. 2010. Triggering Nationalist Violence: Competition and Conflict in Uprisings Against Colonial Rule. *International Security* 35 (2):88–122.

Li, Quan, and Drew Schaub. 2004. Economic Globalization and Transnational Terrorism: A Pooled Time-Series Analysis. *Journal of Conflict Resolution* 48 (2):230–58.

Lyall, Jason. 2010. Do Democracies Make Inferior Counterinsurgents? Reassessing Democracy's Impact on War Outcomes and Duration. *International Organization* 64 (1):167–92.

Mao, Tse-Tung. 1961 [1937]. *On Guerrilla Warfare.* Translated by Samuel B. Griffith. New York: Praeger.

Mason, T. David, Joseph P. Weingarten, and Patrick J. Fett. 1999. Win, Lose, or Draw: Predicting the Outcome of Civil Wars. *Political Research Quarterly* 52 (2):239–68.

McCormick, Gordon H. 2003. Terrorist Decision Making. *Annual Review of Political Science* 6:473–507.

Merari, Ariel. 1993. Terrorism as a Strategy of Insurgency. *Terrorism and Political Violence* 5 (4):213–51.

Metelits, Claire. 2010. *Inside Insurgency: Violence, Civilians, and Revolutionary Group Behavior.* New York: New York University Press.

Minorities at Risk Project. 2009. Minorities at Risk Dataset: "Minority Group Assessments" and "Chronologies." College Park, MD: Center for International Development and Conflict Management. Available at http://www.cidcm.umd.edu/mar/data.asp. Accessed 29 November 2012.

National Consortium for the Study of Terrorism and Responses to Terrorism (START). 2008. Terrorist Organization Profiles (TOPs). Available at http://www.start.umd.edu/start/data_collections/tops/. Accessed 29 November 2012.

Nemeth, Stephen. 2014. The Effect of Competition on Terrorist Group Operations. *Journal of Conflict Resolution* 58 (2):336–62.

Pape, Robert A. 2003. The Strategic Logic of Suicide Terrorism. *American Political Science Review* 97 (3): 343–61.

———. 2005. *Dying to Win: The Strategic Logic of Suicide Terrorism.* New York: Random House.

Pape, Robert A., and James K. Feldman. 2010. *Cutting the Fuse: The Explosion of Suicide Terrorism and How to Stop It.* Chicago: University of Chicago Press.

Sambanis, Nicholas, 2008. Terrorism and Civil War. In *Terrorism, Economic Development, and Political Openness,* edited by Philip Keefer and Norman Loayza, 174–208. Cambridge, UK: Cambridge University Press.

Sánchez-Cuenca, Ignacio, and Luis de la Calle. 2009. Domestic Terrorism: The Hidden Side of Political Violence. *Annual Review of Political Science* 12:31–49.

Satana, Nil S., Molly Inman, and Johanna K. Birnir. 2013. Religion, Government Coalitions, and Terrorism. *Terrorism and Political Violence* 25 (1):29–52.

Schmid, Alex P., and Albert J. Jongman. 1988. *Political Terrorism: A New Guide to Actors, Authors, Concepts, Data Bases, Theories, and Literature.* Rev. ed. Amsterdam: North Holland.

Silke, Andrew. 1996. Terrorism and the Blind Man's Elephant. *Terrorism and Political Violence* 8 (3):12–28.

Stanton, Jessica A. 2009. Strategies of Violence and Restraint in Civil War. PhD diss., Department of Political Science, Columbia University, New York.

———. 2013. Terrorism in the Context of Civil War. *Journal of Politics* 75 (4):1009–22.

Stephan, Maria J., and Erica Chenoweth. 2008. Why Civil Resistance Works: The Strategic Logic of Nonviolent Conflict. *International Security* 33 (1):7–44.

Svensson, Isak. 2007. Fighting with Faith: Religion and Conflict Resolution in Civil Wars. *Journal of Conflict Resolution* 51 (6):930–49.

Thomas, Jakana. 2014. Rewarding Bad Behavior: How Governments Respond to Terrorism in Civil War. *American Journal of Political Science* 58 (4):804–18.

Thornton, Thomas P. 1964. Terror as a Weapon of Political Agitation. In *Internal War: Problems and Approaches,* edited by Harry Eckstein, 71–99. London: Free Press.

Uppsala Conflict Data Program. 2012. UCDP Conflict Encyclopedia. Uppsala, Sweden: Uppsala University. Available at www.ucdp.uu.se/database. Accessed 29 November 2012.

Walter, Barbara F. 2002. *Committing to Peace: The Successful Settlement of Civil Wars.* Princeton, NJ: Princeton University Press.

Wilson, James Q. 1974. *Political Organizations.* Princeton, NJ: Princeton University Press.

Wood, Reed M., and Jacob D. Kathman. 2014. Too Much of a Bad Thing? Civilian Victimization and Bargaining in Civil War. *British Journal of Political Science* 44 (3):1–22.

Martha Finnemore

CHANGING NORMS OF HUMANITARIAN INTERVENTION

Since the end of the Cold War states have increasingly come under pressure to intervene militarily and, in fact *have* intervened militarily to protect citizens other than their own from humanitarian disasters. Recent efforts by NATO to protect Albanian Kosovars in Yugoslavia from ethnic cleansing, efforts to alleviate starvation and establish some kind of political order in Somalia, endeavors to enforce protected areas for Kurds and no-fly zones over Shiites in Iraq, and the huge UN military effort to disarm parties and rebuild a state in Cambodia are all instances of military action whose primary goal is not territorial or strategic but humanitarian.

Realist and neoliberal theories do not provide good explanations for this behavior. The interests these theories impute to states are geostrategic or economic or both, yet many or most of these interventions occur in states of negligible geostrategic or economic importance to the intervenors, Thus no obvious national interest is at stake for the states bearing the burden of the military intervention in most if not all these cases. Somalia is, perhaps, the clearest example of military action undertaken in a state of little or no strategic or economic importance to the principal intervenor. Similarly, in Cambodia, the states that played central roles in the UN military action were, with the exception of China, not states that had any obvious geostrategic interests there by 1989; China, which did have

a geostrategic interest, bore little of the burden of intervening. Realism and neoliberalism offer powerful explanations of the Persian Gulf War but have little to say about the extension of that war to Kurdish and Shiite protection through the enforcement of UN Resolution 688. The United States, France, and Britain have been allowing abuse of the Kurds for centuries. Why they should start caring about them now is not clear.

The recent pattern of humanitarian interventions raises the issue of what interests intervening states could possibly be pursuing. In most of these cases, the intervention targets are insignificant by any usual measure of geostrategic or economic interest. Why, then, do states intervene? This chapter argues that the pattern of intervention cannot be understood apart from the changing normative context in which it occurs. Normative context is important because it shapes conceptions of interest and gives purpose and meaning to action. It shapes the rights and duties states believe they have toward one another, and it shapes the goals they value, the means they believe are effective and legitimate to obtain those goals, and the political costs and benefits attached to different choices.

* * * I examine the role of humanitarian norms in shaping patterns of humanitarian military intervention over the past 180 years and the ways those norms have changed over time creating new patterns of intervention behavior. Three factors, in particular, have changed. Who is human has changed, that is, who can successfully claim humanitarian protection from strong states has changed. In the nineteenth century, only white

From Martha Finnemore, *The Purpose of Intervention: Changing Beliefs about the Use of Force* (Ithaca, NY: Cornell University Press), 52–84. Some of the author's notes have been edited.

Christians received protection; mistreatment of other groups did not evoke the same concern. By the end of the twentieth century, however, most of the protected populations were non-white, non-Christian groups. How we intervene has changed. Humanitarian intervention now must be multilateral in order to be acceptable and legitimate. Since 1945 states have consistently rejected attempts to justify unilateral interventions as "humanitarian"; in the nineteenth century, however, they were accepted. Our military goals and definitions of "success" have also changed. Powerful states in the nineteenth century could simply install a government they liked as a result of these operations. Today we can only install a process, namely elections. Given that elections often do not produce humane and just leaders (despite occasional attempts to manipulate them to do so), this may not be a particularly functional change, but it is a necessary one in the current international normative context.

By "humanitarian intervention" I mean deploying military force across borders for the purpose of protecting foreign nationals from man-made violence. Interventions to protect foreign nationals from natural disasters are excluded from the analysis. I am interested in the changing purpose of force, and, in such cases, militaries are not using force but are deployed in a completely consensual manner for their logistical and technical capabilities. Similarly interventions to protect a state's *own* nationals from abuse are excluded in this analysis. Although international legal scholars once categorized such interventions as humanitarian, these do not present the same intellectual puzzles about interests since protecting one's own nationals is clearly connected to conventional understandings of national interest.[1]

The analysis proceeds in five parts. The first shows that realist and neoliberal approaches to international politics do not provide good explanations of humanitarian intervention as a practice, much less how they have changed over time,

because the interests they emphasize do not seem to correlate with these interventions. A more inductive approach that attends to the role of normative and ethical understandings can remedy this by allowing us to problematize interests and the way they change. In the second section I demonstrate that change has, indeed, occurred by examining humanitarian intervention practices in the nineteenth century and inducing a sketch of the norms governing behavior in that period from both the military actions taken and the way leaders spoke of them. Among the findings is the sharply circumscribed understanding of who was "human" and could successfully claim protection from powerful states. The third section traces the expansion of this definition of "humanity" by examining efforts to abolish slavery, the slave trade, and colonization. Although these were not the only arenas in which people fought to expand the West's definition of "humanity," they were important ones that involved military coercion, and thus they provide insight into intermediate stages in the evolution of links between humanitarian claims and military action. The fourth section briefly reviews humanitarian intervention as a state practice since 1945, paying particular attention to non-cases, that is, cases where humanitarian action could or should have been claimed but was not. These cases suggest that sovereignty and self-determination norms trumped humanitarian claims during the Cold War, a relationship that no longer holds with consistency. They further suggest that unilateral intervention, even for humanitarian purposes, is normatively suspect in contemporary politics and that states will work hard to construct multilateral coalitions for this purpose. The chapter concludes by comparing the goals or end states sought by intervenors in the nineteenth century versus the twentieth and argues that contemporary intervention norms contain powerful contradictions that make "success" difficult to achieve, not for material or logistical reasons but for normative ones.

Understanding Humanitarian Action

Humanitarian intervention looks odd from conventional perspectives on international politics because it does not conform to the conceptions of interest that they specify. Realists would expect to see some geostrategic or political advantage to be gained by intervening states. Neoliberals might emphasize economic or trade advantages for intervenors. These are hard to find in most post-1989 cases. The 1992–93 U.S. action in Somalia was a clear case of intervention without obvious interests. Economically Somalia was insignificant to the United States. Security interests are also hard to find. The United States had voluntarily given up its base at Berbera in Somalia, because advances in communications and aircraft technology made it obsolete for the communications and refueling purposes it once served. Further, the U.S. intervention in that country was not carried out in a way that would have furthered strategic interests. If the United States truly had had designs on Somalia, it should have welcomed the role of disarming the clans. It did not. The United States resisted UN pressure to "pacify" the country as part of its mission. In fact, U.S. officials were clearly and consistently interested not in controlling any part of Somalia but in getting out of the country as soon as possible—sooner, indeed, than the UN would have liked. That some administration officials opposed the Somalia intervention on precisely the grounds that no vital U.S. interest was involved underscores the realists' problem.

The massive intervention under UN auspices to reconstruct Cambodia in the early 1990s presented similar anomalies. Like Somalia, Cambodia was economically insignificant to the intervenors and, with the Cold War ended, was strategically significant to none of the five powers on the Security Council except China, which bore very little of the intervention burden. Indeed, U.S. involvement appears to have been motivated by domestic opposition to the return of the Khmers Rouges on moral grounds—another anomaly for these approaches—rather than by geopolitical or economic interests. Kosovo and Bosnia touched the security interests of the major intervenor, the United States, only derivatively in that those states are in Europe. However, events in these places did not prompt intervention from major European powers, whose interests would presumably be much more involved, despite much U.S. urging. These targets are outside the NATO alliance and hence trigger none of that alliance's security guarantees; in both cases, moreover, intervention served no strong domestic constituency and was militarily and politically risky.

Liberals of a more classical and Kantian type might argue that these interventions were motivated by an interest in promoting democracy and liberal values. After all, the UN's political blueprint for reconstructing these states after intervention has occurred is a liberal one. However, these arguments run afoul of the evidence. The United States consistently refused to take on the state building and democratization mission in Somalia, which liberal arguments would have expected to have been at the heart of U.S. efforts. Similarly the UN stopped short of authorizing an overthrow of Saddam Hussein in Iraq in 1991, even when this was militarily possible and was supported by many in the U.S. armed forces. The United Nations, NATO, and especially the United States have emphasized the humanitarian rather than democratizing nature of these interventions, both rhetorically and in their actions on the ground.

None of these realist or liberal approaches provides an answer to the question: "What interests are intervening states pursuing?" A generous interpretation would conclude that realism and liberalism simply are not helpful in understanding these interventions, since the specification of interests is outside their analysis. To the extent that these approaches *do* specify interests, however, those specifications appear wrong in these cases.

The failure of these approaches leads me to adopt another method of analysis. Lacking any good alternative explanation that casts doubt on them, I take the intervenors' humanitarian claims seriously and try to untangle what, exactly, they mean by "humanitarian intervention," what makes those claims compelling to states, and what constraints exist on this kind of behavior. When intervenors claim humanitarian motives, I want to know what it means to them to be "humanitarian"— what action does that entail (or not entail). I want to know what kinds of claims prompt a humanitarian intervention (and what claims do not). I want to know the extent to which and the ways in which "humanitarianism" competes with (or complements) other kinds of incentives states might have to intervene (or not to intervene). This last point is important. Although there have been a rash of interventions since 1989 that look particularly altruistic, all interventions are prompted by a mixture of motivations in some way. Even if the principal decision maker had only one consideration in mind (which is unlikely), the vast number of people involved in these operations, often people from different intervening states, bring different motivations to bear on the intervention as it unfolds. Humanitarian motivations will interact differently with other state goals, depending on how humanitarian action is defined and what other kinds of goals states have. These definitions may change over time. For example, antidemocratic human rights abusers have now been defined as threats to international peace and security, which might explain why many more humanitarian interventions were undertaken in the 1990s than in any previous ten-year period.[2]

The empirical evidence presented here consistently points to the interwoven and interdependent character of norms that influence international behavior. Humanitarianism—its influence and definition—is bound up in other normative changes, particularly sovereignty norms and human rights norms. Mutually reinforcing and consistent norms appear to strengthen one another; success in one area (such as abolishing slavery) strengthens and legitimates new claims in logically and morally related norms (such as human rights and humanitarian intervention). The relationship identified here between slavery, sovereignty, and humanitarian intervention suggests the importance of viewing norms not as individual "things" floating atomistically in some international social space but rather as part of a highly structured social context. It may make more sense to think of a fabric of interlocking and interwoven norms rather than to think of individual norms concerning a specific issue, as current scholarship, my own included, has been inclined to do. Change in one set of norms may open possibilities for, and even logically or ethically require changes in, other norms and practices. Without attending to these relationships, we will miss the larger picture.[3]

Humanitarian Intervention in the Nineteenth Century

Before the twentieth century virtually all instances of military intervention to protect people other than the intervenor's own nationals involved protection of Christians from the Ottoman Turks.[4] In at least four instances during the nineteenth century European states used humanitarian claims to influence Balkan policy in ways that would have required states to use force—the Greece War for Independence (1821–27); in Syria/Lebanon (1860–61); during the Bulgarian agitation of 1876–78; and in response to the Armenian massacres (1894–1917). Although not all these instances led to a full-scale military intervention, the claims made and their effects an policy in the other cases shed light on the evolution and influence of humanitarian claims during this period. I give a brief account of each incident below, highlighting commonalities and change.

Greek War for Independence (1821–1827)

Russia took an immediate interest in the Greek insurrection and threatened to use force against the Turks as early as the first year of the war. In part its motivations were geostrategic; Russia had been pursuing a general strategy of weakening the Ottomans and consolidating control in the Balkans for years. But the justifications Russia offered were largely humanitarian. Russia had long seen itself as the defender of Orthodox Christians under Turkish rule. Atrocities, such as the wholesale massacres of Christians and sale of women into slavery, coupled with the Sultan's order to seize the Venerable Patriarch of the Orthodox Church after mass on Easter morning, hang him and three Archbishops, and then have the bodies thrown into the Bosphorus, formed the centerpiece of Russia's complaints against the Turks and the justification of its threats of force.[5]

Other European powers, with the exception of France, opposed intervention largely because they were concerned that weakening Turkey would strengthen Russia.[6] However, although the governments of Europe seemed little affected by these atrocities, significant segments of their publics were. A Philhellenic movement had spread throughout Europe, especially in the more democratic societies of Britain, France, and parts of Germany. The movement drew on two popular sentiments: the European identification with the classical Hellenic tradition and the appeal of Christians oppressed by the Infidel. Philhellenic aid societies in Western Europe sent large sums of money and even volunteers, including Lord Byron, to Greece during the war. Indeed, it was a British Captain Hastings who commanded the Greek flotilla that destroyed a Turkish squadron off Salona and provoked the decisive battle at Navarino.[7] Russian threats of unilateral action against the Sultan eventually forced the British to become involved, and in 1827 the two powers, together with Charles X of France in his capacity as "Most Christian King," sent an armada that roundly defeated Ibrahim at Navarino in October 1827.

It would be hard to argue that humanitarian considerations were the only reason to intervene in this case; geostrategic factors were also very important. However, humanitarian disasters were the catalyst for intervention, galvanizing decision makers and powerful domestic elites. Humanitarianism also provided the public justification for intervention, and the episode is revealing about humanitarian intervention norms in several ways. First, it illustrates the circumscribed definition of who was "human" in the nineteenth-century conception. Massacring Christians was a humanitarian disaster; massacring Muslims was not. There were plenty of atrocities on both sides in this conflict. Many of the massacres of Christians by Ottomans were in response to previous massacres of Muslims at Morea and elsewhere in April 1821. For example, Greek Christians massacred approximately eight thousand Turkish Muslims in the town of Tripolitza in 1821. In all, about twenty thousand Muslims were massacred during the war in Greece without causing concern among the Great Powers. Since, under the law of the Ottoman Empire, the Christian Patriarch of Constantinople was responsible for the good behavior of his flock, his execution was viewed justified on grounds of these atrocities against Muslims.[8] The European Powers, however, were impressed only by the murder of Christians and less troubled about the fact that the initial atrocities of the war were committed by the Christian insurgents (admittedly after years of harsh Ottoman rule). The initial Christian uprising at Morea "might well have been allowed to burn itself out 'beyond the pale of civilization'"; it was only the wide-scale and very visible atrocities against Christians that put the events on the agenda of major powers.[9]

Second, intervening states, particularly Russia and France, placed humanitarian factors together with religious considerations at the center for their continued calls for intervention and application of force. As will be seen in other nineteenth-century cases, religion was important in both motivating humanitarian action and defining who is human. Notions about Christian charity supported general humanitarian impulses, but specific religious identifications had the effect of privileging certain people over others. In this case Christians were privileged over Muslims. Elsewhere, as later in Armenia and Bulgaria, denominational differences within Christianity appear important both in motivating action and in restraining it.

Third, the intervention was multilateral. The reasons in this case were largely geostrategic (restraining Russia from temptation to use this intervention for other purposes), but, as subsequent discussion will show, multilateralism as a characteristic of legitimate intervention becomes increasingly important.

Fourth, mass publics were involved. Not only did public opinion influence policy making in a diffuse way, but publics were organized transnationally in ways that strongly foreshadow humanitarian activity by nongovernmental organizations (NGOs) in the late twentieth century. Philhellenism was a more diffuse movement than the bureaucratized NGOs we have now, but the individual Philhellenic societies communicated across national borders and these groups were able to supply both military and financial aid directly to partisans on the ground, bypassing their governments.

Lebanon/Syria (1860–1861)

In May 1860 conflict between Druze and Maronite populations broke out in what is now Lebanon but at the time was Syria under Ottoman rule. Initial rioting became wholesale massacre of Maronite populations, first by the Druze and later by Ottoman troops. The conflict sparked outrage in the French popular press. As early as 1250, Louis IX signed a charter with the Maronite Christians in the Levant guaranteeing protection as if they were French subjects and, in effect, making them part of the French nation. Since then, France had styled itself as the "protector" of Latin Christians in the Levant. Napoleon III thus eagerly supported military intervention in the region at least in part to placate "outraged Catholic opinion" at home. Russia was also eager to intervene, and Britain became involved in the intervention to prevent France and Russia from using the incident to expand.[10]

On August 3, 1860, the six Great Powers (Austria, France, Britain, Prussia, Russia, and Turkey) signed a protocol authorizing the dispatch of twelve thousand European troops to the region to aid the Sultan in stopping violence and establishing order. A letter from the French foreign minister, Thouvenal, to the French ambassador in Turkey stressed that "the object of the mission is to assist stopping, by prompt and energetic measures, the effusion of blood, and [to put] an end to the outrages committed against Christians, which cannot remain unpunished." The protocol further emphasized the lack of strategic and political ambitions of the Powers acting in this matter.[11]

France supplied half of the twelve thousand troops immediately and dispatched them in August 1860. The other states sent token warships and high-ranking officers but no ground troops, which meant that, in the end, the six thousand French troops were the sum total of the intervention force. The French forces received high marks for their humanitarian conduct while in the region, putting a stop to the fighting and helping villagers to rebuild homes and farms. They left when agreement was reached among the Powers for Christian representation in the government of the region.[12]

This case repeats many of the features of the Greek intervention. Again, saving Christians was central to the justification for intervention. Public opinion seems to have some impact, this time on the vigor with which Napoleon pursued an interventionist policy. The multilateral character of the intervention was different, however, in that there was multilateral consultation and agreement on the intervention plan but execution was essentially unilateral.

The Bulgarian Agitation (1876–1878)

In May 1876 Ottoman troops massacred unarmed and poorly organized agitators in Bulgaria. A British government investigation put the number killed at twelve thousand with fifty-nine villages destroyed and an entire church full of people set ablaze after they had already surrendered to Ottoman soldiers. The investigation confirmed that Ottoman soldiers and officers were promoted and decorated rather than punished for these actions.[13] Accounts of the atrocities gathered by American missionaries and sent to British reporters began appearing in British newspapers in mid-June. The reports inflamed public opinion, and protest meetings were organized throughout the country, particularly in the North where W. T. Stead and his paper, the *Northern Echo,* were a focus of agitation.[14]

The result was a split in British politics. Prime Minister Disraeli publicly refused to change British policy of support for Turkey over the matter, stating that British material interests outweighed the lives of Bulgarians.[15] However, Lord Derby, the Conservative foreign secretary, telegraphed Constantinople that "any renewal of the outrages would be more fatal to the Porte than the loss of a battle."[16] More important, former prime minister Gladstone came out of retirement to oppose Disraeli on the issue, making the Bulgarian atrocities the centerpiece of his anti-Disraeli campaign.[17] Although Gladstone found a great deal of support

in various public circles, he did not have similar success in government. The issue barely affected British policy. Disraeli was forced to carry out the investigation mentioned above, and did offer proposals for internal Ottoman reforms to protect minorities—proposals Russia rejected as being too timid.[18]

Russia was the only state to intervene in the wake of the Bulgarian massacres. The treaty that ended the Crimean War was supposed to protect Christians under Ottoman rule. Russia justified her threats of force on the basis of Turkey's violation of these humanitarian guarantees. In March 1877 the Great Powers issued a protocol reiterating demands for the protection of Christians in the Ottoman Empire guaranteed in the 1856 treaty ending the Crimean War. After Constantinople rejected the protocol, Russia sent in troops in April 1877. Russia easily defeated the Ottoman troops and signed the Treaty of San Stefano, which created a large independent Bulgarian state—an arrangement that was drastically revised by the Congress of Berlin.

As in the previous cases, saving Christians was an essential feature of this incident, and Gladstone and Russia's justifications for action were framed in this way. However, military action in this case was not multilateral; Russia intervened unilaterally and, although other powers worried about Russian opportunism and how Russian actions might alter the strategic balance in the region, none said that the intervention was illegitimate or unacceptable because it was unilateral. Public opinion and the media, in particular, were powerful influences on the politics of this episode. Transnational groups, mostly church and missionary groups, were a major source of information for publics in powerful states about the atrocities being committed. These groups actively worked to get information out of Bulgaria and into the hands of sympathetic media outlets in a conscious attempt to arouse public opinion and influence policy in ways that resemble current NGO activist tactics. Although public opinion was not able to change British policy in this case, it was able to make adherence to that policy much more difficult for Disraeli in domestic terms.

Armenia (1894–1917)

The Armenian case offers some interesting insights into the scope of Christianity requiring defense by European powers in the last century. Unlike the Orthodox Christians in Greece and Bulgaria and the Maronites in Syria, the Armenian Christians had no European champion. The Armenian Church was not in communion with the Orthodox Church, hence Armenian appeals had never resonated in Russia; the Armenians were not portrayed as "brothers" to the Russians as were the Bulgarians and other Orthodox Slavs. Similarly, no non-Orthodox European state had ever offered protection nor did they have historical ties as the French did with the Maronites. Thus many of the reasons to intervene in other cases were lacking in the Armenian case.

That the Armenians were Christians, albeit of a different kind, does seem to have had some influence on policy. The Treaty of Berlin explicitly bound the Sultan to carry out internal political reforms to protect Armenians, but the nature, timing, and monitoring of these provisions were left vague and were never enforced. The Congress of Berlin ignored an Armenian petition for an arrangement similar to that set up in Lebanon following the Maronite massacres (a Christian governor under Ottoman rule). Gladstone took up the matter in 1880 when he returned to power but dropped it when Bismarck voiced opposition.[19]

The wave of massacres against Armenians beginning in 1894 was far worse than any of the other atrocities examined here in terms of both the number killed or the brutality of their executions. Nine hundred people were killed and twenty-four villages burned in the Sassum massacres in August 1894. After this the intensity increased. Between fifty thousand and seventy thousand were killed in 1895. In 1896 the massacres moved into Constantinople where, on August 28–29, six thousand Armenians were killed in the capital.[20]

These events were well known and highly publicized in Europe.[21] Gladstone came out of retirement yet again to denounce the Ottomans and called Abd-ul-Hamid the "Great Assassin." French writers denounced him as "the Red Sultan." The European Powers demanded an inquiry, which produced extensive documentation of "horrors unutterable, unspeakable, unimaginable by the mind of man" for European governments and the press.[22] Public opinion pressed for intervention, and both Britain and France used humanitarian justifications to threaten force. However, neither acted. Germany by this time was a force to be reckoned with, and the Kaiser was courting Turkey. Russia was nervous about nationalist aspirations in the Balkans generally and had no special affection for the Armenians, as noted above. Their combined opposition made the price of intervention higher than either the British or French were willing to pay.[23]

These four episodes are suggestive in several ways. They make it very clear that humanitarian intervention is not new in the twentieth century. The role played by what we now call "transnational civil society" or NGOs is also not new. There certainly were far fewer of these organizations and the networks of ties were much thinner, but they did exist and have influence even 180 years ago.

These episodes also say something about the relationship of humanitarian goals to other foreign-policy goals in the period. Humanitarian action was never taken when it jeopardized other articulated goals or interests of a state. Humanitarians were sometimes able to mount considerable pressure on policy makers to act contrary to stated geostrategic interests, as in the case of Disraeli and the Bulgarian agitation, but they never succeeded.

Humanitarian claims did succeed, however, in creating new interests and new reasons for states to act where none had existed. Without the massacre of Maronites in Syria, France would almost certainly not have intervened. It is less clear whether there would have been intervention in the Greek war for independence or in Bulgaria without humanitarian justifications for such interventions. Russia certainly had other reasons to intervene in both cases, but Russia was also the state that identified most with the Orthodox Christians being massacred. Whether the humanitarian claims from fellow Orthodox Christians alone would have been sufficient for intervention without any geostrategic issues at stake is impossible to know. The role of humanitarian claims in these cases thus seems to be constitutive and permissive rather than determinative. Humanitarian appeals created interests where none previously existed and provided legitimate justifications for intervention that otherwise might not have been taken; however, they certainly did not require intervention or override alliance commitments or realpolitik understandings of national security and foreign policy making.

Humanitarian intervention in the nineteenth century could be implemented in a variety of ways. Action could be multilateral, as in the case of Greek independence, unilateral, as when Russia intervened in Bulgaria, or some mixture of the two, as in Lebanon/Syria where intervention was planned by several states but execution was unilateral. As shown below, this variety of forms for intervention changes over time. Specifically the unilateral option for either the planning or execution of humanitarian intervention appears to have disappeared in the twentieth century, and multilateral options have become more elaborate and institutionalized.

Finally, and perhaps most significant, intervenors found reasons to identify with the victims of humanitarian disasters in some important and exclusive way. The minimal rationale for such identification was that the victims to be protected

by intervention were Christians; there were no instances of European powers considering intervention to protect non-Christians. Pogroms against Jews did not provoke intervention. Neither did Russian massacres of Turks in Central Asia in the 1860s.[24] Neither did mass killings in China during the Taiping Rebellion against the Manchus.[25] Neither did mass killings by colonial rulers in their colonies.[26] Neither did massacres of Native Americans in the United States. Often a more specific identification or social tie existed between intervenor and intervened, as between the Orthodox Slav Russians and the Orthodox Slav Bulgarians. In fact, as the Armenian case suggests, the lack of an intense identification may contribute to inaction.

Over time, these exclusive modes of identification changed in European powers. People in Western states began to identify with non-Western populations during the twentieth century with profound political consequences, among them a greater tendency to undertake humanitarian intervention. Longer-standing identifications with Caucasians and Christians continue to be strong. That non-Christians and non-whites are now sometimes protected does not mean that their claims are equally effective as those of Christians and whites. But that their claims are entertained at all, and that these people are sometimes protected, is new. It is not the fact of humanitarian behavior that has changed but its focus. The task at hand is to explain how extending and deepening this identification to other groups changed humanitarian intervention.

The Expansion of "Humanity" and Sovereignty

The expansion of "humanity" between the nineteenth and late twentieth centuries drives much of the change we see in humanitarian intervention behavior, both directly and indirectly. It does this directly by creating identification with and legitimating normative demands by people who previously were invisible in the politics of the West. It contributes to change indirectly through the role it plays in promoting and legitimating new norms of sovereignty, specifically anticolonialism and self-determination. These changes in understandings about humanity and sovereignty obviously do much more than change humanitarian intervention. They alter the purpose of force broadly in world politics, changing the way people think about legitimate and effective uses of state coercion in a variety of areas. Understandings that shape social purpose do not exist, after all, in a vacuum. Social purpose is formed by a dense web of social understandings that are logically and ethically interrelated and, at least to some degree, mutually supporting. Thus changes in one strand of this web tend to have wide effects, causing other kinds of understandings to adjust. Social psychological mechanisms, such as cognitive dissonance, contribute to this process, but so, too, do institutional processes. People who are confronted with the fact that they hold contradictory views will try to adjust their beliefs to alleviate dissonance between them. Similarly lawyers and judges recognize "logical coherence" as a powerful standard for arbitrating between competing normative claims within the law; norms that no longer "fit" within the larger normative fabric of understandings are likely to be rejected in judicial processes and lose the support of associated social institutions.[27]

Like humanitarian intervention, slavery and colonialism were two large-scale activities in which state force intersected with humanitarian claims in the nineteenth century. In many ways slavery was the conceptual opposite of humanitarian intervention: It involved the use of state force to deny and suppress claims about humanitarian need rather than to provide protection. The effort to stamp out the slave trade raises cross-border

humanitarian issues that reveal the limits in when states would use force and provides an interesting comparison with our intervention cases. Colonialism connects views about humanity with understandings about legitimate sovereignty and political organization. Colonialism was justified initially, in part, as a humane form of rule. The West was bringing the benefits of civilization to those in need. Decolonization involved turning this understanding of "humane" politics on its head, and the sovereignty norms that emerged from that struggle are extremely important to the subsequent practices of humanitarian intervention. If, indeed, changes in understandings about "humanity" have broad, interrelated effects, we should expect to see these transformed understandings reshaping states' policies and their use of force in dealing with colonialism.

Abolition of Slavery and the Slave Trade

The abolition of slavery and the slave trade in the nineteenth century were essential to the universalization of "humanity." European states generally accepted and legalized both slavery and the slave trade in the seventeenth and eighteenth centuries, but by the nineteenth century these same states proclaimed these practices "repugnant to the principles of humanity and universal morality."[28] Human beings previously viewed as beyond the edge of humanity—as being property—came to be viewed as human, and with that status came certain, albeit minimal, privileges and protections. For example, states did use military force to suppress the slave trade. Britain was particularly active in this regard and succeeded in having the slave trade labeled as piracy, thus enabling Britain to seize and board ships sailing under non-British flags that were suspected of carrying contraband slaves.[29]

Although in some ways this is an important case of a state using force to promote humanitarian ends, the fashion in which the British framed and justified their actions also speaks to the limits of humanitarian claims in the early to mid-nineteenth century. First, the British limited their military action to abolishing the *trade* in slaves, not slavery itself. No military intervention was undertaken on behalf of endangered Africans in slavery as it had been on behalf of endangered white Christians. Further, although the British public and many political figures contributed to a climate of international opinion that viewed slavery with increasing distaste, the abolition of slavery as a domestic institution of property rights was accomplished in each state where it had previously been legal without other states intervening militarily.[30] Moreover, the British government's strategy for ending the slave trade was to label such trafficking as piracy, which in turn meant the slaves were "contraband," that is, still property. The British justified their actions on the basis of Maritime Rights governing commerce. The practices of slavery and slaveholding themselves did not provoke the same reaction as Ottoman abuse of Christians. This may be because the perpetrators of the humanitarian violations were "civilized" Christian nations (as opposed to the infidel Turks).[31] Another reason was probably that the targets of these humanitarian violations were black Africans, not "fellow [i.e. white] Christians" or "brother Slavs." Thus it appears that by the 1830s black Africans had become sufficiently "human" that enslaving them was illegal inside Europe, but enslaving them outside Europe was only distasteful. One could keep them enslaved if one kept them at home, within domestic borders. Abuse of Africans did not merit military intervention inside another state.

Slavery itself was thus never the cause of military intervention, and, although trade in slaves did provoke some military action, it was limited in both scope and justification. The abolition of slavery was accomplished in most of the world through either domestic mechanisms (sometimes violent ones, as in the United States) or through the transnational advocacy networks that have been described elsewhere or by both these means.[32] Once accomplished, however, the equality norms that defeated slavery norms fed back into later decisions about humanitarian intervention in interesting ways. For example, accusations of racism aimed at Western states that had provided much more attention and aid to Bosnia than Somalia in the early 1990s were important factors in mobilizing support for the intervention in Somalia, particularly from the U.S. government.[33]

Colonization, Decolonization, and Self-Determination

Justifications for both colonization and decolonization offer additional lenses through which to examine changing understandings of who is "human" and how these understandings shape uses of force. Both processes—colonization and its undoing—were justified, at least in part, in humanitarian terms. However, the understanding of what constituted humanity was different in the two episodes in ways that bear on the current investigation of humanitarian intervention norms.

The vast economic literature on colonization often overlooks the strong moral dimension that many of the colonizers perceived and articulated. Colonization was a crusade. It would bring the benefits of civilization to the "dark" reaches of the earth. It was a sacred trust, the white man's burden, and was mandated by God that these Europeans venture out to parts of the globe unknown to them, bringing what they understood to be a better way of life to the inhabitants there. Colonization for the missionaries and those driven by social conscience was a humanitarian undertaking of huge proportions and, consequently, of huge significance.

Colonialism's humanitarian mission was of a particular kind, however. The mission of colonialism was to "civilize" the non-European world—to bring the "benefits" of European social, political, economic, and cultural arrangements to Asia, Africa, and the Americas. Until these peoples were "civilized" they remained savages, barbarians, less than human. Thus, in a critical sense, the core of the colonial humanitarian mission was to *create* humanity where none had previously existed. Non-Europeans became human in European eyes by becoming Christian, by adopting European-style structures of property rights, by embracing European-style territorial political arrangements, by entering the growing European-based international economy.[34]

Decolonization also had strong humanitarian justifications.[35] By the mid-twentieth century normative understandings about humanity had shifted. Humanity was no longer something one could create by bringing civilization to savages. Rather, humanity was inherent in individual human beings. It had become universalized and was not culturally dependent as it was in earlier centuries. Asians and Africans were now viewed as having human "rights," and among these was the right to determine their own political future—the right to self-determination.

Like other major normative changes, the rise of human rights norms and decolonization are part of a larger, interrelated set of changes in the international normative web. Norms do not just evolve; they coevolve. Those studying norm change generally, and decolonization and slavery specifically, have noted several features of this revolutionary process. The first, as indicated above, comes from international legal scholars who have emphasized the power of logical coherence in creating legitimacy in normative structures.[36] Norms that fit logically with other powerful norms are more likely to become persuasive and to shape behavior. Thus changes in core normative structures (in this case, changes toward recognition of human equality within Europe) provided an ethical platform from which activists could work for normative changes elsewhere in society and a way to frame their appeals that would be powerful. Mutually reinforcing and logically consistent norms appear to be harder to attack and to have an advantage in the normative contestations that occur in social life. In this sense, logic internal to norms themselves shapes their development and, consequently, shapes social change.

Applied to decolonization, the argument would be that the spread of these decolonization norms is the result, at least to some extent, of their "fit" within the logical structure of other powerful pre-existing European norms. As liberal beliefs about the "natural" rights of man spread and gained power within Europe, they influenced Europe's relationship with non-European peoples in important ways. The egalitarian social movements sweeping the European West in the eighteenth and nineteenth centuries were justified with universal truths about the nature and equality of human beings. These notions were then exported to the non-European world as part of the civilizing mission of colonialism. Once people begin to believe, at least in principle, in human equality, there is no logical limit to the expansion of human rights and self-determination.[37]

The logical expansion of these arguments fueled attacks on both slavery and colonization. Slavery, more blatantly a violation of these emerging European norms, came under attack first. Demands for decolonization came more slowly and had to contend with the counter claims for the beneficial humanitarian effects of European rule. However, logic alone could not dismantle these institutions. In both cases former slaves and Western-educated colonial elites were instrumental in change. Having been "civilized" and Europeanized, they were able to use Europe's own norms against these institutions. These people undermined the social legitimacy of both slave holders and colonizers simply by being exemplats of "human" non-Europeans who could read, write, worship, work, and function in Western society. Their simple existence undercut the legitimacy of slavery and colonialism within a European framework of proclaimed human equality.

Another feature that channels contemporary normative coevolution is the rational-legal structure in which it is embedded. Increasingly since the nineteenth century international normative understandings have been codified in international law, international regimes, and the mandates of formal international organizations. To the extent that legal processes operate, the logical coherence processes described above will be amplified, since law requires explicit demonstrations of such logical fit to support its claims. International organizations, too, can amplify the power of new normative claims if these are enshrined in their mandates, structure, or operating procedures. For example, the United Nations played a significant role in the decolonization process and the consolidation of anticolonialism norms. Self-determination norms are proclaimed in the UN Charter, but the organization also contained Trusteeship machinery and one-state-one-vote voting structures that gave majority power to the weak, often formerly colonized states, all of which contributed to an international legal, organizational, and normative environment that made colonial practices increasingly illegitimate and difficult to carry out.[38]

Humanitarian Intervention since 1945

Unlike humanitarian intervention practices in the nineteenth century, virtually all the instances in which claims of humanitarian intervention have been made in the post-1945 period concern military action on behalf of non-Christians, non-Europeans, or both. Cambodia, Somalia, Bosnian Muslims, Kurds in Iraq, Albanian Muslims in Kosovo all fit this pattern. The "humanity" worth protecting has widened as a result of the normative changes described above. However, humanitarian intervention practices have also become more limited in a different dimension: Intervening

states often shied away from humanitarian claims during the Cold War when they could have made them. One would think that states would claim the moral high ground in their military actions whenever it was at all credible, and strong humanitarian claims were certainly credible in at least three cases; India's intervention in East Pakistan in the wake of massacres by Pakistani troops; Tanzania's intervention in Uganda toppling the Idi Amin regime; and Vietnam's intervention in Cambodia ousting the Khmers Rouges. Amin and Pol Pot were two of the most notorious killers in a century full of infamous brutal leaders. If states could use humanitarian claims anywhere, it should have been in these cases, yet they did not. In fact, India initially claimed humanitarian justifications on the floor of the United Nations but quickly retracted them, expunging statements from the UN record. Why?

The argument here is that this reluctance stems not from norms about what is "humanitarian" but from norms about legitimate intervention. Although the scope of who qualifies as human has widened enormously and the range of humanitarian activities that states routinely undertake has expanded, norms about intervention have also changed, albeit less drastically. Humanitarian military intervention now must be *multilateral* to be legitimate; without multilateralism, claims of humanitarian motivation and justification are suspect.[39] As we saw in the nineteenth century, multilateralism is not new; it has often characterized humanitarian military action. However, states in the nineteenth century still invoked and accepted humanitarian justifications even when intervention was unilateral (for example, Russia in Bulgaria during the 1870s, and, in part, France in Lebanon). That did not happen in the twentieth century nor has it happened in the twenty-first century. Without multilateralism, states will not and apparently cannot successfully claim humanitarian justification.[40]

The move to multilateralism is not obviously dictated by the functional demands of intervention or military effectiveness. Certainly multilateralism had (and has) important advantages for states. It increases the transparency of each state's actions to others and so reassures states that opportunities for adventurism and expansion will not be used. It can be a way of sharing costs and thus be cheaper for states than unilateral action. However, multilateralism carries with it significant costs of its own. Cooperation and coordination problems involved in such action, an issue political scientists have examined in detail, can make it difficult to sustain multilateral action.[41] Perhaps more important, multilateral action requires the sacrifice of power and control over the intervention. Further, it may seriously compromise the military effectiveness of those operations, as recent debates over command and control in UN military operations suggest.

There are no obvious efficiency reasons for states to prefer either multilateral or unilateral intervention to achieve humanitarian ends. Each type of intervention has advantages and disadvantages. The choice depends, in large part, on perceptions about the political acceptability and political costs of each, which, in turn, depend on the normative context. As is discussed below, multilateralism in the present day has become institutionalized in ways that make unilateral intervention, particularly intervention not justified as self-defense, unacceptably costly, not in material terms but in social and political terms. A brief examination of these "noncases" of humanitarian intervention and the way that states debated and justified these actions provides some insight into the normative fabric of contemporary intervention and the limitations these impose on humanitarian action.

Unilateral Interventions in Humanitarian Disasters[42]

a. *India in East Pakistan (1971).* Pakistan had been under military rule by West Pakistani officials since partition. When the first free elections were held in November 1970, the Awami League won 167 out of 169 parliamentary seats reserved for East Pakistan in the National Assembly. The Awami League had not urged political independence for the East during the elections but did run on a list of demands concerning one-man-one-vote political representation and increased economic autonomy for the East. The government in the West viewed the Awami League's electoral victory as a threat. In the wake of these electoral results, the government in Islamabad decided to postpone the convening of the new National Assembly indefinitely, and in March 1971 the West Pakistani army started killing unarmed civilians indiscriminately, raping women, burning homes, and looting or destroying property. At least one million people were killed, and millions more fled across the border into India.[43] Following months of tension, border incidents, and increased pressure from the influx of refugees, India sent troops into East Pakistan. After twelve days the Pakistani army surrendered at Dacca, and the new state of Bangladesh was established.

As in many of the nineteenth-century cases, the intervenor here had an array of geopolitical interests. Humanitarian concerns were not the only reason, or even, perhaps, the most important reason, to intervene. However, this is a case in which intervention could be justified in humanitarian terms, and initially the Indian representatives in both the General Assembly and the Security Council did articulate such a justification.[44] These arguments were widely rejected by other states, including many with no particular interest in politics on the subcontinent. States as diverse as Argentina, Tunisia, China, Saudi Arabia, and the United States all responded to India's claims by arguing that principles of sovereignty and noninterference should take precedence and that India had no right to meddle in what they all viewed as an "internal matter." In response to this rejection of its claims, India retracted its humanitarian justifications, choosing instead to rely on self-defense to defend its actions.[45]

b. Tanzania in Uganda (1979). This episode began as a straightforward territorial dispute. In the autumn of 1978 Ugandan troops invaded and occupied the Kagera salient—territory between the Uganda–Tanzania border and the Kagera River in Tanzania.[46] On November 1 Amin announced annexation of the territory Nyerere considered the annexation tantamount to an act of war and, on November 15, launched an offensive from the south bank of the Kagera River. Amin, fearing defeat, offered to withdraw from the occupied territories if Nyerere would promise to cease support for Ugandan dissidents and agree not to attempt to overthrow his government. Nyerere refused and made explicit his intention to help dissidents topple the Amin regime. In January 1979 Tanzanian troops crossed into Uganda, and, by April, these troops, joined by some Ugandan rebel groups, had occupied Kampala and installed a new government headed by Yusef Lule.

As in the previous case, there were nonhumanitarian reasons to intervene; but if territorial issues were the only concern, the Tanzanians could have stopped at the border, having evicted Ugandan forces, or pushed them back into Uganda short of Kampala. The explicit statement of intent to topple the regime seems out of proportion to the low-level territorial squabble. However, humanitarian considerations clearly compounded other motives in this case. Tesón makes a strong case that Nyerere's intense dislike of Amin's regime and its abusive practices influenced the scale of the response. Nyerere had already publicly called Amin a murderer and refused to sit with him on the Authority of the East African Community.[47] Tesón also presents strong evidence that the lack of support or material help for Uganda in this intervention from the UN, the Organization of African Unity (OAU), or any state besides Libya suggests tacit international acceptance of what otherwise would have been universally condemned as international aggression because of the human rights record of the target state.[48]

Despite evidence of humanitarian motivations, Tanzania never claimed humanitarian justification. In fact, Tanzania went out of its way to disclaim responsibility for the felicitous humanitarian outcome of its actions. It claimed only that it was acting in response to Amin's invasion and that its actions just happened to coincide with a revolt against Amin inside Uganda. When Sudan and Nigeria criticized Tanzania for interfering in another state's internal affairs in violation of the OAU charter, it was the new Ugandan regime that invoked humanitarian justifications for Tanzania's actions. The regime criticized the critics, arguing that members of the OAU should not "hide behind the formula of non-intervention when human rights are blatantly being violated."[49]

c. Vietnam in Cambodia (1979). In 1975 the Chinese-backed Khmers Rouges took power in Cambodia and launched a policy of internal "purification" entailing the atrocities and genocide now made famous by the 1984 movie *The Killing Fields.* This regime, under the leadership of Pol Pot, was also aggressively anti-Vietnamese and engaged in a number of border incursions during the late 1970s. Determined to end this border activity, the Vietnamese and an anti–Pol Pot army of exiled Cambodians invaded the country in December 1978, succeeded in routing the Khmers Rouges by January 1979, and installed a sympathetic government under the name People's Republic of Kampuchea (PRK).

Again, humanitarian considerations may not have been central to Vietnam's decision to intervene, but humanitarian justifications would seem to have offered some political cover to the internationally unpopular Vietnamese regime. However, like Tanzania, the Vietnamese made no appeal to humanitarian justifications. Instead, they argued that they were only helping the Cambodian people to achieve self-determination against the neocolonial regime of Pol Pot, which had been "the product of the hegemonistic and expansionist policy of the Peking authorities."[50] Even if Vietnam *had* offered humanitarian justifications for intervention, indications are that other states would have rejected them. A number of states mentioned Pol Pot's appalling human rights violations in their condemnations of Vietnam's action but said, nonetheless, that these violations did not entitle Vietnam to intervene. During the UN debate no state spoke in favor of the right to unilateral humanitarian intervention, and several states (Greece, the Netherlands, Yugoslavia, and India) that had previously supported humanitarian intervention arguments in the UN voted for the resolution condemning Vietnam's intervention.[51]

Multilateral Intervention in Humanitarian Disasters

To be legitimate in contemporary politics, humanitarian intervention must be multilateral. The Cold War made such multilateral efforts politically difficult to orchestrate, but, since 1989, several large-scale interventions have been carried out claiming humanitarian justifications as their raison d'être. All have been multilateral. Most visible among these have been the following:

- the U.S., British, and French efforts to protect Kurdish and Shiite populations inside Iraq following the Gulf War;
- the United Nations Transitional Authority in Cambodia (UNTAC) mission to end civil war and to reestablish a democratic political order in Cambodia;
- the large-scale U.S. and UN effort to end starvation and to construct a democratic state in Somalia;
- deployment of UN and NATO troops to protect civilian, especially Muslim, populations primarily from Serbian forces in Bosnia;
- NATO's campaign to stop the ethnic cleansing of Albanian Muslims in the province of Kosovo, Yugoslavia.

Although these efforts have attracted varying amounts of criticism concerning their effectiveness, their legitimacy has received little or no criticism. Further, and unlike their nineteenth-century counterparts, all have been organized through standing international organizations—most often the United Nations. Indeed, the UN Charter has provided the normative framework in which much of the normative contestation over intervention practices has occurred since 1945. Specifically, the Charter enshrines two principles that at times conflict. On the one hand, Article 2 preserves states' sovereign rights as the organizing principle of the international system. The corollary is a near-absolute rule of nonintervention. On the other hand, Article 1 of the Charter emphasizes human rights and justice as a fundamental mission of the United Nations, and subsequent UN actions (among them, the adoption of the Universal Declaration of Human Rights) have strengthened this claim. Gross humanitarian abuses by states against their own citizens, like those discussed in this chapter bring these two central principles into conflict.

In this struggle between principles, the balance seems to have shifted since the end of the Cold War, and humanitarian claims now frequently trump sovereignty claims. States still may not respond to humanitarian appeals, but they do not hesitate because they think such intervention will be denounced internationally as illegitimate. A brief look at the "non-case" of Rwanda illustrates this. Contemporary humanitarian intervention norms do more than just "allow" intervention. The Genocide Convention actually makes action mandatory. Signatories must stop genocide, defined as "acts committed with intent to destroy, in whole or in part, a national, ethnical, racial or religious group."[52] Although the failure of the West to respond to the Rwandan genocide in 1994 shows that humanitarian claims must compete with other interests states have as they weigh the decision to use force, the episode also reveals something about the normative terrain on which these interventions are debated. In contrast to the Cold War cases, no significant constituency was claiming that intervention in Rwanda for humanitarian purposes would have been illegitimate or an illegal breach of sovereignty. States did not fear the kind of response India received when it intervened in East Pakistan. France, the one state to intervene (briefly and with multilateral authorization) was criticized not because the intervention was illegitimate but because its actions aided the *génocidaires* rather than the victims.[53] States understood very well that legally and ethically this case required intervention, and because they did not want to intervene for other reasons, they had to work hard to suppress information and to avoid the word "genocide" in order to sidestep their obligations.[54] When the killing was (conveniently) over, the American president, Bill Clinton, actually went to Rwanda and apologized for his administration's inaction. While the Rwandan case can be viewed pessimistically as a case where ethics were ignored and states did what was convenient, it also reveals that states understood and publicly acknowledged a set of obligations that certainly did not exist in the nineteenth century and probably not during most of the Cold War. States understood that they had not just a right but a duty to intervene in this case. That the Americans apologized substantiates this.[55]

In addition to a shift in normative burdens to act, intervention norms now place strict requirements on the ways humanitarian intervention can be carried out. Humanitarian intervention must be multilateral when it occurs. It must be organized under multilateral consent. Further, it must be implemented with a multilateral force if at all possible. Specifically the intervention force should contain troops from "disinterested" states, usually middle-level powers outside the region of conflict—another dimension of multilateralism not found in nineteenth-century practice.

Contemporary multilateralism thus differs from the multilateral action of the nineteenth century.

The latter was what John Ruggie might call "quantitative" multilateralism and only thinly so.[56] Nineteenth-century multilateralism was strategic. States intervened together to keep an eye on one another and to discourage adventurism or exploitation of the situation for nonhumanitarian gains. Multilateralism was driven by shared fears and perceived threats, not by shared norms and principles. States did not even coordinate and collaborate extensively to achieve their goals. Military deployments in the nineteenth century may have been contemporaneous, but they were largely separate; there was virtually no joint planning or coordination of operations. This follows logically from the nature of multilateralism, since strategic surveillance of one's partners is not a shared goal but a private one.

Recent interventions exhibit much more of what Ruggie calls the "qualitative dimension" of multilateralism. They are organized according to, and in defense of, "generalized principles" of international responsibility and the use of military force, many of which are codified in the UN Charter, in UN Declarations, and in the UN's standard operating procedures. These principles emphasize international responsibilities for ensuring human rights and justice, and dictate appropriate procedures for intervening such as the necessity of obtaining Security Council authorization for action. They also require that intervening forces be composed not just of troops of more than one state but of troops from disinterested states other than Great Powers—not a feature of nineteenth-century action.

Contemporary multilateralism is deeply political and normative, not just strategic. It is shaped by shared notions about when use of force is legitimate and appropriate. Contemporary legitimacy criteria for use of force, in turn, derive from these shared principles, articulated most often through the UN, about consultation and coordination with other states before acting and about multinational composition of forces. U.S. interventions in Somalia and Haiti were not multilateral because the United States needed the involvement of other states for military or strategic reasons. The United States was capable of supplying the forces necessary and, in fact, did supply the lion's share. No other Great Power was particularly worried about U.S. opportunism in these areas so none joined the action for surveillance reasons. These interventions were multilateral for political and normative reasons. To be legitimate and politically acceptable, the United States needed UN authorization and international participation for these operations. Whereas Russia, France, and Britain tolerated one another's presence in operations to save Christians from the infidel Turk, the United States had to beg other states to join it for a humanitarian operation in Haiti.

Multilateral norms create political benefits for conformance and costs for nonconforming action. They create, in part, the structure of incentives states face. Realists or neoliberal institutionalists might argue that in the contemporary world multilateral behavior is efficient and unproblematically self-interested because multilateralism helps to generate political support for intervention both domestically and internationally. However, this argument only begs the question: *Why* is multilateralism necessary to generate political support? It was not necessary in the nineteenth century. Indeed, multilateralism, as currently practiced, was inconceivable in the nineteenth century. As discussed earlier, nothing about the logic of multilateralism itself makes it clearly superior to unilateral action. Each action has advantages and costs to states, and the costs of multilateral intervention have become abundantly clear in recent UN operations. One testament to the power of these multilateral norms is that states adhere to them even when they know that doing so compromises the effectiveness of the mission. Criticisms of the UN's ineffectiveness for military operations are widespread. That UN involvement continues to be a central feature of these operations, despite the UN's apparent lack of military competence, underscores the power of multilateral norms.[57]

Multilateralism legitimizes action by signaling broad support for the actor's goals. Intervenors use it to demonstrate that their purpose in intervening is not merely self-serving and particularistic but is joined in some way to community interests that other states share.[58] Making this demonstration is often vital in mustering international support for an intervention, as India discovered, and can be crucial in generating domestic support as well. Conversely, failure to intervene multilaterally creates political costs. Other states and domestic constituencies both start to question the aims and motives of intervenors when others will not join and international organizations will not bless an operation. These benefits and costs flow not from material features of the intervention but from the expectations that states and people in contemporary politics share about what constitutes legitimate uses of force. Perceptions of illegitimacy may eventually have material consequences for intervenors, but the motivations for imposing those costs are normative.

Both realist and neoliberal analyses fail to ask where incentives come from. They also fail to ask where interests come from. A century ago the plight of non-white, non-Christians was not an "interest" of Western states, certainly not one that could prompt the deployment of troops. Similarly, a century ago, states saw no interest in multilateral authorization, coordination, and use of troops from "disinterested" states. The argument here is that these interests and incentives have been constituted socially through state practice and the evolution of shared norms through which states act.

Conclusion

Humanitarian intervention practices are not new. They have, however, changed over time in some systemic and important ways. First, the definition of who qualifies as human and is therefore deserving of humanitarian protection by foreign governments has changed. Whereas in the nineteenth century European Christians were the sole focus of humanitarian intervention, this focus has been expanded and universalized such that by the late twentieth century all human beings were treated as equally deserving in the international normative discourse. In fact, states are very sensitive to charges that they are "normatively backward" and still privately harbor distinctions. When Boutros-Ghali, shortly after becoming Secretary-General, charged that powerful states were attending to disasters in white, European Bosnia at the expense of non-white, African Somalia, the United States and other states became defensive, refocused attention, and ultimately launched a full-scale intervention in Somalia before acting in Bosnia.

Second, although humanitarian intervention in the nineteenth century was frequently multilateral, it was not necessarily so. Russia, for example, claimed humanitarian justifications for its intervention in Bulgaria in the 1870s; France was similarly allowed to intervene unilaterally, with no companion force to guard against adventurism. Other states did not contest, much less reject, these claims despite the fact that Russia, at least, had nonhumanitarian motives for intervening. They did, however, reject similar claims by India in the twentieth century. By the twentieth century, not only did multilateralism appear to be necessary to claim humanitarian justifications but sanction by the United Nations or some other formal organization was required. The United States, Britain, and France, for example, went out of their way to find authority in UN resolutions for their protection of Kurds in Iraq.

These changes have not taken place in isolation. Changes in humanitarian intervention behavior are intimately connected with other sweeping changes in the normative fabric that have taken place over the past two centuries. Who counts as human has changed, not just for intervention but in all arenas of social life—slavery, colonialism, but also political participation generally at all levels and in most parts of the world. Similarly multilateralism norms are by no means specific to, or even most consequential for, intervention behavior. As Ruggie and his colleagues have amply documented, these norms pervade virtually all aspects of interstate politics, particularly among the most powerful Western states (which are also the most likely and most capable intervenors).[59] The related proliferation of formal institutions and the ever-expanding use of these rational-legal authority structures to coordinate and implement international decision making are also generalized phenomena. These trends have clear and specific impacts on contemporary humanitarian interventions but are also present and powerful in a wide variety of areas of world politics.[60] These interconnections should not surprise us. Indeed, they are to be expected given both the social psychological and institutional mechanisms at work to resolve normative paradoxes and the ways that these extend normative changes to logically and ethically related areas of social life. Changes as fundamental as the ones examined here, namely, changes in who is human and in the multilateral and rational-legal structure of politics, are logically connected to a vast range of political activity and appear again in other cases of intervention. * * *

NOTES

1. Scholars of international law have increasingly made the distinction I make here and have reserved the term "humanitarian intervention" for military protection of foreign citizens, as I do, in order to follow changing state practice. See Anthony Clark Arend and Robert J. Beck, *International Law and the Use of Force: Beyond the UN Charter Paradigm* (New York: Routledge, 1993), esp. chap. 8; and Fernando Tesón, *Humanitarian Intervention: An Inquiry into Law and Morality* (Dobbs Ferry, NY: Transnational, 1988).

2. For more on the way that respect for human rights has become an integral part of contemporary definitions of "security" and how this was accomplished, most visibly at the UN in the 1970s during the anti-apartheid movement, see Audie Klotz, "Norms Reconstituting Interests: Global Racial Equality and U.S. Sanctions against South Africa," *International Organization* 49, no. 3

(summer 1995); 451–78; Michael Barnett, "Bringing in the New World Order: Liberalism, Legitimacy, and the United Nations," *World Politics* (July 1997): 526–51; and Michael Barnett and Martha Finnemore, "The Politics, Power, and Pathologies of International Organizations," *International Organization* 53, no. 4 (1999): 699–732.

3. That the regimes literature, which brought norms back into the study of international politics in the 1980s, defined norms in issue-specific terms probably influenced this orientation in the scholarship. Arguments about interrelationships between norms and the nature of an overarching social normative structure have been made by sociological institutionalists, legal scholars, and, to a lesser extent, scholars of the English school like Gerrit Gong in his discussion of standards of "civilisation" (Gerrit Gong, *The Standard of "Civilisation" in International Society* [Oxford: Clarendon, 1984]). See the discussion of the content of the world polity in George Thomas, John Meyer, Francisco Ramirez, and John Boli, eds., *Institutional Structure: Constituting State, Society, and the Individual* (Newbury Park, CA: Sage, 1987), esp. chap. 1; John Boli and George M. Thomas, eds., *Constructing World Culture: International Nongovernmental Organizations since 1875* (Stanford: Stanford University Press, 1999), esp. chaps. 1–2 and the conclusion. On the kinds of norm relationships that contribute to legitimacy and fairness, see Thomas M. Franck, *The Power of Legitimacy among Nations* (New York: Oxford University Press, 1990); Thomas M. Franck, *Fairness in International Law and Institutions* (New York: Oxford University Press, 1995); and Gong, *The Standard of "Civilisation."*

4. Intervention in the Boxer Rebellion in China (1898–1900) is an interesting related case. I omit it from the analysis here because the primary goal of intervenors was to protect their own nationals, not the Chinese. But the intervention did have the happy result of protecting a large number of mostly Christian Chinese from slaughter.

5. J. A. R. Marriott, *The Eastern Question: An Historical Study in European Diplomacy* (Oxford: Clarendon, 1917), 183–85. Atrocities continued through the more than five years of the conflict and fueled the Russian claims. Perhaps the most sensational of these were the atrocities Egyptian troops committed under Ibrahim when they arrived to quell the Greek insurrection in 1825 for the Sultan (to whom they were vassals). Egyptian troops began a process of wholesale extermination of the Greek populace, apparently aimed at recolonization of the area by Muslims. This fresh round of horrors was cited by European powers for their final press toward a solution.

6. France had a long-standing protective arrangement with eastern Christians, as described below, and had consistently favored armed intervention (*Cambridge Modern History*, 10:193).

7. William St. Clair, *That Greece Might Still Be Free* (London: Oxford University Press, 1972), 81; C. W. Crawley, *The Question of Greek Independence* (New York: Fertig, 1973), 1: Cambridge Modern History, 10:180, 196.

8. Eric Carlton, *Massacres: An Historical Perspective* (Aldershot, Hants., England: Scolar, 1994), Marriott, *The Eastern Question*, 183; *Cambridge Modern History*, 10:178–83.

9. *Cambridge Modern History*, 10:178–79.

10. R. W. Seton-Watson, *Britain in Europe, 1789 to 1914* (New York: Macmillan, 1937), 419–21; Marc Trachtenberg, "Intervention in Historical Perspective," in *Emerging Norms of Justified Intervention*, ed. Laura W. Reed and Carl Kaysen (Cambridge, MA: American Academy of Arts and Sciences, 1993), 23.

11. Louis B. Sohn and Thomas Buergenthal, *International Protection of Human Rights* (Indianapolis: Bobbs-Merrill, 1973), 156–60.

12. A. L. Tiwabi, *A Modern History of Syria* (London: Macmillan, 1969), 131; Seton-Watson, *Britain in Europe*, 421.

13. Mason Whiting Tyler, *The European Powers and the Near East, 1875–1908* (Minneapolis: University of Minnesota Press, 1925), 66 n.; Seton-Watson, *Britain in Europe*, 519–20; Marriott, *The Eastern Question*, 291–92; *Cambridge Modern History*, 12:384.

14. Seton-Watson, *Britain in Europe*, 519.

15. Mercia Macdermott, *A History of Bulgaria, 1393–1885* (New York: Praeger, 1962), 280.

16. *Cambridge Modern History*, 12:384.

17. Tyler, *European Powers and the Near East*, 70. Gladstone even published a pamphlet on the subject, *The Bulgarian Horrors and the Question of the East*, which sold more than two hundred thousand copies, Seton-Watson, *Britain in Europe*, 519; Marriott, *The Eastern Question*, 293.

18. Macdermott, *History of Bulgaria*, 277; Tyler, *European Powers and the Near East*, 21.

19. *Cambridge Modern History*, 12:415–17; Marriott, *The Eastern Question*, 349–51.

20. Of course, these events late in the nineteenth century were only the tip of the iceberg. More than a million Armenians were killed by Turks during World War I, but the war environment obviates discussions of military intervention.

21. Indeed, there were many firsthand European accounts of the Constantinople massacres since execution gangs even forced their way into the houses of foreigners to execute Armenian servants (*Cambridge Modern History*, 12:417).

22. The quotation is from Lord Rosebery as cited in *Cambridge History of British Foreign Policy*, 3:234.

23. *Cambridge Modern History*, 12:417–18; Sohn and Buergenthal, *International Protection of Human Rights,* 181.

24. For more on this topic, see Stanford J. Shaw and Ezel Kural Shaw, *History of the Ottoman Empire and Modern Turkey*, vol. 2, *Reform, Revolution and Republic: The Rise of Modern Turkey* (Cambridge: Cambridge University Press, 1977).

25. Christopher Hibbert, *The Dragon Wakes: China and the West, 1793–1911* (Newton Abbot, Devon, England: Reader's Union, 1971). Hibbert estimates that the three-day massacre in Nanking alone killed more than one hundred thousand people (*The Dragon Wakes*, 303).

26. In one of the more egregious incidents of this kind the Germans killed sixty-five thousand indigenous inhabitants of German Southwest Africa (Namibia) in 1904. See Barbara Harff, "The Etiology of Genocides," in *Genocide and the Modern Age: Etiology and Case Studies of Mass Death*, ed. Isidor Wallimann and Michael N. Dohkowski (New York: Greenwood, 1987), 46, 56.

27. For more social psychological underpinnings, see Alice Eagly and Shelly Chaiken, *The Psychology of Attitudes* (Fort Worth, TX:

Harcourt Brace Jovanovich, 1993). For more on logical coherence in law, see Franck, *The Power of Legitimacy,* esp. chap. 10.

28. Quotation comes from the Eight Power Declaration concerning the Universal Abolition of the Trade in Negroes, signed February 8, 1815, by Britain, France, Spain, Sweden, Austria, Prussia, Russia, and Portugal; quoted in Leslie Bethell, *The Abolition of the Brazilian Slave Trade* (Cambridge: Cambridge University Press, 1970), 14.

29. Bethell, *Abolition of the Brazilian Stave Trade,* chap. 1. In 1850 Britain went so far as to fire on and board ships in Brazilian ports to enforce anti-slave trafficking treaties (Bethell, *Abolition of the Brazilian Slave Trade,* 329–31). One might argue that such action was a violation of sovereignty and thus qualifies as military intervention, but, if so, they were interventions of a very peripheral kind. Note, too, that British public opinion on abolition of the slave trade was not uniform. See Chaim D. Kaufmann and Robert A. Pape, "Explaining Costly International Moral Action: Britain's Sixty-Year Campaign against the Atlantic Slave Trade," *International Organization* 53, no. 4 (1999): 631–68.

30. The United States is a possible exception. One could argue that the North intervened militarily in the South to abolish slavery. Such an argument would presume that (a) there were always two separate states such that the North's action could be understood as "intervention," rather than civil war, and (b) that abolishing slavery rather than maintaining the Union was the primary reason for the North's initial action. Both assumptions are open to serious question. (The Emancipation Proclamation was not signed until 1863 when the war was already half over.) Thus, although the case is suggestive of the growing power of a broader conception of "humanity," I do not treat it in this analysis.

31. For an extended treatment of the importance of the categories "civilized" and "barbarian" on state behavior in the nineteenth century, see Gong, *The Standard of "Civilisation."*

32. Margaret Keck and Kathryn Sikkink, *Activists beyond Borders* (Ithaca, NY: Cornell University Press, 1998), chap. 2; James Lee Ray, "The Abolition of Slavery and the End of International War," *International Organization* 43, no. 3 (1989): 405–39.

33. See Boutros-Ghali's comment in the July 22, 1992, Security Council meeting. Rep. Howard Wolpe made a similar comment in the House Africa Subcommittee hearings on June 23, 1992, about double standards in policy toward Bosnia and Somalia. The black caucus became galvanized around this "double standard" issue and became a powerful lobbying force in the administration, and its influence was felt by General Colin Powell, then chairman of the Joint Chiefs of Staff, among others. For details of the U.S. decision-making process on Somalia, see John G. Sommer, *Hope Restored? Humanitarian Aid in Somalia, 1990–1994* (Washington, DC: Refugee Policy Group, 1994). For a discussion of Boutros-Ghali and Wolpe, see Sommer, *Hope Restored?* 22 n. 63; for a discussion of Powell, see 30 n. 100.

34. Gerrit Gong provides a much more extensive discussion of what "civilization" meant to Europeans from an international legal perspective. See Gong, *The Standard of "Civilisation."*

35. To reiterate, I am making no claims about the causes of decolonization.

36. For an excellent exposition, see Franck, *The Power of Legitimacy,* esp. chap. 10.

37. Neta Crawford, "Decolonization as an International Norm: The Evolution of Practices, Arguments, and Beliefs," in *Emerging Norms of Justified Intervention,* ed. Laura Reed and Carl Kaysen (Cambridge, MA: American Academy of Arts and Sciences, 1993), 37–61 at 53; Neta Crawford, *Argument and Change in World Politics: Ethics, Decolonization, and Humanitarian Intervention* (New York: Cambridge University Press, 2002).

38. Crawford, "Decolonization as an International Norm," 37–61; Crawford, *Argument and Change in World Politics;* Michael Barnett, "The United Nations and the Politics of Peace: From Juridical Sovereignty to Empirical Sovereignty," *Global Governance* 1 (1995): 79–97.

39. Other authors have noted a similar trend in related areas. David Lumsdaine discusses the role of multilateral versus bilateral giving of foreign aid in his *Moral Vision in International Politics: The Foreign Aid Regime, 1949–1989* (Princeton, NJ: Princeton University Press, 1993)].

40. An interesting exception that proves the rule is the U.S. claim of humanitarian justifications for its intervention in Grenada. First, the human beings to be protected by the intervention were not Grenadians but U.S. nationals. Protecting one's own nationals can still be construed as protecting national interests and is therefore not anomalous or of interest analytically in the way that state action to protect nationals of *other* states is. Second, the humanitarian justification offered by the United States was widely rejected in the international community, which underscores the point made here that states are generally suspicious of unilateral humanitarian intervention. See the discussion in Tesón, *Humanitarian Intervention,* 188–200; and Arend and Beck, *International Law and the Use of Force,* 126–28.

41. Significantly, those who are more optimistic about solving these problems and about the utility of multilateral action rely on norms and shared social purpose to overcome these problems. Norms are an essential part both of regimes and multilateralism in the two touchstone volumes on these topics. See Stephen D. Krasner, ed., *International Regimes* (Ithaca, NY: Cornell University Press, 1983); and [John] Ruggie, [ed.,] *Multilateralism Matters* (New York: Columbia University Press, 1993).

42. These synopses are drawn, in large part, from Tesón, *Humanitarian Intervention,* chap. 8; Michael Akehurst, "Humanitarian Intervention," in *Intervention in World Politics,* ed. Hedley Bull (Oxford: Clarendon, 1984), 95–118; and Arend and Beck, *International Law and the Use of Force,* chap. 8.

43. Estimates of the number of refugees vary wildly. The Pakistani government put the number at two million; the Indian government claimed ten million. Independent estimates have ranged from five to nine million. See Tesón, *Humanitarian Intervention,* 182, including n. 163 for discussion.

44. See ibid., 186 n. 187, for the text of a General Assembly speech by the Indian representative articulating this justification. See also Akehurst, "Humanitarian Intervention," 96.

45. Akehurst concludes that India actually had prior statements concerning humanitarian justifications deleted from the Official Record of the UN ("Humanitarian Intervention," 96–97).

46. Amin attempted to justify this move by claiming that Tanzania had previously invaded Ugandan territory.

47. Tesón, *Humanitarian Intervention*, 164.

48. Ibid., 164–67.

49. As quoted in Akehurst, "Humanitarian Intervention," 99.

50. As quoted ibid., 97 n. 17.

51. One reason for the virtual absence of humanitarian arguments in this case, compared to the Tanzanian case, may have been the way the intervention was conducted. Tanzania exerted much less control over the kind of regime that replaced Amin, making the subsequent Ugandan regime's defense of Tanzania's actions as "liberation" less implausible than were Vietnam's claims that it, too, was helping to liberate Cambodia by installing a puppet regime that answered to Hanoi.

52. The definition in Article 2 of the 1948 Genocide Convention lists the following specific acts as included in the term "genocide": "(a) Killing members of the group; (b) Causing serious bodily or mental harm to members of the group; (c) Deliberately inflicting on the group conditions of life calculated to bring about its physical destruction in whole or in part; (d) Imposing measures intended to prevent births within the group; (e) Forcibly transferring children of the group to another group" (Convention on the prevention and punishment of the crime of genocide, Adopted by Resolution 260 (III) A of the United Nations General Assembly on December 9, 1948. Available at http://www.unhchr.ch/html/menu3/b/p _genoci.htm).

53. For particularly damning accounts, see Philip Gourevitch, *We Wish to Inform You That Tomorrow We Will Be Killed with Our Families* (New York: Farrar, Straus and Giroux, 1998), chap. 11; and Samantha Power, *"A Problem from Hell": America and the Age of Genocide* (New York: Basic Books, 2002), chap. 10.

54. The suppression of a cable from the United Nations Assistance Mission in Rwanda (UNAMIR) commander in Kigali, Dallaire, to his superiors at the Department of Peace Operations in New York (then run by Kofi Annan) was a scandal when it was uncovered. See Philip Gourevitch, *We Wish to Inform You*; Michael Barnett, *Eyewitness to a Genocide: The United Nations and Rwanda* (Ithaca, NY: Cornell University Press, 2002).

55. Samantha Power would probably be unimpressed with this change. She argues that the United States has known about virtually every genocide in the twentieth century and never acted to stop any of them. I do not dispute her claim; rather, we are investigating a different question. Power wants to know why the United States has not acted to stop genocide; I want to know why the United States has done any humanitarian intervention at all. See Power, *"A Problem from Hell."*

56. John G. Ruggie, "Multilateralism: The Anatomy of an Institution," in Ruggie, *Multilateralism Matters,* 6.

57. Contemporary multilateralism is not, therefore, "better" or more efficient and effective than the nineteenth-century brand. I contend only that it is different.

58. For a more generalized argument about the ways international organizations enjoy legitimacy of action because they are able to present themselves as guardians of community interests as opposed to self-seeking states, see Michael N. Barnett and Martha Finnemore, *The Power and Pathologies of International Organizations* (Ithaca, NY: Cornell University Press, forthcoming).

59. Ruggie, *Multilateralism Matters.*

60. Barnett and Finnemore, "The Politics, Power, and Pathologies of International Organizations", Barnett and Finnemore, *The Power and Pathologies of International Organizations.*

9

INTERNATIONAL POLITICAL ECONOMY

Economic issues are critical to understanding international relations in the twenty-first century. In the first selection here, a classic from *U.S. Power and the Multinational Corporation* (1975), Robert Gilpin concisely discusses the relationship between economics and politics. He examines the three basic conceptions of political economy (liberalism, radicalism, and mercantilism), comparing their perspectives on the nature of economic relations, their theories of change, and how they characterize the relationship between economics and politics.

Two other classic articles continue to shape thinking about international political economy in very fundamental ways. Stephen D. Krasner's "State Power and the Structure of International Trade" assesses the proposition that global free trade requires leadership by a single, very powerful hegemonic state that has the resources and incentives to forge an open international economic system. Ronald Rogowski's "Political Cleavages and Changing Exposure to Trade" is a bracingly ambitious attempt to explain major trends in domestic political regimes—for example, whether a country's political coalition will be dominated by landowners, industrial capitalists, or the working class—based on how exposed the country is to trade opportunities and threats. These two concise articles show the power of a simple, sharply formulated insight to shed light on a broad range of basic political questions.

Jeffry Frieden's essay "The Governance of International Finance" is a model of how to bring clear, logical theory to bear on a vitally important contemporary problem: the governance pathologies that contributed to the near-collapse of the global financial system in 2008. Daniel W. Drezner then presents evidence to support his view that the governance system for the international economic system worked effectively to contain the global financial crisis.

Robert Gilpin

THE NATURE
OF POLITICAL ECONOMY

The international corporations have evidently declared ideological war on the "antiquated" nation state. . . . The charge that materialism, modernization and internationalism is the new liberal creed of corporate capitalism is a valid one. The implication is clear: the nation state as a political unit of democratic decision-making must, in the interest of "progress," yield control to the new mercantile mini-powers.[1]

While the structure of the multinational corporation is a modern concept, designed to meet the requirements of a modern age, the nation state is a very old-fashioned idea and badly adapted to serve the needs of our present complex world.[2]

These two statements—the first by Kari Levitt, a Canadian nationalist, the second by George Ball, a former United States undersecretary of state—express a dominant theme of contemporary writings on international relations. International society, we are told, is increasingly rent between its economic and its political organization. On the one hand, powerful economic and technological forces are creating a highly interdependent world economy, thus diminishing the traditional significance of national boundaries. On the other hand, the nation-state continues to command men's loyalties and to be the basic unit of political decision making. As one writer has put the issue, "The conflict of our era is between ethnocentric nationalism and geocentric technology."[3]

Ball and Levitt represent two contending positions with respect to this conflict. Whereas Ball advocates the diminution of the power of the nation-state in order to give full rein to the productive potentialities of the multinational corporation, Levitt argues for a powerful nationalism which could counterbalance American corporate domination. What appears to one as the logical and desirable consequence of economic rationality seems to the other to be an effort on the part of American imperialism to eliminate all contending centers of power.

Although the advent of the multinational corporation has put the question of the relationship between economics and politics in a new guise, it is an old issue. In the nineteenth century, for example, it was this issue that divided classical liberals like John Stuart Mill from economic nationalists, represented by Georg Friedrich List. Whereas the former gave primacy in the organization of society to economics and the production of wealth, the latter emphasized the political determination of economic relations. As this issue is central both to the contemporary debate on the multinational corporation and to the argument of this study, this chapter analyzes the three major treatments of the relationship between economics and politics—that is, the three major ideologies of political economy.

From Robert Gilpin, *U.S. Power and the Multinational Corporation* (New York: Basic Books, 1975), chap. 1.

The Meaning of Political Economy

The argument of this study is that the relationship between economics and politics, at least in the modern world, is a reciprocal one. On the one hand, politics largely determines the framework of economic activity and channels it in directions intended to serve the interests of dominant groups; the exercise of power in all its forms is a major determinant of the nature of an economic system. On the other hand, the economic process itself tends to redistribute power and wealth; it transforms the power relationships among groups. This in turn leads to a transformation of the political system, thereby giving rise to a new structure of economic relationships. Thus, the dynamics of international relations in the modern world is largely a function of the reciprocal interaction between economics and politics.

First of all, what do I mean by "politics" or "economics"? Charles Kindleberger speaks of economics and politics as two different methods of allocating scarce resources: the first through a market mechanism, the latter through a budget.[4] Robert Keohane and Joseph Nye, in an excellent analysis of international political economy, define economics and politics in terms of two levels of analysis: those of structure and of process.[5] Politics is the domain "having to do with the establishment of an order of relations, a structure. . . ."[6] Economics deals with "short-term allocative behavior (i.e., holding institutions, fundamental assumptions, and expectations constant). . . ."[7] Like Kindleberger's definition, however, this definition tends to isolate economic and political phenomena except under certain conditions, which Keohane and Nye define as the "politicization" of the economic system. Neither formulation comes to terms adequately with the dynamic and intimate nature of the relationship between the two.

In this study, the issue of the relationship between economics and politics translates into that between wealth and power. According to this statement of the problem, economics takes as its province the creation and distribution of wealth; politics is the realm of power. I shall examine their relationship from several ideological perspectives, including my own. But what is wealth? What is power?

In response to the question, What is wealth?, an economist-colleague responded, "What do you want, my thirty-second or thirty-volume answer?" Basic concepts are elusive in economics, as in any field of inquiry. No unchallengeable definitions are possible. Ask a physicist for his definition of the nature of space, time, and matter, and you will not get a very satisfying response. What you will get is an *operational* definition, one which is usable: it permits the physicist to build an intellectual edifice whose foundations would crumble under the scrutiny of the philosopher.

Similarly, the concept of wealth, upon which the science of economics ultimately rests, cannot be clarified in a definitive way. Paul Samuelson, in his textbook, doesn't even try, though he provides a clue in his definition of economics as "the study of how men and society *choose* . . . to employ *scarce* productive resources . . . to produce various commodities . . . and distribute them for consumption."[8] Following this lead, we can say that wealth is anything (capital, land, or labor) that can generate future income; it is composed of physical assets and human capital (including embodied knowledge).

The basic concept of political science is power. Most political scientists would not stop here; they would include in the definition of political science the purpose for which power is used, whether this be the advancement of the public welfare or the domination of one group over another. In any case, few would dissent from the following statement of Harold Lasswell and Abraham Kaplan:

The concept of power is perhaps the most fundamental in the whole of political science:

the political process is the shaping, distribution, and exercise of power (in a wider sense, of all the deference values, or of influence in general.)[9]

Power as such is not the sole or even the principal goal of state behavior. Other goals or values constitute the objectives pursued by nation-states: welfare, security, prestige. But power in its several forms (military, economic, psychological) is ultimately the necessary means to achieve these goals. For this reason, nation-states are intensely jealous of and sensitive to their relative power position. The distribution of power is important because it profoundly affects the ability of states to achieve what they perceive to be their interests.

The nature of power, however, is even more elusive than that of wealth. The number and variety of definitions should be an embarrassment to political scientists. Unfortunately, this study cannot bring the intradisciplinary squabble to an end. Rather, it adopts the definition used by Hans Morgenthau in his influential *Politics among Nations*: "man's control over the minds and actions of other men."[10] Thus, power, like wealth, is the capacity to produce certain results.

Unlike wealth, however, power cannot be quantified; indeed, it cannot be overemphasized that power has an important psychological dimension. Perceptions of power relations are of critical importance; as a consequence, a fundamental task of statesmen is to manipulate the perceptions of other statesmen regarding the distribution of power. Moreover, power is relative to a specific situation or set of circumstances; there is no single hierarchy of power in international relations. Power may take many forms—military, economic, or psychological—though, in the final analysis, force is the ultimate form of power. Finally, the inability to predict the behavior of others or the outcome of events is of great significance. Uncertainty regarding the distribution of power and the ability of the statesmen to control events plays an important role in international relations.

Ultimately, the determination of the distribution of power can be made only in retrospect as a consequence of war. It is precisely for this reason that war has had, unfortunately, such a central place in the history of international relations. In short, power is an elusive concept indeed upon which to erect a science of politics.

■ ■ ■

The distinction * * * between economics as the science of wealth and politics as the science of power is essentially an analytical one. In the real world, wealth and power are ultimately joined. This, in fact, is the basic rationale for a political economy of international relations. But in order to develop the argument of this study, wealth and power will be treated, at least for the moment, as analytically distinct.

To provide a perspective on the nature of political economy, the next section of the chapter will discuss the three prevailing conceptions of political economy: liberalism, Marxism, and mercantilism. Liberalism regards politics and economics as relatively separable and autonomous spheres of activities; I associate most professional economists as well as many other academics, businessmen, and American officials with this outlook. Marxism refers to the radical critique of capitalism identified with Karl Marx and his contemporary disciples; according to this conception, economics determines politics and political structure. Mercantilism is a more questionable term because of its historical association with the desire of nation-states for a trade surplus and for treasure (money). One must distinguish, however, between the specific form mercantilism took in the seventeenth and eighteenth centuries and the general outlook of mercantilistic thought. The essence of the mercantilistic perspective, whether it is labeled economic nationalism, protectionism, or the doctrine of the German Historical School, is the subservience of the economy to the state and its interests—interests that range from matters of domestic welfare to those of international security. It is this more general meaning of mercantilism that is implied by the use of the term in this study.

■ ■ ■

Three Conceptions of Political Economy

The three prevailing conceptions of political economy differ on many points. Several critical differences will be examined in this brief comparison. (See Table 9.1.)

The Nature of Economic Relations

The basic assumption of liberalism is that the nature of international economic relations is essentially harmonious. Herein lay the great intellectual innovation of Adam Smith. Disputing his mercantilist predecessors, Smith argued that international economic relations could be made a positive-sum game; that is to say, everyone could gain, and no one need lose, from a proper ordering of economic relations, albeit the distribution of these gains may not be equal. Following Smith, liberalism assumes that there is a basic harmony between true national interest and cosmopolitan economic interest. Thus, a prominent member of this school of thought has written, in response to a radical critique, that the economic efficiency of the sterling standard in the nineteenth century and that of the dollar standard in the twentieth century serve "the cosmopolitan interest in a national form."[11] Although Great Britain and the United States gained the most from the international role of their respective currencies, everyone else gained as well.

Liberals argue that, given this underlying identity of national and cosmopolitan interests in a free market, the state should not interfere with economic transactions across national boundaries.

Table 9.1. Comparison of the Three Conceptions of Political Economy

	LIBERALISM	MARXISM	MERCANTILISM
Nature of economic relations	Harmonious	Conflictual	Conflictual
Nature of the actors	Households and firms	Economic classes	Nation-states
Goal of economic activity	Maximization of global welfare	Maximization of class interests	Maximization of national interest
Relationship between economics and politics	Economics should determine politics	Economics does determine politics	Politics determines economics
Theory of change	Dynamic equilibrium	Tendency toward disequilibrium	Shifts in the distribution of power

Through free exchange of commodities, removal of restrictions on the flow of investment, and an international division of labor, everyone will benefit in the long run as a result of a more efficient utilization of the world's scarce resources. The national interest is therefore best served, liberals maintain, by a generous and cooperative attitude regarding economic relations with other countries. In essence, the pursuit of self-interest in a free, competitive economy achieves the greatest good for the greatest number in international no less than in the national society.

Both mercantilists and Marxists, on the other hand, begin with the premise that the essence of economic relations is conflictual. There is no underlying harmony; indeed, one group's gain is another's loss. Thus, in the language of game theory, whereas liberals regard economic relations as a nonzero-sum game, Marxists and mercantilists view economic relations as essentially a zero-sum game.

The Goal of Economic Activity

For the liberal, the goal of economic activity is the optimum or efficient use of the world's scarce resources and the maximization of world welfare. While most liberals refuse to make value judgments regarding income distribution, Marxists and mercantilists stress the distributive effects of economic relations. For the Marxist the distribution of wealth among social classes is central; for the mercantilist it is the distribution of employment, industry, and military power among nation-states that is most significant Thus, the goal of economic (and political) activity for both Marxists and mercantilists is the redistribution of wealth and power.

The State and Public Policy

These three perspectives differ decisively in their views regarding the nature of the economic actors.

In Marxist analysis, the basic actors in both domestic and international relations are economic classes; the interests of the dominant class determine the foreign policy of the state. For mercantilists, the real actors in international economic relations are nation-states; national interest determines foreign policy. National interest may at times be influenced by the peculiar economic interests of classes, elites, or other subgroups of the society; but factors of geography, external configurations of power, and the exigencies of national survival are primary in determining foreign policy. Thus, whereas liberals speak of world welfare and Marxists of class interests, mercantilists recognize only the interests of particular nation-states.

Although liberal economists such as David Ricardo and Joseph Schumpeter recognized the importance of class conflict and neoclassical liberals analyze economic growth and policy in terms of national economies, the liberal emphasis is on the individual consumer, firm, or entrepreneur. The liberal ideal is summarized in the view of Harry Johnson that the nation-state has no meaning as an economic entity.[12]

Underlying these contrasting views are differing conceptions of the nature of the state and public policy. For liberals, the state represents an aggregation of private interests: public policy is but the outcome of a pluralistic struggle among interest groups. Marxists, on the other hand, regard the state as simply the "executive committee of the ruling class," and public policy reflects its interests. Mercantilists, however, regard the state as an organic unit in its own right: the whole is greater than the sum of its parts. Public policy, therefore, embodies the national interest or Rousseau's "general will" as conceived by the political élite.

The Relationship between Economics and Politics; Theories of Change

Liberalism, Marxism, and mercantilism also have differing views on the relationship between economics and politics. And their differences on this issue are directly relevant to their contrasting theories of international political change.

Although the liberal ideal is the separation of economics from politics in the interest of maximizing world welfare, the fulfillment of this ideal would have important political implications. The classical statement of these implications was that of Adam Smith in *The Wealth of Nations*.[13] Economic growth, Smith argued, is primarily a function of the extent of the division of labor, which in turn is dependent upon the scale of the market. Thus he attacked the barriers erected by feudal principalities and mercantilistic states against the exchange of goods and the enlargement of markets. If men were to multiply their wealth, Smith argued, the contradiction between political organization and economic rationality had to be resolved in favor of the latter. That is, the pursuit of wealth should determine the nature of the political order.

Subsequently, from nineteenth-century economic liberals to twentieth-century writers on economic integration, there has existed "the dream . . . of a great republic of world commerce, in which national boundaries would cease to have any great economic importance and the web of trade would bind all the people of the world in the prosperity of peace."[14] For liberals the long-term trend is toward world integration, wherein functions, authority, and loyalties will be transferred from "smaller units to larger ones; from states to federalism; from federalism to supranational unions and from these to superstates."[15] The logic of economic and technological development, it is argued, has set mankind on an inexorable course toward global political unification and world peace.

In Marxism, the concept of the contradiction between economic and political relations was enacted into historical law. Whereas classical liberals—although Smith less than others—held that the requirements of economic rationality *ought* to determine political relations, the Marxist position was that the mode of production does in fact determine the superstructure of political relations. Therefore, it is argued, history can be understood as the product of the dialectical process—the contradiction between the evolving techniques of production and the resistant sociopolitical system.

Although Marx and Engels wrote remarkably little on international economics, Engels, in his famous polemic, *Anti-Duhring*, explicitly considers whether economics or politics is primary in determining the structure of international relations.[16] E. K. Duhring, a minor figure in the German Historical School, had argued, in contradiction to Marxism, that property and market relations resulted less from the economic logic of capitalism than from extraeconomic political factors: "The basis of the exploitation of man by man was an historical act of force which created an exploitative economic system for the benefit of the stronger man or class."[17] Since Engels, in his attack on Duhring, used the example of the unification of Germany through the Zollverein or customs union of 1833, his analysis is directly relevant to this discussion of the relationship between economics and political organization.

Engels argued that when contradictions arise between economic and political structures, political power adapts itself to the changes in the balance of economic forces; politics yields to the dictates of economic development. Thus, in the case of nineteenth-century Germany, the requirements of industrial production had become incompatible with its feudal, politically fragmented structure. "Though political reaction was victorious in 1815 and again in 1848," he argued, "it was unable to prevent the growth of large-scale industry in Germany and the growing participation of German commerce in the world market."[18] In summary, Engels wrote, "German unity had become an economic necessity."[19]

In the view of both Smith and Engels, the nation-state represented a progressive stage in human development, because it enlarged the political realm of economic activity. In each successive economic epoch, advances in technology and an increasing scale of production necessitate an enlargement of political organization. Because the city-state and feudalism restricted the scale of production and the division of labor made possible by the Industrial Revolution, they prevented the efficient utilization of resources and were, therefore, superseded by larger political units. Smith considered this to be a desirable objective; for Engels it was an historical necessity. Thus, in the opinion of liberals, the establishment of the Zollverein was a movement toward maximizing world economic welfare;[20] for Marxists it was the unavoidable triumph of the German industrialists over the feudal aristocracy.

Mercantilist writers from Alexander Hamilton to Frederich List to Charles de Gaulle, on the other hand, have emphasized the primacy of politics; politics, in this view, determines economic organization. Whereas Marxists and liberals have pointed to the production of wealth as the basic determinant of social and political organization, the mercantilists of the German Historical School, for example, stressed the primacy of national security, industrial development, and national sentiment in international political and economic dynamics.

In response to Engels's interpretation of the unification of Germany, mercantilists would no doubt agree with Jacob Viner that "Prussia engineered the customs union primarily for political reasons, in order to gain hegemony or at least influence over the lesser German states. It was largely in order to make certain that the hegemony should be Prussian and not Austrian that Prussia continually opposed Austrian entry into the Union, either openly or by pressing for a customs union tariff lower than highly protectionist Austria could stomach."[21] In pursuit of this strategic interest, it was "Prussian might, rather than a common zeal for political unification arising out of economic partnership, (that) . . . played the major role."[22]

In contrast to Marxism, neither liberalism nor mercantilism has a developed theory of dynamics. The basic assumption of orthodox economic analysis (liberalism) is the tendency toward equilibrium; liberalism takes for granted the existing social order and given institutions. Change is assumed to be gradual and adaptive—a continuous process of dynamic equilibrium. There is no necessary connection between such political phenomena as war and revolution and the evolution of the economic system, although they would not deny that misguided statesmen can blunder into war over economic issues or that revolutions are conflicts over the distribution of wealth; but neither is inevitably linked to the evolution of the productive system. As for mercantilism, it sees change as taking place owing to shifts in the balance of power; yet, mercantilist writers such as members of the German Historical School and contemporary political realists have not developed a systematic theory of how this shift occurs.

On the other hand, dynamics is central to Marxism; indeed Marxism is essentially a theory of social *change*. It emphasizes the tendency toward *dis*equilibrium owing to changes in the means of production, and the consequent effects on the everpresent class conflict. When these tendencies can no longer be contained, the sociopolitical system breaks down through violent upheaval. Thus war and revolution are seen as an integral part of the economic process. Politics and economics are intimately joined.

Why an International Economy?

From these differences among the three ideologies, one can get a sense of their respective explanations for the existence and functioning of the international economy.

An interdependent world economy constitutes the normal state of affairs for most liberal economists. Responding to technological advances in transportation and communications, the scope of the market mechanism, according to this analysis, continuously expands. Thus, despite temporary setbacks, the long-term trend is toward global economic integration. The functioning of the international economy is determined primarily by considerations of efficiency. The role of the dollar as the basis of the international monetary system, for example, is explained by the preference for it among traders and nations as the vehicle of international commerce.[23] The system is maintained by the mutuality of the benefits provided by trade, monetary arrangements, and investment.

A second view—one shared by Marxists and mercantilists alike—is that every interdependent international economy is essentially an imperial or hierarchical system. The imperial or hegemonic power organizes trade, monetary, and investment relations in order to advance its own economic and political interests. In the absence of the economic and especially the political influence of the hegemonic power, the system would fragment into autarkic economies or regional blocs. Whereas for liberalism maintenance of harmonious international market relations is the norm, for Marxism and mercantilism conflicts of class or national interests are the norm.

■   ■   ■

NOTES

1. Kari Levitt, "The Hinterland Economy," *Canadian Forum* 50 (July–August 1970): 163.
2. George W. Ball, "The Promise of the Multinational Corporation," *Fortune*, June 1, 1967, p. 80.
3. Sidney Rolfe, "Updating Adam Smith," *Interplay* (November 1968): 15.
4. Charles Kindleberger, *Power and Money: The Economics of International Politics and the Politics of International Economics* (New York: Basic Books, 1970), p. 5.
5. Robert Keohane and Joseph Nye, "World Politics and the International Economic System," in *The Future of the International Economic Order: An Agenda for Research*, ed. C. Fred Bergsten (Lexington, MA: D. C. Heath, 1973), p. 116.
6. Ibid.
7. Ibid., p. 117.
8. Paul Samuelson, *Economics: An Introductory Analysis* (New York: McGraw-Hill, 1967), p. 5.
9. Harold Lasswell and Abraham Kaplan, *Power and Society: A Framework for Political Inquiry* (New Haven: Yale University Press, 1950), p. 75.
10. Hans Morgenthau, *Politics among Nations* (New York: Alfred A. Knopf), p. 26. For a more complex but essentially identical view, see Robert Dahl, *Modern Political Analysis* (Englewood Cliffs, NJ: Prentice-Hall, 1963).
11. Kindleberger, *Power and Money*, p. 227.
12. For Johnson's critique of economic nationalism, see Harry Johnson, ed., *Economic Nationalism in Old and New States* (Chicago: University of Chicago Press, 1967).
13. Adam Smith, *The Wealth of Nations* (New York: Modem Library, 1937).
14. J. B. Condliffe, *The Commerce of Nations* (New York: W. W. Norton, 1950), p. 136.
15. Amitai Etzioni, "The Dialectics of Supranational Unification" in *International Political Communities* (New York: Doubleday, 1966), p. 147.
16. The relevant sections appear in Ernst Wangerman, ed., *The Role of Force in History: A Study of Bismarck's Policy of Blood and Iron*, trans. Jack Cohen (New York: International Publishers, 1968).
17. Ibid., p. 12.
18. Ibid., p. 13.
19. Ibid., p. 14.
20. Gustav Stopler, *The German Economy* (New York: Harcourt, Brace and World, 1967), p. 11.
21. Jacob Viner, *The Customs Union Issue*, Studies in the Administration of International Law and Organization, no. 10 (New York: Carnegie Endowment for International Peace, 1950), pp. 98–99.
22. Ibid., p. 101.
23. Richard Cooper, "Eurodollars, Reserve Dollars, and Asymmetrics in the International Monetary System," *Journal of International Economics* 2 (September 1972): 325–44.

Stephen D. Krasner

STATE POWER AND THE STRUCTURE OF INTERNATIONAL TRADE

Introduction

In recent years, students of international relations have multinationalized, transnationalized, bureaucratized, and transgovernmentalized the state until it has virtually ceased to exist as an analytic construct. Nowhere is that trend more apparent than in the study of the politics of international economic relations. The basic conventional assumptions have been undermined by assertions that the state is trapped by a transnational society created not by sovereigns, but by nonstate actors. Interdependence is not seen as a reflection of state policies and state choices (the perspective of balance-of-power theory), but as the result of elements beyond the control of any state or a system created by states.

This perspective is at best profoundly misleading. It may explain developments within a particular international economic structure, but it cannot explain the structure itself. That structure has many institutional and behavioral manifestations. The central continuum along which it can be described is openness. International economic structures may range from complete autarky (if all states prevent movements across their borders), to complete openness (if no restrictions exist). * * * I will present an analysis of one aspect of the international economy—the structure of international trade; that is, the degree of openness for the movement of goods as opposed to capital, labor, technology, or other factors of production.

Since the beginning of the nineteenth century, this structure has gone through several changes. These can be explained, albeit imperfectly, by a state-power theory: an approach that begins with the assumption that the structure of international trade is determined by the interests and power of states acting to maximize national goals. The first step in this argument is to relate four basic state interests—aggregate national income, social stability, political power, and economic growth—to the degree of openness for the movement of goods. The relationship between these interests and openness depends upon the potential economic power of any given state. Potential economic power is operationalized in terms of the relative size and level of economic development of the state. The second step in the argument is to relate different distributions of potential power, such as multipolar and hegemonic, to different international trading structures. The most important conclusion of this theoretical analysis is that a hegemonic distribution of potential economic power is likely to result in an open trading structure. That argument is largely, although not completely, substantiated by empirical data. For a fully adequate analysis it is necessary to amend a state-power argument to take account of the impact of past state decisions on domestic social structures as well as on international economic ones. The two major organizers of the structure of trade since the beginning of the nineteenth

From *World Politics* 28, no.3 (April 1976): 317–347.

century, Great Britain and the United States, have both been prevented from making policy amendments in line with state interests by particular societal groups whose power had been enhanced by earlier state policies.

The Causal Argument: State Interests, State Power, and International Trading Structures

Neoclassical trade theory is based upon the assumption that states act to maximize their aggregate economic utility. This leads to the conclusion that maximum global welfare and Pareto optimality are achieved under free trade. While particular countries might better their situations through protectionism, economic theory has generally looked askance at such policies. In his seminal article on the optimal tariff, Harry Johnson was at pains to point out that the imposition of successive optimal tariffs could lead both trading partners to a situation in which they were worse off than under competitive conditions.[1] Neoclassical theory recognizes that trade regulations can also be used to correct domestic distortions and to promote infant industries,[2] but these are exceptions or temporary departures from policy conclusions that lead logically to the support of free trade.

State Preferences

Historical experience suggests that policy makers are dense, or that the assumptions of the conventional argument are wrong. Free trade has hardly been the norm. Stupidity is not a very interesting analytic category. An alternative approach to explaining international trading structures is to assume that states seek a broad range of goals. At least four major state interests affected by the structure of international trade can be identified. They are: political power, aggregate national income, economic growth, and social stability. The way in which each of these goals is affected by the degree of openness depends upon the potential economic power of the state as defined by its relative size and level of development.

Let us begin with aggregate national income because it is most straightforward. Given the exceptions noted above, conventional neoclassical theory demonstrates that the greater the degree of openness in the international trading system, the greater the level of aggregate economic income. This conclusion applies to all states regardless of their size or relative level of development. The static economic benefits of openness are, however, generally inversely related to size. Trade gives small states relatively more welfare benefits than it gives large ones. Empirically, small states have higher ratios of trade to national product. They do not have the generous factor endowments or potential for national economies of scale that are enjoyed by larger—particularly continental—states.

The impact of openness on social stability runs in the opposite direction. Greater openness exposes the domestic economy to the exigencies of the world market. That implies a higher level of factor movements than in a closed economy, because domestic production patterns must adjust to changes in international prices. Social instability is thereby increased, since there is friction in moving factors, particularly labor, from one sector to another. The impact will be stronger in small states than in large, and in relatively less developed than in more developed ones. Large states are less involved in the international economy: a smaller percentage of their total factor endowment is affected by the international market at any given level of openness. More developed states are better able to adjust factors: skilled workers can more easily be moved from one kind of production to another than can unskilled laborers or peasants.

Hence social stability is, *ceteris paribus,* inversely related to openness, but the deleterious consequences of exposure to the international trading system are mitigated by larger size and greater economic development.

The relationship between political power and the international trading structure can be analyzed in terms of the relative opportunity costs of closure for trading partners.[3] The higher the relative cost of closure, the weaker the political position of the state. Hirschman has argued that this cost can be measured in terms of direct income losses and the adjustment costs of reallocating factors.[4] These will be smaller for large states and for relatively more developed states. Other things being equal, utility costs will be less for large states because they generally have a smaller proportion of their economy engaged in the international economic system. Reallocation costs will be less for more advanced states because their factors are more mobile. Hence a state that is relatively large and more developed will find its political power enhanced by an open system because its opportunity costs of closure are less. The large state can use the threat to alter the system to secure economic or noneconomic objectives. Historically, there is one important exception to this generalization—the oil-exporting states. The level of reserves for some of these states, particularly Saudi Arabia, has reduced the economic opportunity costs of closure to a very low level despite their lack of development.

The relationship between international economic structure and economic growth is elusive. For small states, economic growth has generally been empirically associated with openness.[5] Exposure to the international system makes possible a much more efficient allocation of resources. Openness also probably furthers the rate of growth of large countries with relatively advanced technologies because they do not need to protect infant industries and can take advantage of expanded world markets. In the long term, however, openness for capital and technology, as well as goods, may hamper the growth of large, developed countries by diverting resources from the domestic economy, and by providing potential competitors with the knowledge needed to develop their own industries. Only by maintaining its technological lead and continually developing new industries can even a very large state escape the undesired consequences of an entirely open economic system. For medium-size states, the relationship between international trading structure and growth is impossible to specify definitively, either theoretically or empirically. On the one hand, writers from the mercantilists through the American protectionists and the German historical school, and more recently analysts of *dependencia,* have argued that an entirely open system can undermine a state's effort to develop, and even lead to underdevelopment.[6] On the other hand, adherents of more conventional neoclassical positions have maintained that exposure to international competition spurs economic transformation.[7] The evidence is not yet in. All that can confidently be said is that openness furthers the economic growth of small states and of large ones so long as they maintain their technological edge.

From State Preferences to International Trading Structures

The next step in this argument is to relate particular distributions of potential economic power, defined by the size and level of development of individual states, to the structure of the international trading system, defined in terms of openness.

Let us consider a system composed of a large number of small, highly developed states. Such a system is likely to lead to an open international trading structure. The aggregate income and economic growth of each state are increased by an open system. The social instability produced by exposure to international competition is mitigated by the factor mobility made possible by higher levels of development. There is no loss of political power from openness because the costs of closure are symmetrical for all members of the system.

Now let us consider a system composed of a few very large, but unequally developed states. Such a distribution of potential economic power is likely to lead to a closed structure. Each state could increase its income through a more open system, but the gains would be modest. Openness would create more social instability in the less developed countries. The rate of growth for more backward areas might be frustrated, while that of the more advanced ones would be enhanced. A more open structure would leave the less developed states in a politically more vulnerable position, because their greater factor rigidity would mean a higher relative cost of closure. Because of these disadvantages, large but relatively less developed states are unlikely to accept an open trading structure. More advanced states cannot, unless they are militarily much more powerful, force large backward countries to accept openness.

Finally, let us consider a hegemonic system—one in which there is a single state that is much larger and relatively more advanced than its trading partners. The costs and benefits of openness are not symmetrical for all members of the system. The hegemonic state will have a preference for an open structure. Such a structure increases its aggregate national income. It also increases its rate of growth during its ascendency—that is, when its relative size and technological lead are increasing. Further, an open structure increases its political power, since the opportunity costs of closure are least for a large and developed state. The social instability resulting from exposure to the international system is mitigated by the hegemonic power's relatively low level of involvement in the international economy, and the mobility of its factors.

What of the other members of a hegemonic system? Small states are likely to opt for openness because the advantages in terms of aggregate income and growth are so great, and their political power is bound to be restricted regardless of what they do. The reaction of medium-size states is hard to predict; it depends at least in part on the way in which the hegemonic power utilizes its resources. The potentially dominant state has symbolic, economic, and military capabilities that can be used to entice or compel others to accept an open trading structure.

At the symbolic level, the hegemonic state stands as an example of how economic development can be achieved. Its policies may be emulated, even if they are inappropriate for other states. Where there are very dramatic asymmetries, military power can be used to coerce weaker states into an open structure. Force is not, however, a very efficient means for changing economic policies, and it is unlikely to be employed against medium-size states.

Most importantly, the hegemonic state can use its economic resources to create an open structure. In terms of positive incentives, it can offer access to its large domestic market and to its relatively cheap exports. In terms of negative ones, it can withhold foreign grants and engage in competition, potentially ruinous for the weaker state, in third-country markets. The size and economic robustness of the hegemonic state also enable it to provide the confidence necessary for a stable international monetary system, and its currency can offer the liquidity needed for an increasingly open system.

In sum, openness is most likely to occur during periods when a hegemonic state is in its ascendency. Such a state has the interest and the resources to create a structure characterized by lower tariffs, rising trade proportions, and less regionalism. There are other distributions of potential power where openness is likely, such as a system composed of many small, highly developed states. But even here, that potential might not be realized because of the problems of creating confidence in a monetary system where adequate liquidity would have to be provided by a negotiated international reserve asset or a group of national currencies. Finally, it is unlikely that very large states, particularly at unequal levels of development, would accept open trading relations.

These arguments, and the implications of other ideal typical configurations of potential economic power for the openness of trading structures, are summarized in [Table 9.2].

The Dependent Variable: Describing the Structure of the International Trading System

The structure of international trade has both behavioral and institutional attributes. The degree of openness can be described both by the *flow* of goods and by the *policies* that are followed by states with respect to trade barriers and international payments. The two are not unrelated, but they do not coincide perfectly.

In common usage, the focus of attention has been upon institutions. Openness is associated with those historical periods in which tariffs were substantially lowered: the third quarter of the nineteenth century and the period since the Second World War.

Tariffs alone, however, are not an adequate indicator of structure. They are hard to operationalize quantitatively. Tariffs do not have to be high to be effective. If cost functions are nearly identical, even low tariffs can prevent trade. Effective tariff rates may be much higher than nominal ones. Non-tariff barriers to trade, which are not easily compared across states, can substitute for duties. An undervalued exchange rate can protect domestic markets from foreign competition. Tariff levels alone cannot describe the structure of international trade.[8]

A second indicator, and one which is behavioral rather than institutional, is trade proportions—the ratios of trade to national income for different states. Like tariff levels, these involve describing the system in terms of an agglomeration of national tendencies. A period in which these ratios are increasing across time for most states can be described as one of increasing openness.

A third indicator is the concentration of trade within regions composed of states at different levels of development. The degree of such regional

Table 9.2. Probability of an Open Trading Structure with Different Distributions of Potential Economic Power

		SIZE OF STATES		
		RELATIVELY EQUAL		
		SMALL	LARGE	VERY UNEQUAL
Level of Development of States	EQUAL	Moderate-High	Low-Moderate	High
	UNEQUAL	Moderate	Low	Moderate-High

encapsulation is determined not so much by comparative advantage (because relative factor endowments would allow almost any backward area to trade with almost any developed one), but by political choices or dictates. Large states, attempting to protect themselves from the vagaries of a global system, seek to maximize their interests by creating regional blocs. Openness in the global economic system has in effect meant greater trade among the leading industrial states. Periods of closure are associated with the encapsulation of certain advanced states within regional systems shared with certain less developed areas.

A description of the international trading system involves, then, an exercise that is comparative rather than absolute. A period when tariffs are falling, trade proportions are rising, and regional trading patterns are becoming less extreme will be defined as one in which the structure is becoming more open.

Tariff Levels

The period from the 1820s to 1879 was basically one of decreasing tariff levels in Europe. The trend began in Great Britain in the 1820s, with reductions of duties and other barriers to trade. In 1846 the abolition of the Corn Laws ended agricultural protectionism. France reduced duties on some intermediate goods in the 1830s, and on coal, iron, and steel in 1852. The *Zollverein* established fairly low tariffs in 1834. Belgium, Portugal, Spain, Piedmont, Norway, Switzerland, and Sweden lowered imposts in the 1850s. The golden age of free trade began in 1860, when Britain and France signed the Cobden-Chevalier Treaty, which virtually eliminated trade barriers. This was followed by a series of bilateral trade agreements between virtually all European states. It is important to note, however, that the United States took little part in the general movement toward lower trade barriers.[9]

The movement toward greater liberality was reversed in the late 1870s. Austria-Hungary increased duties in 1876 and 1878, and Italy also in 1878; but the main breach came in Germany in 1879. France increased tariffs modestly in 1881, sharply in 1892, and raised them still further in 1910. Other countries followed a similar pattern. Only Great Britain, Belgium, the Netherlands, and Switzerland continued to follow free-trade policies through the 1880's. Although Britain did not herself impose duties, she began establishing a system of preferential markets in her overseas Empire in 1898.[10] The United States was basically protectionist throughout the nineteenth century. The high tariffs imposed during the Civil War continued with the exception of a brief period in the 1890s. There were no major duty reductions before 1914.

During the 1920s tariff levels increased further. Western European states protected their agrarian sectors against imports from the Danube region, Australia, Canada, and the United States, where the war had stimulated increased output. Great Britain adopted some colonial preferences in 1919, imposed a small number of tariffs in 1921, and extended some wartime duties. The successor states of the Austro-Hungarian Empire imposed duties to achieve some national self-sufficiency. The British dominions and Latin America protected industries nurtured by wartime demands. In the United States the Fordney-McCumber Tariff Act of 1922 increased protectionism. The October Revolution removed Russia from the Western trading system.[11]

Dramatic closure in terms of tariff levels began with the passage of the Smoot-Hawley Tariff Act in the United States in 1930. Britain raised tariffs in 1931 and definitively abandoned free trade at the Ottawa Conference of 1932, which introduced extensive imperial preferences. Germany and Japan established trading blocs within their own spheres of influence. All other major countries followed protectionist policies.[12]

Significant reductions in protection began after the Second World War; the United States had foreshadowed the movement toward greater liberality with the passage of the Reciprocal Trade Agreements Act in 1934. Since 1945 there have been seven rounds of multilateral tariff reductions. The first, held in 1947 at Geneva, and the Kennedy Round, held during the 1960s, have been the most significant. They have substantially reduced the level of protection.[13]

The present situation is ambiguous. There have recently been some new trade controls. In the United States these include a voluntary import agreement for steel, the imposition of a 10 percent import surcharge during four months of 1971, and export controls on agricultural products in 1973 and 1974. Italy imposed a deposit requirement on imports during parts of 1974 and 1975. Britain and Japan have engaged in export subsidization. Non-tariff barriers have become more important. On balance, there has been movement toward greater protectionism since the end of the Kennedy Round, but it is not decisive. The outcome of the multilateral negotiations that began in 1975 remains to be seen.

In sum, after 1820 there was a general trend toward lower tariffs (with the notable exception of the United States), which culminated between 1860 and 1879; higher tariffs from 1879 through the interwar years, with dramatic increases in the 1930s; and less protectionism from 1945 through the conclusion of the Kennedy Round in 1967.

Trade Proportions

With the exception of one period, ratios of trade to aggregate economic activity followed the same general pattern as tariff levels. Trade proportions increased from the early part of the nineteenth century to about 1880. Between 1880 and 1900 there was a decrease, sharper if measured in current prices than constant ones, but apparent in both statistical series for most countries. Between 1900 and 1913—and here is the exception from the tariff pattern—there was a marked increase in the ratio of trade to aggregate economic activity. This trend brought trade proportions to levels that have generally not been reattained. During the 1920s and 1930s the importance of trade in national economic activity declined. After the Second World War it increased.

Figure 9.1 presents these findings in greater detail. There are considerable differences in the movement of trade proportions among states. They hold more or less constant for the United States; Japan, Denmark, and Norway (the last not shown on the graph) are unaffected by the general decrease in the ratio of trade to aggregate economic activity that takes place after 1880. The pattern described in the previous paragraph does, however, hold for Great Britain, France, Sweden, Germany, and Italy.

Figure 9.2 shows postwar developments. Because of the boom in commodity prices that occurred in the early 1950s, the ratio of trade to gross domestic product was relatively high for larger states during these years, at least in current prices. It then faltered or remained constant until about 1960. From the early 1960s through 1972, trade proportions rose for all major states except Japan. Data for 1973 and 1974 show further increases. For smaller countries the trend was more erratic, with Belgium showing a more or less steady increase, Norway vacillating between 82 and 90 percent, and Denmark and the Netherlands showing higher figures for the late 1950s than for more recent years. There is then, in current prices, a generally upward trend in trade proportions since 1960, particularly for larger states. This movement is more pronounced if constant prices are used.[14]

Regional Trading Patterns

The final indicator of the degree of openness of the global trading system is regional bloc concentration. There is a natural affinity for some states to trade with others because of geographical

Figure 9.1. Ratio of Trade to Aggregate Economic Activity, Nineteenth Century–1960, at Current Prices

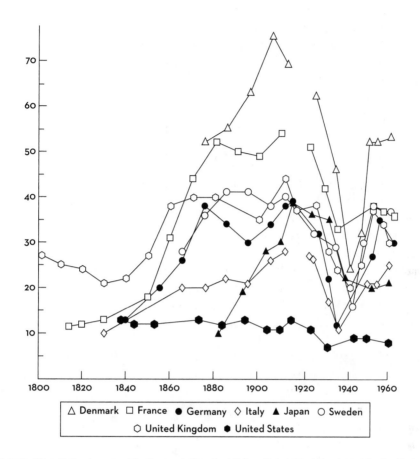

△ Denmark □ France ● Germany ◇ Italy ▲ Japan ○ Sweden
⬡ United Kingdom ⬢ United States

Source: Simon Kuznets, "Quantitative Aspects of the Economic Growth of Nations X. Level and Structure of Foreign Trade: Long-Term Trends," *Economic Development and Cultural Change*, XV (1967), Appendix I. In all cases the mid-points of Kuznets periods were used.

propinquity or comparative advantage. In general, however, a system in which there are fewer manifestations of trading within given blocs, particularly among specific groups of more and less developed states, is a more open one. Over time there have been extensive changes in trading patterns between particular areas of the world whose relative factor endowments have remained largely the same.

Richard Chadwick and Karl Deutsch have collected extensive information on international trading patterns since 1890. Their basic datum is the relative acceptance indicator (RA), which measures deviations from a null hypothesis in which trade between a pair of states, or a state and a region, is precisely what would be predicted on the basis of their total share of international trade.[15] When the null hypothesis holds, the RA indicator is equal to zero. Values less than zero indicate less trade than expected, greater than zero more trade than expected. For our purposes the critical issue is whether, over time, trade tends to become more concentrated as shown by movements away

Figure 9.2. Ratio of Trade to Gross Domestic Product, 1950–1972, at Current Prices

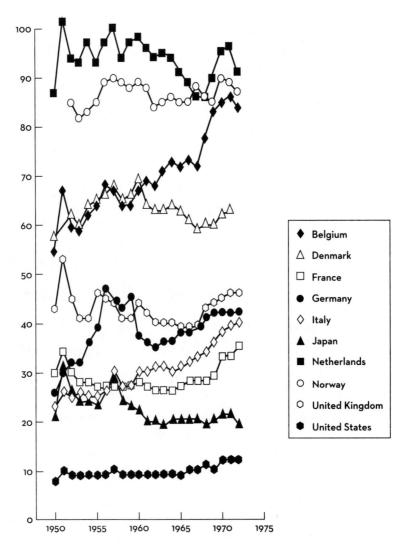

Source: United Nations, *Yearbook of National Account Statistics*, various years.

from zero, or less as shown by movements toward zero.

Table 9.3 [omitted here] presents figures for the years 1890, 1913, 1928, 1938, 1954, and 1958 through 1968, the set collected by Chadwick and Deutsch, for the following pairs of major states and regions: Commonwealth–United Kingdom; United States–Latin America; Russia–Eastern Europe; and France–French speaking Africa. The region's percentage of exports to the country, and the country's percentage of imports from the region, are included along with RA indicators to give some sense of the overall importance of the particular trading relationship.

There is a general pattern. In three of the four cases, the RA value closest to zero—that is the least regional encapsulation—occurred in 1890, 1913, or 1928; in the fourth case (France and French West Africa), the 1928 value was not bettered until 1964. In every case there was an increase in the RA indicator between 1928 and 1938, reflecting the breakdown of international commerce that is associated with the depression. Surprisingly, the RA indicator was higher for each of the four pairs in 1954 than in 1938, an indication that regional patterns persisted and even became more intense in the postwar period. With the exception of the Soviet Union and Eastern Europe, there was a general trend toward decreasing RA's for the period after 1954. They still, however, show fairly high values even in the late 1960s.

If we put all three indicators—tariff levels, trade proportions, and trade patterns—together, they suggest the following periodization.

Period I (1820–1879): Increasing openness—tariffs are generally lowered; trade proportions increase. Data are not available for trade patterns. However, it is important to note that this is not a universal pattern. The United States is largely unaffected: its tariff levels remain high (and are in fact increased during the early 1860s) and American trade proportions remain almost constant.

Period II (1879–1900): Modest closure— tariffs are increased; trade proportions decline modestly for most states. Data are not available for trade patterns.

Period III (1900–1913): Greater openness— tariff levels remain generally unchanged; trade proportions increase for all major trading states except the United States. Trading

patterns become less regional in three out of the four cases for which data are available.

Period IV (1918–1939): Closure—tariff levels are increased in the 1920s and again in the 1930s; trade proportions decline. Trade becomes more regionally encapsulated.

Period V (1945–c. 1970): Great openness— tariffs are lowered; trade proportions increase, particularly after 1960. Regional concentration decreases after 1960. However, these developments are limited to non-Communist areas of the world.

The Independent Variable: Describing the Distribution of Potential Economic Power Among States

Analysts of international relations have an almost pro forma set of variables designed to show the distribution of potential power in the international *political* system. It includes such factors as gross national product, per capita income, geographical position, and size of armed forces. A similar set of indicators can be presented for the international *economic* system.

Statistics are available over a long time period for per capita income, aggregate size, share of world trade, and share of world investment. They demonstrate that, since the beginning of the nineteenth century, there have been two first-rank economic powers in the world economy—Britain and the United States. The United States passed Britain in aggregate size sometime in the middle of the nineteenth century and, in the 1880s, became the largest producer of manufactures. America's lead was particularly marked in technologically advanced industries turning out sewing machines, harvesters, cash registers, locomotives, steam pumps, telephones, and petroleum.[16] Until the First World War, however, Great Britain had a higher per capita income, a greater share of world trade, and a greater share of world investment than any other state. The peak of British ascendance occurred around 1880, when Britain's relative per capita income, share of world trade, and share of investment flows reached their highest levels. Britain's potential dominance in 1880 and 1900 was particularly striking in the international economic system, where her share of trade and foreign investment was about twice as large as that of any other state.

It was only after the First World War that the United States became relatively larger and more developed in terms of all four indicators. This potential dominance reached new and dramatic heights between 1945 and 1960. Since then, the relative position of the United States has declined, bringing it quite close to West Germany, its nearest rival, in terms of per capita income and share of world trade. The devaluations of the dollar that have taken place since 1972 are reflected in a continuation of this downward trend for income and aggregate size.

The relative potential economic power of Britain and the United States is shown in the following two tables.

In sum, Britain was the world's most important trading state from the period after the Napoleonic Wars until 1913. Her relative position rose until about 1880 and fell thereafter. The United States became the largest and most advanced state in economic terms after the First World War, but did not equal the relative share of world trade and investment achieved by Britain in the 1880s until after the Second World War.

Testing the Argument

The contention that hegemony leads to a more open trading structure is fairly well, but not perfectly, confirmed by the empirical evidence presented in the preceding sections. The argument explains the periods 1820 to 1879, 1880 to 1900, and 1945 to 1960. It does not fully explain those from 1900 to 1913, 1919 to 1939, or 1960 to the present.

1820–1879. The period from 1820 to 1879 was one of increasing openness in the structure of international trade. It was also one of rising hegemony. Great Britain was the instigator and supporter of the new structure. She began lowering her trade barriers in the 1820s, before any other state. The signing of the Cobden-Chevalier Tariff Treaty with France in 1860 initiated a series of bilateral tariff reductions. It is, however, important to note that the United States was hardly involved in these developments, and that America's ratio of trade to aggregate economic activity did not increase during the nineteenth century.

Britain put to use her internal flexibility and external power in securing a more open structure. At the domestic level, openness was favored by the rising industrialists. The opposition of the agrarian sector was mitigated by its capacity for adjustment: the rate of capital investment and technological innovation was high enough to prevent British agricultural incomes from falling until some thirty years after the abolition of the Corn Laws. Symbolically, the Manchester School led by Cobden and Bright provided the ideological justification for free trade. Its influence was felt throughout Europe where Britain stood as an example to at least some members of the elite.

Britain used her military strength to open many backward areas: British interventions were frequent in Latin America during the nineteenth century, and formal and informal colonial expansion opened the interior of Africa. Most importantly, Britain forced India into the international economic system.[17] British military power was also a factor in concluding the Cobden-Chevalier Treaty, for Louis Napoleon was more concerned with cementing his relations with Britain than he was in the economic

Table 9.4. Indicators of British Potential Power (Ratio of British value to next highest)

	Per Capita Income	Aggregate Size	Share of World Trade	Share of World Investment*
1860	.91 (US)	.74 (US)	2.01 (FR)	n.a.
1880	1.30 (US)	.79 (1874-83 US)	2.22 (FR)	1.93 (FR)
1900	1.05 (1899 US)	.58 (1899 US)	2.17 (1890 GERM)	2.08 (FR)
1913	.92 (US)	.43 (US)	1.20 (US)	2.18 (1914 FR)
1928	.66 (US)	.25 (1929 US)	.79 (US)	.64 (1921-29 US)
1937	.79 (US)	.29 (US)	.88 (US)	.18 (1930-38 US)
1950	.56 (US)	.19 (US)	.69 (US)	.13 (1951-55 US)
1960	.49 (US)	.14 (US)	.46 (1958 US)	.15 (1956-61 US)
1972	.46 (US)	.13 (US)	.47 (1973 US)	n.a.

* Stock 1870–1913; Flow 1928–1950

Years are in parentheses when different from those in first column.

Countries in parentheses are those with the largest values for the particular indicator other than Great Britain.

Source: Derived from figures in Appendix.

consequences of greater openness. Once this pact was signed, however, it became a catalyst for the many other treaties that followed.[18]

Britain also put economic instruments to good use in creating an open system. The abolition of the Corn Laws offered continental grain producers the incentive of continued access to the growing British market. Britain was at the heart of the nineteenth-century international monetary system which functioned exceptionally well, at least for the core of the more developed states and the areas closely associated with them. Exchange rates were stable, and countries did not have to impose trade barriers to rectify cyclical payments difficulties. Both confidence and liquidity were, to a critical degree, provided by Britain. The use of sterling balances as opposed to specie became increasingly widespread, alleviating the liquidity problems presented by the erratic production of gold and silver.

Foreign private and central banks increasingly placed their cash reserves in London, and accounts were cleared through changing bank balances rather than gold flows. Great Britain's extremely sophisticated financial institutions, centered in the City of London, provided the short-term financing necessary to facilitate the international flow of goods. Her early and somewhat fortuitous adherence to the gold—as opposed to the silver or bimetallic—standard proved to be an important source of confidence as all countries adopted at least a *de facto* gold standard after 1870 because of the declining relative value of silver. In times of monetary emergency, the confidence placed in the pound because of the strength of the British economy allowed the Bank of England to be a lender of last resort.[19]

Hence, for the first three-quarters of the nineteenth century, British policy favored an open international trading structure, and British power helped

Table 9.5. Indicators of U.S. Potential Power (Ratio of U.S. value to next highest)

	Per Capita Income	Aggregate Size	Share of World Trade	Share of World Investment Flows
1860	1.10 (GB)	1.41 (GB)	.36 (GB)	Net debtor
1880	.77 (GB)	1.23 (1883 GB)	.37 (GB)	Net debtor
1900	.95 (1899 GB)	1.73 (1899 GB)	.43 (1890 GB)	n.a.
1913	1.09 (GB)	2.15 (RUS)	.83 (GB)	Net debtor
1928	1.51 (GB)	3.22 (USSR)	1.26 (GB)	1.55 (1911–20 UK)
1937	1.26 (GB)	2.67 (USSR)	1.13 (GB)	5.53 (1930–38 UK)
1950	1.78 (GB)	3.15 (USSR)	1.44 (GB)	7.42 (1951–55 UK)
1960	2.05 (GB)	2.81 (USSR)	2.15 (1958 GB)	6.60 (1956–61 UK)
1972	1.31 (GERM)	n.a.	1.18 (1973 GERM)	n.a.

Years are in parentheses when different from those in first column.

Countries in parentheses are those with the largest values for the particular indicator other than the United States.

Source: Derived from figures in Appendix.

to create it. But this was not a global regime. British resources were not sufficient to entice or compel the United States (a country whose economy was larger than Britain's by 1860 and whose technology was developing very rapidly) to abandon its protectionist commercial policy. As a state-power argument suggests, openness was only established within the geographical area where the rising economic hegemony was able to exercise its influence.

1880–1900. The last two decades of the nineteenth century were a period of modest closure which corresponds to a relative decline in British per capita income, size, and share of world trade. The event that precipitated higher tariff levels was the availability of inexpensive grain from the American Midwest, made possible by the construction of continental railways. National responses varied. Britain let her agricultural sector decline, a not

unexpected development given her still dominant economic position. Denmark, a small and relatively well-developed state, also refrained from imposing tariffs and transformed its farming sector from agriculture to animal husbandry. Several other small states also followed open policies. Germany, France, Russia, and Italy imposed higher tariffs, however. Britain did not have the military or economic power to forestall these policies. Still, the institutional structure of the international monetary system, with the City of London at its center, did not crumble. The decline in trade proportions was modest despite higher tariffs.

1945–1960. The third period that is neatly explained by the argument that hegemony leads to an open trading structure is the decade and a half after the Second World War, characterized by the ascendancy of the United States. During these years the structure of the international trading system became increasingly open. Tariffs were lowered; trade proportions were restored well above interwar levels. Asymmetrical regional trading patterns did begin to decline, although not until the late 1950s. America's bilateral rival, the Soviet Union, remained—as the theory would predict—encapsulated within its own regional sphere of influence.

Unlike Britain in the nineteenth century, the United States after World War II operated in a bipolar political structure. Free trade was preferred, but departures such as the Common Market and Japanese import restrictions were accepted to make sure that these areas remained within the general American sphere of influence.[20] Domestically the Reciprocal Trade Agreements Act, first passed in 1934, was extended several times after the war. Internationally the United States supported the framework for tariff reductions provided by the General Agreement on Tariffs and Trade. American policy makers used their economic leverage over Great Britain to force an end to the imperial preference system.[21] The monetary system established at Bretton Woods was basically an American creation. In practice, liquidity was provided by the American deficit; confidence by the size of the American economy. Behind the economic veil stood American military protection for other industrialized market economies—an overwhelming incentive for them to accept an open system, particularly one which was in fact relatively beneficial.

The argument about the relationship between hegemony and openness is not as satisfactory for the years 1900 to 1913, 1919 to 1939, and 1960 to the present.

1900–1913. During the years immediately preceding the First World War, the structure of international trade became more open in terms of trade proportions and regional patterns. Britain remained the largest international economic entity, but her relative position continued a decline that had begun two decades earlier. Still, Britain maintained her commitment to free trade and to the financial institutions of the City of London. A state-power argument would suggest some reconsideration of these policies.

Perhaps the simplest explanation for the increase in trade proportions was the burst of loans that flowed out of Europe in the years before the First World War, loans that financed the increasing sale of goods. Germany and France as well as Britain participated in this development. Despite the higher tariff levels imposed after 1879, institutional structures—particularly the monetary system—allowed these capital flows to generate increasing trade flows. Had Britain reconsidered her policies, this might not have been the case.

1919–1939. The United States emerged from the First World War as the world's most powerful economic state. Whether America was large enough to have put an open system in place is a moot question. As Tables 9.4 and 9.5 indicate, America's share of world trade and investment was only 26 and 55 percent greater than that of any other state, while comparable figures for Great Britain during the last part of the nineteenth century are 100 percent. What is apparent, though, is that American policy makers made little effort to open the structure of international trade. The call for an open door was a shibboleth, not a policy. It was really the British who attempted to continue a hegemonic role.

In the area of trade, the U.S. Fordney-McCumber Tariff of 1922 increased protection. That tendency was greatly reinforced by the Smoot-Hawley Tariff of 1930 which touched off a wave of protective legislation. Instead of leading the way to openness, the United States led the way to closure.

In the monetary area, the American government made little effort to alter a situation that was confused and often chaotic. During the first half of the 1920s, exchange rates fluctuated widely among major currencies as countries were forced, by the inflationary pressures of the war, to abandon the gold standard. Convertibility was restored in the mid-twenties at values incompatible with long-term equilibrium. The British pound was overvalued, and the French franc undervalued. Britain was forced off the gold standard in September 1931, accelerating a trend that had begun with Uruguay in April 1929. The United States went off gold in 1933. France's decision to end convertibility in 1936 completed the pattern. During the 1930s the monetary system collapsed.[22]

Constructing a stable monetary order would have been no easy task in the political environment of the 1920s and 1930s. The United States made no effort. It refused to recognize a connection between war debts and reparations, although much of the postwar flow of funds took the form of American loans to Germany, German reparations payments to France and Britain, and French and British war-debt payments to the United States. The Great Depression was in no small measure touched off by the contraction of American credit in the late 1920s. In the deflationary collapse that followed, the British were too weak to act as a lender of last resort, and the Americans actually undercut efforts to reconstruct the Western economy when, before the London Monetary Conference of 1933, President Roosevelt changed the basic assumptions of the meeting by taking the United States off gold. American concern was wholly with restoring the domestic economy.[23]

That is not to say that American behavior was entirely obstreperous; but cooperation was erratic and often private. The Federal Reserve Bank of New York did try, during the late 1920s, to maintain New York interest rates below those in London to protect the value of the pound.[24] Two Americans, Dawes and Young, lent their names to the renegotiations of German reparations payments, but most of the actual work was carried out by British experts.[25] At the official level, the first manifestation of American leadership was President Hoover's call for a moratorium on war debts and reparations in June 1931; but in 1932 the United States refused to participate in the Lausanne Conference that in effect ended reparations.[26]

It was not until the mid-thirties that the United States asserted any real leadership. The Reciprocal Trade Agreements Act of 1934 led to bilateral treaties with twenty-seven countries before 1945. American concessions covered 64 percent of dutiable items, and reduced rates by an average of 44 percent. However, tariffs were so high to begin with that the actual impact of these agreements was limited.[27] There were also some modest steps toward tariff liberalization in Britain and France. In the monetary field, the United States, Britain, and France pledged to maintain exchange-rate stability in the Tripartite Declaration of September 1936. These actions were not adequate to create an open international economic structure. American policy during the interwar period, and particularly before the mid-thirties, fails to accord with the predictions made by a state-power explanation of the behavior of a rising hegemonic power.

1960–present. The final period not adequately dealt with by a state-power explanation is the last decade or so. In recent years, the relative size and level of development of the U.S. economy has fallen. This decline has not, however, been accompanied by a clear turn toward protectionism. The Trade Expansion Act of 1962 was extremely liberal and led to the very successful Kennedy Round of multilateral tariff cuts during the mid-sixties. The protectionist Burke-Hartke Bill did not pass. The 1974 Trade Act does include new protectionist aspects, particularly in its requirements for review of the removal of non-tariff barriers by Congress and for stiffer requirements for the imposition of countervailing duties, but it still maintains the mechanism of presidential discretion on tariff cuts that has been the keystone of postwar reductions.

While the Voluntary Steel Agreement, the August 1971 economic policy, and restrictions on agricultural exports all show a tendency toward protectionism, there is as yet no evidence of a basic turn away from a commitment to openness.

In terms of behavior in the international trading system, the decade of the 1960s was clearly one of greater openness. Trade proportions increased, and traditional regional trade patterns became weaker. A state-power argument would predict a downturn or at least a faltering in these indicators as American power declined.

In sum, although the general pattern of the structure of international trade conforms with the predictions of a state-power argument—two periods of openness separated by one of closures—corresponding to periods of rising British and American hegemony and an interregnum, the whole pattern is out of phase. British commitment to openness continued long after Britain's position had declined. American commitment to openness did not begin until well after the United States had become the world's leading economic power and has continued during a period of relative American decline. The state-power argument needs to be amended to take these delayed reactions into account.

Amending the Argument

The structure of the international trading system does not move in lockstep with changes in the distribution of potential power among states. Systems are initiated and ended, not as a state-power theory would predict, by close assessments of the interests of the state at every given moment, but by external events—usually cataclysmic ones. The closure that began in 1879 coincided with the Great Depression of the last part of the nineteenth century. The final dismantling of the nineteenth-century international economic system was not precipitated by a change in British trade or monetary policy, but by the First World War and the Depression. The potato famine of the 1840s prompted abolition of the Corn Laws; and the United States did not assume the mantle of world leadership until the world had been laid bare by six years of total war. Some catalytic external event seems necessary to move states to dramatic policy initiatives in line with state interests.

Once policies have been adopted, they are pursued until a new crisis demonstrates that they are no longer feasible. States become locked in by the impact of prior choices on their domestic political structures. The British decision to opt for openness in 1846 corresponded with state interests. It also strengthened the position of industrial and financial groups over time, because they had the opportunity to operate in an international system that furthered their objectives. That system eventually undermined the position of British farmers, a group that would have supported protectionism if it had survived. Once entrenched, Britain's export industries, and more importantly the City of London, resisted policies of closure.[28] In the interwar years, the British rentier class insisted on restoring the prewar parity of the pound—a decision that placed enormous deflationary pressures on the domestic economy—because they wanted to protect the value of their investments.[29]

Institutions created during periods of rising ascendancy remained in operation when they were no longer appropriate. For instance, the organization of British banking in the nineteenth century separated domestic and foreign operations. The Court of Directors of the Bank of England was dominated by international banking houses. Their decisions about British monetary policy were geared toward the international economy.[30] Under a different institutional arrangement more attention might have been given after 1900 to the need to revitalize the domestic economy. The British state was unable to free itself from the domestic structures that its earlier policy decisions had created, and continued to follow policies appropriate for a rising hegemony long after Britain's star had begun to fall.

Similarly, earlier policies in the United States begat social structures and institutional arrangements that trammeled state policy. After protecting import-competing industries for a century, the United States was unable in the 1920s to opt for more open policies, even though state interests would have been furthered thereby. Institutionally, decisions about tariff reductions were taken primarily in congressional committees, giving virtually any group seeking protection easy access to the decision-making process. When there were conflicts among groups, they were resolved by raising the levels of protection for everyone. It was only after the cataclysm of the depression that the decision-making processes for trade policy were changed. The Presidency, far more insulated from the entreaties of particular societal groups than congressional committees, was then given more power.[31] Furthermore, the American commercial banking system was unable to assume the burden of regulating the international economy during the 1920s. American institutions were geared toward the domestic economy. Only after the Second World War, and in fact not until the late 1950s, did American banks fully develop the complex institutional structures commensurate with the dollar's role in the international monetary system.[32]

Having taken the critical decisions that created an open system after 1945, the American Government is unlikely to change its policy until it confronts some external event that it cannot control, such as a worldwide deflation, drought in the great plains, or the malicious use of petrodollars. In America perhaps more than in any other country "new policies," as E. E. Schattschneider wrote in his brilliant study of the Smoot-Hawley Tariff in 1935, "create new politics,"[33] for in America the state is weak and the society strong.[34] State decisions taken because of state interests reinforce private societal groups that the state is unable to resist in later periods. Multinational corporations have grown and prospered since 1950. International economic policy making has passed from the Congress to the Executive. Groups favoring closure, such as organized labor, are unlikely to carry the day until some external event demonstrates that existing policies can no longer be implemented.

The structure of international trade changes in fits and starts; it does not flow smoothly with the redistribution of potential state power. Nevertheless, it is the power and the policies of states that create order where there would otherwise be chaos or at best a Lockian state of nature. The existence of various transnational, multinational, transgovernmental, and other nonstate actors that have riveted scholarly attention in recent years can only be understood within the context of a broader structure that ultimately rests upon the power and interests of states, shackled though they may be by the societal consequences of their own past decisions.

NOTES

1. Johnson, "Optimum Tariffs and Retaliation," in Harry Johnson, *International Trade and Economic Growth* (Cambridge: Harvard University Press 1967), 31–61.

2. See, for instance, Everett Hagen, "An Economic Justification of Protectionism," *Quarterly Journal of Economics*, Vol. 72 (November 1958), 496–514; Harry Johnson, "Optimal Trade Intervention in the Presence of Domestic Distortions," in Robert Baldwin and others, *Trade. Growth and the Balance of Payments: Essays in Honor of Gottfried Haberler* (Chicago: Rand McNally 1965), 3–34; and Jagdish Bhagwati, *Trade, Tariffs, and Growth* (Cambridge: MIT Press 1969), 295–308.

3. This notion is reflected in Albert O. Hirschman, *National Power and the Structure of Foreign Trade* (Berkeley: University of California Press 1945); Robert W. Tucker, *The New Isolationism: Threat or Promise?* (Washington: Potomac Associates 1972); and Kenneth Waltz, "The Myth of Interdependence," in Charles P. Kindleberger, ed., *The International Corporation* (Cambridge: MIT Press 1970), 205–23.

4. Hirschman (fn. 3), 13–34.

5. Simon Kuznets, *Modern Economic Growth: Rate, Structure, and Spread* (New Haven: Yale University Press 1966), 302.

6. See David P. Calleo and Benjamin Rowland, *America and the World Political Economy* (Bloomington: Indiana University Press 1973), Part II, for a discussion of American thought; Eli Heckscher, *Mercantilism* (New York: Macmillan 1955); and D. C. Coleman, ed., *Revisions in Mercantilism* (London: Methuen 1969), for the classic discussion and a collection of recent articles on mercantilism; Andre Gunder Frank,

Latin America: Underdevelopment or Revolution (New York: Monthly Review 1969); Arghiri Emmanuel, *Unequal Exchange: A Study of the Imperialism of Trade* (New York: Monthly Review 1972); and Johan Galtung, "A Structural Theory of Imperialism," *Journal of Peace Research,* VIII, No. 2 (1971), 81–117, for some representative arguments about the deleterious effects of free trade.

7. See Gottfried Haberler, *International Trade and Economic Development* (Cairo: National Bank of Egypt 1959); and Carlos F. Diaz-Alejandro, "Latin America: Toward 2000 A.D.," in Jagdish Bhagwati, ed., *Economics and World Order from the 1970s to the 1990s* (New York: Macmillan 1972), 223–55, for some arguments concerning the benefits of trade.

8. See Harry Johnson, *Economic Policies Toward Less Developed Countries* (New York: Praeger 1967), 90–94, for a discussion of nominal versus effective tariffs; Bela Belassa, *Trade Liberalization among Industrial Countries* (New York: McGraw-Hill 1967), chap. 3, for the problems of determining the height of tariffs; and Hans O. Schmitt, "International Monetary System: Three Options for Reform," *International Affairs,* L (April 1974), 200, for similar effects of tariffs and undervalued exchange rates.

9. Charles P. Kindleberger, "The Rise of Free Trade in Western Europe 1820–1875," *The Journal of Economic History,* XXXV (March 1975), 20–55; Sidney Pollard, *European Economic Integration 1815–1970* (London: Thames and Hudson 1974), 117; J. B. Condliffe, *The Commerce of Nations* (New York: Norton 1950), 212–23, 229–30.

10. Charles P. Kindleberger, "Group Behavior and International Trade," *Journal of Political Economy,* Vol. 59 (February 1951), 33; Condliffe (fn. 9), 498; Pollard (fn. 9), 121; and Peter A. Gourevitch, "International Trade, Domestic Coalitions, and Liberty: Comparative Responses to the Great Depression of 1873–1896," paper delivered to the International Studies Association Convention, Washington, 1973.

11. Charles P. Kindelberger, *The World in Depression* (Berkeley: University of California Press 1973), 171; Condliffe (fn. 9), 478–81.

12. Condliffe (fn. 9), 498; Robert Gilpin, "The Politics of Transnational Economic Relations," *International Organization,* XXV (Summer 1971), 407; Kindelberger (fn. 11), 132, 171.

13. John W. Evans, *The Kennedy Round in American Trade Policy* (Cambridge: Harvard University Press 1971), 10–20.

14. Figures are available in United Nations, *Yearbook of National Account Statistics,* various years.

15. Richard I. Savage and Karl W. Deutsch, "A Statistical Model of the Gross Analysis of Transaction Flows," *Econometrica,* XXVIII (July 1960), 551–72. Richard Chadwick and Karl W. Deutsch, in "International Trade and Economic Integration: Further Developments in Trade Matrix Analysis," *Comparative Political Studies,* VI (April 1973), 84–109, make some amendments to earlier methods of calculation when regional groupings are being analyzed. These are not reflected in Table 9.3. I am indebted to Professor Deutsch for giving me access to the unpublished data presented in the table.

16. League of Nations, *Industrialization and Foreign Trade* (1945, II.A.10), 13; Mira Wilkins, *The Emergence of Multinational Enterprise* (Cambridge: Harvard University Press 1970), 45–65.

17. John Gallagher and Ronald Robinson, "The Imperialism of Free Trade," *Economic History Review,* 2nd Series, VI (August 1953), 1–15.

18. Kindleberger (fn. 9), 41.

19. Robert Triffin, *The Evolution of the International Monetary System* (Princeton: Princeton Studies in International Finance. No. 12, 1964). 2–20; R. G. Hawtrey, *The Gold Standard in Theory and Practice* (London: Longmans, Green 1947), 69–80; Leland Yeager, *International Monetary Relations* (New York: Harper and Row 1966), 251–61; Sidney E. Rolfe and James Burtle, *The Great Wheel: The World Monetary System, a Reinterpretation* (New York: Quadrangle 1973), 10–11; Condliffe (fn. 9), 343–80.

20. Raymond Aron, *The Imperial Republic* (Englewood Cliffs, NJ: Prentice-Hall 1973), 191; Gilpin (fn. 12), 409–12; Calleo and Rowland (fn. 6), chap. 3.

21. Lloyd Gardner. *Economic Aspects of New Deal Diplomacy* (Madison: University of Wisconsin Press 1964), 389; Gilpin (fn. 12), 409.

22. Triffin (fn. 19), 22–28; Rolfe and Burtle (fn. 19), 13–55; Yeager (fn. 19), 278–317; Kindleberger (fn. 11), 270–71.

23. Kindleberger (fn. 11), 199–224; Yeager (fn. 19), 314; Condliffe (fn. 9), 499.

24. Triffin (fn. 19), 22.

25. Kindleberger (fn. 11), 296.

26. Condliffe (fn. 9), 494–97.

27. Evans (fn. 13), 7.

28. Robert Gilpin, *American Power and the Multinationals: The Political Economy of Foreign Investment* (New York: Basic Books 1975), chap. 3; Kindleberger (fn. 11), 294.

29. Yeager (fn. 19), 279.

30. Condliffe (fn. 9), 347.

31. This draws from arguments made by Theodore Lowi, particularly his "Four Systems of Policy, Politics and Choice," *Public Administration Review,* XXXII (July–August 1972), 298–310. See also E. E. Schattschneider, *Politics, Pressures and the Tariff: A Study of Free Enterprise in Pressure Politics as Shown in the 1929–1930 Revision of the Tariff* (New York: Prentice-Hall 1935).

32. See Janet Kelly, "American Banks in London," Ph.D. diss. (Johns Hopkins University 1975), for a study of the overseas expansion of American banks in the postwar period.

33. Schattschneider (fn. 31), 288.

34. See Peter J. Katzenstein, "Transnational Relations and Domestic Structures: Foreign Economic Policies of Advanced Industrial States," *International Organization,* XXX (Winter 1976), for a suggestive discussion of the impact of the relative power of state and society on foreign economic policy. See also Samuel P. Huntington, "Paradigms of American Politics: Beyond the One, the Two, and the Many," *Political Science Quarterly,* Vol. 89 (March 1974), 16–17, as well as Huntington, *Political Order in Changing Societies* (New Haven: Yale University Press 1968), chap. 2.

Appendix 1. Aggregate Economic Size

Year	Indicator	Unit	Great Britain	United States	France	Germany	Japan
1. 1860	Real Income	millions IU's*	8.34 (1870)	11.25	4.84	5.70	n.a.
2. 1874-83	"	"	11.55 (1883)	14.23	5.88 (1880)	10.54 (1883)	n.a.
3. 1899	GDP	billions 1955 $	34.0	59.0	14.0	29.3	2.80
4. 1913	"	"	42.0	97.0	16.0	37.5	4.80
5. 1929	"	"	42.0	168.0	25.0	40.5	9.10
6. 1937	"	"	50.0	171.0	22.4	46.5	12.99
7. 1950	"	"	54.7	294.0	32.4	31.8	11.1
8. 1955	"	"	63.5	362.5	40.0	49.0	16.5
9. 1957	"	"	66.0	376.0	44.8	55.0	19.8
10. 1960	"	billions current $	71.2	509.0	61.0	72.0	43.1
11. 1963	"	"	84.6	596.0	83.3	96.2	68.1
12. 1969	"	"	109.7	928.0	141.5	153.7	168.0
13. 1972	"	"	153.0	1,159.0	197.7	260.2	299.2

* IU's (International Units): Quantity of goods exchangeable on the average for $1 in the U.S. during 1925–34. Dates are in parentheses when different from those in first column.

Sources for I.1 and I.2:

Lines 1–2: Colin Clark, *The Conditions of Economic Progress* (London: Macmillan 1957), chap. III, Tables 23, 40, 22, 21, 28.

Lines 3–9: Alfred Maizels. *Industrial Growth and World Trade* (Cambridge: Cambridge University Press 1963), 533, 531.

Lines 10–13: *United Nations Statistical Yearbook 1974,* 596–98.

Appendix 2. Percentage of Share of World Trade

Years	United Kingdom*	France	Germany	Russia	United States**	Japan
1720, 1750, 1780	14.1	9.7	10.2	9.4	1.0	n.a.
1820, 1830	21.6	9.9	11.5	6.7	6.0	n.a.
1830, 1840	20.8	10.8	10.2	6.4	6.3	n.a.
1840, 1850	20.1	11.4	8.8	5.3	7.3	n.a.
1850, 1860	22.7	11.3	8.6	4.0	8.3	n.a.
1860, 1870	25.1	10.8	9.2	4.0	8.3	n.a.
1870, 1880	24.0	10.8	9.7	4.5	8.8	n.a.
1880, 1890	22.4	10.2	10.3	3.9	9.8	n.a.
1913	15.5	7.3	12.1	12.8	12.9	n.a.
1928	13.7	6.1	9.3	8.3	17.3	n.a.
1937	14.1	4.8	8.3	7.4	16.0	5.1
1950	11.6	5.3	4.1	n.a.	16.7	1.6
1958	9.3	5.0	7.5	3.9	20.0	2.7
1969	7.0	6.0	10.0	2.0	15.0	6.0
1973	9.0	9.0	16.0	2.0	19.0	9.0

*1913–1937 United Kingdom and Ireland.

**1913–1937 North America.

Sources: 1720–1937: Simon Kuznets, *Modern Economic Growth* (New Haven: Yale University Press 1966), 306–8.

1950–1973: International Monetary Fund, *Direction of Trade,* various years; and United Nations, *Yearbook of International Trade Statistics,* various years.

Ronald Rogowski

POLITICAL CLEAVAGES AND CHANGING EXPOSURE TO TRADE

Why countries have the political cleavages they do and why those cleavages change are among the enduring mysteries of comparative politics. Among the many factors that have been adduced as partial explanations are preexisting cultural and religious divisions, the rapidity and timing of industrialization or of the grant of mass suffrage, the sequence of "crises" of modernization, the electoral system, and—most recently—the product cycle (see, inter alia, Binder et al. 1971; Duverger 1959; Kurth 1979a, 1979b; Lipset and Rokkan 1967; Rokkan 1970, 1981).

Without denying the importance of any of these variables, I want to suggest the relevance of a factor that has, until now, been widely neglected: externally induced changes—in countries with different factor endowments—in exposure to international trade.

To be sure, some studies of individual countries, and even a few comparative inquiries, have argued the significance of changing international trade in particular circumstances: one thinks, in particular, of Abraham 1981, Gerschenkron 1943, Gourevitch 1977 and 1986, Rosenberg 1943, Sunkel and Paz 1973. One author, Cameron (1978), has even suggested a relation, at least in recent decades, between exposure to trade and the rate of growth in state expenditure.

Arguing much more generally, I shall try to show that basic results of the theory of international trade—including, in particular, the well-known

From *The American Political Science Review* 81, no. 4 (December 1987): 1121–37.

Stolper-Samuelson Theorem (Stolper and Samuelson 1941)—imply that increases or decreases in the costs and difficulty of international trade should powerfully affect domestic political cleavages and should do so differently, but predictably, in countries with different factor endowments. Moreover, I shall suggest that these implications conform surprisingly well with what has been observed about patterns of cleavage and about changes in those patterns in a great variety of countries during four periods of global change in exposure to trade, namely the "long" sixteenth century, the nineteenth century, the Depression of the 1930s, and the years since World War II.

Nonetheless, what I present here remains conjectural and preliminary. The evidence I shall be able to advance is suggestive rather than conclusive. It is principally the clarity of the logical case that seems to me to justify further refinement and testing.

The Stolper-Samuelson Theorem

In 1941 Wolfgang Stolper and Paul Samuelson solved conclusively the old riddle of gains and losses from protection (or, for that matter, from free trade). They showed that in any society protection benefits—and liberalization of trade harms—owners of factors in which that society is *poorly* endowed, relative to the rest of the world, as well as producers who use the scarce factors intensively.[1]

Conversely, protection harms—and liberalization benefits—owners of factors the given society holds *abundantly* relative to the rest of the world, and producers who use the abundant factors intensively.[2] Thus, in a society rich in labor but poor in capital, protection would benefit capital and harm labor; and liberalization of trade would benefit labor and harm capital.

So far, the theorem is what it is usually perceived to be: merely a statement, if an important and sweeping one, about the effects of tariff policy. The picture is altered, however, when one realizes that exogenous changes can have exactly the same effects as increases or decreases in protection. A cheapening of transport costs, for example, is indistinguishable in its impact from an across-the-board decrease in every affected state's tariffs (Mundell 1957, 330); so is any change in the international regime that decreases the risks or the transaction costs of trade. The converse is of course equally true: when a nation's external transport becomes dearer, or its trade less secure, it is affected exactly as if it had imposed a higher tariff.

The point is of more than academic interest because we know, historically, that major changes in the risks and costs of international trade have occurred: notoriously, the railroads and steamships of the nineteenth century brought drastically cheaper transportation (Landes 1969, 153–54, 196, 201–2; Hobsbawm 1979, Chap. 3); so, in our own generation, did supertankers, cheap oil, and containerization (Rosecrance 1986, 142). According to the familiar argument of Kindleberger (1973) and others, international hegemony decreases both the risks and the transaction costs of international trade; and the decline of hegemonic power makes trade more expensive, perhaps—as, according to this interpretation, in the 1930s—prohibitively so. Analyzing a much earlier period, the Belgian historian Henri Pirenne (1939) attributed much of the final decline of the Roman Empire to the growing insecurity of interregional, and especially of Mediterranean, trade after 600 A.D.[3]

Global changes of these kinds, it follows, should have had global consequences. The "transportation revolutions" of the sixteenth, the nineteenth, and scarcely less of the mid-twentieth century must have benefited, in each affected country, owners and intensive employers of locally abundant factors and must have harmed owners and intensive employers of locally scarce factors. The events of the 1930s should have had exactly the opposite effect. What, however, will have been the *political* consequences of those shifts of wealth and income? To answer that question we require a rudimentary model of the political process and a somewhat more definite one of the economy.

Simple Models of the Polity and the Economy

I shall assume of domestic political processes only two things: (1) that the beneficiaries of a change will try to continue and accelerate it, while the victims of the same change will endeavor to retard or to halt it; and (2) that those who enjoy a sudden increase in (actual or potential)[4] wealth and income will thereby be enabled to expand their political influence as well (cf. Becker 1983). As regards international trade, (1) implies that the gainers from any exogenous change will seek to continue and to expand free trade, while the losers will seek protection (and, if that fails, imperialism);[5] (2) implies that those who gain, or are positioned to gain, economically from exogenous changes in international trade will increase their political power as well.

Economically, I propose to adopt with minor refinements the traditional three-factor model—land, labor, and capital—and to assume, for now, that the land-labor ratio informs us fully about any country's endowment of those two factors. No country, in other words, can be rich both in land and in labor: a high land-labor ratio implies abundance of land and scarcity of labor; a low ratio signifies the opposite. (I shall later relax this assumption.) Finally, I shall simply define an *advanced* economy as one in which capital is abundant.

This model of factor endowments inevitably oversimplifies reality and will require amendment. Its present simplicity, however, permits us in theory to place any country's economy into one of four cells (see Figure 9.3), according to (1) whether it is advanced or backward and (2) whether its land-labor ratio is high or low. We recognize, in other words, only economies that are (1) capital rich, land rich, and labor poor; (2) capital rich, land poor, and labor rich; (3) capital poor, land rich, and labor poor; or (4) capital poor, land poor, and labor rich.

Political Effects of Increasing Exposure to Trade

I shall now try to demonstrate that the Stolper-Samuelson Theorem, applied to our simple model, implies that increasing exposure to trade must result in *urban-rural conflict* in two kinds of economies and in *class conflict* in the two others.

Consider first the upper right-hand cell of Figure 9.3: the advanced (therefore capital-rich) economy endowed abundantly in labor but poorly in land. Expanding trade must benefit both capitalists and workers; it harms only landowners and the pastoral and agricultural enterprises that use land intensively. Both capitalists and workers—that is to say, almost the entire urban sector—should favor free trade; agriculture should on the whole be protectionist. Moreover, we expect the capitalists and the workers to try, very likely in concert, to expand their political influence. Depending on pre-existing circumstances, they may seek concretely an extension of the franchise, a reapportionment of seats, a diminution in the powers of an upper house or of a gentry-based political elite, or a violent "bourgeois" revolution.

Urban-rural conflict should also arise in backward, labor-poor economies (the lower left-hand cell of Figure 9.3) when trade expands, albeit with a complete reversal of fronts. In such "frontier" societies, both capital and labor are scarce: hence both are harmed by expanding trade and will seek protection. Only land is abundant, and therefore only agriculture culture will gain from free trade. Farmers and pastoralists will try to expand their influence in some movement of a "Populist" and antiurban stripe.

Conversely, in backward economies with low land-labor ratios (the lower right-hand cell of Figure 9.3), land and capital are scarce and labor is abundant. The model therefore predicts *class conflict*: labor will pursue free trade and expanded political power (including, in some circumstances, a workers' revolution); landowners, capitalists, and capital-intensive manufacturers will unite to support protection, imperialism, and a politics of continued exclusion. (Lest the picture of a rising in support of freer markets seem too improbable a priori, I observe at once its general conformity with Popkin's 1979 astute interpretation of the Vietnamese revolution.)

The reverse form of class conflict is expected to arise in the final case, that of an advanced but land-rich economy (the upper left-hand cell of Figure 9.3) under increasing exposure to trade. Because both capital and land are abundant, capitalists, capital-intensive industries, and agriculture will all benefit from, and will endorse, free trade; labor being scarce, workers and labor-intensive industries will embrace protection and (if need be) imperialism. The benefited sectors will seek to expand their political power, if not by disfranchisement then by curtailment of workers' economic prerogatives and suppression of their organizations.

These implications of the theory of international trade (summarized in Figure 9.4) seem clear, but do they in anyway describe reality? I shall address that question more fully below, but for now it is worth observing how closely the experience of three major

Figure 9.3. Four Main Types of Factor Endowments

	Land-Labor Ratio	
	High	**Low**
Advanced Economy	Abundant: Capital, Land Scarce: Labor	Abundant: Capital, Labor Scarce: Land
Backward Economy	Abundant: Land Scarce: Capital, Labor	Abundant: Labor Scarce: Capital, Land

Figure 9.4. Predicted Effects of Expanding Exposure to Trade

	Land-Labor Ratio	
	High	**Low**

Advanced Economy	Class cleavage:
	  Land and capital free-trading, assertive
	  Labor defensive, protectionist
		Urban-rural cleavage:
		  Capital and labor free-trading, assertive
		  Land defensive, protectionist
		    (Radicalism)

Backward Economy	Urban-rural cleavage:
	  Land free-trading, assertive
	  Labor and capital defensive, protectionist
	    (U.S. populism)
		Class cleavage:
		  Labor free-trading assertive
		  Land and capital defensive, protectionist
		    (Socialism)

countries—Germany, Britain, and the United States—conforms to this analysis in the period of rapidly expanding trade in the last third of the nineteenth century; and how far it can go to explain otherwise puzzling disparities in those states' patterns of political evolution.

Germany and the United States were both still relatively backward, that is, capital-poor, societies: both, in fact, imported considerable amounts of capital in this period (Feis 1965, 24–25 and Chap. 3). Germany, however, was rich in labor and poor in land; the United States, of course, was in exactly the opposite position. Again, the demonstration is easy: the United States imported—and Germany exported (not least to the United States)—workers.[6] The theory, of course, predicts class conflict in Germany, with labor the "revolutionary" and free-trading element and with land and capital united in support of protection and imperialism. Surely this description will not ring false to any student of German socialism or of Germany's infamous "marriage of iron and rye."[7] For the United States, conversely, the theory predicts—quite accurately, I submit—urban-rural conflict, with the agrarians now assuming the "revolutionary" and free-trading role and with capital and labor uniting in a protectionist and imperialist coalition. E. E. Schattschneider (1960) or Walter Dean Burnham (1970) could hardly have described more succinctly the history of populism and of the election of 1896.[8]

Britain, on the other hand, was already an advanced economy in the later nineteenth century, one in which capital was so abundant that it was exported in vast quantities (Feis 1965, Chap. 1). That it was also rich in labor is demonstrated by its extensive exports of that factor to the United States, Canada, Australia, New Zealand, and Africa.[9] Britain therefore falls into the upper right-hand quadrant of Figure 9.3 and is predicted to exhibit a rural-urban cleavage, with fronts opposite to those found in the United States: capitalists and labor unite in support of free trade and in demands for expanded political power, while landowners and agriculture support protection and imperialism.

While this picture surely obscures important nuances, it illuminates a crucial difference between Britain and, for example, Germany in this period: in Britain, capitalists and labor *did* unite effectively in the Liberal party and forced an expanded suffrage and curtailment of (still principally landowning) aristocratic power; in Germany, with liberalism shattered (Sheehan 1978), the suffrage for the powerful state parliaments was actually contracted, and—far from eroding aristocratic power—the bourgeoisie grew more and more *verjunkert* in style and aspirations.

Political Effects of Declining Exposure to Trade

When declining hegemony or rising costs of transportation substantially constrict external trade, the gainers and losers are simply the reverse of those under increasing exposure to trade: owners of locally scarce factors prosper, owners of locally abundant ones suffer. The latter, however, can invoke no such simple remedy as protection or imperialism; aside from tentative "internationalist" efforts to restore orderly markets (Gourevitch 1986, Chap. 4), they must largely accept their fate. Power and policy, we expect, will shift in each case toward the owners and intensive users of scarce factors.

Let us first consider the situation of the highly *developed* (and therefore, by our earlier definition, capital-rich) economies. In an economy of this kind with a high land-labor ratio (the upper left-hand cell of Figure 9.3), we should expect intense *class* conflict precipitated by a newly aggressive working class. Land and capital are both abundant in such an economy; hence, under declining trade, owners of both factors (and producers who use either factor intensively) lose. Labor being the only scarce resource, workers are well positioned to reap a significant windfall from the protection that dearer or riskier trade affords; and, according to our earlier assumption, like any other benefited class they will soon try to parlay their greater economic into greater political power. Capitalists and landowners, even if they were previously at odds, will unite to oppose labor's demands.

Quite to the contrary, declining trade in an advanced economy that is labor rich and land poor (the upper right-hand cell of Figure 9.3) will entail *urban-rural* conflict. Capital and labor, being both abundant, are both harmed by the contraction of external trade. Agriculture, as the intense exploiter of the only scarce factor, gains significantly and quickly tries to translate its gain into greater political control.

Urban-rural conflict is also predicted for backward, land-rich countries under declining trade; but here agriculture is on the defensive. Labor and capital being both scarce, both benefit from the contraction of trade; land, as the only locally abundant factor, retreats. The urban sectors unite, in a parallel to the "radical" coalition of labor-rich

Figure 9.5. Predicted Effects of Declining Exposure to Trade

Land-Labor Ratio

	High	Low
Advanced Economy	Class cleavage: Labor gains power. Land and capital lose. (U.S. New Deal)	Urban-rural cleavage: Land gains power. Labor and capital lose. (Western European Fascism)
Backward Economy	Urban-rural cleavage: Labor and capital gain power. Land loses. (South American Populism)	Class cleavage: Land and capital gain power. Labor loses. (Asian & Eastern European Fascism)

developed countries under expanding trade, to demand an increased voice in the state.

Finally, in backward economies rich in labor rather than land, class conflict resumes, with labor this time on the defensive. Capital and land, as the locally scarce factors, gain from declining trade; labor, locally abundant, loses economically and is soon threatened politically.

Observe again, as a first test of the plausibility of these results—summarized in Figure 9.5—how they appear to account for some prominent disparities of political response to the last precipitous decline of international trade, the Depression of the 1930s. The U.S. New Deal represented a sharp turn to the left and occasioned a significant increase in organized labor's political power. In Germany, a depression of similar depth (gauged by unemployment rates and declines in industrial production [Landes 1969, 391]) brought to power first Hindenburg's and then Hitler's dictatorship. In both, landowners exercised markedly greater influence than they had under Weimar (Abraham 1981, 85–115 and Chap. 4; Gessner 1977); and indeed a credible case can be made out that the rural sector was the principal early beneficiary of the Nazi regime (see, inter alia, Gerschenkron 1943, 154–63; Gies 1968; Holt 1936, 173–74, 194ff.; Schoenbaum 1966, 156–63).[10] Yet this is exactly the broad difference that the model would lead us to anticipate if we

accept that by 1930 both countries were economically advanced—although Germany, after reparations and cessions of industrial territory, was surely less abundant in capital than the United States—but the United States remained rich in land, which in Germany was scarce. Only an obtuse observer would claim that such factors as cultural inheritance and recent defeat in war played no role; but surely it is also important to recognize the sectoral impact of declining trade in the two societies.[11]

As regards the less-developed economies of the time, it may be profitable to contrast the Depression's impact on such South American cases as Argentina and Brazil with its effects in the leading Asian country, Japan. In Argentina and Brazil, it is usually asserted (Cardoso and Faletto 1979, 124–26 and Chap. 5; Skidmore and Smith 1984, 59–60; Sunkel and Paz 1973, 352–54), the Depression gave rise to, or at the least strengthened, "Populist" coalitions that united labor and the urban middle classes in opposition to traditional, landowning elites. In Japan, growing military influence suppressed representative institutions and nascent workers' organizations, ruling in the interest—albeit probably not under the domination—of landowners and capitalists (Kato 1974; Reischauer 1974, 186–87, 195–99). (Similar suppressions of labor occurred in China and Vietnam [Clubb 1972, 135–40; Popkin 1979, xix, 215].)

In considering these contrasting responses, should we not take into account that Argentina and Brazil were rich in land and poor in labor (recall the extent of immigration, especially into Argentina), while in Japan (and, with local exceptions, in Asia generally) labor was abundant and land was scarce (respectively, the lower left- and right-hand cells of Figure 9.5)?

A Preliminary Survey of the Evidence

I want now to undertake a more systematic, if still sketchy, examination of the historical evidence that bears on the hypotheses developed here. This effort will serve principally to suggest directions for further research; it can in no way be described as conclusive.

The "Long" Sixteenth Century

It has long been recognized that improvements in navigation and shipbuilding permitted, from about 1450 on, a previously unimagined expansion of trade, which eventuated in the European "discovery" and colonization of the Americas (Cipolla 1965). Among social scientists, Immanuel Wallerstein (1974) has studied this period most intensively; and it is worth emphasizing that the present analysis conforms with essential aspects, and, indeed, permits some clarification, of his.

Within the context of the age, what Wallerstein calls the *core* economies of the new world system—those, essentially, of northwestern Europe—were defined by their abundance in capital and labor, and by their relative scarcity of land. The *periphery* can be described as the exact inverse: rich in land, poor in both capital and—often leading to the adoption of slavery or serfdom—labor. Under expanding trade, the regimes of the core come to be dominated by a "bourgeois" coalition of capital and skilled labor (the Dutch Republic, the Tudors), and of the manufactures that use both intensively; the older, landed elites lose ground. Conversely, in the periphery, land—in the persons of plantation owners and *Gutsherren*—suppresses both capital and labor and, indeed, almost all urban life.

So far the equation seems apt. Can we, however, not go on to define that Wallersteinian chimera, the *semiperiphery* (Wallerstein 1974, 102–7), as comprising economies that fall into the lower right-hand cell of Figure 9.3, economies poor in capital and land, rich in labor? That would, I suspect, accurately describe most of the southern European economies in this period; and it would correctly predict (see again Figure 9.4) the intense class conflict (including the German Peasants War [Moore 1967, 463–67]) and the wholly retrograde and protectionist policies adopted by a peculiarly united class of landowners and capitalists in many of these regions.[12]

The Nineteenth Century

We can again proceed regionally, generalizing on the sketch of Britain, Germany, and the United States developed earlier for this period. For the period just before the great cheapening of transportation—roughly at the middle of the nineteenth century[13]—Britain can stand as the surrogate for the advanced and labor-rich economies of northwest Europe generally, including Belgium, the Netherlands, and northern France (Hobsbawm 1962, Chap. 9; Landes 1969, Chap. 3). For this whole region, as for Britain, the model predicts that expanding trade would engender rural-urban conflict: capitalists and workers, united in support of free trade and greater urban influence, oppose a more traditional and protectionist landed sector. It does not seem to me farfetched to see the powerful liberalism and radicalism of this whole region in the later nineteenth century (Carstairs 1980, 50,

62; Cobban 1965, 21–28, 58–67; Daalder 1973, 196–98; Lorwin 1966, 152–55)—or, for that matter, much of the conflict between secularism and clericalism—in this light.

Almost all of the rest of Europe at the dawn of this period can be compared with Germany: poor in capital and in land, rich in labor.[14] (The land-labor ratio seems as a rule to have declined as one moved from north to south within the economically backward regions of Europe [see figures for 1846 in Bowden, Karpovich, and Usher 1937, 3].) As it does for Germany, the model predicts for these other countries, particularly in southern Europe, class conflict as a consequence of increasing exposure to trade: workers (including agricultural wage laborers) press for more open markets and greater influence; capitalists and landowners unite in support of protection and more traditional rule. In its main aspect, this seems to me only a restatement of a central tendency that has long been remarked, namely that class conflict in the nineteenth century came at an earlier phase of industrialization, and more bitterly, to southern and central than to northwestern Europe (e.g., Lipset 1970, 28–30; Macridis 1978, 485–87; cf. Thomson 1962, 375–78); and it seems to me a more credible account of these regions' extremism than Duverger's (1959, 238) famous invocation of an allegedly more mercurial "Latin" temperament.

The United States, finally, represents the land-rich, but labor- and capital-poor "frontier societies" of this period generally: most of both Americas, Australia, New Zealand, even those parts of central and southern Africa that would soon be opened to commercial agriculture. Here, expanding trade benefits and strengthens landowners and farmers against protectionist capitalists and workers (although, as in the United States, the protectionist forces may still prevail); rural-urban conflict ensues, precipitated by demands from the rural sector.

Again, this does not at first glance appear wide of the mark. In many of the Latin American societies, this period cemented landed rule (Skidmore and Smith 1984, 50; Sunkel and Paz 1973, 306–21); in the United States and Canada, it was characterized by conflicts between the industrial East and the agricultural West (Easterbrook and Aitken 1958, 503–4); in almost wholly agricultural Australia, trade precipitated a cleavage between free-trading landowners and increasingly protectionist rural and urban wage labor (Gollan 1955, esp. 162–69; Greenwood 1955, 216–20).

In all of these cases, as I have emphasized before, other factors were surely at work and important aspects are neglected by the present analysis; but it is essential also not to ignore the benefits and costs of expanding trade to the various sectors.

The Depression of the 1930s

Here the fit between theory and reality seems quite strong. Not only the United States but Canada, Australia, and New Zealand were by this time advanced, land-rich economies. Labor, their only scarce factor, gained from the collapse of international trade: workers became more militant, policy shifted to the left. Most Latin American societies remained land-rich but backward; and for them this was quite generally the period of "Populist" coalitions of the two scarce factors, labor and capital. In developed northern Europe, owners and exploiters of the locally scarce factor of land grew more assertive, and generally more powerful, wherever previous developments had not caused them to disappear; capitalists and workers lost ground. Finally, throughout the backward regions of the world economy, where labor was abundant and land was scarce—not only in Asia but in southern and eastern Europe—labor lost to a renascent coalition of the locally scarce factors of land and capital: in Spain, Italy, Rumania, Hungary, and Poland, to name only the most prominent cases (Carsten 1967, Chaps. 2, 5 and pp. 194–204).

After World War II

Under U.S. hegemony, and with new economies in transportation and communication, the West since World War II has experienced one of history's more dramatic expansions of international trade (Organization for Economic Cooperation and Development [OECD] 1982, 62–63). Again, the theory would lead us to expect different regional consequences.

In the developed, labor-rich and land-poor economies—including now not only most of Europe but Japan—the model would predict an "end of ideology," at least as regards issues of class: labor and capital, both beneficiaries of expanding trade, unite to advance it and to oppose any remaining pretensions to rule by the landowning groups.[15] Conversely, in the land-rich and still underdeveloped economies of Latin America, expanding trade displaces the Depression-era "Populist" coalitions of labor and capital and brings renewed influence to the landed sectors. The areas of Asia and of southern Europe that are economically backward and abundant only in labor experience labor militancy and, in not a few cases, revolutionary workers' movements. Finally, and perhaps more as a statement about the future, the few economies rich in both capital and land—principally those of North America, Australia, and New Zealand—should, as they become seriously exposed to international trade, experience class conflict and a considerable suppression of labor. Capital and agriculture will for the most part unite in support of the free trade that benefits them; labor, as the locally scarce factor, will favor protection and imperialism.

Further Implications

To the extent that the model has gained any credibility from the foregoing brief survey, it may be useful to observe some of its other implications for disciplinary riddles and conjectures. Take first Gerschenkron's (1962) observation, and Hirschman's (1968) subsequent challenge and amendment of it, that "latecomers" to economic development tend to assign a stronger role to the state. From the present perspective, what should matter more, at least among labor-rich economies, is whether development *precedes* or *follows* significant exposure to trade. In an economy that has accumulated abundant capital before it is opened to trade, capital and labor will operate in relative harmony, and little state intervention will be required. Where trade precedes development, assertive labor faces—as it did in Imperial Germany—the united opposition of capitalists and landowners. To the extent that labor wins this struggle, it will require a strong state to administer the economy; to the extent that capital and land prevail, a state powerful enough to suppress labor is needed. Either route leads to a stronger state.

Even this generalization, however, applies only to economies where labor is abundant, and land scarce. Hence Hirschman's observation that "latecomers" in Latin America do not behave as Gerschenkron predicts should not surprise us. Where land is abundant, and labor scarce—as has generally been true of the Americas—"late" economic modernization (i.e., one that follows significant exposure to trade) radicalizes owners of *land* rather than owners of labor. In such "frontier" economies, labor and capital again find themselves in the same political camp, this time in support of protection. In the absence of class conflict, no powerful state is required.

This last point, of course, sheds some light on Sombart's old question, Why is there no socialism in the United States? If this model is right, the question is appropriately broadened to, Why is there no socialism in land-rich economies? Simply put, socialism develops most readily where labor is favored by rising exposure to trade and capital is not; labor is then progressive and capital is reactionary. But labor is never favored by rising trade where it is scarce. Powerful socialist movements, the present model suggests, are confined to backward and labor-rich economies under conditions of expanding trade (the less-developed European societies in the later nineteenth century, Asia after World War II).

A third riddle this approach may help resolve is that of the coalitional basis and aims of the North in the U.S. Civil War.[16] As Barrington Moore, Jr. posed the question in a memorable chapter of *Social Origins of Dictatorship and Democracy* (1967, Chap. 3), What was the connection between *protection* and Free Soil in the platform of the Republican party or of the North more generally, and Why did so broad a coalition support both aims?

If, as seems apparent, labor was scarce in the United States, then the nineteenth century's increasing exposure to trade should have depressed, or at least retarded the advance of, wages. By definition, slaves already received a lower wage than they would voluntarily accept (Else, why coerce them?); and increased trade could reasonably be seen as intensifying, or at least as retarding the demise of, slavery. Conversely, protection in a labor-scarce economy might so raise the general wage level (while, paradoxically, also increasing returns to scarce capital) as to make manumission feasible. Hence to link protection and abolition might seem a wholly sensible strategy. Moreover, because protection in that period would benefit workers and capitalists generally, it could attract the support of a very wide coalition. At least some of the mystery seems dissolved.

Relaxing the Reliance on Land-Labor Ratios

For the sake of logical completeness, and to fill a nagging empirical gap, let us now relax the assumption that the land-labor ratio informs us

completely about the relative abundance of these two factors. We admit, in other words, that a country may be rich or poor in *both* land and labor. Four new cases arise in theory if (as I suspect) rarely in practice (see Figure 9.6): economies may be, as before, advanced or backward (i.e., capital rich or capital poor); but they may now be rich in both land and labor or poorly endowed in both factors.

Two cases—that of the advanced economy rich in both factors and of the backward one poor in both—are theoretically improbable[17] and politically uninteresting: if all factors were abundant relative to the rest of the world, the society would unanimously embrace free trade; if all were scarce, it would agree on protection. Let us consider, then, the remaining two possibilities.

In an advanced economy where both land and labor are scarce, expanding trade will benefit only capital. Agriculture and labor—*green* and *red*—will unite in support of protection and, if need be, imperialism; only capitalists will embrace free trade. When trade contracts in such an economy, the scarce factors of land and labor gain, and capital loses, influence; farmers and peasants are likely to seek expanded mass participation in politics and a radical curtailment of capitalist power.

In a backward economy with abundant land and labor (a possibility considered explicitly by Myint [1958, 323]), change in exposure to trade again mobilizes a coalition of red and green, but with diametrically opposed positions. Expanding trade now *benefits* farmers and workers but harms capitalists; and the labor-landowner coalition pursues a wider franchise, free trade, and disempowerment of capital. Contracting trade, however, benefits only the owners of capital and injures both workers and farmers; again intense conflict between capital and the other two factors is predicted, ending in either a capitalist dictatorship or an anti-capitalist revolution.

It is tempting, if speculative in the extreme, to see in the red-green coalitions of Scandinavia in

Figure 9.6. Predicted Effects on Economies That Are Rich or Poor in Both *Land and Labor*

	Land and Labor both Abundant	Land and Labor both Scarce
Advanced Economy	N/A	Expanding trade: Capital assertive, free-trading Land and labor protectionist, defensive Declining trade: Land and labor gain power. Capital loses.
Backward Economy	Expand trade: Land and labor free-trading, assertive Capital defensive, protectionist Declining trade: Capital gains power. Land and labor lose.	N/A

the 1930s (Gourevitch 1986, 131–35; Hancock 1972, 30–31; Rokkan 1966, 84) the natural response to trade contraction of (by then) capital-rich but land- and labor-poor economies; and, conversely, to view modern Russian history, at least until well after World War II, as that of a backward but land- *and* labor-rich economy,[18] which, in a time of expanding trade, indeed forged an anti-capitalist coalition of peasants and workers and, when trade contracted, experienced (as Stalin's enemies alleged at the time) a dictatorship of state capital over both workers and farmers.

Certainly so long as we cling to the view that land can only be abundant where labor is not, and vice-versa, we can offer no trade-based account of red-green coalitions; indeed, changing exposure to trade must drive the two factors apart, for it always helps the one and hurts the other. On the one hand, this reflects reality—coalitions of labor and agriculture have been rare, and have failed even where much seemed to speak for them (e.g., in U.S. populism and on the German left); on the other, it leaves the few actual red-green coalitions, particularly those that arose in circumstances of

changing exposure to trade, as standing refutations of the model.

Possible Objections

At least three objections can plausibly be raised to the whole line of analysis that I have advanced here:

First and most fundamentally, it may be argued that the effects sketched out here will not obtain in countries that depend only slightly on trade. A Belgium, where external trade (taken as the sum of exports and imports) roughly equals GDP, can indeed be affected profoundly by changes in the risks or costs of international commerce; but a state like the United States in the 1960s, where trade amounted to scarcely a tenth of GDP, will have remained largely immune (OECD 1982, 62–63).

This view, while superficially plausible, is incorrect. The Stolper-Samuelson result obtains at any margin; and, in fact, holders of scarce factors have been quite as devastated by expanding trade in almost autarkic economies—one need think only of the weavers of capital-poor India or Silesia, exposed in the nineteenth century to the competition of Lancashire mills—as in ones previously more dependent on trade. (Cf. Thomson 1962, 163–64, on the vast dislocations that even slight exposure to trade occasioned in previously isolated areas of nineteenth-century Europe.)

Second, one can ask why the cleavages indicated here should persist. In a world of perfectly mobile factors and rational behavior, people would quickly disinvest from losing factors and enterprises (e.g., farming in Britain after 1880) and move to sectors whose auspices were more favorable. Markets should swiftly clear, and a new, if different, political equilibrium should be achieved.

To this, two answers may be given. First, in some cases trade expands or contracts so rapidly as to frustrate rational expectations. Especially in countries that experience a steady series of such exogenous shocks—Europe, for example, since 1840—divisions based on factor endowments (which ordinarily change only gradually)[19] will be repeatedly revived. Second, often enough some factors' privileged access to political influence makes the extraction of rents and subsidies seem cheaper than adaptation: Prussian *Junker,* familiarly, sought (and, rather easily, won) protection rather than adjustment. In such circumstances, adaptation may be long delayed, sometimes with ultimately disastrous consequences.

Finally, it may be objected that I have said nothing about the outcome of these conflicts. I have not done so for the simple reason that I cannot: history makes it all too plain—as in the cases of nineteenth-century Germany and the United States—that the economic losers from trade may win politically over more than the short run. What I have advanced here is a speculation about *cleavages,* not about outcomes. I have asserted only that those who gain from fluctuations in trade will be strengthened and emboldened politically; nothing guarantees that they will win. Victory or defeat depends, so far as I can see, on precisely those institutional and cultural factors that this perspective so resolutely ignores.

Conclusion

I have not claimed that changes in countries' exposure to trade explain all, or even most, of their varying patterns of political cleavage. It would be foolish to ignore the importance of ancient cultural and religious loyalties, of wars and migrations, or of such historical memories as the French Revolution and the *Kulturkamf.* Neither have I offered anything like a convincing empirical demonstration of the modest hypotheses I have advanced; at most, the empirical regularities that I have noted or have taken over from such authorities as Gerschenkron and Lipset can serve to suggest the plausibility of the model and the value of further refinement and testing of it.

I have presented a theoretical puzzle, a kind of social-scientific "thought-experiment" in Hempel's (1965) original sense: a teasing out of unexpected and sometimes counterintuitive implications of theories already widely accepted (Chap. 7). For the Stolper-Samuelson Theorem *is* generally, indeed almost universally, embraced; yet, coupled with a stark and unexceptionable model of the political realm, it plainly implies that changes in exposure to trade must profoundly affect nations' internal political cleavages. Do they do so? If they do not, what is wrong—either with our theories of international trade or with our understanding of politics?

NOTES

1. In fact, the effect flows backward from products and is an extension of the Heckscher-Ohlin theorem: under free trade, countries export products whose manufacture uses locally abundant, and import products whose, manufacture uses locally scarce, factors intensively (cf. Learner 1984, esp. 8–10).

2. Admittedly, this result depends on simplifying assumptions that are never achieved in the real world, among them perfect mobility of factors within national boundaries, a world of only two factors and two goods, and incomplete specialization. Still, as an approximation to reality, it remains highly serviceable (cf. Ethier 1984, esp. 163–64, 181).

3. Later historians have, of course, largely rejected Pirenne's attribution of this insecurity to the rise of Islam and its alleged blockade of

Mediterranean commerce (Havighurst 1958). It can hardly be doubted, however, that the decline of Roman power by itself rendered interregional trade far less secure.

4. As transportation costs fall, states may offset the effect by adopting protection. Owners of abundant factors then still have substantial *potential* gains from trade, which they may mortgage to pressure policy toward lower levels of protection.

5. Countries that lack essential resources can only beggar themselves by protection. Ultimately, those in such a society who seek protection from trade must advocate conquest of the missing resources—as indeed occurred in Japan and Germany in the 1930s.

6. Between 1871 and 1890, just under two million Germans emigrated to points outside Europe; in the same years, some seven million immigrants entered the United States (Mitchell 1978, Tbl. A-5; Williams, Current, and Freidel 1969, 158).

7. The Stolper-Samuelson analysis also helps to clear up what had seemed even to the perspicacious Gerschenkron (1943, 26–27) an insoluble riddle: why the *smallholding* German peasants had quickly become as protectionist as the *Junker*. Not only landowners, we now see, but all enterprises that *used land intensively,* will have been harmed by free trade. On the other hand—and later the distinction will become crucial—agricultural *wage labor* should have been free trading.

8. That the farmers of the Great Plains were hardly prospering in these years is no refutation of the analysis advanced here. Their *potential* gains were great (see n. 4), and their suffering could plausibly be attributed not to expanded trade but to the obstacles or exploitation laid upon that trade by other sectors. As in Marxist analysis, the older relations of production and of politics could be seen as "fetters."

9. Emigrants from the United Kingdom to areas outside Europe totalled 5.1 million between 1871 and 1890 (see Mitchell 1978, Tbl. A-5).

10. Certainly they had been among its earliest and strongest supporters: virtually every study of late Weimar voting patterns (e.g., Brown 1982; Childers 1983; Lipset 1960, 138–48) has found a large rural-urban difference (controlling for such other variables as religion and class) in support for National Socialism.

11. Historians have, of course, often recognized declining trade's sectoral effects on Weimar's final convulsions; the controversial essay of Abraham (1981) is only the best-known example. They may, however, have exaggerated agriculture's woes (see Holt 1936; Rogowski 1982).

12. Sabean (1969, Chap. 3) and Blickle (1981, 76–78) link the Peasants War convincingly to the density and rapid growth of population in the affected areas, i.e., to an increasing abundance of labor.

13. "The world's trade between 1800 and 1840 had not quite doubled. Between 1850 and 1870 it increased by 260 percent" (Hobsbawm 1979, 33).

14. Finer distinctions would require a more precise definition of factor abundance and scarcity. The one commonly accepted for the case of more than two factors stems from Vanek's extension of the Heckscher-Ohlin Theorem (Leamer 1984, 15); it defines a country as abundant (or scarce) in a factor to the extent that its share of world endowment in that factor exceeds (or falls short of) its share

of world consumption of all goods and services. Leamer's (1984, App. D) Factor Abundance Profiles are a tentative effort to apply this definition to present-day economies. To do so with any precision for earlier periods hardly seems possible.

15. Zysman seems to me to have captured the essence of European and Japanese agricultural policy in this period: "The peasantry could be held in place [by subsidies and price supports] even as its economic and social positions were destroyed" (1983, 24).

16. I am grateful to David D'Lugo and Pradeep Chhibber for having raised this issue in seminar discussion.

17. More precisely, they are inconsistent with balanced trade (cf. Leamer 1984, 8–10; Leamer 1987, 14–15).

18. There can be no doubt of Russia's abundance of land: as late as 1960, its population per square kilometer of agricultural land (35.7) was comparable to that of the United States (40.9) or Canada (28.4) and strikingly lower than those of even the more thinly populated nations of western and central Europe (e.g., France, 133; Poland, 146) (World Bank 1983). On the other hand, Myint's (1958, 323–31) insightful analysis suggests how even sparsely populated regions can have great reserves of underemployed labor under conditions of primitive markets and social structures; and he takes episodes of extremely rapid economic growth, such as the USSR exhibited in the 1930s, as putative evidence of such "surplus" labor (Myint 1958, 323–24, 327).

19. The chief exception to this rule arises from extensions of trade to wholly new areas with quite different factor endowments. In 1860, for example, Prussia was abundant in land relative to its trading partners; as soon as the North American plains and the Argentine *pampas* were opened, it ceased to be so. I am grateful to my colleague Arthur Stein for having pointed this out.

REFERENCES

Abraham, David. 1981. *The Collapse of the Weimar Republic.* Princeton: Princeton University Press.

Becker, Gary S. 1983. A Theory of Competition among Pressure Groups for Political Influence. *Quarterly Journal of Economics* 98:371–400.

Binder, Leonard, James S. Coleman, Joseph La-Palombara, Lucian W. Pye, Sidney Verba, and Myron Weiner. 1971. *Crises and Sequences in Political Development.* Princeton: Princeton University Press.

Blickle, Peter. 1981. *The Revolution of 1525: The German Peasants' War from a New Perspective.* Trans. Thomas A. Brady, Jr., and H. C. Erik Midelfort. Baltimore: Johns Hopkins University Press.

Bowden, Witt, Michael Karpovich, and Abbott Payson Usher. 1937. *An Economic History of Europe since 1750.* New York: American Book.

Brown, Courtney. 1982. The Nazi Vote: A National Ecological Study. *American Political Science Review* 76:285–302.

Burnham, Walter Dean. 1970. *Critical Elections and the Mainsprings of American Politics.* New York: W. W. Norton.

Cameron, David R. 1978. The Expansion of the Public Economy: A Comparative Analysis. *American Political Science Review* 72:1243–61.

Cardoso, Fernando Henrique, and Enzo Faletto. 1979. *Dependency and Development in Latin America.* Trans. Marjory Mattingly Urquidi. Berkeley and Los Angeles: University of California Press.

Carstairs, Andrew McLaren. 1980. *A Short History of Electoral Systems in Western Europe.* London: George Allen & Unwin.

Carsten, Francis Ludwig. 1967. *The Rise of Fascism.* Berkeley and Los Angeles: University of California Press.

Childers, Thomas. 1983. *The Nazi Voter: The Social Foundations of Fascism in Germany, 1919–1933.* Chapel Hill: University of North Carolina Press.

Cipolla, Carlo M. 1965. *Guns, Sails, and Empires: Technological Innovation and the Early Phases of European Expansion, 1400–1700.* New York: Pantheon Books.

Clubb, Oliver Edmund. 1972. *Twentieth-Century China.* 2d ed. New York: Columbia University Press.

Cobban, Alfred. 1965. *France of the Republics, 1871–1962.* Vol. 3 of *A History of Modern France.* Harmondsworth: Penguin Books.

Daalder, Hans. 1973. The Netherlands: Opposition in a Segmented Society. In *Political Oppositions in Western Democracies,* ed. Robert Dahl. New Haven: Yale University Press.

Duverger, Maurice. 1959. *Political Parties: Their Organization and Activity in the Modern State.* 2d ed. Trans. Barbara and Robert North. New York: John Wiley & Sons.

Easterbrook, William Thomas, and Hugh G. J. Aitken. 1958. *Canadian Economic History.* Toronto: Macmillan of Canada.

Ethier, Wilfred J. 1984. Higher Dimensional Issues in Trade Theory. In *Handbook of International Economics.* Vol. 1, ed. Ronald W. Jones and Peter B. Kenen. Amsterdam: Elsevier Science.

Feis, Herbert. 1965. *Europe, the World's Banker, 1870–1914.* New York: Norton.

Gerschenkron, Alexander. 1943. *Bread and Democracy in Germany.* Berkeley and Los Angeles: University of California Press.

Gerschenkron, Alexander. 1962. *Economic Backwardness in Historical Perspective.* Cambridge, MA: Harvard University Press.

Gessner, Dieter. 1977. *Agrardepression und Präsidialregierungen in Deutschland 1930 bis 1933.* Düsseldorf: Droste Verlag.

Gies, Horst. 1968. Die nationalsozialistische Machtergreifung auf dem agrarpolitischen Sektor. *Zeitschrift für Agrargeschichte und Agrarsoziologie* 16:210–32.

Gollan, Robin A. 1955. Nationalism, the Labour Movement and the Commonwealth, 1880–1900. In *Australia: A Social and Political History,* ed. Gordon Greenwood. London: Angus & Robertson.

Gourevitch, Peter Alexis. 1977. International Trade, Domestic Coalitions, and Liberty: Comparative Responses to the Crisis of 1873–1896. *Journal of Interdisciplinary History* 8:281–313.

Gourevitch, Peter Alexis. 1986. *Politics in Hard Times: Comparative Response to International Economic Crises.* Ithaca, NY: Cornell University Press.

Greenwood, Gordon. 1955. National Development and Social Experimentation, 1901–1914. In *Australia: A Social and Political History,* ed. author. London: Angus & Robertson.

Hancock, M. Donald. 1972. *Sweden: The Politics of Postindustrial Change.* Hinsdale, IL: Dryden Press.

Havighurst, Alfred F., ed. 1958. *The Pirenne Thesis: Analysis, Criticism, and Revision.* Boston: D. C. Heath.

Hempel, Carl G. 1965. *"Aspects of Scientific Explanation" and Other Essays in the Philosophy of Science.* New York: Free Press.

Hirschman, Albert O. [1968] 1971. The Political Economy of Import-Substituting Industrialization in Latin America. *Quarterly Journal of Economics* 82:2–32. Reprinted in Albert O. Hirschman, *A Bias for Hope: Essays on Development and Latin America.* New Haven: Yale University Press.

Hobsbawm, Eric J. 1962. *The Age of Revolution, 1789–1848.* New York: New American Library.

Hobsbawm, Eric J. 1979. *The Age of Capital, 1848–1875.* New York: New American Library.

Holt, John Bradshaw. 1936. *German Agricultural Policy, 1918–1934: The Development of a National Policy toward Agriculture in Postwar Germany.* Chapel Hill: University of North Carolina Press.

Kato, Shuichi. 1974. Taisho Democracy as the Pre-Stage for Japanese Militarism. In *Japan in Crisis: Essays on Taisho Democracy,* ed. Bernard S. Silberman and H. D. Harootunian. Princeton: Princeton University Press.

Kindleberger, Charles P. 1973. *The World in Depression, 1929–1939.* Berkeley: University of California Press.

Kurth, James R. 1979a. Industrial Change and Political Change: A European Perspective. In *The New Authoritarianism in Latin America,* ed. David Collier. Princeton: Princeton University Press.

Kurth, James R. 1979b. The Political Consequences of the Product Cycle: Industrial History and Political Outcomes. *International Organization* 33:1–34.

Landes, David S. 1969. *The Unbound Prometheus: Technological Change and the Industrial Revolution in Western Europe from 1750 to the Present.* London: Cambridge University Press.

Leamer, Edward A. 1984. *Sources of Comparative Advantage: Theory and Evidence.* Cambridge: MIT Press.

Leamer, Edward A. 1987. Paths of Development in the $3 \times n$ General Equilibrium Model. University of California, Los Angeles. Typescript.

Lipset, Seymour Martin. 1960. *Political Man.* Garden City, NY: Doubleday.

Lipset, Seymour Martin. 1970. Political Cleavages in "Developed" and "Emerging" Politics. In *Mass Politics: Studies in Political Sociology,* ed. Erik Allardt and Stein Rokkan. New York: Free Press.

Lipset, Seymour Martin, and Stein Rokkan. 1967. *Party Systems and Voter Alignments.* New York: Free Press.

Lorwin, Val R. 1966. Belgium: Religion, Class and Language in National Politics. In *Political Opposition in Western Democracies,* ed. Robert Dahl. New Haven, CT: Yale University Press.

Macridis, Roy C. 1978. *Modern Political Systems: Europe.* 4th ed. Englewood Cliffs, NJ: Prentice-Hall.

Mitchell, Brian R. 1978. *European Historical Statistics, 1750–1970.* Abridged ed. New York: Columbia University Press.

Moore, Barrington, Jr. 1967. *Social Origins of Dictatorship and Democracy: Lord and Peasant in the Making of the Modern World.* Boston: Beacon.

Mundell, Robert A. 1957. International Trade and Factor Mobility. *American Economic Review* 47:321–35.

Myint, Hla. 1958. The "Classical Theory" of International Trade and the Underdeveloped Countries. *Economic Journal* 68:317–37.

Organization for Economic Cooperation and Development. 1982. *Historical Statistics 1960–1980.* Paris: OECD.

Pirenne, Henri. 1939. *Mohammed and Charlemagne.* London: Allen & Unwin.

Popkin, Samuel. 1979. *The Rational Peasant: The Political Economy of Rural Society in Vietnam.* Berkeley: University of California Press.

Reischauer, Edwin O. 1974. *Japan: The Story of a Nation.* New York: Alfred A. Knopf.

Rogowski, Ronald. 1982. Iron, Rye, and the Authoritarian Coalition in Germany after 1879. Paper delivered at the annual meeting of the American Political Science Association, Denver, CO.

Rokkan, Stein. 1966. Norway: Numerical Democracy and Corporate Pluralism. In *Political Oppositions in Western Democracies,* ed. Robert Dahl. New Haven: Yale University Press.

Rokkan, Stein. 1970. *Citizens, Elections, Parties.* Oslo: Universitetsforlaget.

Rokkan, Stein. 1981. Territories, Nations, Parties: Toward a Geoeconomic-Geopolitical Model for the Explanation of Changes within Western Europe. In *From National Development to Global Community,* ed. Richard L. Merritt and Bruce M. Russett. London: Allen & Unwin.

Rosecrance, Richard. 1986. *The Rise of the Trading State: Commerce and Conquest in the Modern World.* New York: Basic Books.

Rosenberg, Hans. 1943. Political and Social Consequences of the Great Depression in Europe, 1873–1896. *Economic History Review* 13:58–73.

Sabean, David. 1969. The Social Background to the Peasants' War of 1525 in Southern Upper Swabia. Ph.D. diss., University of Wisconsin.

Schattschneider, Elmer E. 1960. *The Semi-Sovereign People: A Realist's View of Democracy in America.* New York: Holt, Rinehart & Winston.

Schoenbaum, David. 1966. *Hitler's Social Revolution: Class and Status in Nazi Germany 1933–1939.* Garden City, NY: Doubleday.

Sheehan, James J. 1978. *German Liberalism in the Nineteenth Century.* Chicago: University of Chicago Press.

Skidmore, Thomas E., and Peter H. Smith. 1984. *Modern Latin America.* New York: Oxford University Press.

Stolper, Wolfgang Friedrich, and Paul A. Samuelson. 1941. Protection and Real Wages. *Review of Economic Studies* 9:58–73.

Sunkel, Osvaldo, and Pedro Paz. 1973. *El subdesarrollo latinoamericano y la teoria del desarrollo.* 4th ed. Madrid: Siglo veintiuno de España.

Thomson, David. 1962. *Europe since Napoleon.* 2d ed. New York: Alfred A. Knopf.

Wallerstein, Immanuel. 1974. *The Modern World-System: Capitalist Agriculture and the Origins of the European World-Economy in the Sixteenth Century.* New York: Academic.

Williams, Thomas Harry, Richard N. Current, and Frank Freidel. 1969. *A History of the United States since 1865.* 3d ed. Baltimore: Johns Hopkins University Press.

World Bank. 1983. *World Tables.* 3d ed. Vol. 2. Baltimore: Johns Hopkins University Press.

Zysman, John. 1983. *Governments, Markets, and Growth: Financial Systems and the Politics of Industrial Change.* Ithaca, NY: Cornell University Press.

Jeffry Frieden

THE GOVERNANCE OF INTERNATIONAL FINANCE

International finance is at the cutting edge of contemporary international economic integration. Today's global financial markets are of enormous size and can move huge quantities of money around the world with extraordinary speed and massive effect. Their impact was demonstrated with a vengeance during the Great Financial Crisis (GFC) that began at the end of 2007, during which financial markets transmitted economic impulses—many of them highly damaging—from country to country in a matter of days or weeks.

The great economic and political prominence of international financial markets has given rise to extensive discussion of the need to regulate, monitor, or otherwise control their impact on national economies and polities. Indeed, the ranks of those who believe that some form of governance of global finance is desirable are clearly growing. However, even among the more fervent believers in global financial governance, it is not clear how this might be accomplished in a world in which policies are still made almost entirely by nation-states.

* * * I evaluate the state of attempts to provide some financial oversight at the international level that comes close to what exists at the national level. I start below with a summary of the normative argument for international financial governance. The following section provides a brief overview of what has been done to supply something approaching global public goods in this arena. Finally, I move on to analytical approaches to understanding what has been done, and might be done, in global financial governance.

Normative Arguments for Global Financial Governance

Analysts and policymakers make a variety of arguments for some form of international governance of global financial affairs. In this context, governance implies the provision of government-like functions at a level above that of the nation-state. The normative basis for these arguments, then, must be analogous to the rationale for the government provision of public goods at the national level: Because of market failures, things for which there is demand are undersupplied by private actors.

One typical form of argumentation is by analogy. As financial markets grew from being local to being national, there was a need for national public goods involved in overseeing these markets. This led all governments to provide national financial regulation and supervision (discussed below). Financial markets are now global, which means that overseeing the international financial markets must require global public goods. This is the character of many arguments for global financial governance.

An argument for global governance, however, requires that such global public goods cannot

From *Annual Review of Political Science* 19 (June 2016).

adequately be supplied by national governments. In other words, build a case for a truly global governance of international financial relations, it is not enough to show that the goods in question would be undersupplied by the private sector (a justification that would suffice at the national level). For global governance to be justifiable, national governments must be unable, or unwilling, to oversee their financial affairs on their own so as to provide the desired international outcome. In other words, the argument for global governance requires demonstration that not only private actors but also national governments are insufficiently willing or able to provide something that is globally desirable. To take an analogy, in pure welfare terms international trade liberalization does not in itself require global governance inasmuch as it is in the national interest to liberalize unilaterally: Enough of the positive effects of trade liberalization are internalized within the liberalizing country that it has an incentive to undertake the liberalization.[1]

This then means that the argument for global governance must inherently involve political economy considerations. Unlike at the national level, where government provision is justifiable because private supply is insufficient to satisfy demand, at the international level global provision would be justified only if national governments did not have incentives to supply the good—and the incentives to governments are inherently political. Therefore, a normative argument for the global governance of international finance, as of anything else, requires that supporters show that national governments are either technically unable or politically unmotivated to provide the necessary and relevant policies. In this context, we can identify the sorts of interventions that are most commonly, and justifiably, presented as the kinds of global public goods that the global governance of international finance could or should provide.

The overarching public good at stake in this realm is financial stability. Financial markets provide important benefits to society, both domestically and internationally, by moving funds from where they are less needed to where they can be used more productively. However, they are also subject to periodic crises with substantial economic costs. Domestically, national governments have long recognized that systemic stability is unlikely to be provided sufficiently by private actors, and they have intervened in a variety of ways to reduce the threat of financial instability.

A similar logic holds internationally. Financial crises that begin in one country or group of countries are often transmitted to the rest of the world, causing contagious international financial crises (Borio et al. 2014, Lorenzoni 2014). Here the political economy argument for this sort of global public good is clear. Each national government may act to protect its own financial institutions and system, but it stops there. Measures taken to stabilize the international financial system could benefit all countries and all participants; however, no single country has an incentive to undertake the great costs of providing this stability, because no country fully internalizes the externalities. Indeed, if left to their own devices, individual governments may have incentives to encourage behavior by their own financial institutions that might give them a competitive edge but endanger international financial stability—such as engaging in risky lending or secretive banking practices. The fact that countries do not fully internalize both positive and negative externalities in this realm provides a clear and cogent argument for the global provision of global financial governance.[2]

There are many ways of attempting to provide financial stability. Below I examine those that have been most prominent in discussions of the governance of international financial markets.

Lender-of-Last-Resort Facilities

At least since the middle 1800s, it has been understood that financial markets are subject to "panics" or "bank runs," in which doubts about the solvency of financial institutions can lead market participants to withdraw funds (Diamond and Dybvig 1983). These panics can be self-reinforcing, causing otherwise healthy institutions to fail solely due to a potentially misplaced loss of confidence. Such bank runs can also be contagious and snowball into full-blown financial crises with serious costs to society, which means that there are strong welfare arguments for avoiding them. As a result, virtually every government has agreed, in one way or another, to act as an implicit or explicit lender of last resort. This means that it stands ready to provide liquidity to the financial market to keep otherwise solvent financial institutions from being bankrupted by a contagious loss of confidence. This is not an unproblematic policy: The line between insolvency and illiquidity can be unclear, as is the best way for the government to intervene (Grossman and Rockoff 2015). However, the basic principle is well established: Governments need to stand ready to intervene in an emergency to supply funds to financial markets to avoid a descent into panic.

International financial markets are, it turns out, exquisitely susceptible to these sorts of panics. In the international financial system, which is populated by large financial institutions rather than small depositors, panic typically takes the form of a loss of confidence in the ability of other financial institutions to fulfill contracts, even for very short-term (such as overnight) arrangements. The financial components of the crisis that began in 2007 are the modern equivalent of a bank run: With intermediation taking place in markets rather than through banks, the panic that developed was about the inability of markets to reliably allow contracts to be completed and serviced (Gorton 2009). Extraordinary levels of uncertainty made it difficult or impossible even for the largest financial institutions to borrow on the interbank market, which is necessary for them to carry on everyday business.

Today's international financial system is subject to the threat of panics, which means that lender-of-last-resort facilities are desirable. The modern system performs a function that is analogous to that of a traditional national banking system: maturity transformation with fractional reserves, underpinned by a very short-term interbank market.[3] To some extent national governments have addressed the international lender of last resort problem by working out arrangements that require home country authorities to provide these facilities to their financial institutions even when they are operating internationally. However, these arrangements have many weaknesses and vulnerabilities, such as the fact that the commitments involve many different currencies, and most observers agree that some manner of international lender-of-last-resort facilities would be desirable (Landau 2014, Obstfeld 2009).

As in the general case, the political economy case for an international lender of last resort is strong. Such facilities are complex and can be costly to provide in a credible way. Although each national government has powerful reasons to establish lender-of-last-resort facilities domestically to protect its own financial institutions and system, the benefits largely stop at the water's edge. No one government can internalize the full benefits of providing liquidity to the international financial system, which makes the normative case for global provision a powerful one.

Regulatory Harmonization

Financial regulation is a central component of national efforts to provide financial stability. In fact, it can be seen as the counterpart of policies to backstop the financial system, such as the lender of last resort: If governments are providing some sort of insurance to financial markets, they need to attempt to limit moral hazard and adverse selection. But experience has shown that a financial system with inconsistent or discordant regulatory components, whether regionally or functionally, can create serious problems. Major regulatory differences give financial institutions incentives to engage in regulatory arbitrage, designing their operations so as to find the most permissive regulations for each segment of their business.

At the international level, major regulatory differences and private-sector regulatory arbitrage can lead to an accumulation of under-regulated activities. This in turn creates the potential for very large international financial institutions to manipulate regulations so as to put many national regulators and financial systems at risk. It might also lead to regulatory competition with a harmful race to the bottom. And because financial crises in one major financial market are typically transmitted to other markets, lax regulation in one country can cause contagious crises throughout the world.

Just as it is desirable for national financial systems to avoid regulatory fragmentation and contagious financial crises, there is a normative argument for regulatory harmonization at the international level. As with lender-of-last-resort facilities, the argument takes into account the political economy of the issue. Individual national governments do not fully internalize the benefits of tighter regulation, and they may even realize significant costs if business flees for looser jurisdictions. This means that national governments, like private firms, may not have sufficient incentives to provide adequate global regulatory consistency or rigor on their own. The case for some form of global governance, even if only for cooperative arrangements among national authorities, is strong.

This sort of regulatory harmonization can take different forms. Regulators can agree to impose common rules for capital adequacy, that is, how much capital banks have to hold in compared to their outstanding assets (loans and investments). This is meant to impose common standards of prudence on financial institutions. A related measure is to harmonize the treatment of shadow banking activities, that is, the activities of financial institutions that are typically outside of the normal reach of banking regulators. Harmonization can also provide common standards for how national financial authorities are expected to intervene in the case of major bank failures.

Other Sources of Financial Stability

A range of other policies may also stabilize a financial system. Especially in the aftermath of the GFC, there has been much discussion of interventions to either limit the likelihood of financial instability or reduce its effects.

One set of policies that has attracted a great deal of attention is macro prudential regulation (Engel 2015b, Schoenmaker 2014). This approach takes financial regulation to a higher level, requiring regulators to supervise financial institutions and to consider their impact on the entire financial system. This could lead regulators to influence the pace and direction of lending, focusing not simply on the solvency of individual banks but rather on the broader systemic impact of their behavior. Moreover, assessing the macroeconomic impact of individual banks' activities is a complex and potentially controversial task: No bank wants to be denied profit opportunities solely due to nebulous systemic considerations. Nonetheless, the experience of recent financial crises has led many national regulators to take systemic factors much more seriously. Again, the normative case for some form of macroprudential regulation at the global level—or at the least for coordination of national macroprudential policies—is strong. Although national regulators have incentives to take nationally systemic effects seriously, they have no strong reasons to think about the global financial system. Again, the positive externalities are not internalized, and national regulators are unlikely to pay due attention to potential internationally systemic implications of their banks' activities.

Another policy dimension that has generated much discussion recently is the control of cross-border capital flows to limit their impact on domestic, and potentially international, financial conditions. Indeed, the International Monetary Fund (IMF) has indicated that it regards the judicious use of such capital controls as a reasonable response to the threat of financial instability: National authorities might limit inflows to avoid excessive borrowing, and in time of crisis they might limit outflows to avoid currency runs or other destabilizing financial movements. Once more, inasmuch as national financial crises can be contagious, there is a normative basis for some global provision, or at least coordination, of policies to control capital movements. A national government that does not take global effects into consideration could encourage foreign borrowing even if it risks an eventual crisis, especially if many of the costs of the crisis are borne by foreigners (creditors or other countries infected by panic). In this context, policies to limit capital movements would best be designed with global factors in mind, in ways no national government would be inclined to do (Brunnermeier & Sannikov 2015).

Macroeconomic Policy Coordination

Divergences in macroeconomic policies are at the root of many financial difficulties. This is especially the case today, in a world with enormous capital markets and rapid capital flows: Minor differences in macroeconomic conditions can lead to large financial flows that increase those divergences and exacerbate boom-and-bust cycles, which carry substantial social costs. The normative case for macroeconomic policy coordination has been contested: A traditional view would be that responsible macroeconomic policies are unilaterally desirable and their positive effects are fully realized by the country that pursues them, so that the incentives for such policies would be strong enough not to require any international coordination. However,

recent trends have strengthened the argument for coordination, given that uncoordinated national macroeconomic policies could lead to the sorts of regional and global crises that have beset so much of the world over the past 20 years [Engel (2015a), Frieden & Broz (2013), and Frieden et al. (2012) provide overviews; Taylor (2014) presents a mild endorsement from a skeptic]. As with the other policies discussed above, there are strong political economy grounds to justify something other than purely national action: Inasmuch as one country's macroeconomic policies can impose externalities on other countries, there is an argument for a supranational effort to internalize the externalities.

If we accept that financial stability is a public good, and further accept that policies to provide it at the national level create cross-border externalities that are not fully internalized, there is a normative case for providing the global public good of financial stability at a level above that of the nation-state. This global governance might, however, take many forms. The form most similar to national-level government is probably provision by a supranational institution, followed by closely coordinated provision by a coalition of national governments. Global governance could conceivably take the form of provision of the public good by one government, if enough of the benefits were realized by its home country—or if others could somehow compensate it for the job. The governance function could be provided by nongovernmental organizations, such as private, usually corporate, regulatory or standardization bodies.

The form taken by global governance is likely to depend both on the issue area and on the agents involved. One perspective, familiar from the literature on federalism (including the European literature on subsidiarity), emphasizes that the governance structure should reflect the distribution of externalities. So if most of the positive, or negative, effects are realized by one, or a few, nations, they are more likely both to provide the governance and to benefit disproportionately from it. A similar consideration could explain why a highly motivated NGO, or a group of corporations, might have powerful enough incentives to undertake the difficult task of creating a global institution to provide some of these government-like functions. Büthe & Mattli (2011), Koppell (2010), and Pauly & Coleman (2008) all look at this set of issues.

It should be noted that even if analysis provides criteria within which some form of international financial governance constitutes a global public good, it does not necessarily follow that this governance is distributionally neutral. Because the definition of global public goods refers largely to nations and governments, it is perfectly conceivable that some such governance policies and structures could impose net costs on groups or individuals within countries. Moreover, there are many different and distributionally varied ways in which public goods can be supplied. I return to this in much more detail when discussing positive analyses of global governance.

Despite the strong normative argument for international financial governance, we might still doubt that national governments will agree on whether or how to work together to provide global public goods. In a world of independent nation-states, cooperation to provide public goods may be the exception rather than the rule. However, the past 25 years or so provide some surprising evidence of an increasing tendency toward the provision of such global public goods in the financial realm. In the next section, I summarize some of these developments; in the following section, I turn to how we might explain them.

Developments in Global Financial Governance

The international financial system was hit by a series of financial crises in the 1990s, the most prominent of which were the Mexican crisis of 1994 and the East Asian crisis of 1997–1998. In each case, there was substantial contagion within the respective region, and even outside it. Again in each case, there was enough serious concern about the implications for the international financial system that the IMF and the national governments of the major financial centers stepped in to provide hundreds of billions of dollars to bail out the troubled debtor nations and supervise the restructuring of hundreds of billions dollars in private credit. The Mexican and East Asian events were followed in short order by similar, if more isolated, crises in Russia, Turkey, and Argentina.

In the aftermath of these crises, policy makers and observers began serious discussions of what was at the time usually called the international financial architecture. They increasingly shared the belief that financial instability in one country or region could cause serious global problems and required a more explicitly cooperative global response. Depending on the forum and the protagonists, discussions included financial regulation, macroeconomic policies, and adjustment measures.

Several institutional developments reflected the expressed desire for more international consultation and cooperation on financial issues. One was the broadening of the Group of Seven (G7) industrial countries with the creation of the Group of Twenty (G20), which includes some of the largest developing nations. A second was the extension of the mandate of the IMF to include monitoring member states' financial stability and its international implications. This included asking the IMF to issue an annual Global Financial Stability Report and later to focus its surveillance obligations on what was called a Multilateral Consultation on Global Imbalances. Finally, member states expanded the role of the Bank for International Settlements (BIS, of which more below) and established a new Financial Stability Forum to bring together central bankers, finance ministers, and other international financial policy makers to discuss common problems (for summaries of these issues, see Eichengreen 1999, Goldstein 2005).

Despite these innovations, the most significant progress toward global financial governance came under the auspices of the BIS and its Basel Committee on Banking Supervision. This committee was originally made up of regulatory and monetary authorities from 13 principal industrial countries (the G7 plus Belgium, Luxembourg, the Netherlands, Spain, Sweden, and Switzerland). The committee began meeting in the aftermath of the first modern panic-like event, when in 1974 the failure of two mid-sized banks, one German and one American, practically froze the international interbank market (Spero 1980). After a series of agreements to avoid a recurrence of the problem, eventually in 1988 the committee adopted a formal set of harmonized regulatory principles, which came to be called the Basel Accord (and eventually Basel I). The principles were implemented by the committee members by 1992. This was an unprecedented step toward cooperation among national bank supervisors, and it reflected the growing belief that there were clear systemic externalities that could not be addressed without explicit collaboration—an early step toward financial governance at the international level. Over the next decade or so, many other countries claimed to have conformed to the Basel regulatory framework. Starting in the late 1990s, the committee began a substantial revision and enhancement of the standards, eventually leading to a second agreement in 2004 called Basel II. But the implementation of Basel II was interrupted by the eruption of the GFC in 2007.

The GFC provoked a dramatic increase in international attempts to address global financial issues. The crisis graphically demonstrated the depth, breadth, and speed with which financial instability could spread around the world. As financial markets reached near-panic in October 2008, emergency plans were made for an unprecedented meeting of the leaders of the G20 countries. The G20 had been expanded in 1999 to include about a dozen emerging markets (including Brazil, Russia, India, China, South Africa, and Mexico), but its meetings had only been among finance ministers and similar policy makers. The Washington Summit of November 14–15, 2008, brought together the heads of government or state of the G20 members. Among other agreements, the summit, followed about five months later by another one in London, committed members to a coordinated macroeconomic response to the crisis. Although the principal macroeconomic coordination that ensued involved only the major central banks—especially the Federal Reserve, European Central Bank, Bank of England, Bank of Japan, and Bank of Canada—the very high level of representation at the G20 meetings and the inclusion of major emerging markets in the deliberations were significant.

The G20 has become the focus of many of the measures aiming to provide some degree of global financial governance (Véron 2014). It has expanded the Financial Stability Forum, now re-branded the Financial Stability Board (FSB), to include the major emerging markets, and it has overseen substantive discussions over regulatory harmonization as well as attempts to resolve such complex issues as the regulatory and moral hazard problems associated with systemically important financial institutions.

Closely related to the G20's efforts have been the redoubled attempts by the BIS's Basel Committee on Banking Supervision to address the flaws in Basel II that were revealed by the GFC. The committee developed a new, significantly more encompassing, Basel Accord by the end of 2010. There have been substantial revisions since then, and Basel III is unlikely to be fully implemented by major financial centers before 2020 (Basel Comm. Bank. Superv. 2014). Nonetheless, there has definitely been substantial movement toward greater coordination among national regulators and toward the harmonization of regulatory and supervisory standards among the major financial centers.

Meanwhile, central bankers have continued to cooperate at levels that had not been seen before the crisis. This cooperation has developed more or less in tandem with an expansion of the IMF's role, especially through substantial increases in the funds available for crisis lending and emergency liquidity provision. In a variety of ways, the IMF, clearly with the approval of its principal members, is moving in the direction of acting as something like an international lender of last resort. The funds it has available are insufficient to play this role fully, but it can be argued that, in concert with the involvement of national governments, the major national and supranational players in the international financial system take seriously the need for a global lender of last resort and have worked toward that goal [the IMF summarizes its response to the crisis in IMF (2015); its response is evaluated more critically in Indep. Eval. Off. (2014)].

In summary, over the past decade the G20's Financial Stability Board and related institutions, the BIS, the IMF, and the major financial centers have progressed toward providing an international financial governance infrastructure at the global level that resembles national financial management. There are the beginnings of international lender-of-last-resort facilities, of globally harmonized financial supervision and regulation to accompany these facilities, and of systematic collaboration among national authorities and supranational institutions. Even optimists would admit that the progress has been slow, difficult, and partial, and that much remains to be done. But even pessimists would probably accept that there has been more movement in this direction than they had anticipated a decade ago. A most useful summary is in the annual reports of the organization New Rules for Global Finance (e.g., New Rules Glob. Finance 2014).

Analyzing International Financial Governance

We would like to understand the forces that have constrained or enabled the creation of institutions and policies associated with international financial governance. Of course, an understanding of these forces is strongly affected by the theoretical tools used by scholars to analyze the politics of international financial relations. It is to an overview of the different analytical perspectives that I now turn. These perspectives are not necessarily mutually exclusive, but they do tend to focus on different potential sources of government actions (Helleiner & Pagliari 2011 provide a useful summary).

The most simple-minded approach—which is so simple-minded as to not be represented in the scholarly literature—explains governance developments on social welfare grounds, based on the promotion of global efficiency. This is what might be called a functionalist view, in the sense that governance functions grow out of the inherent demand for them. The analytical problem, of course, is that there is no agent, public or private, with a clear incentive to intervene solely in the interests of global social welfare. However, this baseline is important, and in fact somewhat contested.

Although it is common to claim that international financial initiatives are undertaken in the interests of all, as noted above, it is perfectly plausible that such initiatives may have strong distributive effects. These may involve the uneven allocation of costs and benefits among countries: Creditor nations may be able to force debtor nations into bearing a disproportionate share of the burden of adjusting to the aftermath of irresponsible lending, or large countries may be able to constrain small countries to conform to standards that harm them and their private sectors. Even if these initiatives are arrived at voluntarily among member governments, which implies that they benefit all *governments*, there may still be domestic distributive effects within countries. For example, a government might have no compunctions about forcing taxpayers to shoulder the full expense of reckless lending by national financial institutions.

In all these cases, even though there may be social benefits to the financial stability that is enhanced by the policies in question, for individual countries or individuals within countries these benefits may be outweighed by their costs. In other words, both among countries and within countries, there is no guarantee that the governance structures will deliver Pareto improvements. And even where the policies are Pareto improving, there are typically many ways in which they can be structured, with different distributional implications (Krasner 1991 is the classic statement).

Analytically, the fact that these global public goods may not be distributionally neutral— whether the distributional features are international or domestic—provides a mechanism to explain how and why they might be supplied in a world without global government. Again, there is an analogy to the provision of public goods at the national level. Leaving aside political entrepreneurship, which has only weak parallels at the international level, a common explanation for the provision of public goods is that they are promoted by concentrated groups that stand to benefit disproportionately from them. This could be because the public good in question has differential benefits, with much more significant effects on some groups than others (bankers versus farmers, for example). It could also be because the public good comes bundled with private benefits that accrue to a concentrated group (e.g., bankers who get a cartel in return for supporting an independent central bank; see Broz 1998).

At the international level, one could imagine that a global public good might have particularly significant benefits for some country or small group of countries; that it might have particularly significant benefits for concentrated groups within countries; or that it might be closely associated with

private benefits to some countries or groups within countries. The existence of concentrated benefits to domestic groups could provide incentives for a government to pursue the global public good; the existence of concentrated benefits to one country or group of countries could similarly provide them with incentives to undertake the efforts necessary to supply the global public good.

For all these reasons, even scholars who accept the broad desirability of some form of international financial governance look for distributional features of their evolution that explain why such global public goods might be promoted by governments, potentially at significant national cost. One approach emphasizes the extent to which particularly large and important financial centers internalize the benefits of financial stability, which may give their governments incentives enough to play a major role in working toward global governance agreements and structures. In this picture, the disproportional size of a country can give it a disproportional interest in resolving some of the problems that arise in the absence of public goods in the international financial arena.

This approach, then, focuses on the willingness of the governments of the largest financial powers to lead the way in expanding global financial governance, and, typically, on the ability of these governments to use their power to cajole or persuade other governments to follow their lead. In somewhat different ways, for example, Drezner (2007), Kapstein (1989, 1994), Posner (2009), and Simmons (2001) ascribe financial regulatory harmonization to the willingness and ability of countries (or, in the case of the European Union, groups of countries) to use their bargaining power and influence to create a context to which smaller actors are forced to respond, usually by complying with the patterns set by the dominant actors.

The fact that dominant governments can strong-arm others into accepting their version of the public good in question—be it financial regulation, lender-of-last-resort facilities, or something else—does not rule out the possibility that the outcome actually improves the welfare of all governments that sign onto the regime. Although the point is often implicit, it is probably the case that most scholars in this tradition think of the eventual provision of some form of international financial governance as an improvement over its absence. Inasmuch as Pareto improvements come in many distributionally relevant varieties, and the bargaining power of the larger states gives them outsized influence on outcomes, the international governance structures that emerge are likely to be disproportionately favorable to the largest countries. One example is the role of the IMF in resolving debt crises: Although it is probably in the interest of debtor and creditor nations alike to have some mechanism to deal with such crises, Copelovitch (2010) argues that the IMF's behavior is powerfully affected by the influence of the largest creditor nations, and Stone (2011) is even more insistent that formal and informal rules bias international financial institutions heavily toward the interest of the largest states.

A further step away from functionalist logic is to question whether in fact the governance structures improve welfare for all. The most consistent variant of this argument is to note that the agreements to provide this sort of global public good are made by national governments, and that there is little guarantee that a government will be acting in the national interest, however defined. More specifically, national governments may be "captured" in the global financial realm by powerful domestic special interests that want to see international financial agreements bent in their favor, even if this works against the interests of their countrymen. One common argument to this effect is that the shape of global financial cooperation is strongly affected, and perhaps distorted, by the particularistic interests of powerful and internationally engaged private financial institutions. In this sense, what looks to some like global financial governance might also be described as the solidification of a global financial cartel, organized so as to extract resources from those outside the cartel: borrowers and taxpayers, in particular.

For these reasons, many scholars begin their analysis of international financial policies, cooperation, and governance with the concentrated interests of nationally based economic groups, particularly financial institutions. Then they can build up to governments that may or may not have national interests in mind, but that bias their policy orientations toward the concerns of these powerful groups (Oatley & Nabors 1998; Singer 2004, 2007). Returning to the example of the IMF in crisis resolution, Copelovitch (2010) argues that it was not just the interests of the largest countries that were most strongly reflected in IMF policies, but more specifically the interests of the large private financial institutions of these largest countries. At an even more differentiated level, Broz (2005, 2008) shows that support for the actions and institutions of global financial governance are contingent on their domestic distributional impact: The behavior of American legislators in making decisions on these matters is strongly influenced by the economic interests of their constituents.[4]

These first two modes of analysis have a lot in common and are not mutually exclusive. They both tend to assume that international financial cooperation improves global welfare, but they both temper this view with the observation that the results are likely to be strongly biased by power differentials among countries and among groups within countries. Both approaches rely primarily upon the behavior of national states, although they accept that government policy depends on domestic as well as international considerations. Both focus on the economic interests of private actors and/or their reflection in the preferences of national governments.

Many scholars deemphasize economic interests, the actions of governments, or both. "Ideational" approaches to the making of foreign policy have their reflection in the international financial realm, as elsewhere. These analyses tend to emphasize the changing nature of common understandings of the problems faced in international financial relations and of how they might be addressed (prime examples include Blyth 2002, Abdelal 2007, and Chwieroth 2010). Clearly, policy makers and others are influenced by the state of knowledge, or opinion, about these issues. If ideas converge within an epistemic community of experts or technocrats, or within a community of policymakers, this convergence can lead to policy outcomes that might otherwise be unimaginable. The evolution of the views of the IMF in the aftermath of the Asian financial crisis of 1997–1998, and of the more recent GFC, leads some observers to posit that this sort of ideational change can create conditions for a higher degree of global financial governance—whether under the auspices of the IMF or otherwise.

An ideas-based explanation of the management of international financial relations has resonated with many scholars, especially those who are particularly critical of mainstream neoliberal policy prescriptions. One of the more famous variants of this view comes from Washington-based economist John Williamson, who dubbed the IMF–World Bank–US Treasury view of how developing countries should manage their economies the "Washington Consensus" (Williamson 1989). In Williamson's view, a nearly religious attitude toward development policy had biased the recommendations coming from the IMF and the World Bank in ways that were not warranted by theory or evidence. More recently, both scholars and observers, including many politicians, have attacked governmental responses to the GFC, especially in Europe, for an attachment to austerity that they regard as both ideologically motivated and genuinely unwarranted (Blyth 2013 is the canonical statement).

Rather than centering on national politicians who respond to political pressures, a related perspective focuses on international or domestic bureaucrats who respond both to these sorts of ideational factors and to more technocratic considerations. An emphasis on technocratic bureaucracies is especially plausible in the international financial realm, where the problems and potential solutions are technically complex and well beyond the understanding of most citizens and many politicians. This provides an opportunity for experienced and well-informed officials of national governments, international organizations, or even nongovernmental organizations to create strong networks that can affect both national and supranational policies (Bach & Newman 2010, Barnett & Finnemore 2004, Lall 2015, and Porter 2005 are disparate examples of this scholarship). These transnational networks can be particularly powerful if they are able to garner support from individual governments or groups of governments, including those not normally in the inner corridors of international financial power (Gallagher 2014).

Idea-centered and technocrat-centered approaches are often blended. Indeed, some of the influential analyses focus on how ideologically committed technocrats in international institutions guide the course of institutional engagement and policy. At the same time, it is common to suggest that many of these technocratic and ideological biases are motivated by distributionally relevant considerations, for example, in favor of the corporate sector (Blyth 2013 combines aspects of all three).

Developments in international financial politics in the aftermath of the GFC provide an opportunity to see how different perspectives might analyze the course of global financial governance. Some would emphasize the interaction of the major states, especially within the G7, each concerned with nationally specific conditions. This emphasis on interstate strategic interaction could be augmented by seeing how the management group was expanded to the G20—although the extent to which this expansion affected outcomes would be contested.

Related scholarship would emphasize how bargaining among the principal national governments over how to confront the crisis was, and is, strongly constrained by the domestic conditions faced by each of the major players. Foremost among these constraints are the interests and influence of major private financial institutions that operate internationally. The domestic politics of financial regulation and monetary policy is now tightly interwoven with international financial developments, especially in the leading financial centers. There is undoubtedly plenty of evidence for the influence of powerful private-sector players and of national policy makers over the developments in international financial governance since 2008.

Evidence for the importance of changing ideas about the appropriate policies for today's international financial system is also likely to be strong. It is not surprising that an unprecedented level of financial integration and technological change, along with the most serious financial crisis since the 1930s, should give rise to a rethinking of the precepts that have guided policy making. At this point, much of what we know—or think we know—about international finance is up for discussion, and the pathways these discussions take have had, and will have, an impact on policy makers at both the national and the international levels.

Finally, there is little question that the GFC has highlighted the centrality of technically trained policy makers in both national and international institutions. To a great extent, the principal global response to the crisis has been managed by the world's principal central banks, and although central bankers are hardly impervious to political pressure, much of what they have done has been guided by their technocratic training and expertise. At the same time, the crisis has certainly enhanced the role of international institutions in the financial realm. The IMF and the BIS have both played major parts in discussions of how the world may move forward in the aftermath of the crisis.

In short, all of the factors identified by scholars as relevant to the making of international financial governance can be seen as having affected the course of the world's financial order since 2008.

This is hardly surprising: There are good theoretical and empirical reasons for the significance of all of these factors. What remains to be argued is whether one or more of the approaches described here outperforms the others in explaining the course of international financial events.

My summary of recent experience, undoubtedly colored by my own theoretical prejudices, is that we can understand most of the policy reaction to the GFC as a combination of domestic politics and interstate bargaining. Certainly the theoretical novelty of the panic of 2008 and the unprecedented nature of the Eurozone crisis have provided some space for policy entrepreneurship among international bureaucracies and for new ideas. But one of the striking features of the political economy of the crisis is just how similar it looks to previous financial and debt crises (Chinn & Frieden 2011). There has been massive conflict over how the burden of adjustment should be distributed, both among and within countries. The intersection of intercountry bargaining and domestic political conflicts has been particularly prominent in the Eurozone crisis. Although there have been ideas in conflict, and technocrats in the mix, it is hard to escape the conclusion that the cold hard cash at stake, both domestically and internationally, has been the main determinant of the political economy of the crisis.

Conclusion

International financial markets today are extraordinarily large and wield enormous influence over the course of global economic and political affairs. In the wake of the most damaging financial crisis in the last 75 years, it is no wonder that everyone, from policy makers and journalists to scholars, is interested to know if a higher level of international financial governance might avoid a repetition of the past decade's disasters. In a way, current discussions are reminiscent of the debates that took place in the aftermath of previous financial crises and bank panics at the national level, most of which led to an expansion of national financial regulation and supervision.

There are in fact good normative arguments for the development of international mechanisms to limit the damage international financial markets can cause and to enhance their benefits. At the domestic level, financial markets create positive externalities when they work well and negative externalities when they do not, and this creates a demand for management that is undersupplied by the private actors themselves—hence justifying the government's provision of the public goods associated with financial stability. At the international level, no single government has sufficient incentive to supply these global public goods, so their provision would depend on the joint decisions of multiple governments. But whatever the normative and theoretical argument for global public goods, the realities of international and domestic politics make their supply in practice problematic.

Nonetheless, there has unquestionably been movement toward greater global financial governance over the past 25 years, and this movement is in the direction of providing something akin to global public goods in the financial area. This development has taken the form of greater cooperation among the major financial centers, increased harmonization of financial regulations among countries, a more significant role for international financial institutions, and other measures that supply some part of what is typically associated with financial stability at the domestic level.

Scholars have adduced several factors to help explain both progress and obstacles in the path of international financial governance. The realities of collaboration among independent, self-interested nation-states may stand in the way, although if some countries expect to benefit disproportionately from international financial stability they may be more likely to work hard to contribute to it. By the same token, inasmuch as powerful groups—especially private financial institutions—anticipate private benefits from greater international financial governance, they will be inclined to pressure their governments to work in that direction. At the same time, trends in the intellectual understanding of international financial problems and of how they might most effectively be addressed can affect the ways in which national and international policymakers confront the problems they face. This is especially true when the policy makers are united by common technical training and by long experiences of working together either at the national or in international financial institutions.

The international financial system is likely to continue to grow and to expand its influence over both the global economy and the economies of countries. It is just as likely to continue to be subject to periodic tensions and pressures, and at times these tensions will almost certainly erupt into full-blown financial crises. Crises have always been endemic to financial markets, and we have no reason to believe that the near future will be different from the past. National governments have gradually developed ways to limit, though not eliminate, the damage caused by these financial stresses at the domestic level. The evidence of the past several decades is that the world's major governments, along with major international financial institutions, are moving gradually and haltingly in the direction of managing international financial affairs more comprehensively at the global level. This does not necessarily mean that the results of these efforts will be some magical resolution of global problems, or even that they will make most people and most countries better off. But there are prospects for progress in addressing the potential costs of international financial integration and enhancing its positive effects. It is important to understand these prospects and the obstacles to their realization.

NOTES

1. This is not to imply that there are no potential global public goods in the international trade realm. For example, the monitoring and enforcement of agreements might require some form of global governance. Scholars have suggested other such public goods in trade (and the internalization of a terms-of-trade externality). I mean only to point out that trade liberalization does not itself require global governance inasmuch as enough benefits of the national policy are realized within the nation to make the policy nationally desirable.

2. I should note that there is a small public choice–influenced literature that contests the normative case for international financial governance (see, e.g., Vaubel 1983, Dreher & Vaubel 2004).

3. "Maturity transformation" refers to the process whereby financial institutions borrow at short term (i.e., from depositors) and lend at long term (i.e., to mortgage holders). A fractional reserve system is one where banks have only a fraction of the money necessary to cover their liabilities (such as to depositors) available upon demand, on the principle that only a fraction of these liabilities are expected to be called at any given time.

4. Büthe and Mattli 2011 make similar arguments but taken a step farther, to explain why some such governance is delegated directly to the private sector itself.

REFERENCES

Abdelal, Rawi. 2007. *Capital Rules: The Construction of Global Finance*. Cambridge, MA: Harvard University Press.

Bach, David, and Abraham Newman. 2010. Transgovernmental Networks and Domestic Policy Convergence: Evidence from Insider Trading Regulation. *International Organization* 64:505–28.

Barnett, Michael, and Martha Finnemore. 2004. *Rules for the World: International Organizations in Global Politics*. Ithaca, NY: Cornell University Press.

Basel Committee on Banking Supervision. 2014. *A Brief History of the Basel Committee*. Basel: Bank for International Settlements.

Blyth, Mark. 2002. *Great Transformations: Economic Ideas and Institutional Change in the Twentieth Century*. Cambridge, UK: Cambridge University Press.

———. 2013. *Austerity: The History of a Dangerous Idea*. Oxford, UK: Oxford University Press.

Borio, Claudio, Harold James, and Hyung Song Shin. 2014. *The International Monetary and Financial System: A Capital Account Historical Perspective*. Bank for International Settlements Working Paper No. 457. Basel: Bank for International Settlements.

Broz, J. Lawrence. 1998. The Origins of Central Banking: Solutions to the Free Rider Problem. *International Organization* 52, no. 2 (Spring): 231–68.

———. 2005. Congressional Politics of International Financial Rescues. *American Journal of Political Science* 49, no. 3 (July): 479–96.

———. 2008. Congressional Voting on Funding the International Financial Institutions. *Review of International Organizations* 3, no. 4 (December): 351–74.

Brunnermeier, Markus, and Yuliy Sannikov. 2015. International Credit Flows and Pecuniary Externalities. *American Economics Journal: Macroeconomics* 7, no. 1: 297–338.

Büthe, Tim, and Walter Mattli. 2011. *The New Global Rulers: The Privatization Regulation in the World Economy*. Princeton, NJ: Princeton University Press.

Chwieroth, Jeffrey. 2010. *Capital Ideas: The IMF and the Rise of Financial Liberalization*. Princeton, NJ: Princeton University Press.

Copelovitch, Mark. 2010. *The International Monetary Fund in the Global Economy: Banks, Bonds, and Bailouts*. Cambridge, UK: Cambridge University Press.

Diamond, Douglas, and Philip Dybvig. 1983. Bank Runs, Deposit Insurance, and Liquidity. *Journal of Political Economy* 91, no. 3 (June): 401–19.

Dreher, Axel, and Roland Vaubel. 2004. The Causes and Consequences of IMF Conditionality. *Emerging Markets Finance and Trade* 40, no. 3 (May–June).

Drezner, Daniel W. 2007. *All Politics Is Global: Explaining International Regulatory Regimes*. Princeton, NJ: Princeton University Press.

Eichengreen, Barry. 1999. *Toward a New International Financial Architecture*. Washington, DC: Institute for International Economics.

Engel, Charles. 2015a. International Coordination of Central Bank Policy. NBER working paper 20952. Cambridge, MA: NBER.

———. 2015b. Macroprudential Policy in a World of High Capital Mobility. NBER working paper 20951. Cambridge, MA: NBER.

Frieden Jeffry, and J. Lawrence Broz. 2013. The Political Economy of International Monetary Policy Coordination. *I. Handbook of Safeguarding Global Financial Stability: Political, Social, Cultural, and Economic Theories and Models*, Vol. 2, edited by Gerard Caprio, 81–90. Oxford, UK: Elsevier Inc.

Frieden, Jeffry, Michael Pettis, Dani Rodrik, and Ernesto Zedillo. 2012. *After the Fall: The Future of Global Cooperation*. Geneva Report 14. London: Center for Economic Policy Research.

Gallagher, Kevin. 2014. *Ruling Capital: Emerging Markets and the Re-regulation of Cross-Border Finance*. Ithaca, NY: Cornell University Press.

Goldstein, Morris. 2005. The International Financial Architecture. In *The United States and the World Economy: Foreign Economic Policy for the Next Decade*, edited by C. Fred Bergsten, pp. 373–407. Washington, DC: Peterson Institute for International Economics.

Gorton, Gary. 2009. The Panic of 2007. In *Maintaining Stability in a Changing Financial System*, pp. 131–262. Kansas City: Federal Reserve Bank of Kansas City.

Grossman, Richard, and Hugh Rockoff. 2015. *Fighting the Last War: Economists on the Lender of Last Resort*. NBER Working paper 20832 (January). Cambridge, MA: NBER.

Helleiner, Eric, and Stefano Pagliari. 2011. The End of an Era in International Financial Regulation? A Postcrisis Research Agenda. *International Organization* 65 (Winter): 169–200.

Independent Evaluation Office. 2014. *IMF Response to the Financial and Economic Crisis*. Washington, DC: IMF.

International Monetary Fund. 2015. IMF's Response to the Global Economic Crisis. Washington, DC: IMF. Available at http://www.imf.org/external/np/exr/facts/changing.htm.

Kapstein, Ethan B. 1989. Resolving the Regulator's Dilemma: International Coordination of Banking Regulations. *International Organization* 43, no. 2 (Spring): 323–47.

———. 1994. *Governing the Global Economy: International Finance and the State*. Cambridge, MA: Harvard University Press.

Koppell, Jonathan. 2010. *World Rule: Accountability, Legitimacy, and the Design of Global Governance*. Chicago: University of Chicago Press.

Krasner, Stephen D. 1991. Global Communications and National Power: Life on the Pareto Frontier. *World Politics* 43, no. 3 (April): 336–66.

Lall, Ranjit. 2015. Timing as a Source of Regulatory Influence: A Technical Elite Network Analysis of Global Finance. *Regulation and Governance* 9, no. 2 (June): 125–43.

Landau, Jean-Pierre. 2014. International Lender of Last Resort: Some Thoughts for the 21st Century. In *Rethinking the Lender of Last Resort*. BIS Papers Number 79. Basel: Bank for International Settlements.

Lorenzoni, Guido. 2014. International Financial Crises. In *Handbook of International Economics*, vol. 4, edited by Elhanan Helpman, Kenneth Rogoff, and Gita Gopinath. Amsterdam: Elsevier.

New Rules for Global Finance. 2014. *Global Financial Governance and Impact Report 2014*. Washington, DC: New Rules for Global Finance.

Oatley, Thomas, and Robert Nabors. 1998. Redistributive Cooperation: Market Failure, Wealth Transfers, and the Basel Accord. *International Organization* 52, no. 1 (Winter): 35–54.

Obstfeld, Maurice. 2009. Lenders of Last Resort in a Globalized World. *Monetary and Economic Studies* 27 (November): 35–52.

Pauly, Louis, and William Coleman, eds. 2008. *Global Ordering: Institutions and Autonomy in a Changing World*. Seattle: University of Washington Press.

Porter, Tony. 2005. *Globalization and Finance*. Cambridge, UK: Polity Press.

Posner, Elliot. 2009. Making Rules for Global Finance: Transatlantic Regulatory Cooperation at the Turn of the Millennium. *International Organization* 63, no. 4 (Fall): 665–99.

Schoenmaker, Dirk, ed. 2014. *Macroprudentialism*. London: Centre for Economic Policy Research.

Simmons, Beth. 2001. The International Politics of Harmonization: The Case of Capital Market Regulation. *International Organization* 55, no. 3 (Autumn): 589–620.

Singer, David. 2004. Capital Rules: The Domestic Politics of International Regulatory Harmonization. *International Organization* 58, no. 3: 531–65.

Singer, David. 2007. *Regulating Capital: Setting Standards for the International Financial System*. Ithaca, NY: Cornell University Press.

Spero, Joan. 1980. *The Failure of the Franklin National Bank: Challenge to the International Banking System*. New York: Columbia University Press.

Stone, Randall. 2011. *Controlling Institution: International Organizations and the Global Economy*. Cambridge, UK: Cambridge University Press.

Taylor, John. 2014. The Federal Reserve in Globalized World Economy. Federal Reserve Bank of Dallas Globalization and Monetary Policy Institute Working Paper 200. Dallas: Federal Reserve Bank of Dallas.

Vaubel, Roland. 1983. The Moral Hazard of IMF Lending. *The World Economy* 6, no. 3.

Véron, Nicolas. 2014. The G20 Financial Reform Agenda After Five Years. *Bruegel Policy Contribution* 11 (September): 1–9.

Williamson, John. 1989. What Washington Means by Policy Reform. In *Latin American Readjustment: How Much Has Happened*, ed. John Williamson, pp. 7–40. Washington, DC: Institute for International Economics.

Daniel W. Drezner

THE IRONY OF GLOBAL ECONOMIC GOVERNANCE
The System Worked

Introduction

The 2008 financial crisis posed the biggest challenge to the global economy since the Great Depression and provided a severe "stress test" for global economic governance. A review of economic outcomes, policy outputs, and institutional resilience reveals that these regimes performed well during the acute phase of the crisis, ensuring the continuation of an open global economy. Even though some policy outcomes have been less than optimal, international institutions and frameworks performed contrary to expectations. Simply put, the system worked.

During the first ten months of the Great Recession, global stock market capitalization plummeted lower as a percentage of its precrisis level than during the first ten months of the Great Depression.[1] Housing prices in the United States declined more than twice as much as they did during the Great Depression.[2] The global decline in asset values led to aggregate losses of $27 trillion in 2008—a half-year's worth of global economic output.[3] Global unemployment increased by an estimated fourteen million people in 2008 alone.[4] Nearly four years after the crisis, concerns about systemic risk still continue.[5]

The demand for global economic governance structures to perform effectively is at its greatest

Working Paper, Council on Foreign Relations, International Institutions and Global Governance Program (Oct. 2012).

during crises. An open global economy lessens the stagnation that comes from a financial crisis, preventing a downturn from metastasizing into another Great Depression. One of the primary purposes of multilateral economic institutions is to provide global public goods—such as keeping barriers to cross-border exchange low. Even if states are the primary actors in world politics, they rely on a bevy of acronym-laden institutions—the International Monetary Fund (IMF), World Trade Organization (WTO), Bank for International Settlements (BIS), and Group of Twenty (G20)—to coordinate action on the global scale. International institutions can be the policymaker's pacifier. In an anarchic world, these structures reduce uncertainty for all participating actors. When they function well, they facilitate communication and foster shared understanding between policy principals. When they function poorly, a lack of trust and a surfeit of uncertainty stymies responsible authorities from cooperating.

Since the Great Recession began, there has been no shortage of scorn for the state of global economic governance among pundits and scholars.[6] Nevertheless, a closer look at the global response to the financial crisis reveals a more optimistic picture. Despite initial shocks that were more severe than the 1929 financial crisis, national policy elites and multilateral economic institutions responded quickly and robustly. Whether one looks at economic outcomes, policy outputs, or institutional resilience, global economic governance structures have either reinforced or improved upon the status quo since the collapse of the subprime mortgage bubble. To be sure, there remain areas where governance has either faltered or failed, but on the whole, the global regime worked.

How Does Global Economic Governance Work?

Debates about whether global governance works or not usually do not suffer from an abundance of data. More typically, critics of the current system tend to rely on a few stylized facts that are meant to suggest general dysfunction. In recent years, the three events most commonly cited are:[7]

■ *The collapse of the Doha round.* Just before the financial crisis hit its acute phase, last-gasp efforts to the Doha round of WTO negotiations stalled out. Subsequent G20 pledges to abstain from protectionism and complete the Doha round of world trade talks have been as common as they have been toothless. Within the first six months of the financial crisis, seventeen of the twenty countries had violated that pledge, implementing a combined forty-seven measures to restrict trade at the expense of other countries.[8] The current status of the Doha round is so moribund that the Bush administration's last U.S. trade representative advocated abandoning the effort.[9]

■ *The breakdown of macroeconomic policy consensus at the 2010 Toronto G20 summit.* Prior to the Toronto summit, there was a rough consensus among the G20 in favor of government stimulus to keep the global economy afloat. The United States went into that summit to argue for more expansionary monetary and fiscal policy, but came out of it with no consensus. Other countries embraced austerity

policies instead. In the subsequent eighteen months, numerous G20 members accused each other of starting a currency war.

■ *The escalation of Europe's sovereign debt crisis.* As an increasing number of eurozone economies have found their fiscal fortunes collapsing, European institutions have appeared powerless to stop the spreading financial contagion. If the European Union, the single most powerful regional institution in existence, cannot cope with this crisis, why should we expect global governance structures to do better with bigger problems?

These facts are true, but they are not the whole truth. To ascertain the effectiveness of global economic governance after the 2008 financial crisis, it is useful to look at three different levels of analysis. First, what do the policy outcomes look like? How have global output, trade, and other capital flows responded since the start of the Great Recession? Second, what do the policy outputs look like? Have important international institutions provided policies that experts would consider significant and useful in response to the global financial crisis? Finally, have these governance structures demonstrated institutional resiliency and flexibility? A common complaint prior to 2008 was that these institutions had not adapted to the shifting distribution of power. Have these structures maintained their relevance and authority? Have they responded to the shifts in the distribution of power to ensure that the powerful actors continue to buy into existing arrangements?

Policy Outcomes

In looking at outcomes, the obvious question is how well the global economy has recovered from the 2008 crisis, The current literature on economic downturns suggests two factors that impose significant barriers to a strong recovery from the

Great Recession: it was triggered by a financial crisis and it was global in scope. Whether measuring output, per capita income, or employment, financial crashes trigger downturns that last longer and have far weaker recoveries than standard business cycle downturns.[10] Furthermore, the global nature of the crisis makes it extremely difficult for countries to export their way out of the problem. Countries that have experienced severe banking crises since World War II have usually done so when the global economy was largely unaffected. That was not the case for the Great Recession.

The global economy has rebounded much better than during the Great Depression. Economists Barry Eichengreen and Kevin O'Rourke have compiled data to compare global economic performance from the start of the crises (see Figures 9.7 and 9.8).[11] Two facts stand out in their comparisons. First, the percentage drop in global industrial output and world trade levels at the start of the 2008 financial crisis was more precipitous than the falloffs following the October 1929 stock market crash. The drop in industrial output was greater in 2008 nine months into the crisis than it was eighty years earlier after the same amount of time. The drop in trade flows was more than twice as large. Second, the post-2008 rebound has been far more robust. Four years after the onset of the Great Recession, global industrial output is 10 percent higher than when the recession began. In contrast, four years after the 1929 stock market crash, industrial output was at only two-thirds of precrisis levels.

A similar story can be told with aggregate economic growth. According to World Bank figures, global economic output rebounded in 2010 with 2.3 percent growth, followed up in 2011 with 4.2 percent growth. The global growth rate in 2011 was 44 percent higher than the average of the previous decade. Even more intriguing, the

Figure 9.7. World Industrial Production: Great Depression vs. Great Recession

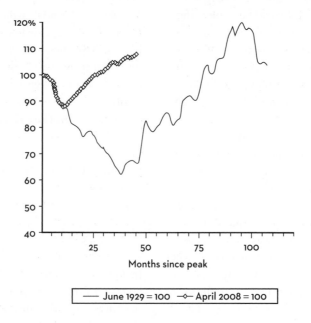

Months since peak

| —— June 1929 = 100   ◇ April 2008 = 100 |

Source: Eichengreen and O'Rourke, "A tale of two depressions redux"

Figure 9.8. World Trade Volumes: Great Depression vs. Great Recession

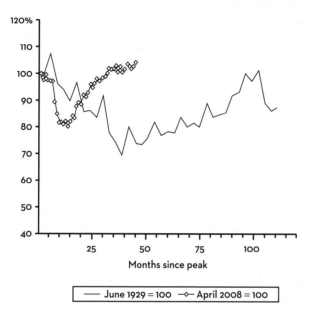

Months since peak

—— June 1929 = 100　—◇— April 2008 = 100

Source: Eichengreen and O'Rourke, "A tale of two depressions redux"

growth continued to be poverty reducing.[12] The World Bank's latest figures suggest that despite the 2008 financial crisis, extreme poverty continued to decline across all the major regions of the globe. And the developing world achieved its first Millennium Development Goal of halving the 1990 levels of extreme poverty.[13]

An important reason for the quick return to positive economic growth is that cross-border flows did not dry up after the 2008 crisis. Again, compared to the Great Depression, trade flows have rebounded extremely well.[14] Four years after the 1929 stock market crash, trade flows were off by 25 percent compared to precrisis levels. Current trade flows, in contrast, are more than 5 percent higher than in 2008. Even compared to other postwar recessions, the current period has seen robust cross-border exchange. Indeed, as a report from CFR's Maurice R. Greenberg Center for Geoeconomic Studies concluded in May 2012, "The

growth in world trade since the start of the [current] recovery exceeds even the best of the prior postwar experiences."[15]

Other cross-border flows have also rebounded from 2008–2009 lows. Global foreign direct investment (FDI) has returned to robust levels. FDI inflows rose by 17 percent in 2011 alone. This put annual FDI levels at $1.5 trillion, surpassing the three-year precrisis average, though still approximately 25 percent below the 2007 peak. More generally, global foreign investment assets reached $96 trillion, a 5 percent increase from precrisis highs. Remittances from migrant workers have become an increasingly important revenue stream to the developing world—and the 2008 financial crisis did not dampen that income stream. Cross-border remittances to developing countries quickly rebounded to precrisis levels and then rose to an estimated all-time high of $372 billion in 2011, with growth rates in 2011 that exceeded those in 2010. Total cross-border remittances were more than $501 billion last year, and are estimated to reach $615 billion by 2014.[16]

Another salient outcome is mass public attitudes about the global economy. A general assumption in public opinion research is that during a downturn, demand for greater economic closure should spike, as individuals scapegoat foreigners for domestic woes. The global nature of the 2008 crisis, combined with anxiety about the shifting distribution of power, should have triggered a fall in support for an open global economy. Somewhat surprisingly, however, the reverse is true. Pew's Global Attitudes Project has surveyed a wide spectrum of countries since 2002, asking people about their opinions on both international trade and the free market more generally.[17] The results show resilient support for expanding trade and business ties with other countries. Twenty-four countries were surveyed both in 2007 and at least one year after 2008, including a majority of the G20 economies. Overall, eighteen of those twenty-four countries showed equal or greater support for trade in 2009 than two years earlier. By 2011, twenty of twenty-four countries showed greater or equal support for trade compared to 2007. Indeed, between 2007 and 2012, the unweighted average support for more trade in these countries increased from 78.5 percent to 83.6 percent. Contrary to expectation, there has been no mass public rejection of the open global economy. Indeed, public support for the open trading system has strengthened, despite softening public support for free-market economics more generally.[18]

The final outcome addresses a dog that hasn't barked: the effect of the Great Recession on cross-border conflict and violence. During the initial stages of the crisis, multiple analysts asserted that the financial crisis would lead states to increase their use of force as a tool for staying in power.[19] Whether through greater internal repression, diversionary wars, arms races, or a ratcheting up of great power conflict, there were genuine concerns that the global economic downturn would lead to an increase in conflict. Violence in the Middle East, border disputes in the South China Sea, and even the disruptions of the Occupy movement fuel impressions of surge in global public disorder.

The aggregate data suggests otherwise, however. A fundamental conclusion from a recent report by the Institute for Economics and Peace is that "the average level of peacefulness in 2012 is approximately the same as it was in 2007."[20] Interstate violence in particular has declined since the start of the financial crisis—as have military expenditures in most sampled countries. Other studies confirm that the Great Recession has not triggered any increase in violent conflict; the secular decline in violence that started with the end of the Cold War has not been reversed.[21]

None of these data suggest that the global economy is operating swimmingly. Growth remains unbalanced and fragile, and has clearly slowed in 2012. Transnational capital flows remain depressed compared to precrisis levels—primarily due to a drying up of cross-border interbank lending in Europe. Currency volatility remains an ongoing concern. Compared to the aftermath of other postwar recessions, growth in output, investment, and employment in the developed world have all lagged behind. But the Great Recession is not like other postwar recessions in either scope or kind; expecting a standard V-shaped recovery was unreasonable. One financial analyst characterizes the current global economy as in a state of "contained depression."[22] The operative word is contained, however. Given the severity, reach, and depth of the 2008 financial crisis, the proper comparison is with the Great Depression. And by that standard, the outcome variables look impressive.

Policy Outputs

It could be that the global economy has experienced a moderate bounce back in spite rather than because of the global policy response. Economists like Paul Krugman and Joseph Stiglitz have been particularly scornful of policymakers and central bankers.[23] In assessing policy outputs, Charles Kindleberger provided the classic definition of what should be done to stabilize the global economy during a severe financial crisis: "(a) maintaining a relatively open market for distress goods; (b) providing countercyclical long-term lending; and (c) discounting in crisis."[24] Serious concerns were voiced in late 2008 and early 2009 about the inability of anyone to provide these kinds of public goods, threatening a repeat of the trade protectionism and beggar-thy-neighbor policies of the 1930s.[25]

By Kindleberger's criteria, however, public goods provision has been quite robust since 2008. On the surface, the open market for distressed goods seemed under threat. The death of the Doha round, the rise of G20 protectionism after the fall 2008 summit, and the explosion of anti-dumping cases that occurred at the onset of the financial crisis suggested that markets were drifting toward closure. According to the WTO's data, antidumping initiations surged by 30 percent in 2008 alone. This surge quickly receded, however. Figure 9.9 shows that by 2011, antidumping initiations had declined dramatically to precrisis levels. Indeed, these cases have fallen to their lowest levels since the WTO's founding in 1995. Both countervailing duty complaints and safeguards initiations have also fallen to precrisis levels.

Some post-2008 measures aren't captured in these traditional metrics of nontariff barriers, but similar results hold. Most of those implemented measures were concentrated in countries that already possessed higher barriers to global economic integration, such as Russia and Argentina. Even including these additional measures, the combined effect of protectionist actions for the first year after the peak of the financial crisis

Figure 9.9. Trade Restrictions, 2006–2011

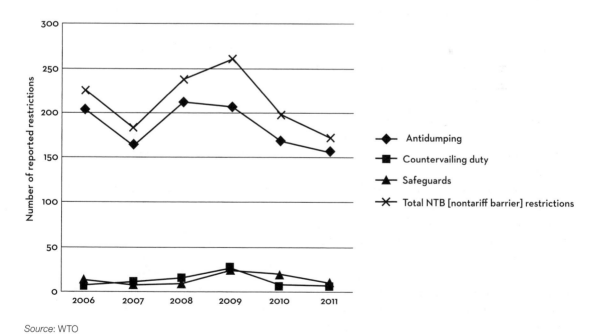

Source: WTO

affected less than 0.8 percent of global trade.[26] Furthermore, the use of these protectionist measures declined additionally in 2010 to cover only 0.2 percent of global trade. Protectionist actions rose again in 2012, but again, the effect of these measures remains modest.[27] The quick turnaround and growth in trade levels show that these measures have not seriously impeded market access.[28] In part, accelerated steps toward trade liberalization at the bilateral and regional levels have blunted the effect of these protectionist actions.

Proponents of trade liberalization embrace the bicycle theory—the belief that unless multilateral trade liberalization moves forward, the entire global trade regime will collapse because of a lack of forward momentum. The past four years suggest that there are limits to that rule of thumb. Recent surveys of global business leaders reveal that concerns about protectionism have stayed at a low level.[29] At a minimum, the bicycle of world trade is still coasting forward at high speed.

From the earliest stages of the financial crisis, there was also concerted and coordinated action among central banks to ensure both discounting and countercyclical lending. The central banks of the major economics began cutting interest rates slowly after the fall of 2007. By the fall of 2008 they were cutting rates ruthlessly and in a coordinated fashion, as Figure 9.10 indicates. According to BIS estimates, global real interest rates fell from an average of 3 percent prior to the crisis to zero in 2012—in the advanced industrialized economies, the real interest rate was effectively negative.[30] At present, the highest interest rate among the major advanced economies is 0.75 percent, offered by the European Central Bank. Not content with lowering interest rates, most of the major central banks also expanded other credit facilities and

Figure 9.10. Major Policy Interest Rates, 2007–2012

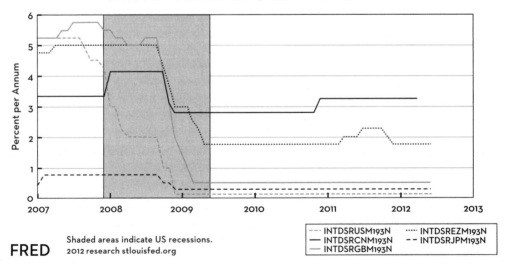

Interest Rates, Discount Rate for United States (INTDSRUSM193N), Interest Rates, Discount Rate for Euro Area (INTDSREZM193N), Interest Rates, Discount Rate for China (INTDSRCNM193N), Interest Rates, Discount Rate for Japan (INTDSRJPM193N), Interest Rates, Discount Rate for United Kingdom (INTDSRGBM193N)

FRED
Shaded areas indicate US recessions.
2012 research stlouisfed.org

INTDSRUSM193N   INTDSREZM193N
INTDSRCNM193N   INTDSRJPM193N
INTDSRGBM193N

Source: St. Louis Federal Reserve Bank

engaged in more creative forms of quantitative easing. Between 2007 and 2012, the balance sheets of the central banks in the advanced industrialized economies more than doubled. BIS acknowledged in its 2012 annual report that "decisive action by central banks during the global financial crisis was probably crucial in preventing a repeat of the experiences of the Great Depression."[31]

Central banks and finance ministries also took coordinated action during the fall of 2008 to try to ensure cross-border lending as to avert currency and solvency crises. In October of that year, the Group of Seven (G7) economies plus Switzerland agreed to unlimited currency swaps in order to ensure liquidity would be maintained in the system. The United States then extended its currency-swap facility to Brazil, Singapore, Mexico, and South Korea. The European Central Bank expanded its swap arrangements for euros with Hungary, Denmark, and Poland. China, Japan, South Korea, and the Association of Southeast Asian Nations (ASEAN) economics broadened the Chang Mai Initiative into an $80 billion swap arrangement to ensure liquidity. The IMF created the Short-Term Liquidity Facility designed to "establish quick-disbursing financing for countries with strong economic policies that are facing temporary liquidity problems."[32] The fund also negotiated emergency financing for Hungary, Pakistan, Iceland, and Ukraine.

Over the longer term, the great powers bulked up the resources of the international financial institutions to provide for further countercyclical lending. In 2009 the G20 agreed to triple the IMF's reserves to $750 billion. In 2012, in response to the worsening European sovereign debt crisis, G20 countries combined to pledge more than $430 billion in additional resources. The World Bank's International Development Association (IDA), which offers up the most concessionary form of lending, also increased its resources. The sixteenth IDA replenishment was a record $49.3 billion—an 18 percent increase of IDA resources from three years earlier. By Kindleberger's criteria, global economic governance worked reasonably well in response to the 2008 financial crisis.

To be sure, there exist global public goods that go beyond Kindleberger's criteria. Macroeconomic policy coordination would be an additional area of possible cooperation, as would coordinating and clarifying cross-border financial regulations. Again, however, the international system acted in these areas after 2008. Between late 2007 and the June 2010 G20 Toronto summit, the major economies agreed on the need for aggressive and expansionary fiscal and monetary policies in the wake of the financial crisis. Even reluctant contributors like Germany—whose finance minister blasted the "crass Keynesianism" of these policies in December 2008—eventually bowed to pressure from economists and G20 peers. Indeed, in 2009, Germany enacted the third-largest fiscal stimulus in the world.[33]

Progress has also been made on regulatory coordination in finance and investment rules. There were developments in two areas in particular: banking regulation and investor protectionism. In the former area, international regulators have significantly revised the Basel core banking principles. At the November 2010 Seoul summit, the G20 approved the Basel III banking standards. Basel III took only two years to negotiate—an extraordinarily brief period given that the Basel II standards took more than six years to hammer out. The new rules, scheduled to be phased in over the rest of this decade, increase the amount of reserve capital banks need to keep on hand and add additional countercyclical capital buffers to prevent financial institutions from engaging in pro-cyclical lending.

Financial sector scholars have debated whether Basel III is a sufficient upgrade in regulatory stringency and whether it will be implemented too slowly or not at all. There is consensus, however, on two points. First, Basel III clearly represents an upgrade over the Basel II standards in preventing bank failures.[34] Second, the dampening effects of the new standards on economic growth are negligible. Furthermore, these standards were approved despite fierce resistance from the global banking industry. In November 2011 the Financial Stability Board designated global systemically important banks that will be required to keep additional capital on hand, and it plans to identify global systemically important nonfinancial institutions by the end of 2012.[35]

Progress was also made in investor protectionism against state-owned enterprises and funds. The rise of sovereign wealth funds prior to 2008 had precipitated a ratcheting up of restrictions to cross-border investment by state-owned enterprises and funds. The Organization of Economic Cooperation and Development (OECD) articulated its own guidelines for recipient countries but warned that unless these funds demonstrated greater transparency, barriers to investment would likely rise even further. In September 2008 an IMF-brokered process approved a set of Generally Accepted Principles and Practices (GAPP) for sovereign wealth funds. These voluntary guidelines—also called the Santiago Principles—consisted of twenty-four guidelines addressing the legal and institutional frameworks, governance issues, and risk management of these funds. Contemporaneous press reports characterized the new rules as "a rare triumph for IMF financial diplomacy."[36] The expert consensus among financial analysts, regulators, and academics was that these principles—if fully implemented—address most recipient country concerns.[37] Since the IMF approved the Santiago Principles, furthermore, investor protectionism has declined.[38]

Institutional Resilience and Flexibility

The degree of institutional resiliency and flexibility at the global level has been rather remarkable. Once the acute phase of the 2008 financial crisis began, the G20 quickly supplanted the G7 and Group of Eight (G8) as the focal point for global economic governance. At the September 2009 G20 summit in Pittsburgh, the member countries explicitly avowed that they had "designated the G20 to be the premier forum for our international economic cooperation."[39] This move addressed the worsening problem of the G8's waning power and relevancy—a problem of which G8 members were painfully aware.[40] The G20 grouping comprises 85 percent of global economic output, 80 percent of global trade, and 66 percent of global population. The G20 is not perfectly inclusive, and it has a somewhat idiosyncratic membership at the margins, but it is a far more legitimate and representative body than the G8.[41] As Geoffrey Garrett puts it, "the G20 is globally representative yet small enough to make consensual decision-making feasible."[42] As a club of great powers, consensus within the G20 should lead to effective policy coordination across a wide range of issues.[43]

To be sure, having the capacity to be an effective body and actually *being* effective are two different things. The perception is that the G20's political momentum stalled out years ago after countries disagreed on macroeconomic imbalances and the virtues of austerity. The reality is a bit more complex. According to the University of Toronto's G20 Information Centre, compliance with G20 commitments actually increased over time. They measured G20 adherence to "chosen priority commitments." Measured on a per country average, G20 members have steadily improved since the 61.5 percent compliance rate for the April 2009 London Summit commitments, rising all the way to 77 percent for the November 2011 Cannes Summit.[44]

An obvious rejoinder is that this kind of assessment inflates compliance because the pledges made at these summits are increasingly modest.[45] It could be that the G20 has simply scaled back its ambitions—even in its "priority commitments"—making compliance easier. There are examples, however, of great powers using the G20 as a means of blunting domestic pressures for greater protectionism—at precisely the moment when the group was thought to be losing its momentum. For example, the G20 has served as a useful mechanism to defuse tensions concerning China's undervalued currency. In response to congressional pressure for more robust action, in April 2010 Treasury secretary Timothy Geithner cited the G20 meetings as "the best avenue for advancing U. S. interests" on China's manipulation of its exchange rate.[46] In June of that year, President Barack Obama sent a letter to his G20 colleagues stressing the importance of "market-determined exchange rates." Three days after the president's letter was sent, the People's Bank of China announced that it would "enhance the RMB exchange rate flexibility." For the next two years, the renminbi nominally appreciated at a rate of 5 percent a year—more so if one factors in the differences in national inflation rates.[47]

Other important financial bodies also strengthened their membership and authority as a response to the 2008 crisis. In March 2009, the Basel Committee on Banking Supervision expanded its membership from thirteen advanced industrialized states to twenty-seven countries by adding the developing country members of the G20. The Financial Stability Forum was renamed the Financial Stability Board in April 2009, was given greater responsibilities for regulatory coordination, and similarly expanded to include the developing country members of the G20 in its membership. During this period the Committee of the Global Financial System also grew in size from thirteen countries to twenty-two members, adding Brazil, China, and India, among others. The Financial Action Task Force on money laundering has added China, India, and South Korea to its grouping over the past five years. Prior to 2008, the G7 countries dominated most of these financial standard-setting agencies.[48] In terms of membership, that is no longer the case.

The International Monetary Fund and World Bank have also changed after the financial crisis, though on the surface that might not appear to be the case. The implicit compact in which a European is given the IMF managing director slot and an American the World Bank presidency has continued over the past two years. Despite the scandals that engulfed Dominique Strauss-Kahn in 2011 and Paul Wolfowitz five years earlier, former French finance minister Christine Lagarde replaced Strauss-Kahn in 2011 and American Jim Yong Kim became the new World Bank president in 2012.

Beneath the surface, however, the bank and the fund have witnessed significant evolution. Power within the IMF is based on quota size, calculated using a complex formula of economic variables. Prior to 2007, the allotment of quotas in the IMF bore little resemblance to the distribution of economic power. This has changed. The most significant step has been two rounds of quota reform in the IMF, the first enacted in 2008 and the second to be completed by the end of this year. The explicit goal of the quota reform was to expand the voting power of advanced developing economies to better reflect the distribution of economic power. Once completed, China will possess the third-largest voting share in the fund and all four of the BRIC (Brazil, Russia, India, and China) economies will be among the ten largest shareholders in the IMF.[49] The World Bank Group underwent a parallel set of reforms. Between 2008 and 2010, the voting power of developing and transition economies within the main World Bank institution (the International Bank for Reconstruction and Development) had been increased by 4.59 percentage points, and China became the third-largest voting member. The International Finance Corporation (IFC) approved an even larger shift of 6.09 percentage points. More important, the bank's development committee agreed that bank and IFC shareholding would be reviewed every five years beginning in 2015, routinizing the process.[50]

While the appointments of Lagarde and Kim might seem retrograde, they came with political bargaining that reflected the greater influence of the advanced developing countries. In both cases, the nominee had to woo developing countries to secure political support in advance of voting. The appointment of Chinese national Min Zhu to be a deputy managing director of the IMF at the same time that Lagarde took over shows a shift in the distribution of senior-level appointments toward the advanced developing economies.

The content of the bank and fund policies has also shifted to better reflect developing country concerns. In a staff paper, the IMF acknowledged that "capital controls may be useful in addressing both macroeconomic and financial stability concerns in the face of inflow surges," a shift from the Washington consensus.[51] As for the bank, Kim's appointment to the presidency in 2012 highlights the shift in priorities. Trained as a doctor and an anthropologist, Kim's entire career has focused entirely on health policy until now. This suggests that the bank will use a more capacious notion of development going forward.

The trade and investment regimes have displayed somewhat less resiliency than global financial governance—but these regimes have not withered on the vine either. The multilateral trade regime in particular would appear to have suffered the most from the Great Recession. The collapse of the Doha round was a severe blow to the World Trade Organization. Nevertheless, the WTO as an institution has endured. Indeed, it has expanded its reach in several ways. Geographically, the WTO finally secured the accession of the Russian Federation, the last G20 nonmember, after a slow-motion, fifteen-year negotiation process. The WTO's dispute settlement mechanism helped contain the spread of protectionist measures that the Great Recession triggered. There is no evidence that compliance with these rulings has waned since 2008; the available evidence suggests that the WTO's dispute settlement arm is still playing a valuable role.[52] The WTO's Government Procurement Agreement (GPA) helped blunt the most blatant parts of the "Buy American" provisions of the 2009 fiscal stimulus, thereby preventing a cascade of fiscal protectionism. Although the GPA is only plurilateral, China is now negotiating to join the agreement. The United States, European Union, and China are

also accelerating talks on a services liberalization agreement that would encompass most of the OECD economies as well as developing countries.

In truth, the Doha round had lost its momentum long before the 2007–2008 financial crisis, and it was effectively moribund before the Great Recession started. What is interesting to note is that the enthusiasm for greater trade liberalization has not lost its momentum, but rather found a new outlet: the explosion of regional and bilateral free trade agreements (FTAs). The traditional expectation that an economic downturn would dampen enthusiasm for greater openness has not been borne out by the data on FTAs. In the four years prior to the collapse of Lehman Brothers, fifty-one FTAs were reported to the World Trade Organization. In the four years since Lehman, fifty-eight free trade agreements have been registered.[53] A transpacific partnership and a transatlantic free trade zone are at preliminary stages of negotiation as well. To be sure, not all of these FTAs were created equal. Some of them have greater coverage of goods than others. Some of them might promote more trade diversion than trade creation. Nevertheless, the patterned growth of these FTAs mirrors how they spread in the late nineteenth century.[54] Although these FTAs do not possess the "most-favored nation" provision that accelerated trade liberalization in the nineteenth century, the political economy of trade diversion still generates competitive incentives for a growth in FTAs, thereby leading to a similar outcome.[55] Through their own shared understandings and dispute settlement mechanisms, they act as an additional brake on protectionist policies.[56]

There is no multilateral investment regime to display resiliency. Instead, investment is governed by a network of bilateral investment treaties (BITs). Compared to the data on free trade agreements, it would appear that the pace of BITs has slowed since 2008. According to United Nations Conference on Trade and Development (UNCTAD) data, an annual average of seventy-eight BITs were

Figure 9.11. Annual Count of Bilateral Investment Treaties, 1960–2011

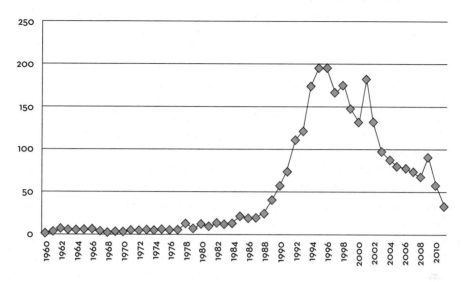

Source: UNCTAD

completed in the three years prior to 2008; only an average of sixty-one per annum were negotiated in the three years after 2008. That indicates a slowdown. A look at the series over the longer term, however, reveals that this slowdown is not surprising. As Figure 9.11 shows, the peak of BIT negotiations took place in the decade after the end of the Cold War. From 1992 to 2001, an annual average of 160 BITs were negotiated. After 2001, however, the number of negotiated BITs declined, following a standard diffusion pattern. Based on that kind of pattern of diffusion, the past three years have seen expected levels of BIT growth.

Why Has the System Worked?

Global economic governance did what was necessary during the Great Recession—but why did the system work? The precrisis observations about sclerotic international institutions and waning

American power did not seem off the mark. How did these actors manage to produce the necessary policy outputs and reforms to stave off systemic collapse? The most commonly provided answer is that the shared sense of crisis spurred the major economies into joint action. The crisis mentality did not lead to sustained cooperation during the Great Depression, however. Significant postwar economic downturns—such as the end of the Bretton Woods regime, the oil shocks of the 1970s, and the failure of the European Exchange Rate Mechanism in the early 1990s—also failed to spur meaningful great power cooperation during the immediate crisis moments. What caused powerful actors to think of the 2008 crisis as a shared one?

A fuller answer will require additional research, but some tentative answers can be proffered here. Power, institutions, and ideas are among the primary building blocks of international relations theory, and each of these factors offers a partial explanation for the performance of global economic governance. Comparing the current situation with the analogous moment during the Great Depression along these three dimensions can help explain why events have unfolded differently this time around. Looking at the distribution of power, for example, the interwar period was truly a moment of great power transition. At the start of the Great Depression, the United Kingdom's lack of financial muscle badly hampered its leadership efforts. Even as it was trying to maintain the gold standard, Great Britain possessed only 4 percent of the world's gold reserves.[57]

In contrast, U.S. power and leadership during the recent crisis turned out to be more robust than expected. This was particularly true in the financial realm. Despite occasional grumblings among the BRICs, the U.S. dollar's hegemony as the world's reserve currency remains unchallenged, giving the United States the financial power that the United Kingdom lacked eight decades ago. Capital surplus countries—such as China—exaggerated the leverage they could obtain from holding large amounts of dollar-denominated reserves.[58] They rapidly discovered that U.S. dollar hegemony bound their interests to the United States on financial issues. While domestic politics might have prevented a more robust U.S. policy response, partisan gridlock did not prevent the United States from pursuing emergency rescue packages (via the 2008 Troubled Assets Relief Program), expansionary fiscal policy (via the 2009 American Recovery and Reinvestment Act), expansionary monetary policy (via interest rate cuts, two rounds of quantitative easing, and Operation Twist), and financial regulatory reform (via the Dodd-Frank Act). These deeds of U.S. leadership helped secure multilateral cooperation on macroeconomic policy coordination for two years, as well as Basel III.

Another way to demonstrate the significance of U.S. leadership is to compare and contrast the finance and trade dimensions. As just noted, U.S. power in the financial realm remained

significant even after the crisis; according to the IMF, in 2010 the United States was responsible for 25 percent of global capital markets. American policy outputs were significant enough to display leadership on these issues. The picture looks very different on trade. U.S. relative power on this issue had faded: U.S. imports as a share of total world imports declined from 18.1 percent of total imports in 2001 to 12.3 percent a decade later. U.S. policy on this issue was inert.[59] The executive branch's trade promotion authority expired, and legislative demands for protectionism spiked. Not surprisingly, the global policy response on trade has been somewhat more muted than on finance.

Despite weaker U.S. power and leadership, the global trade regime has remained resilient—particularly when compared to the 1930s. This highlights another significant factor: the thicker institutional environment. There were very few multilateral economic institutions of relevance during the Great Depression. No multilateral trade regime existed, and international financial structures remained nascent. The last major effort to rewrite the global rules—the 1933 London Monetary and Economic Conference—ended in acrimony.[60] Newly inaugurated president Franklin D. Roosevelt unilaterally took the United States off the gold standard, signaling an end to any attempt at multilateral cooperation.

In contrast, the current institutional environment is much thicker, with status-quo policies focused on promoting greater economic openness. A panoply of preexisting informal and formal regimes was able to supply needed services during a time of global economic crisis. At a minimum, institutions like the G20 functioned as useful focal points for the major economies to coordinate policy responses. International institutions like the Bank of International Settlements further provided crucial expertise to rewrite the global rules of the game. Even if the Doha round petered out, the WTO's dispute settlement mechanism remained in place to coordinate and adjudicate monitoring and enforcement. Furthermore, the status-quo preference for each element of these regimes was to promote greater cross-border exchange within the rule of law. It is easier for international institutions to reinforce existing global economic norms than to devise new ones. Even if these structures were operating on autopilot, they had already been pointed in the right direction.

The final difference between the interwar era and the current day is the state of economic ideas. As the Great Depression worsened during the decade of the 1930s, there was no expert consensus about the best way to resuscitate the economy. Prominent economists like John Maynard Keynes, who had been staunch advocates of free trade a decade earlier, reversed themselves as the depression worsened. There was no agreement on the proper macroeconomic policy response to the downturn, nor was there any agreement about how to fix the broken gold standard.

There has also been a rethinking of causal beliefs after the 2008 financial crisis, but this rethink has been much less severe. Former Federal Reserve chairman Alan Greenspan made headlines when he admitted that his faith in the intellectual edifice of self-correcting markets had collapsed. As previously noted, the IMF has reversed course on the utility of temporary capital controls. Though the Washington consensus might be fraying, it has not been dissolved or replaced by a "Beijing consensus"—indeed, it is far from clear that a Beijing consensus actually exists.[61] Postcrisis surveys of leading economists suggest that a powerful consensus remains on several essential international policy dimensions. For example, the University of Chicago has run an economic experts panel for the past few years. The survey results show a strong consensus on the virtues of freer trade and a rejection of returning to the gold standard to regulate international exchange rates. On the other hand, there is much less consensus on monetary policy and the benefits of further quantitative easing.[62] This absence of agreement reflects a much greater policy debate on the subject, helping to explain why macroeconomic policy coordination has been less robust.

Why the Misperception?

Why is there such a profound gap between perceptions and reality in evaluating the performance of multilateral economic institutions? The simplest explanation is that the core economies—the advanced industrialized democracies—have not rebounded as vigorously as expected. Two trends have marked most postwar global business cycles: economies rebound as vigorously as they drop, and the advanced industrialized states suffer less than the economic periphery. Neither of these trends has held during the Great Recession. As previously noted, the recovery from a financial crisis tends to be longer and slower than standard business-cycle recessions. After the 2008 financial crisis, the recovery has been particularly weak in the advanced industrialized economies. According to the Economist Intelligence Unit, the OECD economies have averaged GDP growth of 0.5 percent between 2008 and 2012. The non-OECD economies have averaged 5.2 percent during the same period. A weak economy feeds perceptions of institutional breakdown. The 2012 Edelman Trust Barometer reflects this phenomenon; contrary to traditional numbers, trust of elite institutions is significantly higher among developing countries than in the developed democracies.[63] Since most analyses of global governance structures have been anchored in the developed world, it is not surprising that this literature suffers from a pessimistic bias.

Pessimism about current economic conditions in the developed world might also be causing analysts to conflate poor domestic and regional governance with poor global governance. The primary causes for domestic economic weakness in the United States, Europe, and Japan are not global in origin—and neither are the best policy responses, Japan's current economic woes are a function of two decades of slack economic growth combined with the aftereffects of the Fukushima disaster. American economic misfortunes have little to do with either the global economy or global economic governance. Indeed, the United States has benefited from the current state of international affairs through lower borrowing costs and higher exports. Domestic political deadlock and uncertainty, on the other hand, have contributed to the anemic U.S. recovery. Already, concerns about the coming fiscal cliff have dampened economic activity.[64] Eroding policy consensus within the Federal Reserve has not helped either. Without more expansionary fiscal and monetary policies, it will take even longer for the necessary private-sector deleveraging to play itself out.

Europe's situation is more complex. To be sure, the Great Recession was the trigger for the eurozone's sovereign debt crisis. The international response to the crisis has been that of a modest supporting role. The IMF has proffered both its technical expertise and financial support in excess of $100 billion to Greece, Portugal, and Ireland. The United States and other major economies have offered to reopen swap lines with the European Central Bank to ensure liquidity. European and national policy responses to the crisis, however, have badly exacerbated the economic situation. Greece's reckless precrisis levels of government spending and borrowing made that economy a ripe target for market pessimism. The initial European bailout package for Greece was woefully inadequate, allowing the crisis to fester. The austerity policies advocated in some quarters have not panned out as expected. The European Central Bank's decision to prematurely raise interest rates in early 2010 helped stall out the nascent recovery on the continent. On the fiscal side of the equation, austerity-related policies have led to a double-dip recession in Great Britain, higher borrowing costs in Spain and Italy, and continued uncertainty about the future of the euro. Europe's fiscal and monetary policies have been less expansionary than in the United States. This, in turn,

has prevented any appreciable private-sector deleveraging in Europe, thereby guaranteeing a longer downturn before any sustained recovery is possible.[65]

The IMF has come under criticism for failing to exert more influence over the eurozone crisis. One official recently resigned, blasting the fund for its European bias and the consensus culture that keeps it from criticizing countries in the middle of lending programs. There are two counterpoints to this argument, however. First, the IMF *has* been critical at various moments during the eurozone crisis. Fund staff issued warnings about the health of the European banks in August 2011, and IMF managing director Lagarde called explicitly for debt sharing among the eurozone in June 2012.[66] The first criticism received significant pushback from the European Central Bank and eurozone governments, and Germany ignored the second criticism. This leads to the second point: it is highly unlikely that national governments would feel compelled to respond to IMF criticism in the absence of a market response. The fund must walk a tightrope between transparent criticism and setting off market panic. This is hardly an ideal vantage point for strong-arming governments with sizable IMF quotas.

A final reason for misperception about global economic governance is exaggerated nostalgia for the past eras of global economic governance. The presumption in much of the commentary on the current global political economy is that both governance structures and hegemonic leadership were better and stronger in the past. Much of this commentary evokes the 1940s, when the creation of the Bretton Woods institutions, backstopped by the United States, ushered in a new era of global governance. The contrast between U.S. leadership then and now seems stark.

This comparison elides some inconvenient facts, however. The late 1940s were indeed the acme of American hegemonic leadership. Even during that peak, however, the United States failed to ratify the Havana Charter that would have created an

International Trade Organization with wider scope than the current WTO. With the Marshall Plan, the United States decided to act outside the purview of Bretton Woods institutions, weakening their influence. After the late forties, American leadership and global financial governance experienced as many misses as hits. The logic of the Bretton Woods system rested on an economic contradiction that became known as the Triffin dilemma. Extravagant macroeconomic policies in the United States, combined with a growing reluctance to accommodate the U.S. position, eroded that global financial order. As the logical contradictions of the Bretton Woods regime became more evident, existing policy coordination mechanisms failed to correct the problem. By 1971, when the United States unilaterally decided to close the gold window, all of the major economies had chosen to ameliorate domestic interests rather than coordinate action at the global level.[67] In ending Bretton Woods, the United States also undercut the IMF's original purpose for existence.

Post-Bretton Woods global economic governance was equally haphazard. An increase in anti-dumping, countervailing duties, and nontariff barriers weakened the rules of the global trading system over the next two decades. Neither the United States nor any global governance structure was able to prevent the Organization of the Petroleum Exporting Countries (OPEC) from raising energy prices from 1973 to 1986.[68] Exchange rates and macroeconomic policy coordination devolved from the IMF to the G7. A predictable cycle emerged: other G7 countries would pressure the United States to scale back its fiscal deficits. In turn, the United States would pressure Japan and West Germany to expand their domestic consumption in order to act as locomotives of growth. Not surprisingly, the most common outcome on the macroeconomic front was a stalemate.[69]

Even perceived successes in macroeconomic policy coordination have had mixed results. The 1985 Plaza Accord helped depreciate the value of the dollar while allowing the yen to rise in value, but it was also the beginning of an unsustainable asset bubble in Japan. In Europe, the creation of the euro would seem to count as an example of successful coordination. The Growth and Stability Pact that was attached to the creation of the common European currency, however, was less successful. Within a year of the euro's birth, five of the eleven member countries were not in compliance; by 2005, the three largest countries in the eurozone were ignoring the pact.[70] Regardless of the distribution of power or the robustness of international institutions, the history of macroeconomic policy coordination is not a distinguished one.[71]

None of this is to deny that global economic governance was useful and stabilizing at various points after 1945. Rather, it is to observe that even during the heyday of American hegemony, the ability of global economic governance to solve ongoing global economic problems was limited.[72] The original point of Kindleberger's analysis of the Great Depression was to discuss what needed to be done during a global economic crisis. By that standard, the post-2008 performance of vital institutions has been far better than extant commentary suggests. Expecting more than an effective crisis response might be unrealistic.

Conclusion

Five years ago, there were rampant fears that waning American power would paralyze global economic regimes. The crisis of the Great Recession exacerbated those fears even further. A review of policy outcomes, policy outputs, and institutional resilience shows a different picture. Global trade and investment levels have recovered from the plunge that occurred in late 2008. A mélange of international coordination mechanisms facilitated the provision of policy outputs from 2008 onward. Existing global governance structures, particularly in finance, have revamped themselves to accommodate shifts in the distribution of power. The World Economic Forum's survey of global experts shows rising confidence in global governance and global cooperation.[73] The evidence suggests that global governance structures adapted and responded to the 2008 financial crisis in a robust fashion. They passed the stress test. The picture presented here is at odds with prevailing conventional wisdom on this subject.

This does not mean that global economic governance will continue to function effectively going forward. It is worth remembering that there were genuine efforts to provide global public goods in 1929 as well, but they eventually fizzled out. The failure of the major economies to assist Austria after the Credit Anstalt bank crashed in 1931 led to a cascade of bank failures across Europe and the United States. The collapse of the 1933 London conference guaranteed an ongoing absence of policy coordination for the next several years.

The start of the Great Depression was bad. International policy coordination failures made it worse. Such a scenario could play out again. There is no shortage of latent or ongoing crises that could lead to a serious breakdown in global economic governance. The IMF's reluctance to take more critical actions to address the eurozone crisis have already prompted one angry resignation letter from an IMF staffer. The summer 2012 drought in the midwestern United States could trigger another spike in food prices. The heated protectionist rhetoric of the 2012 presidential campaign in the United States, or the nationalist rhetoric accompanying China's 2012 leadership transition, could spark a Sino-American trade war. If global economic growth continues to be mediocre, the surprising effectiveness of global economic governance could peter out. Incipient signs of backsliding in the WTO and G20 might mushroom into a true "G-Zero" world.[74]

It is equally possible, however, that a renewed crisis would trigger a renewed surge in policy coordination. As scholar G. John Ikenberry has observed, "the complex interdependence that is unleashed in an open and loosely rule-based order generates some expanding realms of exchange and investment that result in a growing array of firms, interest groups and other sorts of political stakeholders who seek to preserve the stability and openness of the system."[75] The post-2008 economic order has remained open, entrenching these interests even more across the globe. Despite uncertain times, the open economic system that has been in operation since 1945 does not appear to be closing anytime soon.

NOTES

1. Barry Eichengreen and Kevin O'Rourke, "A tale of two depressions," VoxEU.org, March 8, 2010, http://www.voxeu.org/index.php?q=node/3421.
2. Carmen Reinhart and Kenneth Rogoff, *This Time Is Different: Eight Centuries of Financial Folly* (Princeton: Princeton University Press, 2009), p. 226.
3. Charles Roxburgh, Susan Lund, and John Piotrowski, *Mapping global capital markets 2011*, McKinsey Global Institute, August 2011. An Asian Development Bank report also estimates the 2008 decline in asset values to have been twice as large. See Claudio Loser, "Global Financial Turmoil and Emerging Market Economies," Asian Development Bank, March 2009, p. 7.
4. *The Financial and Economic Crisis: A Decent Work Response* (Geneva: International Labour Organization, 2009), p. v.
5. See, for example, the *Financial Times-Economist* Business Barometer, August 2012.
6. See, for example, Richard Samans, Klaus Schwab, and Mark Malloch-Brown, "Running the World, After the Crash," *Foreign Policy* 184 (January/February 2011), pp. 80–83. See also Lee Howell, "The Failure of Governance in a Hyperconnected World," *New York Times*, January 10, 2012.
7. These are by no means the only facts mentioned when talking about the perceived failure of global economic governance. Other examples include the PBOC chairman's March 2009 call for a "super-sovereign currency" to replace the dollar, the failure of the Copenhagen climate change summit in December 2009, and the continuation of the norm whereby a European heads the IMF and an American helms the World Bank. Quite often haplessness at the United Nations is also cited as evidence of the failure of global governance more generally.
8. Elisa Gamberoni and Richard Newfarmer, "Trade Protection: Incipient but Worrisome Trends," World Bank Trade Note No. 37, March 2, 2009.
9. Susan Schwab, "After Doha," *Foreign Affairs*, vol. 90, May/June 2011.
10. Carmen Reinhart and Kenneth Rogoff, "The Aftermath of Financial Crises," in Reinhart and Rogoff, *This Time Is Different: Eight Centuries of Financial Folly* (Princeton: Princeton University Press, 2009); Claessens, Kose, and Terrones, "Financial Cycles: What? How? When?" IMF Working Paper 11/76, April 2011;

Carmen Reinhart and Vincent Reinhart, "After the Fall," NBER Working Paper No. 16334, September 2010; Barry Eichengreen, "Crisis and Growth in the Advanced Economies: What We Know, What We Don't Know, and What We Can Learn from the 1930s," *Comparative Economic Studies* 53 (March 2011), pp. 383–406.

11. Eichengreen and O'Rourke, "A tale of two depressions"; Eichengreen and O'Rourke, "A tale of two depressions redux," VoxEU.org, March 6, 2012, http://www.voxeu.org/article/tale-two-depressions-redux.

12. *World Development Indicators*, World Bank, July 9, 2012.

13. Ibid. See also Shaochua Chen and Martin Rayallion, "An update to the World Bank's Estimate of consumption poverty in the developing world," March 1, 2012; Annie Lowrey, "Dire Poverty Falls Despite Global Slump, Report Finds," *New York Times*, March 6, 2012.

14. Data in this paragraph comes from Eichengreen and O'Rourke, "A tale of two depressions redux."

15. Dinah Walker, "Quarterly Update: The Economic Recovery in Historical Context," Council on Foreign Relations, August 13, 2012.

16. For FDI data, see the OECD/UNCTAD report "Seventh report on G20 investment measures," July 2012. For foreign investment assets, sec Roxburgh, Lund, and Piotrowski, *Mapping Global Capital Markets 2011*, p. 31. For remittance flows, see Dilip Ratha and Ani Silwal, "Remittances flows in 2011: An Update," *Migration and Development Brief* 18, World Bank, April 23, 2012.

17. See data gathered by the Pew Global Attitudes Project, Pew Research Center, 2012, http://www.pewglobal.org/database/?indicator=16&survey=13 &response=Good&20thing&mode=table.

18. On the latter, see data gathered by the Pew Global Attitudes Project, Pew Research Center, 2012, http://www.pewglobal.org/database/?indicator=18 &survey=12&response=Agree&mode=table.

19. See, for example, Paul Rogers, "The Tipping Point?" Oxford Research Group, November 2008; Joshua Kurlantzick, "The World is Bumpy," *New Republic*, July 15, 2009; Rogers Brubaker, "Economic Crisis, Nationalism, and Politicized Ethnicity," in Craig Calhoun and Georgi Derlugian, eds., *The Deepening Crisis: Governance Challenges After Neoliberalism* (New York: New York University Press, 2011), p. 93.

20. Institute for Economics and Peace, *Global Peace Index 2012*, June 2012, p. 37.

21. See, for example, the Human Security Report Project, *Human Security Report* 2009/2010: *The Causes of Peace and the Shrinking Costs of War* (New York: Oxford University Press, 2010).

22. David Levy, "The Contained Depression," Jerome Levy Forecasting Center, April 2012.

23. Paul Krugman, *End This Depression Now!* (New York: W. W. Norton, 2012); Joseph Stiglitz, *The Price of Inequality* (New York: W. W. Norton, 2012).

24. Kindleberger, *The World In Depression*, 292.

25. "The Return of Economic Nationalism," *Economist*, February 5, 2009; Kurlantzick, "The World is Bumpy"; Michael Sesit, "Smoot-Hawley's Ghost Appears as Economy Tanks," *Bloomberg News*, February 19, 2009; Rawi Abdelal and Adam Segal, "Yes, Globalization Passed Its Peak," ForeignAffairs.com, March 17, 2009.

26. Uri Dadush, Shimelse Ali, and Rachel Esplin Odell, "Is Protectionism Dying?" Carnegie Papers in International Economics, May

2011. Furthermore, while these measures are undeniably restrictive in nature, a case can be made that they represent a form of "efficient protectionism": small and symbolic measures that mollify protectionist constituencies in exchange for preserving and strengthening the overall level of economic openness. See C. Fred Bergsten, "A Renaissance for U.S. Trade Policy?" *Foreign Affairs*, vol. 81, November/December 2002.

27. See Simon Evenett, "Débâcle," VoxEU.org, June 14, 2012. As a counter, however, see also Chad Bown, "Import Protection Update," VoxEU.org. August 18, 2012.

28. Dadush, Ali, and Odell, "Is Protectionism Dying?"; Matthieu Bussiere, Emilia Perez-Barreiro, Roland Straub, and Daria Taglioni, "Protectionist Responses to the Crisis: Global Trends and Implications," *World Economy*, vol. 34, May 2011.

29. Between May 2011 and August 2012, a maximum of 13 percent of business executives cited trade protectionism as a serious concern. See the *Financial Times-Economist* Business Barometer, http://www.ft.com/intl/cms/s/0/2648032c-c78d-11e1-8686-00144feab49a.html#axzz23kj5DEaP.

30. Bank of International Settlements, *82nd Annual Report*, June 24, 2012, p. 39.

31. Ibid., p. 41.

32. "IMF Creates Short-Term Liquidity Facility for Market-Access Countries," IMF Press Release No. 08/262, October 29, 2008.

33. Eswar Prasad and Isaac Sorkin, "Assessing the G-20 Stimulus Plans: A Deeper Look," Brookings Institution, March 2009.

34. Adrian Blundell-Wignall and Paul Atkinson, "Thinking Beyond Basel III: Necessary Solutions for Capital and Liquidity," *OECD Journal: Financial Market Trends*, vol. 1, 2010; Nicolas Verou, "Financial Reform after the Crisis: An Early Assessment," Peterson Institute for International Economics Working Paper 12–2, January 2012.

35. It should be noted that some scholars have questioned whether the FSB has the capability and flexibility to impose more rigorous standards on the global financial system. See Stephany Griffith-Jones, Eric Helleiner, and Ngaire Woods, eds., *The Financial Stability Board: An Effective Fourth Pillar of Global Economic Governance?* (Waterloo: Centre for International Governance Innovation, June 2010).

36. Bob Davis, "Foreign Funds Agree to Set of Guiding Principles," *Wall Street Journal*, September 3, 2008.

37. *Minding the GAPP: Sovereign wealth, transparency and the "Santiago Principles,"* Deloitte Touche Tohmatsu, October 2008; Edward Truman, "Making the World Safe for Sovereign Wealth Funds," *Real Time Economic Issues Watch*, October 14, 2008; Cohen and DeLong, *The End of Influence*, p. 89.

38. OECD/UNCTAD, "Seventh Report on G20 investment measures."

39. "G20 to become main economic forum," al-Jazeera, September 28, 2009, http://www.aljazeera.com/news/americas/2009/09/20099252124936203.html.

40. Mark Sobel and Louellen Stedman, "The Evolution of the G-7 and Economic Policy Coordination," U.S. Treasury Department Occasional Paper No. 3, July 2006; Drezner, "The New New World Order," *Foreign Affairs*, vol. 86, March/April 2007.

41. The G20 also has no treaty status or permanent secretariat, but there are theoretical arguments in favor of this informal status. See, for

example, Charles Lipson, "Why are some international agreements informal?" *International Organization*, vol. 45, September 1991.

42. Geoffrey Garrett, "G2 in G20: China, the United States, and the World after the Global Financial Crisis," *Global Policy*, vol. 1, January 2010, p. 29.

43. Daniel W. Drezner, *All Politics is Global: Explaining International Regulatory Regimes* (Princeton: Princeton University Press, 2007).

44. *2011 Cannes G20 Summit Final Compliance Report*, G20 Information Centre, p. 12.

45. George Downs, David Rocke, and Peter Barsoom, "Is the Good News About Compliance Good News About Cooperation?" *International Organization*, vol. 50, June 1996.

46. "Geithner Statement on Delay of Report on China Currency Policies," Real Time Economics, *Wall Street Journal*, April 3, 2010, http://blogs.wsj.com/economics/2010/04/03/geithner-statement-on-delay-of-report-on-china-currency-policies/.

47. David Leonhardt, "As U.S. Currency Rises, U.S. Keeps Up the Pressure," *New York Times*, February 15, 2012. It should be noted, however, that the yuan has depreciated against the dollar for much of 2012.

48. Daniel W. Drezner, "Club Standards and International Finance," in Daniel W. Drezner, *All Politics Is Global.*

49. For more on IMF quota reform, see "IMF Quotas," International Monetary Fund, August 24, 2012.

50. "World Bank Group Reform: An Update," World Bank Group Development Committee, September 30, 2010.

51. Jonathan D. Ostry, Atish R. Ghosh, Karl Habermeier, Marcos Chamon, Mahvash S. Qureshi, and Dennis B.S. Reinhardt, "Capital Inflows: The Role of Controls," IMF Staff Position Note SPN/10/04, International Monetary Fund, February 19, 2010.

52. Alan Beattie, "Decommission the weapons of trade warfare," *Financial Times*, August 8, 2012.

53. "Regional Trade Agreements Information System," World Trade Organization, August 27, 2012, http://rtais.wto.org/UI/Public PreDefRepByEIF.aspx.

54. David Lazer, "The Free Trade Epidemic of the 1860s and Other Outbreaks of Economic Discrimination," *World Politics*, vol. 51, July 1999.

55. See Daniel W. Drezner, *U.S. Trade Strategy: Free Versus Fair?* (New York: Council on Foreign Relations Press, 2006), pp. 71–92, for more on this dynamic.

56. Dadush et al., "Is Protectionism Dying?" pp. 8–9.

57. Jeffry Frieden, "The established order collapses," in Jeffry Frieden, *Global Capitalism: Its Fall and Rise in the Twentieth Century* (New York: W. W. Norton, 2006); Liquat Ahamed, *Lords of Finance: The Bankers Who Broke The World* (New York Penguin, 2009).

58. The arguments in this paragraph draw from Daniel W. Drezner, "Bad Debts: Assessing China's Financial Influence in Great Power Politics," *International Security*, vol. 34, Fall 2009; and Daniel W. Drezner, "Will Currency Follow the Flag?" *International Relations of the Asia-Pacific*, vol. 10, September 2010.

59. Data from WTO: http://stat.wto.org/StatisticalProgram/WSDBStat ProgramHome.aspx, accessed August 2012.

60. Herbert Feis, *1933: Characters in Crisis* (Boston: Little Brown and Company, 1966).

61. Matt Ferchen, "Whose China Model is it Anyway? The contentious search for consensus," *Review of International Political Economy*, forthcoming.

62. On the gold standard and free trade, see "Gold Standard," IGM Forum, University of Chicago Booth School of Business, January 12, 2012; and "Free Trade," IGM Forum, University of Chicago Booth School of Business, March 13, 2012. On monetary policy, see "Monetary Policy," IGM Forum, University of Chicago Booth School of Business, September 29, 2011. For further evidence of the absence of consensus on monetary policy, compare Martin Wolf, "We still have that sinking feeling," *Financial Times*, July 10, 2012, with Mohamed El-Erian, "Central Bankers Can't Save the World," *Bloomberg View*, August 2, 2012. See also Joe Weisenthal, "The Biggest Tragedy in Economics," *Business Insider*, September 7, 2012.

63. Data from the Edelman Trust Barometer can be accessed at http://trust.edelman.com/trust-download/global-results/.

64. Nelson D. Schwartz, "Fearing an Impasse in Congress, Industry Cuts Spending," *New York Times*, August 5, 2012.

65. Reinhart and Rogoff, *This Time Is Different*; Charles Roxburgh, Susan Lund, Toos Daruvala, James Manyika, Richard Dobbs, Ramon Forn, and Karen Croxson, *Debt and Deleveraging: Uneven Progress on the Path to Growth*, McKinsey Global Institute, January 2012.

66. Alan Beattie and Chris Giles, "IMF and curozone clash over estimates," *Financial Times*, August 31, 2011; James Kanter, "IMF Urges Europe's Strongest to Shoulder Burdens of Currency Bloc," *New York Times*, June 21, 2012.

67. Joanne Gowa, *Closing the Gold Window: Domestic Politics and the End of Bretton Woods* (Ithaca: Cornell University Press, 1984).

68. Robert Keohane, "Theory of Hegemonic Stability and Changes in International Economic Regimes, 1967–1977," in Ole Holsti, Randolph Siverson, and Alexander George, eds., *Change in the International System* (Boulder: Westview Press, 1980), pp. 131–62.

69. Robert Putnam and Nicholas Bayne, *Hanging Together: Cooperation and Conflict in the Seven-Power Summits* (Cambridge: Harvard University Press, 1987); David M. Andrews, ed., *International Monetary Power* (Ithaca: Cornell University Press, 2005).

70. Kathryn Dominguez, "The European Central Bank, the Euro, and Global Financial Markets," *Journal of Economic Perspectives*, vol. 20, Fall 2006.

71. Thomas Willett, "Developments in the Political Economy of Policy Coordination," *Open Economies Review*, vol. 10, May 1999.

72. This parallels the recent argument by Robert Kagan that people exaggerate the effectiveness of American hegemony in the past as well. Robert Kagan, *The World America Made* (New York: Knopf, 2012).

73. "Global Confidence Index," World Economic Forum, August 22, 2012, http://www.weforum.org/content/pages/global-confidence-index.

74. Ian Bremmer and Nouriel Roubini, "A G-Zero World," *Foreign Affairs*, vol. 90, March/April 2011; Ian Bremmer, *Every Nation for Itself* (New York: Portfolio/Penguin, 2012).

75. G. John Ikenberry, *Liberal Leviathan* (Princeton: Princeton University Press, 2011), p. 340.

10 HUMAN RIGHTS

For generations, the idea of human rights has been contested. Which rights should be included? Which are excluded? How are rights determined in a culturally diverse world? Amartya Sen develops the argument that human rights need to be viewed as entitlements to capability—the opportunity to have freedom. Eschewing the idea of a fixed listing of capabilities, Sen suggests a process of public reasoning to arrive at an understanding of capability.

Jack Donnelly, in a chapter from *Universal Human Rights in Theory and Practice* (2003), probes whether there can be universal human rights. At the level of concepts, he sees an extensive consensus on a limited set of obligations defined in the Universal Declaration of Human Rights. But, he suggests, the ways these rights are implemented may vary, thus offering logical explanations for the persistence of arguments that rights should vary by culture. In contrast, Makau Mutua, the Harvard-educated former dean of the State University of New York Law School, pulls no punches in arguing that the international human rights regime is an export of Western culture that exploits a harmful metaphor of "Savages, Victims, and Saviors." He seeks to recast human rights thinking along more multicultural lines.

Beth A. Simmons's *Mobilizing for Human Rights* is a meticulous study of whether signing human rights treaties does any good, or whether it is just cheap talk in an effort to distract attention from misbehavior. Mixing statistical evidence with case studies of allegations of Israeli torture of Palestinian detainees and of abuses under a Chilean military dictatorship, this excerpt from Simmons's magisterial book shows that treaties do indeed promote rights compliance, but mainly in partially democratic countries with somewhat independent courts and active civil society organizations. This finding is noteworthy, and so is the impeccable research design that she uses to derive the finding.

Much human rights activism in wealthy countries focuses on civil and political rights. Responding to criticism that Human Rights Watch has neglected economic and social rights, that organization's executive director, Kenneth Roth, lays out criteria for deciding when to treat economic and social demands as rights questions, and when not to.

Amartya Sen

HUMAN RIGHTS AND CAPABILITIES

Introduction

The moral appeal of human rights has been used for varying purposes, from resisting torture and arbitrary incarceration to demanding the end of hunger and of medical neglect. There is hardly any country in the world—from China, South Africa and Egypt to Mexico, Britain and the United States—in which arguments involving human rights have not been raised in one context or another in contemporary political debates.

However, despite the tremendous appeal of the idea of human rights, it is also seen by many as being intellectually frail—lacking in foundation and perhaps even in coherence and cogency. The remarkable co-existence of stirring appeal and deep conceptual scepticism is not new. The American Declaration of Independence took it to be 'self-evident' that everyone is "endowed by their Creator with certain inalienable rights," and 13 years later, in 1789, the French declaration of 'the rights of man' asserted that "men are born and remain free and equal in rights." But it did not take Jeremy Bentham long to insist, in *Anarchical Fallacies*, written during 1791–1792, that "natural rights is simple nonsense: natural and imprescriptible rights [an American phrase], rhetorical nonsense, nonsense upon stilts" (Bentham, 1792/1843, p. 501). That division remains very alive today, and there are many who see the idea of human rights as no more than "bawling upon paper" (to use another of Bentham's barbed descriptions).

From *Journal of Human Development* 6, no. 2 (July 2005), 151–66.

The concepts of human rights and human capabilities have something of a common motivation, but they differ in many distinct ways. It is useful to ask whether considering the two concepts together—capabilities and human rights—can help the understanding of each. I will divide the exercise into four specific questions. First, can human rights be seen as entitlements to certain basic capabilities, and will this be a good way of thinking about human rights? Second, can the capability perspective provide a comprehensive coverage of the content of human rights? Third, since human rights need specificity, does the use of the capability perspective for elucidating human rights require a full articulation of the list of capabilities? And finally, how can we go about ascertaining the content of human rights and of basic capabilities when our values are supposed to be quite divergent, especially across borders of nationality and community? Can we have anything like a universalist approach to these ideas, in a world where cultures differ and practical preoccupations are also diverse?

Human Rights as Entitlements to Capabilities

It is possible to argue that human rights are best seen as rights to certain specific freedoms, and that the correlate obligation to consider the associated duties must also be centred around what others can do to safeguard and expand these freedoms. Since capabilities can be seen, broadly, as freedoms of particular kinds, this would seem to establish a basic connection between the two categories of ideas.

We run, however, into an immediate difficulty here. I have argued elsewhere that 'opportunity' and 'process' are two aspects of freedom that require distinction, with the importance of each deserving specific acknowledgment.[1] While the opportunity aspect of freedoms would seem to belong to the same kind of territory as capabilities, it is not at all clear that the same can be said about the process aspect of freedom.

An example can bring out the *separate* (although not necessarily independent) relevance of both *substantive opportunities* and *freedom of processes*. Consider a woman, let us call her Natasha, who decides that she would like to go out in the evening. To take care of some considerations that are not central to the issues involved here (but which could make the discussion more complex), it is assumed that there are no particular safety risks involved in her going out, and that she has critically reflected on this decision and judged that going out would be the sensible—indeed the ideal—thing to do.

Now consider the threat of a violation of this freedom if some authoritarian guardians of society decide that she must not go out ('it is most unseemly'), and if they force her, in one way or another, to stay indoors. To see that there are two distinct issues involved in this one violation, consider an alternative case in which the authoritarian bosses decide that she must—absolutely *must*—go out ('you are expelled for the evening—just obey'). There is clearly a violation of freedom even here though Natasha is being forced to do exactly what she would have chosen to do anyway, and this is readily seen when we compare the two alternatives 'choosing freely to go out' and 'being forced to go out'. The latter involves an immediate violation of the *process aspect* of Natasha's freedom, since an action is being forced on her (even though it is an action she would have freely chosen also).

The opportunity aspect may also be affected, since a plausible accounting of opportunities can include having options and it can *inter alia* include valuing free choice. However, the violation of the opportunity aspect would be more substantial and manifest if she were not only forced to do something chosen by another, but in fact forced to do something she would not otherwise choose to do. The comparison between 'being forced to go out' (when she would have gone out anyway, if free) and, say, 'being forced to polish the shoes of others at home' (not her favorite way of spending time, I should explain) brings out this contrast, which is primarily one of the opportunity aspect, rather than the process aspect. In the incarceration of Natasha, we can see two different ways in which she is losing her freedom: first, she is being forced to do something, with no freedom of choice (a violation of her process freedom); and second, what Natasha is being obliged to do is not something she would choose to do, if she had any plausible alternative (a violation of her substantive opportunity to do what she would like to do).[2]

It is important to recognize that both processes and opportunities can figure powerfully in the content of human rights. A denial of 'due process' in being, say, sentenced without a proper trial can be an infringement of human rights (no matter what the outcome of the fair trial might be), and so can be the denial of opportunity of medical treatment, or the opportunity of living without the danger of being assaulted (going beyond the exact process through which these opportunities are made real).

The idea of 'capability' (i.e., the opportunity to achieve valuable combinations of human functionings—what a person is able to do or be) can be very helpful in understanding the opportunity aspect of freedom and human rights.[3] Indeed, even though the concept of opportunity is often invoked, it does require considerable elaboration, and capability can help in this elucidation. For example, seeing opportunity in terms of capability allows us to distinguish appropriately between (i) whether a person is actually able to do things she would value *doing*, and (ii) whether she possesses the *means or instruments or permissions* to pursue what she would like to do (her actual ability to do that pursuing may depend on many contingent circumstances). By shifting attention, in particular, toward the former, the capability-based approach resists an overconcentration on means (such as incomes and primary goods) that can be found in some theories of justice (e.g. in the Rawlsian Difference Principle). The capability approach can help to identify the possibility that two persons can have very different substantial opportunities even when they have exactly the same set of means: for example, a disabled person can do far less than an able-bodied person can, with exactly the same income and other 'primary goods.' The disabled person cannot, thus, be judged to be equally advantaged—with the same opportunities—as the person without any physical handicap but with the same set of means or instruments (such as income and wealth and other primary goods and resources).

The capability perspective allows us to take into account the parametric variability in the relation between the means, on the one hand, and the actual opportunities, on the other.[4] Differences in the capability to function can arise even with the same set of personal means (such as primary goods) for a variety of reasons, such as: (1) *physical or mental heterogeneities among persons* (related, for example, to disability, or proneness to illness); (2) *variations in non-personal resources* (such as the nature of public health care, or societal cohesion and the helpfulness of the community); (3) *environmental diversities* (such as climatic conditions, or varying threats from epidemic diseases or from local crime); or (4) *different relative positions vis-à-vis others* (well illustrated by Adam Smith's discussion, in the *Wealth of Nations*, of the fact that the clothing and other resources one needs "to appear in public without shame" depends on what other people standardly wear, which in turn could be more expensive in rich societies than in poorer ones).

I should, however, note here that there has been some serious criticism of describing these substantive opportunities (such as the capability to live one kind of a life or another) as 'freedoms,' and it has been argued that this makes the idea of freedom too inclusive. For example, in her illuminating and sympathetic critique of my *Development as Freedom*, Susan Okin has presented arguments to suggest that I tend "to overextend the concept of freedom."[5] She has argued: "It is hard to conceive of some human functionings, or the fulfilment of some needs and wants, such as good health and nourishment, as freedoms without stretching the term until it seems to refer to everything that is of central value to human beings" (Okin, 2003, p. 292).

There is, certainly, considerable scope for argument on how extensively the term freedom should be used. But the particular example considered in Okin's counter-argument reflects a misinterpretation. There is no suggestion whatever that a functioning (e.g. being in good health or being well nourished) should be seen as freedom of any kind, such as capability. Rather, capability concentrates on the *opportunity* to be able to have combinations of functionings (including, in this case, the opportunity to be well-nourished), and the person is free to make use of this opportunity or not. A capability reflects the alternative combinations of functionings from which the person can choose one combination. It is, therefore, not being suggested at all that being well-nourished is to be seen as a freedom. The term freedom, in the form of capability, is used here to refer to the extent to which the person is free to choose particular levels of functionings (such as being well-nourished), and that is not the same thing as what the person actually decides to choose. During India's struggle for independence from the Raj, Mahatma Gandhi famously did not use that opportunity to be well fed when he chose to fast, as a protest against the policies of the Raj. In terms of the actual functioning of being well-nourished, the fasting Gandhi did not differ from a starving famine victim, but the freedoms and opportunities they respectively had were quite different.

Indeed, the *freedom to have* any particular thing can be substantially distinguished from actually *having* that thing. What a person is free to have—not just what he actually has—is relevant, I have argued, to a theory of justice.[6] A theory of rights also has reason to be involved with substantive freedoms.

Many of the terrible deprivations in the world have arisen from a lack of freedom to escape destitution. Even though indolence and inactivity had been classic themes in the old literature on poverty, people have starved and suffered because of a lack of alternative possibilities. It is the connection of poverty with unfreedom that led Marx to argue passionately for the need to replace "the domination of circumstances and chance over individuals by the domination of individuals over chance and circumstances."[7]

The importance of freedom can be brought out also by considering other types of issues that are also central to human rights. Consider the freedom of immigrants to retain their ancestral cultural customs and lifestyles. This complex subject cannot be adequately assessed without distinguishing between *doing* something and being free to do that thing. A strong argument can be constructed in favor of an immigrant's having the freedom to retain her ancestral lifestyle, but this must not be seen as an argument in favor of her pursuing that ancestral lifestyle whether she herself chooses that pursuit or not. The central issue, in this argument, is the person's freedom to choose how she should live—including the *opportunity* to pursue ancestral customs—and it cannot be turned into an argument for that person specifically pursuing those customs in particular, irrespective of the alternatives she has.[8] The importance of capability—reflecting opportunities—is central to this distinction.

The Process Aspect of Freedom and Information Pluralism

In the discussion so far I have been concentrating on what the capability perspective can do for a theory of justice or of human rights, but I would now like to turn to what it *cannot* do. While the idea of capability has considerable merit in the assessment of the opportunity aspect of freedom, it cannot possibly deal adequately with the process aspect of freedom, since capabilities are characteristics of individual advantages, and they fall short of telling us enough about the fairness or equity of the processes involved, or about the freedom of citizens to invoke and utilise procedures that are equitable.

The contrast of perspectives can be brought out with many different types of illustrations; let me choose a rather harsh example. It is, by now, fairly well established that, given symmetric care, women tend to live longer than men. If one were concerned only with capabilities (and nothing else), and in particular with equality of the capability to live long, it would have been possible to construct an argument for giving men more medical attention than women to counteract the natural masculine handicap. But giving women less medical attention than men for the same health problems would clearly violate an important requirement of process equity, and it seems reasonable to argue, in cases of this kind, that demands of equity in process freedom could sensibly override a single-minded concentration on the opportunity aspect of freedom (and on the requirements of capability equality in particular). While it is important to emphasise the relevance of the capability perspective in judging people's substantive opportunities (particularly in comparison with alternative approaches that focus on incomes, or primary goods, or resources), that point does not, in any way, go against seeing the relevance also of the process aspect of freedom in a theory of human rights—or, for that matter, in a theory of justice.

In this context, I should comment briefly also on a misinterpretation of the general relevance of the capability perspective in a theory of justice. A theory of justice—or more generally an adequate theory of normative social choice—has to be alive both to the fairness of the processes involved and to the equity and efficiency of the substantive opportunities that people can enjoy.[9] In dealing with the latter, capability can indeed provide a very helpful perspective, in comparison with, say, the Rawlsian concentration on 'primary goods.' But capability can hardly serve as the sole informational basis for the *other* considerations, related to processes, that must also be accommodated in normative social choice theory.

Consider the different components of Rawls's (1971) theory of justice. Rawls's 'first principle' of justice involves the priority of liberty, and the first part of the 'second principle' involves process fairness, through demanding that 'positions and offices be open to all.' The force and cogency of these Rawlsian concerns (underlying his first principle and the first part of the second principle) can neither be ignored nor be adequately addressed through relying only on the informational base of capabilities. We may not agree with Rawls's own way of dealing with these issues, but these issues have to be addressed, and they cannot be sensibly addressed within the substantive boundaries of capability accounting.

On the other hand, the capability perspective comes into its own in dealing with the *remainder* of the second principle; namely, 'the Difference Principle'—a principle that is particularly concerned with the distribution of advantages that different people enjoy (a consideration that Rawls tried to capture, I believe inadequately, within the confines of the accounting of 'primary goods'). The territory that Rawls reserved for primary goods, as used in his Difference Principle, would

indeed, I argue, be better served by the capability perspective. That does not, however, obliterate in any way the relevance of the rest of the territory of justice (related to the first principle and the first part of the second principle), in which process considerations, including liberty and procedural equity, figure.

A similar plurality of informational base has to be invoked in dealing with the multiplicity of considerations that underlie a theory of human rights. Capabilities and the opportunity aspect of freedom, important as they are, have to be supplemented by considerations of fair processes and the lack of violation of people's right to invoke and utilize them.

Listing Capabilities

I turn now to the controversial question of the listing of capabilities. In its application, the capability approach allows considerable variations in application. Martha Nussbaum has discussed powerfully the advantages of identifying an overarching 'list of capabilities,' with given priorities. My own reluctance to join the search for such a canonical list arises partly from my difficulty in seeing how the exact lists and weights would be chosen without appropriate specification of the context of their use (which could vary), but also from a disinclination to accept any substantive diminution of the domain of public reasoning. The framework of capabilities helps, in my judgement, to clarify and illuminate the subject matter of public reasoning, which can involve epistemic issues (including claims of objective importance) as well as ethical and political ones. It cannot, I would argue, sensibly aim at displacing the need for continued public reasoning.

Indeed, I would submit that one of the uses of the capability perspective is to bring out the need for transparent valuational scrutiny of individual advantages and adversities, since the different *functionings* have to be assessed and weighted in relation to each other, and the opportunities of having different *combinations* of functionings also have to be evaluated.[10] The richness of the capability perspective broadly interpreted, thus, includes its insistence on the need for open valuational scrutiny for making social judgments, and in this sense it fits in well with the importance of public reasoning. This openness of transparent valuation contrasts with burying the evaluative exercise in some mechanical—and valuationally opaque—convention (e.g. by taking market-evaluated income to be the invariable standard of individual advantage, thereby giving implicit normative priority to institutionally determined market prices).

The problem is not with listing important capabilities, but with insisting on one predetermined canonical list of capabilities, chosen by theorists without any general social discussion or public reasoning. To have such a fixed list, emanating entirely from pure theory, is to deny the possibility of fruitful public participation on what should be included and why.

I have, of course, discussed various lists of capabilities that would seem to demand attention in theories of justice and more generally in social assessment, such as the freedom to be well nourished, to live disease-free lives, to be able to move around, to be educated, to participate in public life, and so on. Indeed, right from my first writings on using the capability perspective (for example, the 1979 Tanner Lecture 'Equality of what?'; Sen, 1980), I have tried to discuss the relevance of specific capabilities that are important in a particular exercise. The 1979 Tanner Lecture went into the relevance of "the ability to move about" (I discussed why disabilities can be a central concern in a way that an income-centered approach may not be able to grasp), along with other basic capabilities, such as "the ability to meet one's nutritional requirements, the wherewithal to be clothed and sheltered, the power to participate in the social life of the community." The contrast between lists of capabilities and commodities was a central concern

in *Commodities and Capabilities* (Sen, 1985a). The relevance of many capabilities that are often neglected were discussed in my second set of Tanner Lectures, given at Cambridge University under the title *The Standard of Living* (Hawthorn, 1987).

My skepticism is about fixing a cemented list of capabilities that is seen as being absolutely complete (nothing could be added to it) and totally fixed (it could not respond to public reasoning and to the formation of social values). I am a great believer in theory, and certainly accept that a good theory of evaluation and assessment has to bring out the relevance of what we are free to do and free to be (the capabilities in general), as opposed to the material goods we have and the commodities we can command. But I must also argue that pure theory cannot 'freeze' a list of capabilities for all societies for all time to come, irrespective of what the citizens come to understand and value. That would be not only a denial of the reach of democracy, but also a misunderstanding of what pure theory can do, completely divorced from the particular social reality that any particular society faces.

Along with the exercise of listing the relevant capabilities, there is also the problem of determining the relative weights and importance of the different capabilities included in the relevant list. Even with a given list, the question of valuation cannot be avoided. There is sometimes a temptation not only to have one fixed list, but also to have the elements of the list ordered in a lexicographic way. But this can hardly work. For example, the ability to be well-nourished cannot in general be put invariably *above* or *below* the ability to be well-sheltered (with the implication that the tiniest improvement of the higher ranked capability will always count as more important than a large change in the lower ranked one). The judgment must take into account the extent to which the different abilities are being realized or violated. Also, the weighting must be contingent on circumstances. We may have to give priority to the ability to be well-nourished when people are dying of hunger in their homes, whereas the freedom to be sheltered may rightly receive more weight when people are in general well-fed, but lack shelter and protection from the elements.

Some of the basic capabilities (with which my 1979 Tanner Lecture was particularly concerned) will no doubt figure in every list of relevant capabilities in every society. But the exact list to be used will have to take note of the purpose of the exercise. There is often good sense in narrowing the coverage of capabilities for a specific purpose. Jean Drèze and I have tried to invoke such lists of elementary capabilities in dealing with 'hunger and public action,' and in a different context, in dealing with India's economic and social achievements and failures (Drèze and Sen, 1989, 2002). I see Martha Nussbaum's powerful use of a given list of capabilities for some minimal rights against deprivation as being extremely useful, in the same practical way. For another practical purpose, we may need quite a different list.

For example, when my friend Mahbub ul Haq asked me, in 1989, to work with him on indicators of human development, and in particular to help develop a general index for global assessment and critique, it was clear to me that we were involved in a particular exercise of specific relevance. So the 'Human Development Index' was based on a very minimal listing of capabilities, with a particular focus on getting at a minimally basic quality of life, calculable from available statistics, in a way that the Gross National Product or Gross Domestic Product failed to capture (United Nations Development Programme, 1990). Lists of capabilities have to be used for various purposes, and so long as we understand what we are doing (and, in particular, that we are getting a list for a particular reason, related to assessment, evaluation, or critique), we do not put ourselves against other lists that may be relevant or useful for other purposes.

All this has to be contrasted with insisting on one 'final list of capabilities that matter.' To decide that some capability will not figure in the list of relevant capabilities at all amounts to putting a zero weight on that capability for every exercise, no matter what the exercise is concerned with, and no matter what the social conditions are. This could be very dogmatic, for many distinct reasons.

First, we use capabilities for different purposes. What we focus on cannot be independent of what we are doing and why (e.g. whether we are evaluating poverty, specifying certain basic human rights, getting a rough and ready measure of human development, and so on).

Second, social conditions and the priorities that they suggest may vary. For example, given the nature of poverty in India as well as the nature of available technology, it was not unreasonable in 1947 (when India became independent) to concentrate on elementary education, basic health, and so on, and to not worry too much about whether everyone can effectively communicate across the country and beyond. However, with the development of the internet and its wide-ranging applications, and the advance made in information technology (not least in India), access to the web and the freedom of general communication has become a very important capability that is of interest and relevance to all Indians.

Third, even with given social conditions, public discussion and reasoning can lead to a better understanding of the role, reach, and the significance of particular capabilities. For example, one of the many contributions of feminist economics has precisely been to bring out the importance of certain freedoms that were not recognized very clearly—or at all—earlier on; for example, freedom from the imposition of fixed and time-honored family roles, or immunity from implicit derogation through the rhetoric of social communication.

To insist on a 'fixed forever' list of capabilities would deny the possibility of progress in social understanding, and also go against the productive role of public discussion, social agitation, and open debates. I have nothing against the listing of capabilities (and take part in that activity often enough), but I have to stand up against any proposal of a grand mausoleum to one fixed and final list of capabilities.

Public Reasoning, Cultural Diversity, and Universality

I turn now to the final question. If the listing of capabilities must be subject to the test of public reasoning, how can we proceed in a world of differing values and disparate cultures? How can we judge the acceptability of claims to human rights and to relevant capabilities, and assess the challenges they may face? How would such a disputation—or a defence—proceed? I would argue that, like the assessment of other ethical claims, there must be some test of open and informed scrutiny, and it is to such a scrutiny that we have to look in order to proceed to a disavowal or an affirmation. The status that these ethical claims have must be ultimately dependent on their survivability in unobstructed discussion. In this sense, the viability of human rights is linked with what John Rawls has called 'public reasoning' and its role in 'ethical objectivity.'[11]

Indeed, the role of public reasoning in the formulation and vindication of human rights is extremely important to understand. Any general plausibility that these ethical claims—or their denials—have is, on this theory, dependent on their ability to survive and flourish when they encounter unobstructed discussion and scrutiny (along with adequately wide informational availability). The force of a claim for a human right would be seriously undermined if it were possible to show that they are unlikely to survive open public scrutiny. But contrary to a commonly offered reason for skepticism and rejection, the case for human rights cannot be discarded simply by pointing to the possibility that in politically and socially repressive regimes, which do not allow open public discussion, many of these human rights are not taken seriously at all.

Open critical scrutiny is essential for dismissal as well as for defence. The fact that monitoring of violations of human rights and the procedure of 'naming and shaming' can be so effective (at least, in putting the violators on the defensive) is some indication of the wide reach of public reasoning when information becomes available and ethical arguments are allowed rather than suppressed.

It is, however, important not to keep the domain of public reasoning confined to a given society only, especially in the case of human rights, in view of the inescapably universalist nature of these rights. This is in contrast with Rawls's inclination, particularly in his later works, to limit such public confrontation within the boundaries of each particular nation (or each 'people,' as Rawls calls this regional collectivity), for determining what would be just, at least in domestic affairs.[12] We can demand, on the contrary, that the discussion has to include, even for domestic justice (if only to avoid parochial prejudices and to examine a broader range of counter-arguments), views also from 'a certain distance.' The necessity of this was powerfully identified by Adam Smith:

> We can never survey our own sentiments and motives, we can never form any judgment concerning them; unless we remove ourselves, as it were, from our own natural station, and endeavour to view them as at a certain distance from us. But we can do this in no other way than by endeavouring to view them with the eyes of other people, or as other people are likely to view them.[13]

Questions are often raised about whether distant people can, in fact, provide useful scrutiny of local issues, given what are taken to be 'uncrossable' barriers of culture. One of Edmund Burke's criticisms of the French declaration of the 'rights of man' and its universalist spirit was concerned with disputing the acceptability of that notion in other cultures. Burke argued that "the liberties and the restrictions vary with times and circumstances, and admit of infinite modifications, that cannot be settled upon any abstract rule."[14] The belief that the universality that is meant to underlie the notion of human rights is profoundly mistaken has, for this reason, found expression in many other writings as well.

A belief in uncrossable barriers between the values of different cultures has surfaced and resurfaced repeatedly over the centuries, and they are forcefully articulated today. The claim of magnificent uniqueness—and often of superiority—has sometimes come from critics of 'Western values,' varying from champions of regional ethics (well illustrated by the fuss in the 1990s about the peerless excellence of 'Asian values'), or religious or cultural separatists (with or without being accompanied by fundamentalism of one kind or another). Sometimes, however, the claim of uniqueness has come from Western particularists. A good example is Samuel Huntington's (1996) insistence that the "West was West long before it was modern," and his claim that "a sense of individualism and a tradition of individual rights and liberties" are "unique among civilized societies." Similarly, no less a historian of ideas than Gertrude Himmelfarb has argued that ideas of 'justice,' 'right,' 'reason,' and 'love of humanity' are "predominantly, perhaps even uniquely, Western values" (1996, pp. 74–75).

I have discussed these diagnoses elsewhere (for example Sen, 1999). Contrary to cultural stereotypes, the histories of different countries in the world have shown considerable variations over time as well as between different groups within the same country. When, in the twelfth century, the Jewish philosopher Maimonedes had to flee an intolerant Europe and its Inquisitions to try to safeguard his human right to stick to his own religious beliefs and practice, he sought shelter in Emperor Saladin's Egypt (via Fez and Palestine),

and found an honored position in the court of this Muslim emperor. Several hundred years later, when, in Agra, the Moghal emperor of India, Akbar, was arguing—and legislating—on the government's duty to uphold the right to religious freedom of all citizens, the European Inquisitions were still going on, and Giordano Bruno was burnt at the stake in Rome, in 1600.

In his autobiography, *Long Walk to Freedom*, Nelson Mandela (1994, p. 21) describes how he learned about democracy and individual rights, as a young boy, by seeing the proceedings of the local meetings held in the regent's house in Mqhekezweni:

> Everyone who wanted to speak did so. It was democracy in its purest form. There may have been a hierarchy of importance among the speakers, but everyone was heard, chief and subject, warrior and medicine man, shopkeeper and farmer, landowner and laborer.

Not only are the differences on the subject of freedoms and rights that actually exist between different societies often much exaggerated, but also there is, typically, little note taken of substantial variations *within* each local culture—over time and even at a point of time (in particular, right now). What are taken to be 'foreign' criticisms often correspond to internal criticisms from non-mainstream groups.[15] If, say, Iranian dissidents are imprisoned by an authoritarian regime precisely because of their heterodoxy, any suggestion that they should be seen as 'ambassadors of Western values' rather than as 'Iranian dissidents' would only add serious insult to manifest injury. Being culturally non-partisan requires respecting the participation of people from any corner of the earth, which is not the same thing as accepting the prevailing priorities, especially among dominant groups in particular societies, when information is extremely restricted and discussions and disagreements are not permitted.

Scrutiny from a 'distance' may have something to offer in the assessment of practices as different from each other as the stoning of adulterous women in the Taliban's Afghanistan and the abounding use of capital punishment (sometimes with mass jubilation) in parts of the United States. This is the kind of issue that made Smith insist that "the eyes of the rest of mankind" must be invoked to understand whether "a punishment appears equitable."[16] Ultimately, the discipline of critical moral scrutiny requires, among other things, "endeavoring to view [our sentiments and beliefs] with the eyes of other people, or as other people are likely to view them" (*The Theory of Moral Sentiments*, III, 1, 2; in Smith, 1976, p. 110).

Intellectual interactions across the borders can be as important in rich societies as they are in poorer ones. The point to note here is not so much whether we are *allowed* to chat across borders and to make cross-boundary scrutiny, but that the discipline of critical assessment of moral sentiments—no matter how locally established they are—*requires* that we view our practices *inter alia* from a certain distance.

Both the understanding of human rights and of the adequacy of a list of basic capabilities, I would argue, are intimately linked with the reach of public discussion—between persons and across borders. The viability and universality of human rights and of an acceptable specification of capabilities are dependent on their ability to survive open critical scrutiny in public reasoning.

Conclusions

To conclude, the two concepts—human rights and capabilities—go well with each other, so long as we do not try to subsume either entirely within the other. There are many human rights for which the capability perspective has much to offer. However, human rights to important process freedoms cannot be adequately analyzed within the capability approach.

Furthermore, both human rights and capabilities have to depend on the process of public reasoning, which neither can lose without serious impoverishment of its respective intellectual content. The methodology of public scrutiny draws on Rawlsian understanding of 'objectivity' in ethics, but the impartiality that is needed cannot be confined within the borders of a nation. We have to go much beyond Rawls for that reason, just as we also have to go beyond the enlightenment provided by his use of 'primary goods,' and invoke, in that context, the more articulate framework of capabilities. The need for extension does not, of course, reduce our debt to John Rawls. Neither human rights nor capabilities would have been easy to understand without his pioneering departures.

NOTES

1. See Sen (2002a), particularly the Arrow Lectures ('Freedom and Social Choice') included there (essays 20–22).

2. An investigation of more complex features of the opportunity aspect and the process aspect of freedoms can be found in the Arrow Lectures ('Freedom and Social Choice') in Sen (2002a, essays 20–22).

3. On the concept of capability, see Sen (1980, 1985a, 1985b), Nussbaum and Sen (1993), and Nussbaum (2000). See also the related theories of substantial opportunities developed by Arneson (1989), Cohen (1989), and Roemer (1996), among other contributions.

4. The relevance of such parametric variability for a theory of justice is discussed in Sen (1990).

5. See Okin (2003, p. 293). On related issues see also Joshua Cohen (1994, especially pp. 278–80), and G. A. Cohen (1995, especially pp. 120–25).

6. See Sen (1980, 1985a, 1985b). In contrast, G. A. Cohen has presented arguments in favor of focusing on achieved functionings—related to his concept of 'midfare'—rather than on capability (see Cohen, 1989, 1993).

7. See Marx (1845–1846/1977, p. 190).

8. There is a substantial difference between: (1) valuing multiculturalism because of the way—and to the extent that—it enhances the freedoms of the people involved to choose to live as they would like (and have reason to like); and (2) valuing cultural diversity *per se*, which focuses on the descriptive characteristics of a social pattern, rather than on the freedoms of the people involved. The contrast receives investigation in the *Human Development Report 2004* (United Nations Development Programme, 2004).

9. On the plurality of concerns that include processes as well as opportunities, which is inescapably involved in normative social choice (including theories of justice), see Sen (1970, 1985b). Since I have often encountered the diagnosis that I propound a "capability-based theory of justice," I should make it clear that this could be true only in the very limited sense of naming something according to one *principal* part of it (comparable with, say, using England for Britain). It is only one part of the informational base of a theory of justice that the capability perspective can expect to fill.

10. I cannot emphasise adequately how important I believe it is to understand that the need for an explicit valuational exercise is an advantage, rather than a limitation, of the capability approach, because valuational decisions have to be explicitly discussed, rather than being derived from some mechanical formula that is used, without scrutiny and assessment. For arguments *against* my position on this issue, see Beitz (1986) and Williams (1987). My own position is more fully discussed in Sen (1999, 2004).

11. See Rawls (1971, 1993, especially pp. 110–13).

12. See particularly John Rawls (1999). See also Rawls's formulation of the original position in *Political Liberalism* (Rawls, 1993, p. 12): "I assume that the basic structure is that of a closed society: that is, we are to regard it as self-contained and as having no relations with other societies. . . . That a society is closed is a considerable abstraction, justified only because it enables us to focus on certain main questions free from distracting details."

13. See Smith (1759/1790, III, 1, 2). Smith (1976, p. 110). I have tried to discuss and extend the Smithian perspective on moral reasoning in Sen (2002b).

14. Quoted in Lukes (1997, p. 238).

15. On this see Nussbaum and Sen (1988).

16. Smith (1978/1982, p. 104).

REFERENCES

Arneson, R. (1989) 'Equality and Equal Opportunity for Welfare,' *Philosophical Studies*, 56, pp. 77–93.

Beitz, C. (1986) 'Amartya Sen's resources, values and development,' *Economics and Philosophy*, 2, pp. 282–90.

Bentham, J. (1792) *Anarchical Fallacies; Being an Examination of the Declaration of Rights Issued during the French Revolution* [Republished in J. Bowring (Ed.) (1843) *The Works of Jeremy Bentham*, volume II, William Talt, Edinburgh].

Cohen, G.A. (1989) 'On the currency of egalitarian Justice,' *Ethics*, 99, pp. 906–44.

Cohen, G.A. (1993) 'Equality of what? On welfare, resources and capabilities,' in M. Nussbaum and A. Sen (Eds.), *The Quality of Life*, Clarendon Press, Oxford.

Cohen, G.A. (1995) 'Review: Amartya Sen's unequal world,' *The New Left Review*, January, pp. 117–29.

Cohen, J. (1994) 'Review of Sen's *Inequality Reexamined*,' *Journal of Philosophy*, 92, pp. 275–88.

Drèze, J. and Sen, A. (1989) *Hunger and Public Action*, Clarendon Press, Oxford.

Drèze, J. and Sen, A. (2002) *India: Participation and Development*, Oxford University Press, Delhi.

Hawthorn, G. (Ed.) (1987) *Amartya Sen et al., The Standard of Living*, Cambridge University Press, Cambridge.

Himmelfarb, G. (1996) 'The illusions of cosmopolitanism,' in M. Nussbaum with respondents (Ed.), *For Love of Country*, Beacon Press, Boston.

Huntington, S. (1996) *The Clash of Civilizations and the Remaking of World Order*, Simon and Schuster, New York.

Lukes, S. (1997) 'Five fabies about human rights,' in M. Ishay (Ed.), *The Human Rights Reader*, Routledge, London.

Mandela, N. (1994) *Long Walk to Freedom*, Little, Brown & Co., Boston.

Marx, K. (1845–1846) *The German Ideology*, with F. Engels [Republished in D. McLellan (Ed.) (1977) *Karl Marx: Selected Writings*, Oxford University Press, Oxford].

Nussbaum, M. (2000) *Women and Human Development: The Capabilities Approach*, Cambridge University Press, Cambridge.

Nussbaum, M. and Sen, A. (1988) 'Internal criticism and Indian rationalist traditions,' in M. Krausz (Ed.), *Relativism: Interpretation and Confrontation*, University of Notre Dame Press, Notre Dame.

Nussbaum, M. and Sen, A. (Eds) (1993) *The Quality of Life*, Clarendon Press, Oxford.

Okin, S. (2003) 'Poverty, Well-being and gender: what counts, who's heard?,' *Philosophy and Public Affairs*, 31, pp. 280–316.

Rawls, J. (1971) *A Theory of Justice*, Harvard University Press, Cambridge, MA.

Rawls, J. (1993) *Political Liberalism*, Columbia University Press, New York.

Rawls, J. (1999) *The Law of Peoples*, Harvard University Press, Cambridge, MA.

Roemer, J.E. (1996) *Theories of Distributive Justice*, Harvard University Press, Cambridge, MA.

Sen, A. (1970) *Collective Choice and Social Welfare*, Holden-Day, San Francisco [Republished by North-Holland, Amsterdam].

Sen, A. (1980) 'Equality of what?,' in S. McMurrin (Ed.), *Tanner Lectures on Human Values*, volume I, Cambridge University Press, Cambridge: University of Utah Press, Cambridge.

Sen, A. (1985a) *Commodities and Capabilities*, North-Holland, Amsterdam.

Sen, A. (1985b) 'Well-being, agency and freedom: the Dewey Lectures 1984,' *Journal of Philosophy*, 82, pp. 169–221.

Sen, A. (1985/1987) *The Standard of Living*, Tanner Lectures, Cambridge University Press, Cambridge.

Sen, A. (1990) 'Justice: means versus freedoms,' *Philosophy and Public Affairs*, 19, pp. 111–21.

Sen, A. (1999) *Development as Freedom*, Knopf, New York: Oxford University Press, New York.

Sen, A. (2002a) *Rationality and Freedom*, Harvard University Press, Cambridge, MA.

Sen, A. (2002b) 'Open and closed impartiality,' *The Journal of Philosophy*, 99, pp. 445–69.

Sen, A. (2004) 'Elements of a theory of human rights,' *Philosophy and Public Affairs*, 32(4), pp. 315–56.

Smith, A. (1759/1790/1976) *The Theory of Moral Sentiments*, revised edition 1790 [Republished by Clarendon Press, Oxford].

Smith, A. (1776/1979) *An Inquiry into the Nature and Causes of the Wealth of Nations*, Clarendon Press, Oxford [Reprinted by Liberty Press, 1981].

Smith, A. (1978/1982) in R. L. Meek, D. D. Raphael and P. G. Stein (Eds.), *Lectures on Jurisprudence*, Clarendon Press, Oxford [Reprinted by Liberty Press, Indianapolis].

United Nations Development Programme (1990) *Human Development Report 1990*, Oxford University Press, Oxford.

United Nations Development Programme (2004) *Human Development Report 2004*, Oxford University Press, Oxford.

Williams, B. (1987) 'The standard of living: interests and capabilities,' in G. Hawthorn (Ed.), *Amartya Sen et al., The Standard of Living*, Cambridge University Press, Cambridge.

Makau Mutua

SAVAGES, VICTIMS, AND SAVIORS
The Metaphor of Human Rights

I. Introduction

The human rights movement[1] is marked by a damning metaphor. The grand narrative of human rights contains a subtext that depicts an epochal contest pitting savages, on the one hand, against victims and saviors, on the other.[2] The savages-victims-saviors (SVS)[3] construction is a three-dimensional compound metaphor in which each dimension is a metaphor in itself.[4] The main authors of the human rights discourse including the United Nations, Western states, international nongovernmental organizations (INGOs), and senior Western academics, constructed this three-dimensional prism. This rendering of the human rights corpus and its discourse is unidirectional and predictable, a black-and-white construction that pits good against evil.

This article attempts to elicit from the proponents of the human rights movement several admissions, some of them deeply unsettling. It asks that human rights advocates be more self-critical and come to terms with the troubling rhetoric and history that shape, in part, the human rights movement. At the same time, the article does not only address the biased and arrogant rhetoric and history of the human rights enterprise, but also grapples with the contradictions in the basic nobility and majesty that drive the human rights project—the drive from the unflinching belief that human beings and the political societies they construct can be governed by a higher morality. This first section briefly introduces the three dimensions of the SVS metaphor and how the metaphor exposes the theoretical flaws of the current human rights corpus.

The first dimension of the prism depicts a savage and evokes images of barbarism. The abominations of the savage are presented as so cruel and unimaginable as to represent their state as a negation of humanity. The human rights story presents the state as the classic savage, an ogre forever bent on the consumption of humans.[5] Although savagery in human rights discourse connotes much more than the state, the state is depicted as the operational instrument of savagery. States become savage when they choke off and oust civil society.[6] The "good" state controls its demonic proclivities by cleansing itself with, and internalizing, human rights. The "evil" state, on the other hand, expresses itself through an illiberal, anti-democratic, or other authoritarian culture. The redemption or salvation of the state is solely dependent on its submission to human rights norms. The state is the guarantor of human rights; it is also the target and *raison d'être* of human rights law.[7]

But the reality is far more complex. While the metaphor may suggest otherwise, it is not the state per se that is barbaric but the cultural foundation of the state. The state only becomes a vampire when "bad" culture overcomes or disallows the development of "good" culture. The real savage, though, is not the state but a cultural deviation from human rights. That savagery inheres in the theory and practice of the one-party state, military

From *Harvard International Law Journal* 42, no. 1 (Winter 2001): 201–45. Some of the author's notes have been omitted.

junta, controlled or closed state, theocracy, or even cultural practices such as the one popularly known in the West as female genital mutilation (FGM),[8] not in the state per se. The state itself is a neutral, passive instrumentality—a receptacle or an empty vessel—that conveys savagery by implementing the project of the savage culture.

The second dimension of the prism depicts the face and the fact of a victim as well as the essence and the idea of victimhood. A human being whose "dignity and worth" have been violated by the savage is the victim. The victim figure is a powerless, helpless innocent whose naturalist attributes have been negated by the primitive and offensive actions of the state or the cultural foundation of the state. The entire human rights structure is both anti-catastrophic and reconstructive. It is anti-catastrophic because it is designed to prevent more calamities through the creation of more victims. It is reconstructive because it seeks to re-engineer the state and the society to reduce the number of victims, as it defines them,[9] and prevent conditions that give rise to victims. The classic human rights document—the human rights report—embodies these two mutually reinforcing strategies. An INGO human rights report is usually a catalogue of horrible catastrophes visited on individuals. As a rule, each report also carries a diagnostic epilogue and recommended therapies and remedies.[10]

The third dimension of the prism is the savior or the redeemer, the good angel who protects, vindicates, civilizes, restrains, and safeguards. The savior is the victim's bulwark against tyranny. The simple, yet complex promise of the savior is freedom: freedom from the tyrannies of the state, tradition, and culture. But it is also the freedom to create a better society based on particular values. In the human rights story, the savior is the human rights corpus itself, with the United Nations, Western governments, INGOs, and Western charities as the actual rescuers, redeemers of a benighted world.[11] In reality, however, these institutions are merely fronts. The savior is ultimately a set of culturally based norms and practices that inhere in liberal thought and philosophy.

The human rights corpus, though well-meaning, is fundamentally Eurocentric,[12] and suffers from several basic and interdependent flaws captured in the SVS metaphor. First, the corpus falls within the historical continuum of the Eurocentric colonial project, in which actors are cast into superior and subordinate positions. Precisely because of this cultural and historical context, the human rights movement's basic claim of universality is undermined. Instead, a historical understanding of the struggle for human dignity should locate the impetus of a universal conception of human rights in those societies *subjected* to European tyranny and imperialism. Unfortunately, this is not part of the official human rights narrative. Some of the most important events preceding the post-1945, United Nations–led human rights movement include the anti-slavery campaigns in both Africa and the United States, the anti-colonial struggles in Africa, Asia, and Latin America, and the struggles for women's suffrage and equal rights throughout the world.[13] But the pioneering work of many non-Western activists[14] and other human rights heroes are not acknowledged by the contemporary human rights movement. These historically important struggles, together with the norms anchored in non-Western cultures and societies, have either been overlooked or rejected in the construction of the current understanding of human rights.

Second, the SVS metaphor and narrative rejects the cross-contamination[15] of cultures and instead promotes a Eurocentric ideal. The metaphor is premised on the transformation by Western cultures of non-Western cultures into a Eurocentric prototype and not the fashioning of a multicultural mosaic.[16] The SVS metaphor results in an "othering" process that imagines the creation of inferior clones, in effect dumb copies of the original. For example, Western political democracy is in effect an organic element of human rights.[17] "Savage" cultures and peoples are seen as lying outside the human rights orbit, and by implication, outside the regime of political democracy. It is this distance from human rights that allows certain cultures to create victims. Political democracy is then viewed as a panacea. Other textual examples anchored in the treatment of cultural phenomena, such as "traditional" practices that appear to negate the equal protection for women, also illustrate the gulf between human rights and non-liberal, non-European cultures.

Third, the language and rhetoric of the human rights corpus present significant theoretical problems. The arrogant and biased rhetoric of the human rights movement prevents the movement from gaining cross-cultural legitimacy.[18] This curse of the SVS rhetoric has no bearing on the substance of the normative judgment being rendered. A particular leader, for example, could be labeled a war criminal, but such a label may carry no validity locally because of the curse of the SVS rhetoric.[19] In other words, the SVS rhetoric may undermine the universalist warrant that it claims and thus engender resistance to the apprehension and punishment of real violators.

The subtext of human rights is a grand narrative hidden in the seemingly neutral and universal language of the corpus. For example, the UN Charter describes its mandate to "reaffirm faith in fundamental human rights, in the dignity and worth of the human person, in the equal rights of men and women and of nations large and small."[20] This is certainly a noble ideal. But what exactly does that terminology mean here? This phraseology conceals more than it reveals. What, for example, are fundamental human rights, and how are they determined? Do such rights have cultural, religious, ethical, moral, political, or other biases? What exactly is meant by the "dignity and worth" of the human person? Is there an essentialized human being that the corpus imagines? Is the individual found in the streets of Nairobi, the slums of Boston, the deserts of Iraq, or the rainforests of

Brazil? In addition to the Herculean task of defining the prototypical human being, the UN Charter puts forward another pretense—that all nations "large and small" enjoy some equality. Even as it ratified power imbalances between the Third World and the dominant American and European powers, the United Nations gave the latter the primary power to define and determine "world peace" and "stability."[21] These fictions of neutrality and universality, like so much else in a lopsided world, undergird the human rights corpus and belie its true identity and purposes. This international rhetoric of goodwill reveals, just beneath the surface, intentions and reality that stand in great tension and contradiction with it.

This article is not merely about the language of human rights or the manner in which the human rights movement describes its goals, subjects, and intended outcomes. It is not a plea for the human rights movement to be more sensitive to non-Western cultures. Nor is it a wholesale rejection of the idea of human rights.[22] Instead, the article is fundamentally an attempt at locating—philosophically, culturally, and historically—the normative edifice of the human rights corpus. If the human rights movement is driven by a totalitarian or totalizing impulse, that is, the mission to require that all human societies transform themselves to fit a particular blueprint, then there is an acute shortage of deep reflection and a troubling abundance of zealotry in the human rights community. This vision of the "good society" must be vigorously questioned and contested.

Fourth, the issue of power is largely ignored in the human rights corpus. There is an urgent need for a human rights movement that is multicultural, inclusive, and deeply political. Thus, while it is essential that a new human rights movement overcome Eurocentrism, it is equally important that it also address deeply lopsided power relations among and within cultures, national economies, states, genders, religions, races and ethnic groups, and other societal cleavages. Such a movement cannot treat Eurocentrism as the starting point and other cultures as peripheral. The point of departure for the movement must be a basic assumption about the moral equivalency of all cultures. Francis Deng has correctly pointed out that to "arrogate the concept [of human rights] to only certain groups, cultures, or civilizations is to aggravate divisiveness on the issue, to encourage defensiveness or unwarranted self-justification on the part of the excluded, and to impede progress toward a universal consensus on human rights."[23]

The fifth flaw concerns the role of race in the development of the human rights narrative. The SVS metaphor of human rights carries racial connotations in which the international hierarchy of race and color is reintrenched and revitalized. The metaphor is in fact necessary for the continuation of the global racial hierarchy. In the human rights narrative, savages and victims are generally non-white and non-Western, while the saviors are white. This old truism has found new life in the metaphor of human rights. But there is also a sense in which human rights can be seen as a project for the redemption of the redeemers, in which whites who are privileged globally as a people—who have historically visited untold suffering and savage atrocities against non-whites—redeem themselves by "defending" and "civilizing" "lower," "unfortunate," and "inferior" peoples. The metaphor is thus laced with the pathology of self-redemption.

As currently constituted and deployed, the human rights movement will ultimately fail because it is perceived as an alien ideology in non-Western societies. The movement does not deeply resonate in the cultural fabrics of non-Western states, except among hypocritical elites steeped in Western ideas. In order ultimately to prevail, the human rights movement must be moored in the cultures of all peoples."[24]

The project of reconsidering rights, with claims to their supremacy, is not new. The culture of rights in the present milieu stretches back at least to the rise of the modern state in Europe. It is that state's monopoly of violence and the instruments of coercion that gave rise to the culture of rights to counterbalance the abusive state.[25] Robert Cover refers to this construction as the myth of the jurisprudence of rights that allows society to both legitimize and control the state.[26] Human rights, however, renew the meaning and scope of rights in a radical way. Human rights bestow naturalness, transhistoricity, and universality to rights. But this article lodges a counterclaim against such a leap. This article is certainly informed by the works of critical legal scholars,[27] feminist critics of rights discourse,[28] and critical race theorists.[29] Still, the approach of this article differs from all three because it seeks to address an international phenomenon and not a municipal, distinctly American question. The critique of human rights should be based not just on American or European legal traditions but also on other cultural milieus. The indigenous, non-European traditions of Asia, Africa, the Pacific, and the Americas must be central to this critique. The idea of human rights—the quest to craft a universal bundle of attributes with which all societies must endow all human beings—is a noble one. The problem with the current bundle of attributes lies in their inadequacy, incompleteness, and wrong-headedness. There is little doubt that there is much to celebrate in the present human rights corpus just as there is much to quarrel with. In this exercise, a sober evaluation of the current human rights corpus and its language is not an option—it is required.[30]

■ ■ ■

II. Development of the Grand Narrative of Human Rights

The Charter of the United Nations, which is the constitutional basis for all UN human rights texts, captures the before-and-after, backward-progressive view of history. It declares human rights an indispensable element for the survival of humankind. It does so by undertaking as one of its principal aims the promotion of "universal respect for, and observance of, human rights and fundamental freedoms for all without distinction as to race, sex, language, or religion."[31] This self-representation of human rights requires moral and historical certainty and a belief in particular inflexible truths. The Universal Declaration of Human Rights (UDHR), the grandest of all human rights documents, endows the struggle between good and evil with historicity in which the defeat of the latter is only possible through human rights.[32] This is now popularly accepted as the normal script of human rights.[33] In fact, there is today an orgy of celebration of this script by prominent scholars who see in it the key to the redemption of humanity.[34] But this grand script of human rights raises a multitude of normative and cultural questions and problems, especially in light of the historical roots of the human rights movement.

Any valid critique must first acknowledge that the human rights movement, like earlier crusades, is a bundle of contradictions. It does not have, therefore, a monopoly on virtue that its most vociferous advocates claim. This article argues that human rights, and the relentless campaign to universalize them, present a historical continuum in an unbroken chain of Western conceptual and cultural dominance over the past several centuries. At the heart of this continuum is a seemingly incurable virus: the impulse to universalize Eurocentric norms and values by repudiating, demonizing, and "othering" that which is different and non-European. By this argument, the article does not mean to suggest that human rights are bad per se or that the human rights corpus is irredeemable. Rather, it suggests that the globalization of human rights fits a historical pattern in which all high morality comes from the West as a civilizing agent against lower forms of civilization in the rest of the world.[35]

Although the human rights movement is located within the historical continuum of Eurocentrism as a civilizing mission, and therefore as an attack on non-European cultures, it is critical to note that it was European, and not non-European, atrocities that gave rise to it. While the movement has today constructed the savage and the victim as non-European, Adolf Hitler was the quintessential savage. The abominations and demise of his regime ignited the human rights movement.[36] Hitler, a white European, was the personification of evil. The Nazi regime, a white European government, was the embodiment of barbarism. The combination of Hitler's gross deviation from the evolving European constitutional law precepts and the entombment of his imperial designs by the West and the Soviet Union started the avalanche of norms known as the human rights corpus.

Nuremberg, the German town where some twenty-two major Nazi war criminals were tried—resulting in nineteen convictions—stands as the birthplace of the human rights movement, with the London Agreement[37] its birth certificate. Originally, the West did not create the human rights movement in order to save or civilize non-Europeans, although these humanist impulses drove the anti-slavery abolitionist efforts of the nineteenth century.[38] Neither the enslavement of Africans, with its barbaric consequences and genocidal dimensions, nor the classic colonization of Asians, Africans, and Latin Americans by Europeans, with its bone-chilling atrocities, were sufficient to move the West to create the human rights movement. It took the genocidal extermination of Jews in Europe—a white people—to start the process of the codification and universalization of human rights norms. Thus, although the Nuremberg Tribunal[39] has been argued by some to be in a sense hypocritical,[40] it is its promise that is significant. For the first time, the major powers drew a line demarcating impermissible conduct by states toward their own people and created the concept of collective responsibility for human rights. But no one should miss the irony of brutalizing colonial powers pushing for the Nuremberg trials and the adoption of the UDHR.

■   ■   ■

Thus, the human rights movement originated in Europe to curb European savageries such as the Holocaust, the abuses of Soviet bloc Communism, and the denials of speech and other expressive rights in a number of Western countries. The movement grew initially out of the horrors of the West, constructing the image of a European savage. The European human rights system, which is now a central attribute of European legal and political identity, is designed to hold member states to particular standards of conduct in their treatment of individuals.[41] It is, as it were, the bulwark against the re-emergence of the unbridled European savage—the phenomenon that gave rise to and fueled the Third Reich.

The human rights corpus, only put into effect following the atrocities of the Second World War, had its theoretical underpinnings in Western colonial attitudes. It is rooted in a deep-seated sense of European and Western global predestination.[42] As put by David Slater, European "belief in the necessity of an imperial mission to civilize the other and to convert other societies into inferior versions of the same" took hold in the nineteenth century.[43] This impulse to possess and transform that which was different found a ready mask and benign cover in messianic faiths. For example, Denys Shropshire, a European Christian missionary, described Africans as "primitive" natives in the "technically barbaric and pre-literary stage of sociological and cultural development."[44] The purpose of the missionary was not "merely to civilize but to Christianize, not merely to convey the 'Gifts of Civilization.' "[45] By the nineteenth century, the

discourse of white over black superiority had gained popularity and acceptance in Europe:

> The advocates of this discourse—[German philosopher Georg] Hegel most typically, but duly followed by a host of 'justifiers'—declared that Africa had no history prior to direct contact with Europe. Therefore the Africans, having made no history of their own, had clearly made no development of their own. Therefore they were not properly human, and could not be left to themselves, but must be "led" towards civilization by other peoples: that is, by the peoples of Europe, especially of Western Europe, and most particularly of Britain and France.[46]

As if by intuition, the missionary fused religion with civilization, a process that was meant to remove the native from the damnation of prehistory and to deliver him to the gates of history. In this idiom, human development was defined as a linear and vertical progression of the dark or backward races from the savage to the civilized, the pre-modern to the modern, from the child to the adult, and the inferior to the superior. * * * The United States, whose history is simply a continuation of the Age of Europe, suffers from this worldview just like its European predecessors. American predestination, as embodied in the Monroe Doctrine, is almost as old as the country itself. President Theodore Roosevelt expressed this sense of predestination when he referred to peoples and countries south of the United States as the "weak and chaotic governments and people south of us" and declared that it was "our duty, when it becomes absolutely inevitable, to police these countries in the interest of order and civilization."[47] * * *

In the last several hundred years, the globe has witnessed the universalization of Eurocentric norms and cultural forms through the creation of the colonial state and the predominance of certain economic, social, and political models. International law itself was founded on the preeminence of four specific European biases: geographic Europe as the center, and Christianity, mercantile economics, and political imperialism as superior paradigms.[48] Both the League of Nations and its successor, the United Nations, revitalized and confirmed European-American domination of international affairs. In the post-War period, non-European states were trusted or mandated to Western powers or became client states of one or another Western state.[49]

Since 1945, the United Nations has played a key role in preserving the global order that the West dominates. A critically important agenda of the United Nations has been the universalization of principles and norms which are European in identity. Principal among these has been the spread of human rights which grow out of Western liberalism and jurisprudence.[50] The West was able to impose its philosophy of human rights on the rest of the world because it dominated the United Nations at its inception.[51] The fallacy of the UDHR, which refers to itself as the "common standard of achievement for all peoples and all nations,"[52] is now underscored by the identification of human rights norms with political democracy. The principal focus of human rights law has been on those rights that strengthen, legitimize, and export the liberal democratic state to non-Western societies.[53]

Some scholars have argued that democratic governance has evolved from a moral prescription to an international legal obligation.[54] According to Thomas Franck, the right to democratic governance is supported by a large normative human rights canon.[55] He asserts that people almost everywhere, including Africa and Asia, "now demand that government be validated by [W]estern-style parliamentary, multiparty democratic process."[56] * * * Franck presents the apparent triumph of liberal democratic nationalism as the free, uncoerced choice of non-Western peoples.

It may appear that Third World states have participated in the legitimization of the human rights corpus, particularly at the United Nations, the institution most responsible for the creation and universalization of human rights norms. However, too much should not be made of this Third World participation in the making of human rights law. The levers of power at the United Nations and other international law-making fora have traditionally been out of the reach of the Third World. And even if they were within reach, it is doubtful that most Third World states actually represent their peoples and cultures. * * *

■　■　■

Today, most of the activities of the ICJ, AI, and the other Western-based INGOs, such as Human Rights Watch (HRW), the Lawyers Committee for Human Rights, and the International Human Rights Law Group, are focused on the Third World. As a consequence, the predominant image of the savage in the human rights discourse today is that of a Third World, non-European person, cultural practice, or state.

At first blush, there appear to be sufficient grounds for the INGOs' unrelenting emphasis on Third World states as the foci for their work. As a general rule, INGOs concentrate their work on the violations of civil and political rights—the species of legal protections associated with a functioning political democracy. Admittedly, there are more undemocratic states in the Third World than in the developed West. Third World despots have acted with impunity. Violations of civil and political rights and the plunder of Third World economies by their leaders are common and flagrant. The spotlight by INGOs here is appropriate, necessary, and welcome, particularly where local advocacy groups and the press have been muzzled or suffocated by the state. There is no doubt that mechanisms for the protections of human rights are more fragile in many Third World states, if they exist at all.

But while this explains the work of INGOs in the Third World, it does not excuse their relative inactivity on human rights violations in the West. Western countries, like the United States, are notorious for their violations of the civil rights of racial minorities and the poor. Although both AI and HRW have haltingly started to breach the publicity and advocacy barriers in these areas,[57] such reports have been sparse and episodic, and have given the impression of a public relations exercise, designed to mute critics who charge INGOs with a lopsided Third World focus.

The ravages of globalization notwithstanding, INGOs have largely remained deaf to calls for advocacy on social and economic rights.[58] There certainly is no sufficient defense for their failure to address the violations of economic and social rights by Western states.[59] * * *

The historical pattern is undeniable. It forms a long queue of the colonial administrator, the Bible-wielding Christian missionary, the merchant of free enterprise, the exporter of political democracy, and now the human rights zealot. In each case the European culture has pushed the "native" culture to transform. The local must be replaced with the universal—that is, the European. * * *

■ ■ ■

The purpose of this article is not to assign ignoble intentions or motivations on the individual proponents, leaders, or participants in the human rights movement. Without a doubt many of the leaders and foot-soldiers of the human rights movement are driven by a burning desire to end human suffering, as they see it from their vantage point. The white American suburban high school or college student who joins the local chapter of AI and protests FGM in far away lands or writes letters to political or military leaders whose names do not easily roll off the English tongue are no doubt drawing partly from a well of noblesse oblige. The zeal to see all humanity as related and the impulse

to help those defined as in need is noble and is not the problem addressed here. A certain degree of human universality is inevitable and desirable. But what that universality is, what historical and cultural stew it is made of, and how it is accomplished make all the difference. What the high school or college student ought to realize is that her zeal to save others—even from themselves—is steeped in Western and European history. If one culture is allowed the prerogative of imperialism, the right to define and impose on others what it deems good for humanity, the very meaning of freedom itself will have been abrogated. That is why a human rights movement that pivots on the SVS metaphor violates the very idea of the sanctity of humanity that purportedly inspires it.

III. The Metaphor of the Savage

Human rights law frames the state as its primary target. Although voluntarily entered into, human rights treaties are binding on the state.[60] The state is both the guarantor and subject of human rights. Underlying the development of human rights is the belief that the state is a predator that must be contained. Otherwise it will devour and imperil human freedom. From this conventional international human rights law perspective, the state is the classic savage.

But it is not the state per se that is predatory, for the state in itself is simply a construct that describes a repository for public power, a disinterested instrumentality ready to execute public will, whatever that may be. There is a high degree of fluidity in the nature of that power and how it is exercised. For instance, a state's constitutional structure could in its configuration require a particular form of democratic government. Or a state's constitution could locate public power in religious bodies and clerics, as has been the case in the

Islamic Republic of Iran.[61] However, a state could, through revolution or some other device, be Islamic today and secular tomorrow. Since the state in this construction appears to be an empty vessel, the savage must be located beyond the state.

The state should be unmasked as being a mere proxy for the real savage. That leaves the historically accumulated wisdom, the culture of a society, as the only other plausible place to locate the savage. I have argued elsewhere that culture "represents the accumulation of a people's wisdom and thus their identity; it is real and without it a people is without a name, rudderless, and torn from its moorings."[62] In this sense, culture is a set of local truths which serve as a guide for life's many pursuits in a society. The validity of a cultural norm is a local truth, and judgment or evaluation of that truth by a norm from an external culture is extremely problematic, if not altogether an invalid exercise.[63] But culture itself is a dynamic and alchemical mix of many variables, including religion, philosophy, history, mythology, politics, environmental factors, language, and economics. The interaction of these variables—both within the culture and through influence by other cultures—produces competing social visions and values in any given society. The dominant class or political interests that capture the state make it the public expression of their particular cultural vision. That is to say, the state is more a conveyer belt than an embodiment of particular cultural norms. The state is but the scaffolding underneath which the real savage resides. Thus, when human rights norms target a deviant state, they are really attacking the normative cultural fabric or variant expressed by that state. The culture, and not the state, is the actual savage. From this perspective, human rights violations represent a clash between the culture of human rights and the savage culture.

The view that human rights is an ideology with deep roots in liberalism and democratic forms of government is now supported by senior human rights academics in the West.[64] The cultural biases of the human rights corpus can only be properly understood if it is contextualized within liberal theory and philosophy. Understood from this position, human rights become an ideology with a specific cultural and ethnographic fingerprint.[65] The human rights corpus expresses a cultural bias, and its chastening of a state is therefore a cultural project. If culture is not defined as some discrete, exotic, and peculiar practice which is frozen in time but rather as the dynamic totality of ideas, forms, practices, and structures of any given society, then human rights, as it is currently conceived, is an expression of a particular European-American culture. The advocacy of human rights across cultural borders is then an attempt to displace the local culture with the "universal" culture of human rights. Human rights, therefore, become the universal culture. It is in this sense that the "other" culture, that which is non-European, is the savage in the human rights corpus and its discourse.

In major international human rights instruments, the "other" culture is quite often depicted as the evil that must be overcome by human rights itself. An example is the Convention on the Elimination of all Forms of Discrimination against Women (CEDAW),[66] which is based on equality and anti-discrimination, the two basic and preeminent norms of the human rights corpus. The most transformatively radical human rights treaty, CEDAW refers to offending "social and cultural patterns"[67] and demands that the state take all appropriate measures to transform attitudes and practices that are inimical to women.[68] The treaty explicitly requires that states seek the "elimination of prejudices and customary and all other practices" that are based on the ideas of the inequality of the sexes.[69]

■　　■　　■

The impression left by the reports and the activities of powerful INGOs is unmistakable. While the West is presented as the cradle of a feminist movement, countries in the South have been constructed as steeped in traditions and practices which are harmful to women. In one of her first reports, Radhika Coomaraswamy, the UN Special Rapporteur on Violence against Women, confirmed this impression when she noted that "[c]ertain customary practices and some aspects of tradition are often the cause of violence against women."[70] She noted that "besides female genital mutilation, a whole host of practices violate female dignity. Foot binding, male preference, early marriage, virginity tests, dowry deaths, sati, female infanticide and malnutrition are among the many practices that violate a woman's human rights."[71] All of these practices are found in non-Western cultures. Images of practices such as FGM, dowry burnings, and honor killings have come to frame the discourse, and in that vein stigmatize non-Western cultures.

Elsewhere, non-European political traditions, which lie outside the liberal tradition and do not yield political democratic structures, are demonized in the text of human rights and its discourse. Take, for example, the view expressed by human rights documents in the area of political participation. Here, the human rights corpus expects all societies to support a pluralist, democratic society. Both the UDHR and the International Covenant on Civil and Political Rights (ICCPR), the two key documents in the area of civil and political rights, are explicit about the primacy of rights of expression and association. They both give citizens the right to political participation through elections and the guarantee of the right to assemble, associate, and disseminate their ideas.[72] This scheme of rights coupled with equal protection and due process rights implies a political democracy or a political society with a regularly elected government, genuine competition for political office, and separation of powers with judicial independence. While it is true that the human rights regime does not dictate the particular permutation or strain of political democracy, it suggests a Western-style liberal democracy nevertheless. Systems of government such as monarchies, theocracies, dictatorships, and one-party states would violate rights of association and run afoul of the human rights corpus.[73] When it rejects non-Western political cultures as undemocratic, the human rights corpus raises the specter of political savagery.

■　　■　　■

Some writers have depicted certain practices as part of a savage culture. In the gruesome conflict following the collapse of Yugoslavia, genocide and other war crimes were perpetrated with chilling callousness. In particular, one of the most horrifying war crimes was the massive rape by Serbs of Muslim Bosnian women, with some reports estimating as many as 20,000 victims.[74] Todd Salzman characterizes these offenses as "an assault against the female gender, violating her body and its reproductive capabilities as a 'weapon of war.'"[75] He traces these atrocities to a savage Serbian patriarchal culture that usurps the female body and reduces the female to "her reproductive capacities in order to fulfill the overall objective of Serbian nationalism by producing more citizens to populate the nation."[76] According to Salzman, this view of the female body is deeply rooted in Serbian culture, the Serbian Orthodox Church, and Serbian official policies.[77] The savage here is located in religion, politics, and culture which the state supports and implements for the purpose of creating "Greater Serbia."

The image of the savage is also painted impressively by INGOs in their work through reporting and other forms of public advocacy. The focus here is not on domestic human rights nongovernmental organizations (NGOs) in the Third World because many simply imitate the practices of their predecessors in the North.[78] Typically, INGOs perform three basic functions: investigation, reporting, and advocacy.[79] The focus of human rights INGOs is usually human rights violations in a Third World country, where the "investigation" normally takes place. Generally, a Western-based INGO—typically based in the political and cultural capitals of the most powerful countries in the West[80]—sends a team of investigators called a human rights mission to a country in the South. The mission lasts anywhere from several days to a few weeks, and collects data and other information on human rights questions from victims, local NGOs, lawyers, local journalists, human rights defenders, and government officials. Information from these local sources is usually cross-checked with other, supposedly more objective sources—meaning Western embassies, locally based Western reporters, and other Western interests such as foundations. Upon returning to the West, the mission systematizes the information and releases it in the form of a report.

The human rights report is a catalogue of abuses committed by the state against liberal values.[81] It criticizes the state for departing from the civil and political rights obligations provided for in the major instruments. Its purpose is to shame the Third World state by pointing out the gulf between the state's conduct and internationally sanctioned civilized behavior. This departure from good behavior is stigmatized and used to paint the state either as a pariah or out-of-step with the rest of the civilized world. Reports normally contain corrective measures and recommendations to the offending state. In many instances, however, the audience of these reports is the West or some other Western institution, such as the European Union. The pleas of the INGO report here pit a First World state or institution against a Third World state or culture. The report asks that the West cut off aid, condition assistance, impose sanctions, and/or publicly denounce the unacceptable conduct of the Third World state.[82] INGOs thus ask First World states and institutions to play a significant role in "taming" and "civilizing" Third World states, even though such a role relies on the power and economic imbalances of the international order which favors the North over the South.[83]

The human rights report also tells another, more interesting, story about the target of the human rights corpus. In this story, the report describes several images of the savage, including the Third World state, the quintessential savage. Human rights literature is replete with images of bloodthirsty Third World despots and trigger-happy police and security forces.

Perhaps in no other area than in the advocacy over FGM is the image of culture as the savage more poignant. The word "mutilation" itself implies the willful, sadistic infliction of pain on a hapless victim, and stigmatizes the practitioners and their cultures as barbaric savages. Descriptions of the practice are so searing and revolting that they evoke images of a barbarism that defies civilization.[84] Although the practice has dissipated over the last several decades, it is still carried out in parts of Africa and the Middle East. Given Western stereotypes of barbaric natives in the "dark" continent,[85] Western advocacy over FGM has evoked images of machete-wielding natives only too eager to inflict pain on women in their societies.

The speed, for example, with which the 1994 mass killings in Rwanda took place, and the weapons used, have come to symbolize in the Western mind the barbarism of Africans. Philip Gourevitch, an American journalist, was one of the instrumental voices in the creation of this portrayal:

> Decimation means the killing of every tenth person in a population, and in the spring and early summer of 1994 a program of massacres decimated the Republic of Rwanda. *Although the killing was low-tech—performed largely by machete—it was carried out at dazzling speed: of an original population of about seven and a half million, at least eight hundred thousand people were killed in just a hundred days. Rwandans often speak of a million deaths, and they may*

be right. The dead of Rwanda accumulated at nearly three times the rate of Jewish dead during the Holocaust. It was the most efficient mass killing since the atomic bombings of Hiroshima and Nagasaki (emphasis added).[86]

These images are critical in the construction of the savage. Human rights opposition and campaigns against FGM, which have relied heavily on demonization, have picked up where European colonial missionaries left off.[87] Savagery in this circumstance acquires a race—the black, dark, or non-Western race. The Association of African Women for Research and Development (AAWORD), by contrast, opposed female circumcision but sharply denounced the racism inherent in Western-led, anti-FGM campaigns:

> This new crusade of the West has been led out of the moral and cultural prejudices of Judaeo-Christian Western society: aggressiveness, ignorance or even contempt, paternalism and activism are the elements which have infuriated and then shocked many people of good will. In trying to reach their own public, the new crusaders have fallen back on sensationalism, and have become insensitive to the dignity of the very women they want to "save."[88]

AAWORD vigorously questioned the motives of Western activists and suggested that they were twice victimizing African women. It stopped just short of asking Western activists to drop the crusade, yet openly denounced the use of the SVS metaphor:

> [Western crusaders] are totally unconscious of the latent racism which such a campaign evokes in countries where ethnocentric prejudice is so deep-rooted. And in their conviction that this is a "just cause," they have forgotten that these women from a different race and a different culture are also *human beings,* and that solidarity can only exist alongside self-affirmation and mutual respect (emphasis in original).[89]

As illustrated by the debate over FGM, advocacy across cultural barriers is an extremely complex matter. Making judgments across the cultural divide is a risky business because the dice are always heavily loaded. Not even the black-white pretense of human rights can erase those risks. But since that is precisely what the human rights movement does—make judgments across cultures—there is an obligation to create truly universal standards. Otherwise, the human rights enterprise will continue to present itself as a struggle between the cultures of non-Western peoples and the "universal" culture of the West.

IV. The Metaphor of the Victim

The metaphor of the victim is the giant engine that drives the human rights movement. Without the victim there is no savage or savior, and the entire human rights enterprise collapses. This section examines the victim from the perspective of the United Nations, human rights treaties, human rights law, and, especially, human rights literature. Also, race and the legacy of colonialism, as intertwined in the victim identity, are examined.

The basic purpose of the human rights corpus is to contain the state, transform society, and eliminate both the victim and victimhood as conditions of human existence. In fact, the human rights regime was designed to respond to both the potential and actual victim, and to create legal, political, social, and cultural arrangements to defang the state. The human rights text and its discourse present political democracy, and its institutions of governance, as the *sine qua non* for a victimless society.

On the international level, the United Nations pursues civilizing campaigns that ostensibly seek to prevent conditions that create human victims, to "save succeeding generations from the scourge of war,"[90] to "establish conditions under which justice" can be maintained,[91] and to "reaffirm faith in fundamental human rights."[92] Human rights treaties are therefore a series of obligations assumed by states to prevent the creation of victims. To accomplish this, the state obligates itself to three basic duties for every basic human right: to avoid depriving, to protect from deprivation, and to aid the deprived.[93] The first duty, being negative, may be the least costly and mainly requires self-restraint; the latter two are positive and demand the expenditure of more resources and the implementation of programs.

Human rights law protects against the invasion of the inherent dignity and worth of the potential victim. Regardless of whether an individual is guilty of some offense, the state is not permitted to violate his fundamental rights without abiding by certain state-created norms. The state's culpability extends to individuals and entities within its jurisdiction, whether or not the violation can be traced directly to it. Thus, for example, the state's failure to prevent or punish domestic violence can be seen as a human rights violation.

In human rights literature, the victim is usually presented as a helpless innocent who has been abused directly by the state, its agents, or pursuant to an offensive cultural or political practice.[94] The most visible human rights victims, those that have come to define the term, are subjected to the now numbingly familiar set of abuses: arbitrary arrest and detention; denial of the rights to speech, assembly, and association; involuntary exile; mass slaughter and genocide; discrimination based on race, ethnicity, religion, gender, and political opinion; and denial of due process.[95] Consider this descriptive report of an incident where Iraqi government soldiers randomly selected Kurdish male villagers and executed them within earshot of their wives, children, and relatives:

The soldiers opened fire at the line of thirty three squatting men from a distance of about 5–10 meters. . . . Some men were killed immediately by rifle fire. Others were wounded, and a few were missed altogether . . . . [S]everal soldiers approached the line of slumped bodies on orders of the lieutenant and fired additional individual rounds as a coup de grace. The soldiers then left the execution site, without burying the bodies or otherwise touching them, according to survivors who lay among the corpses.[96]

A basic characteristic of the victim is powerlessness, an inability for self-defense against the state or the culture in question. The usual human rights narrative generally describes victims as hordes of nameless, despairing, and dispirited masses. To the extent they have a face, it is desolate and pitiful. Many are uneducated, destitute, old and infirm, young, poorly clad, and/or hungry. Many are peasants, the rural and urban poor, marginalized ethnic groups and nationalities, and lower castes, whose very being is a state of divorce from civilization and a large distance from modernity. Many are women and children twice victimized because of their gender and age,[97] and sometimes the victim of the savage culture is the female gender itself.[98]

Another example of the images of helplessness and utter degradation of victims comes from a report by AI, detailing the torture and abuse, including rape, of women in detention in many states around the globe. An account from an Israeli detention center, while not unique, is particularly disturbing:

Dozens of Palestinian women and children detained in the Israeli-Occupied Territories have reportedly been sexually abused or threatened in sexually explicit language during interrogation. Fatimah Salameh was arrested near Nablus in July 1990. Her interrogators allegedly threatened to rape her with a chair leg and told her they would photograph her naked and show the pictures to her family. "They called me a whore and said that a million men had slept with me," she said. Fatimah Salameh agreed to confess to membership in an illegal organization and was sentenced to 14 months' imprisonment.[99]

The language of the human rights reports suggests the need for help—most likely outside intervention—to overcome the conditions of victimization. In many instances, the victims themselves deeply believe in and openly declare their helplessness and plead for outside help. A classic example was the case of the Kosovars who sought Western support in their conflict with the Serbian government of Slobodan Milošević.[100] Individual victims serve as more vivid illustrations of this particular victim syndrome. Tong Yi, a Chinese dissident who was jailed and freed in 1997 partly due to the pressure exerted by HRW and the U.S. government, was profusely grateful to Robert Bernstein, the human rights patriarch and founder of HRW, whom she credited with her release. Despite her torturous time in prison, Yi noted that "[i]f there's a smile on my face, it's because of Bob Bernstein."[101]

The victim must also be constructed as sympathetic and innocent. Otherwise it is difficult to mobilize public outrage against the victimizer. Moral clarity about the evil of the perpetrator and the innocence of the victim is an essential distinction for Western public opinion, for it is virtually impossible to evoke sympathy for a victim who appears villainous, roguish, or unreceptive to a liberal reconstructionist project.[102]

In the case of the Kosovo Albanians, the demon was Milošević, the hated autocrat who has refused to join the democratic-privatization dance currently in vogue in the former Soviet bloc. The NATO intervention may have been more intended to oust him and replace him with a "Good Serb"[103] than to save the Kosovars. The Kosovars and their rag-tag band of fighters were painted as defenders of an innocent population against the cruel repression of Milošević. Although Kosovars are Muslims, the press did not employ the stigma of Islamic fundamentalism to discredit their victim status. In stark contrast to this depiction, Chechen fighters have been portrayed as Islamic zealots and dangerous terrorists responsible for bombings and fundamentalist atrocities in both Chechnya and Russia.[104]

The face of the prototypical victim is nonwhite. With the exception of the wars and atrocities committed in the former Yugoslavia and in Northern Ireland, the most enduring faces of human rights victims have been either black, brown, or yellow. But even in Bosnia and Kosovo the victims were Muslims, not Christians or "typical" white Westerners. The images of the most serious suffering seem to be those of Africans, Asians, Arabs, or Latin Americans. Thus, since the Second World War, the major focus of human rights advocacy by both the United Nations and INGOs has been in the Third World in Latin America, Africa, and Asia.

■   ■   ■

The representations of the victim in human rights literature spring from a messianic ethos in both the INGO and the United Nations. There is a colonial texture to the relationship between the human rights victim and the West. In the colonial project, for example, the colonizer justified his mission by drawing a distinction between the "native" and the "civilized" mind. In one case, which was typical of the encounter between Africa and the West, a European missionary compared what he called the "Bantu mind" to that of a "civilized man":

> It is suggested that the mere possession on the part of the Bantu of nothing but an oral tradition of culture creates a chasm of difference between the Native 'mind' and that of civilized man, and of itself would account for a lack of balance and proportion in the triple psychological function of feeling, thinking and acting, implying that thinking is the weakest of the three and that

feeling is the most dominant. The Native seeks not truth nor works, but power—the dynamical mood.[105]

The view that the "native" is weak, powerless, prone to laziness, and unable on his own to create the conditions for his development was a recurrent theme in Western representations of the "other." Early in the life of the organization, an International Labor Organization report concluded, for example, that indigenous peoples could not by themselves overcome their "backwardness." It noted, "[I]t is now almost universally recognized that, left to their own resources, indigenous peoples would have difficulty in overcoming their inferior economic and social situation which inevitably leaves them open for exploitation."[106] In the culture of the human rights movement, whose center is in the West, there is a belief that human rights problems afflict people "over there" and not people "like us." The missionary zeal to help those who cannot help themselves is one of the logical conclusions of this attitude.

The idea that the human rights corpus is concerned with ordering the lives of non-European peoples has a long history in international law itself. More recent scholarship explores this link between international law and the imposition of European norms, values, ideas, and culture on non-European societies and cultures.[107] Since the inception of the current international legal order some five centuries ago, there have been outright challenges by non-European cultures to the logic, substance, and purpose of international law.[108] The development of human rights has only blunted, but not eliminated, some of those challenges.

V. The Metaphor of the Savior

The metaphor of the savior is constructed through two intertwining characteristics—Eurocentric universalism and Christianity's missionary zeal. This section examines these characteristics and the institutional, international actors who promote liberal democracy as the antidote to human rights abuses.

First, the savior metaphor is deeply embedded in the Enlightenment's universalist pretensions, which constructed Europe as superior and as center of the universe.[109] International law itself is founded on these assumptions and premises.[110] International law has succeeded in governing "states of all civilizations, European and non-European,"[111] and it has become "universal" although some have argued that it bears an ethnocentric fingerprint.[112]

In addition to the Eurocentric focus of human rights, the metaphor of the savior is also located in the missionary's Christian religion. Inherent to any universalizing creed is an unyielding faith in the superiority of at least the beliefs of the proselytizer over those of the potential convert, if not over the person of the convert. The project of universality or proselytism seeks to remake the "other" in the image of the converter. Christianity has a long history of such zealotry. Both empire-building and the spread of Christendom justified the means.

> Crusades, inquisitions, witch burnings, Jew burnings and pogroms, burnings of heretics and gay people, of fellow Christians and of infidels—all in the name of the cross. It is almost as if Constantine, upon his and his empire's conversion to Christianity in the fourth century, uttered a well-fulfilled prophecy when he declared: 'In the name of this cross we shall conquer.' The cross has played the role of weapon time and time again in Christian history and empire building.[113]

In fact, the political-cultural push to universalize one's beliefs can be so obsessive that it has been identified frequently with martyrdom in history.

[T]he supreme sacrifice was to die fighting under the Christian emperor. The supreme self-immolation was to fall in battle under the standard of the Cross. . . . But by the time Christianity was ready to meet Asia and the New World, the Cross and the sword were so identified with one another that the sword itself was a cross. It was the only kind of cross some conquistadores understood.[114]

There is a historical continuum in this impulse to universalize Eurocentrism and its norms and to ratify them under the umbrella of "universalism." Whether it is in the push for free markets, liberal systems of government, "civilized" forms of dress, or in the ubiquity of the English language itself, at least the last five centuries can appropriately be called the Age of Europe. These Eurocentric models have not been content to remain at home. They intrinsically define themselves as eternal truths. Universalization is an essential attribute of their validity. This validation comes partly from the conquest of the "primitive" and his introduction and delivery to "civilization."[115] * * *

■   ■   ■

The impulses to conquer, colonize, save, exploit, and civilize non-European peoples met at the intersection of commerce, politics, law, and Christianity and evolved into the Age of Empire. As put by John Norton Pomeroy, lands occupied by "persons who are not recognized as belonging to the great family of states to whom international law applies" or by "savage, barbarous tribes" belonged as of right upon discovery to the "civilized and Christian nation."[116]

The savior-colonizer psyche reflects an intriguing interplay of both European superiority and manifest destiny over the subject. The "othering" project degrades although it also seeks to save. One example is the manipulative manner in which the British took over large chunks of Africa. Lord Lugard, the British colonialist, described in denigrating language a "treaty-making" ceremony in which an African ruler "agreed" to "British protection." He described this ceremony with both parties "[s]eated cross-legged on a mat opposite to each other on the ground, you should picture a savage chief in his best turn-out, which consists probably of his weapons of war, different chalk colourings on his face, a piece of the skin of a leopard, wild cat, sheep or ox."[117] As put by a European missionary, the "Mission to Africa" was "the least that we [Europeans] can do . . . to strive to raise him [the African] in the scale of mankind."[118] Anghie notes that the deployment of denigrating, demeaning language is essential to the psyche of the savior.[119] * * * Human rights law continues this tradition of universalizing Eurocentric norms by intervening in Third World cultures and societies to save them from the traditions and beliefs that it frames as permitting or promoting despotism and disrespect for human rights itself.

■   ■   ■

Human rights are part of the cultural package of the West, complete with an idiom of expression, a system of government, and certain basic assumptions about the individual and his relationship to society.[120] The spread of the liberal constitution—with its normative assumptions and the political structures it implies—makes human rights an integral part of the Western conception of modern society and its ubiquitous domination of the globe.

Institutionally, saviors constitute a broad range of actors and interests which are driven by a belief in the redemption of non-liberal, usually non-European, societies and cultures from human rights abominations. Such actors include those at the intergovernmental, governmental, and nongovernmental levels.

■   ■   ■

Finally, INGOs constitute perhaps the most important element of the savior metaphor. Conventionally doctrinal, INGOs are the human rights movement's foot soldiers, missionaries, and proselytizers. Their crusade is framed in moral certainty in which "evil" and "good" are as separate as night and day. They claim to practice law, not politics.[121] Although they promote paradigmatic liberal values and norms, they present themselves as neutral, universal, and unbiased. Based in the capitals of the powerful Western states, their staffs are mostly well-educated, usually trained in the law, middle-class, and white.[122] They are very different from the people they seek to save. They are modern-day abolitionists who see themselves as cleansers, single-handedly rooting out evil in Third World countries and cultures by shining light where darkness reigns.

INGOs have also been instrumental in the creation of national NGOs in the Third World. Mandates of many national NGOs initially mirrored those of INGOs. However, in the last decade, many Third World NGOs have started to broaden their areas of concentration and go beyond the INGOs' civil and political rights constraints. In particular, domestic Third World NGOs are now paying more attention to economic and social rights, development, women's rights, and the relationships between transnational corporations and human rights conditions. In spite of this incipient conceptual independence on the part of NGOs, many remain voiceless in the corridors of power at the United Nations, the European Union, the World Bank, and in the dominant media organizations in the West.

INGOs occupy such a high moral plane in public policy discourse that they are rarely the subject of probing critiques. Morally righteous, they are supported by an almost universal consensus that they are the "good guys." Even academia has been slow to reflect seriously on INGOs. INGOs and their supporters see those who question them as naive, at best, and apologists for repressive governments and cultures, at worst. This climate of passivity has a chilling effect on human rights speech, particularly of young, probing scholars and activists. It also encourages a herd mentality and compliance with knee-jerk, governmental human rights strategies, positions, or responses. It certainly does not encourage innovation on the part of the movement.

INGOs also play the role of gatekeepers to powerbrokers in the West, including powerful Western states. Significantly, national NGOs have virtually no financial independence. They rely almost exclusively on funding from Western states, foundations, charities, development agencies, and intergovernmental institutions such as the European Union. In spite of these criticisms of INGOs, many non-Western NGOs expressed appreciation for the work of INGOs at a retreat[123] which discussed the roles of NGOs in the human rights movement. In fact, many sought a more involved approach by INGOs.

> The critics sought a more expanded role of INGOs and not an abandonment of their traditional work. No one at the retreat doubted INGOs' contributions to the growth of the human rights movement as a whole and to heightening consciousness about rights in general, thereby influencing the directions and pace of change. No one doubted the vital importance of INGOs' activities: monitoring, investigative reports, publicity, education, and lobbying or interventions before national and intergovernmental bodies.[124]

The lack of a more vigorous and fundamental disagreement between national NGOs and Western INGOs may speak volumes about the leadership of Third World human rights actors. This complacency also does not take into account locally grown, indigenous, "non–human rights" efforts to oppose repression and fight for political and social change. While it is true that INGOs often spoke and agitated for those who were politically voiceless, especially during the Cold War, it would be a mistake to see local human rights activists as separate from the entire human rights project. Opposing that project would be tantamount to self-repudiation. These so-called human rights activists, local collaborators in the civilizing mission, are drawn primarily from the elite in their own societies and aspire generally to the political, social, and economic models of the West. Many of these activists and their organizations are financially dependent on the West, and rely on connections with Western institutions, including the diplomatic missions in their countries, for their social status.

In the last decade in Africa, however, a more politically educated activist and thinker, one who questions the human rights project more seriously and who seeks a culturally grounded program for social change, has started to emerge.[125] This activist and thinker understands the connections among power relations, human rights, economic domination, and the historical relationships between the West and the rest of the world. Such a thinker is aware of the deep contradictions that mark the human rights enterprise and seeks the construction of a different human rights movement. While this new actor is still being defined, and constitutes but a small fraction of the human rights movement on the African continent, he is now increasingly at the center of innovative thinking and action. At the core of this new activism and thinking is the push for intellectual originality and self-reliance, local and not Western foundation support, and a commitment to challenge all sources of violations, be they local or foreign. This development represents the cultivation of a truly local human rights culture in terms of the definition of rights and their enforcement.

VI. Conclusion

■   ■   ■

The human rights movement must abandon the SVS metaphor if there is going to be real hope in a genuine international discourse on rights. * * *

Ultimately, a new theory of internationalism and human rights, one that responds to diverse cultures, must confront the inequities of the international order. In this respect, human rights must break from the historical continuum—expressed in the metaphor and the grand narrative of human rights—that keeps intact the hierarchical relationships between European and non-European populations. * * *

■   ■   ■

Stepping back from the SVS rhetoric creates a new basis for calculating human dignity and identifies ways and societal structures through which such dignity could be protected or enhanced. Such an approach would not assume, *ab initio*, that a particular cultural practice was offensive to human rights. It would respect cultural pluralism as a basis for finding common universality on some issues. With regard to FGM, for instance, such an approach would first excavate the social meaning and purposes of the practice, as well as its effects, and then investigate the conflicting positions over the practice in that society. Rather than demonizing and finger-pointing, under the tutelage of outsiders and their local supporters, the contending positions would be carefully examined and compared to find ways of either modifying or discarding the practice without making its practitioners feel shameful of their culture and of themselves. The zealotry of the SVS approach leaves no room for a deliberative intra-cultural dialogue and introspection.

The purpose of this article is not to raise or validate the idea of an original, pure, or a superior Third World society or culture. Nor is it to provide a normative blueprint for another human rights corpus, although such a project must be pursued with urgency. Rather, the article is a plea for a genuine cross-contamination of cultures to create a new multicultural human rights corpus. The human rights movement should rethink and re-orient its hierarchical, binary view of the world in which the West leads the way and the rest of the globe follows. Human rights can play a role in changing the unjust international order and particularly the imbalances between the West and the Third World. Still, it will not do so unless it stops working within the SVS metaphor. Ultimately, the quest must be for the construction of a human rights movement that wins for all.

NOTES

1. For the purposes of this article, the "human rights movement" refers to that collection of norms, processes, and institutions that traces its immediate ancestry to the Universal Declaration of Human Rights (UDHR), adopted by the United Nations in 1948. Universal Declaration of Human Rights, G.A. Res. 217(III), U.N. GAOR, 3d Sess., 183d mtg. at 71, U.N. Doc. A/810 (1948) [hereinafter UDHR]. The UDHR, the first human rights document adopted by the United Nations, is the textual foundation of the human rights movement and has been referred to as the "spiritual parent" of most other human rights documents.

2. This oppositional duality is central to the logic of Western philosophy and modernity. As described by David Slater, this binary logic constructs historical imperatives of the superior and the inferior, the barbarian and the civilized, and the traditional and the modern. Within this logic, history is a linear, unidirectional progression with the superior and scientific Western civilization leading and paving the way for others to follow. See generally David Slater, Contesting Occidental Visions of the Global: The Geopolitics of Theory and North-South Relations, *Beyond Law*, Dec. 1994, at 97, 100–01.

3. This article hereinafter refers to the "savages-victims-saviors" metaphor as "SVS." The author uses the term "metaphor" to suggest a historical figurative analogy within human rights and its rhetoric and discourse.

4. Each of the three elements of the SVS compound metaphor can operate as independent, stand-alone metaphors as well. Each of these three separate metaphors is combined within the grand narrative of human rights to compose the compound metaphor.

5. The human rights corpus is ostensibly meant to contain the state, for the state is apparently the *raison d'être* for the corpus. See Henry J. Steiner, The Youth of Rights, 104 *Harv. L. Rev.* 917, 928–33 (1991) (reviewing Louis Henkin, The Age of Rights (1990)). Thus the state is depicted as the "antithesis of human rights; the one exists to combat the other in a struggle for supremacy over society." Makau wa Mutua, Hope and Despair for a New South Africa: The Limits of Rights Discourse, 10 *Harv. Hum. Rts. J.* 63, 67 (1997).

6. In Western thought and philosophy, the state becomes savage if it suffocates or defies civil society. *See generally* John Keane, Despotism and Democracy, in *Civil Society and the State* 35 (John Keane ed., 1988).

7. Mutua, Hope and Despair for a New South Africa: The Limits of Rights Discourse, *supra* note at 67.

8. There has been considerable debate among scholars, activists, and others in Africa and in the West about the proper term for this practice entailing the surgical modification or the removal of some portions of the female genitalia. For a survey of the debate, see Hope Lewis, Between Irua and "Female Genital Mutilation": Feminist Human Rights Discourse and the Cultural Divide, 8 *Harv. Hum. Rts.* J. 1, 4–8 (1995); Hope Lewis & Isabelle R. Gunning, Cleaning Our Own House: "Exotic" and Familial Human Rights Violations, 4 *Buff. Hum. Rts. L. Rev.* 123, 123–24 n. 2 (1998). See also Isabelle R. Gunning. Arrogant Perception, World Traveling and Multicultural Feminism: The Case of Female Genital Surgeries, 23 *Colum. Hum. Rts. L. Rev.* 189, 193 n. 5 (1991–92).

9. The human rights movement recognizes only a particular type of victim. The term "victim" is not deployed popularly or globally but refers rather to individuals who have suffered specific abuses arising from the state's transgression of *internationally recognized human rights*. For example, the human rights movement regards an individual subjected to torture by a state as a victim whereas a person who dies of starvation due to famine or suffers malnutrition for lack of a balanced diet is not regarded as a human rights victim. The narrow definition of the victim in these instances relates in pare to the secondary status of economic and social rights in the jurisprudence of human rights. See generally U.N. ESCOR, 7th Sess., Supp 2, at 82, U.N. Doc. E/1993/22 (1992) (criticizing the emphasis placed upon civil and political rights over economic, social, and cultural rights).

10. The art and science of human rights reporting was pioneered and perfected by Amnesty International (AI), the International Commission of Jurists (ICJ), and Human Rights Watch (HRW), the three oldest and most influential INGOs. Other INGOs as well as domestic human rights groups have mimicked this reporting. On the character, work, and mandate of NGOs and INGOs, see generally Nigel Rodley, The Work of Non-Governmental Organizations in the World-Wide Promotion and Protection of Human Rights, 90/1 *U.N. Bull. Hum. Rts.* 84, 85 (1991), *excerpted in* [Henry J. Steiner & Philip Alston, International Human Rights in Context: Law, Politics, Morals 120 (1996)], at 476–79; Peter R. Baehr, Amnesty International and Its Self-Imposed Limited Mandate, 12 *Neth. Q. Hum. Rts.* 5 (1994); Jerome Shestack, Sisyphus Endures: The International Human Rights NGO, 24 *N.Y.L. Sch. L. Rev.* 89

(1978–79); Theo van Boven, The Role of Non-Governmental Organizations in International Human Rights Standard-Setting: A Prerequisite of Democracy, 20 *Cal. W. Int'l. L.J.* 207 (1989–90).

11. Kenneth Roth, the Executive Director of HRW, underscored the savior metaphor when he powerfully defended the human rights movement against attacks that it had failed to move the international community to stop the 1994 mass killings in Rwanda. He dismissed those attacks as misguided, arguing that they amounted to a call to close "the fire brigade because a building burned down, even if it was a big building." Kenneth Roth, Letter to the Editor, Human-rights abuses in Rwanda, *Times Literary Supp.*, Mar. 14, 1997, at 15. Turning to various countries in Africa as examples, he pointed to the gratitude of Africans, who with the help of the human rights movement, threw off dictatorial regimes and inaugurated political freedom. Id. He argued, further, that in some countries, "like Nigeria, Kenya, Liberia, Zambia, and Zaire [now Democratic Republic of the Congo], the human rights movement has helped numerous Africans avoid arbitrary detention, violent abuse, and other violations." Id.

12. This article contends that the participation of non-European states and societies in the enforcement of human rights cannot in itself universalize those rights. It is important to note that the terms "European" or "Eurocentric" are used descriptively and do not necessarily connote evil or undesirability. They do, however, point to notions of cultural specificity and historical exclusivity. The simple point is that Eurocentric norms and cultures, such as human rights, have either been imposed on, or assimilated by, non-European societies. Thus the current human rights discourse is an important currency of cross-cultural exchange, domination, and valuation.

13. Margaret E. Keck & Kathryn Sikkink, Activists Beyond Borders: Advocacy Networks in International Politics 39–58 (1998).

14. See, e.g., Josiah Mwangi Kariuki, *"Mau Mau" Detainee: The Account by a Kenyan African of His Experiences in Detention Camps, 1953–1960* (1963); Kwame Nkrumah, *Autobiography of Kwame Nkrumah* (1973); Mohandas K. Ghandi, *An Autobiography: The Story of My Experiments with Truth* (1957).

15. The author uses the term "cross-contamination" facetiously here to refer to the idea of "cross-fertilization." Many Western human rights actors see the process of multiculturalization in human rights as contaminating as opposed to cross-fertilizing in an enriching way. For example, Louis Henkin has accused those who advocate cultural pluralism or diversity of seeking to make human rights vague and ambiguous. Louis Henkin, *The Age of Rights*, at X (1990). In other words, he casts cross-fertilization as a negative process, one that is contaminating and harmful to the clarity of human rights.

16. Slater argues that the "Western will to expand was rooted in the desire to colonize, civilize and possess the non-Western society; to convert what was different and enframed as inferior and backward into a subordinated same." Slater, *supra* note 2, at 101.

17. For a discussion on the relationship among human rights, political democracy, and constitutionalism, see Steiner & Alston, *supra* note 10, at 710–25.

18. Since the rhetoric is flawed, those who create and promote it wonder whether it will resonate "out there" in the Third World. The use of the SVS rhetoric is in itself insulting and unjust because it draws from supremacist First World/Third World hierarchies and the attendant domination and subordination which are essential for those constructions.

19. For example, Serbs sympathized with former Yugoslav President Slobodan Milošević possibly because they felt he had been stigmatized by the West. Milošević played to locals' fears of the West and used the arrogance of the discourse to blunt the fact that he is an indicted war criminal. See e.g., Niles Lathem, Defiant Milošević: Hell, No, I won't go!, *N.Y. Post*, Aug. 7, 1999, at 10.

20. UN Charter pmbl.

21. Dianne Otto, Subalternity and International Law: The Problems of Global Community and the Incommensurability of Difference, 5 *Soc. & Legal Stud.* 337, 339–40 (1996).

22. I have argued elsewhere that all human cultures have norms and practices that both violate and protect human rights. Fundamental to this idea is the notion that all cultures construct their view of human dignity. What is needed is not the imposition of a single culture's template of human dignity but rather the mining of all cultures to craft a truly universal human rights corpus. See generally Makau wa Mutua, The Banjul Charter and the African Cultural Fingerprint: An Evaluation of the Language of Duties, 35 *Va. J. Int'l L.* 339 (1995).

23. Francis M. Deng, A Cultural Approach to Human Rights Among the Dinka, in *Human Rights in Africa: Cross-Cultural Perspectives* 261, 261 (Abdullahi A. An-Na'im & Francis M. Deng eds., 1990).

24. But genuine reconstructionists must not be mistaken with cynical cultural manipulators who will stop at nothing to justify repressive rule and inhuman practices in the name of culture. Yash Ghai powerfully exposed the distortions by several states of Asian conceptions of community, religion, and culture to justify the use of coercive state apparatuses to crush dissent, protect particular models of economic development, and retain political power within the hands of a narrow, largely unaccountable political and bureaucratic elite. Yash Ghai, Human Rights and Governance: The Asia Debate, 15 *Austl. Y.B. Int'l L.* 1 (1994).

Such cultural demagoguery is clearly as unacceptable as is the insistence by some Western academics and leaders of the human rights movement that the non-West has nothing to contribute to the human rights corpus and should accept the human rights corpus as a gift of civilization from the West. See Aryeh Neier, Asia's Unacceptable Standard, 92 *Foreign Pol'y* 42 (1993). Henkin has written that the United States viewed human rights "as designed to improve the condition of human rights in countries other than the United States (and a very few like-minded liberal states)." Henkin, *supra* note 15, at 74. Elsewhere, Henkin has charged advocates of multiculturalism and ideological diversity in the reconstruction of human rights with desiring a vague, broad, ambiguous, and general text of human rights, one that would be easily manipulated by regimes and cultures bent on violating human rights. *Id.* at x.

25. *See* Robert M, Cover, Obligation: A Jewish Jurisprudence of the Social Order, 5 *J.L. & Religion* 65 (1987).

26. Id. at 69. *See also* John Locke, *Two Treatises of Government* (Peter Laslett ed., Cambridge University. Press 1988) (1690).

27. For examples of critical legal scholarship, see generally Karl E. Klare, The Public/Private Distinction in Labor Law, 130 *U. Pa. L. Rev.* 1358 (1982); Mark Tushnet, An Essay on Rights, 62 *Tex. L. Rev.* 1363 (1984).

28. For examples of feminist critiques of the law, see generally Frances Olsen, Statutory Rape: A Feminist Critique of Rights Analysis, 63 *Tex. L. Rev.* 387 (1984); Elizabeth M. Schneider, The Dialectic of Rights and Politics: Perspectives from the Women's Movement, 61 *N.Y.U. L. Rev.* 589 (1986).

29. For examples of critical race theory scholarship, see generally *Critical Race Theory: The Key Writings That Formed the Movement* (Kimberlé Crenshaw et al. eds., 1995); Kimberlé Williams Crenshaw, Race, Reform, and Retrenchment: Transformation and Legitimation in Antidiscrimination Law, 101 *Harv. L. Rev.* 1331 (1988). For examples of critical race feminism, an offshoot or critical race theory, see generally *Critical Race Feminism: A Reader* (Adrien Katherine Wing ed., 1997); Leila Hilal, What Is Critical Race Feminism?, 4 *Buff. Hum. Rts. L Rev.* 367 (1997) (reviewing *Critical Race Feminism: A Reader* (Adrien Katherine Wing ed., 1997)).

30. For other probing critiques of the human rights movement, see Raimundo Panikkar, Is the Notion of Human Rights a Western Concept?, 120 *Diogenes* 75 (1982); Bilahari Kausikan. Asia's Different Standard, 92 *Foreign Pol'y* 24 (1993); Josiah A.M. Cobbah, African Values and the Human Rights Debate: An African Perspective, 9 *Hum. Rts. Q.* 309 (1987).

31. UN Charter art. 55(c). See also id. pmbl.

32. The UDHR argues in its preamble that it is the "disregard and contempt for human rights that have resulted in barbarous acts" and that human dignity, freedom, justice, and peace can only be achieved if human rights are respected. See UDHR, *supra* note 1, pmbl.

33. As noted by Mary Ann Glendon, the UDHR "is already showing signs of having achieved the status of holy writ within the human rights movement." Mary Ann Glendon, Knowing the Universal Declaration of Human Rights, 73 *Notre Dame L. Rev.* 1153, 1153 (1998). Glendon also notes that "[c]ults have formed around selected provisions [of the UDHR]." Id.

34. Henkin has called this the "Age of Rights" and asserted, unequivocally, that "[h]uman rights is the idea of our time, the only political-moral idea that has received universal acceptance." Henkin, *supra* note 15, at xvii. Alston has argued that the naming of a claim "as a human right elevates it above the rank and file of competing societal goals" and provides it with "an aura of timelessness, absoluteness, and universal validity." Philip Alston, Making Space for New Human Rights: the Case of the Right to Development, 1 *Harv. Hum. Rts. Y.B.* 3, 3 (1988). See also Thomas M. Franck, The Emerging Right to Democratic Governance, 86 *Am. J. Int'l L.* 46 (1992) (arguing not only for the universality or rights but also, to achieve human rights goals, that human rights law *requires* a Western-style democratic government).

35. I have argued elsewhere that although the human rights corpus is essentially Eurocentric normatively and culturally, it might be redeemed through the process of genuine multiculturalization. See

generally [Makau wa] Mutua, The Ideology of Human Rights, [36 *Va. J. Int'l L.* 589, 594–601 (1996).]

36. As noted by Thomas Buergenthal, the rise and development of the human rights movement "can be attributed to the monstrous violations of human rights of the Hitler era and to the belief that these violations and possibly the war itself might have been prevented had an effective international system for the protection of human rights existed." Thomas Buergenthal, *International Human Rights in a Nutshell* 21 (1995).

37. Agreement for the Prosecution and Punishment of the Major War Criminals of the European Axis, Aug. 8, 1945, 59 Stat. 1544 [hereinafter London Agreement].

38. Howard B. Tolley, Jr., *The International Commission of Jurists: Global Advocates for Human Rights* 7 (1994).

39. The International Military Tribunal at Nuremberg was established in 1945 by the London Agreement, resulting from conferences held among the United States, Britain, France, and the Soviet Union to determine what policies the victorious allies should pursue against the defeated Germans, Italians, and their surrogates. London Agreement, *supra* note 37.

40. See Kenneth Anderson, Nuremberg Sensibility: Telford Taylor's Memoir of the Nuremberg Trials, 7 *Harv. Hum. Rts. J.* 281 (1994) (reviewing Telford Taylor, *Anatomy of the Nuremberg Trials* (1992)). Nuremberg has been criticized for the Allies' selective prosecution of war criminals and their inventiveness of the applicable law. Nuremberg also has been labeled a gross demonstration of the powers of the victors over the vanquished. U.S. Chief Justice Harlan Fiske Stone said the Nuremberg trials had a "false façade of legality" and were "a little too sanctimonious a fraud to meet my old-fashioned ideas." Alpheus Thomas Mason, Harlan Fiske Stone; *Pillar of the Law* 715–16 (1956).

41. The European human rights system, which includes the European Commission on Human Rights and the European Court of Human Rights, is central to the European Union. The system was put in place following the atrocities of the Second World War. *See, e.g.,* Buergenthal, *supra* note 36, at 102–73; Laurence R. Helfer & Anne-Marie Slaughter, Toward a Theory of Effective Supranational Adjudication, 107 *Yale L.J.* 273 (1997).

42. See Slater, *supra* note 2, at 100.

43. Id.

44. Denys W. T. Shropshire, *The Church and Primitive Peoples,* at xiii (1938).

45. Id. at 425.

46. Basil Davidson, *Africa in History,* at xvi (1991).

47. Dana G. Munro, *Intervention and Dollar Diplomacy in the Caribbean 1900–1921,* at 76 (1964). William P. Alford, Exporting "The Pursuit of Happiness," 113 *Harv. L. Rev. 1677,* 1678–79 (2000) (reviewing Thomas Carothers, *Aiding Democracy Abroad: The Learning Curve* (1999)).

48. Mohammed Bedjaoui of the International Court of Justice has written, "This classic international law thus consisted of a set of rules with a geographical bias (it was a European law), a religious-ethical inspiration (it was a Christian law), an economic motivation (it was a mercantilist law), and political aims (it was an imperialist law)." Mohammed Bedjaoui, Poverty of the International Order, in

International Law: A Contemporary Perspective 153, 154 (Richard Falk et al. eds., 1985).

49. See generally Otto, *supra* note 21, at 339–40. Note that the UN Security Council, the only organ of the United Nations that wields real power, has been dominated by the United States, United Kingdom, France, and formerly the Soviet Union. China, the only permanent non-European member of the Security Council, has traditionally been isolated by the three Western powers that control it.

50. *See* Jack Donnelly, Human Rights and Western Liberalism, *in Human Rights in Africa: Cross-Cultural Perspectives, supra* note 23, at 31; Virginia Leary, The Effect of Western Perspectives on International Human Rights, *in Human Rights in Africa: Cross-Cultural Perspectives, supra* note 23, at 15.

51. Antonio Cassese, The General Assembly: Historical Perspective 1945–1989, *in The United Nations and Human Rights: A Critical Appraisal* 25, 31–32 (Philip Alston ed., 1992).

52. UDHR, *supra* note 1, pmbl.

53. The human rights corpus has been concerned mainly with the development of civil and political rights in a scheme that leads to the construction of a liberal state. The application of human rights norms appears to lead to the typology of state governed by the project of constitutionalism. Such a state yields the following key characteristics: the government rests on popular sovereignty; accountability for political leadership by the populace is exercised through various devices such as open, periodic, and competitive elections; government is limited through the separation of powers; the judiciary is independent to safeguard the rule of law; and individual civil and political rights are sanctified. See Steiner & Alston, *supra* note 10, at 710–25.

54. See Franck, *supra* note 34; see also Gregory H. Fox, The Right to Political Participation in International Law, 17 *Yale J. Int'l L.* 539 (1992).

55. Franck, *supra* note 34, at 79.

56. Id. at 49.

57. See *Amnesty Int'l, United States of America: Race, Rights and Police Brutality* (1999); *Human Rights Watch & American Civil Liberties Union, Human Rights Violations in the United States* (1993).

58. For example, HRW recently declined to co-publish a study on trade and human rights [Makau Mutua & Robert Howse, *Protecting Human Rights in a Global Economy: Challenges for the World Trade Organization* (2000)], although it had jointly commissioned it with the Montreal-based International Centre for Human Rights and Democratic Development.

59. HRW is the only major INGO to pay some attention to economic and social rights, although its 1996 policy was so nebulous that it has been relegated to the margins. See Mutua, The Ideology of Human Rights, *supra* note 35, at 619. Although HRW has recently reported on corporations and human rights, such activity remains very restricted and highly unsatisfactory. Here, HRW has taken on "easier" or less stigmatized economic and social rights such as labor rights in the Third World—which Western states now advocate because of pressure from organized labor in their countries—and the atrocities committed by oil companies in complicity with repressive governments. The violations of labor rights around the world—particularly in developing and industrializing countries such as India, Vietnam, and Pakistan, to name a few—have become a sort of a *cause célèbre* in the West. The prominence of these violations in the Western press have increased pressure on them to act. Still, INGOs have not tackled the more difficult questions of official corruption within governments, transnational corporations, and the pernicious effects of globalization on the rights to health, the environment, education, and land. In its most important report of the year, a 517-page tome, HRW only devoted a scant five pages to economic and social rights. *See Human Rights Watch, World Report 2000,* at 464–69 (1999).

60. Human rights treaties are negotiated by states and are meant to bind them. States undertake in human rights treaties to respect the rights contained therein. For example, the International Covenant on Civil and Political Rights (ICCPR) gives individuals a multitude of rights and then declares that "Each State Party . . . undertakes to respect and to ensure to all individuals within its territory and subject to its jurisdiction the rights recognized in the present Covenant." ICCPR, G.A. Res. 2200 (XXI), U.N. GAOR, 21st Sess., Supp. No. 16, at 53, U.N. Doc. A/6316 (1966) (entered into force Jan. 3, 1976). All other human rights treaties have similar obligatory language. Thus, although states voluntarily enter into treaty obligations, they are bound by them once ratified.

61. The Iranian constitution provides for the supremacy of the Islamic Consultative Assembly and the Guardian Council over many areas including legislation and the adoption of international agreements. Iran Const. art, 71–99.

62. Makau Mutua, Returning to My Roots: African "Religions" and the State, in *Proselytizing and Communal Self-Determination in Africa* 169, 170 (Abdullah Ahmed An-Na'im ed., 1999).

63. See Elvin Hatch, Culture and Morality: The Relativity of Values in Anthropology 8 (1983). *See also* The Executive Board, Am. Anthropological Ass'n, *Statement on Human Rights*, 49 *Am. Anthropologist* 539 (1947).

64. *See* Burns H. Weston, Human Rights, 20 *New Encyclopedia Britannica* 656 (15th ed. 1992): Mutua, The Ideology of Human Rights, *supra* note 35; [Henry J.] Steiner, *Political Participation as a Human Right,* [1 Harv. Hum. Rts. Y. B. 77, 79 (1988)]; Henkin, *supra* note 15, at x; Jack Donnelly, *Universal Human Rights in Theory and Practice* (1989); Adamantia Pollis & Peter Schwab, Human Rights: A Western Construct with Limited Applicability, *in Human Rights: Cultural and Ideological Perspectives* 1 (Adamantia Pollis & Peter Schwab eds., 1979); Cassese, *supra* note 51, at 25.

65. Steiner has stated that "[o]bservers from different regions and cultures can agree that the human rights movement, with respect to its language of rights and the civil and political rights that it declares, stems primarily from the liberal tradition of Western thought." Steiner & Alston, *supra* note 10, at 187.

66. Convention on the Elimination of all Forms of Discrimination against Women, 1249 U.N.T.S. 14 (entered into force Sept. 3, 1981).

67. Id. at pt. 1, art. 5(a).

68. See generally Convention on the Elimination of all Forms of Discrimination against Women, *supra* note 66.

69. Id. at pt. 1, art. 5(a).

70. U.N. ESCOR, 50th Sess., Agenda Item 11(a), at para. 67, U.N. Doc. E/CN.4/1995/42 (1994).

71. Id.

72. The following provisions of the ICCPR are illustrative: Article 21 on assembly, Article 22 on freedom of association, Article 25 on political participation, Article 19 on expression, and Article 18 on free thought, conscience, and religion. ICCPR, *supra* note 60. The UDHR includes Article 21 on political participation, Article 20 on assembly, and Article 19 on freedom of opinion and expression. UDHR, *supra* note 1.

73. Steiner, *The Youth of Rights, supra* note 5, at 930–31.

74. *Contemporary Forms of Slavery. Working Paper on the Situation of Systematic Rape, Sexual Slavery and Slavery-like Practices During Wartime. Including Internal Armed Conflict, Submitted by Ms. Linda Chavez in Accordance with Subcommission Decision 1994/109,* U.N. ESCOR, 47th Sess., Agenda Item 16, at 2–3, U.N. Doc. E/CN.4/Sub.2/1995/38 (1995). *See also* M. Cherif Bassiouni & Marcia McCormick, Sexual Violence: An Invisible Weapon of War in the Former Yugoslavia (1996).

75. Todd A. Salzman, Rape Camps as a Means of Ethnic Cleansing: Religious, Cultural, and Ethnic Responses to Rape Victims in the Former Yugoslavia, 20 *Hum. Rts. Q.* 348, 349 (1998).

76. Id. at 349.

77. Id. at 349–52.

78. See, e.g., Mutua, *The Ideology of Human Rights, supra* note 35, at 597.

79. For a helpful overview of the investigative processes of INGOs, see Diane F. Orentlicher, Bearing Witness: The Art and Science of Human Rights Fact-Finding, 3 *Harv. Hum. Rts. J.* 83 (1990).

80. None of the major INGOs have located their headquarters in the Third World. AI is headquartered in London; HRW is based in New York City; ICJ is based in Geneva; the Lawyers Committee for Human Rights is based in New York City; and the International Human Rights Law Group is based in Washington, DC. *See, e.g.,* Mutua, *The Ideology of Human Rights, supra* note 35, at 610–12; Issa G. Shivji, The Concept of Human Rights in Africa 34–35 (1989).

81. See Henry J. Steiner, Diverse Partners: Non-Governmental Organizations in the Human Rights Movement 19 (1991), at 22–25.

82. See, e.g., Africa Watch Committee, Kenya: Taking Liberties 362–82 (1991) (calling on the British and American governments to push Kenya proactively toward democracy and more respect for human rights); Alice Jay, Robert F. Kennedy Mem'l Ctr. for Human Rights, Persecution by Proxy: The Civil Patrols in Guatemala 69–71 (Kerry Kennedy Cuomo et al. eds., 1993) (urging the United States to press Guatemala to abolish and disarm abusive civil patrols).

83. Ian Martin, a former secretary general of AI, has expressed disapproval of advocacy strategies that exploit power imbalances. He has argued that although many powerful Western states appear ready in the aftermath of the Cold War to use their economic power to compel Third World states to comply with human rights, INGOs should be suspicious of such offers. "My contention is that this is a prospect which the human rights movement should view coolly. It should avoid aligning itself with the power relationships of an unjust world and it should recognize the ways in which the cause of human rights requires that those relationships be challenged." Ian Martin, The New World Order: Opportunity or Threat for Human Rights, Edward A. Smith Lecture at the Harvard Law School Human Rights Program (Apr. 14, 1993), available at http://www.law.harvard.edu/programs/HRP/publications/martin.html (visited on Nov. 9, 2000).

84. Of the three forms of female circumcision practiced, two are often described in particularly graphic and cruel language. First, the mildest form is "circumcision proper" in which only the clitoral prepuce is removed. Second, *(e)xcisson* involves the amputation of the whole of the clitoris and all or part of the labia minora. [Third,] *(i)nfibulation,* also known as *Pharaonic circumcision,* involves the amputation of the clitoris, the whole of the labia minora, and at least the anterior two-thirds and often the whole of the medial part of the labia majora. The two sides of the vulva are then stitched together with silk, catgut, or thorns, and a tiny sliver of wood or a reed is inserted to preserve an opening for urine and menstrual blood. The girl's legs are usually bound together from ankle to knee until the wound has healed, which may take anything up to 40 days (italics in original).

World Health Org., A Traditional Practice That Threatens Health—Female Circumcision, 40 *World Health Chron.* 31–32 (1986).

85. Images of African savagery, for example, are standard fare in the American press. Reporting on the killings of eight Western tourists in Uganda in March 1999, a journalist characterized the suspected killers as "100 Rwandan Hutus, screaming and brandishing machetes and guns," and expressed surprise that there were not more fatalities "given the killers' barbarism." Romesh Ratnesar, In Uganda, Vacation Dreams Turn to Nightmares, *Time*, Mar. 15, 1999, at 64.

86. Philip Gourevitch, We Wish to Inform You That Tomorrow We Will Be Killed with Our Families 3 (1998).

87. See generally Lewis & Gunning, *supra* note 8; *Jomo Kenyatta, Facing Mount Kenya: The Tribal Life of the Gikuyu* 130–54 (1953).

88. AAWORD, A Statement on Genital Mutilation, in *Third World—Second Sex: Women's Struggles and National Liberation* 217–18 (Miranda Davies ed., 1983). See also Gunning, *supra* note 8; Yael Tamir, Hands Off Clitoridectomy, *Boston Rev.*, Summer 1996, at 21.

89. AAWORD, *supra* note 88, at 218. As further expressed by Lewis:

A primary concern in African feminist texts is the tendency among Western human rights activists to essentialize the motivations for practicing FGS [Female Genital Surgery] as rooted in either superstition or in the passive acceptance of patriarchal domination. In rejecting these characterizations, African feminists seek to recapture and control the representation of their own cultural heritage.

Lewis, *supra* note 8, at 31.

90. UN Charter, pmbl.

91. Id.

92. Id.

93. Henry Shue, Basic Rights: Subsistence, Affluence and U.S. Policy 52 (1996).

94. Images of the victim painted by a recent AI report on refugees are standard fare. In addition to the gloomy descriptions in the report, accompanying pictures show Rwandan refugees in the wild with their worldly belongings on their heads, Afghan and Sri Lankan "boat people" arriving in Denmark, and Sudanese youths caught between government and rebel forces fleeing on a raft. The images of despair and defeat are overwhelming. Amnesty Int'l, Amnesty International Report 1997 3, 11, 17 (1997).

95. For a recent survey of human rights victims, see Human Rights Watch, Human Rights Watch World Report 2000, *supra* note 59.

96. *Middle East Watch, The Anfal Campaign in Iraqi Kurdistan: The Destruction of Koreme* 46–47 (Andrew Whitley ed., 1993).

97. See Amnesty Int'l, Amnesty International Report 1997, *supra* note 94.

98. See Salzman, *supra* note 94, for descriptions of the female gender as the victim.

99. *Amnesty Int'l, Rape and Sexual Abuse: Torture and Ill Treatment of Women in Detention* 4 (1992).

100. A recent poll of Kosovo Albanians found that 52 percent thought that the 1999 American-led NATO intervention, ostensibly to create an autonomous Kosovo, was the most important event for Kosovo in the second half of the twentieth century. NATO Intervention was the Biggest Event, Say Kosovar Albanians, *Deutsche Presse-Agentur,* Jan. 7, 2000, available in LEXIS, News Library, CURNWS File.

101. Meryl Gordon, *Freedom Fighter,* New York, Nov. 16, 1998, at 42. Incidentally, Robert Bernstein claimed the mantle of the savior without equivocation: "When you meet [a victim] . . . you really personalize it. It's not just some person being beat up. You think, *She could be my daughter." Id.* (emphasis in original).

102. Other factors may, of course, enter the decision-making calculus and drive public opinion and determine whether Western states will intervene. It is unlikely, for example, that the West would rush to intervene in a domestic conflict involving a nuclear power such as Russia. For an example of the calculus of intervention, see Editorial, The Intervention Debate, *The Detroit News,* Jan. 10, 2000, at A8 (discussing the rationale for intervention in Kosovo and Rwanda).

103. For a discussion of the "Good" versus the "Bad" Serb, see Thomas Goltz, An Anti-Ethnic Diatribe, 22 *Wash, Q,* 113, 118–21 (1999).

104. Chechnya Reveals Western Hypocrisy, *Toronto Sun, Nov.* 25, 1999, at 15.

105. Shropshire, *supra* note 44, at xix. Or consider, for example, the repugnant views of Lord Asquith, an arbitrator in the dispute between the Sheikh of Abu Dhabi and Petroleum Development Ltd. In his view, Koranic law was primitive at best:

> [N]o such law can reasonably be said to exist. The Sheikh administers a purely discretionary justice with the assistance of the Koran; and it would be fanciful to suggest that in this very primitive region there is any settled body of legal principles applicable to the construction of modern commercial instruments.

Petroleum Development Ltd. v. Sheikh of Abu Dhabi, 18 I.L.R. 144, 149 (1951).

106. Int'l Labour Org., Conditions of Life and Work of Indigenous Populations of Latin American Countries, Fourth Conference of American States Members of the International Labour Organization, Report II (1949).

107. See Ruth Gordon, Growing Constitutions, 1 *U. Pa. J. Const. L.* 528 (1999); Ruth Gordon, Saving Failed States: Sometimes a Neo-Colonialist Notion, 12 *Am. J. Int'l L. & Pol'y* 903 (1997); Note, Aspiration and Control: International Legal Rhetoric and the Essentialization of Culture, 106 *Harv. L. Rev.* 723 (1993).

108. *See* Christopher Weeramantry & Nathaniel Berman, The Grotius Lectures Series, 14 *Am. U. Int'l. L. Rev.* 1515 (1999).

109. *See* Antony Anghie, Francisco de Vitoria and the Colonial Origins of International Law, 5 *Soc. & Legal Stud.* 321 (1996). For example, not only does the world use the Gregorian calendar, but also time is universally calibrated from Greenwich Mean Time. It is the "centrality" of England in the social and political construction of the world that gave rise to designations of places as the "Middle East," "Far East," "remote," and so on.

110. *See* James Thuo Gathii, International Law and Eurocentricity, 9 *Eur. J. Int'l L.* 184 (1998). See also Nathaniel Berman, Beyond Colonialism and Nationalism? Ethiopia, Czechoslovakia, and "Peaceful Change," 65 *Nordic J. Int'l L.* 421 (1996).

111. S. Prakash Sinha, *Legal Polycentricity and International Law* 15 (1996).

112. For a very insightful and pathbreaking discussion of the ethnocentricity of international law, see Antony Anghie, Finding the Peripheries: Sovereignty and Colonialism in Nineteenth-Century International Law, 40 *Harv. Int'l L.J.* 1 (1999). Antony Anghie writes that:

> the association between international law and universality is so ingrained that pointing to this connection appears tautological. And yet, the universality of international law is a relatively recent development. It was not until the end of the nineteenth century that a set of doctrines was established as applicable to all states, whether these were in Asia, Africa, or Europe.

Id. at 1. He writes, further, that:

> [t]he universalization of international law was principally a consequence of the imperial expansion that took place towards the end of the 'long nineteenth century.' The conquest of non-European peoples for economic and political advantage was the most prominent feature of this period, which was termed by one eminent historian, Eric Hobsbawm, as the 'Age of Empire.'

Id. at 1–2. See also Christopher Weeramantry, *Nauru: Environmental Damage Under International Trusteeship* (1992).

113. Matthew Fox, *A Spirituality Named Compassion and the Healing of the Global Village, Humpty Dumpty and Us* 112 (HarperSanFrancisco 1990) (1979).

114. Thomas Merton, Conjectures of a Guilty Bystander 87 (1966).

115. See, e.g., Chris Tennant, Indigenous Peoples, International Institutions, and the International Legal Literature from 1945–1993, 16 *Hum. Rts.* Q. 1 (1994) (reviewing literature on indigenous peoples and concluding, among other things, that indigenous peoples have been represented as the "other" that needs saving by the West).

116. John Norton Pomeroy, *Lectures on International Law in Time of Peace* 96 (Theodore Salisbury Woolsey ed., 1886). Similarly, Edward Said has identified this European predestination in the construction of Orientalism as the "corporate institution of dealing with the Orient—dealing with it by making statements about it, authorizing views of it, describing it, by teaching it, settling it, ruling over it: in short, Orientalism as a Western style for dominating, restructuring, and having authority over the Orient." Edward Said, *Orientalism* 3 (1978).

117. *See* Frederick Lugard, Treaty-Making in Africa, 1 *Geographical J.* 53, 53–54 (1893).

118. A. H. Barrow, *Fifty Years in West Africa* 29 (1900).

119. Anghie, *Finding the Peripheries, supra* note 112, at 7.

120. It is useful here to refer to Steiner's discussion of the connections among liberalism, constitutionalism, and human rights. He notes that all three concepts are linked in that human rights, as it is known today, would not be possible without liberal thought and the notion of constitutionalism. *See* Steiner & Alston, *supra* note 10, at 187–92, 710–12.

121. See Thomas Carothers, Democracy and Human Rights: Policy Allies or Rivals, 17 *Wash.* Q. 106, 109 (1994).

122. *See* Mutua, *The Ideology of Human Rights, supra* note 35, at 613–16.

123. The retreat was composed of human rights activists associated with INGOs. It was held June 5–10, 1989, on the island of Crete, Greece. Steiner, Diverse Partners, *supra* note 81.

124. *Id.,* at 22.

125. Two examples of such politically educated African human rights scholars and activists are James Thuo Gathii, Assistant Professor, Graduate School of Management, Rutgers University, and Obiora Chinedu Okafor, Assistant Professor of Law, Carleton University.

Jack Donnelly
HUMAN RIGHTS AND CULTURAL RELATIVISM

Cultural relativity is an undeniable fact; moral rules and social institutions evidence astonishing cultural and historical variability. The doctrine of cultural relativism holds that some such variations cannot be legitimately criticized by outsiders. I argue, instead, for a fundamentally universalistic approach to internationally recognized human rights.

In most recent discussions of cultures or civilizations[1]—whether they are seen as clashing, converging, or conversing—the emphasis has been on differences, especially differences between the West and the rest. From a broad cross-cultural or intercivilizational perspective, however, the most striking fact about human rights in the contemporary world is the extensive overlapping consensus on the Universal Declaration of Human Rights. * * * Real conflicts do indeed exist over a few internationally recognized human rights. There are numerous variations in interpretations and modes of implementing internationally recognized human rights. Nonetheless, I argue that culture[2] poses only a modest challenge to the contemporary normative universality of human rights.

1. Defining Cultural Relativism

When internal and external judgments of a practice diverge, cultural relativists give priority to the internal judgments of a society. In its most extreme form, what we can call *radical cultural relativism* holds that culture is the sole source of the validity of a moral right or rule.[3] *Radical universalism*, by contrast, would hold that culture is irrelevant to the (universal) validity, of moral rights and rules. The body of the continuum defined by these end points can be roughly divided into what we can call strong and weak cultural relativism.

Strong cultural relativism holds that culture is the principal source of the validity of a right or rule. At its furthest extreme, strong cultural relativism accepts a few basic rights with virtually universal application but allows such a wide range of variation that two entirely justifiable sets of rights might overlap only slightly.

Weak cultural relativism, which might also be called strong universalism, considers culture a secondary source of the validity of a right or rule. Universality is initially presumed, but the relativity of human nature, communities, and rules checks potential excesses of universalism. At its furthest extreme, weak cultural relativism recognizes a comprehensive set of prima facie universal human rights but allows limited local variations.

We can also distinguish a qualitative dimension to relativist claims. Legitimate cultural divergences from international human rights norms might be advocated concerning the *substance* of lists of human rights, the *interpretation* of particular rights, and the *form* in which those rights are implemented. * * * I will defend a weak cultural relativist (strong universalist) position that permits deviations from international human

From *Universal Human Rights in Theory and Practice* (Ithaca: Cornell University Press, 2003), Chap. 6, 89–106.

rights norms primarily at the level of form or implementation.

2. Relativity and Universality: A Necessary Tension

Beyond the obvious dangers of moral imperialism, radical universalism requires a rigid hierarchical ordering of the multiple moral communities to which we belong. The radical universalist would give absolute priority to the demands of the cosmopolitan moral community over other ("lower") communities. Such a complete denial of national and subnational ethical autonomy, however, is rare and implausible. There is no compelling moral reason why peoples cannot accept, say, the nation-state, as a major locus of extrafamilial moral and political commitments. And at least certain choices of a variety of moral communities demand respect from outsiders—not uncritical acceptance, let alone emulation, but, in some cases at least, tolerance.

But if human rights are based in human nature, on the fact that one is a human being, how can human rights be relative in any fundamental way? The simple answer is that human nature is itself relative. * * * There is a sense in which this is true even biologically. For example, if marriage partners are chosen on the basis of cultural preferences for certain physical attributes, the gene pool in a community may be altered. More important, culture can significantly influence the presence and expression of many aspects of human nature by encouraging or discouraging the development or perpetuation of certain personality traits and types. Whether we stress the "unalterable" core or the variability around it—and however we judge their relative size and importance—"human nature," the realized nature of real human beings, is as much a social project as a natural given.

But if human nature were infinitely variable, or if all moral values were determined solely by culture (as radical cultural relativism holds), there could be no human rights (rights that one has "simply as a human being") because the concept "human being" would have no specificity or moral significance. As we saw in the case of Hindu India, * * * some societies have not even recognized "human being" as a descriptive category. The very names of many cultures mean simply "the people" (e.g., Hopi, Arapahoe), and their origin myths define them as separate from outsiders, who are somehow "not-human."

Such views, however, are almost universally rejected in the contemporary world. For example, chattel slavery and caste-based legal and political systems, which implicitly deny the existence of a morally significant common humanity, are almost universally condemned, even in the most rigid class societies.

The radical relativist response that consensus is morally irrelevant is logically impeccable. But many people do believe that such consensus strengthens a rule, and most think that it increases the justifiability of certain sorts of international action. In effect, a moral analogue to customary international law seems to operate. If a practice is nearly universal and generally perceived as obligatory, it is required of all members of the community. Even a weak cosmopolitan moral community imposes substantive limitations on the range of permissible moral variation.

Notice, however, that I contend only that there are a few cross-culturally valid moral *values*. This still leaves open, the possibility of a radical cultural relativist denial of human *rights*. Plausible arguments can be (and have been) advanced to justify alternative mechanisms to guarantee human dignity. But few states today attempt such an argument. In all regions of the world, a strong commitment to human *rights* is almost universally proclaimed. Even where practice throws that commitment into question, such a widespread rhetorical "fashion" must have some substantive basis.

That basis * * * lies in the hazards to human dignity posed by modern markets and states. The political power of traditional rulers usually was substantially limited by customs and laws that were entirely independent of human rights. The relative technological and administrative weakness of traditional political institutions further restrained abuses of power. In such a world, inalienable entitlements of individuals held against state and society might plausibly be held to be superfluous (because dignity was guaranteed by alternative mechanisms), if not positively dangerous to important and well-established values and practices.

Such a world, however, exists today only in a relatively small number of isolated areas. The modern state, even in the Third World, not only has been freed from many of the moral constraints of custom but also has a far greater administrative and technological reach. It thus represents a serious threat to basic human dignity, whether that dignity is defined in "traditional" or "modern" terms. In such circumstances, human rights seem necessary rather than optional. Radical or unrestricted relativism thus is as inappropriate as radical universalism.[4] Some kind of intermediate position is required.

3. Internal Versus External Judgments

Respect for autonomous moral communities would seem to demand a certain deference to a society's internal evaluations of its practices, but to commit ourselves to acting on the basis of the moral judgments of others would abrogate our own moral responsibilities. The choice between internal and external evaluations is a moral one, and whatever choice we make will be problematic.

Where internal and external judgments conflict, assessing the relative importance attached to those judgments may be a reasonable place to start in seeking to resolve them. Figure 10.1 offers a simple typology.

Case 1—morally unimportant both externally and internally—is uninteresting. Whether or not one maintains one's initial external condemnation is of little intrinsic interest to anyone. Case 2—externally unimportant, internally very important—is probably best handled by refusing to press the negative external judgment. To press a negative external judgment that one feels is relatively unimportant when the issue is of great importance internally usually will be, at best insensitive. By the same token, Case 3—externally very important, internally unimportant—presents the best occasion to press an external judgment (with some tact).

Case 4, in which the practice is of great moral importance to both sides, is the most difficult to handle, but even here we may have good reasons to press a negative external judgment. Consider, for example, slavery. Most people today would agree that no matter how ancient and well established the practice may be, to turn one's back on the enslavement of human beings in the name of cultural relativity would reflect moral obtuseness, not sensitivity. Human sacrifice, trial by ordeal, extrajudicial execution, and female infanticide are other cultural practices that are (in my view rightly) condemned by almost all external observers today.

Underlying such judgments is the inherent universality of basic moral precepts, at least as we understand morality in the West. We simply do not believe that our moral precepts are for us and us alone. This is most evident in Kant's deontological universalism. But it is no less true of the principle of utility. And, of course, human rights are also inherently universal.

Figure 10.1. Type Conflicts over Culturally Relative Practices

	Internal judgment of practice	
	Morally unimportant	Morally very important
External judgment of practice — Morally unimportant	Case 1	Case 2
External judgment of practice — Morally very important	Case 3	Case 4

In any case, our moral precepts are *our* moral precepts. As such, they demand our obedience. To abandon them simply because others reject them is to fail to give proper weight to our own moral beliefs (at least where they involve central moral precepts such as the equality of all human beings and the protection of innocents).

Finally, no matter how firmly someone else, or even a whole culture, believes differently, at some point—slavery and untouchability come to mind—we simply must say that those contrary beliefs are wrong. Negative external judgments may be problematic. In some cases, however, they are not merely permissible but demanded.

4. Concepts, Interpretations, Implementations

In evaluating arguments of cultural relativism, we must distinguish between variations in substance, interpretation, and form. Even very weak cultural relativists—that is, strong universalists—are likely to allow considerable variation in the form in which rights are implemented. For example, whether free legal assistance is required by the right to equal protection of the laws usually will best be viewed as largely beyond the legitimate reach of universal standards. Important differences between strong and weak relativists are likely to arise, however, at the levels of interpretation and, especially, substance.

A. Substance or Concept

The Universal Declaration generally formulates rights at the level of what I will call the *concept,* an abstract, general statement of an orienting value. "Everyone has the right to work, to free choice of employment, to just and favorable conditions of work and to protection against unemployment" (Art. 23). *Only* at this level do I claim that there is a consensus on the rights of the Universal Declaration, and at this level, most appeals to cultural relativism fail.

It is difficult to imagine arguments against recognizing the rights of Articles 3–12, which include life, liberty, and security of the person; the guarantee of legal personality, equality before the law, and privacy, and protections against slavery, arbitrary arrest, detention, or exile, and inhuman or degrading treatment. These are so clearly connected to basic requirements of human dignity, and are stated in sufficiently general terms, that virtually every morally defensible contemporary form of social organization must recognize them (although perhaps not necessarily as inalienable rights). I am even tempted to say that conceptions of human nature or society that are incompatible with such rights are almost by definition indefensible in contemporary international society.

Civil rights such as freedom of conscience, speech, and association may be a bit more relative. Because they assume the existence and positive evaluation of relatively autonomous individuals, they may be of questionable applicability in strong, thriving traditional communities. In such communities, however, they would rarely be at issue. If traditional practices truly are based on and protect culturally accepted conceptions of human dignity, then members of such a community will not have the desire or the need to claim such rights. In the more typical contemporary case, however, in which relatively autonomous individuals face modern states, it is hard for me to imagine a defensible conception of human dignity that does not include almost all of these rights. A similar argument can be made for the economic and social rights of the Universal Declaration.

In twenty years of working with issues of cultural relativism, I have developed a simple test that I pose to skeptical audiences. Which rights in the Universal Declaration, I ask, does your society or culture reject? Rarely has a single full right (other than the right to private property) been rejected. Never has it been suggested to me that as many as four should be eliminated.

Typical was the experience I had in Iran in early 2001, where I posed this question to three different audiences. In each case, discussion moved quickly to freedom of religion, and in particular atheism and apostasy by Muslims (which the Universal Declaration permits but Iran prohibits).[5] Given the continuing repression of Iranian Bahais—although, for the moment at least, the apparent end to executions—this was quite a sensitive issue. Even here, though, the challenge was not to the principle, or even the right, of freedom of religion (which almost all Muslims support) but to competing "Western" and "Muslim" conceptions of its limits. And we must remember that *every* society places some limits on religious liberty. In the United States, for example, recent court cases have dealt with forced medical treatment for the children of Christian Scientists, live animal sacrifice by practitioners of santaria, and the rights of Jehovah's Witnesses to evangelize at private residences.

We must be careful, however, not to read too much into this consensus at the level of the concept, which may obscure important disagreements concerning definitions and implicit limitations. Consider Article 5 of the Universal Declaration: "No one shall be subjected to torture or to cruel, inhuman or degrading treatment or punishment." The real controversy comes over definitions of terms such as "cruel." Is the death penalty cruel, inhuman, or degrading? Most European states consider it to be. The United States does not. We must recognize and address such differences without overstating their importance or misrepresenting their character.

Implicit limits on rights may also pose challenges to universalist arguments. Most of the rights in the Universal Declaration are formulated in categorical terms. For example, Article 19 begins: "Everyone has the right to freedom of opinion and expression." To use the hackneyed American example, this does not mean that one can scream "Fire!" in a crowded theater. All rights have limits.[6] But if these limits differ widely and systematically across civilizations, the resulting differences in human rights practices might indeed be considerable.

Are there systematic differences in definitions of terms across civilizations? Do cultures differ systematically in the standard limits they put on the exercises of rights? And if these differences are systematic, how significant are they? I have suggested that the answers to these questions are largely negative. For reasons of space—as well as the fact that such negative arguments cannot be conclusively established—I leave this claim as a challenge. Critics may refute my argument with several well-chosen examples of substantial cultural variation either at the level of concepts or in systematic variations at the level of interpretation that undermine the apparent conceptual consensus. So far, at least, I have not encountered anyone capable of presenting such, a pattern of contradictory evidence, except in the case of small and relatively isolated communities.[7]

B. Interpretations

What ought to count, for example, as adequate protection against unemployment? Does it mean a guaranteed job, or is it enough to provide compensation to those who are unemployed? Both seem to me plausible interpretations. Some such variations in interpreting rights seem not merely defensible but desirable, and even necessary.

Particular human rights are like "essentially contested concepts," in which there is a substantial but rather general consensus on basic meaning coupled with no less important, systematic, and apparently irresolvable conflicts of interpretations (Gallie 1968). In such circumstances, culture provides one plausible and defensible mechanism for selecting interpretations (and forms).

We should also note that the Universal Declaration lists some rights that are best viewed as interpretations. For example, the right of free and full consent of intending spouses reflects an interpretation of marriage over which legitimate

controversy is possible. Notice, however, that the right (as stated in Sec. 2 of Art. 16) is subordinate to the right to marry and to found a family (over which, at this highest level of generality, there is little international dispute). Furthermore, some traditional customs, such as bride price, provide alternative protections for women that address at least some of the underlying concerns that gave rise to the norm of free and full consent.

I would suggest, however, that defensible variations in interpretations are likely to be relatively modest in number. And not all "interpretations" are equally plausible or defensible. They are *interpretations* not free associations or arbitrary, let alone self-interested, stipulations. The meaning of, for example, "the right to political participation" is controversial, but an election in which a people were allowed to choose an absolute dictator for life ("one man, one vote, once," as a West African quip put it) is simply indefensible.

We must also note that considerable divergences in interpretation exist not only between but also *within* cultures or civilizations. Consider, for example, differences within the West between Europe and the United States on the death penalty and the welfare state. Japan and Vietnam have rather different interpretations of the rights to freedom of speech and association, despite being East Asians.

Even where there are variations between two cultures, we still need to ask whether culture in fact is the source of cause of these differences. I doubt that we are actually saying much of interest or importance when we talk of, say, Japan as Asian. Consider the common claim that Asian societies are communitarian and consensual and Western societies are individualistic and competitive. What exactly is this supposed to explain, or even refer to, in any particular Asian or Western country? Dutch or Norwegian politics is at least as consensual as Thai politics. The Dutch welfare state is in its own way as caring and paternalistic as the most traditional of Japanese employers. Such examples, which are easily multiplied, suggest that even where variations in practice exist, culture does much less explanatory work than most relativists suggest—or at least that the "culture" in question is more local or national rather than regional or a matter of civilization.

C. Implementation or Form

Just as concepts need to be interpreted, interpretations need to be implemented in law and political practice. To continue with the example of the right to work, what rate of unemployment compensation should be provided, for how long, in what circumstances? The range of actual and defensible variation here is considerable—although limited by the governing concept and interpretation.

Even a number of rights in the International Human Rights Covenants involve specifications at the level of form. For example, Article 10(2)(b) of the International Covenant on Civil and Political Rights requires the segregation of juvenile defendants. In some cultures the very notion of a juvenile criminal defendant (or a penitentiary system) does not exist Although there are good reasons to suggest such rules, to demand them in the face of strong reasoned opposition seems to me to make little sense—so long as the underlying objectives are realized in some other fashion.

Differences in implementations, however, often seem to have little to do with culture. And even where they do, it is not obvious that cultural differences deserve more (or less) respect than differing implementations attributable to other causes (e.g., levels of economic development or unique national historical experiences).

I stress this three-level scheme to avoid a common misconception. My argument is for universality only at the level of the concept. The Universal Declaration insists that all states share a limited but important range of obligations. It is, in its own words, "a common standard of achievement for all peoples and all nations." The ways in which these rights are implemented, however, so long as they fall within the range of variation consistent with the overarching concept, are matters of legitimate variation. * * *

This is particularly important because most of the "hot button" issues in recent discussions have occurred at the level of implementation. For example, debates about pornography are about the limits—interpretation or implementation—of freedom of expression. Most Western countries permit the graphic depiction of virtually any sex act (so long as it does not involve and is not shown to children). Many others countries punish those who produce, distribute, or consume such material. This dispute, however, does not suggest a rejection of human rights, the idea of personal autonomy, or even the right to freedom of speech.

We should also note that controversy over pornography rages internally in many countries. Every country criminalizes some forms of pornography, and most countries—Taliban Afghanistan being the exception that proves the rule—permit some depictions of sexual behavior or the display of erotic images that another country has within living memory banned as pornographic. Wherever one draws the line, it leaves intact both the basic internationally recognized human right to freedom of speech and the underlying value of personal autonomy.

D. Universality within Diversity

There are at least three ways in which rights that vary in form and interpretation can still be plausibly described as "universal." First, and most important, there may be an overlapping consensus * * * on the substance of the list, despite diversity in interpretations and implementations. Second, even where there are differences at the level of substance or concept, a large common core may exist with relatively few differences "around the edges." Third, even where substantial substantive disagreements occur, we might still be justified in speaking of universal rights if there are strong statistical regularities and the outliers are few and clearly overshadowed by the central tendency.

In contemporary international society, I think that we can say that there are few far outliers (e.g., North Korea) at least at the level of agreed-on concepts. I would admit that overlapping conceptual consensus often is thin. Nonetheless, I think that we can fairly (although not without controversy) say that variations at the level of concepts are infrequent. Somewhat more contentious is the claim that I would also advance that the range of diversity in standard interpretations is modest and poses relatively few serious international political disputes.

We do not face an either-or choice between cultural relativism and universal human rights. Rather, we need to recognize both the universality of human rights and their particularity and thus accept a certain *limited* relativity, especially with respect to forms of implementation. We must take seriously the initially paradoxical idea of the relative universality of internationally recognized human rights.[8]

5. Explaining the Persistence of Culturalist Arguments

If my argument for relative universality is even close to correct, how can we explain the persistence of foundational appeals to culture? If we could explain this puzzle, both for the relativist arguments * * * and for the claims about human rights in traditional societies, * * * the plausibility of a universalist perspective would be enhanced. At least six explanations come to mind.

First, it is surprisingly common for even otherwise sophisticated individuals to take the particular institutions associated with the realization of a right in their country or culture to be essential to that right. Americans, in particular, seem to have unusually great difficulty in realizing that the way we do things here is not necessarily what international human rights norms require.

Second, narrow-minded and ham-handed (Western, and especially American) international human rights policies and statements exacerbate these confusions. Consider Michael Fay, an American teenager who vandalized hundreds of thousands of dollars worth of property in Singapore. When he was sentenced to be publicly caned, there was a furor in the United States. President Clinton argued, with apparently genuine indignation, that it was abominable to cane someone, but he failed to find it even notable that in his own country people are being fried in the electric chair. If this indeed is what universalism means—and I hasten to repeat that it is not—then of course relativism looks far more attractive.

The legacy of colonialism provides a third important explanation for the popularity of relativist arguments. African, Asian, and Muslim (as well as Latin American) leaders and citizens have vivid, sometimes personal, recollections of their sufferings under colonial masters. Even when the statements and actions of great powers stay within the range of the overlapping consensus on the Universal Declaration, there is understandable (although not necessarily justifiable) sensitivity to external pressure. (Compare the sensitivity of the United States to external criticism even in the absence of such a historical legacy.) When international pressures exceed the bounds of the overlapping consensus, that sensitivity often becomes (justifiably) very intense.

Fourth, arguments of relativism are often rooted in a desire to express and foster national, regional, cultural, or civilizational pride. It is no coincidence that the "Asian values" debate * * * took off in the wake of the Asian economic miracle and dramatically subsided after the 1977 financial crisis.

The belief that such arguments have instrumental efficacy in promoting internationally recognized human rights is a fifth important reason. For example, Daniel Bell plausibly argues that building human rights implementation strategies on local traditions (1) is "more likely to lead to long term commitment to human rights"; (2) "may shed light on the groups most likely to bring about desirable social and political change"; (3) "allows the human rights activist to draw on the most compelling justifications"; (4) "may shed light on the appropriate attitude to be employed by human rights activists"; and (5) "may also make one more sensitive to the possibility of alternative" mechanisms for protecting rights (1996: 657–59). I would insist only that we be clear that this is a practical, not a theoretical, argument; that we operate with a plausible theory of culture and an accurate understanding of the culture in question; and that we not assume that culture trumps international norms. "To realize greater social justice on an international scale, activists and intellectuals must take culture seriously, but not in the totalizing, undifferentiated way in which some leaders of non-Western nations have used it as a trump card" (L. Bell 2001: 21).

This leads to the sixth, and perhaps the most important, explanation for the prevalence of culturalist arguments, namely, that they are used by vicious elites as a way to attempt to deflect attention from their repressive policies. And well-meaning Westerners with a well-developed sense of the legacy of Western colonialism indirectly support such arguments when they shy away from criticizing arguments advanced by non-Westerners

even when they are empirically inaccurate or morally absurd.

6. Culture and Politics

So far I have proceeded, in line with the standard assumption of cultural relativists, by treating "cultures" as homogenous, static, all-encompassing, and voluntarily accepted "things," the substance of which can be relatively easily and uncontroversially determined. None of these assumptions is defensible.

A. Identifying a "Culture"

Cultures are anything but homogenous. In fact, differences *within* civilizations often are as striking and as important as those between civilizations. "The Western tradition," for example, includes both Caligula and Marcus Aurelius, Francis of Assisi and Torquemada, Leopold II of Belgium and Albert Schweitzer, Jesus and Hitler—and just about everything in between.

We thus face a difficult problem even in determining what is to count as evidence for a claim of the form "civilization x holds belief y." Political authorities are but one (very problematic) source of evidence of the views and practices of a civilization. Nor can we rely on authoritative texts. For example, the Christian Bible has significantly shaped Western civilization. But even when particular practices do not diverge from what one might expect from reading this "foundational" text and setting aside the fact that such expectations change with time, place, and reader—few Western practices are adequately explained in terms of, let alone reducible to, those texts.[9]

Even the long-established practice of leading states may diverge significantly from the norms and values of the civilization of which they are a part. The United States, for example, is in many ways a very *atypical* Western country in its approach to economic and social rights. In characterizing and comparing civilizations, we must not mistake some particular expressions, however characteristic, for the whole. For example, Christianity and secularism are arguably equally important to modern Western civilization. And the balance between secular and religious forces, values, and orientations varies dramatically with time, place, and issue in "the West."

Such cautions are especially important because culturalist arguments regularly rely on appeals to a distant past, such as the precolonial African village, Native American tribes, and traditional Islamic societies. The traditional culture advanced to justify cultural relativism far too often no longer exists—if it ever did in the idealized form in which it is typically presented. In the Third World today we usually see not the persistence of "traditional" culture in the face of "modern" intrusions, or even the development of syncretic cultures and values, but rather disruptive "Westernization," rapid cultural change, or people enthusiastically embracing "modern" practices and values.[10] And the modern nation-states and contemporary nationalist regimes that have replaced traditional communities and practices cannot be judged by standards of a bygone era.

We must also be careful to distinguish "civilization" or "culture" from religion and politics. The United States is a state, a political entity, not a civilization. Islam is not a civilization but a religion, or, as many believers would put it, a true and comprehensive way of life that transcends culture or civilization. An "Islamic civilization"—centered on Mecca and running, say, from the Maghreb to the Indus—does not include all Muslims, or even all majority Muslim countries. The broader Muslim world, running from Dakar to Jakarta, may be an international political unit of growing interest or importance, but it certainly is not a culture or civilization. And tens of millions of Muslims live outside of even this community.

B. The Politics of Cultural Relativism

Cultures are not merely diverse but are contested. In fact, contemporary anthropologists increasingly depict "cultures" not as "things" but as sites of contestation. "Rather than simply a domain of sharing and commonality, culture figures here more as a site of difference and contestation, simultaneously ground and stake of a rich field of cultural-political practices" (Gupta and Ferguson 1997: 5).

> Culture is usually viewed by the new cultural theorists as contested—a social context in which power struggles are constantly waged over the meaning and control of what Pierre Bourdieu has called "symbolic capital" as well as over more overtly material forms of wealth and power. In short, culture is not a given, but rather a congeries of ways of thinking, believing, and acting that are constantly in the state of being produced; it is contingent and always unstable, especially as the forces of "modernity" have barreled down upon most people throughout the world over the course of the twentieth century. (Bell, Nathan, and Peleg 2001: 11)
>
> All forms of cultural relativism fundamentally fail to recognize culture as an ongoing historic and institutional process where the existence of a given custom does not mean that the custom is either adaptive, optimal, or consented to by a majority of its adherents. Culture is far more effectively characterized as an ongoing adaptation to a changing environment rather than as a static superorganic entity. In a changing environment, cultural practices routinely outlive their usefulness, and cultural values change either through internal dialogue within the cultural group or through cross-cultural influences. (Zechenter 1997: 332–33)

"Culture" is constructed through selective appropriations from a diverse and contested past and present. Those appropriations are rarely neutral in process, intent, or consequences. Cultural relativist arguments thus regularly obscure often troubling realities of power and politics.

Arguments of cultural relativism are far too often made by (or on behalf of) economic and political elites that have long since left traditional culture behind. Even when this represents an admirable effort to retain or recapture cherished traditional values, it is at least ironic to see "Westernized" elites warning against the values and practices they have adopted. There is also more than a hint of a troubling, even tragic, paternalism. For example, "villagization" in Tanzania, which was supposed to reflect traditional African conceptions, was accomplished only by force, against the strong opposition of much of the population.

Even such troubling sincerity is unfortunately rare. Government officials denounce the corrosive individualism of Western values—while they line their pockets with the proceeds of massive corruption, drive imported luxury automobiles, and plan European or American vacations. Leaders sing the praises of traditional communities—while they wield arbitrary power antithetical to traditional values, pursue development policies that systematically undermine traditional communities, and replace traditional leaders with corrupt cronies and party hacks. Rigged elections, military dictatorships, and malnutrition caused by government incentives to produce cash crops rather than food are just a few of the widespread abuses of internationally recognized human rights that do not express, but rather infringe, indigenous cultural values.

In traditional cultures—at least the kinds of traditional cultures that might justify deviations from international human rights standards—people are not victims of the arbitrary decisions of rulers whose principal claim to power is their control of

modern instruments of force and administration. Traditional customs and practices usually provide each person with a place in society and a certain amount of dignity and protection. Furthermore, rulers and ruled (and rich and poor) usually are linked by reciprocal bonds. The human rights violations of most Third World regimes are as antithetical to such cultural traditions as they are to "Western" human rights conceptions.

Relativist arguments became particularly perverse when they support a small elite that has arrogated to itself the "right" to speak for "its" culture or civilization, and then imposes its own self-interested views and practices on the broader society—invoking cultural relativism abroad while ruthlessly trampling on local customs. Consider, for example, Suharto and his cronies in Indonesia, who sought to cloak their version of modern state-based repression and crony capitalism in the aura of traditional culture. In Zaire, President Mobutu created the practice of *salongo*, a form of communal labor with a supposedly traditional basis, which was in fact essentially a revival of the colonial, practice of corvee labor (Callaghy 1980: 490). Macias Nguema of Equatorial Guinea, perhaps the most vicious ruler independent black Africa has seen, called himself "Grand Master of Popular Education, Science, and Traditional Culture," a title that might be comical were the situation not so tragic.

7. Dialogue over Real Differences

The above discussion is intentionally one-sided. I have drawn attention to commonalities and minimized (real) differences. But even if I am correct about the extent of those differences, we must not confuse overlapping consensus with homogeneity.

Furthermore, the fact that differences are *relatively* minor, in the context of the full body of internationally recognized human rights, does not mean that they are unimportant, especially at the level of day-to-day polities. Question about such issues as capital and corporal punishment, the limits of religious liberty, and the dimensions of gender equality merit intensive discussions both within and between states and civilizations.

Should traditional notions of "family values" and gender roles be emphasized in the interest of children and society, or should families be conceived in more individualistic and egalitarian terms? What is the proper balance between rewarding individual economic initiative and redistributive taxation in the interest of social harmony and support for disadvantaged individuals and groups? At what point should the words or behaviors of deviant or dissident individuals be forced to give way the interests or desires of society?

Questions such as these, which in my terminology involve conflicting interpretations, involve vital issues of political controversy in virtually all societies. In discussing them we must often walk the difficult line between respect for the other and respect for one's own values. * * * Here I want to consider a relatively easy case—slavery—in an unconventional way.

Suppose that in contemporary Saudi Arabia a group were to emerge arguing that because slavery was accepted in the early Muslim world it should be reinstituted in contemporary Saudi Arabia. I am certain that almost all Saudis, from the most learned clerics to the most ordinary citizens, would reject this view. But how should these individuals be dealt with?

Dialogue seems to me the appropriate route, so long as they do not attempt to *practice* slavery. Those in the majority who would remonstrate these individuals for their despicable views have, I think, an obligation to use precisely such forceful moral terms. Nonetheless, freedom of belief and speech requires the majority to tolerate these views, in the minimal sense of not imposing legal liabilities on those who hold or express

them. Should they attempt to practice slavery, however, the force of the law is appropriately applied to suppress and punish this practice. Condemnation by outsiders also seems appropriate, although so long as the problem is restricted to expressions of beliefs only in Saudi Arabia there probably will be few occasions for such condemnations.

But suppose that the unthinkable were to occur and the practice of slavery were reintroduced in Saudi Arabia—not, let us imagine, as a matter of law, but rather through the state refusing to prosecute slave-holders. Here we run up against the state system and the fact that international human rights law gives states near total discretion to implement internationally recognized human rights within their own territories.

One might argue that slavery is legally prohibited as a matter of *jus cogens*, general principles of law, and customary (as well as treaty) law. But coercive international enforcement is extraordinarily contentious and without much legal precedent. Outsiders, however, remain bound by their own moral principles (as well as by international human rights norms) to condemn such practices in the strongest possible terms. And foreign states would be entirely justified in putting whatever pressure, short of force, they could mobilize on Saudi Arabia to halt the practice.

This hypothetical example illustrates the fact that *some* cultural practices, rather than deserve our respect, demand our condemnation. It also indicates, though, that some beliefs, however despicable, demand our toleration—because freedom of opinion and belief is an internationally recognized human right. So long as one stays within the limits of internationally recognized human rights, one is entitled to at least a limited and grudging toleration and the personal space that comes with that. But such individuals are *owed* nothing more.

Many cases, however, are not so easy. This is especially true where cultures are undergoing substantial or unusually rapid transformation. In much of the Third World we regularly face the problem of "modem" individuals or groups who reject traditional practices. Should we give priority to the idea of community self-determination and permit the enforcement of customary practices against modern "deviants" even if this violates "universal" human rights? Or should individual self-determination prevail, thus sanctioning claims of universal human rights against traditional society?

In discussing women's rights in Africa, Rhoda Howard suggests an attractive and widely applicable compromise strategy (1984: 66–68). On a combination of practical and moral grounds, she argues against an outright ban on such practices as child betrothal and widow inheritance, but she also argues strongly for national legislation that permits women (and the families of female children) to "opt out" of traditional practices. This would permit individuals and families to, in effect, choose the terms on which they participate in the cultures that are of value to their lives. Unless we think of culture as an oppressive external force, this seems entirely appropriate.

Conflicting practices, however, may sometimes be irreconcilable. For example, a right to private ownership of the means of production is incompatible with the maintenance of a village society in which families hold only rights of use to communally owned land. Allowing individuals to opt out and fully own their land would destroy the traditional system. Even such conflicts, however, may sometimes be resolved, or at least minimized, by the physical or legal separation of adherents of old and new values, particularly with practices that are not material to the maintenance or integrity of either culture.

Nevertheless, a choice must sometimes be made, at least by default, between irreconcilable practices. Such cases take us out of the realm in which useful general guidelines are possible. Fortunately, though, they are the exception rather than the

rule—although no easier for that fact to deal with when they do arise.

It would be dangerous either to deny differences between civilizations where they do exist or to exaggerate their extent or practical importance. Whatever the situation in other issue areas, in the case of human rights, for all the undeniable differences, it is the similarities across civilizations that are more striking and important Whatever our differences, now or in the past, all contemporary civilizations are linked by the growing recognition of the Universal Declaration as, in its own words, "a common standard of achievement for all peoples and all nations." Or, as I prefer to put it, human rights are relatively universal.

NOTES

1. Civilizations seems to be emerging as the term of choice in UN-based discussions. 2001 was designated the United Nations Year of Dialogue Among Civilizations. For a sampling of UNESCO sources, see http://www.unesco.org/dialogue2001/en/culturer.htm. I use "culture" and "civilization" more or less interchangeably, although I think that a useful convention would be to treat civilizations as larger or broader: for example, French culture but Western civilization.

2. * * * I begin by taking at face value the common understanding of culture as static, unitary, and integral. * * *

3. I am concerned here only with cultural relativist views as they apply to human rights, although my argument probably has applicability to other relativist claims.

4. We can also note that radical relativism is descriptively inaccurate. Few people anywhere believe that their moral beliefs rest on nothing more than tradition. The radical relativist insistence that they do offers an implausible (and unattractive) account of the nature and meaning of morality.

5. Gender equality, perhaps surprisingly, did not come up (although these were elite, English-speaking audiences, and Iran has, self-consciously, made considerable progress on women's rights issues in recent years). But even when it does, dispute usually focuses on the meaning of nondiscrimination or on particular practices, such as equal rights in marriage.

6. Logically, there can be at most one absolute right (unless we implausibly assume that rights never conflict with one another).

7. The general similarity of regional human rights instruments underscores this argument. Even the African Charter of Human and Peoples' Rights, the most heterodox regional treaty, differs largely at the level of interpretation and, in substance or concept, by addition (of peoples' rights) rather than by subtraction.

8. Coming at a similar perspective from the other end of the spectrum, Richard Wilson notes that human rights, and struggles over their implementation, "are embedded in local normative orders and yet are caught within webs of power and meaning which extend beyond the local" (1997: 23). Andrew Nathan has recently described this orientation as "tempered universalism" (2001).

9. To cite one example of misplaced textualism, Roger Ames (1997) manages to devote an entire article to "the conversation on Chinese human rights" that manages to make only a few passing, exceedingly delicate, mentions of events since 1949. China and its culture would seem to have been unaffected by such forces as decades of brutal party dictatorship or the impact of both socialism and capitalism on land tenure and residence patterns. In fact, although he cites a number of passages from Confucius, Ames does not even attempt to show how traditional Confucian ideas express themselves in contemporary Chinese human rights debates.

10. None of this should be surprising when we compare the legal, political, and cultural practices of the contemporary West with those of ancient Athens, medieval Paris, Renaissance Florence, or even Victorian London.

REFERENCES

Ames, Roger. 1997. "Continuing the Conversation on Chinese Human Rights." *Ethics and International Affairs* 11: 177–205.

Bell, Daniel A. 1996. "The East Asian Challenge to Human Rights: Reflections on an East-West Dialogue." *Human Rights Quarterly* 18 (August): 641–67.

Bell, Lynda, Andrew J. Nathan, and Ilan Peleg. 2001. "Introduction: Culture and Human Rights." In *Negotiating Culture and Human Rights.* Edited by Lynda Bell, Andrew J. Nathan, and Ilan Peleg. New York: Columbia University Press.

Bell, Lynda S. 2001. "Who Produces Asian Identity? Discourses, Discrimination, and Chinese Peasant Women in the Quest for Human Rights." In *Negotiating Culture and Human Rights.* Edited by Lynda Bell, Andrew J. Nathan, and Ilan Peleg. New York: Columbia University Press.

Gallie, W. B. 1968. "Essentially Contested Concepts." In *Philosophy and the Historical Understanding.* New York: Schocken Books.

Gupta, Akhil, and James Ferguson. 1997. "Culture, Power, Place: Ethnography at the End of an Era." In *Culture, Power, Place: Explorations in Critical Anthropology.* Edited by Akhil Gupta and James Ferguson. Durham: Duke University Press.

Howard, Rhoda E. 1984. "Women's Rights in English-Speaking Sub-Saharan Africa." In *Human Rights and Development in Africa.* Edited by Claude E. Welch Jr. and Ronald I. Meltzer. Albany: State University of New York Press.

Kant, Immanuel. 1983. *Perpetual Peace and Other Essays.* Translated by Ted Humphrey. Indianapolis: Hackett.

Nathan. 2001. "Universalism: A Particularistic Account." In *Negotiating Culture and Human Rights.* Edited by Lynda Bell, Andrew J. Nathan, and Ilan Peleg. New York: Columbia University Press.

Wilson, Richard. 1997. "Introduction." In *Human Rights, Culture and Context: Anthropological Perspectives.* Edited by Richard Wilson. London: Pluto Press.

Zechenter, Elizabeth M. 1997. "In the Name of Cultural Relativism and the Abuse of the Individual." *Journal of Anthropological Research* 53 (Fall): 319–47.

Beth A. Simmons

FROM *MOBILIZING FOR HUMAN RIGHTS*

Human rights underwent a widespread revolution internationally over the course of the twentieth century. The most striking change is the fact that it is no longer acceptable for a government to make sovereignty claims in defense of egregious rights abuses. The legitimacy of a broad range of rights of individuals vis-à-vis their own government stands in contrast to a long-standing presumption of internal sovereignty: the right of each state to determine its own domestic social, legal, and political arrangements free from outside interference. And yet, the construction of a new approach has taken place largely at governments' own hands. It has taken place partially through the development of international legal institutions to which governments themselves have, often in quite explicit terms, consented.

■　■　■

* * * Treaties are the clearest statements available about the content of globally sanctioned decent rights practices. * * * Treaties serve notice that governments are *accountable*—domestically and externally—for refraining from the abuses proscribed by their own mutual agreements. Treaties signal a seriousness of intent that is difficult to replicate in other ways. They reflect politics but they also shape political behavior, setting the

stage for new political alliances, empowering new political actors, and heightening public scrutiny.

When treaties alter politics in these ways, they have the potential to change government behaviors and public policies. It is precisely because of their potential power to constrain that treaty commitments are contentious in domestic and international politics. Were they but scraps of paper, one might expect every universal treaty to be ratified swiftly by every government on earth, which has simply not happened. Rather, human rights treaties are pushed by passionate advocates—domestically and transnationally—and are opposed just as strenuously by those who feel the most threatened by their acceptance. This study deals with both the politics of treaty commitment and the politics of compliance. It is the latter, of course, that has the potential to change the prospects for human dignity around the world.

■　■　■

The Argument in Brief

Treaties reflect politics. Their negotiation and ratification reflect the power, organization, and aspirations of the governments that negotiate and sign them, the legislatures that ratify them, and the groups that lobby on their behalf. But treaties also *alter politics,* especially in fluid domestic political settings. Treaties set visible goals for public policy and practice that alter political coalitions and the strength, clarity, and legitimacy of their demands.

From Beth A. Simmons, *Mobilizing for Human Rights: International Law in Domestic Politics* (New York: Cambridge University Press, 2009). Some of the author's notes have been omitted.

Human rights treaties matter most where they have domestic political and legal traction. This * * * is largely about the conditions under which such traction is possible.

Why should a government commit itself to an international legal agreement to respect the rights of its own people? The primary reason is that the government anticipates its ability and willingness to comply. Governments participate in negotiations, sign drafts, and expend political capital on ratification in most cases because they support the treaty goals and generally want to implement them. They tend to drag their feet in negotiating treaties they find threatening, potentially costly, or socially alienating. Polities participate most readily and enthusiastically in treaty regimes that reflect values consonant with their own. In this sense, the treaty-making and ratifying processes "screen" the participants themselves, leaving a pool of adherents that *generally* are likely to support their goals. Were this not the case, treaty ratification would be empirically random and theoretically uninteresting—a meaningless gesture to which it would be impossible to attach political, social, or legal significance. If we expect treaties to have effects, we should expect them to be something other than random noise on the international political landscape.[1]

Treaties are not perfect screens, however—far from it. Motives other than anticipated compliance influence some governments to ratify, even if their commitments to the social purposes of the agreement are weak. The single strongest motive for ratification in the absence of a strong value commitment is the preference that nearly all governments have to avoid the social and political pressures of remaining aloof from a multilateral agreement to which most of their peers have already committed themselves. As more countries—especially regional peers—ratify human rights accords, it becomes more difficult to justify nonadherence and to deflect criticism for remaining a nonparty. Figuratively, a treaty's mesh widens as more and more governments pass through the ratification screen.

Treaties are also imperfect screens because countries vary widely in their treaty-relevant national institutions. Legal traditions, ratification procedures, and the degree of decentralization impact the politics of the treaty-acceptance process. Because governments sometimes anticipate that ratification will impose political costs that they are not ready to bear, they sometimes self-screen. Despite general support for the goals of a human rights accord, opposition may form in powerful political subunits (states or provinces) that have traditionally had jurisdiction in a particular area (e.g., the death penalty in the United States). Sympathetic governments may self-screen if the costs of legal incorporation are viewed as too high or too uncertain. They may also self-screen if the ratification hurdle is high relative to the value they place on joining a particular treaty regime. The point is this: Two governments with similar values may appear on opposite sides of the ratification divide because of their domestic institutions rather than their preferences for the content of the treaty itself. Treaties may act as screens, but domestic institutions can do so as well.

The most significant claim this book makes is that, regardless of their acknowledged role in generally separating the committed human rights defenders from the worst offenders, treaties also play a crucial constraining role. As in the case of their screening function, they constrain imperfectly but perceptibly. The political world differs in important ways on either side of the ratification act. The main reason is one that institutionalists have recognized since the publication of Robert Keohane's seminal work: Regimes focus actors' expectations. To be sure, the focus can begin to shift during the treaty negotiations.[2] Expectations can begin to solidify further as more governments express commitment to an emerging standard—the process of legitimation emphasized by scholars of international norms and their spread.[3] But expectations regarding a particular government's behavior change qualitatively when that government publicly expresses its commitment to be legally bound to a specific set of rules. Treaties are perhaps the best instrument available to sovereign states to sharpen the focus on particular accepted and proscribed behaviors. Indeed, they are valued by sovereign states as well as nongovernmental actors for precisely this reason. Treaties constrain governments because they help define the size of the *expectations gap* when governments fail to live up to their provisions. This expectations gap has the power to alter political demands for compliance, primarily from domestic constituencies, but sometimes by the international community as well.

The three domestic mechanisms I explore in the following pages are the ability of a treaty to effect elite-initiated agendas, to support litigation, and to spark political mobilization. I think of these mechanisms as ranging from the most to the least elite of processes. In the simplest case, treaties can change the national agenda simply because they raise questions of ratification and hence implementation. International law raises the question: Do we move to ratify and to implement? In many cases, treaties insert issues into national politics that would not have been there in the absence of international politics. Governing elites can initiate compliance, with practically no public participation, if they value international cooperation on the issue the treaty addresses. Treaties are important in these cases, because the national agenda would have been different in the absence of international negotiations.

International treaties also provide a resource in litigation should the government be less than eager to comply. The availability of this mechanism depends on the nature of the domestic legal system and the quality of the courts. Litigation is a possibility where treaties have the status of law in the domestic legal system (or where they have been implemented through enforceable domestic statutes) and where the courts have a degree of political independence. Even in these cases, litigation cannot force compliance. It can only raise the political costs of government resistance by legitimating through indigenous legal institutions the demand to comply. In countries with a strong rule of law tradition, an adverse court ruling can add weight to the pressures a government will experience to comply.

Finally, a public treaty commitment can be important to popular mobilization to demand compliance. Treaties provide political, legal, and social resources to individuals and groups whose goal is to hold governments to their promises. In these pages, I will argue that explicit legal commitments raise the expected value of social mobilization by providing a crucial tangible resource for nascent groups and by increasing the size of the coalition with stakes in compliance. What is more, this effect is greatest in countries that are neither stable democracies (where most rights are already protected and the motive to mobilize is relatively low) nor stable autocracies (where the likelihood of successful mobilization is low if the rights the treaty addresses are seen in any way as challenging status quo governing arrangements). Key here is the legitimating function of an explicit public commitment to a global standard. That commitment is used strategically by demandeurs to improve the rights in which they have an interest.

The central point is this: The political environment most (though not all) governments face differs on either side of the ratification divide. These changes are subtle, and they are often conditional. They involve changes that give relatively weak political actors important tangible and intangible resources that raise the political costs governments pay for foot-dragging or for noncompliance. These changes are not drastic, but they may be enough to encourage women's groups in Japan, supported by a few Diet members who otherwise might not have seized the cause, to press for legislation to address the most egregious forms of employment discrimination in that country. These changes are sometimes just enough to give a small rights interest group in Israel enough legal ammunition to argue before the Supreme Court that "moderate physical pressure" is not allowed under the Convention Against Torture and Other Cruel, Inhumane or Degrading Treatment or Punishment (CAT) and to turn the political tables by requiring the Israeli legislature explicitly (and, one can assume, to their embarrassment) to pass legislation to the contrary. No one, this author in particular, believes that signing a treaty will render a demonic government angelic. But under some circumstances, a public international legal commitment can alter the political costs in ways that make improvements to the human condition more likely.

The argument developed in this book is also conditional. Treaties vary by virtue of the rights practices they are attempting to influence. Some can directly impact the perceived ability of the government to maintain political control. The International Covenant on Civil and Political Rights (ICCPR) and the CAT are two examples that potentially have serious governing consequences for a ruling regime. Broad political rights can empower political opposition; the use of torture can be strategically employed to retain political control or to glean information from various enemies of the state. Governments are much more likely to disregard an international commitment if doing so is perceived in any way to endanger their grip on power or the "stability" of the broader polity. Other accords are less likely to threaten a government's political or security goals. The Convention on the Elimination of All Forms of Discrimination Against Women (CEDAW) and the Convention on the Rights of the Child (CRC) are much more important for their social impact than their direct political implications. Most governments—with the possible exception of theocracies whose doctrines embrace the political and social subordination of women—are far less likely to have a crucial political stake in assuring or withholding rights for women and children than they are to have the uninhibited freedom to oppress political opposition. The more a treaty addresses issues clearly related to

the ability of the government to achieve its central political goals, the weaker we should expect the treaty's effect to be.

Finally, quintessentially political treaties, such as the CAT and the ICCPR, are likely to have their greatest mobilization effects precisely where the conditions exist to gain significant domestic political traction. Treaties alter politics; they do not cause miracles. They supplement and interact with domestic political and legal institutions; they do not replace them. Extremely stable domestic political institutions will not be much affected by a political human rights treaty commitment. On the one hand, in stable autocracies, they are largely irrelevant. Potential political actors simply do not have the resources to effectively demand change. Treaties may have effects if transnational coalitions are thereby empowered,[4] but the chain of demands is attenuated and likely to be weak. This obvious fact is what causes some scholars to conclude that human rights treaties do not have positive effects.[5] On the other hand, in stable democracies, treaties may be readily accepted, but they are often redundant. Because political rights are largely protected—and have been in living memory—treaty ratification adds very little political activity to that already established around domestically guaranteed protections. The point is that treaties have significant effects, but they do not have the same effects everywhere.

I argue that even the most politically sensitive human rights treaties have significant positive effects in those countries where political institutions have been unstable. Treaties alter politics through the channel of social mobilization, where domestic actors have the motive and the means to form and to demand their effective implementation. In stable autocracies, citizens have the motive to mobilize but not the means. In stable democracies, they have the means but generally lack a motive. Where institutions are most fluid, however, the expected value of importing external political rights agreements is quite high.[6] Rights beneficiaries have a clear incentive to reach for a legal instrument the content and status of which are unlikely to change regardless of the liberality of the current government. They also have a basic capacity to organize and to press for treaty compliance. In many cases, these more volatile polities have experienced at least a degree of political participation and enjoyed some modicum of democratic governance. It is precisely in these polities that we should expect ratification of the more political human rights treaties to influence political coalitions, demands, and ultimately government practices. One of the most significant findings of this book is that even the most politically sensitive human rights treaties have positive effects on torture and repression for the significant number of countries that are neither stable democracies nor stable autocracies. International law matters most where domestic institutions raise the expected value of mobilization, that is, where domestic groups have the motive and the means to demand the protection of their rights as reflected in ratified treaties.

■   ■   ■

Humane Treatment: The Prevalence and Prevention of Torture

Cruelty is perhaps the most difficult human interaction to regulate. Whether inflicted on alleged criminals, ethnic minorities, political opposition, or enemies of the nation, torture and inhumane treatment involve relationships of power and vulnerability that frequently resist external intervention. Torture is often one despicable act in a broader, frequently violent, political drama. Perpetrators sometimes view their actions as justified when placed in their broader context. What hope is there for international legal commitments to influence the torture and inhumane treatment of detainees held by public authorities? * * *

The previous [sections] have demonstrated that international legal agreements have had a positive, though limited, effect on the human rights practices of some governments. The crucial difference between gender or children's issues * * * and torture is that the latter is often perceived to have a critical bearing on the ability of the government to maintain order, security, and its own political power. [These sections] will examine whether, and under what conditions, international legal commitments can influence governments' most repressive and coercive tactics to achieve political goals. As we shall see, this is an area in which even the most democratic governments have preferred to retain a degree of discretion, though the ban in international law is absolute.

* * * The first section discusses the problem of torture. Unfortunately, torture is widespread and, for reasons to be discussed, extremely difficult to detect and eliminate. The next section discusses international legal efforts to address this problem. While the prohibition against torture is now widely considered a part of customary international law, one global treaty in particular—the Convention Against Torture and Other Cruel, Inhuman or Degrading Treatment or Punishment (the CAT)—defines and *categorically proscribes* the kinds of practices with which we are concerned here. The third section reviews what researchers now know about the scourge of officially sanctioned or permitted torture. Thanks to data that have been systematically gathered by such NGOs as Amnesty International and by some government agencies (the U.S. Department of State,[7] for example), it has been possible to research the coercive tactics that most governments would prefer to keep hidden from the broader international community.

The centerpiece * * * is an empirical investigation of what role, if any, international law has played in conditioning governmental use of torture. Few scholars or practitioners would expect an external legal obligation to have much leverage over a government intent on coercively cowing its own people into submission by employing extreme physical or psychological cruelty. But the findings * * * are surprising in this regard. As many skeptics would assume, there are certainly conditions under which treaty commitments matter not a (statistically detectable) whit to the governments that use these horrific political practices. But probing deeper reveals something quite interesting: Governments of polities that are partially accountable or in democratic transition are much less likely to use torture if they have made a public CAT commitment than similarly situated governments that have not. This process is examined in the context of Chile, where a brutal regime ratified the CAT before an election and then discovered just how powerful a tool it could be in the hands of activists. I then turn to the case of Israel, a democratic country but one embattled and conflicted over the issue of how to treat individuals held in detention by state security forces. In both of these cases, the evidence suggests that explicit international legal commitments can provide a mechanism allowing citizens to grasp their rights when their governments might prefer harsh repression. International law has its most important consequences in those—by now quite numerous—polities that have had at least a taste of democratic accountability and refuse to allow their governments to turn back.

Torture and International Law

THE NATURE OF THE PROBLEM

Without a doubt, the use of torture by state officials is one of the most horrifying human rights violations imaginable.[8] The use of severe physical or psychological coercion can be sensational but more often it is insidious, as officials deny or minimize and justify their practices in the name of a higher national or political purpose. Despite offending states' efforts to obscure such practices, the right to be free from torture is often listed as one of the physical integrity rights most commonly violated.[9] By some accounts, despite a decade-long campaign by NGOs to expose such practices, by the early 1990s torture continued to be practiced in more than half of the world's countries.[10] The fates of torturers' victims are not usually well known. Some are (intentionally) made to disappear; others remain at a vicious government's mercy for years. Some survive to see a new regime that effectively renounces such policies. Others flee, looking for sanctuary in a new location. By some estimates, 5 to 35 percent of the world's 20 million refugees have experienced torture.[11] And lest we imagine torture to be limited to a few brutal areas of the world, it is important to note that no region is immune. Appalling photos from the Abu Graib prison in Iraq have reminded Americans of the crucial importance of vigilance against the insidious abuse of prisoners. Even Europe, with the strongest legal regime of any region, still presents some surprisingly disturbing cases.[12]

The practice of torture is centuries old[13] and calls for explanation. Torture is broadly understood to mean the deliberate infliction of violence involving severe mental or physical suffering. The purpose of torturing an individual can vary: Jack Donnelly and others have noted that such explanations range from sadism to national security.[14] Psychologists and social psychologists concentrate on the immediate environmental and personal conditions that stimulate individuals to intentionally inflict pain on others. Social psychologists have analyzed the use of torture as they do other forms of human aggression, noting that stress, risk, group conflict, physical discomfort, and the belief that cherished values are at stake are conditions that can provoke the use of intentional pain on detainees.[15] Sociologists have analyzed torture as an institution used to "deculturate" a society by silencing the dominant group's cultural enemies and breaking down rival cultural identities.[16] Perhaps this is why some studies suggest that physically harsh repression is more prevalent in culturally and racially diverse societies than in more homogeneous ones.[17] Political scientists have tended to analyze torture as a practice used to achieve particular political or governing goals, especially as a means of maintaining order, security, or power by cowing political opposition. In the United States, torture has most recently been discussed as a way to "exploit [detainees] for actionable intelligence"[18] essential to the country's national security.[19] Social scientists have tried to explain why torture is appallingly widespread and to model the conditions under which it can become increasingly sadistic.[20]

The use of torture is a very difficult phenomenon to study in an objective and systematic way. Given the negative connotation modern societies attach to the use of intentionally painful coercive practices, completely frank discussions about official torture are extraordinarily rare. Even governments that have accepted the obligation under the CAT to report to the Committee Against Torture hardly expose their shortcomings gladly; more complete disclosures are usually left to "shadow reports" submitted by various nongovernmental human rights organizations.[21] Simply put: Every government has an incentive to minimize the seriousness of their own abuses; ironically, it is the most open governments that are most likely to allow the kind of access from which the more highly critical shadow reports can be written.[22] Furthermore, even if we can all agree that torture is abhorrent, people differ over exactly what it is. Whether a particular practice constitutes "maltreatment," "abuse," or is serious enough to be termed "torture" can be highly contentious in all but the most extreme cases.

Controlling the practice of torture—even among governments willing to do so—is quite difficult because of the highly decentralized way in which it is carried out. Certainly, torture is more likely to be systematic and widespread where governments encourage or condone such practices. But even when they do not, even when official policy actively opposes torture, the act of torture itself may be carried out in innumerable police stations, detention centers, or prisons around a country. It can be very difficult to make official policy effective in such highly decentralized settings. In their study of Latin American transitions, Ellen Lutz and Kathryn Sikkink found that although torture was explicitly prohibited by treaty and implemented in domestic legislation, eliminating such practices lagged behind progress in other, less legalized but more public areas, such as democratic elections. They point precisely to this problem of decentralization, noting that even a government that *wants* to comply with legal prohibitions against torture may find it difficult to control the actions taken in multiple police precincts across a country.[23]

INTERNATIONAL LEGAL EFFORTS TO PROHIBIT TORTURE

The prohibition against torture has been a part of the international human rights regime since its post–World War II inception. The UDHR addressed torture in Article 5, which states, "No one shall be subjected to torture or to cruel, inhuman or degrading treatment or punishment."[24] But because the declaration is a broad statement of principles, it neither defines torture nor provides any hint of enforcement. The first treaty to mention torture in peacetime was the ICCPR, whose Article 7 provides that "No one shall be subjected to torture or to cruel, inhuman or degrading treatment or punishment." In light of Nazi practices in the 1930s and 1940s, Article 7 went on to provide that "In particular, no one shall be subjected without his free consent to medical or scientific experimentation." As discussed in Chapter 5, the ICCPR created the Human Rights Committee and, for the first time, began a system of oversight (largely through state reporting). The ICCPR did not enter into force until 1976, however, and by that time, a concerted effort was underway, led by Amnesty International, to draft and promulgate a convention specifically designed to eliminate torture.[25]

From 1972, Amnesty International was a central advocate for, and ultimately an influential architect of, the international legal regime to ban torture.[26] Amnesty's campaign focused on key national legislatures (for example, the U.S. Congress), as well as the UN, in essence urging these bodies to take the problem much more seriously. Amnesty succeeded in arranging a joint UN–NGO Conference for the Abolition of Torture in 1973, which by most accounts was successful in publicizing the issue.[27] Soon thereafter, the governments of Sweden and the Netherlands took an especially active role, urging the UNGA to pass the Declaration on the Protection of All Persons from Being Subjected to Torture and Other Cruel, Inhuman, or Degrading Treatment or Punishment in December 1975.[28] The first article contained, in embryonic form, the definition of torture that would eventually make its way into the world's first binding treaty devoted to the subject. This declaration also proclaimed torture to be unjustifiable under any circumstances[29]—language that eventually became enshrined in treaty law.

The CAT is without doubt the premiere universal effort on the part of the international community to guarantee individuals a right to be free from torture and to ban its practice. On 4 February 1985, the convention was opened for signature at UN headquarters in New York City. Representatives of twenty-five states signed early that year.[30]

The CAT is the first international and legally binding effort to define torture. Article 1, paragraph 1 says:

Torture means any act by which severe pain or suffering, whether physical or mental, is intentionally inflicted on a person for such purposes as obtaining from him or a third person information or a confession, punishing him for an act he or a third person has committed or is suspected of having committed, or intimidating or coercing him or a third person, or for any reason based on discrimination of any kind, when such pain or suffering is inflicted by or at the instigation of or with the consent or acquiescence of a public official or other person acting in an official capacity. It does not include pain or suffering arising only from, inherent in or incidental to lawful sanctions.[31]

Article 2 makes it clear that the prohibition contained in the treaty is absolute. The convention is aimed at *official* or *officially condoned* or permitted torture.[32] Torture cannot be justified under any circumstances, including war, internal political instability, or any other public emergency,[33] nor can it be justified by orders from a superior public authority.[34]

■   ■   ■

The CAT takes three approaches to enforcement. First, it establishes universal jurisdiction for the crime of torture. Article 5 of the treaty requires nations either to extradite or to prosecute alleged torturers within their boundaries, *regardless of where their crimes took place.*[35] In theory, this means that torturers have no place to hide; they can be held legally accountable for their actions if they enter the jurisdiction of any party to the treaty. Article 5 was successfully used in Pinochet's prosecution, for example, illustrating that heads of state are not immune from the CAT's provisions.[36] In practice, of course, governments may be reluctant to prosecute torturers for political reasons, especially if they are former heads of state.[37] Nonetheless, most analysts have hailed universal jurisdiction as an important and innovative way to enforce the treaty's provisions.[38]

The CAT also contains two optional enforcement mechanisms. First, any state party may declare under Article 21 that it "recognizes the competence of the Committee to receive and consider communications to the effect that a State Party claims that another State Party is not fulfilling its obligations under this Convention." The committee is directed under Article 21 to handle such complaints in a dispute settlement rather than an enforcement mode. Its decisions are not binding on either party. Despite the fact that 53 states have to date made an Article 21 declaration,[39] this procedure has *never* been invoked.

The second optional enforcement mechanism is for state parties to declare themselves bound under Article 22 ". . . to recognize the competence of the Committee to receive and consider communications from or on behalf of individuals subject to its jurisdiction who claim to be victims of a violation by a State Party of the provisions of the Convention."[40] Such a declaration, in effect, gives individuals standing to complain about a state's behavior to the Committee Against Torture. Some 56 states have made such a declaration, and as of April 2004, the committee has received 241 complaints. Sweden, Switzerland, and Canada head the list of countries complained against, indicating that this provision may be most relevant to those individuals already in possession of a fairly strong sense of their rights.[41]

THE STATE OF RESEARCH

Relatively little cross-national research has been done to try to explain the prevalence and patterns of state-sponsored torture, and attention to the role of international legal commitments has been even more scant. * * *

Only two studies have addressed the role of international law in affecting governments' physical integrity rights violations, and only one of these deals specifically with torture. Linda Camp Keith's study of the ICCPR found differences across signatories and nonsignatories, but found no improvement in physical integrity rights among signatories before and after treaty ratification.[42] The only study to directly examine the effect of the CAT on practices that are specifically banned by that convention is that of Oona Hathaway. Her work does not support the proposition that making a commitment to the CAT has much effect on the propensity to torture. Quite the contrary: She concluded her study by noting that "the torture and genocide conventions appear to have the smallest impact on human rights practices of all the universal conventions."[43] * * *

Hathaway's explanation for the CAT's null effect is that governments ratify human rights conventions to express their symbolic support for their principles as well as to reduce criticism attendant upon remaining formally outside the conventions. But compliance theorists have noted the logical oddities in such an argument, at least as a general explanation. The single most puzzling problem is why any government would sign an international treaty thinking that this would be sufficient to deflect criticism from their practices.[44] As I have [previously] argued, the empirical record with respect to treaty ratification seems to suggest a completely different dynamic: NGOs have campaigned hard for ratification (notably Amnesty International in the case of the CAT)[45] because they believe it will give them greater moral, legal, and political leverage over states than would have been the case otherwise. The evidence does not seem to support the contention that ratification alone satisfies antitorture groups that their mission has been accomplished.

A more reasonable expectation is that an international commitment to eschew the practice of torture is effective under some conditions and not under others. *Some* governments may ratify the CAT for expressive purposes; these are likely to be those polities already quite committed to the treaty's provisions. They do not need an international commitment to influence their policies: A credible commitment to abstain from torture can be generated from within the domestic political system itself. The Swedens, Netherlands, and Costa Ricas of the world may sign as an expression of their commitment to humane treatment and their desire to influence others to do the same,[46] but so many internal checks on torture are in place that an international treaty is superfluous. On the other hand, *some* governments may believe (wrongly in many if not most cases) that ratification will earn them some cheap credit with the international community. In both cases, ratification should not be expected to alter behavior significantly: Those with the best records will continue to eschew torture, while the few looking for cheap international kudos will continue to behave badly. Under these conditions, the motives for signing and the propensity to torture will differ radically, but the behavioral observation—no apparent treaty effect—will be the same.

Many governments are neither stable compliers nor cynical signers. They rule polities with *some* experience with democratic principles and human rights. Their populations have in many cases had *some* exposure to the rule of law, as well as a degree of governmental accountability, and value international obligations as a way to help secure greater human rights guarantees. As I have argued, [earlier], international legal instruments can mobilize individuals and groups to demand their rights under the treaty's provision. This is especially true in the case of torture. Experiences of pain and loss cut to the core of everyday lives, and when such suffering is the result of torture, these feelings can occupy a prominent place in the domains of public opinion and issue activism.[47] Civil society is *provokable* in these countries, and citizens have enough freedom to be able to act according to their values and in their perceived interests. In these cases, one might expect a convention against torture to have real effects on government practices.

There are good theoretical reasons to take another look at the effect of ratification of the CAT,

specifying clearly the conditions under which we might expect it to have real consequences for the polity. Torture is about political and social control. The CAT should have its strongest positive effects in places where control is contested—where politics are most unstable and precarious for the governing elite. Neither stable democracies nor complete autocracies fit this description. Rather, we should expect a commitment to the CAT to matter most where political regimes are in flux. The next section tests this idea and reveals treaty effects that earlier studies have obscured.

Data and Methods

THE DEPENDENT VARIABLE: TORTURE SCALE

As defined by the CAT, torture is the intentional and coercive inflicting of severe pain or suffering by a government authority acting in his or her official capacity on another person or persons. The CAT specifically excludes pain or suffering caused by "lawful sanctions." Two sources have long collected information useful in developing a torture measure: NGOs (Amnesty International, in particular) and the U.S. Department of State. Oona Hathaway's work depended on the latter, which does not differ significantly from information collected by nongovernmental sources. Indeed, the Department of State to a large extent bases its own reports on information supplied at least in part by NGOs.[48] Since her measure is designed specifically to tap compliance with the CAT, I have extended Hathaway's data through 2002.

The dependent variable is a five-category measure that captures the pervasiveness of the practice of torture by government officials.[49] The worst cases (Category 1) are those in which torture (including severe beatings) was considered "prevalent" and "widespread."[50] The next category (Category 2) includes cases in which torture was considered "common," there were widespread reports of beatings to death, or other beatings and other forms of abusive treatment were quite routine. The third category involves those cases in which there was some reference (without specified frequency) to maltreatment, or common beatings or isolated reports of severe beatings (e.g., to death). The fourth category includes those cases in which abuses were occasional or there were possible cases of beatings (though never to death). And finally, the fifth category involves the best cases, those in which serious abuses were never reported, though isolated cases of a less serious nature were on rare occasions reported and responded to with disciplinary action. Table 10.1 summarizes the criteria used for the torture scale.

Figure 10.2 gives a sense of how torture practices have compared with CAT ratification since 1985. Apparently, the number of treaty adherents has increased even as the global average of torture practices has deteriorated. The question addressed here, though, is whether committing to the CAT improves practices among the committed or whether there are any conditions under which commitment improves practices, controlling for other explanations and influences. If governments are influenced by their international legal commitments, we should see a positive relationship, indicative of improvement, when countries ratify the CAT.

CONDITIONING EFFECTS: REGIME TYPE AND JUDICIAL INSTITUTIONS

The central hypothesis of this chapter is that human rights treaties need at least some domestic political traction to have significant positive effects. They are not likely to change behavior in countries with stable dictatorships or in countries that reliably ensure the political accountability of leaders and other agents of the state. Legal constraints are largely ignored in the former and are redundant in the latter. * * * I distinguish three kinds of historical regime experiences. First, I distinguish countries that have been stable democracies for the entire post–World War II period or, if newly independent since 1945, democratic for their whole independent existence. I code them as "stable democracies" if their democracy score never goes below 8 in the polity dataset during the post–World War II period. Next, countries are never democratic if they have never had a democracy score above 5. I would expect a treaty commitment to have very little effect in either of these cases. That leaves the unstable, transitionally or partially democratic "middle"—a category that includes a large number of countries * * * Many of these are countries transitioning toward democracy; a smaller number are moving in the opposite direction. A few are fairly stable partial democracies. I run additional tests later to see whether volatility or partial democracy seems to account most fully for the observed effects of the CAT in this cluster of regimes.

THE STATISTICAL MODELS

One of the most serious problems associated with trying to estimate treaty effects accurately is that, with a few exceptions, the same factors that lead to ratification are likely to explain compliance * * *. Thus, it is important to use a statistical model that endogenizes the ratification choice itself and to "identify" the model with instruments that can help distinguish ratification from compliance. Two of the most reliable factors that influence ratification, as we have seen, are the nature of the legal system[51] and treaty ratification of other states in the region. These are the two variables I use to explain ratification in the first equation of a two-stage least squares model. The second-stage equation tests the hypotheses for the CAT's influence that were developed previously. I expect the CAT to improve torture practices; hence, we should expect a positive relationship between the CAT and the torture scale. * * *

Table 10.1. Torture Prevalence: The Dependent Variable

NOTE: IN EACH CASE, AT LEAST ONE OF THE FOLLOWING MUST BE TRUE:

Type of Activity	Category 1	Category 2	Category 3	Category 4	Category 5
Psychological mistreatment		Frequent, often	Used without reference to frequency	Sometimes, occasional	Isolated reports with disciplinary response
Rough handling, other abuse		Frequent, routine	Regular brutality, severe maltreatment of prisoners	Sometimes, occasional	Isolated reports with disciplinary response
Beatings		Frequent, routine	Common (or not uncommon), numerous reports	Allegations or indications (any reported—regardless of redress)	Isolated reports with disciplinary response
Torture	Prevalent, widespread, repeated, methodical	Common, several reports, numerous allegations	Some, occasional (unless redressed)	Unsubstantiated; unlikely true; isolated, with redress	None
Abused to death	Common, frequent, many, widespread	Some, occasional incidents, several reports	Isolated reports	None	None

Note: This presentation inverts the original scale so that higher scores represent better practices.

Source: Hathaway 2002.

Figure 10.2. CAT Ratifications and the Torture Scale

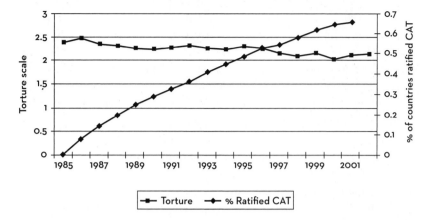

Source: Ratification status for the CAT: Office of the UN Commission for Human Rights, http://www.ohchr.org/english/countries/ratification /9.htm. Torture Scale (measuring torture prevalence): Hathaway 2002 (inverted scale).

■   ■   ■

CONTROLS

A series of control variables are included in all specifications to reduce the possibility of erroneously attributing causal significance to ratification of the CAT. Certainly, the basic causal explanations for the prevalence of torture are not likely to be an international legal commitment, but rather institutional and social features of each country, as well as each government's perceived threats to national security or to its hold on political power. No one should expect international law to overcome these basic conditions; rather, the question is, once we control for these conditions, does a treaty commitment make any difference to the prevalence of torture on the margins?

A first set of controls speaks to the country's domestic institutions. The primary hypotheses have to do with degree of democratic accountability and the rule of law, but other domestic institutions could matter as well. Most important here are institutions that make it difficult for a government to torture its citizens without some resistance. Besides regime characteristics, accountability could plausibly be influenced by a free press. Torture is much less likely to be widespread in countries in which the press can expose and criticize the government without censorship or fear of reprisals or harassment. A free press can both expose abuse and remind a people that its government is violating international accords to which it is legally committed.[52] * * *

National truth commissions can be used in exceptional circumstances to try to address the widespread use of torture and related rights abuses. A truth commission is a domestically generated effort to come to terms with an oppressive and violent past. The creation of such a commission presumably signals a commitment to acknowledge past abuses, set the record straight, and place the country on a more just path. Truth commissions can certainly be aimed at injustices other than torture, but they are frequently set up specifically to address egregious human rights abuses.[53] If they are successful, we might expect torture practices to be ameliorated once a commission is established.* * *

The second set of controls relate to a country's security situation. One of the classic justifications for using coercive tactics against detainees is either to silence or to wrench information from various groups or individuals the government considers its or the country's enemies. War also gives rise to physical and social conditions that are linked to individual aggression.[54] Even countries that eschew torture under normal circumstances can find justifications for its use when the nation is at war.[55] Practically every study on human rights notes that they deteriorate during wartime.[56] We should therefore expect the use of torture to spread and become more intense during a violent conflict. Indicators for both international and civil wars are therefore included in the following analysis.* * *

A third set of controls relate to potential external levers of influence over a country's torture practices. Countries that receive large amounts of foreign aid or that trade extensively with wealthy democracies could be discouraged from using brutal interrogation practices if these partners publicize these practices and/or threaten sanctions. I therefore include overseas development aid as a proportion of GDP and the total number of preferential trade agreements as potential sources of external leverage over rights practices.

Among potential external levers, the international community working through the UN has developed mechanisms to investigate, expose, and embarrass governments about their repressive practices. Three major UN mechanisms could potentially have an influence on a country's propensity to torture.[57] The first is the UNGA's use of specific resolutions criticizing a country by name for some aspect of its human rights record.* * *

The second mechanism the international community has at its disposal for influencing countries' most egregious human rights practices is what is known as a 1503 Investigation.* * *

[The aim of this procedure] is to identify countries in which serious abuses are occurring rather than provide a remedy for those complaining of human rights violations.[58]

Third, since the 1980s, the special rapporteur on torture has been available to provide visits to countries that evidence indicates have indulged in torture on a systematic basis.* * *

Finally, I control for a country's developmental level, as measured by its GDP per capita, the size of its population (a large population could explain Amnesty International's ability to tally up large numbers of torture cases), and average regional trends (average torture score in the region in the previous period).

Statistical Findings

PARTIALLY DEMOCRATIC/ TRANSITION REGIMES

The first point that these analyses confirm is that committing one's state to honor the CAT does not have a positive effect on torture practices in all kinds of regimes. *The CAT does not have unconditional effects.*[59] In fact, in a lightly controlled model * * *, the CAT appears to be mildly *negative* (though not significantly so). But if ratifying the CAT appears to have no positive effect across the board, it does seem to have important effects *under certain political conditions.* Whereas we might not expect a CAT commitment to have much of an effect in a stable democracy—with well-developed and highly stable channels of political accountability— and while it may not be realistic to expect an international legal obligation to matter much in a polity that has never experienced any degree of political accountability, we can test the proposition that *ratifying the CAT helps significantly to reduce torture in polities with some experience with or prospect for a degree of political accountability.* These are the regimes in which domestic groups and stakeholders have both the motive and the means to organize to demand compliance with the CAT.

[Analysis suggests] that the CAT may indeed have an important impact on the severity of torture practices for countries with only moderately accountable institutions. * * * There is practically no influence of ratifying the CAT in stable democracies * * * and countries that have never been democratic* * *. It is fairly clear that ratifying the CAT does not help much in stable democracies or stable autocracies. For the most part, there is no significant difference within these categories between ratifiers and nonratifiers.[60] In fact, for countries that have never been democratic, the model with a full set of controls suggests that ratification likely has no effect whatsoever. Evidently, these are the governments most likely to believe that they can ratify the CAT strategically.

The results for countries in transition provide a sharp contrast. For these countries, it is fairly clear that those that ratify the CAT are much more likely to improve their practices (reduce their incidence of torture) than transitional countries that do not. Statistically speaking, we can be fairly confident (about 94 percent confident) that among transitional countries, CAT ratifiers' practices become much better than those of nonratifiers. Ratification of the CAT is associated with almost a 40 percent increase in the likelihood that a country will improve by one category on the torture scale. Among the control variables, the only consistent explanation appears to be the importance of information, as indicated by the strong positive effect of a relatively free press. The use of truth commissions may also be associated with future reductions in the use of torture, increasing the chances of moving from one category on the scale by about 15 percent. Surprisingly, neither international nor civil wars mattered significantly in these specifications for the transition countries. Nor did any of the UN mechanisms have much impact in these countries.

■   ■   ■

It is natural to wonder, what drives the "transitional" result: the fact that the country is partially democratic, and thus individuals and groups have both the motives and the means to demand greater respect and protection from their government? Or is it that they are unstable, and treaties—especially treaties guaranteeing a right not to be tortured—are a way to stabilize antitorture norms? In order to get at the mechanism involved, we can implement two further tests. The first tests for the hypothesis that the CAT has most traction under moderate levels of democratic accountability. I created an interaction term for moderate levels of democracy and interacted it with CAT ratification.[61] Moderate democracies thus defined were much more likely to improve their torture practices than moderate democracies without such a commitment* * *. The same relationship did not hold for either full democracies or full autocracies. * * *

THE COURTS: POSSIBILITIES FOR LITIGATION

The data suggest—they of course do not prove—that when a government makes a formal and public commitment to abide by the provisions of the CAT, under certain conditions it is likely to do so. The conditions under which CAT ratification was most likely to affect actual practices were conditions of partial democratization. I have theorized that these are the conditions under which groups and individuals have both the motive and the means to mobilize to demand that their rights be respected.

A second mechanism * * * was litigation. Treaties are law in most countries; as such, they are available at least in theory as a way to make a legal case against practices state agents use to hold "dangerous" persons while in custody. This should be true, however, only if a country's courts are not a sham. If they are politically controlled by the government, no citizen or activist would consider it worthwhile to launch a case to try to get the CAT enforced against a brutal government able to pull all judicial strings.

It is possible to test for the plausibility of litigation as a mechanism by examining the relationship between CAT ratification, torture practices, and judicial independence. The proxy used here for judicial independence is * * * a measure of the rule of law collected by the World Bank broadly reflecting perceptions of the quality of judicial institutions as well as law and order in each country. While we should be cognizant of its weaknesses as a measure of judicial independence, this proxy provides one (noisy) cut at the question of whether the CAT is more likely to matter in countries where the courts are more likely to be respected.

A certain degree of judicial independence, competence, and credibility is necessary if the courts are to be a mechanism available for the enforcement of international treaty commitments. To be sure, countries with the most highly developed rule of law norms are unlikely to be among the worst torturers in the first place. If we see large improvements in torture practices in countries with the weakest court systems, we should seek the explanation outside of the court system itself. If the courts are an important enforcement mechanism, we should see the top tier and possibly the middle tier of high-scoring rule of law countries making improvements after ratification.[62]

[Analysis] shows that ratification is associated with significant improvements in torture practices—but not universally. * * * Among countries with very weak legal systems, ratification makes no difference whatsoever * * *. Similarly, there is not much difference within high rule of law countries between those that have ratified and those that have not * * *. In fact, if anything, it looks like nonratifiers have better torture records among high rule of law states than nonratifiers, but the relationship is inconsistent and not statistically reliable. The picture is very different among the mid-level set of countries * * *. Where the rule of law is reasonably well developed and the courts are

fairly independent of governmental control, chances are good that CAT ratification has indeed served to improve practices on average and controlling for many other alternative explanations. * * *

Thus, there may be some basis to conclude that the CAT has had an important impact on a considerable subset of countries in which stakeholders and other activists have the motive and the means to mobilize politically to demand compliance with the CAT and to use the CAT in domestic legal struggles over the meaning and use of torture. The following section discusses two examples of how this treaty became important in domestic law and politics, eventually contributing to the amelioration of torture practices on the part of government agents.

Chile and Israel: Experiences with the CAT

To illustrate the kinds of political and legal dynamics that could be behind the broad trends documented previously, it is useful to look at an example of how the CAT has made its way into domestic politics and litigation. The case of Chile illustrates the role that this convention can play in a partial or transitional democracy. First, it shows that human rights activists strategically deployed international legal norms to gain adherents and to strengthen the legitimacy of their opposition to Augusto Pinochet's military regime. However, they were hobbled in this early effort by a paucity of ratified treaties and the uselessness of litigation by a conservative, regime-controlled court system. Second, it illustrates that rights activists did want international legal commitments to bind their government. In fact, by the mid-1980s, several groups were specifically and publicly demanding CAT ratification—often at significant personal risk. Third, the CAT was highly relevant to local law development well into the transition period and beyond. Once the courts were reformed (circa 1997), and particularly once the CAT's power was demonstrated by the arrest and extradition of Pinochet himself, litigation involving the CAT grew significantly Furthermore, there is some evidence that torture practices in Chile were ameliorated at around this time as well. Overall, the case is useful in suggesting the importance of both the mobilization and litigation mechanisms discussed earlier.

Israel, of course, is a fairly stable democracy, and activists were motivated almost immediately upon Israel's ratification to use the CAT to bolster court cases alleging the use of torture and to embarrass the government by pointing to the treaty as an authoritative statement regarding the definition and the unconditional prohibition of torture. Crucial here was the Committee Against Torture's official view that many of the practices used in detention did in fact constitute torture. Once the Supreme Court of Israel rendered its landmark decision (1999) incorporating this view, the ball was back in the Israeli politician's court: They could choose to legalize those practices, but at the peril of making Israel the only country in the world to legalize torture. In both of these cases, the treaty was important in changing the way in which individuals held in government detention were treated.

CHILE: DEMOCRATIC TRANSITION, JUDICIAL REFORM, AND THE LEGAL EMPOWERMENT OF THE CAT

Chile is a case in which the treaty's commitments interact with democratic transition and institutional reform. Despite a comparatively long history of democratic governance, Chile is a country whose recent past has been marred by widespread use of torture perpetrated by the military and sanctioned by the highest levels of government. In 1973, a military junta led by General Augusto Pinochet overthrew the government of Salvador Allende and ruthlessly rooted out—tortured and murdered—political opponents and sympathizers with the left. For most of its rule, Pinochet's junta was not formally constrained by international

human rights treaties, although throughout the period his government was accused of grave breaches of customary international law related to crimes against humanity and serious human rights abuses. Yet, human rights organizers—and, significantly, the political opposition to the junta—drew to a considerable extent on international law norms and rhetoric to legitimate demands for an end to human rights abuses and torture. The junta ratified the CAT in 1988—just before the election in which Pinochet would lose his official grasp on government. Not only would the CAT be the legal instrument responsible for Pinochet's extradition to face torture charges, it would also inspire litigation in Chilean courts that would cumulatively contribute to significant improvements in Chilean law and ultimately practice. Torture has not been eradicated from the country, but the CAT has been very useful in bringing attention to the problem, reducing the overt reliance on "states of exception," and reducing torturers' calculations that they will escape responsibility for their actions through amnesty, statutes of limitations, or protection in sympathetic military courts.

The domestic opposition to the repressive tactics of the junta, whose goal was to crush socialism, was led by the moral authority of the outspoken Catholic Church. The church early on had a legal strategy for responding to the crushing repression of Pinochet's military dictatorship.[63] As early as October 1973, a religious-cum-legal alliance against the repression developed under the coleadership of Catholic and Lutheran bishops. They founded the Cooperative Committee for Peace in Chile (COPACHI), which focused initially on providing legal defense in the courts-martial cases as well as in cases of political firings. Expanding from a mere 8 employees to over 100 less than a year after its founding, COPACHI began to investigate a broad range of rights violations. By 1974, when a Mexican newspaper reported that COPACHI was keeping records on fundamental human rights violations, the organization was viewed by the government as in a threatening alliance with the political opposition. That year, COPACHI filed some 1,568 habeas corpus petitions on behalf of persons held in government detention, with the intent of both documenting these cases and delegitimating the government's practices. * * *

■ ■ ■

* * * In the 1970s, however, the international human rights regime was far less developed than it would become toward century's end. To be sure, the UDHR was available, and human rights organizations in Chile made reference to its norms on a regular basis. But in Chile, the status of the ICCPR was contested. ICCPR ratification was one of the last actions taken by Allende's regime before its overthrow. The UN records the date of Chile's ratification as 1972, but the position of the junta was that it had never been implemented in Chilean law and therefore was not a legally constraining document. Furthermore, the CAT did not exist when Pinochet came to power, though some accounts credit the widespread torture and disappearance under his rule with provoking the international community to address torture specifically. The international legal and institutional environment for human rights was fairly thin in the mid-1970s; still, rights groups appealed to an international audience to apply pressure directly on the Chilean government, as described well by Margaret Keck and Kathryn Sikkink.[64]

That Chile had ratified and implemented in domestic law few international human rights treaties was legally beside the point anyway, since during Pinochet's dictatorship the courts were hardly independent of the government and were largely sympathetic to right-wing ideologies. "During the first seven and a half years of authoritarian rule," according to a recent study by Lisa Hilbink, "the decisions of Chile's high courts overwhelmingly

favored the perspectives and policies of the regime's leadership."[65] * * *

■ ■ ■

The Sebastian Acevedo Movement Against Torture was one of the first groups to organize antitorture demonstrations publicly.[66] Demonstrators spearheaded by the Acevedo Movement used international legal instruments to focus their demands for human rights protections just as soon as these were available. In parallel with the UN debate and adoption of the CAT, local activists fastened on torture as the specific focus of their protest. In December 1983, "A peaceful demonstration against torture held by laymen and religious persons" was reported by local radio to have been violently repressed in Santiago. Demonstrators "chant[ed] and pray[ed] . . . demanding an end to torture." They "presented a declaration stating that everyone knows that the CNI [National Information Center] illegally detains persons, . . . and tortures them."[67] According to reports, "pedestrians spontaneously joined the demonstrators in their demand to end torture." *Carabineros*—the uniformed Chilean national police force—responded violently to this and other demonstrations focused on detentions and torture by the CNI. On 29 May 1984, *carabineros* beat antitorture demonstrators, "who were marching in silence . . . against any type of physical and harmful torture."[68] The Sebastian Acevedo Movement Against Torture staged a series of short, spontaneous demonstrations, displaying signs reading "Yes to Life; No to Torture."[69] In August 1984, 100 demonstrators from the Sebastian Acevedo Movement Against Torture demonstrated, reading an open letter addressed to Interior Minister Sergio Onofre Jarpa urging him to publicly state his opposition to torture.[70] Calls by the Alliance for Democracy for the intervention of the judicial branch to investigate allegations of torture went unheeded.

Activists continued to appeal to whatever international legal instruments were available to them to oppose civil rights violations and brutal treatment by government agents. Almost every December in the 1980s, activists from several rights organizations demonstrated in Santiago to commemorate the anniversary of the UDHR, reading the charter aloud in public and demanding the government's adherence.[71] * * *

■   ■   ■

For reasons that scholars have not yet been able to document convincingly, Chile finally did ratify the CAT in September 1988. General Pinochet himself signed the instrument of ratification. Three important reservations were entered upon ratification: that the convention would not be enacted until after 11 March 1990; that it would not be applied retroactively; and that Chile did not recognize the commission's jurisdiction over its internal affairs. Spain and other countries formally objected to these reservations, complaining that they were contrary to the objectives and intention of the international agreement.

Why did a regime infamous for the torture of detainees ratify a convention that bars these practices under all circumstances? No scholar has yet analyzed the ratification specifically, but Darren Hawkins's research implies that it may have been yet another legitimacy-seeking tactic by a junta that was in any case split on how much to concede to its political opposition.[72] The government's public justification was that ratification merely reflected its long-term commitment to human rights. According to the presidential secretary, the decision was "consistent with the principles of the government, maintaining an unchanged policy of preventing and punishing those illegal actions, and with preserving the Constitution and the law."[73] Coming only weeks before the national plebiscite that would determine whether Pinochet would remain in power another eight years, there is a good chance that ratification was a tactic (ultimately unsuccessful) to gain electoral support.[74]

Furthermore, the government may have thought that its treaty reservations as well as the national amnesty laws would protect any government or military officials from being held accountable. In any event, at the time—and with attention on the upcoming plebiscite on renewing Pinochet's term as president and passage of the constitution—little was made of the ratification. It merits one factual line in most treatments of Chile's human rights history and its transition to democracy.[75]

It is probably safe to infer that Pinochet's government ratified the CAT anticipating that it would pose no serious threat to his freedom or his mode of governance. If so, his miscalculation began with the results of the plebiscite itself. Despite harassment of the opposition and attacks on the critical media, on 5 October 1988, Pinochet lost the national plebiscite, with nearly 55 percent of Chilean voters rejecting his plan to remain in power. Within weeks, the opposition coalesced around Patricio Aylwin as its candidate for the coming year's presidential elections.

Aylwin was among the leaders of the opposition that as early as 1978 had explicitly built their vision of Chilean political life around the UDHR. The UDHR was integrated into the opposition coalition's platform and represented a clear break with Chile's compromised rights practices.[76] The opposition party proposed several key judicial reforms meant to protect the rights of the detained, including the jurisdiction of ordinary courts in human rights cases, amnesty for political prisoners, and pardons for those who had not committed blood crimes. They also proposed that ratified international human rights treaties be raised to the status of constitutional law in Chile.[77] In 1989, one of the 54 constitutional changes introduced by the opposition added a line to Article 5 making it a duty of the state to respect and promote the human rights guaranteed by the constitution and by international treaties ratified by Chile.[78] On 30 July 1989, these constitutional reforms were approved by a whopping 85.7 percent of the Chilean electorate.[79]

The electoral success of the opposition did not make the democratic transition easy or human rights unquestionably secure. After all that dissidents had endured, Pinochet was still quite popular in Chile: He had won about 40 percent of the recent vote, and the political right still held the balance of power in the legislature. Moreover, the opposition was faced with an essentially hostile judiciary; the Supreme Court, in particular, was sympathetic to right-wing ideology and to the goals if not all of the methods of the military government.[80] * * *

Several rulings in the 1990s illustrate the refusal of the Supreme Court to alter fundamentally their perspective on accountability for torture. They upheld the national amnesty law, finding that while international treaties had constitutional status in Chilean law, they could not be applied retroactively to extinguish national amnesty protections. Similarly, during the first half of the 1990s, the court refused to allow civilian courts to handle cases accusing military officers, which afforded them the protection of "in-house" military justice. Finally, the court almost always interpreted the national amnesty law as preventing the prosecution of crimes under international law. These positions made it almost impossible for many years to hold perpetrators of torture responsible for their acts.

The watershed year for the litigation of torture cases was 1998. In 1997, the Eduardo Frei government moved to propose and implement a number of reforms, and important shifts in the nature of court decisions began to surface in a very short time.[81] Most importantly, General Pinochet was arrested in London in 1998 while on a fleeting visit there. He was arrested and held, ironically, only because Chile had in 1988 ratified the CAT, which required either the prosecution or the extradition of alleged torturers to jurisdictions willing to prosecute. As a result of judicial reform and the example of the extraordinary reach of the CAT, litigation in Chilean courts began to change drastically. The number of cases alleging or in some way related to torture increased significantly.[82]

Torture cases began appearing in much greater numbers in the Supreme Court and the Appeals Court of Santiago by 2003. In many more cases, the courts are relying on the CAT to make decisions. These trends are clear in Figure 10.3.

■ ■ ■

The CAT is highly relevant to the question of prosecuting torturers. Hence, the Appeals Court of Santiago cited the CAT in several decisions relating to the national amnesty law. In 1994 the Appeals Court found a way to reduce the amnesty's reach in certain unresolved cases by ruling that kidnapping is a continuing and permanent offense ("qualified kidnapping") until the bodies of the victims are found and, as such, continues past the time limit set by these amnesty laws, making such crimes subject to laws and treaties in force at present.[83] In 2007, the Appeals Court rendered an even more significant decision, holding that under the military government there was a systematic pattern of state violence—including torture—that violated fundamental human rights norms. The court held that the state has an affirmative obligation to prosecute and sanction crimes against humanity and cannot grant amnesty to perpetrators of these abuses, as established in multiple human rights documents, among them the Genocide Convention and the CAT.[84] In both of these cases, the CAT was central in supplying the Appeals Court with a clear rationale for setting aside national amnesty laws and establishing judicial principles of accountability.

Only recently has the Supreme Court begun to agree that international legal obligations to which Chile is party make a blanket national amnesty legally untenable. In an important case in 2006, the Supreme Court made explicit use of the CAT to rule that Chile's amnesty law cannot be applied to crimes against humanity.[85] International treaties, including the CAT, were binding in national law, the court held; thus, even if an individual might otherwise be absolved under the national amnesty,

Figure 10.3. Chilean Court Cases on Torture: Supreme Court, Constitutional Tribunal, and Appeals Court of Santiago

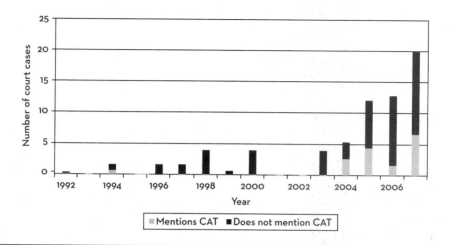

these obligations required judicial punishment.[86] The Supreme Court has made use of the CAT as well as general principles of international law to establish the principle that there are no statutory limits in the case of grave rights violations such as torture.[87] The CAT has also been used to make the case for compensation to victims or their families for torture committed during the Pinochet era.[88] Overall, the CAT has been especially useful in Chilean law to establish the limits of amnesty and the rules relating to criminal responsibility under the military regime.

■ ■ ■

Did the possibility of torture litigation—appealing to the CAT in Chilean courts—have any effect on torture practices in the country? It will never be possible to know the definitive answer to that question. But the evidence is suggestive. The torture index does begin to improve in Chile in 1999—just as it becomes clear that the CAT is highly relevant to how international and hence Chilean law is equipped to deal with the atrocities of the Pinochet

regime.[89] The most noticeable improvement on the torture scale did not come in the first decade of the country's democratic transition. Rather, it came when the utility of the CAT became clear and the courts had undergone crucial reforms. Under these circumstances, international law became available to Chilean activists to hold their government accountable for torture, past and current.

ISRAEL: AN EMBATTLED DEMOCRACY

Israel is an interesting case: It is a highly democratic country and a country that the World Bank scores well but not at or near the top of the countries they have rated on their rule of law scale. Israel also faces security threats that make interrogation of terrorist and criminal suspects a serious issue. It is a good case for illustrating the ways in which international treaty commitment can gain traction through the mobilization of activists employing a strategy of litigation. The fact that the Israeli Supreme Court is so easy for individuals to access made the strategy possible. This combination of factors gave the CAT special traction in

Israeli domestic politics and institutions, which in turn provided some impetus for revising coercive practices that the international community had described as torture.

Israel is a democracy, and there is no particular reason to think that a treaty banning torture should have much impact in a democratic country, which is far less likely to practice torture in the first place. Israel provides an interesting case study because it is an outlier: a stable democracy with a recent history of harsh interrogation practices that many would describe as torture. It is a good case to compare with those of transitioning and politically unstable regimes. In particular, it is interesting to observe the ways in which ratification of the CAT opened up political as well as legal space within Israel for critics of government practices. Once Israel had ratified the CAT (in 1991), domestic political groups mobilized and made strategic use of Israel's own institutional strengths: relatively independent and competent courts. As a result, Israeli interrogation practices have moderated, though they are still far from perfect.

Israeli law has addressed the issue of torture since passage of the Prevention of Terrorism Act (1948) shortly after the inception of the state. Controversial regulations dating from 1977 permitted "moderate physical pressure" in the interrogation of terrorist suspects, but it was not until 1987—and the eruption of the intifada—that the government's policies were systematically assessed by the Landau Commission Report. After an investigation undertaken in response to a five-year prison sentence for a Palestinian man that was based largely on a forced confession, the commission controversially concluded that the use of "moderate physical" and "non-violent psychological" pressure by the General Security Services (Shin Bet) was acceptable against Palestinians suspected of security offences. The report—details of which were never made public—contained interrogation guidelines allowing for "a moderate measure of physical pressure," which nonetheless "must never reach the level of torture."[90]

The report of the Landau Commission was part of a broader effort in the late 1980s to address the limits of permissible practices for interrogating individuals in the custody of public authorities. Israel signed the CAT in 1986, just before the 1987 outbreak of the first intifada. Partially in response to growing internal and external pressures (and despite an uptick in security concerns), the government ratified in October 1991, with some reservations.[91] Two important human rights changes in the Basic Law followed in 1992.[92] These changes provided political and legal opportunities for activists to demand further change in policy and practice. Israel's dualist legal system meant that the CAT itself could not be enforced in national courts in the absence of implementing legislation,[93] but ratification of the CAT became an important point of leverage in the lobbying campaign to bring Israel's penal code into conformity with the nation's public international commitment.[94] Both international and local human rights organizations campaigned in the early 1990s for an amendment to the Israeli Penal Code (Article 277), which allowed physical pressure. The Prohibition of Torture Bill was amended in 1996 to bring its wording into conformity with the CAT, but it would be years before its provisions became law.[95]

Meanwhile, allegations of abusive interrogation practices were becoming a more common feature of the nightly news.[96] In 1993, the evening news told the story of Hassan Zubeidi, a 34-year-old grocer from Anabta on the West Bank, who had allegedly been beaten comatose by Shin Bet. This case and others sent the government into a flurry of activity that it hoped would deflect concern. In April the government announced that a ministerial committee had tightened up the 1987 Landau Commission guidelines for Shin Bet interrogators. In June a bill banning torture was proposed by several members of parliament, and the justice minister, David Libai, appointed a committee to study the proposal. Public protest was limited, partly because Israelis continued to view Shin Bet as crucial to Israel's security.[97]

Figure 10.4. Torture Litigation in Israel

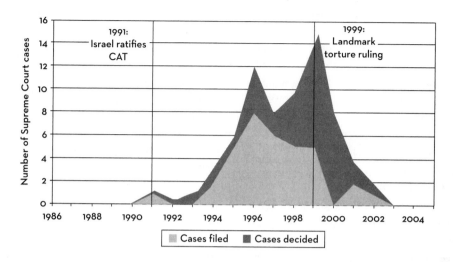

Note: In all cases, plaintiffs are Palestinians and NGOs on their behalf (mainly the Public Committee against Torture in Israel and the Center for the Defense of the Individual). The defendant is the General Security Service (GSS) (in some cases, the minister of defense and the police were additional defendants). In one case, the defendant was the commander of Israeli Defense Forces in the West Bank.

Source: Israeli Supreme Court, CD-ROM.

While hardly sparking a mass social movement, the human rights issues—raised in stark fashion in the aftermath of the intifada—fueled a burst of organized activism. By one count, only one human rights NGO existed in Israel before December 1987, and about fifteen of the twenty-five rights NGOs currently operating in Israel were established in the years immediately following.[98] In the Occupied Territories, only one rights organization existed before the intifada, and about six other rights organizations were established within a very short period following its eruption.[99] One of the most important groups formed was the Public Committee Against Torture, which spearheaded much of the legal activity discussed below. Links with international rights groups were forged, from Amnesty International and Middle East Watch to the International Commission of Jurists and Physicians for Human Rights.[100] International rights discourse peppered their press releases, human rights reports, and correspondence with Israeli authorities (government, military, civil administration).[101]

Israeli activists chose an explicit strategy of legal contestation in their efforts to stamp out their government's practice of what many considered torture. "Politically motivated Palestinian and Israeli lawyers used the legal terrain as a site of resistance to reform or to transform the way the state exercises power," according to one astute observer.[102] This strategy is clearly reflected in the number of cases alleging torture that were brought to the Israeli Supreme Court in the 1990s. Figure 10.4 illustrates this explosion of cases. * * *

■   ■   ■

Israel's struggle with terrorism over the course of the 1990s made it hard for the government to eschew completely the continued use of moderate physical pressure against suspects. In September

1994, critics of such practices gained support from some politicians on the right when members of an alleged Jewish terror cell were arrested and some alleged physical or mental violence while under interrogation.[103] After a wave of deadly suicide bombings in 1994, the government was reported to have given Shin Bet permission to use force in interrogations, although the service was required to seek permission from a ministerial commission every three months for the continued use of moderate physical pressure against terrorist suspects.[104] Efforts to codify the conditions under which such pressure could be used were roundly criticized by Amnesty International and other groups as proposals to "legalize torture in Israel and the occupied territories."[105] While the government argued in favor of flexibility under extenuating circumstances, Amnesty International cited the nonderogable nature of the CAT's Article II.[106]

The Israeli government responded to its critics in two ways: necessity and compliance. "The main duty of the government is to protect its citizens," said Uri Dromi, the chief government spokesman in late 1995, "and therefore we have to resort to methods that are not so nice. In other circumstances we would not do it, but we are faced with a very dangerous enemy, and it is the enemy not only of Israel but of the free world."[107] At the same time, the government expressed its desire to comply with the CAT it had ratified five years before. In defending a legislative proposal to set guidelines on the use of physical pressure in interrogations in early 1996, Minister of Justice David Libai noted that "The [proposed] methods used during interrogations will be in line with the International Convention against torture and will not lead to suffering or great pain. . . . This law will give clear regulations on acceptable methods, which will help Shin Bet agents avoid mistaken initiatives."[108] * * *

In a short while, the experts comprising the Committee Against Torture were to allege otherwise. Israel's techniques became a target of the committee's concern after a 1996 Israeli Supreme Court ruling gave interrogators more leeway in using physical means to uncover information on terrorism.[109] * * *

By 1998, the government and activists in alliance with the UN Committee Against Torture were at an impasse, with the former claiming that specific Israeli practices did not and the latter claiming that they did constitute torture. The most decisive way remaining to settle the issue was to apply to the highest legal authority in Israel to decide this very issue. * * *

■　■　■

The landmark case came on 7 September 1999, and the decision was unanimous. The court held that:

> . . . a reasonable investigation is necessarily one free of torture, free of cruel, inhuman treatment of the subject and free of any degrading handling whatsoever. There is a prohibition on the use of "brutal or inhuman means" in the course of an investigation. . . . Human dignity also includes the dignity of the suspect being interrogated. . . . This conclusion is in perfect accord with (various) International Law treaties—to which Israel is a signatory—which prohibit the use of torture, "cruel, inhuman treatment" and "degrading treatment." . . . These prohibitions are "absolute." There are no exceptions to them and there is no room for balancing. Indeed, violence directed at a suspect's body or spirit does not constitute a reasonable investigation practice.[110]

The court went on to say that particular practices were not permitted according to these prohibitions:

> . . . we declare that the GSS does not have the authority to "shake" a man, hold him in the "Shabach" position . . . , force him into a "frog

crouch" position and deprive him of sleep in a manner other than that which is inherently required by the interrogation.[111]

Initial reactions to the ruling were very optimistic, almost ebullient.[112] The Israeli human rights organization B'Tselem characterized the decision as putting "an end to torture in Israel,"[113] while the Palestinian human rights group LAW declared that the decision "outlawed torture."[114] Once the amazement wore off, reactions to the High Court decision were much more restrained.[115] While certain practices—such as violent shaking, certain painful positions, and prolonged hooding—were declared to be torture by the court, the door was also left open for these issues to be legalized through parliamentary legislation.

It was only a matter of months before conservative members of the Knesset moved to do so. In November 1999 approximately 64 members of the 120-member Israeli parliament introduced a bill specifically authorizing the GSS to use physical pressure in interrogation. The author of the bill acknowledged that the bill would be "introducing torture into the law of the State of Israel" and that the provisions he proposed violated international law and Israel's treaty obligations.[116] As it turns out, however, legislating torture in a democratic forum is politically not very feasible. Antitorture lobbyists turned out in numbers, and the bill did not pass.

What are the larger implications of torture litigation in Israel? The Israeli Supreme Court did not ban torture, as many would have liked to see it do. On the other hand, torture has never been legitimated through a parliamentary decision of the Knesset, despite security threats that might have made it expedient to do so. Activists and monitors continue to criticize certain aspects of Israel's interrogation practices. And yet, even Israel's critics recognize that practices have improved. Peter Burns of the ten-member UN Committee Against Torture told reporters in 2001 that "There is absolutely

no question that the high court ruling has had an impact."[117] Now, instead of speaking in terms of flagrant violations, the committee focuses on the ways in which Israel's compliance is incomplete. "In the absence of a defined crime of torture in terms consistent with the Convention we feel there are gaps, [and] that certain types of conduct slip through the net," Burns said. This assessment comports with the evidence used to assess torture practices in this chapter. While their practices have improved one category on the torture scale since 1999, Israel is still a country in which detainee abuse is on balance not uncommon.

International law played a crucial supporting role in this episode. Mobilization in Israel on the issue of the treatment of detainees followed ratification of the CAT, and used the fact and language of that commitment to articulate an undeniable proposition: Israel was obligated by international convention not to engage in torture. The key problem was that the government disagreed that that is what its agents were doing. And here the convention played another crucial role: It bolstered the judgment that particular practices were beyond the pale. Ratification entailed reporting to the Committee Against Torture; reporting spawned counter-reports and eventually a formal decision of the committee that particular practices were in breach of an international commitment. By 1999, a fairly independent High Court felt that it could not avoid a ruling on the legality of the practices in question. While it did not appeal directly to international law in its decision, the court was constrained by the interpretation of the CAT by its authoritative implementation committee. The solution chosen was to declare Israel's practices inconsistent with existing law, which the court acknowledged could be changed by legislative means—a move that itself served to diffuse conservative opposition. Effectively, Israel's voluntarily assumed CAT obligation put normative and legal constraints on

Israeli politics and institutions that impacted practices and made wholesale violation of international torture standards untenable.

Conclusions

The ban on torture is the strongest international legal prohibition contained in any human rights treaty. By ratifying the CAT, governments expressly acknowledge that there are no conditions under which the use of severe physical or psychological pain by public authorities is justified. Yet, despite such clear prohibitory language, there is little quantifiable evidence that signing a treaty makes it so. Torture is appallingly widespread. Even if we take into account the likelihood that information on torture has improved over the course of the past two decades, and even if we concede that standards of what constitutes torture may be getting tougher, there are still far too many cases in which governments are willing to ignore or even to condone detainee treatment that is illegally harsh.

The initial evidence casts some doubt on the ability of treaty commitments to alter this basic reality. Indicators of torture seem to have gotten worse over time even as the number of CAT signatories increased. The *unconditional* effects of ratifying the CAT were, if anything, negative, indicating that it is quite common for governments to perform *worse* on this scale once they have ratified the CAT. It is important to reiterate the opening observations * * *: The decentralized and secretive nature of this offense makes it difficult to study, let alone to stop. Some governments practice torture out of self-constructed "necessity," justifying their practices with references to security and the public or national interest.

It is wrong to conclude, however, that the CAT has failed to improve the treatment of government-held detainees. This [analysis] revealed the ability of a treaty commitment to influence positively government behavior in moderately democratic and transitional regimes, of which there are many. Chile is a good example of how this can work out in practice. This [analysis] has also found some impact in countries whose legal systems are at least moderately well equipped to enforce international treaty commitments. Israel is a good example of how this can happen. The main finding * * * is that a CAT commitment significantly improves the treatment of detainees in countries with at least moderate levels of public accountability. CAT ratification resonates in those polities; individuals and groups who may have good reason to fear mistreatment of themselves, their families, their countrymen, or other humans by the government have strong incentives to mobilize to implement the international ban in domestic law. The domestic politics that mobilize around the issue are likely key to the treaty's gaining traction in the local polity.

The factors that drive torture are many, and many are far more important than a treaty commitment. The use of torture can become distressingly embedded in a local culture of brutality and can be very difficult to dislodge. Consistently, the most significant explanation for torture in every model in this [analysis] was practices in past years. Governments often continue their "law enforcement" efforts as they have for decades, unless demands from a mobilized public begin to elicit a reexamination of policy. Then, too, governments tend to maintain good practices until a national security threat justifies the rougher handling of detainees. It is clear that many factors conspire to create an environment where torture flourishes, from military conflicts to a gagged press.

As Jack Donnelly has written, ". . . the key to change in state practices probably lies not in any one type or forum of activity but in the mobilization of multiple, complementary channels of influence."[118] A treaty commitment has an important role to play in polities where complementary channels of influence—public demands, foreign pressures, powerful and well-respected courts—come together to demand an end to torture. As this [analysis] has shown, that is most likely to be the case in polities that have experienced both public accountability and its breach. For many countries over the course of the past three decades, the CAT has provided a focal norm and a stabilizing standard from which vigilant polities have insisted their governments not retreat.

NOTES

1. Simmons and Hopkins 2005.
2. Chayes and Chayes 1993.
3. Finnemore and Sikkink 1998.
4. Keck and Sikkink 1998.
5. Hathaway 2002.
6. Moravcsik 2000.
7. Some of the practices that the State Department reports have condemned in other countries have, ironically, been approved by the United States in the interrogation of alleged terrorists. See Malinowski 2005.
8. Several books provide an account of the history of torture; see, for example, Dunér 1998.
9. Cingranelli and Richards 1999a.
10. Basoglu 1993.
11. Baker 1992; Kane and Peterson 1995.
12. Cassese 1996.
13. See Ross 2005.
14. Becker and Becker 2001; Donnelly 1998; Worden 2005.
15. Dunér 1998.
16. Sironi and Branche 2002; Slaughter 1997.
17. Walker and Poe 2002.
18. Article 15–16, Investigation of the 800th Military Police Brigade, paragraph 6. Text of the report, investigated under the direction of Maj. Gen. Antonio M. Taguba, can be found at http://www.msnbc.msn.com/id/4894001/ (accessed 30 June 2008).
19. Danner 2004.
20. Wantchekon and Healy 1999.
21. The United Kingdom's report to the Committee Against Torture is criticized by Amnesty International for not acknowledging that authorities had "violated the prohibition against the use of statements obtained through torture as evidence in any proceedings, except against a person accused of torture." See http://web.amnesty.org/library/Index/ENGEUR450292004?open&;of=ENG-GBR (accessed 30 June 2008). The U.S. report to the Committee Against Torture, for example, is criticized by the World Organization for Human Rights USA for "side-step[ping] and downplay[ing] the reality that as a matter of official policy the United States has been encouraging the use of torture of detainees on a systematic and widespread basis, and seeking to justify these major violations of international human rights standards as a necessary tool to combat terrorism." See http://www.humanrightsusa.org/modules.php?op=modload&name=News&file=article&sid=32 [inactive link].
22. Goodman and Jinks 2003.
23. Lutz and Sikkink 2000.
24. UDHR, Article 5.
25. For a discussion of the development of the UN regime with respect to torture, see Clark 2001:37–69.
26. On the role of NGOs in drafting the CAT, see Baehr 1989; Burgers 1989; Burgers and Danelius 1988; Clark 2001; Korey 1998; Lippman 1994; Tolley 1989. Korey describes this campaign as ". . . one of the most successful initiatives ever undertaken by an NGO" (1998:171).
27. See, for example, Leary 1979.
28. UNGA 9 December 1975 (resolution 3452 [XXX]). Text can be found at http://unhchr.ch/html/menu3/b/h_comp38.htm (accessed 23 August 2005).
29. CAT, Article 3.
30. Afghanistan, Argentina, Belgium, Bolivia, Costa Rica, Denmark, Dominican Republic, Ecuador, Finland, France, Greece, Iceland, Italy, Luxembourg, Netherlands, Norway, Panama, Portugal, Senegal, Spain, Sweden, Switzerland, United Kingdom, Uruguay, and Venezuela.
31. CAT, Article 1, para. 1.
32. On the other hand, the Tokyo declaration, adopted by the World Medical Association in 1975, defines torture as ". . . the deliberate, systematic, or wanton infliction of physical or mental suffering by one or more persons acting alone or on the orders of any authority, to force another person to yield information, to make a confession, or for any other reason." World Medical Association Declaration Guidelines for Medical Doctors Concerning Torture and Other Cruel, Inhuman, or Degrading Treatment or Punishment in Relation to Detention and Imprisonment (Declaration of Tokyo). Adopted by the 29th World Medical Assembly, Tokyo, Japan, October 1975.
33. CAT, Article 2.2. Text of the CAT can be found at http://www.hrweb.org/legal/cat.html.
34. CAT, Article 2.3. For a defense of the nonderogable nature of this prohibition, see Lukes 2006.
35. CAT, Article 5. Sweden and a group of NGOs—notably the International Association of Penal Law and the ICJ—were especially influential in including universal jurisdiction language in the CAT. See Burgers and Danelius 1988; Hawkins 2004; Rodley 1999.
36. Bosco 2000.
37. See Solomon 2001.
38. On the importance of universal jurisdiction in the CAT, see Boulesbaa 1999; Hawkins 2004; Rodley 1999.
39. Declarations can be found at http://www.unhchr.ch/html/menu2/6/cat/treaties/convention-reserv.htm (accessed 30 June 2008).
40. CAT, Article 22.
41. Statistics (current as of 30 April 2004) on individual complaints under Article 22 can be found at http://www.unhchr.ch/html/menu2/8/stat3.htm (accessed 30 June 2008).

42. Keith 1999.

43. Hathaway 2002:1988.

44. Goodman and Jinks 2003.

45. A point made by many observers of NGO priorities and the CAT ratification record; see Claude and Weston 1992; Forsythe 1985; van Boven 1989–1990.

46. See, for example, the discussion regarding the desire to influence others to sign as a motivation in Ratner 2004.

47. Jennings 1999.

48. For a discussion of how the U.S. Department of State reports are compiled, see De Neufville 1986; Valencia-Weber and Weber 1986.

49. For a detailed discussion of the criteria used, see Hathaway 2002. These categories are greatly preferable to counting instances of torture or abuse, which several researchers have noted give a false [sense] of accuracy; see Goldstein 1986; Stohl et al. 1986. The use of this scale comports with Thomas Pogge's notion of individuals' right to institutions that secure access to a particular right. Pogge asserts, for example, that whether an individual enjoys the human right against torture turns not on whether the individual is actually tortured, but rather on the probability that that individual will be tortured under the prevailing social conditions, which are roughly what this scale captures (2002:65).

50. Hathaway's (2002) coders also looked for terms such as "repeated," "methodical," "routine," and "frequent."

51. Common law countries are much less likely to ratify a human rights treaty * * *, but they are no more or less likely to engage in torture. In fact, common law countries average 2.3 on the torture scale, while all other counties average 2.2—a statistically indistinguishable and substantively insignificant difference.

52. On the role of the press generally in exposing human rights abuses, see Husarska 2000.

53. Bronkhorst 1995; Hayner 1994, 2001.

54. Sironi and Branche 2002.

55. For an excellent book on the French use of and justification for torture during the Algerian War, see Maran 1989.

56. See, for example, Apodaca 2001; Haas 1994; Hamburg 2000; Ignatieff 2001; Poe and Tate 1994; Poe et al. 1999.

57. For a discussion of these and other "enforcement" mechanisms, see Donnelly 1998. Legal scholars have considered these mechanisms "international secondary soft law"; see Shelton 1997.

58. For a general discussion of these mechanisms, see Tardu 1980. For a case study that provides some evidence that debate and resolutions adopted by the Human Rights Commission under these procedures has had some influence on China, see Kent 1999.

59. This confirms the reported findings in Hathaway 2002.

60. It is important to note, though, that stable democracies still tend to be at the very good end of the torture scale: about 85 percent of stable democracies' torture observations were in the top two categories. Among stable democracies, not a single observation fell in the worst category. Lithuania, Jamaica, and Israel were the only stable democracies to have had more than one observation in the second to the lowest category. Neither Lithuania nor Jamaica had ratified the CAT; Israel, on the other hand, had.

61. For purposes of this test, moderate democracies are those years scoring between 3 and 8 on the polity scale, inclusive. Full autocracies are those that scored 1 or 2, and full democracies are those that scored 9 or 10.

62. Kaufmann et al. 2008:10. See the description at http://papers.ssrn.com/so13/papers.cfm?abstract_id=1148386.

63. The Catholic Church in Chile's role in defending human rights deserves much more attention than can be devoted to it in these pages. In Mara Loveman's words, "The Church as an institution provided a 'moral shield' for human rights work through its domestic influence as a source of legitimacy and its international symbolic, moral, and political weight" (1998:494).

64. Keck and Sikkink 1998.

65. Hilbink 2007:129.

66. Cleary 1997:15.

67. "Torture Demonstrations 'Violently Repressed,'" Santiago Radio Cooperativa, 14 December 1983; FBIS PY142234. See also "Denunciations of Torture Gain Strength," Paris, AFP; 14 December 1983; FBIS PY160125.

68. "Carabineros 'Beat' Anti-Torture Demonstrators," Santiago Radio Cooperativa, 29 May 1984. FBIS PY292225. See also "Relatives of Missing Detainees March in Santiago," Santiago Radio Cooperativa, 23 May 1984. FBIS PY240242; and "Catholic Episcopate Calls for Halt to Torture," Madrid EFE, 25 April 1985. FFBIS PY260345.

69. "Santiago Demonstration Protests Torture," Santiago Radio Cooperativa, 19 July 1984. FBIS PY1912115.

70. "Demonstrators Protest Torture Near La Moneda," Paris, AFP. 22 August 1984. PY230242. On the significance of the Acevedo movement for Chile's position on torture, see Hawkins 2002:ch. 5.

71. "Demonstrations Mark Human Rights Day in Santiago," Porto Alegre Radio Guiaba, FBIS PY110149. See also "Human Rights Demonstration Prompts Arrest," Santiago Radio Chilena, 10 December 1985. FBIS PY110135.

72. Hawkins 2002:4–5.

73. "Chile: Pinochet Signs OAS and UN Conventions on Torture," BBC Summary of World Broadcasts, 17 September 1988, part 4.

74. This was the view of the Chilean Human Rights Commission, as reported by Shirley Christian. "Violent Scenes as Torture Is Banned," *Sydney Morning Herald* (Australia); source: *New York Times*, 17 September 1988.

75. America's Watch, for example, reported the ratification with practically no comment (U.S.) 1988:106. Five years later, even the 1993 Report of the Chilean National Commission on Truth and Reconciliation neglected to mention that Chile had ratified the CAT in 1988. There is a section on "Norms, Concepts, and Criteria" in which torture is mentioned, but the UDHR is the only human rights document cited. The only section that mentions anything Chile has ratified is that on "Laws of War or International Humanitarian Law," referring to Chile's ratification of the 1949 Geneva Conventions. See Berryman 1993:27–29. One reason might be that the CAT requires prosecution, which is not the purpose or strategy of the Truth and Reconciliation Commission.

76. Brito 1997:110.

77. Brito 1997:120.

78. Hilbink 2007:179–80, fn 6.

79. Brito 1997:102.

80. Brito 1997:108.

81. Hilbink 2007:185.

82. Lutz and Sikkink 2001.

83. Appeals Court of Santiago, 30 September 1994; Chile Lexis-Nexis database.

84. Appeals Court of Santiago, 18 December 2007, Rol 11801-2006; Chile Lexis-Nexis database.

85. Supreme Court, 30 May 2006, Rol 3215-2005; Chile Lexis-Nexis database.

86. Supreme Court, 6 June 2006, Rol 1528-2006 00; Chile Lexis-Nexis database.

87. Supreme Court, 5 September 2007, Rol 6525-2006; Chile Lexis-Nexis database. In this case, however, the torturer was given an "attenuated sentence," which they held to be permissible under the treaty. Furthermore, in 18 October 2007, Rol 4691-2007 the court seemed to contradict itself, arguing that there is no treaty or general norm of international law that proscribes statutory limits. The minority argued strenuously nevertheless that the state was under an obligation—represented by the CAT and other treaties—to prosecute torturers regardless of the amnesty.

88. Compensation is addressed in Article 14 of the CAT. Such compensation has not been without controversy in Chile. See Kevin G. Hall, "Chilean Torture Victims Demand Compensation, Prosecution." 13 December 2004. http://www.soaw.org/newswire_detail.php _detail.php?id=642 (accessed 30 June 2008).

89. The torture scale improves from 3 to 2 in 1999, indicating a move from fairly regularized brutality to cases of isolated incidents.

90. For a discussion of the contents of the Landau Commission Report, see Grosso 2000.

91. Source: http://www2.ohchr.org/english/law/cat-ratify.htm (accessed 2 July 2008).

92. Laursen 2000:440.

93. Grosso 2000:319. This does not mean that international law has no effects on Israeli law. For a discussion of the possibilities, see Benvenisti 1994.

94. See Ray 2000:46; Clark 2000–1; Grosso 2000; St. Amand 1999–2000.

95. Ray 2000:46.

96. In general, the relative openness of the Israeli political system, with its lack of press censorship, meant that many of the most egregious abuses were in fact fairly easy to document. In 1992, five reports showed that, since the intifada began, between 2,000 and 3,000 detainees had been beaten, hooded, deprived of sleep, or made to stand in boxes no bigger than their bodies for hours. See Caroline Moorehead, "The Court to Rule on Use of Torture in Israel," *The Independent* (London), 21 April 1993; International news, p. 11.

97. Joel Greenberg, "Israel Rethinks Interrogation of Arabs," *New York Times*, Section 1, p. 3, 14 August 1993.

98. Gordon 2004.

99. Hanafi and Tabar 2004.

100. In the summer of 1993, a series of physicians' organizations—including the Israeli Medical Association and the Association of Israeli-Palestinian Physicians for human rights—publicly refused to cooperate with the government in its interrogation practices. See Joel Greenberg, "Israel Rethinks Interrogation of Arabs," *New York Times*, Section 1, p. 3, 14 August 1993.

101. Gordon and Berkovitch n.d.:12.

102. Hajjar 2001:24.

103. *The Economist,* 1 October 1994, p. 58.

104. Agence France Presse, "Israel to Legalise Use of Force Against Palestinian Prisoners," International news, 23 January 1996.

105. United Press International, 23 October 1995, "Amnesty Says Israel to Legalize Torture."

106. Abed Jaber, "UN Concerned by Torture in Israel," United Press International, 23 October 1995. See also Derek Brown, "Making Torture Legal," *The Guardian,* foreign page, p. 9, 23 October 1995.

107. Derek Brown, "Making Torture Legal," *The Guardian,* foreign page, p. 9, 23 October 1995.

108. Agence France Presse, "Israel to Legalise Use of Force Against Palestinian Prisoners," International news, 23 January 1996.

109. *New York Times,* "UN Panel Rules Israel Uses Torture." 10 May 1997, p. A6.

110. Judgment on the Interrogation Methods applied by the GSS; The Supreme Court of Israel, sitting as the High Court of Justice; Cases H.C. 5100/94, H.C. 4054/95, H.C. 6536/95, H.C. 5188/96, H.C. 7563/97, H.C. 7628/97, H.C. 1043/99, para. 23. Text available at http://www.derechos.org/human-rights/mena /doc/torture.html (accessed 14 August 2008).

111. Id., paragraph 40 (accessed 14 August 2008).

112. "The High Court decision brings an end to an inglorious chapter in Israel's history, in which the state authorized Shin Bet interrogators to use torture methods in their work on the grounds of security needs." *Ha'aretz,* editorial, 7 September 1999. See also Deborah Sontag, "Court Bans Most Use of Force in Interrogations," *New York Times,* 7 September 1999, p. A1.

113. Press Release, B'Tselem, 6 September 1999.

114. LAW, "After 18 Months, Israeli High Court Outlaws Torture," 7 September 1999.

115. St. Amand (1999–2000:683) asserts that the decision was a tiny legal step and notes that there was no explicit reference to the international prohibition contained in the CAT; see also Mandel 1999:313.

116. Aryeh Dayan, "A Ticking Time Bomb in the Knesset: Some 64 MKs Have Signed a Bill Specifically Authorizing the Shin Bet to Use Torture Under Certain Conditions—Despite the Fact That Israel Has Signed an International Treaty Prohibiting It," *Ha'aretz,* 1 November 1999.

117. Peter Capella, "UN Panel Urges Israel to Eliminate Torture." Agence France Presse, 23 November 2001. See also Elizabeth Olson, "Citing Some Progress, U.N. Panel on Torture Urges Israel to Take More Steps," *New York Times,* 24 November 2001, p. A8.

118. Donnelly 1998:85.

REFERENCES

Apodaca, Claire. 2001. Global Economic Patterns and Personal Integrity Rights after the Cold War. *International Studies Quarterly* 45(4): 587–602.

Baehr, P. R. 1989. The General Assembly: Negotiating the Convention on Torture. In *The United Nations in the World Political Economy: Essays in Honour of Leon Gordenker*, edited by David P. Forsythe and Leon Gordenker, 36–53. Basingstoke, England: Macmillan.

Baker, R. 1992. Psychological Consequences for Tortured Refugees Seeking Asylum and Refugee Status in Europe. In *Torture and Its Consequences: Current Treatment Approaches*, edited by Metin Basoglu, 83–106. Cambridge: Cambridge University Press.

Basoglu, Metin. 1993. Prevention of Torture and Care of Survivors: An Integrated Approach. *Journal of the American Medical Association* 270(5): 606–11.

Becker, Lawrence C., and Charlotte B. Becker. 2001. *Encyclopedia of Ethics,* 2nd ed. New York: Routledge.

Benvenisti, Eyal. 1994. The Influence of International Human Rights Law on the Israeli Legal System: Present and Future. *Israel Law Review* 28(1): 136–53.

Berryman, Phillip. 1993. *Report of the Chilean National Commission on Truth and Reconciliation.* South Bend, IN: Notre Dame University Press.

Bosco, David. 2000. Dictators in the Dock. *The American Prospect*: 14 August 2000, 26–29.

Boulesbaa, Ahcene. 1999. *The U.N. Convention on Torture and the Prospects for Enforcement.* International Studies in Human Rights, V. 51. The Hague: Martinus Nijhoff.

Brito, Alexandra Batahona de. 1997. *Human Rights and Democratization in Latin America: Uruguay and Chile.* Oxford, New York: Oxford University Press.

Bronkhorst, Daan. 1995. *Truth and Reconciliation: Obstacles and Opportunities for Human Rights.* Amsterdam: Amnesty International, Dutch Section.

Burgers, Jan Herman, 1989. An Arduous Delivery: The United Nations Convention against Torture. In *Effective Negotiation: Case Studies in Conference Diplomacy.* edited by Johan Kaufmann, 45–52. Dordrecht, the Netherlands: Martinus Nijhoff.

Burgers, Jan Herman, and Hans Danelius. 1988. *The United Nations Convention Against Torture: A Handbook on the Convention Against Torture and Other Cruel, Inhuman, or Degrading Treatment or Punishment.* Dordrecht, the Netherlands: Martinus Nijhoff.

Cassese, Antonio. 1996. *Inhuman States: Imprisonment, Detention and Torture in Europe Today.* Oxford: Polity Press.

Chayes, Abram, and Antonia Handler Chayes. 1993. On Compliance. *International Organization* 47(2): 175–205.

Cingranelli, David L., and David L. Richards. 1999. Measuring the Level, Pattern, and Sequence of Government Respect for Physical Integrity Rights. *International Studies Quarterly* 43(2): 407–18.

———. 1999b. Respect for Human Rights after the End of the Cold War. *Journal of Peace Research* 36(5): 511–34.

Clark, Ann Marie. 2001. *Diplomacy of Conscience; Amnesty International and Changing Human Rights Norms.* Princeton, NJ: Princeton University Press.

Clark, Melissa. 2000–1. Israel's High Court of Justice Ruling on the General Security Service Use of "Moderate Physical Pressure": An End to the Sanctioned Use of Torture? *Indiana Comparative and International Law Review* 11(1): 145–82.

Claude, Richard Pierre, and Burns H. Weston. 1992. *Human Rights in the World Community: Issues and Action,* 2nd ed. Philadelphia: University of Pennsylvania Press.

Cleary, Edward L. 1997. *The Struggle for Human Rights in Latin America.* Westport, CT: Praeger.

Danner, Mark. 2004. *Torture and Truth: America, Abu Ghraib, and the War on Terror.* New York: New York Review of Books.

De Neufville, Judith Innes. 1986. Human Rights Reporting as a Policy Tool—An Examination of the State Department Country Reports. *Human Rights Quarterly* 8(4): 681–99.

Donnelly, Jack. 1998. *International Human Rights,* 2nd ed. Boulder, CO: Westview Press.

Dunér, Bertil, ed. 1998. *An End to Torture: Strategies for Its Eradication.* London, New York: Zed Books; St. Martin's Press.

Finnemore, Martha, and Kathryn Sikkink. 1998. International Norm Dynamics and Political Change. *International Organization* 52(4): 887–918.

Forsythe, David P. 1985. The United Nations and Human Rights. *Political Science Quarterly* 100(2): 249–69.

Goldstein, Judith. 1986. The Political Economy of Trade: Institutions of Protection. *American Political Science Review* 80(1): 161–84.

Goldstein, Robert J. 1986. The Limitations of Using Quantitative Data in Studying Human Rights Abuses. *Human Rights Quarterly* 8(4): 607–27.

Goodman, Ryan, and Derek Jinks. 2003. Measuring the Effects of Human Rights Treaties. *European Journal of International Law* 13:171–83.

Gordon, Neve, ed. 2004. *From the Margins of Globalization: Critical Perspectives on Human Rights.* Lanham, MD: Lexington Books.

Grosso, Catherine M. 2000. International Law in the Domestic Arena: The Case of Torture in Israel. *Iowa Law Review* 86:305–37.

Haas, Michael. 1994. *Improving Human Rights.* Westport, CT: Praeger.

Hajjar, Lisa. 2001. Human Rights in Israel/Palestine: The History and Politics of a Movement. *Journal of Palestine Studies* 30(4): 21–38.

Hamburg, David. 2000. Human Rights and Warfare: An Ounce of Prevention Is Worth a Pound of Cure. In *Realizing Human Rights: Moving from Inspiration to Impact,* edited by Samantha Power and Graham T. Allison, 321–36, New York: St. Martin's Press.

Hanafi, Sari, and Linda Tabar. 2004. Donor Assistance, Rent-Seeking and Elite Formation. In *State Formation in Palestine: Viability and Governance During a Social Transformation,* edited by Mushtaq H. Khan, 215–38. London, New York: Routledge.

Hathaway, Oona. 2002. Do Human Rights Treaties Make a Difference? *Yale Law Journal* III: 1935–2042.

Hawkins, Darren G. 2002. *International Human Rights and Authoritarian Rule in Chile: Human Rights in International Perspective V. 6.* Lincoln: University of Nebraska Press.

———. 2004. Explaining Costly International Institutions: Persuasion and Enforceable Human Rights Norms. *International Studies Quarterly* 48(4): 779–804.

Hayner, Priscilla B. 1994. Fifteen Truth Commissions—1974 to 1994: A Comparative Study. *Human Rights Quarterly* 16(4): 597–655.

———. 2001. *Unspeakable Truths: Confronting State Terror and Atrocity.* New York: Routledge.

Hilbink, Lisa. 2007. *Judges Beyond Politics in Democracy and Dictatorship: Lessons from Chile.* Cambridge: Cambridge University Press.

Husarska, Anna. 2000. "Conscience Trigger": The Press and Human Rights. In *Realizing Human Rights: Moving from Inspiration to Impact,* edited by Samantha Power and Graham T. Allison, 337–50. New York: St. Martin's Press.

Ignatieff, Michael. 2001. Human Rights as Politics. In *Human Rights as Politics and Idolatry,* edited by Michael Ignatieff and Amy Gutmann, 3–52. Princeton, NJ: Princeton University Press.

Jennings, M. Kent. 1999. Political Responses to Pain and Loss. *American Political Science Review* 92(113): 1–13.

Kane, Hal, and Jane A. Peterson. 1995. *The Hour of Departure: Forces That Create Refugees and Migrants.* Worldwatch Paper 125. Washington, DC: Worldwatch Institute.

Kaufmann, Daniel, Aart Kraay, and Massimo Mastruzzi. 2008. *Governance Matters VII: Aggregate and Individual Governance Indicators, 1996–2007.* Washington, DC: World Bank. Available at http://papers.ssrn.com/sol3/papers.cfm?abstract_id=1148386 (accessed 8 June 2009).

Keck, Margaret E., and Kathryn Sikkink. 1998. *Activists Beyond Borders: Advocacy Networks in International Politics.* Ithaca, NY: Cornell University Press.

Keith, Linda Camp. 1999. The United Nations International Covenant on Civil and Political Rights: Does It Make a Difference in Human Rights Behavior? *Journal of Peace Research* 36(1): 95–118.

Kent, Ann. 1999. *China, the United Nations, and Human Rights.* Philadelphia: University of Pennsylvania Press.

Korey, William. 1998. *NGOs and the Universal Declaration of Human Rights: A Curious Grapevine.* New York: St. Martin's Press.

Laursen, Andreas. 2000. Israel's Supreme Court and International Human Rights Law: The Judgement on Moderate Physical Pressure. *Nordic Journal of International Law* 69(4): 413–47.

Leary, Virginia A. 1979. A New Role for Non-Governmental Organizations in Human Rights: A Case Study of Non-Governmental Participation in the Development of Norms of Torture. In *UN Law/Fundamental Rights,* edited by Antonio Cassese, 197–210. Alphen aan den Rijn, the Netherlands: Sitjhoff & Noordhoff.

Lippman, Matthew. 1994. The Development and Drafting of the United Nations Convention Against Torture and Other Cruel, Inhuman or Degrading Treatment or Punishment. *Boston College International and Comparative Law Review* 17:275–335.

Loveman, Mara. 1998. High-Risk Collective Action: Defending Human Rights in Chile, Uruguay, and Argentina. *The American Journal of Sociology* 104(2): 477–525.

Lukes, Steven. 2006. Liberal Democratic Torture. *British Journal of Political Science* 36:1–16.

Lutz, Ellen L., and Kathryn Sikkink. 2000. International Human Rights Law and Practice in Latin America. *International Organization* 54(3): 633–59.

———. 2001. The Justice Cascade: The Evolution and Impact of Foreign Human Rights Trials in Latin America. *Chicago Journal of International Law* 2(1): 1–33.

Malinowski, Tom. 2005. Banned State Department Practices. In *Torture: Does It Make Us Safer? Is It Ever OK? A Human Rights Perspective,* edited by Kenneth Roth, Minky Worden, and Amy D. Bernstein, 139–44. New York: New Press.

Mandel, Michael. 1999. Democracy and the New Constitutionalism in Israel. *Israel Law Review* 33(2): 259–321.

Maran, Rita. 1989. *Torture: The Role of Ideology in the French–Algerian War.* New York: Praeger.

Moravcsik, Andrew. 2000. The Origins of Human Rights Regimes: Democratic Delegation in Postwar Europe. *International Organizations* 54(2): 217–52.

Poe, Steven C., and C. Neal Tate. 1994. Repression of Human Rights to Personal Integrity in the 1980s: A Global Analysis. *American Political Science Review* 88(4): 853–72.

Poe, Steven C., Neal Tate, and Linda Camp Keith. 1999. Repression of the Human Right to Personal Integrity Revisited: A Global Crossnational Study Covering the Years 1976–1993. *International Studies Quarterly* 43:291–315.

Pogge, Thomas Winfried Menko. 2002. *World Poverty and Human Rights: Cosmopolitan Responsibilities and Reforms.* Malden, MA: Blackwell.

Ratner, Steven R. 2004. Overcoming Temptations to Violate Human Dignity in Times of Crisis: On the Possibilities for Meaningful Self-Restraint. *Theoretical Inquiries in Law (Online Edition)* 5(1): Article 3. Available at http://www.bepress.com/til/default/vol5/iss1/art3 (accessed 8 June 2009).

Ray, June. 2000. Human Rights Protection and the Rule of Law: Case Studies in Israel and Egypt. In *The Rule of Law in the Middle East and the Islamic World: Human Rights and the Judicial Process,* edited by Eugene Cottan and Mai Yamani, 43–50. London, New York: I. B. Tauris.

Rodley, Nigel S. 1999. *The Treatment of Prisoners Under International Law,* 2nd ed. New York: Oxford University Press.

Ross, James. 2005. A History of Torture. In *Torture: Does It Make Us Safer? Is It Ever OK? A Human Rights Perspective,* edited by Kenneth Roth, Minky Worden, and Amy D. Bernstein, 3–17. New York: New Press. Distributed by W. W. Norton.

Schou, Nina. 2000. Instances of Human Rights Regimes. In *Delegating State Powers: The Effect of Treaty Regimes on Democracy and Sovereignty,* edited by Thomas M. Franck, 209–54. Ardsley, NY: Transnational Publishers.

Shelton, Dinah. 1997. Compliance with International Human Rights Soft Law. In *International Compliance with Nonbinding Accords,* edited by Edith Brown Weiss, 119–43. Washington, DC: American Society of International Law.

Simmons, Beth A., and Daniel J. Hopkins. 2005. The Constraining Power of International Treaties: Theory and Methods. *American Political Science Review* 99(4): 623–31.

Sironi, Francoise, and Raphaelle Branche. 2002. Torture and the Borders of Humanity. *International Social Science Journal* 54(174): 539–48.

Slaughter, Joseph. 1997. A Question of Narration: The Voice in International Human Rights Law. *Human Rights Quarterly* 19(2): 406–30.

Solomon, Aaron. 2001. The Politics of Prosecutions Under the Convention Against Torture. *Chicago Journal of International Law* 20(2): 309–13.

St. Amand, Matthew G. 1999–2000. Public Committee Against Torture in *Israel v. The State of Israel et al.:* Landmark Human Rights Decision by the Israeli High Court of Justice or Status Quo Maintained? *North Carolina Journal of International and Comparative Regulation* 25:655–84.

Stohl, Michael, David Carleton, George A. Lopez, and Stephen Samuels. 1986. State Violation of Human Rights: Issues and Problems of Measurement. *Human Rights Quarterly* 8(4): 592–606.

Tardu, Maxime. 1980. United Nations Responses to Gross Violations of Human Rights: The 1503 Procedure. *Santa Clara Law Review* 20:559.

Tolley, Howard. 1989. Popular Sovereignty and International Law—ICJ Strategies for Human Rights Standard Setting. *Human Rights Quarterly* 11(4): 561–85.

USIP. 2001a. *U.S. Human Rights Policy toward Africa.* Washington, DC: United States Institute of Peace.

———. 2001b. *U.S. Human Rights Policy toward Latin America.* Washington, DC: United States Institute of Peace.

Valencia-Weber, Gloria, and Robert J. Weber. 1986. El-Salvador: Methods Used to Document Human-Rights Violations. *Human Rights Quarterly* 8(4): 731–70.

van Boven, Theo. 1989–1990. The Role of Non-Governmental Organizations in International Human Rights Standard Setting: A Prerequisite of Democracy. *California Western International Law Journal* 20(2): 207–25.

Walker, Scott, and Steven C. Poe. 2002. Does Cultural Diversity Affect Countries' Respect for Human Rights? *Human Rights Quarterly* 24(1): 237–63.

Wantchekon, Leonard, and Andrew Healy. 1999. The "Game" of Torture. *Journal of Conflict Resolution* 43(5): 596–609.

Worden, Minky. 2005. Torture Spoken Here: Ending Global Torture. In *Torture: Does It Make Us Safer? Is It Ever OK? A Human Rights Perspective,* edited by Kenneth Roth, Minky Worden, and Amy D. Bernstein, 79–105. New York: New Press.

Kenneth Roth

DEFENDING ECONOMIC, SOCIAL, AND CULTURAL RIGHTS

Practical Issues Faced by an International Human Rights Organization

Over the last decade, many have urged international human rights organizations to pay more attention to economic, social and cultural (ESC) rights. I agree with this prescription, and for several years Human Rights Watch has been doing significant work in this realm.[1] However, many who urge international groups to take on ESC rights have a fairly simplistic sense of how this is done. Human Rights Watch's experience has led me to believe that there are certain types of ESC issues for which our methodology works well and others for which it does not. In my view, understanding this distinction is key for an international human rights organization such as Human Rights Watch to address ESC rights effectively. Other approaches may work for other types of human rights groups, but organizations such as Human Rights Watch that rely foremost on shaming and the generation of public pressure to defend rights should remain attentive to this distinction.

During the Cold War, ESC rights tended to be debated in ideological terms. This consisted of the West stressing civil and political rights while the Soviet bloc (in principle if not in practice) stressed ESC rights. Many in the West went so far as to deny the very legitimacy of ESC issues as rights. Aryeh Neier, the former head of Human Rights Watch and now the president of the Open Society Institute, is perhaps the leading proponent of this view—most recently in his memoirs, *Taking Liberties*.[2] Certainly, interesting philosophical debates can be had about whether the concept of human rights should embrace positive as well as negative rights.[3] Since consensus in such debates is probably unattainable, the international human rights movement, in my view, has no choice but to rest on a positive-law justification for its work. That is, unless there are concrete and broadly understandable reasons to deviate from existing law, we must defend human rights law largely as written if we are to have any legitimacy and force to our work. That law, of course, codifies civil and political as well as ESC rights.[4]

That said, I must admit to finding the typical discussion of ESC rights rather sterile. I have been to countless conferences and debates in which advice is freely offered about how international human rights organizations must do more to protect ESC rights. Fair enough. Usually, the advice reduces to little more than sloganeering. People lack medical care; therefore, we should say that their right to health has been violated. People lack shelter; therefore, we should say that their right to housing has been violated. People are hungry; therefore, we should say that their right to food has been violated. Such "analysis," of course, wholly ignores such key issues as who is responsible for the impoverished state of a population, whether

From *Human Rights Quarterly* 26, no. 1 (February 2004): 63–73.

the government in question is taking steps to progressively realize the relevant rights, and what the remedy should be for any violation that is found. More to the point, for our purposes, it also ignores which issues can effectively be taken up by international human rights organizations that rely on shaming and public pressure and which cannot.

There are obviously various ways to promote ESC rights. One way is simply to encourage people to insist on respect for these rights. The language of rights can be a powerful organizing tool. But given that respect for ESC rights often requires the reallocation of resources, the people who have the clearest standing to insist on a particular allocation are usually the residents of the country in question. Outsiders such as international human rights organizations are certainly free to have a say in such matters. In an imperfect world in which the fulfillment of one ESC right is often at the expense of another, however, their voice insisting on a particular tradeoff has less legitimacy than that of the country's residents. Why should outsiders be listened to when they counsel, for example, that less be spent on health care and more on education—or even that less be spent on roads, bridges or other infrastructure deemed important for long-term economic development, and more on immediate needs?

I would suggest that merely advocating greater respect for ESC rights—simply adding our voice to that of many others demanding a particular allocation of scarce resources—is not a terribly effective role for international human rights groups such as Human Rights Watch. By expending our accumulated moral capital, we may well be listened to more than others in the short term, but that moral capital does not accumulate through our voice alone (why should our opinion count more than others?) but through our investigative and reporting methodology. It is a finite resource that can dissipate rapidly if not grounded in our methodological strength.

I am aware that similar tradeoffs of scarce resources can arise in the realm of civil and political

rights. Building prisons or creating a judicial system can be expensive. However, my experience has been that international human rights organizations implicitly recognize these tradeoffs by avoiding recommendations that are costly. For example, Human Rights Watch in its work on prison conditions routinely avoids recommending large infrastructure investments. Instead, we focus on improvements in the treatment of prisoners that would involve relatively inexpensive policy changes.[5] Similarly, our advocacy of due process in places such as Rwanda with weak and impoverished judicial systems implicitly takes account of the practical limitations facing the country leading us to be more tolerant of prosecutorial compromises such as *gacaca* courts than we would be in a richer country.[6]

A second way to promote ESC rights is through litigation—or, of greater relevance to most countries, by promoting the legislation that would make it possible to enforce ESC rights in court. It is clearly in the interest of those who believe in ESC rights that these rights be codified in enforceable national law. Many countries have such laws in various forms—be they guarantees of a minimum level of income (minimum wage or welfare), food, housing, or health care—but too many countries do not. International human rights organizations might press governments to adopt the legislation—the statutory rights—needed to make litigation a meaningful tool to enforce ESC rights. That is inevitably useful, but it is a procedural device that still falls significantly short of actual implementation. When it comes to deciding which ESC rights should be implemented first, or which tradeoffs among competing economic demands should be made, the advocacy of legislation does not give international human rights organizations any greater standing to address the concrete realization of ESC rights.

Similar shortcomings plague efforts by international human rights organizations to press governments to adopt national plans to progressively realize ESC rights.[7] Even though such plans would facilitate enforcement through public shaming for failure to live up to the plan, the international human rights movement is poorly placed to insist on the specifics of the plan.

Another way to promote ESC rights is by providing technical assistance to governments. Many development organizations perform this service, and presumably international human rights organizations could as well. But as in the realm of civil and political rights, technical assistance works only when governments have the will to respect ESC rights but lack the means or know-how to do so. This assistance thus is ill-suited to address the most egregious cases of ESC rights abuse—the area where, as in the civil and political rights realm, international human rights organizations would presumably want to focus. Indeed, the provision of technical assistance to a government that lacks a good-faith desire to respect rights can be counter-productive by providing a facade of conscientious striving that enables a government to deflect pressure to end abusive practices.

In my view, the most productive way for international human rights organizations, like Human Rights Watch, to address ESC rights is by building on the power of our methodology. The essence of that methodology, as I have suggested, is not the ability to mobilize people in the streets, to engage in litigation, to press for broad national plans, or to provide technical assistance. Rather, the core of our methodology is our ability to investigate, expose, and shame. We are at our most effective when we can hold governmental (or, in some cases, nongovernmental) conduct up to a disapproving public. Of course, we do not have to wait passively for public morality to coalesce on a particular issue; we can do much to shape public views by exposing sympathetic cases of injustice and suggesting a moral analysis for understanding them. In the end, the principal power of groups like Human Rights Watch is our ability to hold official conduct up to scrutiny and to generate public outrage. The relevant public is best when it is a local one—that is, the public of the country in question. Surrogate publics can also be used if they have the power to shape the policies of a government or institution with influence over the officials in question, such as by conditioning international assistance or trade benefits, imposing sanctions, or pursuing prosecution.

Although there are various forms of public outrage, only certain types are sufficiently targeted to shame officials into action. That is, the public might be outraged about a state of affairs—for example, poverty in a region—but have no idea whom to blame. Or it might feel that blame is dispersed among a wide variety of actors. In such cases of diffuse responsibility, the stigma attached to any person, government, or institution is lessened, and with it the power of international human rights organizations to effect change. Similarly, stigma weakens even in the case of a single violator if the remedy to a violation—what the government should do to correct it—is unclear.

In my view, to shame a government effectively—to maximize the power of international human rights organizations like Human Rights Watch—clarity is needed around three issues: violation, violator, and remedy. We must be able to show persuasively that a particular state of affairs amounts to a violation of human rights standards, that a particular violator is principally or significantly responsible, and that a widely accepted remedy for the violation exists. If any of these three elements is missing, our capacity to shame is greatly diminished. We tend to take these conditions for granted in the realm of civil and political rights because they usually coincide. For example, one can quibble about whether a particular form of mistreatment rises to the level of torture, but once a reasonable case is made that torture has occurred, it is fairly easy to determine the violator (the torturer as well as the governments or institutions that permit the torturer to operate with impunity) and the remedy (clear directions to stop torture, prosecution to back these up, and various prophylactic measures, such as ending incommunicado detention).

In the realm of ESC rights, the three preconditions for effective shaming operate much more independently. (For these purposes, I exclude the right to form labor unions and bargain collectively since while codified in the International Covenant on Economic, Social and Cultural Rights (ICESCR), this right functions more as a subset of the civil and political right to freedom of association.)[8] I accept, for the sake of this argument, that indicia have been developed for subsistence levels of food, housing, medical care, education, etc.[9] When steady progress is not being made toward realizing these subsistence levels, one can presumptively say that a "violation" has occurred.

But who is responsible for the violation, and what is the remedy? These answers flow much less directly from the mere documentation of an ESC rights violation than they do in the civil and political rights realm. For example, does responsibility for a substandard public health system lie with the government (through its corruption or mismanagement) or with the international community (through its stinginess or indifference). If the latter, which part of the international community? The answer is usually all of the above, which naturally reduces the potential to stigmatize any single actor.

Similar confusion surrounds discussions of appropriate remedies. Vigorously contested views about "structural adjustment" are illustrative. Is structural adjustment the cause of poverty, through its forced slashing of public investment in basic needs, or is it the solution by laying the groundwork for economic development? Supporting evidence can be found on both sides of this debate. When the target of a shaming effort can marshal respectable arguments in its defense, shaming usually fails.

The lesson I draw from these observations is that when international human rights organizations such as Human Rights Watch take on ESC rights,

we should look for situations in which there is relative clarity about violation, violator, and remedy.

Broadly speaking, I would suggest that the nature of the violation, violator, and remedy is clearest when it is possible to identify arbitrary or discriminatory governmental conduct that causes or substantially contributes to an ESC rights violation. These three dimensions are less clear when the ESC shortcoming is largely a problem of distributive justice. If all an international human rights organization can do is argue that more money be spent to uphold an ESC right—that a fixed economic pie be divided differently—our voice is relatively weak. We can argue that money should be diverted from less acute needs to the fulfillment of more pressing ESC rights, but little reason exists for a government to give our voice greater weight than domestic voices. On the other hand, if we can show that the government (or other relevant actor) is contributing to the ESC shortfall through arbitrary or discriminatory conduct, we are in a relatively powerful position to shame: we can show a violation (the rights shortfall), the violator (the government or other actor through its arbitrary or discriminatory conduct), and the remedy (reversing that conduct).

What does this mean in practice? To illustrate, let us assume we could demonstrate that a government was building medical clinics only in areas populated by ethnic groups that tended to vote for it, leaving other ethnic groups with substandard medical care. In such a case, an international human rights organization would be in a good position to argue that the disfavored ethnic groups' right to health care is being denied. This argument does not necessarily increase the resources being made available for health care, but it at least ensures a more equitable distribution. Since defenders of ESC rights should be concerned foremost with the worst-off segments of society, that redistribution would be an advance. Moreover, given that the government's supporters are not likely to be happy about a cutback in medical care, enforcement of a nondiscriminatory approach stands a reasonable chance of increasing health-related resources overall.

To cite another example, imagine a government that refuses to apply available resources for the benefit of its population's health. (South African President Thebo Mbeki's long refusal to allow donated nevirapine or AZT to be given to HIV-infected mothers to prevent mother-to-child transmission of the disease comes to mind.) A credible case can be made that such a government is acting arbitrarily—that it is not making a sincere effort to deploy available resources to progressively realize the ESC rights of its people. Again, by investigating and exposing this arbitrary conduct, an international human rights organization would have all the elements it needs to maximize the impact of its shaming methodology—a violation (the ESC shortcoming), a violator (the government acting arbitrarily), and the remedy (end the arbitrary conduct). Once more, there is no need to argue for more money to be spent or for a different allocation of available money (areas where there is little special power to the voice of international rights organizations), since in the case of arbitrary conduct the money is available but is being clearly misspent.

To cite yet another example, Human Rights Watch recently investigated conditions facing child farm workers in the United States. Had we been forced to delve into details about the appropriate maximum level of danger or pesticide exposure, or the appropriate number of working hours per day, we would have been in the amorphous realm of costs and benefits and thus lacked the clarity needed for effective shaming. However, we were able to show that child farm workers stand virtually alone in being excluded from the laws regulating working conditions for children in the United States. In making this revelation, we were able to demonstrate that U.S. laws governing child farm workers were both arbitrary (the exception was written in an era when the family farm was predominant; it has little relevance to the agribusiness that typifies the field today) and discriminatory (most of the parents of today's farmworker children are immigrants, politically an easy category to ignore).[10]

Education has been a productive area for this approach as well. For example, Human Rights Watch has been able to show that governments' failure to address violence against certain students (girls in South Africa, gays and lesbians in the United States) or bonded child labor (in India and Egypt) discriminatorily deprives these disfavored children of their right to education.[11]

If one accepts that international human rights organizations like Human Rights Watch are at our most powerful in the realm of ESC rights when we focus on discriminatory or arbitrary conduct rather than matters of pure distributive justice, guidance for our ESC work is provided. An important part of our work should be to shape public opinion gradually so that it tends to see ESC issues not only in terms of distributive justice but also in terms of discriminatory or arbitrary conduct. For example, governments' failure to provide universal primary education would seem to be a classic case of distributive justice—there is not enough money to go around, so governments cannot provide education to all children. Human Rights Watch is considering a project that would focus on the practice of funding education in such circumstances through school fees. We would hope to argue that this is a discriminatory and arbitrary way of funding education because it has the foreseeable effect of excluding children from poor families. If we succeed in promoting this perspective, we hope to transform the debate from one on which international human rights organizations have had little if any impact to one in which our ability to stigmatize and hence shape public policy on education would be much enhanced.

We used the same approach to highlight the neglect of "AIDS orphans" in Kenya. The provision of care for children without parents, while classically a state responsibility, is frequently limited by scarce resources. In Kenya, as in many African countries, the responsibility was typically delegated to, and accepted by, the extended family. However, given the devastation of the AIDS crisis, extended families increasingly are unable to bear this burden, leaving many of these orphans destitute. By demonstrating that the classic state approach to the problem had become arbitrary (it was no longer working in light of the AIDS pandemic) and discriminatory (it falls on a group of people who are already stigmatized, AIDS-affected families), Human Rights Watch succeeded in generating significant pressure on the Kenyan government and international organizations to recognize and address the problem.[12]

Similar efforts might be made to address issues of corruption. For example, if it can be shown that government officials are pocketing scarce public resources or wasting them on self-aggrandizing projects rather than meeting ESC needs, international human rights organizations can use our shaming capacity to enlarge the size of the economic pie without entering into more detailed discussions about how that pie should be divided to realize ESC rights.

In making these observations, I recognize that there are certain realms where international human rights organizations might be able to take on distributive justice questions more directly. If the issue is not how a foreign government divides a limited economic pie, but rather how much money a Northern government or an international financial institution spends on international assistance for the realization of ESC rights, Northern-based international human rights organizations speak less as an outside voice and more as a domestic constituent. Even then, given our relative weakness at mobilizing large numbers of people at this stage in our evolution, pressure simply to spend more, rather than stigmatization over arbitrary or discriminatory spending, is less likely to resonate with

decision makers. That is all the more true when Northern governments point to the failure of many needy governments to establish sufficient transparency and public accountability to reasonably assure that international assistance will be well spent. As noted, the international human rights movement's ability to shame diminishes significantly if the target has a credible rebuttal.

To conclude, let me offer a hypothesis about the conduct of international human rights organizations working on ESC rights. It has been clear for many years that the movement would like to do more in the ESC realm. Yet despite repeated professions of interest, its work in this area remains limited. Part of the reason, of course, is expertise; the movement must staff itself somewhat differently to document shortfalls in such matters as health or housing than to record instances of torture or political imprisonment. But much of the reason, I suspect, is a sense of futility. International human rights activists see how little impact they have in taking on matters of pure distributive justice so they have a hard time justifying devoting scarce institutional resources for such limited ends. However, if we focus our attention on ESC policy that can fairly be characterized as arbitrary or discriminatory, I believe our impact will be substantially larger. And there is nothing like success to breed emulation.

Thus, when outsiders ask international human rights organizations such as Human Rights Watch to expand our work on ESC rights, we should insist on a more sophisticated and realistic conversation than has been typical so far. It is not enough, we should point out, to document ESC shortcomings and to declare a rights violation. Rather, we should ask our interlocutors to help us identify ESC shortcomings in which there is relative clarity about the nature of the violation, violator, and remedy, so that our shaming methodology will be most effective. As we succeed in broadening the number of governmental actions that can be seen in this way, we will go a long way toward enhancing the ESC work of the international human rights movements—work that, we all realize, is essential to our credibility.

Coincidentally, international development and humanitarian organizations are increasingly adopting the view that poverty and severe deprivation is a product less of a lack of public goods than of officially promoted or tolerated policies of social exclusion. That insight meshes well with the approach I have outlined for promoting ESC rights. A lack of public goods tends to be a matter of distributive justice. In ESC right terms, however, policies of social exclusion tend to have a relatively clear violation, violator, and remedy. If development and humanitarian organizations indeed move in this direction, it portends useful partnerships with international human rights organizations such as Human Rights Watch.

NOTES

1. *See* the Human Rights Watch website on Economic, Social, and Cultural Rights at www.hrw.org/esc.

2. Aryeh Neier, Taking Liberties: Four Decades in the Struggle for Rights xxix–xxx (2003).

3. See Isaiah Berlin, Four Essays on Liberty 122–34 (1969) for more on the concepts of positive and negative freedom. See also, e.g., Amartya Sen, Development as Freedom (1999); Martha Nussbaum, Women and Human Development: The Capabilities Approach (2000) (discussing this debate within a contemporary human rights framework).

4. See International Covenant on Civil and Political Rights, adopted 16 Dec. 1966, G.A. Res. 2200 (XXI), U.N. GAOR, 21st Sess., Supp. No. 16, U.N. Doc. A/6316 (1966), 999 U.N.T.S. 171 (entered into force 23 Mar 1976); International Covenant on Economic, Social, and Cultural Rights, adopted 16 Dec. 1966, G.A. Res. 2200 (XXI), U.N. GAOR, 21st Sess., Supp. No. 16, U.N. Doc. A/6316 (1966), 993 U.N.T.S. 3 (entered into force 3 Jan. 1976) (hereinafter ICESCR); see also Universal Declaration of Human Rights, adopted 10 Dec. 1948, G.A. Res. 217A (III), U.N. GAOR, 3d Sess. (Resolutions, part 1), at 71, U.N. Doc. A/810 (1948), reprinted in 43 *Am. J. Int'l L.* Supp. 127 (1949).

5. See, e.g., Human Rights Watch, Prison Conditions in South Africa (1994); Human Rights Watch, Out of Sight: Super-Maximum Security Confinement in the United States Vol. 12 (2000); Human Rights Watch, Prison Conditions in Japan (1995); Human Rights Watch, Prison Conditions in Czechoslovakia (1989); Human Rights Watch, Prison Conditions in Czechoslovakia: An Update (1991); Human Rights Watch, Prison Conditions in Poland: An Update (1988); Human Rights Watch, Prison Conditions in Poland: An Update (1991).

6. See, e.g., Press Release, Human Rights Watch, Rwanda: Elections May Speed Genocide Trials: But New System Lacks Guarantees of Rights (4 Oct. 2001) available at www.hrw.org/press/2001/10/rwanda1004.

7. *See* ICESCR, *supra* note 4, art. 2:

> Each State Party to the present Covenant undertakes to take steps, individually and through international assistance and co-operation, especially economic and technical, to the maximum of its available resources, with a view to achieving progressively the full realization of the rights recognized in the present Covenant by all appropriate means, including particularly the adoption of legislative measures.

See also General Comment No. 3, Comm. on Econ., Soc. Cultural Rts., 5th Sess., Annex III, UN Doc. E/1991/23 (1990) (interpreting the meaning of the progressive-realization requirement).

8. See ICESCR, *supra* note 4.

9. See, e.g., Masstricht Guidelines on Violations of Economic, Social and Cultural Rights, adopted 22–26 Jan. 1997, reprinted in The Masstricht Guidelines on Violations of Economic, Social and Cultural Rights, 20 *Hum. Rts. Q.* 691 (1998); The Limburg Principles on the Implementation of the International Covenant on Economic, Social and Cultural Rights, adopted 8 Jan. 1987, U.N. ESCOR, Comm'n on Hum. Rts., 43rd Sess., Agenda Item 8, U.N. Doc. E/CN.4/1987/17/Annex (1987), reprinted in The Limburg Principles on the Implementation of the International Covenant on Economic, Social and Cultural Rights, 9 *Hum. Rts. Q.* 122 (1987); Draft Guidelines: A Human Rights Approach to Poverty Reduction Strategies, adopted 10 Oct. 2002, U.N. OHCHR.

10. Human Rights Watch, Fingers to the Bone: United States Failure to Protect Child Farmworkers 55–73 (2000).

11. Human Rights Watch, Hatred in the Hallways: Violence and Discrimination Against Lesbian, Gay, Bisexual, and Transgender Students in U.S. Schools 3–7 (2001); Press Release, Human Rights Watch, South Africa: Sexual Violence Rampant in Schools: Harassment and Rape Hampering Girls' Education (27 Mar. 2001) available at www.hrw.org/press/2001/03/sa–0327; Human Rights Watch, Underage and Unprotected: Child Labor in Egypt's Cotton Fields (2001); Human Rights Watch, The Small Hands of Slavery: Bonded Child Labor in India 14–19 (1996).

12. Human Rights Watch, In the Shadow of Death: HIV/AIDS and Children's Rights in Kenya (2001).

11 TRANSNATIONAL ISSUES

Reflecting the worldwide interconnectedness that is now called "globalization," transnational concerns have become part of the global agenda. Such concerns include the environment, pollution, population, health, and international crime. For many transnational issues, the interests, rights, and responsibilities of the individual, the state, and the international community may be incompatible or even diverge. Do the rights of the individual take precedence over the rights of the community in the use of land and natural resources? Does a couple have the right of unlimited procreation when resources are limited? In his pathbreaking 1968 article, Garrett Hardin posits in unequivocal terms that the pursuit of individual interests may not necessarily lead to the common good.

Climate change is a quintessential example of a "tragedy of the commons." The whole earth is affected, and the efforts of people and governments worldwide are needed to solve the problem. Scott Barrett asks "Why Have Climate Negotiations Proved So Disappointing?" He argues that the temptation of states to "free ride" on the efforts of others is exacerbated by the high cost of the remedies, uncertainty about the point at which the climate will tip to disaster, and the difficulty of organizing reciprocity when cooperation of many stakeholders is needed. Barrett thinks the successful Montreal agreement banning gases that deplete the atmosphere's ozone layer offers a model of how to create incentives to limit carbon emissions that cause global climate change.

Global problems may also be caused by misguided social practices. Valerie M. Hudson and Andrea M. den Boer trace the numerous social ills that stem from a population imbalance between men and women and the cultural practices that contribute to this imbalance. Some of the phenomena with partial roots in this gender disparity, such as terrorism and migration, can have transnational and international consequences.

New communications and information technologies are also having international and transnational effects. Jon R. Lindsay's essay evaluates claims about the potential for cyberwarfare and computer espionage to disrupt U.S.-Chinese relations.

Finally, Laurie Garrett draws lessons for the reform of international health systems from their failure to respond effectively to the challenges posed by the Ebola epidemic in Africa. This scathing critique of the World Health Organization should be read alongside the article by Michael Barnett and Martha Finnemore in chapter 5 on "The Politics, Power, and Pathologies of International Organizations."

Garrett Hardin
THE TRAGEDY OF THE COMMONS

The population problem has no technical solution; it requires a fundamental extension in morality.

At the end of a thoughtful article on the future of nuclear war, Wiesner and York[1] concluded that: "Both sides in the arms race are . . . confronted by the dilemma of steadily increasing military power and steadily decreasing national security. *It is our considered professional judgment that this dilemma has no technical solution.* If the great powers continue to look for solutions in the area of science and technology only, the result will be to worsen the situation."

I would like to focus your attention not on the subject of the article (national security in a nuclear world) but on the kind of conclusion they reached, namely that there is no technical solution to the problem. An implicit and almost universal assumption of discussions published in professional and semipopular scientific journals is that the problem under discussion has a technical solution. A technical solution may be defined as one that requires a change only in the techniques of the natural sciences, demanding little or nothing in the way of change in human values or ideas of morality.

In our day (though not in earlier times) technical solutions are always welcome. Because of previous failures in prophecy, it takes courage to assert that a desired technical solution is not possible. Wiesner and York exhibited this courage; publishing in a science journal, they insisted that the solution to the problem was not to be found in the natural sciences. They cautiously qualified their

statement with the phrase, "It is our considered professional judgment. . . ." Whether they were right or not is not the concern of the present article. Rather, the concern here is with the important concept of a class of human problems which can be called "no technical solution problems," and, more specifically, with the identification and discussion of one of these.

It is easy to show that the class is not a null class. Recall the game of tick-tack-toe. Consider the problem, "How can I win the game of tick-tack-toe?" It is well known that I cannot, if I assume (in keeping with the conventions of game theory) that my opponent understands the game perfectly. Put another way, there is no "technical solution" to the problem. I can win only by giving a radical meaning to the word "win." I can hit my opponent over the head; or I can drug him; or I can falsify the records. Every way in which I "win" involves, in some sense, an abandonment of the game, as we intuitively understand it. (I can also, of course, openly abandon the game—refuse to play it. This is what most adults do.)

The class of "No technical solution problems" has members. My thesis is that the "population problem," as conventionally conceived, is a member of this class. How it is conventionally conceived needs some comment. It is fair to say that most people who anguish over the population problem are trying to find a way to avoid the evils of overpopulation without relinquishing any of the privileges they now enjoy. They think that farming the seas or developing new strains of wheat will solve the problem—technologically. I try to show here that the solution they seek cannot be found. The population problem cannot be solved

From *Science* 162, no. 3859 (Dec. 13, 1968), 1243–48.

in a technical way, any more than can the problem of winning the game of tick-tack-toe.

What Shall We Maximize?

Population, as Malthus said, naturally tends to grow "geometrically," or, as we would now say, exponentially. In a finite world this means that the per capita share of the world's goods must steadily decrease. Is ours a finite world?

A fair defense can be put forward for the view that the world is infinite; or that we do not know that it is not. But, in terms of the practical problems that we must face in the next few generations with the foreseeable technology, it is clear that we will greatly increase human misery if we do not, during the immediate future, assume that the world available to the terrestrial human population is finite. "Space" is no escape.[2]

A finite world can support only a finite population; therefore, population growth must eventually equal zero. (The case of perpetual wide fluctuations above and below zero is a trivial variant that need not be discussed.) When this condition is met, what will be the situation of mankind? Specifically, can Bentham's goal of "the greatest good for the greatest number" be realized?

No—for two reasons, each sufficient by itself. The first is a theoretical one. It is not mathematically possible to maximize for two (or more) variables at the same time. This was clearly stated by von Neumann and Morgenstern,[3] but the principle is implicit in the theory of partial differential equations, dating back at least to D'Alembert (1717–1783).

The second reason springs directly from biological facts. To live, any organism must have a source of energy (for example, food). This energy is utilized for two purposes: mere maintenance and work. For man, maintenance of life requires about 1600 kilo-calories a day ("maintenance calories"). Anything that he does over and above merely staying alive will be defined as work, and is supported by "work calories" which he takes in. Work calories are used not only for what we call work in common speech; they are also required for all forms of enjoyment, from swimming and automobile racing to playing music and writing poetry. If our goal is to maximize population it is obvious what we must do: We must make the work calories per person approach as close to zero as possible. No gourmet meals, no vacations, no sports, no music, no literature, no art. . . . I think that everyone will grant, without argument or proof, that maximizing population does not maximize goods. Bentham's goal is impossible.

In reaching this conclusion I have made the usual assumption that it is the acquisition of energy that is the problem. The appearance of atomic energy has led some to question this assumption. However, given an infinite source of energy, population growth still produces an inescapable problem. The problem of the acquisition of energy is replaced by the problem of its dissipation, as J. H. Fremlin has so wittily shown.[4] The arithmetic signs in the analysis are, as it were, reversed; but Bentham's goal is still unobtainable.

The optimum population is, then, less than the maximum. The difficulty of defining the optimum is enormous; so far as I know, no one has seriously tackled this problem. Reaching an acceptable and stable solution will surely require more than one generation of hard analytical work—and much persuasion.

We want the maximum good per person; but what is good? To one person it is wilderness, to another it is ski lodges for thousands. To one it is estuaries to nourish ducks for hunters to shoot; to another it is factory land. Comparing one good with another is, we usually say, impossible because goods are incommensurable. Incommensurables cannot be compared.

Theoretically this may be true; but in real life incommensurables *are* commensurable. Only a criterion of judgment and a system of weighting are needed. In nature the criterion is survival. Is it better for a species to be small and hide-able, or large and powerful? Natural selection commensurates the incommensurables. The compromise achieved depends on a natural weighting of the values of the variables.

Man must imitate this process. There is no doubt that in fact he already does, but unconsciously. It is when the hidden decisions are made explicit that the arguments begin. The problem for the years ahead is to work out an acceptable theory of weighting. Synergistic effects, nonlinear variation, and difficulties in discounting the future make the intellectual problem difficult, but not (in principle) insoluble.

Has any cultural group solved this practical problem at the present time, even on an intuitive level? One simple fact proves that none has: there is no prosperous population in the world today that has, and has had for some time, a growth rate of zero. Any people that has intuitively identified its optimum point will soon reach it, after which its growth rate becomes and remains zero.

Of course, a positive growth rate might be taken as evidence that a population is below its optimum. However, by any reasonable standards, the most rapidly growing populations on earth today are (in general) the most miserable. This association (which need not be invariable) casts doubt on the optimistic assumption that the positive growth rate of a population is evidence that it has yet to reach its optimum.

We can make little progress in working toward optimum poulation size until we explicitly exorcize the spirit of Adam Smith in the field of practical demography. In economic affairs, *The Wealth of Nations* (1776) popularized the "invisible hand," the idea that an individual who "intends only his own gain," is, as it were, "led by an invisible hand to promote . . . the public interest."[5] Adam Smith did not assert that this was invariably true, and perhaps neither did any of his followers. But he contributed to a dominant tendency of thought that has ever since interfered with positive action based on rational analysis, namely, the tendency to assume that decisions reached individually will, in fact, be the best decisions for an entire society. If this assumption is correct it justifies the continuance of our present policy of laissez-faire in reproduction. If it is correct we can assume that men will control their individual fecundity so as to produce the optimum population. If the assumption is not correct, we need to reexamine our individual freedoms to see which ones are defensible.

Tragedy of Freedom in a Commons

The rebuttal to the invisible hand in population control is to be found in a scenario first sketched in a little-known pamphlet[6] in 1833 by a mathematical amateur named William Forster Lloyd (1794–1852). We may well call it "the tragedy of the commons," using the word "tragedy" as the philosopher Whitehead used it[7]: "The essence of dramatic tragedy is not unhappiness. It resides in the solemnity of the remorseless working of things:" He then goes on to say, "This inevitableness of destiny can only be illustrated in terms of human life by incidents which in fact involve unhappiness. For it is only by them that the futility of escape can be made evident in the drama."

The tragedy of the commons develops in this way. Picture a pasture open to all. It is to be expected that each herdsman will try to keep as many cattle as possible on the commons. Such an arrangement may work reasonably satisfactorily for centuries because tribal wars, poaching, and disease keep the numbers of both man and beast well below the carrying capacity of the land. Finally, however, comes the day of reckoning, that is, the day when the long-desired goal of social stability becomes a reality. At this point, the inherent logic of the commons remorselessly generates tragedy.

As a rational being, each herdsman seeks to maximize his gain. Explicitly or implicitly, more or less consciously, he asks, "What is the utility *to me* of adding one more animal to my herd?" This utility has one negative and one positive component.

1) The positive component is a function of the increment of one animal. Since the herdsman receives all the proceeds from the sale of the additional animal, the positive utility is nearly +1.

2) The negative component is a function of the additional overgrazing created by one more animal. Since, however, the effects of overgrazing are shared by all the herdsmen, the negative utility for any particular decision-making herdsman is only a fraction of −1.

Adding together the component partial utilities, the rational herdsman concludes that the only sensible course for him to pursue is to add another animal to his herd. And another; and another. . . . But this is the conclusion reached by each and every rational herdsman sharing a commons. Therein is the tragedy. Each man is locked into a system that compels him to increase his herd without limit—in a world that is limited. Ruin is the destination toward which all men rush, each pursuing his own best interest in a society that believes in the freedom of the commons. Freedom in a commons brings ruin to all.

Some would say that this is a platitude. Would that it were! In a sense, it was learned thousands of years ago, but natural selection favors the forces of psychological denial.[8] The individual benefits as an individual from his ability to deny the truth even though society as a whole, of which he is a part, suffers. Education can counteract the natural tendency to do the wrong thing, but the inexorable succession of generations requires that the basis for this knowledge be constantly refreshed.

A simple incident that occurred a few years ago in Leominster, Massachusetts, shows how perishable the knowledge is. During the Christmas shopping season the parking meters downtown were covered with plastic bags that bore tags reading: "Do not open until after Christmas. Free parking courtesy of the mayor and city council." In other words, facing the prospect of an increased demand for already scarce space, the city fathers reinstituted the system of the commons. (Cynically, we suspect that they gained more votes than they lost by this retrogressive act.)

In an approximate way, the logic of the commons has been understood for a long time, perhaps since the discovery of agriculture or the invention of private property in real estate. But it is understood mostly only in special cases which are not sufficiently generalized. Even at this late date, cattlemen leasing national land on the western ranges demonstrate no more than an ambivalent understanding, in constantly pressuring federal authorities to increase the head count to the point where overgrazing produces erosion and weed-dominance. Likewise, the oceans of the world continue to suffer from the survival of the philosophy of the commons. Maritime nations still respond automatically to the shibboleth of the "freedom of the seas." Professing to believe in the "inexhaustible resources of the oceans," they bring species after species of fish and whales closer to extinction.[9]

The National Parks present another instance of the working out of the tragedy of the commons. At present, they are open to all, without limit. The parks themselves are limited in extent—there is only one Yosemite Valley—whereas population seems to grow without limit. The values that visitors seek in the parks are steadily eroded. Plainly, we must soon cease to treat the parks as commons or they will be of no value to anyone.

What shall we do? We have several options. We might sell them off as private property. We might keep them as public property, but allocate the right to enter them. The allocation might be on the basis of wealth, by the use of an auction system. It might be on the basis of merit, as defined by some agreed-upon standards. It might be by lottery. Or it might be on a first-come, first-served basis, administered to long queues. These, I think, are all the reasonable possibilities. They are all objectionable. But we must choose—or acquiesce in the destruction of the commons that we call our National Parks.

Pollution

In a reverse way, the tragedy of the commons reappears in problems of pollution. Here it is not a question of taking something out of the commons, but of putting something in—sewage, or chemical, radioactive, and heat wastes into water; noxious and dangerous fumes into the air; and distracting and unpleasant advertising signs into the line of sight. The calculations of utility are much the same as before. The rational man finds that his share of the cost of the wastes he discharges into the commons is less than the cost of purifying his wastes before releasing them. Since this is true for everyone, we are locked into a system of "fouling our own nest," so long as we behave only as independent, rational, free-enterprisers.

The tragedy of the commons as a food basket is averted by private property, or something formally like it. But the air and waters surrounding us cannot readily be fenced, and so the tragedy of the commons as a cesspool must be prevented by different means, by coercive laws or taxing devices that make it cheaper for the polluter to treat his pollutants than to discharge them untreated. We have not progressed as far with the solution of this problem as we have with the first. Indeed, our particular concept of private property, which deters us from exhausting the positive resources of the earth, favors pollution. The owner of a factory on the bank of a stream—whose property extends to the middle of the stream—often has difficulty seeing why it is not his natural right to muddy the waters flowing past his door. The law, always behind the times, requires elaborate stitching and fitting to adapt it to this newly perceived aspect of the commons.

The pollution problem is a consequence of population. It did not much matter how a lonely American frontiersman disposed of his waste. "Flowing water purifies itself every 10 miles," my grandfather used to say, and the myth was near enough to the truth when he was a boy, for there were not too many people. But as population became denser, the natural chemical and biological recycling processes became overloaded, calling for a redefinition of property rights.

How to Legislate Temperance?

Analysis of the pollution problem as a function of population density uncovers a not generally recognized principle of morality, namely: *the morality of an act is a function of the state of the system at the time it is performed.*[10] Using the commons as a cesspool does not harm the general public under frontier conditions, because there is no public; the same behavior in a metropolis is unbearable. A hundred and fifty years ago a plainsman could kill an American bison, cut out only the tongue for his dinner, and discard the rest of the animal. He was not in any important sense being wasteful. Today, with only a few thousand bison left, we would be appalled at such behavior.

In passing, it is worth noting that the morality of an act cannot be determined from a photograph. One does not know whether a man killing an elephant or setting fire to the grassland is harming others until one knows the total system in which his act appears. "One picture is worth a thousand words," said an ancient Chinese; but it may take 10,000 words to validate it. It is as tempting to ecologists as it is to reformers in general to try to persuade others by way of the photographic shortcut. But the essen[c]e of an argument cannot be photographed: it must be presented rationally—in words.

That morality is system-sensitive escaped the attention of most codifiers of ethics in the past. "Thou shalt not . . ." is the form of traditional ethical directives which make no allowance for particular circumstances. The laws of our society follow the pattern of ancient ethics, and therefore are poorly suited to governing a complex, crowded, changeable world. Our epicyclic solution is to augment statutory law with administrative law. Since it is practically impossible to spell out all the conditions under which it is safe to burn trash in the back yard or to run an automobile without smog-control, by law we delegate the details to bureaus. The result is administrative law, which is rightly feared for an ancient reason—*Quis custodiet ipsos custodes?*—"Who shall watch the watchers themselves?" John Adams said that we must have "a government of laws and not men." Bureau administrators, trying to evaluate the morality of acts in the total system, are singularly liable to corruption, producing a government by men, not laws.

Prohibition is easy to legislate (though not necessarily to enforce); but how do we legislate temperance? Experience indicates that it can be accomplished best through the mediation of administrative law. We limit possibilities unnecessarily if we suppose that the sentiment of *Quis custodiet* denies us the use of administrative law. We should rather retain the phrase as a perpetual reminder of fearful dangers we cannot avoid. The great challenge facing us now is to invent the corrective feedbacks that are needed to keep custodians honest. We must find ways to legitimate the needed authority of both the custodians and the corrective feedbacks.

Freedom to Breed Is Intolerable

The tragedy of the commons is involved in population problems in another way. In a world governed solely by the principle of "dog eat dog"—if

indeed there ever was such a world—how many children a family had would not be a matter of public concern. Parents who bred too exuberantly would leave fewer descendants, not more, because they would be unable to care adequately for their children. David Lack and others have found that such a negative feedback demonstrably controls the fecundity of birds.[11] But men are not birds, and have not acted like them for millenniums, at least.

If each human family were dependent only on its own resources; *if* the children of improvident parents starved to death; *if,* thus, overbreeding brought its own "punishment" to the germ line—*then* there would be no public interest in controlling the breeding of families. But our society is deeply committed to the welfare state,[12] and hence is confronted with another aspect of the tragedy of the commons.

In a welfare state, how shall we deal with the family, the religion, the race, or the class (or indeed any distinguishable and cohesive group) that adopts overbreeding as a policy to secure its own aggrandizement?[13] To couple the concept of freedom to breed with the belief that everyone born has an equal right to the commons is to lock the world into a tragic course of action.

Unfortunately this is just the course of action that is being pursued by the United Nations. In late 1967, some 30 nations agreed to the following[14]:

> The Universal Declaration of Human Rights describes the family as the natural and fundamental unit of society. It follows that any choice and decision with regard to the size of the family must irrevocably rest with the family itself, and cannot be made by anyone else.

It is painful to have to deny categorically the validity of this right; denying it, one feels as uncomfortable as a resident of Salem, Massachusetts, who denied the reality of witches in the seventeenth century. At the present time, in liberal quarters, something like a taboo acts to inhibit criticism of the United Nations. There is a feeling that the United Nations is "our last and best hope," that we shouldn't find fault with it; we shouldn't play into the hands of the archconservatives. However, let us not forget what Robert Louis Stevenson said: "The truth that is suppressed by friends is the readiest weapon of the enemy." If we love the truth we must openly deny the validity of the Universal Declaration of Human Rights, even though it is promoted by the United Nations. We should also join with Kingsley Davis[15] in attempting to get Planned Parenthood-World Population to see the error of its ways in embracing the same tragic ideal.

Conscience Is Self-Eliminating

It is a mistake to think that we can control the breeding of mankind in the long run by an appeal to conscience. Charles Galton Darwin made this point when he spoke on the centennial of the publication of his grandfather's great book. The argument is straightforward and Darwinian.

People vary. Confronted with appeals to limit breeding, some people will undoubtedly respond to the plea more than others. Those who have more children will produce a larger fraction of the next generation than those with more susceptible consciences. The difference will be accentuated, generation by generation.

In C. G. Darwin's words: "It may well be that it would take hundreds of generations for the progenitive instinct to develop in this way, but if it should do so, nature would have taken her revenge, and the variety *Homo contracipiens* would become extinct and would be replaced by the variety *Homo progenitivus*."[16]

The argument assumes that conscience or the desire for children (no matter which) is hereditary—but hereditary only in the most general formal sense. The result will be the same whether the attitude is transmitted through germ cells, or exosomatically, to use A. J. Lotka's term. (If one denies the latter possibility as well as the former, then what's the point of education?) The argument has here been stated in the context of the population problem, but it applies equally well to any instance in which society appeals to an individual exploiting a commons to restrain himself for the general good—by means of his conscience. To make such an appeal is to set up a selective system that works toward the elimination of conscience from the race.

Pathogenic Effects of Conscience

The long-term disadvantage of an appeal to conscience should be enough to condemn it; but has serious short-term disadvantages as well. If we ask a man who is exploiting a commons to desist "in the name of conscience," what are we saying to him? What does he hear?—not only at the moment but also in the wee small hours of the night when, half asleep, he remembers not merely the words we used but also the nonverbal communication cues we gave him unawares? Sooner or later, consciously or subconsciously, he senses that he has received two communications, and that they are contradictory: (i) (intended communication) "If you don't do as we ask, we will openly condemn you for not acting like a responsible citizen"; (ii) (the unintended communication) "If you *do* behave as we ask, we will secretly condemn you for a simpleton who can be shamed into standing aside while the rest of us exploit the commons."

Everyman then is caught in what Bateson has called a "double bind." Bateson and his co-workers have made a plausible case for viewing the double bind as an important causative factor in the genesis of schizophrenia.[17] The double bind may not always be so damaging, but it always endangers the mental health of anyone to whom it is applied. "A bad conscience," said Nietzsche, "is a kind of illness."

To conjure up a conscience in others is tempting to anyone who wishes to extend his control beyond the legal limits. Leaders at the highest level succumb to this temptation. Has any President during the past generation failed to call on labor unions to moderate voluntarily their demands for higher wages, or to steel companies to honor voluntary guidelines on prices? I can recall none. The rhetoric used on such occasions is designed to produce feelings of guilt in noncooperators.

For centuries it was assumed without proof that guilt was a valuable, perhaps even an indispensable, ingredient of the civilized life. Now, in this post-Freudian world, we doubt it.

Paul Goodman speaks from the modern point of view when he says: "No good has ever come from feeling guilty, neither intelligence, policy, nor compassion. The guilty do not pay attention to the object but only to themselves, and not even to their own interests, which might make sense, but to their anxieties."[18]

One does not have to be a professional psychiatrist to see the consequences of anxiety. We in the Western world are just emerging from a dreadful two-centuries-long Dark Ages of Eros that was sustained partly by prohibition laws, but perhaps more effectively by the anxiety-generating mechanisms of education. Alex Comfort has told the story well in *The Anxiety Makers*[19]; it is not a pretty one.

Since proof is difficult, we may even concede that the results of anxiety may sometimes, from certain points of view, be desirable. The larger question we should ask is whether, as a matter of policy, we should ever encourage the use of a technique the tendency (if not the intention) of which is psychologically pathogenic. We hear much talk these days of responsible parenthood; the coupled words are incorporated into the titles of some organizations devoted to birth control. Some people

have proposed massive propaganda campaigns to instill responsibility into the nation's (or the world's) breeders. But what is the meaning of the word responsibility in this context? Is it not merely a synonym for the word conscience? When we use the word responsibility in the absence of substantial sanctions are we not trying to browbeat a free man in a commons into acting against his own interest? Responsibility is a verbal counterfeit for a substantial *quid pro quo*. It is an attempt to get something for nothing.

If the word responsibility is to be used at all, I suggest that it be in the sense Charles Frankel uses it.[20] "Responsibility," says this philosopher, "is the product of definite social arrangements." Notice that Frankel calls for social arrangements—not propaganda.

Mutual Coercion Mutually Agreed Upon

The social arrangements that produce responsibility are arrangements that create coercion, of some sort. Consider bank-robbing. The man who takes money from a bank acts as if the bank were a commons. How do we prevent such action? Certainly not by trying to control his behavior solely by a verbal appeal to his sense of responsibility. Rather than rely on propaganda we follow Frankel's lead and insist that a bank is not a commons; we seek the definite social arrangements that will keep it from becoming a commons. That we thereby infringe on the freedom of would-be robbers we neither deny nor regret.

The morality of bank-robbing is particularly easy to understand because we accept complete prohibition of this activity. We are willing to say "Thou shalt not rob banks," without providing for exceptions. But temperance also can be created by coercion. Taxing is a good coercive device. To keep downtown shoppers temperate in their use of parking space we introduce parking meters for short periods, and traffic fines for longer ones. We need not actually forbid a citizen to park as long as he wants to; we need merely make it increasingly expensive for him to do so. Not prohibition, but carefully biased options are what we offer him. A Madison Avenue man might call this persuasion; I prefer the greater candor of the word coercion.

Coercion is a dirty word to most liberals now, but it need not forever be so. As with the four-letter words, its dirtiness can be cleansed away by exposure to the light, by saying it over and over without apology or embarrassment. To many, the word coercion implies arbitrary decisions of distant and irresponsible bureaucrats; but this is not a necessary part of its meaning. The only kind of coercion I recommend is mutual coercion, mutually agreed upon by the majority of the people affected.

To say that we mutually agree to coercion is not to say that we are required to enjoy it, or even to pretend we enjoy it. Who enjoys taxes? We all grumble about them. But we accept compulsory taxes because we recognize that voluntary taxes would favor the conscienceless. We institute and (grumblingly) support taxes and other coercive devices to escape the horror of the commons.

An alternative to the commons need not be perfectly just to be preferable. With real estate and other material goods, the alternative we have chosen is the institution of private property coupled with legal inheritance. Is this system perfectly just? As a genetically trained biologist I deny that it is. It seems to me that, if there are to be differences in individual inheritance, legal possession should be perfectly correlated with biological inheritance—that those who are biologically more fit to be the custodians of property and power should legally inherit more. But genetic recombination continually makes a mockery of the doctrine of "like father, like son" implicit in our laws of legal inheritance. An idiot can inherit millions, and a

trust fund can keep his estate intact. We must admit that our legal system of private property plus inheritance is unjust—but we put up with it because we are not convinced, at the moment, that anyone has invented a better system. The alternative of the commons is too horrifying to contemplate. Injustice is preferable to total ruin.

It is one of the peculiarities of the warfare between reform and the status quo that it is thoughtlessly governed by a double standard. Whenever a reform measure is proposed it is often defeated when its opponents triumphantly discover a flaw in it. As Kingsley Davis has pointed out,[21] worshippers of the status quo sometimes imply that no reform is possible without unanimous agreement, an implication contrary to historical fact. As nearly as I can make out, automatic rejection of proposed reforms is based on one of two unconscious assumptions: (i) that the status quo is perfect; or (ii) that the choice we face is between reform and no action; if the proposed reform is imperfect, we presumably should take no action at all, while we wait for a perfect proposal.

But we can never do nothing. That which we have done for thousands of years is also action. It also produces evils. Once we are aware that the status quo is action, we can then compare its discoverable advantages and disadvantages with the predicted advantages and disadvantages of the proposed reform, discounting as best we can for our lack of experience. On the basis of such a comparison, we can make a rational decision which will not involve the unworkable assumption that only perfect systems are tolerable.

Recognition of Necessity

Perhaps the simplest summary of this analysis of man's population problems is this: the commons, if justifiable at all, is justifiable only under conditions of low-population density. As the human population has increased, the commons has had to be abandoned in one aspect after another.

First we abandoned the commons in food gathering, enclosing farm land and restricting pastures and hunting and fishing areas. These restrictions are still not complete throughout the world.

Somewhat later we saw that the commons as a place for waste disposal would also have to be abandoned. Restrictions on the disposal of domestic sewage are widely accepted in the Western world; we are still struggling to close the commons to pollution by automobiles, factories, insecticide sprayers, fertilizing operations, and atomic energy installations.

In a still more embryonic state is our recognition of the evils of the commons in matters of pleasure. There is almost no restriction on the propagation of sound waves in the public medium. The shopping public is assaulted with mindless music, without its consent. Our government is paying out billions of dollars to create supersonic transport which will disturb 50,000 people for every one person who is whisked from coast to coast three hours faster. Advertisers muddy the airwaves of radio and television and pollute the view of travelers. We are a long way from outlawing the commons in matters of pleasure. Is this because our Puritan inheritance makes us view pleasure as something of a sin, and pain (that is, the pollution of advertising) as the sign of virtue?

Every new enclosure of the commons involves the infringement of somebody's personal liberty. Infringements made in the distant past are accepted because no contemporary complains of a loss. It is the newly proposed infringements that we vigorously oppose; cries of "rights" and "freedom" fill the air. But what does "freedom" mean? When men mutually agreed to pass laws against robbing, mankind became more free, not less so. Individuals locked into the logic of the commons are free only to bring on universal ruin; once they see the necessity of mutual coercion, they become free to

pursue other goals. I believe it was Hegel who said, "Freedom is the recognition of necessity."

The most important aspect of necessity that we must now recognize, is the necessity of abandoning the commons in breeding. No technical solution can rescue us from the misery of overpopulation. Freedom to breed will bring ruin to all. At the moment, to avoid hard decisions many of us are tempted to propagandize for conscience and responsible parenthood. The temptation must be resisted, because an appeal to independently acting consciences selects for the disappearance of all conscience in the long run, and an increase in anxiety in the short.

The only way we can preserve and nurture other and more precious freedoms is by relinquishing the freedom to breed, and that very soon. "Freedom is the recognition of necessity"—and it is the role of education to reveal to all the necessity of abandoning the freedom to breed. Only so, can we put an end to this aspect of the tragedy of the commons.

NOTES

1. J. B. Wiesner and H. F. York, *Sci. Amer.* 211 (No. 4), 27 (1964).
2. G. Hardin, *J. Hered.* 50, 68 (1959); S. von Hoernor, *Science* 137, 18 (1962).
3. J. von Neumann and O. Morgenstern, *Theory of Games and Economic Behavior* (Princeton Univ. Press, Princeton, NJ, 1947), p. 11.
4. J. H. Fremlin, *New Sci.*, No. 415 (1964), p. 285.
5. A. Smith, *The Wealth of Nations* (Modern Library, New York, 1937), p. 423.
6. W. F. Lloyd, *Two Lectures on the Checks to Population* (Oxford Univ. Press, Oxford, England, 1833), reprinted (in part) in *Population, Evolution, and Birth Control*, G. Hardin, Ed. (Freeman, San Francisco, 1964), p. 37.
7. A. N. Whitehead, *Science and the Modern World* (Mentor, New York, 1948), p. 17.
8. G. Hardin, Ed. *Population, Evolution, and Birth Control* (Freeman, San Francisco, 1964), p. 56.
9. S. McVay, *Sci. Amer.* 216 (No. 8), 13 (1966).
10. J. Fletcher, *Situation Ethics* (Westminster, Philadelphia, 1966).
11. D. Lack, *The Natural Regulation of Animal Numbers* (Clarendon Press, Oxford, 1954).

12. H. Girvetz, *From Wealth to Welfare* (Stanford Univ. Press, Stanford, CA, 1950).
13. G. Hardin, *Perspec. Biol. Med.* 6, 366 (1963).
14. U. Thant, *Int. Planned Parenthood News*, No. 168 (February 1968), p. 3.
15. K. Davis, *Science* 158, 730 (1967).
16. S. Tax, Ed., *Evolution after Darwin* (Univ. of Chicago Press, Chicago, 1960), vol. 2, p. 469.
17. G. Bateson, D. D. Jackson, J. Haley, J. Weakland, *Behav. Sci.* 1, 251 (1956).
18. P. Goodman, *New York Rev. Books* 10(8), 22 (23 May 1968).
19. A. Comfort, *The Anxiety Makers* (Nelson, London, 1967).
20. C. Frankel, *The Case for Modern Man* (Harper, New York, 1955), p. 203.
21. J. D. Roslansky, *Genetics and the Future of Man* (Appleton-Century-Crofts, New York, 1966), p. 177.

Scott Barrett

WHY HAVE CLIMATE NEGOTIATIONS PROVED SO DISAPPOINTING?

I'm grateful to the organizers for proposing this question for my title, because it's important. People often complain that the climate negotiations have been disappointing, only to wring their hands and say that we must do better. But unless we know the *reasons* why the negotiations have been disappointing, we won't know *how* to do better. Using a medical metaphor, if our diagnosis of the illness is wrong, our recommended treatment is unlikely to heal the patient. Indeed, the wrong treatment may only make the patient sicker.

One of the striking things about the climate negotiations is that the negotiators have admitted that they have failed to meet their own goal.

In the Framework Convention on Climate Change, adopted in 1992, parties agreed that atmospheric concentrations of greenhouse gases should be stabilized "at a level that would prevent dangerous anthropogenic interference with the climate system." Later, in the non-binding Copenhagen Accord adopted in 2009, countries recognized "the scientific view that the increase in global temperature should be below 2 degrees Celsius." Finally, in Cancun in 2010, the parties to the Framework Convention reaffirmed this goal, but added that it may need to be strengthened, limiting temperature rise to 1.5°C.

From "Sustainable Humanity, Sustainable Nature: Our Responsibility." Proceedings of the Joint Workshop 2–6 May, 2014. Extra Series 41. Vatican City, 2015, 261–76.

After Copenhagen, countries submitted pledges for reducing their emissions. However, analysis by Rogelj et al. (2010) shows that even an optimistic reading of these pledges implies that mean global temperature will surpass the 2°C temperature change target.

The negotiators agree with this assessment. In Durban in 2011, they noted "*with grave concern* the significant gap between the aggregate effect of Parties' mitigation pledges in terms of global annual emissions of greenhouse gases by 2020 and aggregate emission pathways consistent with having a likely chance of holding the increase in global average temperature below" the agreed threshold. Rogelj et al. (2010: 1128) describe this behavior as being "equivalent to racing toward a cliff and hoping to stop just before it."

Note that the Copenhagen pledges are voluntary. It's possible that they'll be exceeded. As bad as things look now, they could turn out to be worse.

The problem isn't disagreement about what should be done. Support for the 2°C goal is universal. The problem is that this is a global goal. Every one is responsible for meeting it, meaning that no country is responsible for meeting it. Limiting climate change requires very broad cooperation. It requires *collective action*.

The reason collective action has eluded us so far is that reducing emissions is a prisoners' dilemma game. Each country is better off when *all* countries reduce their emissions substantially. But each country has only a small incentive to reduce its *own* emissions.

The Kyoto Protocol asks some countries to reduce their emissions beyond "business as usual," and so confronts the prisoners' dilemma head on. But Kyoto has failed in its mission to limit emissions.[1] The Copenhagen Accord, by focusing on the need to avoid "dangerous" climate change, has tried to reframe the problem. Will Copenhagen succeed? Reframing is the right strategy. But we need a different framing. Although my main purpose is to explain why the negotiations have been disappointing, I also want to suggest how an understanding of this failure can provide insights into how we might do better. Countries are currently trying to negotiate a new kind of climate agreement for adoption in 2015. My paper ends by suggesting how a different framing of the climate collective action problem could turn the negotiations around. The climate negotiations needn't be as disappointing as they have been so far.

The "Dangerous" Climate Change Game

Here is a way to think about the "dangerous" climate change game. Let's say that there exists a red line for "danger," and that countries know what this red line is. For example, it might be the 2°C goal. Let's also say that the impact of crossing this threshold is expected to be so severe relative to the costs of staying clear of it that all countries, collectively, prefer to stay clear of it. Then it's obvious what countries should do if they act collectively: they should limit concentrations of greenhouse gases to avoid crossing the red line.

The problem, of course, is that countries don't act collectively. They're sovereign. They act independently. So, we should ask: What *incentives* do countries have to stay within the good side of the red line?

Under reasonable assumptions, the game I have just described is not a prisoners' dilemma. It's a "coordination game" with two Nash equilibria (Barrett 2013).[2] In one, countries stay just within the "safe" zone. In the other, they breeze past the tipping point, making catastrophe inevitable. In general, game theory has trouble predicting how countries will behave in a coordination game. However, since the "bad" Nash equilibrium is so obviously bad, staying within the red line is focal (Schelling 1960). Moreover, with the help of a treaty, countries can virtually guarantee that they will coordinate around the "good" Nash equilibrium.

Here is how the treaty should be written. It should assign to every country an emission limit, with each country's limit chosen to ensure that, when all the limits are added up, concentrations stay within the "safe" zone. The limits should also be chosen to ensure that every country is better off staying within its assigned limit, given that all the other countries stay within *their* assigned limits. Finally, the agreement should only enter into force if ratified by every country.

The beauty of such a treaty is that it makes every country pivotal. If every other country behaves as required, each country has an incentive to behave as required. The reason: even the slightest slip up guarantees catastrophe.

This treaty, like all good treaties, transforms the game. In the treaty participation game, every country has a dominant strategy to participate. Why? Every country has nothing to lose by joining. If the agreement fails to enter into force, each country would be free to act as it pleased. If the agreement were to enter into force, however, then it would be binding on all parties, and catastrophe would be avoided—the outcome every country prefers. Every country is thus always better off participating.

How would the emission limits for individual countries be chosen? This is the bargaining problem. If countries were "symmetric," bargaining would be simple. Technically, a wide variety of allocations would satisfy the requirements I described above, but an equal allocation would be focal, and for that reason is to be expected. Asymmetry makes bargaining more complex, but so long as collective action promises all countries an aggregate gain, there will exist an allocation of responsibility that will be acceptable to every country (this allocation won't be unique and may require side payments, but these are relatively minor points compared with the imperative to avoid catastrophe).

The threat of catastrophe simplifies the negotiation problem. It makes each county's promise to stay within its agreed limits *credible.*

The vulnerability in this game isn't the behavior of the countries. It is the credibility of the *science*—in particular, the science of locating the critical tipping point.

In the dangerous climate change game, it would be irrational for any country to exceed its assigned amount of emissions when doing so would cause atmospheric concentrations to cross the catastrophic tipping point. In this case, free rider deterrence depends on the credibility of *Nature's* threat to tip a critical geophysical system. Yes, in the dangerous climate change game, Nature is an important player.

The Importance of Scientific Uncertainty

What would countries need to do collectively to prevent dangerous climate change?

The Copenhagen Accord says:

To achieve the ultimate objective of the Convention to stabilize greenhouse gas concentration in the atmosphere at a level that would prevent dangerous anthropogenic interference with the climate system, we shall, recognizing *the scientific view that the increase in global temperature*
should be below 2 degrees Celsius [emphasis added], on the basis of equity and in the context of sustainable development, enhance our long-term cooperative action to combat climate change.[3]

Why defer to the "scientific view"? The reason is that it simplifies the negotiations. It allows negotiators to bargain over individual country shares.

However, while scientists warned of "climate disaster" before the Framework Convention was adopted (see, in particular, Mercer 1978), I think the Framework Convention caused scientists to focus on this question at least as much as previous scientific research caused negotiators to focus on it.

Reference to "*the* scientific view" [emphasis added] implies that there is strong agreement among scientists about the threshold. There isn't. The only "scientific view" that I detect in the literature is that thresholds are likely to exist.[4]

Although temperature thresholds are uncertain, the uncertainties involved in choosing a target are even greater than this. The Framework Convention specifies the target in terms of concentrations, not temperature, and converting temperature to concentrations introduces an additional layer of uncertainty—something known as "climate sensitivity" (Roe and Baker 2007). Moreover, we don't know the quantity of global emissions (expressed, perhaps, as a cumulative sum) needed to meet any particular concentration target, due to uncertainty in the carbon cycle. For example, there is uncertainty about how much of the CO_2 emitted will be taken up by soils and the oceans. The fifth assessment report by the Intergovernmental Panel on Climate Change calculates a global "budget" in terms of cumulative emissions that will keep temperature change within 2°C, but all of these values are probabilistic. Even if we knew for certain that 2°C were the true red line for climate change (and we don't know this), countries would have to decide how to balance the cost of reducing emissions with reductions in the risk of crossing the red line.

The Dangerous Climate Change Game with Uncertain Thresholds

Uncertainty about the threshold for "danger" changes the climate change game fundamentally.

Consider a very simple game—no treaty. In stage 1, countries choose their emission levels independently. In stage 2, Nature chooses the tipping point. When making their choices in stage 1, the players know the probability density function for the tipping point. What they don't know is which value under this function will be chosen by Nature—the "true" value for the tipping point.

An example will make this clear. Rockström et al. (2009) argue that atmospheric CO_2 concentrations should be constrained "to *ensure* [emphasis added] the continued existence of the large polar ice sheets." They note that the paleoclimatic record implies "that there is a critical threshold between 350 and 550 ppmv," and interpret this as saying that if concentrations are limited to 350 ppmv, then the ice sheets will be preserved, whereas if concentrations rise to 550 ppmv, then the ice sheets will be lost. In between these values there is a chance that the ice sheets will disappear, with the probability increasing with the concentration level. (For reference, last month's reading from Mona Loa was about 399.65 ppmv; at the start of the industrial revolution, concentrations were about 280 ppmv; when the Framework Convention was adopted they were 356 ppmv).

Assume that the probability density function is uniform over the range (350,550).[5] Assume also that the expected aggregate benefit of reducing the threat of catastrophe exceeds the cost. What should countries do? Under reasonable assumptions (Barrett 2013), the collective-best outcome is to limit concentrations to 350 ppmv. This implements the "precautionary principle." Acting independently, however, countries have incentives to reduce

emissions only up to the point where their expected *individual* marginal benefit equals marginal cost—under reasonable assumptions, a substantially smaller value. Indeed, very simple calculations show that it will probably pay individual countries to abate so little that will they blow right past the critical threshold. They will cross the 550 ppmv line, guaranteeing catastrophe.

You might think this is just theory and that country representatives wouldn't be this dumb. I think there are good reasons to take the prediction seriously.

Astrid Dannenberg and I have tested these predictions in the experimental lab with real people playing for real money (Barrett and Dannenberg 2012). Putting people into groups of 10, we find that when the threshold is certain, 18 out of 20 groups avoid catastrophe.[6] By contrast, when the threshold is uncertain, catastrophe occurs with probability 100% for 16 out of 20 groups and with probability no less than 80% for the rest.[7]

How sensitive are these results? Intuitively, there should exist a critical amount of uncertainty such that if uncertainty were greater than this amount, catastrophe would be bound to occur, whereas if uncertainty were less than this, catastrophe would be avoided. This is exactly what the theory predicts (Barrett 2013), and in further experiments (Barrett and Dannenberg 2014a), Astrid Dannenberg and I have shown that this result is also robust. To the left of a critical "dividing line" for threshold uncertainty, we find that catastrophe is avoided with high probability almost all the time. Just to the right of the dividing line, by contrast, catastrophe occurs with probability 100% This research suggests that negotiators can't rely on science to solve their collective action problem. Even the new science of "early warning signals" won't be able to shrink uncertainty by enough to transform the behavior of nation states.

This research is helpful, I think, because it is completely consistent with the behavior we are observing in the real world. As noted before, countries have agreed to limit temperature change to 2°C, but they have pledged emission reductions that virtually guarantee overshooting of this target.

If the science of climate change were much more certain, the prospect of catastrophe would give countries the discipline they needed to act in their collective-best interest. It would make the dangerous climate change game a coordination game. Scientific uncertainty makes the emission reductions game a prisoners' dilemma. The most important thing about a prisoners' dilemma is that the collective-best outcome cannot be sustained by non-cooperative behavior. It requires enforcement, something that the international system is very bad at doing.

A Climate Doomsday Machine

It is tempting to consider an analogy to nuclear arms control. Herman Kahn (1961: 107) proposed construction of a Doomsday Machine,

> a device whose function is to destroy the world. This device is protected from enemy action (perhaps by being situated thousands of feet underground) and then connected to a computer, in turn connected to thousands of sensory devices all over the United States. The computer would be programmed so that if, say, five nuclear bombs exploded over the United States, the device would be triggered and the world destroyed. Barring such problems as coding errors (an important technical consideration), this machine would seem to be the 'ideal' [deterrent]. If Khrushchev ordered an attack, both Khrushchev and the Soviet population would be automatically and efficiently annihilated.

A Climate Doomsday Machine would connect all the world's nuclear bombs to a computer, which in turn would be linked to a sensor at the top of Mona Loa in Hawaii. This is where readings are taken of atmospheric concentrations of greenhouse gases. Today, as noted before, the concentration level is about 400 ppmv. The computer could be programmed to destroy the world should this level top, say, 500 ppmv. With the trigger for catastrophe being certain, theory and experimental evidence strongly suggest that this device would give the world all the encouragement needed to stay within 500.

Of course, I'm not seriously proposing this. The proposal is unacceptable.[8] However, the idea behind it is worth thinking about. The Doomsday Machine is a purely strategic device. Its sole purpose is to change the incentives countries have to rein in their emissions and save the world from dangerous climate change. It works by transforming the prisoners' dilemma into a coordination game. Thinking about it begs the question: Are there *acceptable* strategic approaches that could have a similar effect? I shall return to this point later in the paper.

Framing Reconsidered

Has a focus on "dangerous" climate change really made no difference? Under certain conditions, theory suggests that uncertainty about the threshold could mean that behavior won't change at all, even though the consequences of failing to act will be much worse because of the threat of catastrophic climate change (Barrett 2012).

But is this result to be believed? Many predictions of analytical game theory are disproved in the experimental lab. For example, cooperation in a prisoners' dilemma typically exceeds the Nash equilibrium prediction (though the level of cooperation declines rapidly as the players learn that their efforts to cooperate are not reciprocated). In a one-shot test of the theory, Astrid Dannenberg and I found that cooperation was higher for the prisoners' dilemma with an uncertain threshold for "catastrophe" compared to a prisoners' dilemma without any risk of "catastrophe" (Barrett and Danenberg 2014b). This suggests that, given the risk from "dangerous" climate change, the wording of Article II of the Framework Convention has probably helped (though it is the real risk rather than the wording that would affect behavior). Unfortunately, our experiment also showed that the additional cooperation wasn't enough to prevent catastrophe from occurring.

Strategies of Reciprocity

My description of the dangerous climate change game left out the role of an international agreement. I explained before that a treaty could change the incentives in the game with a certain threshold, ensuring coordination. Could a treaty help overcome the incentive to free ride when the threshold is very uncertain? Theory suggests that an agreement would help very little (Barrett 2013). The reason is the difficulty of enforcing an agreement to limit emissions.

Atmospheric concentrations of CO_2 are determined by the aggregate behavior of *all* countries (as mediated by the carbon cycle). Strategies of reciprocity work very well in two-player games. They work less well when the number of players is large.

In the climate change game, how many players really matter? Some countries are bigger emitters than others. However, the top ten emitters account for only about two-thirds of total emissions, and stabilizing concentrations requires driving global net emissions to zero, necessitating the engagement of nearly *all* countries.[9]

The temptation to free ride is further aggravated by the high marginal cost of reducing emissions substantially. It is sometimes argued that reducing emissions is cheap. If this were true, however, collective action would be easy.

Another problem is the lack of correlation between a country's contribution to emissions and its vulnerability to climate change. To illustrate, William Nordhaus (2011) has calculated that the "social cost of carbon" is more than twice as large for Africa, a continent of more than 50 states, as it is for the United States. Moreover, this gap is growing. Yet, Africa's emissions are tiny when compared to those of the United States. Africa is both more vulnerable to climate change and less able to prevent it from occurring.

Finally, globalization amplifies the incentives to free ride. Abatement by a single country or coalition of countries will tend to shift emissions toward the countries that fail to act—a phenomenon known as "leakage."

It is well known that infinitely repeated play of the prisoners' dilemma can allow the full cooperative outcome to be sustained as a (subgame perfect) Nash equilibrium, provided discount rates are sufficiently low. The reason is that, should a country "cheat" on an agreement to limit emissions, the others can reciprocate. This suggests that cooperation should be easy.

The flaw in this perspective is that it considers only the interests of individual countries. It ignores these countries' collective interests.

Imagine that all the world's countries come together and negotiate an agreement that maximizes their collective interests. Later, one country announces that it will withdraw. This withdrawal would harm the other states, and they would like to punish this country (or, better yet, threaten to punish it, hoping to deter its withdrawal). In the context of a treaty, they would naturally *cooperate* to punish the deviant country. To deter a deviation, their punishment must be big enough that the deviant would be better off remaining in the agreement than withdrawing and facing the punishment. But the punishment must also be credible. Given that this country has withdrawn, the remaining $N-1$ countries must be better off when they impose the punishment than when they do not impose it (or when they impose a weaker punishment). Because so many countries remain in the agreement, it will only pay these countries to cut their abatement a little. A larger punishment wouldn't be credible. A small punishment, however, would be too little to deter a defection. Continuing in this way, it is easy to see that an agreement to limit emissions is only self-enforcing if the number of countries participating is very small. For then, should one country withdraw, the remaining countries would have an incentive to drop their abatement significantly. However, once participation shrinks to such a low level, the treaty achieves very little.

It may be possible for countries to sustain a high level of participation, but this would only be true if the gains to cooperation were small. It may also be possible to sustain a high level of participation if the ambition of the treaty were set very low. What isn't possible is for countries to sustain a high degree of cooperation when the gains from cooperation are very large.[10]

I have so far focused on participation. What about compliance? A flaw in the approaches to enforcement taken previously is that they either ignore participation (as in Chayes and Chayes 1995) or fail to distinguish between participation and compliance (as in Downs, Rocke, and Barsoon 1996). Under the rules of international law, countries are free to choose whether or not to participate in a treaty. However, the countries that choose to participate are legally obligated to comply with it (*pacta sunt servanda,* meaning "agreements must be kept"). The easiest way to avoid needing to comply is therefore not to participate in the first place—or to withdraw after becoming a party. From the perspective of game theory, the problem is coming up with a credible punishment that is large enough to deter non-participation. Once this is done, deterring non-compliance is easy. Remember, larger deviations can only be deterred by larger punishments, and larger punishments are less credible. What's the biggest harm a party could ever do?

Behaving as it would were it not a party to the agreement (any bigger harm would not be credible). So, if the parties can deter non-participation, they can easily deter a smaller deviation of non-compliance. From both perspectives, then, deterring non-participation is the binding constraint on enforcement (Barrett 2003).

This is theory. Is the reasoning compelling? I know of no example from international cooperation that challenges this perspective. The World Trade Organization might appear to be an exception, but trade isn't a global public good. Trade is a bilateral activity, and strategies of reciprocity are very effective in sustaining cooperation amongst pairs of players. The Montreal Protocol on protecting the ozone layer might appear to be another exception, but as I shall explain later, this treaty works very differently.

Enforcement of the Kyoto Protocol

The Kyoto Protocol looks at climate change as a prisoners' dilemma, demands that certain countries cooperate, and then does nothing about enforcement.

How do we know this? The United States participated in the Kyoto negotiations. President Clinton signed the treaty. However, the United States never ratified Kyoto. One reason for this is that there were no consequences to the United States for not ratifying the agreement. Non-participation by the United States was not deterred.

Canada ratified Kyoto, but failed to adopt the domestic legislation needed to implement its obligations. As a consequence, Canada's emissions exceeded the limit set by Kyoto limit. Once in this situation, Canada had three options. It could buy permits or offsets to stay in compliance; it could stay in the agreement and be in non-compliance; or it could withdraw from the agreement. In contrast to the first option, withdrawal would be costless. In contrast to the second option, withdrawal would not violate international law. Not surprisingly, Canada decided to withdraw. The Kyoto Protocol could not deter Canada from withdrawing.

Compliance with the Kyoto Protocol by other parties is uneven (Haita 2012). However, there are ways to get around compliance. For example, Japan is maneuvering to achieve compliance partly by purchasing "assigned amount units" from Ukraine, when Ukraine's emissions are well below its "assigned amounts." In other words, in buying these units from Ukraine, Japan can comply without emissions being reduced anywhere. This may seem crazy but the treaty was written to allow this trading in "hot air."

Finally, countries like China and India are not subject to limits on their emissions. They participate in Kyoto. They comply with it. But Kyoto does not require that these countries do anything.

Overall, did Kyoto contribute to meeting the objectives of the Framework Convention? Did it reduce global emissions? Econometric analysis of the Kyoto Protocol by Rahel Aichele and Gabriel Felbermayr (2012: 351) shows that Kyoto did reduce the emissions of participating countries. However, its effect on *global* carbon emissions "has been statistically indistinguishable from zero."

The most important indicator of whether the objectives of the Framework Convention are being met is whether the growth in atmospheric concentrations is slowing. It isn't. If anything, the rate of increase has gone up.[11] We are no closer now to addressing this great problem than we were more than twenty years ago when the Framework Convention was adopted.

Pivot: From Kyoto to Paris

The Copenhagen talks were supposed to provide a successor agreement to the Kyoto Protocol. They failed.

A new agreement is now being negotiated under the "Durban Platform." It is supposed to be ready for adoption by 2015, when the parties to the Framework Convention meet in Paris. It is supposed to be implemented by 2020.

Since Kyoto's emission limits ended in 2012, this leaves a gap of eight years. To fill the gap, Kyoto was given an extension in the form of the Doha Amendment (which has yet to enter into force). However, it is a further sign of Kyoto's failings that Japan, New Zealand, and Russia declared their intention not to participate this time around.[12]

The new agreement being negotiated now won't repeat all of Kyoto's mistakes, but there is no indication yet that it will improve much on what countries would have done in the absence of cooperation. Kyoto referred to its emission limits as "commitments." However, countries were never truly committed to meeting these limits; they couldn't be committed to meeting these limits so long as Kyoto lacked the means to compel parties to do more than they were willing to do unilaterally. It is a sign of where the current round of negotiations are going that in Durban countries agreed to negotiate a new "protocol, legal instrument or agreed outcome with legal force," and that in the recent Warsaw talks they agreed to negotiate "contributions" rather than "commitments."

The world clearly needs a new model for cooperation on climate change.

Why the Montreal Protocol Succeeded

Kyoto lacks a strategic design. The emissions targets and timetables were chosen in the expectation that they would be met. No consideration was given to whether the treaty created *incentives* for them to be met.

The Montreal Protocol, negotiated to protect the stratospheric ozone layer, was designed very differently. Remarkably, while the Montreal Protocol was not intended to reduce greenhouse gases, it has been much more successful at doing this than the Kyoto Protocol. It turns out that ozone in the stratosphere is a greenhouse gas (protecting the ozone layer will thus add to climate change), as are the chemicals that deplete stratospheric ozone (reducing these emissions will thus help mitigate climate change) and many of their substitutes (use of these will thus add to climate change). Calculations by Velders et al. (2007) show that, by phasing out the ozone-depleting substances that double as greenhouse gases, the Montreal Protocol has done four times as much to limit atmospheric concentrations as the Kyoto Protocol aimed to do.

Why did Montreal succeed where Kyoto failed? A key reason for its success is the threat to restrict trade—in particular, a ban on trade in controlled substances between parties and non-parties (Barrett 2003). The most important motive for the trade restriction was to enforce participation in the agreement (Benedick 1998:91). If participation could be enforced, then trade leakage would be eliminated; moreover, compliance could also be enforced (Barrett 2003). Crucially, the trade restrictions in the Montreal Protocol are a strategic device. Their purpose was not to be used; their purpose was to change behavior.

How do the trade restrictions work? Imagine that very few countries are parties to an agreement to limit emissions, and your country is contemplating whether or not to join. If you join, you will have to reduce your emissions. Your country will pay the cost, and the benefits will be diffused; the incentives to free ride will not be blunted. If, in addition, you are now also prohibited from trading with non-parties—the vast majority of countries—then you will be doubly harmed. By joining, you not only forfeit the benefits of free riding; you also lose the gains from trade.

Now imagine that almost every other country is a party to the same agreement. If you join, you still lose the benefits of free riding. But now you are able to trade with the vast majority of countries. If the gains from trade exceed the loss from free riding, your country will be better off joining. Put differently, if every country is a party to such an agreement, none will wish to withdraw. The agreement will sustain full participation by means of a self-enforcing mechanism—the trade restriction. Most remarkably, in equilibrium, trade will never be restricted, just as the Doomsday Device would never be detonated. It is the credible threat to restrict trade (detonate the device) that disciplines behavior.

Notice that a key feature of this strategy is that "enough" countries participate in the agreement. If too few participate, none will want to participate. If enough participate, everyone will want to participate. Somewhere in between there exists a "tipping point" for participation. Once this tipping point has been identified, the treaty only needs to coordinate participation—something treaties can do very easily. As I said before, treaties need to ensure that countries are steered towards the desired outcome. In the Montreal Protocol, this was achieved by the minimum participation clause (Barrett 2003).

The trade restrictions are an acceptable alternative to the Doomsday Machine. Like the Doomsday Machine, trade restrictions transform the prisoners' dilemma into a coordination game.

Coordination in Climate Treaties

The Montreal Protocol could be amended to achieve more for the climate. Hydrofluorocarbons (HFCs) do not deplete the ozone layer, and so are not currently regulated by the Montreal Protocol. However, HFCs are a very potent greenhouse gas—one of the six gases controlled by the Kyoto Protocol. Kyoto has done very little to limit HFCs. In May 2011, the United States, Canada, and Mexico proposed amending the Montreal Protocol to control HFCs. If adopted, such an amendment would represent a significant departure from the approach taken so far to address climate change. It would mean addressing one piece of the problem, rather than all of it in a comprehensive way. And it would likely involve using trade restrictions for purposes of enforcement. I want to underline that the application of trade restrictions is purely strategic. Other proposals for trade restrictions in climate policy are very different; their purpose is to be *used*, not to alter behavior strategically (Barrett 2011).

There are other opportunities for transforming the climate change game from a prisoners' dilemma into a coordination game, especially the application of technology standards (Barrett 2003, 2006).

Let me give one example. Another greenhouse gas known as perfluorocarbons or PFCs is emitted in the process of manufacturing aluminum. Apparently, these emissions can be eliminated if the anodes being used now are replaced with inert anodes. According to the United States Environmental Protection Agency's webpage, "This technology is being pursued aggressively through a joint R&D program that has been established between the aluminum industry and the U.S. Department of Energy in its Industrial Technology Program."[13] The new anode is expected to be available in ten to fifteen years.

Here, then, is a suggestion. A new agreement should be negotiated requiring that producers adopt the new technology, and that all parties agree to import aluminum only from countries that participate in the agreement. This approach creates a "tipping" phenomenon. Provided enough countries join the agreement, all will want to join it. Why? To be outside the agreement when most countries are inside means not being able to trade in aluminum with most of the world.

This proposal for aluminum would be different from Montreal. The trade restriction would be based on a process standard, not a product standard. However, I believe it would still be effective.

I also believe it would be compatible with the WTO, partly because of the exemptions allowed under Article XX, but also because it would be adopted by a multilateral agreement.

A final point. Another reason Montreal works is that it includes side payments to address related equity issues. Side payments could also be included in an agreement establishing an aluminum production standard. As in Montreal, any side payments should be based on the "incremental costs" of adopting the standard. Transfers should be small, and the countries giving the money should know what they are getting for their money.

Again, this is just one example of how the negotiations could be made more effective.[14] My aim here is not to develop a comprehensive approach to future climate negotiations but to suggest a new direction. If the negotiators understood their job as needing to achieve coordination, and to think strategically, they would achieve more—and the climate negotiations wouldn't prove so disappointing.

NOTES

1. See, especially, research by Aichele and Felbermayr (2012), discussed later in this paper, which takes into account the effect of Kyoto on trade "leakage."
2. In a coordination game, people want to do what others are doing. A car may be driven on the left or right side of the road. So, on which side of the road should you drive? The answer depends on where everyone else is driving. In Italy, it's obvious that you should drive on the right. In the UK, it's obvious that you should drive on the left. These different outcomes (driving on the left and driving on the right) are each a "Nash equilibrium." Given that others are driving on the left (right), each driver chooses to drive on the left (right).
3. The Copenhagen Accord was written somewhat hastily, and this temperature target is identified without reference to a base level of temperature. In Cancun the following year, negotiators clarified that the temperature reference target was the pre-industrial level.
4. Rapid changes in temperature have been observed in the paleoclimatic record, an example being the Younger Dryas; see Broecker (1997).
5. This means that the probability that the threshold lies between 350 and 400 ppmv is the same as the probability that the threshold lies between 400 and 450 ppmv, between 450 and 500 ppmv, and

between 500 and 550 ppmv. It also means that the probability that the threshold lies below 350 or above 550 ppmv is zero.

6. In each of the two failing groups, just one individual, a bad apple, caused the trouble, pledging to contribute his or her fair share and then choosing to contribute nothing.

7. Interestingly, theory predicts that uncertainty about the *impact* of crossing a critical threshold should make no difference to collective action (Barrett 2013), another prediction confirmed in the experimental lab (Barrett and Dannenberg 2012). It is only uncertainty about the tipping point that matters, and this is a purely scientific matter.

8. Nor did Kahn recommend the Doomsday Machine: "If one were presenting a military briefing advocating some special weapon system as a deterrent . . . the Doomsday Machine might seem better than any alternative system; nevertheless, it is unacceptable." (Kahn 1961: 104–05).

9. Unless, that is, substantial amounts of carbon are removed from the atmosphere.

10. All of these points are developed in detail in Barrett (2003).

11. The data can be found at http://www.esrl.noaa.gov/gmd/ccgg/trends/.

12. The European Union will participate, because this agreement only requires that Europe meet the target it declared it would meet unilaterally. The new government in Australia has introduced legislation to repeal the previous government's climate legislation, a sign that Australia may not ratify the Doha Amendment.

13. http://www.epa.gov/aluminum-pfc/resources.html.

14. For other examples of sectoral approaches to reducing emissions, see Barrett (2011).

REFERENCES

Aichele, Rahel and Gabriel Felbermayr (2012). "Kyoto and the Carbon Footprint of Nations," *Journal of Environmental Economics and Management* 63: 336–54.

Barrett, Scott (2003). *Environment and Statecraft: The Strategy of Environmental Treaty-Making,* Oxford: Oxford University Press.

Barrett, S. (2006). "Climate Treaties and 'Breakthrough' Technologies." *American Economic Review (Papers and Proceedings)* 96(2): 22–25.

Barrett, Scott (2011). "Rethinking Climate Change Governance and Its Relationship to the World Trading System," *The World Economy* 34(11): 1863–82.

Barrett, Scott (2013). "Climate Treaties and Approaching Catastrophes," *Journal of Environmental Economics and Management,* 66(2): 235–50.

Barrett, Scott and Astrid Dannenberg (2012). "Climate Negotiations Under Scientific Uncertainty," *Proceedings of the National Academy of Sciences,* 109(43): 17372–376.

Barrett, Scott and Astrid Dannenberg (2014a). "Sensitivity of Collective Action to Uncertainty about Climate Tipping Points," *Nature Climate Change* 4: 36–39.

Barrett, Scott and Astrid Dannenberg (2014b). "Negotiating to Avoid 'Gradual' versus 'Dangerous' Climate Change: An Experimental Test of Two Prisoners' Dilemmas," in Todd L. Cherry, Jon Hovi, and Dave McEvoy (eds.), *Toward a New Climate Agreement: Conflict, Resolution, and Governance,* London: Routledge.

Benedick, R. E. (1998). *Ozone Diplomacy: New Directions in Safeguarding the Planet,* Enlarged Edition, Cambridge, MA: Harvard University Press.

Broecker, W. S. (1997). "Thermohaline Circulation, the Achilles Heel of Our Climate System: Will Man-Made CO_2 Upset the Current Balance?" *Science* 278:1582–88.

Chayes, A. and A. H. Chayes (1995), *The New Sovereignty.* Cambridge, MA: Harvard University Press.

Downs, G. W., D. M. Rocke, and P. N. Barsoon (1996). "Is the Good News About Compliance Good News About Cooperation?" *International Organization* 50: 379–406.

Environmental Protection Agency (2006). *Global Mitigation of Non-CO2 Greenhouse Gases,* Washington, DC: EPA.

Haita, Corina (2012). "The State of Compliance in the Kyoto Protocol," International Center for Climate Governance; http://www.iccgov .org/FilePagineStatiche/Files/Publications/Reflections/12 _Reflection_December_2012.pdf.

Kahn, Herman (1961). "The Arms Race and Some of Its Hazards," in Donald G. Brennan (ed.), *Arms Control, Disarmament, and National Security,* New York: George Braziller, pp. 89–121.

Mercer, J. H. (1978). "West Antarctic Ice Sheet and CO2 Greenhouse Effect: A Threat of Disaster," *Nature* 271: 321–25.

Nordhaus, William (2011). "Estimates of the Social Cost of Carbon: Background and Results from the RICE-2011 Model." Cowles Foundation Discussion Paper No. 1826, Yale University.

Rockström, J., W. Steffen, K. Noone, Å. Persson, S. Chapin III, E. F. Lambin, T. M. Lenton, M. Scheffer, C. Folke, H. J. Schellnhuber, B. Nykvist, C. A. de Wit, T. Hughes, S. van der Leeuw, H. Rodhe, S. Sörlin, P. K. Snyder, R. Costanza, U. Svedin, M. Falkenmark, L. Karlberg, R. W. Corell, V. J. Fabry, J. Hansen, B. Walker, D. Liverman, K. Richardson, P. Crutzen, and J. A. Foley (2009). "A Safe Operating Safe for Humanity," *Nature* 461: 472–75.

Roe, G. H. and M. B. Baker (2007). "Why Is Climate Sensitivity So Unpredictable?" *Science* 318: 629–32.

Rogelj, J., J. Nabel, C. Chen, W. Hare, K. Markmann, M. Meinshausen, M. Schaeffer, K. Macey, and N. Höhne (2010). "Copenhagen Accord Pledges are Paltry," *Nature* 464: 1126–28.

Schelling, T. C. (1960). *The Strategy of Conflict.* Cambridge, MA: Harvard University Press.

Velders, G.J.M., S. O. Anderson, J. S. Daniel, D. W. Fahey, and M. McFarland (2007). "The Importance of the Montreal Protocol in Protecting Climate," *Proceedings of the National Academy of Sciences* 104 (12): 4814–19.

Valerie M. Hudson and Andrea M. den Boer
MISSING WOMEN AND BARE BRANCHES: GENDER BALANCE AND CONFLICT

The emerging subfield of "security demographics" examines the linkages between population dynamics and the security trajectories of nation-states. For the last five to ten years, researchers have examined the security aspects of such topics as the demographic transition, the sub-replacement birth rates of developed economies, the proportion of young men as compared to older men in the population, the effects of legal and illegal immigration, and the effects of pandemics such as AIDS and drug-resistant tuberculosis. We hope to add the variable of gender balance to the discussion: are societies with an abnormal ratio between men and women less secure?

Missing Women

In two areas of the world such imbalances have become fairly significant in the last half-century: 1) Russia and several former Warsaw Pact nations, where we find a deficit of adult males,[1] and 2) Asia—particularly India, China, and Pakistan—where we find a deficit of women, including female infants and children. We will let other scholars research the link between a deficit of males and national security. Our research, as explained in *Bare Branches: The Security Implications of Asia's Surplus Male Population* (MIT Press, 2004), focuses

From the Environmental Change and Security Program Report, Issue 11 (2005): 20–24.

on the deficit of females in Asia. Standard demographic analysis readily confirms this abnormal deficit.[2] If we compare overall population sex ratios, the ratio for, say, Latin America is 98 males per 100 females (using 2000 U.S. Census Bureau figures), but the corresponding figure for Asia is 104.4 males per 100 females. But one must also keep in mind the sheer size of Asia's population: India and China alone comprise approximately 38 percent of the world's population. Thus, the overall sex ratio of the world is 101.3, despite the fact that the ratios for the rest of the world (excluding Oceania) range from 93.1 (Europe) to 98.9 (Africa).

Birth sex ratios in several Asian countries are outside of the established norm of 105–107 boy babies born for every 100 girl babies. The Indian government's estimate of its birth sex ratio is approximately 113 boy babies born for every 100 girl babies, with some locales recording ratios of 156 and higher (India Registrar General, 2001). The Chinese government states that its birth sex ratio is approximately 119, though some Chinese scholars have gone on record that the birth sex ratio is at least 121 (China State Statistical Bureau, 2001).[3] Again, in some locations, the ratio is higher; for example, the island of Hainan's birth sex ratio is 135. Other countries of concern include Pakistan, Bangladesh, Nepal, Bhutan, Taiwan, Afghanistan, and South Korea.[4]

Another indicator of gender imbalance is early childhood mortality. Boys typically have a higher early childhood mortality rate, which virtually cancels out their numerical advantage by age five. Boys' higher mortality is tied to sex-linked genetic mutations, such as hemophilia, as well as higher death rates from common childhood diseases, such as dysentery. However, in some of the Asian nations mentioned above, early childhood mortality rates for girls are actually higher than boys' (United Nations Population Division, 1998). Furthermore, orphanages house more girls than boys in these nations.[5]

What forces drive the deficit of females in Asian nations such as India and China? Why are their birth sex ratios so abnormal? Why are early childhood mortality rates for girls higher than those for boys? Why are most children in orphanages girls? How do we account for the disappearance of so many women—estimated conservatively at over 90 million missing women in seven Asian countries alone (see Table 11.1)?

Some scholars assert that there may be a physical cause at work preventing female births, such as the disease hepatitis B, antigens of which have been associated with higher birth sex ratios (Oster, 2005). While this may well be a contributing factor, it is worth considering the experience of the municipality of Shenzhen in southern China. Alarmed at the rising birth sex ratio, which reached 118 in 2002, local officials instituted a strict crackdown on black market ultrasound clinics. Offering up to 2,000 yuan for tips, officials then vigorously prosecuted and imprisoned the owners and technicians. By 2004, the birth sex ratio had dropped to 108 ("Shenzhen's newborn sex ratio more balanced," 2005).

Accounts such as this support the thesis that the modern gender imbalance in Asia, as with historical gender imbalances in Asia and elsewhere, is largely a man-made phenomenon.[6] Girls are being culled from the population, whether through prenatal sex identification and female sex-selective abortion, or through relative neglect compared to male offspring in early childhood (including abandonment), or through desperate life circumstances that might lead to suicide.

The gender imbalance in Asia is primarily the result of son preference and the profound devaluation of female life. This value ordering is not confined to Asia; why, then, is the deficit of women found there almost exclusively? Historically, of course, the culling of girls was not confined to Asia; evidence for this practice can be found on every continent. And practices are changing in some Asian nations: Japan normalized its sex ratios in the 20th century, and in South Korea, the deficit has been decreasing over time (Dickemann, 1975; South Korea National Statistics Office, 2001).

But this excellent question can only be answered through a multifactorial cultural analysis that examines variables such as religious prohibitions or sanctions; patrilocality (couples living with the husband's family); the duty of male offspring to support aged parents; dowry, hypergyny, and caste purity in India; the effect of interventions such as China's one-child policy; and the web of incentives and disincentives surrounding the issue of prenatal sex determination technology.[7]

Bare Branches

What effect will this deficit of females have on the security trajectory of nations? Anthropologist Barbara D. Miller (2001) has termed the preservation of a balanced sex ratio a "public good" that governments overlook at their peril. Will it matter to India and China that by the year 2020, 12–15 percent of their young adult males will not be able to "settle down" because the girls that would have grown up to be their wives were disposed of by their societies instead? With each passing year between now and 2020 (or even further), both the proportion and the number of young adult males that exceed the number of young adult females in China and India will increase (Hudson & den Boer, 2004). The Chinese have a special term for such young men: *guang guner*, or "bare branches"—branches of

Table 11.1. Number of Missing Women for Selected Asian Countries Using Census Data

Country	Year	Actual Number of Males	Actual Number of Females	Actual Sex Ratio	Expected Sex Ratio	Expected Number of Women	Missing Women
Afghanistan	2000	11,227,000	10,538,000	106.5	96.4	11,646,266	1,108,266
Bangladesh	2001	65,841,419	63,405,814	103.8	99.6	66,105,842	2,700,028
China	2000	653,550,000	612,280,000	106.7	100.1	652,897,103	40,617,103
India	2001	531,277,078	495,738,169	107.2	99.3	535,022,234	39,284,065
Pakistan	1998	68,873,686	63,445,593	108.6	99.2	69,429,119	5,983,526
South Korea	2000	23,068,181	22,917,108	100.7	100.0	23,068,181	151,073
Taiwan	2000	11,386,084	10,914,845	104.3	100.2	11,363,357	448,512
Total							90,292,573

Sources: Afghanistan—United Nations Population Division, *World Population Prospects: The 2002 Revision,* http://www.un.org/esa /population/publications/wpp2000/annex-tables.pdf; Bangladesh—Bangladesh Bureau of Statistics, *Population Census, 2001: Preliminary Report,* http://www.bbsgov.org; China—National Bureau of Statistics of the People's Republic of China, "Communiqué on Major Figures of the 2000 Population Census," No. 1, April 23, 2002, http://www.stats.gov.cn/english/newrelease/statisticalreports/200204230084 .htm; India—Office of the Registrar General, *Census of India, 2001, Series 1: India, Paper 1 of 2001: Provisional Population Totals* (New Delhi: India, 2001), http://www.censusindia.net/results; Pakistan—Population Census Organization, Statistics Division, Government of Pakistan, "1998 Census of Pakistan," http://www.pap.org.pk/population/sec2.htm; South Korea—National Statistical Office, *Republic of Korea Census Population, 2000,* http://www.nso.go.kr; and Taiwan—Statistical Bureau of Taiwan, *Historical Comparison of the Census Results, 2000,* http://www.stat.gov.tw.

Note: From *Bare Branches: The Security Implications of Asia's Surplus Male Population* (page 62), by Valerie M. Hudson and Andrea M. den Boer, 2004, Cambridge, MA: MIT Press. Copyright 2004 by Belfer Center for Science and International Affairs. Reprinted with permission.

the family tree that will never bear fruit, but which may be useful as "bare sticks," or clubs.

The Chinese elision between bare branches and truncheons echoes our argument: men who are not provided the opportunity to develop a vested interest in a system of law and order will gravitate toward a system based on physical force, in which they hold an advantage over other members of society. Furthermore, in a system with too few women, the men who marry are those with higher socio-economic status. The men unable to marry are poorer, less educated, less skilled, and less likely to be employed. These men are already at risk for establishing a system based on physical force in order to obtain by

force what they cannot obtain legitimately. Without the opportunity to establish a household, they may not transition from potential threats to potential protectors of society. The rate of criminal behavior of unmarried men is many times higher than that of married men; marriage is a reliable predictor of a downturn in reckless, antisocial, illegal, and violent behavior by young adult males (Mazur & Michalek, 1998). If this transition cannot be effected for a sizeable proportion of a society's young men, the society is likely to become less stable.[8]

Statistical evidence for the linkage between gender imbalance and conflict includes several excellent studies that have demonstrated a strong correlation between state-level sex ratios and state-level rates of violent crime in India (Oldenburg, 1992; Dreze & Khera, 2000). States with high sex ratios, such as Uttar Pradesh, have much higher violent crime rates than states with more normal sex ratios, such as Kerala. Historical case studies abound, since abnormal sex ratios are not a new phenomenon. The nineteenth century Nien rebels came from a very poor region in China with a sex ratio of at least 129 men per 100 women. At first, relatively smaller groups of men coalesced to form smuggling and extortion gangs. Eventually, these gangs banded together to form larger armies, wresting territory from imperial control. It took the emperor years to subdue this rebellion.

We must not overlook sociological theory and experimental evidence, as well. For example, scholars have studied the behavior of unattached young males, noting their propensity to congregate with others like them and to engage in dominance displays in such groups. Sociologists have found that the "risky shift" in group behavior, where a group is willing to take greater risks and engage in more reckless behavior than an individual member of the group, is much more pronounced in groups comprised solely of unattached young adult males (Johnson, Stemler, & Hunter, 1977).

After examining the evidence, some predictions can be made for societies with rising sex ratios: crime rates will increase; the proportion of violent crime will increase; rates of drug use, drug smuggling, weapons smuggling, trafficking, and prostitution will increase (see Hudson & den Boer, 2004). The society might develop domestic and international chattel markets that kidnap and traffic women within the country and across borders. For example, the shortage of marriage-age women in China is fueling a brisk business in trafficked brides from North Korea (Demick, 2003).

We must also examine the reaction of the government. Historically, we have found that as governments become aware of the negative consequences of a growing number of bare branches, most governments are motivated to do something. In the past, "doing something" meant thinning the numbers of bare branches, whether through fighting, sponsoring the construction of large public works necessitating dangerous manual labor, exporting them to less populated areas, or co-opting them into the military or police. One sixteenth century Portuguese monarch sent his army, composed primarily of noble and non-noble bare branches, on one of the later crusades to avoid a crisis of governance; more than 25 percent of that army never returned, and many others were seriously wounded (Boone, 1983, 1986).

We find that the need to control the rising instability created by the increasing numbers of bare branches has led governments to favor more authoritarian approaches to internal governance and less benign international presences. In many ways, a society's prospects for democracy and peace are diminished in step with the devaluation of daughters.

How will this play out in twenty-first century Asia? Gender imbalance does not cause war or conflict per se, but it can aggravate it. Will the internal instability caused by substantial numbers of bare branches (by 2020, 28 million in India—the same or more in China) overshadow external security concerns for the governments of these nations? Some potentially unstable situations spring to mind: the feuding countries of Pakistan and India have gender imbalances, as do China and Taiwan; and the resource-rich Russian Far East faces an influx of Chinese workers while Russia continues to lose men (Radyuhin, 2003).

How will gender imbalances affect the potential for democracy in China and the evolution of democracy in India? The gender imbalances of these two countries will not remain solely their problem, as alone they comprise more than one-third of the world's population. The status of women in these nations could become an important factor in both domestic and international security in Asia, with possible implications for the entire international system.

The Chinese government is acting on this linkage. In July 2004, they announced their desire to normalize the birth sex ratio by the year 2010, and in January 2005, they announced programs to provide old-age pensions to parents of girls. Only time will tell if these and other interventions will achieve their desired ends. In the meantime, the horse has left the barn for at least the next 20 years, for there is no way to undo the birth sex ratios of previous years. Have these Asian nations discovered the value of female life too late? The whole world is waiting to see whether bare branches will be given the opportunity to grow again.

NOTES

1. In Russia and its former satellites, drug and alcohol abuse, as well as tuberculosis and AIDS, have dramatically increased the mortality rate for adult males—recent U.S. Census Bureau (2005) figures estimate that there are 10 million fewer men than women in Russia alone. This, in turn, has fueled female emigration, supporting not only a vigorous "mail-order bride" business, but also increasingly sophisticated and far-flung transnational prostitution and human trafficking networks.

2. There are established ranges of normal variation in overall population sex ratios, as well as early childhood and birth sex ratios. These ratios are adjusted for country-specific circumstances such as, for example, maternal mortality rates and infant mortality rates. Using official census data, we can determine if there are fewer women than could reasonably be expected. Of course, there are perturbing variables: for example, many of the Gulf states have very abnormal sex ratios favoring males due to the high number of guest workers, predominantly male, that labor in the oil economies of these states. Once we take these types of factors into account, we find that the deficit of females in Asia is a real phenomenon (Hudson & den Boer, 2004).

3. Additional information provided by the director of the Chinese Academy of Social Sciences via e-mail, concerning the *Nando Times* article, "China Reportedly Has 20 Percent More Males Than Females," dated January 7, 1999.

4. No data are available for North Korea.

5. Other statistics also factor into the observed gender imbalance. In the West, for example, male suicides far outnumber female suicides. But in countries with deficits of women, female suicides outnumber male suicides. In fact, approximately 55 percent of all female suicides in the world are Chinese women of childbearing age (Murray & Lopez, 1996).

6. For more examples, please see Hudson and den Boer (2004).

7. For a more complete cultural analysis of these practices in Asia, please see Hudson and den Boer (2004), Bossen (2000), Miller (2001), and Sen (1990).

8. Note that this transition is also less likely in societies with a deficit of males; in such societies, men need not marry or form permanent attachments to obtain food, shelter, sexual services, domestic services, and so forth. In that respect, societies with too few men and societies with too many men share some characteristics. Furthermore, societies in which marriage age is generally delayed for men can also produce instability; for example, the average age at first marriage for men in Egypt is now 32 (Diane Singerman, personal communication, July 19, 2004).

REFERENCES

Boone, James L. (1983). "Noble family structure and expansionist warfare in the Late Middle Ages." In Rada Dyson-Hudson & Michael A. Little (Eds.), *Rethinking human adaptation: Biological and cultural models* (pp. 79–86). Boulder, CO: Westview.

Boone, James L. (1986). "Parental investment and elite family structure in preindustrial states: A case study of late medieval–early modern Portuguese genealogies." *American Anthropologist 88*(4), 859–78.

Bossen, Laurel. (2000). "Women and development." In Robert Gamer (Ed.), *Understanding contemporary China* (pp. 309–30). Boulder, CO: Lynne Rienner Publishers.

China State Statistical Bureau. (2001). *Major figures of the 2000 population census.* Beijing: China Statistics Press.

Demick, Barbara. (2003, August 18). "N. Korea's brides of despair." *Los Angeles Times.* Retrieved November 10, 2005, from http://www2.gol.com/users/coynerhm/n_koreas_brides_of_despair.htm.

Dickermann, Mildred. (1975). "Demographic consequences of infanticide of man." *Annual Review of Ecology and Systematics 6*, 107–37.

Dreze, Jean, & Reetika Khera. (2000). "Crime, gender, and society in India: Insights from homicide data." *Population and Development Review 26*(2), 335–52.

Hudson, Valerie M., & Andrea M. den Boer. (2004). *Bare branches: The security implications of Asia's surplus male population.* Cambridge, MA: MIT Press.

India Registrar General. (2001). *Census of India, 2001, Series 1: India, Paper of 2001: Provisional population totals.* New Delhi, India: Office of the Registrar General.

Johnson, Norris R., James G. Stemler, & Deborah Hunter. (1977). "Crowd behavior as 'risky shift': A laboratory experiment." *Sociometry 40*(2), 183–87.

Mazur, Allan, & Joel Michalek. (1998). "Marriage, divorce, and male testosterone." *Social Forces, 77*(1), 315–30.

McDonald, Hamish. (1991, December 26). "Unwelcome sex." *Far Eastern Economic Review 154*(52), 18–19.

Miller, Barbara D. (2001). "Female-selective abortion in Asia: Patterns, policies, and debates." *American Anthropologist 103*(4), 1083–95.

Murray, Christopher J. L., & Alan D. Lopez (Eds.). (1996). *The global burden of disease: A comprehensive assessment of mortality and disability from diseases, injuries, and risk factors in 1990 and projected to 2020.* Cambridge, MA: Harvard University Press.

Oldenburg, Philip. (1992). "Sex ratio, son preference, and violence in India: A research note." *Economic and Political Weekly 27*(49–50), 2657–62.

Oster, Emily. (2005, December). "Hepatitis B and the case of the missing women." *Journal of Political Economy 113*(6), 1163–1216. Retrieved November 4, 2005, from http://www.people.fas.harvard.edu/~eoaster/hepb.pdf.

Radyuhin, Vladamir. (2003, September 23). "A Chinese 'invasion.'" *The Hindu,* Retrieved November 7, 2005, from http://www.worldpress.org/Asia/1651.cfm#down.

Sen, Amartya. (1990, December 20). "More than 100 million women are missing." *New York Review of Books 37*(20), 61–66.

"Shenzhen's newborn sex ratio more balanced." (2005, April 15). *Shenzhen Daily.* Retrieved November 10, 2005, from english.people.com.cn/200504/15/eng20050415_181218.html.

South Korea National Statistics Office. (2001). *2001 report of the National Statistical Office of South Korea.* Seoul: National Statistics Office.

United Nations Population Division. (1998). *Too young to die: Genes or gender.* New York: United Nations.

United States Census Bureau. (2005). *International database summary demographic data for Russia.* Retrieved November 4, 2005, from http://www.census.gov/cgi-bin/ipc/idbsum.pl?cty=RS.

Jon R. Lindsay

THE IMPACT OF CHINA ON CYBERSECURITY

The ubiquity and interconnectedness of computers in global commerce, civil society, and military affairs create crosscutting challenges for policy and conceptual confusion for theory. The challenges and confusion in cybersecurity are particularly acute in the case of China, which has one of the world's fastest growing internet economies and one of its most active cyber operations programs. In 2013 U.S. National Security Adviser Tom Donilon singled out Chinese cyber intrusions as "not solely a national security concern or a concern of the U.S. government," but also a major problem for firms suffering from "sophisticated, targeted theft of confidential business information and proprietary technologies . . . emanating from China on an unprecedented scale."[1] One U.S. congressman alleged that China has "established cyber war military units and laced the U.S. infrastructure with logic bombs." He suggested that "America is under attack by digital bombs."[2] The discourse on China and cybersecurity routinely conflates issues as different as political censorship, unfair competition, assaults on infrastructure, and internet governance, even as all loom large for practical cyber policy. Although they involve similar information technologies, there is little reason to expect different political economic problems to obey the same strategic logic, nor should one necessarily expect China to enjoy relative advantage in all spheres.

Indeed, the intelligence leaks from Edward Snowden in 2013 underscored the sophistication and extent of internet surveillance by the United States and its allies against targets worldwide, including in China.[3] The Snowden revelations not only invigorated debate about the balance between security and privacy in a democracy but also undercut the moral force of American complaints about Chinese penetration of commercial, government, and defense networks.[4] Chinese writers hasten to compare the United States to "a thief crying stop thief."[5] Meanwhile U.S. officials attempt to distinguish between acceptable data collection for national security and unacceptable criminal economic espionage.[6] Notably, a May 2014 grand jury indicted five alleged members of the Chinese People's Liberation Army (PLA) on several counts of industrial espionage, but omitted mentioning that the same PLA unit targets military interests as well.[7] Chinese critics reject the American distinction between legitimate and illegitimate internet surveillance and deny allegations of hacking. They also call for the restriction of American internet firms from the Chinese domestic market in order to protect Chinese infrastructure from subversion.[8] Cyber operations and the rhetorical reactions to them on both sides of the Pacific have undermined trust in the Sino-American relationship.[9]

Exaggerated fears about the paralysis of digital infrastructure and growing concerns over competitive advantage exacerbate the spiral of mistrust. Closer consideration of domestic factors within China and China's strategic interaction with the United States reveals a more complicated yet less worrisome situation. This article argues that for every type of purported Chinese cyber threat, there

From *International Security* 39, no. 3 (Winter 2014/15): 7–47.
Some of the author's notes have been edited.

are also serious Chinese vulnerabilities and Western strengths that reinforce the political status quo. Cyberwar between the United States and China, much like U.S.–China conventional war, is highly unlikely. Nevertheless, the economically driven proliferation of information technology enables numerous instances of friction to emerge below the threshold of violence. From a technical perspective, cyber operations are often thought to be inexpensive and effective, but there are underappreciated institutional costs involved in their employment. Moreover, even if actors can overcome the operational barriers associated with ambitious cyber penetrations, they still have incentives to moderate the intensity of their exploitation in order to preserve the benefits that make exploitation worthwhile in the first place. This logic culminates in a relentlessly irritating but indefinitely tolerable stability in the cyber domain. China and the United States can look forward to chronic and ambiguous intelligence-counterintelligence contests across their networks, even as the internet facilitates productive exchange between them.

■　　■　　■

Cybersecurity and International Relations

Claims about Chinese cyber threats fall at the intersection of two different debates, one about the impact of information technology on international security and the other about the political and economic future of a rising power. The technological debate centers on whether ubiquitous networks create revolutionary dangers or just marginal evolutions of computer crime, signals intelligence, and electronic warfare.[10] One side of this debate argues that interconnected infrastructure and easily accessible hacking tools make advanced industrial powers particularly vulnerable to serious disruption from weaker states or even nonstate

actors.[11] The other side argues that the defense industry and national security establishment greatly exaggerate the cyber threat.[12] The political debate offers contrasting liberal and realist interpretations of China's meteoric growth.[13] One side argues that China is increasingly integrated into the global economy and international institutions and, furthermore, that the Communist government is committed to growth and stability to maintain its legitimacy.[14] The other side argues that Chinese military modernization and the relative decline of the United States heighten the potential for opportunistic aggression, miscalculation in a crisis, or preventive war.[15] The very existence and magnitude of a shift in relative power is also a matter of debate.[16]

Technological and political questions become entangled in cybersecurity discourse, because the internet facilitates the expansion of trade while providing new tools for subversion. The novelty of cyber operations and the ambiguity of China's developmental trajectory compound the uncertainty. It is possible, however, to turn this practical ambiguity to analytical advantage. By taking the extremes of the conceptual debates that frame cyber policy discussions and combining them orthogonally, one can describe four ideal-type threat narratives that clarify the capabilities and motivations shaping cyber behavior. Each category in the typology makes different assumptions about what is possible and probable, technologically and politically.

Figure 11.1 presents each threat, along with counterarguments that I develop below.[17] The "open internet" quadrant describes a more or less cooperative political environment of connected states willing to tolerate a variety of minor threats. The internet has the potential to enhance liberal trade and discourse, but computer fraud and authoritarian censorship undermine this promise. The "contested cyberspace" quadrant describes a situation where competitive states engage in intelligence collection and harassment using evolutionary adaptations of familiar security practices. Discourse in this quadrant focuses less on the risks of a "cyber

Figure 11.1. A Typology of Cyber Threat Narratives

	Evolutionary Technology	Revolutionary Technology
Cooperative Political Environment	**Open Internet** Assumption: The Internet enhances the value of social and economic exchange. Threat: State censorship and survelliance violate human rights and reduce trust in the internet. Counterargument: Prioritization of informaion control over technical defence exposes China to foreign and domestic cyber attack.	**Cybersecurity Norms** Assumption: States must adopt common norms to protect the internet from catastrophe. Threat: Authoritarian "Internet sovereignty" norms imperil the liberal "multistakeholder" system. Counterargument: The institutional status quo is durable, and China cannot credibly commit to its proposed norms.
Competitive Political Environment	**Contested Cyberspace** Assumption: Cyber technology improves intelligence collection methods and opportunities. Threat: Chinese cyber espionage is systematically eroding the competitiveness of Western firms. Counterargument: Absorption of stolen data is a nontrivial obstacle, and Western Intelligence also exploits China.	**Cyber Warfare** Assumption: Cyberspace is a dangerous, asymmetric, offense dominant warfighting environment. Threat: China can paralyze U.S. military command and control and civilian infrastructure at low cost. Counterargument: China's cyber capabilities do not live up to Chinese rhetoric, and "informatization" exposes China to attack.

Pearl Harbor" and more on a "death by a thousand cuts" through Chinese espionage. The "cyberwarfare" quadrant is the culmination of the most pessimistic interpretations of technology and politics, where conflict-prone actors wield revolutionary cyber capabilities. Because U.S. power projection, like the U.S. economy, depends heavily on computer networks for command and control, many analysts worry that Chinese cyber attacks could blunt or dissuade U.S. intervention in an East Asia crisis. The final "cybersecurity norms" quadrant describes a more indirect threat emerging through international overreaction to the direct threats described in the other categories. The reform of internet governance predicated on Chinese "internet sovereignty" might, as many Western observers fear, legitimize authoritarian control and undermine the cosmopolitan promise of the "multi-stakeholder" system.[18]

At best, each narrative highlights different political, espionage, military, and institutional threats. At worst, they are mutually inconsistent, in which case some of them should be discounted or reconciled. All are present to some degree in political debate about China and cybersecurity, and they are often conflated. By identifying different assumptions about threat characterizations, one can also pose counterarguments in each category that either question the magnitude of the Chinese threat or point out countervailing Western advantages.

Political Threats to the Open Internet

Almost from its inception, the internet fostered hopeful expectations that connectivity might deliver economic and political liberalization for user populations, if not the outright transformation of digital society into a cosmopolitan utopia.[19] Economic drag from criminal hacking and information control by governments, however, challenge the techno-libertarian ideal. In particular, state censorship and surveillance target domestic and expatriate dissidents and minority groups, thus posing a digital threat to human rights.[20] As China uses the internet more intensively and as the internet becomes increasingly Chinese, the global internet provides a channel for China's illiberal domestic politics to challenge liberal interests abroad.[21] These are important concerns, but they are only part of the picture: state internet control efforts do generate limited threats to civil society, but they can also inadvertently undermine the state's defense against other types of threats.

Unbundling Openness

Economic openness promotes growth, but China sees political openness as a threat to its legitimacy. As President Xi Jinping states, development and security go together like "two wings of a bird and two wheels of an engine," and therefore "[c]yberspace should be made clean and chipper."[22] In advanced industrial countries, networked computers have enhanced profit and performance in every sector from manufacturing to transportation, service, entertainment, governance, and public safety.[23] Similarly for China, internet-enabled supply chains tie its production lines into the global economy while information technology facilitates the modernization of infrastructure and boosts export-led growth.[24] Chinese "netizens" (*wangmin*)—more than 600 million users as of 2013—enjoy expanded access to entertainment, shopping, gossip, and news.[25] To the degree that civil society exists in China, it does so predominantly online. As a 2010 State Council white paper asserts, however, "China advocates the rational use of technology to curb dissemination of illegal information online."[26] The result is the most sophisticated internet censorship architecture in the world (i.e., "the Great Firewall of China"). The government requires internet service providers to block politically sensitive websites and searches and to employ human censors to remove offending social media posts or guide discussion in more politically acceptable directions. Domestic security services often single out dissidents, domestic and expatriate alike, for more aggressive online harassment and service denial attacks.[27] China is the foremost counterexample to the myth that the borderless internet undermines the power of the state.[28]

Whereas the Western notion of cybersecurity emphasizes technical threats, China places greater weight on ideological threats. The Chinese notion of information security (*xinxi anquan*), accordingly, includes control of information content as well as, if not more than, technical network security (*wangluo anquan*) against malware. In 2010 the director of the State Council Information Office and External Propaganda Department of the Chinese Communist Party (CCP) linked "hostile foreign forces" and subversive "universal values" to internet penetration: "As long as our country's internet is linked to the global internet, there will be channels and means for all sorts of harmful foreign information to appear on our domestic internet."[29] An authoritative 2013 CCP directive "on the current state of the ideological sphere" warns more pointedly of "accelerating infiltration of the internet" by "Western anti-China forces and internal 'dissidents.'"[30]

CCP internet control is not absolute, however. Netizens playfully exploit Mandarin homophones to evade or ridicule censors.[31] The phenomenon of the "human flesh search" (*renrou sousuo*) or crowd-sourced vigilantism targets disgraced citizens and corrupt officials for public humiliation. While unruly behavior encourages the state to crack down on individuals branded as "rumor mongers," CCP officials tolerate internet discussion to identify brewing unrest or lapses in party discipline.[32] Thus censors do not block all criticism of the state, but only that which the CCP fears might mobilize public demonstration and dissent.[33]

China's Fragmented Cyber Defenses

The CCP's obsession with political "information security" has so far not translated into effective technical "network security."[34] Cybercrime thrives amid a fragmented bureaucracy. Lax and uneven law enforcement emboldens Chinese cybercriminals to prey on domestic targets and creates a blatantly open online underground economy in China. Chinese cybercriminals target Chinese victims given the relatively low risk of domestic police action; by comparison, Eastern Europe cybercriminals tend to avoid hacking at home, instead focusing their predation abroad. Stolen usernames and passwords, financial data, video game accounts, and hacker tools can be bought and sold openly on Chinese social media forums such as Baidu and Tencent QQ. By one estimate, cybercrime damage to the economy exceeded $830 million and affected more than 20 percent of users and websites in 2011 alone.[35] Rampant cybercrime is a result, in part, of China's below-average cyber defenses.[36] Importantly, networks exposed to criminal predation are also vulnerable to foreign exploitation, because state intelligence services use some of the same technology and methods.

Cyber policy coordination among defense, law enforcement, and regulatory agencies is a challenge in any state, but China's lack of governmental transparency makes a hard problem worse. * * *

Numerous agencies under the State Council are responsible for the implementation of policy and the regulation of information technology in China. The People's Liberation Army, subordinate to the CCP rather than the state, has considerable military and intelligence cyber capacity as well as civilian regulatory responsibility (e.g., in the transportation sector). Provincial governments, furthermore, enjoy substantial de facto autonomy and compete fiercely for patronage. In response to a glut of funding for SILG initiatives, expenditure in China's information security industry grew from $527 million in 2003 to $2.8 billion in 2011. In the assessment of one industry observer, however, this expansion was marred by a "lack of overall planning," "decentralization of decisionmaking power," and a "lack of adequate communication."[37] * * *

■   ■   ■

Intelligence Threats in Contested Cyberspace

The open internet quadrant in Figure 11.1 is populated by digital evolutions of crime and illiberal domestic control in an international environment of broadly shared interests. The contested cyberspace quadrant, in turn, contains a more competitive environment in which actors adapt information technology for intelligence purposes. Since the introduction of the telegraph in the mid-nineteenth century and with every innovation in telephony, radio, and computation since, the sophistication of techniques for electronic interception and deception has increased without, however, creating lasting decisive advantages.[38] An intelligence contest is never one-sided, because the target reacts with operational security and counterintelligence measures, which in turn raise the political and technical barriers for attackers reliant on covert advantage. The mere fear of counterintelligence compromise can be as inhibiting as actual defenses. The novelty of computer network exploitation (CNE) lies mainly in the scope and diffusion of classic intelligence-counterintelligence contests. By virtue of the internet's reach and ubiquity, private firms and other nongovernmental organizations are increasingly involved in the sort of intelligence activities—as both participants and targets—that were once mainly the purview of state security agencies.

The exposure of profitable Western firms to Chinese espionage online raises particular concerns about the future competitiveness of such companies. A U.S. National Intelligence Estimate in early 2013 reportedly described Chinese CNE as a serious and persistent economic threat to U.S. firms and government institutions.[39] * * * Chinese espionage activity alone, however, cannot produce this result. To realize competitive advantage, China needs to be able to absorb and apply the data it steals. Moreover, the United States is also a formidable intelligence actor, which can be expected to offset Chinese advantages to some degree. The category of contested cyberspace highlights the increasing intensity of intelligence competition, not a clear advantage for one side or the other.

■   ■   ■

Obstacles to the Absorption of Stolen Data

Remote access to target networks is only the first step toward developing an intelligence advantage, much less downstream competitive advantage. Although Western cyber defenders can observe the exfiltration of petabytes of data to Chinese servers, they cannot so readily measure China's ability to use the data. It is possible, for example, that operators in the Third Department of the PLA General

Staff are simply rewarded for the number of foreign targets penetrated and terabytes exfiltrated, with little attention to the satisfaction of the intelligence customer, thereby creating lots of measurable CNE with little improvement in national competitiveness. The acquisition, absorption, and application of foreign information from any source is a complicated process. Transaction costs at every step along the way caused by information overload, analytic misinterpretation, or bureaucratic silos can undermine the translation of stolen data into new production knowledge and successful competition in the marketplace.

Technology transfer by any means is both a priority and a challenge for China. The MLP promotes a policy of "indigenous innovation" (*zizhu chuangxin*), which involves "enhancing original innovation through co-innovation and re-innovation based on the assimilation of imported technologies."[40] This policy involves a four-part process for converting foreign technology into remade domestic variants that Chinese sources describe as "introduce, digest, assimilate, and re-innovate" (IDAR). * * *

China faces major challenges in converting foreign inputs into innovative output given the notoriously compartmentalized and hierarchical nature of Chinese bureaucracy, underdeveloped high-end equipment manufacturing capacity, and chronic dependence on foreign technology and know-how. Reliance on Russia for fighter jet engines despite years of access to technical design information and assistance from Russian technicians is a particularly notable but hardly unique example in the Chinese defense industry. Foreign expertise is only one input in the overall innovation process, which also requires "hard" factors such as materials, universities, skilled labor, laboratories, and factories, as well as "soft" factors such as leadership, regulation, contract enforcement, standards and protocols, and an innovative culture. The utility of even the best CNE is sensitive to the performance of the rest of these factors working in synergy, and China still has far to go in integrating them.[41]

Similar considerations extend from economic to defense competitiveness. * * * The Soviet Union's reliance on systematic industrial espionage to catch up with the West provides a cautionary tale: the Soviet system became optimized for imitation rather than innovation and was thus locked into a form of second-place dependency, even as it shortened research and development timelines.[42] Chinese espionage can potentially narrow the gap with the West, but only at the price of creating dependency through investment in a large-scale absorption effort. * * *

■ ■ ■

Chinese espionage is impressive in its scope, but it does not translate easily into industrial absorption, which is a prerequisite for competitive advantage. Furthermore, U.S. intelligence appears to be more technically adept, even if its target set differs somewhat from China's. Both sides are engaged in commercial and intelligence contests using a range of political, economic, and technical tools. Charges of unfair competition and attempts to redress it will remain a chronic feature of U.S.–China relations. There is no reason to expect the side playing catch-up to realize an enduring advantage for technical reasons alone.

Military Threats of Cyberwarfare

Just as the social context of exploitation and adversary counteraction combine to blunt the potential of cyber espionage, similar challenges in operational weaponization and strategic interaction constrain the potency of more disruptive cyber threats. Yet conventional wisdom holds that a multitude of technical factors favor offense over defense in cyberspace and that the difficulty of attribution

undermines the credibility of deterrence; therefore, weaker actors can attack the control systems of superior adversaries to achieve levels of physical disruption possible previously only through kinetic bombing. As President Obama writes in a *Wall Street Journal* opinion article, "Computer systems in critical sectors of our economy—including the nuclear and chemical industries—are being increasingly targeted. . . . In a future conflict, an adversary unable to match our military supremacy on the battlefield might seek to exploit our computer vulnerabilities here at home. Taking down vital banking systems could trigger a financial crisis. The lack of clean water or functioning hospitals could spark a public health emergency. And as we've seen in past blackouts, the loss of electricity can bring businesses, cities and entire regions to a standstill."[43] A number of former U.S. government officials have even likened the advent of cyberweapons to a new atomic age and have wondered why a catastrophic cyberattack has not yet occurred. Chinese military doctrine similarly envisions cyberwarfare to be a low-cost, long-range, highly effective counter to a superior adversary.[44] There are reasons, however, to doubt the PLA's ability to implement these ideas or to defend itself against cyberattacks launched by a superior adversary.

Chinese Cyber Doctrine

The aggressive tenor of Chinese writings on cyberwarfare and the copious APT activity described above are the major sources of evidence that Western analysts usually offer to characterize the Chinese cyberwarfare threat. Official Chinese military doctrine and sources in Chinese military professional literature consistently describe cyberwarfare as a revolutionary development in military affairs. Senior Col. Ye Zheng, author of books published by the Chinese Academy of Military Science entitled *On Informationalized Warfare* and *Information Warfare Course*, writes, "Although the main melody of the times—peace and development—is still playing strongly, the dark spirit of network warfare is lurking in the sky above humanity." This rhetorical construction implies that the cyber revolution undermines Deng Xiaoping's diagnosis of the largely stable nature of the international environment. Ye singles out the United States for experimenting with cyberweapons such as Stuxnet (used in the attack on Iranian enrichment infrastructure) and hints at the prospect of more to come: "[J]ust as nuclear war was the strategic warfare of the industrial age, network warfare will be the strategic warfare of the information age. It has already become a 'top level' form of operation that is highly destructive and relates to national security and survival."[45] * * * Information operations are considered so vital for the limited high-technology wars the PLA envisions fighting that information supremacy is thought to be a precondition for gaining military supremacy anywhere else. The PLA's general strategic principle of "active defense" stresses offensive operations to seize the initiative. The authoritative *Science of Campaigns* thus states that the beginning of a network war will determine its outcome: "Whoever strikes first prevails."[46] PLA strategists assert that the vital targets of an advanced technology adversary are its information systems, and by attacking them covertly from beyond the range of enemy weapon systems it is possible to cause paralysis of the enemy's organization, strategic decisionmaking, and national economy. * * * Chinese writers argue that a relatively weaker PLA can achieve information superiority against a stronger military only as long as it is able to launch paralyzing strikes at the beginning of a conflict.

■　　■　　■

Chinese Cyber Capabilities

Although Chinese writers emphasize the revolutionary potential of cyberwarfare, episodes of Chinese aggression in cyberspace have been more mundane.

China's "hacker wars" flare up during episodes of tension in Chinese foreign relations, as between Taiwan and the mainland between 1996 and 2004 in the wake of Taiwanese elections, between the United States and China following the 1999 bombing of the Chinese embassy in Belgrade and the 2001 EP-3 spy plane collision, and between China and Japan throughout the past decade during controversies involving the Yasukuni Shrine and the Senkaku/Diaoyu Islands.[47] Nationalist hackers (as distinguished from PLA units) deface foreign websites and launch temporary distributed denial of service attacks. Nationalist online outbursts may take place with the tacit consent or encouragement of the Chinese government, yet patriotic "hacktivism" is essentially just another form of symbolic protest. There has been speculation that PLA "cyber militias" associated with Chinese universities maintain a more potent reserve capability, but one study of open sources suggests that they are oriented toward more mundane educational and network defense activities.[48]

The majority of known PLA cyber operations are CNE for intelligence rather than computer network attacks to cause disruption.[49] Nevertheless, many analysts worry that CNE is "only a keystroke away" from CNA, thereby generating dangerous ambiguity between intelligence gathering and offensive operations. Intrusion techniques developed for industrial espionage might be used to plant more dangerous payload code into sensitive controllers or constitute reconnaissance for future assaults. Chinese probing of critical infrastructure such as the U.S. power grid is aggressive, to be sure, so a latent potential for the PLA to convert CNE into CNA cannot be discounted.[50] The discovery of access vectors and exploitable vulnerabilities, however, is only the first step to achieving effective reconnaissance of a target, and effective reconnaissance is just one step toward planning and controlling a physically disruptive attack. The most significant historical case of kinetic CNA to date, the Stuxnet attack on Iran's enrichment infrastructure, suggests that painstaking planning, careful rehearsals, and sophisticated intelligence are required to control a covert disruption.[51] The U.S. military also considered using cyberattacks to take down Libya's air defense system in 2011, but reportedly it would have taken too long to develop the option.[52] The latency between CNE and CNA is more complicated than generally assumed.

The PLA does have access to considerable resources, human capital, and engineering skill, so it might in principle overcome operational barriers to weaponization, but its observed operational focus and experience are concentrated on intelligence operations. * * *

The Downside of "Informatization"

China's ambition to become a world-class military power will lead the PLA to become more like the U.S. military in its dependence on networks and space assets. This modernization will undermine the asymmetry of vulnerability thought to make cyberweapons so dangerous to the United States and instead put some of the PLA's own most sophisticated systems at risk. PLA antiaccess capabilities against U.S. power projection also include antiship ballistic missiles, cruise missile boats, antisatellite weapons, and fifth-generation aircraft. The PLA requires traditional forces, moreover, for other missions that might require warfighting, military operations other than war, or coercive diplomacy (a role ill-suited for secret and intangible cyberweapons). China's goal of "winning local wars under the conditions of informatization" requires the PLA to "enhance [its] warfighting capabilities based on information systems."[53] This transformation into a modern "informatized" force, inspired in no small part by American RMA ideals and force structure, entails greater reliance on C4ISR systems and computer networks. Yet China's pursuit of the promise of the RMA will also reveal its liabilities.

In imagining and planning for a potential war with the United States, the PLA has to worry about the demonstrated ability and willingness of the U.S. military to conduct cyber operations on the battlefield (in Iraq and Afghanistan) and in covert action (e.g., the Stuxnet attack). * * * The United States already has, while China still struggles to develop, the institutional complements and experience required to plan and control cyber operations in synchrony with the larger battle. * * * If the military utility of cyber warfare is actually more limited than Chinese doctrine writers seem to believe, then conventional considerations about military effectiveness (e.g., the balance of power as well as skill in combined arms warfare and joint operations) should be expected to dominate strategic calculation and operational interaction in any conflict.

Two considerations complicate this discounting of the potency of cyberwarfare. First is the problem of misperception. The assumption that cyberwarfare is a potent, low-cost means for achieving an advantage is widespread in Chinese military writing. Although the RMA debate over whether information technology is an evolutionary complement or a revolutionary disruption in warfare is prominent in Western cyber literature, it is virtually absent in Chinese writings. Given the complexity of the cyber operating environment (i.e., remote intrusions through layers of heterogeneous technical systems and imperfectly understood organizational practices), there is nontrivial potential for an attacker to become confused, deceived, or compromised, especially against more ambitious and sensitive targets. There is also little Chinese discussion of the unintended consequences and collateral damage risks of cyber operations—for example, that one's own malware might cause blowback or harm friendly civilian infrastructure.[54]

Second, and related, is the risk of inadvertent escalation. Chinese doctrine stresses that striking first and striking hard against the most important networked targets is essential, because victory at the beginning of a war will determine its end. These beliefs are false.[55] Yet they could lead the PLA to authorize preemptive cyber strikes on high-value targets such as U.S. satellites or the civilian power grid in the false hope that these would paralyze or intimidate an adversary. The contrast between offense-dominant cyber dogma and a more complicated reality recalls the mismatch between "the cult of the offensive" before World War I and the defensive advantages of machine guns and barbed wire.[56] Preemptive PLA cyberattacks that fizzle could be worse than nothing at all if they reveal hostile intent and thereby encourage U.S. "cross domain" retaliation with more kinetic weapons. Conversely, U.S. commanders who wrongly fear the existence of a PLA "assassin's mace" in cyberspace may be tempted to preemptively strike PLA assets by the same first-mover logic. This possibility is particularly troubling in light of the PLA Second Artillery's dual command of both conventional antiship ballistic missiles and nuclear forces. Misperception of cyber offense dominance, heightened by the secrecy of cyber capabilities on both sides, is a recipe for U.S.—China crisis instability.[57] At the same time, the PLA's cautious and probing behavior in recent years during tensions with China's neighbors is at odds with its doctrinal musing about rapid operations. * * *

■   ■   ■

Conclusion

Overlap across political, intelligence, military, and institutional threat narratives makes cybersecurity a challenging policy problem, which can lead to theoretical confusion. For each category, I have argued that the threat from China is exaggerated whereas the threat to China is underappreciated. By prioritizing political information control over technical cyber defense, China has inadvertently degraded the economic efficiency of its networks and exposed them to foreign infiltration. Although China also actively infiltrates Western networks, its ability to absorb stolen data is questionable, especially at the most competitive end of the value chain, where the United States dominates. Similarly, China's military cyber capacity cannot live up to its aggressive doctrinal aspirations, even as "informatization" creates vulnerabilities that more experienced foreign cyber operators can attack. Outmatched by the West, China has resorted to a strategy of institutional reform, but it benefits too much from multistakeholder governance to pose a credible alternative. The secrecy of cyber capabilities and operations on all sides makes it difficult to estimate with confidence the magnitude of the gap between China and the United States in the balance of cyber power, but it is potentially growing, not shrinking.

My examination of the case of China provides further support for critics of the cyber revolution thesis. The social context of exploitation matters tremendously for cyber performance. The more ambitious the infiltration, the greater the reliance on technical expertise, reliable intelligence, and organizational capacity to contend with mounting complexity and risk of compromise. This stands in contrast to the popular and erroneous belief that hacking is cheap and easy. It is a mistake to infer conclusions about high-impact cyber operations from more prosaic and plentiful cybercrime. Cyberspace enables numerous variations on familiar themes in political demonstration, crime, propaganda, signals intelligence, and electronic warfare, and it diffuses these activities widely. But cyber capabilities work as complements to power, not substitutes for it, and they are certainly not revolutionary game changers. This finding effectively shrinks two of the four quadrants in my typology, leaving only the evolutionary end of the technological threat spectrum. The normative politics of internet governance return to the open internet quadrant (where they have always been), and cyberwarfare collapses largely into contested cyberspace. Military cyber operations will emphasize exploitation for intelligence over disruption, even as the latter plays an adjunct role in combined arms warfare and covert action. The main problem of cybersecurity thus reduces to the evolving pursuit of marginal and deceptive advantage amid the benefits of open interconnection. Hallmarks of this development include continuous and sophisticated intelligence contests, the involvement and targeting of civilian entities, enduring great power advantage relative to weaker states and nonstate actors, noisy symbolic protest, and complicated politics of institutional design.

∎   ∎   ∎

As long as dense interconnection and economic interdependence remain mutually beneficial for powers such as the United States and China, they will be able to tolerate the irritants that they will inevitably inflict on one another. The modern intelligence-counterintelligence contest plays out in a complicated sociotechnical space where states take advantage of economic cooperation and hedge against security competition. If their broader mutual interest frays, however, then cyberwarfare becomes just one facet of a more serious strategic problem involving more dangerous means. Exaggeration of the cyber threat feeds spirals of mistrust, which make this undesirable outcome slightly more likely.

The United States and China should discuss the interaction of cybersecurity and traditional military force in depth and take steps to limit misunderstandings about the other's intentions. They might even learn to interpret chronic cyber friction as a sign that more truly dangerous threats have been constrained. Contrary to conventional wisdom, the emergence of complex cyber threats may be a positive development in the tragic history of international politics: the bad news about cybersecurity is good news for global security.

NOTES

1. Tom Donilon, "The United States and the Asia-Pacific in 2013," Asia Society, New York, March 11, 2013 (Washington, DC: White House, March 2013), http://www.whitehouse.gov/the-press-office/2013/03/11/remarks-tom-donilon-national-security-advisory-president-united-states-a.

2. Charles Cooper, "House Hearing: U.S. Now Under Cyber Attack," CNET, April 24, 2012, http://news.cnet.com/8301-1009_3-57420229-83/house-hearing-u.s-now-under-cyber-attack/.

3. Jeffrey T. Richelson, ed., "The Snowden Affair: Web Resource Documents the Latest Firestorm over the National Security Agency," *National Security Archive Electronic Briefing Book* (Washington, DC: National Security Archive, George Washington University, September 4, 2013), http://www2gwu.edu/~nsarchiv/NSAEBB/NSAEBB436/.

4. See, for example, Office of the National Counterintelligence Executive, *Foreign Spies Stealing US Economic Secrets in Cyberspace: Report to Congress on Foreign Economic Collection and Industrial Espionage 2009–2011* (Washington, DC: Office of the National Counterintelligence Executive, October 2011).

5. Zhong Sheng, "The United States Bears Primary Responsibility for Stopping Cyber War," *People's Daily Online,* February 7, 2013.

6. For example, the United States forbids "the collection of foreign private commercial information or trade secrets . . . to afford a competitive advantage to U.S. companies and U.S. business sectors commercially." See Office of the Press Secretary, White House, "Signals Intelligence Activities," Presidential Policy Directive/PPD-28 (Washington, DC: White House, January 17, 2014).

7. U.S. Department of Justice, Office of Public Affairs, "U.S. Charges Five Chinese Military Hackers for Cyber Espionage against U.S. Corporations and a Labor Organization for Commercial Advantage," press release, May 19, 2014, http://www.justice.gov/opa/pr/2014/May/14-ag-528.html. For further details on the Second Bureau of the PLA General Staff Department Third Bureau (3/PLA), see Mandiant, "APT1: Exposing One of China's Cyber Espionage Units" (Alexandria, VA: Mandiant, February 2013), http://intelreport.mandiant.com/Mandiant_APT1_Report.pdf.

8. Michael D. Swaine, "Chinese Views on Cybersecurity in Foreign Relations," *China Leadership Monitor,* September 20, 2013, http://carnegieendowment.org/2013/09/20/chinese-views-on-cybersecurity-in-foreign-relations.

9. Kenneth G. Lieberthal and Wang Jisi, "Addressing U.S.-China Strategic Distrust" (Washington, DC: Brookings Institution, March 2012).

10. For collections of perspectives on both sides of the debate, see Franklin D. Kramer, Stuart H. Starr, and Larry K. Wentz, eds., *Cyberpower and National Security* (Washington, DC: Potomac, 2009); and Derek S. Reveron, ed., *Cyberspace and National Security: Threats, Opportunities, and Power in a Virtual World* (Washington, DC: Georgetown University Press, 2012). For balanced introductions to cybersecurity policy, see P. W. Singer and Allan Friedman, *Cybersecurity and Cyberwar: What Everyone Needs to Know* (New York: Oxford University Press, 2014); and National Research Council, *At the Nexus of Cybersecurity and Public Policy:*

Some Basic Concepts and Issues (Washington, DC: National Academies Press, 2014).

11. See, inter alia, Gregory J. Rattray, *Strategic Warfare in Cyberspace* (Cambridge, MA: MIT Press, 2001); Scott Borg, "Economically Complex Cyberattacks," *IEEE Security and Privacy Magazine,* Vol. 3, No. 6 (November/December 2005), pp. 64–67; Richard A. Clarke and Robert K. Knake, *Cyber War: The Next Threat to National Security and What to Do about It* (New York: Ecco, 2010); Joel Brenner, *America the Vulnerable: Inside the New Threat Matrix of Digital Espionage, Crime, and Warfare* (New York: Penguin, 2011); Joseph S. Nye Jr., "Nuclear Lessons for Cyber Security?" *Strategic Studies Quarterly,* Vol. 5, No. 4 (Winter 2011), pp. 18–36; Timothy J. Junio, "How Probable Is Cyber War? Bringing IR Theory Back In to the Cyber Conflict Debate," *Journal of Strategic Studies,* Vol. 36, No. 1 (February 2013), pp. 125–33; Dale Peterson, "Offensive Cyber Weapons: Construction, Development, and Employment," *Journal of Strategic Studies,* Vol. 36, No. 1 (February 2013), pp. 120–24; and Lucas Kello, "The Meaning of the Cyber Revolution: Perils to Theory and Statecraft," *International Security,* Vol. 38, No. 2 (Fall 2013), pp. 7–40.

12. On cyber threat inflation, see Myriam Dunn Cavelty, "Cyber-Terror—Looming Threat or Phantom Menace? The Framing of the US Cyber-Threat Debate," *Journal of Information Technology & Politics,* Vol. 4, No. 1 (February 2008), pp. 19–36; Sean Lawson, "Beyond Cyber-Doom: Assessing the Limits of Hypothetical Scenarios in the Framing of Cyber-Threats," *Journal of Information Technology & Politics,* Vol. 10, No. 1 (February 2013), pp. 86–103; and Erik Gartzke, "The Myth of Cyberwar: Bringing War in Cyberspace Back Down to Earth," *International Security,* Vol. 38, No. 2 (Fall 2013), pp. 41–73.

13. Alastair Iain Johnston, "Is China a Status Quo Power?" *International Security,* Vol. 27, No. 4 (Spring 2003), pp. 5–56; Aaron L. Friedberg, "The Future of U.S.-China Relations: Is Conflict Inevitable?" *International Security,* Vol. 30, No. 2 (Fall 2005), pp. 7–45; Thomas J. Christensen, "Fostering Stability or Creating a Monster? The Rise of China and U.S. Policy toward East Asia," *International Security,* Vol. 31, No. 1 (Summer 2006), pp. 81–126; Robert S. Ross and Zhu Feng, eds., *China's Ascent: Power, Security, and the Future of International Politics* (Ithaca, NY: Cornell University Press, 2008); and M. Taylor Fravel, "International Relations Theory and China's Rise: Assessing China's Potential for Territorial Expansion," *International Studies Review,* Vol. 12, No. 4 (December 2010), pp. 505–32.

14. Barry Naughton, *The Chinese Economy: Transitions and Growth* (Cambridge, MA: MIT Press, 2007); Daniel W. Drezner, "Bad Debts: Assessing China's Financial Influence in Great Power Politics," *International Security,* Vol. 34, No. 2 (Fall 2009), pp. 7–45.

15. John J. Mearsheimer, *The Tragedy of Great Power Politics* (New York: W. W. Norton, 2001), pp. 360–402 and Jonathan Kirshner, "The Tragedy of Offensive Realism: Classical Realism and the Rise of China," *European Journal of International Relations,* Vol. 18, No. 1 (March 2012), pp. 53–75.

16. Christopher Layne, "The Waning of U.S. Hegemony—Myth or Reality? A Review Essay," *International Security,* Vol. 34, No. 1 (Summer 2009), pp. 147–72; Michael Beckley, "China's Century? Why America's Edge Will Endure," *International Security,* Vol. 36, No. 3 (Winter 2011/12), pp. 41–78; Randall L. Schweller and Xiaoyu Pu, "After Unipolarity: China's Visions of International Order in an Era of U.S. Decline," *International Security,* Vol. 36, No. 1 (Summer 2011), p. 41–72; and Alastair Iain Johnston, "How New and Assertive Is China's New Assertiveness?" *International Security,* Vol. 37, No. 4 (Spring 2013), pp. 7–48.

17. Because this article evaluates the Chinese cyber threat—primarily to the United States—this typology emphasizes interactions among nation-states. Nonstate actors loom large in cyber discourse, and indeed, criminal and "hacktivist" threats create headaches even in the cooperative "open internet" quadrant. The most worrisome cyber activity observed to date, however, has been driven by states (e.g., PLA espionage and U.S. covert action). For an argument about how the cyber revolution diffuses power beyond the state, see Joseph S. Nye Jr., *The Future of Power* (New York: PublicAffairs, 2011), pp. 113–52.

18. The term "multistakeholder" system is widely used by practitioners to describe the mélange of academic, corporate, regulatory, and nongovernmental actors in contemporary internet governance.

19. Vincent Mosco, *The Digital Sublime: Myth, Power, and Cyberspace.* (Cambridge, MA: MIT Press, 2005); and Janet Abbate, *Inventing the Internet* (Cambridge, MA: MIT Press, 1999).

20. Sarah McKune, " 'Foreign Hostile Forces': The Human Rights Dimension of China's Cyber Campaigns," in Jon R. Lindsay, Tai Ming Cheung, and Derek S. Reveron, eds., *China and Cybersecurity: Espionage, Strategy, and Politics in the Digital Domain* (New York: Oxford University Press, forthcoming).

21. According to the World Bank's World Development Indicators, in 2012 China had nearly a quarter of the global internet population (23 percent), more than double that of the United States (10 percent) and more than that of the entire European Union (15 percent). See World Bank, "World Development Indicators" (Washington, DC: World Bank, July 2014), http://data.worldbank.org/data-catalog/world-development-indicators.

22. "Xi Jinping Leads Internet Security Group," Xinhua news agency, February 27, 2014, http://news.xinhuanet.com/english/china/2014-02/27/c_133148273.htm.

23. James W. Cortada, *The Digital Hand,* 3 vols. (Oxford: Oxford University Press, 2008). The so-called productivity paradox of the 1990s has been resolved through improved measurement of the relationship between computation and growth.

24. By one estimate, the internet contributed on average 21 percent of gross domestic product (GDP) growth from 2004 to 2009 for early adopters such as Germany, Japan, Sweden, and the United States (up from 10 percent during the previous decade) and a more modest 3 percent for later adopters such as Brazil, China, and India.

25. China Internet Network Information Center, "Statistical Report on Internet Development in China" (Beijing: China Internet Network Information Center, July 2013), p. 3.

26. State Council Information Office, "The Internet in China" (Beijing: State Council Information Office, June 8, 2010).

27. Ronald Deibert et al., eds., *Access Contested: Security, Identity, and Resistance in Asian Cyberspace* (Cambridge, MA: MIT Press, 2012).

28. Jack L. Goldsmith and Tim Wu, *Who Controls the Internet? Illusions of a Borderless World* (New York: Oxford University Press, 2006); and Daniel W. Drezner, "The Global Governance of the Internet: Bringing the State Back In," *Political Science Quarterly*, Vol. 119, No. 3 (Fall 2004), pp. 477–98.

29. McKune, "Foreign Hostile Forces."

30. The Central Committee of the CCP General Office's "Document 9" also describes "Western freedom, democracy, and human rights" as a "political tool" "adopted by Western anti-China forces" amounting to a "serious form of political opposition." The full title of the April 2013 document is "Communiqué on the Current State of the Ideological Sphere." See ibid.

31. One widespread internet meme features contests between the "grass mud horse" (*caonima*) and "river crabs" (*hexie*), which are tonal puns on a vulgar insult and the word for ideological "harmonization," respectively. See Nigel Inkster, "China in Cyberspace," *Survival*, Vol. 52, No. 4 (August/September 2010), pp. 55–66. This is an internet-era manifestation of the logic described by James C. Scott, *Weapons of the Weak: Everyday Forms of Peasant Resistance* (New Haven, CT: Yale University Press, 2008).

32. Guobin Yang, *The Power of the Internet in China: Citizen Activism Online* (New York: Columbia University Press, 2009); and Susan L. Shirk, ed., *Changing Media, Changing China* (Oxford: Oxford University Press, 2011).

33. Gary King, Jennifer Pan, and Margaret E. Roberts, "How Censorship in China Allows Government Criticism but Silences Collective Expression," *American Political Science Review*, Vol. 107, No. 2 (May 2013), pp. 326–43.

34. For a contrasting argument that censorship architecture improves Chinese situational awareness and thus cyber defense for at least some types of technical threats at national gateways, see Robert Sheldon, "The Situation Is Under Control: Cyberspace Situational Awareness and the Implications of China's Internet Censorship," *Strategic Insights*, Vol. 10, No. 1 (Spring 2011), pp. 36–51.

35. Zhuge Jianwe et al., "Investigating the Chinese Online Underground Economy," in Lindsay, Cheung, and Reveron, *China and Cybersecurity*.

36. For an evaluation of legal and regulatory frameworks, technical infrastructure, industrial applications, and the economic and social context of cyberspace usage for twenty countries, see Economist Intelligence Unit, "Cyber Power Index" (McLean, VA: Booz Allen Hamilton, December 2011), http://www.boozallen.com/insights /2012/01/cyber-power-index. China scored 34.6 on a 100-point scale; this can be compared with the United States at 75.4, Germany at 68.2, Japan at 59.3, Brazil at 38.6, Russia at 31.7, and India at 28.3. A more recent study scored China at 58.4 out of 100 and the United States at 86.3. See Tobias Feakin, Jessica Woodall, and Klée Aiken, "Cyber Maturity in the Asia-Pacific Region 2014" (Barton: International Cyber Policy Centre, Australian Strategic Policy Institute, April 2014). Because the two studies' methodologies are different, it is hard to say whether China has improved very much.

37. Wang Chuang, "Xinxi-ānquán: Zhèngcè hùháng chǎnyé zhuàngdà" [Information security: Policy driving industrial growth], *China Electronics News*, October 9, 2012.

38. Daniel R. Headrick, *The Invisible Weapon: Telecommunications and International Politics, 1851–1945* (New York: Oxford University Press, 1991).

39. Ellen Nakashima, "U.S. Said to Be Target of Massive Cyber-Espionage Campaign," *Washington Post*, February 10, 2013. The U.S. intelligence community has also released unclassified official reports alleging high levels of economic espionage originating in China, as well as Russia and other countries. See Office of the National Counterintelligence Executive, *Foreign Spies Stealing US Economic Secrets in Cyberspace*.

40. Government of the People's Republic of China, "National Medium- and Long-Term Plan for the Development of Science and Technology (2006–2020)," quoted in [James] McGregor, "China's Drive for 'Indigenous Innovation[': A Web of Industrial Policies" (Washington, DC: Global Intellectual Property Center, U.S. Chamber of Commerce, 2010)], p. 4.

41. Tai Ming Cheung, "The Chinese Defense Economy's Long March from Imitation to Innovation," *Journal of Strategic Studies*, Vol. 34, No. 3 (June 2011), pp. 325–54.

42. Central Intelligence Agency, "Soviet Acquisition of Militarily Significant Western Technology: An Update" (Langley, VA: Central Intelligence Agency, September 1985), http://www.dtic.mil/dtic/tr /fulltext/u2/a160564.pdf.

43. Barack Obama, "Taking the Cyberattack Threat Seriously," *Wall Street Journal*, July 19, 2012.

44. Kevin Pollpeter, "Controlling the Information Domain: Space, Cyber, and Electronic Warfare," in Ashley J. Tellis and Travis Tanner, eds., *Strategic Asia 2012–13; China's Military Challenge* (Seattle, WA: National Bureau of Asian Research, 2012), pp. 163–96.

45. Ye Zheng and Zhao Baoxian, "Wǎngluò zhàn, zenme zhàn" [How do you fight a network war?], *China Youth Daily*, June 3, 2011.

46. Quoted in [Kevin] Pollpeter, "Chinese Writings on Cyberwarfare and Coercion," [in Lindsay, Cheung, and Reveron, *China and Cybersecurity*,] p. 142.

47. Desmond Ball, "China's Cyber Warfare Capabilities," *Security Affairs*, Vol. 17, No. 2 (Winter 2011), pp. 81–103; and Scott J. Henderson, *The Dark Visitor: Inside the World of Chinese Hackers* (Fort Leavenworth, Kans.: Foreign Military Studies Office, 2007).

48. Robert Shelden and Joe McReynolds, "Civil-Military Integration and Cybersecurity: A Study of Chinese Information Warfare Militias," in Lindsay, Cheung, and Reveron, *China and Cybersecurity*.

49. For background on CNE and CAN, see William A. Owens, Kenneth W. Dam, and Herbert S. Lin, eds., *Technology, Policy, Law, and Ethics Regarding U.S. Acquisition and Use of Cyberattack Capabilities* (Washington, DC: National Academies Press, 2009).

50. The primary example cited as motivating this fear appears to be Chinese intrusion into a company that monitors North American oil and gas pipelines; technical characteristics of the intrusion suggested that it was just a case of economically motivated espionage. See Nicole Perlroth, David E. Sanger, and Michael S. Schmidt, "As Hacking against U.S. Rises, Experts Try to Pin Down Motive," *New York Times*, March 4, 2013.

51. [Jon R.] Lindsay, "Stuxnet and the Limits of Cyber Warfare," [*Security Studies*, Vol. 22, No. 3 (August 2013).]

52. Ellen Nakashima, "U.S. Accelerating Cyberweapon Research," *Washington Post,* March 18, 2012.

53. State Council Information Office, "The Diversified Employment of China's Armed Forces" (Beijing: State Council Information Office, April 2013), http://news.xinhuanet.com/english/china/2013-04/16/c_132312681.htm.

54. Pollpeter, "Chinese Writings on Cyberwarfare and Coercion."

55. For the strategic argument on this point, see Gartzke, "The Myth of Cyberwar."

56. Jack L. Snyder, *The Ideology of the Offensive: Military Decision Making and the Disasters of 1914* (Ithaca, NY: Cornell University Press, 1984); and Stephen Van Evera, *Causes of War: Power and the Roots of Conflict* (Ithaca, NY: Cornell University Press, 1999).

57. David C. Gompert and Martin Libicki, "Cyber Warfare and Sino-American Crisis Instability," *Survival.* Vol. 56, No. 4 (August/September 2014), pp. 7–22; and Avery Goldstein, "First Things First: The Pressing Danger of Crisis Instability in U.S.–China Relations," *International Security,* Vol. 37, No. 4 (Spring 2013), pp. 49–89.

Laurie Garrett

EBOLA'S LESSONS

In a biological sense, last year's Ebola epidemic, which struck West Africa, spilled over into the United States and Europe, and [had by October 2015] led to more than 27,000 infections and more than 11,000 deaths, was a great surprise. Local health and political leaders did not know of the presence of the hemorrhagic fever virus in the 35,000-square-mile Guinea Forest Region, and no human cases had ever been identified in the region prior to the outbreak. Its appearance in the tiny Guinean village of Meliandou in December 2013 went unnoticed, save as a domestic tragedy for the Ouamouno family, who lost their toddler son Emile to a mysterious fever. Practically all the nonbiological aspects of the crisis, however, were entirely unsurprising, as the epidemic itself and the fumbling response to it played out with deeply frustrating predictability. The world has seen these mistakes before.

Humanity's first known encounter with Ebola occurred in 1976, with an outbreak in the village of Yambuku, Zaire (now the Democratic Republic of the Congo), and surrounding areas. A horrible unknown disease suddenly started causing internal bleeding, high fevers, sometimes hallucinations and deranged behavior, and often death; it was eventually named Ebola after a nearby river. Back then, science lacked today's tool kit for the rapid identification and genetic analysis of viruses, not to mention meaningful antivirus treatments, biotechnology, sophisticated HAZMAT suits, and cell phones. Considerable courage, combined with a fair amount of swagger and medical savvy, was the key trait of the couple of dozen foreigners who

From *Foreign Affairs* 94 (September/October 2015): 80–107.

swooped in to assist the local disease fighters. Most were veterans of battles against other microbes, such as smallpox or yellow fever, but had not previously worked together. Karl Johnson, a virologist at the U.S. Centers for Disease Control and Prevention (CDC), took charge, and the multinational group operated as a team of rivals, jockeying for their respective institutional or national stature in the loosely governed investigation.

Conducting its work under the brutal dictatorship of Mobutu Sese Seko, the group's every small achievement, from corralling air transport to communicating with the CDC's headquarters in Atlanta, was a near miracle. But within a few months, the virus was identified, the Belgian Catholic mission hospital at the center of the outbreak was closed, quarantines were enacted, and the epidemic ended. Almost 300 people had died.

The world's second serious confrontation with Ebola came 19 years later, in 1995, when the disease again broke out in Zaire—this time in Kikwit, a community of nearly half a million people spread out along the edges of a vast rainforest in what amounted to a giant village of mud roads, with no running water, no electricity, no phones, no media of any kind, and only the crudest of medical facilities. I took up temporary residence in Kikwit during the epidemic, reporting on how it played out. There was (and still is) only one paved road out of town, the N1, heading around 300 miles due west to Kinshasa and 550 miles southeast to Mwene-Ditu. At the time, Mobutu held Zaire in his clutches and used its national treasury as his family's personal account; he would die two years later, and the nation would discover its bank vaults were empty. When the mysterious disease plaguing the community was finally confirmed as Ebola, the despot had his military cut off access to the highway, leaving the people of Kikwit to suffer on their own.

The global response boiled down to the Zairean doctor Jean-Jacques Muyembe-Tamfun and his medical team; three physicians from Médecins Sans Frontières (MSF, or Doctors Without Borders); three World Health Organization (WHO) officials; and about two dozen clinicians and scientists from the CDC, France's Institut Pasteur, Belgium's Institute of Tropical Medicine, South Africa's National Institute for Virology (now the National Institute for Communicable Diseases), and other Western agencies and academic centers. Supplies and funds were scarce, electricity was available only by using generators, and there were no rapid diagnostic tools, medicines, or vaccines available.

The Kikwit epidemic ended after around nine months, having killed 250 people. Afterward, the leader of the global response, David Heymann, an American employed by the CDC but temporarily working at the WHO's headquarters in Geneva, returned to Switzerland with a list of frustrations. Some of his concerns mirrored those of Johnson in fighting Ebola 19 years earlier: there was still no vaccine, no treatment, no field diagnostic tools, limited supplies of protective gear, nearly nonexistent local health-care systems and trained medical personnel, no clear lines of national and global authority for epidemic response, few qualified scientists capable of and interested in being deployed, no international law governing actions inside countries lacking the capacity to stop epidemics on their own, and no money. Heymann had scoured Europe looking for funds to get his team and supplies to Kikwit. The WHO had not been able to help much, and in the end, the German airline Lufthansa provided free travel and logistical support.

Yet another 19 years on, when I visited Liberia in late 2014, I found that little had improved. Although there had been at least 16 more Ebola outbreaks across the Congo basin and Uganda in the interim, the world had not developed any new technical or medical tools for addressing the virus. Treatment was only incrementally more sophisticated than it had been back in 1995, it was still impossible to rapidly diagnose infections, and there was still no vaccine.

Same Old Story

The 1976 Yambuku outbreak came at a time of tremendous optimism in the fields of global health and Western medicine. The previous decades had seen the development and widespread use of a host of remarkably effective vaccines. They had brought horrors such as diphtheria, measles, pertussis, polio, rubella, and tetanus down to insignificant levels in rich countries, offering the hope that immunization campaigns in poor countries could eliminate the diseases entirely. New antibiotics kept appearing on the market, pushing the prices of older stalwarts, such as penicillin and tetracycline, further down toward affordability in poor countries. The medical establishment in the United States was growing in size and sophistication, producing specialists offering treatments for rare forms of cancer, obscure inherited disorders, and deep psychiatric afflictions. The pharmaceutical industry was at the beginning of an enormous boom. And the WHO was successfully straddling both sides of the Cold War, garnering support from the Soviet Union and the United States.

But 1976 was also a year of harbingers of bad things to come. There was not just Ebola's emergence in Yambuku. The United States struggled with two strange new outbreaks of its own, of swine flu and Legionnaires' disease. In addition, the sexual revolution was spreading across Europe and North America, with increases in unprotected sex leading to a rising incidence of sexually transmitted diseases such as gonorrhea, herpes, and syphilis. Within five years, physicians in the

United States would note a set of new, fatal symptoms among hemophiliacs, gay men, and intravenous drug users; the disease would eventually be called acquired immune deficiency syndrome, or AIDS, caused by the human immunodeficiency virus, or HIV.

In what became known as the swine flu fiasco, the Ford administration and the American public health establishment overreacted to the death of a U.S. Army private from the disease. The fatality was isolated, but it led to a panic and a national immunization campaign. Convinced that a massive pandemic was on the way, Congress indemnified the vaccine industry. Immunizations were hastily rushed into production; amid claims of contamination and side effects, years of lawsuits followed. The episode left policymakers skeptical about trusting their health-care professionals and determined never again to indemnify drug makers; manufacturers, in turn, ran for cover, and some drug companies shed their vaccine production lines entirely. An infuriated Congress convened hearings to rake the CDC over the coals, forcing the resignation of the agency's director.

Six months after the death of the army private, 34 hotel guests attending an American Legion convention in Philadelphia died from a mysterious illness (later dubbed Legionnaires' disease). The inability of the CDC and Pennsylvania health authorities to rapidly determine what had happened further undermined policymakers' confidence, and when the cause of the disease turned out to be a previously unknown species of bacteria lurking in the air-conditioning system, the public was shocked. If the age of infectious diseases was past, how could a new bacterial ailment appear, go undiagnosed for months, and prove tough to treat with antibiotics?

AIDS would, of course, prove the greatest challenge—to human hubris, the pharmaceutical and research communities, and international global health governance. Shortly after his first visit to Liberia to see the Ebola epidemic firsthand last August, the CDC's current director, Thomas Frieden, told reporters, "I will say that in the 30 years I've been working in public health, the only thing like this has been AIDS, And we have to work now so that this is not the world's next AIDS." Frieden was referring not to the disease itself but to the world's disastrous response to it. For two decades, as the AIDS pandemic unfolded in country after country, governments and general populations almost always proved more interested in attacking the subpopulations at greatest risk for the disease than in fighting the virus itself. Children infected by HIV-contaminated blood transfusions were banned from schools, the homes of hemophiliacs were burned, masses of gay men died with little attention from the heterosexual communities around them, intravenous drug users were denied sterile syringes, female prostitutes were imprisoned or denied access to health care, and many medical and dental providers refused to allow HIV-positive individuals access to care unrelated to their infections.

From the perspective of HIV prevention, in nearly every country in the world, the 1980s and 1990s were long, ugly decades during which the virus spread relentlessly, with AIDS eventually ranking as the third-largest pandemic in world history (after the Black Death and the 1918 influenza pandemic). In comparing Ebola and AIDS, Frieden was not forecasting that Ebola would infect 60 million people, as HIV has; rather, he was indicating that the ignorant, inept, and cruel response to AIDS was being mirrored by events unfolding in West Africa in 2014.

During the 1980s, the WHO failed to recognize the importance of HIV and AIDS. Inside its Geneva headquarters, some experts exhibited as much prejudice against the populations at great risk for AIDS—especially homosexuals—as did the general public. For a brief time in the mid-1980s, its Global Program on AIDS (GPA) thrived, led by the epidemiologist Jonathan Mann. But WHO insiders grumbled and complained about the millions of dollars in AIDS funds Mann was raising and about the dire (and, in retrospect, mostly accurate) forecasts his group was issuing. A common refrain among insider critics was, "Since more people die of diarrhea—or cancer, or hypertension, or malaria, or whatever—than of AIDS, why is it getting so much money and media attention?" Heeding the grousing, the WHO's director general, Hiroshi Nakajima, forced Mann's resignation, slashed the AIDS budget, and eventually shut down the GPA, essentially walking away from the largest pandemic in modern history.

Since then, the global response to the rise of new pathogens has continued to be limited, uncoordinated, and dysfunctional. From SARS to MERS, H5N1 to H1N1 to H7N9, the story has been similar. Poor nations are unable to detect new diseases quickly and bring them swiftly under control. Rich nations generally show only marginal interest in outbreaks until the microbes seem to directly threaten their citizens, at which point they hysterically overreact. Governments look after their own interests, cover up outbreaks, hoard scarce pharmaceutical supplies, prevent exports of life-saving medicines, shut borders, and bar travel.

The global health infrastructure has shown itself to be weak, fractured, prone to infighting, and more interested in searching for technological silver bullets than engaging in the hard slog of social mobilization and classic local public health work. And through it all, the WHO has struggled to remain credible, as its financial resources have shrunk, tensions have grown between its Geneva headquarters and its regional offices, and rival multilateral organizations have taken control over much of the global health action and agenda.

"I Thought I Knew Fear"

By mid 2015, the nation of Liberia [was] returning to its normal, pre-Ebola life. This is in sharp contrast to the horrors of fall [2014] when every nook and cranny of the country was in the grip of the disease and people were literally dying in the streets of Monrovia for lack of hospital beds and treatment centers. Nearly 500 new cases a week were detected in the country during late September and early October. * * *

Charts of the rates of infection and fatalities show that Liberia's plague was on its downward course before the world mobilized to help. With heroic assistance from MSF, the International Committee of the Red Cross, a few other foreign humanitarian and religious organizations, and small teams of foreign scientists and public health experts, Liberia was able to turn the tide of its epidemic largely without the UN Mission for Ebola Emergency Response (UNMEER), the U.S. military, or the promised hundreds of millions of dollars' worth of World Bank and multinational aid. As late as the end of February 2015, after the worst of the crisis had passed, less than half of the finances, personnel, and supplies promised by the global community had actually materialized on the ground. If the aid had arrived earlier, the epidemic would undoubtedly have been contained faster and with fewer fatalities.

There was no good reason to believe that Liberia would be able to acquit itself so well in managing its catastrophe. When the crisis struck, Liberia, one of the poorest nations on earth, barely had a health-care and hospital system or even a method for processing public-sector payrolls. It ranked 175 out of 187 countries in the UN's Human Development Index, had an official unemployment rate of more than 80 percent, and a total GDP of only $1.95 billion. Less than half of the population was functionally literate, a third of the country's women had never set foot in a classroom, and fewer than five percent of households could, by African Development Bank standards, be labeled middle class. And in fact, if not for a smattering of dedicated officials and medical personnel, together with the good sense of local villagers, Liberia might still be in crisis.

■   ■   ■

Not in My Backyard

On September 16, [2014] Obama announced his decision to deploy around 3,000 U.S. military personnel to West Africa to fight the epidemic and committed $750 million to the effort. On a visit to the CDC's headquarters, Obama pledged a series of additional commitments from Washington, pointedly adding, "But this is a global threat, and it demands a truly global response. International organizations just have to move faster than they have up until this point. More nations need to contribute experienced personnel, supplies, and funding that's needed, and they need to deliver on what they pledge quickly. Charities and individual philanthropists have given generously, and they can make a big difference."

It was the middle of September when the world finally began to reckon with the reality of what was happening in West Africa. The UN Security Council declared Ebola an international threat, the General Assembly echoed the cry the next day, and the CDC released a forecast predicting exponential growth to more than a million cases by February absent major international intervention. The World Bank and the White House pressured countries around the world to pony up resources; the UN estimated the costs of stopping the epidemic at just under $1 billion and created a new Ebola task force, UNMEER; and according to a report in *The New York Times*, the World Bank's president, Jim Yong Kim, chastised Chan for the WHO's failed response during a meeting of international health officials at the bank's headquarters. (Through a WHO spokesperson, Chan declined a request to be interviewed for this article.)

The first small U.S. Army team arrived in Liberia on September 17 to assess the situation; hundreds more U.S. military personnel would arrive in October, and a field hospital dedicated to the care of health-care workers themselves would open in early November. In Sierra Leone, the British military mobilized, deploying at about the same time as the U.S. Army did in Liberia. Both built elite-care Ebola treatment facilities. But the U.S. Army's facilities went operational only after Liberia's epidemic had started winding down, and most received no patients. The Sierra Leone epidemic, in contrast, lagged months behind Liberia's, and British forces saw many Ebola patients, including at least one from their own ranks. UNMEER, meanwhile, put its first official boots on the ground in the region on September 29, coordinating humanitarian activities akin to those executed by UN agencies during famines and after natural disasters.

While all of this was happening, however, attention in the West shifted away from Africa and toward the enemy within. On September 24, a Liberian man named Thomas Duncan came down with Ebola while visiting his fiancée in Dallas, Texas, and soon two of Duncan's attending nurses were infected. (Duncan died on October 8; both nurses were eventually cured.) A nurse in Spain, meanwhile, contracted the disease from a patient who had been brought home from Africa for treatment, showing that both the United States and Europe were potentially at risk. The reaction was swift and hysterical, with a host of prominent Americans issuing calls to ban travelers from the three Ebola-afflicted countries and self-proclaimed experts warning about the possibility that the virus might be able to spread through the air. Ebola coverage became a staple of cable television and talk radio and even figured prominently in the U.S. midterm elections (as a telling sign of the global chaos supposedly sparked by Obama's foreign policy failures).

African observers hardly knew what to think. "We were saddened by the reaction in America," Sirleaf later told me. "We understand the fear. We live with fear. But the risk was minimal [for Americans]." To put the world reaction in perspective, on September 28, when the Liberian epidemic was at what later proved to be its peak, Twitter users were posting Ebola-related messages at the rate of about a few dozen per minute. In the days after Duncan was officially diagnosed, on September 30, the rate rose to around 6,300 messages per minute.

Ironically, it was during just this period that Liberia's epidemic started to abate. Many factors played a role in defeating it, including a remarkable U.S. mobilization; great improvements in laboratory testing and diagnostic speed; the construction of Ebola treatment units, which allowed infected individuals to be isolated; and the virtual elimination of unsafe burials and the imposition of mandatory cremations. But officials in the Sirleaf government repeatedly acknowledged actions taken by the Liberian citizenry at large. "We need to give credit to the public for what has been done," one of Sirleaf's political advisers, Emmanuel Dolo, told me. "And we have to say that we cannot let that go."

For example, rural communities realized that Ebola was coming from outsiders, especially villagers returning from Monrovia and other big cities. So without any push from the government, communities took matters into their own hands, setting up temporary isolation places (usually designated houses or sheds), in which they ordered visitors and returnees from the cities to be quarantined. After months of struggling with traditional burial practices, rural residents began bringing their dead to authorities. And the Liberian Ministry of Health deployed an army of thousands of contact tracers—young men and women hired temporarily to track down all known associates of confirmed Ebola patients and fatalities. In local villages, I found village chiefs taking control: ordering families to bring out their sick and dead, commanding safe burials, and searching for ways to feed quarantined households.

When I visited the Liberian town of Jene-Wonde, nestled along the border with Sierra Leone, the chief was ordering young men to dig a well and build a fence to enclose a newly refurbished clinic, made of wattle and thatch. Chebe Sano, a middle-aged woman with a quiet, commanding presence, was the chief of the roughly 700 residents and led the creation of a three-room Ebola community care center, designed to house a dozen people in quarantine. Sano didn't wait for the Liberian government or a group of nonexistent doctors to take action. She knew that her people's plague could be stopped only if the infected were separated from the rest of the population. With advice from a handful of the CDC's Epidemic Intelligence Service officers, Sano simply took tough quarantine steps that eventually stopped Jene-Wonde's horror.

"It is the communities in Liberia that turned this around. The thing that kept us going," Gbanya explained to the WHA in Geneva in May 2015, "is we knew, we need to do the best we can to save Mama Liberia." But she admonished the delegates from 194 nations to maintain international vigilance. "It's not over until it's over in our sister countries, Guinea and Sierra Leone," she said. "When a disease hits your neighbor's front door, be aware that it can come to your backdoor."

Who Needs the WHO?

The WHO performed so poorly during the crisis that there is a question of whether the world actually needs it. The answer is yes, it does—but in a revised form, with a clearer mandate, better funding, more competent staff, and less politicization. The agency should be clearly at the apex of the global health architecture, not jockeying for command of epidemic response with other organizations, as happened last year. But with power comes responsibility, and the WHO needs to merit its position, not simply assume it. If the WHO is going to remain the world's central authority on global health issues—which it should, because there needs to be one, and it has the most legitimate claim to perform such a role—it needs to concentrate on its core competencies and be freed from the vast array of unrealistic, unprioritized, and highly politicized mandates that its member states have imposed. Rather than wasting resources duplicating the responsibilities and expertise of other agencies, it should scale back to providing technical expertise and advice in areas such as tuberculosis, malaria, HIV/AIDS, and child immunizations. And although the World Bank offers financial backing and advice on many programs having to do with health, its own expertise is primarily about money: it should not be competing with the WHO on providing guidance for handling outbreaks of infectious diseases but rather be helping finance the measures a competent WHO argues are necessary. Ban, the UN secretary-general, should convene private meetings with the leaders of the World Bank, the WHO, and several dozen other relevant agencies and institutions to develop plans for a more coherent and efficient response to future epidemics.

This year's WHA was obsessed with trying to learn lessons from the crisis and featured a great deal of questioning of the WHO's basic credibility, given the organization's inadequate response. It may not represent an existential crisis, but as the former Oxfam chief executive Barbara Stocking told the gathering, it is surely the WHO's "defining moment." Stocking is chair of the Ebola Interim Assessment Panel, which Chan created to offer an objective appraisal of the organization's response to the outbreak. If the director general had hoped for a mild rebuke, she must have been sorely disappointed. In July, the panel published its final report; it was devastating.

The Ebola outbreak revealed, Stocking's panel concluded, that the WHO was incapable of responding to emergencies in a timely fashion and lacked the credibility to enforce the IHR, its own instrument. The WHO's leadership was alarmingly slow to respond to the unfolding crisis, the panel reported, because the organization "does not have a culture of rapid decision-making and tends to adopt a reactive, rather than a proactive, approach to emergencies." The panel lamented that senior

WHO officials failed to adequately react to warnings of the outbreak's growing seriousness that they received from within the organization and from outside sources, especially MSF. "WHO must re-establish its pre-eminence as the guardian of global public health; this will require significant changes throughout WHO," the panel's report stated. It went on to recommend twenty-one major reforms, affecting nearly every aspect of the organization, including strengthening GOARN, significantly increasing funding to improve the ability of member countries to respond to disease emergencies, and placing all of the WHO's disparate emergency-response units into a single chain of command.

The WHO's executive board, meanwhile, had delivered its own harsh critique of the agency back in January. There is a "clear gap in the WHO's mission and structure," it stated, with "no clear lines of decision-making or dedicated funding in place [leading to] a slow, uncoordinated response to the Ebola outbreak." Not only did the WHO fail to implement the IHR in a timely fashion, the executive board concluded, but it also did too little to prevent nations from taking steps in violation of the IHR that isolated and stigmatized the affected countries. At the height of the crisis, most other African countries banned people from and trade with Guinea, Liberia, and Sierra Leone; Australia and Canada declined all visa requests from the region; all but two commercial air carriers and all airfreight services ceased flights to the area; and insurance companies declined to pay for air rescue services. All such actions were in violation of the IHR, yet the WHO appeared powerless and inept in response, unable to enforce its own regulations.

The executive board's and the assessment panel's reports both insist that epidemic prevention should be the core function of the WHO: if the agency cannot credibly lead in a disease crisis, it might not merit donor support. But as MSF's Liu said on the sidelines of an Ebola meeting in Dakar in June, "The reality today is if Ebola were to hit on the scale it did in August and September, we would hardly do much better than we did the last time around."

In response to the assessment panel's report, the WHO issued a statement claiming that it was "already moving forward on some of the panel's recommendations." A few days later, I spoke with Bruce Aylward, a WHO assistant director general who was deeply involved in the Ebola response and who distinguished himself as one of the first members of the senior leadership to realize that the organization's response was lagging. Aylward acknowledged the validity of many of the complaints lodged by the executive board and the assessment panel but argued that many of the WHO's critics fail to appreciate just how difficult a position the WHO is in and underestimate how much the organization relies on buy-in and consensus from its member states. "I think the issue is, what is the purpose [of the WHO]? And are the member states in agreement on that purpose? Where do they want the organization to land?" he said. "We're in an extremely dangerous position, being pressured to make incremental changes until member states are assuaged, but not so much change that the organization, internally, revolts." But he conceded that the WHO "has got to evolve, to be more than a mere technical organization. It must be a health emergency manager."

That idea is now the subject of heated debate among global health experts and policymakers. Some argue that the WHO cannot credibly fulfill its role as an emergency manager. But no one has identified an alternative agency that could realistically take on the job. The only way the WHO can hope to do so is by enlarging GOARN and expanding its mandate, allowing it to operate as a semiautonomous unit that controls its own budget, overseen by an independent governing board and protected by a firewall separating its science-based decisions from the vagaries of international politics.

Another important step the WHO should take is to plan for a competent, quickly deployable, international volunteer medical corps. Composed of doctors, nurses, lab technicians, epidemiologists, and other professionals necessary for handling a humanitarian crisis, such a corps should be voluntary and multinational, with thousands of trained and registered people ready to be summoned into service on short notice when the next emergency arises. When crises are so obviously recurring and predictable, there is simply no reason that each one should be met with a similarly ad hoc, uncoordinated, amateurish response, sluggish when it matters most and panicked when problems have already escalated.

Even were such a corps to exist, however, it would still need to get to the crisis quickly, something that is a much greater problem than most people realize. As soon as the Ebola epidemic was confirmed, the only air travel of any kind between the affected countries was provided by the UN Humanitarian Assistance Service, which was available only to UN agencies and authorized others. Under the 1944 Convention on International Civil Aviation, sovereign states may close their airspace due to adverse conditions such as bad weather or conflict, and airlines may cancel flights for their own marketing or risk-assessment rationales. The convention offers no means for a sovereign state to compel airlines to service it, nor for an airline to override an airspace closure. The International Civil Aviation Organization should revisit these issues, paying special attention to encouraging airlines to maintain reasonable services to countries facing health crises.

As a result of these difficulties with air travel, it was hard for people and supplies to get to the epidemic and practically impossible to coordinate responses across all three countries. Medical volunteers from the developed world who tried to help out, meanwhile, found themselves discriminated against by airlines or subject to mandatory quarantines when they tried to come home, which was not only unfair but also a clear deterrent to such help, rather than the facilitation and support of it that the situation required.

The WHO and the U.S. State Department, accordingly, should figure out how to ensure that such problems do not arise in future crises. Among other things, this will mean scrutinizing the air transport agreements the CDC has with commercial carriers for the emergency transport of personnel, supplies, and dangerous microbe samples. The world cannot rely on standard market operations to proceed as usual during a crisis, and so authorities need to lock in appropriate arrangements beforehand.

Another area requiring advance attention is the availability and use of experimental medicines, vaccines, and rapid diagnostic tools. All three were lacking during the recent crisis, even though promising drugs, immunizations, and point-of-care instant diagnostics are in various stages of development. The WHO's innovation team has been bogged down for months in ethics debates and arguments over how vaccine trials might be properly executed, and with the epidemic waning, it is possible that nothing will actually get into field trials in time to be tested against actually existing Ebola. Together with the pharmaceutical, scientific, medical ethics, and biotechnology communities, the WHO should create policy templates for future rapid action—now, before the next crisis hits, rather than being forced to deal with such matters in the heat of the moment.

In the end, the world must come to grips with the fact that future epidemics are not just likely but also inevitable and prepare to deal with them more effectively. As Nabarro, the UN's special envoy on Ebola, recently put it to me, "There will be more: one, because people are moving around more; two, because the contact between humans and the wild is on the increase; and maybe because of climate change. The worry we always have is that there will be a really infectious and beastly bug that comes along."

Some major authorities have argued that the real problem is less epidemic response than the availability of basic public health programs—that the Ebola crisis would never have developed to catastrophic proportions if Guinea, Liberia, and Sierra Leone had universally accessible health-care systems. This is simply not true. Good health care should indeed be considered a basic human right, but even if it were available everywhere, outbreaks of strange new diseases and viruses would still occur—just look at SARS in Toronto and Singapore in 2003, MRSA and other drug-resistant bacterial diseases in hospitals across the United States today, and MERS in Saudi Arabia, to name a few.

On the other hand, there is simply no question that the problems Gbanya and her colleagues have had to grapple with go well beyond crisis response. The health-care systems of Guinea, Liberia, and Sierra Leone were in terrible shape before the Ebola epidemic struck, and they will be in worse shape after the epidemic has passed, having lost a significant number of health-care professionals to the disease. Across Liberia now stand empty Ebola treatment units that are little more than tented wooden platforms wrapped in plastic sheets. With the return of the rainy season this summer, those expensive emergency isolation facilities will be washed away, leaving no permanent improvement in local medical systems.

"A weak health system was struggling before Ebola," Gbanya told me. "After Ebola, health-care service delivery will be difficult. And the costs will be three times as high. Why? Because of all the protective equipment, all the training, the emergency-response system. At this stage, we have the opportunity to think what sort of investment can equal medium-term improvement in Liberia. We're not going to have a country anymore if we keep getting Ebola." And so it comes back to money. The world will get what it pays for—and right now, that is not very much.

CREDITS

Francis Fukuyama: "The End of History?" Originally published in *The National Interest* (Summer 1989). Reprinted by permission of Francis Fukuyama.

Laurie Garrett: "Ebola's Lessons: How the WHO Mishandled the Crisis" republished with permission of the Council on Foreign Relations, from *Foreign Affairs* Vol. 94 (Sept./Oct. 2015). Copyright © 2015 by the Council on Foreign Relations, Inc; permission conveyed through Copyright Clearance Center, Inc.

Robert Gilpin: "The Nature of Political Economy," from *U.S. Power and the Multinational Corporation: The Political Economy of Foreign Direct Investment*, pp. 20–33. Copyright © 1975 by Basic Books, Inc. Reprinted by permission of Basic Books, a member of Perseus Books Group.

Garrett Hardin: From "The Tragedy of the Commons," *Science* 162 (Dec, 13, 1968), 1243–1248. Reprinted with permission from AAAS.

Valerie M. Hudson and Andrea M. den Boer: "Missing Women and Bare Branches: Gender Balance and Conflict," from *Environmental Change and Security Program Report*, Issue 11 (2005), pp. 20–24. Reprinted by permission of the Woodrow Wilson International Center for Scholars; Table from "Missing Women and Bare Branches" originally published as Table 2.4, p. 62 in *Bare Branches: The Security Implications of Asia's Surplus Male Population* by Valerie M. Hudson & Andrea M. den Boer. © 2004 Massachusetts Institute of Technology, by permission of The MIT Press.

Samuel Huntington: "The Clash of Civilization" republished with permission of the Council on Foreign Relations, from *Foreign Affairs* Vol. 72, No. 3 (Summer 1993). Copyright © 1993 by the Council on Foreign Relations, Inc; permission conveyed through Copyright Clearance Center, Inc.

G. John Ikenberry: Chapter 1: "Crisis of the Old Order" republished with permission of Princeton University Press from *Liberal Leviathan*. Copyright © 2011 by Princeton University Press, pp. 1–27, 31–32; permission conveyed through Copyright Clearance Center, Inc.

Robert Jervis: "Hypotheses on Misperception," from *World Politics* Vol. 20, No. 3 (April 1968), pp. 454–479. Copyright © 1968 Trustees of Princeton University. Reprinted with the permission of Cambridge University Press; "Cooperation under the Security Dilemma," from *World Politics* Vol. 30, No. 2 (January 1978), pp. 167–214. Copyright © 1978 Trustees of Princeton University. Reprinted with the permission of Cambridge University Press.

Immanuel Kant: From *Perpetual Peace and Other Essays on Politics, History, and Morals*, translated by Ted Humphrey. Copyright © 1983 by Hackett Publishing Company, Inc. Reprinted by permission of Hackett Publishing Company, Inc. All rights reserved.

Margaret E. Keck and Kathryn Sikkink: "Transnational Advocacy Networks in International Politics," republished with permission of Cornell University Press from *Activists Beyond Borders: Advocacy Networks in International Politics*. Copyright © 1998 by Cornell University, pp. 1–3, 9–11, 16–18, 25–26, 32–34, 104–110, 119–120; permission conveyed through Copyright Clearance Center, Inc.

George Kennan: "The Sources of Soviet Conduct," reprinted with permission of the Council on Foreign Relations, from *Foreign Affairs* Vol. 25, No. 4 (July 1947). Copyright © 1947 by the Council on Foreign Relations, Inc.; permission conveyed through Copyright Clearance Center, Inc.

Robert O. Keohane: Republished with permission of Princeton University Press, from *After Hegemony: Cooperation and Discord in the World Political Economy*. Copyright © 1984 by Princeton University Press, pp. 7–10, 85–98, 111–16; permission conveyed through Copyright Clearance Center, Inc.

Stephen D. Krasner: Excerpts from "Sharing Sovereignty: New Institutions for Collapsed and Failing States." *International Security*, 29:2 (Fall 2004), pp. 85–120. © 2004 by the President and Fellows of Harvard College and the